# ADVANCED ACCOUNTING:
## An Organizational Approach

A Volume in the Wiley Series in Accounting and Information Systems

# Advanced Accounting:
## An Organizational Approach

**FOURTH EDITION**

**NORTON M. BEDFORD**
University of Illinois

**KENNETH W. PERRY**
University of Illinois

**ARTHUR R. WYATT**
Arthur Andersen & Co.

**JOHN WILEY & SONS**
New York  Chichester  Brisbane  Toronto

Copyright © 1961, 1967, 1973, and 1979, by John Wiley & Sons, Inc.

All rights reserved. Published simultaneously in Canada.

Reproduction or translation of
any part of this work beyond that permitted by Sections
107 and 108 of the 1976 United States Copyright
Act without the permission of the copyright
owner is unlawful. Requests for permission
or further information should be addressed to
the Permissions Department, John Wiley & Sons.

*Library of Congress Cataloging in Publication Data:*

Bedford, Norton M.
  Advanced accounting: an organizational approach.

  Includes index.
  1. Accounting. I. Perry, Kenneth W., joint author.
  II. Wyatt, Arthur R., joint author. III. Title.

HF5635.B4152 1979     657'.046     78-6961
ISBN 0-471-02927-0

Printed in the United States of America
10 9 8 7 6 5 4 3 2 1

# About the Authors

Norton M. Bedford is the Arthur Young Distinguished Professor and Head of the Department of Accountancy at the University of Illinois. Professor Bedford has taught graduate and undergraduate courses in accounting theory, accounting research and accounting practice, and related courses during his academic years.

Professor Bedford earned his Ph.D. from Ohio State University and taught for three years at Washington University before joining the University of Illinois. He has served as President of the American Accounting Association and on the Board of Directors of the American Institute of Certified Public Accountants. He has written extensively and lectured throughout the world. Currently he is a member of the Board of Trustees of the Financial Accounting Foundation.

Many of the concepts and procedures included in *Advanced Accounting* were developed from discussions with practicing accountants and were expanded to conform with accounting theory developments in order to bring to the student an organized view of the material appropriate for a textbook on advanced accounting.

Kenneth W. Perry is the Alexander Grant Professor at the University of Illinois. He earned his Ph.D. from the University of Illinois and has been on the faculty of that institution since 1950. He has taught on a visiting basis at Berea College, University of Kentucky, Northeastern University, Parsons College, Florida A & M University, and the University of Virginia.

Professor Perry was selected as Eastern Kentucky University's 1969 Outstanding Alumnus. He was the first (1972) recipient of the Excellence in Teaching Award given by the Alumni Association of the College of Commerce and Business Administration of the University of Illinois. He was the recipient of the American Accounting Association's Outstanding Educator Award for 1974 and was a Beta Gamma Sigma Distinguished Scholar for 1977-1978. He has authored or coauthored several books and has had numerous articles published in various professional periodicals.

Arthur R. Wyatt was born in Aurora, Illinois, and was graduated with high honors from the University of Illinois, where he later received an M.S. and a Ph.D. degree. He taught accountancy at the University of Illinois for fifteen years and was named professor of accountancy in 1960.

In 1966 Mr. Wyatt joined the international public accounting firm of Arthur Andersen & Co. He was admitted to the firm as a partner in 1968, and currently is Director—Accounting Principles and a member of the firm's Committee on Accounting and Auditing Standards. He was closely associated with the projects and deliberations of the Accounting Principles Board. Since 1973 he has been a member of the Accounting Standards Executive Committee of the AICPA and he is currently chairman of that Committee. He is also a member of the Financial Accounting Standards Advisory Council and of the Screening Committee on Emerging Problems of the Financial Accounting Standards Board.

Mr. Wyatt is the author of numerous articles and books, including *Accounting Research Study NO. 5,* "A Critical Study of Accounting for Business Combinations," published by the American Institute of Certified Public Accountants. He has been active for a number of years in the American Accounting Association and is a past editor of *The Illinois CPA*. He currently is a member and secretary of the Board of Trustees of the City Colleges of Chicago.

# Preface

The subject matter of advanced accounting is expanding rapidly both conceptually and in the scope of application. *Statements* of the Financial Accounting Standards Board, accounting releases of the Securities and Exchange Commission, and pronouncements by other influential groups have provided authoritative support for these developments. The inclusion in this edition of these newer developments required an adjustment and expansion of prior editions, but the basic organizational structure of all editions has been retained.

As noted in previous editions, the problem of providing textbook material suitable in content, level, and method for training and education in accountancy is rather involved. Constantly changing activities in the practice of the profession, coupled with divergent and conflicting philosophies of education, must be evaluated in some manner if a textbook is to contribute to the development of accounting education. The recent, rapid, and widespread changes in our economy have revealed a pressing need for additional educational material to support the further development and expansion of the profession of accounting.

We believe that a distinction must be drawn between *training* for accounting and *education* for accounting. To us, *training* means any process which emphasizes proficiency in the application of a set of rules to selected business situations. On the other hand, by *education* for accounting we mean the process whereby an understanding of the concepts and principles of accounting is sought. This second approach is based on the assumption that it is not possible to train a student to act expertly in all possible business situations, and that the objective of accounting education is to provide a broad framework of concepts and principles so that a graduate is better equipped to handle any general accounting situation than to meet one specific problem.

Some accounting textbooks are concerned primarily with the methods of accounting, giving little attention to the principles underlying the mechanistic procedures. Others are directed and devoted to the concepts and underlying economic conditions that govern the procedures of accounting. We believe a void now exists about midway between these two categories. It is toward this midway level, skewed slightly on the conceptual side, that this textbook is directed.

The justification for the development of another edition of a textbook at this level rests on both educational and professional needs. Failure to adjust an accounting curriculum to an educational level, wherein concepts, reasoning, and understanding are of the essence of the program of study, will lead ultimately to a decline in the quality of students interested in the field. More directly, the profession of accounting is changing and expanding, and with change has come the realization on the part of practitioners of the profession that the educational process should provide a broad approach to the practice of accounting.

On the other hand, the broad educational requirements of an accountant should not hinder the development of rather complete familiarity with the procedures and the rules of accounting. It is singular that personnel representatives of the larger public accounting firms speak of the need for broad training for accounting but frequently employ the technically proficient student. It must be concluded that both attributes are desired, and this textbook has been developed to provide such an education.

It is an accepted "law of learning" that the student retains best that which is presented within a logically consistent framework. To provide for this retention feature, we organized the materials of advanced accounting to provide a logical learning sequence in five parts:

Part I. Formation of the business organization.
Part II. Maintenance of the business organization.
Part III. Expansion of the business organization.
Part IV. Contraction of the business organization.
Part V. Liquidation of the business organization.

This arrangement of materials resulted from the observation that intermediate accounting is concerned largely with the operations of a going concern, but advanced accounting is mainly the story of accounting problems arising from activities that provide an organizational unit for operations.

In addition to changing the sequence in which familiar materials are introduced, this edition adds certain new and uptdated materials to the teaching area of advanced accounting. In Part II, covering maintenance of the organizational unit, the materials concerning business risk and price-level fluctuations contain new developments in accounting. Also, in Part III, concerning business expansion, the accounting procedure leading up to decision making on expansion problems is new to an advanced accounting course. The more extended treatment of reorganizations of all types in Part IV represents material that we believe significant in the light of current economic conditions.

This textbook was written upon the assumption that the student of advanced accounting has had sufficient mathematics to handle simple computations in the area of statistics, compound interest, and annuities. Recognizing, however, that this assumption may not always be warranted, an appendix on the fundamentals

*Preface*

of actuarial science has been included. It is our belief that an advanced accounting textbook should include some background accounting material to furnish an orderly transition to the advanced material. Toward this end, the opening chapters review certain fundamental accounting concepts that are necessary to establish the background for the advanced discussion.

This revised edition also incorporates many significant changes in accounting thinking and business practice, which developed subsequent to the original edition. For example, the use of long-term leases to effect a variety of transactions has increased rapidly in recent years. The principal issues in accounting for leases, both as an asset and as a liability, are discussed. The positions expressed in opinions of the Accounting Principles Board and *Statements* of the Financial Accounting Standards Board have been incorporated in the discussion where appropriate. To meet the demand for additional problem materials, the number of problems has been increased substantially. Finally, as everyone acquainted with advanced accounting knows, recently enunciated accounting principles reflect the emergence of a more complex methodology and the narrowing of alternative principles. These necessary adjustments have been made in the present edition. Irrelevant material has been deleted. Problems have been modernized and expanded and, for those interested in sitting for the CPA examination, an appendix covering governmental accounting is included.

We express our appreciation for the reactions of students, faculty members, and practitioners who have contributed to the present edition. Again we are grateful to the American Institute of Certified Public Accountants for permitting us to use C.P.A. examination problem material.

NORTON M. BEDFORD
KENNETH W. PERRY
ARTHUR R. WYATT

# Contents

**Part I   FORMATION OF THE BUSINESS ORGANIZATION**

1  **The Conceptual and Theoretical Background / 3**

   The role of accounting; External conditions affecting accounting, Scarce means, Standards of equity, Rational and prudent conduct, Fundamental assumptions of accounting, Usefulness, Entity, Price, Continuity or going concern, Periodicity, Principles and standards of accounting; Social significance of accounting; Accounting view of the enterprise—Proprietary versus entity theory. *Forms of business organization:* The proprietorship, Legal aspects of proprietorships, Accounting aspects of proprietorship formation, The partnership, Legal aspects of partnerships; Accounting aspects of partnership formation, The corporation, Legal aspects of corporations, Accounting aspects of corporate formation, The trust, Powers of trustees, Accounting for the formation of a trust, The cooperative, The joint venture, Accounting aspects of joint ventures, Uncompleted ventures, Miscellaneous venture combinations.

2  **Valuation of Assets / 30**

   Acquisition cost valuation, Problems of asset valuation, Acquisition cost versus realizable value. *Valuation of cash and direct claims to cash:* Realizable value—Reporting date versus future date, Materiality and realizable valuation, Valuation of long-term receivables; The use of current market value, Cash surrender value, Summary of valuation of cash and claims to cash items, Valuation of accounts receivable, Valuation of notes receivable, Valuation of long-term receivables arising from a sale, Procedures in valuation of receivables. *Valuation of service resources:* Discounts in valuation, Exchange of service resources for other service resources, Contributed service resources,

xi

Leased resources; Asset classification and recognition, Classification, Recognition. *Application of principles:* Illustration—Partnership formed from proprietorship; Goodwill, Partnership goodwill, Corporation goodwill, Problems in partnership goodwill and bonus; Economic valuation of enterprise assets.

### 3  Valuation of Equities / 64

*Equities as claims vs. equities as sources:* Valuation of creditorship equities, Varying recognition dates; Lease liabilities; Estimated liabilities, Time of retirement. *Summary: liability valuation:* Valuation of owners' equities; Source versus claim—summarization. *Classification of equities:* Classification of liabilities; Classification of ownership equities—proprietorship; Classification of ownership equities—partnership, Partners' capital and risk, Valuation of partners' capital; Classification of ownership equities—corporation; Financing the enterprise, Trading on the equity, Short-term versus long-term financing; Variations in classification of stockholders' equity; Supplementary data.

## Part II  MAINTENANCE OF THE BUSINESS ORGANIZATION

### 4  Accounting for Insurable Business Risks / 93

*Insurable asset risks:* Fire insurance; Fire loss account, Book value of fixed assets destroyed or damaged, Book value or estimated cost of inventories destroyed or damaged, Salvage, Insurance settlement. Coinsurance clause, Contribution clause, Mortgage clause. Business interruption insurance. *Insurable employee risks:* Life insurance, Participating, Nonparticipating; Ordinary life insurance, Cash surrender value, Accounting for cash surrender value, Insurance settlements, Financial statement presentation; Group life insurance, Group plans. *Miscellaneous insurable employee risks:* Health insurance, Accounting for health insurance; Workmen's compensation and employers' liability insurance, Cost of workmen's compensation insurance, Accounting for workmen's compensation, Unexpired workmen's compensation insurance account, Miscellaneous policy provisions; Fidelity bonds. *Self-insurance:* Accounting for self-insured risks, Accrual basis, Reporting of provision (reserve) for self-insurance; Nonaccrual basis. *Accounting for pension costs:* Nonaccrual basis, Cost of pension plans, Funded Versus unfunded plans, Past and prior service costs.

### 5  Accounting for the Administration of Income / 123

*Income measurement versus income administration:* Interest charges as a distribution of income, Interest charges as an expense; *Allocation of income:* Allocation of income—partnerships, Allocation according to capital ratio, Allocation according to specified ratio, Allocation of partnership losses, Salary allowance, Interest allowance, Salary, interest, and ratio; Allocation of income—corporations, Appropriated income; Allocation of income—estates and trusts, Illustration: charge and discharge statement—as to income. *Distribution of income:* Accounting for undistributed income, Nondisclosure of undistributed income, Stock dividends as a means of disclosure, Appropriations as a means of disclosure; Nature of a distribution of income; Determination of time of distribution; Legal aspects of asset severance, Scrip dividend, Bonds as a distribution of income, Stock dividend; Valuation of distribution of income, Illustration—dividend in kind.

## 6 Valuation of the Enterprise / 149

*Methods of valuation:* Valuation at acquisition cost less allocation for usage; Valuation by earning power, Theoretical approach, Practical approach, Valuation by appraisal, Accounting for appraisals, Valuation in terms of common dollars, Common-dollar valuation illustrated. *Valuation of partnerships:* No valuation adjustment recorded; Purchase of an interest from one partner, Purchase of an interest from several partners, Adjustment of capital accounts, Distribution of cash, Purchase price equals book value, Purchase price less than book value, Purchase price more than book value; Valuation adjustment recorded, Purchase price less than book value, Purchase price more than book value; Special problems if valuation adjustments are not recorded; Illustration. *Special enterprise valuation problems:* Refunding bonds outstanding, Alternative plans available, The discounting process, Accounting for refunding of bonds; Valuation of bonds payable, Bond premium or bond discount, Determination of issuance price, Determination of effective interest cost. Accounting for interest costs; Valuation of fixed assets, Discounting process applied to depreciation, Interest methods.

## Part III  EXPANSION OF THE BUSINESS ORGANIZATION

### 7 Investment for Expansion / 199

*Accounting data for investment decisions:* Role of accounting, Total annual cost and revenue, Differential costing, Utilization costing, Measuring utilization cost, Rate of return; Nonaccounting considerations; Illustration using accounting data for expansion planning; Limitations and qualifications. *Financing plans—general:* Estimating funds from internal sources, Utilizing nonincome operational funds; Capitalizing retained earnings, Recognition by accounting entries, Recognition by stock dividend, Recorded at par value, Recorded at market value, Proper accounting treatment, Recognition by stock split-up, Summary. *External financing of expansion:* New partner as a source of funds, Bonus to old partners, Bonus to new partner, Bonus procedure summarized, Bonus procedure evaluated, Goodwill to old partners, Goodwill to new partner, Goodwill to all partners. *Expansion and financing as one activity:* Methods of expansion.

8 **Expansion by Branch Operations / 231**

Separate ledgers, Factory ledger, Private ledger. *Branch accounting concepts and procedures:* Establishing the branch, Working fund, Separate ledger, Establishing the branch, Operations of the branch, Merchandise billed above cost, Shipments to branch, Branch sales, Illustration — branch accounting, Interbranch transfers; Combined financial statements; Foreign branches.

9 **Expansion by Subsidiary Companies / 257**

*The subsidiary company:* Reasons for subsidiary companies. *Consolidated statements:* When to consolidate, Controlling financial interest, Majority-owned subsidiary, Control without stock ownership, Homogeneous operations, Different fiscal periods, Consolidation policy; Limitations of consolidated statements, Minority stockholders, Creditors, Financial analysts; Unconsolidated subsidiaries; Theories of consolidated statements; Summary.

10 **Consolidated Statements at Date of Acquisition / 272**

Basic consolidating procedures, Elimination of reciprocal elements, Establishment of reciprocity, Consolidation of nonreciprocal elements; Types of statements consolidated; Consolidated statement of financial position at date of acquisition, 100% ownership, Illustration A-1 — 100% ownership acquired at book value, Basic procedure; Illustration A-2 — 100% ownership acquired at more than book value. Basic procedure; Illustration A-3 — 100% ownership acquired at less than book value, Basic procedure; Consolidated goodwill; Less than 100% ownership, Illustration B-1 — less than 100% ownership acquired at book value, Basic procedure, Statement presentation of minority interest, Reconciliation of illustrations B-1 and A-1; Illustration B-2 — less than 100% ownership acquired at more than book value, Basic procedure, Reconciliation of illustrations B-2 and A-2; Illustration B-3 — less than 100% ownership acquired at less than book value, Basic procedure, Reconciliation of illustrations B-3 and A-3; Miscellaneous intercompany items; Consolidated statement of retained earnings at acquisition date; Accounting for the difference between cost and book value of subsidiary stock acquired.

11 **Consolidated Statements Subsequent to Date of Acquisition — Investment Carried at Cost / 300**

Methods of carrying investments in subsidiaries. *Cost method:* Consolidated statement of financial position — investment carried at cost, Basic consolidating procedure, Establishment of reciprocity; 100% ownership, Illustration A-$1_1$ — 100% ownership acquired at book value, Basic procedure, The establishment of reciprocity, The elimination of reciprocals, The consolidation of nonreciprocals; Illustration A-$2_1$ — 100% ownership acquired at more than book value, Basic procedure; Illustration A-$3_1$ — 100% ownership acquired at less than book value, Basic procedure; Less than 100% ownership, Illustration

B-1₁—less than 100% ownership acquired at book value, Basic procedure; illustration B-2₁—less than 100% ownership acquired at more than book value, Basic procedure; Illustration B-3₁—less than 100% ownership acquired at less than book value, Basic procedure; Consolidated statement of income and retained earnings—investment carried at cost, Illustration C-1, Basic procedure; Illustration C-2, Basic procedure, Trial balance approach; illustration D-1, Illustration D-2, Illustration D-3.

## 12  Consolidated Statements Subsequent to Date of Acquisition—Investment Not Carried at Cost / 334

*Equity method:* Consolidated statement of financial position—equity method, Basic consolidating procedure, 100% ownership—illustration A-1₁₍ₐ₎, 100% ownership acquired at book value, Basic procedure; Illustration A-2₁₍ₐ₎, 100% ownership acquired at more than book value, Basic procedure; Illustration A-3₁₍ₐ₎, 100% ownership acquired at less than book value, Basic procedure; Less than 100% ownership—Illustration B-1₁₍ₐ₎, less than 100% ownership acquired at book value, Basic procedure; Illustration B-2₁₍ₐ₎ less than 100% ownership acquired at more than book value, Basic procedure; Illustration B-3₁₍ₐ₎, less than 100% ownership acquired at less than book value, Basic procedure; Consolidated statement of income and retained earnings—investment carried at equity, Illustration C-1₁, Basic procedure; Illustration C-2₁, Basic procedure. Trial balance approach, Illustration D-1₁, Illustration D-2₁, Illustration D-3₁.

## 13  Consolidated Statements—Intercompany Profit Transactions / 364

*Intercompany inventory transactions:* 100% ownership of selling affiliate; Less than 100% ownership in selling affiliate; One hundred per cent elimination, Entire amount eliminated from consolidated retained earnings, Elimination divided between consolidated retained earnings and the minority interest, Work sheet illustration, Trial balance approach. *Intercompany fixed asset transactions:* Nondepreciating fixed assets; Depreciating fixed assets, Trial balance approach. *Intercompany bond transactions:* 100% elimination from consolidated retained earnings, 100% elimination prorated between consolidated retained earnings and minority interest, Trial balance approach.

## 14  Consolidated Statements—Intercompany Stock Transactions / 398

*Acquisition of subsidiary stock:* Acquisition of control and the date of acquisition; Purchase of subsidiary stock subsequent to acquisition of control; Purchase of subsidiary stock at interim dates; Interim acquisition of control, Interim purchase subsequent to acquisition of control. *Disposal of subsidiary stock:* Complete disposal; Partial disposal, partial disposal at an interim date,

Effect of partial disposals on consolidated goodwill, Effect of partial disposals on subsequent consolidations. *Subsidiary stock transactions:* Issuance of additional shares of subsidiary stock, Issuance by sale, Sale at book value, Sale above book value, Basic procedure, Sale below book value, Basic procedure; Subsidiary stock distributions, Capitalization considered as part of consolidated paid-in capital, Capitalization considered as part of consolidated retained earnings; Treasury stock transactions; Preferred stock, At date of acquisition, Subsequent to date of acquisition.

## 15 Consolidated Statements—Indirect Ownership and Mutual Stockholdings / 446

*Indirect ownership:* Major and minor parents, First illustration, Second illustration; Connecting affiliates, First illustration, Second illustration; Combination of major and minor parents and a connecting affiliate. *Mutual stockholdings:* Mutual stockholdings between subsidiaries, First illustration, Second illustration; Mutual stockholdings between parent and subsidiary; Mutual stockholdings between subsidiaries and between the parent and subsidiaries; Mutual stockholdings as treasury stock. Effect of indirect ownership and mutual stockholdings on intercompany-profit eliminations: Indirect ownership—major and minor parent, Indirect ownership—connecting affiliate, Mutual stockholdings, Combination of indirect ownership and mutual stockholdings.

## 16 Consolidated Statements—Comprehensive Review / 478

*Consolidation at date of acquisition;* Summary. *Consolidation subsequent to date of acquisition:* Summary. *Intercompany profit transactions:* Intercompany profits in inventories, Intercompany profits in fixed assets, Summary. *Intercompany stock transactions:* Disposal of subsidiary stock, Acquisition of additional subsidiary stock, Effects of intercompany stock transactions upon subsequent consolidations, Summary; Indirect ownership and mutual stockholdings, Major and minor parent, Connecting affiliate, Mutual stockholdings, Summary; Trial balance approach, Summary.

## 17 Consolidated Statements Reexamined / 526

Limitations, Disclosure, Additional problems. *Consolidation policies:* Criteria for consolidation, Legal considerations, Economic considerations; The meaning of control, reexamination of the control concept, Large block of minority interest; Conclusion on consolidation policy. *Statement presentation:* Valuation of consolidated assets. Dual valuation, Imputed valuation, Unresolved valuation problems, Amortization of goodwill, Reexamination of the valuation of consolidated assets; Intercompany gains and losses; Valuation of minority interest, Illustration; Valuation of consolidated retained earnings, Statement of changes in consolidated retained earnings—illustrated, Change in parent company's percent of ownership of subsidiary; Change in composition of consolidated entity; Unconsolidated subsidiaries.

## 18 Expansion by Foreign Operations / 554

Domestic company with foreign transactions; Foreign sales, Foreign purchases, Realized versus unrealized exchange gain or loss, Assets transmitted for sale in a foreign country, Assets transmitted for use in a foreign country, Assets transmitted versus assets acquired in a foreign country, Foreign operations; Foreign branches, Translation rates, Monetary assets and liabilities, Nonmonetary assets and liabilities, Reciprocal accounts, Nominal accounts, Exchange gain or loss, Realized gains and losses, Unrealized gains and losses; Foreign branch accounting illustrated; Foreign subsidiaries, Translation rates; Consolidation of foreign subsidiaries illustrated.

## 19 Expansion by Combination / 584

*Precombination considerations:* Types of business combinations; Definitions; Basic accounting distinctions; Pooling-of-interests accounting; Purchase accounting; Summary; Classification of the combination transaction; Practice since *APB Opinion No. 16;* Pro forma statements; Pro forma statement illustrated, Accounting for business combinations—an example; Impact on subsequent financial statements; Accounting for combinations—a reevaluation; Distribution of securities.

# Part IV CONTRACTION OF THE BUSINESS ORGANIZATION

## 20 Disinvestment / 621

Enterprise contraction, Accounting for contraction. *Asset realization:* Accounting for asset realization, Sale for cash and for interest-bearing securities, Sale for noninterest-bearing securities, Determination of cash equivalent of securities, Interest earned—straight-line approach, Interest earned—actuarial approach, Sale for stock of acquiring corporation. *Asset revaluation:* Decline in economic values, Accounting for decline in economic values, Decline in value due to obsolescence, Accounting for decline due to obsolescence. *Debt retirement:* Retirement of short-term debt, Early extinguishment of long-term debt; Retirement of bonds outstanding—at par, Retirement of bonds outstanding—at a premium, Refunding of bonds outstanding, Alternatives to debt retirement. *Residual equity retirements:* Retirement or sale of partnership interest, Basis of settlement with retiring partner, illustration, Adherence to cost principle, Revaluation of assets, Recognition of goodwill, Bonus to retiring partner, Deferred settlement on retirement; Payment of corporate liquidating dividend, Accounting for a liquidating dividend; Reacquisition of corporation's own stock, Reporting of stock reacquired, Stock reacquired at issue price, Stock reacquired at less than issue price, Stock reacquired at more than issue price; Retirement of one or more classes of stock, Exercise of call option, Use of an agent to effect retirement, Retirement without a call option. *Summary.*

## 21 Reorganizations / 654

Legal background, Acounting background. *Quasi reorganization:* Characteristics, Upward versus downward revaluations, Revaluations in a quasi reorganization; Illustration of quasi reorganization, Adjustment of assets, Adjustment of equities, Adjustments of both assets and equities. Dating of retained earnings. *Financial reorganizations:* Securing an extension of time for payments to creditors; Asset exchange for debt, Refinancing of debt, Refinancing at face value. Refinancing with a call premium, Unamortized discount or premium on issue outstanding, Immediate write-off, Amortization over life of original issue, Amortization over life of new issue; Creditor committee; Equity receivership, Legal procedures, Accounting procedures; Reorganizations under bankruptcy act, Legal procedures, Accounting procedures, Illustration — reorganization of F Corporation, Summary.

# Part V  LIQUIDATION OF THE BUSINESS ORGANIZATION

## 22  Proprietorship Liquidation / 689

Reasons for a business liquidation, Liquidation procedures; Bankruptcy, Insolvency versus bankruptcy, Involuntary bankruptcy, Acts of bankruptcy, General bankruptcy procedure, Summary. *Liquidation of proprietorships:* Liquidation because of death of the proprietor, Role of the accountant, General legal procedures, Duties of executor, Realization and liquidation by an executor; Accounting for estate liquidation, Opening accountability records, Entries in accountability records, Pro forma entries for estate liquidation, Estate principal versus estate income, Estate principal and income problems, Classification of estate expenditures; Accounting for proprietorship liquidation; Executor's report to the court.

## 23  Partnership Liquidation / 723

Causes of partnership dissolution; Accounting for liquidation of a partnership; Death of a partner; Liquidation of a partnership after complete realization of assets, Group 1 illustrations, Group 2 illustrations, Group 3 illustrations; Liquidation of a partnership by installment, General rules for distribution of cash, Illustrations; Miscellaneous problems, Advance planning for cash distributions.

## 24 Corporate Liquidation / 770

Reasons for corporate dissolution, Corporate liquidation versus dissolution; Tax considerations, Types of corporate liquidations, Corporate liquidation by trustee; Significance of current values, Example of presentation, Reporting deficiency in resources, Additional considerations. *Receivership in equity:* Receivership accounting, General concepts, Basic procedures, Receiver's reports. Termination of receivership. Realization and liquidation statement, Illustration, Closing out the receivership, Summary.

**Appendix A. Actuarial Science: Compound Interest and Probability / 807**

**Appendix B. Governmental (Fund) Accounting / 851**

**Appendix T. Tables of Amounts and Present Values / 876**

**Appendix TH. Table of Area Under Normal Curve / 885**

# PART ONE:
# Formation of the Business Organization

# 1
# The Conceptual and Theoretical Background

Accounting has found its greatest field of usefulness in measuring, recording, classifying, summarizing, communicating, and interpreting the economic events of individual business units. In fact, accounting is primarily a method of analyzing the various economic activities of an enterprise. This description of accounting embodies a number of significant features: accounting includes a data-recording system; the records contain factual and analyzed data; these data result from economic activities—transactions in a broad sense; the economic activities are those of the enterprise for which the records are maintained; and the data from accounting, when properly interpreted, are useful in evaluating the accountability function of an enterprise and in reaching forward-looking business decisions.

## The Role of Accounting

Accounting serves a number of roles in our economic society. Most generally, accounting's role is described as the measurement of enterprise economic activities and the accumulation of data useful for performance evaluation and decision-making. These roles are rather broadly stated, but greater insight into the real impact of accounting can come only from a more precise identification of the roles that it plays in an economic society.

Many authorities agree that in a competitive economic society effective management of the scarce resources of land, labor, and capital determines in large measure the success of an enterprise. Effective management involves timely and well-informed decisions concerning the resources that are available to an enterprise. As our economic society has mushroomed in complexity in recent years, management has begun to rely to an increasing degree on accounting data and reports as bases for reaching decisions on important matters. Some areas of managerial decisions for which accounting information has proved useful include potential avenues of expansion, either through acquisitions, new product development, or new territory development; potential avenues of capital accumulation, either through sales of stock, long-term borrowing, leasing, or retention of earned income; potential avenues of allocating the resources available among competing demands for such things as new products, new markets, new techniques, and research; and potential alternatives for minimization of the impact of taxation.

On the other hand, accounting serves an additional role of considerable importance in an economic society. Through accounting data and reports, we are provided with a basis for evaluation of the performance of the business unit. Investors and credit grantors have a direct interest in the evaluation of performance, since these groups provide the land and capital for management to utilize in their business unit. A further responsibility exists: In any economic society there is a genuine need for society to be able to evaluate the performance of those who guide the utilization of the scarce resources available for economic effort. Accounting provides the basis for evaluation of the effectiveness of use of these resources.

The significance of these roles creates a substantial responsibility for accounting to provide data and reports of maximum usefulness. The information that accounting provides must be reliable and factual; it must be relevant to the business unit being reported on; it must be presented in a form adaptable to analysis and interpretation. These responsibilities impose on accounting the necessity to develop concepts, techniques, and procedures that will provide reliable information on business activity. These concepts, techniques, and procedures must also give recognition to the environment in which accounting activity is expected to operate. A brief look at some aspects of this environment may help to explain further the nature and role of accounting.

## External Conditions Affecting Accounting

Accounting is a product of its environment. Like other aspects of our society, it is affected by, and in turn has an effect upon, the environmental conditions existing at any time. The environmental, or external, conditions that have a direct influence on accounting are too numerous to identify completely or to discuss in detail. Social attitudes, legal conditions, business practices, economic concepts, and moral and ethical standards all have an influence on shaping the direction of accounting actions. Some external conditions seem to have had a more direct impact on accounting development, however, and these bear specific consideration.[1]

**Scarce Means.** The fundamental external condition which finds considerable expression in accounting is the fact that man lives in a world of scarce economic means. The existence of income measurement as the indicator of success in

---

[1] For a more complete discussion of some of the ideas developed here and in the following section, see *A Statement of Basic Accounting Postulates and Principles,* Center for International Education and Research in Accounting, Urbana, Illinois, 1964.

economic activities is directly related to this fact. Assets find expression on statements of financial condition principally because they have value to the enterprise, and this value arises from the fact of scarcity. Emphasis on control, protection of property, and reduction of waste and inefficiency are all related to the scarcity of resources. It is difficult to visualize the shape that accounting would take in an environment in which economic scarcity was not a fact of life.

**Standards of Equity.** The fact that man has developed certain laws and standards of conduct to control human behavior is another environmental condition affecting accounting. Current legal and ethical ideas of property and other rights provide boundaries of a sort for accounting actions. Thus, in providing data that may be used by conflicting interests, accounting accepts standards of equity and fairness, both legal and moral, that already exist in its environment. Accounting does not make its own laws or establish its own standards of equity. Rather, accounting finds within its environment the existing standards to determine equity among the varying interests in the enterprise. These standards condition to some extent the direction of accounting actions.

**Rational and Prudent Conduct.** As an economic society increases in complexity, certain individuals with property (capital) are moved to entrust the custodianship and control of all or a part of their property to others. In fact, this is one of the important characteristics of a complex economy—the utilization of the property of others in an economic endeavor. Those entrusted with the use of the property are assumed to act rationally and within the accepted bounds of honesty and fairness unless there is evidence to the contrary. This condition of rational and prudent conduct is important to accounting primarily because of the incomplete nature of many transactions at any given time. The fact that rational and prudent conduct is an expected pattern of behavior means that accounting can place reliance on data flowing from transactions. There is no need to examine the motivation and authenticity of every transaction in the absence of evidence suggesting irrational or irresponsible conduct.

## Fundamental Assumptions of Accounting

A thorough understanding of the nature and role of accounting in an economic society requires consideration of the conceptual framework and certain fundamental assumptions. The term "accounting postulates" has been used to describe the underlying assumptions of accounting which are generally accepted as valid. These fundamental assumptions provide a basis for reasoning in the development of accounting principles and other important concepts in accounting. Each postulate has an important place in the theory and practice of accounting. While it is true that we may learn to carry out many technical or mechanical aspects of accounting without a thorough understanding of these postulates, it is also true that the resolution of many difficult problems requires a sound grounding in these important accounting ideas. Reference to these postulates should be helpful in circumstances in which two or more approaches to an accounting issue appear to be justifiable.

Because accounting is utilitarian and constantly adjusts to changing economic conditions, these postulates of accounting are more in the nature of general assumptions than in the nature of fixed and unyielding axioms. Although no authoritative listing of the fundamental accounting assumptions has been widely accepted, most of the following have fairly widespread recognition.

**Usefulness.** The basic assumption is that accounting data and reports must provide useful information to a wide number of users having different interests. Although this may appear to be a self-evident proposition, it is important that it be clearly expressed and well understood. Accounting information of an enterprise is not aimed at one single user of financial and economic reports. Rather, accounting data have wide usefulness and, therefore, emphasis must be placed on their validity and reliability so that their usefulness is not impaired.

**Entity.** Economic activity is engaged in by a business unit, an entity, which is separate and distinct from the owners of the business unit. These entities constitute units of accountability around which accounting interest centers. This proposition has greatly influenced the development of accounting. It has allowed for the extension of accounting to cover transactions between the business unit and the owners. Overall, it seems appropriate to suggest that the entity concept has contributed much to the rather amazing growth of accounting as a technique for collecting and recording economic data in a systematic manner. Of central importance here is recognition that an accounting report relates to one specific business unit or entity. This postulate has considerable impact on financial reporting and also has an impact on the boundaries of accounting.

**Significant Activities.** Accounting is concerned only with the significant economic activities of an entity, though accounting procedures are heavily concerned with exchange transactions, and with those other activities whose results are essentially the same as exchange transactions, between the entity and other enterprises or individuals. This postulate introduces one type of boundary of accounting. Accounting is concerned with specific entities, and only with certain activities of those entities. The activities that are of interest to accounting are frequently evidenced by transactions—exchanges of economic values between the entity and others. Certain other activities of substance—for example, the passage of time in connection with accrued interest, fires, thefts, or the imposition of taxes—possess attributes that make them appear to be essentially the same as transactions. Also, revaluations may at times provide significant information. Accounting includes these activities within its area of interest.

**Price.** The money price associated with the transactions or other significant activities of the enterprise provides an appropriate basis for recording accounting data. The price generated by transactions of the enterprise with other enterprises or individuals is relevant to the enterprise, is objectively determinable, and provides useful data to facilitate subsequent analysis. This postulate is sometimes phrased in such a way as to indicate that accounting assumes that the price level is stable or that the monetary unit is stable. Such an assumption is inappropriate for accounting. The postulate as stated does not limit accounting data to the acquisition price or historical cost. Rather, it asserts that transaction-price data hold a significant place in accounting. During times of changing price levels, modifications and adjustments of price data may be desirable or even essential. When such conditions exist, disclosure of any adjustments made and their effects on the data reported is important.

**Continuity or Going Concern.** Underlying many accounting procedures is the assumption that the enterprise will continue to operate in the future in much the same manner as it has operated in the past unless persuasive evidence exists to the contrary. Since a substantial number of the transactions of the enterprise are in a somewhat indeterminate status at any reporting date, accounting needs to make some assumption as to the future of the enterprise. For example, receivables are not collected, items in inventory have not been sold, fixed assets possess unexpired usefulness. Some anticipation of the future disposition of these assets is necessary. Although it has been proposed that accounting measures should assume liquidation of the enterprise, accounting normally assumes that an entity will continue to exist.

**Periodicity.** The uninterrupted flow of economic activity of an enterprise can be identified with specific periods in which the enterprise operates. Implicit in this postulate is the need of users of accounting data for timely reporting of the results of activities of the period. Two distinct views prevail: (1) activities involving changes in the value of assets and liabilities should be reported or (2) activities involving changes in revenue and expense should be reported. Also implicit is the idea that each transaction of an enterprise has a peculiar relevance to a specified time period. Many difficult problems in accounting have their source in this idea that the uninterrupted life of an enterprise can be divided into time periods and specific transactions identified with a given period on some reasonable basis.

## Principles and Standards of Accounting

Much controversy exists within the accounting profession regarding the nature and role of accounting standards and principles. In theory, principles are commonly derived from certain fundamental assumptions, axioms, or postulates. Such derivation generally relies upon logical reasoning, or deductive analysis. Thus, accounting principles should, it would seem, flow from the basic postulates of accounting with due recognition being accorded the environmental conditions within which accounting operates.

In actuality, however, accounting principles—or at least those propositions of accounting that carry the status of accounting standards—have developed out of accounting practice, very largely in an inductive manner. As business has taken on novel or at least different aspects, accountants have developed practices, methods, procedures, and rules for their analysis and interpretation. As these practices, methods, procedures, and rules come to be more widely recognized and accepted as useful aspects of accounting, they come, in the mass, to be recognized as "generally accepted accounting principles" or "standards." Thus, the main test that any proposition must meet to warrant the label "accounting principles" has been the test of general acceptance.

It is at this point that accounting theory and accounting practice diverge. Most accountants would agree that accounting principles should be derived in logical fashion from the underlying postulates of the field. Likewise, most accountants would agree that accounting principles are derived from the mass of practices, methods, procedures, and rules that gain the label of general acceptability.

A number of topics generally discussed in elementary and intermediate accounting indicate the absence of fully logical analysis. For example, the existence of FIFO, LIFO, and average cost methods of inventory pricing with all appearing to be equally acceptable in any situation appears somewhat illogical. Again, the acceptability of straight-line, double declining balance, and sum-of-the-years' digits as depreciation methods with little regard for the nature of the asset or its physical absorption raises certain questions regarding accounting principles. Subsequent sections of this book examine additional areas of accounting in which the generally accepted principle appears to suffer from a lack of logic.

Over the years considerable effort has been aimed at clarifying accounting principles and eliminating those that appear inappropriate, and more of such effort will be necessary. At the same time, changes in business practices have required new accounting methods and procedures that have gained the status of generally accepted accounting principles even though they are not logically derived from more basic underlying postulates of accounting. Attempts to relate specific accounting practices, methods, procedures, and rules to the basic postulates should be fruitful for the student. Such analyses will pinpoint areas of weakness in accounting theory, areas on which more effort must be expended if accounting is to serve the economic society most effectively.

## Social Significance of Accounting

From the social standpoint, accounting may be conceived of as part of the mechanism that enables management to use enterprise data in directing economic action. As a result, economic resources are directed to profitable uses and are used in an efficient manner to produce the goods and services needed by society. Consumers benefit from better products at lower prices, and the entire economy benefits by having produced more goods and services than it might have produced otherwise.

As the economy becomes more complex through increases in the size of organizational units, through increased demand generated by larger populations, through advances in technology, and through greater interaction on the part of government planning, the challenge to accounting increases in like manner. In recent years many of the challenges have been met by utilization of the computer, and increased activity in this direction by accounting is certain. Complexity and challenge, however, do not minimize the necessity for a full grasp of basic ideas in accounting. Rather, the need for fuller understanding must increase so that maximum benefit may be derived from the computer and from other sophisticated tools of analysis.

The relatively rigid boundaries of accounting which have been widely accepted in the past need reappraisal. The interpretive function of accounting encompasses concepts that extend beyond the entity. Social and economic planning contemplates broader implications than the single entity. Accounting data, generated by economic activities of the entity, but interpreted in the light of broader social, regional, and politico-economic implications, will play an increasingly significant role in reaching decisions on complex issues.

The directing force in the production and distribution of goods and services to consumers is the central management of the entity. This management coordinates the utilization of land, properties, and labor in an effective manner. Management provides organization to the entity and, in fact, enables the entity to take on the necessary aspects of an operating organization. Because of the need for an understanding of the social features of accounting and since accounting is one of the chief tools used by management to solve enterprise problems, it is perhaps only logical that an advanced study of accounting be approached from a study of the various problems faced by a business organization from its inception to its possible termination. Organizations may be profit- or nonprofit-oriented and may take several forms — proprietorships, partnerships, corporations, trusts, joint ventures — but the business corporation is unquestionably the most significant to our economy. Accordingly, in this book primary emphasis is placed on the corporate form of organization, although peculiar problems associated with the other forms of organization are also discussed.

## Accounting View of the Enterprise — Proprietary Versus Entity Theory

The accounting concept of the business organization is that it is a distinct being or entity in and of itself. The entity postulate contributes to this concept and is consistent with many facts of economic activity. Transactions are entered into and consummated by the organization as a unit separate and distinct from identifiable parts of the organization. The view of the enterprise as an entity is simply an extension of this concept. In accounting parlance this concept is frequently referred to as the "enterprise entity concept."

Recognition and general acceptance of this view of the enterprise are relatively recent. Prior to the 1930's, a different view, the proprietary theory, had widespread acceptance. In fact, much of the breakthrough in accounting thought on the nature of the accounting entity can be traced back to this time when the question of the proper accounting entity was a topic of discussion. According to the entity theory, the assets belong to the entity, and the liabilities and equities represent sources of the assets, whether in the form of capital stock, a note payable, or any other type of equity. Even when equities are viewed as claims to assets rather than sources of assets, the entity theory is a valid concept.

According to the proprietary theory, the assets of the enterprise are owned effectively by the shareholders (or other owners), and the liabilities are considered as liabilities of the shareholders. In the case of the sole proprietorship and the partnership, the proprietary theory is pretty much in accordance with the legal facts of the situation. Partners and proprietors may well have to pay business liabilities out of personal assets if the business cannot pay them. Legally the debts of the business are a liability of the partners or proprietors, and the assets of the business really belong to the partners or proprietors.

In the case of the corporation, however, the legal facts of the situation support the entity theory. The shareholders of the corporation assume no liability for the debts of the corporation and cannot withdraw assets from the corporation without corporate approval and action.

The law thus provides no clear-cut support for either the entity theory or the proprietary theory. It supports both theories in different circumstances, which is not a desirable situation from an accounting point of view. To make the basic postulates of accounting depend upon the type of legal form of the business allows an inconsistency in accounting procedures which is held to be undesirable. While accountants might contend that the corporate form of business dominates business activity to such a degree that the accounting unit should always be the separate entity, many accounting procedures are based on the proprietary theory. For example, the income of a business is computed as the income accruing to the shareholders, rather than as the income accruing to all creditors and equity holders. Interest charges are considered to be an expense of operations, but dividends on all types of capital stock are considered to be a distribution of income under the proprietary theory. Both interest and dividends would be a distribution of income under the entity theory. Contemporary accounting practice in the reporting of income thus conforms to the proprietary theory. But in the basic accounting equation that assets equal equities, the concept of the accounting unit as a separate and distinct entity prevails.

It is the opinion of the authors that the entity theory conforms more closely to the economic reality of business operations. Prior to the growth of the corporate form of business enterprise, the proprietary theory was undoubtedly the economic reality of business operations, and it still dominates accounting practice in many areas. Thus it appears that accounting procedures are in a period of transition from those based on the proprietary theory to those based on the entity theory. This causes some confusion to students learning accounting procedures, because it precludes consistent reasoning from one accepted base.

With this background in mind, let us now turn to a description and analysis of the problems involved in accounting for the formation of the various forms of business organizations or entities.

# FORMS OF BUSINESS ORGANIZATION

## The Proprietorship

A business owned entirely by one individual is frequently referred to as a single proprietorship. In early times the manufacture of goods and the sale of goods and services were conducted on a much smaller scale than they are at present. Large amounts of capital were not necessary and, as a result, the dominant type of business organization was the single proprietorship. As the small entrepreneurial system of Adam Smith's day evolved into the capitalistic enterprise system of today, more capital was needed than one person could provide or would be willing to risk. As a consequence, other forms of business organization such as the partnership and corporation took on added importance. Even today, however, there are still many units of small size. In the United States the number of single proprietorships exceeds that of all other types of ownership.

**Legal Aspects of Proprietorships.** From the legal standpoint there is not much involved in the formation, operation, and dissolution of a proprietorship. To form a proprietorship, since no contractual arrangement or charter is necessary, all the owner has to do is to obtain the necessary operating license(s), and he is ready to start operations.

In certain types of business, it may be necessary for a man to establish proof of his ability in the field of business he is entering. For example, a pharmacist, a lawyer, a doctor, or a certified public accountant generally must pass an examination before opening an office. Also, certain types of businesses, such as a barber shop, may be subjected to special regulations. In some states a certificate of doing business has to be filed if the company has a special trade name. Essentially, however, the process of forming a sole proprietorship is one of gathering the funds, deciding what to do, and acquiring facilities to carry on the business. During operations, the only legal requirements to be met are the usual federal, state, and local regulatory agency requirements such as the filing of various tax returns. If the owner of a single proprietorship desires to discontinue his business, he may do so without consulting anyone. No other kind of business organization can be dissolved so easily.

**Accounting Aspects of Proprietorship Formation.** The procedure of establishing a recording system for a proprietorship has been discussed in elementary accounting. The most important consideration in the process is the recognition, classification, and valuation of the various assets and equities of the new enterprise. In general, assets are recognized as a part of the entity at the time of transfer to it, are classified and grouped according to their legal or physical form, and are valued at their fair market value on the date they are contributed to the business. Equities are recognized and classified on similar bases, but are valued on the basis of their ultimate claim to assets or on the basis of the value of the assets contributed by the equity interests.

In the formation of any business, sound financing requires that attention be directed to certain fundamental considerations. Some considerations on which the accountant may be called for information, are the following:

1. The best source of funds for the business.
2. The best use to which funds should be directed.
3. Selection of assets for effective liquidity and maximum earning capacity.

Normally, anyone forming a new business would conduct a thorough investigation of the need for the proposed business venture. This investigation might include market surveys of consumer needs, review of the availability of supplies, employees, and materials, and a study of financing methods appropriate for the undertaking. These planning procedures normally provide data that can be developed into an accounting budget or report. Usually, projected (pro forma) balance sheets and income statements for a number of years in the future may be used to convey to the prospective owner an articulated view of anticipated activities of the business.

Once these considerations have been evaluated and resolved by the prospective new business owner, the process of recording the actual formation of a proprietorship follows the procedures outlined in elementary accounting.

## The Partnership

The partnership form of business organization is used for a variety of reasons. Typical of the conditions that may lead to the formation of a partnership are the following:

1. The capital requirements of a business enterprise may exceed the amount of capital that may be raised by a single proprietor or the amount of capital that an individual may wish to invest in a particular venture when he would have no one to help him assume risks.
2. A single proprietor, partnership, or business organization may wish to obtain or retain the talents or services of others.
3. For some reason, frequently professional in nature, a group of people may wish to form a business organization where limited liability, as found in the corporate form of business organization, is undesirable.

**Legal Aspects of Partnerships.** The Uniform Partnership Act, which has been adopted by a majority of the states, defines a partnership as "an association of two or more persons to carry on as co-owners a business for profit." A "person," as defined by the Act, includes individuals, partnerships, corporations, and other associations.

A partnership may be "general" or "limited." In the general partnership, each partner has unlimited liability, that is, he may be liable personally for all of the organization's debts. In the limited partnership, however, the liability of a certain partner or partners is limited to a particular amount. Limited partnerships cannot be formed in all states; in those states permitting them, *at least one* partner must be a general partner.

Since a partnership is based on a contract between two or more persons, it is important, although not necessarily a legal requirement, that special attention be given to the drawing up of the partnership agreement. This agreement is generally referred to as the "Articles of Copartnership." In order to avoid unnecessary and perhaps costly litigation at some later date, the Articles should contain all of the terms of the agreement relating to the formation, operation, and dissolution of the partnership. For example, these terms should include provisions such as those below.

1. Amount and nature of capital to be invested by each partner, and the basis of valuation for assets other than cash.
2. Basis of division of profits and losses.
3. Rate and other details concerning the calculation of interest, if any, to be charged each partner on withdrawals and to be allowed on capital.
4. Conditions under which the partnership might be terminated before the time originally designated.

Since the partnership agreement is essentially a legal matter, partners are well advised to seek legal counsel prior to forming the partnership.

**Accounting Aspects of Partnership Formation.** Establishing a data-recording system for a partnership differs little from opening the books of a proprietorship. Similar recognition points and classification schemes are used, but the determination of fair market value of assets and equities is more objective, just because all partners must agree on the valuation, and not as subjective as in the case of the sole proprietor. A partner contributing assets to a partnership may want his assets valued high, and those contributed by his fellow partners valued low. In arriving at an appropriate valuation, major emphasis would normally be placed upon the fair market value of the assets at the time of their contribution to the partnership. The problem of asset valuation in the formation of a partnership is generally solved by mutual agreement among the partners. Such agreements normally reflect fair market value of the assets contributed by the various partners. Where a suitable fair market value is not available, the partners must reach some agreement on an acceptable valuation. The role of the accountant in this process is one of disclosing fully the implications of different valuations. Equity among partners, in partnership formations, is essential for a lasting partnership. After contributed assets have been valued correctly, the entries to open the records of the partnership would be recorded as set forth in elementary accounting.

## The Corporation

In early business ventures the conflict of interests between creditors and owners was relatively nonexistent, since the resources upon which the enterprise operated consisted almost entirely of owner contributions. Few, if any, resources were provided by either long-term or short-term creditors. Among other factors, the social and religious ideas of the time were unfavorable to lending which, in turn, tended to keep borrowing at a minimum. At the end of a venture, debts were paid and the residue divided among the joint contributors or partners. Any creditors that might have existed were protected because they generally contributed a relatively small portion of the capital, and because of the unlimited liability of each of the venturers.

After continuing partnerships began to replace ventures, it was not long before business organizations with special charters made their appearance. One important feature of some of these charters was that they limited ownership liability. With the appearance of limited ownership liability, contributions by the owners became the essential margin of protection for creditors. As a result, careful and accurate accounting became more important to creditors.

The desire of security holders, particularly shareholders, to limit their liability and perhaps their responsibility appears to have been one of the most powerful forces contributing to the growth of the business unit from the owner-manager type of Adam Smith's day into the corporate form of organization as it now exists. In the modern corporation, resources are contributed and business risks are assumed usually by absentee owners. The appointment of agents, frequently referred to as "professional managers," for business purposes by absentee owners is very common. These agents may operate at a great distance from their principals, who exercise their control largely through reports rendered to them periodically. In order to be of much significance, these reports must, of course, be rendered on the basis of the corporation as a separate entity.

**Legal Aspects of Corporations.** As defined by Chief Justice Marshall in the *Dartmouth College* case, a corporation is "an artificial being, invisible, intangible, and existing only in contemplation of law." Since it is a legal entity, it must be created either by specific action of a legislative body or by application of the authority provided by a statute passed by such body. The corporation, therefore, functions as a distinct entity within a legal framework. Most states have an act, typically entitled "The Business Corporation Act," which should be studied thoroughly and complied with carefully when organizing, operating, or dissolving a corporation. A corporate charter granted by the state gives the entity certain rights and privileges and at the same time imposes certain duties and responsibilities.

The corporation laws of the state together with the "Articles of Incorporation" constitute the charter of the corporation. The Articles consist of a written statement embodying specific information required by state statutes such as the name of the corporation, names and addresses of the incorporators, the purpose or purposes for which the corporation is organized, the minimum amount of capital with which the entity will start business, and details regarding the shares of capital stock authorized for issuance. Information with respect to capital stock should include, in addition to the number of shares of each class of stock, the par value, if any, as well as a statement of the preferences, qualifications, limitations, and restrictions of each class. In addition to those prescribed by statute, the Articles may include provisions for the regulation of the internal affairs of the corporation, such as specific restriction on distributions of earnings.

**Accounting Aspects of Corporate Formation.** Starting the accounting record of a corporation differs little from opening the books of a proprietorship or partnership. Assuming proper recognition, classification, and valuations of contributed assets and equities, the records of the corporation would be opened in the manner explained in elementary accounting.

The process of forming an entirely new corporation requires (1) state authorization, (2) issuance of shares of stock, and (3) acquisition of assets; whereas the incorporation of an existing enterprise may require only (1) state authorization and (2) the issuance of shares of stock.

Securing state authorization normally requires three or more persons to file an application for a charter with the incorporating agency of the state in which incorporation is sought. Normally, upon approval of the application by the state and the filing of a copy of the charter with the clerk of the county where the principal office of the corporation is located, the corporation comes into existence. Authorization to issue shares of stock is often a part of the approved charter.

Selling authorized shares of stock may be done either (1) *directly* by the incorporators of the corporation or (2) *indirectly* through an investment banking syndicate or selling group. In selling very large issues, registration with the Securities and Exchange Commission may be required.

When common shares alone are issued to the corporation organizers in payment for their investment in the company, few equity problems arise. Normally, each share of stock received represents a proportionate share of the value of all assets invested. When several classes of securities are issued, however, the problem of an equitable allocation of the different types of securities is more involved. To illustrate the nature of the problem, assume that A, B, and C form a corporation by contributing the following assets to the corporation.

|  | A | B | C | Total |
|---|---|---|---|---|
| Cash | $ 50,000 | $ 50,000 | $ 50,000 | $150,000 |
| Goodwill | — | — | 40,000 | 40,000 |
| Tangible Assets | 50,000 | 100,000 | 10,000 | 160,000 |
| Total | $100,000 | $150,000 | $100,000 | $350,000 |

Assume that the corporation is authorized to issue:

(a) Preferred stock ($100 par) paying 6%, noncumulative
(b) Common stock (no par)
(c) Bonds paying 5%

Assume that A, B, and C agree that income shall be distributed in a 2:3:2 ratio and that they also want to protect the initial contribution of each investor. They decide to issue bonds for the cash contribution and preferred stock, which is preferred on liquidation up to $100, for the tangible assets. They also want to distribute common shares equally so that each will have the same voting power. This plan provides no payment to C for the goodwill contribution. Another class of nonvoting second preferred stock might solve the problem. Not being authorized to issue a second preferred stock, A, B, and C will have to settle for something less than an ideal solution.

In making recommendations for a solution, it may be appropriate to suggest bonds to provide security, preferred stock to provide security upon liquidation and a right in excess earnings in the form of dividend participation rights, and common stock (as much as possible) to provide appropriate voting rights. There is, of course, no one solution. The different interests and wishes of each participant must be considered. For different participants and for different situations, different suggestions are appropriate.

## The Trust

A trust is an entity formed by depositing a sum of money or other resources in the custody of another entity, often a bank, with direction to invest these resources for the benefit of a beneficiary. It differs from a corporation principally in that the trustee is restricted in the use of the resources. The trust entity arises whenever property is held by a trustee for the benefit of another. The *trustee* holds legal title to the property but must use it for the benefit of the *beneficiary*. A trust may be created by a will—a testamentary trust—wherein assets left to a beneficiary are assigned to a trustee to use for the benefit of the beneficiary. Also, a trust may be created by a trust agreement or indenture under which a living grantor assigns specific assets to a trustee for use for the benefit of a designated beneficiary. This living trust is referred to as an "inter vivos" trust.

**Powers of Trustees.** A person who occupies a position of confidence toward others by holding assets to which another has a beneficial title or who receives and controls income of another is known as a "fiduciary." A trustee is a fiduciary.

The powers and duties of the trustee are derived both from the provisions of the document creating the trust (will, deed of trust, agreement, or court decree) and from the general laws on the trust relationship. The general powers and duties of the trustee are:

1. To take and retain possession of the trust property.
2. To invest and reinvest trust funds appropriately. Not all property is recognized as proper for trust investments, and what constitutes proper trust investments varies. Almost universally, however, bonds of the United States government, bonds of the state in which the trust is administered, and certain first mortgages on improved real property are recognized as proper trust investments.
3. To pay the expenses of the trust.
4. To distribute the trust property to those who are to receive it.

# 1 / The Conceptual and Theoretical Background

As a fiduciary the trustee is *accountable* for his actions to the beneficiary. He is responsible for all contracts made for the trust, but is not responsible for loss by theft, embezzlement, or accident if he has taken the precautions a prudent businessman would take in guarding his own property.

**Accounting for the Formation of a Trust.** The objective of trust accounting is directed to a significant degree to the keeping of accounts in such a manner that the trustee can prove he has accounted for the assets assigned to him and has used them appropriately. This type of accounting has been referred to as fiduciary accounting.

In recording trust transactions, care must be exercised to distinguish between transactions changing the *trust principal,* which represents the resources to be turned over to a designated beneficiary at the termination of the trust, and *trust income,* which represents the earnings of the trust that are distributable to the designated income beneficiary during the existence of the trust. The distinction between the two does not rest on the need for maintaining a certain amount of monetary value as the principal. Rather the principal is looked upon as a group of assets that must be separated from the assets that represent undistributed income. This physical concept of principal rather than monetary value raises a number of problems in distinguishing between principal and income. For example, the gain on the sale of an investment of principal funds would be considered as part of principal, whereas the interest received from the investment would be income. The result of treating certain gains as principal and other gains as income calls attention to the need for different accounting concepts of income in accounting for trusts.

A trust is formed by turning over to the trustee the assets that represent the principal of the trust. For example, assume that Mr. A. T. Enden died leaving in trust certain assets, the income from which is to go to his wife until the time of her death, but with a provision that the principal shall be turned over to his son and the trust terminated at the death of the wife. Normally, an inventory of these resources is filed with a court. The values accepted by the court in the inventory must be used by the trustee in accounting for the trust principal. Assume that the trust resources, valued at the court-accepted inventory, in the illustration above are:

|  |  |
| --- | --- |
| Cash | $20,000 |
| Investments: |  |
| Stock of Company ZTA | 15,000 |
| Bonds of the Q Company | 8,000 |
| Real estate | 42,000 |
| Total | $85,000 |

The entry to open the accounts of the trust would be:

|  |  |
| --- | --- |
| Cash | $20,000 |
| Stock of Company ZTA | 15,000 |

|  |  |  |
|---|---|---|
| Bonds of the Q Company | 8,000 | |
| Real estate | 42,000 | |
| Trust principal | | $85,000 |

The record-keeping procedures in accounting for trusts typically involves a cash receipts journal, a cash disbursements journal, a general journal, and a ledger with several subsidiary ledgers. Controlling accounts are used extensively in trust accounting. The "investment" account in the general ledger of a trust would be supported by detailed subsidiary ledgers and schedules.

Subject to these few introductory provisions, an accountant familiar with basic accounting can quickly develop a suitable record-keeping system for a trust.

## The Cooperative

Cooperatives are of a variety of types with a variety of provisions regarding their operations. Their typical feature is the banding together of a group of consumers for the objective of saving for themselves the profits which otherwise would accrue to other forms of business organizations, by buying from the cooperative rather than from another business organization.

Because of the variety of types and operations of cooperatives, accounting for such a business organization may vary. The essential requirement in accounting for the formation of the cooperative is to designate clearly the investment made by each member of the cooperative. In the case of an apartment building owned by occupants who provide the initial investment and pay as rent only the necessary management costs, the accounting records should reveal the total investment with the owner-occupants listed individually as participants in the cooperative. The entry would be:

|  |  |  |
|---|---|---|
| Building | xxxx | |
| J. A. Adams | | xxxx |
| T. T. Baker | | xxxx |
| Others | | xxxx |

Accounting for cooperatives is similar in principle to the accounting for other types of business organizations. Because they pose no particular accounting problems, they are not treated further in this textbook.

The accounting principles followed for each of these business organizations, both in the formative stages and in subsequent operations, are consistent in large measure with the postulates previously enumerated. The accounting records are maintained from the viewpoint of the entity, entries are largely based on transactions and at prices appropriate to the transaction, adjustments and analyses are based on the assumption the enterprise will continue to operate, and reports are rendered periodically for the information of all users.

The next type of business organization to be considered differs from the foregoing and, as a result, certain accounting aspects are different.

Certain aspects of the types of business organizations discussed to this point are presented in tabular form on page 19.

|  | Proprietorship | Partnership | Corporation | Trust | Cooperative |
| --- | --- | --- | --- | --- | --- |
| 1. Number of owners per entity | One | Two or more | Two or more; generally many | One or more | Several |
| 2. Legal requirements | Informal | Contractual | State authorization and charter | Formal, by trust agreement | Generally contractual |
| 3. Asset valuation at inception | Fair value | Fair value | Fair value | Fair value | Fair value |
| 4. Owners' liability | Unlimited | Unlimited, generally | Limited | Fiduciary only | Generally limited |
| 5. Owners' equity accounts | Capital Drawing | Capital Drawing | Capital Additional Paid-in Capital Retained Earnings | Trust Capital | Capital Fund Retained Earnings |

## The Joint Venture

Historically, the joint venture form of business operation — and organization — has been important. In early times it meant little more than an association of individuals who united their resources, or part of them, for some specific venture — for example, sending a ship from London to the East Indies for trading purposes. As a rule, the venture was one that required a larger capital than any one of the individuals possessed, or it involved risks too great for any one of them to assume in total.

The occasional associations for a specific venture remained fairly common down to the eighteenth century, and in fact were the forerunners of the modern-day partnership. These associations, because of their contractual and impersonal character, contributed to the close relationship of the business unit as the accounting unit. After several decades of relatively little importance in our economy, the joint venture returned in the late 1950's and early 1960's. The "joint venturers" of today, however, are corporations rather than individuals. The motivations remain somewhat the same — sharing of risks, accumulation of capital, merging of know-how — with the added impact of international business via partners spanning the continents. Today's joint ventures are many times called "50%-owned companies" wherein two corporations each own 50% of the venture. The venture, however, is deemed a separate accounting entity.

**Accounting Aspects of Joint Ventures.** In a number of instances, accounting for joint ventures parallels accounting for a partnership or corporation, particularly for many of the "50%-owned companies" noted above. In other instances, however, accounting for joint ventures differs from normal accrual accounting. Generally, the differences are related to the fact that some joint ventures have a stipulated or indefinite, but limited, life-span. When this characteristic of the venture exists, the postulate of continuity or going concern is not appropriate and the inapplicability of any postulate in a given situation can well suggest, or even necessitate, modifications in otherwise acceptable accounting practices.

Venture accounting is sometimes distinguished from accrual accounting in terms of the manner of recognizing income and allocating costs. However, several aspects of accrual accounting may exist in venture accounting. The differences that do exist are related to the absence of the continuity postulate. The limited nature of the venture's life, as well as some uncertainties that are characteristic of many venture operations, suggest that items normally subject to deferral or accrual should be recognized in the accounts on a completed transaction basis.

**Uncompleted Ventures.** If a venture is not completed at the date that financial statements are to be prepared, balances in venture accounts remaining after appropriate recognition of any gains or losses should be disclosed. Normally, the balances in uncompleted ventures are debits representing the unconsumed assets of the venture in which each of the participating organizations has an investment.

On the books of each of the participating organizations where a separate set of books is maintained for the venture, the investment account reflects the equity of the particular participant in the venture. Where separate books are not maintained for the venture, each participant's investment account reflects the full balance of the venture which is offset by separate accounts for the equity of the other participants. On a statement of financial position, only the equity of the reporting participant should be included as an asset of that particular participant. When separate books are not maintained, the balance of the joint venture account must be offset by the equities of the other participants, as follows:

| Investment: | |
|---|---|
| Joint venture | $31,000 |
| Less: Other participants' equity | 27,000 |
| Equity in joint venture | $4,000 |

**Miscellaneous Venture Combinations.** Miscellaneous business and non-business combinations of a temporary nature similar to joint ventures are rather common. The combining together of a group of investment bankers for underwriting and selling a specific issue of corporate securities is one of the better known forms of a temporary business combination. Other combinations of this type include real estate development projects and similar large-scale activities requiring more resources than one company might have or be willing to invest, or in some instances to combine the special resources of different companies. In general, the accounting procedures used in joint-venture accounting can be readily adapted to various types of miscellaneous venture combinations.

## PROBLEMS

### Problem 1-1

Mr. T. A. Hoyer owned a building, some tools, and office equipment. On January 1, 1980, he decided to go into the TV repair business. On that date his accountant prepared the following list of assets with which Mr. Hoyer started operations.

| | Cost to Mr. Hoyer | Depreciated Cost on Jan. 1, 1980 | Fair Market Value on Jan. 1, 1980 |
|---|---|---|---|
| Building | $8,000 | $6,000 | $17,000 |
| Tools | 1,500 | 1,200 | 1,000 |
| Office equipment | 800 | 800 | 1,200 |
| Cash | | | 10,000 |

On January 2, 1980, Mr. Hoyer obtained an operating license from the City Hall for $10, purchased 10 TV sets on account for $800, and opened the shop for business. To provide for emergency demands for cash, he discussed his project with the local bank and made arrangements to borrow money if the need should arise.

*Required:*
(1) At what amount should these activities be recorded at the formation of the sole proprietorship. Why?
(2) Give the entries necessary to record the formation of the business if it were incorporated and 2,000 shares of $10 par value stock issued for the assets.
(3) Is the arrangement to borrow money a significant activity of the new entity? If so, how should it be recorded?

## Problem 1-2

Don Freeman has operated a small manufacturing plant for several years. His accounting records have been maintained on an accrual basis. His inventory has been priced consistently on a LIFO basis, no estimate has been made for doubtful receivables, and depreciation has been taken on an accelerated basis. On January 1, 1980, the book value of his assets is $80,000. Late in 1979 he rejected the offer of a competitor of $115,000 for his business. Subsequently, Freeman decided to expand and to admit Rich Jones as a full partner. Jones contributed $70,000 in cash and newly acquired machinery of $30,000.

*Required:*
(1) Discuss the accounting problems the new partners would face in the formation of the partnership.
(2) Does the continuity concept find application in this situation? Discuss.

## Problem 1-3

Upon the death of his father, Mr. H. D. Dugan took over his father's small furniture store. At the time of death the following assets of the store were transferred to the son.

|  | Fair Market Value at Time of Death | Valuation on the Father's Books |
|---|---|---|
| Cash | $ 6,000 | $ 6,000 |
| Accounts receivable | 12,000 | 15,000 |
| Notes receivable | 33,000 | 37,000 |
| Merchandise (furniture) | 32,000 | 32,000 |
| Store building (one-third interest) | 15,000 | 12,000 |
| Store equipment | 10,000 | 2,000 |

The store building was valued at $45,000. It was owned equally by the father and two widows. The widows agree to a continuous lease of their portion of the building.

*Required:*
(1) Should the store be valued at $45,000 with the equity of the two widows shown as liabilities? Should the store be shown at $15,000 only?

(2) Give recording entries necessary to set up the new proprietorship for the son, Mr. H. D. Dugan.
(3) Is the death of an owner sufficient grounds for abandoning the going-concern concept and starting a new entity for accounting purposes? Explain.

## Problem 1-4

The Control Specialty Company is planning a public sale of securities. Tentative plans are to issue 175,000 of its 75 cent par common stock at $5 per share. The shares are to be offered by an investment syndicate and an $0.80 per share commission is to be paid. In addition, the Company has agreed to pay $30,000 expenses of the underwriting group.

Control Specialty was organized one year ago to acquire from Analysis Photo, Inc., assets consisting of certain patents and inventions in the electromechanical, electronic, and photographic fields. The Company intends to put into production certain devices and systems based on these assets and to continue developmental and research work. Net proceeds of the sale of stock, assuming all shares are sold, is estimated at $700,000. Of the net proceeds, $160,000 will be supplied to subcontractors for tools, jigs, dies, and models in connection with the production of three devices; $250,000 will be used for working capital; $30,000 will be paid to the predecessor company for certain development expenses; $140,000 for inventories and work in process; $95,000 for continuing research and development; and $25,000 for advertising and sales promotion.

Control Specialty now has outstanding 325,000 common shares, of which 250,000 were issued to Analysis Photo, Inc., for its assets. Analysis Photo, Inc., had spent $350,000 in research and development costs at the time that the patents and inventions were acquired by Control Specialty. Kelly Foster is president and treasurer of Control Specialty and also owns 54% of Analysis Photo, Inc. Analysis Photo Inc., owns 250,000 of the Control Specialty outstanding shares.

*Required:*
(1) Explain how Control Specialty Company was formed.
(2) Why is Control Specialty planning to issue additional shares?
(3) Give the entry or entries to record the issuance of stock and use of proceeds, assuming that the plans are carried out.
(4) What accounting problems are suggested by the relationship of Control Specialty, Analysis Photo, Inc. and Kelly Foster? Does this relationship violate standards of equity accepted in accounting?

## Problem 1-5

The Illini Shoppes of Urbana has filed a registration statement with the Securities and Exchange Commission to register 200,000 shares of common stock to be offered to the public. The underwriters are to make the offering at $3 per share, with a 40 cent selling commission to the underwriter. Illini Shoppes also will issue the underwriter warrants to purchase 15,000 common shares at $3 for a period of 5 years and to pay up to $15,000 of the expenses of sale.

The Company is engaged primarily in the operation of snack counters, bars, refreshment stands, and entertainment centers both on a franchise and a management basis. The Company has 150,000 shares of stock outstanding in the hands of two owners, Robert Cargo and James Niebuhr.

Net proceeds of the sale of the 200,000 shares to the public are estimated at $500,000. They will be applied first to repay a $70,000 bank loan. Remaining proceeds will pay a loan from Daniel Dorr of $60,000, with interest; will purchase $20,000 for equipment and installation at four new locations; will be added to working capital at the additional locations; and will be held in reserve for expansion.

*Required:*
(1) Assume that the balance sheet of Illini Shoppes of Urbana just prior to the new issue reported current assets of $40,000 and net fixed assets of $275,000. Prepare a pro forma balance sheet as it would look if the new issue were sold and invested as indicated.
(2) What was the book value per share prior to the sale? Following the sale?
(3) Should it be easier or more difficult for the Illini Shoppes of Urbana to borrow after the sale? Why? Does the $500,000 of estimated receipts from sale of the 200,000 shares of stock represent reliable and factual information that is acceptable for accounting purposes? Explain.

## Problem 1-6

Koss, Wright, and Burke organized a syndicate to bid for the Pesotum Seeders professional football franchise. Each of the 12 members of the syndicate pledged $300,000 toward the purchase price, and the State Bank of Sidney extended a line of credit up to $12,000,000. The bid of the syndicate of $14,100,000 was successful.

Koss, Wright, and Burke then formed the Seeders Eleven Corporation with an authorized common stock of 2,000,000 shares at $5 par value. Each of the 12 members of the original syndicate received 80,000 shares for his $300,000 investment. Of the remaining shares, 800,000 were offered to the public by an investment syndicate at a price of $7 per share, with the investment syndicate to receive $0.60 per share for commission and expenses. After $500,000 was reserved for working capital, the proceeds of the stock issuances were used to reduce the line of credit at the State Bank of Sidney.

The resources and rights of Pesotum Seeders included a roster of 40 players, a 30-year old stadium, the right to play in the Central Football League, rights to television and radio broadcasts, equipment for concessions, and 30 acres of land used for parking. Of these assets the stadium had a net book value of $1,500,000 on the books of Pesotum Seeders, the land was carried at $60,000, and the depreciated cost of the equipment was $40,000.

*Required:*
  (1) Prepare a balance sheet for the syndicate immediately after receiving its bid for Pesotum Seeders.
  (2) Prepare entries for the sale of stock to the syndicators and the public.
  (3) Discuss how the various resources and rights of Pesotum Seeders should be reported on the books of Seeders Eleven Corporation.

## Problem 1-7

Transactions between the enterprise and other enterprises or individuals provide the raw data of accounting. Each of the following activities of an enterprise may be considered in relation to the transaction concept:

(a) Sale of merchandise for cash.
(b) Sale of merchandise on account, terms 1/20, n/60.
(c) Sale of merchandise on account, terms 36 months.
(d) Purchase of an asset with a 5-year life on January 2, 1980.
(e) Use of the asset in (d) during 1980.
(f) Accrual of interest on a note receivable held by the enterprise.
(g) A theft of merchandise.
(h) An increase in market value of long-term securities.
(i) Hiring a new accountant.

*Required:*
  (1) Are each of the activities above transactions?
  (2) Would each be the basis for an accounting entry? Why?
  (3) What significant activities took place that are not transactions?

## Problem 1-8

(a) The Drake Company sells about one-third of its merchandise for cash, one-third on 30-day open account, and one-third on a 3-year installment plan. An entry is made at the time of each sale because each is considered a transaction of the enterprise.

*Required:*
  Discuss similarities and differences in accounting for the three types of sales in view of the continuity and periodicity postulates of accounting.

(b) The Drake Company uses fixed assets in manufacturing which are sometimes superseded in usefulness by new inventions.

*Required:*
  In view of the continuity and periodicity postulates, discuss some of the more important issues the Drake Company must consider in accounting for these assets.

## Problem 1-9

The General Supermarkets Company has been expanding rapidly, both in terms of new store openings and increased volumes. Since its management early adopted a policy of owning its stores and underlying real estate, the Company has reached a point where it has a relatively high debt level, as shown by the following condensed balance sheet.

### General Supermarkets Company

| | | | |
|---|---|---|---|
| Cash and receivables | $ 18,000,000 | Current liabilities | $ 30,000,000 |
| Inventories | 40,000,000 | Long-term debt | 105,000,000 |
| Land | 12,000,000 | Stockholders' equity | 36,000,000 |
| Buildings (net) | 80,000,000 | | |
| Equipment (net) | 21,000,000 | | |
| | $171,000,000 | | $171,000,000 |

The management has organized a new company, General Realty Company, to which it intends to sell all of its land and buildings for $120,000,000. General Realty will then lease these properties to General Supermarkets Company, generally for 30 years with renewal options at rentals that will cover principal, interest, taxes, insurance, and a profit element. General Realty will obtain a bank loan for $95,000,000 and will raise the remaining $25,000,000 by a stock offering, $10,000,000 of which will be subscribed by General Supermarkets Company. General will use the net proceeds of the sale to reduce its long-term debt to $10,000,000 and to apply the remaining proceeds to its current liabilities.

*Required:*
(1) Prepare a balance sheet for General Supermarkets to reflect the transactions above.
(2) What alternatives are possible to account for the gain on the sale of properties?
(3) How will General Supermarkets' income statement differ after the sale from what was previously reported?
(4) Why would General Supermarkets Company enter into this transaction? Does elimination of the long-term debt and recognition of a gain result in a fair financial presentation?

## Problem 1-10

Messrs. Amber, Brown, and Kreem have formed a corporation known as the ABK Company. The Corporation has been authorized to issue:

(a) 2,000 shares of $100 par nonvoting 6% preferred stock.
(b) 10,000 shares of $10 stated value voting common stock.
(c) $100,000 of 5% bonds.

Net assets to be contributed to ABK Company by the three organizers are:

|  | Amber | Brown | Kreem |
|---|---|---|---|
| Miscellaneous assets | $60,000 | $120,000 | $80,000 |
| Current liabilities | 10,000 | 30,000 | 20,000 |
| Net assets contributed | $50,000 | $ 90,000 | $60,000 |
| Average annual earnings | $ 2,790 | $ 5,010 | $ 3,300 |

The three organizers request advice on how to issue the three types of securities to each person so as to provide for each the same right in assets and income, and the same security as to risk, as existed prior to the formation of the Corporation. Also, they want to share equally in voting control of the Corporation.

*Required:*
(1) Draw up a suggested plan for issuing securities to the three organizers. Your investigation reveals that similar companies in the industry are financed (excluding current liabilities) about 30% by bonds and 70% by stock.
(2) Point out the weaknesses and advantages of your plan in terms of accounting standards of equity.

## Problem 1-11

Messrs. A. J. Cromley and E. B. Martin have decided to go into business together. Assets to be contributed by each are:

|  | Cromley | Martin |
|---|---|---|
| Cash | $ 6,000 | $ 8,000 |
| Merchandise | 18,000 | 7,000 |
| Building | –0– | 30,000 |
| Equipment | 12,000 | 3,000 |
| Other assets | 6,000 | 4,000 |
|  | $42,000 | $52,000 |

*Required:*
(1) Give the entries to record the formation of the new company, if
   (a) a partnership is formed.
   (b) a corporation is formed and $90,000 of par value common stock is issued as payment for the assets.
(2) How many shares of stock would be given each investor if the $90,000 stock was $50 par value stock?

## Problem 1-12

The Ida-Far Company is a joint venture recently formed by Idaho Construction Company and Farina Associates to construct a $120,000,000 dam in the southwestern United States. The Project is expected to take four years to complete and will be managed by Idaho Construction Company, which owns a 60% interest in the Ida-Far joint venture. Farina Associates, which owns 40% of the joint venture, will provide engineers and certain specialized equipment. The contract resulted from a low bid of $120,000,000 on a fixed-price basis.

The project will require certain items of heavy construction machinery as well as smaller items of relatively expensive equipment. Monthly reports will be rendered to the venturers by the joint venture, including engineering estimates of stages of completion. Profits will be shared in the ownership ratios.

*Required:*
(1) Will it be possible to prepare income statements for the Ida-Far Company before the completion of the contract?
(2) Should normal approaches to calculation of depreciation be altered for this joint venture? Why?
(3) Discuss other accounting issues of significance for Ida-Far Company.

## Problem 1-13

Three companies, A, B, and C, combine to form a joint venture to develop a product to compete with a new industry which poses an increasing threat to the products regularly sold by A, B, and C. Company A is to manage the venture. Transactions of the venture were:

Jan. 6, 1980 — Fixed assets to be used in making the product were contributed by B — $90,000. Patents and processes contributed by C — $30,000.
Jan. 10, 1980 — A purchased $10,000 of materials and $1,500 of supplies for the venture.
Jan. 31, 1980 — A paid monthly expenses — $6,000.
Feb. 28, March 31, April 30, May 31, and June 30 — A paid monthly expenses of $5,000, $7,000, $6,000, $6,000 and $12,000, respectively.
July 15 — A spent $15,000 for advertising of the new product.
July 31 — Sales for cash were $5,000. Monthly expenses were $14,000.
August 15 — B contributed $15,000 additional materials.

Sales and expenses, all paid for or received by A were:

|  | August | September | October | November | December |
|---|---|---|---|---|---|
| Sales | $ 7,000 | $10,000 | $20,000 | $30,000 | $40,000 |
| Expenses | 15,000 | 14,000 | 16,000 | 12,000 | 10,000 |

On December 31, the assets in the hands of the venture, other than cash, were:

| Merchandise | $ 1,000 |
|---|---|
| Supplies | 200 |
| Fixed assets (net after depreciation) | 80,000 |
| Patents and processes | 10,000 |

Profits and losses are to be shared equally by the three participating companies.

*Required:*
(1) Compute the profit or loss accruing to each company for the year's activities.

(a) Assuming that the venture is not incorporated.
(b) Assuming that the venture is incorporated.
(2) If the venture is considered unsuccessful and is to be dissolved, how much of each venture resource would A turn back to companies B and C.
(3) What external (environmental) conditions, fundamental assumptions, and principles were accepted in your answers to requirements (1) and (2)?

## Problem 1-14

The firms of Jones and Company, Smith and Associates, and Black and Black and Company, form a syndicate to purchase and sell on an equal basis $600,000 face value of bonds of the Border Company. The bonds are sold to the underwriters at 98 and are to be issued to investors at 100. The sales commission is 1%, and the expenses are to be paid by the syndicate.

Operations of the syndicate were as follows:

1. The bonds were purchased for cash, each of the three participating companies putting up one-third of the money.
2. Expenses of $1,200 were paid by Jones and Company for the syndicate.
3. Bonds sold by the participants were:

| | |
|---|---|
| Jones & Co. @ 100 | $199,000 |
| Smith and Associates @ 100 | 180,000 |
| Black & Co. @ 100 | 197,000 |
| Total | $576,000 |

4. Unsold bonds are assigned equally to the three underwriters.
5. Cash settlement after allocating commissions and profits among the three participants was made and the venture was terminated.

*Required:*
Prepare the journal entries for each of the three firms to account for the underwriting operations.

# 2

# Valuation of Assets

The process by which a new business entity acquires assets involves a financing function and an investing function. The financing function refers to the acquisition of cash from investors and creditors of the enterprise. The investing function refers to the acquisition of economic resources needed for business operations in exchange for cash. Both functions are telescoped into one transaction when assets are acquired on credit or by an equity investment. Because the two functions involve the acquisition of two types of assets, money resources and economic resources, both common and distinct valuation principles apply to them.

## Acquisition Cost Valuation

Newly acquired assets of both types become a part of the operating capacity of the enterprise, and must enter the accounting record in some manner. A rather fundamental concept, covered in elementary textbooks in accounting, is that these assets should be recorded (valued) at their fair value on their acquisition date. Without evidence to the contrary, it must be assumed that buyer and seller both acted rationally and that at acquisition the fair value is best represented by acquisition cost. This means that the acquired assets should be entered in the accounting records at the dollar consideration or equivalent given up to acquire the assets on the acquisition date. This concept is sometimes referred to as the valuation of assets in terms of historical or original cost.

Many of the problems of asset valuation would be eliminated if the foregoing elementary concept were accepted completely by accountants. Actually, many economic resources are acquired directly with a promise to pay cash later. This situation exists when purchases are made on account. In other situations, owners often contribute economic resources directly rather than cash. Thus investors and creditors often supply economic resources directly to the enterprise. The enterprise may also acquire economic resources in exchange for other economic resources. Determination of the dollar consideration given to acquire the new assets poses a real problem in these circumstances. In addition, situations arise wherein departure from the acquisition cost valuation appears to be not only warranted, but advisable. This would normally be the case when acquisition cost clearly does not reflect fair value at the acquisition date. When departure from acquisition cost is appropriate, care must be exercised to distinguish between fair value at acquisition and fair value at some other date. Adjustment to the latter is a "revaluation" process not relevant to the initial valuation of acquired assets.

**Problems of Asset Valuation.** There are three main problems involved in the valuation of assets. In question form they are:

1. When shall accountants recognize on the books of account that assets have been acquired?
2. At what amounts shall assets recognized be valued?
3. Inasmuch as it is impossible to keep a separate asset account for each asset acquired, how should the various assets recognized be combined or classified?

Overriding these problems is the fundamental issue of the nature of an asset. There is a need to know the characteristics that make a thing or process an asset. The elementary view that an asset is anything of value owned by the enterprise is not particularly useful in the more advanced problems of accounting. A somewhat broader view would be to consider assets as of two rather distinct types:

1. General purchasing power in the form of cash and direct claims to cash.
2. Command over specific resources embodying services that are to be used in the operations of the enterprise.

The second type of asset arises because the nature of business activity is to acquire economic resources at one time but not to use them completely until a later date. As a result, at any one time the bulk of the assets of the enterprise will be of service to the enterprise in its future operations.

**Acquisition Cost Versus Realizable Value.** As previously mentioned, general accounting procedure suggests that the assets of an enterprise be valued at fair value measured in terms of the cash or cash equivalent required to acquire the assets. While this basis is generally used for the service resources of the enterprise, many accountants endeavor to value the cash and direct claims-to-cash portion of assets at the amount of cash that will be provided by these items. Economists and others at times suggest that all assets — service resources as well as cash and claims to cash — should be valued according to the amount of cash that will be realized ultimately by their use. Accountants have hesitated to accept this view as a concept capable of implementation in valuing service resources. Acquisition cost rather than realizable value has seemed more real. In the case of receivables that represent a direct claim to cash, however, accountants think in terms of realizable value. Estimated uncollectibles are deducted to arrive at the estimated cash to be realized on the receivables.

## VALUATION OF CASH AND DIRECT CLAIMS TO CASH

Cash and direct claims to cash, such as notes and accounts receivable, bonds receivable, and government securities, are generally recorded at an amount representing their cash equivalent on the date acquired. When direct claims to cash such as notes and bonds are acquired for cash, the distinction between an investment and a direct claim to cash may become blurred, and it is frequently assumed that the cash equivalent refers to acquisition cost. In some instances, receivables such as 30-day accounts receivables are measured by the amount of cash to be collected at some future date.

The justification for this different valuation of direct claims to cash seems to lie in the length of the waiting period before cash will be realized and in the amount involved. If the waiting period is relatively short and if the amount of the variation is not especially large, there seems to be no objection to measuring the claim to cash in terms of the total cash that will be provided in the reasonably near future. When the waiting period is long, the amount involved material, or when the interest charge for waiting is not included in the face amount of the claim to cash (as with an interest-bearing note), valuation is usually made on the basis of the sale price or cash equivalent on the date the asset is acquired.

When the variation between the present and future cash equivalent to be received is material, practice varies in disclosing the receivable as one net amount or in two partially offsetting accounts.

For example, assume that a company sells merchandise, with a sale price of $950, in exchange for a $1,000 bond of the buying company. The entry to record this sale would be:

| | | |
|---|---|---|
| Bonds receivable | $950 | |
| Sales | | $950 |

But, if the same company sells merchandise, with a sales price of $950, in exchange for a noninterest-bearing note receivable in the face amount of $1,000, the entry would be:

| | | |
|---|---|---|
| Notes receivable | $1,000 | |
| Sales | | $950 |
| Unearned interest income | | 50 |

Since the unearned interest income or revenue is normally deducted from the face amount of the note on a balance sheet, both procedures provide in substance the same valuation.

### Realizable Value — Reporting Date Versus Future Date

At each reporting date an attempt is generally made to value cash and claims to cash items at an approximation of the cash that the various assets will provide. This valuation commonly requires an adjustment of the recorded amount. The basic problem, and one that is frequently overlooked, lies in distinguishing clearly the two possible modifications of the original valuation:

## 2 / Valuation of Assets

1. The amount of cash that the assets will provide as of the balance sheet or reporting date.
2. The amount of cash that the assets will provide at some future date.

Thus, for certain types of receivables, such as accounts receivable and some short-term notes, valuation at the amount of cash that will be provided at some future date is accepted. Consequently, the recording of estimated uncollectible accounts and the deduction of this amount from accounts receivable on the balance sheet accomplishes a receivable valuation in terms of estimated cash to be provided at some future date. On the other hand, certain long-term notes and bonds receivable, which also represent direct claims to cash, are valued in terms of the amount of cash that could be provided on the reporting date. This latter valuation is sometimes further modified, in a somewhat inconsistent manner, for fluctuations in market valuations. A bond receivable which a company expects to hold for a relatively short period, initially valued at the cash equivalent required to acquire the bond, is valued at its cash equivalent on the reporting date only when the market (selling price) price is below the original or previously modified valuation. This procedure for valuing receivables is an application of the time-honored, though logically inconsistent, "cost or market, whichever is lower" rule.

**Materiality and Realizable Valuation.** From the discussion above one should not conclude that the accountant expends considerable effort at each reporting date to make certain that each cash or claim-to-cash item is valued at its cash equivalent at the reporting date or at some future date. While such a valuation might be desirable from a theoretical standpoint, implementation would involve numerous minor adjustments of an insignificant nature. For receivables it might be considered desirable to adjust normal accounts for estimated bad debts, estimated discounts still available, estimated costs of collecting the receivables, estimated administrative costs of booking and billing, and, possibly, for the interest that could have been earned if the receivables had been in the form of cash as of the reporting date. Carried to this extreme, the valuation of accounts receivable at their cash equivalent on the reporting date might appear somewhat as shown below.

CURRENT ASSETS:
| | | | |
|---|---|---|---|
| Cash | | | $2,000.00 |
| Accounts receivable | | $8,000.00 | |
| Less: Bad debt allowance | $100.00 | | |
| Sales discounts available | 20.00 | | |
| Estimated collection costs | 10.00 | | |
| Booking costs | 5.00 | | |
| Implicit interest allowance | 15.00 | | |
| Miscellaneous adjustments | 8.00 | 158.00 | |
| Cash equivalent of accounts receivable | | | 7,842.00 |

Such an extremely detailed presentation is difficult to justify on the basis of disclosure of materially significant information. It should be recognized, however, that the bad debt allowance, which is an adjustment normally made, is similar in nature to the other items listed. The purpose of each is, partially at least, to modify the acquisition price of the receivables toward an amount closer to cash equivalent on the reporting date.

The important point to recognize is that adjustments of the recorded cash equivalent (of cash and claims to cash) are made in the interest of reporting these items at an approximation of the cash they will provide. Numerous other possible adjustments are not regularly made, principally because the additional accuracy that would result is not particularly significant. Consistent valuation over a period of time is more to be desired than an attempt at excessive accuracy. This conclusion, of course, is subject to the standard that no material aspect of valuation may be omitted in determination of asset valuation.

**Valuation of Long-Term Receivables.** The concept that accountants value cash and claims to cash at the amount of cash that will be provided by the immediate sale of these items does not apply to long-term receivables. Typical of the conventional procedures is the accounting for bonds receivable. Bonds are normally recorded at their acquisition cost and then periodically adjusted upward or downward as the discount or premium on purchase is amortized in some systematic and rational manner. The following example illustrates this process:

On January 1, 1979, Company A purchases for $9,600 bonds of Company B that have a maturity value of $10,000 on December 31, 1982. At the time of acquisition of this investment receivable, Company A would make this entry:

| | | |
|---|---|---|
| Investment in bonds of B | $9,600 | |
| Cash | | $9,600 |

Company A officials expect to hold these bonds until maturity. If the bonds were to be accounted for in a manner similar to that used for the various service resources of an enterprise, such as machinery or materials, no adjustment of this initial valuation would be made until the resources were disposed of. That is, the asset would continue to be carried at cost; however, accountants generally adjust the acquisition cost of bonds receivable when such cost differs from the maturity value. At the end of each year the bonds would be "revalued" until, at maturity date, they would reveal a value of $10,000. If Company A elects to make such "revaluation," more commonly called amortization of the purchase discount, by the straight-line process, the adjustment entry December 31, 1979 (and each subsequent December 31 until maturity) would be:

| | | |
|---|---|---|
| Investment in bonds of B | $100 | |
| Interest income | | $100 |

As a result of this entry, Company A would report the bonds receivable from B at $9,700 on December 31, 1979. Similarly, the bonds would be reported at an additional $100 each December 31 until maturity. At maturity the bonds would be reported at their cash equivalent at that date of $10,000.

The procedure above indicates that accountants value long-term receivables on a basis different from that used in the valuation of service resources. Acquisition cost is not strictly followed. Likewise, the modification in value is not governed by the cash equivalent of the bonds at the reporting date. Market values are reported only parenthetically, if at all. The governing concept appears to be to modify the acquisition cost in order to get the bonds receivable to a cash equivalent value at maturity date. Thus, we might say that accountants initially value long-term receivables at acquisition cost, but that they may subsequently be revalued in order to obtain their cash equivalent value at maturity date. At reporting dates between acquisition and maturity, the bonds will be reported at a "going-concern value" between the acquisition cost and the maturity value.

## The Use of Current Market Value

Some evidence of accountants' support for the valuation of cash and claims to cash in terms of the amount of cash that the item will provide on the reporting date is found in the common usage of cost or market, whichever is lower, for claims to cash not expected to be held until maturity. To illustrate this practice, we can again refer to the example in the preceding section.

If Company A acquires $10,000 maturity value of Company B bonds on January 1, 1979, for $9,600, the following entry would be made, even if Company A did not intend to hold these bonds until their December 31, 1982, maturity date:

| | | |
|---|---|---|
| Investment in bonds of B | $9,600 | |
| Cash | | $9,600 |

If Company A does not intend to hold these bonds until their maturity date, there appears to be little reason to amortize the bond discount over the period remaining until maturity. Thus, the valuation of the asset is not guided by an attempt to base the asset value on the amount of cash to be provided at some future date. For an asset of this type, at any balance sheet date the accountant has a choice of adhering to the acquisition cost, as reflected by the entry made at acquisition, or of modifying the acquisition cost in an attempt to approach the cash equivalent at the balance sheet date. If one were to follow logically the previously indicated concept of valuing claims to cash at their cash equivalent, we might expect to find the bonds reported at their market value at the reporting date. While support appears to be growing for the view that market value should also be used when higher than cost, the general practice currently followed by accountants is to use market value only when the market price of bonds is below acquisition cost. As a result, temporary investments are commonly reported at acquisition cost or at cash (market) equivalent at the reporting date, whichever value is lower.

It might be noted at this point that the selling market price rather than the buying market price is used for this revaluation purpose. Where no market price exists, bid price by buyers is used in preference to the asked price by sellers of the security. Because bid price is used, the inference is that accountants endeavor to value these receivables in terms of their cash equivalent as of the balance sheet date.

Thus, for the bonds of Company B in the example above, at December 31, 1979 the acquisition cost would be $9,600. If the asked price by sellers were 95½ and the bid price by buyers 94½, the choice of values for the bonds would be: acquisition value, $9,600; selling market value, $9,550; or buying market value, $9,450. Applying the cost or market, whichever is lower, rule, and using the bid price as the market value, the bonds of Company B would be valued at $9,450 for balance sheet purposes.

**Cash Surrender Value.** Further evidence of acceptance by accountants of the concept that claims to cash should be valued in terms of the cash that could be realized on the reporting date is found in the valuation of insurance policies that have a cash surrender feature. Assume that Company A decided on January 1, 1979 to take out a $100,000 life insurance policy on the life of the president with the company designated as beneficiary. Also assume that the annual premium on this policy is $3,000, and that upon payment of the third annual premium the initial cash surrender value of $600 arises. The following entries might be made:

| Jan. 1, 1979 | Insurance expense | $3,000 | |
| --- | --- | --- | --- |
| | Cash | | $3,000 |
| Jan. 1, 1980 | Insurance expense | $3,000 | |
| | Cash | | $3,000 |
| Jan. 1, 1981 | Insurance expense | $2,400 | |
| | Cash surrender value of life insurance | 600 | |
| | Cash | | $3,000 |

Each subsequent year the $3,000 premium would be apportioned (1) to record the increase in the cash surrender value and (2) to record the remainder as the insurance expense for that year.[1] The asset, cash surrender value of life insurance, would thereby be reported periodically in terms of the cash that could be received on the reporting date through surrender of the policy.

**Summary of Valuation of Cash and Claims-to-Cash Items.** The amount at which cash and direct claims to cash should be valued may be summarized in this manner:

1. Cash, which may best be defined as anything that will be accepted by a commercial bank for deposit at the face amount of the negotiable instrument, should be valued at the amount of cash that could be disposed of on the

---

[1] The procedure above may be questioned on theoretical grounds that the initial $600 cash surrender value is applicable to the entire three-year period rather than entirely to the third year. Thus, we might find some support for allocating the $600 as follows: $400 to correction of prior years' income and $200 to reduction of the current year's expense. Further discussion of this subject will be found in Chapter Four.

reporting date. In the case of cash not readily available for disposition, such as cash tied up in an insolvent bank, some adjustment is required. A simple reclassification to remove the amount from disposable cash may be all that is required. At times the actual value of the "frozen" cash may have to be reduced for reporting purposes, but this action would normally require objective evidence that less than the amount carried will subsequently be realized.

2. Direct claims to cash take several forms. They may be in the form of:

   a. Immediate claims to cash, as in the case of surrender value of life insurance policies; savings deposits, where the funds are technically not available for immediate disbursements but in fact can be readily obtained; and United States savings bonds. Normally, these items are to be valued at an amount equal to the cash that could be claimed on the reporting date.

   b. Claims to cash due in the near future, such as accounts and notes receivable. These items are valued at an amount equal to the cash that will be realized on the claim. Normally, adjustments are made only for bad debts and, in a few cases where the amount involved is material, for sales discounts available. Possible additional adjustments that would make the amount reported approach more closely the actual realizable cash at the reporting date (and also sharpen the determination of net income) are currently passed over because of immateriality and difficulties in computation.

   c. Claims to cash due in the distant future, such as bonds receivable. Normally, these items are valued at a computed amount somewhat representative of the claim to cash on a going-concern basis as of the reporting date. It is sometimes stated that the appropriate valuation for these items is amortized cost. This is an indirect method of saying that cost is not the correct valuation, but that by amortizing cost—in order to achieve face value by maturity date—an approximation of the cash equivalent is achieved on the reporting date from a going-concern viewpoint. In those instances in which the intent of management is to dispose of the receivable by sale prior to its maturity date, so that the ultimate cash to be realized is unknown, it is customary accounting practice to value the receivable at cost, provided such cost is below the market price at the reporting date. When the market price is below cost, the market valuation is generally used.

The following paragraphs illustrate some of the problems in the valuation of specific claims to cash.

**Valuation of Accounts Receivable.** The ABC Company sells on account merchandise at an invoice price of $1,000, terms 5/10, net 30. At the time of the sale, two possible bases for valuing this receivable exist: (1) the amount of the cash claim the receivable represents at the date of the sale, or (2) the amount of the cash claim the receivable represents if the customer does not take the discount available. Theoretically, strict adherence to the view that cash and direct claims to cash should be valued at their cash equivalent would require an entry to record the sale as follows:

| | | |
|---|---|---|
| Accounts receivable | $950 | |
| Sales | | $950 |

Practically, however, many companies follow the practice of recording the receivable at the invoice amount, as follows:

| | | |
|---|---|---|
| Accounts receivable | $1,000 | |
| Sales | | $1,000 |

In the first entry, where the receivable is recorded at the net amount, if the discount available does lapse, through expiration of the discount period, an entry would be required to restate the receivable to the corrected amount, as follows:

| | | |
|---|---|---|
| Accounts receivable | $50 | |
| Sales discounts not taken | | $50 |

As far as the valuation of the receivable is concerned, the following question should be asked: Does the gross procedure result in a material misrepresentation of the valuation of the receivable? In general, accountants have decided that such a procedure is not a material departure from theoretical accuracy and that recording at the gross amount is a satisfactory representation of the valuation of the receivable. The gross procedure does lend itself to ease in recording and in verification, since the booking would involve the actual invoice amounts without adjustment for possible discounts. At present, many businesses bill customers at net in recognition of the high frequency of discounts taken. Under these business conditions the booking of receivables at the net price would seem to be practical and would also achieve more theoretically proper asset values.

**Valuation of Notes Receivable.** Assume that the ABC Company accepts a $1,000 note bearing interest at 3% and due in 60 days in payment for a sale of merchandise. At the sale date, the note could be sold at a discount rate of 6%. At the date of the sale, the question arises as to the appropriate valuation of the note and the sale.

Five possible valuations are represented by the following entries:

(1)

| | | |
|---|---|---|
| Notes receivable | $1,005 | |
| Sales | | $1,000 |
| Unearned interest income | | 5 |

This entry values the asset at its total eventual cash equivalent and reports as sales revenue the face amount of the asset received in exchange.

(2)

| | | |
|---|---|---|
| Notes receivable | $1,005 | |
| Sales | | $994.95 |
| Unearned interest income | | 10.05 |

## 2 / Valuation of Assets

This entry values the asset at its total eventual cash equivalent, reports sales at an amount equal to the discounted maturity value ($1,005 at 6% for 60 days) of the asset received, and reports unearned interest income at the amount of interest to be earned over the 60-day holding period of the note.

(3)
| | | |
|---|---|---|
| Notes receivable | $994.95 | |
| Sales | | $994.95 |

(4)
| | | |
|---|---|---|
| Notes receivable | $1,000 | |
| Sales | | $994.95 |
| Unearned interest income | | 5.05 |

These two alternative entries value the sale at its cash equivalent at the sale date as in Entry (2). Entry (3) values the note directly at its cash equivalent while Entry (4) uses the offsetting contra account to adjust the note valuation to its face value.

(5)
| | | |
|---|---|---|
| Notes receivable | $1,000 | |
| Sales | | $1,000 |

This entry values the asset at its face value and the sale in like terms. Any interest for waiting would be recognized when earned and/or received according to the terms of the note.

Normally, explicit interest payments, such as 3% in Entry (1) above, are not included as a part of the receivable until the explicit interest has been earned by the passage of time. Even when the interest receivable is granted a valuation, it is generally not included as a part of the valuation of the note, but is classified separately as interest receivable. Thus, the claim to cash represented by interest receivable is not normally reported as an asset until the passage of time has produced an existing claim. This procedure is consistent with the concept of valuing cash items at their cash equivalent at the reporting date.

The face amount of the note is commonly accepted as the appropriate valuation of the note, as in Entries (4) and (5) above. This valuation is justified on the ground that it does not result in any material distortion from valuation of the claim to cash in existence at the reporting date. Entries (2), (3), and (4) above report the sale at its theoretically appropriate amount, the cash equivalent of the asset received in exchange. Since sales revenue is considered earned at the date of the sale, whereas interest revenue is not earned until the passage of time, this refinement in the measurement of sales is appropriate. Entry (2) above includes the explicit interest in the asset, but Entry (3) excludes all interest from the asset amount. Entry (4) is the preferable alternative, since it reports as sales the cash equivalent of the asset received, as an asset the face amount of the note received, and as unearned interest the implicit interest in the note. If the amount is not significant, Entry (5) may be satisfactory. Of course, at any subsequent reporting date, accrued interest on the note would be reported as a receivable and as income.

The example above illustrates that theoretical accuracy is sometimes sacrificed for practical ease in recording. On a consistent basis, however, the use of the fourth alternative above results in reasonably satisfactory measurement of assets (and income) in a practicably justifiable manner.

**Valuation of Long-Term Receivables Arising from a Sale.** Assume that the ABC Company accepts a noninterest-bearing note due in three years, having a face amount of $10,000, in payment for a sale of land. The question then arises as to the appropriate valuation of the note. *APB Opinion No. 21,* "Interest on Receivables and Payables," requires imputation of the interest implicit in the face of a note when stated interest rates differ from market rates. If the market rate of interest is 6%, so that on exchange the note could be sold for $8,396.19, the note or bond should be valued as follows:

(1)

| | | |
|---|---|---|
| Notes receivable | $8,396.19 | |
| Sales | | $8,396.19 |

Because of the large amount of the contra valuation account "Unearned interest income," some accountants prefer the following entry.

(2)

| | | |
|---|---|---|
| Notes receivable | $10,000.00 | |
| Sales | | $8,396.19 |
| Unearned interest income | | 1,603.81 |

An erroneous valuation of the note and sale at the gross amount would result in the following entry:

(3)

| | | |
|---|---|---|
| Notes receivable | $10,000.00 | |
| Sales | | $10,000.00 |

The effect of recording such a transaction at the gross amount is to anticipate revenue by including as sales the interest implicit in the face of the noninterest-bearing note. Where this amount of interest is material, the cash equivalent valuation is necessary to provide a fair assignment of the implicit interest to the period in which it is earned. To treat as sales that which is properly interest revenue, if material, may cause investors to make erroneous judgments as to the nature and profitability of the entity.

In a more realistic situation, a seller may accept in payment of a sale a note bearing interest at a rate that is well below the prevailing market rate of interest and then insist that both the sale and the note should be valued at the face amount of the note and recorded in the manner used in Entry (3) above. Correctly, when a $10,000 three-year 3% note is received for the sale of land when the prevailing market rate of interest is 6%, sales should be recorded in the manner used in Entry (1) above at the fair value of the note, as follows:

|  |  |  |
|---|---|---|
| Notes receivable | $9,244.77 | |
| Sales | | $9,244.77 |

or as in Entry (2) above, as follows:

|  |  |  |
|---|---|---|
| Notes receivable | $10,000 | |
| Sales | | $9,244.77 |
| Unearned interest income | | 755.23 |

Computation
(a) Present value of $10,000 due in three years discounted at 6%     $8,396.19
(b) Present value of $300 a year for three years (3% of $10,000)
    discounted at 6%                                                      848.58
    Market value of note                                                $9,244.77

**Procedures in Valuation of Receivables.** To some extent, the valuation of receivables in practice is dictated more by the manner in which the receivable is acquired than by adherence to the concept that receivables should be valued at their cash equivalent on the reporting date.

If the receivable arises as a result of a loan of money by the company, which is the essential nature of the purchase of a bond, as noted previously, there is a supposition on the part of the accountant that the valuation of the exchange is expressed in terms of the cash exchanged to acquire the receivable. Thus, the incoming asset is valued in terms of the outgoing asset. However, if the receivable arises as a result of a sale or a contribution, the view of the accountant shifts decidedly to the concept that realizable cash is the proper valuation. Thus, the incoming asset is valued in terms of its cash equivalent at the acquisition date. The strong support for the view that receivables should be valued in terms of the cash equivalent claim suggests that valuation in terms of cash exchanged to acquire the receivable may be based on a supposition that cost price properly reflects realizable cash on the acquisition date.

It is imperative that a student of accountancy understand the conceptual background of accounting procedures in order to cope with unusual situations that may arise. He also needs a thorough knowledge of customary procedures of accounting practice. As far as receivables are concerned, the procedures of accounting may be generalized by stating that unless cash is exchanged to acquire the receivable, the proper valuation is the cash equivalent claim of the receivable on the reporting date. An exception is that, for convenience in recording, a receivable due to be converted into cash within a short period of time may be valued at the cash ultimately to be received, provided such a procedure does not materially depart from the valuation on the reporting date. For example, if a company made a $1,000 sale and received in exchange a $1,000 noninterest-bearing note due in 15 days, in terms of cash or cash equivalent value, if interest is 6% per year, the proper valuation of the note is $997.50 ($1,000 less 6% of $1,000 for 15 days). Because the interest element involved is not material, for convenience in recording, the note may be valued at the cash ultimately to be received, $1,000.

On the other hand, if the interest involved were material, the proper valuation would be the discounted amount.

## VALUATION OF SERVICE RESOURCES

Contrary to the conceptual valuation of cash and direct claims to cash in terms of the cash to be *realized* by the asset, the valuation of service resources such as buildings, materials, and labor is based on their fair value, which is normally measured in terms of the cash or cash equivalent *invested* in them. Such a valuation is referred to as acquisition cost or as historical cost.

At the procedural level this concept is sometimes expressed: Assets, except cash and receivables, should be valued at the total of all costs required to have the asset available for use. There are, however, several departures from this procedural rule, and these departures can generally be explained in terms of materiality or in terms of difficulties of measurement. Typical of these departures is the procedure of charging to the period as expense freight-in and purchasing costs on material acquisitions, rather than deferring these items to the future as inventoriable costs. The student has been subjected to these procedures at the elementary and intermediate level of accountancy education. It now becomes necessary to establish an understanding of the concepts underlying these procedures.

The essential problem involved in implementing the concept that service resources should be valued in terms of invested cash or cash equivalent at acquisition is the determination of the amount of cash equivalent invested. When the investment is in terms of cash, the problem involved is one of classifying the acquisitions in a significant manner. The problem of classification will be discussed later. In those instances where the investment is not a cash outlay, but involves either the promise to pay cash at a later date or the exchange of other assets, determination of the amount of the investment presents a more difficult problem.

**Discounts in Valuation.** Assume that the ABC Company purchases a machine on account at an invoice amount of $1,000 terms 2/10, net 30. It is quite apparent that as of the date of acquisition the cash obligation is only $980. Acceptance of the view that service resources acquired should be measured in terms of the cash equivalent outlay required to obtain them indicates that the correct valuation of the machine would be $980. If the discount is not taken and an additional $20 is paid out, the additional expenditure should be charged off as an expense of the period. In practice, refinements such as this illustration poses may be ignored if the amount involved is not substantial enough to cause material distortion of the valuation.

**Exchange of Service Resources for Other Service Resources.** (Reciprocal Transfer of Nonmonetary Assets.) As prescribed in *APB Opinion No. 29,* a reciprocal transfer results in the acquisition of nonmonetary assets or services or the satisfying of liabilities by surrendering other nonmonetary assets or services or incurring other obligations. Thus an exchange of inventories, property, plant and equipment, or liabilities for rent collected in advance or any combination thereof would represent a nonmonetary exchange transaction. The Accounting Principles Board concluded that, in general, accounting for nonmonetary transactions should be based on the fair value of the asset surrendered to obtain the acquired asset. Fair value refers to the estimated realizable values in cash transactions of the same or similar assets, quoted market prices, independent appraisals, and other available evidence of the cash equivalent of the assets given up. The fair value of the asset received should be used to measure the cost of the acquired nonmonetary asset if such value is more clearly evident than the fair value of the asset surrendered. If neither the fair value of a nonmonetary asset transferred nor the fair value of a nonmonetary asset received in exchange is determinable within reasonable limits, the recorded (booked) amount of the nonmonetary asset transferred out may be the only available measure of the transaction.

To illustrate the valuation of reciprocal transfers, assume that Company A transfers Merchandise X to Company B in exchange for Merchandise Y. If Merchandise X could readily be sold for $1,200 or has a quoted sales price at which similar items of merchandise have been sold of $1,200, the $1,200 would be fair value and Merchandise Y would be recorded on the books of Company A at $1,200. If Merchandise X should have no well-established fair value, but it is clearly evident that the fair value of Merchandise Y is $1,300, the transaction would be valued at $1,300 and Merchandise Y would be recorded at the $1,300. If major uncertainties exist about the fair value of both X and Y but Company A does have Merchandise X recorded at a booked value of $1,050, then acquired Merchandise Y may have to be valued at $1,050.

**Contributed Service Resources.** The valuation of assets contributed by a sole proprietor or by partners in a partnership has been discussed. The term "fair market value" was used to designate a reasonable measure of the proper cash or cash equivalent valuation. More accurate measures of "fair market value" are often available for corporations than for proprietorships or partnerships. When service resources are contributed by stockholders or owners of the enterprise in exchange for stock, the normal rule is that the services acquired should be valued at the cash that could have been obtained if the shares of stock or other ownership equity had been issued for cash. Actually, the determination of the cash equivalent exchanged in this manner is often not possible, so recourse to other methods of valuation is necessary. As a substitute, the cash equivalent price of the resources received may be used as a basis of valuation. In many cases neither the market price of the stock issued nor the cash equivalent of the resources acquired is readily determinable to a satisfactory degree. As a consequence, it is generally accepted accounting procedure to assume that the exchange is an exchange of equal values and that valuation should be determined by the more readily and accurately determinable *estimate* of the cash equivalent of either the stock issued or the resources acquired. The procedures involved in recording this type of transaction have been discussed in intermediate accounting.

The valuation of service resources acquired frequently requires the use of estimates. With a variety of estimates available, it is only through the exercise of sound judgment that the most appropriate value estimate may be determined. The accountant, who frequently must provide management with sound advice in this area, must exercise considerable care in preparing his recommendations and must also be cognizant of the possible long-run effects of these recommendations. For example, when capital stock is issued in exchange for a building, the accountant must recognize that the effect of the value-estimate determined to be proper will be reflected through several subsequent income statements, as the value-estimate for the building is amortized through depreciation entries. The accountant must consider carefully the various alternatives prior to presenting management with his considered recommendation on the proper value for the assets involved.

**Leased Resources.** A number of unusual problems arise when an enterprise uses resources leased from others. A lease agreement generally involves the right to use a resource for a part, or all, of its estimated useful life in exchange for regular rental payments. Generally, the user of the resource (lessee) does not obtain title to the resource from the owner (lessor). Historically, the lessee has not recorded leased resources as assets. Thus, rental payments for the use of leased resources are charged to expense as a cost of operations in the period incurred. Some accountants argue, however, that a lease agreement transfers to the lessee the right to use a resource (an asset) in exchange for an obligation to make rental payments (a liability). These accountants would require accounting recognition by lessees for all leases, or for all leases whose term runs beyond a relatively short period, say, a year or more.

In its *Statement No. 13*, the Financial Accounting Standards Board concluded that those leases that convey to the lessee substantially all of the service potential in an asset should be capitalized as assets and liabilities. For leases meeting the criteria set forth in *Statement No. 13*, a strong case can be made for recognizing the substance of the lease rather than relying on its legal form. Here the resource leased should be recognized as an asset, the valuation of it being the discounted amount of future lease rental payments, less the portion of the payments for such things as taxes or insurance. A liability for a like amount should also be recorded. The amount capitalized for the leased resource should be allocated as an amortization charge over the useful life of the resource or over the initial period of the lease, depending on whether the lease is virtually the same as an installment purchase of the property.

If a machine were leased for a 10-year period under a contract to pay $5,000 a year rental for the first three years, $3,000 a year for the next five, and $1,000 a year for the last two with an option to purchase or to renew at a nominal amount, and the machine had an expected useful life of 10 years, the lease arrangement is essentially the equivalent of an installment purchase of the machine. Assuming a 6% market rate of interest, the discounted amount of the future lease payment at acquisition would be computed as follows:

(a)  Present value of $5,000 a year for 3 years discounted at 6% . . . . . . . . . . . $13,365.06

(b) Present value of $3,000 a year for 5 years deferred three years and discounted at 6% .................................................. 10,610.34
(c) Present value of $1,000 a year for 2 years discounted at 6% deferred 8 years ..................................................... 1,150.29
   Asset valuation         $25,125.69

The entry to record the acquisition would be

| | | |
|---|---|---|
| Machinery—acquired by lease | $25,125.69 | |
| Lease obligation | | $25,125.69 |

The entries to record the amortization of the machinery and the lease payment in the first year would be

(1)

| | | |
|---|---|---|
| Depreciation—leased machinery | $2,512.57 | |
| Acc. depr.—leased machinery | | $2,512.57 |

(2)

| | | |
|---|---|---|
| Lease obligation on machinery | $3,492.46 | |
| Interest expense | 1,507.54 | |
| Cash | | $5,000.00 |

The lessor of leased property also faces problems in accounting for resources that it leases. Depending on the basic nature of the lease, the lessor may treat the lease as a sale or as a financing arrangement. If the lessor, such as a lease-finance company, a bank, or an insurance company, signs a lease that is primarily a financing arrangement, the "financing" accounting method is used, and the asset "contract receivable for equipment rentals" is debited for the aggregate rentals called for in the lease. Unearned finance charges or interest included in the aggregate rentals should be shown as a deduction from the receivable.

If the lessor is a manufacturer or dealer, the lease may be a marketing arrangement that is substantially equivalent to a sale. The aggregate rentals called for in the lease would be reported as a receivable, the present value of the rentals would be reported as a sale, and the difference would be deducted from the receivable as unearned interest income. The carrying amount of the leased resource would be charged to cost of sales, so that gross profit would be the difference between the present value of the rentals and the carrying amount of the resource.

If the lessor, such as an owner-operator of a building or a short-term automotive equipment lessor, signs a lease that primarily involves an arrangement to provide services for a rental receipt, the "operating" accounting method is used and the asset "property leased to others" is debited for the cost of the property. Income is recognized as rental revenue over the term of the lease.

To illustrate the valuation procedures, if a lessor buys property from a manufacturer for $10,000 and rents the property to Company A for 10 years at $1,360 a year rental after which it will have no salvage value, the following entries would be made under the "operating" method and the "financing" method.

                    (1) "Operating" Method
Property leased to others                    $10,000
    Property                                              $10,000

                    (2) "Financing" Method
Contract receivable for equipment
    rentals                                   $13,600
        Property                                          $10,000
        Unearned interest income                           3,600

If the property had cost the manufacturer $8,000 and he leased (sold) it under the same terms, he would make the following entry:

                    (3) "Sales" Method
Contract receivable for equipment
    rentals                                   $13,600
Cost of sales                                   8,000
    Sales                                                 $10,000
    Finished goods                                          8,000
    Unearned interest income                                3,600

## Asset Classification and Recognition

**Classification.** There are two aspects to the problem of classification of assets. One relates to the question of how various acquisitions of resources should be classified. A typical example would be the question of whether an expenditure to add a new electric system should be classified as building, machinery, fixtures, or in some other manner. Another example is the question of how to classify expenditures of the removal of an old building. There is no one answer to these problems of classification. It has been suggested, however, that resources to be used together should be classified together. In the case of the electric system, if it were expected that it would be used over the entire life of the building, it should be classified as part of the building. If, on the other hand, the use of the system were to be restricted to a special type of machine, the cost of the system should be added to the cost of the machine. Expected use often dictates the proper classification of many resources.

Service resources are generally classified according to a natural usage, such as buildings, machinery, and the like, but this manner of classification is not necessarily the most useful. In some situations it may be more appropriate to classify service resources according to the function to be performed by the use of the services, such as in the case of delivery services (which might include trucks and other natural objects used in the delivery function), warehousing (which might include building, fixtures, and other natural objects used in the warehousing function), and other functional activities. In practice, the natural classification is most often used because it is more objective and does not lend itself to being changed by managerial intent.

The second aspect of asset classification relates to the question of how specific assets should be presented in financial statements. Discussion of asset classification, other than for the reporting of leased resources, has been covered in elementary and intermediate courses. Disclosure of leased resources in the financial statements of the lessee generally depends on the nature of the lease. If the lease agreement transfers substantially all the service potential in the asset, the discounted value of future lease rental payments is capitalized as an asset. This asset would normally be reported as a fixed asset, with a related reduction for estimated depreciation to date on the capitalized value.

The lessor of resources generally will report as an asset a lease that transfers substantially all the service potential in the asset, among the receivables, with separate disclosure if amounts are material. Other leases are more in the nature of operating leases in which the lessor retains the normal risks or rewards of ownership. Costs invested in the leased resources are properly reported with or near property, plant, and equipment as a separately disclosed item, where material.

**Recognition.** The time at which assets should be recognized by the enterprise varies from situation to situation, but, in general, recognition that an asset has been acquired turns on the passage of legal title to the asset to the acquiring enterprise. Exceptions to this general rule arise when title has not legally passed, but when evidence exists that the asset is essentially or constructively owned. An example of this would be the situation under a conditional purchase, where the economic facts indicate that acquisition has taken place, even though legal title to the resource has not been acquired. Similarly, certain leases involve a commitment by the lessee to acquire substantially all the services embodied in the asset. Such a lease is considered an economic resource of the lessee, even though title has not passed.

Underlying this general idea of the time for recognizing assets on the books of record is the practical point that assets may be recorded as acquired when certain types of business papers, such as invoices from sellers, are available as evidence of the acquisition. This practical procedure, which does not always represent legal passage of title, often requires adjustments at the reporting date to assure that only assets that meet the more fundamental test of being owned are reported.

## APPLICATION OF PRINCIPLES

The concepts and standards set forth in this book for recording assets rest on the concept that assets should be stated in terms of the reporting enterprise. Thus, the cash or cash equivalent should be in terms of the investment made by the company to acquire the assets and not stated at the valuation that some previous owner may have placed on them.

### Illustration — Partnership Formed from Proprietorship

Assume that A is a sole proprietor having the following assets, among others, valued at cost to him:

| | |
|---|---|
| Building | $30,000 |
| Equipment | 10,000 |
| Inventory | 18,000 |
| Total | $58,000 |

If A decides to form a partnership with B and contributes the assets above to the partnership, the proper valuation of the assets would not necessarily be their cost to A, but should be their cost to the partnership. This cost would normally be determined by bargaining between A and B. If the bargain agreement does not disclose this valuation, it is customary to accept current market price as the proper valuation of the assets. In the instance above, if the fair market value of the assets were some other amounts, these amounts would be the basis for an entry on the books of the new enterprise. If the building were considered to be worth $45,000, the equipment $8,000, and the inventory $18,000, the entry on the books of the partnership to record the admission of A to the partnership would be:

| | | |
|---|---|---|
| Building | $45,000 | |
| Equipment | 8,000 | |
| Inventory | 18,000 | |
| A, Capital | | $71,000 |

This same principle applies if a corporation is formed to take over the assets of another corporation, a partnership, or a sole proprietorship. Likewise, as noted in Chapter One, it would seem that an individual having personal assets that he proposes to use in his sole proprietorship business would follow the procedure of revaluing the personal assets to their market valuation as of the time the assets are turned over to the business. Actually, this refinement is often ignored on the grounds that the personal assets and the proprietorship assets both belong to the individual and should be valued at cost to the individual, rather than at cost to the business. This departure from principle seems to have considerable support in practice in order to assure a more objective basis for the valuation of proprietorship assets.

The need for valuing partnership contributed assets at fair market value rather than at cost to the individual making the contribution may be demonstrated in the following example. Assume that A contributed assets that cost him $58,000 (as noted first above) and B contributed cash of $58,000. If the assets contributed by A had a market value of $71,000 (as noted later above), it is immediately apparent that A has contributed more than 50% of the total asset values. If A had sold the assets for the $71,000, he personally would have recognized a gain of $13,000. On the other hand, if A contributed the assets to the partnership at his original cost of $58,000, and if the partnership subsequently sold these assets for $71,000, the resulting gain of $13,000 would be divided between the partners in their income-sharing ratio. If such ratio were 50% to each partner, A would be given credit for only $6,500 of the gain to the partnership. To avoid this inequity, or the reverse when market price is below cost to the original owner, the accounting principle that assets should be valued at their cost to the acquiring enterprise is generally accepted in practice.

## 2 / Valuation of Assets

The foregoing illustration may be explained more clearly by indicating the entries that would appear on the books of the partnership if A allowed his contribution to be valued at his cost of $58,000.

(1)
| | | |
|---|---|---|
| Building | $30,000 | |
| Equipment | 10,000 | |
| Inventory | 18,000 | |
|     A, Capital | | $58,000 |

(2)
| | | |
|---|---|---|
| Cash | $58,000 | |
|     B, Capital | | $58,000 |

By the foregoing entries each partner has been given a capital credit of $58,000. Assume now that the partnership sells the assets contributed by A for $71,000. The entries to record the sale and to allocate the income realized would be:

(1)
| | | |
|---|---|---|
| Cash | $71,000 | |
|     Building | | $30,000 |
|     Equipment | | 10,000 |
|     Inventory | | 18,000 |
|     Gain on sale of assets | | 13,000 |

(2)
| | | |
|---|---|---|
| Gain on sale of assets | $13,000 | |
|     A, Capital | | $6,500 |
|     B, Capital | | 6,500 |

This clearly demonstrates that A has, in fact, contributed to B the sum of $6,500, or one-half the profit that had existed on A's personal assets prior to the transfer of these assets to the partnership.

Now let us assume that the partnership does not resell the assets, but uses them in producing goods and services that are subsequently sold. Even under this alternative an inequity will arise, since partnership expenses will be lower by $13,000 than they would otherwise have been. That is, as the service resources contributed by A are used up by the partnership, $13,000 less cost will be charged to operations than if the assets had been recorded at their cash equivalent to the partnership of $71,000. This will result in an income greater than that actually earned by the partnership in the amount of the $13,000. If this additional income is divided on a 50-50 basis, A will have, in effect, contributed $6,500 of his income to B. This is one-half the unrealized profit that existed on A's assets at the date of contribution of the assets to the partnership.

## Goodwill

At times an individual may have assets valued at cost which have a higher market valuation but which are worth more than either of these amounts to a new enterprise that is being formed. The owners of the new business may then agree to allow the individual contributing these assets a capital credit greater than the market value of the assets contributed. One reason for the increased valuation may be the moral and professional reputation or the ability and "know-how" of the contributing individual to use the assets profitably. In a situation such as this, accountants are reluctant to place a valuation other than fair market value on the assets contributed. The excess contribution often is construed to be goodwill.

The typical definition of goodwill runs in terms of the excessive earning power attributable not to the individual assets of the entity but to the entity itself. It has been referred to as "going-value" because its existence depends upon the continued operations of the entity. It cannot be sold as a separate asset but attaches to the combination and use made of the tangible assets as a whole. In a more realistic sense, goodwill is also held to attach to individuals or groups of individuals within the entity. It has been referred to also as a "master valuation" account. In this sense it refers to the additional value attaching to the individual assets because they are in organized form as a business enterprise. This concept of goodwill represents an additional valuation to enterprise assets. This additional valuation would not be recorded under the normal accounting valuations of assets. For purposes of this textbook, goodwill will be considered as embodying one or more or all of these various views of the nature of goodwill.

**Partnership Goodwill.** To illustrate this treatment, assume that A has assets that cost him $58,000, but that have a market value of $71,000 on the date they are contributed to the partnership, and that B agrees to give A credit for a $90,000 contribution. B also agrees to contribute cash of $90,000 for a 50% interest in the new partnership. The presumption, following the reasoning in the paragraph above, would be that A has contributed goodwill of $19,000, as well as the assets to be recorded at $71,000. The formation of the partnership would be recorded as follows:

(1)
| | | |
|---|---|---|
| Building | $45,000 | |
| Equipment | 8,000 | |
| Inventory | 18,000 | |
| Goodwill | 19,000 | |
| A, Capital | | $90,000 |

(2)
| | | |
|---|---|---|
| Cash | $90,000 | |
| B, Capital | | $90,000 |

The result of this recording is that each partner has a 50% equity in the partnership assets, and that these assets include $19,000 goodwill. Many businessmen wish to avoid having the intangible asset "goodwill" appear in their records and on their reports. Accordingly, in practice the procedure of allocating the goodwill to the other assets is at times followed. It is apparent, however, that any allocation of the goodwill to individual assets may be largely an arbitrary procedure. Therefore, if goodwill is not to be recorded, an equitable alternative would be for one partner to give a capital bonus to the partner bringing in the goodwill. Acceptance of the bonus concept would mean that the partner not contributing goodwill (partner B above) would allow the other partner (A) to take capital credit for some of his (B's) contribution.

The following illustration indicates the bonus procedure. A contributes the individual assets of $71,000 and goodwill of $19,000, while B contributes $90,000 cash. It is evident that both partners have made an equal contribution. Total assets are $180,000, which includes the $19,000 of goodwill. If goodwill is not to be recognized as an asset, the total assets of the partnership will be $161,000 ($180,000 − $19,000) and, if partners' capitals are to be equal, each should be credited for $80,500. If B contributes $90,000 of cash and receives credit for only $80,500, and if A contributes recognized assets of only $71,000 and receives a capital credit of $80,500, it is apparent that B has given a bonus in capital to A, and that goodwill will not be recorded on the books of the partnership. The entries to record the foregoing example would be as follows:

(1)
| | | |
|---|---|---|
| Building | $45,000 | |
| Equipment | 8,000 | |
| Inventory | 18,000 | |
| A, Capital | | $71,000 |

(2)
| | | |
|---|---|---|
| Cash | $90,000 | |
| B, Capital | | $80,500 |
| A, Capital | | 9,500 |

**Corporation Goodwill.** It is acceptable accounting procedure to recognize goodwill as an asset under partnership accounting, but similar situations in corporation accounting are, in effect, handled according to the bonus procedure. Substituting in the foregoing example, assume that 500 shares of $100 par value stock are issued to both A and B in exchange for their asset contributions. The entries to record the formation of the corporate enterprise would be

(1)
| | | |
|---|---|---|
| Building | $45,000 | |
| Equipment | 8,000 | |
| Inventory | 18,000 | |
| Capital stock (issued to A) | | $50,000 |
| Capital in excess of par | | 21,000 |

(2)
| | | |
|---|---|---|
| Cash | $90,000 | |
| Capital stock (issued to B) | | $50,000 |
| Capital in excess of par | | 40,000 |

Since capital in excess of par attaches equally to each share of stock outstanding, it is apparent that the equity of each individual at book value would be the

$50,000 of capital stock plus one-half of the excess (or $30,500), for a total equity of $80,500. This is the result also obtained under the partnership procedure when the bonus alternative was used.

It should not be assumed that corporations never recognize goodwill as an asset. When a corporation pays cash for goodwill, or whenever stock is issued for assets, both tangible and intangible, and one of the assets is specifically determined to be goodwill, the goodwill is recognized as an asset. In addition, a special type of goodwill frequently arises through the procedures involved in the preparation of consolidated statements. Goodwill from consolidation may appear on consolidated financial statements if the parent corporation has acquired a controlling interest in the stock of another (subsidiary) corporation at a cost price in excess of the book value of the shares of stock acquired. Goodwill from consolidation, as well as the entire area of preparation of consolidated statements, is discussed later, beginning with Chapter Nine.

**Problems in Partnership Goodwill and Bonus.** Occasionally the intentions of partners in reaching an agreement on their respective interests in a partnership are not clearly discernible. The interest each partner is to have in the partnership, whether or not goodwill is to be recognized, and, if goodwill is involved, the amount to be recognized, are questions that sometimes are difficult to resolve.

Thus, for example, the agreement may indicate that A is to contribute tangible assets of $60,000, that B is to contribute tangible assets of $80,000, and that the two partners are to share equally in the partnership assets. While these points of agreement may appear clear enough at first glance, further study indicates that it is impossible to determine whether both A and B contributed goodwill which is to be recognized or whether the bonus procedure is to be used. If the bonus procedure is to be used, the entries would be:

(1)
| | | |
|---|---|---|
| Assets | $60,000 | |
| A, Capital | | $60,000 |

(2)
| | | |
|---|---|---|
| Assets | $80,000 | |
| A, Capital | | $10,000 |
| B, Capital | | 70,000 |

If, however, the partners agree that B contributes no goodwill, and if the partners have agreed to have equal capital in the partnership, then A must have contributed goodwill of $20,000. The entries would be:

(1)
| | | |
|---|---|---|
| Assets | $60,000 | |
| Goodwill | 20,000 | |
| A, Capital | | $80,000 |

## 2 / Valuation of Assets

(2)

| | | |
|---|---|---|
| Assets | $80,000 | |
| B, Capital | | $80,000 |

If the partners should indicate that only $10,000 of goodwill is to be recognized, but that each partner is to have a 50% equity in the enterprise, both goodwill and bonus appear to exist. The entries would be:

(1)

| | | |
|---|---|---|
| Assets | $60,000 | |
| Goodwill | 10,000 | |
| A, Capital | | $70,000 |

(2)

| | | |
|---|---|---|
| Assets | $80,000 | |
| B, Capital | | $75,000 |
| A, Capital | | 5,000 |

## Economic Valuation of Enterprise Assets

Earlier in the chapter it was stated that for recording purposes accountants value service resource assets at the cash or cash equivalent invested in these assets, but tend to value cash and direct claims to cash at the amount of cash to be received from such assets. Some economists and others maintain that proper valuations of all assets should be in terms of the cash to be received from such assets. Invested cost to them has little significance, for the only significant value of an asset is the cash or cash equivalent that it can provide. Since at any date the cash potential of each asset is unknown, the cash to be received must be estimated. Because the cash equivalent requires estimation, it is apparent that economic valuations include a large amount of subjective opinion.

Another fundamental difference between recorded accounting and "economic" valuation lies in the different approaches to the valuation of an enterprise. Economic valuations are based on a view of the enterprise itself as a single asset and provide for the valuation of the enterprise in terms of the net receipts expressed in terms of cash or cash equivalent which the enterprise will provide over its life. Accounting, of course, considers individual assets as valuation units, and the sum of the asset values is one measure of the value of the enterprise.

The variation between the accounting summation valuation of the enterprise assets and the economic valuation is attributed to (1) the difference in the market values of the individual assets and their cost (unrealized gain or loss) and (2) the difference in the market value of the enterprise as a whole and the sum of the market value of the individual assets (goodwill). This relationship is portrayed below for an enterprise to be merged with another firm, where the value of the enterprise assets as a going concern determined by discounting net cash receipts is $100,000, although the sum of the market value of the individual assets is $80,000 (asset A — $20,000 + asset B — $50,000 + asset C — $10,000) and the accounting cost summation valuation is $70,000 (asset A − $30,000 + asset B − $30,000 + asset C − $10,000).

| | | |
|---|---:|---:|
| Economic valuation (going concern) | | $100,000 |
| Market valuation (individual assets) | $80,000 | 80,000 |
| Goodwill | | $ 20,000 |
| Accounting valuation (individual assets) | 70,000 | |
| Unrealized appreciation of asset values | $10,000 | |

## PROBLEMS

### Problem 2-1

The following information relates to the purchase of an asset that was paid for by a trade-in of an old asset and the balance in cash:

| | |
|---|---:|
| List price of the new asset | $10,000 |
| Cash payment | 5,800 |
| Cost of old asset | 8,000 |
| Depreciation accrued—old asset | 5,000 |
| Second hand market value—old asset | 3,600 |

*Required:*
(1) You are to prepare entries to show three different methods of recording the transaction.
(2) Following each entry give an explanation of the reasoning behind that method of recording and indicate the circumstances in which it might be appropriate. (AICPA adapted)

### Problem 2-2

During 1979, the following transactions between the Warehouse Company and the Investment Company were reported.

1. Warehouse Company completed construction of a warehouse building on its own land in June at a cost of $500,000. Construction was financed by a construction loan from the Central Savings Bank.
2. On July 1, Investment Company bought the building from Warehouse for $500,000. Warehouse used the $500,000 to pay its construction loan.
3. On July 1, Investment Company borrowed $500,000 from Central Savings Bank to be repaid quarterly over four years plus interest at 8%. A mortgage was placed on the building to secure the loan and Warehouse Company signed as a guarantor of the loan.
4. On July 1, Warehouse Company signed a noncancelable 10-year lease of the warehouse building from Investment Company. The lease specified that Warehouse would pay $75,000 per year for 10 years, payable in advance on

July 1, and provided an option to Warehouse, exercisable at the end of the 10-year period, either to (1) purchase the building for $100,000, or (2) renew the lease for an additional 15 years at $25,000 per year and purchase the building for $10,000 at the end of the renewal period. The lease specified that $12,000 of the annual payment would be for insurance, taxes, and maintenance for the following 12 months; if the lease were renewed, $13,000 of each annual payment would be for insurance, taxes, and maintenance.

5. The building has a useful life of 40 years and should be depreciated under a straight-line method (assume no salvage value).
6. Warehouse and Investment negotiated the lease for a return of 9%.

*Required:*

For the December 31, 1980, balance sheets of both Warehouse and Investment, compute the following

(1) Prepaid insurance, taxes, and maintenance.
(2) "Building" on books of lessee.
(3) "Building" on books of lessor.
(4) Current liabilities and receivables on the lease.
(5) Any other balance sheet disclosures necessary to account for the lease.

(AICPA adapted)

## Problem 2-3

1. Present briefly the arguments for using each of the following valuation bases for reporting assets in the balance sheet:
   a. Market value or realizable value.
   b. Original cost, or original cost less estimated depreciation.
   c. Appraised value.
2. Explain the relation of the "going-concern concept" to each of the bases of valuation listed above.

(AICPA adapted)

## Problem 2-4

ABC Corporation purchased a machine in 1979, trading in an older machine of a similar type. The old machine, which was acquired in 1966, had a cost basis of $77,250 but was written up $47,750 to $125,000 in 1970 with a corresponding credit made to surplus from unrealized appreciation. In subsequent years this appreciation amount has been partially amortized. Both the old and new machines have an estimated 20-year life, and reappraisal of the old machine did not affect its estimated life. ABC Corporation takes one-half year of depreciation in years of acquisition and disposal.

The terms of purchase provided for a trade-in allowance of $25,000 and called for a cash payment of $125,000 or 12 monthly payments of $11,000 each. ABC Corporation chose to accept the latter alternative. Other expenses incurred in connection with the exchange were as follows:

Payroll charges:
| | |
|---|---|
| Removal of old machine | $ 800 |
| Repairs to factory floor | 700 |
| Installation of new machine | 900 |

Invoices received:
| | |
|---|---|
| Sales engineer who supervised installation 40 hours at $10.00 | 400 |
| Hotel, meals, travel, etc. for sales engineer | 200 |
| Freight in—new machine | 1,100 |
| Freight out—old machine | 1,000 |

*Required:*

Prepare entries to reflect the exchange on the books of ABC on a basis acceptable for federal income tax purposes. Show all computations clearly labeled.

(AICPA adapted)

## Problem 2-5

Messrs. R. T. Robbins and C. A. Taylor decide to go into partnership. The two partners contribute the assets listed below and accept the values indicated:

| | Robbins' Valuation | Taylor's Valuation | Accepted for Partnership |
|---|---|---|---|
| Cash | $10,000 | $10,000 | $ 20,000 |
| Building | 40,000 | –0– | 60,000 |
| Merchandise | | 12,000 | 12,000 |
| Equipment | | 10,000 | 28,000 |
| Goodwill | | 1,000 | 5,000 |
| Total | $50,000 | $33,000 | $125,000 |

*Required:*
(1) If Taylor were forming a sole proprietorship, should the $1,000 of goodwill Mr. Taylor believes he has be accepted as an asset?
(2) Give the entry to record the formation of the partnership.

## Problem 2-6

N. M. Cleary and W. B. Bonnell operated separate proprietorships with results for 1979, considered typical, as follows:

| December 31, 1979 | Cleary | Bonnell |
|---|---|---|
| Total assets | $100,000 | $120,000 |
| Liabilities | 10,000 | 20,000 |
| Proprietorship | $ 90,000 | $100,000 |
| Earnings in 1979 | $ 18,000 | $ 15,000 |

As separate businesses, the two companies earned a total of $33,000 ($18,000 plus $15,000). Both men agree that if the two companies were combined as a partnership, total income would increase about $6,000 to an average of $39,000. The partners agree that the excess $6,000 would be contributed equally by each company.

The two men decide to form the partnership. They believe an appropriate rate of return for the partnership would be 15%. From this they conclude that if $39,000 represents 15%, 100% of the business would be $260,000. Since the combined net assets of the separate companies is only $190,000 ($90,000 + $100,000), the partners agree to recognize $70,000 of goodwill.

*Required:*
Give the entries to set up the partnership books.

## Problem 2-7

V. N. Smith and A. K. Brown own separate businesses with operating results substantially as follows:

|  | Smith | Brown |
|---|---|---|
| Assets | $80,000 | $30,000 |
| Liabilities | none | none |
| Proprietorship | $80,000 | $30,000 |
| Earnings each year | $ 8,000 | $ 8,000 |

It is agreed by both men that Mr. Brown's high earnings, $8,000 a year on a $30,000 investment, are due to the goodwill that attaches to his company.

The men agree that on the formation of a partnership, the $50,000 of goodwill which they decide Mr. Brown has (calculated by assuming that the $8,000 represents a 10% return on the investment, so 100% of the investment would be $80,000, of which $30,000 is represented by tangible assets and $50,000 by goodwill) should be considered, but they do not want to put it on the books. They decide to have Mr. Smith give Mr. Brown a bonus of an appropriate amount when the partnership is formed and to recognize no goodwill.

*Required:*
(1) Give the entry to record the formation of the partnership.
(2) Discuss the appropriateness of the bonus procedure.

## Problem 2-8

The Alpha Company purchased a store building for $100,000. Immediately thereafter, $10,000 was spent to remodel the store front. In the opinion of competent real estate firms, the expenditure of this additional $10,000 did not add to the "resale value" of the building—that is, this building, which was purchased for $100,000, could not be resold for more than that amount, even though the additional $10,000 was spent in improving the store front.

What is your advice regarding the accounting treatment of this $10,000 expenditure? *Discuss fully.* (AICPA adapted)

### Problem 2-9

A small but growing road building contractor would like to bid on a contract to rebuild and surface 10.6 miles of road. The job is considerably larger than any he has attempted in the past and, if he wins the contract, he estimates that he will need a $100,000 line of credit for working capital.

The contractor's most recent statement of financial position shows that he has a net worth of $170,000, of which $110,000 represents the book value of road building equipment. Most of the equipment was acquired a few years ago at a bankruptcy sale. The equipment has a fair value several times as great as book value.

The contractor knows that his bank will not give him a $100,000 line of credit on the basis of a position statement (balance sheet) that shows his net worth at $170,000. He wants to adjust his accounting records to show the current fair value of the equipment and to prepare a revised position statement.

*Required:*
(1) List the factors that, alone or in combination, may have caused the difference between the book value and the current fair value of the equipment.
(2) The current fair value of fixed assets may be estimated by using one of the following methods:
   (a) Reproduction cost.
   (b) Replacement cost.
   (c) Capitalization of earnings.

Describe each of the three methods of estimating the current fair value of fixed assets and discuss the possible limitations of each.

(3) Discuss the propriety of adjusting the accounting records to show the fair value of the equipment and of preparing a revised position statement.

(AICPA adapted)

### Problem 2-10

The abbreviated balance sheet of the B. E. Ornot Company on December 31, appears as follows:

| Current assets | $100,000 | Liabilities | $ 80,000 |
|---|---|---|---|
| Fixed assets | 300,000 | Stockholders' equity | 320,000 |
| | $400,000 | | $400,000 |

On this date the Ornot Company signed a contract with a large company to take all of Ornot's output, for which it would be paid net receipts (receipts over cash disbursements) of $60,000 a year for an indefinite period in the future.

*Required:*
(1) Assuming that money is worth 10%, what is the capitalized "going-concern" value of the assets of the Company?

(2) Account for the difference between the $400,000 valuation of the assets and the capitalized value. Assume that unrealized appreciation on the fixed assets is $63,000.

## Problem 2-11

Give the journal entry to record the following transactions:

1. A sale was made in exchange for a $1,000 note receivable, bearing interest at 3% a year, due in one year. On the date of sale, the bank discount rate used for discounting notes receivable was 6%.
2. On December 31, the Cam Company sold for $100,000 merchandise on account with terms of 2/10, n/30. The Company prepares financial statements as of December 31 of each year. Annual sales of the Company, if the $100,000 is included will be $185,000.

## Problem 2-12

Assume that R. U. Semhi and I. C. Haff contributed the following assets to the partnership of Semhi and Haff.

|  | Semhi | Haff | Accepted for Partnership |
|---|---|---|---|
| Cash | $11,000 | $12,000 | $23,000 |
| Building | 18,000 | –0– | 25,000 |
| Equipment | –0– | 9,000 | 8,000 |
| Goodwill (Mr. Semhi knows a considerable number of future customers, which will increase the earnings of the new partnership about $1,000 a year above what they would otherwise be. The two partners agree to value this intangible asset at an amount equal to 4 times the estimated exess earnings of $1,000.) |  |  | 4,000 |
| Total | $29,000 | $21,000 | $60,000 |

For purposes of the partnership, the assets contributed by each partner would be:

|  | Semhi | Haff |
|---|---|---|
| Cash | $11,000 | $12,000 |
| Building | 25,000 | –0– |
| Equipment | –0– | 8,000 |
| Goodwill | 4,000 | –0– |
| Total | $40,000 | $20,000 |

The partners are reluctant to have goodwill on the books of the partnership.

*Required:*
Give the journal entries to record the formation of the partnership.

## Problem 2-13

The Per Pet Yule Corporation was formed on July 1, 1979, by a charter from the Secretary of State, and was authorized to issue 100,000 shares of $50 par value common stock. The three incorporators, Messrs. Ace, Black, and Cash each contributed one section of land and each took 100 shares of stock in payment. On the date the land was turned over to the Corporation, it had a fair market value as follows:

|  | Fair Market Value |
| --- | --- |
| Land contributed by Mr. Ace | $ 4,000 |
| Land contributed by Mr. Black | 3,800 |
| Land contributed by Mr. Cash | 4,100 |
| Total | $11,900 |

*Required:*
(1) Mr. Ace suggests that you value each section of land at $5,000 and issue the stock at par. As an accountant, would you follow this procedure? Explain.
(2) Give the most appropriate entry to record the acquisition of the land and the issuance of the 300 shares of stock.

## Problem 2-14

The main office of the Doral Company is on land valued at $6,000,000. Depreciation on the building has been taken at $250,000 a year for 30 years. The building cost $10,000,000, and its book value is now down to $2,500,000. An appraisal indicates that the property has a market value of $15,000,000. The Doral Company receives an offer to buy it on a 25-year leaseback basis for $15,000,000. The lease is to yield a 7% return to the buyer and to provide options for Doral to repurchase at the end of 25 years for $6,000,000 or to exercise as desired three 10-year lease extensions at 60% of the initial term rental. Assume that Doral will have to pay a 25% capital gains tax and a 52% ordinary income tax. Rent is to be paid annually in advance.

*Required:*
(1) Compute the annual rental to be paid by Doral.
(2) Should Doral accept the offer to buy?

## Problem 2-15

Select the *best* answer for each of the following items:

1. Jones sold land to Smith for $200,000 cash and a noninterest-bearing note with a face amount of $800,000. The fair value of the land at the date of sale was $900,000. Jones should value the note receivable at
   a. $900,000.
   b. $800,000.
   c. $700,000.
   d. $1,000,000.

2. On April 30, 1979, White sold land with a book value of $600,000 to Black for its fair value of $800,000. Black gave White a 12%, $800,000 note secured only by the land. At the date of sale, Black was in a very poor financial position and its continuation as a going concern was very questionable. White should
   a. Use the cost recovery method of accounting.
   b. Record the note at its discounted value.
   c. Record a $200,000 gain on the sale of the land.
   d. Fully reserve the note.

3. On April 1, 1978, Austin Corporation sold equipment costing $1,000,000 with accumulated depreciation of $250,000 to its wholly owned subsidiary, Cooper Company, for $900,000. Austin was depreciating the equipment on the straight-line method over 20 years with no salvage value, which Cooper continued. In consolidation at March 31, 1979, the cost and accumulated depreciation, respectively, are
   a. $1,000,000 and $300,000.
   b. $900,000 and $50,000.
   c. $900,000 and $60,000.
   d. $750,000 and $50,000.

4. On June 30, 1979, the Ingalls Corporation sold equipment for $420,000 which had a net book value of $400,000 and a remaining life of 10 years. That same day the equipment was leased back at $1,000 per month for 5 years with no option to renew the lease or repurchase the equipment. Ingalls' rent expense for this equipment for the six months ended December 31, 1979, would be
   a. $5,000.
   b. $4,000.
   c. $6,000.
   d. $(14,000).

5. The Ackley Company exchanged 100 shares of Burke Company common stock, which Ackley was holding as an investment, for a piece of equipment from the Flynn Company. The Burke Company common stock, which had been purchased by Ackley for $30 per share, had a quoted market value of $34 per share at the date of exchange. The piece of equipment had a recorded amount on Flynn's books of $3,100. What journal entry should Ackley have made to record this exchange?

|     |                                              | Debit  | Credit |
| --- | -------------------------------------------- | ------ | ------ |
| a.  | Equipment                                    | $3,000 |        |
|     | Investment in Burke                          |        |        |
|     | Company common stock                         |        | $3,000 |
| b.  | Equipment                                    | 3,100  |        |
|     | Investment in Burke                          |        |        |
|     | Company common stock                         |        | 3,000  |
|     | Other income                                 |        | 100    |
| c.  | Equipment                                    | 3,100  |        |
|     | Other expense                                | 300    |        |
|     | Investment in Burke                          |        |        |
|     | Company common stock                         |        | 3,400  |
| d.  | Equipment                                    | 3,400  |        |
|     | Investment in Burke                          |        |        |
|     | Company common stock                         |        | 3,000  |
|     | Other income                                 |        | 400    |

Items 6 and 7 are based on the following information:

Taft Co. sells Lee Co. a machine, the usual cash price of which is $10,000, in exchange for an $11,800 noninterest-bearing note due three years from date.

6. If Taft records the note at $10,000, the overall effect will be
    a. A correct sales price and correct interest revenue.
    b. A correct sales price and understated interest revenue.
    c. An understated sales price and understated interest revenue.
    d. An overstated sales price and understated interest revenue.

7. If Lee records the asset and note at $11,800, the overall effect will be
    a. A correct acquisition cost and correct interest expense.
    b. A correct acquisition cost and understated interest expense.
    c. An understated acquisition cost and understated interest expense.
    d. An overstated acquisition cost and understated interest expense.

8. On January 2, 1979, MacAngus Co., as lessor, leased machinery to Yen Co. for $1,000 per year for ten years. The machinery is manufactured by MacAngus at a cost of $4,000 and has a normal selling price of $6,000. If Yen Co. had borrowed money to purchase the machinery outright, it would have had to pay interest at 12%. The estimated salvage value of the machinery at the end of its ten years of useful life is $1,000.

The present value of $1 for 10 periods at 12% per period is $.322.

The present value of an annuity of $1 per period for 10 periods at 12% per period is $5.650.

Assume that this lease is, in substance, an installment sale of the property by MacAngus. *Ignoring income taxes,* the amount of gross profit that MacAngus should recognize at the date the lease is signed is
    a. $2,000.
    b. $1,650.
    c. $650.
    d. $1,328.

9. On January 2, 1974, Lewis Corporation issued $1,000,000 of 8% bonds at 98 due December 31, 1983. Legal and other costs of $30,000 were incurred in connection with the issue. Interest on the bonds is payable annually each December 31. The $30,000 issue costs are being deferred and amortized on a straight-line basis over the 10-year term of the bonds. The discount on the bonds is also being amortized on a straight-line basis over the 10 years (straight-line being immaterially different in effect from the preferable "interest method").

The bonds are callable at 101 (that is, at 101% of face amount), and on January 2, 1979, Lewis called $500,000 face amount of the bonds and retired them.

*Ignoring income taxes,* the amount of loss, if any, to be recognized by Lewis as a result of retiring the $500,000 of bonds in 1979 is
- a. $0.
- b. $5,000.
- c. $10,000.
- d. $17,500.

10. Burke Company issued a note solely in exchange for cash. Assuming that the items listed below differ in amount, the present value of the note at issuance is equal to the
- a. Face amount.
- b. Face amount discounted at the prevailing interest rate for similar notes.
- c. Proceeds received.
- d. Proceeds received discounted at the prevailing interest rate for similar notes.

# Valuation of Equities

Equity refers to the rights or interests in some entity or activity. In accounting, the rights or interests are the financial interests and, traditionally, accountants have referred to the interests of an owner in an enterprise as the equity of the entity. Shares of stock have been referred to as capital or owners' equity. As the contractual rights of various types of stockholders and bondholders have increasingly narrowed the difference between rights of creditors and rights of owners, the view has developed that "equities" is a broad term encompassing the investments by both creditors and owners in the enterprise, and thereby includes both the liabilities and the owners' equity in the enterprise. Although numerous differences exist between liabilities and an owner's interest, both are essentially sources of or claims to funds needed to develop and operate the business enterprise. The different types of equities are considered separately, although certain problems of valuation are common to all types of equities.

## VALUATION OF CREDITORSHIP EQUITIES

The basic unsettled question in the valuation of equities is whether equities represent (1) a claim or right to the assets of an enterprise, or (2) a source of or interest in the assets of the business. The distinction between the two points of view may be illustrated by assuming that a firm issues $100,000 of bonds at a discount of $5,000, so that the company receives only $95,000 in cash. Whether equities are considered a claim to assets or a source of assets, the entry to record the issuance of the bonds is:

| | | |
|---|---|---|
| Cash | $95,000 | |
| Discount on bonds payable | 5,000 | |
| Bonds payable | | $100,000 |

The distinction between the two views arises when the results of this transaction are disclosed in a balance sheet. If the creditorship equity is considered to represent the source of assets, and if the sale of the bonds has provided only $95,000 in cash, the bond discount should be shown on the balance sheet as a deduction from bonds payable, as follows:

| Assets | | Equities | |
|---|---|---|---|
| Cash | $95,000 | Bonds payable | $100,000 |
| | | Less: | |
| | X X X X | Bond discount | 5,000 |
| | | Bondholders' contribution | $95,000 |
| | X X X X | | X X X X |
| | XXXX | | XXXX |

If the creditorship equity is considered a claim to the assets, bonds payable may be shown at $100,000 (the amount of assets eventually to be claimed) and the bond discount treated as prepaid interest:

| Assets | | Equities | |
|---|---|---|---|
| Cash | $95,000 | Bonds payable | $100,000 |
| Bond discount | 5,000 | | |
| | X X X X | | X X X X |
| | XXXX | | XXXX |

In the past, accountants have almost uniformly treated bond discount as an asset and classified it as a deferred charge. In terms of fair value, however, at the time of issue the bonds have a market value equal to the cash they provide. Market value is also the amount that would have to be paid out at the issue date to retire the bonds. The economic reality is that at the issue date the economic claim to assets is equal to the resources provided, so the two notions of valuing liabilities may be viewed as a single notion: value liabilities at the amount of resources to be paid out discounted to the time the liability is incurred. This notion is a modification of the view that liabilities are claims to assets, and it provides a rationale for viewing liabilities as claims to assets. On a balance sheet, bond discount should be deducted from the face amount of bonds payable.

More broadly, when liabilities are viewed as claims, three broad types of liabilities must be recognized:

A. Money obligations—specified amount payable.
   1. Specified payee payable at specific date for purchases of goods and services.
   2. Specified payee payable at specific date for borrowed money and interest thereon.
   3. Undesignated payee payable at specified date (bearer bonds).
   4. Undesignated payee payable at no one specified date (unregistered serial bonds).
   5. Specified payee payable at no one specified date.

B. Money obligations—estimated amount payable to undesignated parties at unknown times (product guarantee warranties).
C. Product or service obligations—to be delivered to designated or undesignated entities at known or unknown times.

## Problems of Liability Valuation

There are two main limitations to the concept that creditorship equities should be valued in terms of the claims to assets. These limitations are:

1. Creditorship equities or liabilities vary in the degree and nature of their claim to assets and in time when they have to be paid. Tax liabilities normally have a higher priority than a liability to pay a pledged contribution to a college. A claim against assets due immediately may be more pressing than one due in six months. Claims that can be deferred by extension or renewal are different from claims that must be paid when due. Claims to goods and services are different from claims to cash. Claims with a specific prior claim against specific assets are different from those with only general claims against assets. Despite somewhat imprecise disclosure of varying types of claims, the general concept of a claim to assets seems to provide useful information to report users.
2. The notion that liabilities are obligations of the entity and claims to assets is interpreted by some readers to mean that all claims against assets are recorded. But many claims cannot be recorded, which raises the issue of whether certain claims will be paid out of future assets or from assets on hand. An illustration of this limitation is periodic bond interest requirements which will have to be paid in the future. Legally and contractually, the annual or semi-annual bond interest requirement represents a claim to company assets, yet accepted accounting procedures involve recording the claim of the bonds but not the claim of bond interest until the interest has accrued.

Conceptually, liabilities are recorded when obligations to pay out cash, transfer assets, or render services in the future are recognized as having been imposed through law or other action or contracted for in exchanges. Ideally, they should be measured at amounts established at the time of imposition or exchange discounted to the time of the event. Departures of an immaterial nature are readily accepted in practice.

Excluded from the concept of a recorded liability are most executory contracts. Such exchanges of promises between contracting parties represent offsetting assets and liabilities and "the right of offset" is assumed to apply until one party performs under the contract.

Despite this limitation to the scope of liabilities as claims, the claims notion is future action-oriented, in that liabilities indicate future disbursement activities, and provides more information to accounting report users than would a statement indicating the source of assets.

**Varying Recognition Dates.** It is seldom appropriate accounting procedure to report all of the interest that will have to be paid on a bond issue as a liability at the date the bond is issued. From a claim point of view the total interest liability is just as valid a claim against assets as is the face amount of the bond. In fact, most of the interest liability will have to be paid off prior to the payment of the maturity amount of the bond. The explanation for this seemingly inadequate disclosure lies in the accounting guideline or principle to the effect that a claim cannot exist until the activity causing the claim has been recognized. This principle results in the accounting recognition of similar liabilities at different dates dependent on the circumstances in a given situation. To illustrate, "wages payable" earned but not due to be paid to an employee for a month would be recognized as a liability. A similar obligation to be paid on the same date for work to be done next week would not be recognized. It would be considered an executory contract. The point to be noted is that a statement of entity liabilities is not a statement of future disbursements to be made. Departures from these general principles prevail in recording lease liabilities and estimated liabilities.

## Lease Liabilities

Commitments of a business enterprise under long-term lease agreements pose a variety of accounting problems. Traditionally, accounting for leases involved simply an entry to record the periodic rental payments. Gradually, disclosure of lease obligations in financial statement footnotes gained a measure of acceptance. Recognition has come more recently that some leases are in essence installment purchases of property and that these leases should be accounted for in relation to their substance as a purchase.

*Financial Accounting Standard No. 13* by the Financial Accounting Standards Board distinguishes between capital leases and operating leases. This accounting standard provides that a lease meeting one or more of certain criteria is a capital lease for which the obligation of the lessee is a liability.[1] The lessee's liability is the present value of the minimum lease payment using his incremental borrowing rate (the rate the lessee would have to pay to borrow the funds to purchase the asset) unless he can determine the lessor's implicit interest rate and it is lower. The capital lease obligation is disclosed as a liability in a balance sheet, as illustrated below, with disclosure in a footnote of the annual future minimum lease payments.

*Company XYZ*
*Balance Sheet*

| Assets | | Liabilities | |
|---|---|---|---|
| x x x | x x | Current liabilities: | |
| | | Obligations under capital | |
| | | leases (note A) | x x x |
| | | Noncurrent liabilities: | |
| | | Obligations under capital | |
| | | leases (note A) | x x x |

[1] See *FAS No. 13*, page 9, for a list of the criteria.

The rationale for this accounting procedure is the fact that leases have increasingly come to be used as a financing vehicle for the acquisition of long-lived service resources. Recognition of the total obligation under the lease terms on a discounted basis appears to represent a better accounting procedure for certain leases than either footnote disclosure or a simple entry to record rental payments.

To illustrate the determination of a lease liability and its disclosure in a balance sheet, assume that the Lee Company leases a machine from the Sell Company under a three-year noncancelable contract at a rental of $500 a quarter, payable at the beginning of each quarter. To assure proper maintenance of the machine, the lease contract provides that the lessee (the Lee Company) must guarantee a residual value of $2,000 at the end of the three-year life. Any value above $2,000 goes to the lessee. Assume further that the lease is renewable at the option of the lessee at a fair rental based on the life and efficiency of the machine at the end of the three-year period. Had the Lee Company chosen to borrow funds and buy the machine, an interest rate of 8% per year over the three-year period would have been paid, reflecting the Lee Company's incremental borrowing rate.

The criteria for classifying the lease as a capital lease (the meeting of any one or more establishes the lease as a capital lease), as set forth in Paragraphs 7a, b, c, and d of *FAS No. 13*, indicates that the lease is a capital lease, because the present value of the minimum lease payments exceeds 90% of the fair value of the property at the inception of the lease.

The present value of the minimum lease payments would be computed as follows, if discounted at the incremental borrowing rate of 8%.

|  | Undiscounted Amount | Discounted Amount |
|---|---|---|
| Minimum rental payments over the three-year period ($500 × 12 quarters) | $6,000.00 | $5,393.42 |
| Lease guarantee of residual value at the end of the lease | 2,000.00 | 1,576.99 |
| Total minimum lease payment | $8,000.00 | $6,970.41 |
| Fair value of the machine at the start of the lease |  | $7,000.00 |
| Minimum lease payments as a percentage of fair value ($6,970.41/7000) times 100 = |  | 99.58% |

Because the present value of the lease is below fair value at the date of the start of the lease, the Lee Company would report its liability at $6,970.41 disaggregated into a current liability portion of $1,941.95 (present value of first year's lease payments) and a noncurrent liability portion of $5,028.46.

## Estimated Liabilities

Estimated liabilities represent claims that are expected to fall due in the future, even though at the reporting date the exact amount of the claim may not be known. Although no liability in the legal sense may exist at the reporting date — on the basis of past transactions and experience, as well as of future expectations — recognition of the estimated liability can be justified.

Underlying many estimated liabilities is some type of a contingent loss. *FAS No. 5* defines a contingency "as an existing condition, situation, or set of circumstances involving uncertainty as to possible gain or loss to an enterprise that will ultimately be resolved when one or more future events occur or fail to occur." Other estimated liabilities are not contingencies in the foregoing sense because, though the amounts are estimated, there is nothing uncertain about the fact that the obligations have been incurred. The accrual of amounts owed for utility services is an example of the latter type of estimated liability.

Examples of estimated liabilities based on loss contingencies are (1) pending or threatened litigation, (2) risk of loss of enterprise property by threats of expropriation, and (3) obligations related to product warranties. *FAS No. 5* requires that an estimated loss from a loss contingency be accrued if (1) "it is probable that ... a liability had been incurred at the date of the financial statements," and (2) "the amount of the loss can be reasonably estimated."

A common situation indicating recognition of an estimated liability evolves from selling products under terms including a money-back guarantee. At any year-end it is evident that some refund claims will be made in the future on sales agreements entered into during the past year. On the basis of past experience, expected sales volume, and other variables, an estimate can be determined for future refunds from the past year's sales. The amount so determined will be reported on the statement of financial position as a liability (Estimated Liability on Product Guarantee) and in the income statement as an expense (Loss on Product Guarantee).

The Estimated Liability on Product Guarantee is similar to other creditorship equities in that it more closely represents a claim on assets than a source of assets. Other estimated liabilities are sometimes reported in a similar manner on the statement of financial position. Thus, liabilities under pension plans and tax obligations are at times based on estimates and reported as liabilities even though actual amounts due may not be known accurately.

As was noted in the discussion on lease liabilities, recognition of certain liabilities at estimated amounts appears to represent a sound accounting procedure. Although not all the normal tests of liability classification are met by lease commitments or by various estimated claims, financial reporting appears to be more complete with inclusion of these items as liabilities.

**Time of Retirement.** The need to distinguish between the amount of claim at the time of the initial exchange, the amount at the reporting date, and the amount that will have to be paid off ultimately influences the valuation of the equities. To illustrate, assume that Company X purchased merchandise on account at an invoice amount of $1,000, terms 2/10, n/30. This purchase may be recorded:

| | | |
|---|---|---|
| Purchases (merchandise) | $1,000 | |
| Accounts payable | | $1,000 |

If financial statements are to be prepared on the day following the purchase, a question arises as to the correct valuation of the accounts payable. On the reporting date the correct liability is $980, but if the Company never takes discounts, or if there is no intention to take this discount, the amount that will ultimately have to be paid is $1,000. Current accounting practice would sanction the reporting of a liability of either $1,000 or of $980 on the grounds that at any annual reporting date the amount of the difference, relative to other income statement and balance sheet items, is not material. The amount reported would generally be determined by the method of recording the liability initially, gross or net.

On the other hand, assume that the liability is in the form of bonds payable issued at a discount of $6,000 which are callable on the balance sheet date for $105,000, and have an ultimate maturity amount due of $100,000. Here a question may arise as to the proper amount that should be used for valuing the liability. Normally, accountants have assumed a going-concern point of view and have valued the bonds at the maturity amount with an appropriate amortization of the bond discount. If a definite intention to call the bonds shortly after the balance sheet date existed, the call price of $105,000 would likely be used. Even though the current market price of the bonds may indicate that the bonds could, at least in part, be retired well below the maturity value of the bonds, in the absence of clear evidence of an intent to retire the bonds, accountants would report the liability at the maturity value with a supplemental disclosure of the amount of the unamortized bond discount.

## SUMMARY: LIABILITY VALUATION

Accountants generally view creditorship equities as claims to assets valued at the amount of economic resources or services to be provided to other entities in the future, discounted to the time the liability is incurred. Since accountants do not show *all* claims to assets of an enterprise on a given balance sheet, a more accurate summary might be that, to the extent creditorship equities are recognized on a balance sheet, accountants tend to conceive of them as general claims to the assets also reported. The amount of the claim is established at the time of the exchange transaction and represents the amount to be transferred to another entity in the future, sometimes discounted and sometimes estimated.

## VALUATION OF OWNERS' EQUITIES

As indicated above, the valuation of liabilities tends to run in terms of ultimate claims against assets that the equity commands. The reverse has been true of the owners' equity. There has been support for the view that stockholders' equity should be valued in terms of the contributions made by the equity holders. Typical of this treatment is the accounting procedure of presenting preferred stock on the balance sheet at par less applicable discount on the stock. A similar example is found in the failure to include as a portion of preferred stock equity any dividend

## 3 / Valuation of Equities

in arrears that may exist until the dividend is declared payable by the board of directors of the company. The fact that accountants have accepted the source point of view in valuing ownership equities may be illustrated by assuming that a corporation issues 1,000 shares of $100 par preferred stock at $98 per share. The entry to record the sale of this stock would be:

| | | |
|---|---|---|
| Cash | $98,000 | |
| Discount on preferred stock | 2,000 | |
| Preferred stock | | $100,000 |

The point of view that ownership equities are valued to represent the source of assets is revealed by the balance sheet presentation, which indicates that $98,000 was contributed by stockholders, as follows:

| Assets | | Equities | |
|---|---|---|---|
| Cash | $98,000 | Preferred stock | $100,000 |
| | | Less: | |
| | | Discount on sale | 2,000 |
| | | Stockholders' contribution | $98,000 |
| | $98,000 | | $98,000 |

The basis for the source valuation of owners' equity is the legal and economic recognition of it as a residual interest in the economic resources of an enterprise that remains after deducting economic obligations. As a residual interest, the amount claimed by an ownership equity is somewhat uncertain, so valuation in terms of the amount claimed is difficult, though desirable. Advocates of the current exit value model for valuing assets cite as one of the advantages of their proposal the fact that ownership equity measures will then reflect the amount the owner could claim if the equity were liquidated. Other accounting authorities have expressed an interest in developing the concept of ownership equity as a claim to assets for accounting purposes. The dominant accounting view, held by advocates of the historical-cost accounting model, the general price-level adjusted accounting model, and most conceptions of the current value model is that ownership equities can be measured only as sources of enterprise funds—the amount to be claimed is too uncertain.

When more than one class of stock is outstanding, when options or warrants to acquire common stock exist, or when convertible securities are outstanding, the determination of the relative rights of various types of equity holders in the residual interest becomes somewhat involved. For example, at any point in time, there is a need to recognize the potential reallocation of the value of equity-holder rights when additional shares of stock may be issued as a result of the exercising of warrants or the converting of senior securities to common stock. To illustrate the situation involved, assume that the right-hand side of the balance sheet of the Pure Pak Company includes the following:

| | |
|---|---|
| Bonds payable, 7% convertible | $10,000,000 |
| Common stock (100,000 shares) | 1,000,000 |
| Retained earnings | 6,000,000 |

If the bondholders have the right to convert each $1,000 bond to 20 shares of common stock, and if they have not yet made any conversion, the book value per share of common stock is $70. Should the bondholders convert to common stock, the book per share then outstanding would be $57 or approximately a 19% dilution of the equity rights of each share of common stock. A large number of options and warrants outstanding with rights to purchase new common stock at a price below $70 could have the same dilutive effect.[2]

The problem of reallocation of the value of equity-holders' rights has become of concern as capital structures have become complex and have included potentially dilutive convertible securities, options, warrants, or other rights that may on a per-share basis materially dilute the book value of common stock outstanding. The concept that a security may be the equivalent of common stock has evolved and is now used in computing earnings per share. Although it is not now applicable to balance sheet disclosures, it may be used in the analysis of common-share values for decision making. In addition to convertible debt, convertible preferred stock, and stock options and warrants, common stock may be diluted by special purchase contracts—for example, right to buy common stock if it reaches a certain price—, participating securities and two-class common stock—for example, participating preferred stock—, and contingent shares—for example, shares that will be issued at a low price or no price if some contingent event occurs.

Although balance sheet valuation of the possible reallocation of the value of equity-holders' rights may not be feasible, the financial statements should disclose sufficient information to enable statement readers to make judgments as to the present and potential value of the various residual interests. Specifically, financial statements should include a description of the rights and privileges of each type of security outstanding. For example, dividend and liquidation privileges should be disclosed, as should participation rights, call prices, conversion ratios, warrant exercise prices, and similar situations that might significantly dilute the rights of any equity holder.

## VALUATION OF ALL EQUITIES—THE SOURCE VERSUS CLAIM ISSUE

There is evidence that accountants value creditorship or liability equities as claims against the enterprise present or future assets. There is no implication that the claim attaches only to the assets currently recorded by the accountant. When it is apparent that liability equities will be paid from currently recorded assets, there is a tendency to value such equities at an amount equal to the claim existing at the reporting date. It is not uncommon, however, to find departures from this con-

---

[2] It should be noted that outstanding common stock equivalent might also have dilutive effect on market price if conversion occurred or options were exercised unexpectedly.

cept when the amount involved is not material. Thus, cash discounts available on unpaid accounts payable are usually disregarded in arriving at the financial statement valuation for accounts payable.

On the other hand, when the liability will in all probability be paid out of the future assets of the enterprise, customary accounting practice reveals the amount that will ultimately have to be paid, as in the case of long-term debt. Accompanying this valuation of long-term liabilities is the view that a liability should not be recognized if prior to its payment there will be a contribution of services or assets to the enterprise by action of the equity interest. Thus, wages to be paid employees for work in the near future do not become a liability until the employees render the services required. Similarly, bond interest does not become a liability until the money borrowed has been used for the period of time for which the interest accrues.

The view that ownership equities should be valued from the source of assets point of view has been the general rule in accounting practice. Some proponents of value accounting propose that all equities be valued at current values.

## CLASSIFICATION OF EQUITIES

### Classification of Liabilities

There are numerous ways in which liabilities may be classified, to disclose different characteristics and information about liabilities, such as:

1. According to the time they are due for payment.
2. By the name of the entity to whom payment will be made.
3. According to the nature of the document evidencing the liability.

There seems to be some agreement, as far as published reports are concerned, that the most useful information is disclosed when liabilities are classified according to the nature of the liability, such as accounts payable, notes payable, bonds payable, accrued items, and special items payable by a descriptive title. For balance sheet purposes, to provide information about payment due date, these items are then grouped under the headings of current or long-term liabilities. The following selections from the Securities and Exchange Commission's classification of liabilities for commercial and industrial companies under Regulation S-X (released June 23, 1972) is illustrative of current practice guidelines.

(1) *Rule 3-12. Current Liabilities.*

Obligations which are payable within one year or whose liquidation is reasonably expected to require the use of existing current assets (see Rule 3-11) or the creation of other current liabilities shall be classed as current liabilities. However, if the normal operating cycle of the company is longer than one year, generally recognized trade practices may be followed with respect to the exclusion of items such as customers' deposits and deferred income, provided an appropriate explanation of the circumstances is made.

(2) 25. *Accounts and notes payable.* — (a) State separately amounts payable to (1) banks, for borrowings; (2) trade creditors; (3) parents and subsidiaries; (4) other affiliates and other persons the investments in which are accounted for by the equity method; (5) underwriters, promoters, directors, officers, employees, and principal holders (other than affiliates) of equity securities of the person and its affiliates; and (6) others. Exclude from (5) amounts for purchases from such persons subject to usual trade terms, for ordinary travel expenses, and for other such items arising in the ordinary course of business. With respect to (3) and (4), state separately in the registrant's balance sheet the amounts which in the related consolidated balance sheet are (i) eliminated and (ii) not eliminated.

(b) If the aggregate amount of notes payable exceeds 10 percent of the aggregate amount of payables, the above information shall be set forth separately for accounts and notes payable.

(3) 26. *Accrued liabilities.* — State separately (a) payrolls; (b) taxes, including current portion of deferred income taxes; (c) interest; and (d) any other material items, indicating any liabilities to affiliates.

(4) 27. *Other current liabilities.* — State separately (a) dividends declared; (b) current portion of bonds, mortgages and similar debt; and (c) any other item in excess of 5 percent of total current liabilities, indicating any such liability to affiliates. Remaining items may be shown in one amount.

(5) 29. *Bonds, mortgages and similar debt.* — State separately here, or in a note referred to herein, each issue or type of obligation and such information as will indicate (a) the general character of each type of debt including the rate of interest; (b) the date of maturity, or if maturing serially, a brief indication of the serial maturities, such as "maturing serially from 1980 to 1990"; (c) if the payment of principal or interest is contingent, an appropriate indication of such contingency; (d) a brief indication of priority; (e) if convertible, the basis; and (f) the combined aggregate amount of maturities and sinking fund requirements for all issues, each year for the five years following the date of the balance sheet. For amounts owed to affiliates, state separately in the registrant's balance sheet the amounts which in the related consolidated balance sheet are (1) eliminated and (2) not eliminated.

(6) 30. *Unamortized debt discount.* — The amount applicable to debt issues . . . shall be deducted from or added to the face amounts of the issues under the particular caption either individually or in the aggregate, . . .

(7) 32. *Other long-term debt.* — Include under this caption all amounts of long-term debt not provided for. . . . State separately amounts payable to persons specifying any material item. Indicate the extent that the

3 / Valuation of Equities    75

debt is collateralized. Show here, or in a note referred to herein, the information required under caption 29.
(8) 33. *Other liabilities.* — State separately any item not properly classed as one of the preceding liability captions which is in excess of 5 percent of the total of liabilities.
(9) 35. *Deferred credits.* — State separately amounts for (a) deferred income taxes, (b) deferred tax credits, and (c) material items of deferred income. The current portion of deferred income taxes shall be included under caption 26.

The details of the classification of liabilities are considered more extensively in elementary and intermediate accounting textbooks.

## Classification of Ownership Equities — Proprietorship

The formation of a sole proprietorship normally involves the setting aside of assets by an individual to be used in the business enterprise. The valuation of such assets is the sum of the valuation of all the assets contributed to the enterprise, and this sum in turn measures the initial valuation of the proprietor's capital account. Thus, the capital account is measured by the initial or restated valuation of the assets contributed to the enterprise and is a reflection of the source of certain of the assets to the firm.

To a creditor, the capital account of the proprietorship is a reflection of the investment of the proprietor which may be expected to remain in the enterprise on a rather permanent basis. A *personal* account separate from the capital account is normally used to record current withdrawals and the accumulation of earnings to he withdrawn.

The income earned by the proprietorship should be credited to the personal account if such income is to be withdrawn or has previously been withdrawn. Should it become apparent that any credit or debit balances in the personal account are permanent or intended to be permanent, such balances should be transferred to the capital account.

It is sometimes contended that the personal account should always be closed out to the capital account and the separate classification of the two elements of proprietor equity abandoned, because a sole proprietor is personally liable for all debts of the business. However, creditors are frequently interested not only in the debt-paying ability of the owner of the business, but also in the debt-paying ability of the business as a separate entity. Many reasons may explain this point of view, but the fact that such a view does exist suggests that the capital account of the enterprise should reflect only the more or less permanent capital of the firm.

## Classification of Ownership Equities — Partnership

Like the sole proprietor, each partner in a partnership has his equity interest disclosed by using two accounts: a capital account and a drawing (or personal) account. In the balance sheet these two accounts might be presented as follows:

| Assets | | Equities | | |
|---|---|---|---|---|
| Various | x x x x x x | Liabilities | | x x x x x x |
| | | Owners' equity: | | |
| | | A, Capital | x x x x x | |
| | | A, Drawing (credit) | x x x x | x x x x x |
| | | B, Capital | x x x x x | |
| | | B, Drawing (debit) | x x x x | x x x x x |
| | XXXXXX | | | XXXXXX |

At the time of formation of a partnership, the partnership agreement sometimes provides that the partners shall share in profits and losses of the enterprise in a ratio different from their capital contributions. This type of agreement may present a problem of determining the proper valuation in the capital accounts of the partners. Other problems resulting from this situation will be discussed in later chapters dealing with the distribution of partnership income.

Assume that A and B form a partnership, with A contributing $40,000 and B contributing $20,000 with the understanding that profits and losses are to be shared equally. In recording the contribution by the partners, accountants would ignore the profit-and-loss sharing agreement and would record the capital contributions as follows:

| | | |
|---|---|---|
| Assets | $60,000 | |
| A, Capital | | $40,000 |
| B, Capital | | 20,000 |

**Partners' Capital and Risk.** Care should be taken, however, in interpreting the meaning of such recording. The capital balances above do not mean that A is risking $40,000 and B only $20,000. To the extent that B does have additional personal assets, which may be needed to settle partnership claims, he may be assuming a risk greater than the $20,000 investment indicates. This may be illustrated by assuming that the partnership loses the entire $60,000. The loss would be distributed equally to the partners in accordance with the profit-and-loss ratio, as follows:

| | | |
|---|---|---|
| A, Capital (Drawing) | $30,000 | |
| B, Capital (Drawing) | 30,000 | |
| Assets | | $60,000 |

As a result of this distribution of the loss, the capital accounts of the partners appear as follows:

| A, Capital | | B, Capital | |
|---|---|---|---|
| $30,000 | $40,000 | $30,000 | $20,000 |

Thus, B owes the partnership the sum of $10,000, while A has a capital claim of $10,000. The final result of the partnership would be that B would contribute

$10,000 of his personal assets to satisfy his debt to the partnership, and A would take this $10,000 in settlement of his claim against the partnership. Thus, each partner would bear the risk of the partnership in accordance with the profit-and-loss sharing ratio.

**Valuation of Partners' Capital.** A well-established accounting procedure is to record partnership equities at an amount equal to the contribution made by the partners. In situations where partners contribute assets other than cash, certain problems may arise in applying this rule. From the preceding chapter we know that assets should be valued at their fair market value at the time of their contribution to the partnership. The determination of fair market value, however, often involves an estimation and is therefore frequently subject to question. As a result, the accountant should have the partners reach an agreement on the valuation of the assets contributed by each partner before attempting to provide a valuation of the respective capital accounts of the partners. To illustrate, assume that A contributes assets with a market valuation of $10,000, and B contributes assets with a fair market valuation of $15,000. A contends and B agrees, however, that to the partnership the special type of assets contributed by A are worth $12,000. The fact that the two partners agree is normally presumptive evidence that the $12,000 valuation is appropriate, and A should be given credit in his capital account for the $12,000 contribution. The following entry reflects the agreement reached:

| Assets | $27,000 | |
|---|---|---|
| A, Capital | | $12,000 |
| B, Capital | | 15,000 |

In some instances, however, the evidence may clearly indicate that the $12,000 value is not proper, that the assets contributed by A have a fair market value of only $10,000, and that the agreement between A and B is in reality an agreement that B is giving A a bonus for joining the partnership. Here, a revaluation of the assets might not be appropriate, but the capital accounts should be divided on the ratio agreed on by the partners. Thus, in the example in the previous paragraph, the partners may agree that A is to receive 12/27 of the capital contribution and B is to receive 15/27. The fair value of the total assets contributed would be $25,000, and A would receive credit for more than this $10,000 because of the bonus received, while B would receive credit for less than his $15,000 contribution because of the bonus given. The following entry reflects this distribution:

| Assets | $25,000 | |
|---|---|---|
| A, Capital | | $11,111.11 |
| B, Capital | | 13,888.89 |

Some accountants would contend that the valuation in the previous situation can best be accomplished by recognizing as goodwill the difference between the fair market value of the assets contributed by the partners and the value agreed on by the partners. In the example above, the goodwill would be $2,000

($27,000 − $25,000). But, unless the income and loss sharing ratio is the same as the capital ratio, the $2,000 as it is written off will be charged against the partners in a proportion different from that used under the bonus procedure. However, the goodwill alternative is seldom used for situations of this kind. Normally, the valuation agreed on by the partners is acceptable, but if the accountant has reason to question such a valuation, he should encourage the partners to use the bonus procedure indicated above, since it would be more satisfactory and equitable to both of the partners.

## Classification of Ownership Equities — Corporation

There is some agreement that corporation ownership equities should be valued at an amount equal to the assets contributed to the enterprise, with the ownership equities thereby being treated as a record of the source of assets. Several problems arise in determining the accounts to be used and the method of presenting the accounts to provide useful information in the balance sheet.

The shares of stock evidencing ownership equity of a corporation are frequently assigned a par or stated value. These shares may then be issued to the stockholders for assets valued at an amount other than the par or stated value of the stock issued. In this type of situation the difference between the par or stated value of the stock issued and the value of the assets received is normally recorded by the use of an adjunct or contra account to the capital stock account.

From an accounting point of view there seems to be little reason to use adjunct and contra accounts. The asset contribution of the stockholders could be reported in the capital stock account, with this account then reflecting the owners' equity from assets contributed. However, the procedure is well established in practice, and in addition has legal backing in many states. The legal support undoubtedly lends impetus to its continuance in accounting practice. The legal implication normally associated with the procedure is that par or stated value per share represents the permanent capital of the corporation. This permanent capital serves as a buffer of protection for the creditors of the enterprise, since it cannot be distributed legally in the form of dividends and thereby weaken the security behind any loan extended by a creditor. In many states any asset contribution by the stockholders in excess of the par or stated value of the stock issued is available for certain types of dividend distribution. This excess appears to have less permanence as capital than does the par or stated value. Whether stock is issued above or below par will depend, in part, on the way the entity is financed.

## SELECTION OF EQUITIES — FINANCING THE ENTERPRISE

The problem of suitable financing for a business enterprise is complex, and the role of accounting in this analysis is involved. The student of accountancy must be familiar with the overall problem. Essentially, the problem involved is determining the source from which the business enterprise should derive its assets for operational purposes. Contributing to the complexity of the problem is the practical fact that for most corporate enterprises no one source will provide all the funds needed by the enterprise. Creditors will not supply all the funds, either on policy grounds or because of the risk involved. For most enterprises some funds must be acquired from the owners of the business before creditors will make loans. But the amount to be secured from creditors versus the amount to be acquired from owners is only a small aspect of the problem, for there are various types of creditor loans with varying degrees of maturity and varying types of security, and in addition there are varying types of ownership equities. Furthermore, the most suitable financing arrangement for one firm is not necessarily the most appropriate for another similar firm. Financing plans will differ among industries and among enterprises within any given industry.

**Trading on the Equity.** Normally, the financing plan adopted is initiated by representatives of the owners of the enterprise. Although the owners might desire to rely rather heavily on creditor financing, through bonds or long- or medium-term bank notes, excessive financing with creditor money means assumption of heavy, and possibly excessive, risk by the owners. Most creditor financing carries with it a heavy risk of loss by the owners if interest payments are not maintained. Recognizing this risk element in creditor financing, the owners might decide to finance largely or fully with owner capital. Greater use of owner financing may reduce the enterprise owners' rate of return on invested capital.

If an enterprise is able to earn a higher rate of return on all its assets than it has to pay in interest for creditor financing, there is an incentive to finance in part through use of creditor financing. An example may demonstrate this more clearly. Assume that Company A acquires assets of $100,000 by issuing $80,000 of bonds and $20,000 of stock. Assume that the bonds bear interest at 8%. If the company should earn exactly 8% on the $100,000, or $8,000, the bondholders and the stockholders would receive an identical return on their respective investments:

|  | Bonds (8%) | Stock |
|---|---|---|
| Amount of financing | $80,000 | $20,000 |
| Portion of $8,000 return on assets | 6,400 | 1,600 |
| Rate of return on investment | 8% | 8% |

Now assume that the enterprise earns $10,000 on its assets, an increase of 25% over the amount earned in the first example. The creditors (bondholders) will still receive $6,400 in interest, and the remaining $3,600 will be applicable to the owners (stockholders). This $3,600 return on the $20,000 owner investment will mean a return to the owners of 18% on invested capital:

|  | Bonds (8%) | Stock |
|---|---|---|
| Amount of financing | $80,000 | $20,000 |
| Portion of $10,000 return on assets | 6,400 | 3,600 |
| Rate of return on investment | 8% | 18% |

Thus borrowing at 8% in order to earn 10% on the assets borrowed proves to be advantageous to the owners.

On the other hand, if earnings decreased 20% from those in the first example, to $6,400, the owners would earn nothing on their investment, because the entire $6,400 would be needed to pay the bondholders their interest:

|  | Bonds (8%) | Stock |
|---|---|---|
| Amount of financing | $80,000 | $20,000 |
| Portion of $6,400 return on assets | 6,400 | –0– |
| Rate of return on investment | 8% | –0– |

Here, borrowing at 8% in order to earn 6.4% on the assets borrowed does not prove to be advantageous to the owners.

This process of financing the enterprise by borrowing, whereby the owners undergo the risk of excessive loss or excessive gain, is known as trading on the equity or *leverage*. Excessive trading on the equity (excessive borrowing) can make investment in stock quite a risky undertaking.

**Short-term Versus Long-term Financing.** The question of whether borrowing should be on a short-term or a long-term basis largely resolves itself into the length of time required to convert the assets acquired back into a liquid form. If the assets are to be converted into cash through sale in the near future, as in the case of merchandise, short-term financing may be appropriate. On the other hand, if the assets acquired will not be sold or used up in production within a relatively short period of time, short-term financing might be inappropriate. Thus, the acquisition of long-lived assets is commonly financed by long-term borrowing.

In summary, the decision on the most appropriate method of financing depends, in part at least, on (1) the prospects that the firm will have funds available to repay the financing source when due, and (2) the prospects of having stable and sufficient earnings to cover the cost of carrying the obligation, in the form of interest or dividend payments. While the final decision on the financing plan rests on the owners of the enterprise, both as to type and length of the financing, the accountant can render valuable service to the owners through the preparation of analyses that disclose the effects, both short-term and long-term, of the alternative plans under consideration.

## VARIATIONS IN DISCLOSURE OF STOCKHOLDERS' EQUITY

The presentation of the status of the equities of a business enterprise to interested parties is normally accomplished through the use of the balance sheet. The equities are frequently classified in a manner that reveals various types of information about the enterprise, not all of which are accounting-oriented. As an illustration of this, there is a tendency in the law to assume that the capital stock of the corporation represents a buffer of assets that cannot be reduced until the creditors are satisfied. This means that no distribution to stockholders should be made which would result in the reduction of the capital stock below its legal amount. Implementation of this concept would require that premium and discount on

## 3 / Valuation of Equities

capital stock, treasury stock, and other adjunct and contra items to the capital stock account be separately disclosed, possibly in the following manner:

*Stockholders' equity:*

| | | | |
|---|---|---|---|
| Capital stock (1,000 shares, $100 par) | | | $100,000 |
| Capital in excess of par: | | | |
|     Premium on stock sold | | $ 4,000 | |
|     Less: Discount on stock sold | | 1,000 | |
| | | 3,000 | |
|     Increase from appraisal of assets | | 12,000 | |
|     Total | | $15,000 | |
| Retained earnings: | | | |
|     Accumulated earnings | $12,000 | | |
|     Less: Treasury stock (at cost) | 4,000 | | |
|     Unrestricted | | 8,000 | |
|     Total equity in excess of par | | | 23,000 |
| Total Stockholders' equity | | | $123,000 |

This type of presentation of the stockholders' equity conveys the impression that capital stock of $100,000 is permanently invested in the business and will not be withdrawn until liquidation. As such, it serves as a buffer of protection for creditors in that losses by the firm up to $100,000 could be absorbed by the company before the creditors would be unable to get back their loaned money.

If the state law provides that dividends can be paid only out of retained earnings, the effect is to include the capital in excess of par value as part of the buffer protection for the creditors. Thus, in the preceding illustration the $15,000 capital in excess of par value could be added to the capital stock to give a permanent capital equity of $115,000.

Currently, the trend in stockholder equity presentation is to use accounting concepts rather than legal concepts of net worth. The result is a classification of stockholder equity as either contributed capital or accumulated earnings. A revision of the stockholders' equity section presented above might be:

*Stockholders' equity:*

| | | |
|---|---|---|
| Capital stock (1,000 shares, $100 par) | | $100,000 |
|     Less: Treasury stock (at par) | | 4,000 |
|     Capital stock outstanding, at par | | 96,000 |
|     Premium on stock sold | $4,000 | |
|     Less: Discount on stock sold | 1,000 | 3,000 |
|     Contributed capital | | 99,000 |
| Increase from appraisal of assets | | 12,000 |
| Retained earnings: | | |
|     Restricted by treasury stock | $4,000 | |
|     Unrestricted | 8,000 | |
|     Total Retained earnings | | 12,000 |
| Total Stockholders' equity | | $123,000 |

## Supplementary Data

Whatever the classification used in a financial statement, the purpose of the information disclosure determines the appropriate presentation. Full disclosure requires that shareholders receive additional information to supplement the data provided in the balance sheet. This development seems to have arisen in part because of the wide variation between book value and market value of shares of stock. There are, of course, several reasons for the variation between book value and market value. In part, the difference may arise from company policy as to the capital versus maintenance charges of the firm—some capital investments are often charged off as maintenance expense, or vice versa—and to overcome any question of this point, a statement of the capital maintenance policy of the firm is sometimes included in the reports to stockholders. Unrecognized appreciation of assets may also contribute to a variation between book value and market value per share. Indication of the unrealized appreciation of assets is sometimes made in financial statements by reporting the dates at which specific assets were purchased and also reporting specific and general index numbers to permit additional interpretation by the readers of the accounting reports. Other factors contributing to the variation between book value and market value, such as particularly promising sales market outlook for the future, are more difficult to disclose objectively.

While a definite trend in financial reporting is to disclose all material data necessary to make the statements not misleading, accountants still generally require "objective" evidence of its existence before reporting supplementary data. Increasing demand for informative disclosures presents accountants with a real challenge as they attempt to improve financial reporting.

## PROBLEMS

### Problem 3-1

The controller of Lafayette Corporation has requested assistance in determining equities and income for presentation in the Corporation's statement for the year ended September 30, 1980. As currently calculated, the Corporation's net income is $400,000 for fiscal year 1979-1980. The controller has indicated that the income figure might be adjusted and distinct equities recognized for some of the following transactions which were recorded by charges or credits directly to retained earnings (the amounts are net of applicable income taxes):

1. The sum of $375,000, applicable to a breached 1976 contract, was received as a result of a lawsuit. Prior to the award, legal counsel was uncertain about the outcome of the suit.
2. A gain of $300,000 was realized on the sale of a subsidiary.
3. A gain of $80,000 was realized on the sale of treasury stock.
4. A special inventory write-off of $150,000 was made, of which $125,000 applied to goods manufactured prior to October 1, 1979.

## 3 / Valuation of Equities

Your working papers disclose the following opening balances and transactions in the Corporation's capital stock accounts during the year:

1. Common stock (at October 1, 1979, stated value $10, authorized 300,000 shares; effective December 1, 1979, stated value $5, authorized 600,000 shares):
   Balance, October 1, 1979—issued and outstanding 60,000 shares.
   December 1, 1979—60,000 shares issued in a 2 for 1 stock split.
   December 1, 1979—280,000 shares (stated value $5) issued at $39 per share.
2. Treasury stock—common:
   March 1, 1980—purchased 40,000 shares at $38 per share.
   April 1, 1980—sold 40,000 shares at $40 per share.
3. Stock purchase warrants, Series A (initially, each warrant was exchangeable with $60 for one common share; effective December 1, 1979, each warrant became exchangeable for two common shares at $30 per share):
   October 1, 1979—25,000 warrants issued at $6 each.
4. Stock purchase warrants, Series B (each warrant is exchangeable with $40 for one common share):
   April 1, 1980—20,000 warrants authorized and issued at $10 each.
5. First mortgage bonds, 5½%, due 1995 (nonconvertible; priced to yield 5% when issued):
   Balance October 1, 1979—authorized, issued and outstanding—the face value of $1,400,000).
6. Convertible debentures, 7%, due 1999 (initially each $1,000 bond was convertible at any time until maturity into 12½ common shares; effective December 1, 1979 the conversion rate became 25 shares for each bond):
   October 1, 1979—authorized and issued at their face value (no premium or discount) of $2,400,000.

The following table shows market prices for the Corporation's securities and the assumed bank prime interest rate during 1979/1980:

|  | Price (or Rate) at | | | Average for Year Ended |
|---|---|---|---|---|
|  | October 1, 1979 | April 1, 1980 | September 30, 1980 | September 30, 1980 |
| Common stock | 66 | 40 | 36¼ | 37½* |
| First-mortgage bonds | 88½ | 87 | 86 | 87 |
| Convertible debentures | 100 | 120 | 119 | 115 |
| Series A Warrants | 6 | 22 | 19½ | 15 |
| Series B Warrants | — | 10 | 9 | 9½ |
| Bank prime interest rate | 8% | 7¾% | 7½% | 7¾% |

*Adjusted for stock split.

*Required:*

Prepare a schedule of Corporation equities as they should be presented in the Corporation's statement for the year ended September 30, 1980.

## Problem 3-2

The equity holders of a business entity usually are considered to include both creditors and owners. These two classes of equity holders have some characteristics in common, and sometimes it is difficult to make a clear-cut distinction between them. Examples of this problem include (1) convertible debt and (2) debt issued with stock purchase warrants. While both examples represent debts of a corporation, there is a question as to whether there is an ownership interest in each case that requires accounting recognition.

*Required:*
- (a) 1. What are alternative accounting treatments for the proceeds from convertible debt? Explain.
  2. Which treatment is preferable? Explain.
- (b) 1. What are alternative accounting treatments for the proceeds from debt issued with stock purchase warrants? Explain.
  2. Which treatment is preferable? Explain.

(AICPA adapted)

## Problem 3-3

Messrs. A, B, and C each went to a bank to borrow $100 cash, for 60 days. The bank charged each 6% annual interest. The three men elected to borrow as follows:

1. Mr. A decided to give the bank a $101.1 noninterest-bearing note payable which the bank discounted.
2. Mr. B gave the bank a $100 note payable bearing interest at 6.06% a year which the bank discounted.
3. Mr. C gave the bank a $100.50 note payable bearing interest at 3% a year which the bank discounted.

*Required:*
- (a) What is the liability in each case
  - (1) At the time the money is borrowed?
  - (2) At the time the money is to be repaid?
- (b) (1) What liability should be shown on each man's balance sheet immediately after borrowing the money?
  - (2) Would your answer be different if $1,000,000 had been borrowed instead of $100? Explain.

## Problem 3-4

The Horace Corporation has an opportunity to acquire a substantial amount of its raw materials at what it considers to be a favorable price. The terms of this pur-

## 3 / Valuation of Equities

chase, the invoice price of which is $12,000 are 3/10, n/60. After expiration of 60 days, interest is charged by the supplier on any unpaid balance at the rate of 1½% per month. Since the Horace Corporation's operations are very seasonal in nature, the expectation is that it will be 9 months from the date of this purchase before payment could be made.

The president of the Horace Corporation has arranged with his bankers to obtain a 9-month loan to cover this purchase. He would obtain this loan at 9% interest and receive the proceeds just in time to be entitled to his purchase discount. The face of the note would be equal to the amount due his supplier at that date.

*Required:*
(1) Is it advantageous to borrow at the bank? Support your answer.
(2) At what amount and in what manner should the liability for this purchase be reported (*a*) if the purchase is made on open account and (*b*) if the bank borrowing is utilized? Reconcile or rationalize any difference.
(3) At what amount should the purchase of materials be recorded under each alternative means of payment?
(4) Would your answer to (3) be different if the purchase involved machinery rather than raw materials? Why?

## Problem 3-5

The Retail Department Store received a deposit from a customer of $300 in payment for a television set. Not having the television set on hand, the accountant made the following entry:

|  |  |  |
|---|---|---|
| Cash | $300 |  |
| Customer's deposit liability |  | $300 |

Actually the $300 represents the price of the television set and a one-year service guarantee contract. It is estimated that the television set will cost $160 and the service guarantee will cost $40.

The department sales manager claims the only liability the store has is $200 ($160 and $40).

*Required:*
(1) Answer the sales manager's claim.
(2) Assume that the television set is delivered; should the liability for the service contract be $40 or $60?

## Problem 3-6

The Thursday Realty Company purchased land from Mr. R. T. Ring. The terms of the sale were that Mr. Ring would accept as payment a house owned by Thursday. On December 31, 1980, Mr. Ring had transferred the land, and the Realty Company had a liability on that date to deliver the house. The house had cost the Company $20,000 three years ago and has an estimated fair market value on December 31, 1980, of $24,000. The land has an estimated fair market value of $24,500.

*Required:*
(1) What amount should be shown as the liability on the December 31, 1980, statement of financial position of the Thursday Company?
(2) Give the entry required when the land was transferred on December 27, 1980.
(3) Give the entry required to pay the liability on January 10, 1981, when the house is transferred to Mr. Ring.

## Problem 3-7

(*a*) The Dawson Company sold a $1,000,000 par value issue of first-mortgage bonds on July 1, 1980 at 98½. The bonds are due in 40 years and bear interest at an annual rate of 8%, interest payable each July 1. The Dawson Company has a June 30 fiscal year-end.

*Required:*
(1) Prepare the journal entry to record the sale of bonds July 1, 1980.
(2) Discuss two alternative amounts to report as long-term bond liability immediately after the sale of the bonds.
(3) Determine all amounts to be reported on a balance sheet of the Dawson Company at June 30, 1981, and explain how they would be classified.
(4) How much interest will the Dawson Company pay over the life of the bonds? Since all of this interest is due and payable before the bonds themselves are due, why is the total interest to be paid not reported as a liability on each balance sheet date?

(*b*) The Pearson Company decides to create a real estate subsidiary to finance and construct a new office building for the Company. The building cost is estimated at $5,000,000. The Pearson Company signs a lease with its subsidiary for 25 years with an option to renew for a like period. The rental rate per year is $450,000, payable one year in advance on each January 2. It includes an estimated $150,000 to cover real estate taxes, insurance, and related executory contracts. The residual value of the building at the end of 25 years is estimated at $1,000,000 and nothing at the end of 50 years.

*Required:*
(1) What amount will the Pearson Company report in its income statement each year as the cost of using this building? What item or items would replace this amount in an income statement if the Pearson Company owned the building?
(2) In a balance sheet of the Pearson Company at each December 31 what liability will be reported in connection with this building and/or its lease?
(3) If this transaction were considered to be, in essence, a purchase of the building, how should the transaction be given effect in the Pearson Company financial statements if the cost of capital for Pearson is 8% a year?

Assuming a depreciation rate of 5% a year, give the entries required to account for the lease arrangement in the first two years.

(4) Assume an interest rate of 10% per year and that the building can be purchased for cash at the end of the 25th year for $1,000,000. How would the lessee record the lease as a capital lease?

## Problem 3-8

Jones and Smith decide to form a partnership, and to share income or loss equally. Assets contributed to the partnership, valued at fair market value, were: Jones, $20,000; Smith, $12,000. Partners agree that the total ownership equity is to be $32,000 ($20,000 plus $12,000). Both recognize, however, that Smith is also bringing in goodwill of $6,400. They request that the "bonus" procedure be used to provide an equitable determination of partners' capital accounts.

*Required:*

Should the $6,400 be allocated to partners in the capital ratio or the income-or-loss ratio? Demonstrate by assuming that the goodwill will last two years and income before amortization of goodwill is $5,000 each year.

## Problem 3-9

Income taxes have been 48% of income before income taxes. The ABC Company's earnings after taxes have averaged $6,000 on a $100,000 capital stock. The Company is considering refinancing by issuing $50,000 of 8% bonds and reducing capital stock by $50,000 (i.e., the stockholders would exchange $50,000 of stock for $50,000 of bonds).

*Required:*
(a) Compute the change in company income after taxes by adopting the refinancing plan.
(b) Under what conditions is the proposed refinancing appropriate?

## Problem 3-10

The Albert Holmes Company entered into a lease agreement according to which it would pay at the end of each year $20,000 a year for a 20-year lease on a building. One of the creditors contends the $400,000 ($20,000 times 20 years) is a liability. He points out that after 20 years the building will have no value. In effect, he claims that the Company bought the building and is paying for it at the rate of $20,000 a year and that the lease agreement is just like a bond liability and should be shown as a liability.

*Required:*
(1) Should the lease be shown as a liability?
(2) Assuming that the Company could borrow money for 8% annual interest and the Company officials want to know how much money they would have to put up as one sum now to make the lease payments, compute the amount.

## Problem 3-11

The ownership interest in a corporation is customarily reported in the statement of financial position as shareholders' equity.

*Required:*
(1) List the principal transactions or items that reduce the amount of retained earnings. (Do not include appropriations of retained earnings.)
(2) In the stockholders' equity section of the balance sheet, a distinction is made between contributed capital and earned capital. Why is this distinction made? Discuss.  (AICPA adapted)

## Problem 3-12

From the following information prepare the stockholders' equity section of the Roy Ann Company on December 31, 1980, according to (*A*) the legal aspects of the stockholders' equity and (*B*) contributed and earned equity.

| | | |
|---|---:|---:|
| Capital stock issued—1000 shares ($100 par) | | $100,000 |
| Premium on issue listed above | | 5,000 |
| Retained earnings to 12/31/80 | $80,000 | |
| Less stock dividend issued (200 shares) | 20,000 | 20,000 |
| | 60,000 | |
| Balance, 12/31/80 | | 60,000 |
| Treasury stock (at cost) 200 shares | | (19,000) |
| Total | | $166,000 |

## Problem 3-13

The Mulliken Company operated in 1980 with assets having a book value of $5,000,000. These assets had been obtained as follows: initial contribution by stockholders, $2,000,000; earnings retained in prior years; $1,500,000; debts to trade creditors, including accruals, $700,000; an intermediate term bank loan at 8% for $800,000, dated January 15, 1979 and due December 31, 1983. Interest is paid annually.

In 1980 the Mulliken Company reported net income after taxes of $245,000 on sales of $4,900,000. Its board of directors is contemplating a major productive expansion estimated to cost $1,500,000. If the decision is made to proceed with these plans, the facility will enter production at the end of 1981. It is expected to generate additional sales of $2,000,000 annually on which the return after depreciation—an interest element of 8% of the facility's cost—and taxes is expected to be 20% greater than on present sales.

*Required:*
(1) Determine the advantage to stockholders of trading on the equity in 1980 if the Mulliken Company traded on the equity in that year.
(2) Determine the advantage to the stockholders of trading on the equity in 1982 assuming the expansion capital was borrowed at 8% and that in 1981

and 1982 the Mulliken Company distributed net income of the prior year as dividends.

## Problem 3-14

The Claire Company has the following financial plan:

| | |
|---|---|
| Current liabilities (average interest cost, 1%) | $2,000,000 |
| Long-term debt (7½%) | 4,000,000 |
| Common stock—contributed equity | 4,000,000 |
| Retained earnings | 2,000,000 |

The Company's gross margin averages 30% of sales, and its operating expenses, including taxes but exclusive of interest, are 25% of sales. Dividends of $400,000 have been paid each of the past 6 years, being $4 per share. Sales average $15,000,000 per year.

The long-term debt is callable at par and is due in 12 years. The board of directors of the Claire Company is contemplating issuing additional stock to get the dollars to call the debt. It is expected that 40,000 shares would be needed.

*Required:*
(1) Determine the benefit, if any, to the stockholders from trading on the equity.
(2) Determine the benefit, if any, to the stockholders from trading on the equity after the stock issue. Also determine the effect of the issue on return on stockholders' equity.
(3) Assuming the existing dividend rate is to be maintained, discuss the contemplated stock issue considering trading on the equity and cost of capital.

*Note:*
For additional problems, see the Appendix—particularly Problems AP– 12, 14, 15, 28, 30.

# PART TWO:
# Maintenance of the Business Organization

# 4

# Accounting for Insurable Business Risks

The formation of an organization is the first step in the successful operation of a business. Once the business organization has been successfully formed, management must direct its efforts to maintaining that organization if the business is to continue operations. Maintenance of a business involves not only profitable operations on a current basis but also providing for business risks, effectively administering income, and maintaining the business as a unified operating unit.

The first three chapters of this textbook have been directed to the problems arising from the formation of a business organization. Some of the accounting problems involved in recording the operations of a business are covered in intermediate accounting. The accounting aspects of other features that accompany the maintaining of the business organization are covered in the next three chapters of this text.

Possibly the most involved feature encountered by management in maintaining a business is the element of risk. Business organizations constantly face the risk of loss—loss of assets by fire, storm, theft, accident, or other casualties; loss of employees by sickness, accident, or death; and loss of earning power by changes in product demand or technological change. Any single loss may be ruinous if the resulting financial burden falls entirely upon the individual firm concerned. In modern society, however, many of these risks may be shifted, for a fee, to a burden-assuming organization. These risks are usually referred to as insurable risks.

The problem of risk management is most involved. To place the accounting features of the problem in proper perspective, a distinction should be made between losses due to uncertainty—i.e., losses of such an unusual nature that they cannot be anticipated, and losses due to risk—i.e., losses that past experience indicates can be predicted within a long period of time.

This chapter is confined to the accounting problems involved in handling *risk*. That is, it is confined to a discussion of the usual risks that a business enterprise encounters because of its existence and continuation. For discussion purposes these risks are classified as:

1. Insurable asset risks.
2. Insurable employee risks.
3. Miscellaneous insurable risks.

**INSURABLE ASSET RISKS**

It is more or less general practice for business concerns to insure their destructible assets against loss by fire, storm, theft, accident, and other casualties with an insurance company. However, business organizations for one reason or another may elect to assume these risks themselves rather than obtaining insurance by paying someone else to assume them. The accounting issues arising when insurance is not obtained, sometimes called "self-insurance," are covered in a separate section of this chapter.

When an insured asset is damaged, destroyed, or lost—as, for example, when an insured building burns—the relevant accounts must be adjusted and settlement with the insurance company must be effected. The maximum amount recoverable, according to the standard insurance policy, is the cash value of the asset involved, or what it would cost to repair or replace it, with due allowance for the condition of the asset on the date of destruction, damage, or loss. This maximum recoverable amount is frequently referred to as the replacement value of the property, and is, for insurance purposes, termed "insurable value." Regardless of the face amount of the policy, therefore, the insured cannot legally expect to recover more from the insurance company than the insurable value. In the event that the insured and insurer cannot agree as to the insurable value, such value is determined by appraisers as provided for in the policy. In some instances the amount recoverable is also limited by some special feature such as a "deductible clause" in the case of automobile insurance or a "coinsurance clause" in the case of fire insurance.

**Fire Insurance**

The purpose of fire insurance, of course, is to protect the insured against loss resulting from a fire. A particular fire loss is predicated on the sound value of the property involved at the time the loss is sustained and not at the time of issuance of the insurance policy. The insurance company, in most instances, is liable for any loss caused directly or indirectly by the fire. Thus, a loss sustained by the insured from smoke, water, removal damage, or falling walls is usually covered, as well as any direct loss from the fire. However, only property that is specifically included in the policy is protected. Fire insurance coverage may be obtained for buildings, building contents (such as machinery, equipment, and inventories), and other miscellaneous property. The accounting treatment necessary when insurance premiums are purchased and amortized is normally considered in elementary textbooks.

## Fire Loss Account

In the event of fire, as previously indicated, all relevant accounts must be adjusted and settlement with the insurance company effected. In order to centralize the accounting involved when a fire occurs, a "Fire Loss" account is generally used. This account, which is a special profit and loss account, is charged with all costs and expenses and credited with all revenues resulting from the fire in order to measure the net effect of the fire. Thus, the essential features of this account are similar to the usual profit and loss summary account. A typical Fire Loss account is:

*Debited for:*
1. Book value of fixed assets destroyed or damaged.
2. Book value or estimated cost of inventories destroyed or damaged.
3. Expense related to the fire.

*Credited for:*
1. Salvage.
2. Insurance settlement.

**Book Value of Fixed Assets Destroyed or Damaged.** Since the Fire Loss account is charged with all costs and expenses related to a particular fire loss, the undepreciated cost of any fixed asset involved should be closed to this account. The undepreciated cost, frequently termed "book" or "carrying" value, is, of course, the difference between the cost of the asset and the accumulated depreciation, which is the balance in the accrued depreciation account if this account is up to date. Consequently, the asset and the related accumulated depreciation must both be transferred to the Fire Loss account. This is usually accomplished by using a compound entry such as the following (assuming that a building that originally cost $100,000, with an estimated useful life of 20 years and no anticipated scrap value, is destroyed by fire at the end of the 15th year):

| | | |
|---|---|---|
| Fire loss | $25,000 | |
| Accrued depreciation of building | 75,000 | |
| Building | | $100,000 |

**Book Value or Estimated Cost of Inventories Destroyed or Damaged.** If the Fire Loss account is to be debited for all costs and expenses of a particular fire, the cost of any inventory destroyed should be closed to this account. The determination of the cost to be transferred to the Fire Loss account depends upon the system of inventory accounting in use. If a good perpetual system is in use, the determination of book value is relatively simple since the stock ledger cards and other records provide the necessary information. However, in instances where inventories are accounted for on a periodical basis only, the problem may be more difficult, since it may be neither feasible nor possible to take a physical count.

When the only inventory system in use is a periodical one, there is at least one method that permits the computation of an estimated inventory valuation without a physical count. It is frequently referred to as the "gross profit method" or gross profit test. The gross profit method is based on the supposition that under like conditions a business will make approximately the same percent of gross profit in any one period of time as in any other similar period of time. Its use is based on the assumption that the cost of goods available for sale, minus the cost of goods sold, is equal to the cost of goods on hand. Therefore, if sales reduced to cost are deducted from the cost of goods available for sale, the result will be the inventory that should be on hand. To illustrate the computation, assume that a business, which normally makes 30% gross profit based on selling price, had a beginning inventory of $100,000 and purchases of $500,000, both at cost, and sales of $400,000 up to the date of fire:

| | | |
|---|---|---|
| Beginning inventory (at cost) | | $100,000 |
| Purchases (at cost) | | 500,000 |
| Goods available (at cost) | | 600,000 |
| Less: Cost of sales (estimated cost): | | |
| Sales | $400,000 | |
| Less gross profit (30%) | 120,000 | 280,000 |
| Approximate cost of goods on hand | | $320,000 |

If the inventory were completely destroyed by the fire, the amount calculated, $320,000, would be closed to the Fire Loss account. Likewise, if the inventory were estimated to have been 40% destroyed in the fire, $128,000 (40% of $320,000) would be charged to the Fire Loss account.

**Salvage.** Since the Fire Loss account is credited for all revenues related to a particular fire, any proceeds from salvage should be credited to this account. If the salvaged assets are to be repaired or rebuilt and put back in use, the particular asset account should be debited and the Fire Loss account credited with the estimated value. Occasionally the insurance company personally takes care of small repairs. In this case no entry is necessary on the insured's books.

**Insurance Settlement.** The Fire Loss account is credited for the proceeds of the settlement received from the insurance company. It is obvious, of course, that the insurance company will not pay more than the face of the policy, and as was emphasized earlier, the maximum recoverable amount is limited to the insurable value of the asset at the date of fire. Many fire insurance policies, however, also have an additional limiting feature called the coinsurance clause.

**Coinsurance Clause.** Since most assets when burned are only partially destroyed, many businesses would take out only enough insurance to cover the usual or average loss if they were not encouraged by the insurance company to do otherwise. The object of the coinsurance clause, therefore, is to encourage the insured to take out and to maintain a certain amount of coverage or else be a coinsurer with the insurance company. Consequently, many policies on business property provide that, unless the insured carries insurance that totals a certain percent (frequently 80%) of the insurable value, the insurance company shall be liable for only a portion of any loss sustained by the insured.

In the case of a coinsurance clause, the insured may recover from the insurance company that portion of the loss which the amount of insurance carried bears to the amount of insurance that should be carried according to the coinsurance clause. The amount recoverable from the insurance company may be stated proportionately or as a formula, as follows:

1. *Stated as a proportion:*

    The amount recoverable is to the loss as the amount of insurance carried is to the amount of insurance that should be carried.

2. *Stated as a formula:*

$$\frac{\text{Amount of insurance carried}}{\text{Amount of insurance that should be carried}} \times \text{Loss} = \text{Amount Recoverable}$$

The following examples illustrate the use of the formula in determining the amount recoverable, assuming an 80% coinsurance clause. In Examples $E$ and $F$ it should be noted that the amount recoverable will never exceed the amount of the loss or the face of the policy.

| | | |
|---|---|---:|
| A. | Insurable value | $100,000 |
| | Insurance carried | 80,000 |
| | Amount that should be carried (80% × $100,000) | 80,000 |
| | Amount of loss | 60,000 |
| | Amount recoverable $\left(\dfrac{80{,}000}{80{,}000} \times \$60{,}000\right)$ | $ 60,000 |
| B. | Insurable value | $100,000 |
| | Insurance carried | 70,000 |
| | Amount that should be carried (80% × $100,000) | 80,000 |
| | Amount of loss | 60,000 |
| | Amount recoverable $\left(\dfrac{70{,}000}{80{,}000} \times \$60{,}000\right)$ | $ 52,500 |
| C. | Insurable value | $100,000 |
| | Insurance carried | 60,000 |
| | Amount that should be carried (80% × $100,000) | 80,000 |
| | Amount of loss | 60,000 |
| | Amount recoverable $\left(\dfrac{60{,}000}{80{,}000} \times \$60{,}000\right)$ | $ 45,000 |
| D. | Insurable value | $100,000 |
| | Insurance carried | 50,000 |
| | Amount that should be carried (80% × $100,000) | 80,000 |
| | Amount of loss | 60,000 |
| | Amount recoverable $\left(\dfrac{50{,}000}{80{,}000} \times \$60{,}000\right)$ | $ 37,500 |

E. 
| | |
|---|---|
| Insurable value | $100,000 |
| Insurance carried | 90,000 |
| Amount that should be carried (80% × $100,000) | 80,000 |
| Amount of loss | 60,000 |
| Amount recoverable $\left(\dfrac{90,000}{80,000} \times \$60,000\right) = \$67,500$ | $ 60,000* |

F. 
| | |
|---|---|
| Insurable value | $100,000 |
| Insurance carried | 80,000 |
| Amount that should be carried (80% × $100,000) | 80,000 |
| Amount of loss | 90,000 |
| Amount recoverable $\left(\dfrac{80,000}{80,000} \times \$90,000\right) = \$90,000$ | $ 80,000† |

*Amount recoverable limited to the amount of loss.
†Amount recoverable limited to the amount of insurance carried.

**Contribution Clause.** When a particular asset is insured with several different insurance companies, each company whose policy contains a contribution clause is liable for only a pro-rata share of a loss. If all of the policies have the same coinsurance clause, recovery is obtained from the different companies in proportion to the face of each policy. However, if the policies have different coinsurance clauses, the amount of recovery from the different companies is obtained by multiplying the loss by a fraction, the numerator of which is the face of the individual policy, and the denominator of which is the higher of (1) the face of all policies, or (2) the amount required under the coinsurance clause of the particular policy. To illustrate, assume that an asset having an insurable value of $200,000 is insured under the policies described below, and that a loss of $100,000 is incurred. If the policies contain the same coinsurance clauses, recovery would be made as follows:

| Policy | Insurance Carried | C. I. Clause | Fraction | Loss | Amount Collectible |
|---|---|---|---|---|---|
| No. 1 | $ 60,000 | $180,000 | 60/180 | $100,000 | $33,333.33 |
| No. 2 | 75,000 | 180,000 | 75/180 | 100,000 | 41,666.67 |
| No. 3 | 30,000 | 180,000 | 30/180 | 100,000 | 16,666.67 |
| | $165,000 | | | | $91,666.67 |

If the policies contain different coinsurance clauses, the recoverable portion of the loss would be allocated as follows:

| Policy | Insurance Carried | C. I. Clause | Fraction | Loss | Amount Collectible |
|---|---|---|---|---|---|
| No. 1 | $ 60,000 | $180,000 | 60/180 | $100,000 | $33,333.33 |
| No. 2 | 75,000 | 175,000 | 75/175 | 100,000 | 42,857.14 |
| No. 3 | 30,000 | 160,000 | 30/165 | 100,000 | 18,181.82 |
| | $165,000 | | | | $94,372.29 |

**Mortgage Clause.** Most mortgaged property is required by the mortgagee to be insured. Consequently, fire insurance companies have formulated a standard mortgage clause which is included in the policy when appropriate. When included in the policy, it provides that the settlement of a fire loss be paid to the mortgagee to the extent of his interest and any remaining balance be paid to the mortgagor. For example, if property mortgaged for $20,000 is fully insured and a $24,000 fire loss settlement is made, $20,000 is payable to the mortgagee and $4,000 to the mortgagor. Since the amount paid to the mortgagee reduces the amount owed by the mortgagor, both parties are protected by a single policy. The following entry illustrates how this settlement would be recorded on the mortgagor's books:

| | | |
|---|---|---|
| Cash | $ 4,000 | |
| Mortgage payable | 20,000 | |
| Fire loss | | $24,000 |

## Business Interruption Insurance

In addition to protection from losses arising as the result of fire, an insured may protect his assets against other losses or damages arising from various occurrences. Some of the risks that are commonly insured against are sprinkler leakage, boiler explosion, and business interruption. Insurance policies on risks such as these vary. Except for business interruption, however, most provide protection only against loss directly connected with the risk or hazard covered in the policy. Thus, a fire insurance policy will provide protection for assets covered against loss of fire. A business enterprise, however, could well suffer a greater loss from indirect effects of the fire than from the direct fire damage. For example, the loss resulting from the interruption of profitable operations could easily be greater than the value of the property destroyed by the fire.

To cover these indirect losses, fire loss policies, as well as policies covering other types of property damage, are commonly drawn to contain a provision known as business interruption insurance. Inclusion of a business interruption provision in property damage policies will indemnify the insured for indirect losses resulting from damage to the insured business property. Policy provisions may differ widely in this area, but a business interruption provision might compensate the insured for loss of profits caused by the interruption of business activity, outlays for various expenses such as salaries, payroll, and other contractual-type expenses such as rent, interest, and utility charges which necessarily continue while a business is shut down during the replacement period following the property destruction. The policy is normally explicit on the extent of coverage and on the manner in which the loss of profits is to be determined. Past history and projections of the future usually form the basis for this determination.

Business interruption insurance, often referred to as use and occupancy insurance, is concerned not with the material loss of property but with the loss of ability to use the property. Proceeds from such insurance are used to pay dividends to stockholders and interest to creditors, and to retain essential employees on the payroll. Essentially it does that which the company would have done had there been no interruption of business operations. To have a business interruption insurable interest, there must be more than a mere loss of use of destroyed property; there must be an expectation of business revenues to cover net income, fixed charges, and operating expenses had the property damage not occurred. Unless this revenue prospect exists, business interruption insurance is not applicable.

Various types of business interruption insurance policies may be written. Policies related to special situations are not uncommon. For example, a manufacturer may be largely dependent upon one source of supply for raw materials or component parts. The manufacturer may insure himself against the possible loss from interruption to his business arising from an interruption in the flow of materials or parts for any one of a number of causes.

## INSURABLE EMPLOYEE RISKS

A business organization encounters certain employee risks merely because of its existence. It must face still others if it is to continue as a going concern. As in the case of asset risks, however, most employee risks are insurable. The lives of employees may be insured, the health of employees may be insured, and their capacity to work and earn a living is also insurable.

### Life Insurance

Life insurance provides for the payment of a definite sum of money at the insured's death or, in the case of an endowment policy, at some determinable future date if the insured is still living. This provision for payment is made by the insurance company in return for the policyholder's agreement to pay periodically a sum of money (the premium) to the insurance company. Life insurance premiums are payable in advance and may be payable on an annual, semi-annual, quarterly, or monthly basis. The shorter rates are proportionately greater, since they include an element of interest and administrative costs, and most companies buy life insurance on an annual basis.

**Participating.** A particular life insurance policy may be participating or nonparticipating. If the policy is a participating one, the premium rate is fixed at an amount somewhat greater than is needed under normal conditions to pay for the cost of providing the insurance, and as a result of the participating feature, the policyholder gets a refund or dividend. The dividend is based on actual operating experience together with an estimate of future needs. The dividend, which is usually available after premiums for the first two or three years have been paid, represents that portion of the premium not needed by the insurance company for (1) benefit payments, (2) possible contingencies, and (3) operating expenses. Deducting the yearly dividend from the regular annual premium gives the policyholder his yearly net cost. Premiums paid should be *charged* to the insurance account and dividends received should be *credited* thereto. Frequently dividends are used to reduce future premiums. In this case the net cost is the amount of the premium, and no entry is required for the dividend.

**Nonparticipating.** In a nonparticipating policy, the premium rate is fixed at an amount that approximates as closely as possible the amount needed to pay for the cost of providing the insurance. No dividend or refund is received by the policyholder. Thus, the periodic premium is the actual cost to the policyholder for the period.

## Ordinary Life Insurance

Although individual life insurance policies may be classified in many different ways, from the standpoint of the business organization there are basically two methods of providing this type of employee insurance, namely:

1. Ordinary life insurance.
2. Group life insurance.

Ordinary life insurance can be used to meet almost every conceivable type of business need in which protection of human life values and loss of earning power are at stake. It is frequently used in the business world to insure the lives of business executives and other key employees for the benefit of the particular business. This makes it possible to compensate to some degree for the loss that might be sustained from the death of one of the key members of the organization. In partnerships and in small or closely held corporations the lives of all part-owners are frequently insured. This makes it possible, when a partner or stockholder dies, to pay, with a minimum amount of delay, his beneficiary or beneficiaries a prearranged or determinable price for his interest in the business. It enables the surviving partners or stockholders to continue the business without undue interruption, and it avoids unnecessary delay in settlement or liquidation.

When a business takes out an ordinary life insurance policy on its key personnel, it usually retains the right to name the beneficiary. In case the business is named as beneficiary, the premiums are not a deductible item for income tax purposes, although from a going-concern viewpoint they are operating expenses. Occasionally, the insured is given the right to name the beneficiary, in which case the premiums are generally considered to be additional salary.

**Cash Surrender Value.** The value of a life insurance policy is measured primarily on its ability to meet the basic objective for which it is purchased. In addition, however, most policies (other than the usual term policy) have additional values, one of which is the cash value or, as it is frequently termed, "cash surrender value." The cash value of a life insurance policy is the sum of money that the insurance company will owe to a policyholder who purchases insurance on a particular type of premium plan, if and when he stops paying premiums. It is a value that is guaranteed in the insurance contract. When premium payments are stopped, the policyholder has various options as to the cash surrender value. For example, he may request that the amount be used to cover, or insure, his life on a term basis for as long as the cash surrender value will last. Or, he may request that the insurance company pay him the cash surrender value in cash. A policy usually has no cash value until it has been in force two or three years.

A cash loan is available from the insurance company on ordinary life-time or endowment policies after the policy has been in effect one, two, or three years, depending upon the particular policy. This is known as the policy loan provision and permits the policyholder to borrow any amount up to the cash surrender value of the policy. Policies contain a table that shows the contractual loan and surrender values at various anniversary dates, for example:

**Table 4-A**  Cash Values

| End of Policy Year | Cash Value | End of Policy Year | Cash Value |
|---|---|---|---|
| 1 | $ –0– | 6 | $3,600 |
| 2 | –0– | 7 | 4,500 |
| 3 | 1,500 | 8 | 5,500 |
| 4 | 2,100 | 9 | 6,600 |
| 5 | 2,800 | etc. | |

***Accounting for Cash Surrender Value.***  Since after a certain period of time most life insurance policies have a determinable cash value, many business organizations like to reflect this value on their books and in their financial statements. When recording these values, the accounting problems revolve around (1) the proper distinction between capital and revenue expenditures, and (2) the proper determination and allocation of insurance expense to the period benefiting therefrom.

When accounting for the cash value of a policy, part of the annual premium is treated as a capital charge (debited to an asset account), and part of it as a revenue charge (debited to an expense account). As indicated earlier in the case of a participating policy, the insurance expense for a particular year is the annual premium minus the dividend received. However, when cash surrender values are recorded, the yearly expense is the annual premium minus the sum of the dividend received and the increase in cash surrender value. The following entries illustrate the accounting involved, assuming a life insurance policy of $100,000, annual premium of $3,000, and assuming Table 4-A to be the applicable table of cash values:

FIRST YEAR

| | | |
|---|---|---|
| Life insurance | $3,000 | |
|   Cash | | $3,000 |
| (to record annual premium payment) | | |
| Income summary | $3,000 | |
|   Life insurance | | $3,000 |
| (to close life insurance expense) | | |

## 4 / Accounting for Insurable Business Risks

### Second Year

| | | |
|---|---:|---:|
| Life insurance | $3,000 | |
|   Cash | | $3,000 |
| (to record annual premium payment) | | |
| Cash | $ 100 | |
|   Life insurance | | $ 100 |
| (received $100 life insurance dividend) | | |
| Income summary | $2,900 | |
|   Life insurance | | $2,900 |
| (to close life insurance expense) | | |

### Third Year

| | | |
|---|---:|---:|
| Life insurance | $3,000 | |
|   Cash | | $3,000 |
| (to record annual premium payment) | | |
| Cash | $ 100 | |
|   Life insurance | | $ 100 |
| (received $100 life insurance dividend) | | |
| Cash surrender value of life insurance | $1,500 | |
|   Life insurance | | $ 500 |
|   Correction of prior years' profits[1] | | 1,000 |
| (to record cash surrender value at the end of the third year) | | |
| Income summary | $2,400 | |
|   Life insurance | | $2,400 |
| (to close life insurance expense) | | |

### Fourth Year

| | | |
|---|---:|---:|
| Life insurance | $3,000 | |
|   Cash | | $3,000 |
| (to record annual premium payment) | | |
| Cash | $ 100 | |
|   Life insurance | | $ 100 |
| (received $100 life insurance dividend) | | |
| Cash surrender value of life insurance | $ 600 | |
|   Life insurance | | $ 600 |
| (to record the increase in cash surrender value) | | |
| Income summary | $2,300 | |
|   Life Insurance | | $2,300 |
| (to close life insurance expense) | | |

---

[1] Although the division of the credit of $1,500 into two parts, one to reduce the current year's expense account and the balance to record the portion relating to the overstatement of prior years' expenses, may be theoretically proper, general practice would normally involve a credit to the current year's expense account for the entire amount. This procedure may be supported on the grounds of materiality, since the initial cash value would normally not be large enough to create a distortion of the income for a given year.

**Insurance Settlements.** The accounting treatment necessary when recording a life insurance settlement by the insurance company depends upon whether the company has properly recorded the cash surrender value as an asset. The cash surrender value should be recorded as it arises, but if the value has not been entered on the books, the proper accounting treatment upon receipt of the cash would be to debit cash and credit a nonrecurring income account with the amount. When the cash surrender value has been recorded on the books, however, settlement requires the removal of the Cash Surrender Value account from the books. To illustrate, assume $100,000 settlement and $60,000 balance in the related Cash Surrender Value account:

| | | |
|---|---|---|
| Cash | $100,000 | |
|    Cash surrender value of life insurance | | $60,000 |
|    Proceeds from life insurance, less cash surrender value | | 40,000 |

**Financial Statement Presentation.** Cash surrender value is usually classified on the balance sheet as a noncurrent asset and is frequently placed in the long-term investment section. It should not be classified as a current asset unless there are definite plans to cancel the policy, thereby collecting the proceeds within the next operating cycle.

## Group Life Insurance

Group life insurance, as the name implies, is a form of insurance whereby a group of people is insured under one policy. The usual group life insurance policy permits a number of people, usually the employees of a business organization, to be insured without medical examination. The amount of insurance available to each employee is generally about one year's salary or earnings. A master contract is issued to the employer with each employee receiving a certificate giving the amount of his insurance, the name of his beneficiary, and a summarization of his rights and benefits.

Group life insurance is usually issued on the term basis, that is, the premium buys current protection only and does not buy permanent protection. However, in recent years various types of group permanent life insurance plans have been developed whereby an employee leaving his employer retains some part of his group protection as fully paid permanent insurance. The employee also usually has the right to buy an individual policy equal to the balance of his group protection without evidence of insurability.

**Group Plans.** Some group life insurance plans are contributory and others are noncontributory. In the case of contributory plans the employer and employee share the cost of the insurance, the employee's portion being deducted from his earnings and the balance of the premium being paid by the employer. When the plan is a noncontributory one, the employer pays the entire cost. The accounting treatment of both plans is illustrated in the following entries, assuming $100,000 payroll before insurance deductions, and total insurance cost of $2,000.

In the case of the contributory plan the cost is divided equally between the employee and employer:

(1) *Contributory plan:*

| | | |
|---|---|---|
| Salaries and wages | $100,000 | |
|    Group insurance withholdings | | $ 1,000 |
|    Accrued payroll | | 99,000 |
| Group insurance withholdings | $ 1,000 | |
| Insurance expense | 1,000 | |
|    Cash | | $ 2,000 |

(2) *Noncontributory plan:*

| | | |
|---|---|---|
| Salaries and wages | $100,000 | |
|    Accrued payroll | | $100,000 |
| Insurance expense | $ 2,000 | |
|    Cash | | $ 2,000 |

## MISCELLANEOUS INSURABLE EMPLOYEE RISKS

### Health Insurance

One of the numerous employee fringe benefits which has become rather common in recent years deals with health insurance coverage. Employers may purchase health and hospitalization coverage on a group basis for their employees at a premium rate per employee somewhat lower than the employee would pay for similar coverage on an individual basis. The employer may pay the entire premium cost, or the employees may assume part of the premium cost through periodic payroll deductions. The policy coverage normally includes reimbursements to the employee for all or part of the costs incurred in connection with diseases or illnesses requiring individual attention or hospitalization. Normally, the fact of employement need bear no relationship to the disease or illness for coverage to exist. Insurance coverage on employment-connected accidents or injuries is discussed in the following section on workmen's compensation insurance.

**Accounting for Health Insurance.** The accounting problems of health insurance are not very involved. Premium payments may be monthly, quarterly, or annually, depending upon the policy terms, and the premiums may be charged either to an expense or to a prepaid expense account when paid. If the employees contribute to the premium cost through payroll deductions, the payroll accounting procedure must provide for the employee withholding according to the terms of the plan. Amounts withheld should be credited either to the account charged when the employer pays the premiums, or to an accrued liability account that will subsequently be closed to the insurance expense account. The difference between the premiums paid and the employee withholdings represents the cost of the health insurance plan to the employer.

### Workmen's Compensation and Employers' Liability Insurance

In general, workmen's compensation insurance protects employers from liabilities that might arise under various state workmen's compensation laws. Prior to the enactment of the various state laws dealing with workmen's compensation, employees encountered considerable difficulty in recovering from employers for injuries or loss of wages occasioned by accidents arising in connection with their employment. Now most states have workmen's compensation laws which provide for the receipt of fixed sums, partial wages, or other compensations for various accidents arising during the course of employment. While the laws vary from state to state, in general they provide for compensation to employees for accidents, occupational diseases, and loss of employment arising therefrom during the course of employment. Thus, employers are subject to heavy potential liability under these laws. It is only natural that some form of workmen's compensation insurance would be developed to share the business risks arising under the state laws.

Workmen's compensation insurance policies generally provide that the insurance company will assume the risks that the employer is subject to under the specific state law on workmen's compensation. In addition, workmen's compensation insurance also generally provides protection to the employer for legal action brought by employees to recover damages for personal injuries. Because state laws vary considerably and because the terms of specific insurance policies may also be rather diverse, the accountant must become familiar with both the risks to which the business enterprise is subject and the provisions that various policies may include for insuring adequately against these risks.

**Cost of Workmen's Compensation Insurance.** The cost of workmen's compensation policies varies directly with the degree of risk involved in the jobs of the employees covered by the policies. The insurance company will evaluate the risk by reference to past accident experience of the occupation involved, with some modification based upon the particular insured's accident experience and safety devices in operation. Thus, a company that emphasizes employee safety and that develops a good safety record over the years will effect a saving in insurance costs.

Even though the insured may have employees engaging in various kinds of occupations, all employees may be covered by the same policy. Thus, the P Corporation, a roofing contractor, may have employees who are roofers, a rather hazardous occupation, sheet metal workers, concrete finishers, and some clerical staff. The insurance company will establish a rate per $100 of payroll which is applicable to each employee group. As with most insurance, premiums on workmen's compensation policies are established in advance of the period of coverage. Since workmen's compensation rates are stated at so much per $100 of payroll, an estimate of the premium on a policy requires an estimate of the payroll for the policy period by employee classes. In general, the payroll estimates are made by the insured on the basis of his past experience and the outlook for the future.

4 / *Accounting for Insurable Business Risks*

**Accounting for Workmen's Compensation.** Assume that the P Corporation takes out a new workmen's compensation policy on May 1, and that the total premium is based on the following schedule:

| Classification | Estimated Annual Payroll | Rate per $100 | Estimated Premium |
|---|---|---|---|
| Roofers | $60,000 | $6.36 | $3,816.00 |
| Sheet metal workers | 60,000 | 2.21 | 1,326.00 |
| Concrete finishers | 15,000 | 3.44 | 516.00 |
| Clerical office employees | 20,000 | .10 | 20.00 |
| Total | | | $5,678.00 |

This table shows that the standard premium estimate is $5,678.00 for the policy year, and this is the basis upon which the P Corporation will pay its premium. Under some policies this premium would be payable in full at the start of the policy year. In other policies a deposit would be made on May 1, with the remaining balance being paid periodically over the policy life. For example, the P Corporation may pay an initial installment deposit of $1,419.50 (¼ of annual estimated premium) on May 1, and nine subsequent payments of $473.17 each, beginning June 1. The entry for the advance premium payment would be:

| | | |
|---|---|---|
| Unexpired insurance—workmen's compensation | $1,419.50 | |
| Cash | | $1,419.50 |

Since the premium payments are based upon the payroll of the different employee classifications, the P Corporation must organize its payroll records in such a manner as to provide the data necessary to determine the expense (premium earned by insurance company) applicable to each fiscal period. Payroll records must show wages earned separately for each class of employees so that the computations of earned premiums can be made.

Assume that at the end of May the payroll records show the following data for wages earned in May. The earned premium may be calculated in the manner indicated:

| Classification | May Payroll | Rate per $100 | Premium Earned |
|---|---|---|---|
| Roofers | $8,000 | $6.36 | $508.80 |
| Sheet metal workers | 5,400 | 2.21 | 119.34 |
| Concrete finishers | 1,800 | 3.44 | 61.92 |
| Clerical office employees | 1,700 | .10 | 1.70 |
| Total Earned Premium | | | $691.76 |

If monthly financial statements are prepared, the following entry (or working paper adjusting entry) would record the expense for May:

| | | |
|---|---|---|
| Insurance expense—workmen's compensation | $691.76 | |
| Unexpired insurance—workmen's compensation | | $691.76 |

If the P Corporation's accounting system provides for accumulation of costs by departments, or by functions, the expense charge above could be recorded as four separate charges to appropriately named expense accounts. At the end of each period a similar entry would be made on the basis of the wages earned in that period as reflected in the payroll records.

**Unexpired Workmen's Compensation Insurance Account.** Because the terms of the policy normally provide for payment of the premium at a more rapid rate than the premium is earned by the insurance company, the Unexpired Insurance—Workmen's Compensation account will normally contain a debit balance at the end of each accounting period. A debit balance is commonly reported as a prepaid expense, although there is some justification for reporting the item as a receivable from the insurance company. Toward the end of the policy year the Unexpired Insurance account may show a credit balance. This credit balance would arise when the wages earned during the policy year exceeded the estimates upon which the premium was based. A credit balance should be reported as a current payable item.

Final settlement of the premium on a workmen's compensation policy is made subsequent to the end of the policy year and is based on an audit of the insured's payroll records conducted by representatives of the insurance company. On the basis of this audit, the insurance company will refund any unearned premium arising when actual wages have been less than the estimate upon which the premium was based. Likewise, if the actual wages have exceeded the original estimate, and if the insured has not modified his original payment plan, the insured will be billed for the premium due.

**Miscellaneous Policy Provisions.** Workmen's compensation policies may contain various provisions that create problems in determining the expense properly applicable to a given accounting period. For example, the rates per $100 upon which the premium is based may be set high enough to provide for a periodic dividend to the insured based upon the amount of earned premium. Frequently the extent of this dividend is not known at the end of the insured's accounting period. Another provision may deal with the retrospective review of the premium. For example, a policy may provide that the insurance company reserves the right to review in retrospect the insured's accident experience during the policy year and, on the basis of this review, to revise upward or downward the previously established premium rate. Again, the end of an accounting period it is difficult for the insured to determine the proper expense, since the effectiveness of this retrospective provision may not be known until after the policy year ends a few months later.

## Fidelity Bonds

Employers may protect themselves to some degree from the risk of loss resulting from the dishonesty of their employees. Such protection takes the form of fidelity bonds under which a surety company agrees to reimburse the insured for losses from theft, embezzlement, etc., perpetrated by dishonest employees. Fidelity bonds may be issued in various forms to cover a variety of insurable risks. Thus, an employer may purchase a bond on a specific employee, on a specific position without reference to a specific individual, or on several specific employees or specific positions detailed in the bond schedule.

Prompt notice must be made by the insured of losses falling within the coverage of the bond. Likewise, specific time limits are commonly imposed by the bonds on the period within which claims must be filed or suits instituted for recovery of losses. When a loss becomes known by the employer, he should meet the provisions of the policy for filing the claim, determine the amount of loss if possible, and adjust his accounts so that the loss is carried in a suspense-type account until final disposition of the claim is made.

## SELF-INSURANCE

Business insurance provides a method whereby certain types of business losses may be borne by a large number of firms, rather than by the particular firm upon which a loss chances to fall in the first instance. As indicated earlier, the insurance company acts as a clearing house and effects the distribution of the losses for a fee. In some instances, however, a business organization may be justified in assuming its own insurable risks. When a firm is in such a position that it can effect a distribution of risks and the clearing of losses, it may save the operating cost of the insurance company, which frequently amounts to as much as one-half of the ordinary premium. A firm that assumes one or more of its own insurable risks is technically uninsured. However, in common parlance, the firm is said to be "self-insured."

### Accounting for Self-Insured Risks

**Accrual Basis.** Prior to the issuance in 1975 of *Financial Accounting Standards Board Statement No. 5,* "Accounting for Contingencies," many companies that elected to assume one or more of their own insurable risks accounted for the "cost" associated with the risk assumption on the accrual basis, much as any other cost would be treated. The amount of periodic accrual was often related to what the insurance premiums would have been had insurance been purchased. The offset to the cost accrual was a "provision" account (often called a "reserve for self-insurance") reported among the liabilities on the balance sheet.

*FASB Statement No. 5* established criteria for the accounting recognition of losses in advance of their actual incurrence. These criteria are:

a) Information available prior to issuance of the financial statements indicates that it is probable that an asset had been impaired or a liability had been incurred at the date of the financial statements. It is implicit in this condition that it must be probable that one or more future events will occur confirming the fact of the loss.

b) The amount of loss can be reasonably estimated.[1]

[1] *Statement of Financial Accounting Standards No. 5,* "Accounting for Contingencies," March 1975, Financial Accounting Standards Board, Stamford, Connecticut.

Under *Statement No. 5*, few uninsured risks meet the criterion for accrual accounting. In some cases, workmen's compensation claims may not be insured under circumstances where periodic estimates can reasonably be made for claims filed and even for accidents incurred for which claims have not been filed. The following entries illustrate the accounting involved:

| | | |
|---|---|---|
| Workmen's compensation expense | $46,000 | |
|    Provision for uninsured risks | | $46,000 |
|       (to accrue for estimated costs of workmen's compensation claims and injuries) | | |
| Provision for uninsured risks | $ 8,500 | |
|    Cash | | $ 8,500 |
|       (to settle workmen's compensation claim of G. Martz) | | |

**Reporting of Provision for Uninsured Risks.** The financial statement treatment of the Provision for Uninsured Risks account poses some problems. In the example above, the charge offsetting the account was closed to income at year-end. Thus, the credit account represents insurance charges of past years expected to be absorbed by future operations as losses occur. While the nature of the account does not meet all the tests of a liability, it would appear that the account is more like an estimated liability (similar to Estimated Liability on Product Guarantee, discussed in Chapter Three) than any other type of account. Past operating periods have been charged for amounts estimated to be necessary to meet future charges, and the unabsorbed balance of the Provision for Uninsured Risks may be classified on the financial statements as a liability reported between the long-term liabilities and the stockholders' (partners') equity.

**Nonaccrual Basis.** When a company elects to assume one or more of its own insurable risks and the loss contingency involved is not of a nature that will permit the criteria specified in *FASB Statement No. 5* to be met, any losses should be recorded as they are incurred. Generally, it is advisable to disclose uninsured risks and to explain what may be significant, irregular, and infrequently recurring losses. Under the standards of *Statement No. 5*, therefore, a company is not able to spread out, or smooth, the effects of risk losses that are uninsured unless the specified criteria are met.

## ACCOUNTING FOR PENSION COSTS

In recent years increased emphasis has been placed on employee pension plans. This has been a result not only of social security legislation but also of the increased recognition that pension plans fall within the scope of collective bargaining. In addition to the economic and social ramifications, this trend has created additional problems for the accountant. Since there is usually a certain amount of insurable risk associated with a pension plan, the accounting treatment involved is included at this time.

**Cost of Pension Plans.** The provisions and terms of pension plans vary widely. In some plans the employees make contributions in addition to the amounts contributed by employers. In some plans the employees become eligible for benefits after a short employment period, while in other plans an employment period of several years may be specified before an employee is entitled to any rights under the plan. Other variables that enter into the estimates of pension costs include the level of payments on retirement, employee turnover, anticipated future compensation levels, employee mortality estimates, earnings anticipated from pension fund investments, and related benefits (such as social security) with which the pension plan may be integrated. The Employee Retirement Income Security Act (ERISA) of 1975 standardized to some extent certain variables in pension plans.

The accounting for pension costs varied widely prior to the issuance of *Accounting Principles Board Opinion No. 8* in November 1966. This *Opinion* narrowed the different accounting methods and provided, in part, that:

1. The cost of a pension plan should be accounted for on the assumption that the company will continue to provide benefits. Thus pension costs are to be recognized annually and are not considered to be discretionary (that is, provided for in profitable years only).
2. The entire cost of benefit payments ultimately to be made should be charged against income; no portion of such cost should be charged directly against retained earnings.
3. Estimates and assumptions as to the future may be changed as experience evolves, for example, mortality estimates may be revised, funds contributed may earn at a higher or lower rate. These changes are classified as actuarial gains and losses, and they should be given effect in the provision for pension cost in a consistent manner that reflects the long-range nature of pension cost.

**Funded Versus Unfunded Plans.** Pension plans may be funded or unfunded. The funding procedure to be used in any given situation is dependent on the size of the company, its objectives, its desire to eliminate or minimize administrative and actuarial work, its expectancy of turnover, and the like.

In the case of a funded plan the funding transaction is recorded by charging a prepaid or deferred account such as "Unamortized Pension Payments." This is then systematically amortized and charged to income. In the case of an unfunded plan, costs should be accrued. The estimated accrual is recorded by charging an expense account and crediting a "provision" account. When pension payments are made to the employees, the "provision" account is charged.

**Past and Prior Service Costs.** When a pension plan is adopted, it is common to make certain benefits retroactive in the sense that employees receive credits toward pension benefits for past years' services as if the pension plan had been in effect in those past years. The cost of these credits is called *past service* *cost.* Likewise, when pension plans are revised, increased benefits are commonly provided, and the cost to be incurred for these benefits is called *prior service cost.*

One of the major accounting problems related to pension plans concerns past and prior service costs. APB *Opinion No. 8* recommends that both past and prior service costs be charged to income of current and future periods as a part of the periodic determination of pension expense. Specific formulas are provided to set the minimum and maximum extremes in determining the annual charge to income for pension costs. This treatment of past and prior service cost recognizes that even though these costs are based on past services performed, they are incurred in contemplation of present and future services. Since present and future periods will benefit, the costs are appropriately borne by those periods.

*Opinion No. 8* provides that the difference between the amount charged against income in current and prior periods and the amount that has been paid to a pension fund or otherwise should be shown in the balance sheet as accrued or prepaid pension cost. In some cases, a company will have a legal obligation for pension costs in excess of amounts paid or accrued. The excess should be reported in the balance sheet as both a liability and a deferred charge. Unfunded past and prior service costs are not liabilities to be shown in the balance sheet except to the extent that a legal obligation exists in relation to these costs at the balance sheet date. In some cases, employees become entitled to benefits that are not contingent on the employee's continuing in the service of the employer. These benefits are called *vested benefits,* and to the extent that the actuarially computed value of these vested benefits exceeds the pension fund plus any net balance sheet accruals for pension costs, the excess should be disclosed in a footnote.

## PROBLEMS

### Problem 4-1

During your audit of the XYZ Company, which closes its books on December 31, you examine the life insurance policies, premium receipts, and confirmations returned by the insurance companies in response to your request for information. You find that the Company paid premiums during the year on the following policies insuring the life of Wilson Jones, president of the XYZ Company:

| Sole Owner and Beneficiary | Face Amount of Policy | Premium Paid in 1980 | Date of Annual Premium Payment | Cash Surrender Value Dec. 31 1980 | Cash Surrender Value Dec. 31 1979 |
|---|---|---|---|---|---|
| 1. XYZ Company | $100,000 | $2,500 | June 30 | $32,000 | $30,000 |
| 2. Hattie T. Jones, wife of Wilson Jones | 50,000 | 1,600 | Sept. 30 | 15,000 | 14,000 |
| 3. XYZ Company | 100,000 | 3,600 | Dec. 31 | 22,000 | 19,000 |

*Required:*

Indicate how you would present the facts regarding these policies on the balance sheet of the XYZ Company at December 31, 1980, including supporting computations as part of your answer. Give the justification for the treatment which you propose, including an explanation of the disposition of the premiums paid.

(AICPA adapted)

## Problem 4-2

A fire at the Spillville plant of Domby Distilleries, Inc., completely destroyed a building on July 1, 1980. Domby had insured the building against fire with two companies under the following three-year policies:

| Company | Face | Coinsurance Clause | Unexpired Premium 1/1/80 | Date of Expiration |
|---------|------|--------------------|--------------------------|--------------------|
| X | $ 80,000 | 80% | $ 800 | 8/31/80 |
| Y | 120,000 | 80% | 1,200 | 8/31/80 |

An umpire set the insurable value at the date of the fire at $260,000 and the loss at $255,000. In spite of this ruling, there proved to be no net salvage value recoverable from the building. The building was carried on the books of Domby at a cost of $200,000 less accumulated depreciation charged to operations to date of fire of $40,000.

*Required:*
(1) Compute the amount recoverable under each insurance policy and the total amount recoverable. You must set forth the formula that you use in making your computation.
(2) Compute the balance of the "Fire Loss" account after such of the data above as affect it have been recorded. Label clearly the various elements entering into your computation. (AICPA adapted)

## Problem 4-3

On January 1, 1979, Mort paid $3,000 for a three-year fire insurance policy. As of December 31, 1980, a question arose as to the amount of prepaid insurance that should be shown on Mort's balance sheet.

One proposal was to show prepaid insurance at $600, which was the short-rate cancellation value of the policy on December 31, 1980.

A second proposal was to show prepaid insurance at $1,000, representing one-third of the original premium cost.

A third proposal was to show prepaid insurance at $1,200, which is the one-year premium cost for a policy for the same amount as the policy in force.

*Required:*

Discuss each of the proposals in terms of its acceptability, the general principle underlying it, and its effect on reported income.

(AICPA adapted)

## Problem 4-4

Adams, Baker, Charles, and Day are partners. Their interest in the capital and their profit and loss ratios are as follows:

| | |
|---|---|
| Adams | 40% |
| Baker | 30% |
| Charles | 20% |
| Day | 10% |

To provide a means whereby the remaining partners might purchase a deceased partner's interest from his estate, a life insurance program was inaugurated whereby life insurance proceeds would be paid to the remaining partners in proportion to their percentage ownership in the partnership. Since each partner was in effect insuring the life of each of the other partners, it was agreed that no partner would pay any part of the premiums on policies covering his own life.

In 1979 the premium on all policies amounted to $9,000, which was charged as an expense on the books and thereby deducted from the year's profits. The profit was then credited to each partner in proportion to his ownership percentage.

Investigation of the insurance premiums revealed the following:

| | |
|---|---|
| Premium on the life of Adams | $3,500 |
| Premium on the life of Baker | 1,400 |
| Premium on the life of Charles | 2,300 |
| Premium on the life of Day | 1,800 |

*Required:*

You are to prepare the correcting entry that should be made to the partners' capital accounts in order to reflect properly the agreement as to the insurance. Present supporting computations in good form.

(AICPA adapted)

## Problem 4-5

The Delta Tire Company suffered rather heavy fire damage on April 1, 1980. To support a claim for recovery for loss of inventory in the fire, the following data were available:

| | |
|---|---|
| Inventory on January 1, 1980 | $115,000 |
| Sales delivered to date of fire | 225,000 |
| Purchases received to date of fire | 126,000 |
| Goods in transit at date of fire | 24,000 |
| Freight on goods received to date of fire | 4,000 |
| Inventory of salable merchandise immeditaely after fire | 40,000 |
| Face of policy (80% coinsurance clause) | 80,000 |
| Annual premium, paid October 1, 1979 | 1,680 |
| Average rate of gross profit in 1977–79 was 40% | |

The Company adjusts and closes its books annually at December 31.

## 4 / Accounting for Insurable Business Risks

*Required:*
(1) Determine the inventory destroyed at April 1, 1980.
(2) Providing the insurance company agreed to settle on the valuation in (1), determine the amount of settlement.

## Problem 4-6

The Richter Manufacturing Company had a fire January 2, 1980, that severely damaged the building it rented for its manufacturing operations; 80% of the fixed assets and all of the inventories were destroyed. The Company's office was located in another building and was not damaged. On April 1, 1980, when the Company resumed operations, you were asked to assist in filing a loss claim under the Company's business interruption insurance policy.

The following information is available:

1. The profit and loss portion of the Company's trial balance prior to closing at December 31, 1979, is as follows:

|  |  |  |
|---|---:|---:|
| Sales |  | $600,000 |
| Sales returns and allowances | $ 4,900 |  |
| Raw materials inventory, 1-1-79 | 44,000 |  |
| Raw materials inventory, 12-31-79 |  | 30,000 |
| Finished goods inventory, 1-1-79 | 10,000 |  |
| Finished goods inventory, 12-31-79 |  | 10,000 |
| Purchases of raw materials | 340,000 |  |
| Freight in | 5,000 |  |
| Direct labor | 55,000 |  |
| Factory heat, light, and power | 24,100 |  |
| Manufacturing supplies | 8,000 |  |
| Rent—factory | 12,000 |  |
| Office salaries | 34,000 |  |
| Manufacturer sales representatives' commissions | 28,600 |  |
| Administrative and general expense | 51,000 |  |
| Depreciation: |  |  |
|    Machinery and equipment | 24,000 |  |
|    Office furniture and fixtures | 5,900 |  |
| Bad debts | 6,000 |  |
| Purchase discounts |  | 6,500 |
| Interest income—U.S. Treasury bonds |  | 2,300 |
| Net loss |  | 3,700 |
|  | $652,500 | $652,500 |

2. The Company has business interruption insurance under a gross earnings policy with the following features:

   (a) Recovery under the policy is limited to the reduction in "Insured Gross Earnings" directly resulting from such interruption of business less

charges and expenses that do not necessarily continue during interruption of business.
(b) "Insured Gross Earnings" are defined as the sum of
1. Total net sales value of production, and
2. Total net sales of merchandise purchased for resale,
Less the direct cost of
1. Raw stock from which such production is derived,
2. Materials and supplies consumed directly in the manufacturing operations, and
3. Merchandise sold and services purchased from outsiders for resale which do not continue under contract.
(c) In determining "Insured Gross Earnings," due consideration shall be given to the experience of the business before the date of damage or destruction and the probable experience thereafter had no loss occurred.
(d) By additional investigations you determine that "total net sales value of production" may be interpreted as the net proceeds from the sales of goods manufactured by the Company.
(e) The policy is in the amount of $125,000 with a 70% coinsurance clause.

3. Company policy on pricing finished goods inventory results in a reasonably consistent valuation at 80% of selling price.
4. Neither sales nor production is seasonal in nature.
5. The terms of the building lease provide no rental payments need be made for periods during which the premises are not fit for occupancy.
6. The Company paid all employees their base salaries and wages from January 1 to April 1, 1980.
7. Depreciation was recorded on the straight-line method, and no assets were fully depreciated.

*Required:*
(1) Prepare a schedule computing the amount of the Richter Manufacturing Company's "Insured Gross Earnings" based on the year ended December 31, 1979. Compute the limitation, if any, on the insurance company's liability imposed by the coinsurance clause.
(2) Prepare a schedule computing the amount of fire loss due to lost gross earnings. Determine the amount of the fire loss, if any, to be absorbed by the Richter Manufacturing Company. (AICPA adapted)

## Problem 4-7

The Mulliken Corporation is a small manufacturing company producing a highly flammable cleaning fluid. On May 31, 1979 the Corporation had a fire which completely destroyed the processing building and the in-process inventory; some of the equipment was saved.

The cost of the fixed assets destroyed and their related allowances for depreciation at May 31, 1979 were:

4 / Accounting for Insurable Business Risks    117

Building, cost $40,000; allowance $24,667.
Machinery and equipment, cost $15,000; allowance $4,375.

At present prices the cost to replace the destroyed property would be: building, $80,000; machinery and equipment, $37,500. At the time of the fire it was determined that the destroyed building was 62.5% depreciated, and the destroyed machinery and equipment were 33.3% depreciated. The insurable value of all the building, machinery, and equipment was determined to be $75,000.

After the fire a physical inventory was taken. The raw materials were valued at $30,000, the finished goods at $60,000, and supplies at $5,000.

The inventories on January 1, 1979 consisted of:

| | |
|---|---|
| Raw materials | $ 15,000 |
| Work in process | 50,000 |
| Finished goods | 70,000 |
| Supplies | 2,000 |
| Total | $137,000 |

A review of the accounts showed that sales and gross profit for the last 5 years were:

| | Sales | Gross Profit |
|---|---|---|
| 1974 | $300,000 | $ 86,200 |
| 1975 | 320,000 | 102,400 |
| 1976 | 330,000 | 108,900 |
| 1977 | 250,000 | 62,500 |
| 1978 | 280,000 | 84,000 |

The sales for the first 5 months of 1979 were $150,000. Raw material purchases were $50,000. Freight on purchases was $5,000. Direct labor for the first 5 months was $40,000; for the past 5 years manufacturing overhead was 50% of direct labor.

Insurance on the property and inventory was carried with three companies. Each policy included an 80% coinsurance clause. The amount of insurance carried with the various companies was:

| | Buildings, Machinery, and Equipment | Inventories |
|---|---|---|
| Company A | $30,000 | $38,000 |
| Company B | 20,000 | 35,000 |
| Company C | 15,000 | 15,000 |

The cost of cleaning up the debris was $7,000. The value of the scrap salvaged from the fire was $600.

*Required:*
(1) Compute the value of inventory lost.
(2) Compute the expected recovery from each insurance company.

(AICPA adapted)

## Problem 4-8

The City Wholesale Company lost its entire inventory of merchandise and its furniture and fixtures by fire early in January, 1980, before completing the physical inventory that was being taken as of December 31, 1979. The following information was taken from the books of the Company as of December 31, 1977, 1978, and 1979:

|  | Dec. 31, 1977 | Dec. 31, 1978 | Dec. 31, 1979 |
|---|---|---|---|
| Inventory, January 1 | $ 35,304 | $ 42,380 | $ 45,755 |
| Purchases | 160,842 | 164,426 | 174,433 |
| Purchase returns and allowances | 9,163 | 8,021 | 10,015 |
| Sales | 185,904 | 196,603 | 203,317 |
| Sales returns and allowances | 3,325 | 2,402 | 2,212 |
| Wages | 15,271 | 17,743 | 18,356 |
| Salaries | 7,500 | 8,000 | 9,000 |
| Taxes, other than income | 2,647 | 3,732 | 3,648 |
| Rent | 4,800 | 5,400 | 5,400 |
| Insurance | 915 | 967 | 982 |
| Light, heat, water | 1,012 | 1,134 | 1,271 |
| Advertising | 2,875 | 4,250 | 2,680 |
| Interest expense | 3,365 | 2,755 | 3,020 |
| Depreciation expense | 1,125 | 1,255 | 1,280 |
| Furniture and fixtures, net of depreciation | 9,150 | 10,065 | 10,570 |
| Miscellaneous expenses | 6,327 | 6,634 | 6,897 |

*Required:*

(1) From the information above estimate the book amount of inventory destroyed by the fire, assuming that there were no transactions after December 31, 1979.

(2) On the basis of such estimate and the book value of the furniture and fixtures, determine the amount due from each insurance company in settlement of the total loss of the assets under the following concurrent policies, each containing an 80% coinsurance clause:

|  | Policy on Inventory | Policy on Furniture |
|---|---|---|
| A Company | $20,000 | $2,000 |
| B Company | 15,000 | 3,000 |
| L and D Company | 10,000 | 3,000 |

(3) Assuming that the fire loss was 50% of the amounts used in (2), determine the amount due from each company under the same three policies.

(AICPA adapted)

## Problem 4-9

The Fletcher Manufacturing Company had a fire on October 1, 1979, at one of its warehouses. A survey after the fire disclosed that the building was a 60% loss and the inventory stored in the building was also a 60% loss. Records disclosed that sales since the first of the year, at an average markup of 50% on cost, were $450,000. Purchases during the same period totaled $313,000, while the inventory at the start of the year had been $75,000. Expenses per the records were: transportation-in, $8,000; storage costs, $4,000; transportation-out, $6,000. The building had a cost of $720,000, and an estimated life of 30 years, and it was 40% depreciated at January 1, 1979. The Company adjusts for depreciation, insurance, and other deferred and accrued items on a semi-annual basis at June 30 and December 31 each year.

The insurance adjusters and company officials agree to estimate the value of the inventory by employing the average rate of gross profit. They also agree that the building was worth $600,000 at the date of the fire.

Insurance coverage on the building and contents was as follows:

| Company | Policy Face | Coinsurance Clause | Date Paid | Annual Premium Amount |
|---------|-------------|--------------------|-----------|----------------------|
| X | $200,000 | None | 3/1/79 | $600 |
| Y | 150,000 | 90% | 7/1/79 | 480 |
| Z | 250,000 | 85% | 11/1/78 | 780 |

*Required:*
(1) Determine the settlement to be made by each insurance company.
(2) Prepare journal entries to record the events connected with the fire and the recoveries from the insurance companies.

## Problem 4-10

At December 31, 1980, the Vaughn Production Company had the following account in its general ledger:

Unexpired Insurance—Workmen's Compensation

| 1980 | | | | 1980 | | | |
|------|---|---|---|------|---|---|---|
| Jan. 1 | Balance | $ 900 | | Jan. 31 | Est. expense for month | | $300 |
| Mar. 1 | Deposit | 1,000 | | Feb. 28 | " " " " | | 300 |
| Apr. 1 | Monthly payment | 375 | | Mar. 31 | " " " " | | 300 |
| Apr. 16 | Final for 1979 | 280 | | Apr. 30 | " " " " | | 300 |
| May 1 | Monthly payment | 375 | | May 31 | " " " " | | 300 |
| June 1 | Monthly payment | 375 | | June 30 | " " " " | | 300 |
| July 1 | Monthly payment | 375 | | July 31 | " " " " | | 300 |
| Aug. 1 | Monthly payment | 375 | | Aug. 31 | " " " " | | 300 |
| Sep. 1 | Monthly payment | 375 | | Sep. 30 | " " " " | | 300 |
| Oct. 1 | Monthly payment | 375 | | Oct. 31 | " " " " | | 300 |
| Nov. 1 | Monthly payment | 375 | | Nov. 30 | " " " " | | 300 |
| | Bal. $1,580 | | | Dec. 31 | " " " " | | 300 |

The workmen's compensation policy runs from March 1 to February 28, and the premium is payable ¼ at March 1, the balance in eight equal monthly installments. A final audit and billing is made each March for the past year. At December 31, 1980, the following data are taken from the Vaughn Co. policy and payroll records:

| Classification | Rate per $100 | Payroll Estimate 3/1/80 to 3/1/81 | Estimated Premium | Actual Payroll of Company Year—1980 3/1/80 to 12/31/80 | |
|---|---|---|---|---|---|
| AB | $3.20 | $80,000 | $2,560 | $82,000 | $70,000 |
| CD | 2.10 | 40,000 | 840 | 35,600 | 30,400 |
| EF | 1.20 | 50,000 | 600 | 54,400 | 47,600 |
|  |  |  | $4,000 |  |  |

*Required:*
(1) Determine the proper balance in the account above at December 31, 1980.
(2) Prepare a journal entry to adjust account to correct balance and to adjust the expense account.
(3) On what basis could the expense account as adjusted in the entry above be criticized for being inaccurate?

## Problem 4-11

The partnership of Banks, Baker, and Long carried a joint policy insuring the lives of each partner for $50,000. The partnership was the beneficiary, with proceeds from any settlement being credited to the surviving partners. On August 1, 1980, the annual premium of $3,600 was paid. On that date the cash surrender value of the policy was $12,000. The cash surrender value had been $10,800 on August 1, 1979, and was to become $13,500 on August 1, 1981. On September 15, 1980, a check for $120 is received as a dividend for the policy year ended August 1, 1980. On March 1, 1981, Mr. Baker died.

*Required:*
Prepare journal entries necessary on August 1, 1980, September 15, 1980, December 31, 1980, and March 1, 1981.

## Problem 4-12

The Sloan Manufacturing Company has a workmen's compensation policy with a policy year ending each December 31, the same date as the end of the Company's fiscal year. At December 31, 1979, the Unexpired Workmen's Compensation Insurance account had a credit balance of $624.60. On January 15, 1980, the initial premium payment was made on the policy covering the year 1980. The policy calls for four quarterly payments based on the annual payroll estimate. Final settlement is made by adjustment after an annual audit. The final audit for the year

1979 resulted in a receipt by the Company of a debit memo from the insurance company of $620.10. The following table presents the information regarding the 1980 policy:

| Classification | Rate per $100 | Estimated Annual Payroll | Estimated Annual Premium |
|---|---|---|---|
| Machinists | $1.66 | $150,000 | $2,490 |
| Helpers | 1.28 | 100,000 | 1,280 |
| Storeroom | .48 | 70,000 | 336 |
| Clerical | .09 | 80,000 | 72 |
| Total | | | $4,178 |

During the first quarter of 1980, wages earned by the various wage classifications were:

| Classification | January | February | March |
|---|---|---|---|
| Machinists | $10,000 | $10,600 | $12,400 |
| Helpers | 7,600 | 7,800 | 8,400 |
| Storeroom | 5,000 | 5,000 | 5,400 |
| Clerical | 6,500 | 6,500 | 6,600 |

At the end of each month the premium earned by the insurance company is recorded prior to the preparation of the monthly statements.

*Required:*
(1) Prepare journal entries to record the payment made to the insurance company on January 15 and to record the monthly adjusting entries.
(2) What is the balance of the Unexpired Insurance account on March 31? What does it represent?

## Problem 4-13

The C Company is planning a pension system for certain of its employees. It wishes to provide funds for meeting the payments under the pension plan and asks you for assistance.

The Company does not contemplate making any pension payments under the plan until January 1, 1990. Payments in 1990 and thereafter to the present group of covered employees are expected as follows:

| January 1, 1990 | $ 5,000 | January 1, 1997 | $22,000 |
|---|---|---|---|
| 1991 | 7,000 | 1998 | 17,000 |
| 1992 | 10,000 | 1999 | 12,000 |
| 1993 | 14,000 | 2000 | 8,000 |
| 1994 | 16,000 | 2001 | 5,000 |
| 1995 | 20,000 | 2002 | 2,000 |
| 1996 | 25,000 | 2003 | 2,000 |

Starting on January 1, 1980, and continuing for ten years, the Company will deposit $9,000 a year in a special fund. On January 1, 1979, the Company wishes to make a lump sum deposit of an amount sufficient to provide the remaining funds needed for meeting the pensions. It is expected that all of the funds above will earn 5% interest compounded annually during the entire life of the fund.

*Required:*

You are to compute the amount of payment that should be made on January 1, 1979. Show all supporting computations. Use the tables in the appendix.

(AICPA adapted)

*Note:*

For additional problems see the Appendix—particularly Problems AP– 26 and 29.

# Accounting for the Administration of Income

In this chapter some of the accounting problems involved in the administration of income so as to maintain the enterprise and the rights of various equity holders will be examined. Administration of income refers to the assignment, allocation, or distribution of recognized income to various equity interests in the enterprise. It should not be confused with the managerial use of the increased assets represented by the income measurement. Managerial use of assets acquired from income operations and other sources is revealed in the Statement of Changes in Financial Position, and is typically discussed in intermediate accounting textbooks. Accounting for the administration of income refers to the accounting disclosure of the disposition of the income. It is concerned with the maintenance of fair treatment of the various equity interests, and with the nature of different rights in income.

Accounting for the administration of income is not unrelated to the managerial disposition of the assets generated by income, since the way in which the assets are used will bear on the nature of an equity holder's rights in income. If assets generated are invested in fixed assets by management, the income right of an equity holder may represent less of a prospect of receiving a cash distribution than it would if the assets were held as cash.

There are three major problem areas associated with income administration:

1. The problem of distinguishing income measurement from income administration. Income measurement provides data for an income report, whereas the results of income administration are normally disclosed in the balance sheet.
2. The problem of allocating the income appropriately to interested parties so that creditor and owner rights are reflected in the accounting records. In the case of a partnership this involves allocating partnership income to the accounts of the separate partners.

3. The problem of distributing the income to the income recipients. At issue is the question of when a distribution of income occurs. The solution seems to center on the question of whether or not there has been a severance of assets to the benefit of the investors.

## INCOME MEASUREMENT VERSUS INCOME ADMINISTRATION

The area of administration of income is closely related to income measurement, since certain deductions that are made in arriving at a "net income" figure may actually involve distribution of income, which is one phase of the administration of income. For example, the interest payment for borrowed funds is usually reported as a deduction in the measurement of net income, yet it also may be considered from the standpoint of the enterprise to represent a distribution of the income accruing to creditors. The problem becomes involved when income that has been allocated to one group of equity holders is reallocated in a subsequent period, as, for example, when debt is extinguished prior to maturity at a gain or loss. *Financial Accounting Standard No. 4* requires that "gain or loss from extinguishment of debt ... shall be aggregated and, if material, classified as an extraordinary item." Since the effect of an early retirement of a debt below its book value is to transfer a portion of the debtors claim to a stockholders claim to assets, it is more a reallocation of income and investment claims than it is income to the separate distinct entity independent of its equity holders.

**Interest Charges as a Distribution of Income.** The concept of the enterprise as an entity distinct from any particular equity interest is not always followed consistently in practice. In fact, under the change in assets and liabilities view, income is defined as the change in the owners' equity other than capital changes. The revenue and expense view of income is compatible both with the view that income is the increase in assets of an enterprise and with the view that it is the increase in the ownership equity, as traditionally portrayed in the annual reports of business firms. For purposes of income administration, however, there are advantages to the view that entity income is independent of the source of the funds used to create the income. For example, if income is conceived to be the increase in assets which the enterprise has realized, interest payments, like dividend payments, represent a distribution of assets for the use of funds.

To illustrate the point, assume that Company A is formed by securing $10,000 from bondholders and $10,000 from stockholders. To Company A, as a separate accounting entity, both the bondholders and the stockholders represent a source of funds for operating the business. If income is conceived as a measure of the success with which management has been able to use the contributed funds, it would appear that all costs of acquiring the funds should be in the nature of distributions of income. In more specific terms, if Company A used the $20,000 to buy merchandise, fixtures, and similar operating assets, and then used up one-half of the acquired facilities to provide a revenue of $12,000, it may be contended that its operating income would be $2,000, as follows:

| | |
|---|---:|
| Increase in assets (cash or cash equivalent) | $12,000 |
| Decrease in assets (merchandise, fixtures, and similar items) | 10,000 |
| Excess of increase over decrease in assets (accruing to all investors) | $ 2,000 |

For income administration purposes, the $2,000 represents the increase in assets accomplished through the use of assets originally contributed by all investors, an increase commonly recognized as operating income. The Company would then have to distribute $800 of this increase in the form of interest (assuming that the $10,000 bonds bore interest at 8%), just as it would probably pay out some amount to the stockholders as dividends. To corporate management, both the interest and dividends would be considered distributions of the income as payment for the use of funds contributed for business use. Part of the process of income administration involves selecting financing methods that distribute income in the long-run interests of the enterprise.

If the $800 interest charge is considered to be an expense of the enterprise, the income of Company A would be $1,200 ($2,000 minus $800). The $1,200 would represent the income accruing to the stockholders. Those who contend that interest should not be reported as expense reason that the value created by the Company is measured by the increase in assets before interest payments, and that interest payments represent merely a distribution of the increase in assets to the creditor investors. In addition, inclusion of interest as an expense may hinder comparisons of different companies, because one company may be financed entirely by owner funds while another company may have relied heavily on borrowed funds. Since the source of assets used does not seem to have any necessary effect on how well the assets are used, it may be contended that the method of financing a business should not influence the measurement of income.

**Interest Charges as an Expense.** Contrary to the position that interest is a distribution of income is the view that the income of a business entity is the amount earned for the owners of the business. Because interest does represent a payment that must be paid before the owners have a claim to any of the earnings of the company, it is contended that interest—at least to the owners—is as much an expense as any other payment the company might have to make to provide an income for the owners. By this line of reasoning, interest payments are properly a deduction in determining the net income of the owners.

There is, of course, a basis for the position that interest payments represent a distribution of income and not an expense. However, this position has not been adopted extensively in accounting practice. Most enterprises include interest as an expense, and even the income tax regulations support this practice. A noticeable trend exists, however, for a company to report "income before interest charges" and "income after interest charges." The separate disclosure of interest as an expense indicates that if interest is an expense, it is an expense of a rather special nature.

## ALLOCATION OF INCOME

The allocation of income refers to the recognition of the right of various types of creditors and investors to the income of an entity. Because allocation problems differ with the type of business organization involved, allocation of income will be discussed by types of organization.

### Allocation of Income — Partnerships

The allocation of partnership income should be made in accordance with the partnership agreement as to how income and losses should be divided. If the partnership agreement is silent on this point, the assumption supported by legal decisions is that income and losses shall be allocated equally to each partner. This rule holds regardless of the amount of time devoted by each partner to the operation of the business or the amount of capital invested by each partner. For example, one partner with no invested capital may be entitled to a share of the income or loss equal to that of partners with invested capital.

For illustrative purposes, assume that A, B, and C are in partnership with capital invested of $20,000, $30,000, and $40,000, respectively. Income for the year, after interest charges, amounts to $15,000. In T-account form the books of the partnership might appear as follows:

| Assets | Liabilities | A, Capital |
|---|---|---|
| $125,000 | | $20,000 |
| | $20,000 | |

| B, Capital | C, Capital | Income Summary |
|---|---|---|
| | | |
| $30,000 | $40,000 | $15,000 |

If the partnership agreement is silent on the matter of income allocation, or if the agreement specifies equal allocation to each partner, income and losses should be allocated equally to each partner. The appropriate entry to close the Income Summary account would be:

| | | |
|---|---|---|
| Income summary | $15,000 | |
| A, Drawing | | $5,000 |
| B, Drawing | | 5,000 |
| C, Drawing | | 5,000 |

**Allocation According to Capital Ratio.** On the other hand, if the partnership agreement provides that income and losses shall be allocated in accordance with the capital ratio, the $15,000 would be allocated 2/9 to A (A's capital of $20,000 over the total partnership capital of $90,000), 3/9 to B, and 4/9 to C, so that the entry to allocate the $15,000 balance in the Income Summary account would be:

| | | |
|---|---|---|
| Income summary | $15,000 | |
| A, Drawing | | $3,333.33 |
| B, Drawing | | 5,000.00 |
| C, Drawing | | 6,666.67 |

When the partnership agreement provides that income and losses shall be allocated in accordance with the capital ratio, the agreement must also state which capital ratio shall be used, since capital balances may change from time to time. For example, the capital balances to be used in determining the capital ratio might be one of the following:

1. The capital balances at the time of the start of the partnership.
2. The capital balances as of any arbitrary date set forth in the partnership agreement.
3. The capital balances in the partnership accounts as of the start of the period when the profit or loss is incurred.
4. The average capital balances maintained by each partner during the period. If this method is to be used, the partnership agreement should also indicate the manner in which the average capital is to be computed. One satisfactory way to determine the average capital is to compute the average daily capital balances in the following manner:

   Assume that A had a capital balance of $40,000 on January 1 of the operational year, withdrew $30,000 on June 30, and invested an additional $10,000 on December 1. His average capital for the year could be computed by multiplying the various balances in his capital account by the number of days he carried each balance and then dividing the sum of the total by 365 days, as follows:

   | Balance | Number of Days Carried | Sum |
   |---|---|---|
   | $40,000 | 181 | $7,240,000 |
   | 10,000 | 154 | 1,540,000 |
   | 20,000 | 30 | 600,000 |
   | Total | 365 | $9,380,000 |

   Daily Average = $25,700 ($9,380,000 divided by 365)

   Average capitals for the other two partners might be computed in a similar manner and the appropriate ratio be computed from such averages. Other methods of computing average capitals might involve the monthly balances, or a simple division of the sum of the beginning capital balance plus the ending capital balance by 2. In the case of A, the latter computation would be $40,000 + $20,000 divided by 2, to give an average capital of $30,000.
5. The capital balances in the partnership accounts as of the end of the period. When this method is used, the partnership agreement should state whether or not drawing accounts are to be closed to the capital accounts before or after computing the capital balances. If B has a credit balance in his capital account of $30,000, but has a debit balance in his drawing account of $10,000, it is obvious that a decision on the disposition of the drawing account should be made before the capital balance can be computed.

**Allocation According to Specified Ratio.** At times the partnership agreement may set forth a definite ratio according to which income and losses are to be allocated among the partners. In the illustration above, there is no reason why the partnership agreement could not state that profits and losses are to be allocated to A, B, and C in a 50%, 30%, and 20% ratio, respectively. In such a situation the entry to close the Income Summary account would be:

| | | |
|---|---|---|
| Income summary | $15,000 | |
| A, Drawing | | $7,500 |
| B, Drawing | | 4,500 |
| C, Drawing | | 3,000 |

***Allocation of Partnership Losses.*** It should be noted that the agreement regarding the manner in which income is to be allocated to partners applies also if the partnership has a loss. For example, if A, B, and C have agreed to share income and losses on a 5:3:2 ratio, respectively, and if the partnership reported a $12,000 loss, resulting in a debit balance in the Income Summary account of this amount, the entry to allocate the loss would be:

| | | |
|---|---|---|
| A, Drawing | $6,000 | |
| B, Drawing | 3,600 | |
| C, Drawing | 2,400 | |
| Income summary | | $12,000 |

***Salary Allowance.*** In those instances where one of the partners assumes administrative operation of the partnership, it is not uncommon for the partnership agreement to provide the operating partner a salary for his work. Such a salary is normally not considered to be a partnership expense, but is considered to be a method of allocating income. For example, assume that the ABC partnership reports an income of $15,000, but the partnership agreement calls for a salary allowance of $6,000 to A, after which any balance is to be allocated equally to the partners. The entry to close the balance of the Income Summary account would be:

| | | |
|---|---|---|
| Income summary | $15,000 | |
| A, Drawing | | $9,000 |
| B, Drawing | | 3,000 |
| C, Drawing | | 3,000 |
| (A's $9,000 reflects his $6,000 salary plus his ⅓ of the remaining profit of $9,000 or $3,000) | | |

Once a partnership agreement provides that a salary is to be allowed one partner, the salary portion of the income must be allocated to the partner even if the income of the partnership is less than the salary allowance. The debit balance in the Income Summary account after such a salary allowance would then be allocated as a loss to the partners in the appropriate profit-and-loss sharing ratio. In the illustration above, if the partnership had reported an income of only $3,000, instead of $15,000, the entry to close the Income Summary account would be:

## 5 / Accounting for the Administration of Income

| | | |
|---|---|---|
| Income summary | $3,000 | |
| B, Drawing | 1,000 | |
| C, Drawing | 1,000 | |
|     A, Drawing | | $5,000 |
| (A's $5,000 credit reflects his $6,000 salary less his ⅓ of the remaining loss of $3,000, or $1,000) | | |

At times the partnership agreement will not stipulate a specific dollar salary allowance, but will express the salary as a percentage of the net income. For example, the partnership agreement may provide that A be allowed a salary of 30% of net income (but not of a loss). A question then arises as to whether or not the 30% figure is to be applied to the net income before the salary allowance or to the net income after the salary allowance. The question is: Is the salary allowance to be deductible in arriving at the income figure on which the salary will be based? Although it is generally agreed that partnership income is that existing before the salary allowance, the partnership agreement may indicate an intent that the salary allowance be based on the amount existing after the salary allowance. To illustrate, assume that the ABC partnership reports an income of $12,000 and the partnership agreement provides that A is to be allowed a salary of 20% of the income. If the 20% is to be applied to the income before the salary allowance, the entry to close the Income Summary account would be:

| | | |
|---|---|---|
| Income summary | $12,000 | |
|     A, Drawing | | $5,600 |
|     B, Drawing | | 3,200 |
|     C, Drawing | | 3,200 |
| (A's $5,600 reflects his $2,400 salary plus his ⅓ of the remaining profit of $9,600, or $3,200) | | |

On the other hand, if the partnership agreement stipulates that the salary allowance shall be 20% of the income after the salary, the computation of the salary allowance becomes more involved. The $12,000 is no longer the income on which the salary is based. The $12,000 now is equal to the net income plus the salary. Thus, it could be said that the $12,000 is equal to net income plus 20% of net income, or is equal to 120% of net income. On this basis, the following computation may be made to determine the salary allowance:

$12,000 = 120% of net income
$100 = 1% of net income ($12,000 ÷ 120)
$10,000 = 100% of net income (100 × $100)

The salary allowance would then be 20% of the net income ($10,000), or $2,000. In this case the entry to allocate the $12,000 credit balance in the Income Summary account would be:

|  |  |  |
|---|---|---|
| Income summary | $12,000 |  |
|   A, Drawing |  | $5,334 |
|   B, Drawing |  | 3,333 |
|   C, Drawing |  | 3,333 |

(A's $5,334 reflects his
$2,000 salary plus his ⅓
of the remaining profit of
$10,000, or $3,334)

**Interest Allowance.** In order to compensate a partner for providing more capital to the partnership than provided by other partners, partnership agreements often provide that in the process of allocating partnership income an allowance shall first be made for interest on the invested capital. As in the case of allocation of income according to the ratio of capital balances, the agreement should indicate which capital balance is to be used as a basis for computing the interest allowance. Once the agreement has been reached to allow interest on capital in allocating income, the allowance must be made even if it reduces the balance in the Income Summary account to a debit balance to be allocated to the partners in the regular profit-and-loss sharing ratio.

As an illustration, assume that the ABC partnership agreement provides that interest of 10% shall be allowed on the balance in the capital accounts at the end of the year. Assume that capital balances at the end of the year were: A, $20,000; B, $40,000; and C, $50,000; and that income was $10,000. If the allocation of the income other than the interest allowance is unspecified in the partnership agreement, the balance after the interest allowance should be divided equally among the partners. As a result, the allocation of the $10,000 of income would be:

|  |  |  |
|---|---|---|
| Income summary | $11,000 |  |
|   A, Drawing |  | $2,000 |
|   B, Drawing |  | 4,000 |
|   C, Drawing |  | 5,000 |

(to allocate interest on the basis
of ending capital balances)

|  |  |  |
|---|---|---|
| A, Drawing | $333 |  |
| B, Drawing | 333 |  |
| C, Drawing | 334 |  |
|   Income summary |  | $1,000 |

(to allocate debit balance
resulting in Income Summary
after allocation of interest,
⅓ to each partner)

**Salary, Interest, and Ratio.** The ABC Partnership books on December 31, 1981, in T-account form appear as follows:

## 5 / Accounting for the Administration of Income

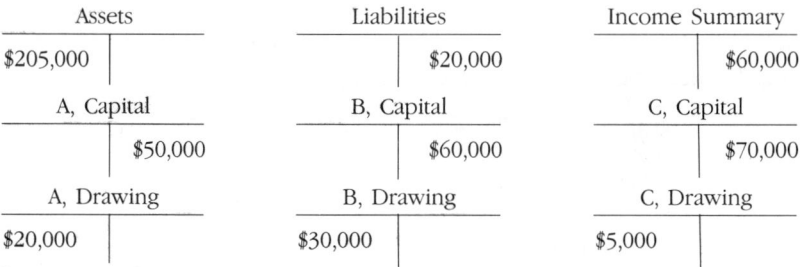

| Assets | Liabilities | Income Summary |
|---|---|---|
| $205,000 | $20,000 | $60,000 |
| **A, Capital** | **B, Capital** | **C, Capital** |
| $50,000 | $60,000 | $70,000 |
| **A, Drawing** | **B, Drawing** | **C, Drawing** |
| $20,000 | $30,000 | $5,000 |

Reference to the partnership agreement indicates that A is to be allowed a salary of 20% of the income after salary; that interest is to be allowed on partners' capital at a rate of 20% on the capital balances at the end of the year; that partners are to be allowed a drawing of $10,000 a year with the understanding that any withdrawal by a partner in excess of the $10,000 shall represent a capital withdrawal; and that any income or loss balance shall be divided equally among the partners.

In more involved computations to determine the allocation of income among partners, it is sometimes helpful to set up a schedule somewhat as follows:

ABC PARTNERSHIP
COMPUTATIONS FOR ALLOCATION OF 1981 INCOME

| Allocation Bases | A | B | C | Total Allocated |
|---|---|---|---|---|
| Salary (1) | $10,000 | | | $10,000 |
| Interest (2) | 8,000 | $ 8,000 | $14,000 | 30,000 |
| Ratio (3) | 6,666 | 6,667 | 6,667 | 20,000 |
| Total | $24,666 | $14,667 | $20,667 | $60,000 |

(1) The salary allowance is computed as follows:

Income before salary = net income + salary
$60,000 = net income + 20% of net income
$60,000 = 120% of net income
$50,000 = net income
$10,000 = salary (20% of net income)

(2) The interest computations would be:

For A: 20% of $40,000 ($50,000 capital less $10,000 excess drawing).
For B: 20% of $40,000 ($60,000 capital less $20,000 excess drawing).
For C: 20% of $70,000 ($70,000 capital. C had no excess drawing and receives no credit for drawings less than allowed amount).

(3) The profit remaining after allocation of the salary and the interest on capital account would be $20,000 ($60,000 − $40,000). This $20,000 will be apportioned equally among the partners.

From such a schedule it is then possible to formulate quite easily the entries to allocate the balance in the Income Summary account to the drawing accounts and to close the drawing accounts to the capital accounts, if such is desired:

| | | |
|---|---:|---:|
| Income summary | $60,000 | |
| A, Drawing | | $24,666 |
| B, Drawing | | 14,667 |
| C, Drawing | | 20,667 |
| A, Drawing | $ 4,666 | |
| B, Capital | 15,333 | |
| C, Drawing | 15,667 | |
| A, Capital | | $ 4,666 |
| B, Drawing | | 15,333 |
| C, Capital | | 15,667 |

## Allocation of Income — Corporations

As noted previously, interest paid on borrowed capital by an enterprise normally is reported in the income statement as a deduction prior to the determination of net income. Thus, the process of accruing interest charges and establishing the liability for interest charges results in an automatic provision in the accounting records of the amount earned by creditor investors. The income then reported is the net income to stockholders, and the problem becomes one of allocating corporate income to the various groups of stockholders. If a corporation has only common stock outstanding, there is no need to allocate income, since each share of common stock has an equal right to its proportionate share of the income of the corporation.

In those cases, however, where the corporation has both preferred and common stock outstanding, an allocation of income between the two classes of stock might be appropriate, especially when the preferred stock is cumulative. In the absence of any allocation of retained income, no indication exists as to which stockholders the retained income pertains. Nevertheless, current accounting practice does not provide for the allocation of stockholder income among the different classes of stock. As a result the retained earnings of a corporation represents the income allocated to all classes of shares outstanding.

**Appropriated Income.** In recent years some modifications have been noted in the unsegregated nature of corporate income. The annual reports of some companies provide for an accounting appropriation of retained earnings to report preferred dividends in arrears. Others use footnotes to disclose the arrearage. It is the opinion of the authors that accounting practice would be improved by allocating corporate retained earnings, by the use of appropriation accounts, among the different classes of stock outstanding.

The practice of making appropriations of retained earnings for various purposes may be considered in the nature of an allocation of income. This may best be explained by an illustration. Assume that Corporation X has an accumulated income of $50,000. If this is reported in one amount as retained earnings, readers of the financial statements may not be informed about any intended utilization by the corporate management of the assets generated by this income. Statement readers may conclude that a distribution to stockholders is imminent, when in reality the assets may have been used in the expansion of productive facilities. In recognition of this situation many corporations have attempted to reveal the extent to which the earnings are to be used for purposes other than for distribution to the stockholders. Typical of segregations along this line are provisions for specific contingencies. Assume that Corporation X decides to retain $20,000 of the $50,000 accumulated earnings for future lawsuit contingency. It might advise the stockholders and other readers of the Corporation's statements of this action by reducing the amount in the Retained Earnings account and setting up another account under the title of Appropriation for Pending Lawsuit. The entry to record such an allocation of retained earnings would be:

| | | |
|---|---|---|
| Retained earnings | $20,000 | |
| Appropriation for pending lawsuit | | $20,000 |

The new account would be reported in the balance sheet as a part of retained earnings, as follows:

CORPORATION X BALANCE SHEET

| Assets | | | Equities | | |
|---|---|---|---|---|---|
| Various | | xxxxxx | Liabilities | | xxxxxx |
| | | | Stockholders' equity: | | |
| | | | Capital stock | xxxxxx | |
| | | | Retained earnings: | | |
| | | | Appropriated for pending lawsuit | 20,000 | |
| | | | Unappropriated | 30,000 | |

Whether or not the process of setting up retained earnings appropriations represents an attempt to allocate income, it is evident that the ultimate effect of the procedure is similar to the process of allocating income.

## Allocation of Income — Estates and Trusts

The distinction between the determination of income and the allocation of income normally is not made in the typical reports of executors and administrators of estates and trusts. Rather, both the reporting of income and the allocation of it which has been made may be disclosed in a Charge and Discharge Statement — As to Income. In effect, the allocation of income between beneficiary and remainderman, who gets the principal, is accomplished by legal ruling or court order specifying the expense and revenue items that accrue to principal and those that accrue to income. Further details of the distinction between principal and income in the area of estates and trusts are considered in Chapter Twenty-Two. The expense and revenue items allocated to the income beneficiary may be reflected in a Charge and Discharge Statement—As to Income. Although this statement is not used extensively in practice, it suffices as an educational technique to indicate the accounting problem involved in determining and allocating trust or estate income accruing to the income beneficiary.

Essentially, a Charge and Discharge Statement—As to Income is a statement presented by the executor or administrator of the income of a trust or estate. The income accrues to the income beneficiary, and all expenses of providing this income are deductible in determining distributable income to the beneficiary. The typical form is:

ESTATE OF JOHN JONES<br>
DAVID JONES, EXECUTOR<br>
CHARGE AND DISCHARGE STATEMENT—AS TO INCOME<br>
FROM (DATE OF DEATH) TO (DATE OF REPORT)

| | | | |
|---|---|---|---|
| *I Charge Myself:* | | | |
| Income (Detail by sources) | | | $ x x x x x x |
| *I Credit Myself:* | | | |
| Expense (Detail by types) | $x x x x x x | | |
| Distributions of income (Detail) | | x x x x x | x x x x x x |
| *Balance of Undistributed Income* | | | $ x x x x x |
| Balance composed of: | | | |
| Cash—income | | $ x x x | |
| Other | | x x | $ x x x x x |

There is an implication inherent in this statement that the undistributed income is income allocated to the beneficiary. No further allocation of income is considered appropriate unless there are several income beneficiaries and the undistributed income assets are being held for specific beneficiaries. In this latter case, an allocation of the income among these beneficiaries is appropriate.

It must be reiterated that the foregoing charge and discharge statement is not used extensively in the specific form illustrated. Reports rendered by executors and trustees conform to the requirements of the court or trust agreement under which they operate. Furthermore, it must be emphasized that the courts and trust agreements have defined income differently than accountants do in reporting business income. As noted, courts often hold that gain or loss on the sale of stocks and bonds, property, and other items that constitute the principal of the estate or trust are not income but a revaluation of principal. Also, court rules are not uniform on whether or not accrued items are includable as expense or income. This area will be covered more completely in subsequent chapters.

**Illustration: Charge and Discharge Statement—As to Income.** To illustrate the preparation of the Charge and Discharge Statement—As to Income, assume that X dies on January 18, 1980, and Mr. Q is appointed to administer his estate. Assume further that the transactions undertaken by Mr. Q are as follows:

5 / *Accounting for the Administration of Income*     135

(1) Collected interest on estate bonds—$2,000. (One-half of this interest had accrued prior to the death of X.)
(2) Sold estate bonds at a gain of $900.
(3) Collected dividends on stock, declared payable January 20, 1980, and actually paid on February 3, 1980—$4,000.
(4) Rent earned since January 18, 1980, on estate property rented to a wholesale firm—$19,000.
(5) Depreciation on building rented—$2,000.
(6) Miscellaneous expenses paid—$1,200.
(7) Administrator's salary—$3,000.
(8) Payments made to income beneficiary—$8,000.

The Charge and Discharge Statement reflecting the events listed above might appear as follows:

ESTATE OF MR. X

MR. Q ADMINISTRATOR

CHARGE AND DISCHARGE STATEMENT—INCOME

JANUARY 18, 1980 TO JULY 17, 1980

*I Charge Myself:*

| | | |
|---|---:|---:|
| Interest income (1) | $ 1,000 | |
| Dividends on stock (3) | 4,000 | |
| Rental income (4) | 19,000 | $24,000 |

*I Credit Myself:*

| | | |
|---|---:|---:|
| Depreciation expense (5) | $ 2,000 | |
| Miscellaneous expense (6) | 1,200 | |
| Administrator's salary (7) | 3,000 | |
| Distribution to income beneficiary (8) | 8,000 | 14,200 |
| **Balance of Undistributed Income** | | $ 9,800 |

Balance composed of:

| | | |
|---|---:|---:|
| Cash | $11,800 | |
| Less: Due to estate principal for depreciation on building rented | 2,000 | $ 9,800 |

Mr. Q (Signed)
Administrator

The numbers in parentheses in the report above identify the item with the event listed previously. One-half the interest received in Item (1) pertains to the principal of the estate and would not be reflected on this report as to income. Likewise, the gain in Item (2) would normally accrue to the estate principal and not to income.

## DISTRIBUTION OF INCOME

Allocation of income is the process of assigning to the various equity interests their claims to the assets generated by the income. As has been indicated, the process of assigning the income to an investor claimant may be somewhat involved. It should be recognized, however, that the allocation process is not the only problem involved in distributing income. Possibly more important is the problem of determining when and in what amount there has been a distribution of assets to the investors entitled to the income. The problems encountered may be described in question form as:

1. What accounting is necessary to disclose the intent of management not to distribute the allocated income?
2. What is a distribution of income?
3. When does a distribution of income take place?
4. What is the amount or valuation to be assigned to any distribution of income?

## Accounting for Undistributed Income

There are several reasons why a firm may choose not to distribute all of the income that has been generated in a given operating period. The more distinctly different reasons include the following:

*Legal restrictions* — such as a state law prohibiting a corporation from paying dividends when a sum equal to the retained earnings is invested in treasury stock. The amount invested in treasury stock measures the restriction on distributable retained earnings.

*Contractual agreements* — such as an agreement with the trustee for outstanding bonds to accumulate retained earnings up to the amount of the bonds payable, or to restrict income distribution in such a manner that an amount equal to the bond liability will be built up by the maturity date of the bonds.

*Business decisions* — such as expansion of productive facilities, maintenance of same level of operations in periods of rising prices, and various types of contingencies.

Whatever the reason for the nondistribution of the income, the problem of revealing that the income is not to be distributed must be faced by the accountant. In the case of partnership accounting, the decision to leave the allocated income in the firm on a more or less permanent basis normally is reflected in the accounts by closing out the drawing account to the capital account. Amounts carried forward in drawing accounts would normally be assumed to reflect temporary investments. In the case of corporations, a decision to retain the earnings in the firm may involve (1) taking no accounting action, (2) the issuance of a stock dividend, or (3) the appropriation of retained earnings.

**Nondisclosure of Undistributed Income.** Some authorities have suggested that accountants avoid the problem of disclosure of the intent not to distribute income by doing nothing. Avoiding the problem may contribute to consistency in reporting, and thus be considered desirable, but such avoidance actually contributes nothing toward meeting what is a legitimate desire on the part of report readers. Investors and others want to be informed if the income is not to be distributed and, further, they would like to know why no distribution will occur. The desire for such information seems to be reasonable.

**Stock Dividends as a Means of Disclosure.** If it is the intent of management to postpone distribution of income indefinitely, the management may consider it desirable to capitalize all or part of the income retained in the enterprise. In the case of a corporation this is generally accomplished through the issuance of a stock dividend. To illustrate this procedure, assume that the X Corporation has 1,000 shares of common stock outstanding (par $100) and has retained earnings of $60,000. The management of the X Corporation may recognize that a good portion of the assets generated by these earnings is committed to the operations of the enterprise on a more or less permanent basis. For example, it may recognize that $20,000 of the retained earnings has been invested in fixed assets and that the business operations have expanded to such a degree that the $20,000 is permanent capital. In order to disclose this condition more clearly, the management may declare a stock dividend of 15%. The dividend represents 15% of the capital stock outstanding and would amount to 150 shares, each share having an assumed market value of $135, or $20,250 to be capitalized. The entries to record this process of capitalizing retained earnings are:

| | | |
|---|---|---|
| Retained earnings | $20,250 | |
|   Stock dividend payable | | $20,250 |
| (to record declaration of the stock dividend) | | |
| Stock dividend payable | $20,250 | |
|   Capital stock | | $15,000 |
|   Capital in excess of par | | 5,250 |
| (to record issuance of stock in connection with stock dividend) | | |

The effect of this process is to reduce the retained earnings by $20,250 and to increase permanent capital by $20,250. Essentially, this is similar to the process used when the drawing accounts of a partnership are closed to the capital accounts. In either instance the end result is equivalent to the enterprise having acquired additional long-term capital from the owner interests.

**Appropriations as a Means of Disclosure.** In many instances the failure to distribute income is attributable to less permanent decisions. When the absence of the distribution of income is temporary, corporations—but not partnerships—may employ the process known as appropriation of retained earnings to disclose the temporary retention of assets generated by earnings. For example, continuing the foregoing illustration, assume that X Corporation, which will have a $39,750 balance of retained earnings after declaration of the stock dividend, plans to invest $6,000 in treasury stock; has an agreement with the trustee for the bonds outstanding to set aside $10,000 to protect the security of the bonds; and plans to expand facilities to take advantage of a temporary shutdown of competing firms, estimating that $15,000 should be retained in the firm for this purpose. These decisions may be reflected in the accounting records by reducing the balance in the Retained Earnings account and setting up appropriations for each of the needs through appropriation of retained earnings, in the following manner:

| | | |
|---|---|---|
| Retained earnings | | $31,000 |
| Provision for investment in treasury stock | | $ 6,000 |
| Provision for bond protection | | 10,000 |
| Provision for expansion of facilities | | 15,000 |

The entry above has no immediate effect on the assets of the enterprise, but it does disclose the intent of management as to the use of portions of the assets generated by past earnings. Thus, the management of the X Corporation is disclosing its intention to use $31,000 of the assets generated by past earnings for three purposes. To the extent of the $31,000 management is also indicating that cash dividends will not be paid at present. Investors and others are thus able to understand, to some extent at least, what the management of the X Corporation intends to do, or has done, with the past income. Properly employed, the procedure of appropriating retained income can enhance disclosure of certain management decisions.

## Nature of a Distribution of Income

The essential characteristics of a distribution of income is that a severance of assets takes place, and that these assets pass from the control of the enterprise to the control of the investors. The major question from an accounting viewpoint lies in the determination of the time that the shift in control takes place.

When a physical transfer of some of the assets of the enterprise to the investor has been made, there seems to be little question that a severance of assets has taken place and that some of the income has been distributed. In the case of partnerships, estates and trusts, and certain other forms of business, distributions of income are not recognized until the physical severance of assets has taken place. In the case of corporations, however, the physical severance of assets does not appear to be as important in determination of the timing of a distribution of income. For corporations the distribution of income is commonly recognized as a fact as soon as the obligation to make the severance is legally in existence.

## Determination of Time of Distribution

**Legal Aspects of Asset Severance.** The legal obligation to make a severance of assets in connection with the distribution of income arises as soon as a board of directors of a corporation formally declares an intent to pay the dividend. Thus it becomes appropriate for accountants to recognize the distribution of income on the date that the dividends are declared by the directors. To illustrate, assume that the X Corporation on February 16, 19X2, declared a cash dividend payable to stockholders of record (those who have their names recorded as owners of the stock) on March 2, 19X2, with payment to be made on March 18, 19X2. The distribution of income would be recognized on February 16 by the following entry:

    Dividends declared (Retained earnings)    $5,000
        Dividends payable                              $5,000

**Scrip Dividend.** The legal test for recognition of the distribution of income is also commonly applied when it is the intention of the corporate board of directors to declare a scrip dividend, a note dividend, or even a bond dividend. Thus, the distribution of income may precede the severance of assets to the extent that the intent of the board of directors is formalized in advance of the actual date of severance of the assets. For example, assume that the X Corporation does not have sufficient cash currently available to distribute a cash dividend, but wishes to distribute some of the income to the investors. The Corporation may decide to issue a scrip dividend (a promise to pay a certain sum at some future date). Scrip dividends normally may be negotiated by the investor-recipients in much the same manner as any negotiable instrument. The severance of assets would be recognized on the date the board of directors declared the dividend. If the scrip dividend were declared on February 16, 19X2, payable to stockholders of record on March 5, 19X2, to be issued on March 26, 19X2, but to be redeemed in cash on June 23, 19X2, the dividend would be recorded on February 16, 19X2, as follows:

    Dividends declared (Retained earnings)    $5,000
        Scrip dividend payable                        $5,000

**Bonds as a Distribution of Income.** Presumably, if a corporation were to issue as a dividend distribution its own bonds not due until many years in the future, accountants would recognize the distribution of income on the date the board of directors declared the dividend. Some accountants would question recognition of the income distribution at this date in view of the fact that physical severance of assets from the control of the corporation will not take place until the distant future. These accountants would emphasize that recognition of the income distribution at the date of legal declaration is merely a convenience and that the distribution actually arises coincident with the physical severance of assets. When the time lag between legal declaration and physical severance is minor, use of the legal date is satisfactory. When the time lag becomes material, however, recognition of the income distribution should await the physical severance of assets. This line of reasoning appears to have merit. It is the opinion of the authors, however, that bonds issued as a dividend represent a distribution of income in that the owners of the bonds have received a senior claim to assets of the company. Severance of assets is considered to have proceeded to the point where recognition of the fact may be appropriate.

**Stock Dividend.** In many respects the payment of an ordinary stock dividend (a dividend declared payable in shares identical to those on which the dividend is based) appears to be similar to a bond dividend. However, conventional accounting does not recognize a stock dividend to be a distribution of income, but a restriction of earnings available for distribution. This treatment is supported by the arguments that no distribution of assets has, in fact, occurred and that no such distribution was intended on declaration of a stock dividend. In fact, declaration of a stock dividend is frequently notice to the owner interests that management feels that assets generated by past operations are permanently necessary to the future business operations and thus will not be available for distribution directly to the stockholders.

## Valuation of Distribution of Income

The physical characteristics of distributions of income may be:

1. Cash.
2. Promises to pay cash in the near future.
3. Promises to pay cash in the distant future.
4. Securities of other corporations.
5. Productive assets, other than cash, owned by the company.
6. Merchandise.

In the case of a cash dividend, the proper valuation of the distribution is the amount of cash paid out. In the case of the promises to pay cash at some future date, the amount of the distribution is measured at the amount of cash that will have to be paid out, excluding any interest to be paid on such obligations. In cases where the interest to be paid on such obligations is in the face amount of the promise to pay cash later, as would be the case if a 20-year noninterest-bearing bond were issued as a dividend, it is appropriate to value the dividend at the current cash value of the promise to pay cash later. When the distribution is to be in the form of assets other than cash, problems arise as to the amount of the distribution that has taken place. Theoretically, the proper rule would be to value the distribution at the cash or cash equivalent distribution. However, this amount is not always readily determinable, in which case approximations must be used. Even when the amount is determinable, values arrived at in other ways are commonly used.

**Illustration—Dividend in Kind.** To illustrate the difficulty of valuing the distribution of income in noncash form, assume that X Corporation declares a dividend payable in merchandise and in securities of other corporations that the Corporation owns. The merchandise is carried on the books of the X Corporation at a cost valuation of $6,000, but it has a market valuation ranging from $8,000 to $10,000, depending upon whether it is sold to a wholesaler or to a retailer. The securities are carried on the books at a cost valuation of $11,000, but they have a market valuation of $20,000. It is estimated, however, that it will cost $1,000 to sell them. It is evident that the valuation finally decided on will be an approximation of the cash equivalent of the assets being distributed. Although there is some thought that the most practical procedure is to value the distribution at cost or at the value at which it is carried on X Corporation's records, it is evident that such a procedure may represent an undesirable valuation. The board of directors may intend to distribute a greater portion of earnings than is represented by the cost of the assets to be distributed. More realistic is the fact that the fair value of the assets distributed is above cost.

*APB Opinion No. 29* requires that this nonreciprocal transfer of nonmonetary assets be recorded at the fair value of the asset distributed if the fair value is objectively measurable and would be clearly realizable to the distributing entity in an outright sale at or near the time of the distribution. Assuming that X Corporation regularly sells to retailers, valuation of the dividend in kind at net realizable value is appropriate as illustrated below:

| | | |
|---|---|---|
| Merchandise | $ 4,000 | |
| Securities | 8,000 | |
| Gain on revaluation of merchandise and securities (retained earnings) | | $12,000 |
| (to revalue merchandise and securities to their realizable value for dividend payment purposes.) | | |
| Dividends declared (retained earnings) | $29,000 | |
| Dividends payable in merchandise | | $10,000 |
| Dividends payable in securities | | 19,000 |

The Gain on Revaluation account would eventually be closed to the Retained Earnings account.

## PROBLEMS

### Problem 5-1

Company A and Company B each have total assets of $100,000. Reported incomes for each company were $10,000 and $8,000, respectively. Although Company B's earnings were $2,000 less than those of Company A, one of Company B's expenses was a $3,000 interest expense charge for payment on B's 8% bonds outstanding. Company A has $15,000 of current liabilities and B has $10,000 of such items.

*Required:*
(1) What rate of return was earned on the stockholders' equity in each company?
(2) What rate of return was earned on the total assets?
(3) Under what conditions would you feel that a better figure of B's earnings should be something other than $8,000 with distinctive disclosure of the allocation of the income?

### Problem 5-2

C, D, and E are partners. In 1980, earnings of the partnership were $30,000. For each case below indicate how much of the income would be allocated to each partner.

*Case A* — The partnership agreement is silent on how profit or loss is to be shared.

*Case B* — The partnership agreement specifies profits or losses are to be shared according to the capital ratio existing at the start of the year. Capital accounts of C, D, and E on January 1, 1980, were $50,000, $70,000, and $30,000.

*Case C* — E is allowed a salary of $10,000 for running the business. Any balance is to be divided among the partners in the ratio of 2 : 2 : 1 to C, D, and E, respectively.

*Case D* — C is to be allowed a salary of 50% of partnership income after the salary allowance. The balance of any gain or loss is to be shared equally.

*Case E* — D is allowed a salary of $10,000 and each partner is allowed a 20% return on his capital as of 1/1/80 (see Case B above).

## Problem 5-3

In T-account form, selected accounts for the G and H partnership as they appear on December 31, 1979, are as follows:

| G, Capital | | H, Capital | |
|---|---|---|---|
| | 1/1/79 $50,000 | | 1/1/79 $30,000 |
| | 6/30/79 10,000 | | |

| G, Drawing | | H, Drawing | |
|---|---|---|---|
| 3/31/79 $8,000 | $10,000 | 6/30/79 $6,000 | $10,000 |
| | | 7/31/79 6,000 | |

| Partners' Salaries | | Income Summary | |
|---|---|---|---|
| $20,000 | | | $30,000 |

The partnership agreement provides that withdrawals in excess of the salary allowance shall be treated as withdrawals of capital. It further provides that income or loss after salary allowances shall be divided in accordance with the twelve-months average capital ratios.

*Required:*
(1) Compute the amount of income allocated to each partner.
(2) Give the entry or entries to close the books of the partnership.

## Problem 5-4

The partnership agreement of Adams and Larrson provides that income and losses shall be shared according to the capital ratio at the beginning of each year. It further provides that each partner may draw up to $10,000 a year. Withdrawals in excess of $10,000 are subject to a 10% penalty payable to the partnership but settled in the allocation of income at the end of the year. Selected accounts for the partnership on December 31, 1980, are:

## 5 / Accounting for the Administration of Income

| Adams, Capital | | Larrson, Capital | |
|---|---|---|---|
| | 1/1/80 $100,000 | | 1/1/80 $60,000 |
| | 6/30/80 20,000 | | |

| Adams, Drawing | | Larrson, Drawing | |
|---|---|---|---|
| $9,000 | | $15,000 | |

| Income Summary | |
|---|---|
| | $30,000 |

*Required:*
(1) Compute the allocation of the $30,000 of income to the partners.
(2) Prepare a statement of changes in capital for 1980.

## Problem 5-5

Partnership contracts usually specify a profit-and-loss ratio. They may also provide for such additional income-and-loss sharing features as salaries, bonuses, and interest allowances on invested capital.

*Required:*
(1) What is the objective of income-and-loss sharing arrangements? Why may there be a need for features in addition to the profit-and-loss ratio? Discuss.
(2) Discuss the arguments for recording salary and bonus allowances to partners as charges to operations.
(3) What are the arguments against treating partnership salary and bonus allowances as expenses? Discuss.
(4) In addition to its other profit-and-loss sharing features, a partnership agreement may state that "interest is to be allowed on invested capital." List the additional provision that should be included in the partnership agreement so that "interest to be allowed on invested capital" can be computed. (AICPA adapted)

## Problem 5-6

Hook and Fill formed a partnership on January 1, 1978, and agreed to share income and losses, as follows:

| | Hook | Fill | Income (Loss) |
|---|---|---|---|
| 1978 | 60% | 40% | $ 30,000 |
| 1979 | 50% | 50% | $(10,000) |
| 1980 | 40% | 60% | $ 20,000 |

On January 1, 1981, it was discovered that:
A. The ending inventory on December 31, 1978, should have been $10,000 instead of $1,000.

B. Excessive depreciation of $2,000 a year has been charged on a machine acquired January 1, 1979.

*Required:*
Give the entry to correct the accounting records on January 1, 1981.

## Problem 5-7

The preclosing trial balance of the Jow Dones Company on December 31, 1980, contains the following accounts:

| | |
|---|---:|
| Cash | $ 10,000 |
| Accounts receivable | 62,000 |
| Stock of the XYZ Company—500 shares | 40,000 |
| Merchandise 12/31/80 | 78,000 |
| Treasury stock, common—200 shares (at cost) | 18,000 |
| Prepaid insurance | 2,200 |
| Land | 17,800 |
| Building, less accumulated depreciation | 130,000 |
| Machinery, less accumulated depreciation | 100,000 |
| Equipment, less accumulated depreciation | 40,000 |
| Accounts payable | 35,000 |
| Notes payable—due 3/1/87 | 20,000 |
| Sales | 300,000 |
| Cost of goods sold | 200,000 |
| Selling expenses | 50,000 |
| Administrative expenses | 20,000 |
| Interest charges | 1,000 |
| Common stock—issued (par $100) | 400,000 |
| Retained earnings | 14,000 |

The Company has decided tentatively to pay a 10% dividend. They are somewhat concerned, however, regarding (1) whether or not they have sufficient cash on hand to pay the dividend, (2) the legal restriction that dividends shall not reduce retained earnings below the amount invested in treasury stock, and (3) the possibility of issuing the stock of the XYZ Company as the dividend in view of the $60 per share at which the stock is currently selling.

*Required:*
(1) Compute the maximum amount of dividend that might be paid legally.
(2) Compute the amount of dividend that might be paid in view of the cash position of the Company.
(3) Compute the maximum dividend that might be paid of XYZ stock, if the stock is valued at $60 per share for dividend purposes.
(4) Assume that the Company declared a 5% dividend, but before the dividend was paid, another 10 shares of their own stock were purchased as treasury stock at $92 per share. Give the journal entry to set up the divi-

dend declaration and the subsequent acquisition of the additional 10 shares.

## Problem 5-8

Evan W. Moore died on March 1, 1981, leaving the following estate:

| | |
|---|---|
| Bonds (market value) | $20,000 |
| Stock (market value) | 32,000 |
| Real estate (market value) | 26,000 |
| Bank account | 18,000 |
| Total | $96,000 |

*Additional Information:*
1. The bonds (face amount, $25,000) bear interest at the rate of 4% payable semi-annually on February 1, August. 1.
2. Debts of the decedent at time of death were $300.
3. $2,500 was spent for the funeral.
4. Death taxes and fees came to $8,200.
5. The stock was sold on July 2, after receiving a dividend of $1,200 on July 1, for $36,000.

*Required:*
Prepare a Charge and Discharge Statement—As to Income for the period March 1, 1981, to July 15, 1981.

## Problem 5-9

Michael Dunlap, a retired partner of a public accounting partnership, died on July 3, 1981. At the time of his death his estate included the following assets:

| | |
|---|---|
| Bank checking account | $ 2,400 |
| Bank savings account | 8,600 |
| Equity in partnership (3/5 of equity at retirement) | 36,000 |
| Common stocks (market value) | 42,000 |
| Apartment building (fully rented) (insurance value) | 124,000 |
| | $213,000 |

Between July 3 and October 31, 1981, the following events took place in connection with Mr. Dunlap's estate:
(a) Dividends received on common stock were $410.
(b) Rentals received on apartment building totaled $5,600.
(c) Funeral costs paid were $2,800.
(d) $12,000 was received from Mr. Dunlap's former partnership, representing 1/5 of his equity at his retirement date.
(e) Operating expenses on the apartment building were $1,400.
(f) Debts due at death (unrelated to the assets above) and paid, $800.

(g) Administrator's fees paid were $1,200.
(h) Interest earned on savings account, $810.
(i) Depreciation on apartment building, $1,800.
(j) Property taxes on the apartment building, about $2,400 per year.

*Required:*
Prepare a Charge and Discharge Statement—As to Income for the period July 3, 1981 to October 31, 1981.

## Problem 5-10

The Carson-Allyn Company has been pressed for dividends by its common stockholders. The Company's stockholders' equity account on December 31, 1981, appears as follows:

|  |  |
|---|---|
| Common stock |  |
| 10,000 shares (no par) | $980,000 |
| Retained earnings | 630,000 |
| Total | $1,610,000 |

Stockholders have agreed to accept a dividend in kind, composed of stock of the Abbet-Lincoln Company and merchandise regularly sold by the Carson-Allyn Company, and a 10% stock dividend. The assets and stock to be issued are valued as follows:

|  | On Books Of Carson-Allyn | Market Value Date Dividend Declared |
|---|---|---|
| Abbet-Lincoln stock | $33,000 | $ 49,000 |
| Merchandise | 18,000 | 8,000 |
| Stock dividend | (Book value) | 210,000 |

*Required:*
(1) How should the declaration and payment of the dividend be recorded?
(2) One of the auditors objects to the valuation given the dividend in merchandise. He maintains it allows Carson-Allyn to avoid a $10,000 loss which they would otherwise have to report. Do you agree with the auditor?

## Problem 5-11

The AUDP Company paid a dividend in its own bonds. The bonds have a face amount of $10,000 but the current market price at the time the dividend was declared was $8,900. At the time the dividend was paid the market value of the bonds was $8,700.

*Required:*
Record the declaration and payment of the dividend.

## Problem 5-12

At the regular meeting of the board of directors of the May Corporation a dividend payable in the stock of the June Corporation is to be declared. The stock of the June Corporation is recorded on the books at cost, $87,000; market value of the stock is $100,000.

*Required:*
(1) Discuss the propriety of the two methods of recording the dividend liability, including in your discussion an analysis of the circumstances under which each might be acceptable.
(2) The property dividend declaration might state that "corporate property is being distributed as a dividend," or it might state that "corporate property is being distributed in payment of the dividend liability." Discuss briefly the significance of the wording of the property dividend declaration and its effect upon the stockholder receiving the dividend. (AICPA adapted)

## Problem 5-13

In the suburbs of New Orleans a few years ago a group of immigrants formed a corporation. Having invested the sum of $30,000, which represented the life savings of a number of the group, they were most interested in getting back their investment. During its first year of operations, the corporation made an income of $5,000 and distributed cash of $3,000 to the stockholders. Not one of the investors considered the $3,000 as income. All looked on it as a partial return of their investment. When an internal revenue agent sought to collect an income tax on the $3,000, they asked how they could have any income until they recovered their investment.

*Required:*
How did the internal revenue agent "know" the $3,000 was a dividend? On what assumption was the distribution a distribution of income?

## Problem 5-14

Superior Products, Inc. for the first time is including a 5-year summary of earnings and dividends per share in its 1980 annual report to stockholders. At January 1, 1976 the Corporation had issued 7,000 shares of 8% cumulative, nonparticipating, $100 par value preferred stock and 40,000 shares of $10 par value common stock, of which 108 shares of preferred and 4,000 shares of common stock were held in the treasury.

Dividends were declared and paid semi-annually on the last day of June and December. Cash dividends paid per share of common stock and net income for each year were:

| | 1976 | 1977 | 1978 | 1979 | 1980 |
|---|---|---|---|---|---|
| Net income (loss | $126,568 | $(11,812) | $47,148 | $115,824 | $193,210 |
| Dividend on Common: | | | | | |
| June 30 | .40 | .11 | .10 | .40 | .60 |
| December 31 | .48 | .11 | .30 | .40 | .40 |

In addition, a 10% stock dividend was declared and distributed on all common stock (including treasury shares) on April 1, 1978 and common was split 5 for 1 on October 1, 1980. The Corporation has met a sinking-fund requirement to purchase and retire 140 shares of its preferred stock on October 1 of each year, beginning in 1979, using any available treasury stock. On July 1, 1977 the Corporation purchased 400 shares of its common stock and placed them in the treasury and on April 1, 1979 issued 5,000 shares of common stock to officers, using treasury stock to the extent available.

*Required:*

a. Prepare a schedule showing the computation of preferred stock dividends paid semi-annually and annually for the 5 years. Use the following columnar headings:

| Year | Half (1st or 2nd) | Number of Shares Purchased and Retired | Outstanding | Dividends Paid Semi-annually | Annually |
|------|-------------------|----------------------------------------|-------------|------------------------------|----------|

b. Prepare a schedule that shows for each of the 5 years the cash dividends paid to common stockholders and the average number of shares of common stock outstanding after adjustment for the stock dividend and split. Use the following format.

| Dividend Date | Shares of Common Stock In Treasury | Outstanding | Dividends Paid Per Share | Total | Common Stock Adjusted for: 10% Stock Dividend | 5 for 1 Stock Split |
|---------------|-----------------------------------|-------------|--------------------------|-------|----------------------------------------------|---------------------|
| 6/30/76 | | | | | | |
| 12/31/76 | | | | | | |

Total for year

Average for year

(Continue this format for remaining 4 years)

c. Prepare a 5-year financial summary presenting for each year:
1. Net income and dividends paid and
2. Earnings and dividends per share for common stock.

(AICPA adapted)

# Valuation of the Enterprise

The problem of maintaining an existing organizational unit and assuring its continuation has various aspects. The two preceding chapters have been concerned with the problems of providing for business risk and the problems of income administration. Another problem of maintaining the enterprise relates to the maintenance of the "values" entrusted to the enterprise. It is to this aspect of enterprise maintenance that this chapter is directed.

**METHODS OF VALUATION**

The problem of valuing a business entity may be approached by examining the various methods of valuation. Better-known business methods of valuation, all used to some extent in practice, include:

1. Valuation at acquisition costs less allocation for portions used ("historical cost" basis).
2. Valuation by capitalization of the earning power of the enterprise ("present value" basis).
3. Valuation by appraisal ("current cost" and "current exit value" bases).
4. Valuation at acquisition costs adjusted to common dollar amounts ("General Purchasing Power Units" basis)

**Valuation at Acquisition Cost Less Allocation for Usage**

The attempt to value an enterprise by valuing the individual assets and liabilities in terms of their acquisition cost has several limitations. Uninitiated readers of financial statements frequently conclude, erroneously, that a summation of the asset dollar amounts reported on the statements represents the value of the enterprise. This misunderstanding exists in spite of the fact that accountants have been most insistent that such a list of assets is not a statement of value, of individual assets or of the total enterprise.

The other main limitation to this valuation method is that it is a measure of commitments of value made by management in the past whereas the greater information need of financial statement readers is for current or future values. Despite these limitations, the acquisition cost method is used extensively because of the inability to know future values and the variety of "current" values—for example, sales value versus purchase market value. The use of this method of valuation involves several questions, including the following:

1. What is the correct amount of the cost of acquiring a particular asset?
2. When should an asset acquired be recorded?
3. How much of an asset is used up in an accounting period?

The problem of valuation of individual assets and liabilities is the typical approach to valuation used in beginning and intermediate accounting textbooks. In addition, Chapters Two and Three of this text deal with various problems in valuation of individual assets and equity items.

## Valuation by Earning Power

One method of valuing enterprise total assets that seems to have considerable support both in theory and in practical financial analysis is the capitalization of earning-power approach. In its theoretical framework the term means that an enterprise is worth the amount of net receipts it can provide. For example, if a firm can earn regularly $10,000 a year indefinitely, the amount an investor would pay for the right to receive this annual $10,000 return would depend upon the market rate of interest for funds put in similar types of ventures. Since the market rate of interest includes a payment for the risk that the anticipated receipts will not materialize, the risk associated with a venture will influence the valuation of the enterprise. Assume that a 10% annual return is demanded by investors. From this it follows that:

> If $10,000 is equal to 10% of the worth of the enterprise, then 100%, or the total worth of the enterprise, is $100,000.

This method of determining the value of an enterprise is based on the assumption that the $10,000 annual income will continue indefinitely and that the rate of risk appropriate for the enterprise will likewise remain at 10%.

If one assumes that the enterprise will not continue indefinitely, valuation in terms of earning power shifts to valuation in terms of the present value of the net receipts to be provided over the known or estimated life of the enterprise. Crude estimates of such net receipts derived by adding depreciation back to net income imply that no asset will be replaced. For example, if depreciation were $3,000 a year, it would be incorrect to add this to the $10,000 of net income and estimate annual net receipts of $13,000 a year indefinitely. On the other hand, if the enterprise were to dissolve at the end of the life of the fixed assets (assume 10 years),

6 / *Valuation of the Enterprise*

it would then be correct to compute the present value of the $13,000 of annual receipts discounted at 10% for 10 years ($79,879.37) and contend that according to the earning-power method, the enterprise value was $79,879.37.

**Theoretical Approach.** The preceding process of determining the valuation of the enterprise is a shortcut process of determining the sum of the present

**Table 6-A**

| No. of Years Income is Deferred | Annual Income to be Received | Rate of Capitalization | Present Value of Income | |
|---|---|---|---|---|
| 1 | $10,000 | 5% | $9,523.81 | |
| 2 | 10,000 | 5% | 9,070.29 | |
| 3 | 10,000 | 5% | 8,638.38 | |
| 4 | 10,000 | 5% | 8,227.02 | |
| 5 | 10,000 | 5% | 7,835.26 | |
| 6 | 10,000 | 5% | 7,462.15 | |
| 7 | 10,000 | 5% | 7,106.81 | |
| 8 | 10,000 | 5% | 6,768.39 | |
| 9 | 10,000 | 5% | 6,446.09 | |
| 10 | 10,000 | 5% | 6,139.13 | |
| Present value of $10,000 a year for 10 years at interest of 5% | | | | $ 77,217.33 |
| 11 | $10,000 | 5% | $5,846.79 | |
| 12 | 10,000 | 5% | 5,568.37 | |
| 13 | 10,000 | 5% | 5,303.21 | |
| 14 | 10,000 | 5% | 5,050.68 | |
| 15 | 10,000 | 5% | 4,810.17 | |
| 16 | 10,000 | 5% | 4,581.12 | |
| 17 | 10,000 | 5% | 4,362.97 | |
| 18 | 10,000 | 5% | 4,155.21 | |
| 19 | 10,000 | 5% | 3,957.34 | |
| 20 | 10,000 | 5% | 3,768.89 | |
| Present value of $10,000 a year for a second 10-year period at interest of 5% | | | | $ 47,404.75 |
| Present value of $10,000 a year for 20 years at 5% | | | | $124,622.08 |
| Present value of $10,000 a year for 30 years at 5% | | | | $153,724.46 |
| Present value of $10,000 a year for 40 years at 5% | | | | $171,590.86 |
| Present value of $10,000 a year for 50 years at 5% | | | | $182,559.26 |
| Present value of $10,000 a year for 90 years at 5% | | | | $197,522.62 |
| Present value of $10,000 a year for 100 years at 5% | | | | $198,479.10 |

value of each year's annual income or net receipts at the date of valuation. Present value refers to the worth now of the $10,000 to be received at a future date. If the $10,000 is to be received one year from now, and if the rate of interest involved is 5%, the present value of the $10,000 would be $9,523.81. (See Present Value of 1 Table in Appendix.) If the $9,523.81 were invested at 5% a year, it would amount to $10,000 at the end of a year. In a similar manner the present value of $10,000 not to be received for two years can be computed as $9,070.29. If the present value of $10,000 a year forever is computed and the summation made of the resulting present values, the result would be the total present value of the enterprise. This approach to approximating the valuation of the business entity has considerable theoretical merit and frequent application in practical situations, such as in the determination of a price to be paid at the time of sale of an enterprise to new owners.

To illustrate that enterprise value is the present value of the future income to be received, assume that the firm will receive an income of $10,000 a year indefinitely and that the rate of risk is 5%. Table 6-A shows that each successive $10,000 has a smaller present value and must ultimately approach zero. Consequently, as the time period over which the $10,000 a year is to be received increases, the present value of such an annuity increases toward the maximum of $200,000, which is the present value of $10,000 a year at 5% forever, or in perpetuity (see Table 6-A).

If one assumes that the enterprise will not have continuous existence or that earnings per year will not be constant, an estimation of future receipts or future net income by years is necessary. Since estimates of the future are necessarily somewhat uncertain, typically different possible receipts are recognized as possible though a greater probability may attach to one over others. The determination of value of an enterprise under these conditions can best be explained with an illustration.

Assume that the estimates of future net receipts for the Rocket Company over its short life, the expected rates of return, and the probability of each are as follows.

|  |  | Probability of Occurrence |  |  |
| --- | --- | --- | --- | --- |
| Expected Net Receipts: | Year 1 | Year 2 | Year 3 | Year 4 |
| $10,000 | .00 | .10 | .10 | .20 |
| 15,000 | .10 | .20 | .30 | .50 |
| 20,000 | .30 | .30 | .40 | .30 |
| 25,000 | .60 | .40 | .20 | .00 |
| Total | 1.00 | 1.00 | 1.00 | 1.00 |
| Expected Rate of Return |  |  |  |  |
| (Per year) |  |  |  |  |
| 5% | .50 | .30 | .20 | .10 |
| 10% | .40 | .40 | .40 | .20 |
| 15% | .10 | .30 | .40 | .70 |
| Total | 1.00 | 1.00 | 1.00 | 1.00 |

# 6 / Valuation of the Enterprise

The expected value of both net receipts and rate of return may be computed by multiplying the respective probabilities by the possible amounts, as follows.

Anticipated net receipts

| Amount | | Year 1 | | Year 2 | | Year 3 | | Year 4 |
|---|---|---|---|---|---|---|---|---|
| $10,000 | × | .00 = 0 | × | .10 = $ 1,000 | × | .10 = $ 1,000 | × | .20 = $ 2,000 |
| $15,000 | × | .10 = $ 1,500 | × | .20 = 3,000 | × | .30 = 4,500 | × | .50 = 7,500 |
| $20,000 | × | .30 = 6,000 | × | .30 = 6,000 | × | .40 = 8,000 | × | .30 = 6,000 |
| $25,000 | × | .60 = 15,000 | × | .40 = 10,000 | × | .20 = 5,000 | × | .00 = 0 |
| Expected (Average) value | | $22,500 | | $20,000 | | $18,500 | | $15,500 |

Anticipated rates of return

| 5% | × | .50 = 2.5 | × | .30 = 1.5 | × | .20 = 1.0 | × | .10 = .5 |
|---|---|---|---|---|---|---|---|---|
| 10% | × | .40 = 4.0 | × | .40 = 4.0 | × | .40 = 4.0 | × | .20 = 2.0 |
| 15% | × | .10 = 1.5 | × | .30 = 4.5 | × | .40 = 6.0 | × | .70 = 10.5 |
| Expected (Average) value = | | 8.0% | | 10.0% | | 11.0% | | 13.0% |

Discounting the expected value of future net receipts at the expected value of the future discount rates, the value of the enterprise may be computed as follows.

1. Reduce Year 4 expected value to its value at end of Year 3:

$$\$15,500 \times \frac{100}{113} = \$13,717$$

2. Add Year 3 expected value = 18,500
3. Reduce the balance of $32,217 to its value at end of Year 2:

$$\$32,217 \times \frac{100}{111} = \$29,024$$

4. Add Year 2 expected value = 20,000
5. Reduce the balance of $49,024 to its value at end of Year 1:

$$\$49,024 \times \frac{100}{110} = \$44,567$$

6. Add Year 1 expected value = 22,500
7. Reduce the balance of $67,067 to its value at start of Year 1:

$$\$67,067 \times \frac{100}{108} = \$62,099. \text{ (Present value)}$$

Because expected values are averages, the confidence in the $62,099 valuation is less than it would have been had the net receipts and discount rate been known with certainty. Without going into a statistical analysis of the dispersion around the expected value, present value might also be computed in terms of the most pessimistic and most optimistic estimates to provide a range of possible values for the Rocket Company, computed as follows:

*Most pessimistic estimate:*

|  | Year 1 | Year 2 | Year 3 | Year 4 |
|---|---|---|---|---|
| Net receipts | $15,000 | $10,000 | $10,000 | $10,000 |
| Discount rate | 15% | 15% | 15% | 15% |

$$\text{Present value} = \frac{1 - \frac{1}{(1+.15)^3}}{.15}(10,000)\left(\frac{1}{1.15}\right) + \frac{1}{1.15}(15,000)$$

$$= (2.28322512)(10,000)(.86956522)$$
$$+ (.86956522)(15,000)$$

$$= \underline{\$32,897.61}$$

*Most optimistic estimate:*

|  | | | | |
|---|---|---|---|---|
| Net receipts | $25,000 | $25,000 | $25,000 | $20,000 |
| Discount rate | 5% | 5% | 5% | 5% |

$$\text{Present value} = \left\{\left[\left(20,000 \times \frac{1}{1.05} + 25,000\right) \times \frac{1}{1.05} + 25,000\right]\right.$$
$$\left. \times \frac{1}{1.05} + 25,000\right\} \times \frac{1}{1.05}$$

$$= \underline{\$84,535.25}$$

The illustration emphasizes an extreme situation where the value of the enterprise is placed somewhere between $32,897.61 and $84,535 with an average expected value of $62,099. If the estimates of future receipts and interest rates were more certain, the wide range of possible values could be avoided.

It is frequently proposed that for all reasonable valuation purposes, extreme values should be eliminated and that a determination of the expected value and the values above and below it equal to two standard deviations would be an adequate representation of the value of the enterprise.

To illustrate this theoretical proposal, assume that the expected value of annual earnings of the Rocket Company is $10,000 with a standard deviation of $500 and that the expected value of future interest rates is 10% with a standard deviation of ½%. The capitalized value of Rocket Company would be

$$\text{Upper value (two standard deviations)} = \frac{11,000}{.09} = \$122,222$$

$$\text{Expected value} = \frac{10,000}{.10} = \$100,000$$

$$\text{Lower value (two standard deviations)} = \frac{9,000}{.11} = \$ 81,818$$

Because of the nondeterministic measure resulting from the capitalization of fluctuating annual earning power, the expected value is proposed as the proper valuation. This in effect is the equivalent of the valuation initially developed when it was assumed an enterprise can regularly earn $10,000 a year indefinitely and the risk factor is 10%.

**Practical Approach.** A general practical application of this concept of valuing an enterprise substitutes an average of annual earnings over a relatively short period for the concept of indefinite continuation of the earnings at the amount of assumed earning power. Typically, the assumed earning power to be capitalized is the average of annual earnings over the past 3 to 5 years of operations. For example, the worth of Company A could be computed as follows, using the earnings of the past four years as a base:

| | |
|---|---|
| First year | $20,000 |
| Second year | 22,000 |
| Third year | 17,000 |
| Fourth year | 21,000 |
| | $80,000 |

By dividing the total of the past four years' earnings, $80,000, by 4, an average annual earnings of $20,000 results. If the normal rate of return (risk element) in this type of industry is 20%, the worth of Company A would be computed as $100,000 ($20,000 = 20%, so $100,000 = 100%). In effect, the valuation of $100,000 is based on an assumption that Company A will earn $20,000 a year indefinitely.

Some authorities contend that earnings after taxes and interest should be capitalized to determine the proper valuation of the stockholders' equity. Others contend the proper valuation should be based upon earnings after taxes but before interest to determine the appropriate valuation of the total assets of the company. A few authorities suggest that the proper valuation results from capitalizing earnings before taxes and interest. This merely reflects the need to develop different valuations of the enterprise for different purposes.

## Valuation by Appraisal

The process of appraisal has not been and probably never can be reduced to formulae to a sufficient degree to provide a precise unequivocal valuation of an enterprise or a piece of property. Essentially it is an estimate and its accuracy depends upon the competence and integrity of the appraiser. Appraisers usually think of value in three ways:

1. *The current cost approach,* wherein the objective is to determine the current cost of reproduction or replacement of a property less depreciation. It implies the use of exact or highly similar material in the determination of reproduction cost. Alternatively, replacement cost, the cost of a facility with the same service capacity as the one under valuation, may be used. The current cost approach implies itemizing the materials and equipment that comprise the enterprise and applying current replacement prices to them.
2. *The current value or market data approach,* wherein an estimate of the value of a property is made by comparing it with similar properties that have been sold recently or are in the market. The value derived by this approach is assumed to approximate "the price at which a willing seller would sell and a willing buyer would buy, neither being under abnormal pressure."

3. *Present value or the income approach,* wherein an estimate of the net income or future potential benefits of enterprise property is capitalized by discounting expected future net receipts to the reporting date.

Combining the results of the three approaches into a final appraisal valuation requires consideration of the purpose of the appraisal, the type of business or property, the reliability of the data, and similar factors. Different valuations are needed for different purposes. For insurance purposes, reproduction cost is given greater weight than the other values. For a going-concern valuation, the income approach is emphasized. In the determination of liquidation value, the sales price as estimated by the market data approach is sought. The value most commonly sought in an appraisal is market value.

Normally, the valuation of an enterprise by appraisal implies an appraisal of assets. Such appraisal would generally have two characteristics: (1) the dollar value attached to the assets would be determined by human estimate; and (2) the valuation of the enterprise would be determined by a summation of the various asset values after appraisal. Thus, valuation of an enterprise by appraisal is somewhat related to the first method of valuation discussed above, a valuation arrived at by summation of acquisition costs less portions allocated to past operations; "current values," or more accurately, "appraised values," are substituted for acquisition costs.

Although valuation of an enterprise by appraisal has practical usefulness in a variety of business situations, accountants have been reluctant to incorporate the results of appraisals into the accounting records of an enterprise. They have required more objective evidence as a condition precedent to the recording of a business event. It should be noted, however, that competent and experienced appraisers may well determine values for given assets which could be as acceptable as those determined in the marketplace. The recent SEC call for replacement cost valuation may tend to encourage the use of appraisals.

**Accounting for Appraisals.** The accounting procedures for recording appraisals is generally considered in intermediate accounting textbooks and will not be illustrated here. Although accountants have not used appraisal values in accounting records, they have used appraisals for business purposes. On many occasions when the valuation of enterprise assets and liabilities is desired, appraisals are most helpful. For example, in determining the adequacy of insurance coverage, the management of an enterprise must be aware constantly of changing asset values. Periodic appraisals in terms of current replacement cost are most helpful to give an indication of the adequacy of existing coverage. Likewise, in pledging collateral in borrowing agreements, an enterprise may well desire to have its collateral-assets appraised at realizable value or, more properly, the lending agency may desire such an appraisal. The accountant recognizes numerous valid uses of appraisals, both in the valuation of an enterprise as a unit and in the valuation of its specific elements.

Because the two appraisal values (replacement cost and realizable value) differ for the same resource or entity, practical appraisers have developed the notion of

6 / *Valuation of the Enterprise*

a "fair" or "just" value purportedly representing the exchange price that should prevail given a willing buyer and willing seller each fully informed. This value normally falls between replacement cost and realizable value.

## Valuation in Terms of Common Dollars

In recognition of the fluctuations in the value of the monetary unit, some accountants, economists, and businessmen have suggested that the proper valuation of the enterprise may be achieved only by adjusting the historical cost, replacement cost, or realizable value to some uniform-dollar measuring unit. The procedure in this process may be likened to the translation of foreign currency into a domestic currency. The process of uniform-dollar accounting converts all dollar valuations to a common or uniform dollar. It should be distinguished from accounting for specific price-level (market value) changes of individual products. Common-dollar accounting adjusts for changes in the value of the dollar, but market value changes in the price of individual products reflect changes in the value of the product and may occur whether or not the value of the dollar has changed.

Normally, the conversion of historical or acquisition cost dollars is accomplished by means of index numbers. The most comprehensive index of the general price level in the United States is the *Gross National Product Implicit Price Deflator*, issued quarterly by the Office of Business Economics of the Department of Commerce. Normally, historical cost data are adjusted to the general purchasing power of the dollar at the latest balance sheet date. As a result, the adjustment can be made by multiplying the historical valuation by the ratio of the index on the balance sheet date to the index on the acquisition date. For example, assume that for each of four years the appropriate index numbers to be used for conversion are as follows:

| 1979 | 90  | 1981 | 115 |
|------|-----|------|-----|
| 1980 | 110 | 1982 | 110 |

Acquisition costs and the year of acquisition of assets to be converted are as follows:

| 1979 | $10,000 | 1981 | $10,000 |
|------|---------|------|---------|
| 1980 | 10,000  | 1982 | 10,000  |

If all acquisition costs expressed in terms of one year's prices, say, year 1982, are desired, the conversion process to convert all dollars to the dollar in existence in 1982 would be:

| 1979 | $10,000 times 110/ 90, or | $12,222 |
|------|---------------------------|---------|
| 1980 | 10,000 times 110/110, or  | 10,000  |
| 1981 | 10,000 times 110/115, or  | 9,565   |
| 1982 | 10,000 times 110/110, or  | 10,000  |
|      | Total, in terms of 1982 dollars | $41,787 |

Thus, the total acquisition cost of the assets, $40,000, would be modified on a common-dollar basis to $41,787 in terms of year 1982 dollars.

The valuation of assets in terms of common dollars has the advantage of eliminating the change in the value of money from the amount at which the asset is reported. The main limitation to this process of valuation is the inadequacy of any one set of index numbers to make an adjustment appropriate for all situations. If the intent of the adjustment is to indicate replacement cost of the assets, an index number reflecting the specific price-level changes of similar assets would be needed. If the objective is to adjust for general changes in the purchasing power of money, the general index number would be appropriate.

**Common-Dollar Valuation Illustrated.** Comparative balance sheets and an income statement for the Landy Corporation are presented below:

BALANCE SHEET
DECEMBER 31

| Assets | 1980 | 1979 | Increase or Decrease* |
|---|---|---|---|
| Cash | $11,000 | $ 10,000 | $1,000 |
| Receivables | 16,000 | 18,000 | 2,000* |
| Merchandise | 19,000 | 16,000 | 3,000 |
| Land | 20,000 | 20,000 | — |
| Building | 30,000 | 30,000 | — |
| Allowance for depr., Building | (12,000) | (11,000) | (1,000) |
| Equipment | 25,000 | 25,000 | — |
| Allowance for depr., Equipment | (10,000) | (7,500) | (2,500) |
| Total assets | $99,000 | $100,500 | $1,500* |
| Equities | | | |
| Accounts payable | $ 9,000 | $ 12,000 | $3,000* |
| Bonds payable | 20,000 | 20,000 | — |
| Capital stock | 50,000 | 50,000 | — |
| Retained earnings | 20,000 | 18,500 | 1,500 |
| Total equities | $99,000 | $100,500 | $1,500* |

*Income Statement for 1980*

| | | |
|---|---|---|
| Sales | | $125,000 |
| Cost of goods sold: | | |
|   Inventory, January 1 | $ 16,000 | |
|   Purchases | 93,000 | |
| | $109,000 | |
|   Inventory, December 31 | 19,000 | |
| | $ 90,000 | |
| Operating expenses, excluding depreciation | 17,000 | |
| Depreciation | 3,500 | |
| Interest charges | 1,000 | |
| Income taxes | 7,000 | |

6 / *Valuation of the Enterprise*  159

|  |  |
|---|---|
| Total expenses | $118,500 |
| Income | $ 6,500 |
| Dividends paid | 5,000 |
| Increase in retained earnings | $ 1,500 |

*General Price Index Numbers Prevailing at Date Various Assets and Equities Arose*

| Date | Item Acquired | Index No. |
|---|---|---|
| 12/31/67 | Building | 80 |
| 12/31/65 | Land | 70 |
| 12/31/75 | Equipment | 90 |
| 12/31/64 | Capital stock issued | 60 |
| Nov. and Dec. 1979 | 12/31/79 Merchandise | 104 |
| Nov. and Dec. 1980 | 12/31/80 Merchandise | 106 |
| Average, 1980 | Appropriate 1980 operating items | 105 |
| 12/31/79 | December 31, 1979 Balance sheet | 107 |
| 12/15/80 | Dividends and interest paid | 109 |
| 12/31/80 | December 31, 1980 Balance sheet | 108 |

The procedures below could be followed to prepare statements adjusted to the general price level existing as of December 31, 1980:

A. The dollar amounts of dates other than December 31, 1980, may be converted to their equivalent amount of December 31, 1980 dollars by multiplying them by the ratio of the 12/31/80 index to the index prevailing at the other dates.

B. Converting the Income Statement (nearest $100):

(1) Sales are assumed to have been sold throughout the year, when the average index was 105. This amount may be converted to 12/31/80 dollars, as follows:
108/105 times $125,000 =                                                       $128,600

(2) Cost of goods sold:

| | |
|---|---|
| Merchandise 12/31/79 = 108/104 × $16,000 = | $ 16,600 |
| Purchases 108/105 × $93,000 = | 95,700 |
| Total | $112,300 |
| Merchandise 12/31/80 = 108/106 × $19,000 = | 19,400 |
| Adjusted cost | $ 92,900 |

(3) Operating expenses, excluding depreciation:
$17,000 × 108/105 =                                                                          $ 17,500

(4) Depreciation:

| | |
|---|---|
| Building—$1,000 × 108/80 = 1,350 or | $ 1,300 |
| Equipment—$2,500 × 108/90 = | 3,000 |
| Total depreciation | $ 4,300 |

(5) Interest charges (paid once a year):
$1,000 \times 108/109 = \$991$ or $\qquad$ \$ 1,000

(6) Income taxes (assuming that this item is paid throughout the year):
$7,000 \times 108/105 =$ $\qquad$ \$ 7,200

(7) Dividends paid:
$5,000 \times 108/109 = \$4,953$ or $\qquad$ \$ 5,000

Comparative income statements adjusted and unadjusted, might be presented as follows:

*Income Statement for 1980*

|  | Unadjusted for Price-Level Changes |  | Adjusted to 12/31/80 Price Level | Price-Level Increase Decrease* |
|---|---|---|---|---|
| Sales |  | $125,000 | $128,600 | $3,600 |
| Cost of goods sold: |  |  |  |  |
| Inventory 1/1/80 | $ 16,000 |  | $ 16,600 |  |
| Purchases | 93,000 |  | 95,700 |  |
|  | $109,000 |  | $112,300 |  |
| Inventory 12/31/80 | 19,000 |  | 19,400 |  |
|  | $ 90,000 |  | $ 92,900 | 2,900 |
| Operating expenses | 17,000 |  | 17,500 | 500 |
| Depreciation | 3,500 |  | 4,300 | 800 |
| Interest charges | 1,000 |  | 1,000 | — |
| Income taxes | 7,000 |  | 7,200 | 200 |
| Total expenses |  | $118,500 | $122,900 | $4,400 |
| Income |  | $ 6,500 | $ 5,700 | $ 800 |
| Dividends paid |  | 5,000 | 5,000 | — |
| Increase in retained earnings |  | $ 1,500 | $ 700 | $ 800* |

C. Converting the balance sheets (nearest $100):

(1) Cash on 12/31/80 is stated in terms of the price level prevailing on 12/31/80 and would remain $\qquad$ $11,000

Cash on 12/31/79 had a greater purchasing power on 12/31/79 than it would have had on 12/31/80. Adjustment for equivalent purchasing power would be:
$10,000 \times 108/107 =$ $\qquad$ 10,100

(2) Receivables would be converted similar to cash:
12/31/80 Receivable = $16,000 \times 108/108 =$ $\qquad$ $16,000
12/31/79 Receivable = $18,000 \times 108/107 =$ $\qquad$ 18,200

(3) Inventories would be converted as shown in the cost of goods sold:
12/31/79 Inventory = $16,000 \times 108/104 =$ $\qquad$ $16,600
12/31/80 Inventory = $19,000 \times 108/106 =$ $\qquad$ 19,400

6 / *Valuation of the Enterprise*

(4) Land as converted, would appear in both balance sheets as:
$20,000 × 108/70 =     $30,900

(5) Building and building depreciation would be:
Building (both years) = $30,000 × 108/80 =     $40,500

Accumulated depreciation:
12/31/79—$11,000 × 108/80 =     14,900
12/31/80—$12,000 × 108/80 =     16,200

(6) Equipment and equipment depreciation:
Equipment (both years)—$25,000 × 108/90 =     $30,000

Accumulated depreciation:
12/31/79—$ 7,500 × 108/90 =     9,000
12/31/80—$10,000 × 108/90 =     12,000

(7) Accounts payable would be converted on the same basis as current receivables and cash:
12/31/80 a/c payable = $ 9,000 × 108/108 =     $ 9,000
12/31/79 a/c payable = $12,000 × 108/107 =     12,100

(8) Bonds payable:
12/31/80 payable = $20,000 × 108/108 =     $20,000
12/31/79 payable = $20,000 × 108/107 =     20,200

(9) Capital stock would be the converted purchasing power contributed to the Company, for both years:
$50,000 × 108/60 =     $90,000

(10) Retained earnings may be computed as the amount needed to balance the balance sheet. Since this procedure may include unrealized gains or losses, it might better be labeled "Additional stockholder equity."

Comparative adjusted balance sheets would be as follows:

BALANCE SHEET
AS OF DECEMBER 31
ADJUSTED TO 12/31/80 PRICE LEVEL

| Assets | 1980 | 1979 | Increase or Decrease* |
|---|---|---|---|
| Cash | $ 11,000 | $ 10,100 | $ 900 |
| Receivables | 16,000 | 18,200 | 2,200* |
| Merchandise | 19,400 | 16,600 | 2,800 |
| Land | 30,900 | 30,900 | — |
| Building | 40,500 | 40,500 | — |
| Allowance for depr., Building | (16,200) | (14,900) | (1,300) |
| Equipment | 30,000 | 30,000 | — |
| Allowance for depr., Equipment | (12,000) | (9,000) | (3,000) |
| Total assets | $119,600 | $122,400 | $2,800* |

|  |  |  |  |
|---|---:|---:|---:|
| Equities |  |  |  |
| Accounts payable | $ 9,000 | $ 12,100 | $3,100* |
| Bonds payable | 20,000 | 20,200 | 200* |
| Capital stock | 90,000 | 90,000 | — |
| Additional stockholder equity | 600 | 100 | 500 |
| Total equities | $119,600 | $122,400 | $2,800* |

In *Statement No. 3,* the Accounting Principles Board of the American Institute of Certified Public Accountants suggests the following steps in preparing general price-level adjusted financial statements:

*Step 1.* Identify monetary and nonmonetary assets and liabilities. Monetary assets are those stated in terms of a money amount to be received or paid regardless of changes in price levels. Investments in long term receivables on a temporary basis would normally not be included as a monetary asset. Nor would a convertible debt outstanding be considered a monetary liability if conversion to common stock were expected.

*Step 2.* Analyze all nonmonetary items in the balance sheet of the current year to determine when the component money amounts originated.

*Step 3.* Analyze all revenue, expense, gain, and loss items in the income statement of the current year, and all dividends and other changes in retained earnings during the year, to determine when the amounts originated that ultimately resulted in the charges and credits in the statements of income and retained earnings.

*Step 4.* Restate the nonmonetary items.

*Step 5.* Restate the monetary items in the balance sheet at the beginning of the first year.

*Step 6.* Apply the "cost or market" rule after restatement to the items to which it applies before restatement. This is necessary because market may be below or above some restated costs even though it is not below or above historical-dollar cost.

*Step 7.* Compute the general price-level gain or loss for the current year.

*Step 8.* "Roll forward" the restated statements of the prior year to dollars of current general purchasing power. The purpose of this step is to restate previously restated financial statements of a prior period to the current dollar equivalent. The procedure involves multiplying each item in the previously restated statements by the ratio of the current general price level to the general price level of the earlier period.

In order to simplify the calculations, *Statement No. 3* suggests that conversion factors (multiplier) be developed to restate amounts to the 12/31/80 dollars. This involves dividing the 12/31/80 index of 108 by each of the other index numbers, as follow.

6 / *Valuation of the Enterprise*                                                                 163

| Date or Time Period | Index No. | Ratio | Conversion Factor |
|---|---|---|---|
| 12–31–67 | 80 | 108/80 | 1.3500 |
| 12–31–65 | 70 | 108/70 | 1.5429 |
| 12–31–75 | 90 | 108/90 | 1.2000 |
| 12–31–64 | 60 | 108/60 | 1.8000 |
| Nov. and Dec. 1979 | 104 | 108/104 | 1.0385 |
| Nov. and Dec. 1980 | 106 | 108/106 | 1.0189 |
| Average, 1980 | 105 | 108/105 | 1.0286 |
| 12–31–79 | 107 | 108/107 | 1.0093 |
| 12–31–80 | 108 | 108/108 | 1.0000 |
| 12–15–80 | 109 | 108/109 | .9908 |

Applying these conversion factors to the data for the Landy Corporation will produce adjusted balance sheets and income statements similar to the ones presented in the preceding section. *APB Statement No. 3* provides, however, that general price-level gain or loss on monetary items be included in the restated income statement. The computation of this general price-level gain or loss follows:

|  | 12–31–79 Reported | Restated to 12–31–80 $'s | 12–31–80 12–31–80 $'s |
|---|---|---|---|
| Net monetary items: |  |  |  |
| Cash | $10,000 | $10,100 | $11,000 |
| Receivables | 18,000 | 18,200 | 16,000 |
| Accounts payable | (12,000) | (12,100) | (9,000) |
| Bonds payable | (20,000) | (20,200) | (20,000) |
| Balance | $ (4,000) | $ (4,000) | $ (2,000) |

|  | Historical | Restated |
|---|---|---|
| Computation of gain or loss: |  |  |
| Net monetary items on 12/31/79 | $ (4,000) | $ (4,000) |
| Add (monetary increases): |  |  |
| Current sales | 125,000 | 128,600 |
| Total available | $121,000 | $124,600 |
| Less (monetary decreases): |  |  |
| Purchases | 93,000 | 95,700 |
| Operating expenses | 17,000 | 17,500 |
| Interest charges | 1,000 | 1,000 |
| Income taxes | 7,000 | 7,200 |
| Dividends | 5,000 | 5,000 |
| Total decreases | $123,000 | $126,400 |
| Net monetary items on 12–31–80 | $ (2,000) | $ (1,800) |

General price-level loss by restatement = [(2,000) − (1,800)] $200.00.

The resulting restated income statement for 1980, with the monetary gain or loss reflected in the income statement, would appear as follows:

LANDY CORPORATION
GENERAL PRICE-LEVEL ADJUSTED STATEMENT
OF INCOME AND RETAINED EARNINGS
FOR 1980

| | | |
|---|---:|---:|
| Sales | | $128,600 |
| Cost of goods sold | $92,900 | |
| Operating expenses | 17,500 | |
| Depreciation—Building | 1,300 | |
| Depreciation—Equipment | 3,000 | |
| Interest charges | 1,000 | |
| Income taxes | 7,200 | |
| General price-level loss | 200 | |
| Total expenses | | 123,100 |
| Net income | | $ 5,500 |
| Dividends paid | | 5,000 |
| Increase in retained earnings | | $ 500 |

The distinction between monetary and nonmonetary gains and losses must be kept clearly in mind. A monetary gain or loss is an economic gain or loss, whereas the nonmonetary gain or loss is merely the result of valuing a resource in terms of a different measuring unit. To illustrate the difference, assume that two assets are owned on December 31, 1980, when the GNP Deflator is 140, and are held until December 31, 1981, when the Deflator is 147. The ratio of the 1981 index to the 1980 index is 1.050. The assets as valued on 12–31–80 could be restated to the 12–31–81 dollar by multiplying each value by 1.05, as follows:

| Asset | 12–31–80 Dollars | Ratio of Deflators | 12–21–81 Dollars |
|---|---|---|---|
| Cash | $5,000 | 1.05 | $5,250 |
| Land | $5,000 | 1.05 | $5,250 |

Now these two $250 write-ups are quite different, for if the $5,000 cash were held for the year, it would still be $5,000, having automatically changed its economic value until it is worth only $5,000 12–31–81 dollars. There is not $5,250 on hand on 12–31–81 and because the $5,000 in 12–31–80 was worth the equivalent of $5,250 12–31–81 dollars, the monetary asset has undergone an economic loss of value of $250. This economic loss is just as real as any loss that could be realized.

On the other hand, the nonmonetary write-up ("gain") of $250 on the land is merely a restatement of the historical cost of the land from 12–31–80 dollars to 12–31–81 dollars. The measuring unit has changed and that alone would not change the value of the land.

Because of the "real" and "unreal" nature of monetary and nonmonetary gains and losses, the former should be considered in evaluating company economic success or failure.

In times of a rising general price level, real monetary gains can be realized by reducing resources of a monetary form and by increasing liabilities. In times of a falling general price level, the opposite procedure is appropriate.

6 / *Valuation of the Enterprise*    **165**

In subsequent periods when the general price level then prevailing indicates that a different value of money exists, the foregoing statements can be "rolled forward" to the new dollar value for comparisons over time. For example, if the GNP Implicit Price Deflator were 110 on December 31, 1981, the foregoing statements could be rolled forward by multiplying each item by the ratio 110/108. This would adjust the statements to 12–31–81 dollars, and they could be compared with General Price Level Statements for 1981.

Although there is considerable merit in uniform-dollar accounting (the use of general price-level statements), it has not been extended to use in practice. It is, however, quite feasible and can be done in a quite objective manner. Such objectivity and feasibility do not apply to specific price-level adjustments, which are more in the nature of current market value accounting.

## VALUATION OF PARTNERSHIPS

As indicated earlier, a partnership is a group of individuals banded together as one business enterprise. When a partner withdraws from a partnership or when a partner is admitted to partnership, a new partnership is created and the old partnership is dissolved. The problem of valuing the enterprise arises every time there is an admission or withdrawal of a partner. Valuation is necessary at each of these times to determine how much must be paid out to the withdrawing partner or how much the new partner should pay in for a share of the partnership. When one or more members of the existing partnership sells all or a portion of his interest(s) in the partnership to a new partner, two alternatives exist for adjustment of the valuation of the partnership:

1. No adjustment of asset values recorded.
2. Adjustment of asset values is recorded on the basis of the sale price of the partnership interest sold.

### No Valuation Adjustment Recorded

**Purchase of an Interest from One Partner.**   In some instances one partner will sell out his interest to a new partner. In these instances there are no assets flowing in and out of the partnership, since the only change from the point of view of the partnership is a change in the composition of the partners. For example, assume that C, with a partnership capital of $8,000, sells out his interest in the partnership to D for $10,000. C must have the consent of the other partners to sell out to D, but assuming that such approval is obtained, the only entry on the books of the partnership would be:

|  |  |  |
|---|---|---|
| C, Capital | $8,000 |  |
| D, Capital |  | $8,000 |

The price at which C sold to D is not recorded on the books of the partnership. The partnership continues as before except for the change in owners. As far as the valuation of the enterprise is concerned, if no adjustment of individual asset values is made, there is an implication that the original acquisition price of the assets continues to represent the appropriate valuation of the enterprise.

## Purchase of an Interest from Several Partners.

***Adjustment of Capital Accounts.*** Another common change in partnership ownership arises when several of the partners sell a partial interest to a new incoming partner. Again, the distinction between an investment of assets into the partnership and the buying out of a former partner's interest must be maintained. In this instance the sale involves a transfer of part of several partners' interests directly to the incoming partner. The asset transfer will be between the old partners and the incoming partner, and the partnership as an enterprise will have no change in assets.

For illustrative purposes, assume that the new partner D is buying a one-third interest from the original partners. The one-third interest here means one-third of the capital and one-third of the income or loss. Because partners may share profits and losses in a ratio other than the capital ratio, it is important that the incoming partner make certain that he is buying both capital interest and profit and loss interest. The transfer of each former partner's capital to the incoming partner will depend upon the agreement reached by the old partners regarding the amount of capital and profit-and-loss interest to be transferred by each partner. Since the new partner is to receive a one-third interest, it is apparent that in total the old partners will have to transfer one-third of their capital to the capital credit of the incoming partner. But the amount of the one-third which each old partner is to sell depends upon agreement among the old partners.

In the illustration below, assume that each old partner is to transfer one-third of his individual interest in the partnership, both capital and profit-and-loss sharing interests, to D. The capital accounts and the profit-and-loss sharing ratio of the old partners prior to selling an interest to the new partner were as follows:

| Partner | Capital | Profit and Loss Ratio |
|---|---|---|
| A | $ 50,000 | 50% |
| B | 40,000 | 30% |
| C | 30,000 | 20% |
| Total | $120,000 | 100% |

Assume that D is to join the partnership and is to pay $40,000 to the old partners for a one-third interest in the capital of the partnership and a one-third interest in profits and losses. The portion of each old partner's capital account to be transferred to D would be computed as follows:

| Partner | Capital | ⅓ to D | P&L Ratio | ⅓ to D |
|---|---|---|---|---|
| A | $ 50,000 | $16,667 | 50% | 16⅔% |
| B | 40,000 | 13,333 | 30% | 10% |
| C | 30,000 | 10,000 | 20% | 6⅔% |
| Total | $120,000 | $40,000 | 100% | 33⅓% |

The entry to record the sale of the old partners' interests to the new partner would be:

| | | |
|---|---|---|
| A, Capital | $16,667 | |
| B, Capital | 13,333 | |
| C, Capital | 10,000 | |
|     D, Capital | | $40,000 |

After recording the admission of the new partner, the capital accounts and profit and loss sharing ratio would be:

| Partner | Capital | Profit and Loss Ratio |
|---|---|---|
| A | $ 33,333 | 33⅓% |
| B | 26,667 | 20% |
| C | 20,000 | 13⅓% |
| D | 40,000 | 33⅓% |
| Total | $120,000 | 100% |

It should be noted that had D purchased one-third of the capital only, and had the agreement remained silent as to the sharing of profit and loss, D would have received a profit and loss sharing interest of 25% rather than 33⅓%. Partnership law provides that when the partnership agreement is silent as to the profit and loss sharing ratio, profits and losses are to be divided equally. Normally, the partnership agreement provides that a sale of capital includes the sale of partners' interests in undistributed profits or withdrawals. Thus, had A, B, and C in the illustration above had credits or debits in their Drawing accounts, such would also be transferred by a sale of one-third of the capital. In those instances, where the partnership agreement specifies that withdrawals in excess of profits or profits in excess of withdrawals shall not become part of capital, balances in the Drawing account are not closed to capital. Normally, the total capital of a partnership can be changed only by consent of all of the old partners.

**Distribution of Cash.** The foregoing illustration indicates the essential accounting procedures of recording the continuation of the enterprise when partners are changed. The problem of dividing the cash paid by the new partner among the old partners must also be considered. Three possibilities may arise:

1. New partner pays book value for his interest ($40,000).
2. New partner pays less than book value ($35,000).
3. New partner pays more than book value ($42,000).

**Purchase Price Equals Book Value.** If the payment equals book value, the cash is distributed among the old partners at the amount of capital transferred by each old partner. In the illustration, this would be computed, assuming a purchase price of $40,000, as follows:

| Partner | Capital Transferred | Cash to be Received |
|---|---|---|
| A | $16,667 | $16,667 |
| B | 13,333 | 13,333 |
| C | 10,000 | 10,000 |
| Total | $40,000 | $40,000 |

***Purchase Price Less than Book Value.*** If the payment to the old partners is less than the book value transferred, it is apparent that cash cannot be distributed in accordance with the capital transfers. The loss (difference between book value and cash paid) must be deducted in the old partnership profit and loss sharing ratio from the book value of the capital transferred in order to determine the cash distribution, as follows:

| Partner | Capital Transfer | Less Loss | Cash to be Received |
|---|---|---|---|
| A | $16,667 | $2,500 | $14,167 |
| B | 13,333 | 1,500 | 11,833 |
| C | 10,000 | 1,000 | 9,000 |
| Total | $40,000 | $5,000 | $35,000 |

The loss of $5,000, which is the difference between the book value acquired by the incoming partner ($40,000) and the cash paid ($35,000), is allocated to the old partners in the profit-and-loss sharing ratio existing prior to the admission of the new partner. The reasoning supporting this allocation is that the old partners have sustained a loss that has not been recorded on the books. Had it been recorded, it would have been allocated in the profit-and-loss sharing ratio prevailing in the past when the old partnership existed. Since profit-and-loss sharing ratios apply whether or not a gain or loss is recorded, it is equitable to allocate the loss to the old partners in the profit-and-loss sharing ratio existing during the period when the loss arose.

***Purchase Price More than Book Value.*** If the payment to the old partners is more than the book value of the capital transferred, an unrecorded gain exists. Although it is not necessary to record this gain on the books of the partnership, the gain must be allocated to the old partners in order to distribute the cash received from the incoming partner. Assuming that the incoming partner D paid $42,000 to acquire a one-third interest in the partnership capital of $120,000, a $2,000 gain accrues to the old partners. This gain would be allocated in the old partnership profit-and-loss sharing ratio, in order to determine the distribution of the cash, as follows:

| Partner | Capital Transfer | Plus Gain | Cash to be Received |
|---|---|---|---|
| A | $16,667 | $1,000 | $17,667 |
| B | 13,333 | 600 | 13,933 |
| C | 10,000 | 400 | 10,400 |
| Total | $40,000 | $2,000 | $42,000 |

## Valuation Adjustment Recorded

The foregoing was based on the assumption that the proper valuation of enterprise assets was in terms of acquisition cost. That is, no adjustments were made to the asset values on the books of the partnership, even though the price paid for an interest by an incoming partner was not necessarily equal to the book value of the capital interest acquired. Some authorities suggest that the proper valuation of the enterprise should reflect the value of the assets indicated by the price paid by the new partner in buying a portion of the old partners' interests. This suggestion may be supported by pointing out that the purchase price arrived at for the sale would be based on an appraisal, an approximation of the earning power of the enterprise, or on some other approach to the valuation of the enterprise. The purchase price is considered to be an appropriate valuation of the partnership interest being transferred. If such purchase price exceeds book value, the assumption is that the assets and the capital of the partnership are undervalued and should be revalued upward, or that the partnership includes a goodwill element that is not reflected on the books. On the other hand, if the purchase price is below book value, the assumption is that the partnership assets are overstated and should be revalued downward.

Using the same facts as in the previous illustration, assume that the price paid by the incoming partner is used as a basis for departure from the acquisition cost valuation of the assets.

**Purchase Price Less than Book Value.** If the new partner pays only $35,000 for a capital interest with a $40,000 book value, it appears that $40,000 of assets are overstated by $5,000, if the purchase price is an accepted valuation. For the $120,000 of assets, the overstatement would be three times as large ($120,000 divided by $40,000), or $15,000. Thus, the book value of the net assets exceeds the accepted valuation, as evidenced by the purchase price, by $15,000. This $15,000 overvaluation should be recorded as a loss and allocated to the old partners' accounts in the old profit-and-loss sharing ratio, as follows:

| | | |
|---|---|---|
| A, Capital | $7,500 | |
| B, Capital | 4,500 | |
| C, Capital | 3,000 | |
| Assets | | $15,000 |

The particular asset accounts to be written down from their acquisition cost basis would depend upon a review, or appraisal, of all asset valuations to determine which should be revalued. After recognizing this as a loss, the capital accounts of the old partners and the one-third portion of the capital account that each contributes to the incoming partner would be as follows:

| Partner | Capital | ⅓ to New Partner | Capital Balance After Transfer |
|---|---|---|---|
| A | $ 42,500 | $14,167 | $28,333 |
| B | 35,500 | 11,833 | 23,667 |
| C | 27,000 | 9,000 | 18,000 |
| Total | $105,000 | $35,000 | $70,000 |

The entry to record the transfer of capital to the new partner would be:

| | | |
|---|---|---|
| A, Capital | $14,167 | |
| B, Capital | 11,833 | |
| C, Capital | 9,000 | |
| D, Capital | | $35,000 |

The cash distribution would be identical to the capital transferred. It should be noted that this cash distribution is identical to the distribution that resulted when no valuation adjustment was used in determining the distribution of the cash (see p. 168).

**Purchase Price More than Book Value.** If the new partner pays $42,000 for a capital interest with a book value of $40,000, it appears that the book value of the assets is understated by $2,000 on $40,000 of the partnership assets. The total undervaluation would be three times this amount, or $6,000, on assets of $120,000 represented by partnership capital. Following the concept that the purchase price establishes a sound basis for valuing the enterprise, the unrecorded valuation of $6,000 should be recorded and allocated to the old partners in their profit-and-loss sharing ratio. The entry to record this valuation would be:

| | | |
|---|---|---|
| Goodwill (or Assets) | $6,000 | |
| A, Capital | | $3,000 |
| B, Capital | | 1,800 |
| C, Capital | | 1,200 |

While it would be more desirable theoretically to adjust the appropriate asset accounts upward, frequently a "goodwill" account is debited for the undervaluation. This debit is supported by the argument that it is not possible to designate specifically which of the individual assets are undervalued. After recording this gain, the capital accounts of the old partners, and the one-third each contributes to the incoming partner, would be:

| Partner | Capital | ⅓ to New Partner | Capital Balance After Transfer |
|---|---|---|---|
| A | $ 53,000 | $17,667 | $35,333 |
| B | 41,800 | 13,933 | 27,867 |
| C | 31,200 | 10,400 | 20,800 |
| Total | $126,000 | $42,000 | $84,000 |

The entry to record the transfer of capital to the new partner would be:

| | | |
|---|---|---|
| A, Capital | $17,667 | |
| B, Capital | 13,933 | |
| C, Capital | 10,400 | |
| D, Capital | | $42,000 |

The distribution of cash among the old partners would be equal to the capital transferred. This is the same distribution that resulted when the acquisition cost

6 / *Valuation of the Enterprise*  171

valuation of the enterprise was used in determining the distribution of cash (see p. 168).

## Special Problems if Valuation Adjustments are Not Recorded

From the foregoing adjustment it should not be concluded that the decision on whether to record the valuation adjustment has no effect on any partner's respective interest in the partnership. The partners' respective interests will be affected by the decision to record or not to record the revaluation if either of the following conditions exist:

1. The new profit-and-loss sharing ratio of the old partners among themselves is different from the ratio existing prior to the admission of the new partner.
2. The new partner acquires a profit-and-loss ratio different from his capital ratio.

When the revaluation is not recorded and either of the conditions above exists, and there is actual realization in a subsequent period of the gain or loss evidenced by the purchase price of the new partner, a different allocation to the partners will result than if the revaluation had been recorded on the partnership books at the date of admission of the new partner.

**Illustration.** Assume that D acquires a one-third interest in the profits and losses of the enterprise and one-third of the existing partners' capital for $35,000, that the total capital is $120,000, and that no adjustment is made for the overvaluation of the assets and capital interests of the partnership. Also, assume that A, B, and C agree to share their remaining 66⅔% of the profits and losses as follows:

$$A = 25\%$$
$$B = 25\%$$
$$C = 16⅔\%$$

If, immediately after formation of the new partnership, certain assets were sold at a loss of $15,000, the following balances would result in the various partners' capital accounts:

| Partner | Capital Balance | D Acquires ⅓ | Capital Balance | Share of Loss | Balance |
|---|---|---|---|---|---|
| A | $ 50,000 | ($16,667) | $ 33,333 | ($3,750) | $ 29,583 |
| B | 40,000 | ( 13,333) | 26,667 | ( 3,750) | 22,917 |
| C | 30,000 | ( 10,000) | 20,000 | ( 2,500) | 17,500 |
| D | — | 40,000 | 40,000 | ( 5,000) | 35,000 |
| Total | $120,000 | — | $120,000 | ($15,000) | $105,000 |

A comparison of the final balances above with those resulting in the example on page 169, in which the loss evidenced by D's acquisition price was recorded, reveals the following:

| Partner | Ending Balance, Above | Ending Balance if Revaluation Recorded, page 169 | Difference Increase (Decrease) |
|---|---|---|---|
| A | $ 29,583 | $ 28,333 | $1,250 |
| B | 22,917 | 23,667 | (750) |
| C | 17,500 | 18,000 | (500) |
| D | 35,000 | 35,000 | — |
| Total | $105,000 | $105,000 | — |

The comparison indicates that by recording no valuation adjustment at the time of D's admission to the partnership, A benefited by $1,250 at the expense of B ($750) and C ($500), when the loss was actually realized. This benefit to A arose because A's share of the loss in the new partnership was less, proportionately, than under the old agreement. The reverse would have resulted from a gain situation. A similar inequity would arise if D's profit and loss ratio differed from his capital ratio.

Thus, in addition to reflecting more current asset values, recording a valuation adjustment at the date a new partner acquires an interest in a partnership may also be supported on the grounds of equity to all parties. If the price paid for the partnership interest is not representative of the current value of the assets, such a conclusion is not valid.

## SPECIAL ENTERPRISE VALUATION PROBLEMS

Accountants are frequently called on to provide guidance in business problems that may not bear directly on accounting entries. Some of these problem areas involve the process of valuation of specific asset or equity elements of the enterprise. The process of valuation at acquisition cost for individual items within the firm is one approach used in valuing specific items. Another approach involves appraisals. In connection with certain items normally appearing as equities on financial statements, accountants may find it appropriate to employ approaches to valuation other than acquisition cost or appraisal.

### Refunding Bonds Outstanding

In the case of long-term bonds outstanding, several valuations of this equity are possible, each suitable for different purposes. Possible valuations include (1) face amount of the bonds, (2) callable amount of the bonds, and (3) a discounted amount. The discounted amount is useful for several purposes. It may be particularly appropriate if an enterprise is considering refunding existing bonds prior to their maturity date. For example, assume that the Lynn Company has outstanding bonds in a maturity amount of $200,000. The bonds are due in 10 years, bear interest at a rate of 8%, and are callable at any time by the Lynn Company at 108. The current market rate of interest is such that the Lynn Company believes that refunding bonds can be issued at a rate of 6%. The question involved is whether the Company should refund the outstanding bond issue. The cost of refunding, aside from interest charges, will amount to about $1,000 to print the new bonds, $20,000 to call the old bonds, and $9,000 to issue the new bonds.

**Alternative Plans Available.** The simplest approach to this problem is to determine the present value, discounted at the appropriate current market rate of interest, of the cash requirements of the alternatives available. Assume that the new bonds will have a life equal to the remaining life of the old bonds. The three alternatives are:

1. Do not refund.
2. Deposit a sum with a trustee to provide for the payments required over the life of the old bonds and issue new bonds.
3. Call the old bonds and issue new bonds.

Assume a deposit with a trustee will earn 5% per year and that the current market rate of interest on bonds of this type is 6% a year. The three costs are:

1. Present value of requirements of old bonds:
   a. $16,000 a period for 10 periods at 6%   = $117,761.39
   b. $200,000 due in 10 periods at 6%   = 111,678.96   $229,440.35
2. Present value of trust requirements of old bonds:
   a. $16,000 a period for 10 periods at 5%   = $123,547.76
   b. $200,000 due in 10 years at 5%   = 122,782.65
   c. Cost of printing and issuing new bonds   = 10,000.00   $256,330.41
3. Present cost to call old bonds and issue new bonds:
   a. Call price ($200,000 at 108)   = $216,000.00
   b. Call expenses   = 20,000.00
   c. Cost of printing and issuing new bonds   = 10,000.00   $246,000.00

The valuations indicate that the most economical decision is not to refund the old bonds. The cost of not refunding is $16,559.65 ($246,000.00 − $229,440.35) less costly than the next most expensive alternative.

Notice that the book valuation of the old bonds is not relevant to the refunding decision, except for the possibility that a tax loss will be sustained.

Related to the decision of refunding is the question of when investment in treasury bonds is appropriate. As indicated above, the present value of the $200,000 bonds is $229,440.35 or $1,147.20 for each $1,000 bond. If the Lynn Company does have cash to invest and the market price of the bond is below $1,147.20 (quoted 114¾), the option of buying treasury bonds is a better investment than leaving the bonds outstanding. However, an alternative investment of available cash could be even more profitable than an investment in treasury bonds. Thus the present value of the requirements of the old bonds merely represents a maximum price above which no treasury bond should be purchased.

**The Discounting Process.** At this point further explanation of the discounting process may be in order. This process, which involves the discounting of future known amounts, is explained more fully in the Appendix. The method used in the illustration above is similar to the procedure used earlier (pp. 151–154) in arriving at a value for an asset in terms of its capitalized earning power. In effect, the annual interest payments of $16,000 represent an annuity of $16,000 a year payable by the Company to the bondholders for 10 years, while the $200,000 maturity amount represents a future sum that the Company will pay the bondholders. Using the tables of present value in the Appendix, and discounting at 6% the rate at which it is assumed funds can currently be invested, the following computations can be made.

The present value of an annuity of $1.00 a period for 10 periods at 6% equals $7.36008705. Since the annuity is $16,000 a period rather than $1.00, it is necessary to multiply the $7.36008705 by $16,000 to determine the present value of an annuity of $16,000 a period for 10 periods. When the multiplication is performed, the result indicates that the sum of $117,761.39 would have to be deposited today (present value) at 6% interest per period in order to pay out $16,000 each year for the next 10 years.

To determine the amount that would have to be deposited now in order to have $200,000 at the end of the 10 years, the amount necessary to pay off the maturity amount of the bonds, it is necessary to refer to the table of Present Value of 1 in the Appendix. Referring to this table, the present value of $1.00 to be received in 10 periods, if the interest rate is 6%, is $.55839478. Since it is $200,000 rather than $1.00 to be received in 10 years, it is necessary to multiply the $.55839478 by $200,000 to determine the present value of the maturity amount of the bonds. Multiplication indicates that this valuation is $111,678.96. This means that $111,678.96 would have to be deposited so that in 10 years $200,000 would be available, assuming a 6% annual interest rate. Since the present value of the interest payments is $117,761.39, the present sum of all the money to be deposited with a trustee would be the sum of these two amounts, or $229,440.35.

**Accounting for Refunding of Bonds.** To illustrate the recording process when bonds are refunded, assume that the bonds in the foregoing illustration were callable at 101, or at a cost of $202,000. Assume further that the cost to call the old bonds is $8,000 and the $10,000 cost of issuing new ones is absorbed by the underwriter to whom the new bonds are issued for $190,000. Under these conditions, the total cash equivalent required to refund would be $220,000. Since the cost of refunding is now less than the cost of not refunding $229,440.35, the Company might refund, providing that other considerations would not make such a decision inadvisable. It should be recognized that numerous considerations other than comparative costs influence the decision on refunding. These considerations include the income-tax impact from refunding as opposed to leaving the old bonds outstanding.

Assuming that the decision to refund is made, the entry to record the issuance of the new bonds might be:

| | | |
|---|---|---|
| Cash | $190,000 | |
| Bond discount | 10,000 | |
|     Bonds payable | | $200,000 |

The entry to record the retirement of the old bonds will depend upon the value at which they are being carried on the books. For illustrative purposes, assume that the old bonds were carried in the accounts at a maturity amount of $200,000 but with a related unamortized bond discount and expense account of $19,000. The entry to record the call of the old bonds would be:

| | | |
|---|---|---|
| Bonds payable | $200,000 | |
| Loss on retirement of bonds | 29,000 | |
| Bond discount | | $ 19,000 |
| Cash | | 210,000 |

*Financial Accounting Standard No. 4* requires that the $29,000 loss on early extinguishment of debt be treated as an extraordinary item, net of related income tax effect, in an income report. This is an exception to the criteria for extraordinary items established in *APB Opinion No. 30* in that it is not unusual in nature and occurs rather frequently.

### Valuation of Bonds Payable

Two other valuations of bonds payable are book value and market price. At the time bonds are issued, these two valuations may be the same, but at any time subsequent to that date different valuations would be the normal situation. The market price valuation will change because of a number of factors. Book value will change as the premium or discount on the bonds is amortized.

**Bond Premium or Bond Discount.** The price at which bonds can be issued depends upon two factors: (1) the interest rate that the company agrees to pay, generally referred to as the *nominal* rate of interest, and (2) the interest rate that investors will demand before investing in the bonds, generally referred to as the *effective* rate of interest. The relationship between the two rates will indicate whether the bonds will be issued at a discount or at a premium. For example, assume that the Jean Brown Company decides to issue $100,000 face amount of bonds at 6%, payable 3% twice a year, due in 10 years. These bonds are being issued at a nominal rate of 6% or a rate of 3% every six months. If investors who might buy the bonds have the opportunity to make a similar investment elsewhere and earn 4% every six months, it is obvious that the prospect of selling the 6% bonds at par is rather remote, and it may be expected that the bonds would sell at a discount. On the other hand, if the market rate of interest for ventures of a similar risk were 2% every six months, it is apparent that investors would want very much to acquire the bonds paying 3% every six months and would bid up the price of these bonds until they would be sold at a premium.

**Determination of Issuance Price.** The price at which bonds could be issued may be determined through the use of compound interest tables. To illustrate the process of estimating the price at which bonds may be issued, assume that the BT Company decides to issue bonds in the face amount of $100,000. Such bonds are to bear annual interest of 6%, interest payable twice a year, and they are to mature in 20 years. An examination of the security markets indicates that bonds bearing a risk somewhat similar to that involved in the current issue of bonds are selling at a price to yield an effective rate of interest of 2% every six months. As a result, it may be assumed that the bonds of the BT Company can be sold at an effective rate of 2% every six months—that is, at a price to yield the purchaser a 2% return every six months. The computation of the price at which the bonds would sell requires recognition that the bond involves two types of money payments: (1) an annuity of $3,000 every six months for 20 years, and (2) a promise to pay $100,000 at the end of a 20-year period. The determination of the price of the bonds resolves itself into the question of how much should be paid now to receive the annuity of $3,000 each six months and the future $100,000 if money invested in this type of risk earns 2% every six months.

Referring to the compound interest tables in the Appendix, it can be determined that the price to be paid for an annuity of $1.00 a period of 40 periods, if the interest rate is 2% a period, is $27.35547924. For an annuity of $3,000 every six months for 20 years (40 "periods"), the price would be 3,000 times larger, or $82,066.44. For the second phase of the problem, the compound interest tables indicate that to have $1.00 at the end of 40 six-month periods, if the interest rate is 2% every six months, it would be necessary to deposit $.45289042. To have $100,000, the sum of $45,289.04 should be deposited. Since the bonds will provide both the annuity of $3,000 and the future $100,000, the price of the bonds would then be:

Present value of an annuity of $3,000 every six months for 20
  years, if interest is assumed to be 2% every six months .................$ 82,066.44
Present value of $100,000 at the end of a 20-year period, if interest
  is assumed to be 2% every six months ............................. 45,289.04
Total (Price of the bonds) $127,355.48

For each $1,000 bond the price would be $1,273.5548, and the bonds would probably be quoted at 127.35548. The entry to record the issuance of the bonds, assuming no issue cost, would be:

| | | |
|---|---|---|
| Cash | $127,355.48 | |
|     Bonds payable | | $100,000.00 |
|     Premium on bonds | | 27,355.48 |

**Determination of Effective Interest Cost.** After the bonds have been issued, $3,000 of interest will be paid each six months, but all of the $3,000 should not be considered an expense. Part of the $3,000, in effect, represents a return of part of the premium of $27,355.48. The proper interest charge for a period would be computed by taking 2% of the carrying value of the bonds (maturity amount plus unamortized premium or minus unamortized discount). For the first interest period in the illustration above the interest expense would be $2,547.11 (2% of $127,355.48). The difference between this expense and the $3,000 payment or $452.89, would be applied to reduce the amount of the premium on the bonds.

For the second six-month period the carrying value of the bonds would be smaller by $452.89, and the effective interest on this smaller balance at 2% would be $2,538.05 (2% of $126,902.59). The amortization of the premium in this period would be $461.95 ($3,000 less $2,538.05). Table 6-B indicates the proper interest expense and the valuation of the bonds resulting from the use of the effective rate to amortize the premium on the bonds:

**Table 6-B**

| End of Period | Interest Paid | Effective Interest | Carrying Value of Bonds Payable |
|---|---|---|---|
| 0 | 0 | 0 | $127,355.48 |
| 1 | $3,000.00 | $2,547.11 | 126,902.59 |
| 2 | 3,000.00 | 2,538.05 | 126,440.64 |
| 3 | 3,000.00 | 2,528.81 | 125,969.45 |
| 4 | 3,000.00 | 2,519.39 | 125,488.84 |
| — | — | — | — |
| 39 | 3,000.00 | 2,038.83 | 100,980.39 |
| 40 | 3,000.00 | 2,019.61 | 100,000.00 |

**Accounting for Interest Costs.** The entries each six months to record the proper interest charges and the appropriate amortization of the premium are illustrated below for the first two six-month periods:

```
End of first six months:
  Premium on bonds              $ 452.89
  Bond interest expense         2,547.11
    Cash                                    $3,000.00
End of second six months:
  Premium on bonds              $ 461.95
  Bond interest expense         2,538.05
    Cash                                    $3,000.00
```

Contrary to the straight-line method of amortizing bond discount or premium, the effective rate method of amortization results in a different amount to be amortized each period. Under straight-line amortization, each of the 40 six-month entries would be:

```
Premium on bonds ($27,355.48 ÷ 40)    $ 683.89
Bond interest expense                 2,316.11
  Cash                                          $3,000.00
```

Although the straight-line method of amortization of bond premium or discount is often used, the effective rate method of amortization appears to provide a more realistic valuation of the bonds outstanding.

## Valuation of Fixed Assets

The valuation of fixed assets acquired was discussed in Chapter Two. But as it has been observed, "All fixed assets are on an irresistible march to the junk heap." So it becomes necessary to depreciate the fixed assets of an enterprise if management is to be advised regarding whether or not the business is being maintained. The process of straight-line and other depreciation methods has been considered in elementary accounting textbooks.

Once the discounting process of valuation is understood, it can be used in the valuation of almost any phase of the enterprise. Although it is seldom, if ever, used in the area of depreciation in practice, the concept underlies a number of discussions on depreciation and warrants the attention of the student of advanced accounting.

**Discounting Process Applied to Depreciation.** Essentially, the concept underlying the discounting process as applied to depreciating assets involves the recognition that assets are composed of services, some of which are extracted for use by the enterprise during each period of operation. From this point of view the purchase of a depreciable asset involves the purchase of a series of services to be used over a period of time. Since the services embodied in the assets are acquired in advance of their use, an enterprise may suffer a loss of interest by having funds tied up in such services in advance of their utilization. The loss of interest may be compensated for if the price of the services to be used in the future is lower than that of the services to be used immediately.

To illustrate, assume that the CUP Company pays $2,775.09 for a machine which will last three years, and will be utilized at the same rate in each of the three years. Assuming no scrap value, the $2,775.09 represents the cost of three years' services from the machine. At 4% interest, this sum is the present value of $1,000 of services each year, determined as follows:

| | |
|---|---:|
| Present value of $1,000 to be received at the end of one period, if the interest rate is 4% | $ 961.54 |
| Present value of $1,000 to be received at the end of two periods, if the interest rate is 4% | 924.56 |
| Present value of $1,000 to be received at the end of three periods, if the interest rate is 4% | 888.99 |
| Total | $2,775.09 |

Since different prices have been paid for the services to be received in different years, it might be concluded that the depreciation each year on the basis of cost should be $961.54, $924.56, and $888.99, respectively. Straight-line depreciation would, of course, result in an annual depreciation charge of $925.03.

Application of the discounting process to depreciation accounting gives rise to the need for considering imputed interest, the interest that could have been earned if the dollars invested in the long-lived asset had been invested directly in an interest-generating asset. Determination of the annual depreciation charge and the credit to the allowance account would include imputed interest when the discounting method is used.

**Interest Methods.** Two main procedures, known as the sinking fund method and the annuity method, might find application in this concept of depreciation accounting. These two methods are discussed in some detail in the Appendix.

# PROBLEMS

## Problem 6-1

The Bass Company statement of financial position as of December 31, 1980, shows total assets having a book value of $6,000,000 and total liabilities of $2,500,000. Recent feelers have been received by the board of directors concerning a possible sale of the business. The board is of the opinion that the business as a going enterprise is worth considerably more than the amount reported on the statement of financial position. As evidence they cite the past five years' earnings, which have been reported as follows:

| | |
|---|---|
| 1976 | $500,000 |
| 1977 | 120,000 |
| 1978 | 580,000 |
| 1979 | 595,000 |
| 1980 | 605,000 |

In 1977 the Company wrote off completely $400,000 of goodwill when it was determined that this "goodwill" had in fact never existed, even though it had been paid for. Interest costs average $60,000 per year.

*Required:*

Prepare a brief report for the board of directors of the Bass Company discussing several possible values for their business. Include estimates for both the total assets and the stockholders' equity. Assume that the risk element, or normal rate of return, is about 8% in the industry.

## Problem 6-2

A somewhat condensed statement of financial position of the Fisher Corporation is presented below:

FISHER CORPORATION
STATEMENT OF FINANCIAL POSITION
DECEMBER 31, 1980

*Assets*

| | |
|---|---:|
| Cash in bank and on hand | $ 300,000 |
| Receivables (less estimated uncollectibles) | 2,600,000 |
| Inventories (at LIFO cost; replacement market $6,600,000) | 4,000,000 |
| Investment in Rayburn Company (at cost) | 1,200,000 |
| Plant, machinery, and equipment (at depreciated cost) | 8,000,000 |
| Total | $16,100,000 |

*Liabilities and Equities*

| | |
|---|---:|
| Current liabilities | $ 2,900,000 |
| Long-term debt, 5%, due 7–1–1999 | 4,000,000 |
| Stockholders' contributed equity | 2,000,000 |
| Earnings reinvested in the business | 7,200,000 |
| Total | $16,100,000 |

Additional information of interest includes: (1) the Investment in Rayburn Company was made several years ago and represents 70% of Rayburn's outstanding common stock. Net book value of Rayburn's assets on its balance sheet is $10,000,000 at December 31, 1980. (2) During 1980 an appraisal of plant, machinery, and equipment for insurance purposes indicated a replacement cost new of $21,000,000 and an insurable value of $12,500,000. (3) Receivables appear fairly valued. (4) Average net income, after interest and taxes, for the past five years has been $2,430,000. (5) The long-term debt was incurred in 1980. (6) Rayburn Company has paid no dividends since Fisher Corporation acquired its interest.

*Required:*
(1) Assuming that a normal rate of return is 9%, approximate the value of the Fisher Corporation.
(2) Construct a pro forma statement of financial position to give effect to the value of the enterprise determined in (1).
(3) Discuss some unknown factors in the situation which make justification of *any* value estimate for the Fisher Corporation a difficult task.

## Problem 6-3

Comparative balance sheets of the Hardeen Company on December 31, 1980 and 1981, are presented below:

| Assets | December 31, 1980 | December 31, 1981 | Increase (Decrease) |
|---|---:|---:|---:|
| Cash | $ 160,000 | $ 150,000 | $(10,000) |
| Receivables | 400,000 | 500,000 | 100,000 |
| Merchandise | 600,000 | 700,000 | 100,000 |
| Fixed assets | 3,600,000 | 3,800,000 | 200,000 |
| Less: Allowance for depreciation | (900,000) | (1,000,000) | (100,000) |
| Total assets | $3,860,000 | $4,150,000 | $290,000 |
| | | | |
| Equities | | | |
| Accounts payable | $ 200,000 | $ 100,000 | $(100,000) |
| Bonds payable | 500,000 | 400,000 | (100,000) |
| Common stock | 3,000,000 | 3,000,000 | — |
| Retained earnings | 160,000 | 650,000 | 490,000 |
| Total equities | $3,860,000 | $4,150,000 | $290,000 |

6 / *Valuation of the Enterprise*

An analysis of the physical facts underlying the accounts and the changes therein during the year reveals the following:

1. The general price level remained substantially unchanged during the year.
2. The physical number of items of merchandise (a one-product company) decreased from 100,000 to 80,000.
3. Replacement cost new of $3,600,000 of the fixed assets on December 31, 1981, ($200,000 additional were acquired on December 30, 1981) was conservatively placed at $1,800,000.
4. A cash dividend of $270,000 was paid on December 15, 1981.

On January 15, 1981, the management of Hardeen Company is sued by one of its stockholders. The stockholder contends that management has paid out as dividends a substantial sum of the Company's capital. Because he has to pay an income tax on the dividend received, the stockholder is suing the management of Hardeen for recovery of the income tax.

*Required:*

You are engaged by the stockholder to prepare a report that he can use to prove that most of the $18,000 he received in dividends and on which he has to pay a 60% income tax represents a distribution of capital. He reports to you confidentially that had the fixed assets been replaced new on December 31, 1980, they would have cost $2,400,000.

Prepare the requested report indicating the amount for which he should sue.

## Problem 6-4

Abbreviated information on the activities of the Kart Company is presented below:

|  | December 31 |  |  |  |
| --- | --- | --- | --- | --- |
|  | 1978 | 1979 | 1980 | 1981 |
| Total assets | $600,000 | $620,000 | $700,000 | $650,000 |
| Bonds payable | 100,000 | 100,000 | 50,000 | 50,000 |
| Stockholders' equity: |  |  |  |  |
| Capital stock | 400,000 | 400,000 | 400,000 | 400,000 |
| Retained earnings | -0- | 30,000 | 50,000 | 40,000 |

|  | For the Year |  |  |  |
| --- | --- | --- | --- | --- |
|  | 1978 | 1979 | 1980 | 1981 |
| Net income to stockholders | -0- | $50,000 | $50,000 | $30,000 |
| Bond interest charges | 3,000 | 6,000 | 3,000 | 3,000 |
| Dividends paid | -0- | 20,000 | 30,000 | 40,000 |

Mr. A. R. Kart owns all of the stock of the Company and plans to sell it to Mr. C.A. Norse. The two men agree that the price of the stock will be based on the value of the assets. It is agreed further that the value of the assets shall be determined by capitalizing the earning power at 8%. Earnings for this purpose shall be the average earnings of the years 1979 and 1980. Each man computes the price to be paid for the stock, as follows:

| Mr. A. R. Kart | $625,000 |
|---|---|
| Mr. C. A. Norse | 461,250 |

*Required:*

(1) Compute the amount to be paid for the stock according to the agreement. Present your computation in an explanatory report.

(2) Assuming that the sale is to take place on December 31, 1981, and that it is further agreed between the two men that any "goodwill" arising as a result of the calculated sale price shall be valued at 50% of the computed amount, compute the sales price of the stock.

## Problem 6-5

Balance sheets for the Zanadir Company for 1980 and 1981 and an income statement for 1981 are presented below:

BALANCE SHEET AS OF DECEMBER 31

| Assets | 1980 | 1981 |
|---|---|---|
| Cash | $ 20,000 | $ 21,000 |
| Receivables | 30,000 | 35,000 |
| Merchandise | 15,000 | 20,000 |
| Fixed assets | 320,000 | 320,000 |
| Allowance for depreciation | (80,000) | (96,000) |
| Total assets | $305,000 | $300,000 |

| Equities | | |
|---|---|---|
| Current liabilities | $ 55,000 | $ 30,000 |
| Capital stock | 200,000 | 200,000 |
| Retained earnings | 50,000 | 70,000 |
| Total equities | $305,000 | $300,000 |

*Income Statement, 1981*

| | | |
|---|---|---|
| Sales | | $400,000 |
| Cost of Goods Sold: | | |
|   Inventory: January 1 | $ 15,000 | |
|   Purchases | 205,000 | |
|   Available | $220,000 | |
|   Inventory: December 31 | 20,000 | |
|     Cost of goods sold | $200,000 | |
| Operating expenses, excl. depreciation | 109,000 | |
| Depreciation | 16,000 | |
| Income taxes | 35,000 | |
|   Total expenses | | $360,000 |
| Income | | 40,000 |
| Dividends paid, June 15 and December 15 | | 20,000 |
| Increase in retained earnings | | $ 20,000 |

## 6 / Valuation of the Enterprise

*Additional data:*
1. The fixed assets were acquired, as follows:

| Asset | Date Acquired | Accumulated Depreciation | Annual Depreciation | Cost |
|---|---|---|---|---|
| Land | Jan. 1, 1955 | $ –0– | $ –0– | $ 40,000 |
| Building | Jan. 1, 1966 | 40,000 | 2,500 | 100,000 |
| Equipment | July 1, 1978 | 35,000 | 10,000 | 100,000 |
| Fixtures | Jan. 1, 1976 | 21,000 | 3,500 | 80,000 |
| Total | | $96,000 | $16,000 | $320,000 |

2. Price Index Numbers, presumed to reflect the increase in the general price level, are:

| Date | Index No. |
|---|---|
| 1/1/55 | 40 |
| 1/1/66 | 70 |
| 1/1/67 | 70 |
| 1/1/76 | 100 |
| 7/1/78 | 110 |
| Average, December, 1980 | 112 |
| Average, December, 1981 | 113 |
| December 31, 1980 | 110 |
| December 31, 1981 | 112 |
| Average, 1980 | 111 |
| Average, 1981 | 113 |
| June 15, 1981 | 110 |
| December 15, 1981 | 113 |

3. The capital stock was issued as follows:

| | |
|---|---|
| January 1, 1955 | $ 40,000 |
| January 1, 1967 | 160,000 |
| Total | $200,000 |

4. Inventories, receivables, and current liabilities on the year-end balance sheets were all acquired or incurred in December.

*Required:*
(In all parts, round each conversion to the nearest $100.)
(1) Prepare an income statement for 1981 adjusted to the December 31, 1981, price level.
(2) Prepare comparative balance sheets, adjusted to the December 31, 1981, price level.
(3) Prepare comparative balance sheets, adjusted to the December 31, 1980, price level.

## Problem 6-6

To obtain a more realistic appraisal of his investment, Martin Arnett, your client, has asked you to adjust certain financial data of The Glo-Bright Company for price-level changes. On January 1, 1978, he invested $50,000 in the Glo-Bright Company in return for 10,000 shares of common stock. Immediately after his investment, the trial balance appeared as follows:

|  | Dr. | Cr. |
|---|---|---|
| Cash and receivables | $ 65,200 | $ |
| Merchandise inventory | 4,000 | |
| Building | 50,000 | |
| Accumulated depreciation—building | | 8,000 |
| Equipment | 36,000 | |
| Accumulated depreciation—equipment | | 7,200 |
| Land | 10,000 | |
| Current liabilities | | 50,000 |
| Capital stock, $5 par | | 100,000 |
| | $165,200 | $165,200 |

Balances in certain selected accounts as of December 31 of each of the next three years were as follows:

|  | 1978 | 1979 | 1980 |
|---|---|---|---|
| Sales | $39,650 | $39,000 | $42,350 |
| Inventory | 4,500 | 5,600 | 5,347 |
| Purchases | 14,475 | 16,350 | 18,150 |
| Operating expenses (excluding depr.) | 10,050 | 9,050 | 9,075 |

Assume the 1978 price level as the base year and that all changes in the price level take place at the beginning of each year. Further assume that the 1979 price level is 10% above the 1978 price level and that the 1980 price level is 10% above the 1979 level.

The building was constructed in 1974 at a cost of $50,000 with an estimated life of 15 years. The price level at that time was 80% of the 1978 price level. The equipment was purchased in 1976 at a cost of $36,000 with an estimated life of 10 years. The price level at that time was 90% of the 1978 price level.

The LIFO method of inventory valuation is used. The original inventory was acquired during the year in which the building was constructed and was maintained at a constant $4,000 until 1978. In 1978 a gradual buildup of the inventory was begun in anticipation of an increase in the volume of business.

Arnett considers the return on his investment as the dividend he actually receives. In 1980 Glo-Bright paid cash dividends in the amount of $8,000.

On July 1, 1979 there was a reverse stock split-up of the Company's stock in the ratio of one-for-ten.

*Required:*
(1) Compute the 1980 earnings per share of common stock in terms of 1978 dollars.
(2) Compute the percentage return on investment for 1978 and 1980 in terms of 1978 dollars.

(AICPA adapted)

## Problem 6-7

A and B are in partnership with capital accounts on the books of $16,000 and $20,000, respectively. The partners share profit and loss equally.

*Required:*
For each case described below give the journal entry to record the change in partnership interest in the partnership.

*Case 1.* A sold his interest in the partnership to C for $24,000.
*Case 2.* A sold his interest in the partnership to C for $15,000.
*Case 3.* A sold one-half of his interest in the partnership to C for $9,000.
*Case 4.* A and B equally sell C a one-third interest in the partnership for $15,000.
*Case 5.* A sells B one-half of his profit-and-loss sharing ratio for $5,000 cash.

## Problem 6-8

Selected accounts of the partnership of A, B, and C on December 31, 1980, before final closing of the books are presented below:

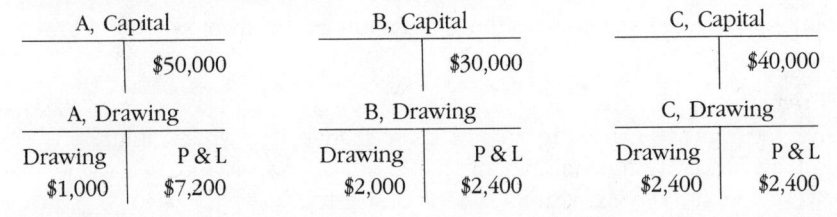

| A, Capital | B, Capital | C, Capital |
|---|---|---|
| $50,000 | $30,000 | $40,000 |

| A, Drawing | | B, Drawing | | C, Drawing | |
|---|---|---|---|---|---|
| Drawing | P & L | Drawing | P & L | Drawing | P & L |
| $1,000 | $7,200 | $2,000 | $2,400 | $2,400 | $2,400 |

On December 31, 1980, the partners agree to sell D a one-fourth interest for $50,000 cash.

*Required:*
(1) Give the journal entry necessary to record the sale of the old partners' interest to the new partner.
   (*a*) Assuming that no goodwill is to be recognized on the books.
   (*b*) Assuming that goodwill should be recognized on the books.
(2) Prepare a schedule showing how the $50,000 cash should be distributed to the old partners.
(3) Assume that the partners agree to share profits equally (25% to each partner) after D is admitted. By how much might A, B, and C question the distribution of any gain or loss if the business were then sold to Mr. X for $230,000 cash — if goodwill were not recognized when D was admitted to partnership.

## Problem 6-9

A and B are in partnership with capitals of $10,000 and $83,000, respectively. Income or loss is shared equally. The partners sell C a one-third interest in the partnership for $10,000 cash.

*Required:*
  (1) Give the journal entry to record the admission of C to the partnership.
  (2) Prepare a schedule for distributing the $10,000 in cash to the old partners.

## Problem 6-10

R. J. Adams owns a small manufacturing company in the Middle West. On December 31, 1979, his capital account was $120,000. On this date he sold a one-third interest (both capital and income and loss ratio) to C. A. Baker for $50,000. The two partners accept the valuation of $50,000 for a one-third interest for purposes of the partnership and value the combined capital accounts at $150,000. On December 31, 1980, when the capital accounts have increased to $55,000 for Baker and $110,000 for Adams, Adams sold R. W. Calvin a one-fourth interest (both capital and income-and-loss ratio) for $45,000. Because the relative income-and-loss ratio was not changed, no revaluation of the accounts was made when Calvin entered the partnership. On December 31, 1981, when the capital accounts had increased to $59,000 for Baker, $43,000 for Calvin and $75,000 for Adams, the partnership was changed to a corporation. Because the income and loss sharing ratio was in effect changed when common stock was issued for the respective capital accounts, it was agreed that the business should be revalued, and an amount of $201,000 was the resulting valuation of the owners' equity in the corporation.

*Required:*
  Give the journal entries to record each change in owners' interest over the period, and indicate the number of shares of common stock each owner would receive if the stock were issued at $100 a share.

## Problem 6-11

The H. W. Barker Company has bonds payable outstanding of $100,000 on which an unamortized bond discount exists on January 1, 1980, of $4,000. The bonds are selling in the market at 95 and are callable at 103 at any time.

*Required:*
  At what valuation should the bonds be shown on the balance sheet of this date? Discuss.

## Problem 6-12

The JWM Corporation has outstanding a $2,000,000 debenture bond issue on which the interest rate is 5½%. The bonds were sold 6 years ago at 101½ and are due 14 years from the present date. The bonds are listed on the New York Bond

Exchange and were recently quoted at 94. They are widely held. The bonds are callable at 106 for one more year, at 105 for the subsequent three years, at 104 for three additional years, and at 102½ thereafter to maturity.

*Required:*
(1) Indicate the probable amount at which the bonds are carried on the statement of financial position of the JWM Corporation.
(2) Discuss possible alternative valuations for these bonds, indicating circumstances under which any alternative valuation might have significance for management.

## Problem 6-13

The Melgar Company purchased a tract of land as an investment in 1977 for $100,000; late in that year the Company decided to construct a shopping center on the site. Construction began in 1978 and was completed in 1980; one-third of the construction was completed each year. Melgar originally estimated the costs of the project would be $1,200,000 for materials, $750,000 for labor, $150,000 for the variable overhead, and $600,000 for depreciation.

Actual costs (excluding depreciation) incurred for construction were:

|  | 1978 | 1979 | 1980 |
|---|---|---|---|
| Materials | $418,950 | $434,560 | $462,000 |
| Labor | 236,250 | 274,400 | 282,000 |
| Variable overhead | 47,250 | 54,208 | 61,200 |

Shortly after construction began, Melgar sold the shopping center for $3,000,000 with payment to be made in full on completion in December 1980. One hundred and fifty thousand dollars of the sales price was allocated for the land.

The transaction was completed as scheduled and now a controversy has developed between the two major stockholders of the Company. One feels the Company should have invested in land because a high rate of return was earned on the land. The other feels that the original decision was sound and that changes in the price level that were not anticipated affected the original cost estimates.

You are engaged to furnish guidance to these stockholders in resolving the controversy. As an aid, you obtain the following information:

1. Using 1977 as the base year, price-level indices for relevant years are: 1974 = 90, 1975 = 93, 1976 = 96, 1977 = 100, 1978 = 105, 1979 = 112, and 1980 = 120.
2. The Company allocated $200,000 per year for the depreciation of fixed assets allocated to this construction project; of that amount $25,000 was for a building purchased in 1974 and $175,000 was for equipment purchased in 1976.

*Required:*
a. Prepare a schedule to restate in base-year (1977) costs the actual costs, including depreciation, incurred each year. Disregard income taxes and assume that each price-level index was valid for the entire year.

b. Prepare a schedule comparing the originally estimated costs of the project with the total actual costs for each element of cost (material, labor, variable overhead, and depreciation) adjusted to the 1977 price level.
c. Prepare a schedule to restate the amount received on the sale in terms of base-year (1977) purchasing power. The gain or loss should be determined separately for the land and the building in terms of base-year purchasing power and should exclude depreciation.

(AICPA adapted)

## Problem 6-14

Skadden, Inc., a retailer, was organized during 1978. Skadden's management has decided to supplement its December 31, 1981 historical-dollar financial statements with general price-level financial statements. The following general ledger trial balance (historical dollar) and additional information have been furnished:

SKADDEN, INC.
TRIAL BALANCE
DECEMBER 31, 1981

|  | Debit | Credit |
|---|---|---|
| Cash and receivables (net) | $ 540,000 | $ |
| Marketable securities (common stock) | 400,000 | |
| Inventory | 440,000 | |
| Equipment | 650,000 | |
| Equipment—Accumulated depreciation | | 164,000 |
| Accounts payable | | 300,000 |
| 6% First-mortgage bonds, due 1995 | | 500,000 |
| Common stock, $10 par | | 1,000,000 |
| Retained earnings, December 31, 1980 | 46,000 | |
| Sales | | 1,900,000 |
| Cost of sales | 1,508,000 | |
| Depreciation | 65,000 | |
| Other operating expenses and interest | 215,000 | |
| | $3,864,000 | $3,864,000 |

1. Monetary assets (cash and receivables) exceeded monetary liabilities (accounts payable and bonds payable) by $445,000 at December 31, 1980. The amounts of monetary items are fixed in terms of numbers of dollars regardless of changes in specific prices or in the general price level.
2. Purchases ($1,840,000 in 1981) and sales are made uniformly throughout the year.
3. Depreciation is computed on a straight-line basis, with a full year's depreciation being taken in the year of acquisition and none in the year of retirement. The depreciation rate is 10% and no salvage value is anticipated. Acquisitions and retirements have been made fairly evenly over each year and the re-

tirements in 1981 consisted of assets purchased during 1979 which were scrapped. An analysis of the equipment account reveals the following:

| Year | Beginning Balance | Additions | Retirements | Ending Balance |
|------|-------------------|-----------|-------------|----------------|
| 1979 | —                 | $550,000  | —           | $550,000       |
| 1980 | $550,000          | 10,000    | —           | 560,000        |
| 1981 | 560,000           | 150,000   | $60,000     | 650,000        |

4. The bonds were issued in 1979 and the marketable securities were purchased fairly evenly throughout 1981. Other operating expenses and interest are assumed to be incurred evenly throughout the year.
5. Assume that Gross National Product Implicit Price Deflators (1966 = 100) were as follows:

|                  |       | Index | Conversion Factors (1981 4th Qtr. = 1.000) |
|------------------|-------|-------|--------------------------------------------|
| Annual Averages  |       |       |                                            |
|                  | 1978  | 113.9 | 1.128                                      |
|                  | 1979  | 116.8 | 1.100                                      |
|                  | 1980  | 121.8 | 1.055                                      |
|                  | 1981  | 126.7 | 1.014                                      |
| Quarterly Averages |     |       |                                            |
| 1980             | 4th   | 123.5 | 1.040                                      |
| 1981             | 1st   | 124.9 | 1.029                                      |
|                  | 2nd   | 126.1 | 1.019                                      |
|                  | 3rd   | 127.3 | 1.009                                      |
|                  | 4th   | 128.5 | 1.000                                      |

*Required:*
a. Prepare a schedule to convert the Equipment account balance at December 31, 1981 from historical-cost to general price-level adjusted dollars.
b. Prepare a schedule to analyze in historical dollars the Equipment—Accumulated Depreciation account for the year 1981.
c. Prepare a schedule to analyze in general price-level dollars the Equipment—Accumulated Depreciation account for the year 1981.
d. Prepare a schedule to compute Skadden, Inc.'s general price-level gain or loss on its net holdings of monetary assets for 1981 (ignore income tax implications). The schedule should give consideration to appropriate items on or related to the balance sheet and the income statement.

(AICPA adapted)

## Problem 6-15

Ratio analysis is often applied to test the reasonableness of the relationships among current financial data against those of prior financial data. Given prior financial relationships and few key amounts, a CPA could prepare estimates of current financial data to test the reasonableness of data furnished by his client.

Argo Sales Corporation has in recent years maintained the following relationships among the data on its financial statements:

| | | |
|---|---|---|
| 1. | Gross profit rate on net sales | 40% |
| 2. | Net profit rate on net sales | 10% |
| 3. | Rate of selling expenses to net sales | 20% |
| 4. | Accounts receivable turnover | 8 per year |
| 5. | Inventory turnover | 6 per year |
| 6. | Acid-test ratio | 2 to 1 |
| 7. | Current ratio | 3 to 1 |
| 8. | Quick-asset composition: 8% cash, 32% marketable securities, 60% accounts receivable | |
| 9. | Asset turnover | 2 per year |
| 10. | Ratio of total assets to intangible assets | 20 to 1 |
| 11. | Ratio of accumulated depreciation to cost of fixed assets | 1 to 3 |
| 12. | Ratio of accounts receivable to accounts payable | 1.5 to 1 |
| 13. | Ratio of working capital to stockholders' equity | 1 to 1.6 |
| 14. | Ratio of total debt to stockholders' equity | 1 to 2 |

The Corporation had a net income of $120,000 for 1981 which resulted in earnings of $5.20 per share of common stock. Additional information includes the following:

1. Capital stock authorized, issued (all in 1968), and outstanding:
    Common, $10 per share par value, issued at 10% premium
    Preferred, 6% nonparticipating, $100 per share par value, issued at a 10% premium
2. Market value per share of common at December 31, 1981: $78
3. Preferred dividends paid in 1981: $3,000
4. Times interest earned in 1981: 33
5. The amounts of the following were the same at December 31, 1981 as at January 1, 1981: inventory, accounts receivable, 5% bonds payable—due 1980, and total stockholders' equity.
6. All purchases and sales were "on account."

*Required:*
   a. Prepare in good form the condensed (1) balance sheet and (2) income statement for the year ending December 31, 1981, presenting the amounts you would expect to appear on Argo's financial statements (ignoring income taxes). Major captions appearing on Argo's balance sheet are: Current Assets, Fixed Assets, Intangible Assets, Current Liabilities, Long-term Liabilities, and Stockholders' Equity. In addition to the accounts divulged in the problem, you should include accounts for Prepaid Expenses, Accrued Expenses, and Administrative Expenses. Supporting computations should be in good form.
   b. Compute the following for 1981 (show your computations):
   1. Rate of return on stockholders' equity.
   2. Price-earnings ratio for common stock.

3. Dividends paid per share of common stock.
4. Dividends paid per share of preferred stock.
5. Yield on common stock.

(AICPA adapted)

## Problem 6-16

Published financial statements of United States companies are currently prepared on a stable-dollar assumption, even though the general purchasing power of the dollar has declined considerably because of inflation in recent years. To account for this changing value of the dollar, many accountants suggest that financial statements should be adjusted for general price-level changes. Three independent, unrelated statements regarding general price-level adjusted financial statements follow. Each statement contains some fallacious reasoning.

*Statement I* The accounting profession has not seriously considered price-level adjusted financial statements before because the rate of inflation usually has been so small from year to year that the adjustments would have been immaterial in amount. Price-level adjusted financial statements represent a departure from the historical cost basis of accounting. Financial statements should be prepared from facts, not estimates.

*Statement II* If financial statements were adjusted for general price-level changes, depreciation charges in the earnings statement would permit the recovery of dollars of current purchasing power and, thereby, equal the cost of new assets to replace the old ones. General price-level adjusted data would yield statement-of-financial-position amounts closely approximating current values. Furthermore, management can make better decisions if general price-level adjusted financial statements are published.

*Statement III* When adjusting financial data for general price-level changes, a distinction must be made between monetary and nonmonetary assets and liabilities, which, under the historical cost basis of accounting, have been identified as "current" and "noncurrent." When using the historical cost basis of accounting, no purchasing-power gain or loss is recognized in the accounting process, but when financial statements are adjusted for general price-level changes, a purchasing-power gain or loss will be recognized on monetary and nonmonetary items.

*Required:*
Evaluate each of the independent statements, identify the areas of fallacious reasoning in each, and explain why the reasoning is incorrect. Complete your discussion of each statement before proceeding to the next statement.

(AICPA adapted)

## Problem 6-17

1. William desires to purchase a one-fourth capital and profit and loss interest in the partnership of Eli, George, and Dick. The three partners agree to sell William one-fourth of their respective capital and profit-and-loss interests in exchange for a total payment of $40,000. The capital accounts and the respective percentage interests in profits and losses immediately before the sale to William follow:

   |  | Capital Accounts | Percentage Interests in Profits and Losses |
   | --- | --- | --- |
   | Eli | $ 80,000 | 60% |
   | George | 40,000 | 30 |
   | Dick | 20,000 | 10 |
   | Total | $140,000 | 100% |

   All other assets and liabilities are fairly valued and implied goodwill is to be recorded prior to the acquisition by William. Immediately after William's acquisition, what should be the capital balances of Eli, George, and Dick, respectively?
   
   a. $60,000; $30,000; $15,000.
   b. $69,000; $34,500; $16,500.
   c. $77,000; $38,500; $19,500.
   d. $92,000; $46,000; $22,000.

The following balance sheet is for the AdGenDa partnership. The partners, Ad, Gen, and Da, share profits and losses in the ratio of 5:3:2, respectively.

| Cash | $ 30,000 |
| --- | --- |
| Other assets | 270,000 |
|  | $300,000 |
| Liabilities | $ 70,000 |
| Ad, Capital | 140,000 |
| Gen, Capital | 80,000 |
| Da, Capital | 10,000 |
|  | $300,000 |

2. The assets and liabilities are fairly valued on the balance sheet above and the partnership wishes to admit Melvin as a new partner with a one-fifth interest *without* recording goodwill or bonus. How much should Melvin contribute in cash or other assets?
   
   a. $36,800.
   b. $46,000.
   c. $57,500.
   d. $60,000.

3. Pat, Helma, and Diane are partners with capital balances of $50,000, $30,000, and $20,000, respectively. The partners share profits and losses equally. For an investment of $50,000 cash, MaryAnn is to be admitted as a partner with a one-fourth interest in capital and profits. On the basis of this information, the amount of MaryAnn's investment can **best** be justified by which of the following?
   a. MaryAnn will receive a bonus from the other partners upon her admission to the partnership.
   b. Assets of the partnership were overvalued immediately prior to MaryAnn's investment.
   c. The book value of the partnership's net assets was less than their fair value immediately prior to MaryAnn's investment.
   d. MaryAnn is apparently bringing goodwill into the partnership and her capital account will be credited for the appropriate amount.

4. The partnership of Wayne and Ellen was formed on February 28, 1979. At that date the following assets were contributed:

|  | Wayne | Ellen |
|---|---|---|
| Cash | $25,000 | $ 35,000 |
| Merchandise | — | 55,000 |
| Building | — | 100,000 |
| Furniture and equipment | 15,000 | — |

   The building is subject to a mortgage loan of $30,000, which is to be assumed by the partnership. The partnership agreement provides that Wayne and Ellen share profits or losses 25% and 75%, respectively. Ellen's capital account at February 28, 1979, would be
   a. $190,000.
   b. $160,000.
   c. $172,500.
   d. $150,000.

5. On the basis of the same facts described in Item 4, if the partnership agreement provides that the partners initially should have an equal interest in partnership capital with no contribution of intangible assets, Wayne's capital account at February 28, 1979, would be
   a. $100,000.
   b. $115,000.
   c. $200,000.
   d. $230,000.

6. Partners Allen, Baker, and Coe share profits and losses 50:30:20, respectively. The balance sheet at April 30, 1979, follows:

| Assets: | |
|---|---|
| Cash | $ 40,000 |
| Other assets | 360,000 |
| | $400,000 |

Liabilities and Capital:

| | |
|---|---|
| Accounts payable | $100,000 |
| Allen, Capital | 74,000 |
| Baker, Capital | 130,000 |
| Coe, Capital | 96,000 |
| | $400,000 |

The assets and liabilities are recorded and presented at their respective fair values.

Jones is to be admitted as a new partner with a 20% capital interest and a 20% share of profits and losses in exchange for a cash contribution. **No** goodwill or bonus is to be recorded. How much cash should Jones contribute?
 a. $60,000.
 b. $72,000.
 c. $75,000.
 d. $80,000.                    (AICPA adapted)


## Problem 6-18

Select the *best* answer for each of the following items:

1. On January 2, 1979, the Mannix Corporation mortgaged one of its properties as collateral for a $1,000,000, 7%, five-year loan. During 1979, the general price level increased evenly, resulting in a 5 percent rise for the year.

   In preparing a balance sheet expressing financial position in terms of the general price level at the end of 1979, at what amount should Mannix report its mortgage note payable?
    a. $950,000.
    b. $1,000,000.
    c. $1,025,000.
    d. $1,050,000.

2. The historical-dollar balance sheet of the Rhuda Company showed the original cost of depreciable assets as $5,000,000 at December 31, 1979, and $6,000,000 at December 31, 1980. These assets are being depreciated on a straight-line basis over a 10-year period with *no* salvage value. Acquisitions of $1,000,000 were made on January 1, 1980. A full year's depreciation was taken in the year of acquisition.

   Rhuda presents general price-level financial statements as supplemental information to their historical-dollar financial statements. The December 31, 1979, depreciable assets balance (before accumulated depreciation) restated to reflect December 31, 1980, purchasing power was $5,800,000. What amount of depreciation expense should be shown in the general price-level income statement for 1980 if the general price-level index was 100 at December 31, 1979, and 110 at December 31, 1980?

6 / *Valuation of the Enterprise* 195

    a.   $600,000.
    b.   $660,000.
    c.   $670,000.
    d.   $690,000.

3. Cole corporation retired an issue of bonds before its maturity date through a direct exchange of securities. The best value for Cole to assign to the new issue of debt is the
   a. Maturity value of the new issue.
   b. Net carrying value of the old issue.
   c. Present value of the new issue.
   d. Maturity value of the old issue.

**Items 4, 5, and 6** are based on the following information:

The following schedule lists the general price-level index at the end of each of the five indicated years:

| | |
|---|---|
| 1976 | 100 |
| 1977 | 110 |
| 1978 | 115 |
| 1979 | 120 |
| 1980 | 140 |

4. In December 1979, the Meetu Corporation purchased land for $300,000. The land was held until December 1980, when it was sold for $400,000. The general price-level statement of income for the year ended December 31, 1980, should include how much gain or loss on this sale?
   a. $20,000 loss.
   b. $20,000 general price-level loss.
   c. $50,000 gain.
   d. $100,000 gain.

5. On January 1, 1977, the Silver Company purchased equipment for $300,000. The equipment was being depreciated over an estimated life of 10 years on the straight-line method, with *no* estimated salvage value. On December 31, 1980, the equipment was sold for $200,000. The general price-level statement of income prepared for the year ended December 31, 1980, should include how much gain or loss from this sale?
   a. $10,600 loss.
   b. $16,000 gain.
   c. $20,000 gain.
   d. $52,000 loss.

6. An analysis of the Gallant Corporation's "Machinery and equipment" account as of December 31, 1980, follows:

        *Machinery and Equipment*

| | |
|---|---:|
| Acquired in December 1977 | $400,000 |
| Acquired in December 1979 | 100,000 |
| Balance | $500,000 |

*Accumulated Depreciation*

| | |
|---|---:|
| On equipment acquired in December 1977 | $160,000 |
| On equipment acquired in December 1979 | 20,000 |
| Balance | $180,000 |

A general price-level balance sheet prepared as of December 31, 1980, should include machinery and equipment *net* of accumulated depreciation of
a. $284,848.
b. $360,000.
c. $398,788.
d. $448,000.

*Note:*
For additional problems, see the Appendix—particularly Problems AP-16 through AP-22.

# PART THREE:
# Expansion of the Business Organization

# 7

# Investment for Expansion

Business growth has been one of the well-recognized characteristics of American industry. Small companies have grown large and other companies have merged into one company to be a part of a larger enterprise. A review of this growth reveals that the expansion has been accomplished in a variety of ways. The next several chapters of this text are directed to the accounting aspects of such expansion. This chapter covers the accounting involved when an enterprise expands by buying additional operating assets. In general, the process involves two fairly distinct phases:

1. Selecting desirable areas for investment.
2. Selecting desirable methods of financing.

At times the two phases are combined into one. For example, when a firm issues some of its own stock in exchange for the assets of a going business, both phases are accomplished by the one transaction. But the fact that one transaction covers both the financing and investing of the funds does not basically alter or minimize the accounting involved.

The function of accounting in the area of business expansion is to provide (1) information useful in reaching a decision on the most appropriate investment of funds, and (2) information useful in selecting an appropriate method of financing the investment. Information of this nature is needed regardless of whether the expansion is to be accomplished in a single- or multi-step transaction.

The accounting process of providing data for making decisions on future activities of the enterprise will be the same regardless of the type of business organization. The process of financing the investment, however, raises different types of accounting problems depending upon the type of business organization involved in the expansion plans. Some of these problems are examined in the following sections.

## ACCOUNTING DATA FOR INVESTMENT DECISIONS

The process by which management makes decisions on such questions as adding a new product, changing territories, and selecting new production or marketing methods may be divided into three steps, as follows:

1. Recognition of the possible courses of action.
2. Evaluation of each course of action.
3. Determination of the best course of action.

### Role of Accounting

Normally, the role of accounting in this process lies in the second step, wherein the cost and revenue aspects of specific possibilities are considered. The function of accounting in this area is one of collecting appropriate financial information on the various possibilities under consideration and presenting comparative reports on all of them. The collecting of the data includes gathering estimates from a variety of sources and using available data on past experiences. Normally, the comparative reports on the possibilities are in terms of the costs that are expected to be incurred and the revenues that, it is anticipated, will be realized adjusted for the time element. Reports prepared on such bases are sometimes referred to as pro forma reports.

The function of providing information for evaluating possible courses of action may be most involved, depending as it does on estimates of future events of varying degrees of reliability and certainty. In providing information in this area, the accountant employs certain analytical techniques. Some of the more common are:

1. Total cost and revenue comparisons.
2. Differential cost and revenue comparisons.
3. Utilization cost comparisons.
4. Rate of return comparisons.

The techniques are employed by the accountant in varying degrees of preciseness. The discussion to follow is an introduction to some basic features of these techniques.

**Total Annual Cost and Revenue.** The technique of comparing total average annual operating revenues and expenses is simple and widely used. It does not include as a cost the imputed interest element of investments, but serves as a general guide for investment decisions. To illustrate this form of presentation, assume that two proposals for action for the coming year are under consideration. Average annual costs and revenue of each plan are estimated and presented as follows:

COMPARATIVE COST AND REVENUE REPORT
FOR 19XX OPERATIONS
UNDER PLANS A AND B

|  | Plan A | Plan B |
|---|---|---|
| Revenues obtainable under both Plan A and Plan B | $320,000 | $320,000 |
| Additional revenue of Plan A | 80,000 | — |
| Additional revenue of Plan B | — | 120,000 |
| Total revenue | $400,000 | $440,000 |

|  | Plan A | Plan B |
|---|---|---|
| Fixed costs under both plans | $100,000 | $100,000 |
| Variable costs common to both plans | 150,000 | 150,000 |
| Additional cost of Plan A | 20,000 | — |
| Additional cost of Plan B | — | 70,000 |
| Total costs | $270,000 | $320,000 |
| Estimated annual income | $130,000 | $120,000 |

On the basis of estimated revenues and costs, it appears that Plan A is the preferable plan, since it will result in $10,000 more net income than Plan B. This conclusion utilizes a total cost comparison and is based upon the difference in net income resulting from the comparative figures.

**Differential Costing.** At times the total cost and revenue techniques may be modified or simplified. Since it is the *difference* in income or cost that is of significance in problems of determining the most appropriate expansion program, a comparison that emphasizes the differences may be more useful in making the final decision. This difference is normally referred to as *differential* cost. Thus the costs and revenues in the foregoing illustration could have been measured in terms of the differential costs and revenues.

In analyses utilizing the differential cost approach, the plan that is used as a basis for comparison frequently involves the assumption that the plant would be left idle. The alternative plans involve the assumption that the plant would be utilized in production. Modifying the foregoing illustration to measure the results of the alternative plans in terms of differential costs and revenues, the calculation would be as follows:

|  | Plan A | Plan B | Difference |
|---|---|---|---|
| Revenue obtainable if plant is not left idle | $400,000 | $440,000 | $40,000 |
| Variable cost if plant is used in accordance with plan | 170,000 | 220,000 | 50,000 |
| Differential income (measured as the increase in income resulting if the plant is not left idle) | $230,000 | $220,000 | $10,000 |

The results should be read in the following manner: Plan A will provide $10,000 more income than Plan B and will provide $230,000 more income than if the plant were left idle. Plan B will provide $10,000 less income than Plan A and will provide $220,000 more income than if the plant were left idle. If the plant had been left idle, the company would have lost its fixed costs of $100,000, so that if Plan A provides a net income of $130,000, Plan A in reality provides $230,000 more income than would result from leaving the plant idle.

The use of differential costs and revenues in selecting among various possible plans is advantageous in that the computation problem is somewhat less involved than it is under the total cost and revenue approach. Likewise, the resulting differentials may provide a more useful basis for making comparisons.

**Utilization Costing.** The use of past acquisition costs in developing comparative costs for possible expansion plans under examination may not provide an adequate basis for reaching a decision. At times the unused acquisition cost of an asset does not measure appropriately the sacrifice involved in carrying out the plan. To illustrate, assume that Company A purchased some machines for $40,000 a few years ago. Once the machines have been purchased, their value to the enterprise lies either in the value of their production or in their net disposal price. In this case, assume that the machines at present have a book value of $30,000 (one-fourth of their original estimated life having expired), and a net disposal value of $10,000. The $10,000 may be described as the utilization cost[1] of the machines used to carry out the plan, if the machines are used up fully in carrying out the plan. If only a part of the machines is used in the plan, utilization cost of the plan would be measured as the difference between the net estimated disposal value of the machines before and after the plan is carried out. Assuming that the machines are to be used up in carrying out the plan under consideration, the $10,000 disposal value (rather than the $30,000 of unexpired acquisition cost) would be included in the estimated costs of carrying out the plan. That is, $10,000 is the dollar value *foregone* by the continued use of the machines. Utilization cost is represented by the dollars *foregone* by continued utilization of an asset already owned by an enterprise. In this example, utilization cost is equal to the net disposal price of the asset used.

To illustrate the significance of the difference between the $30,000 of unexpired acquisition cost and the $10,000 of utilization cost, assume that the total differential costs of two plans *before* considering the use of the machines are:

$$\begin{array}{ll} \text{Plan X} & \$180,000 \\ \text{Plan Y} & 200,000 \end{array}$$

Plan X requires the use of the machines; Plan Y does not. If the machines are included at their unamortized acquisition cost, or $30,000, the total cost of Plan X

---

[1] Utilization cost is a concept that is more commonly used in economics than in accounting. In general, this concept refers to the economic value involved in the use or utilization of a given asset or property. This value is referred to as the utilization cost of the asset.

becomes $210,000, and the implication is that Plan Y has a favorable cost differential of $10,000. Actually, this conclusion is not proper because the machines are worth only $10,000, and this amount, their utilization cost, should be used for comparative purposes in determining the most appropriate plan. If the $10,000 utilization cost is used in the example above, the result would be a total differential cost of Plan X of $190,000, leaving a favorable cost differential for Plan X of $10,000.

When utilization cost data (which differ from acquisition cost only when the machines or other resources are already on hand and do not have to be acquired) are used, it should be noted that the only sacrifice involved in adopting Plan X is the $180,000 of cash to be expended and the $10,000 of cash foregone by using the machines rather than by selling them, whereas Plan Y requires a total outlay of $200,000 in cash. The difference between the $30,000 of unexpired acquisition cost and the $10,000 of utilization cost is considered to be a loss previously sustained but not recognized on the books.

This "loss" arises because of the difference between the normal accounting concept of depreciation, which allocates the cost of an asset over its period of useful life, and an alternative concept of depreciation, which is aimed more at valuing the assets in use at various reporting dates. Depreciation charges under the normal accounting concept do not purport to measure the declining value of assets through use nor the declining value arising from technological changes. However, in evaluating alternative *future* uses for assets on hand, the disposal value, or utilization cost, may be of greater significance than book value arising from the accounting concept of depreciation. Any difference between book value and disposal value may be considered as a loss (or gain) without, however, implying that the past depreciation charges have been inappropriate in view of the facts known at the time such charges were made. It should also be recognized that utilization cost may at times be greater than undepreciated cost; nevertheless, it would be the more appropriate cost to use in analyses of this type.

**Measuring Utilization Cost.** In the preceding illustration, utilization cost was measured in terms of net disposal price. Disposal price refers to the highest of immediate sales price, future sales price discounted back to the present, or the net sales prices of the items of output discounted back to the present which the resources would provide if not used in the plan under review. In many cases, however, utilization cost should be measured in terms of replacement cost. The use of replacement cost is appropriate whenever evidence exists to indicate that if the resources on hand are used in the plan in question, it will be necessary to replace these resources at some future date. In this situation, utilization cost reflects the present value of the cash sacrificed by having used the resource in the plan under review. The cash is considered as sacrificed, since it will have to be paid out to make the replacement for future operations.

To illustrate this situation, assume that Romine Company has under consideration two plans, one of which will require the use and consumption of certain properties, while the other plan will not involve the utilization of these properties. In addition, if the properties are used up completely, as the illustration assumes, in carrying out the first plan, replacement of the properties will be necessary in coming months. Exclusive of the properties in question, the alternative plans have differential costs of:

|  |  |
|---|---|
| Plan A | $1,600,000 |
| Plan B | 1,900,000 |

The properties that would be utilized under Plan A have a book value to Romine of $250,000, but would realize only $150,000 cash (after selling expenses) if sold. If the properties were used, or sold, an outlay of $400,000 would be necessary in a few months to replace them for subsequent operations.

An analysis of the facts above would indicate the following:

1. If unamortized acquisition cost of the properties is used to arrive at Plan A's total cost, Plan A would be preferable. Its total differential cost, $1,850,000 ($1,600,000 plus $250,000), would be less than the cost of Plan B. However, as noted above, the use of past acquisition costs is usually not appropriate in making decisions involving alternatives for the future.
2. If the present cash value of the properties is used in the comparision, Plan A again emerges as the best plan. The total cost of Plan A would be $1,750,000 ($1,600,000 plus the $150,000 foregone by using the existing properties). This cost is $150,000 less than the differential cost of Plan B.
3. However, if replacement cost of the properties is used as the proper measure of the cost for comparative purposes, neither the $250,000 nor the $150,000 accurately reflects the sacrifice involved in using up the properties. The sacrifice involved in using up the properties is $400,000, and the total cost of Plan A becomes $2,000,000 ($1,600,000 plus $400,000). Now Plan B appears to be preferable, since an outlay of $1,900,000 is more economical than an outlay of $1,600,000 today, plus an additional $400,000 to replace properties used in addition to the $1,600,000.

In this example, replacement cost appears to be the most suitable measure of the utilization cost of the properties. The decision on the appropriate plan to select may well hinge on the value attached to properties, or assets, currently in use which may be utilized for one plan but not for an alternative and which, if used, will require replacement for subsequent operations.

In general, utilization cost is measured in terms of net disposal price (selling price less cost to sell), unless it is necessary to replace the resources so used. When replacement is necessary, replacement cost may be the appropriate measure of utilization cost.

**Rate of Return.** Although analysis of expansion or investment alternatives in terms of differential costs or utilization costs may provide the basis for an eventual decision, neither of these approaches to the problem should be considered to be the only, or in some situations, the most appropriate, approach possible.

Each of these analytical tools results in an evaluation of the alternatives in terms of the quantity of income arising from each alternative. Quantity of income is not necessarily the only criterion to use in the evaluation of alternative plans of action.

One basic investment criterion that is often not revealed by comparisons that merely indicate the quantity of income is the rate of income earned on the investment in the project. At times, rate of income earned, or rate of return on investment, provides a better measure of the various alternatives than does comparative quantities of income. Analyses relying solely on comparisons of total income may lead to unwise decisions, particularly if the plan leading to the larger total income requires a disproportionately larger investment.

For example, assume that Plan P will provide an income of $10,000, but will require an investment of $100,000, while Plan Q is expected to provide an income of $8,000, but requires only a $50,000 investment. On the basis of the data available, it appears that Plan P would provide a return of 10% on investment, whereas Plan Q would provide a return of 16%. Plan Q, since it yields a larger rate of return, may be the more profitable plan, assuming the Company has at least $100,000 to invest. Under this plan Romine could earn $8,000 on a $50,000 investment. If the additional $50,000 could be invested at a rate of return in excess of 4%, the total return on the $100,000 would be greater than if Plan P were adopted. If the second $50,000 could be invested at 5%, for example, an income of $2,500 would result from this investment. When the $2,500 is added to the $8,000 return on the first $50,000 investment, a total income of $10,500 is provided under Plan Q, as opposed to $10,000 under Plan P.

The following table indicates the desirability of Plan Q, assuming that $100,000 is available for investment:

|  | Investment | Return | Rate of Return |
|---|---|---|---|
| Plan P | $100,000 | $10,000 | 10% |
| Plan Q—Basic Plan | $ 50,000 | $ 8,000 | 16% |
| Investment of balance of the $100,000 | 50,000 | 2,500 | 5% |
| Total | $100,000 | $10,500 | 10.5% |

The rate of return on investment is one of the more important criteria used to evaluate alternative expansion or investment opportunities. Rate of return comparisons rely heavily on accurate revenue and cost estimates and commonly involve considered judgments on application of overhead, administrative, and other fixed and variable costs to the plans under consideration.

## Nonaccounting Considerations

One important point that has not been mentioned in the preceding sections concerns the degree of certainty of any estimated return and/or estimated costs used as the basis for management decision. Although estimates for one plan may provide both a greater income and a greater rate of return than some alternative plan, the apparently more profitable plan may also involve greater risk or uncertainty. The degree of risk may be such as to cause management to select the plan with the smaller income as being preferable to the more risky plan. The accountant can, in part, provide for some of the risks by making allowances for them as costs, but the more practical procedure is to leave these subjective evaluations to management, or disclose them in terms of statistical probabilities.

## Illustration Using Accounting Data for Expansion Planning

The Zerat Company is engaged in the manufacture and sale of lighting equipment. The Company is considering two expansion plans. One plan would increase the volume of present operations; the other plan would involve expansion through adding a new product. Differential costs and revenues, measured from current operational levels, for the two possibilities are:

|  | Volume Expansion | New Product Expansion |
|---|---|---|
| Incremental (additional) revenue | $50,000 | $80,000 |
| Differential costs (includes both variable costs that require cash outlays and fixed costs with a utilization cost) | 30,000 | 50,000 |
| Differential Income | $20,000 | $30,000 |

Assuming that revenue is not realized until the end of the year in each case, and assuming that the outlays for the differential costs must be invested at the beginning of the year, it appears that the Company will need an added investment of $30,000 if volume is expanded and will realize an income of $20,000 on this investment, or a return of 66⅔%. If the new product is added, the additional investment of $50,000 will yield a return of $30,000, or a rate of return of 60%. Although expansion by addition of the new product will produce the greater differential income, this expansion alternative does not provide as great a rate of return as does expansion through additional volume. Likewise, since expansion by addition of a new product will involve a greater additional cost outlay than will volume expansion, the new product plan entails a greater degree of risk to the Zerat Company. The lower rate of return and the greater risk element could cause the management to decide to expand through a volume increase, even though this alternative does not hold promise of providing the greater differential income.

## Limitations and Qualifications

The exact procedure by which management reaches a decision among various expansion alternatives varies widely in practice. Some managements refuse to use estimated cost and revenue data unless they are based on past historical costs of the company. Other managements plan without formally estimating the costs and revenues of different plans. In addition, many techniques not presented at this point may be utilized by management, techniques with which the accountant should become familiar before entering into this highly specialized area of accounting. Advanced textbooks in cost and management accounting should be consulted by those interested in the more specific techniques and procedures useful as aids to management in the process of making decisions on the future activities of the company.

## FINANCING PLANS—GENERAL

Funds for carrying out plans for expansion may be generated internally through operations of the enterprise or externally through borrowing or additional owner equity contributions. Profitable operations produce funds as the result of revenues being in excess of the costs and expenses chargeable against those revenues. However, funds generated internally by operations are not necessarily limited to the amount that is reported as net income. As a general rule, the funds generated by operations exceed net income, since some costs and expenses chargeable against revenues in a period commonly do not require outlays of funds in the period. Thus, depreciation charges act to reduce net income reported in a period, and properly so. However, no current payout is required as a consequence of the depreciation charge. The result insofar as generation of funds is concerned is that operations produce funds in excess of reported net income. The conclusion is valid, then, that operations will generate more funds than indicated by the net income reported to the extent of any noncash charges, such as depreciation.

Although profitable operations generate funds internally, the availability of these funds for expansion purposes is affected by numerous managerial decisions. These funds are available to management for whatever needs seem most pressing. Dividend payments, asset replacement, and reductions in indebtedness, for example, may absorb portions of the internally generated funds. Management may decide to use funds not used for such purposes to effect expansion plans. It should be evident that the balance of the Retained Earnings account is not a very good indication of the amount of funds available for expansion. The balance of this account merely represents past net income less dividend distributions. We must look to the left-hand side of the statement of financial position to determine even in a general way the availability of internally generated funds at any given date.

Accountants assist management in many ways in reaching decisions among alternative investments for expansion, whether financed by internally or externally generated funds. Statements reporting the changes in financial position in any period may be useful in providing a record of past decisions. Cash budgets or forecasts of cash receipts and expenditures assist management by indicating the extent to which funds will be available for various purposes in coming periods. Supplementary schedules, reports, and evaluations may help management to isolate the relevant differences among alternative plans. Once expansion decisions are made, accountants devise appropriate means of reporting the results of these decisions, through footnotes, reserves established out of retained earnings, or other disclosure avenues.

The following portions of this section discuss several aspects of financial expansion from internally generated funds.

### Estimating Funds from Internal Sources

The process of estimating, or forecasting, the funds that will be available for expansion purposes from internal operations involves estimating period income, deductions from it for any revenue not in cash form, and additions to it for any expenses not requiring a current outlay of cash. The result will be the amount of funds provided by operations. Dividends and other claims to such operational funds should then be deducted to arrive at the funds available for expansion. The activities of accountants in the area of budgeting and cash forecasting are treated more fully in textbooks specializing in those areas.

**Utilizing Nonincome Operational Funds.** In a very real sense, funds acquired from operations in addition to those evidenced by net income represent only a temporary source of funds. While depreciation and similar noncash expenses do, in effect, augment cash resources from operations in excess of net income, such cash resources may have to be used to replace depreciable assets as they wear out or become obsolete. If these funds are used for expansion purposes, additional funds will have to be obtained from other sources to replace assets now in use if operations are to continue at the present level. For this reason, it seems desirable to consider the financing of expansion from operating funds provided in excess of income as being in the nature of temporary financing.

In one aspect, however, nonincome funds provided by operations do represent a permanent source of funds. This situation exists when a new business is started. New buildings and other new assets will not have to be replaced for a relatively long period of time, and any new assets purchased with the funds generated by operations in excess of the net income (depreciation charges) will in turn provide operating funds through additional depreciation charges. The ultimate result of this method of expansion is that with a given investment a firm may acquire and operate a substantially greater investment in assets.

To illustrate, assume that Company A invests $100,000 in a new plant. Also assume that each year the plant revenues and costs, including depreciation, are exactly equal. Thus, the funds generated by operations are equal to the depreciation charges, assuming no other noncash revenues or costs. Also assume that the plant has a life of 10 years, so that in the first year the depreciation will be $10,000, which is equal to the total revenue less all other costs. Income is zero. Company A is in a position to expand facilities by using the $10,000 nonincome operational funds. Plant assets to start the second year would then be $110,000. Table 7-A indicates the expansion possibilities through application of nonincome operational funds.

7 / *Investment for Expansion*

The illustration indicates that with a $100,000 original investment a company can expand from nonincome operational sources of funds to an investment of $182,000 of plant assets, if all assets have a life of 10 years. It should be noted that the rate of growth is not uniform, since funds provided by this source are not uniform until the company is rather mature and until additions are equal to withdrawals of assets from the company.

## Capitalizing Retained Earnings

Retained earnings represent another source of funds for expansion. When dividend payments or withdrawals by partners or proprietors are less than income after taxes, the excess of the income over these distributions becomes additional retained income. Likewise, the enterprise will have available for various uses the assets generated by the profitable operations. Retained earnings, therefore, indicate the extent to which operations have generated assets in excess of distributions to owners, disregarding for the moment noncash income charges, such as depreciation.

**Table 7-A**

| Year | Plant Investment | Accumulated Depreciation | Annual Depreciation | Replacement | Removed From Use |
|---|---|---|---|---|---|
| 1  | $100,000 | –0–      | $10,000 | –0–     | –0–      |
| 2  | 110,000  | $10,000  | 11,000  | –0–     | –0–      |
| 3  | 121,000  | 21,000   | 12,100  | –0–     | –0–      |
| 4  | 133,100  | 33,100   | 13,310  | –0–     | –0–      |
| 5  | 146,410  | 46,410   | 14,641  | –0–     | –0–      |
| —  | —        | —        | —       | —       | —        |
| 9  | 214,358  | 114,358  | 21,436  | –0–     | –0–      |
| 10 | 235,794  | 135,794  | 23,579  | $23,579 | $100,000 |
| —  | —        | —        | —       | —       | —        |
| 20 | 182,871  | 82,871   | 18,287  | 18,287  | 23,579   |
| —  | —        | —        | —       | —       | —        |
| 30 | 181,408  | 81,408   | 18,141  | 18,141  | 18,287   |
| —  | —        | —        | —       | —       | —        |
| 40 | 181,741  | 81,741   | 18,174  | 18,174  | 18,141   |
| —  | —        | —        | —       | —       | —        |
| 50 | 181,807  | 81,807   | 18,181  | 18,181  | 18,174   |

The assets generated by profitable operations may be used for numerous business purposes—to increase inventories, to finance sales through lengthening credit terms, to augment cash resources, to expand plant facilities, and to meet many other business needs. Regardless of the use of the assets, the account reflecting the retained income (proprietor, personal; partner, drawing; retained earnings) continues to suggest, to many people at least, the extent of past earnings that are available for distribution to owners. Obviously, however, if the assets resulting from past earnings have been utilized for other business purposes, they are not available for distribution. This is particularly true, of course, if the assets have been employed to expand plant facilities.

**Recognition by Accounting Entries.** Thus the owners or management of the enterprise may desire to have their accounting records and reports reflect a decision to use assets from past income to expand productive facilities, to increase inventories permanently, etc. When it is decided to capitalize earnings permanently, the accountant should record this income administration decision as discussed in Chapter Five.

For example, a corporation that in the past has had earnings in excess of cash dividend payments, or one that at present is earning a higher income than the board of directors desires to distribute, may declare a stock dividend. The declaration of a stock dividend is commonly prompted by a desire on the part of the board of directors to give the stockholders some evidence of their part of the accumulated past earnings without actually distributing cash or other property considered necessary to future business operations. A stock dividend is normally declared as a percentage of the total shares then outstanding. Generally, the stock dividend distribution is of a relatively small portion of additional stock, e.g., 2%, 5%, or 10%. Distributions of additional stock representing a substantial percentage of outstanding shares are sometimes erroneously referred to as stock dividends. Such distributions will be discussed at a later point.

**Recorded at Par Value.** Assume that the following information is pertinent to the operations of the Bangor Corporation at December 31, 1980:

| | |
|---|---:|
| Capital stock, 1,000,000 shares authorized, 300,000 shares outstanding, par value $10 | $3,000,000 |
| Retained earnings | 3,240,000 |
| Net income for 1980 | 450,000 |
| Cash dividend payments for 1980 | $.60 per share |

Also, assume that the outlook for the Bangor Corporation is favorable, but that the cash requirements will be relatively heavy in coming months. The board of directors might decide through the medium of a stock dividend to give the stockholders greater evidence of the past year's profits than the $.60 per share cash dividend. The stock dividend percentage is dependent upon many factors, such as the amount of earnings the board desires to capitalize, the market price of the stock, and long-range plans for future distributions.

From an accounting viewpoint, the basic problem lies in the determination of the valuation to be placed upon the shares of stock to be distributed. If the Bangor Corporation board of directors decides to issue a 4% stock dividend, 12,000 additional shares of stock will be issued (4% of 300,000 shares outstanding). The par value of the shares issued will be $120,000, and the following entry would be made to record the issuance of these shares, if the shares are to be valued at par.

## 7 / Investment for Expansion

        Retained earnings                $120,000
            Capital stock                               $120,000

It must be emphasized that valuation at par is normally not an acceptable procedure and would be used only when no objective means are available to indicate the fair value of the additional shares issued.

**Recorded at Market Value.** The entry above uses par value as the valuation for the stock issued, even though the market value of the shares issued would likely be different from the par value of $10. The board of directors may intend, however, that these additional shares be considered as a distribution of earnings to the extent of the market value of the shares received. The recipient stockholders might tend to view the value of these shares at the same amount. Thus, if the market value of the Bangor Corporation stock is, for example, $22 per share at the date of payment of the dividend, the following entry would be made if the shares are to be valued at market:

        Retained earnings (12,000 × $22)      $264,000
            Capital stock (12,000 × $10)                 $120,000
            Capital in excess of par                        144,000

This entry transfers to a "paid-in capital" basis the market value of the shares issued and reduces the retained earnings by the same amount.

The significance of the different valuation illustrated in the entries is evident. If the par value per share is capitalized, $120,000 of earnings is capitalized; if the market value is capitalized, $264,000 of earnings is capitalized. If the par value basis is used, the difference of $144,000 remains in retained earnings and is presumably available for a subsequent distribution.

**Proper Accounting Treatment.** If the board of directors looks upon the stock dividend as tangible evidence of past earnings to the extent of the market value of the shares distributed, it would seem that the board should determine the number of shares to be issued by dividing the projected market price per share of stock at the date of the distribution into the amount of earnings it desires to capitalize. If this is done, the entry to record the distribution should be made at the fair market value of the shares distributed, as in the entry above.

**Recognition by Stock Split-up.** It was mentioned above that the stock dividend distribution was generally of a relatively small portion of additional stock. At times, a corporation may decide to increase substantially the number of shares outstanding. In most instances such a decision would be motivated largely by a desire to reduce the market price of the shares and thereby achieve a wider interest in and market for the shares. Stock distributions of an amount large enough to affect materially the market price of the stock are normally described as a stock split or stock split-up. A stock split-up, therefore, should have at least two essential characteristics:

1. The number of shares distributed should be substantial in relation to the shares outstanding.
2. The market value per share of the corporation's stock should be markedly affected by the split-up.

Thus, in a two-for-one split-up it would be expected that the market price after the split-up would be roughly one-half the market price prior to the split-up.

Another characteristic of a split-up that prevailed until recent years was that the split-up involved a reduction in the par or stated value of the shares. For example, the Bangor Corporation might have decided to have a two-for-one stock split-up to be effected by reducing the par value per share from $10 to $5. After the split-up was effected, the Corporation would have had 600,000 shares of $5 par value stock outstanding. The total par value outstanding would have been $3,000,000, the same as before the split-up. However, the stockholders' equity would have been spread over twice as many shares, and presumably the market price of the shares would have reflected this halving of the value of each share. No accounting entry would have been required to record such a split-up, since the only changes made were to reduce the par value per share and to increase the number of shares outstanding. It is obvious that a stock split-up effected in this manner does not result in a capitalization of any retained earnings.

In recent years the term "stock split-up" has been used to describe an issuance by a corporation of its own stock to its stockholders without consideration to the corporation. Such action has been prompted mainly by a desire to increase the number of outstanding shares to effect a reduction in market price of the stock and, thereby, to obtain wider distribution and improved marketability of the stock. If the split is effected as a dividend instead of a "pure split," in which par value is proportionately reduced, an entry is required to record the transaction to the extent occasioned by legal requirements. For example, had the Bangor Corporation issued a 100% stock dividend instead of reducing par value from $10 to $5, the following entry would have been required:

| | | |
|---|---|---|
| Retained earnings | $3,000,000 | |
|     Capital stock (300,000 × $10) | | $3,000,000 |

Occasionally a stock split has some of the characteristics of a "pure split" and some of the characteristics of a stock dividend. For example, the Bangor Corporation might have effected their split by distributing two shares for every one outstanding while reducing the par value from $10 to $7.50. In order to fulfill the legal requirement of having par value in the Capital Stock account, the following entry would have been required:

| | | |
|---|---|---|
| Retained earnings | $1,500,000 | |
|     Capital stock | | $1,500,000 |

With 600,000 shares outstanding with a par value of $7.50 per share, $4,500,000 would have been required in the Capital Stock account. Since only $3,000,000 was in the account prior to the split, an additional $1,500,000 would have been needed to meet the legal requirement.

**Summary.** The development of the current concept distinguishing a stock split-up from a stock dividend is based on the *intent* of management. If the primary intent of management is to give the stockholders additional evidence of their equity in past earnings, the distribution is considered to be a dividend. If the primary intent of management is to increase the marketability of the stock, the distribution is considered to be a stock split-up. The American Institute of Certified Public Accountants and the New York Stock Exchange have established a somewhat objective standard as a guide to the determination of the intent of management. This standard indicates that, in order to increase the marketability of stock appreciably, a distribution must be greater than 20% to 25% of the stock outstanding prior to the distribution.

## EXTERNAL FINANCING OF EXPANSION

Obtaining funds from external sources for expansion of an enterprise requires consideration of many of the same factors involved in formation of an enterprise. Since this problem area was discussed in Chapter Three, the student is referred to that chapter for the overall considerations involved. There are, however, a few accounting problems peculiar to expansion of an enterprise, particularly in the partnership form of organization, which are not faced at the time of formation.

### New Partner as a Source of Funds

The preceding chapter contained a discussion of the problems involved in the valuation of a partnership when a new partner is admitted to the partnership by purchasing an interest from one or more of the partners of the existing partnership. In that discussion it was assumed that no new assets were invested in the partnership, but that the amount paid in by the incoming partner was distributed among those partners who had sold all or part of their partnership interests. The discussion involved what is commonly called the purchase of a partnership interest.

At times, an existing proprietorship or partnership may desire to add to its operating assets either through the investment of additional assets by the existing proprietor or partners or by a new individual or individuals who would become a partner or partners in the new partnership. Certain problems exist in determining the accounting treatment of the additional investment. The following paragraphs discuss the accounting problems for what is commonly called the investment in a partnership.

In those cases where the incoming partner invests an amount equal to the book value of the capital account credit received by making the investment, the problem is quite simple. The entry to record the investment requires a debit to the assets contributed and a credit to the new partner's capital account for the amount contributed. For example, assume that A and B are in partnership with capital accounts of $30,000 each. C is admitted to the partnership with a one-third capital interest by investing $30,000 into the partnership. In this instance C will contribute $30,000 and will receive a credit to his capital account for one-third of the resulting total partnership capital ($90,000), or $30,000. The entry to record this acquisition of funds by the partnership would be:

| | | |
|---|---|---|
| Cash | $30,000 | |
|     C, Capital | | $30,000 |

On the other hand, if C were to invest the $30,000 for a one-fourth or a one-half capital interest, he would receive a credit in his capital account in an amount different from the $30,000 he contributes. The total capital equity of the new partnership would amount to $90,000, and if C were to receive a capital credit for one-fourth, he would have credited to his capital account $22,500, even though he contributed $30,000. Similarly, if he acquires a one-half interest in the new partnership, he would have a capital credit of $45,000 for his $30,000 investment.

There are two approaches to the accounting treatment of this type of problem. One approach assumes that the old partners either give or receive a bonus when the new partner is admitted. The other approach assumes that either the new partner or the old partners have additional asset values to recognize. Frequently this additional asset value is assigned to goodwill.

**Bonus to Old Partners.** If a new partner invests an amount different from the amount of capital credit he receives, and if the new partnership decides not to recognize additional asset values, the new investment must involve a bonus to one or more of the partners. In the foregoing illustration, if C were admitted to a one-fourth interest in the new partnership by making an investment of $30,000 in cash, but receiving in return a capital credit of $22,500 (¼ of $90,000), the conclusion is drawn that C gave a bonus of $7,500 to the old partners. This conclusion appears valid since the partnership received $7,500 in excess of the equity to be shown in the new partner's capital account. This bonus is divided between the two old partners in their profit-and-loss sharing ratio. If A and B had been sharing profits ⅔ and ⅓, respectively, the $7,500 credit would be allocated to their capital accounts in that proportion. The entry to admit C to partnership under this situation would be:

| | | |
|---|---|---|
| Cash | $30,000 | |
|     A, Capital | | $ 5,000 |
|     B, Capital | | 2,500 |
|     C, Capital | | 22,500 |

**Bonus to New Partner.** On the other hand, if C were admitted to the partnership with a one-half capital interest by contributing $30,000, his capital account credit would be $45,000 (½ of the $90,000 partners' capital equity). The inference is that the old partners gave the new partner a bonus for joining the partnership. The bonus contribution made by the old partners will require a transfer of a portion of the credit in their capital accounts to the capital account of the new partner. The bonus given by the old partners, like the bonus received, is

7 / Investment for Expansion

assumed to be contributed in the profit-and-loss sharing ratio of the old partners, unless there is an agreement to share the bonus otherwise. Assuming that the old partners share profits on a ⅔ and ⅓ ratio, respectively, the bonus of $15,000 ($45,000 capital credit of C less cash contributed by C of $30,000) would be divided $10,000 to A and $5,000 to B. The entry to record the admission of C under these circumstances would be:

| | | |
|---|---|---|
| Cash | $30,000 | |
| A, Capital | 10,000 | |
| B, Capital | 5,000 | |
| C, Capital | | $45,000 |

**Bonus Procedure Summarized.** The procedure for recording the admission of a new partner when additional asset values are not to be recognized may be summarized as follows:

1. Determine the total capital by adding to the capital accounts of the old partners the contribution made by the new partner.
2. Determine the new partner's share of the total capital of the new partnership by multiplying his percent or fraction of capital interest of the partnership by the total partnership capital equity. The resulting amount is the credit that will be made to the capital account of the incoming partner.
3. If the credit to the capital account of the new partner is *less* than the contribution made by him, it is assumed that the new partner gave a bonus to the old partners in the amount of the difference between the contribution made and the capital credit received. The bonus is allocated to the old partners in their profit-and-loss sharing ratio.
4. If the credit to the capital account of the new partner is *more* than the contribution made by him, it is assumed that the old partners gave a bonus to the new partner in the amount of the difference between the contribution made and the capital credit received. The bonus is charged against the old partners in their profit-and-loss sharing ratio.

**Bonus Procedure Evaluated.** In theory it would seem that the profit-and-loss sharing ratio upon which the bonus to a new partner is allocated should be that which will prevail in the future activities of the partnership, rather than the profit-and-loss ratio existing in the previous partnership. Such a conclusion appears warranted if it is recognized that the apparent reason the old partners gave the bonus was in recognition of the excessive earnings that will prevail in the future through the admission of the new partner. As the higher income is earned in the future, the old partners should recover their bonus contribution in the form of the higher earnings, and these earnings will be allocated to capital accounts in the future profit-and-loss sharing ratio. If the future "excess" earnings are allocated in some ratio different from the allocation for the bonus given at the time of admission of the new partner, an apparent inequity may result. That is, a partner may receive credit for a smaller (or greater) share of excess profits than he, in effect, paid for through the bonus to the new partner.

On the other hand, it is contended that if the old partners receive a bonus, this bonus should be allocated in the past profit and loss sharing ratio of the old partners. The reasoning supporting this conclusion suggests that the bonus being paid to the old partners has been earned by them in the past. However, this reasoning does not appear especially valid, since the incoming partner undoubtedly feels that it is a portion of the future higher earnings that he is buying when he enters the business. Thus, it would seem to follow that it is the future earning power that the old partners are selling for the bonus. If future earning power is the basis for the bonus to the old partners, it would seem that this type of bonus should be divided in the future profit-and-loss ratio of the old partners.

It should be noted, however, that, in spite of the apparent soundness of allocating the bonus resulting from an investment in a partnership in the profit-and-loss ratio that will exist in the new partnership, such procedure is not commonly followed. In general, such bonuses are allocated on the basis of the profit and loss ratio existing in the predecessor partnership.

**Goodwill to Old Partners.** Instead of using the bonus procedure, which gives the incoming partner a capital credit in an amount different from his contribution to the partnership, a goodwill account is sometimes used to account for the difference between the asset contribution and the share of total capital equity acquired. In the preceding illustration where A and B each had a capital of $30,000 and C was admitted to a one-fourth capital interest by paying in an additional $30,000, it is possible to reason that if C paid $30,000 for a one-fourth interest, the total partnership capital should be four times $30,000, or $120,000. Since the book value of the assets after C's contribution is only $90,000, it is apparent that additional asset value exists. Although the value should be assigned to appropriate assets, for convenience the amount is often classified as goodwill. Since C will receive a capital credit of $30,000 if the total partnership capital equity is $120,000, it appears that the $30,000 of goodwill is something that the old partners have created. The capital credit resulting from the recognition of the $30,000 of goodwill should be allocated to the old partners in proportion to their profit and loss sharing ratio in the old partnership. If the profit and loss ratio was ⅔ and ⅓ to A and B, respectively, the $30,000 goodwill would be recorded as follows:

| | | |
|---|---|---|
| Goodwill | $30,000 | |
|     A, Capital | | $20,000 |
|     B, Capital | | 10,000 |

(to recognize goodwill created by the old partners prior to admission of the new partner)

The admission of the new partner would be recorded as follows:

| | | |
|---|---|---|
| Cash | $30,000 | |
|     C, Capital | | $30,000 |

After this information has been recorded, the capital accounts of the three partners would be as follows:

|   |          |
|---|----------|
| A | $ 50,000 |
| B | 40,000   |
| C | 30,000   |
| Total | $120,000 |

The capital ratio of the three partners would be: A, 5/12; B, 4/12; and C, 3/12. Unless the partnership agreement specifically states that this ratio shall be used for the division of profits and losses, care must be taken not to use it for this purpose. The principles of allocating income have been discussed in Chapter Five.

**Goodwill to New Partner.** The new partner, as well as the old partners, may have goodwill to be recognized. The new partner is assumed to have brought in goodwill whenever, under the bonus procedure, he would receive a capital credit in excess of his contribution. For example, in the foregoing illustration, if C is to receive a 50% interest in the total capital equity of $120,000 by paying in only $30,000, it is apparent that C is to receive a capital credit in excess of his contribution. From this, it is concluded that C brought in goodwill that should be recognized in the accounts. The computation of the amount of goodwill is based on the assumption that the two old partners have no goodwill, and, since their 50% of the new partnership is $60,000 (their capital equity), the 50% C will own must be carried at the same equity valuation. Since C contributed $30,000 of this in cash, it is concluded that the other $30,000 is goodwill contributed along with the cash. The entry to admit C under this situation would be:

|   |   |   |
|---|---|---|
| Cash | $30,000 |   |
| Goodwill | 30,000 |   |
|     C, Capital |   | $60,000 |

After this information has been recorded, the capital accounts of the new partnership would be:

| Partner | Capital | Capital Ratio |
|---|---|---|
| A | $ 30,000 | 25% |
| B | 30,000 | 25% |
| C | 60,000 | 50% |
| Total | $120,000 | 100% |

It should be noted that the foregoing conclusion that the old partners should have a capital credit of 25% each was based solely on the fact that this represents the ratio of capitals maintained by the old partners in their former partnership. Actually, of course, the withdrawal or admission of a partner automatically dissolves an old partnership, and a completely new agreement has to be drawn up for the new partnership. Unless there are unusual circumstances, it may be assumed that the relationship that existed between the old partners will, as far as they are concerned, continue in the same proportion in the new partnership.

**Goodwill to All Partners.** At times a new partner may be admitted without the agreement affording any clear indication as to whether a bonus is being given or goodwill is presumed to exist. When the agreement is silent on this matter, it is impossible to conclude that the inclusion of either is proper to the exclusion of the other. Either approach may be justified. For purposes of consistency with corporate accounting, however, it would appear that the bonus procedure is more appropriate, since corporate accounting does not recognize goodwill when a new stockholder acquires stock. For example, assume that the stock of the X Corporation has a par value of $100 per share and a book value of $130 per share. If an additional share is issued at $150, the entry would be:

| | | |
|---|---|---|
| Cash | $150 | |
| Capital stock | | $100 |
| Premium on stock | | 50 |

Since the premium is divided equally among all stockholders, the new stockholder in effect contributes a bonus to the old stockholders, the bonus being the $20 in excess of book value.

Another apparently ambiguous situation arises when a new partner is admitted to a specified interest in a specified total capital equity by contributing a given sum, but without any indication whether the goodwill or bonus procedure is to be used. However, in this case, it may be possible to determine which of these is to be recognized. For example, assume that C is admitted to a one-fourth capital interest in a partnership by paying in $30,000 in cash. The old partners have capital accounts of $40,000 each. It is agreed that the total capital equity of the new partnership shall be $160,000. In this case, if C is to have a one-fourth interest, he should have a capital credit of $40,000. Since he has contributed only $30,000, he should have an additional credit of $10,000. The two old partners will have a capital equity of 75% in the new partnership, or an equity of $120,000. Since their present capital accounts amount to only $80,000, it is apparent that they need an additional credit of $40,000. Since both the old partners and the new partner are to receive additional credits to their capital accounts, it is apparent that the bonus procedure cannot be used and goodwill must be recognized, as follows:

| | | |
|---|---|---|
| Cash | $30,000 | |
| Goodwill | 10,000 | |
|    C, Capital | | $40,000 |
| Goodwill | $40,000 | |
|    A, Capital | | $30,000 |
|    B, Capital | | 10,000 |
| (assumes A and B share profit and loss in a ¾, ¼ ratio.) | | |

## EXPANSION AND FINANCING AS ONE ACTIVITY

Although the decision to expand and the financing of such expansion are best viewed as separate problems, much of business practice combines the two into one activity. Thus, for example, an enterprise may purchase on account additional facilities for expansion, or it may issue capital stock in exchange for expansion facilities. At times, the method of financing affects the cost comparisons used in reaching a decision on whether or not to expand. The following example indicates the close relationship that frequently exists between the decision to expand and the financing alternatives available.

Assume that Company A, which at present has operating assets totaling $2,000,000, is considering expansion of facilities and has two financing plans under consideration: (1) long-term borrowing of $1,500,000 at an annual interest cost of 7%; (2) sale of additional stock for $1,500,000. The cost and revenue estimates are presented as follows:

|  | Present Operations | Under Expansion Long-Term Borrowing | Under Expansion Sale of Stock |
|---|---|---|---|
| Revenues | $1,000,000 | $1,800,000 | $1,800,000 |
| Fixed costs | $ 400,000 | $ 600,000 | $ 600,000 |
| Variable costs | 400,000 | 800,000 | 800,000 |
| Interest costs |  | 105,000 |  |
| Total costs | $ 800,000 | $1,505,000 | $1,400,000 |
| Estimated net income | $ 200,000 | $ 295,000 | $ 400,000 |

Although various factors influence a final decision on whether or not to expand, management should recognize the following relationships in the illustration above. Present operations are returning 10% net income on assets in use ($200,000 net income divided by $2,000,000 total assets). Expansion via the long-term borrowing route will produce $95,000 additional income after interest charges, but return on total assets will fall to 8.43% ($295,000 net income divided by $3,500,000 total assets). The rate of return to stockholders, however, would increase because of the higher income accruing to them without any increase in stockholders' equity. Expansion via the sale-of-stock route will produce $200,000 additional income and will increase return on total assets to 11.43% ($400,000 divided by $3,500,000). Whether the average rate of return to stockholders will increase, however, depends on the manner in which the initial $2,000,000 of assets was financed. If $1,000,000 were provided by liabilities, the former rate of return to stockholders would have been 20% ($200,000 divided by $1,000,000). If the initial $2,000,000 of assets were provided by stockholders, the former rate of return to stockholders would have been 10% ($200,000 divided by $2,000,000). By computing the rate of return to stockholders from the additional $1,500,000, one can determine whether the average rate of return to stockholders will increase or decrease if expansion via sale of stock is undertaken.

Regardless of the accounting analysis, management may make a decision based on other considerations. For example, management may discard the idea of financing the possible expansion by borrowing, deciding that the additional risk involved to stockholders will not be compensated for by the additional income generated. They may decide that expansion through a stock sale looks favorable.

Continuing with this illustration, however, a different conclusion might be reached. Assume that Company A at present has $750,000 of stock outstanding and also has $250,000 of retained earnings. The Company is, therefore, earning a 20% return on the stockholders' equity ($200,000 net income divided by $1,000,000 stockholders' equity). If expansion proceeds by sale of stock, the stockholders' equity will increase to $2,500,000, and earnings to stockholders will increase to $400,000. However, return on stockholders' equity will fall to 16% ($400,000 divided by $2,500,000). In view of this decline in rate of return on investment, management may decide to forego any expansion at this time in the hope that more favorable situations will develop in the future.

In more recent years, financing by means of convertile debt securities, which are convertible into common stock of the issuing company at a specified price at the option of the holder, has been used. Because of the opportunity to acquire common at a specified price at a subsequent date when market price of the stock is higher, buyers of securities have placed a premium on convertible debt securities. This has enabled the issuing company to place a lower interest rate on the convertible securities than would be necessary if straight debt securities were issued. Convertible debt securities are also favored by issuers because in the long run, as debts are converted, it is a means of capital stock financing.

Although it might appear that accounting for the economic reality of convertible debt would require a separation of the proceeds from such an issue into a straight debt portion and a paid-in capital portion, the inseparability of the debt and the conversion option in the one security results in an accounting treatment of convertible debt securities as debt.

In the preceding illustration, if $1,500,000 of convertible debt were issued, an interest rate of 5% might be placed on the debt. This rate would result in a 9.29% ($325,000 revised net income divided by $3,500,000 total assets) return on total assets and a higher rate of return to stockholders until conversion occurred.

In order to separate the debt and options to purchase common stock at a specified price within some specified time period, some companies issue in one package debt with detachable warrants to purchase stock. In this situation, the expectation is that the debt will be paid at maturity, since it cannot be converted. The proceeds from such a package issue of debt and stock purchase warrants should be allocated to the two elements for accounting purposes. The allocation should be based on the relative fair value of the debt without the warrants and of the warrants alone at the time the package is issued. The portion allocated to the warrants should be accounted for as paid-in capital.

To illustrate accounting for this method of financing, assume that an interest rate of 5% is placed on the bonds in the foregoing illustration but that detachable warrants to purchase common stock are included as part of the issue. Assume that proceeds of the package issue are $1,460,000 and that immediately after issue the relative fair value of the bonds and warrants is 90 to 10. The entry to record the issue would be:

| | | |
|---|---|---|
| Cash | $1,460,000 | |
| Bond discount | 186,000 | |
| Bonds payable | | $1,500,000 |
| Paid-in capital | | 146,000 |

Notice that the effect of this method of financing on earnings is very similar to the effect of a convertible debt issue. (The computation of the return on assets and stockholders' equity is left as an exercise for the student.)

This illustration may give some small indication of the complexities of a decision regarding possible expansion. It is frequently advisable for management to separate the analysis of the expansion activity and the financing activity into two parts, but at times the two phases of the overall problem must be merged for proper consideration.

## METHODS OF EXPANSION

Expansion of an enterprise may follow several routes. For example, a company may expand by using existing facilities at a more rapid rate, thus increasing the turnover of resources. This method may require no additional financing. On the other hand, it may require an additional investment if additional assets are required for the increased rate of operations. Thus if a substantial increase in inventories is necessary to the increased volume, additional short-term borrowing may be necessary.

Expansion may involve the outright purchase or construction of additional facilities for additional volume, either of the existing product or of new products. Expansion may be accomplished by forming a separate branch to facilitate the expansion process, or by purchasing the assets of a going concern. Another expansion approach might find a company merging its assets with another company, either creating a new company or retaining one of the merging companies as the surviving company. Another expansion device involves the purchase of a substantial portion of the voting stock of another company, and through this transaction, the purchaser gains control of additional productive facilities. This latter area represents the area wherein consolidated statements, as accountants use the term, are commonly prepared. This area is discussed in detail in subsequent chapters.

## PROBLEMS

### Problem 7-1

The M. Co., manager of an office building, is considering putting in certain concessions in the main lobby. An accounting study produces the following estimates, on an average annual basis:

|  |  |  |
|---|---|---|
| Salaries | | $ 7,000 |
| Licenses and payroll taxes | | 200 |
| Cost of merchandise sold: | | |
|    Beginning inventory | $ 2,000 | |
|    Purchases | 40,000 | |
|    Available | $42,000 | |
|    Ending inventory | 2,000 | 40,000 |
| Share of heat, light, etc. | | 500 |
| Pro-rata building depreciation | | 1,000 |
| Concession advertising | | 100 |
| Share of company administrative expense | | 400 |
| Sales of merchandise | | 49,000 |

The investment in equipment, which would last 10 years, would be $2,000.

As an alternative, a catering company has offered to lease the space for $750 per year, for 10 years, and to put in and operate the same concessions at no cost to the M. Co. Heat and Light are to be furnished by the office building at no additional charges.

What is your advice to the M. Co.? Explain fully.     (AICPA adapted)

## Problem 7-2

The Walter Company management is considering various alternative plans for improving its profit picture. Below is a condensed income statement of the Company for 1980:

|  |  |  |
|---|---|---|
| Sales | | $2,000,000 |
| Cost of sales | | 1,400,000 |
| Gross profit | | 600,000 |
| Selling expenses | $180,000 | |
| Administrative expenses | 220,000 | 400,000 |
| Income from operations | | $ 200,000 |

During 1980 the entire productive facilities were not used, and it is estimated that a cost of $15,000 applicable to the unused facilities is included in the statement above. The following data are developed with respect to a possible plan for the coming year, involving substantially full utilization of the plant facilities:

|  |  | Plan 1 |
|---|---|---|
| Total sales expected | | $2,400,000 |
| Cost of sales | | 1,670,000 |
| Gross profit | | 730,000 |
| Selling expenses | $230,000 | |
| Administrative expenses | 240,000 | 470,000 |
| Income from operations | | $ 260,000 |

7 / *Investment for Expansion*   223

The Company anticipates that it can sell whatever volume is produced, within the foregoing range of production. In 1980 total fixed costs were $600,000.

It is determined that the book value of the idle facilities at December 31, 1980, was $135,000, that these facilities are worth $40,000 if sold, and that if they are utilized, they will have their useful life shortened by one-third over that anticipated during 1980 idleness. The costs stated above for the alternative plan do not include recognition of this accelerated depreciation through utilization of the idle facilities.

*Required:*

On the basis of these facts only, determine whether the Walter Company should move to "Plan 1" or should produce in 1981 on a basis comparable to that of 1980. Support your conclusion.

## Problem 7-3

Paul and Taylor, operating as a partnership, desire to expand their operations by securing additional capital from new sources. Ridley accepts an offer to become an equal partner with Paul and Taylor. Ridley will invest $50,000 in the partnership and will have a one-third interest in the profits and in the capital of the partnership. At the date of investment the capital balances of Paul and Taylor are $38,000 and $42,000, respectively. The partners are undecided as to how they should reflect the investment of Ridley in their accounts. Ridley insists that his capital credit be $50,000; Paul insists that the total capital shall not exceed the net assets on the books prior to the admission of Ridley plus Ridley's investment; Taylor insists that the present balance in his capital account equals one-third of the net assets of the partnership after Ridley's investment.

*Required:*

Prepare a journal entry, or entries, to reflect the desires of the three partners. Describe the result, as to whether the entry involves goodwill or bonus, and whether the goodwill or bonus applies to the old or new partners. If your recommendation were requested as to the most advisable entry, which would you recommend? Why?

## Problem 7-4

The board of directors of the Mortsaw Corporation has been considering an expansion of existing facilities to take advantage of favorable market conditions for its products. During 1980 the Company earned a net income after taxes of $200,000 on sales of $4,000,000. Depreciation on facilities used in 1980 totaled $150,000 and was the only noncash charge against 1980 income. For each of the first five years after completion of the expansion program, sales are expected to average $5,600,000 and produce a net income after taxes, but without regard to finance costs, of $305,000. The new facilities are expected to take one year to construct, will cost $1,125,000, and will have an estimated useful life of 25 years. Once the new facilities are operating, the Company expects to have to carry increased inventories of $300,000, build-up of which would occur during the latter part of the construction period and in the six months following completion of the facilities. At January 1, 1981, the only available cash not required for the existing level of operations is about equal to that generated by 1980 operations. Existing facilities, which are being depreciated on a 25-year life, will not begin to require replacement until January 1, 1984, at which date it is estimated replacement will total $100,000 per year for five years and $200,000 per year thereafter, on an average basis.

Three board members with divergent views on the expansion plans present you with their ideas:

Mr. M. does not want to begin expansion until such time as sufficient cash is on hand, or will be on hand by completion of the facilities, to pay for the costs of expansion. All three board members agree that about 80% of cash generated by operations in 1981 and subsequent years will be available for expansion.

Mr. S. wants to build immediately by obtaining an intermediate-term bank loan for $1,200,000, which is available at 5% interest, to be liquidated by funds obtained from operations.

Mr. W. wants to wait until January 1, 1983, to begin construction, borrowing at that date at 5% the amount necessary after utilizing cash estimated to be available from operations at that date. Liquidation of the loan would proceed as indicated by Mr. S.

*Required:*

You are to summarize the effects on the Company of each of these views, including time delay for construction, comparable costs, etc.

## Problem 7-5

The Savoy Company was contemplating expansion, and the management was determined to explore fully the possibilities of utilizing internally generated funds for the expansion costs. Company officials listed the following items in considering possible sources of expansion funds:

| | |
|---|---:|
| Average annual net income (after dividends) | $100,000 |
| Average annual depreciation charges | 80,000 |
| Accumulated depreciation | 450,000 |
| Retained earnings | 900,000 |
| Average annual mortgage reduction | 60,000 |
| Average annual interest charges | 20,000 |

*Required:*

Draft a brief report to explain to the Savoy management how each of the items above would affect their cash needs, and determine how much cash the Company might expect to have available on an annual basis to use for expansion.

## Problem 7-6

The directors of the Weygandt Corporation are considering the issuance of a stock dividend. They have asked you to discuss the proposed action by answering the questions below.

## 7 / Investment for Expansion

*Required:*
(1) What is a stock dividend? How is a stock dividend distinguished from a stock split-up
   (*a*) from a legal standpoint?
   (*b*) from an accounting standpoint?
(2) For what reasons does a corporation usually declare a stock dividend? A stock split-up?
(3) Discuss the amount, if any, of retained earnings to be capitalized in connection with a stock dividend. (AICPA adapted)

## Problem 7-7

Austin and Bradford are partners. They share profits equally and have equal investments. The partnership's net assets are carried on the books at $20,000. Crane is admitted to the partnership with a one-third interest in profits and net assets. Crane pays $9,000 cash into the partnership for his interest.

Prepare journal entries to show three possible methods of recording on the partnership books the admission of Crane. State the conditions under which each method would be appropriate.

## Problem 7-8

The Capital Budget Committee of the Walton Corporation was established to appraise and screen departmental requests for plant expansions and improvements at a time when these requests totaled $10 million. The Committee thereupon sought your professional advice and help in establishing minimum performance standards which it would demand of these projects in the way of anticipated rates of return before interest and taxes.

The Walton Corporation is a closely held family corporation in which the stockholders exert an active and unified influence on the management. At this date, the Corporation has no long-term debt and has 1,000,000 shares of common stock outstanding. It is currently earning $5 million (net income before interest and taxes) per year. The applicable tax rate is 50%.

Should the projects under consideration be approved, management is confident that the $10 million of required funds can be obtained either:

1. By borrowing—via the medium of an issue of $10 million, 4% 20-year bonds.
2. By equity financing—via the medium of an issue of 500,000 shares of common stock to the general public. It is anticipated that the onwership of these 500,000 shares would be widely dispersed and scattered.

The Company has been earning 12½% return after taxes. The management and the dominant stockholders consider this rate of earnings to be a fair capitalization rate (8 times earnings) as long as the Company remains free of long-term debt. An increase to 15%, or 6⅔ times earnings, would constitute an adequate adjustment to compensate for the risk of carrying $10 million of long-term debt. They believe that this reflects, and is consistent with, current market appraisals.

*Required:*
(1) Prepare columnar schedules comparing minimum returns, considering interest, taxes, and earnings ratio, which should be produced by each alternative to maintain the present capitalized value per share.
(2) What minimum rate of return on new investment is necessary for each alternative to maintain the present capitalized value per share?

(AICPA adapted)

## Problem 7-9

Ace Publishing Company is in the business of publishing and printing guide books and directories. The board of directors has engaged you to make a cost study to determine whether the Company is economically justified in continuing to print, as well as publish, its books and directories. You obtain the following information from the Company's cost accounting records for the preceding fiscal year:

|  | Departments |  |  |  |
| --- | --- | --- | --- | --- |
|  | Publishing | Printing | Shipping | Total |
| Salaries and wages | $275,000 | $150,000 | $25,000 | $450,000 |
| Telephone and telegraph | 12,000 | 3,700 | 300 | 16,000 |
| Materials and supplies | 50,000 | 250,000 | 10,000 | 310,000 |
| Occupancy costs | 75,000 | 80,000 | 10,000 | 165,000 |
| General and administrative | 40,000 | 30,000 | 4,000 | 74,000 |
| Depreciation | 5,000 | 40,000 | 5,000 | 50,000 |
|  | $457,000 | $553,700 | $54,300 | $1,065,000 |

*Additional data:*

(a) A review of personnel requirements indicates that, if printing is discontinued, the publishing department will need one additional clerk at $4,000 per year to handle correspondence with the printer. Two layout men and a proofreader will be required at an aggregate annual cost of $17,000; other personnel in the printing department can be released. One mailing clerk, at $3,000, will be retained; others in the shipping department can be released. Employees whose employment was being terminated would immediately receive, on the average, three months' termination pay. The termination pay would be amortized over a five-year period.
(b) Long-distance telephone and telegraph charges are identified and distributed to the responsible department. The remainder of the telephone bill, representing basic service at a cost of $4,000, was allocated in the ratio of 10 to publishing, 5 to print, and 1 to shipping. The discontinuance of printing is not expected to have a material effect on the basic service cost.
(c) Shipping supplies consist of cartons, envelopes, and stamps. It is estimated that the cost of envelopes and stamps for mailing material to an outside printer would be $5,000 per year.
(d) If printing is discontinued, the Company would retain its present building but would sublet a portion of the space at an annual rental of $50,000.

Taxes, insurance, heat, light, and other occupancy costs would not be significantly affected.
(e) One cost clerk would not be required ($5,000 per year) if printing is discontinued. Other general and administrative personnel would be retained.
(f) Included in administrative expenses is interest expense on a 5% mortgage loan of $500,000.
(g) Printing and shipping room machinery and equipment having a net book value of $300,000 can be sold without gain or loss. These funds in excess of termination pay would be invested in marketable securities earning 5%.
(h) The Company has received a proposal for a five-year contract from an outside printing concern, under which the volume of work done last year would be printed at a cost of $550,000 per year.
(i) Assume continued volume and prices at last year's level.

*Required:*
Prepare a statement setting forth in comparative form the costs of operation of the printing and shipping departments under the present arrangement and under an arrangement in which inside printing is discontinued. Summarize the net saving or extra cost in case printing is discontinued.  (AICPA adapted)

## Problem 7-10

A manufacturing company, in order to improve its relationship with its principal supplier of raw materials, decides to acquire some of its common stock. The following terms are finally agreed upon: The supply company is to be issued 5,000 shares of the manufacturing company's no-par common stock. This stock has a stated value of $25 per share and is currently selling in small lots at approximately $45 per share. In return for these 5,000 shares, the supply company will give the manufacturing company 2,000 of its $100 par value common stock now held in its treasury. The supply company's stock is currently quoted at about $90 per share. The supply company has 25,000 shares of common issued and it will all be outstanding after completion of the exchange.

Discuss fully the reasons for and against at least three bases of valuation which might be considered by the manufacturing company for recording the 2,000 shares of supply company stock it will receive. Exclude income tax considerations.

## Problem 7-11

A variety of alternative plans, each requiring additional capital investment, is under consideration by officials of the Sheehan Company. The details of four plans are presented below:

|  | Plan 1 | Plan 2 | Plan 3 | Plan 4 |
| --- | --- | --- | --- | --- |
| Capital investment required | $100,000 | $200,000 | $250,000 | $50,000 |
| Additional cost, not including interest | 2,000 | 4,000 | 5,000 | 1,000 |
| Additional income | 10,000 | 20,000 | 25,000 | 5,000 |

The Company has $100,000 available for investment. Any additional amounts are estimated to be available at 5% interest. Any amounts not utilized for expansion will be invested at an expected return of 4%.

The officials are interested in which plan appears to be the most appropriate, in terms of differential income, return on investment, risk, etc.

*Required:*

Prepare an analysis to provide the management with the basis for deciding among the alternative plans.

## Problem 7-12

The balance sheet below pertains to the Kolar and Green partnership at April 30, 1980:

| Cash | $ 50,000 | Liabilities | | $ 60,000 |
|---|---|---|---|---|
| Other assets | 170,000 | Kolar, capital | $100,000 | |
| Goodwill | 20,000 | Green, capital | 80,000 | 180,000 |
| | $240,000 | | | $240,000 |

Kolar and Green share profits and losses equally. To obtain additional working capital the partners have offered a share of the business to Burnside in return for his cash investment. The following alternative possibilities have been worked out by Burnside:

1. Burnside invests $56,000 for a one-fourth interest in the total capital of $240,000.
2. Burnside invests $56,000 for a one-third interest in a total capital of $236,000.
3. Burnside invests $56,000 for a one-fourth interest in the total capital of $260,000.
4. Burnside invests $56,000 for a one-fourth interest in the partnership, receiving a capital credit of $56,000.

*Required:*

Prepare journal entries to express each of the alternatives above on the books of the partnership.

## Problem 7-13

The Mosher Company has certain idle facilities which it is contemplating using for production under one alternative plan (Plan 1) being considered for the coming year. The facilities have a book value of $100,000. A recent offer to buy the facilities for $40,000 has been received by the Mosher Company. Another alternative plan (Plan 2) under consideration would not use these facilities. If the facilities are used in Plan 1, it is anticipated they will have no further use to the Company. Although the date of their replacement is uncertain at the present time, the Company officials anticipate that replacement of the facilities would require an outlay of $160,000. A recent appraisal of the value of all properties of the Mosher Company indicates a value of $60,000 for these facilities.

Company officials have determined that the differential cost of the two plans, excluding any consideration of the facilities discussed above, would be:

|  |  |
|---|---|
| Plan 1 | $700,000 |
| Plan 2 | 820,000 |

*Required:*
Based on the data above only, which plan would you recommend? Why?

## Problem 7-14

Leddy and Giller have operated as a partnership for a number of years. At June 30, 1980, their balance sheet appeared as below:

LEDDY & GILLER
BALANCE SHEET, JUNE 30, 1980

| Assets |  | Liabilities |  |
|---|---|---|---|
| Cash | $ 5,000 | Accounts payable | $ 34,000 |
| Receivables | 30,000 | Accrued liabilities | 6,000 |
| Inventories | 60,000 | Mortgage payable | 80,000 |
| Equipment (net) | 80,000 | Leddy, capital | 75,000 |
| Building (net) | 90,000 | Giller, capital | 70,000 |
|  | $265,000 |  | $265,000 |

Peters is interested in becoming a partner on equal terms with Leddy and Giller. The partners do not wish to have any goodwill exist on their books, and they have carefully studied their various asset values to determine the basis for Peters' investment. It is agreed that prior to admission of Peters the receivables should be reduced to $27,000, the equipment to $70,000, and the inventory should be written up to $66,000. Peters agrees to invest $75,000 for a one-third interest in the partnership. The partners agree that all capital accounts shall be equal after this investment.

*Required:*
Prepare journal entries necessary to reflect the data above. How much cash should Giller pay Leddy on a personal basis?

## Problem 7-15

The Keyser Corporation sells computer services to its clients. The Company completed a feasibility study and decided to obtain an additional computer on January 1, 1981. Information regarding the new computer follows:

(*a*) The purchase price of the computer is $230,000. Maintenance, property taxes, and insurance will be $20,000 per year. If the computer is rented, the annual rate will be $85,000 plus 5% of annual billings. The rental price includes maintenance.

(b) Owing to competitive conditions, the Company believes it will be necessary to replace the computer at the end of 3 years with one that is larger and more advanced. It is estimated that the computer will have a resale value of $110,000 at the end of 3 years. The computer will be depreciated on a straight-line basis for both financial reporting and income tax purposes.

(c) The income tax rate is 50%.

(d) The estimated annual billing for the services of the new computer will be $220,000 during the first year and $260,000 during each of the second and third years. The estimated annual expense of operating the computer is $80,000 in addition to the expense mentioned above. An additional $10,000 of start-up expenses will be incurred during the first year.

(e) If it decides to purchase the computer, the Company will pay cash. If the computer is rented, the $230,000 can be otherwise invested at a 15% rate of return.

(f) If the computer is purchased, the amount of investment recovered during each of the three years can be reinvested immediately at a 15% rate of return. Each year's recovery of investment in the computer will have been reinvested for an average of six months by the end of the year.

(g) The present value of $1.00 due at a constant rate during each year and discounted at 15% is:

| Year | Present Value |
|---|---|
| 0–1 | $.93 |
| 1–2 | .80 |
| 2–3 | .69 |

The present value of $1.00 due at the end of each year and discounted at 15% is:

| End of Year | Present Value |
|---|---|
| 1 | $.87 |
| 2 | .76 |
| 3 | .66 |

*Required:*

(1) Prepare a schedule comparing the estimated annual income from the new computer under the purchase plan and under the rental plan. The comparison should include a provision for the opportunity cost of the average investment in the computer during each year.

(2) Prepare a schedule showing the annual cash flows under the purchase plan and under the rental plan.

(3) Prepare a schedule comparing the present values of the cash flows under the purchase plan and under the rental plan.

(4) Comment on the results obtained in parts (1) and (3). How should the computer be financed? Why? (AICPA adapted)

# 8

# Expansion by Branch Operations

Previous chapters of this book have been directed primarily to the accounting problems involved in organizing and developing a company at one central location. It is commonplace in business, however, to find a company spread over a large geographic area with several plants and offices located at various points in the area. Such decentralization may be stimulated by several factors, such as a need to be near a source of supply for raw materials, or by a belief that the impact of depressions, wars, and other contingencies may be lessened by such decentralization. One compelling reason for decentralization is to be near the customers or markets that the company products are attempting to attract.

The development and growth of the marketing process has stimulated the development of large business organizations with a national market for their products. For a typical enterprise this expansion may have taken place somewhat as follows. First, salesmen are assigned a wider and wider area as the market for the company's products expands. This process of expansion has several limitations. As a result, the next step might be the establishment of various sales agencies from which salesmen might operate and through which local customers could be provided with a permanent contact point in dealing with the company. The typical sales agency may carry samples of company products and be financed by a working fund from the home office.

The next step in the expansion process might be the establishment of an almost autonomous branch. The functions and responsibilities of a branch vary considerably, but normally the branch carries for sale merchandise that may be sold for cash or on account. Responsibility for cash receipts and expenses of various kinds may be assigned to the branch. The functions of the head office may include centralized purchasing or production, shipments to the branch of goods purchased or produced, and general direction, as opposed to specific direction, of branch activities.

## Separate Ledgers

As a company spreads itself geographically, it is not uncommon for its accounting system to become decentralized also. One common method of decentralizing accounting activities is to separate from the general ledger those accounts that deal with the decentralized or separated activities. In a sense, this separate ledger is similar to a subsidiary ledger, since one impetus to establishment of subsidiary ledgers is a subdivision or decentralization of accounting activities. Both a separate ledger and a subsidiary ledger represent the withdrawal from the general ledger of selected accounts and the *substitution* for them of one account into which are summarized all the balances of the withdrawn accounts.

A distinction between these two accounting decentralizations may be drawn on the basis of the nature of the separated accounts. Where the separated accounts are similar in nature, such as accounts receivable or accounts payable, they normally are assumed to represent a subsidiary or detailed record of the control account in the general ledger. Where the accounts withdrawn from the general ledger are not similar in nature, that is, where some of the accounts may be assets, some liabilities, expenses, or incomes, the accounts are assumed to represent a separate ledger. Typical illustrations of separate ledgers are:

(1) Factory ledger.
(2) Private ledger.
(3) Branch office ledger.

**Factory Ledger.** The factory ledger is used most frequently in manufacturing enterprises in which the production plant is located physically some distance from the central office. Thus, the impetus to establish the factory ledger may have arisen from a decentralization of enterprise activities. The factory ledger comprises those accounts containing a detailed record of the factory operations. These accounts, and subsequent analyses of them, are necessary for efficient operation of the plant, but the accounts are of little or no concern to the central office on a day-to-day operating basis. On the books of the central office, the account "Factory Ledger" is used as a substitute for the various factory ledger accounts that would otherwise appear in the general ledger. This account is a summary account for all of the activities of the factory.

**Private Ledger.** Another example of a separate ledger is the so-called "private ledger." Although little used now, the private ledger is a means whereby confidential information, such as executive salaries, dividend payments, and bonuses might be removed from the general ledger and accounted for in greater privacy. A summary account, "Private Ledger," is substituted for the various accounts removed from the general ledger. The confidential information is then placed in the private ledger.

# BRANCH ACCOUNTING CONCEPTS AND PROCEDURES

According to sound principles of management, the division of responsibility within an enterprise should be clearly delineated along organizational lines. This principle applies equally well to accounting procedures. One might expect that the accounting procedures of a branch office should provide sufficiently detailed information to permit centralized management to hold branch management responsible for branch activities. Practically, this concept cannot always be applied fully to branch activities because of the difficulty of assigning responsibility to an organizational unit of this nature. In practice, branch accounting procedures may not be in full accord with the principle of organizational responsibility noted above, but to the extent possible they should be consistent with this principle.

Essentially, branch accounting endeavors to account for certain of the assets, revenues, expenditures, and liabilities of the company. It attempts to account for all such items for which the branch may be responsible. The concept of controllable expenditures seems to represent the substance of the underlying objective of branch accounting procedures.

In some branch organizations almost all assets and expenditures are held to be the responsibility of the branch manager. Thus, in this type of organization, branch accounting would include accounting for depreciation of branch equipment, and the accountable assets of the branch would include those assets used in the branch operations. More often, branch managers are held responsible for only a portion of the total branch expenditures with the home office assuming the responsibility for the uncontrollable (fixed) expenses. In this type of branch-home office organization depreciation on branch fixed assets, as well as other expenses not controllable by the branch manager, would not be accounted for by the branch, but would be included in the home office or central accounting system.

In summary, the transactions encompassed by branch accounting procedures depend in part upon the responsibility of the branch manager and in part upon the ability of the branch accounting system to provide information on those activities that are subject to the control of the branch manager.

## Establishing the Branch

When a business enterprise decides to establish a branch outlet, a decision must also be made regarding the accounting system that the branch outlet is to maintain. As noted above, the branch manager may be given relatively little responsibility, in which case he may be provided with a working fund of cash and be expected to establish records that will account for this fund of cash. On the other hand, the branch manager may be given relatively great responsibility, in which case he may establish a separate ledger to account for the transactions in which his branch engages.

**Working Fund.** If the home office is to maintain the detailed records pertaining to the operations of the branch, and if it provides the branch with a working fund of cash, the accounting problems of establishing the branch are relatively simple. Under this system the home office transactions with the branch will involve transmission of merchandise for resale to the branch and the remittance to the home office by the branch of the branch receipts. These transactions would not pass through the branch records. Likewise, major expenditures of the branch will be paid directly by the home office upon receipt of an invoice approved by the branch manager. All branch revenues are deposited intact in a bank by the branch to the credit of the home office. Thus, effective control of the cash rests with the home office. The working fund of cash is used by the branch to meet small branch expenditures. This manner of branch operations provides the home office with fairly complete control over expenditures and receipts of the branch, yet it permits the branch to incur such costs as it deems advisable.

In practice the foregoing procedure is more often used when a sales agency is in operation than it is with a separate branch operation. Accounting for home office-branch transactions under the procedure above would be similar to the procedure of establishing a working fund for a salesman. For example, if the home office were to send the branch $1,000 as a working fund, and if this sum were the only asset transferred to the branch (salesman or sales agency), appropriate accounting on the books of the home office would be:

| | | |
|---|---|---|
| Branch working fund | $1,000 | |
| Cash | | $1,000 |

If the branch or agency should decide to maintain a ledger, even though the limited nature of their accounting needs may indicate that such is not appropriate, the entry should be:

| | | |
|---|---|---|
| Cash | $1,000 | |
| Due to home office | | $1,000 |

As expenses are paid, the branch or agency would debit the expense accounts and credit cash appropriately. For example, if the agency purchases $50 of supplies, the entry should be:

| | | |
|---|---|---|
| Supplies | $50 | |
| Cash | | $50 |

The home or central office would make no record of this transaction until it is reported by the agency. At that time the entry on the books of the home office would be:

| | | |
|---|---|---|
| Supplies | $50 | |
| Branch working fund (or cash if working fund is replenished) | | $50 |

Revenues of the branch or agency need not be recorded by the branch. The central office could record such sales directly, as follows:

| | | |
|---|---|---|
| Cash (receipt acknowledged by bank) | $50 | |
| Sales (branch or agency) | | $500 |

**Separate Ledger.** If the branch is to maintain a separate ledger to account for its transactions, a few modifications in the normal accounting procedures arise because of the home office-branch relationship. Normally, both the branch and the home office will maintain some record of the assets of the branch. The home office typically uses one account, "Branch Office," into which are charged all asset resources for which the branch has accounting responsibility. This account also receives credits as the branch is relieved of accounting responsibility by making remittances to the home office. The "Branch Office" account represents a control account on the books of the home office. This account controls the branch ledger, a separate ledger generally maintained at the branch. The separate ledger provides a detailed record of the information summarized in the controlling account, "Branch Office."

The branch, in order to maintain double-entry accounting, sets up a "Home Office" account, the balance of which represents the home office equity (residual equity) in the branch. The "Home Office" account is credited with all assets contributed by or accruing to the home office, the offsetting debit going to a specific asset or expense account. The account is charged when the branch is relieved of an amount due to the home office, generally through a direct remittance to the home office.

**Establishing the Branch.** Assume that the Pier Corporation of Chicago desires to establish a branch in the city of Urbana, Illinois, by transferring to the branch certain of the activities formerly performed at the Chicago office. The home office wants the branch to be responsible for all assets used by the branch in performing its function. Assuming that the branch receives a building valued at $10,000, equipment valued at $22,000, and inventory with a $31,000 book value, the appropriate entries to record this information would be as follows:

On the Books of the Home Office

| | | |
|---|---|---|
| Branch Office | $63,000 | |
| Building | | $10,000 |
| Equipment | | 22,000 |
| Inventory | | 31,000 |

On the Books of the Branch Office

| | | |
|---|---|---|
| Building | $10,000 | |
| Equipment | 22,000 | |
| Inventory | 31,000 | |
| Home Office | | $63,000 |

It will be observed that from a combined, or consolidated, point of view the Home Office account and the Branch Office account are reciprocal. Both should be eliminated when the accounts of the branch are to be merged with those of the home office in the preparation of combined financial reports. Stated another way, the Branch Office account on the books of the home office is eliminated, and the details supporting this account, as reflected in the separate branch ledger, are substituted.

**Operations of the Branch.** Where the branch maintains a separate double-entry ledger, the recording procedure for home office-branch transactions requires entries on the books of both the home office and the branch. Branch transactions that do not directly involve the home office require entries only on the books of the branch. Continuing the illustration of the Pier Corporation, entries are presented below to record the more common branch operating transactions. For comparative purposes the entries on both sets of books are presented.

(*a*) *Transaction*. The home office ships $2,000 of merchandise to the branch.

ON HOME OFFICE BOOKS:

| | | |
|---|---|---|
| Branch Office | $2,000 | |
|     Merchandise | | $2,000 |

ON BRANCH BOOKS:

| | | |
|---|---|---|
| Merchandise | $2,000 | |
|     Home Office | | $2,000 |

(*b*) *Transaction*. The branch purchases $500 of merchandise and $100 of supplies for cash.

ON HOME OFFICE BOOKS:

No entry.

ON BRANCH BOOKS:

| | | |
|---|---|---|
| Merchandise | $500 | |
| Supplies | 100 | |
|     Cash | | $600 |

(*c*) *Transaction*. The branch sells merchandise on account, $1,500.

ON HOME OFFICE BOOKS:

No entry.

ON BRANCH BOOKS:

| | | |
|---|---|---|
| Accounts receivable | $1,500 | |
|     Sales | | $1,500 |

(*d*) *Transaction*. The branch pays salaries of $300, records depreciation of $100, and determines the cost of merchandise sold for the period to be $700.

ON HOME OFFICE BOOKS:

No entry.

ON BRANCH BOOKS:

| | | |
|---|---|---|
| Salaries | $300 | |
| Depreciation | 100 | |
| Cost of merchandise sold | 700 | |
|     Cash | | $300 |
|     Allowance for depreciation | | 100 |
|     Merchandise | | 700 |

(e) *Transaction*. The branch closes its books and reports profit or loss to the home office.

ON BRANCH BOOKS:

| | | |
|---|---|---|
| Sales | $1,500 | |
|     Income summary | | $1,500 |
| Income summary | $1,200 | |
|     Supplies | | $ 100 |
|     Salaries | | 300 |
|     Depreciation | | 100 |
|     Cost of merchandise sold | | 700 |
| Income summary | $300 | |
|     Home Office | | $300 |

ON HOME OFFICE BOOKS:

| | | |
|---|---|---|
| Branch office | $300 | |
|     Branch profit and loss | | $300 |

(f) *Transaction*. The branch sends the home office $200 cash.

ON HOME OFFICE BOOKS:

| | | |
|---|---|---|
| Cash | $200 | |
|     Branch office | | $200 |

ON BRANCH BOOKS:

| | | |
|---|---|---|
| Home office | $200 | |
|     Cash | | $200 |

A study of the transactions and entries above discloses that the entries on the books of the branch are very similar to those that any enterprise might have. Instead of a "capital" or similar owners' account, the residual equity of the branch is recorded in the "Home Office" account. Branch profit and loss is determined in the normal manner, and the resulting profit or loss is closed to the Home Office account. Distributions by the branch to the home office reduce the equity of the home office in the branch and are so recorded through a charge to Home Office.

The "Branch Office" account in the home office ledger may be considered as a type of investment account. The balance at any closing date indicates the amount due from the branch or the amount the home office has invested in the branch. At any date the "Branch Office" account and the "Home Office" account should contain *reciprocal* balances. The procedure to follow when these accounts do not contain reciprocal balances at a closing date is discussed in a subsequent section.

**Merchandise Billed Above Cost.** While the home office may charge the branch at cost for merchandise shipped to the branch, frequently the home office will buy merchandise for the branch and will bill such merchandise to the branch at a price other than cost. Under this procedure the branch manager will not know the cost of the merchandise he sells, and thus will not be aware of the profit the branch is earning. Although this is a dubious justification at best, a distinct advantage from this procedure may accrue to the home office if the branch is billed at selling price for merchandise shipped by the home office. Billing the branch at selling price provides the home office with continuous information on the inventory of the branch. Branch sales reported to the home office will be deducted from shipments to the branch, both being valued at selling price, and the resulting balance should be the branch inventory in terms of selling price. Periodic comparisons of the inventory so determined with a physical inventory taken at the branch provide a measure of control of branch inventories.

**Shipments to Branch.** The accounting procedure for recording shipments to the branch by the home office depends upon whether the home office maintains perpetual inventory records. Assume that the home office sends merchandise that cost $1,000 to a branch, but transfers it to the branch at a selling price of $1,500. The appropriate entry on the books of the home office to record the shipment would be:

If the home office maintains perpetual inventory records:

| | | |
|---|---|---|
| Branch office | $1,500 | |
|    Merchandise | | $1,000 |
|    Unrealized margin in | | |
|      branch inventory | | 500 |

Since the Merchandise account is carried at cost, any entries to it for shipments to the branch should be made at cost. The credit to "Unrealized Margin in Branch Inventory" represents the difference between the billed price and the cost price of the merchandise. As the merchandise is sold by the branch, the unrealized margin becomes "realized," and the account is adjusted to recognize the realized margin when the branch reports its sales to the home office.

If the home office does not maintain perpetual inventory records:

| | | |
|---|---|---|
| Branch office | $1,500 | |
|    Shipments to branch | | $1,500 |

The "Shipments to Branch" account is used to record at selling price all shipments of merchandise to the branch. The disposition of this account will be discussed in the following section.

Regardless of the recording on the books of the home office, the entry on the branch books would be:

| | | |
|---|---|---|
| Merchandise from home office | $1,500 | |
| Home office | | $1,500 |

**Branch Sales.** Branch accounting for sales of merchandise billed from the home office at a price above cost is identical with the recording procedure for sales of any other type of merchandise. For example, if the branch sold for cash 40% of the $1,500 merchandise received from the home office (cost $1,000), the entry appropriate for the branch books would be:

| | | |
|---|---|---|
| Cash | $600 | |
| Sales | | $600 |

The home office would not be advised of this sale until it was reported by the branch, normally at the close of an accounting period. When the home office receives the report of the branch sale, an entry must be made to record the profit realized by the branch through the sale. If the home office follows a *perpetual inventory system,* the entry will recognize that portion of the previously entered "Unrealized Margin in Branch Inventory" which is no longer unrealized. Thus if 40% of the merchandise shipped to the branch in the example above is sold, the entry on the home office books to record the profit realized through the sale would be:

| | | |
|---|---|---|
| Unrealized margin in branch inventory | $200 | |
| Branch profit and loss | | $200 |

If the home office inventories are adjusted only *periodically,* an entry must be made to record the realized profit and also to record the unrealized profit applicable to the merchandise still unsold at the branch. A suitable procedure to record these facts on the home office books would be:

| | | |
|---|---|---|
| Shipments to branch | $1,500 | |
| Purchases | | $1,000 |
| Branch profit and loss | | 200 |
| Unrealized margin in branch inventory | | 300 |

The "Unrealized Margin in Branch Inventory" account is a valuation account that is deducted from the merchandise inventory on a combined balance sheet of the branch and the home office in order to reduce the inventory to cost.

Determination of the income or loss of the branch requires that the income or loss reported by the branch be added to the realized margin recorded by the home office in the "Branch Profit and Loss" account.

**Illustration—Branch Accounting.** The Brown Company establishes a branch in the town of Deerville on February 2, 1979. On this date the home office transfers to the branch the following assets:

| | |
|---|---|
| Cash | $ 5,000 |
| Equipment | 12,000 |

On February 15 the home office sends $8,000 of merchandise to the branch, but bills it to the branch at $12,000. (The home office does not maintain perpetual inventory records.)

On February 28 the branch pays for the following items:

| | |
|---|---|
| Merchandise | $500 |
| Supplies | 200 |
| Salaries | 800 |

During March the branch activities are:

| | |
|---|---|
| Sales—on account | $5,000 |
| Sales—cash | 4,500 |
| Salaries | 1,000 |
| Cash transferred to home office | 3,000 |

On March 31 branch inventories are:

| | |
|---|---|
| Merchandise from home office | $3,000 |
| Merchandise purchased | 200 |
| Supplies | 100 |

Depreciation on branch equipment for the two-month period is $200.

On March 31 the branch reports its operation to the home office and closes its books. The home office also closes its books on March 31. The facts above would be recorded on the books of the branch and home office in the following manner:

| BRANCH BOOKS | | | HOME OFFICE BOOKS | | |
|---|---|---|---|---|---|
| | | *Feb. 2, 1979* | | | |
| Cash | $ 5,000 | | Branch office | $17,000 | |
| Equipment | 12,000 | | Cash | | $ 5,000 |
|   Home office | | $17,000 | Equipment | | 12,000 |
| | | *Feb. 15, 1979* | | | |
| Merchandise from | | | Branch office | $12,000 | |
|   home office | $12,000 | | Shipments to | | |
|   Home office | | $12,000 |   branch | | $12,000 |
| | | *Feb. 28, 1979* | | | |
| Merchandise | $500 | | No entry. | | |
| Supplies | 200 | | | | |
| Salaries | 800 | | | | |
|   Cash | | $1,500 | | | |

## 8 / Expansion by Branch Operations

| BRANCH BOOKS (Cont'd) | | | HOME OFFICE BOOKS (Cont'd) | | |
|---|---|---|---|---|---|
| | | *March, 1979* | | | |
| Accounts receivable | $5,000 | | No entry. | | |
| Cash | 4,500 | | | | |
|   Sales | | $9,500 | | | |
| | | *March, 1979* | | | |
| Home office | $3,000 | | Cash | $3,000 | |
| Salaries | 1,000 | |   Branch office | | $3,000 |
|   Cash | | $4,000 | | | |
| | | *March 31, 1979* | | | |
| Cost of goods sold | $9,300 | | No entry. | | |
|   Merchandise from home office | | $9,000 | | | |
|   Merchandise | | 300 | | | |
| | | *March 31, 1979* | | | |
| Supplies expense | $100 | | No entry. | | |
|   Supplies | | $100 | | | |
| Depreciation expense | $200 | | No entry. | | |
|   Allowance for depreciation | | $200 | | | |
| Sales | $9,500 | | No entry. | | |
|   Income summary | | $9,500 | | | |
| Income summary | $11,400 | | No entry. | | |
|   Salaries | | $1,800 | | | |
|   Cost of goods sold | | 9,300 | | | |
|   Supplies expense | | 100 | | | |
|   Depreciation expense | | 200 | | | |
| Home office | $1,900 | | Branch profit and loss | $1,900 | |
|   Income summary | | $1,900 | |   Branch office | | $1,900 |
| No entry. | | | Shipments to branch | $12,000 | |
| | | |   Branch profit and loss | | $3,000 |
| | | |   Unrealized margin in branch inventory | | 1,000 |
| | | |   Purchases | | 8,000 |
| No entry. | | | Branch profit and loss | $1,100 | |
| | | |   Income summary | | $1,100 |

From the March 31 entries above, it can be seen that as far as the branch manager is concerned, the branch suffered an operating loss of $1,900 during the period. However, $1,900 is not the actual loss, since the merchandise shipped to the branch by the home office was billed at an amount in excess of cost. The difference between cost price and billed price could be analyzed as follows:

$8,000 merchandise cost billed to branch at $12,000 = $4,000 markup
$3,000 of merchandise billed remains in inventory at
  end of period. $3,000 ÷ $12,000 (total shipped) = ¼
Thus ¼ of markup is unrealized at period end = $1,000
  ¾ of markup is realized at period end = $3,000

Since the $3,000 portion of the markup has been earned by the branch through its sales, the actual branch profit is $1,100 ($3,000 less $1,900 loss). This is the amount closed to the Income Summary account in the final entry on the home office books above.

**Interbranch Transfers.** Occasionally the home office may order one branch to transfer merchandise received from a different branch, or from the home office, to another branch. While generally accepted accounting procedure includes as a cost of merchandise the freight charges of acquiring merchandise held for resale, this procedure is subject to modification when the freight charges are excessive owing to an indirect method of shipping. In such cases the excessive freight would be charged off as a loss.

To illustrate, assume that the home office sent to Branch A $1,000 worth of merchandise on which the home office paid freight charges of $120. Later the home office directed Branch A to send the merchandise to Branch B. To accomplish this shipment, A was required to pay $100 of freight charges. Had the merchandise been shipped directly to Branch B from the home office, the freight charges would have been $150. The foregoing activities would be recorded on the three sets of books as follows:

BRANCH A BOOKS

| | | |
|---|---|---|
| Merchandise from home office | $1,000 | |
| Merchandise from home office | 120 | |
|   Home office | | $1,120 |
|   (to record receipt of merchandise from home office and to include freight charges as a part of merchandise cost) | | |
| Home office | $1,220 | |
|   Merchandise from home office | | $1,120 |
|   Cash | | 100 |
|   (to record transfer of merchandise to Branch B and to charge home office for merchandise and cash given up to make transfer) | | |

BRANCH B BOOKS

| | | |
|---|---|---|
| Merchandise from home office | $1,000 | |
| Merchandise from home office | 150 | |
|   Home office | | $1,150 |

(to record receipt of merchandise from Branch A as directed by home office and to include as cost appropriate freight charges)

HOME OFFICE BOOKS

| | | |
|---|---:|---:|
| Branch "A" | $1,120 | |
|     Shipments to branches | | $1,000 |
|     Cash | | 120 |
| (to record shipment of merchandise to Branch A and to charge the branch for freight charges) | | |
| | | |
| Branch "B" | $1,150 | |
| Interbranch transfer loss | 70 | |
|     Branch "A" | | $1,220 |

(to record transfer of merchandise to Branch B by charging B for the merchandise cost plus freight of $150. To give Branch A credit for the merchandise transfer and freight charges from home office to A of $120 and from A to B of $100. Total freight charges were $220, but only $150 is inventoriable, and $70 loss must be recognized by the home office)

## Combined Financial Statements

When the branch and the home office maintain separate ledgers, the preparation of financial statements for the combined operations requires a combination of the trial balances or the respective statements, as the case may be, of the separate entities. The process of combining financial statements is a rather simple one in most instances. The purpose of the combined report is to show the assets, equities, income, and expenses as if they pertained to a single entity. Thus, it would seem logical to combine like asset, equity, income, and expense accounts to get a combined statement. In addition to combining like accounts, the combination process must deal with the Home Office account on the books of the branch and the Branch Office account on the books of the home office. Normally, these accounts are reciprocal to each other, i.e., they contain balances of like dollar amounts, but one has a credit balance and the other a debit balance. When the accounts are in reciprocal balance, one may be eliminated against the other without upsetting the combined trial balance or financial statements. At times, however, these accounts will not be reciprocal, generally because various in-transit items have not been recorded properly on each set of books. If the Branch Office and the Home Office are not in reciprocal balance, it is necessary to adjust one or both accounts for the items in transit so that the reciprocal relationship will be achieved.

The illustration on page 244 indicates the combining procedure.

## TRIAL BALANCE
### DECEMBER 31, 1980

|  | Branch Dr. | Branch Cr. | Home Office Dr. | Home Office Cr. | Adjustments and Eliminations Dr. | Adjustments and Eliminations Cr. | Combined Trial Balance Dr. | Combined Trial Balance Cr. |
|---|---|---|---|---|---|---|---|---|
| Cash | $ 3,000 | | $ 12,000 | | $ 2,000(1) | | $ 17,000 | |
| Receivables | 4,000 | | 17,000 | | | | 21,000 | |
| Inventory | 5,000 | | 15,000 | | | | 20,000 | |
| Fixed assets | 10,000 | | 95,000 | | | | 105,000 | |
| Allowance for depreciation | | $ 2,000 | | $ 20,000 | | | | $ 22,000 |
| Accounts payable | | 1,000 | | 8,000 | | | | 9,000 |
| Branch office | | | 24,000 | | | $22,000(2) | | |
| | | | | | | 2,000(1) | | |
| Home office | | 22,000 | | | 22,000(2) | | | |
| Sales | | 18,000 | | 105,000 | | | | 123,000 |
| Unrealized margin in branch inventory | | | | 10,000 | 7,500(3) | | | 2,500 |
| Cost of goods sold | 15,000 | | 50,000 | | | | 65,000 | |
| Expenses | 6,000 | | 25,000 | | | | 31,000 | |
| Capital stock | | | | 50,000 | | | | 50,000 |
| Retained earnings | | | | 45,000 | | | | 45,000 |
| Branch profit and loss | | | | | | 7,500(3) | | 7,500 |
| Totals | $43,000 | $43,000 | $238,000 | $238,000 | $31,500 | $31,500 | $259,000 | $259,000 |

(1): The $2,000 adjustment was necessary because the branch had recorded a transfer of $2,000 cash to the home office. The home office had not recorded this in-transit cash.
(2): This entry eliminates the reciprocal accounts.
(3): This entry adjusts the Unrealized Margin in Branch Inventory account. The home office had shipped merchandise costing $10,000 to the branch at a price 100% above cost ($5,000 of the $20,000 billed price remains in the branch inventory).

As may be noted in the footnotes to the work sheet, three entries were required in the combining process. Entry (1) was required to establish reciprocity between the $22,000 balance in the Home Office account in the branch trial balance and the $24,000 balance in the Branch Office account in the home office trial balance. As indicated in Footnote (1), the $2,000 adjustment is necessary because the branch had recorded a transfer of $2,000 cash to the home office but the home office had not recorded this in-transit item. In journal form the entry is:

| | | |
|---|---|---|
| Cash | $2,000 | |
|     Branch office | | $2,000 |

Entry (2) eliminates the reciprocal balances that now exist in the Branch Office account and the Home Office account. Once reciprocity has been established, elimination is accomplished merely by debiting the account with the credit balance (the Home Office account) and crediting the account with the debit balance (the Branch Office account) as follows:

| | | |
|---|---|---|
| Home office | $22,000 | |
|     Branch office | | $22,000 |

Entry (3) adjusts the Unrealized Margin in Branch Inventory account. As indicated in Footnote (3), the home office had shipped merchandise costing $10,000 to the branch at a price 100% above cost, or $20,000. With one-fourth of the merchandise still in the branch inventory on the combination date, one-fourth ($2,500) of the intra-company profit has not yet been realized, whereas three-fourths ($7,500) has been realized. Since the entire $10,000 intra-company profit was provided for at the date of the shipment, the Unrealized Margin in Branch Inventory account must be reduced to $2,500. The realized portion ($7,500) of the intra-company profit is transferred to the Branch Profit and Loss account. In journal form the entry is:

| | | |
|---|---|---|
| Unrealized margin in branch inventory | $7,500 | |
|     Branch profit and loss | | $7,500 |

## Foreign Branches

It is not uncommon for a company to establish a branch in a foreign country. The procedures in accounting for such a branch are similar to those for a domestic branch, except that in the preparation of combined statements and the recording of the branch income it is necessary to translate the foreign currency into dollars. This translation process becomes somewhat involved when the foreign exchange rate is constantly fluctuating. Under a constant exchange rate the process is quite simple.

Possibly the ideal approach would be to translate foreign currency valuations at the rate that will apply when the assets are to be transferred back to the home office. Since this rate is obviously unknown at any date prior to transfer, accountants must use existing rates or rates that have existed in the past. For example, to translate the fixed assets and accumulated depreciation, accountants normally use the rate existing at the time such items were acquired or incurred by the branch. Use of this rate is in accord with the cost principle which holds that assets should be valued at their acquisition value and not at their realizable value. Short-term assets and liabilities, which are readily transferable to or from the home office, should be translated at the current rate of exchange. Use of this rate is based on the belief that items shortly to be realized in cash and transferable should be valued at an approximation of cash equivalent at the reporting date. Operational activities, such as sales and expenses, which occur throughout the operational period are translated at the average exchange rate for the period on the grounds that they were transferable at different rates during the period and the average rate is most appropriate.

Since various exchange rates may be used to translate a trial balance in a foreign currency into dollars, it would be unlikely that the trial balance in dollars would have equal debits and credits following translation. The amount necessary to make the trial balance in dollars balance is considered to be a gain or loss from exchange. This gain or loss may be closed out each period, or it may be carried forward in the financial statements to be offset in future periods. Foreign operations are covered in detail in Chapter Eighteen.

## PROBLEMS

### Problem 8-1

The Pacific Import Company, which operates a branch in a nearby city, has had a change in its accounting department. The new chief accountant found the trial balance as of December 31, 1979, which is presented below, as well as the other information which follows:

| Debits | Home Office | Branch |
|---|---|---|
| Cash | $ 15,000 | $ 2,000 |
| Accounts receivable | 20,000 | 17,000 |
| Inventory, December 31, 1979 | 30,000 | 8,000 |
| Fixed assets, net | 150,000 | |
| Branch office | 44,000 | |
| Cost of sales | 220,000 | 93,000 |
| Expenses | 70,000 | 41,000 |
| | $549,000 | $161,000 |

| Credits | | |
|---|---|---|
| Accounts payable | $ 23,000 | |
| Mortgage payable | 50,000 | |
| Capital stock | 100,000 | |
| Retained earnings, January 1, 1979 | 26,000 | |

|  |  |  |
|---|---:|---:|
| Sales | 350,000 | $150,000 |
| Accrued expenses |  | 2,000 |
| Home office |  | 9,000 |
|  | $549,000 | $161,000 |

## Additional information:

1. The branch receives all of its merchandise from the home office. The home office bills goods to the branch at 125% of cost. During 1979 the branch was billed for $105,000 on shipments from the home office.
2. The home office credits sales for the invoice price of goods shipped to the branch.
3. On January 1, 1979, the inventory of the home office was $25,000. The branch books showed a $6,000 inventory.
4. The home office billed the branch for $12,000 on December 31, 1979, representing the branch's share of expenses paid at the home office. The branch has not recorded this billing.
5. All cash collections made by the branch are deposited in a local bank to the account of the home office. Deposits of this nature included the following:

| Amount | Date Deposited by Branch | Date Recorded by Home Office |
|---|---|---|
| $5,000 | December 28, 1979 | December 31, 1979 |
| 3,000 | December 30, 1979 | January 2, 1980 |
| 7,000 | December 31, 1979 | January 3, 1980 |
| 2,000 | January 2, 1980 | January 5, 1980 |

6. Expenses incurred locally by the branch are paid from an imprest bank account which is reimbursed periodically by the home office. Just prior to the end of the year the home office forwarded a reimbursement check in the amount of $3,000 which was not received by the branch office until January 1980.
7. It is not necessary to make provisions for federal income taxes.

## Required:

(1) Prepare a columnar work sheet for Pacific Import Company and its branch with columns for "Trial balance," "Adjustments and eliminations," "Branch income statement," "Home office income statement," and "Balance sheet." Complete the work sheet and explain all adjustments and eliminations. The Company wishes to follow generally accepted accounting principles.

(2) Prepare a reconciliation of branch office and home office accounts, showing the corrected book balances.

(AICPA adapted)

## Problem 8-2

The Swain Company of Madison established a branch store in Neenah on February 1, 1980. The branch was to receive substantially all merchandise for resale from the home office, maintain its own cash account, make sales and collections, and periodically remit cash to the home office. During the remainder of 1980 the home office sent the branch $4,000 in cash and $60,000 in merchandise at cost. The branch made cash sales of $26,000; sales on account of $44,000, of which ¾ was collected with a 2% discount allowed, and ½ the remainder was uncollected at December 31, 1980. Unsold merchandise was costed at $8,000 at year-end. The branch purchased $3,200 additional merchandise for cash, had expenses of $8,200, all of which was paid except $400, and sent the home office sums totaling $52,000.

*Required:*
(1) Prepare summary entries for the facts above on the books of both the branch and the home office.
(2) Prepare branch closing entries at December 31, 1980.
(3) Prepare a branch profit and loss statement for the period ended December 31, 1980.


## Problem 8-3

The Kibler Corporation decided to set up a branch operation in Central City. Shipments of merchandise to the branch totaled $72,000, which included a 20% markup on cost. The Corporation regularly uses a periodical method of inventory determination.

The branch operations for the period are summarized below:

| | |
|---|---|
| Sales on account | $62,000 |
| Sales for cash | 10,000 |
| Collections on account (at 99%) | 59,400 |
| Expenses paid | 9,000 |
| Purchases of merchandise for cash | 4,000 |
| Expenses unpaid | 800 |
| Inventory on hand, year-end; 90% from home office | 8,000 |
| Remittances to home office | 54,000 |

*Required:*
(1) Prepare entries for the data above on the books of both the branch and the home office.
(2) Prepare closing entries for the branch at year-end.
(3) Prepare entries to take up branch profit and loss on home office books and to reflect the correct profit for the period.

## Problem 8-4

The Nussbaum Company has a branch in Aurora. Prior to the current year, operations at the branch were not voluminous and the home office and current accounts had never been reconciled. At year-end the accounts appear as follows:

### HOME OFFICE

| | | | | | |
|---|---|---|---|---|---|
| 4–1 | Expenses paid by branch, allocated to home office | $ 4,200 | 1–1 | Balance | $ 5,900 |
| | | | 1–10 | Merchandise received | 12,600 |
| 11–1 | Equipment repairs— to home office | 300 | 4–15 | Merchandise received | 18,400 |
| 12–1 | Cash remitted to home office | 36,600 | 8–20 | Merchandise received | 20,600 |
| | | | 12–31 | Profit for year | 2,600 |

### BRANCH OFFICE

| | | | | | |
|---|---|---|---|---|---|
| 1–1 | Balance | $ 8,400 | 1–3 | Remittance received | $ 2,500 |
| 1–8 | Merchandise shipped | 12,600 | 12–4 | Cash received from branch | 36,600 |
| 4–10 | Merchandise shipped | 18,400 | | | |
| 8–10 | Merchandise shipped | 20,600 | | | |
| 10–1 | Equipment shipped to branch | 6,300 | | | |
| 12–26 | Cash to branch for expenses | 5,200 | | | |

*Required:*
(1) Prepare a statement reconciling the Branch Office and Home Office accounts as of the end of the year.
(2) Prepare any adjusting entries necessary on the books of the branch and of the home office.

## Problem 8-5

The Irish Sales Company has had a branch in a nearby city for several years. At the end of each year the branch submits to the home office a copy of its trial balance to be used in preparation of combined financial statements. The trial balances of the home office and branch are presented below.

The home office regularly bills shipments to the branch at 125% of cost.

*Required:*
(1) Prepare closing entries for the branch, adjusting entries for the home office pertaining to the branch, and home office closing entries.
(2) Prepare a work sheet to produce a combined balance sheet.

IRISH SALES COMPANY
TRIAL BALANCE DECEMBER 31, 1980

|  | Home Office |  | Branch |  |
|---|---|---|---|---|
| Cash | $ 6,000 |  | $ 1,500 |  |
| Accounts receivable | 14,000 |  | 6,000 |  |
| Branch office | 18,600 |  |  |  |
| Inventory, December 31, 1979 | 15,000 |  | 5,000 |  |
| Unrealized margin in branch inv. |  | $ 1,000 |  |  |
| Equipment (net) | 26,000 |  | 8,000 |  |
| Accounts payable |  | 12,000 |  | $ 900 |
| Capital stock |  | 50,000 |  |  |
| Retained earnings |  | 10,000 |  |  |
| Sales |  | 236,600 |  | 82,000 |
| Purchases | 260,000 |  |  |  |
| Expenses | 45,000 |  | 6,000 |  |
| Shipments to branch |  | 75,000 |  |  |
| Home office |  |  |  | 18,600 |
| Merchandise from home office |  |  | 75,000 |  |
|  | $384,600 | $384,600 | $101,500 | $101,500 |
| Inventory, December 31, 1980 | $ 17,000 |  | $ 6,000 |  |

## Problem 8-6

The Covington Sports Store operates a branch in Appleton. The trial balances for the branch and the home office at December 31, 1980, are presented below.

COVINGTON SPORTS STORE
HOME OFFICE TRIAL BALANCE

| Cash | $ 2,000 |  |
|---|---|---|
| Accounts receivable | 6,000 |  |
| Inventory 1/1/80 | 22,000 |  |
| Fixtures (net) | 10,000 |  |
| Branch office | 16,000 |  |
| Accounts payable |  | $ 4,000 |
| Covington, capital |  | 40,000 |
| Sales |  | 180,000 |
| Shipments to branch |  | 42,000 |
| Purchases | 172,000 |  |
| Selling expenses | 18,000 |  |
| Administrative expenses | 20,000 |  |
|  | $266,000 | $266,000 |

## Covington Sports Store
### Branch Trial Balance

| | | |
|---|---:|---:|
| Cash | $ 2,500 | |
| Inventory, 1/1/80 | 6,480 | |
| Fixtures (net) | 7,800 | |
| Accounts payable | | $ 1,000 |
| Home office | | 16,000 |
| Purchases | 3,000 | |
| Shipments from home office | 42,000 | |
| Sales | | 50,000 |
| Selling expenses | 4,000 | |
| Administrative expenses | 1,220 | |
| | $ 67,000 | $ 67,000 |

All merchandise shipped to the branch by the home office was priced out at cost plus 20%. The home office reduced its inventory account directly at December 31, 1979, for any unrealized profit in the branch inventory at that date.

All the branch inventory at January 1, 1980, had been acquired from the home office, but at December 31, 1980, the inventory of $7,500 was 20% acquired from outsiders and 80% acquired from the home office. The home office inventory at December 31, 1980 was $20,000.

*Required:*
(1) Prepare entries to adjust and close the books of the branch and of the home office.
(2) Prepare a work sheet to produce a combined balance sheet.

## Problem 8-7

The following trial balances were taken from the records of the Bowers Company and its branch at Springfield on December 31, 1980:

| | Home Office Dr. | Home Office Cr. | Branch Dr. | Branch Cr. |
|---|---:|---:|---:|---:|
| Cash | $ 4,200 | | $ 1,500 | |
| Receivables | 16,000 | | 4,000 | |
| Inventory 1/1/80 | 25,000 | | 7,500 | |
| Branch office | 21,000 | | | |
| Equipment (net) | 60,000 | | 6,500 | |
| Accounts payable | | $ 13,000 | | |
| Unreal. profit in branch inv. | | 1,500 | | |
| Home office | | | | $18,500 |
| Capital stock | | 70,000 | | |
| Retained earnings | | 28,700 | | |
| Sales | | 180,000 | | 63,000 |

|  | Home Office | | Branch | |
|---|---|---|---|---|
|  | Dr. | Cr. | Dr. | Cr. |
| Merchandise from home office |  |  | 46,000 |  |
| Purchases | 190,000 |  | 5,000 |  |
| Merchandise to branch |  | 48,000 |  |  |
| Advertising | 10,000 |  | 6,000 |  |
| Utilities | 7,000 |  | 1,800 |  |
| Other expenses | 6,000 |  | 2,000 |  |
| Discounts (net) | 2,000 |  | 1,200 |  |
|  | $341,200 | $341,200 | $81,500 | $81,500 |

*Other pertinent facts available:*

1. Cash remitted by the branch at December 31, 1980, not received by the home office, was $4,500.
2. Approximately ¼ of the branch accounts receivable are uncollectible.
3. Merchandise shipped by the home office at 12/29/80, not received by the branch at 12/31/80, $2,000.
4. Branch advertising bill paid by the home office and charged to "Advertising" was $4,000. The branch bookkeeper recorded this properly upon receipt of interoffice memo.
5. Home office inventory at December 31, 1980, $27,500.
6. Branch inventory on hand at December 31, 1980, was $6,000, of which $4,000 was received from the home office.
7. The branch had failed to record $500 depreciation at year-end.
8. For the past several years all merchandise shipped from the home office had been marked on a standard "cost-plus" basis. At 1/1/80, 80% of the branch inventory consisted of home office shipments.

*Required:*
(1) Prepare a work sheet to reflect the adjustments necessary at year-end for the preparation of a combined profit-and-loss statement and a combined balance sheet.
(2) Prepare the combined statements for the year.

## Problem 8-8

The trial balance of the Mexican Branch of the Swingin Machine Company as of December 31, 1980, is presented below:

MEXICAN BRANCH — SWINGIN MACHINE COMPANY
TRIAL BALANCE, DECEMBER 31, 1980

|  | Pesos | |
|---|---|---|
| Cash | 40,800 |  |
| Receivables | 6,200 |  |
| Allowance for bad debts |  | 400 |
| Inventory 1/1/80 | 8,000 |  |
| Equipment | 12,000 |  |

|  |  |  |
|---|---|---|
| Allowance for depr. of equipment |  | 2,400 |
| Accounts payable |  | 800 |
| Home office |  | 60,600 |
| Mdse. from home office | 36,000 |  |
| Sales |  | 52,000 |
| Purchases | 2,000 |  |
| Selling expenses | 4,000 |  |
| Depreciation on equipment | 1,200 |  |
| Administrative expenses | 6,000 |  |
|  | 116,200 | 116,200 |

*Additional data:*

A. Exchange rates of dollars per peso at various dates were:

| December 31, 1980 | $ .05 |
|---|---|
| December 31, 1979 | .07 |
| Average rate for 1980 | .055 |
| January 2, 1978 (date equipment acquired) | .08 |

B. Balances per home office books, December 31, 1980:

| Branch office | $ 3,000 |
|---|---|
| Shipments to branch | 1,980 |

*Required:*

Translate the 12/31/80 trial balance of the Mexican Branch into dollars.

## Problem 8-9

The Beach Company has a branch in England, and at December 31, 1980, the branch submitted the following trial balance in pounds sterling to the home office:

THE BEACH CO.—LONDON BRANCH
TRIAL BALANCE, DECEMBER 31, 1980

|  | Dr. | Cr. |
|---|---|---|
| Cash | £ 2,000 |  |
| Receivables | 6,000 |  |
| Inventory, 1/1/80 | 10,000 |  |
| Equipment | 40,000 |  |
| Prepaid insurance | 600 |  |
| Accounts payable |  | £ 3,000 |
| Allowance for depr. of equipment |  | 10,000 |
| Home office |  | 60,200 |
| Sales |  | 180,000 |
| Purchases | 130,000 |  |
| Insurance expense | 600 |  |
| Depreciation expense | 2,000 |  |

|  | Dr. | Cr. |
|---|---|---|
| Selling expense | 20,000 | |
| Other expense | 12,000 | |
| Remittances to home office | 30,000 | |
|  | £253,200 | £253,200 |
| Inventory, 12/31/80 | £ 12,000 | |

The exchange rates at various dates were determined to be:

| December 31, 1980 | $1.40 per £1 |
|---|---|
| December 31, 1979 | 1.85 per £1 |
| Date equipment was acquired | 2.20 per £1 |
| Average rate for 1980 | 1.45 per £1 |

Reciprocal account balances on the home office books at 12/31/80 are found to be:

| Branch office | $83,800 |
|---|---|
| Remittances from branch | 40,000 |

*Required:*

Translate the trial balance above into dollars and prepare financial statements in dollars for the London Branch at December 31, 1980.

## Problem 8-10

On January 2, 1980, the Bakle Company established a branch in Catlin. All merchandise to be sold through the Catlin branch was to be sent from the home office and was to be billed to the branch at cost plus 20%. At December 31, 1980, the branch submitted the following trial balance:

| Cash | $ 800 | |
|---|---|---|
| Receivables | 4,200 | |
| Fixtures (net) | 3,000 | |
| Accounts payable | | $ 600 |
| Home office | | 9,400 |
| Sales | | 100,000 |
| Shipments to branch | 90,000 | |
| Expenses | 12,000 | |
|  | $110,000 | $110,000 |

At the same date the home office bookkeeper drew off the following trial balance from his ledger:

| Cash | $ 18,000 |
|---|---|
| Receivables | 30,000 |
| Inventory | 38,000 |
| Prepaid expenses | 2,000 |
| Machinery (net) | 92,000 |
| Fixtures (net) | 16,000 |
| Branch office | 14,400 |

8 / *Expansion by Branch Operations*     **255**

|  |  |  |
|---|---:|---:|
| Payables |  | $ 4,800 |
| Capital stock |  | 120,000 |
| Retained earnings |  | 45,200 |
| Sales |  | 475,000 |
| Purchases | 420,000 |  |
| Shipments to branch |  | 93,000 |
| Expenses | 107,600 |  |
|  | $738,000 | $738,000 |

The home office bookkeeper, recognizing that certain adjustments appeared necessary prior to preparation of combined financial statements, ascertained the following:

1. Ending inventories, per physical count, at 12/31/80:

    | | |
    |---|---|
    | Home office | $36,000 |
    | Branch | 6,600 |

2. Shipments to Branch, 12/31/80, not received by branch until 1/3/81, $3,000.
3. Expenses paid by the home office for the branch and charged to "Expenses" on home office books, $2,400. No entry made by branch.
4. Receipt of cash by home office from branch, credited to "Accounts Receivable" by home office, $2,000.

*Required:*
(1) Prepare a work sheet to reflect any adjusting entries based upon the information above needed to prepare a combined profit and loss statement and a combined balance sheet.
(2) Prepare the combined statements for the year.

## Problem 8-11

The trial balances of the home office and branch office of The Illioskee Company appear below:

THE ILLIOSKEE COMPANY
FOR THE YEAR ENDED DECEMBER 31, 1980

|  | Home | Branch |
|---|---:|---:|
| Cash | $ 17,000 | $ 200 |
| Inventory | 23,000 | 11,550 |
| Sundry assets | 200,000 | 48,450 |
| Branch office | 60,000 |  |
| Purchases | 190,000 |  |
| Purchases from home office |  | 105,000 |
| Freight in from home office |  | 5,500 |
| Sundry expenses | 42,000 | 24,300 |
|  | $532,000 | $195,000 |

|  | Home | Branch |
|---|---|---|
| Sundry liabilities | $ 35,000 | $ 3,500 |
| Home office |  | 51,500 |
| Sales | 155,000 | 140,000 |
| Sales to branch | 110,000 |  |
| Allowance for markup in branch inventory | 1,000 |  |
| Capital stock | 200,000 |  |
| Retained earnings | 31,000 |  |
|  | $532,000 | $195,000 |

An audit at December 31, 1980 disclosed the following:

(a) The branch office deposits all cash receipts in a local bank for the account of the home office. The audit work sheet for the cash cut-off revealed the following:

| Amount | Deposited by Branch | Recorded by Home Office |
|---|---|---|
| $1,050 | December 27, 1980 | December 31, 1980 |
| 1,100 | December 30, 1980 | January 2, 1981 |
| 600 | December 31, 1980 | January 3, 1981 |
| 300 | January 2, 1981 | January 6, 1981 |

(b) The branch office pays expenses incurred locally from an imprest bank account that is maintained with a balance of $2,000. Checks are drawn once a week on this imprest account and the home office is notified of the amount needed to replenish the account. At December 31 an $1,800 reimbursement check was mailed to the branch office.

(c) The branch office receives all of its goods from the home office. The home office bills the goods at cost plus a markup of 10% of cost. At December 31 a shipment with a billing value of $5,000 was in transit to the branch. Freight costs are typically 5% of billed values. Freight costs are considered to be inventoriable costs.

(d) The trial balance opening inventories are shown at their respective costs to the home office and to the branch office. The inventories at December 31, excluding the shipment in transit, are:

| Home office, at cost | $30,000 |
|---|---|
| Branch office, at billing value | 10,400 |

*Required:*

Prepare a work sheet that will be useful in the preparation of a combined statement of financial position, a branch income statement, and a home office income statement. The branch income statement should be prepared on the home office cost. Disregard income taxes. (AICPA adapted)

# 9

# Expansion by Subsidiary Companies

The methods by which business organizations expand vary considerably. In some instances expansion is accomplished merely by attracting the customers of another organization. This method, frequently referred to as "intensive" expansion, may or may not result in geographic expansion. Normally, however, expansion involves an increase in the geographic market area of the expanding organization. Such expansion may be accomplished by sending out salesmen, by establishing sales agencies and by setting up branches as discussed in the preceding chapter. This method of expansion is frequently referred to as "extensive" expansion.

Several reasons have been given in support of both methods. One economic reason commonly cited is the economy of large-scale operations. It is not uncommon to encounter the statement that the efforts of management to acquire the benefits of large-scale operations explain the advent of the corporation, which allowed one management to collect vast resources under one central control. Even the corporation has not proved adequate in many cases, according to some business leaders, to provide all the capital needed for desirable expansions. As a consequence, other means have been developed by which management can effectively control large masses of economic resources in order to realize economies in the mass production and distribution of goods and services. The next several chapters consider some of the problems involved in accounting for expansion by corporations which acquire financial interests in other companies.

## THE SUBSIDIARY COMPANY

One of the more common means employed by business organizations to gather together mass resources under one central control is the acquisition of enough of the outstanding voting stock of another company to control the activities of the second company. In this manner the acquiring organization gains control over the resources of the acquired company by a smaller investment than would be required to purchase the resources outright. The parent company (company that purchases the stock) needs to buy only enough stock of the subsidiary company (company whose stock is purchased) to assure the election of officers who will comply with the plans of the management of the parent company. As a maximum the investment required for this type of expansion would be that needed to acquire only one share over 50% of the voting stock of the subsidiary company. Many times the cost of this investment would be a price well below that required to purchase the assets directly from the subsidiary company.

To illustrate, assume that the condensed statement of financial position of Company B appeared as follows:

| Assets |  | $600,000 | Liabilities | $200,000 |
|---|---|---|---|---|
|  |  |  | Capital stock (3,000 shares) | 300,000 |
|  |  |  | Retained earnings | 100,000 |
| Total |  | $600,000 | Total | $600,000 |

Company A attempted to buy all of the assets of Company B. The price asked was $890,000. One of the stockholders of Company B agreed to sell 1,600 shares of B stock to Company A for $300,000. By buying the 1,600 shares of stock, Company A could place on the board of directors enough members to control Company B and all of its assets.

## Reasons for Subsidiary Companies

Although expansion can and does take place by methods other than through the acquisition or creation of subsidiaries, several reasons exist, nevertheless, why subsidiaries (separate legal entities) are used in the expansion process. They include:

1. The parent company's competitive position may be enhanced by the acquisition of capital stock of a competitor.
2. A constant supply of raw materials may be assured when control of a supplying company is obtained.
3. The legal provisions of some states or nations may be such as to make it desirable to acquire an existing corporation or create a new corporation in the particular state or nation rather than to register as a foreign corporation in that state or nation.
4. The acquisition of assets in an amount equal to those owned by a subsidiary may require a greater investment than is necessary to obtain control of the subsidiary.
5. Income tax regulations may make it desirable to acquire or create several corportions rather than to have one large corporation.

6. The acquisition of control of an existing company may bring with it the management of the existing organization, and the background and experience of this management may make the acquisition of control advantageous.
7. The acquisition of a subsidiary may provide additional customers for the products of the parent.

## CONSOLIDATED STATEMENTS

Accountants generally recognize that at times it is necessary to depart from the concept that the separate legal entity is the proper accounting entity for financial statements. One of the most obvious of the departures is to be found in the consolidated statement—a statement prepared to reflect the combined resources or activities of a parent company and its subsidiary or subsidiaries. Under consolidated reporting the resources and activities of more than one separate legal entity are combined as resources and activities of one entity—the consolidated entity. Consolidated reporting emphasizes the economic entity rather than the legal entity.

As indicated by the American Institute of Certified Public Accountants in *Accounting Research Bulletin No. 51*, the purpose of consolidated statements is to present (primarily for the benefit of the stockholders and creditors of the parent company) the financial position and results of operations of a parent company and its subsidiaries as if the group were a single company with one or more branches or divisions. There is a presumption in the Institute's position that consolidated statements are more meaningful than separate company statements and that they normally are necessary for a fair presentation when one of the companies in the group directly or indirectly has a controlling financial interest in the other companies.

### When to Consolidate

As a general rule, ownership by one company, directly or indirectly, of over 50% of the outstanding voting shares of another company is a condition pointing toward consolidation. There are, however, exceptions to this rule. The exceptions include conditions where:

1. Control is likely to be temporary.
2. Control does not rest with the parent company, even though over 50% of the oustanding voting stock is owned (as, for instance, where a subsidiary is in legal reorganization or bankruptcy).
3. The amount of the shares of a subsidiary not owned by the parent is substantial; it may be desirable to issue separate statements to provide more useful information.
4. A subsidiary is so different in operations from the activities of other subsidiaries and the parent company (as might be the case with a finance com-

pany subsidiary and a group of manufacturing subsidiaries) it might be desirable to leave the nonhomogeneous subsidiary out of the consolidated report, though its operations should be otherwise disclosed in the report.

5. The resources of a subsidiary (such as a bank or an insurance company) are not available for use throughout the consolidated group owing to restrictions imposed by law.
6. A subsidiary is in a foreign country under currency restrictions that prevent realization of the resources in the subsidiary by the parent.

**Controlling Financial Interest.** A minimum criterion in deciding whether consolidation is appropriate is the existence of a centralized controlling financial interest. Such control refers to the ability of the parent company's management to direct the operational policies of the subsidiary. In this respect it is necessary to distinguish between a company that owns the stock of another company for purposes of control and a company that owns the stock of another company only as an investment. Without the existence of a controlling financial interest, consolidation is not appropriate.

The essential question is whether or not control actually exists. Does the parent company actually possess and exercise the power to make decisions for the subsidiary? If so, consolidation is proper. The possession and exercise of such power implies an integration of activities of the two organizations into one economic unit, one business enterprise. Effective and continuing control is more likely to exist where there is substantial stock ownership.

**Majority-Owned Subsidiary.** As indicated previously, the usual condition for a controlling financial interest is the ownership by one company, directly or indirectly, of over 50% of the outstanding voting stock of another company. It is not uncommon for two companies to create jointly a third company with each of the promoting companies receiving 50% of the stock of the new company. If such a company were included in the consolidated reports of the two parent companies, the assets and liabilities of the third company would appear on the consolidated reports of both. If less than 50%-owned companies are consolidated, their resources and results of operations may appear on the consolidated reports of more than two parent companies. The consolidation of only majority-owned subsidiaries eliminates this possibility.

**Control Without Stock Ownership.** It is often recognized that control of a business enterprise may be exercised without owning any of the stock of the company. Typical of this type of control is the lease agreement, in which the lessor retains control of leased property, or bond agreement, under which the provisions of the indenture may place much of the control of the company in the hands of the bondholders' trustee. Some accountants contend that control of another company by any means requires that the controlled company be included in the consolidated report. The idea underlying this position is that a consolidated report should report on all of the resources and activities under the control of one centralized management. Theoretically, there may be much to support this position but, from a practical standpoint, there is considerable reluctance to prepare consolidated statements except where ownership of the stock of the subsidiary does exist.

**Homogeneous Operations.** It is frequently suggested that companies should not be consolidated unless their operations are so interrelated as to be similar or complementary to each other. Support for this view is still found in current practice where, for example, an individual nonhomogeneous subsidiary is excluded from the consolidation of a group of homogeneous companies. Actually, of course, the operations of many modern business organizations are quite diverse. In fact, diversification is to a great extent the modern trend in business organization and operation. For this and other reasons there is general recognition that companies heterogeneous in operations and structure may be reported upon more adequately in a consolidated report than by a large group of separate statements.

**Different Fiscal Periods.** At times it is suggested that consolidation is not appropriate when a subsidiary and its parent company have different fiscal periods. Actually, the existence of different fiscal periods does not pose a particularly difficult problem. Normally, interim reports may be prepared by the subsidiary for consolidation purposes. Such interim reports may be prepared by adjusting the regular annual report or by developing interim statements that conform to the fiscal period of the parent company.

**Consolidation Policy.** As indicated in *Bulletin 51,* in deciding upon a consolidation policy, the aim should be to make the financial presentation that is most meaningful in light of the circumstances. The statement reader should be given information suitable to his needs, but he should not be burdened with unnecessary detail. Thus, even though a group of companies is heterogeneous in character, it may be better to consolidate than to present a large number of separate statements. On the other hand, separate statements may be more appropriate for a subsidiary if the presentation of financial information concerning the particular subsidiary would be more informative to stockholders and creditors of the parent company than would the inclusion of the subsidiary in a consolidation. For example, separate statements may be required for a subsidiary that is a bank or an insurance company and may be more appropriate for a finance company where the parent and the other subsidiaries are engaged in manufacturing operations. Since there are no hard and fast rules governing all possible situations as to the inclusion or exclusion of a given subsidiary, the consolidation policy followed in any given situation should be disclosed. In many instances this disclosure may be presented in the headings or bodies of the statements, whereas footnote disclosure is required in other situations.

## Limitations of Consolidated Statements

Although consolidated statements have a very real usefulness for purposes of presenting a composite picture of the financial position and operating results of a group of affiliated companies, they cannot be regarded as properly taking the place of statements for the individual companies for certain purposes. Consolidated statements ignore important legal relationships and present statements of an "economic entity." Where there are important interests in the individual companies, consolidated statements may be of limited usefulness to (1) minority stockholders, (2) creditors, and (3) financial analysts.

**Minority Stockholders.** Minority stockholders of a subsidiary can obtain very little information of value from consolidated statements, for such statements do not detail the assets, equities, income, and expenses of the individual subsidiary. For such information, minority stockholders must turn to the separate company statements.

**Creditors.** The creditors of each company in a consolidated group are primarily concerned with the financial position and earnings of the specific debtor company. Most companies having subsidiaries issue consolidated reports, and as indicated earlier, it is generally presumed that the consolidated report is the basic report and separate statements only supplementary. Creditors of a subsidiary company, however, have rights only against the subsidiary company. As the following illustration indicates, a consolidated statement may be misleading to a creditor.

Assume that Company A owns 100% of the outstanding voting stock of Company B. Condensed balance sheets of the two companies as separate entities reflect:

|  | Company A | Company B |
|---|---|---|
| *Assets* | | |
| Investment in B | $ 80,000 | |
| Other assets | 810,000 | $200,000 |
| | $890,000 | $200,000 |
| *Equities* | | |
| Liabilities | $290,000 | $120,000 |
| Capital stock | 600,000 | 80,000 |
| | $890,000 | $200,000 |

It is apparent from the balance sheet of Company B that the outstanding debt is equal to 60% of the total assets whereas the same relationship for Company A is about 33%. Creditors are interested in the amount of asset protection they have behind loans they make. A consolidated balance sheet for the two companies would appear as follows:

CONSOLIDATED BALANCE SHEET

| | |
|---|---:|
| Assets ($810,000 and $200,000) | $1,010,000 |
| Liabilities | $ 410,000 |
| Capital stock | 600,000 |
| Total | $1,010,000 |

The consolidated balance sheet indicates that the relationship of debt to total assets is about 41%, which may suggest to the creditors of the subsidiary company that they have greater asset protection than legally exists.

Creditorship information disclosed in a consolidated statement may be inadequate or limited both from the short-term as well as long-term creditor viewpoint. For example, since a consolidated statement is a composite, a weak current position in one of the affiliated companies may be bolstered by a strong current position in another affiliate. Likewise, bond indentures frequently require the maintaining of specified ratios of current assets to current liabilities, and provide penalties for nonconformance. The ordinary consolidated balance sheet does not give the bondholders of individual companies information from which they can determine whether the requirements are being fulfilled, nor can the stockholders see whether their company is in any jeopardy because of default.

Although consolidated statements may be of limited usefulness to creditors, especially creditors of the individual subsidiaries, this is not necessarily in and of itself sufficient reason for exclusion of a subsidiary from the consolidation. Limitations of consolidated statements for creditor purposes, however, may be such as to require additional disclosure (footnote disclosure, etc.) of information useful to creditors.

**Financial Analysts.** By its very nature a consolidated statement may fail to reveal information pertinent to the financial analyst. For example, to include as current assets, land of a real estate company, bread of a bakery company, and finished chemicals of a chemical company in a consolidated statement of financial position—all as inventory—may disclose little to a particular investor. In part because of this situation and in part because of other limitations, many companies issue both consolidated and separate company reports.

The exclusion of banks and insurance companies from consolidation with other nonfinancial companies is sometimes based upon the distorting effect that their inclusion would presumably have upon an analysis of the financial statements. While much has been said about the distorting effect on financial ratios and relationships that could result from an analysis of only consolidated statements, the importance of this distortion may be overemphasized. For example, when top management has the power to transfer resources from one affiliated company to another in the consolidated group, financial ratios and relationships resulting from the consolidated statements may more accurately reflect the economic facts of the situation than similar ratios and relationships determined from separate company statements. The latter ratios and relationships could be unrepresentative because of the ability of top management to change quickly any one affiliate's financial condition.

Illustrative of this situation would be a subsidiary company with a current ratio of ½ to 1 ($50,000 of current assets to $100,000 of current liabilities) but a parent company with a current rate of 3 to 1 ($300,000 to $100,000). The ability of the subsidiary to pay its current liabilities is not properly represented by the ½ to 1 ratio if the parent company is in a position to transfer any needed current assets to the subsidiary.

Consolidated statements may be of limited value to the financial analyst if they fail to reflect adequately the activities of top management. For example, top management (parent company's management) may for various reasons treat a given affiliate as an investment at one time and as a part of the consolidated group at another time. Or, top management may direct its energies to the development of an affiliated company less than 50% owned but very effectively controlled. In this regard, some criticism may be directed to the adequacy of the over 50% standard for inclusion, but in terms of a compromise between objectivity and subjectivity (it is an observable fact whether or not over 50% of the stock is owned, while the existence of control may be subjective), it has been accepted as one of the most reasonable standards for consolidation yet suggested.

## Unconsolidated Subsidiaries

It is possible to distinguish two types of unconsolidated subsidiaries: (1) companies controlled by less than 50% ownership of the voting stock, and (2) companies over 50% owned but excluded from consolidation as exceptions to the general rule. On the consolidated report, unconsolidated subsidiaries should appear as investments. The proper valuation of these investments, according to the Accounting Principles Board's *Opinion No. 18,* is cost plus (minus) the parent's share of the subsidiary's undistributed earnings (losses) since acquisition. (As we shall see in Chapter Twelve, this method of carrying an investment is known as the *equity method.*)

To illustrate, assume that the parent company owns 60% of a subsidiary company that is not included in the consolidation. The investment in the stock of the subsidiary would then appear on the consolidated statement of financial position as an investment as follows:

        Investment in subsidiary         $XXXXX

Assuming that subsequent to acquisition the unconsolidated subsidiary earns and does not distribute $30,000, proper valuation of the "Investment in Subsidiary" account on the consolidated statement of financial position would require that 60% of the $30,000 be added to the investment account.

Illustrative of the process by which unconsolidated subsidiaries are reported is that of the Caterpillar Tractor Company, which in a recent report included in its consolidated financial statements the account "Investment in Caterpillar Credit Corporation" in the amount of $7,964,917. The assets and liabilities of all other subsidiaries were combined to provide the consolidated report. Because the Caterpillar Credit Corporation was not included in the consolidation, a separate report for the Credit Corporation was attached to the annual report. A footnote to the consolidated report disclosed the following information:

> The financial positions of the Company's wholly owned subsidiaries, except Caterpillar Credit Corporation, have been consolidated with that of the parent company. The investment in Caterpillar Credit Corporation is carried at cost plus the profit retained by the subsidiary.

## Theories of Consolidated Statements

Before turning to the procedures and analyses involved in preparing consolidated statements, attention should be given to alternatives regarding the nature of consolidations which are discussed at theoretical levels. Although knowledge of these theories will contribute little directly to the problem of knowing current practice, they do set forth alternative objectives. There are two essential ideas on the nature of consolidated reports, as follows:

1. Consolidated reports are prepared from the point of view of the stockholders of the parent company. This is usually called the *proprietary theory*.
2. Consolidated reports are prepared from the point of view of the total resources under the control of the top management of the group of companies. They are, therefore, for the use of all stockholders of all of the consolidated companies. This is known as the *entity theory*.

The first theory dominates accounting practice and represents the theory under which the procedures and analyses outlined in this textbook are presented.

A distinction between the procedures of the two theories can best be explained by an example. Assume that Company A purchased 80% of the voting stock of Company B for $80,000 and that at the date of purchase the net assets (assets less liabilities) of Company B totaled $50,000. According to the first theory, the $80,000 represents the price paid for 80% of the net assets of Company B. Since the price paid ($80,000) exceeds the book value of the net assets acquired (80% of $50,000 or $40,000), the assets acquired may be revalued upward by the amount of the excess payment. The consolidated balance sheet would report the assets at $80,000 or would report the excess over book value ($80,000 − $40,000 = $40,000) in a special account so that the full $80,000 would appear on the consolidated balance sheet as the proper valuation for 80% of the net assets of the subsidiary. From the point of view of the stockholders of the parent company, the $80,000 represents their cost of the assets.

Under this theory, however, the remaining 20% of the net assets of the subsidiary would appear on the consolidated balance sheet at their net book value of $10,000.

Under the entity theory, however, the 20% of the net assets would be revalued upward to $20,000 to make it comparable with the valuation given the other assets. This theory holds that the basis for the valuation used in reporting the assets accruing to the stockholders of the parent company should be applied to the assets accruing to the minority stockholders of Company B. Assume the following condensed financial statements:

|  | Separate Company Reports | |
|---|---|---|
| *Assets* | A | B |
| Investment in B | $ 80,000 | |
| Other assets | 430,000 | $70,000 |
| Total | $510,000 | $70,000 |
| *Equities* | | |
| Liabilities | $ 60,000 | $20,000 |
| Capital stock | 450,000 | 50,000 |
| Total | $510,000 | $70,000 |

Consolidated balance sheets prepared under each of the two theories would be as follows:

|  | ENTITY THEORY | | PROPRIETARY THEORY |
|---|---|---|---|
| *Assets* | | | |
| Assets of A | | $430,000 | $430,000 |
| Assets of B: | | | |
|   Assets claimed by B creditors | $20,000 | | $20,000 |
|   Assets claimed by A stockholders: | | | |
|     Book value | 40,000 | | 40,000 |
|     Additional cost | 40,000 | | 40,000 |
|   Assets claimed by B stockholders: | | | |
|     Book value | 10,000 | | 10,000 |
|     Write-up to other assets | 10,000 | | — |
| | | 120,000 | 110,000 |
| Total | | $550,000 | $540,000 |
| *Equities* | | | |
| Liabilities (60,000 and 20,000) | | $ 80,000 | $ 80,000 |
| Capital stock (A's) | | 450,000 | 450,000 |
| Minority interest (B's) | | 20,000 | 10,000 |
| Total | | $550,000 | $540,000 |

## Summary

The nature of consolidated reports has been described as a process of reporting on the activities of an entity larger than the separate legal company. The standard for inclusion of companies within the consolidation has been established as the ownership of over 50% of the voting stock of the subsidiary company with exception to the rule for certain foreign subsidiaries, banks, insurance companies, and finance companies. Limitations to consolidations are not as severe as they might seem at first glance. Finally, the possibility of the preparation of consolidated

## PROBLEMS

### Problem 9-1

1. State briefly the purpose of preparing consolidated financial statements.
2. State the relationship among business organizations that makes the preparation of consolidated financial statements advisable. (AICPA adapted)

### Problem 9-2

In the preparation of consolidated financial statements of a parent corporation and its subsidiaries a decision must be reached concerning the inclusion or exclusion of each of them as a member of the consolidated group. A common criterion is the percentage of voting stock owned by the parent company.

1. What is the significance of the percentage of voting stock ownership in justifying the inclusion of a subsidiary company in a consolidated statement?
2. List other criteria upon which the decision to consolidate or not may also rest.
(AICPA adapted)

### Problem 9-3

Consolidated statements are frequently presented for a parent company and its subsidiary or subsidiaries. There are a number of reasons for their use in presenting financial data. However, such statements are subject to several limitations in the usual situation. State and explain the limitations of consolidated statements.
(AICPA adapted)

### Problem 9-4

The Acme Company as of December 31, 1980, had assets of $500,000 and liabilities of $300,000. Its net earnings for 1980 amounted to $80,000. The assets included all of the stock of Excelsior Company which was acquired late in 1979 for $25,000. Excelsior sustained a net loss of $17,500 in 1980. There were no intercompany transactions except that Acme guaranteed a bank loan of Excelsior in the amount of $20,000.

In preparing statements of Acme, would you disclose the 1980 transaction concerning Excelsior Company:

1. Not at all.
2. By a footnote disclosing Acme's contingent liability.
3. By setting up a receivable from Excelsior and a payable to the bank.
4. By preparing consolidated statements.
5. By writing down the investment in Excelsior to $7,500.

Discuss, giving reasons for the alternatives selected and those rejected by you.
(AICPA adapted)

## Problem 9-5

In 1970 the K Company purchased on the open market, for $75,000, 1,000 shares of the S Company's common stock, of which more than 100,000 shares were then outstanding. During the ensuing years dividends were paid regularly and fluctuations in the market value of the stock were relatively insignificant, with a general upward tendency. At the close of the K Company's fiscal year ended October 31, 1980, the S Company stock was quoted at 150, and the company's latest annual report for its fiscal year ended June 30, 1980, shows a book value per share of approximately $165. Although a manufacturing concern, the K Company has a substantial investment in the securities of other companies. It neither controls nor participates in the direction of these other companies.

The president of the K Company proposes to increase the asset value of S Company stock on the K Company's books to $150 per share.

Discuss this proposal, indicating how the K Company's financial statements would be affected if it is carried out, and the reasons for and against its adoption.

(AICPA adapted)

## Problem 9-6

Discuss in detail the distinguishing features of the entity theory of consolidated reports.

## Problem 9-7

The Y & P Music Company, a Washington corporation, operates two retail music stores, one located in Seattle, Washington, and the other in Tacoma, Washington. Each store maintains a separate set of accounting records; intercompany transfers or transactions are recorded in an intercompany account carried on each set of records.

Purchases of major items of inventory, such as organs and pianos, are made under a financial arrangement with a local bank advancing 90% of the invoice price and the Company paying 10%. If the bank notes remains unpaid at the end of 90 days, the Company is required to pay an additional 10% of the invoice price as a payment on the note.

In August, the Seattle store purchased an organ for which the seller's draft in the amount of $6,300 was sent to The First National Bank of Seattle, which refused to finance the purchase of the instrument. Arrangements were made through the Tacoma store with The Citizens Bank of Tacoma to provide the financing. The bank lent Tacoma 90% of the invoice price, or $5,670, which Tacoma deposited and credited to notes payable. The Seattle store drew a check payable to the Tacoma store for $630, or 10% of the invoice price, charging Tacoma intercompany account on its books. Tacoma took up the deposit crediting the intercompany account carried with Seattle.

Tacoma, using the 10% received from Seattle and the 90% advanced by the bank, drew a check payable to The First National Bank of Seattle in full payment of the draft, charging notes payable.

In November, Seattle made the second payment of $630 directly to the Tacoma bank, charging Tacoma intercompany account, and also notified the Tacoma bookkeeper that the payment had been made. Tacoma took up the transaction charging organ purchases and crediting Seattle. In December Seattle paid off the balance of the note charging organ purchases.

*Required:*
State adjusting entries to be recorded on each set of books correcting the account balances. (AICPA adapted)

## Problem 9-8

The use of consolidated financial statements for reporting to stockholders is common. Under some conditions, however, it is desirable to exclude a subsidiary from consolidated reports.

*Required:*
List the conditions under which a subsidiary should be excluded from consolidation statements. (AICPA adapted)

## Problem 9-9

Select from the alternatives presented "all" of those that correctly complete each of the numbered statements. Note that some of the questions may contain more than one correct statement.

1. Consolidated statements are used to present the result of operations and the financial position of:

    (a) A company and its branches.
    (b) A company and its subcontractors.
    (c) A company and its subsidiaries.
    (d) Any group of companies with related interests.
    (e) None of the above.

2. Consolidated statements are intended primarily for the benefit of:

    (a) Stockholders of the parent company.
    (b) Taxing authorities.
    (c) Management of the parent company.
    (d) Creditors of the parent company.
    (e) None of the above.

3. A consolidated statement for X, Y, and Z is proper if:

    (a) X owns 100% of the outstanding common stock of Y and 49% of Z; Q owns 51% of Z.
    (b) X owns 100% of the outstanding common stock of Y; Y owns 75% of Z.
    (c) X owns 100% of the outstanding common stock of Y and 75% of Z. X

bought the stock of Z one month before the statement date, and sold it six weeks later.
- (*d*) There is no interrelation of financial control among X, Y, and Z. However, they are contemplating the joint purchase of 100% of the outstanding common stock of W.
- (*e*) X owns 100% of the outstanding common stock of Y and Z. Z is in bankruptcy.

4. H is the parent company and would probably treat K as an investment and not a consolidated subsidiary in the proposed consolidated statement of H, J, and K if:

- (*a*) H and J manufacture electronic equipment; K manufactures ball bearings.
- (*b*) H and J manufacture ball-point pens; K is a bank.
- (*c*) K has assets of $1,000,000 and an outstanding bond issue of $750,000. H holds the bonds.
- (*d*) Same as (*c*), except that outsiders hold the bonds.
- (*e*) None of the above.

5. Parent company P has a fiscal year ending June 30, 1980. Subsidiary S's fiscal year ends May 31, 1980. Therefore:

- (*a*) A consolidated statement cannot properly be prepared for P and S.
- (*b*) S's May 31, 1980 statement can be used for consolidation with P's June 30, 1980 statement, provided disclosure (or some recognition) is made of any June event that materially affected S.
- (*c*) If the consolidated statement is permissible, it will be dated June 30, 1980.
- (*d*) If the consolidated statement is permissible, it will be dated May 31, 1980.
- (*e*) None of the above.

6. P owns 90% of the stock of S. W owns 10% of S's stock. In relation to P, W is considered as:

- (*a*) An affiliate.
- (*b*) A subsidiary not to be consolidated.
- (*c*) A minority interest.
- (*d*) A holding company.
- (*e*) None of the above.

7. Company P had 300,000 shares of stock outstanding. It owned 75% of the outstanding stock of T. T owned 20,000 shares of P's stock. In the consolidated balance sheet, Company P's outstanding stock may be shown as:

- (*a*) 280,000 shares.
- (*b*) 300,000 shares less 20,000 shares of treasury stock.

(c) 300,000 shares.
(d) 300,000 shares footnoted to indicate that T holds 20,000 shares.
(e) None of the above.

8. The preferable method of presenting subsidiaries not consolidated in financial statements is:

   (a) At market value, adjusted through income.
   (b) At market value, adjusted through retained earnings.
   (c) At cost, plus the parent's share of the subsidiaries' net income (or minus the net loss) since acquisition, adjusted annually through income.
   (d) At cost, plus the parent's share of the subsidiaries' net income (or minus the net loss) adjusted annually through retained earnings.
   (e) At consolidated group's equity in net realizable value of assets of subsidiaries not consolidated.

9. P and its subsidiaries, T and V, have issued combined statements for a number of years. In connection with a proposed bank loan, P has been requested to present a statement to the bank that will indicate P's financial position at December 31, 1980. The following will supply the desired information:

   (a) A copy of the consolidated statement at December 31, 1980.
   (b) A copy of P's financial statement at December 31, 1980 on which the investments in T and V are reported at the current carrying value.
   (c) A copy of the consolidated statement and of the separate parent company (P) statement, both at December 31, 1980.
   (d) A copy of the consolidated statement at December 31, 1980, modified so that one column is used for P and other columns for T and V.
   (e) A copy of separate financial statements of P, T, and V as of December 31, 1980.

10. The stockholders of S sold all of its common stock, 1,000 shares, to Company P, receiving in return 5,000 shares of Company P stock. On the day prior to the sale, P stock sold for $40 per share; S stock sold for $195 per share. P stock has a par value of $20 per share. S stock has a par value of $50 per share. The investment by P may be recorded on its books at:

    (a) $200,000, only.
    (b) $195,000, only.
    (c) $100,000.
    (d) $50,000.
    (e) Either $200,000 or $195,000.    (AICPA adapted)

# 10

# Consolidated Statements at Date of Acquisition

The preceding chapter dealt with a variety of consolidation policies that might be adopted by different companies. Different consolidation policies normally require the application of different consolidating procedures. As indicated in *Opinion No. 22* of the Accounting Principles Board, it is important that consolidated reports disclose the consolidation policy followed by the company. This disclosure may be indicated by the wording of the report headings, revealed in information in the statements, or stated in footnotes. Company policy indicates the extent to which particular procedures are used, but some procedures are rather generally employed regardless of a given company's consolidation policy. It is to these procedures that the next several chapters are directed.

## Basic Consolidating Procedures

Mechanically, the preparation of consolidated statements is based on certain basic procedures. Although the application of these procedures may vary somewhat from situation to situation, essentially it remains the same. In summary form the procedures are:

1. Elimination of reciprocal elements.
2. Consolidation of nonreciprocal elements.

**Elimination of Reciprocal Elements.** Since consolidated statements are prepared for the purpose of reporting the combined resources, equities, and operations of a group of closely related companies, intercompany items reciprocal in nature such as intercompany payables and receivables must be eliminated. This is necessary in order both to avoid double counting and to eliminate any profits

10 / *Consolidated Statements at Date of Acquisition* 273

recognized on intercompany transactions that are unrealized, at the date of consolidation, from the viewpoint of the affiliated group as an entity. For example, if Company A owns Company B, and Company B owes Company A $10,000 for merchandise that cost A $8,000 and that is still in B's possession, the $10,000 receivable and payable must be eliminated. Likewise, the $2,000 intercompany profit in the valuation of inventory at $10,000 rather than $8,000 must be eliminated when A and B are viewed as one economic unit. If these eliminations were not made, it would appear that the consolidated group owed itself $10,000, and it would also appear that the group made a profit by selling to itself.

One of the more important, if not the most important, intercompany relationships is that existing between the investment account on a parent company's statement of financial position and the stockholders' equity section on a subsidiary company's statement of financial position. Since the parent company's investment account (an asset) is merely a claim against the net assets (represented by the stockholders' equity section) of the subsidiary, they are reciprocal in nature, and an elimination is in order. As was the case in Chapter Eight, when the assets of the branch were substituted for the Branch Office account on the home office statement, a similar substitution is made in the case of a parent and subsidiary when consolidating. When the parent's share of a subsidiary's stockholders' equity is eliminated against the investment account, as will be noted later, in reality the parent company's share of the subsidiary's net assets is substituted for the investment account.

**Establishment of Reciprocity.** Before reciprocal elements can be eliminated, they must, of course, be reciprocal. Consequently, if for any reason reciprocity does not exist between one or more sets of intercompany accounts in which it should exist, reciprocity must be established before the consolidating procedure, as outlined above, can be effected. Reconciliation problems may include such things as goods in transit, cash in transit, interest income and interest expense, and dividends receivable and dividends payable. As will be noted in subsequent chapters, reciprocity must frequently be established between the investment account on a parent company's statement of financial position and the stockholders' equity section on a subsidiary company's statement of financial position.

**Consolidation of Nonreciprocal Elements.** In order to reflect the combined resources, equities, and operations of an affiliated group, nonreciprocal elements must be included in the consolidated statements. Nonreciprocal like items are combined in the statements and nonreciprocal unlike items are shown separately. For example, if Company A has cash of $6,000 and Company B has cash of $10,000, the cash reported on the consolidated statement of financial position would be $16,000. If Company A owns U.S. Government bonds of $25,000 and Company B owns no such bonds, the bonds would be reported as a separate item of $25,000 on the consolidated statement.

## Types of Statements Consolidated

Current financial reporting for individual business organizations emphasizes four basic statements, namely, the statement of financial position, the income statement, the statement of retained earnings, and the statement of changes in financial position. Although differences in title, content, and form of each of these statements are found in practice, there is considerable agreement as to the basic need of each when reporting financial data. These four statements are also the ones most frequently consolidated. If consolidated statements are prepared as of the date of organization or acquisition of the subsidiary by the parent, however, the preparation of a consolidated income statement or a consolidated statement of changes in financial position is not possible, since the companies have not operated as a unit. The consolidated statement of changes in financial position will not be considered to any extent in the following discussion since that statement is generally dealt with in intermediate accounting textbooks and consolidation does not create any unique problems in preparation.

Regardless of when consolidated statements are prepared, the basic procedure is essentially the same, that is (1) eliminate reciprocals, and (2) consolidate nonreciprocals. However, the study of consolidations is perhaps best approached by emphasizing the time of consolidating. This approach is important because if the statements are consolidated at some date subsequent to acquisition, adjustments may be necessary in order to establish reciprocity. Consequently, this textbook emphasizes the *date* of the consolidated statements, and the technique of their preparation is studied in the following sequence:

*First.* At date of acquisition:

1. Statement of financial position.
2. Statement of retained earnings.

*Second.* At a date subsequent to acquisition:

1. Statement of financial position.
2. Income statement.
3. Statement of retained earnings.

## Consolidated Statement of Financial Position at Date of Acquisition

A consolidated statement of financial position is a statement showing as of a given date the combined financial condition of a group of closely related companies viewed as a unit. Consequently, such a statement reflects the assets and equities of the consolidated companies as they would appear to an outsider who considered the separate legal organizations as one economic unit. The technique of combining the assets and equities as of the date of acquisition is demonstrated in the following illustrations which, since control may be obtained by less than 100% ownership, are categorized according to whether (a) 100% ownership exists, or (b) less than 100% ownership exists.

## 10 / Consolidated Statements at Date of Acquisition

**100% Ownership.** In the process of acquiring 100% interest in a subsidiary, a parent company may pay:

1. Book value for the interest acquired.
2. More than book value for the interest acquired.
3. Less than book value for the interest acquired.

In all of the three situations the acquisition is recorded on the books of the parent company at cost. The typical entry would be

| | | |
|---|---|---|
| Investment in Company B | $XXXXXX | |
| Cash | | $XXXXXX |

***Illustration A-1:*** *100% Ownership Acquired at Book Value.* Assume that as of January 1, 1980, Company A acquires 100% ownership in Company B for $150,000, which is also the book value of the interest acquired. The following individual company statements reflect the financial position of the respective companies as of the date of acquisition, and the consolidated statement shows the financial position after consolidation:

### COMPANY A
### STATEMENT OF FINANCIAL POSITION
### JANUARY 1, 1980

| | | | |
|---|---:|---|---:|
| Current assets | $ 80,000 | Current liabilities | $ 20,000 |
| Investment in B | 150,000 | Fixed liabilities | 100,000 |
| Fixed assets (net) | 400,000 | Stockholders' equity: | |
| | | Capital stock | 400,000 |
| | | Retained earnings | 110,000 |
| | $630,000 | | $630,000 |

### COMPANY B
### STATEMENT OF FINANCIAL POSITION
### JANUARY 1, 1980

| | | | |
|---|---:|---|---:|
| Current assets | $ 40,000 | Current liabilities | $ 10,000 |
| Fixed assets (net) | 120,000 | Stockholders' equity: | |
| | | Capital stock | 100,000 |
| | | Retained earnings | 50,000 |
| | $160,000 | | $160,000 |

**Basic Procedure.** As indicated earlier, the basic procedure involved in consolidating financial statements is (1) to eliminate reciprocals, and (2) to consolidate nonreciprocals. In this instance the only reciprocal elements involved are: (1) on the subsidiary's statement, the portion of B's ownership equity owned by A, and (2) on the parent company's statement, the parent company's investment in B. The *work sheet* entry for the elimination expressed in journal form is:

| | | |
|---|---:|---:|
| Capital stock (Company B) | $100,000 | |
| Retained earnings (Company B) | 50,000 | |
|    Investment in B (Company A's account) | | $150,000 |
| (to eliminate Company B's stockholders' equity against the investment account) | | |

The nonreciprocal elements are consolidated by adding them where necessary and extending them to the consolidated statement as illustrated in the following working papers:

COMPANY A AND SUBSIDIARY COMPANY B
CONSOLIDATED WORKING PAPERS
STATEMENT OF FINANCIAL POSITION

JANUARY 1, 1980

| | Company A | Company B | Eliminations Debit | Eliminations Credit | Consolidated Financial Position |
|---|---:|---:|---:|---:|---:|
| *Assets* | | | | | |
| Current assets | $ 80,000 | $ 40,000 | | | $120,000 |
| Investment in B | 150,000 | | | $150,000 | |
| Fixed assets (net) | 400,000 | 120,000 | | | 520,000 |
| | $630,000 | $160,000 | | | $640,000 |
| *Equities* | | | | | |
| Current liabilities | $ 20,000 | $ 10,000 | | | $ 30,000 |
| Fixed liabilities | 100,000 | | | | 100,000 |
| Stockholders' equity: | | | | | |
|   Capital stock | 400,000 | 100,000 | $100,000 | | 400,000 |
|   Retained earnings | 110,000 | 50,000 | 50,000 | | 110,000RE |
| | $630,000 | $160,000 | $150,000 | $150,000 | $640,000 |

In statement form the last column of the working papers would be presented as follows:

COMPANY A AND SUBSIDIARY COMPANY B
CONSOLIDATED STATEMENT OF FINANCIAL POSITION

JANUARY 1, 1980

| | | | | |
|---|---:|---|---:|---|
| Current assets | $120,000 | Current liabilities | | $ 30,000 |
| Fixed assets (net) | 520,000 | Fixed liabilities | | 100,000 |
| | | Stockholders' equity: | | |
| | |   Capital stock | | 400,000 |
| | |   Retained earnings | | 110,000 |
| | $640,000 | | | $640,000 |

## 10 / Consolidated Statements at Date of Acquisition

**Illustration A-2:** *100% Ownership Acquired at More Than Book Value.* A parent company may pay more than book value for the stock it acquires when purchasing an equity in a subsidiary. Since a share of stock represents an undivided interest in the net assets and the earning power of the company, payment in excess of book value (net assets) may be due to such factors as (1) market value of stock may be related to the value of the enterprise rather than the cost of the individual assets, and (2) individual assets may be undervalued on the books.

The difference between the purchase price and the book value of the stock acquired should be analyzed carefully. If the difference is attributed to specific assets on the books of the subsidiary, it should be allocated to them. If the difference represents the price paid for intangible assets not recorded on the books of the subsidiary, these assets should be recorded as assets of the consolidated company. Any difference not assignable to specific items should be included with consolidated assets appropriately described.

To demonstrate the procedures of consolidation, it is assumed in this textbook, unless stipulated otherwise, that any payment in excess of book value should be allocated to the intangible asset, "Goodwill." Consequently, when statements of financial position are consolidated, goodwill may arise if a parent pays more than book value for the stock purchased.

Assume the same general situation as used in the preceding illustration, except that Company A acquires 100% ownership in Company B for $170,000. Since the book value acquired by Company A is only $150,000, there is an excess payment of $20,000 for "goodwill." The consolidating procedure is as follows:

COMPANY A
STATEMENT OF FINANCIAL POSITION

JANUARY 1, 1980

| | | | |
|---|---|---|---|
| Current assets | $ 60,000 | Current liabilities | $ 20,000 |
| Investment in Company B | 170,000 | Fixed liabilities | 100,000 |
| Fixed assets (net) | 400,000 | Stockholders' equity: | |
| | | Capital stock | 400,000 |
| | | Retained earnings | 110,000 |
| | $630,000 | | $630,000 |

COMPANY B
STATEMENT OF FINANCIAL POSITION

JANUARY 1, 1980

| | | | |
|---|---|---|---|
| Current assets | $40,000 | Current liabilities | $ 10,000 |
| Fixed assets (net) | 120,000 | Stockholders' equity: | |
| | | Capital stock | 100,000 |
| | | Retained earnings | 50,000 |
| | $160,000 | | $160,000 |

**Basic Procedure.** The basic procedure is the same as in Illustration A-1, that is, eliminate the reciprocal elements and consolidate the nonreciprocal elements. However, since there is no element reciprocal to the $20,000 payment for goodwill, it cannot be eliminated, and as a result it is extended along with other assets to the consolidated statement as the cost to the consolidated entity of purchased goodwill. The *work sheet* entry for the elimination is the same as in Illustration A-1, that is:

| | | |
|---|---|---|
| Capital stock (Company B's) | $100,000 | |
| Retained earnings (Company B's) | 50,000 | |
| Investment in B (Company A's account) | | $150,000 |
| (to eliminate Company B's stockholders' equity against the investment account) | | |

The nonreciprocal elements are consolidated as they were in the preceding illustration. In the working papers that follow, note how the nonreciprocal element of the investment account is extended to the consolidated statement as (G) goodwill.

COMPANY A AND SUBSIDIARY COMPANY B
CONSOLIDATED WORKING PAPERS
STATEMENT OF FINANCIAL POSITION
JANUARY 1, 1980

| | Company A | Company B | Eliminations Debit | Eliminations Credit | Consolidated Financial Position |
|---|---|---|---|---|---|
| **Assets** | | | | | |
| Currents assets | $ 60,000 | $ 40,000 | | | $100,000 |
| Investment in B | 170,000 | | | $150,000 | 20,000G |
| Fixed assets (net) | 400,000 | 120,000 | | | 520,000 |
| | $630,000 | $160,000 | | | $640,000 |
| **Equities** | | | | | |
| Current liabilities | $ 20,000 | $ 10,000 | | | $ 30,000 |
| Fixed liabilities | 100,000 | | | | 100,000 |
| Stockholders' equity: | | | | | |
| Capital stock | 400,000 | 100,000 | $100,000 | | 400,000 |
| Retained earnings | 110,000 | 50,000 | 50,000 | | 110,000RE |
| | $630,000 | $160,000 | $150,000 | $150,000 | $640,000 |

**Illustration A-3:** 100% *Ownership Acquired at Less Than Book Value.* A parent company may pay less than book value for the stock it acquires when purchasing an equity in a subsidiary. Payment of less than book value may arise from a variety of reasons, such as an advantageous purchase, or because the subsidiary's earning power does not justify payment of book value for its shares.

# 10 / Consolidated Statements at Date of Acquisition

When the cost of a parent's interest in a subsidiary is less than the book value acquired, the accounting treatment of the difference should parallel in reverse the treatment used when a parent company pays more than book value for its interest. Accordingly, to the extent that the difference is considered to be attributable to specific assets, it should be allocated to them, with corresponding adjustments of the depreciation and amortization. In some circumstances there may be a remaining difference, a sort of "negative goodwill," which the Institute recommends be shown in a credit account until taken into income in future periods on a reasonable and systematic basis.

Since it is impossible to allocate the excess—whether it be a form of positive or negative goodwill—without all of the facts, unless specific information is given, the following procedures are used in this textbook to demonstrate the basic techniques of consolidation. If any positive goodwill exists on the statements being consolidated or if any results from consolidation, negative goodwill is deducted therefrom to the extent possible. However, if no positive goodwill exists on the statements being consolidated and if none results from consolidation of other subsidiaries, the unallocated excess of book value over cost is presented in an account entitled "Excess of Subsidiary Book Value Over Cost." Likewise, if positive goodwill exists, but it is insufficient to offset all negative goodwill, it is used to offset as much negative goodwill as possible, and the balance of the excess of book value over cost is disclosed in the account.

Assume the same facts as used in Illustration A-1, except that Company A acquires 100% ownership in Company B for $140,000. Since the book value acquired by Company A is $150,000, negative goodwill of $10,000 is assumed to exist.

### Company A
### Statement of Financial Position
#### January 1, 1980

| | | | |
|---|---|---|---|
| Current assets | $ 90,000 | Current liabilities | $ 20,000 |
| Investment in Company B | 140,000 | Fixed liabilities | 100,000 |
| Fixed assets (net) | 400,000 | Stockholders' equity: | |
| | | Capital stock | 400,000 |
| | | Retained earnings | 110,000 |
| | $630,000 | | $630,000 |

### Company B
### Statement of Financial Position
#### January 1, 1980

| | | | |
|---|---|---|---|
| Current assets | $ 40,000 | Current liabilities | $ 10,000 |
| Fixed assets (net) | 120,000 | Stockholders' equity: | |
| | | Capital stock | 100,000 |
| | | Retained earnings | 50,000 |
| | $160,000 | | $160,000 |

**Basic Procedure.** The basic procedure is the same as in the two preceding illustrations—that is, eliminate the reciprocal elements and consolidate the non-reciprocal elements. However, since there is no element in the investment account reciprocal to the $10,000 excess of book value acquired over cost, the $10,000 cannot be eliminated and therefore must be extended to the consolidated statement. The *work sheet* entry for the elimination is the same as in the preceding illustrations, that is:

| | | |
|---|---|---|
| Capital stock (Company B's) | $100,000 | |
| Retained earnings (Company B's) | 50,000 | |
|     Investment in B (Company A's account) | | $150,000 |
| (to eliminate Company B's stockholders' equity against the investment account) | | |

COMPANY A AND SUBSIDIARY COMPANY B
CONSOLIDATED
WORKING PAPERS
STATEMENT OF FINANCIAL POSITION
JANUARY 1, 1980

| | Company A | Company B | Eliminations Debit | Eliminations Credit | Consolidated Financial Position |
|---|---|---|---|---|---|
| *Assets* | | | | | |
| Current assets | $ 90,000 | $ 40,000 | | | $130,000 |
| Investment in B | 140,000 | | | $150,000 | (10,000)G* |
| Fixed assets (net) | 400,000 | 120,000 | | | 520,000 |
| | $630,000 | $160,000 | | | $640,000 |
| *Equities* | | | | | |
| Current liabilities | $ 20,000 | $ 10,000 | | | $ 30,000 |
| Fixed liabilities | 100,000 | | | | 100,000 |
| Stockholders' equity: | | | | | |
|   Capital stock | 400,000 | 100,000 | $100,000 | | 400,000 |
|   Retained earnings | 110,000 | 50,000 | 50,000 | | 110,000RE |
| | $630,000 | $160,000 | $150,000 | $150,000 | $640,000 |

*The excess of book value acquired over cost.

In statement form the last column of the working papers would be presented as follows:

COMPANY A AND SUBSIDIARY COMPANY B
CONSOLIDATED STATEMENT OF FINANCIAL POSITION
JANUARY 1, 1980

| | | | |
|---|---|---|---|
| Current assets | $130,000 | Current liabilities | $ 30,000 |
| Fixed assets (net) | 520,000 | Fixed liabilities | 100,000 |

|  |  |  |
|---|---|---|
|  | Excess of subsidiary book value over cost | 10,000 |
|  | Stockholders' equity: |  |
|  | Capital stock | 400,000 |
|  | Retained earnings | 110,000 |
| $650,000 |  | $650,000 |

## Consolidated Goodwill

Consolidated goodwill consists of (a) the goodwill already appearing on the books of the constituent companies plus (b) any goodwill not recorded on the books of the constituent companies but which arises when consolidating because the parent company paid more than book value for an interest in a subsidiary, and minus (c) any negative goodwill resulting when consolidating because the parent company paid less than book value for its interest in a subsidiary. If the negative goodwill exceeds the positive goodwill, the excess is considered as a deferred credit to income.

**Less Than 100% Ownership.** When a parent company acquires less than 100% ownership in a subsidiary, it shares the ownership with the other stockholders whose stock it does not acquire. These outside stockholders (outside in the sense that they are not in the consolidated group) are usually referred to as the minority interest. Since the minority interest has a proportionate equity along with the majority interest (the parent company's interest) in the subsidiary, the subsidiary's stockholders' equity is composed essentially of two elements, namely, (1) the parent company's, and (2) the minority interest's.

When consolidating, the parent company's element of the subsidiary's stockholders' equity is eliminated and the minority interest's element thereof is consolidated. As in the case of 100% ownership, three distinct situations may arise when less than 100% ownership exists. They are:

1. Less than 100% ownership acquired at book value.
2. Less than 100% ownership acquired at more than book value.
3. Less than 100% ownership acquired at less than book value.

**Illustration B-1:** *Less than 100% Ownership Acquired at Book Value.* Assume that as of January 1, 1980, Company A acquires a 90% ownership in Company B for $135,000, which is also the book value of the equity acquired. The following individual statements reflect the financial position of the respective companies as of the date of acquisition, and the consolidated statement shows how they would appear when consolidated:

COMPANY A
STATEMENT OF FINANCIAL POSITION
JANUARY 1, 1980

| Current assets | $ 95,000 | Current liabilities | $ 20,000 |
|---|---|---|---|
| Investment in Company B | 135,000 | Fixed liabilities | 100,000 |

| | | |
|---|---:|---:|
| Fixed assets (net) | 400,000 | |
| Stockholders' equity: | | |
| Capital stock | | 400,000 |
| Retained earnings | | 110,000 |
| | $630,000 | $630,000 |

COMPANY B
STATEMENT OF FINANCIAL POSITION
JANUARY 1, 1980

| | | | |
|---|---:|---|---:|
| Current assets | $ 40,000 | Current liabilities | $ 10,000 |
| Fixed assets (net) | 120,000 | Stockholders' equity: | |
| | | Capital stock | 100,000 |
| | | Retained earnings | 50,000 |
| | $160,000 | | $160,000 |

COMPANY A AND SUBSIDIARY COMPANY B
CONSOLIDATED WORKING PAPERS
STATEMENT OF FINANCIAL POSITION

JANUARY 1, 1980

| | Company A | Company B | Eliminations Debit | Eliminations Credit | Consolidated Financial Position |
|---|---:|---:|---:|---:|---:|
| *Assets* | | | | | |
| Current assets | $ 95,000 | $ 40,000 | | | $135,000 |
| Investment in B | 135,000 | | | $135,000 | |
| Fixed assets (net) | 400,000 | 120,000 | | | 520,000 |
| | $630,000 | $160,000 | | | $655,000 |
| *Equities* | | | | | |
| Current liabilities | $ 20,000 | $ 10,000 | | | $ 30,000 |
| Fixed liabilities | 100,000 | | | | 100,000 |
| Stockholders' equity: | | | | | |
| Capital stock: | | | | | |
| Company A | 400,000 | | | | 400,000 |
| Company B | | 100,000 | $ 90,000 | | 10,000MI* |
| Retained earnings: | | | | | |
| Company A | 110,000 | | | | 110,000RE |
| Company B | | 50,000 | 45,000 | | 5,000MI* |
| | $630,000 | $160,000 | $135,000 | $135,000 | $655,000 |

*These two elements represent the 10% interest of the outsiders in Company B. Since Company B has a stockholders' equity of $150,000, the minority interest's claim against it is $15,000 (10% of $150,000) which is composed of two elements; $5,000 equity in retained earnings and $10,000 equity in capital stock.

**Basic Procedure.** Again the basic procedure involved is the same as in the previous illustrations: (1) eliminate reciprocals, and (2) consolidate nonreciprocals. In this instance the only reciprocal element is the parent company's claim against the stockholders' equity of the subsidiary, which is represented by the investment account on the parent's statement. The *work sheet* entry for the elimination expressed in journal form is:

| | | |
|---|---|---|
| Capital stock (90% of Company B's) | $90,000 | |
| Retained earnings (90% of Company B's) | 45,000 | |
| Investment in B (Company A's account) | | $135,000 |
| (to eliminate 90% of Company B's stockholders' equity against the investment account) | | |

The nonreciprocal elements are consolidated by extending them to the consolidated statement. Note the extension of the nonreciprocal element of Company B's capital stock and retained earnings as minority interest. In statement form the consolidated statement of financial position would appear as follows:

COMPANY A AND SUBSIDIARY COMPANY B
CONSOLIDATED STATEMENT OF FINANCIAL POSITION
JANUARY 1, 1980

| | | | |
|---|---|---|---|
| Current assets | $135,000 | Current liabilities | $ 30,000 |
| Fixed assets (net) | 520,000 | Fixed liabilities | 100,000 |
| | | Minority interest | 15,000 |
| | | Stockholders' equity: | |
| | | Capital stock | 400,000 |
| | | Retained earnings | 110,000 |
| | $655,000 | | $655,000 |

**Statement Presentation of Minority Interest.** Minority interest is usually presented either in or just above the parent company's stockholders' equity section on the consolidated statement of financial position. Current practice tends to present it just above the stockholders' equity section. In published statements it is frequently shown as one amount. The Securities and Exchange Commission, however, requires it to be detailed in reports to them: a separation is made between the minority interest in the capital stock and in the surplus elements of the subsidiary.

**Reconciliation of Illustrations B-1 and A-1.** Since, before consolidating, total assets and total equities of Company A and Company B are exactly the same in Illustrations B-1 and A-1, it might seem that when consolidated the total assets and equities on the consolidated statements should be the same. However, this is not the case. In Illustration B-1 the assets and equities total $655,000, respectively, whereas in Illustration A-1 they total $640,000, respectively. The $15,000 difference in total assets is due, of course, to the fact that Company A uses only

$135,000 of its assets to acquire a 90% interest instead of using $150,000 to acquire a 100% interest. The difference of $15,000 remains a part of the current assets of Company A and is included in the consolidated statement. The $15,000 difference in total equities represents the claim of the minority stockholders in the stockholders' equity of Company B. Since this is an outside claim against the consolidated group, it must be reflected on the consolidated statement.

**Illustration B-2:** *Less Than 100% Ownership Acquired at More Than Book Value.* As in the case of 100% ownership, a parent company may pay more than book value when it acquires less than 100% ownership in a subsidiary.

Assume the same facts as in Illustration B-1, except that Company A acquires a 90% interest in Company B for $155,000. Since the book value acquired by Company A is only $135,000 (90% of $150,000) there is an excess payment of $20,000 for goodwill. The consolidating procedure is illustrated as follows:

COMPANY A
STATEMENT OF FINANCIAL POSITION
JANUARY 1, 1980

| | | | |
|---|---|---|---|
| Current assets | $ 75,000 | Current liabilities | $ 20,000 |
| Investment in Company B | 155,000 | Fixed liabilities | 100,000 |
| Fixed assets (net) | 400,000 | Stockholders' equity: | |
| | | Capital stock | 400,000 |
| | | Retained earnings | 110,000 |
| | $630,000 | | $630,000 |

COMPANY B
STATEMENT OF FINANCIAL POSITION
JANUARY 1, 1980

| | | | |
|---|---|---|---|
| Current assets | $ 40,000 | Current liabilities | $ 10,000 |
| Fixed assets (net) | 120,000 | Stockholders' equity: | |
| | | Capital stock | 100,000 |
| | | Retained earnings | 50,000 |
| | $160,000 | | $160,000 |

COMPANY A AND SUBSIDIARY COMPANY B
CONSOLIDATED WORKING PAPERS
STATEMENT OF FINANCIAL POSITION
JANUARY 1, 1980

| | Company A | Company B | Eliminations Debit | Eliminations Credit | Consolidated Financial Position |
|---|---|---|---|---|---|
| *Assets* | | | | | |
| Current assets | $ 75,000 | $ 40,000 | | | $115,000 |
| Investment in B | 155,000 | | | $135,000 | 20,000G |
| Fixed assets (net) | 400,000 | 120,000 | | | 520,000 |
| | $630,000 | $160,000 | | | $655,000 |

## Equities

|  | | | | | |
|---|---|---|---|---|---|
| Current liabilities | $ 20,000 | $ 10,000 | | | $ 30,000 |
| Fixed liabilities | 100,000 | | | | 100,000 |
| Stockholders' equity: | | | | | |
| Capital stock: | | | | | |
| Company A | $400,000 | | | | 400,000 |
| Company B | | 100,000 | $ 90,000 | | 10,000MI |
| Retained earnings: | | | | | |
| Company A | 110,000 | | | | 110,000RE |
| Company B | | 50,000 | 45,000 | | 5,000MI |
| | $630,000 | $160,000 | $135,000 | $135,000 | $655,000 |

**Basic Procedure.** Again the basic procedure is the same: (1) eliminate reciprocals and (2) consolidate nonreciprocals. In this instance, the only elimination necessary is the parent's claim in the stockholders' equity of the subsidiary against the investment account. The *work sheet* entry is the same as in Illustration B-1:

| | | |
|---|---|---|
| Capital stock (90% of Company B's) | $90,000 | |
| Retained earnings (90% of Company B's) | 45,000 | |
| Investment in B (Company A's account) | | $135,000 |
| (to eliminate 90% of Company B's stockholders' equity against the investment account) | | |

The nonreciprocal elements are consolidated by adding them where necessary and extending them to the consolidated statement as in the previous illustrations. In statement form the consolidated statement would appear as follows:

COMPANY A AND SUBSIDIARY COMPANY B
CONSOLIDATED STATEMENT OF FINANCIAL POSITION
JANUARY 1, 1980

| | | | |
|---|---|---|---|
| Current assets | $115,000 | Current liabilites | $ 30,000 |
| Fixed assets (net) | 520,000 | Fixed liabilities | 100,000 |
| Goodwill | 20,000 | Minority interest | 15,000 |
| | | Stockholders' equity: | |
| | | Capital stock | 400,000 |
| | | Retained earnings | 110,000 |
| | $655,000 | | $655,000 |

**Reconciliation of Illustrations B-2 and A-2.** In Illustration B-2 the assets and equities after being consolidated total $655,000, respectively, whereas in Illustration A-2 they total $640,000, although the individual statements have exactly the same totals before consolidating and the same amount of goodwill is involved. The $15,000 difference in total assets arises from the fact that Company A pays $155,000 for a 90% interest in B instead of $170,000 for a 100% interest therein. The $15,000 difference in total equities represents the claim of the minority interest in the stockholders' equity of Company B (10% of $150,000).

**Illustration B-3:** *Less Than 100% Ownership Acquired at Less Than Book Value.* As in the case of 100% ownership, a parent company may pay less than book value when it acquires less than 100% ownership. Assume the same facts as in Illustration B-1, except that Company A acquires a 90% interest in Company B for $125,000. Since the book value acquired by Company A is $135,000 (90% of $150,000), an excess of book value over cost of $10,000 is indicated.

COMPANY A
STATEMENT OF FINANCIAL POSITION
JANUARY 1, 1980

| | | | |
|---|---|---|---|
| Current assets | $105,000 | Current liabilities | $ 20,000 |
| Investment in Company B | 125,000 | Fixed liabilities | 100,000 |
| Fixed assets (net) | 400,000 | Stockholders' equity: | |
| | | Capital stock | 400,000 |
| | | Retained earnings | 110,000 |
| | $630,000 | | $630,000 |

COMPANY B
STATEMENT OF FINANCIAL POSITION
JANUARY 1, 1980

| | | | |
|---|---|---|---|
| Current assets | $40,000 | Current liabilities | $10,000 |
| Fixed assets (net) | 120,000 | Stockholders' equity: | |
| | | Capital stock | 100,000 |
| | | Retained earnings | 50,000 |
| | $160,000 | | $160,000 |

COMPANY A AND SUBSIDIARY COMPANY B
CONSOLIDATED WORKING PAPERS
STATEMENT OF FINANCIAL POSITION
JANUARY 1, 1980

| | Company A | Company B | Eliminations Debit | Eliminations Credit | Consolidated Financial Position |
|---|---|---|---|---|---|
| *Assets* | | | | | |
| Current assets | $105,000 | $ 40,000 | | | $145,000 |
| Investment in B | 125,000 | | | $135,000 | (10,000)G |
| Fixed assets (net) | 400,000 | 120,000 | | | 520,000 |
| | $630,000 | $160,000 | | | $655,000 |
| *Equities* | | | | | |
| Current liabilities | $ 20,000 | $ 10,000 | | | $ 30,000 |
| Fixed liabilities | 100,000 | | | | 100,000 |
| Stockholders' equity: | | | | | |
| Capital stock: | | | | | |
| Company A | 400,000 | | | | 400,000 |

# 10 / Consolidated Statements at Date of Acquisition

| | | | | | | |
|---|---|---|---|---|---|---|
| Company B | | 100,000 | $ 90,000 | | | 10,000MI |
| Retained earnings: | | | | | | |
| Company A | 110,000 | | | | | 110,000RE |
| Company B | | 50,000 | 45,000 | | | 5,000MI |
| | $630,000 | $160,000 | $135,000 | $135,000 | | $655,000 |

**Basic Procedure.** The basic procedure is still essentially the same: eliminate the parent company's claim in the subsidiary's stockholders' equity against the investment account, and consolidate nonreciprocals. The *work sheet* entry for the elimination remains exactly the same as in Illustrations B-1 and B-2:

| | | |
|---|---|---|
| Capital stock (90% of Company B's) | $90,000 | |
| Retained earnings (90% of Company B's) | 45,000 | |
| Investment in B (Company A's account) | | $135,000 |
| (to eliminate 90% of Company B's stockholders' equity against the investment account) | | |

In statement form the consolidated statement of financial position would appear as follows:

COMPANY A AND SUBSIDIARY COMPANY B
CONSOLIDATED STATEMENT OF FINANCIAL POSITION
JANUARY 1, 1980

| | | | |
|---|---|---|---|
| Current assets | $145,000 | Current liabilities | $ 30,000 |
| Fixed assets (net) | 520,000 | Fixed liabilities | 100,000 |
| | | Excess of subsidiary book value over cost | 10,000 |
| | | Minority interest | 15,000 |
| | | Stockholders' equity: | |
| | | Capital stock | 400,000 |
| | | Retained earnings | 110,000 |
| | $665,000 | | $665,000 |

**Reconciliation of Illustrations B-3 and A-3.** In Illustration B-3 the assets and equities total $665,000, respectively, on the consolidated statement, whereas in Illustration A-3 they total $650,000, although the individual statements have exactly the same totals before consolidating and the same amount of negative goodwill is involved. The $15,000 difference in total assets arises from the fact that Company A pays $125,000 for 90% interest in B instead of $140,000 for 100% interest. The $15,000 difference in total equities represents the minority interest's claim against the stockholders' equity of Company B (10% of $150,000), and since all outside equities are reflected on the consolidated statement, this claim must be presented.

## Miscellaneous Intercompany Items

As indicated earlier, intercompany pairs of accounts, reciprocal in nature, must be eliminated in order to avoid double counting from the point of view of the affiliated group as an entity. Among the types of intercompany accounts falling into this category are receivable-payable accounts, such as accounts receivable and accounts payable, notes receivable and notes payable, and dividends receivable and dividends payable.

In the preparation of a consolidated statement of financial position, intercompany receivables and payables are eliminated by work sheet entries that debit the payables and credit the receivables. The effect of such elimination is to restrict consolidated receivables and payables to those resulting from transactions with parties outside the affiliated group. The work sheet entries may be illustrated by using a partial work sheet and assuming that Company A (parent) and Company B (90% owned subsidiary) are being consolidated and that (*a*) Company A owes Company B $5,000 on open account, (*b*) Company A holds Company B's note for $10,000, and (*c*) Company B has declared but not paid a $20,000 dividend.

COMPANY A AND SUBSIDIARY COMPANY B
CONSOLIDATED WORKING PAPERS
STATEMENT OF FINANCIAL POSITION
JANUARY 1, 1980

|  | Company A | Company B | Eliminations Debit | Eliminations Credit | Consolidated Financial Position |
|---|---|---|---|---|---|
| *Assets* | | | | | |
| Accounts receivable |  | $ 6,000 |  | $ 5,000A | $ 1,000 |
| Notes receivable | $ 10,000 |  |  | 10,000B |  |
| Dividends | 18,000 |  |  | 18,000C |  |
| *Equities* | | | | | |
| Accounts payable | $ 7,000 |  | $ 5,000A |  | $ 2,000 |
| Notes payable |  | $ 10,000 | 10,000B |  |  |
| Dividends payable |  | 20,000 | 18,000C |  | 2,000 |

It should be noted that when only a portion of the intercompany account is reciprocal, only that portion is eliminated and the nonreciprocal element is consolidated. For example, in Entry (C), since Company A has only a 90% interest in Company B, only 90% or $18,000 of B's Dividends Payable account is eliminated. The other 10% or $2,000 is not eliminated.

## Consolidated Statements of Retained Earnings at Acquisition Date

Unconsolidated retained earnings statements provide supporting detail for two successive unconsolidated statements of financial position. Likewise, consolidated retained earnings statements provide supporting detail for two successive consolidated statements of financial position. For example, a consolidated statement of retained earnings provides an analysis of the changes in consolidated retained earnings in a given fiscal period. Since at the date of acquisition the consolidated entity has had no period of operations, consolidated retained earnings is identical with the parent company's retained earnings. This is due to the elimination of the parent's share of the subsidiary's retained earnings, and the inclusion of the minority interest's share in the consolidated statement of financial position as minority interest.

To illustrate, assume the same conditions as given in Illustration A-1. Also assume that the following retained earnings statements were prepared as of the date of acquisition.

|  | COMPANY A STATEMENT OF RETAINED EARNINGS JANUARY 1, 1980 | COMPANY B STATEMENT OF RETAINED EARNINGS JANUARY 1, 1980 |
|---|---|---|
| Retained earnings 1/1/79 | $100,000 | $44,000 |
| Net income (1979) | 10,000 | 6,000 |
| Retained earnings 1/1/80 | $110,000 | $50,000 |

Since 100% of Company B's retained earnings is eliminated, the consolidated retained earnings is composed entirely of Company A's retained earnings of $110,000.

Assume the same basic situation as in Illustration B-1 which, in essence, is that Company A acquires 90% ownership in Company B at book value. Also assume that the retained earnings statements prepared were the same as those used in the preceding illustration. Ninety percent of the subsidiary's retained earnings is eliminated, as follows:

| | | |
|---|---|---|
| Capital stock (90% of Company B's) | $90,000 | |
| Retained earnings (90% of Company B's) | 45,000 | |
| Investment in B (Company A's account) | | $135,000 |
| (to eliminate 90% of Company B's stockholders' equity against the investment account) | | |

Although only $45,000 is eliminated from the subsidiary's retained earnings, it will be recalled that the other $5,000 is consolidated as minority interest (see page 282). Consequently, the consolidated retained earnings is the same as the parent company's retained earnings of $110,000.

## Accounting for the Difference between Cost and Book Value of Subsidiary Stock Acquired

Accounting for the difference between the cost of the investment in a subsidiary and the book value of the stock acquired is somewhat more involved than that suggested in the preceding demonstrations of the consolidating procedures.

Proponents of the cost theory of asset valuation maintain that the proper cost of assets is their cost to the consolidated entity. This view, which generally conforms to current practice, provides for the following treatment of the difference between cost of the investment and the book value of the assets acquired:

*If cost exceeds book value:*

1. Assign the excess to specifically identifiable tangible assets for which it is evident that a price in excess of their book value was paid.
2. Recognize as assets those specifically identifiable intangible assets for which it is evident a price was paid.
3. Recognize any difference not accounted for by either (1) or (2) as the "Excess of Cost Over Subsidiary Book Value." According to APB *Opinion 17,* the amount so recognized should be amortized by systematic charges to income over the period benefited. *Opinion No. 17* further states that the amortization period should not exceed 40 years.

If the difference is assigned to depreciable or amortizable assets in the allocation process, expenses of the consolidated entity will include appropriate depreciation or amortization of the allocated difference.

*If book value exceeds cost:*

1. Assign the difference to specifically identifiable tangible assets for which it is evident that the price paid was below their book value.
2. Assign the difference to specifically identifiable intangible assets for which it is evident that the price paid was below their book value.
3. Any difference not accounted for in (1) or (2) should be allocated proportionally against the remaining balances of the noncurrent assets (except long-term investments in marketable securities).
4. Recognize any difference not accounted for in either (1), (2), or (3) as negative goodwill in an account properly entitled "Excess of Subsidiary Book Value Over Cost." As indicated in *Opinion No. 16,* negative goodwill should not be recognized unless the noncurrent assets (other than long-term investments in marketable securities) are reduced to zero value. According to *Opinion No. 17,* the amount so recognized should be taken into income in future periods on a reasonable and systematic basis.

Because amortization policies vary widely in practice, unless specifically stipulated otherwise, 10-year, straight-line amortization is assumed in this text for the amortization of both an excess of cost over book value and an excess of book value over cost. Likewise, as was indicated earlier, if specific information is not given regarding the assignment of a difference between cost and book value, for *textbook purposes* we shall consider the entire difference to be either "positive" or "negative" goodwill.

The amortization of the difference between the cost and the book value of subsidiary stock acquired is ordinarily handled in the accounts in one of two ways. It is either (1) set up in a separate account with the periodic amortizations reflected therein, or (2) left in the investment account with the periodic amortizations reflected therein. To illustrate, assume that $20,000 of positive goodwill is being amortized on a straight-line basis over 10 years.

(1)

| | | |
|---|---|---|
| Amortization expense | $2,000 | |
| Goodwill | | $2,000 |

(2)

| | | |
|---|---|---|
| Amortization expense | 2,000 | |
| Investment in Company B | | 2,000 |

Either approach is acceptable, but for purposes of simplicity the latter generally will be used in this textbook.

## PROBLEMS

### Problem 10-1

From the following data prepare a consolidated statement of financial position at the date of acquisition of 80% of the subsidiary's stock, showing the amount of goodwill and the minority interest:

At the date of acquisition the subsidiary's stockholders' equity was composed of $100,000 capital stock and $40,000 retained earnings. The parent company paid $130,000 for its investment in the subsidiary. The capital stock of the parent was $1,000,000; retained earnings, $200,000; and total net assets (including the investment in the subsidiary), $1,200,000.

### Problem 10-2

Determine the amount of goodwill in each of the following cases:

| | Cost of Investment | Percent of Ownership | Subsidiary's Stockholders' Equity* Retained Earnings | Capital Stock |
|---|---|---|---|---|
| Case 1 | $120,000 | 100% | $20,000 | $100,000 |
| Case 2 | 140,000 | 100% | 30,000 | 100,000 |
| Case 3 | 132,000 | 100% | 40,000 | 100,000 |
| Case 4 | 135,000 | 90% | 50,000 | 150,000 |
| Case 5 | 195,000 | 90% | 60,000 | 150,000 |
| Case 6 | 195,000 | 90% | 70,000 | 150,000 |

*At date of acquisition.

### Problem 10-3

In each of the following cases the data were compiled at the date of acquisition. In each situation determine:

(1) The amount of goodwill involved in the acquisition.
(2) The amount of minority interest at the date of acquisition.

|  | Cost of Investment | Percent of Ownership | Subsidiary's Stockholders' Equity Retained Earnings | Capital Stock |
|---|---|---|---|---|
| Case 1 | $230,000 | 100% | $35,000 | $200,000 |
| Case 2 | 240,000 | 100% | 40,000 | 200,000 |
| Case 3 | 190,000 | 100% | (18,000)* | 200,000 |
| Case 4 | 276,000 | 80% | 40,000 | 300,000 |
| Case 5 | 288,000 | 80% | 60,000 | 300,000 |
| Case 6 | 240,000 | 80% | (10,000)* | 300,000 |

*Deficit.

## Problem 10-4

Consolidate the following statements of financial position of Companies A and B, assuming that:

1. Company A purchases all of the stock of Company B for $100,000 cash.
2. Company A purchases all of the stock of Company B for $108,000 cash.
3. Company A purchases 90% of the stock of Company B for $100,000 cash.
4. Company A purchases 80% of the stock of Company B for $75,000, paying $25,000 cash and giving a note for the balance.

STATEMENT OF FINANCIAL POSITION
DECEMBER 31, 1980

| Assets | Co. A | Co. B | Equities | Co. A | Co. B |
|---|---|---|---|---|---|
| Current assets | $350,000 | $ 20,000 | Current liabilities | $ 50,000 | $ 10,000 |
| Fixed assets (net) | 400,000 | 90,000 | Fixed liabilities | 100,000 | |
|  |  |  | Stockholders' equity: | | |
|  |  |  | Capital stock | 500,000 | 80,000 |
|  |  |  | Retained earnings | 100,000 | 20,000 |
|  | $750,000 | $110,000 |  | $750,000 | $110,000 |

## Problem 10-5

Prepare a consolidated statement of financial position for A Company and its subsidiaries, B Company and C Company. The following condensed statements show the financial position of the three companies as of September 30, 1980, the date A Company acquired its interests in the subsidiaries.

## 10 / Consolidated Statements at Date of Acquisition

### A Company

| | | | |
|---|---|---|---|
| Assets | $249,000 | Liabilities | $150,000 |
| Stock of B (par) | 60,000 | Capital stock | 225,000 |
| Stock of C (par) | 81,000 | Retained earnings | 15,000 |
| | $390,000 | | $390,000 |

### B Company

| | | | |
|---|---|---|---|
| Assets | $175,000 | Liabilities | $ 80,000 |
| | | Capital stock | 75,000 |
| | | Retained earnings | 20,000 |
| | $175,000 | | $175,000 |

### C Company

| | | | |
|---|---|---|---|
| Assets | $100,000 | Liabilities | $ 20,000 |
| Deficit | 10,000 | Capital stock | 90,000 |
| | $110,000 | | $110,000 |

## Problem 10-6

On December 31, 1980, A Company purchased 90% of B Company for $280,000, 80% of C Company for $284,000, and 75% of D Company for $60,000. The statements of financial position of the various companies immediately following the acquisitions were:

| Assets | A Company | B Company | C Company | D Company |
|---|---|---|---|---|
| Cash | $1,256,000 | $ 50,000 | $ 20,000 | $ 25,000 |
| Accounts receivable (net) | 300,000 | 10,000 | 4,000 | 8,000 |
| Inventories | 900,000 | 125,000 | 70,000 | 150,000 |
| Land | 1,000,000 | 20,000 | 30,000 | 25,000 |
| Buildings (net) | 2,000,000 | 300,000 | 400,000 | 100,000 |
| Investment in B Company | 280,000 | | | |
| Investment in C Company | 284,000 | | | |
| Investment in D Company | 60,000 | | | |
| | $6,080,000 | $505,000 | $524,000 | $308,000 |
| *Equities* | | | | |
| Accounts payable | $ 200,000 | $ 30,000 | $ 20,000 | $ 20,000 |
| Notes payable | 180,000 | 70,000 | 50,000 | 200,000 |
| Bonds payable | 100,000 | 100,000 | 100,000 | |
| Capital stock | 5,000,000 | 200,000 | 250,000 | 100,000 |
| Retained earnings (deficit) | 600,000 | 105,000 | 104,000 | (12,000) |
| | $6,080,000 | $505,000 | $524,000 | $308,000 |

Prepare a consolidated statement of financial position as of the date of acquisition.

## Problem 10-7

Using the following data taken from the records of Companies A, B, and C on March 1, 1980, the date Company A acquired its investment in B and C, prepare a consolidated statement of financial position.

| Assets | A Company | B Company | C Company |
|---|---|---|---|
| Current assets | $ 770,000 | $440,000 | $490,000 |
| Investments: | | | |
|   4,200 shares of B stock | 550,000 | | |
|   5,520 shares of C stock | 700,000 | | |
| Fixed assets (net) | 1,780,000 | 400,000 | 460,000 |
| | $3,800,000 | $840,000 | $950,000 |
| *Equities* | | | |
| Current liabilities | $ 600,000 | $120,000 | $ 80,000 |
| Fixed liabilities | 200,000 | 80,000 | 120,000 |
| Capital stock (par $100) | 2,500,000 | 500,000 | 600,000 |
| Capital in excess of par | 100,000 | 40,000 | 60,000 |
| Retained earnings | 400,000 | 100,000 | 90,000 |
| | $3,800,000 | $840,000 | $950,000 |

## Problem 10-8

When a business is purchased as an entity, the price paid often differs from the equity shown by the records of the vendor.

Explain fully why the sale value of a going business may differ from the book value even where acceptable accounting practices have been followed in keeping the accounts of the business.    (AICPA adapted)

## Problem 10-9

What is "negative goodwill"? Explain the conditions under which it is found and its treatment on the financial statements, indicating at least two methods of presentation, and the circumstances under which each would be appropriate.

(AICPA adapted)

## Problem 10-10

On December 31, 1980, P Company acquired all of the capital stock of S-1, and 95% of the capital stock of S-2. Immediately after the acquisitions the statements of financial position appeared as follows:

| Assets | P Company | S-1 | S-2 |
|---|---|---|---|
| Cash | $ 180,000 | $ 25,000 | $ 20,000 |
| Accounts receivable | 95,000 | 45,000 | 40,000 |
| Notes receivable | 30,000 | 20,000 | 10,000 |

|  | | | |
|---|---:|---:|---:|
| Inventories | 100,000 | 30,000 | 50,000 |
| Investment in S-1 | 140,000 | | |
| Investment in S-2 | 160,000 | | |
| Land | 80,000 | 30,000 | 40,000 |
| Buildings (net) | 200,000 | 130,000 | 120,000 |
| Goodwill | 30,000 | | |
| | $1,015,000 | $280,000 | $280,000 |

| Equities | P Company | S-1 | S-2 |
|---|---:|---:|---:|
| Accounts payable | $ 120,000 | $ 38,000 | $ 80,000 |
| Notes payable | 20,000 | 90,000 | 40,000 |
| Bonds payable | 100,000 | | |
| Capital stock | 500,000 | 100,000 | 100,000 |
| Capital in excess of par | 115,000 | 62,000 | |
| Retained earnings (deficit) | 160,000 | (10,000) | 60,000 |
| | $1,015,000 | $280,000 | $280,000 |

Intercompany relationships:

S-1 owed S-2 $5,000 on an open account.
S-2 owed P Company $4,000 on open account.
P Company owed S-1 $7,000 on open account.
S-2 held S-1's note for $10,000.

Prepare a consolidated statement of financial position.

## Problem 10-11

At December 31, 1980, the balance sheet of Company A was as follows:

| | | | |
|---|---:|---|---:|
| Cash | $ 50,000 | Payables | $1,750,000 |
| Receivables, less reserves | 300,000 | Accruals | 450,000 |
| Inventories | 1,600,000 | Common stock, 10,000 | |
| Prepayments | 47,000 | shares | 1,000,000 |
| Fixed assets (net) | 2,003,000 | Retained earnings | 800,000 |
| | $4,000,000 | | $4,000,000 |

An appraisal as of that date, which was carefully considered and approved by the boards of directors of Company A and Company B, placed a total replacement value, less sustained depreciation, of $3,203,000 on the fixed assets of Company A.

Company B's condensed balance sheet at December 31, 1980 showed:

| | | | |
|---|---:|---|---:|
| Cash and investments | $ 7,000,000 | Payables | $ 7,872,000 |
| (including stock of A) | | | |
| Receivables, less reserves | 2,400,000 | Accruals | 1,615,000 |
| Inventories | 11,200,000 | Common stock, 100,000 | |
| Prepayments | 422,000 | shares | 10,000,000 |
| Fixed assets, less reserves | 18,978,000 | Retained earnings | 20,513,000 |
| | $40,000,000 | | $40,000,000 |

Company B offered to purchase all the assets of Company A, subject to its liabilities, as of December 31, 1980, for $3,000,000. However, 40% of the stockholders of Company A objected to the price on the grounds that it did not include any consideration for goodwill, which they believed to be worth at least $500,000. A counter-proposal was made, and final agreement was reached on the basis that Company B acquired 60% of the common stock of Company A at a price of $300 a share.

Prepare a consolidating statement as at December 31, 1980, of the two companies.

(AICPA adapted)

## Problem 10-12

You are engaged to audit the Apex Company and its subsidiary, Apex Sales Co., as of December 31, 1980. During the course of the audit you discover that the balances of the intercompany accounts do not agree.

The Apex Company manufactures fountain pens which it sells to its subsidiary at cost plus 20%. The subsidiary then sells the fountain pens to jewelry stores.

Shown below is a copy of the intercompany account ledger sheets.

Discussion with company employees developed the following explanation of references found on the ledger accounts:

SR—Sales register and invoice number.
CR—Cash receipts book.
CD—Cash disbursements book.
VR—Voucher register, receiving report number, and Apex Company invoice number.
RG—Returned goods register and debit memo number.

A review of the inventory observation working papers discloses the following information:

*Observation at Apex Sales Co. on December 31, 1980:*

1. Last shipment prior to the physical inventory was billed on invoice No. 17882 dated December 31, 1980.
2. No returned merchandise was received from the Apex Sales Co. during the month of December 1980.
3. The last receiving report used in December 1980 was No. 59742 dated December 30, 1980.

*Observation at Apex Sales Co. on December 31, 1980:*

1. Last shipment prior to the physical inventory was billed on invoice No. 77843 dated December 31, 1980.

10 / *Consolidated Statements at Date of Acquisition*

2. The last shipment of merchandise returned to the Apex Company in December 1980 was entered on debit memo No. 74 dated December 31, 1980.
3. The last receiving report *used* in December 1980 was No. 34337 dated December 31, 1980 for merchandise billed on Apex invoice 17879.

You are to prepare in good form:

(1) A reconciliation of the intercompany accounts.
(2) The journal entries required by each company to:
   (*a*) Adjust the intercompany accounts.
   (*b*) Adjust the inventories that are based on physical inventories taken December 31, 1980 valued by each of the two companies at its cost.

ACCOUNT IN THE APEX COMPANY GENERAL LEDGER
INTERCOMPANY ACCOUNT — APEX SALES CO.

| Date | Reference | Amount | Date | Reference | Amount |
|---|---|---|---|---|---|
| Total Forwarded | | $178,683.00 | Total Forwarded | | $123,867.00 |
| Dec. 26 | SR 17877 | 1,950.00 | Dec. 26 | CR | 3,567.00 |
| 27 | SR 17878 | 1,194.00 | 29 | CR | 31,127.00 |
| 28 | SR 17879 | 2,183.00 | 31 | Balance | 28,189.00 |
| 29 | SR 17880 | 849.00 | | | |
| 31 | SR 17882 | 1,891.00 | | | |
| | | $186,750.00 | | | $186,750.00 |

ACCOUNT IN THE APEX SALES CO. GENERAL LEDGER
INTERCOMPANY ACCOUNT — APEX COMPANY

| Date | Reference | Amount | Date | Reference | Amount |
|---|---|---|---|---|---|
| Total Forwarded | | $127,434.00 | Total Forwarded | | $176,508.00 |
| Dec. 28 | CD | 31,127.00 | Dec. 26 | VR 34333 – 17876 | 2,175.00 |
| 31 | CD | 19,777.00 | 28 | VR 34334 – 17877 | 1,950.00 |
| 31 | RG 74 | 2,329.00 | 29 | VR 34335 – 17878 | 1,194.00 |
| 31 | Balance | 6,318.00 | 31 | VR 34336 – 17881 | 3,647.00 |
| | | | 31 | VR 34340 – 17883 | 1,511.00 |
| | | $186,985.00 | | | $186,985.00 |

(AICPA adapted)

## Problem 10-13

From the following information prepare a consolidated statement of financial position of Holding Co. and its wholly owned subsidiary as of July 31, 1980.

On June 30, 1980, A & Co. partnership (profits and losses shared equally), and X Corp. consummated a consolidation agreement pursuant to the terms of which Consolidated Co., newly organized and incorporated with an authorized capital of

20,000 shares of $100 par value common stock, acquired for its common stock issued in the amount of $950,000 to A & Co. and $550,000 to X Corp. certain net assets of the respective companies as follows:

A & Co.—All net assets (including buildings at an appraised sound value of $1,100,000), excluding notes payable.

X Corp.—All net assets, excluding buildings.

The statements of financial position of A & Co. and X Corp. as of June 30, 1980, before consolidation are condensed as follows:

| Assets | A & Co. | X Corp. |
|---|---|---|
| Cash | $ 25,000 | $ 125,000 |
| Accounts receivable | 165,000 | 500,000 |
| Inventory | 150,000 | 435,000 |
| Land | 50,000 | |
| Buildings (net) | 1,000,000 | 125,000 |
| Machinery (net) | 250,000 | 15,000 |
| Patents | 10,000 | |
| | $1,650,000 | $1,200,000 |

| Equities | | |
|---|---|---|
| Accounts payable | $ 300,000 | $ 500,000 |
| Notes payable | 100,000 | |
| Mortgage payable | 600,000 | |
| Capital accounts: | | |
| Partner A | 450,000 | |
| Partner B | 200,000 | |
| Capital stock | | 800,000 |
| Retained earnings (deficit) | | (100,000) |
| | $1,650,000 | $1,200,000 |

On July 1, 1980, A & Co. conveyed 1,000 shares of common stock of Consolidated Co. to the note holders in full settlement of their claims and immediately thereafter distributed the remaining shares of such common stock to the partners in dissolution. On the same date, after the consolidation, in order to provide Consolidated Co. with working capital, A alone (the recipient of his partnership share of Consolidated stock) contributed to Consolidated Co. 10% of the stock so received by him. Such contributed stock was sold by Consolidated Co. on July 25, 1980, for $105 per share.

During July 1980, as a result of operations, the net assets of Consolidated Co. increased by $25,000 represented by increase in cash. For purposes of this problem, assume other balance sheet accounts did not change during July.

On July 31, 1980, the stockholders of Consolidated Co. sold their interests to Holding Co. A statement of financial position of Holding Co. at July 31, 1980, after acquisition of 100% of the issued and outstanding stock of Consolidated Co. was as follows:

HOLDING CO.
STATEMENT OF FINANCIAL POSITION
JULY 31, 1980

| Assets | | Equities | |
|---|---|---|---|
| Investment in | | Capital stock | $2,000,000 |
|   Consolidated Co. | $1,600,000 | Retained earnings | 350,000 |
| Securities—other | 600,000 | | |
| Cash | 150,000 | | |
| | $2,350,000 | | $2,350,000 |

(AICPA adapted)

# 11

# Consolidated Statements Subsequent to Date of Acquisition — Investment Carried at Cost

The preparation of consolidated statements subsequent to the date of acquisition is essentially the same as at the date of acquisition, that is, (1) eliminate reciprocals, and (2) consolidate nonreciprocals. However, when consolidating subsequent to the date of acquisition, it is frequently necessary to establish reciprocity between the parent company's investment account and the subsidiary's stockholders' equity before reciprocals can be eliminated. The establishment of reciprocity in any given situation is dependent upon the parent company's method of carrying the investment account. Although the method used by the parent company will affect the unconsolidated statements and likewise the consolidating procedure, it will not affect the consolidated statements.

**Methods of Carrying Investments in Subsidiaries.** Although many variations exist, the investment account is carried either (1) at cost, or (2) at something other than cost. The cost method is illustrated in this chapter.

## COST METHOD

When the cost method is used, cost is recorded in the investment account at the time the investment is originally made and remains the basis of the account until it is either partially or completely disposed of or until some fundamental change in conditions makes it clearly apparent that the value originally assigned can no longer be justified. Under this method the parent's share of the increases and decreases in the subsidiary's stockholders' equity is not recognized in the accounting records.

The following entries, which would be recorded in the *parent company's books,* illustrate the accounting involved when the investment account is carried at cost:

(1) January 1, 1980, Company A purchases an 80% interest in Company B for $140,000

    Investment in Company B    $140,000
        Cash    $140,000

(2) December 31, 1980, Company B reports $40,000 net income for 1980.
    No entry made by parent.

(3) March 15, 1981, Company B pays $10,000 dividend.
    Cash    $8,000
        Dividend income    $8,000

(4) December 31, 1981, Company B reports $20,000 net loss for 1981.
    No entry made by parent.

If the subsidiary sustains a loss that appears to be permanent, it would be appropriate to adjust the investment account accordingly. Also, if the subsidiary pays a cash dividend out of earnings existing prior to the date the parent acquired the stock, the investment account should be adjusted. To continue the illustration above, assume that in 1982 Company B pays dividends of $20,000 and later in the year suffers an uninsured fire loss of $70,000. The entries on the *books of Company A* would be:

(1) Cash    $16,000
    Dividend income    $8,000
    Investment in Company B    8,000
    (to record 80% of cash dividend paid by B of which $8,000 was from retained earnings created prior to January 1, 1980, and not earned by Company A)

(2) Fire loss by Company B    $56,000
    Investment in Company B    $56,000
    (to recognize A's share of the permanent loss sustained by B as a result of a fire: 80% of $70,000)

## Consolidated Statement of Financial Position— Investment Carried at Cost

**Basic Consolidating Procedure.** As indicated earlier, the basic procedure when consolidating statements subsequent to acquisition is essentially the same as when consolidating at the date of acquisition, except that it may be necessary to establish reciprocity before it is possible to eliminate reciprocals. For example, if the parent company carries the investment account at cost, and if the stockholders' equity of the subsidiary has changed since acquisition, the investment account on the parent's statement and the parent's claim against the stockholders' equity of the subsidiary will not have the same relationship that existed at acquisition. Consequently, before eliminations can be properly made, reciprocity must be established. The basic consolidating procedure when consolidating subsequent to the date of acquisition, therefore, includes:

1. The establishment of reciprocity, if necessary.
2. The elimination of reciprocals.
3. The consolidation of nonreciprocals.

**Establishment of Reciprocity.** Reciprocity is established by a work sheet entry or entries which are frequently referred to as adjusting entries. When the investment account is carried at cost and the subsidiary's stockholders' equity has changed (either increased or decreased) since acquisition, reciprocity could conceivably be established by either (1) adjusting the subsidiary's stockholders' equity back to the date of acquisition, or (2) adjusting the investment account up to the date of consolidation. For example, assume that Company A acquired 100% ownership of Company B for $100,000 at a time when Company B's stockholders' equity was $100,000. If at the end of one year Company B's stockholders' equity has increased to $120,000 (assume that the entire increase is currently reflected in retained earnings) and Company A carries the investment account at cost ($100,000), reciprocity could be established by either of the following work sheet entries:

(1) Retained earnings (Company B's)                   $20,000
      Retained earnings (Company A's)                                     $20,000

(2) Investment in B                                            $20,000
      Retained earnings (Company A's)                                       $20,000

Although both methods produce the same end result, the latter approach is the one generally used and is the one presented in this textbook. It should be noted that if reciprocity were not established in this case, when the elimination is made, $120,000 of the subsidiary's stockholders' equity would be eliminated against the investment account of $100,000. The result would reflect $20,000 negative goodwill; actually, there was no goodwill of any type associated with the purchase since Company A paid $100,000 for a book value of $100,000.

The technique of consolidating the assets and equities of two or more related companies subsequent to the date of acquisition, when the investment is carried at cost, is examined in this chapter. As in the preceding chapter, the presentation distinguishes between (1) whether 100% ownership exists, or (2) whether less than 100% ownership exists.

## 100% Ownership

**Illustration A-1$_1$: 100% Ownership Acquired at Book Value.** Assume that as of January 1, 1980, Company A acquired 100% ownership in Company B for

$150,000, which was also the book value of the interest acquired (see Illustration A-1, page 275). The following individual statements reflect the financial positions of the respective companies one year later, and the consolidated statement column of the working papers on page 304 shows the financial position after consolidation:

COMPANY A
STATEMENT OF FINANCIAL POSITION
DECEMBER 31, 1980

| | | | |
|---|---|---|---|
| Current assets | $100,000 | Current liabilities | $ 30,000 |
| Investment in Company B | 150,000 | Fixed liabilities | 100,000 |
| Fixed assets (net) | 450,000 | Stockholders' equity: | |
| | | Capital stock | 400,000 |
| | | Retained earnings | 170,000 |
| | $700,000 | | $700,000 |

COMPANY B
STATEMENT OF FINANCIAL POSITION
DECEMBER 31, 1980

| | | | |
|---|---|---|---|
| Current assets | $ 80,000 | Current liabilities | $ 20,000 |
| Fixed assets (net) | 110,000 | Stockholders' equity: | |
| | | Capital stock | 100,000 |
| | | Retained earnings | 70,000 |
| | $190,000 | | $190,000 |

**Basic Procedure.** As indicated earlier, the basic procedure when consolidating subsequent to the date of acquisition includes:

1. The establishment of reciprocity, if necessary.
2. The elimination of reciprocals.
3. The consolidation of nonreciprocals.

**The Establishment of Reciprocity.** Since the investment account on the parent company's statement reflects acquisition cost and the subsidiary statement reflects the subsidiary's stockholders' equity at a date subsequent to acquisition, reciprocity must be established. This is accomplished by adjusting the investment account so that it will reflect the parent company's share of any increase or decrease in the subsidiary's stockholders' equity since acquisition. Company B's stockholders' equity has increased $20,000 (from $150,000 to $170,000). In order to establish reciprocity, because Company A owns 100% of Company B, the entire increase must be taken into consideration. Reciprocity is established through the following *work sheet* entry:

## Company A and Subsidiary Company B
### Consolidated Working Papers
### Statement of Financial Position
### December 31, 1980

| | Company A | Company B | Adjustments Debit | Adjustments Credit | Eliminations Debit | Eliminations Credit | Consolidated Financial Position |
|---|---|---|---|---|---|---|---|
| **Assets** | | | | | | | |
| Current assets | $100,000 | $ 80,000 | | | | | $180,000 |
| Investment in B | 150,000 | | $20,000 | | | $170,000 | |
| Fixed assets (net) | 450,000 | 110,000 | | | | | 560,000 |
| | $700,000 | $190,000 | | | | | $740,000 |
| **Equities** | | | | | | | |
| Current liabilities | $ 30,000 | $ 20,000 | | | | | $ 50,000 |
| Fixed liabilities | 100,000 | | | | | | 100,000 |
| Stockholders' equity: | | | | | | | |
| Capital stock: | | | | | | | |
| Company A | 400,000 | | | | | | 400,000 |
| Company B | | 100,000 | | | $100,000 | | |
| Retained earnings: | | | | | | | |
| Company A | 170,000 | | | $20,000 | | | 190,000RE |
| Company B | | 70,000 | | | 70,000 | | |
| | $700,000 | $190,000 | $20,000 | $20,000 | $170,000 | $170,000 | $740,000 |

11 / *Investment Carried at Cost*   305

    Investment in B      $20,000
        Retained earnings (Company A's)      $20,000
    (to recognize the parent company's share of the increase in the subsidiary's stockholders' equity since acquisition)

### The Elimination of Reciprocals.

    Capital stock (Company B's)      $100,000
    Retained earnings (Company B's)      70,000
        Investment in B      $170,000
    (to eliminate 100% of B's stockholders' equity against the investment account)

### The Consolidation of Nonreciprocals.

The nonreciprocal elements are consolidated by adding them where necessary and extending them to the consolidated statement, as is done when consolidating at the date of acquisition. It should be recognized that the consolidated statement of financial position is prepared from the final column of the consolidated working papers.

### Illustration A-2$_1$: 100% Ownership Acquired at More Than Book Value.

Assume that as of January 1, 1980, Company A acquired 100% ownership in Company B for $170,000, which was $20,000 more than the book value acquired (see Illustration A-2, page 277). In the following work sheet, the first two columns reflect the financial positions of the respective companies *two* years later, and the final column reflects the financial position after consolidation. (As was pointed out in the preceding chapter, unless indicated otherwise, a 10-year amortization period is assumed in this text for the amortization of both an excess of cost over book value and an excess of book value over cost. For purposes of simplicity, straight-line amortization is used.)

BASIC PROCEDURE

(1) *Establishment of reciprocity:*

    Investment in B      $15,000
        Retained earnings (Company A's)      $15,000
    (work sheet entry to recognize A's 100% interest in B's $15,000 increase in stockholders' equity since date of acquisition)

(2) *Elimination of reciprocals:*

    Capital stock (Company B's)      $100,000

## Company A and Subsidiary Company B
### Consolidated Working Papers
### Statement of Financial Position
#### December 31, 1981

| | Company A | Company B | Adjustments Debit | Adjustments Credit | Eliminations Debit | Eliminations Credit | Consolidated Financial Position |
|---|---|---|---|---|---|---|---|
| **Assets** | | | | | | | |
| Current assets | $120,000 | $ 90,000 | | | | | $210,000 |
| Investment in B | 166,000 | | $15,000 | | | $165,000 | 16,000G |
| Fixed assets (net) | 444,000 | 105,000 | | | | | 549,000 |
| | $730,000 | $195,000 | | | | | $775,000 |
| **Equities** | | | | | | | |
| Current liabilities | $ 40,000 | $ 30,000 | | | | | $ 70,000 |
| Fixed liabilities | 90,000 | | | | | | 90,000 |
| Stockholders' equity: | | | | | | | |
| Capital stock: | | | | | | | |
| Company A | 400,000 | | | | | | 400,000 |
| Company B | | 100,000 | | | $100,000 | | |
| Retained earnings: | | | | | | | |
| Company A | 200,000 | | | $15,000 | | | 215,000RE |
| Company B | | 65,000 | | | 65,000 | | |
| | $730,000 | $195,000 | $15,000 | $15,000 | $165,000 | $165,000 | $775,000 |

## 11 / Investment Carried at Cost

| | | |
|---|---|---|
| Retained earnings (Company B's) | 65,000 | |
|    Investment in B | | $165,000 |

(work sheet entry to eliminate 100% of B's stockholders' equity against the investment account)

(3) *Consolidation of nonreciprocals:*

Nonreciprocal items are consolidated as they have been in previous illustrations. However, notice that the nonreciprocal portion of the investment account that is extended to the consolidated statement as goodwill is $4,000 less than the amount of goodwill computed at the date of acquisition. This is as it should be, since two years' (2 × 1/10 × $20,000) amortization has been taken. It should also be noted that consolidated retained earnings is composed of the parent company's retained earnings plus the parent company's share of the increase in the subsidiary's retained earnings since the date of acquisition.

**Illustration A-3$_1$: 100% Ownership Acquired at Less Than Book Value.** Assume that as of January 1, 1980, Company A acquired 100% ownership in Company B for $140,000, which was $10,000 less than the book value acquired (see Illustration A-3, page 278). In the work sheet on page 308, the first two columns reflect the financial position of Companies A and B *three* years after acquisition, and the final column reflects the financial position after consolidation.

BASIC PROCEDURE

(1) *Establishment of reciprocity:*

| | | |
|---|---|---|
| Retained earnings (Company A's) | $14,000 | |
|    Investment in B | | $14,000 |

(work sheet entry to recognize A's 100% interest in B's $14,000 decrease in stockholders' equity since acquisition)

(2) *Elimination of reciprocals:*

| | | |
|---|---|---|
| Capital stock (Company B's) | $100,000 | |
| Retained earnings (Company B's) | 36,000 | |
|    Investment in B | | $136,000 |

(work sheet entry to eliminate 100% of B's stockholders' equity against the investment account)

(3) *Consolidation of nonreciprocals:*

Nonreciprocals are consolidated as they were previously. However, it should be noted that the nonreciprocal portion of the investment account is extended to the

**308** EXPANSION OF THE BUSINESS ORGANIZATION

COMPANY A AND SUBSIDIARY COMPANY B
CONSOLIDATED WORKING PAPERS
STATEMENT OF FINANCIAL POSITION
DECEMBER 31, 1982

|  | Company A | Company B | Adjustments Debit | Adjustments Credit | Eliminations Debit | Eliminations Credit | Consolidated Financial Position |
|---|---|---|---|---|---|---|---|
| *Assets* | | | | | | | |
| Current assets | $100,000 | $ 70,000 | | | | | $170,000 |
| Investment in B | 143,000 | | | $14,000 | | $136,000 | (7,000)G |
| Fixed assets (net) | 427,000 | 100,000 | | | | | 527,000 |
| | $670,000 | $170,000 | | | | | $690,000 |
| *Equities* | | | | | | | |
| Current liabilities | $ 50,000 | $ 34,000 | | | | | $ 84,000 |
| Fixed liabilities | 80,000 | | | | | | 80,000 |
| Stockholders' equity: | | | | | | | |
| Capital stock: | | | | | | | |
| Company A | 400,000 | | | | | | 400,000 |
| Company B | | 100,000 | | | $100,000 | | |
| Retained earnings: | | | | | | | |
| Company A | 140,000 | | | | | | 126,000RE |
| Company B | | 36,000 | $14,000 | | 36,000 | | |
| | $670,000 | $170,000 | $14,000 | $14,000 | $136,000 | $136,000 | $690,000 |

consolidated statement as $7,000 negative goodwill, which is the amount computed at the date of acquisition ($10,000) minus three years' amortization ($3,000).

## Less Than 100% Ownership

When a parent company acquires less than 100% ownership in a subsidiary, as indicated in the preceding chapter, it shares the ownership with the minority interest. When consolidation takes place subsequent to the date of acquisition, as well as at the date of acquisition, the parent company's equity in the subsidiary's stockholders' equity is eliminated and the minority interest's equity therein is consolidated. Again, as in the case of 100% ownership, three distinct situations may arise when less than 100% ownership exists, namely:

1. Less than 100% ownership acquired at book value.
2. Less than 100% ownership acquired at more than book value.
3. Less than 100% ownership acquired at less than book value.

**Illustration B-1₁: Less Than 100% Ownership Acquired at Book Value.** Assume that as of January 1, 1980, Company A acquired a 90% interest in Company B for $135,000, which was also the book value of the interest acquired at that date (see Illustration B-1, page 281). The following individual statements reflect the financial positions of the respective companies one year later, and the consolidated statement column of the working papers on page 310 the financial position after consolidation:

COMPANY A
STATEMENT OF FINANCIAL POSITION
DECEMBER 31, 1980

| | | | |
|---|---|---|---|
| Current assets | $115,000 | Current liabilities | $ 30,000 |
| Investment in B | 135,000 | Fixed liabilities | 100,000 |
| Fixed assets (net) | 450,000 | Stockholders' equity: | |
| | | Capital stock | 400,000 |
| | | Retained earnings | 170,000 |
| | $700,000 | | $700,000 |

COMPANY B
STATEMENT OF FINANCIAL POSITION
DECEMBER 31, 1980

| | | | |
|---|---|---|---|
| Current assets | $ 80,000 | Current liabilities | $ 20,000 |
| Fixed assets (net) | 110,000 | Stockholders' equity: | |
| | | Capital stock | 100,000 |
| | | Retained earnings | 70,000 |
| | $190,000 | | $190,000 |

## Company A and Subsidiary Company B
## Consolidated Working Papers
## Statement of Financial Position
## December 31, 1980

| | Company A | Company B | Adjustments Debit | Adjustments Credit | Eliminations Debit | Eliminations Credit | Consolidated Financial Position |
|---|---|---|---|---|---|---|---|
| **Assets** | | | | | | | |
| Current assets | $115,000 | $ 80,000 | | | | | $195,000 |
| Investment in B | 135,000 | | $18,000 | | | $153,000 | |
| Fixed assets (net) | 450,000 | 110,000 | | | | | 560,000 |
| | $700,000 | $190,000 | | | | | $755,000 |
| **Equities** | | | | | | | |
| Current liabilities | $ 30,000 | $ 20,000 | | | | | $ 50,000 |
| Fixed liabilities | 100,000 | | | | | | 100,000 |
| Stockholders' equity: | | | | | | | |
| Capital stock: | | | | | | | |
| Company A | 400,000 | | | | | | 400,000 |
| Company B | | 100,000 | | | $ 90,000 | | 10,000MI |
| Retained earnings: | | | | | | | |
| Company A | 170,000 | | | $18,000 | | | 188,000RE |
| Company B | | 70,000 | | | 63,000 | | 7,000MI |
| | $700,000 | $190,000 | $18,000 | $18,000 | $153,000 | $153,000 | $755,000 |

## Basic Procedure

(1) *Establishment of reciprocity:*

| | | |
|---|---|---|
| Investment in B | $18,000 | |
|     Retained earnings (Company A's) | | $18,000 |

(work sheet entry to recognize A's 90% interest in the $20,000 increase in B's stockholders' equity since acquisition)

(2) *Elimination of reciprocals:*

| | | |
|---|---|---|
| Capital stock (Company B's) | $90,000 | |
| Retained earnings (Company B's) | 63,000 | |
|     Investment in B | | $153,000 |

(work sheet entry to eliminate 90% of B's stockholders' equity against the investment account)

(3) *Consolidation of nonreciprocals:*

In this illustration it should be noted that the nonreciprocal elements of the subsidiary's stockholders' equity are extended to the consolidated statement as minority interest. If the minority interest of Illustration B-1 is compared with this illustration, it will be seen that the minority interest has increased $2,000, from $15,000 to $17,000. This is, of course, due to the minority interest's 10% claim against the $20,000 increase in B's stockholders' equity.

**Illustration B-2₁: Less than 100% Ownership Acquired at More Than Book Value.** Assume that on January 1, 1980, Company A acquired a 90% interest in Company B for $155,000. At the date of acquisition, Company B had a stockholders' equity of $150,000. Since Company A acquired a 90% interest, it acquired book value of $135,000 (90% of $150,000) for its investment (see Illustration B-2, page 284). The working papers on page 312 show how the individual statements of financial position would be consolidated *two* years later.

## Basic Procedure

(1) *Establishment of reciprocity:*

| | | |
|---|---|---|
| Investment in B | $13,500 | |
|     Retained earnings (Company A's) | | $13,500 |

(work sheet entry to recognize A's 90% interest in the $15,000 increase in B's stockholders' equity since acquisition)

COMPANY A AND SUBSIDIARY COMPANY B
CONSOLIDATED WORKING PAPERS
STATEMENT OF FINANCIAL POSITION
DECEMBER 31, 1981

|  | Company A | Company B | Adjustments Debit | Adjustments Credit | Eliminations Debit | Eliminations Credit | Consolidated Financial Position |
|---|---|---|---|---|---|---|---|
| *Assets* |  |  |  |  |  |  |  |
| Current assets | $135,000 | $ 90,000 |  |  |  |  | $225,000 |
| Investment in B | 151,000 |  | $13,500 |  |  | $148,500 | 16,000G |
| Fixed assets (net) | 444,000 | 105,000 |  |  |  |  | 549,000 |
|  | $730,000 | $195,000 |  |  |  |  | $790,000 |
| *Equities* |  |  |  |  |  |  |  |
| Current liabilities | $ 40,000 | $ 30,000 |  |  |  |  | $ 70,000 |
| Fixed liabilities | 90,000 |  |  |  |  |  | 90,000 |
| Stockholders' equity: |  |  |  |  |  |  |  |
| Capital stock: |  |  |  |  |  |  |  |
| Company A | 400,000 |  |  |  |  |  | 400,000 |
| Company B |  | 100,000 |  |  | $90,000 |  | 10,000MI |
| Retained earnings: |  |  |  |  |  |  |  |
| Company A | 200,000 |  |  | $13,500 |  |  | 213,500RE |
| Company B |  | 65,000 |  |  | 58,500 |  | 6,500MI |
|  | $730,000 | $195,000 | $13,500 | $13,500 | $148,500 | $148,500 | $790,000 |

*11 / Investment Carried at Cost*

(2) *Elimination of reciprocals:*

| | | |
|---|---:|---:|
| Capital stock (Company B's) | $90,000 | |
| Retained earnings (Company B's) | 58,500 | |
|     Investment in B | | $148,500 |

(work sheet entry to eliminate 90% of B's stockholders' equity against the investment account)

(3) *Consolidation of nonreciprocals:*

All nonreciprocal elements are consolidated as usual. However, in this instance the nonreciprocal portion of the investment account is extended to the consolidated statement as goodwill, and the nonreciprocal elements of Company B's stockholders' equity are extended as minority interest. It should be noted that the amounts of goodwill in Illustration B-2 and B-2$_1$ differ by $4,000, which is equal to two years' amortization. However, the minority interest has increased from $15,000 to $16,500, which is due, of course, to 10% of the $15,000 increase in Company B's stockholders' equity since acquisition.

**Illustration B-3$_1$: Less than 100% Ownership Acquired at Less Than Book Value.** Assume that as of January 1, 1980, Company A acquired a 90% interest in Company B for $125,000. At the date of acquisition Company B had a stockholders' equity of $150,000. Since Company A acquired a 90% interest, it acquired book value of $135,000 (90% of $150,000) for its investment (see Illustration B-3, page 286). In the work sheet on page 314 the first two columns reflect the financial positions of the respective companies *three* years after acquisition, and the final column reflects the financial position after consolidation.

BASIC PROCEDURE

(1) *Establishment of reciprocity:*

| | | |
|---|---:|---:|
| Retained earnings (Company A's) | $12,600 | |
|     Investment in B | | $12,600 |

(work sheet entry to recognize A's 90% interest in B's $14,000 decrease in stockholders' equity since acquisition)

(2) *Elimination of reciprocals:*

| | | |
|---|---:|---:|
| Capital stock (Company B's) | $90,000 | |
| Retained earnings (Company B's) | 32,400 | |
|     Investment in B | | $122,400 |

(work sheet entry to eliminate 90% of B's stockholders' equity against the investment account)

(3) *Consolidation of nonreciprocals:*

## Company A and Subsidiary Company B
### Consolidated Working Papers
### Statement of Financial Position
#### December 31, 1982

| | Company A | Company B | Adjustments Debit | Adjustments Credit | Eliminations Debit | Eliminations Credit | Consolidated Financial Position |
|---|---|---|---|---|---|---|---|
| **Assets** | | | | | | | |
| Current assets | $115,000 | $ 70,000 | | | | | $185,000 |
| Investment in B | 128,000 | | | $12,600 | | $122,400 | (7,000)G |
| Fixed assets (net) | 427,000 | 100,000 | | | | | 527,000 |
| | $670,000 | $170,000 | | | | | $705,000 |
| **Equities** | | | | | | | |
| Current liabilities | $ 50,000 | $ 34,000 | | | | | $ 84,000 |
| Fixed liabilities | 80,000 | | | | | | 80,000 |
| Stockholders' equity: | | | | | | | |
| Capital stock: | | | | | | | |
| Company A | 400,000 | | | | | | 400,000 |
| Company B | | 100,000 | | | $ 90,000 | | 10,000MI |
| Retained earnings: | | | | | | | |
| Company A | 140,000 | | $12,600 | | | | 127,400RE |
| Company B | | 36,000 | | | 32,400 | | 3,600MI |
| | $670,000 | $170,000 | $12,600 | $12,600 | $122,400 | $122,400 | $705,000 |

Nonreciprocal elements are extended to the consolidated statement as usual. However, it should be noted that the nonreciprocal portion of the investment account is extended to the consolidated statement as negative goodwill, and the nonreciprocal elements of Company B's stockholders' equity are extended as minority interest. The $7,000 negative goodwill is the amount computed at the date of acquisition ($10,000) minus three years' amortization. It should also be noted that the minority interest has decreased $1,400 ($15,000 minus $13,600). This is due to the minority interest's 10% of the $14,000 decrease in the subsidiary's stockholders' equity since the date of acquisition.

## Consolidated Statement of Income and Retained Earnings— Investment Carried at Cost

When a group of affiliated companies is reported for, a consolidated income statement, frequently accompanied by a consolidated statement of retained earnings, is usually prepared and presented along with the consolidated statement of financial position. The consolidated income statement, of course, shows how the consolidated income arose, whereas the consolidated statement of retained earnings serves as a link between the consolidated statement of financial position and the consolidated income statement. These statements may be prepared and presented separately or they may be combined. Combined preparation and presentation is used in this textbook since this approach permits ease of comparison and reconciliation of the two statements.

In order to prepare a consolidated income or retained earnings statement for a group of affiliated companies composed of legally separate entities and to reflect therein the group as one economic unit, all intercompany income and retained earnings transactions must be eliminated. The remaining transactions will then reflect only transactions with outsiders. The basic consolidating procedure, therefore, is essentially the same as that used when preparing consolidated statements of financial position: (1) eliminate intercompany transactions through work sheet entries and (2) consolidate nonintercompany transactions. However, after the nonintercompany transactions are consolidated, an additional step is required in the preparation of consolidated income statements. Total net income must be apportioned between the majority or controlling interest and the minority interest.

The following illustrations show how this basic procedure is applied under varying conditions. Although the general facts remain the same, certain specific conditions are changed in each instance. The general situation is the one used in Illustrations B-1 and B-1$_1$: that Company A acquired 90% of the outstanding stock of Company B as of January 1, 1980.

### Illustration C-1. *Specific Assumptions:*

A. Company A sold Company B $20,000 worth of merchandise.
B. Company B paid Company A $400 interest.
C. Company B reported a net income of $20,000 for 1980.

COMPANY A AND SUBSIDIARY COMPANY B
CONSOLIDATED WORKING PAPERS
STATEMENT OF INCOME AND RETAINED EARNINGS
YEAR ENDED DECEMBER 31, 1980

| Credits | Company A | Company B | Eliminations | Consolidated Income | Consolidated Retained Earnings |
|---|---|---|---|---|---|
| Net sales | $800,000 | $200,000 | $20,000A | $980,000 | |
| Interest income | 6,000 | | 400B | 5,600 | |
| Totals | $806,000 | $200,000 | $20,400 | $985,600 | |
| *Debits* | | | | | |
| Cost of sales | $590,000 | $130,000 | $20,000A | $700,000 | |
| Depreciation | 80,000 | 26,000 | | 106,000 | |
| Interest expense | 6,000 | 2,000 | 400B | 7,600 | |
| Other expenses | 10,000 | 2,000 | | 12,000 | |
| Federal income taxes | 60,000 | 20,000 | | 80,000 | |
| Net income | 60,000 | 20,000 | | 80,000 | |
| Totals | $806,000 | $200,000 | $20,400 | $985,600 | |
| Retained earnings | | | | | |
| 1/1/80 | $110,000 | $50,000 | | | $110,000* |
| Net income (1980) | 60,000 | 20,000 | | | |
| Retained earnings | | | | | |
| 12/31/80 | $170,000 | $70,000 | | | |
| Apportionment of net income: | | | | | |
| Net income | | | | $80,000 | |
| Minority interest (10% of $20,000) | | | | 2,000 | |
| Consolidated interest (remainder) | | | | $78,000 | 78,000 |
| Consolidated retained earnings 12/31/80 | | | | | $188,000† |

*Note:* Consolidated retained earnings at date of acquisition is composed entirely of the parent company's retained earnings.
†*Proof:* Parent company's $170,000 plus 90% of B's $20,000 increase since acquisition.

BASIC PROCEDURE

(1) *Elimination of intercompany transactions:*

                                                    *A*

    Sales                                                           $20,000
        Cost of sales                                          $20,000
    (work sheet elimination of intercompany sales)

## 11 / Investment Carried at Cost

B
Interest income $400
  Interest expense $400
(work sheet elimination of intercompany interest)

(2) *Consolidation of nonintercompany transactions:*

Nonintercompany items are consolidated by extending them to the consolidated income statement.

(3) *Apportionment of net income:*

Minority interest (10% of Company B's $20,000)
Majority interest (90% of Company B's $20,000 plus Company A's $60,000).

The last two columns of the working papers may be presented in statement form as follows:

COMPANY A AND SUBSIDIARY COMPANY B
CONSOLIDATED STATEMENT OF INCOME
AND RETAINED EARNINGS
YEAR ENDED DECEMBER 31, 1980

*Income:*
| | | |
|---|---:|---:|
| Net sales | $980,000 | |
| Interest income | 5,600 | |
| Gross income | $985,600 | $985,600 |

*Costs and Expenses:*
| | | |
|---|---:|---:|
| Cost of sales | $700,000 | |
| Depreciation | 106,000 | |
| Interest expense | 7,600 | |
| Other expenses | 12,000 | |
| Federal income taxes | 80,000 | |
| Total costs and expenses | $905,600 | 905,600 |
| Net income | | $ 80,000 |
| Minority interest | | 2,000 |
| *Consolidated Net Income* | | $ 78,000 |
| Consolidated retained earnings 1/1/80 | | 110,000 |
| Consolidated retained earnings 12/31/80 | | $188,000 |

**Illustration C-2.** *Specific Assumptions:*

A. Company A sold Company B $20,000 worth of merchandise.
B. Company B paid Company A $400 interest.
C. Company B declared and paid $10,000 dividends.
D. Company B reported a net income of $30,000 for 1980.

COMPANY A AND SUBSIDIARY COMPANY B
CONSOLIDATED WORKING PAPERS
STATEMENT OF INCOME AND RETAINED EARNINGS
YEAR ENDED DECEMBER 31, 1980

| Credits | Company A | Company B | Eliminations | Consolidated Income | Consolidated Retained Earnings |
|---|---|---|---|---|---|
| Net sales | $791,000 | $210,000 | $20,000A | $981,000 | |
| Interest income | 6,000 | | 400B | 5,600 | |
| Dividend income | 9,000 | | 9,000C | | |
| Totals | $806,000 | $210,000 | $29,400 | $986,600 | |
| *Debits* | | | | | |
| Cost of sales | $590,000 | $130,000 | $20,000A | $700,000 | |
| Depreciation | 80,000 | 26,000 | | 106,000 | |
| Interest expense | 6,000 | 2,000 | 400B | 7,600 | |
| Other expenses | 10,000 | 2,000 | | 12,000 | |
| Federal income taxes | 60,000 | 20,000 | | 80,000 | |
| Net income | 60,000 | 30,000 | 9,000C | 81,000 | |
| Totals | $806,000 | $210,000 | $29,400 | $986,600 | |
| Retained earnings 1/1/80 | $110,000 | $50,000 | | | $110,000* |
| Dividends paid (1980) | | (10,000) | | | |
| Net income (1980) | 60,000 | 30,000 | | | |
| Retained earnings 12/31/80 | $170,000 | $70,000 | | | |

| Apportionment of net income: | | |
|---|---|---|
| Net income | $81,000 | |
| Minority interest (10% of $30,000) | 3,000 | |
| Consolidated interest (remainder) | $78,000 | 78,000 |
| Consolidated retained earnings 12/31/80 | | $188,000† |

*Note:* Consolidated retained earnings at date of acquisition is composed entirely of the parent company's retained earnings.
†*Proof:* Parent company's $170,000 plus 90% of B's $20,000 increase since acquisition.

BASIC PROCEDURE

(1) *Elimination of intercompany transactions:*

A

Sales $ 20,000
　　Cost of sales $ 20,000
(work sheet elimination of intercompany sales)

## 11 / Investment Carried at Cost

### B

| | | |
|---|---|---|
| Interest income | $ 400 | |
| Interest expense | | $ 400 |
| (work sheet elimination of intercompany interest) | | |

### C

| | | |
|---|---|---|
| Dividend income | $ 9,000 | |
| Net income | | $ 9,000 |
| (work sheet elimination of intercompany dividend) | | |

(2) *Consolidation of nonintercompany transactions:*

Nonintercompany items are consolidated by extending them to the consolidated income statement.

(3) *Apportionment of net income:*

Minority interest (10% of Company B's $30,000)
Majority interest (90% of Company B's $30,000 plus Company A's $60,000 minus $9,000 intercompany income).

The last two columns of the working papers may be presented in statement form as follows:

COMPANY A AND SUBSIDIARY COMPANY B
CONSOLIDATED STATEMENT OF INCOME
AND RETAINED EARNINGS
YEAR ENDED DECEMBER 31, 1980

| | | |
|---|---:|---:|
| *Income:* | | |
| Net sales | $981,000 | |
| Interest income | 5,600 | |
| Gross income | $986,000 | $986,600 |
| *Costs and Expenses:* | | |
| Cost of sales | $700,000 | |
| Depreciation | 106,000 | |
| Interest expense | 7,600 | |
| Other expenses | 12,000 | |
| Federal income taxes | 80,000 | |
| Total costs and expenses | $905,600 | 905,600 |
| Net income | | $ 81,000 |
| Minority interest | | 3,000 |
| *Consolidated Net Income* | | $ 78,000 |
| Consolidated retained earnings 1/1/80 | | 110,000 |
| Consolidated retained earnings 12/31/80 | | $188,000 |

*Illustration D-1*

COMPANY A AND SUBSIDIARY COMPANY B

CONSOLIDATED WORKING PAPERS

DECEMBER 31, 1980

|  | Company A | Company B | Eliminations Debit | Eliminations Credit |
|---|---|---|---|---|
| *Debits* | | | | |
| Current assets | $ 115,000 | $ 80,000 | | |
| Investment in B | 135,000 | | | $135,000*C* |
| Fixed assets (net) | 450,000 | 110,000 | | |
| Cost of sales | 590,000 | 130,000 | | 20,000*A* |
| Depreciation | 80,000 | 26,000 | | |
| Interest expense | 6,000 | 2,000 | | 400*B* |
| Other expenses | 10,000 | 2,000 | | |
| Federal income taxes | 60,000 | 20,000 | | |
| | $1,446,000 | $370,000 | | |
| *Credits* | | | | |
| Current liabilities | $ 30,000 | $ 20,000 | | |
| Fixed liabilities | 100,000 | | | |
| Net sales | 800,000 | 200,000 | $ 20,000*A* | |
| Interest income | 6,000 | | 400*B* | |
| Capital stock: | | | | |
| Company A | 400,000 | | | |
| Company B | | 100,000 | 90,000*C* | |
| Retained earnings: | | | | |
| Company A 1/1/80 | 110,000 | | | |
| Company B 1/1/80 | | 50,000 | 45,000*C* | |
| | $1,446,000 | $370,000 | $155,400 | $155,400 |

Income credits
Income debits
Net income
Apportionment of net income:
  Minority interest:
    Subsidiary income credits     $200,000
    Subsidiary income debits      180,000
    Subsidiary net income     $ 20,000
    Minority interest (10%)       2,000

Consolidated net income (remainder)
Retained earnings 12/31/80
Minority interest 12/31/80
  *A:*  To eliminate intercompany sales.
  *B:*  To eliminate intercompany interest.
  *C:*  To eliminate 90% of B's stockholders' equity against the investment account.

*11 / Investment Carried at Cost*

COMPANY A AND SUBSIDIARY COMPANY B

CONSOLIDATED WORKING PAPERS

(CONTINUED — ILLUSTRATION D-1)

|  Consolidated Income | Consolidated Retained Earnings | Minority Interest | Consolidated Financial Position |
|---|---|---|---|
|  |  |  | $195,000 |
|  |  |  | 560,000 |
| $700,000 |  |  |  |
| 106,000 |  |  |  |
| 7,600 |  |  |  |
| 12,000 |  |  |  |
| 80,000 |  |  |  |
| $905,600 | –0– | –0– | $755,000 |
|  |  |  | $ 50,000 |
|  |  |  | 100,000 |
| $980,000 |  |  |  |
| 5,600 |  |  |  |
|  |  |  | 400,000 |
|  |  | $10,000 |  |
|  | $110,000 |  |  |
|  |  | 5,000 |  |
| $985,600 |  |  |  |
| 905,600 |  |  |  |
| $ 80,000 |  |  |  |
| 2,000 |  | 2,000 |  |
| $ 78,000 | 78,000 |  |  |
|  | $188,000 |  | 188,000RE |
|  |  | $17,000 | 17,000MI |
|  |  |  | $755,000 |

321

*Illustration D-2*

## Company A and Subsidiary Company B
## Consolidated Working Papers
## December 31, 1981

|  | Company A | Company B | Adjustments and Eliminations* Debit | Credit |
|---|---:|---:|---:|---:|
| *Debits* |  |  |  |  |
| Current assets | $ 205,000 | $154,000 |  |  |
| Investment in B | 135,000 |  | $18,000(1) | $153,000A |
| Fixed assets (net) | 460,000 | 100,000 |  |  |
| Cost of sales | 650,000 | 170,000 |  |  |
| Depreciation | 85,000 | 28,000 |  |  |
| Interest expense | 6,000 |  |  |  |
| Other expenses | 14,000 | 3,000 |  |  |
| Federal income taxes | 75,000 | 45,000 |  |  |
|  | $1,630,000 | $500,000 |  |  |
| *Credits* |  |  |  |  |
| Current liabilities | $ 60,000 | 30,000 |  |  |
| Fixed liabilities | 100,000 |  |  |  |
| Net sales | 900,000 | 300,000 |  |  |
| Capital stock: |  |  |  |  |
|   Company A | 400,000 |  |  |  |
|   Company B |  | 100,000 | 90,000A |  |
| Retained earnings: |  |  |  |  |
|   Company A 1/1/81 | 170,000 |  |  | 18,000(1) |
|   Company B 1/1/81 |  | 70,000 | 63,000A |  |
|  | $1,630,000 | $500,000 | $171,000 | $171,000 |

| | | |
|---|---|---:|
| Income credits | | |
| Income debits | | |
| Net income | | |
| Apportionment of net income: | | |
|   Minority interest: | | |
|     Subsidiary income credits | | $300,000 |
|     Subsidiary income debits | | 246,000 |
|     Subsidiary net income | | $ 54,000 |
|     Minority interest (10%) | | 5,400 |

Consolidated net income (remainder)

Retained earnings 12/31/81
Minority interest 12/31/81

  (1): To establish reciprocity by recognizing A's 90% interest in the $20,000 increase in B's stockholders' equity from the date of acquisition to the beginning of the current period.

  A: To eliminate 90% of B's stockholders' equity (as of the beginning of the period) against the investment account.

COMPANY A AND SUBSIDIARY COMPANY B
CONSOLIDATED WORKING PAPERS
(Continued — Illustration D-2)

| Consolidated Income | Consolidated Retained Earnings | Minority Interest | Consolidated Financial Position |
|---|---|---|---|
|  |  |  | $359,000 |
|  |  |  | 560,000 |
| $ 820,000 |  |  |  |
| 113,000 |  |  |  |
| 6,000 |  |  |  |
| 17,000 |  |  |  |
| 120,000 |  |  |  |
| $1,076,000 | –0– | –0– | $919,000 |
|  |  |  | $ 90,000 |
|  |  |  | 100,000 |
| $1,200,000 |  |  |  |
|  |  |  | 400,000 |
|  |  | $10,000 |  |
|  | $188,000 |  |  |
|  |  | 7,000 |  |
| $1,200,000 |  |  |  |
| $1,076,000 |  |  |  |
| $ 124,000 |  |  |  |
| 5,400 |  | 5,400 |  |
| $ 118,600 | 118,600 |  |  |
|  | $306,600 |  | 306,600RE |
|  |  | $22,400 | 22,400MI |
|  |  |  | $919,000 |

*Here and in later chapters adjustments and eliminations will be placed in the same work sheet columns. In order to distinguish between them, adjustments will be *numbered* and eliminations will be *lettered*.

*Illustration D-3*

COMPANY A AND SUBSIDIARY COMPANY B

CONSOLIDATED WORKING PAPERS, DECEMBER 31, 1982

|  | Company A | Company B | Adjustments and Eliminations Debit | Credit |
|---|---|---|---|---|
| *Debits* |  |  |  |  |
| Inventories 1/1/82 | $ 70,000 | $ 40,000 |  |  |
| Other current assets | 208,000 | 158,000 |  |  |
| Investment in B | 135,000 |  | $ 66,600(2) | $201,600 B |
| Fixed assets (net) | 490,000 | 105,000 |  |  |
| Purchases | 700,000 | 200,000 |  |  |
| Depreciation | 84,000 | 30,000 |  |  |
| Other expenses | 100,000 | 70,000 |  |  |
| Dividends paid | 32,000 | 10,000 |  | 9,000 A |
|  | $1,819,000 | $613,000 |  |  |
| Inventories 12/31/82 |  |  | 150,000(1) |  |
| *Credits* |  |  |  |  |
| Current liabilities | $ 90,000 | $ 39,000 |  |  |
| Fixed liabilities | 100,000 |  |  |  |
| Net sales | 980,000 | 350,000 |  |  |
| Dividend income | 9,000 |  | 9,000 A |  |
| Capital stock: |  |  |  |  |
| Company A | 400,000 |  |  |  |
| Company B |  | 100,000 | 90,000 B |  |
| Retained earnings: |  |  |  |  |
| Company A 1/1/82 | 240,000 |  |  | 66,600(2) |
| Company B 1/1/82 |  | 124,000 | 111,600 B |  |
|  | $1,819,000 | $613,000 |  |  |
| Inventories 12/31/82 | $ 90,000 | $ 60,000 |  | 150,000(1) |
|  |  |  | $427,200 | $427,200 |

Income credits
Income debits
Net income
Apportionment of net income:
  Minority interest:
    Subsidiary income credits    $410,000 — Sales + End Inv
    Subsidiary income debits    340,000
    Subsidiary net income    $ 70,000
    Minority interest (10%)    7,000
Consolidated net income (remainder)

Retained earnings 12/31/82

Minority interest 12/31/82
  (1): To record ending inventories.
  (2): To establish reciprocity by recognizing A's 90% interest in the $74,000 increase in B's stockholders' equity from the date of acquisition to the beginning of the current period.
  A: To eliminate intercompany dividends.
  B: To eliminate 90% of B's stockholders' equity against the investment account.

COMPANY A AND SUBSIDIARY COMPANY B

CONSOLIDATED WORKING PAPERS (Continued — Illustration D-3)

| Consolidated Income | Consolidated Retained Earnings | Minority Interest | Consolidated Financial Position |
|---|---|---|---|
| $ 110,000 | | | |
| | | | $ 366,000 |
| | | | 595,000 |
| 900,000 | | | |
| 114,000 | | | |
| 170,000 | | | |
| | $ 32,000 | $ 1,000 | |
| | | | 150,000 |
| $1,294,000 | $ 32,000 | $ 1,000 | $1,111,000 |
| | | | $ 129,000 |
| | | | 100,000 |
| $1,330,000 | | | |
| | | | 400,000 |
| | | $10,000 | |
| | $306,600 | | |
| | | 12,400 | |
| 150,000 | | | |
| 1,480,000 | | | |
| 1,294,000 | | | |
| $ 186,000 | | | |
| 7,000 | | 7,000 | |
| $ 179,000 | 179,000 | | |
| | $485,600 | | |
| | 32,000 | | |
| | $453,600 | | |
| | | $29,400 | |
| | | 1,000 | |
| | | $28,400 | |
| | | | 453,600RE |
| | | | 28,400MI |
| | | | $1,111,000 |

## Trial Balance Approach

In the preceding illustrations consolidated statements have been prepared from the financial statements of the respective companies involved. This procedure is frequently used in practice. However, consolidated statements may be prepared from trial balances as well as from the financial statements. Regardless of the approach used, the basic procedure remains the same: establish reciprocity when necessary, eliminate reciprocals, and consolidate nonreciprocals.

The examples presented illustrate the basic procedure involved in three slightly different, but fundamentally important, situations:

**Illustration D-1:** This illustration is based on the same basic data used in Illustrations B-1, B-1$_1$, and C-1. (The illustration is on pages 320–321.)

**Illustration D-2.** The general situation in this illustration is the same as that used in Illustration D-1: that Company A acquired 90% of the outstanding stock of Company B as of January 1, 1980. However, in this instance consolidation is taking place at the end of 1981 instead of at the end of 1980. It is also assumed that no intercompany transactions arose in 1981. (The illustration is on pages 322–323.)

In this illustration particular attention should be given to the establishment of reciprocity. When the trial balance approach is used, reciprocity must be established as of the beginning of the period rather than as of the end of the period, as is the procedure when the statement approach is used. This modification in the basic procedure is necessary because consolidated net income is added to the beginning balance of consolidated retained earnings in the working papers. If reciprocity were established as of the end of the period, the parent company's share of a subsidiary's earnings for the period would be taken into consolidated retained earnings twice. The basic procedure when using the trial balance approach, therefore, includes:

1. The establishment of reciprocity, if necessary, as of the beginning of the period.
2. The elimination of reciprocals.
3. The consolidation of nonreciprocals.

**Illustration D-3.** The general situation in this illustration is the same as the one used in Illustrations D-1 and D-2: that Company A acquired 90% of the outstanding stock of Company B as of January 1, 1980. However, in this instance consolidation is taking place at the end of 1982 rather than 1980 or 1981, and Companies A and B submit unadjusted trial balances rather than adjusted ones. Particular attention should be given not only to the establishment of reciprocity but also to the treatment of inventories. In addition to the data in the respective trial balances, Company A reports an ending inventory of $90,000 and Company B one of $60,000. (The illustration is on pages 324–325.)

## PROBLEMS

## Problem 11-1

Using the following basic data and the specific assumption given in each instance, for each case:

(a) Prepare the work sheet entry(ies) necessary when establishing reciprocity as of 12/31/80.
(b) Prepare the work sheet entry(ies) necessary when eliminating reciprocals as of 12/31/80.
(c) Determine the amount of goodwill (positive or negative) as of 12/31/80.
(d) Determine the amount of minority interest as of 12/31/80.
(e) Determine the amount of consolidated retained earnings as of 12/31/80.

BASIC DATA

|  | Company X | Company Y | Company Z |
|---|---|---|---|
| Balances as of 1/1/78 |  |  |  |
| Capital stock | $200,000 | $75,000 | $60,000 |
| Retained earnings (deficit) | 100,000 | 40,000 | (10,000) |
| Capital in excess of par | 20,000 | 15,000 | 5,000 |
| Balances as of 12/31/80 |  |  |  |
| Capital stock | $200,000 | $75,000 | $60,000 |
| Retained earnings | 190,000 | 75,000 | 15,000 |
| Capital in excess of par | 20,000 | 15,000 | 5,000 |

*Case 1.* Assume that Company X acquired 90% of the stock of Company Y for $120,000 as of 1/1/78. Company X carries its investment in Y at *cost*.

*Case 2.* Assume that Company X acquired 80% of the stock of Company Z for $40,000 as of 1/1/78. Company X carries its investment in Z at *cost*.

*Case 3.* Assume that Company X acquired 80% of the stock of Company Y and 90% of the stock of Company Z for $105,000 and $46,000, respectively, as of 1/1/78. Company X carries these investments at *cost*.

*Case 4.* Assume that Company Y acquired 75% of the stock of Company Z for $35,000 as of 1/1/78. Company Y carries its investment in Z at *cost*.

*Note:* All cases are independent.

## Problem 11-2

From the following data determine in each case:

1. Minority interest at date of acquisition and at the date of consolidation.
2. Goodwill (either positive or negative) at date of acquisition and at the date of consolidation.
3. Consolidated retained earnings at date of acquisition and at the date of consolidation.

Assume that the parent company's retained earnings amount to $200,000 in all cases.

### Subsidiary Company

|  | Company and % Owned |  | Cost | Acquisition Date 1/1/77 |  | Consolidation Date 12/31/80 |  |
|---|---|---|---|---|---|---|---|
|  |  |  |  | Capital Stock | Retained Earnings | Capital Stock | Retained Earnings |
| Case 1 | A | 90% | $140,000 | $100,000 | $50,000 | $100,000 | $70,000 |
| Case 2 | B | 85% | 104,000 | 100,000 | 30,000 | 100,000 | 20,000 |
| Case 3 | C | 80% | 56,000 | 50,000 | 20,000 | 50,000 | 20,000 |
| Case 4 | D | 100% | 100,000 | 50,000 | 40,000 | 50,000 | 55,000 |

### Problem 11-3

XYZ, Incorporated, purchased an 80% interest in the ABC Company on January 1, 1980, for $140,000. The stockholders' equity of the ABC Company on January 1, 1980, was composed of capital stock, $100,000, and retained earnings, $60,000. XYZ, Incorporated, carries the investment account at cost. On December 31, 1980, the ABC Company announced a profit of $20,000 for 1980 and at the same time declared and paid a dividend of $30,000.

*Required:*
(1) Show in entry form how the dividend should be recorded on the books of XYZ, Incorporated.
(2) What is the amount of goodwill from consolidation as of (*a*) January 1, 1980, and (*b*) December 31, 1980?
(3) What is the amount of minority interest as of (*a*) January 1, 1980, and (*b*) December 31, 1980?

### Problem 11-4

Company A purchases 80% of the stock of Company B for $160,000. Company B has outstanding stock of $100,000 and retained earnings of $100,000. Company B subsequently earns a profit of $10,000 and distributes a dividend of $30,000. Company A records the receipt of dividends by a debit to Cash and a credit to Retained Earnings of $24,000.

*Required:*
(1) Assuming that the investment is carried at cost, give the correct entry which should have been made on Company A's books to record the receipt of the dividend.
(2) Discuss fully the faults of the original entry.
(3) Assume that Company A purchased only 5% of the stock of B as a temporary investment and that B subsequently earns $10,000 and distributes a

dividend of $30,000. State how Company A should record receipt of the dividend. If the principle applicable is different from that applicable in (1), give the reason.

(AICPA adapted)

## Problem 11-5

From the following statements and data:

1. Prepare a consolidated statement of financial position, and
2. Prove the goodwill elements. (Assume that goodwill is not being amortized at this time.)

|  | A | B | C | D | E |
|---|---|---|---|---|---|
| *Assets* | Company | Company | Company | Company | Company |
| Current assets | $ 960,000 | $ 50,000 | $ 80,000 | $ 76,000 | $ 60,000 |
| Subsidiaries (cost): |  |  |  |  |  |
| B Company (90%) | 88,000 |  |  |  |  |
| C Company (80%) | 42,000 |  |  |  |  |
| D Company (70%) | 60,000 |  |  |  |  |
| E Company (60%) | 35,000 |  |  |  |  |
| Other assets | 410,000 | 80,000 | 75,000 | 35,000 | 45,000 |
|  | $1,595,000 | $130,000 | $155,000 | $111,000 | $105,000 |
| *Equities* |  |  |  |  |  |
| Current liabilities | $ 310,000 | $ 24,000 | $ 85,000 | $ 16,000 | $ 61,000 |
| Fixed liabilities | 200,000 |  |  |  |  |
| Capital stock | 500,000 | 75,000 | 60,000 | 60,000 | 50,000 |
| Retained earnings (deficit) | 585,000 | 31,000 | 10,000 | 35,000 | (6,000) |
|  | $1,595,000 | $130,000 | $155,000 | $111,000 | $105,000 |

Stockholders' equities as of date of acquisition:

|  | B | C | D | E |
|---|---|---|---|---|
| Capital stock | $ 75,000 | $ 60,000 | $ 60,000 | $ 50,000 |
| Retained earnings (deficit) | 21,000 | (5,000) | 14,000 | 12,000 |

## Problem 11-6

Company A acquired a 90% interest in Company B and an 80% interest in Company C on January 1, 1980. Company A carries its investments in these companies at cost. From the following data prepare working papers in columnar form showing (1) consolidated income for 1980, and (2) consolidated retained earnings as of December 31, 1980.

STATEMENT OF INCOME

FOR THE YEAR ENDED DECEMBER 31, 1980

|  | Company A | Company B | Company C |
|---|---|---|---|
| Income: |  |  |  |
| Sales (net) | $1,478,000 | $150,800 | $162,000 |
| Dividends | 20,000 |  |  |
| Interest | 12,000 | 1,200 |  |
|  | $1,510,000 | $152,000 | $162,000 |
| Deductions: |  |  |  |
| Cost of sales | $ 750,000 | $ 74,000 | $ 77,000 |
| Selling expenses | 300,000 | 29,000 | 32,000 |
| General expenses | 150,000 | 14,000 | 13,000 |
| Taxes | 166,000 | 15,000 | 16,000 |
|  | $1,366,000 | $132,000 | $138,000 |
| Net Income | $ 144,000 | $ 20,000 | $ 24,000 |

STATEMENT OF RETAINED EARNINGS

AS OF DECEMBER 31, 1980

|  | Company A | Company B | Company C |
|---|---|---|---|
| Balance 1/1/80 | $ 463,000 | $68,000 | $51,000 |
| Net income for year | 144,000 | 20,000 | 24,000 |
| Dividends paid | (30,000) | (10,000) | (12,000) |
| Balance 12/31/80 | $577,000 | $78,000 | $63,000 |

*Intercompany transactions:*

(1) Company A purchased merchandise from Company B for $50,000.
(2) Company B purchased merchandise from Company C for $15,000.
(3) Company C paid Company A $600 interest.

## Problem 11-7

From the following comparative statements of financial position prepare:

1. A consolidated statement of financial position as of December 31, 1979, the date Company A acquired a 90% interest in Company B, and
2. A consolidated statement of financial position as of December 31, 1980.

COMPANY A

STATEMENT OF FINANCIAL POSITION

| Assets | Dec. 31, 1979 | Dec. 31, 1980 |
|---|---|---|
| Current assets | $200,000 | $240,000 |
| Investment in Company B (Cost) | 72,000 | 70,020 |
| Property, plant, and equipment (net) | 340,000 | 310,000 |
| Other assets | 4,000 | 6,980 |
|  | $616,000 | $627,000 |

## 11 / Investment Carried at Cost

### Equities

| | | |
|---|---:|---:|
| Current liabilities | $200,000 | $170,000 |
| Capital stock | 200,000 | 200,000 |
| Retained earnings | 216,000 | 257,000 |
| | $616,000 | $627,000 |

### COMPANY B
### STATEMENT OF FINANCIAL POSITION

| Assets | Dec. 31, 1979 | Dec. 31, 1980 |
|---|---:|---:|
| Current assets | $22,000 | $47,000 |
| Property, plant, and equipment (net) | 45,000 | 42,000 |
| Other assets | 9,000 | 10,000 |
| | $76,000 | $99,000 |

| Equities | | |
|---|---:|---:|
| Current liabilities | $18,000 | $20,000 |
| Capital stock | 50,000 | 50,000 |
| Retained earnings | 8,000 | 29,000 |
| | $76,000 | $99,000 |

## Problem 11-8

Prepare consolidated working papers with columns for income, retained earnings, minority interest, and financial position for the year ended December 31, from the following data:

Ninety-two percent of the stock of Co. S was acquired for $145,000 in 1979, when Co. S's stockholders' equity was composed of $50,000 retained earnings and $100,000 capital stock

### ADJUSTED TRIAL BALANCES
### DECEMBER 31, 1980

| Debits | Co. P | Co. S |
|---|---:|---:|
| Merchandise inventory | $ 40,000 | $ 20,000 |
| Investment in Co. S | 143,600 | |
| Other assets | 520,000 | 270,000 |
| Cost of sales | 390,000 | 140,000 |
| Expenses | 111,400 | 65,000 |
| Dividends paid | 20,000 | 10,000 |
| | $1,225,000 | $505,000 |

| Credits | | |
|---|---:|---:|
| Sales | $ 620,000 | $245,000 |
| Dividend income | 9,200 | |
| Liabilities | 290,000 | 90,000 |
| Capital stock | 200,000 | 100,000 |
| Retained earnings, 1/1/80 | 105,800 | 70,000 |
| | $1,225,000 | $505,000 |

## Problem 11-9

From the following data prepare consolidated working papers with columns for income, retained earnings, minority interest, and financial position for the year ended December 31, 1980:

TRIAL BALANCES
DECEMBER 31, 1980

| Debits | Company A | Company B |
|---|---|---|
| Inventories 1/1/80 | $ 60,000 | $ 32,000 |
| Investment in Company B | 168,480 | |
| Other assets (net) | 630,000 | 285,000 |
| Purchases | 395,000 | 145,000 |
| Expenses | 126,520 | 68,000 |
| Dividends paid | 18,000 | 6,000 |
| | $1,398,000 | $536,000 |

| Credits | | |
|---|---|---|
| Sales | $ 605,840 | $258,000 |
| Dividend income | 5,160 | |
| Liabilities | 280,000 | 70,000 |
| Capital stock | 300,000 | 100,000 |
| Retained earnings 1/1/80 | 207,000 | 108,000 |
| | $1,398,000 | $536,000 |

| Inventories, December 31, 1980 | Company A | $64,000 |
|---|---|---|
| | Company B | 29,000 |
| | | $93,000 |

Eighty-six percent of the stock of Company B was acquired for $170,000 on January 1, 1979, when Company B's stockholders' equity was composed of $80,000 retained earnings and $100,000 capital stock.

## Problem 11-10

From the following data prepare a consolidated statement of financial position as of June 30, 1980:

| Assets | A Company | B Company | C Company |
|---|---|---|---|
| Cash | $ 10,000 | $ 6,000 | $ 2,500 |
| Notes receivable | 7,000 | 3,000 | |
| Accounts receivable | 36,000 | 15,000 | 7,500 |
| Merchandise inventories | 20,000 | 10,000 | 5,000 |
| Investments: | | | |
| B Company | 30,000 | | |
| C Company | 28,000 | | |

## 11 / Investment Carried at Cost

|  |  |  |  |
|---|---|---|---|
| Land | 18,000 |  | 5,000 |
| Buildings, plant, and equipment | 76,000 | 35,000 | 35,000 |
| Deficit |  |  | 4,000 |
| Totals | $225,000 | $69,000 | $59,000 |

### Liabilities and Capital

|  |  |  |  |
|---|---|---|---|
| Notes payable | $ 12,000 | $ 6,000 | $ 8,000 |
| Accounts payable | 18,000 | 7,500 | 9,000 |
| Bonds payable | 50,000 | 15,000 |  |
| Accumulated depreciation | 25,000 | 9,000 | 7,000 |
| Capital stock | 100,000 | 25,000 | 35,000 |
| Retained earnings | 20,000 | 6,500 |  |
| Totals | $225,000 | $69,000 | $59,000 |

The holding company acquired 90% of the capital stock of the B Company, July 1, 1977, at a cost of $26,100, and later arbitrarily increased the book value of this asset to $30,000, crediting the increase to retained earnings. Eighty percent of the capital stock of C Company was acquired at a cost of $28,000 when that company was organized, July 1, 1978.

The intercompany accounts at June 30, 1980, were as follows:

A Company held notes of the B Company for $3,000 and the C Company for $4,000.

B Company held a note of the C Company for $3,000.

A Company owed an open account to the B Company $4,000 and to the C Company $2,500.

The retained earnings accounts of the subsidiary companies, analyzed, were as follows:

|  | B Company | C Company |
|---|---|---|
| Balance, July 1, 1977 | $4,000 |  |
| Profit, 1977–1978 | 3,000 |  |
| Balance, July 1, 1978 | $7,000 |  |
| Profit or loss, 1978–1979 | −1,500 | −$5,000 |
| Balance, July 1, 1979 | $5,500 | −$5,000 |
| Profit, 1979–1980 | 1,000 | 1,000 |
| Balance, June 30, 1980 | $6,500 | −$4,000 |

# 12

# Consolidated Statements Subsequent to Date of Acquisition — Investment Not Carried at Cost

The answer to the question of when earnings and losses of a company are realized by owners of the company's stock is not clear-cut when a parent-subsidiary relationship exists. The normal accounting rule that income on a stock investment is not realized until a dividend is declared may not be applicable in this case, since the payment of a dividend by a subsidiary company may depend on the orders of the parent company. In a sense the earnings of the subsidiary may be available to the parent company at any time. This has led some parent companies to carry their investment in a subsidiary as though earnings of the subsidiary applicable to the parent's investment had been realized by the parent as soon as earned by the subsidiary. This method of carrying the investment is normally referred to as the "equity" or "book value" method. As we saw in Chapter Nine, the Accounting Principles Board in *Opinion No. 18* recommends the use of the equity method for unconsolidated subsidiaries. The Board's endorsement of the equity method in these cases will undoubtedly lead to its wider use.

## EQUITY METHOD

When the equity method is used, the investment is recorded at cost when acquired. In contrast to the cost method, however, under the equity method the parent company's share of increases and decreases in the subsidiary's stockholders' equity is reflected on the parent company's books by periodic entries. Thus, if a parent company owns 90% of the outstanding stock of a subsidiary, it will debit its investment account and credit an income account for 90% of the income reported by the subsidiary.

The following example illustrates the periodic entries that would be recorded on the parent company's books when the equity method is used. For comparative purposes, the cost method is also illustrated.

(1) January 1, 1980, Company A purchases a 90% interest in Company B for $150,000.
(2) December 31, 1980, Company B reports $50,000 net income for 1980.
(3) March 31, 1981, Company B pays $20,000 dividend.
(4) December 31, 1981, Company B reports $10,000 loss for 1981.

|  | Equity Method |  |  | Cost Method |  |
|---|---|---|---|---|---|
| (1) | Purchase |  |  |  |  |
|  | Investment in Co. B | $150,000 |  | Same entry |  |
|  | Cash |  | $150,000 |  |  |
| (2) | 1980 Net Income |  |  |  |  |
|  | Investment in Co. B | $45,000 |  | No entry |  |
|  | Subsidiary income |  | $45,000 |  |  |
| (3) | Dividend Received |  |  |  |  |
|  | Cash | $18,000 |  | Cash | $18,000 |
|  | Investment in Co. B |  | $18,000 | Dividend income | $18,000 |
| (4) | 1981 Net Loss |  |  |  |  |
|  | Subsidiary loss | $9,000 |  | No entry |  |
|  | Investment in Co. B |  | $9,000 |  |  |

## Consolidated Statement of Financial Position—Equity Method

**Basic Consolidating Procedure.** As indicated in the preceding chapter, the basic procedure when consolidating statements of financial position after the date of acquisition is essentially the same as when consolidating at the date of acquisition: (1) eliminate reciprocals, and (2) consolidate nonreciprocals. When the investment is carried at cost, however, reciprocity between the parent's investment and the subsidiary stockholders' equity usually must be established before elimination is possible. This is not always the case when the equity method is used. If *all* increases and decreases in the subsidiary's stockholders' equity have been reflected on the parent company's books, reciprocity already exists. If for some reason all of the subsidiary increases and decreases have not been reflected on the parent company's books, reciprocity must be established. For example, if the subsidiary has declared but not paid a dividend, and if the parent makes no entry until the dividend is paid, an adjustment would be necessary in order to establish reciprocity. The parent would have no account on its books reciprocal to the dividend payable on the subsidiary's books, and likewise the decrease in the subsidiary's retained earnings would not be reflected on the parent's books. Thus the basic consolidating procedure is essentially the same when either the cost or the equity method is used, that is:

1. Establish reciprocity, if necessary.
2. Eliminate reciprocals.
3. Consolidate nonreciprocals.

The following illustrations demonstrate the techniques of consolidating statements of financial position after the date of acquisition when the equity method is used. In these illustrations the same general conditions are assumed to exist as were used in the preceding chapter, as follows:

A. 100% Ownership:
  (1) Purchased at book value.
  (2) Purchased at more than book value.
  (3) Purchased at less than book value.

B. Less than 100% Ownership:
  (1) Purchased at book value.
  (2) Purchased at more than book value.
  (3) Purchased at less than book value.

## 100% Ownership

**Illustration A-1$_{1(a)}$: 100% Ownership Acquired at Book Value.** Assume the same facts as used in Illustration A-1$_1$ (page 302), that as of January 1, 1980, Company A acquired 100% ownership in Company B for $150,000, which was also the book value of the interest acquired. In the following work sheet the first two columns reflect the financial positions of the respective companies *one* year later, and the final column reflects the financial position after consolidation.

BASIC PROCEDURE

(1) *Establishment of reciprocity, if necessary:*

   Since Company A has taken up the $20,000 increase in Company B's stockholders' equity since acquisition ($150,000 to $170,000), reciprocity exists and no adjustment is necessary.

(2) *Elimination of reciprocals:*

A

| | | |
|---|---|---|
| Capital stock (Company B's) | $100,000 | |
| Retained earnings (Company B's) | 70,000 | |
| Investment in B | | $170,000 |

(work sheet entry to eliminate 100% of B's stockholders' equity against the investment account)

## 12 / *Investment Not Carried at Cost*

It should be noted that this is the same elimination that was made in Illustration A-1$_1$ when the investment account was carried at cost. This is so because the establishment of reciprocity reconciles the two methods.

(3) *Consolidation of nonreciprocals:*

The nonreciprocal elements are consolidated by extending them to the consolidated statement as is done when the investment account is carried at cost. Although the individual company statements are different, the consolidated statements are exactly the same whether the investment is carried at cost or at equity.

COMPANY A AND SUBSIDIARY COMPANY B
CONSOLIDATED WORKING PAPERS
STATEMENT OF FINANCIAL POSITION
DECEMBER 31, 1980

| Assets | Company A | Company B | Adjustments & Eliminations Debit | Adjustments & Eliminations Credit | Consolidated Financial Position |
|---|---|---|---|---|---|
| Current assets | $100,000 | $ 80,000 | | | $180,000 |
| Investment in B | 170,000 | | | $170,000A | |
| Fixed assets (net) | 450,000 | 110,000 | | | 560,000 |
| | $720,000 | $190,000 | | | $740,000 |
| **Equities** | | | | | |
| Current liabilities | $ 30,000 | $ 20,000 | | | $ 50,000 |
| Fixed liabilities | 100,000 | | | | 100,000 |
| Stockholders' equity: | | | | | |
| Capital stock: | | | | | |
| Company A | 400,000 | | | | 400,000 |
| Company B | | 100,000 | $100,000A | | |
| Retained earnings: | | | | | |
| Company A | 190,000 | | | | 190,000RE |
| Company B | | 70,000 | 70,000A | | |
| | $720,000 | $190,000 | $170,000 | $170,000 | $740,000 |

**Illustration A-2$_{1(a)}$: 100% Ownership Acquired at More Than Book Value.** Assume the same facts as used in Illustration A-2$_1$ (page 305), that as of January 1, 1980, Company A acquired 100% ownership in Company B for $170,000, which was $20,000 more than the book value acquired. The following work sheet reflects the financial position of the respective companies *two* years later and how they would appear when consolidated at that time:

COMPANY A AND SUBSIDIARY COMPANY B
CONSOLIDATED WORKING PAPERS
STATEMENT OF FINANCIAL POSITION
DECEMBER 31, 1981

|  | Company A | Company B | Adjustments & Eliminations Debit | Adjustments & Eliminations Credit | Consolidated Financial Position |
|---|---|---|---|---|---|
| *Assets* | | | | | |
| Current assets | $120,000 | $ 90,000 | | | $210,000 |
| Investment in B | 181,000 | | | $165,000A | 16,000G |
| Fixed assets (net) | 444,000 | 105,000 | | | 549,000 |
| | $745,000 | $195,000 | | | $775,000 |
| *Equities* | | | | | |
| Current liabilities | $ 40,000 | $ 30,000 | | | $ 70,000 |
| Fixed liabilities | 90,000 | | | | 90,000 |
| Stockholders' equity: | | | | | |
| Capital stock: | | | | | |
| Company A | 400,000 | | | | 400,000 |
| Company B | | 100,000 | $100,000A | | |
| Retained earnings: | | | | | |
| Company A | 215,000 | | | | 215,000RE |
| Company B | | 65,000 | 65,000A | | |
| | $745,000 | $195,000 | $165,000 | $165,000 | $775,000 |

BASIC PROCEDURE

(1) *Establishment of reciprocity:*

Since Company A has taken up its share (100% of $15,000) of Company B's increase in stockholders' equity since acquisition ($150,000 to $165,000), reciprocity exists and no adjustment is needed.

(2) *Elimination of reciprocals:*

*A*

| | | |
|---|---|---|
| Capital stock (Company B's) | $100,000 | |
| Retained earnings (Company B's) | 65,000 | |
| Investment in B | | $165,000 |

(work sheet entry to eliminate 100% of B's stockholders' equity against the investment account)

(3) *Consolidation of nonreciprocals:*

Nonreciprocals are consolidated as they have been in preceding illustrations. It should be noted, however, that the nonreciprocal portion of the investment account extended to the consolidated statement is $16,000, which is $4,000 (two years' amortization) less than the amount computed at the date of acquisition.

## Illustration A-3₁(ₐ): 100% Ownership Acquired at Less Than Book Value.

The facts in Illustration A-3₁ (page 307), that on January 1, 1980, Company A acquired 100% ownership of Company B for $140,000, which was $10,000 less than the book value acquired, are used in the following discussion. In the work sheet the first two columns reflect the financial positions of Companies A and B *three* years after acquisition, and the final column reflects the financial position after consolidation.

COMPANY A AND SUBSIDIARY COMPANY B
CONSOLIDATED WORKING PAPERS
STATEMENT OF FINANCIAL POSITION
DECEMBER 31, 1982

| Assets | Company A | Company B | Adjustments & Eliminations Debit | Adjustments & Eliminations Credit | Consolidated Financial Position |
|---|---|---|---|---|---|
| Current assets | $100,000 | $ 70,000 | | | $170,000 |
| Investment in B | 129,000 | | | $136,000A | (7,000)G |
| Fixed assets (net) | 427,000 | 100,000 | | | 527,000 |
| | $656,000 | $170,000 | | | $690,000 |
| *Equities* | | | | | |
| Current liabilities | $ 50,000 | $ 34,000 | | | $ 84,000 |
| Fixed liabilities | 80,000 | | | | 80,000 |
| Stockholders' equity: | | | | | |
| Capital stock: | | | | | |
| Company A | 400,000 | | | | 400,000 |
| Company B | | 100,000 | $100,000A | | |
| Retained earnings: | | | | | |
| Company A | 126,000 | | | | 126,000RE |
| Company B | | 36,000 | 36,000A | | |
| | $656,000 | $170,000 | $136,000 | $136,000 | $690,000 |

BASIC PROCEDURE

(1) *Establishment of reciprocity:*

No entry is necessary since reciprocity already exists.

(2) *Elimination of reciprocals:*

                            A

Capital stock (Company B's)               $100,000
Retained earnings (Company B's)         36,000
    Investment in B                                         $136,000
(work sheet entry to eliminate 100% of B's stockholders' equity against the investment account)

(3) *Consolidation of nonreciprocals:*

Consolidation of nonreciprocals is the same as in preceding illustrations. Notice, however, that the nonreciprocal portion of the elimination against the investment account is $3,000 (three years' amortization) less than the amount computed at the date of acquisition.

## Less Than 100% Ownership

**Illustration B-1$_{1(a)}$: Less Than 100% Ownership Acquired at Book Value.** Assume the same basic facts as used in Illustration B-1$_1$ (page 309), that on January 1, 1980, Company A acquired a 90% interest in Company B for $135,000. This was also the book value at that date of the interest acquired. In the following work sheet the first two columns reflect the financial position of the respective companies *one* year later, and the final column reflects the financial position after consolidation.

COMPANY A AND SUBSIDIARY COMPANY B
CONSOLIDATED WORKING PAPERS
STATEMENT OF FINANCIAL POSITION
DECEMBER 31, 1980

|  | Company A | Company B | Adjustments & Eliminations Debit | Adjustments & Eliminations Credit | Consolidated Financial Position |
|---|---|---|---|---|---|
| *Assets* | | | | | |
| Current assets | $115,000 | $ 80,000 | | | $195,000 |
| Investment in B | 153,000 | | | $153,000A | |
| Fixed assets (net) | 450,000 | 110,000 | | | 560,000 |
|  | $718,000 | $190,000 | | | $755,000 |
| *Equities* | | | | | |
| Current liabilities | $ 30,000 | $ 20,000 | | | $ 50,000 |
| Fixed liabilities | 100,000 | | | | 100,000 |
| Stockholders' equity: | | | | | |
| Capital stock: | | | | | |
| Company A | 400,000 | | | | 400,000 |
| Company B | | 100,000 | $ 90,000A | | 10,000MI |
| Retained earnings: | | | | | |
| Company A | 188,000 | | | | 188,000RE |
| Company B | | 70,000 | 63,000A | | 7,000MI |
|  | $718,000 | $190,000 | $153,000 | $153,000 | $755,000 |

## 12 / Investment Not Carried at Cost

### Basic Procedure

(1) *Establishment of reciprocity:*

Because Company A has taken up its share (90%) of the $20,000 increase in Company B's stockholders' equity since acquisition ($150,000 to $170,000), reciprocity exists and therefore no adjustment is necessary.

(2) *Elimination of reciprocals:*

A

| | | |
|---|---|---|
| Capital stock (Company B's) | $90,000 | |
| Retained earnings (Company B's) | 63,000 | |
|    Investment in B | | $153,000 |

(work sheet entry to eliminate 90% of B's stockholders' equity against the investment account)

(3) *Consolidation of nonreciprocals:*

Nonreciprocals are consolidated in the usual manner. It should be noted that the nonreciprocal elements of the subsidiary's stockholders' equity are extended to the consolidated statement as minority interest. If the minority interest in this illustration is compared with that in Illustration B-1₁ where the cost method was in use, it will be seen that the minority interest is the same regardless of the method used for carrying the investment account.

### Illustration B-2₁₍ₐ₎: Less Than 100% Ownership Acquired at More Than Book Value.

Assume the same basic facts as used in Illustration B-2 (page 284), that on January 1, 1980, Company A acquired a 90% interest in Company B for $155,000, which was $20,000 more than the book value acquired. The individual statements in the work sheet on page 342 reflect the financial position as reported by the respective companies on December 31, 1981. However, a $10,000 dividend declared by Company B as of December 31, 1981, is not reflected on Company A's statement.

### Basic Procedure

(1) *Establishment of reciprocity:*

(1)

| | | |
|---|---|---|
| Dividends receivable | $9,000 | |
|    Investment in B | | $9,000 |

(work sheet entry to recognize A's share of B's dividend declared December 31, 1981)

(2) *Elimination of reciprocals:*

A

| | | |
|---|---|---|
| Dividends payable | $9,000 | |
|    Dividends receivable | | $9,000 |

(work sheet entry to eliminate dividends receivable and dividends payable)

|   | B |   |   |
|---|---|---|---|
| Capital stock (Company B's) | | $90,000 | |
| Retained earnings (Company B's) | | 58,500 | |
| Investment in B | | | $148,500 |
| (work sheet entry to eliminate 90% of B's stockholders' equity against the investment account) | | | |

(3) *Consolidation of nonreciprocals:*

Nonreciprocals are consolidated in the usual manner. It should be noted that the nonreciprocal element of the subsidiary's stockholders' equity is extended to the consolidated statement as minority interest. If the minority interest in this illustration is compared with that in Illustration B-2$_1$ where the cost method is used, it will be seen that the minority interest is the same regardless of the method used for carrying the investment account.

COMPANY A AND SUBSIDIARY COMPANY B

CONSOLIDATED WORKING PAPERS

STATEMENT OF FINANCIAL POSITION

DECEMBER 31, 1981

| Assets | Company A | Company B | Adjustments & Eliminations Debit | Adjustments & Eliminations Credit | Consolidated Financial Position |
|---|---|---|---|---|---|
| Cash | $ 35,000 | $ 40,000 | | | $ 75,000 |
| Inventories | 100,000 | 50,000 | | | 150,000 |
| Dividends receivable | | | $ 9,000(1) | $9,000A | |
| Investment in B | 173,500 | | | { 9,000(1) <br> 148,500B | 16,000G |
| Fixed assets (net) | 444,000 | 105,000 | | | 549,000 |
| | $752,500 | $195,000 | | | $790,000 |
| *Equities* | | | | | |
| Accounts payable | $ 40,000 | $ 20,000 | | | $ 60,000 |
| Dividends payable | | 10,000 | 9,000A | | 1,000 |
| Fixed liabilities | 90,000 | | | | 90,000 |
| Stockholders' equity: | | | | | |
| Capital stock: | | | | | |
| Company A | 400,000 | | | | 400,000 |
| Company B | | 100,000 | 90,000B | | 10,000MI |
| Retained earnings: | | | | | |
| Company A | 222,500 | | | | 222,500RE |
| Company B | | 65,000 | 58,500B | | 6,500MI |
| | $752,500 | $195,000 | $166,500 | $166,500 | $790,000 |

## 12 / Investment Not Carried at Cost

**Illustration B-3**₁₍ₐ₎**: Less Than 100% Ownership Acquired at Less Than Book Value.** Assume the same basic facts as used in Illustration B-3₁ (page 313), that on January 1, 1980, Company A acquired a 90% interest in Company B for $125,000, which was $10,000 less than the book value acquired. The individual statements in the following work sheet reflect the financial position as reported by the respective companies as of December 31, 1982. However, during 1982 Company B charged a $10,000 correction of an error directly to retained earnings. Since Company A has taken up its share of Company B's 1982 income (loss) as reported on Company B's income statement, this item is not reflected on Company A's books.

COMPANY A AND SUBSIDIARY COMPANY B
CONSOLIDATED WORKING PAPERS
STATEMENT OF FINANCIAL POSITION
DECEMBER 31, 1982

| Assets | Company A | Company B | Adjustments & Eliminations Debit | Adjustments & Eliminations Credit | Consolidated Financial Position |
|---|---|---|---|---|---|
| Current assets | $115,000 | $ 70,000 | | | $185,000 |
| Investment in B | 124,400 | | | $ 9,000(1) 122,400A | (7,000)G |
| Fixed assets (net) | 427,000 | 100,000 | | | 527,000 |
| | $666,400 | $170,000 | | | $705,000 |
| **Equities** | | | | | |
| Current liabilities | $ 50,000 | $ 34,000 | | | $ 84,000 |
| Fixed liabilities | 80,000 | | | | 80,000 |
| Stockholders' equity: | | | | | |
| Capital stock: | | | | | |
| Company A | 400,000 | | | | 400,000 |
| Company B | | 100,000 | $ 90,000A | | 10,000MI |
| Retained earnings: | | | | | |
| Company A | 136,400 | | 9,000(1) | | 127,400RE |
| Company B | | 36,000 | 32,400A | | 3,600MI |
| | $666,400 | $170,000 | $131,400 | $131,400 | $705,000 |

BASIC PROCEDURE

(1) *Establishment of reciprocity:*

(1)

| | | |
|---|---|---|
| Retained earnings (Company A's) | $9,000 | |
| Investment in B | | $9,000 |

(work sheet entry to recognize Company A's share
of Company B's $10,000 correction of an error)

Since this item was not included in the determination of Company B's net income, and since Company A took up its share of B's reported net income, this item is not reflected on A's separate statement.

(2) *Elimination of reciprocals:*

A

| | | |
|---|---|---|
| Capital stock (Company B's) | $90,000 | |
| Retained earnings (Company B's) | 32,400 | |
|     Investment in B | | $122,400 |

(work sheet entry to eliminate 90% of B's stockholders' equity against the investment account)

(3) *Consolidation of nonreciprocals:*

Nonreciprocals are consolidated in the usual manner. It should be noted that the nonreciprocal element of the subsidiary's stockholders' equity is extended to the consolidated statement as minority interest. If the minority interest in this illustration is compared with that in Illustration B-3$_1$ where the cost method is used, it will be seen that the minority interest is the same regardless of the method used for carrying the investment account.

### COST AND EQUITY METHODS COMPARED

| COST METHOD | EQUITY METHOD |
|---|---|
| (1) Stock acquisition is recorded at cost. | (1) Stock acquisition is recorded at cost. |
| (2) Subsidiary earnings are *not* recorded on parent company's books | (2) Subsidiary earnings accruing to parent are recorded on parent company's books. |
| (3) Subsidiary earnings accruing to parent are recognized on the consolidated working papers by an adjusting entry. | (3) Subsidiary earnings are already recorded. |
| (4) Consolidated statements are the same as if the *equity method* had been used. | (4) Consolidated statements are the same as if the *cost method* had been used. |

## Consolidated Statement of Income and Retained Earnings — Investment Carried at Equity

The technique involved in the preparation of consolidated statements of income and retained earnings when the equity method is used is essentially the same as when the cost method is used, that is (1) eliminate intercompany transactions, and (2) consolidate nonintercompany transactions. However, since the parent recognizes the increases and decreases in subsidiary's stockholders' equity by periodic entries, there may be more intercompany accounts to eliminate than when the cost method is used.

The following illustrations are based on the same data as used in Chapter Eleven in Illustrations C-1 and C-2. The general situation is that Company A acquired 90% of the outstanding stock of Company B as of January 1, 1980.

## Illustration C-1$_1$.  *Specific Assumptions:*

A. Company A sold Company B $20,000 worth of merchandise.
B. Company B paid Company A $400 interest.
C. Company B reported a net income of $20,000 for 1980.

COMPANY A AND SUBSIDIARY COMPANY B
CONSOLIDATED WORKING PAPERS
STATEMENT OF INCOME AND RETAINED EARNINGS
YEAR ENDED DECEMBER 31, 1980

|  | Company A | Company B | Eliminations | Consolidated Income | Consolidated Retained Earnings |
|---|---|---|---|---|---|
| *Credits* | | | | | |
| Net sales | $800,000 | $200,000 | $20,000A | $980,000 | |
| Interest income | 6,000 | | 400B | 5,600 | |
| Income from B | 18,000 | | 18,000C | | |
| Totals | $824,000 | $200,000 | $38,400 | $985,600 | |
| *Debits* | | | | | |
| Cost of sales | $590,000 | $130,000 | $20,0000A | $700,000 | |
| Depreciation | 80,000 | 26,000 | | 106,000 | |
| Interest expense | 6,000 | 2,000 | 400B | 7,600 | |
| Other expenses | 10,000 | 2,000 | | 12,000 | |
| Federal income taxes | 60,000 | 20,000 | | 80,000 | |
| Net income | 78,000 | 20,000 | 18,000C | 80,000 | |
| Totals | $824,000 | $200,000 | $38,400 | $985,600 | |
| Retained earnings 1/1/80 | $110,000 | $ 50,000 | | | $110,000* |
| Net income (1980) | 78,000 | 20,000 | | | |
| Retained earnings 12/31/80 | $188,000 | $ 70,000 | | | |

*Note:* Consolidated retained earnings at date of acquisition is composed entirely of the parent company's retained earnings.

Apportionment of net income:
| | | |
|---|---:|---:|
| Net income | $80,000 | |
| Minority interest (10% of $20,000) | 2,000 | |
| Consolidated interest (remainder) | $78,000 | 78,000 |
| Consolidated retained earnings 12/31/80 | | $188,000 |

BASIC PROCEDURE

(1) *Elimination of intercompany transactions:*

A

| | | |
|---|---:|---:|
| Sales | $20,000 | |
|    Cost of Sales | | $20,000 |
| (work sheet elimination of intercompany sales) | | |

B

| | | |
|---|---:|---:|
| Interest income | $ 400 | |
|    Interest expense | | $ 400 |
| (work sheet elimination of intercompany interest) | | |

C

| | | |
|---|---:|---:|
| Income from B | $18,000 | |
|    Net income | | $18,000 |
| (work sheet elimination of intercompany income) | | |

(2) *Consolidation of nonintercompany transactions:*

   Nonintercompany items are consolidated by extending them to the consolidated income statement.

(3) *Apportionment of net income:*

   Minority interest (10% of Company B's $20,000).
   Majority interest (90% of Company B's $20,000 plus Company A's $78,000 minus $18,000 intercompany).

As is the case when the investment is carried at cost, the last two columns of the working papers may be presented in statement form as follows:

COMPANY A AND SUBSIDIARY COMPANY B

CONSOLIDATED STATEMENT OF INCOME
AND RETAINED EARNINGS

YEAR ENDED DECEMBER 31, 1980

*Income:*

| | | |
|---|---:|---:|
| Net sales | $980,000 | |
| Interest income | 5,600 | |
|    Gross income | $985,600 | $985,600 |

12 / *Investment Not Carried at Cost*     347

*Costs and Expenses:*

| | | |
|---|---:|---:|
| Cost of sales | $700,000 | |
| Depreciation | 106,000 | |
| Interest expense | 7,600 | |
| Other expenses | 12,000 | |
| Federal income taxes | 80,000 | |
| Total costs and expenses | $905,600 | 905,600 |
| Net income | | $ 80,000 |
| Minority interest | | 2,000 |
| *Consolidated Net Income* | | $ 78,000 |
| Consolidated retained earnings 1/1/80 | | 110,000 |
| Consolidated retained earnings 12/31/80 | | $188,000 |

## Illustration C-2$_1$. *Specific Assumptions:*

A. Company A sold Company B $20,000 of merchandise at cost.
B. Company B paid Company A $400 interest.
C. Company B reported a net income of $30,000 for 1980.
D. Company B declared and paid $10,000 dividends.

COMPANY A AND SUBSIDIARY COMPANY B
CONSOLIDATED WORKING PAPERS
STATEMENT OF INCOME AND RETAINED EARNINGS
YEAR ENDED DECEMBER 31, 1980

| | Company A | Company B | Eliminations | Consolidated Income | Consolidated Retained Earnings |
|---|---:|---:|---:|---:|---:|
| *Credits* | | | | | |
| Net sales | $791,000 | $210,000 | $20,000A | $981,000 | |
| Interest income | 6,000 | | 400B | 5,600 | |
| Income from B | 27,000 | | 27,000C | | |
| Totals | $824,000 | $210,000 | $47,400 | $986,600 | |
| *Debits* | | | | | |
| Cost of sales | $590,000 | $130,000 | $20,000A | $700,000 | |
| Depreciation | 80,000 | 26,000 | | 106,000 | |
| Interest expense | 6,000 | 2,000 | 400B | 7,600 | |
| Other expenses | 10,000 | 2,000 | | 12,000 | |
| Federal income taxes | 60,000 | 20,000 | | 80,000 | |
| Net income | 78,000 | 30,000 | 27,000C | 81,000 | |
| Totals | $824,000 | $210,000 | $47,400 | $986,600 | |

|  |  |  |  |  |
|---|---:|---:|---:|---:|
| Retained earnings 1/1/80 | $110,000 | $ 50,000 |  | $110,000 |
| Dividends paid (1980) |  | (10,000) |  |  |
| Net income (1980) | 78,000 | 30,000 |  |  |
| Retained earnings 12/31/80 | $188,000 | $ 70,000 |  |  |

| Apportionment of net income: |  |  |
|---|---:|---:|
| Net income | $ 81,000 |  |
| Minority interest (10% of $30,000) | $ 3,000 |  |
| Consolidated interest (remainder) | $ 78,000 | 78,000 |
| Consolidated retained earnings 12/31/80 |  | $188,000 |

Company A and Subsidiary Company B

Consolidated Statement of Income
and Retained Earnings

Year Ended December 31, 1980

*Income:*

| | | |
|---|---:|---:|
| Net sales | $981,000 | |
| Interest income | 5,600 | |
| Gross income | $986,600 | $986,600 |

*Cost and Expenses:*

| | | |
|---|---:|---:|
| Cost of sales | $700,000 | |
| Depreciation | 106,000 | |
| Interest expense | 7,600 | |
| Other expenses | 12,000 | |
| Federal income taxes | 80,000 | |
| Total costs and expenses | $905,600 | 905,600 |
| Net income | | $ 81,000 |
| Minority interest | | 3,000 |
| *Consolidated Net Income* | | $ 78,000 |
| Consolidated retained earnings 1/1/80 | | 110,000 |
| Consolidated retained earnings 12/31/80 | | $188,000 |

Basic Procedure

(1) *Elimination of intercompany transactions:*

                                             A

| | | |
|---|---:|---:|
| Sales | $20,000 | |
|     Cost of sales | | $20,000 |
| (work sheet elimination of intercompany sales) | | |

## 12 / Investment Not Carried at Cost

### B

| | | | |
|---|---|---|---|
| Interest income | | $ 400 | |
| Interest expense | | | $ 400 |

(work sheet elimination of intercompany interest)

### C

| | | | |
|---|---|---|---|
| Income from B | | $27,000 | |
| Net income | | | $27,000 |

(work sheet elimination of intercompany income)

(2) *Consolidation of nonintercompany transactions:*

Nonintercompany items are consolidated by extending them to the consolidated income statement

(3) *Apportionment of net income:*

Minority interest (10% of Company B's $30,000).
Majority interest (90% of Company B's $30,000 plus Company A's $78,000 minus $27,000 intercompany).

The last two columns of the working papers may be presented in statement form as shown on page 348.

## Trial Balance Approach

A trial balance approach, as illustrated in Chapter Eleven when the investment is carried at cost, may also be used when preparing consolidated statements if the investment is carried on some basis other than cost. Regardless of the method used in carrying the investment and regardless of the approach used when consolidating the basic procedure remains the same: establish reciprocity if necessary, eliminate reciprocals, and consolidate nonreciprocals.

The following examples illustrate the basic procedure involved when the investment is carried at something other than cost, in this case, equity. Again, three slightly different, but fundamentally important, situations are illustrated. In these examples particular attention should be given to the establishment of reciprocity.

**Illustration D-$1_1$.** This illustration (pp. 350–351) is based on the same basic data used in Illustrations B-1, B-$1_{1(a)}$, and C-$1_1$.

**Illustration D-$2_1$.** The general situation in this illustration (pp. 352–353) is the same as that in Illustration D-$1_1$: that is, Company A acquired 90% of the outstanding stock of Company B as of January 1, 1980. However, in this instance consolidation is taking place at the end of 1981 instead of at the end of 1980.

*Illustration D-1[1]*

COMPANY A AND SUBSIDIARY COMPANY B

CONSOLIDATED WORKING PAPERS

DECEMBER 31, 1980

|  | Company A | Company B | Adjustments and Eliminations Debit | Credit |
|---|---|---|---|---|
| *Debits* |  |  |  |  |
| Current assets | $ 115,000 | $ 80,000 |  |  |
| Investment in B | 153,000 |  |  | $ 18,000(1) |
|  |  |  |  | 135,000C |
| Fixed assets (net) | 450,000 | 110,000 |  |  |
| Cost of sales | 590,000 | 130,000 |  | 20,000A |
| Depreciation | 80,000 | 26,000 |  |  |
| Interest expense | 6,000 | 2,000 |  | 400B |
| Other expenses | 10,000 | 2,000 |  |  |
| Federal income taxes | 60,000 | 20,000 |  |  |
|  | $1,464,000 | $370,000 |  |  |
| *Credits* |  |  |  |  |
| Current liabilities | $ 30,000 | $ 20,000 |  |  |
| Fixed liabilities | 100,000 |  |  |  |
| Net sales | 800,000 | 200,000 | $ 20,000A |  |
| Interest income | 6,000 |  | 400B |  |
| Income from B | 18,000 |  | 18,000(1) |  |
| Capital stock: |  |  |  |  |
| Company A | 400,000 |  |  |  |
| Company B |  | 100,000 | 90,000C |  |
| Retained earnings: |  |  |  |  |
| Company A 1/1/80 | 110,000 |  |  |  |
| Company B 1/1/80 |  | 50,000 | 45,000C |  |
|  | $1,464,000 | $370,000 | $173,400 | $173,400 |

Income credits
Income debits
Net income
Apportionment of net income:
  Minority interest:
    Subsidiary income credits                $200,000
    Subsidiary income debits                 180,000
    Subsidiary net income                     $ 20,000
    Minority interest (10%)                    2,000
Consolidated net income (remainder)
Retained earnings 12/31/80
Minority interest 12/31/80

(1): To establish reciprocity as of the beginning of the period.
A:   To eliminate intercompany sales.
B:   To eliminate intercompany interest.
C:   To eliminate 90% of B's stockholders' equity against the investment account.

COMPANY A AND SUBSIDIARY COMPANY B

CONSOLIDATED WORKING PAPERS

(Continued — Illustration D-1$_1$)

|  Consolidated Income | Consolidated Retained Earnings | Minority Interest | Consolidated Financial Position |
|---|---|---|---|
|  |  |  | $195,000 |
|  |  |  | 560,000 |
| $700,000 |  |  |  |
| 106,000 |  |  |  |
| 7,600 |  |  |  |
| 12,000 |  |  |  |
| 80,000 |  |  |  |
| $905,600 | −0− | −0− | $755,000 |
|  |  |  | $ 50,000 |
|  |  |  | 100,000 |
| $980,000 |  |  |  |
| 5,600 |  |  |  |
|  |  |  | 400,000 |
|  |  | $10,000 |  |
|  | $110,000 |  |  |
|  |  | 5,000 |  |
| $985,600 |  |  |  |
| 905,600 |  |  |  |
| $ 80,000 |  |  |  |
| 2,000 |  | 2,000 |  |
| $ 78,000 | 78,000 |  |  |
|  | $188,000 |  | 188,000RE |
|  |  | $17,000 | 17,000MI |
|  |  |  | $755,000 |

351

*Illustration D-2*[1]

COMPANY A AND SUBSIDIARY COMPANY B
CONSOLIDATED WORKING PAPERS
DECEMBER 31, 1981

|  | Company A | Company B | Adjustments and Eliminations Debit | Credit |
|---|---|---|---|---|
| *Debits* |  |  |  |  |
| Current assets | $ 205,000 | $154,000 |  |  |
| Investment in B | 201,600 |  |  | $ 48,600(1) |
|  |  |  |  | 153,000*A* |
| Fixed assets (net) | 460,000 | 100,000 |  |  |
| Cost of sales | 650,000 | 170,000 |  |  |
| Depreciation | 85,000 | 28,000 |  |  |
| Interest expense | 6,000 |  |  |  |
| Other expense | 14,000 | 3,000 |  |  |
| Federal income taxes | 75,000 | 45,000 |  |  |
|  | $1,696,600 | $500,000 |  |  |
| *Credits* |  |  |  |  |
| Current liabilities | $ 60,000 | $ 30,000 |  |  |
| Fixed liabilities | 100,000 |  |  |  |
| Net sales | 900,000 | 300,000 |  |  |
| Income from B | 48,600 |  | $ 48,600(1) |  |
| Capital stock: |  |  |  |  |
| Company A | 400,000 |  |  |  |
| Company B |  | 100,000 | 90,000*A* |  |
| Retained earnings: |  |  |  |  |
| Company A 1/1/81 | 188,000 |  |  |  |
| Company B 1/1/81 |  | 70,000 | 63,000*A* |  |
|  | $1,696,600 | $500,000 | $201,600 | $201,600 |

Income credits
Income debits

Net income
Apportionment of net income:
  Minority interest:

|  |  |
|---|---|
| Subsidiary income credits | $300,000 |
| Subsidiary income debits | 246,000 |
| Subsidiary net income | $ 54,000 |
| Minority interest (10%) | 5,400 |

Consolidated net income (remainder)
Retained earnings 12/31/81
Minority interest 12/31/81

(1) To establish reciprocity as of the beginning of the period.
*A*: To eliminate 90% of B's stockholders' equity against the investment account.

COMPANY A AND SUBSIDIARY COMPANY B

CONSOLIDATED WORKING PAPERS

(Continued — Illustration D-2₁)

| Consolidated Income | Consolidated Retained Earnings | Minority Interest | Consolidated Financial Position |
|---|---|---|---|
| | | | $359,000 |
| | | | |
| | | | 560,000 |
| $ 820,000 | | | |
| 113,000 | | | |
| 6,000 | | | |
| 17,000 | | | |
| 120,000 | | | |
| $1,076,000 | –0– | –0– | $919,000 |
| | | | |
| | | | $ 90,000 |
| | | | 100,000 |
| $1,200,000 | | | |
| | | | |
| | | | 400,000 |
| | | $10,000 | |
| | $188,000 | | |
| | | 7,000 | |
| | | | |
| $1,200,000 | | | |
| 1,076,000 | | | |
| $ 124,000 | | | |
| | | | |
| 5,400 | | 5,400 | |
| $ 118,600 | 118,600 | | |
| | $306,600 | | 306,600RE |
| | | $22,400 | 22,400MI |
| | | | $919,000 |

Illustration D-3[1]

COMPANY A AND SUBSIDIARY COMPANY B

CONSOLIDATED WORKING PAPERS, DECEMBER 31, 1982

|  | Company A | Company B | Adjustments and Eliminations Debit | Credit |
|---|---|---|---|---|
| *Debits* |  |  |  |  |
| Inventories 1/1/82 | $ 70,000 | $ 40,000 |  |  |
| Other current assets | 208,000 | 158,000 |  |  |
| Investment in B | 255,600 |  | $ 9,000(2) | $ 63,000(3) <br> 201,600A |
| Fixed assets (net) | 490,000 | 105,000 |  |  |
| Purchases | 700,000 | 200,000 |  |  |
| Depreciation | 84,000 | 30,000 |  |  |
| Other expenses | 100,000 | 70,000 |  |  |
| Dividends paid | 32,000 | 10,000 |  | 9,000(2) |
|  | $1,939,600 | $613,000 |  |  |
| Inventories 12/31/82 |  |  | 150,000(1) |  |
| *Credits* |  |  |  |  |
| Current liabilities | $ 90,000 | $ 39,000 |  |  |
| Fixed liabilities | 100,000 |  |  |  |
| Net sales | 980,000 | 350,000 |  |  |
| Income from B | 63,000 |  | 63,000(3) |  |
| Capital stock: |  |  |  |  |
| Company A | 400,000 |  |  |  |
| Company B |  | 100,000 | 90,000A |  |
| Retained earnings: |  |  |  |  |
| Company A 1/1/82 | 306,600 |  |  |  |
| Company B 1/1/82 |  | 124,000 | 111,600A |  |
|  | $1,939,600 | $613,000 |  |  |
| Inventories 12/31/82 | $ 90,000 | $ 60,000 |  | $150,000(1) |
|  |  |  | $423,600 | $423,600 |

Income credits
Income debits
Net income
Apportionment of net income:
  Minority interest:
    Subsidiary income credits        $410,000
    Subsidiary income debits         340,000
      Subsidiary net income         $ 70,000
        Minority interest (10%)          7,000
Consolidated net income (remainder)
Retained earnings 12/31/82
Minority interest 12/31/82

  (1): To record ending inventories.
  (2) and (3): To establish reciprocity as of the beginning of the period.
  A: To eliminate 90% of B's stockholders' equity against the investment account.

COMPANY A AND SUBSIDIARY COMPANY B
CONSOLIDATED WORKING PAPERS (Continued — Illustration D-3$_1$)

|  Consolidated Income  |  Consolidated Retained Earnings  |  Minority Interest  |  Consolidated Financial Position  |
|---|---|---|---|
| $ 110,000 |   |   |   |
|   |   |   | $ 366,000 |
|   |   |   |   |
|   |   |   | 595,000 |
| 900,000 |   |   |   |
| 114,000 |   |   |   |
| 170,000 |   |   |   |
|   | $ 32,000 | $ 1,000 |   |
|   |   |   | 150,000 |
| $1,294,000 | $ 32,000 | $ 1,000 | $1,111,000 |
|   |   |   | $ 129,000 |
|   |   |   | 100,000 |
| $1,330,000 |   |   |   |
|   |   |   | 400,000 |
|   |   | $10,000 |   |
|   | $306,600 |   |   |
|   |   | 12,400 |   |
| 150,000 |   |   |   |
| $1,480,000 |   |   |   |
| 1,294,000 |   |   |   |
| $ 186,000 |   |   |   |
| 7,000 |   | 7,000 |   |
| $ 179,000 | 179,000 |   |   |
|   | $485,600 |   |   |
|   | 32,000 |   |   |
|   | $453,600 |   | 453,600RE |
|   |   | $29,400 |   |
|   |   | 1,000 |   |
|   |   | $28,400 | 28,400MI |
|   |   |   | $1,111,000 |

As noted previously, particular attention should be given to the establishment of reciprocity. When the trial balance approach is used, reciprocity must be established as of the beginning of the period rather than at the end, as is the case under a statement approach.

**Illustration D-3₁.** The general situation in this illustration is the same as that in Illustrations D-1₁ and D-2₁: that is, Company A acquired 90% of the outstanding stock of Company B as of January 1, 1980. However, in this instance consolidation is taking place at the end of 1982, and Companies A and B submit unadjusted trial balances rather than adjusted ones. In addition to the data in the respective trial balances, Company A reports an ending inventory of $90,000 and Company B one of $60,000. (The illustration is on pages 354–355.)

## PROBLEMS

### Problem 12-1

Using the following data, and assuming that the equity method is being used, determine in each case:

1. Minority interest at date of acquisition (12/31/78) and at the date of consolidation (12/31/80).
2. Goodwill (either positive or negative) at date of acquisition and at the date of consolidation.
3. Carrying value of the investment at the date of consolidation.

| Company and % Owned | | Cost | Acquisition Date Capital Stock | Retained Earnings | Consolidation Date Capital Stock | Retained Earnings |
|---|---|---|---|---|---|---|
| Case 1 | A  90% | $200,000 | $100,000 | $120,000 | $100,000 | $130,000 |
| Case 2 | B  80% | 64,000 | 80,000 | –0– | 80,000 | 15,000 |
| Case 3 | C  70% | 59,000 | 40,000 | 50,000 | 40,000 | 30,000 |
| Case 4 | D  100% | 175,000 | 60,000 | 90,000 | 60,000 | 130,000 |

### Problem 12-2

A Company acquired an 81% interest in the B Company for $20,000 less than its book value. In the 10-year period that followed the acquisition, B Company earned profits aggregating $196,000 and paid dividends of $75,000. The minority interest at the conclusion of the 10-year period was $95,000. Assuming that A Company carries its investment in B on the equity basis and that goodwill is not being amortized at this time, determine:

1. The cost of the investment, and
2. The amount at which the investment was carried at the conclusion of the 10-year period.

## Problem 12-3

Using the following basic data and the specific assumptions given in each instance, for each case:

1. Determine the carrying value of the investment account as of December 31, 1980.
2. Prepare the work sheet entry(ies) necessary when eliminating reciprocals as of December 31, 1980.
3. Determine the amount of goodwill (positive or negative) as of December 31, 1980.
4. Determine the amount of minority interest as of December 31, 1980.
5. Determine the amount of consolidated retained earnings as of December 31, 1980.

### BASIC DATA

|  | Company X | Company Y | Company Z |
|---|---|---|---|
| **Balances as of 1/1/78:** |  |  |  |
| Capital stock | $400,000 | $150,000 | $120,000 |
| Capital in excess of par | 50,000 | 35,000 | 20,000 |
| Retained earnings (deficit) | 200,000 | 80,000 | (25,000) |
| Dividends paid: 1978 | 20,000 | 7,500 |  |
| 1979 | 20,000 | 7,500 |  |
| **Balances as of 12/31/80:** |  |  |  |
| Capital stock | $400,000 | $150,000 | $120,000 |
| Capital in excess of par | 50,000 | 35,000 | 20,000 |
| Retained earnings | 236,000 | 104,000 | 13,000 |

*Case 1.* Assume that Company X acquired 84% of the stock of Company Y for $238,500 as of January 1, 1978. Company X carries its investment in Y on the *equity* basis.

*Case 2.* Assume that Company X acquired 88% of the stock of Company Z for $84,000 as of January 1, 1978. Company X carries its investment in Z on the *equity* basis.

*Case 3.* Assume that Company X acquired 92% of the stock of Company Y and 82% of the stock of Company Z for $250,000 and $91,000, respectively, as of January 1, 1978. Company X carries these investments on the *equity* basis.

*Case 4.* Assume that Company Y acquired 95% of the stock of Company Z for $105,000 as of January 1, 1978. Company Y carries its investment in Z at *cost.*
*Note:* All cases are independent.

## Problem 12-4

From the following statements and data:

1. Prepare a consolidated statement of financial position, and
2. Prove the goodwill elements.

| Assets | Parent | S-1 | S-2 | S-3 | S-4 |
|---|---|---|---|---|---|
| Current assets | $ 650,000 | $22,000 | $40,000 | $ 25,000 | $ 37,000 |
| Subsidiary investments: | | | | | |
| S-1* (100%) | 62,000 | | | | |
| S-2* ( 95%) | 64,350 | | | | |
| S-3* ( 90%) | 49,800 | | | | |
| S-4* ( 80%) | 67,200 | | | | |
| Other assets | 809,400 | 64,000 | 59,000 | 95,000 | 80,000 |
| | $1,702,750 | $86,000 | $99,000 | $120,000 | $117,000 |
| *Equities* | | | | | |
| Current liabilities | $ 300,000 | $30,000 | $24,000 | $ 60,000 | $ 42,000 |
| Capital stock | 1,000,000 | 20,000 | 25,000 | 80,000 | 35,000 |
| Retained earnings (deficit) | 402,750 | 36,000 | 50,000 | (20,000) | 40,000 |
| | $1,702,750 | $86,000 | $99,000 | $120,000 | $117,000 |

Stockholders' equities as of date of acquisition (four years ago):

| | S-1 | S-2 | S-3 | S-4 |
|---|---|---|---|---|
| Capital stock | $20,000 | $25,000 | $80,000 | $35,000 |
| Retained earnings (deficit) | 40,000 | 45,000 | (50,000) | 25,000 |

Cost of investment at date of acquisition:

| | S-1 | S-2 | S-3 | S-4 |
|---|---|---|---|---|
| | $70,000 | $55,000 | $20,000 | $60,000 |

*Parent company uses the equity method of accounting for the investments in subsidiaries.

## Problem 12-5

The Parent Company acquired a 70% interest in B Company and a 75% interest in C Company as of January 1, 1980. The Parent Company carries its investment in these companies on the equity basis. From the following data prepare working papers in columnar form showing (1) consolidated income for 1980, and (2) consolidated retained earnings as of December 31, 1980.

STATEMENT OF INCOME

YEAR ENDED DECEMBER 31, 1980

| | Parent | B Company | C Company |
|---|---|---|---|
| *Income:* | | | |
| Sales (net) | $1,225,000 | $395,000 | $202,000 |
| Dividends | 7,000 | 1,000 | 100 |
| Income from subsidiaries | 36,000 | | |
| Gross income | $1,268,000 | $396,000 | $202,100 |
| *Deductions:* | | | |
| Cost of sales | 610,000 | 205,000 | 86,000 |
| Selling expenses | 290,000 | 85,000 | 68,000 |

|                          |            |            |            |
|--------------------------|-----------:|-----------:|-----------:|
| General expenses         | 160,000    | 47,000     | 13,100     |
| Taxes                    | 106,000    | 29,000     | 15,000     |
|                          | $1,166,000 | $366,000   | $182,100   |
| Net Income               | $ 102,000  | $ 30,000   | $ 20,000   |

STATEMENT OF RETAINED EARNINGS

YEAR ENDED DECEMBER 31, 1980

|                      | PARENT    | B Company | C Company |
|----------------------|----------:|----------:|----------:|
| Balance 1/1/80       | $405,000  | $58,000   | $41,000   |
| Net income for year  | 102,000   | 30,000    | 20,000    |
| Dividends paid       | (24,000)  | (10,000)  | (6,000)   |
|                      | $483,000  | $78,000   | $55,000   |

Intercompany transactions:

(1) B Company made sales to C Company of $40,000 and to the Parent Company of $20,000.
(2) The Parent Company borrowed $10,000 on a note from C Company and $20,000 on open account from B Company.

## Problem 12-6

Prepare consolidated working papers with columns for income, retained earnings, minority interest, and financial position for the year ended December 31, 1980, from the following data:

Eighty-eight percent of the stock of Company S was acquired for $200,000 on January 1, 1979, when Company S's stockholders' equity was composed of $100,000 retained earnings and $100,000 capital stock.

ADJUSTED TRIAL BALANCES

DECEMBER 31, 1980

|                           | Co. P       | Co. S     |
|---------------------------|------------:|----------:|
| *Debits*                  |             |           |
| Merchandise inventory     | $ 80,000    | $ 28,000  |
| Investment in Co. S       | 212,800     |           |
| Other assets              | 730,000     | 315,000   |
| Cost of sales             | 690,000     | 152,000   |
| Expenses                  | 234,800     | 73,000    |
| Dividends paid            | 25,000      | 10,000    |
|                           | $1,972,600  | $578,000  |
| *Credits*                 |             |           |
| Sales                     | $1,212,000  | $290,000  |
| Liabilities               | 210,000     | 58,000    |
| Capital stock             | 300,000     | 100,000   |
| Retained earnings, 1/1/80 | 250,600     | 130,000   |
|                           | $1,972,600  | $578,000  |

## Problem 12-7

From the following comparative statements of financial position prepare:

1. A consolidated statement of financial position as of December 31, 1979, the date Company A acquired a 75% interest in Company B for $154,000, and
2. A consolidated statement of financial position as of December 31, 1980.

### COMPANY A
### STATEMENT OF FINANCIAL POSITION

|  | Dec. 31, 1979 | Dec. 31, 1980 |
|---|---|---|
| *Assets* | | |
| Current assets | $ 890,000 | $ 960,000 |
| Investment in Company B | 154,000 | 189,600 |
| Other assets | 100,000 | 102,400 |
|  | $1,144,000 | $1,252,000 |
| *Equities* | | |
| Current liabilities | $ 220,000 | $ 260,000 |
| Other liabilities | 100,000 | 120,000 |
| Capital stock | 500,000 | 500,000 |
| Retained earnings | 324,000 | 372,000 |
|  | $1,144,000 | $1,252,000 |

### COMPANY B
### STATEMENT OF FINANCIAL POSITION

|  | Dec. 31, 1979 | Dec. 31, 1980 |
|---|---|---|
| *Assets* | | |
| Current assets | $110,000 | $125,000 |
| Other assets | 260,000 | 270,000 |
|  | $370,000 | $395,000 |
| *Equities* | | |
| Current liabilities | $120,000 | $107,000 |
| Other liabilities | 50,000 | 40,000 |
| Capital stock | 150,000 | 150,000 |
| Retained earnings | 50,000 | 98,000 |
|  | $370,000 | $395,000 |

## Problem 12-8

From the following data prepare consolidated working papers with columns for income, retained earnings, minority interest, and financial position for the year ended December 31, 1980:

## 12 / Investment Not Carried at Cost

Eighty-four percent of the stock of Company B was acquired for $325,000 on January 1, 1979, when Company B's stockholders' equity was composed of $170,000 retained earnings and $200,000 capital stock.

### Trial Balances
### December 31, 1980

|  | Company A | Company B |
|---|---|---|
| **Debits** | | |
| Inventories 1/1/80 | $ 180,000 | $ 90,000 |
| Investment in Company B | 352,980 | |
| Other assets (net) | 1,890,000 | 585,000 |
| Purchases | 1,187,000 | 425,000 |
| Expenses | 376,420 | 182,000 |
| Dividends paid | 45,000 | 15,000 |
| | $4,031,400 | $1,297,000 |
| **Credits** | | |
| Sales | $1,515,000 | $ 667,000 |
| Liabilities | 996,400 | 210,000 |
| Capital stock | 900,000 | 200,000 |
| Retained earnings, 1/1/80 | 620,000 | 220,000 |
| | $4,031,400 | $1,297,000 |
| Inventories, December 31, 1980: Company A | $205,000 | |
| Company B | | 110,000 |
| | | $315,000 |

## Problem 12-9

P, a holding company, owns 90% of the capital stock of M and 80% of the capital stock of O. On April 15, 1980, M sold merchandise to O for $50,000, and received from O five noninterest-bearing notes of $10,000 each, due respectively on May 15, June 15, July 15, August 15, and September 15, 1980. On April 15, M discounted the notes due May 15 and June 15, respectively, with its bank, being credited with the proceeds of $19,925. The other three notes it held. In consolidating the accounts of the three companies at the close of the fiscal year ended April 30, 1980, how should the transactions involving the notes be handled? Give reasons for your answer.

(AICPA adapted)

## Problem 12-10

From the following data prepare consolidated working papers with columns for income, retained earnings, minority interest, and financial position for the year ended December 31, 1980.

TRIAL BALANCES
DECEMBER 31, 1980

|  | Company S | Company S-1 | Company S-2 | Company S-3 |
|---|---|---|---|---|
| *Debits* | | | | |
| Inventories 1/1/80 | $ 205,000 | $ 60,000 | $ 52,000 | $ 75,000 |
| Investments in subsidiaries (equity) | 463,600 | | | |
| Other assets (net) | 1,600,000 | 270,000 | 245,000 | 265,000 |
| Purchases | 780,000 | 190,000 | 183,000 | 215,000 |
| Expenses | 260,000 | 63,000 | 87,000 | 108,000 |
| Dividends paid | 24,000 | 6,000 | | 5,000 |
|  | $3,332,600 | $589,000 | $567,000 | $668,000 |
| *Credits* | | | | |
| Sales | $1,210,000 | $282,000 | $212,000 | $338,000 |
| Liabilities | 712,000 | 120,000 | 195,000 | 175,000 |
| Capital stock | 400,000 | 100,000 | 75,000 | 100,000 |
| Retained earnings, 1/1/80 | 1,010,600 | 87,000 | 85,000 | 55,000 |
|  | $3,332,600 | $589,000 | $567,000 | $668,000 |

Inventories, December 31, 1980:
Company S    $228,000
Company S-1    67,000
Company S-2    65,000
Company S-3    87,000
            $447,000

Ninety-five percent of the stock of S-1 was acquired for $142,000 on April 1, 1976, when S-1's stockholders' equity was composed of $100,000 capital stock and $42,000 retained earnings.

Ninety percent of the stock of S-2 was acquired for $138,000 on July 1, 1976, when S-2's stockholders' equity was composed of $75,000 capital stock and $63,000 retained earnings.

Eighty-five percent of the stock of S-3 was acquired for $148,000 on October 1, 1976, when S-3's stockholders' equity was composed of $100,000 capital stock and $75,000 retained earnings.

## Problem 12-11

Financial accounting usually emphasizes the economic substance of events even though the legal form may differ and suggest different treatment. For example, under accrual accounting, expenses are recognized when they are incurred (substance) rather than when cash is disbursed (form).

Although the feature of substance over form exists in most generally accepted accounting principles and practices, there are times when form prevails over substance.

## 12 / Investment Not Carried at Cost

*Required:*

For each of the following topics, discuss the underlying theory in terms of both substance and form, i.e., substance over form and possibly form over substance in some cases. Each topic should be discussed independently.

(1) Consolidated financial statements.
(2) Equity method of accounting for investments in common stock.

(AICPA adapted)

**Problem 12-12**

The North Salem Company has supplied you with information regarding two investments that were made during 1979 as follows:

- On January 1, 1979, North Salem purchased for cash 40% of the 500,000 shares of voting common stock of the Yorktown Company for $2,400,000 representing 40% of the net worth of Yorktown. Yorktown's net income for the year ended December 31, 1979, was $750,000. Yorktown paid dividends of $0.50 per share in 1979. The market value of Yorktown's common stock was $14 per share on December 31, 1979. North Salem exercised significant influence over the operating and financial policies of Yorktown.
- On July 1, 1979, North Salem purchased for cash 15,000 shares representing 5% of the voting common stock of the Mahopac Company for $450,000. Mahopac's net income for the six months ended December 31, 1979, was $350,000 and for the year ended December 31, 1979, was $600,000. Mahopac paid dividends of $0.30 per share each quarter during 1979 to stockholders of record on the last day of each quarter. The market value of Mahopac's common stock was $32 per share on January 1, 1979, and $34 per share on December 31, 1979.

*Required:*
1. As a result of these two investments, what should be the balance in the "Investments" account for North Salem at December 31, 1979? Show supporting computations in good form. *Ignore income taxes and deferred tax considerations in your answer.*
2. As a result of these two investments, what should be the income reported by North Salem for the year ended December 31, 1979? Show supporting computations in good form. *Ignore income taxes and deferred tax considerations in your answer.* (AICPA adapted)

# 13

# Consolidated Statements — Intercompany Profit Transactions

In the preceding chapters intercompany accounts reciprocal in nature were eliminated in the consolidating process. For example, intercompany payables were eliminated against intercompany receivables and intercompany sales against intercompany cost of sales. In many instances, however, intercompany transactions result in a profit or loss to the selling affiliate. This chapter will consider this aspect of the transactions as it affects the consolidating process.

Intercompany profits or losses may be defined as those profits or losses which, on sales to affiliates, have not been actually realized from the consolidated viewpoint through subsequent sales to parties outside the affiliated group. If the consolidated statements are to reflect the financial position and the operating results of a group of affiliated companies as one economic unit, intercompany profits and losses not realized from the consolidated standpoint must be eliminated. Strictly speaking, this would require the elimination of only the net income or loss recognized on the sale. Most accountants, however, assume that intercompany profit or loss for consolidation purposes refers to gross profit, and it is this amount rather than the net amount which is normally eliminated on consolidation. A reasonable position seems to be that gross profit may be eliminated unless evidence indicates that certain cost elements, such as transportation charges, should be included in the inventory. In that event elimination of less than a full gross profit may be appropriate.

Since different types of intercompany profit transactions have differing effects upon subsequent consolidated statements, the problems involved in eliminating intercompany profits or losses can best be examined by classifying and studying them in accordance with their sources, such as:

1. Intercompany inventory transactions.
2. Intercompany fixed asset transactions.
3. Intercompany bond transactions.

## INTERCOMPANY INVENTORY TRANSACTIONS

When merchandise is sold by one affiliate to another, it may be necessary to eliminate not only the intercompany sale and purchase, and the receivable and payable, if appropriate, but also the profit as well. Any profit or loss recognized by the selling affiliate on merchandise that has not been subsequently sold to customers outside the affiliated group has not been realized from a consolidated standpoint and should be eliminated. For example, if affiliate A sells $100,000 worth of merchandise to affiliate B at a $10,000 profit, A would recognize the $10,000 profit on the sale in its separate statements for the period. From the standpoint of A as a separate legal entity, this is realistic. When the consolidated group is being considered as one economic unit, however, the entire $10,000 profit cannot be recognized as having been earned unless all of the intercompany merchandise has been sold to outsiders. If any of the merchandise is in B's inventory at the date of consolidation, some of the profit recognized by A has not been realized from the standpoint of the consolidated group and an elimination of it must be made.

Although there is more or less unanimity among accountants as to the necessity for eliminating intercompany profits in inventories, there is not complete agreement as to the amount of gross profit that should be eliminated or how it should be eliminated. If the affiliate reporting the profit is 100% owned (from the consolidated standpoint the parent is considered as 100% owned), there is general agreement that 100% of the intercompany gross profit should be eliminated. However, if the affiliate reporting the profit is less than 100% owned, there are at least two distinct views as to the amount to be eliminated.

### 100% Ownership of Selling Affiliate

In the case of 100% ownership of the selling affiliate, accountants are more or less in agreement that all of the intercompany gross profit should be eliminated when consolidating. For example, if affiliate B has in its inventory $40,000 of merchandise purchased from 100% owned affiliate A, on which A made a 10% gross profit, $4,000 intercompany profit should be eliminated.

Theoretically the elimination should result in a reduction of the selling company's income or retained earnings and the buying company's inventory. Practically the elimination is usually made against the consolidated retained earnings and the buying company's inventory. Both procedures will give the same result. When the parent company takes up the $4,000 profit (directly if it is the selling company or when establishing reciprocity if it is not the selling company) consolidated retained earnings is increased. Consequently, the elimination may be made against the consolidated retained earnings and the appropriate inventory account. Both are overstated from the standpoint of the consolidated group as one economic unit. In lieu of a direct credit to the inventory account a special contra account such as "Provision for Intercompany Profit in Inventory" may be used. The work sheet entry would be:

| | | |
|---|---|---|
| Retained earnings (Parent company's) | $4,000 | |
| Inventory (Company B's) or Provision for intercompany profit in inventory | | $4,000 |
| (to eliminate unrealized intercompany profit in Company B's inventory) | | |

This elimination would reduce Company B's inventory to consolidated cost. It would also remove $4,000 of unrealized profit from consolidated retained earnings. Although this $4,000 has been realized from the standpoint of Company A as a separate legal entity, it has not been realized from the standpoint of the consolidated group as a single economic unit.

### Less than 100% Ownership in Selling Affiliate

Although accountants generally agree on the amount of the elimination in the case of 100% ownership in the selling affiliate, they do not always agree completely on the amount to be eliminated when the selling affiliate is less than 100% owned. There are at least two distinct views. One group of accountants would eliminate 100% of the intercompany profit, whereas another group would eliminate only that amount represented by the percentage of the selling company that is owned by the consolidated group. Although the latter view has received a certain amount of support in the past, *Accounting Research Bulletin No. 51* recommends 100% elimination, and that approach is advocated in this textbook.

### One Hundred Percent Elimination

The view that accountants should eliminate 100% of unrealized intercompany gross profits when a minority interest is present finds much support in practice as well as in *Bulletin No. 51*. For example, a recent survey of consolidation practices conducted by the American Institute of Certified Public Accountants (AICPA) indicates that a great majority of companies eliminate all of the intercompany profit, regardless of the existence of a minority interest. Although 100% elimination can be supported from the practical viewpoint on such bases as conservatism and materiality, it can also be supported theoretically on the grounds that an entity should not be permitted to write up assets when merchandise is transferred from one department or division to another. From a consolidated entity point of view, the separate companies are similar to departments or divisions of a single company.

According to *Bulletin No. 51*, the elimination of all of the intercompany profit in the case of less than 100% ownership may be charged against consolidated retained earnings, or may be divided between the consolidated retained earnings and the minority interest. Both procedures are illustrated in the following examples.

**Entire Amount Eliminated from Consolidated Retained Earnings.** The elimination of the entire amount of the intercompany profit from consolidated retained earnings finds much support in practice, probably because it is expedient and simple in application. From another point of view, however, this may not be the better approach. For example, should 100% of the profit be eliminated from consolidated retained earnings when only 90% has been taken up? Assume that Company A has $50,000 worth of merchandise purchased at 25% above cost from Company B, a 90% owned subsidiary. When establishing reciprocity the parent company would take up 90% of the $10,000 intercompany profit or $9,000. Assuming for illustrative purposes that the only profit reported by Company B is the $10,000 intercompany profit, the work sheet entry establishing reciprocity would be:

| | | |
|---|---|---|
| Investment in Company B | $9,000 | |
|     Retained earnings (Parent's) | | $9,000 |
| (to recognize Company A's share of the increase in Company B's stockholders' equity since the date of acquisition) | | |

However, $10,000 would be eliminated if the entire amount of intercompany profit is eliminated from consolidated retained earnings by:

| | | |
|---|---|---|
| Retained earnings (Parent's) | $10,000 | |
|     Inventory (Company A's) | | $10,000 |
| (to eliminate intercompany profit in inventories) | | |

Although logically it may not seem correct to eliminate more from consolidated retained earnings than has been entered therein, from a practical standpoint, based on expediency and materiality, it may be justified.

**Elimination Divided Between Consolidated Retained Earnings and the Minority Interest.** Some accountants advocate dividing the elimination of 100% of the intercompany profit between consolidated retained earnings and the minority interest. For example, assuming that the facts are the same as noted previously where, at the time of consolidating, Company A has $50,000 worth of merchandise purchased at 25% above cost from Company B, a 90% owned affiliate, the *work sheet* eliminating entry would be:

| | | |
|---|---|---|
| Retained earnings (Parent's) | $9,000 | |
| Retained earnings (Company B's) | 1,000 | |
|     Inventory (Company A's) | | $10,000 |
| (to eliminate intercompany profit in inventories) | | |

Theoretically this approach appears to be more appropriate, since the portion eliminated from consolidated retained earnings is the same as that included therein. When reciprocity was established, $9,000 was credited to consolidated retained earnings; thus if the elimination is prorated, only $9,000 is removed. This is in contrast to the $10,000 elimination in the case where all intercompany profit is eliminated from consolidated retained earnings.

Some accountants object to charging the minority interest for its pro rata share of intercompany profits. They contend that from the standpoint of the minority interest (as part of a separate legal entity), its share of the intercompany profit has been realized. Granted that this is true, the profit has not, however, been realized from the standpoint of the consolidated group as one economic unit. When consolidating, regardless of where they are currently reflected, *all* intercompany profits recognized but not realized should be eliminated.

**Work Sheet Illustration.** Assume that Company A owns 80% of Company B and 90% of Company C, and that C sells merchandise to B at a $10,000 profit and B sells it to A at another $8,000 profit. All of the merchandise is in A's inventory at the end of the year, and the inventory reported by A is overstated by $18,000 from the point of view of the consolidated entity.

If the entire gross profit were eliminated against the retained earnings of the parent company, the *work sheet* entry would be:

| | | |
|---|---|---|
| Retained earnings (Parent's) | $18,000 | |
| Inventory | | $18,000 |

If the gross profit is to be allocated to the minority interests for their share of the intercompany profit, it would be necessary to compute the appropriate eliminations, as follows:

| | | To Be Eliminated Against Retained Earnings | | |
|---|---|---|---|---|
| | Total | A | B | C |
| First Sale | $10,000 | $ 9,000 | | $1,000 |
| Second Sale | 8,000 | 6,400 | $1,600 | |
| Total | $18,000 | $15,400 | $1,600 | $1,000 |

In journal form the *work sheet* eliminations would be:

| | | |
|---|---|---|
| Retained earnings (Parent's) | $15,400 | |
| Retained earnings (B's) | 1,600 | |
| Retained earnings (C's) | 1,000 | |
| Inventory | | $18,000 |

To illustrate the elimination procedure, the working papers for the consolidated statement of financial position in which separate company statements are included is presented on page 369. The separate statements are based on the assumption that all profits on the intercompany sales have been recorded. Reciprocity has been established.

**Trial Balance Approach.** When a trial balance approach is being used to consolidate financial statements, eliminating entries for intercompany profits in inventories are dependent on: (1) whether a perpetual inventory system is in use, (2) whether adjusted or unadjusted trial balances are being consolidated, and (3) whether the intercompany profit is being eliminated from the beginning or ending inventory. If a perpetual inventory system is in use or if adjusted trial balances are being consolidated, the cost of goods sold is reflected in a Cost of Goods Sold

## 13 / Consolidated Statements—Intercompany Profit Transactions

|  | A | C | B | Eliminations Debit | Eliminations Credit | Consolidated Statement of Financial Position |
|---|---|---|---|---|---|---|
| *Assets* |  |  |  |  |  |  |
| Investment in C | $160,000 |  |  |  | $135,000B | $ 25,000G |
| Investment in B | 240,000 |  |  |  | 224,000C | 16,000G |
| Inventory | 160,000 | $ 80,000 | $ 30,000 |  | 18,000A | 252,000 |
| Other assets | 350,000 | 110,000 | 270,000 |  |  | 730,000 |
|  | $910,000 | $190,000 | $300,000 |  |  | $1,023,000 |
| *Equities* |  |  |  |  |  |  |
| Liabilities | $150,000 | $ 40,000 | $ 20,000 |  |  | $ 210,000 |
| Capital stock—A | 600,000 |  |  |  |  | 600,000 |
| Retained earnings—A | 160,000 |  |  | $ 15,400A |  | 144,600RE |
|  |  |  |  | 90,000B |  |  |
| Capital stock—C |  | 100,000 |  | 45,000B |  | 10,000MI |
|  |  |  |  | 1,000A |  |  |
| Retained earnings—C |  | 50,000 |  | 160,000C |  | 4,000MI |
| Capital stock—B |  |  | 200,000 | 64,000C |  | 40,000MI |
| Retained earnings—B |  |  | 80,000 | 1,600A |  | 14,400MI |
|  | $910,000 | $190,000 | $300,000 | $377,000 | $377,000 | $1,023,000 |

or similar account, and the ending inventory is reflected on the trial balance. To eliminate $10,000 intercompany profit in the ending inventory the following entry would be made:

| | | |
|---|---|---|
| Cost of goods sold | $10,000 | |
|     Inventory | | $10,000 |

If a perpetual inventory system is not in use and if unadjusted trial balances are being consolidated, it is necessary to make an adjustment in the working papers to record the ending inventory. Assuming that there is a $100,000 ending inventory, the entry to record it on an unadjusted trial balance would be:

| | | |
|---|---|---|
| Inventory (statement of financial position) | $100,000 | |
|     Inventory (statement of income) | | $100,000 |

If $10,000 intercompany profits is to be eliminated, the entry should be:

| | | |
|---|---|---|
| Inventory (statement of income) | $10,000 | |
|     Inventory (statement of financial position) | | $10,000 |

The same result could be obtained by simply recording the ending inventory net of intercompany profit as follows:

| | | |
|---|---|---|
| Inventory (statement of financial position) | $90,000 | |
|     Inventory (income statement) | | $90,000 |

To illustrate the procedure for eliminating intercompany profit in beginning inventories under a trial balance approach, assume an intercompany profit of $15,000. If a perpetual inventory system is in use or if adjusted trial balances are being consolidated, the eliminating entry would be:

| | | |
|---|---|---|
| Retained earnings (Parent's) | $15,000 | |
|     Cost of goods sold | | $15,000 |

If a perpetual inventory system is not in use and if unadjusted trial balances are being consolidated, the elimination entry would be:

| | | |
|---|---|---|
| Retained earnings (Parent's) | $15,000 | |
|     Inventory (beginning) | | $15,000 |

## INTERCOMPANY FIXED ASSET TRANSACTIONS

When fixed assets are sold by one affiliate to another at a profit, any intercompany profit unrealized at the date of consolidation should be eliminated. Intercompany profits in fixed assets, like intercompany profits in inventories, are not considered realized from the consolidated point of view until the asset has been transferred to outsiders. Intercompany profits in nondepreciating fixed assets are not realized until a sale to an outsider takes place. However, depreciating fixed assets are different from inventories and nondepreciating fixed assets in that physical transference as such is not necessary. Intercompany profits in depreciating fixed assets are realized by the process of depreciation as well as by a sale to outsiders.

The reasoning supporting this procedure may be described as follows:

1. Depreciation represents a portion of the useful life of the fixed assets that has been used up.
2. Any intercompany profit on the portion of the fixed asset assigned as depreciation is realized when the goods or services produced by use of the asset are sold to outsiders.
3. The depreciation is a measure of the contribution of the asset in making and disposing of the products sold during the period. This means that part of the payment for the products was payment for the contribution provided by the services in the depreciation. Thus, depreciation is sold when the products are sold and intercompany profit is realized at that time.

## Nondepreciating Fixed Assets

The problems created by intercompany profits in nondepreciating fixed assets are basically the same as those created by intercompany profits in inventories. As long as the nondepreciating fixed asset is held within the consolidated group, any intercompany profit on it should be eliminated in consolidated reports. The problems with nondepreciating fixed assets, as with inventories, are how much to eliminate and how it should be eliminated. There is more or less unanimity among accountants that 100% of the intercompany profit should be eliminated, but there is some disagreement as to how the elimination should be effected. Theoretically, as in the case of intercompany profits in inventories, the elimination should be prorated between consolidated retained earnings and minority interest. Practically, however, expediency, materiality, and conservatism may justify eliminating the entire amount from consolidated retained earnings. There is a small minority of accountants who would eliminate only the percent of consolidated interest in the selling affiliate.

The following examples illustrate the *work sheet* entries required when eliminating (1) 100% from consolidated retained earnings, and (2) 100% prorated between consolidated retained earnings and minority interest. The similarity between these entries and those for intercompany profits in inventories should be noted. It should also be noted that in the case of nondepreciating fixed assets the elimination remains the *same* as long as the asset is held by a particular affiliate.

In each illustration, assume that the asset (land) is currently carried at a cost of $100,000 and that the seller in each instance made a 20% profit based on the selling price.

100% Elimination from Consolidated Retained Earnings

1. Parent sells to Company B (90% owned subsidiary):

|  | End of 1st Year | End of 2nd Year | End of Each Subsequent Year |
|---|---|---|---|
| Retained earnings (Parent's) | $20,000 | $20,000 | $20,000 |
| Land |  $20,000 | $20,000 | $20,000 |

2. Company B's (90% owned subsidiary) sells to parent:

|  | End of 1st Year | End of 2nd Year | End of Each Subsequent Year |
|---|---|---|---|
| Retained earnings (Parent's) | $20,000 | $20,000 | $20,000 |
| Land | $20,000 | $20,000 | $20,000 |

3. Company B (90% owned subsidiary) sells to Company C (80% owned subsidiary):

|  | End of 1st Year | End of 2nd Year | End of Each Subsequent Year |
|---|---|---|---|
| Retained earnings (Parent's) | $20,000 | $20,000 | $20,000 |
| Land | $20,000 | $20,000 | $20,000 |

4. Company B (90% owned subsidiary) sells to Company C (80% owned subsidiary), which in turn sells to Company D (70% owned subsidiary):

|  | End of 1st Year | End of 2nd Year | End of Each Subsequent Year |
|---|---|---|---|
| Retained earnings (Parent's) | $36,000* | $36,000* | $36,000* |
| Land | $36,000 | $36,000 | $36,000 |

*20% × $100,000 = $20,000
 20% ×    80,000 =  16,000
                  $36,000

### 100% ELIMINATION PRORATED BETWEEN CONSOLIDATED RETAINED EARNINGS AND MINORITY INTEREST

1. Parent sells to Company B (90% owned subsidiary):

|  | End of 1st Year | End of 2nd Year | End of Each Subsequent Year |
|---|---|---|---|
| Retained earnings (Parent's) | $20,000 | $20,000 | $20,000 |
| Land | $20,000 | $20,000 | $20,000 |

2. Company B (90% owned subsidiary) sells to parent:

|  | End of 1st Year | End of 2nd Year | End of Each Subsequent Year |
|---|---|---|---|
| Retained earnings (Parent's) | $18,000 | $18,000 | $18,000 |
| Retained earnings (B's) | 2,000 | 2,000 | 2,000 |
| Land | $20,000 | $20,000 | $20,000 |

3. Company B (90% owned subsidiary) sells to Company C (80% owned subsidiary):

|  | End of 1st Year | End of 2nd Year | End of Each Subsequent Year |
|---|---|---|---|
| Retained earnings (Parent's) | $18,000 | $18,000 | $18,000 |

|  | | | |
|---|---|---|---|
| Retained earnings (B's) | 2,000 | 2,000 | 2,000 |
| Land | $20,000 | $20,000 | $20,000 |

4. Company B (90% owned subsidiary) sells to Company C (80% owned subsidiary), which in turn sells to Company D (70% owned subsidiary):

|  | End of 1st Year | End of 2nd Year | End of Each Subsequent Year |
|---|---|---|---|
| Retained earnings (Parent's) | $30,400 | $30,400 | $30,400 |
| Retained earnings (C's) | 4,000† | 4,000† | 4,000† |
| Retained earnings (B's) | 1,600* | 1,600* | 1,600* |
| Land | $36,000 | $36,000 | $36,000 |

*10% × $16,000 = $1,600
†20% × $20,000 = $4,000

## Depreciating Fixed Assets

Since intercompany profits in depreciating fixed assets are normally realized through the depreciation process, the consolidating problems revolve around and are closely related to the depreciation process. Basically, the problem is one of determining how much of the intercompany profit has been realized through depreciation and how much has not been realized. That which has not been realized as of the date of consolidation must be eliminated.

Realization through the depreciation process means that as the asset is consumed (expiration of useful life) in production or through service, its cost, which would include intercompany profit, is passed on to outsiders through the depreciation charge. Since depreciation from an accounting standpoint is primarily a matter of allocating the cost of an asset over its useful life, realization of any intercompany profit on such asset is essentially a matter of recognizing this profit as being realized over the same period of time. For example, if, after an intercompany profit transaction has taken place, an asset with a useful life of 10 years is depreciated on a straight-line basis, 1/10 of the intercompany profit is considered realized each year. At the end of seven years 7/10 of the intercompany profit will have been realized and 3/10 unrealized. Likewise, at the end of nine years 9/10 will have been realized and 1/10 will be unrealized.

When consolidating, in addition to eliminating the unrealized portion from consolidated retained earnings, the asset and its related accrued depreciation must be reduced to cost from a consolidated standpoint. This may be illustrated by assuming that Company P (parent) sells to Company A (100% owned subsidiary) for $100,000 (cost to Company P, $80,000) equipment with an estimated useful life of 10 years. At the end of the fourth year 40% of the intercompany profit has been realized and 60% has not been realized. To reduce all accounts to a consolidated cost basis, $12,000 (60% of $20,000) unrealized profit must be eliminated from consolidated retained earnings; $20,000 must be removed from the asset account; and the depreciation taken on the intercompany profit element of the asset during the four-year period must also be removed from the accrued depreciation account. In entry form the elimination would be:

| | | |
|---|---|---|
| Retained earnings (Parent's) (60% of $20,000) | $12,000 | |
| Accrued depreciation (40% of $20,000) | 8,000 | |
| Equipment (100% of $20,000) | | $20,000 |

When entered in the work sheet this entry would eliminate the $12,000 unrealized profit from consolidated retained earnings, leaving in it the $8,000 realized portion. The $8,000 charged to accrued depreciation reduces this account to $32,000 ($40,000 − $8,000), which states it on a consolidated cost basis. Finally, the $20,000 credit to the asset account reduces it to $80,000, which is consolidated cost. After this entry the book value of the asset is $48,000 ($80,000 − $32,000), which is the same as it would have been if no intercompany profit had been made. However, if no elimination had been made, the book value would have been $60,000 ($100,000 − $40,000).

Here, as in the case of intercompany profits in inventories and in nondepreciating fixed assets, there is some disagreement among accountants as to how much profit to eliminate and in some cases how it should be eliminated. Most accountants agree that 100% of the unrealized profit should be eliminated, but they do not all agree as to exactly how the elimination should be made. Again, as in the case of inventories and nondepreciating fixed assets, theory would seem to require a proration between consolidated retained earnings and minority interest. From the practical standpoint, however, simplicity and materiality warrant total elimination from consolidated retained earnings. Although the authors favor (especially from a logical standpoint) the theoretical treatment, both methods are illustrated in the examples on pages 376–379.

Assume in each illustration that the asset (equipment) is currently carried at a cost of $100,000 and that the seller in each instance made a 20% profit based on the selling price. Also assume that depreciation is computed on a straight-line basis, using an estimated useful life of 10 years. In each of the examples the elimination accomplishes three things: (1) it eliminates the unrealized profit from consolidated retained earnings, (2) it reduces the accrued depreciation account to a consolidated cost basis, and (3) it reduces the asset to the consolidated basis.

**Trial Balance Approach.** To illustrate the elimination needed to prepare a consolidated statement of income as well as a consolidated statement of financial position, assume that (1) Company A owns 80% of Company B, (2) Company A has a $40,000 asset purchased from B on which B made a profit of $10,000, (3) the asset has a life of 10 years from the date of sale and A has depreciated it for 4 years, and (4) the books of Company A have not been closed at the end of the fourth year.

The overstatement of depreciation expense on fixed assets, including intercompany profits, is eliminated by the following *work sheet* entry:

| | | |
|---|---|---|
| Accrued depreciation | $1,000 | |
| Depreciation expense | | $1,000 |

(This entry would be required each year over the life of the asset because the depreciation charged by the buying affiliate on its separate books would be $1,000 too high each year.)

Abbreviated trial balance working papers for consolidated statements would appear as shown:

### A AND B
### CONSOLIDATED WORKING PAPERS FOR YEAR 4

|  | Trial Balance A | Trial Balance B | Eliminations Debit | Eliminations Credit | Consolidated Income Statement | Consolidated Financial Position |
|---|---|---|---|---|---|---|
| **Debits** | | | | | | |
| Fixed asset | $40,000 | | | $10,000B | | $30,000 |
| Depreciation expense | 4,000 | | | 1,000A | $ 3,000 | |
| Other debits | XXXX | XXXX | | | XXXX | XXXX |
|  | $XXXX | $XXXX | | | $XXXX | $XXXX |
| **Credits** | | | | | | |
| Retained earnings—A | $100,000 | | $ 7,000B | | | $93,000 |
| Accumulated depreciation | 16,000 | | 1,000A | | | 12,000 |
|  | | | 3,000B | | | |
| Other credits | XXXX | XXXX | | | XXXX | XXXX |
|  | $XXXX | $XXXX | | | $XXXX | $XXXX |

This example illustrates the point that when the trial balance approach is used, the current year's portion of the elimination is made against the expense account rather than against the Retained Earnings account. Had the books been closed, the retained earnings of A would have absorbed the additional $1,000 of excess depreciation. The eliminating entry would then have been:

| | | |
|---|---|---|
| Retained earnings (A's) | $6,000 | |
| Accrued depreciation | 4,000 | |
| Fixed asset | | $10,000 |

## INTERCOMPANY BOND TRANSACTIONS

Intercompany bond transactions are considered separately from short-term debtor-creditor relationships because there is a greater likelihood that gains or losses may be recognized on these transactions. Since gains or losses may arise, the consolidating problem is composed basically of two elements: (1) the intercompany receivable and payable, and (2) the intercompany profit or loss.

## 100% Elimination from Consolidated Retained Earnings

1. Parent sells to Company B (90% owned subsidiary):

| | Date of Sale | End of 1st Year | End of 2nd Year | End of 10th Year |
|---|---|---|---|---|
| Retained earnings (Parent's) | $20,000* | $18,000* | $16,000* | $——* |
| Accrued depreciation | —* | 2,000* | 4,000* | 20,000 |
| Equipment | $20,000 | $20,000 | $20,000 | $20,000 |

*The relationship between the amount of intercompany profit realized and the amount of depreciation taken on the intercompany cost as of any particular date should be noted. For instance, at the date of sale no depreciation has been taken and none of the intercompany profit has been realized, whereas at the end of the first year $2,000 of depreciation has been taken and $2,000 of the intercompany profit has been realized. By the end of the tenth year, all the depreciation has been taken and all of the profit has been realized.

2. Company B (90% owned subsidiary) sells to the parent:

| | Date of Sale | End of 1st Year | End of 2nd Year | End of 10th Year |
|---|---|---|---|---|
| Retained earnings (Parent's) | $20,000 | $18,000 | $16,000 | $—— |
| Accrued depreciation | —— | 2,000 | 4,000 | 20,000 |
| Equipment | $20,000 | $20,000 | $20,000 | $20,000 |

13 / *Consolidated Statements—Intercompany Profit Transactions* 377

3. Company B (90% owned subsidiary) sells to Company C (80% owned subsidiary):

|  | Date of Sale | End of 1st Year | End of 2nd Year | End of 10th Year |
|---|---|---|---|---|
| Retained earnings (Parent's) | $20,000 | $18,000 | $16,000 | $— |
| Accrued depreciation | — | 2,000 | 4,000 | 20,000 |
| Equipment | $20,000 | $20,000 | $20,000 | $20,000 |

4. Company B (90% owned subsidiary) sells to Company C (80% owned subsidiary), which in turn sells to Company D (70% owned subsidiary):

|  | Date of Sale | End of 1st Year | End of 2nd Year | End of 10th Year |
|---|---|---|---|---|
| Retained earnings (Parent's) | $36,000† | $32,400 | $28,800 | $— |
| Accrued depreciation | — | 3,600‡ | 7,200 | 36,000 |
| Equipment | $36,000 | $36,000 | $36,000 | $36,000 |

†20% × $100,000 = $20,000
20% × $ 80,000 = 16,000
$36,000

‡10% × $36,000 = $3,600

## 100% ELIMINATION PRORATED BETWEEN CONSOLIDATED
### RETAINED EARNINGS AND MINORITY INTEREST

1. Parent sells to Company B (90% owned subsidiary):

| | Date of Sale | End of 1st Year | End of 2nd Year | End of 10th Year |
|---|---|---|---|---|
| Retained earnings (Parent's) | $20,000 | $18,000 | $16,000 | $— |
| Accrued depreciation | — | 2,000 | 4,000 | 20,000 |
| Equipment | $20,000 | $20,000 | $20,000 | $20,000 |

The parent is considered to be 100% owned from the standpoint of the consolidation. Consequently, since the parent is making the sale in this situation, no minority interest is involved.

2. Company B (90% owned subsidiary) sells to parent:

| | Date of Sale | End of 1st Year | End of 2nd Year | End of 10th Year |
|---|---|---|---|---|
| Retained earnings (Parent's) | $18,000 | $16,200 | $14,400 | $— |
| Retained earnings (B's) | 2,000 | 1,800 | 1,600 | — |
| Accrued depreciation | — | 2,000 | 4,000 | 20,000 |
| Equipment | $20,000 | $20,000 | $20,000 | $20,000 |

In this situation it should be noted that the unrealized portion of the intercompany profit is divided between the consolidated retained earnings and the minority interest in proportion to the consolidated interest and the minority interest in the selling affiliate—90% and 10%.

## 13 / Consolidated Statements—Intercompany Profit Transactions

3. Company B (90% owned subsidiary) sells to Company C (80% owned subsidiary):

| | Date of Sale | End of 1st Year | End of 2nd Year | End of 10th Year |
|---|---|---|---|---|
| Retained earnings (Parent's) | $18,000 | $16,200 | $14,400 | $— |
| Retained earnings (B's) | 2,000 | 1,800 | 1,600 | — |
| Accrued depreciation Equipment | — | 2,000 | 4,000 | 20,000 |
| | $20,000 | $20,000 | $20,000 | $20,000 |

It should be noted that Illustrations 2 and 3 are identical. This condition exists because Company B is the seller in both cases.

4. Company B (90% owned subsidiary) sells to Company C (80% owned subsidiary), which in turn sells to Company D (70% owned subsidiary):

| | Date of Sale | End of 1st Year | End of 2nd Year | End of 10th Year |
|---|---|---|---|---|
| Retained earnings (Parent's) | $30,400* | $27,360 | $24,320 | $— |
| Retained earnings (B's) | 1,600† | 1,440 | 1,280 | — |
| Retained earnings (C's) | 4,000‡ | 3,600 | 3,200 | — |
| Accrued depreciation Equipment | — | 3,600 | 7,200 | 36,000 |
| | $36,000 | $36,000 | $36,000 | $36,000 |

*90% × $16,000 = $14,400
80% × $20,000 = $16,000
$30,400

†10% × $16,000 = $1,600

‡20% × $20,000 = $4,000

When one affiliate holds bonds of another affiliate, the intercompany-held bonds are essentially treasury bonds and from the standpoint of the consolidated group should be treated as such. The consolidation problem is one of offsetting the asset account of the bondholder against the liability account of the issuer. Since treasury bonds are normally deducted from the liability account on the statement of financial position, the bond investment account would normally be extended to the consolidated column on the work sheet and presented on the consolidated statement of financial position in a manner similar to the following illustration:

| | | |
|---|---:|---:|
| Bonds Payable | $600,000 | |
| Less: Bonds held by affiliated company | 100,000 | |
| Bonds outstanding | | $500,000 |

When intercompany bonds are both issued and acquired at par, no unusual problems occur, other than to treat them as treasury bonds. This is true, of course, because the carrying value (par) is the same (and therefore reciprocal) on both the issuer's and buyer's books. Bonds are not always bought and sold at par, however, and the intercompany accounts may not be reciprocal. When this condition exists, reciprocity must be established before the asset account is "offset" against the liability account. In addition, whenever bonds of an affiliate are acquired from an outsider at some price other than the carrying value on the selling affiliate's books, a gain or loss from the consolidated standpoint has been realized and must be recognized when consolidating. For example, if Company A (100% owned affiliate) sells $100,000 worth of bonds at par to an outsider and Company B (100% owned affiliate) acquires one-half of them immediately for 102, there has been a $1,000 loss from the consolidated standpoint because $51,000 ($50,000 @ 102) was used to reduce a debt to an outsider of $50,000.

In the study of intercompany bond transactions it should be recognized that when bonds are purchased as an investment they are normally recorded at cost. As a result, any premium or discount involved is reflected in the cost. On the other hand, when bonds are issued, they are normally recorded at par and any premium or discount involved is recorded separately. As a consequence, the amortization of any premium or discount on bonds purchased is accomplished by writing the bond investment account up or down to par over the remaining life of the bonds; whereas any premium or discount on the issuance of bonds is amortized by writing off the separately recorded premium or discount over the life of the bonds. In both instances the amortization results in either a charge or a credit to the income account of the individual company. As a consequence of the amortization process, a gain or loss on intercompany bond transactions will eventually find its way into consolidated retained earnings. In this respect the amortization process has an effect similar to the depreciation process as related to intercompany profits in fixed assets. That is, an intercompany gain or loss on bond transactions is realized over the amortization period. If amortization is on a straight-line basis, realization will be on a straight-line basis. If amortization is on some other basis, realization will be on that same basis.

It is generally agreed by accountants that intercompany gains and losses on intercompany bond transactions, like intercompany profits in inventories and fixed assets, should be eliminated. Accountants do not always agree as to how much gain or loss should be eliminated and just how the elimination should be effected. Although there is substantial agreement that 100% of an intercompany gain or loss should be eliminated, there is some disagreement as to how the elimination should be made. Theoretically, as in the case of intercompany profits in inventories and fixed assets, the elimination should be prorated between consolidated retained earnings and minority interest. From a practical standpoint, however, simplicity and materiality may justify eliminating the entire amount from consolidated retained earnings. Here again a small minority of accountants would eliminate only the percent of the consolidated interest in any intercompany gain or loss.

Regardless of the amount to be eliminated, the elimination consists of three basic steps, namely:

1. Write the bond investment account up or down to par.
2. Write off the appropriate amount of unamortized bond discount or premium.
3. Plug the balancing figure to consolidated retained earnings or prorate it between consolidated retained earnings and the minority interest.

**100% Elimination from Consolidated Retained Earnings.** Assume that Company A owns 80% of the stock of Company B. Company B has outstanding $100,000 of bonds with an unamortized premium of $3,000. Company A purchases $50,000 of the bonds for $49,000 or at a $1,000 discount.

If 100% of the elimination is to be made against consolidated retained earnings, the *work sheet* entry for the elimination would be:

| | | |
|---|---|---|
| Bonds of B | $1,000 | |
| Premium on bonds payable | 1,500 | |
| Retained earnings (A's) | | $2,500 |

The portion of the consolidated working papers reflecting the eliminations is presented below:

| | Co. A | Co. B | Adjustments & Eliminations Debit | Credit | Consolidated Financial Position |
|---|---|---|---|---|---|
| *Debits* | | | | | |
| Bonds of B | $49,000 | | $1,000A | | $ 50,000TB |
| *Credits* | | | | | |
| Bonds payable | | $100,000 | | | 100,000 |
| Premium on bonds payable | | 3,000 | 1,500A | | 1,500 |
| Retained earnings (Parent's) | XXXX | | | $2,500A | |

**100% Elimination Prorated Between Consolidated Retained Earnings and Minority Interest.** Assume the same facts as those presented in the preceding illustration. The resulting gain of $2,500 is to be prorated between the minority interest and the consolidated retained earnings. Other than this, the solution is the same. Thus, the *work sheet* entry for the elimination would be:

| | | |
|---|---|---|
| Bonds of B | $1,000 | |
| Premium on bonds payable | 1,500 | |
|    Retained earnings (A's) | | $2,200* |
|    Retained earnings (B's) | | 300** |

*100% of 1,000 plus 80% of 1,500
**20% of 1,500

**Trial Balance Approach.** To illustrate the work sheet procedure for eliminating intercompany gains or losses when the consolidated income statement and the consolidated statement of financial position are prepared, assume the same facts as those used above and assume in addition that the bonds had a remaining life of 10 years after the date of reacquisition. One year after A acquired the bonds, assuming that the bonds were purchased at the start of the fiscal year in the example, the accounts would have the balances revealed in the following work sheet.

| | Trial Balance | | Eliminations | | Consolidated | |
|---|---|---|---|---|---|---|
| | Co. A | Co. B | Debit | Credit | Income Statement | Financial Position |
| *Debits* | | | | | | |
| Bonds of B | $49,100 | | | $ 900*A* | | $ 50,000TB |
| *Credits* | | | | | | |
| Bonds payable | | $100,000 | | | | $100,000 |
| Premium on bonds payable | | 2,700 | 1,080*A* | | | |
| | | | 270*C* | | | 1,350 |
| Bond premium | | | 30*C* | | | |
|   amortized | | 300 | 120*B* | | $150 | |
| Income-amortization | | | | | | |
|   of bonds | 100 | | 100*B* | | | |
| Retained earnings—A | XXXX | | | $1,980*A* | | |
| | | | | 220*B* | | XXXX |
| Retained earnings—B | | XXXX | | 300*C* | | XXXX |

*A:* To write the investment in bonds of B up to par and to write off appropriate premium on bonds sold (80% of 50% of $2,700) and to credit the sum of the two to retained earnings of A.

*B:* To eliminate the one year's amortization of the bond investment and to eliminate the appropriate portion of the one year's premium on bonds sold (80% of 50% of $300) and to credit the sum of the two to retained earnings of A.

*C:* To eliminate the minority stockholders' interest in the bond premium amortized in the year (20% of 50% of $300) and in the premium on bonds sold (20% of 50% of $2,700) and to credit the sum of the two to retained earnings of B (minority interest).

The solution above eliminates 100% of the intercompany gain and prorates it to consolidated retained earnings and minority interest. Assuming that there is 100% elimination from consolidated retained earnings, the *work sheet* entries would be:

*A*

| | | |
|---|---|---|
| Bonds of B | $ 900 | |
| Premium on bonds payable | 1,350 | |
|    Retained earnings (A's) | | $2,250 |

*B*

| | | |
|---|---|---|
| Income-amortization of bonds | $ 100 | |
| Bond premium amortized | 150 | |
|    Retained earnings (A's) | | $ 250 |

*C*

No entry

## PROBLEMS

### Problem 13-1

Company A owns 80% of the stock of Company B and 90% of the stock of Company C. Company A carries the investment accounts at cost. Intercompany sales of merchandise are made at a gross profit of 25% on cost unless otherwise indicated. Show in journal entry form the eliminations that would be necessary for intercompany profits on merchandise when preparing a consolidated statement of financial position in each case below, assuming that:

1. One hundred percent is eliminated from consolidated retained earnings.
2. One hundred percent is eliminated prorata from consolidated retained earnings and minority interest.

  *Case 1.* Merchandise owned by Co. A, sold by Co. B, $20,000
  *Case 2.* Merchandise owned by Co. B, sold by Co. A, $25,000.
  *Case 3.* Merchandise owned by Co. C, sold by Co. B, $30,000.
  *Case 4.* Merchandise owned by Co. A, sold by Co. B, $20,000; Co. C originally sold this merchandise to Co. B for $15,000.

### Problem 13-2

On December 31, 1971, the Barr Company completed the construction of a building for the Able Company. The charge for the construction was $900,000. Cost of the construction was $720,000. The useful life of the building was estimated at 40 years.

Indicate in journal entry form the elimination that would be necessary for intercompany profit when preparing a consolidated statement of financial position as of December 31, 1981, in each case below assuming that:

1. One hundred percent is eliminated from consolidated retained earnings.
2. One hundred percent is eliminated prorata from consolidated retained earnings and minority interest.

Case 1. Barr is the parent owning 100% of Able.
Case 2. Barr is the parent owning 90% of Able.
Case 3. Able is the parent owning 100% of Barr.
Case 4. Able is the parent owning 90% of Barr.

## Problem 13-3

The Baker Company issued $100,000 par value 4% bonds on January 1, 1980, at 97, interest payable June 30 and December 31. The bonds mature on January 1, 1990.

The Alpha Company acquired 40% of the bonds in the open market on December 31, 1980, for $40,450.

Indicate in journal entry form the eliminations that would be necessary for intercompany gain or loss when preparing a consolidated statement of financial position as of December 31, 1981, in each case below assuming that:

1. One hundred percent is eliminated from consolidated retained earnings.
2. One hundred percent is eliminated prorata from consolidated retained earnings and minority interest.

Case 1. Baker is the parent owning 100% of Alpha.
Case 2. Baker is the parent owning 90% of Alpha.
Case 3. Alpha is the parent owning 100% of Baker.
Case 4. Alpha is the parent owning 90% of Baker.

## Problem 13-4

Company P owns 80% of the stock of Company Y and 90% of the stock of Company Z. Both holdings were acquired prior to 1975 and are carried at *cost*. From the following information prepare in journal entry form any adjustments and eliminations necessary when preparing a consolidated statement of financial position as of December 31, 1980:

1. Company P has in its inventory merchandise of $48,300 acquired from Company Z. Merchandise is sold by Company Z at 15% above cost.
2. Company Y has in its inventory merchandise of $7,000 acquired from Company P. The cost of the merchandise to Company P was $4,000.
3. Company P owns $10,000 (par value) of Company Y bonds. The investment in bonds as of December 31, 1980, is carried at $9,600. Bonds are carried at this date by Company Y at 103½.

4. Company P owns equipment of $40,000 acquired from Company Y at the end of March, 1980. The equipment was constructed by Company Y and was sold to Company P at a gross profit of 25% based on the selling price. The equipment is being depreciated on a 10-year basis. Depreciation is computed to the nearest month.

## Problem 13-5

From the following data prepare working papers for consolidated statements for the year ended December 31, 1980:

Eighty percent of the capital stock of Company B was acquired for $148,000 in 1978, when Company B had retained earnings of $70,000. Company A carries its investment in Company B by the equity method.

Company A regularly buys merchandise from Company B. The December 31, 1979, inventory of Company A included merchandise acquired from Company B for $24,000; the December 31, 1980, inventory of Company A includes merchandise acquired from Company B for $21,000. During 1980 Company A made purchases from Company B totaling $63,000. Company B sells merchandise to Company A at 20% above cost.

TRIAL BALANCES
DECEMBER 31, 1980

| Debits | Company A | Company B |
|---|---|---|
| Inventories 1/1/80 | $ 130,000 | $ 110,000 |
| Investment in Company B | 173,600 | |
| Other assets (net) | 780,000 | 460,000 |
| Purchases | 570,000 | 330,000 |
| Expenses | 187,400 | 110,000 |
| Dividends paid | 16,500 | 5,000 |
| | $1,857,500 | $1,015,000 |

| Credits | | |
|---|---|---|
| Sales | $ 890,000 | $ 530,000 |
| Liabilities | 417,500 | 275,000 |
| Capital stock | 300,000 | 100,000 |
| Retained earnings 1/1/80 | 250,000 | 110,000 |
| | $1,857,500 | $1,015,000 |

| Inventories, December 31, 1980: | | |
|---|---|---|
| Company A | | $ 105,000 |
| Company B | | 80,000 |
| | | $ 185,000 |

## Problem 13-6

From the following data prepare working papers for consolidated statements for the year ended December 31, 1980:

Stock of Company S was acquired for $160,000 in 1978, when Company S had retained earnings of $60,000. During 1980, Company P made purchases from Company S totaling $45,000. The December 31, 1979, inventory of Company P included merchandise acquired from Company S at $22,500; the December 31, 1980, inventory of Company P includes merchandise acquired from Company S at $10,500. Company S sells merchandise to Company P at 25% above cost.

TRIAL BALANCES

DECEMBER 31, 1980

|  | Company P | Company S |
|---|---|---|
| *Debits* |  |  |
| Inventories | $ 90,000 | $ 70,000 |
| Investment in Company S (90%) | 156,800 |  |
| Other assets (net) | 740,000 | 410,000 |
| Cost of goods sold | 530,000 | 290,000 |
| Expenses | 168,200 | 95,000 |
| Dividends paid | 21,000 | 6,000 |
|  | $1,706,000 | $871,000 |
| *Credits* |  |  |
| Sales | $ 770,000 | $370,000 |
| Dividend income | 5,400 |  |
| Liabilities | 430,000 | 320,000 |
| Capital stock | 300,000 | 100,000 |
| Retained earnings, 1/1/80 | 200,600 | 81,000 |
|  | $1,706,000 | $871,000 |

## Problem 13-7

ITEM A—Corporation X manufactures at a finished cost of $20.00 per unit and sells to Corporation Y @ $25.00 per unit. Corporation Y leaves its inventory in the warehouse of Corporation X, withdrawing only as needed and pays to Corporation X storage at the rate of 50¢ per unit per month. The quantity in the inventory of Corporation Y at December 31 was purchased six months previously. Corporation Y resells at $40.00, FOB shipping point, which is the same price at which Corporation X sells to others.

ITEM B—Corporation X owns and operates a mine from which Item B is extracted. The average cost of mining Item B is $5.00 per ton. The cost of the mine and development thereof is subject to depletion at the rate of $2.50 per ton. The cost of loading on freight cars averages $1.00 per ton. Corporation Y purchases from Corporation X at cost, FOB the mine, and transports to its plant, paying freight of $1.50 per ton. Corporation X sells approximately 75% of its mined product to others at a price of $15.00 per ton, FOB the mine, and Corporation Y sells at a substantial profit after refinement.

ITEM C—Corporation X buys manufacturing supplies at a price of $50.00 per unit less trade discounts of 10/10/20. A portion of the supplies purchased by Corporation X are resold to Corporation Y at a price of $41.00, FOB Corporation Y's plant. The freight, paid by Corporation X, amounts to 50¢ per unit. Corporation Y does not have access to the market from which Corporation X buys.

ITEM D—Corporation X manufactures this item at the average cost of $29.00 per unit and sells its total output to Corporation Y @ $35.00 per unit, FOB Corporation X's plant, under terms of a firm contract. The freight amounts to $2.00 per unit. The amount obtainable from Corporation X is only about 50% of the quantity required by Corporation Y. The balance of Corporation Y's requirements are obtained from other sources at a price of $32.50 per unit, FOB Y's plant. Y resells this item at a price that yields $34.00 per unit after allowing for sales and handling expense.

ITEM E—Corporation X manufactures at a cost of $6.00 per unit and sells to Corporation Y and others @ $5.00 per unit, FOB Corporation X's plant. The freight to Y's plant amounts to 75¢ per unit. Corporation Y processes this item and sells at a profit.

*Required:*

Consider that there were 10 units of each of the five items in the inventory of *each corporation* at the end of their concurrent fiscal years. You are to show the proper valuation at the lower of cost or market for inventory purposes in the financial statements and to explain in connection with each valuation the reason for using it. Answer for each item separately.

(1) In the financial statements of Corporation X and Corporation Y assuming that there is no relation between the two corporations.
(2) In the consolidated financial statements assuming that Corporation Y is a wholly owned subsidiary of Corporation X.        (AICPA adapted)

## Problem 13-8

Company P, a manufacturer of earth-moving equipment, sells 10 units at its regular selling price of $18,000 each (cost is $12,000 each) to its wholly owned subsidiary, Company S, on September 1, 1980. Company S is an *unconsolidated subsidiary,* carried on Company P's books as an investment at a value adjusted for Company S earnings.

Both Company P and Company S are on the accrual basis and use a calendar-year accounting period.

Company S was incorporated on July 1, 1980, and its capital stock of $25,000 was sold to P at par. It paid for the equipment purchased from Company P by obtaining a four-year, 6% bank loan on September 1, 1980 for the entire purchase price. The units purchased were leased to Company O, a nonaffiliated company, and the lease was assigned as collateral for the bank loan. The loan is payable in equal monthly principal installments on the first of each month plus interest for the preceding month, starting October 1, 1980. (Interest is computed on a 30-day, 360-day year basis.)

Company S depreciates the equipment on the basis of actual hours used, using a 12,000-hour operating life per unit.

The lease agreement with Company O is dated September 1, 1980, and runs for four years. It provides for rental payments starting October 1, 1980, based on the actual number of hours used the preceding calendar month. Rent is to be computed at the rate of $1.80 per hour, with a minimum monthly rental of $2,500, and a maximum total rental of $216,000. Hours operated were: September, 4,000; October, 5,000; November, 5,500; December 3,500.

Do not consider federal income taxes in connection with this problem.

1. What is the amount of gross profit that Company P should report on its income statement for 1980 as realized from the sale? State your reasoning.
2. Assuming that this is Company S's only business activity, what is its net income for 1980? (Give your supporting computations in good form.)
3. What is the carrying value of Company S on Company P's books at December 31, 1980?

(AICPA adapted)

## Problem 13-9

During its fiscal year ended October 31, 1980, the S Company, a wholly owned subsidiary of the P Company, sold to the latter, at a profit, materials which it used in constructing a new building for its own use.

State (1) how the profit on the sales of these materials should be treated in preparing the consolidated financial statements of the P Company and its subsidiary as of October 31, 1980, and for the year then ended, respectively, and (2) how it should be treated in preparing financial statements in subsequent years.

(AICPA adapted)

## Problem 13-10

From the following trial balances and additional information as of December 31, 1980, you are to prepare working papers showing the consolidated income of P and its subsidiary.

|  | P Company Debit | P Company Credit | S Company Debit | S Company Credit |
|---|---|---|---|---|
| Cash | $ 23,940 |  | $ 30,000 |  |
| Accounts receivable | 94,000 |  | 60,000 |  |
| Inventory 1/1/80 | 105,000 |  | 51,000 |  |
| Investment in stock of S | 174,060 |  |  |  |
| Investment in bonds of S | 51,800 |  |  |  |
| Other assets | 445,000 |  | 210,000 |  |
| Current liabilities |  | $ 163,000 |  | $ 17,100 |
| Bonds payable, 5% |  |  |  | 200,000 |
| Deferred bond premium |  |  |  | 5,400 |
| Sales |  | 630,000 |  | 340,000 |

|  |  |  |  |  |
|---|---|---|---|---|
| Purchases | 485,000 |  | 300,000 |  |
| Operating expenses | 92,000 |  | 70,000 |  |
| Other expenses | 22,000 |  | 15,500 |  |
| Interest and dividends |  | 12,800 |  |  |
| Dividends paid | 20,000 |  | 10,000 |  |
| Retained earnings 1/1/80 |  | 107,000 |  | 84,000 |
| Common stock |  | 600,000 |  | 100,000 |
|  | $1,512,800 | $1,512,800 | $746,500 | $746,500 |

*Additional information:*
(1) The investment in stock of S Co. represents a 90% interest, which was acquired January 1, 1980, for $175,000. At the same time, $50,000 face amount of bonds of S was acquired for $52,000. These bonds had been issued in 1970 at 106 and are due January 1, 1990. S Co. has recorded the amortization of the bond premium applicable to 1980 as an adjustment of interest expense. The stock and the bonds were not purchased from the S Co. but from the public.
(2) Included in the Purchases account of S Co. is a total of $180,000 of goods bought from P Co. at 120% of cost to P Co. The closing inventory of S Co. is estimated to include the same proportion of these purchases as of other purchases.
(3) Inventories at December 31, 1980, at cost to each company, were:

P Co.—$80,000
S Co.—$45,000

(AICPA adapted)

## Problem 13-11

To facilitate its production of signal flares and equipment, Flare, Inc., on January 1, 1980, purchased the entire capital stock of Metals, Inc., for $875,000, and Tool, Inc., for $1,200,000.

The trial balances of the three companies at December 31, 1980, were as follows:

|  | Flare, Inc. | Metals, Inc. | Tool, Inc. |
|---|---|---|---|
| *Debits* |  |  |  |
| Cash | $ 80,000 | $ 58,000 | $ 70,000 |
| Notes receivable | 100,000 | 50,000 | 25,000 |
| Notes receivable, Flare, Inc. |  |  | 15,000 |
| Accounts receivable: |  |  |  |
| Customers | 420,000 | 190,000 | 380,000 |
| Metals, Inc. | 25,000 |  | 30,000 |
| Inventories, January 1, 1980: |  |  |  |
| Raw materials | 150,000 | 105,000 | 160,000 |

|  |  |  |  |
|---|---:|---:|---:|
| Work in process | 80,000 | 70,000 | 75,000 |
| Finished goods | 90,000 | 65,000 | 80,000 |
| Investments: |  |  |  |
|   Flare, Inc., bonds |  | 102,000 |  |
|   Metals, Inc., stock | 875,000 |  |  |
|   Tool, Inc., stock | 1,200,000 |  |  |
| Land | 150,000 | 35,000 | 90,000 |
| Buildings | 400,000 | 100,000 | 280,000 |
| Machinery and equipment | 350,000 | 165,000 | 380,000 |
| Purchases | 650,000 | 400,000 | 510,000 |
| Labor | 450,000 | 320,000 | 370,000 |
| Manufacturing expenses | 235,000 | 210,000 | 242,500 |
| Selling expenses | 70,000 | 35,000 | 80,000 |
| Administrative expenses | 60,000 | 30,000 | 30,000 |
| Dividends paid | 150,000 | 25,000 | 40,000 |
| Totals | $5,535,000 | $1,960,000 | $2,857,500 |

*Credits*

|  |  |  |  |
|---|---:|---:|---:|
| Notes payable to: |  |  |  |
|   Banks | $ 72,000 | $ 30,000 | $ 20,000 |
|   Tool, Inc. | 15,000 |  |  |
| Accounts payable: |  |  |  |
|   Trade | 120,000 | 135,000 | 290,000 |
|   Flare, Inc. |  | 25,000 |  |
|   Tool, Inc. |  | 30,000 |  |
| Bonds payable | 306,000 |  |  |
| Allowance for depreciation | 145,000 | 80,000 | 150,000 |
| Sales | 1,750,000 | 1,000,000 | 1,507,500 |
| Dividends received | 65,000 |  |  |
| Capital stock | 3,000,000 | 500,000 | 800,000 |
| Retained earnings, January 1, 1980: | 62,000 | 160,000 | 90,000 |
| Totals | $5,535,000 | $1,960,000 | $2,857,500 |

For a number of years, the three companies had traded with each other, and at December 31, 1979, there were included in the raw material inventory of Flare, Inc., goods purchased from Metals, Inc., valued at $60,000 which cost Metals, Inc., $40,000. Likewise, on that date, the raw material inventory of Metals, Inc., included goods purchased from Tool, Inc., for $75,000 which cost Tool, Inc. $50,000 to produce.

The intercompany sales for the year ended December 31, 1980, were as follows:

|  | Selling Price | Cost to Produce |
|---|---:|---:|
| Tools, Inc., to Metals, Inc. | $200,000 | $160,000 |
| Metals, Inc., to Flare, Inc. | 375,000 | 300,000 |

An analysis of the December 31, 1980, inventories revealed the following information:

|  | Raw Materials | Work in Process | Finished Goods |
|---|---|---|---|
| Flare, Inc. | $280,000 | $95,000 | $135,000 |
| Intercompany profit included in above | 20,000 | 5,000 | 4,000 |
| Metals, Inc. | $175,000 | $80,000 | $145,000 |
| Intercompany profit included in above | 30,000 | 6,000 | 5,000 |
| Tool, Inc. | $210,000 | $85,000 | $105,000 |

On July 1, 1980, Flare, Inc., sold to Metals, Inc., $100,000 first-mortgage 5% bonds at 102. At the same time, the remainder of the issue, or $200,000, was sold through a broker for $204,000. The bonds mature June 30, 1985. The interest, payable semi-annually, had not been paid at December 31, 1980.

*Required:*
Consolidated working papers at December 31, 1980, with columns for income, retained earnings, and financial position. (Assume that goodwill is not to be amortized at this time.)

## Problem 13-12

The individual and consolidated statements of Companies X and Y for the year ending December 31, 1980, are as shown below.

X Company purchased its 70% interest in Y Company several years ago. X Company sells its product in part to Company Y for further processing, and in part to other firms. The inventories of Y Company included an intercompany markup at both the beginning and end of the year. Cash transfers are made between the companies according to working capital needs.

Early in 1980, Y Company purchased $100,000 face value of the bonds of X Company as a temporary investment. These bonds are carried on Y's books at cost.

*Required:*
On the basis of the information you can develop from an analysis of the individual and consolidated statements, answer the following questions. Show clearly all computations necessary to support your answers.

(1) Does X Company carry its "Investment in Y" on the cost or equity (accrual) basis? State the reason for your conclusion.

|  | X Company | Y Company | Consolidated |
|---|---|---|---|
| Cash and receivables | $ 35,000 | $108,000 | $ 97,400 |
| Inventories | 40,000 | 90,000 | 122,000 |
| Plant (net) | 460,000 | 140,000 | 600,000 |
| Appraisal increase in plant (net) |  |  | 50,000 |
| Investment in Y | 245,000 |  | –0– |
| X bonds owned |  | 103,000 | –0– |
|  | $780,000 | $441,000 | $869,400 |
| Current payables | $ 70,000 | $ 23,000 | $ 53,000 |
| Dividends payable | 10,000 | 8,000 | 12,400 |
| Mortgage bonds | 200,000 | 50,000 | 150,000 |
| Capital stock | 300,000 | 200,000 | 300,000 |
| Retained earnings | 200,000 | 160,000 | 231,000 |
| Minority interest |  |  | 123,000 |
|  | $780,000 | $441,000 | $869,400 |
| Sales | $600,000 | $400,000 | $760,000 |
| Cost of sales | 360,000 | 280,000 | 403,000 |
| Gross profit | 240,000 | 120,000 | 357,000 |
| Operating expense | 130,000 | 54,000 | 184,000 |
| Operating profit | 110,000 | 66,000 | 173,000 |
| Interest income | 1,800 | 5,000 | 1,800 |
| Dividend income | 11,200 | –0– | –0– |
| Total | $123,000 | $ 71,000 | $174,800 |
| Interest expense | 10,000 | 3,000 | 8,000 |
| Provision for income taxes | 56,000 | 34,000 | 90,000 |
| Nonrecurring loss |  |  | 3,000 |
| Minority share |  |  | 5,400 |
| Net income | $ 57,000 | $ 34,000 | $ 68,400 |
| Dividends | 20,000 | 16,000 | 24,800 |
| Transfer to retained earnings | $ 37,000 | $ 18,000 | $ 43,600 |

(2) The "Appraisal increase" represents a revaluation of the *total* of Y Company's assets on the basis of the price paid by X Company for its interest in Y. What was the balance of Y's "Retained earnings" at date of acquisition?

(3) Prepare a reconciliation schedule that will explain clearly the difference between X Company's "Retained earnings" at December 31, 1980, $200,000, and the "Consolidated retained earnings" at December 31, 1980, $231,000.

(4) What is the nature of the "Nonrecurring loss" on the consolidated income statement? Show the consolidating elimination entry from which it originated.

(5) Show the amounts of intercompany debts, excluding the bonds, and show which company is the debtor and which is the creditor in each instance.
(6) Prepare a schedule reconciling the sum of the "Cost of Sales" of X and Y individually with the "Consolidated cost of sales." Show clearly the intercompany markup in the beginning and ending inventories of Y Company and how you determined the amounts. (AICPA adapted)

## Problem 13-13

The P Corporation bought from its wholly owned subsidiary for $16,000 certain equipment which was carried on the books of the subsidiary at a cost of $31,000 with accumulated depreciation of $17,000.

State the effect on the consolidated balance sheet of the purchase of equipment from the subsidiary. State specifically what eliminating entries, if any, should be made on the consolidating work sheet used for preparation of the consolidated financial statements.

On January 1, 1980, the S Corporation issued $200,000 of 10-year 4% bonds. These were sold at 98, and expenses of issue were $2,400. Interest is payable January 1 and July 1. In March 1983, the P Corporation acquired 80% of the outstanding stock of S. On March 31, 1984, the P Corporation purchased on the market $100,000 face value of S Corporation's 4% bonds at 90 and accrued interest.

You are to state what eliminating entries should be made as a result of the bond transactions on the consolidating work sheets used for preparation of the consolidated statements at December 31, 1984. *Give a brief explanation of the purpose or reason for each entry you make.* (AICPA adapted)

## Problem 13-14

The Ohio Manufacturing Company on January 1, 1980, acquired 90% of the capital stock of the Wabash Company and on January 1, 1982, 80% of the capital stock of Company X. Following are the trial balances of the companies at December 31, 1982:

| Debits | Ohio Mfg. Co. | Wabash Co. | Company X |
|---|---|---|---|
| Cash | $ 78,300 | $ 8,000 | $ 28,500 |
| Accounts receivable, customers | 132,500 | 87,000 | 50,000 |
| Current account, Wabash Co. | 10,000 | | |
| Current account, Company X | 7,500 | | 6,000 |
| Inventories, January 1, 1982: | | | |
| Raw materials | 175,000 | 30,000 | 22,000 |
| In process | 140,000 | 20,000 | 20,000 |
| Finished goods | 130,000 | 25,000 | 15,000 |

Investments:

| | | | |
|---|---:|---:|---:|
| Wabash Company stock (90%) | 194,000 | | |
| Company X stock (80%) | 48,200 | | |
| Bonds, Company X | | 10,000 | |
| Land | 20,000 | 5,000 | 10,000 |
| Buildings | 50,000 | 40,000 | 20,000 |
| Machinery and equipment | 225,000 | 180,000 | 100,000 |
| Prepaid accounts | 5,000 | 4,000 | 2,000 |
| Material purchases | 1,300,000 | 550,000 | 320,000 |
| Direct labor | 800,000 | 400,000 | 100,000 |
| Indirect manufacturing labor | 50,000 | 30,000 | 10,000 |
| Taxes (other than federal taxes on income) | 6,000 | 4,000 | 2,000 |
| Insurance | 800 | 600 | 200 |
| Repairs | 4,700 | 3,000 | 1,800 |
| Manufacturing supplies and expense | 5,000 | 4,000 | 2,500 |
| Sales returns and allowances | 10,000 | 4,000 | 2,000 |
| Selling expense | 100,000 | 60,000 | 25,000 |
| General and administrative expense | 75,000 | 40,000 | 25,000 |
| Bond interest | | | 6,000 |
| Dividends paid | | 20,000 | 5,000 |
| Totals | $3,567,000 | $1,530,600 | $767,000 |

### Credits

| | | | |
|---|---:|---:|---:|
| Accounts payable | $ 75,000 | $ 70,000 | $ 38,000 |
| Current account, Ohio Mfg. Co. | | 10,000 | 7,500 |
| Current account, Wabash Co. | | | 6,000 |
| Accrued accounts | 154,500 | 46,500 | 9,500 |
| Bonds payable | | | 100,000 |
| Allowance for bad debts | 2,500 | 1,500 | 1,000 |
| Allowance for depreciation | 75,000 | 60,000 | 45,000 |
| Sales | 2,600,000 | 1,120,000 | 500,000 |
| Interest income | | 600 | |
| Rent of factory equipment to Company X | | 2,000 | |
| Capital stock | 500,000 | 200,000 | 50,000 |
| Retained earnings, January 1, 1982 | 160,000 | 20,000 | 10,000 |
| Totals | $3,567,000 | $1,530,600 | $767,000 |

Inventories at December 31, 1982 were as follows:

| | Ohio Mfg. Co. | Wabash Co. | Company X |
|---|---:|---:|---:|
| Raw materials | $190,000 | $40,000 | $20,000 |
| In process | 150,000 | 25,000 | 25,000 |
| Finished goods | 140,000 | 30,000 | 20,000 |
| Totals | $480,000 | $95,000 | $65,000 |

During the year 1982, Company X sold to the Ohio Manufacturing Company $150,000 worth of goods and to the Wabash Company $100,000 worth. The Wabash Company sold to the Ohio Manufacturing Company goods to the amount of $400,000.

The inventories at January 1, 1982, contained profits as follows on sales by the Wabash Company to the Ohio Manufacturing Company:

| | |
|---|---|
| Raw materials | $2,000 |
| In process | 1,000 |
| Finished goods | 600 |

The inventories at December 31, 1982, contained the following profits made on intercompany sales:

| | On sales by Wabash Co. to Ohio Mfg. Co. | On sales by Company X to Ohio Mfg. Co. | On sales by Company X to Wabash Co. |
|---|---|---|---|
| Raw materials | $2,500 | $1,000 | $ 800 |
| In process | 1,200 | 800 | 600 |
| Finished goods | 800 | 600 | 400 |
| Totals | $4,500 | $2,400 | $1,800 |

Each prior year the parent company had taken up in the investment account its share of the subsidiary's profit. Such entry had not yet been made for 1982. All dividends received, including those received from both companies in 1982, had been credited to the respective investment accounts. Goodwill is being amortized on a straight-line basis over 10 years.

Depreciation and prepaid and accrued accounts have been properly accounted for. Federal taxes on income may be ignored. Allowances for bad debts are considered sufficient.

Prepare consolidated financial statements, submitting complete working papers showing the consolidating process.

## Problem 13-15

On January 1, 1975, the X Manufacturing Company acquired for $1,000,000 in cash all the capital stock of the Y Coal Company. On that date the statement of financial position of the Y Coal Company was as follows:

*Assets*

| | |
|---|---|
| Coal lands, less depletion | $400,000 |
| Other assets (valued in accordance with the accounting practice of both companies) | 300,000 |
| | $700,000 |

*Liabilities and Capital*

| | |
|---|---|
| Liabilities | $100,000 |
| Capital stock | 500,000 |
| Retained earnings | 100,000 |
| | $700,000 |

The operations of the Y Coal Company are confined to the mining of coal for the exclusive use of the X Manufacturing Company. No inventories of coal are carried by the Y Coal Company, as all coal mined is immediately charged to the X Manufacturing Company at a profit of 50 cents a ton after charging 10 cents a ton to the mining cost for depletion.

The books of the two companies are kept on the same accounting basis but independently of each other and without regard to the requirements of possible consolidation of the statements of financial position.

On December 31, 1980, such a consolidation was contemplated for the first time, and on that date the statement of financial position of the Y Coal Company was as follows:

*Assets*

| | |
|---|---:|
| Coal lands, less depletion | $300,000 |
| Amount due from X Company | 200,000 |
| Other assets | 250,000 |
| | $750,000 |

*Liabilities*

| | |
|---|---:|
| Liabilities | $100,000 |
| Capital stock | 500,000 |
| Retained earnings | 150,000 |
| | $750,000 |

Depletion provided by the Y Company was based on the cost of the coal land to Y at the date of acquisition ($500,000) and the estimated number of tons of coal in the lands (5,000,000). The estimated number of tons of coal in the lands at January 1, 1975, was 4,000,000. Between that date and December 31, 1980, 1,000,000 tons were mined.

The investment by X Company in Y Company was carried at December 31, 1980, at cost to the X Company ($1,000,000). On that date the accounts of X Company showed that an amount of $150,000 was due to the Y Company, and the difference between this amount and the amount of $200,000 shown as receivable by the Y Company was accounted for as follows:

| | |
|---|---:|
| Cash in transit | $40,000 |
| Inventory in transit (5,000 tons at $2) | 10,000 |
| | $50,000 |

The inventory of the X Company contains 5,000 tons of coal (exclusive of the 5,000 tons in transit) at $2 a ton, plus transportation cost, which includes the profit of 50 cents a ton (already mentioned) to the Y Company.

There are no intercompany accounts, relations, or transactions other than those indicated in this problem.

Prepare in journal entry form the adjustments and eliminations necessary when preparing consolidated statements on December 31, 1980.

(AICPA adapted)

## Problem 13-16

On October 1, 1978, the Arba Company acquired a 90% interest in the common stock of Braginetz Company on the open market for $750,000; the book value was $712,500 at that date. Since the excess could not be attributed to the undervaluation of any specific assets, Arba reported $37,500 of consolidated goodwill on its consolidated balance sheet at September 30, 1979. During fiscal 1980 it was decided that the Braginetz goodwill should be amortized in equal amounts over 10 years beginning with fiscal 1980.

On October 1, 1979, Arba purchased new equipment for $14,500 from Braginetz. The equipment cost Braginetz $9,000 and had an estimated life of 10 years as of October 1, 1979. Arba uses the sum-of-the-years'-digits depreciation method for both financial and income tax reporting.

During fiscal 1981, Arba had merchandise sales to Braginetz of $100,000; the merchandise was priced at 25% above Arba's cost. Braginetz still owes Arba $17,500 on open account and has 20% of this merchandise in inventory at September 30, 1981.

On August 1, 1981, Braginetz borrowed $30,000 from Arba by issuing 12, $2,500, 9%, 90-day notes. Arba discounted four of the notes at its bank on August 31 at 6%.

*Required:*

For each of the following items give the elimination entry (including explanation) that should be made on the working papers for the preparation of the indicated consolidated statement(s) at September 30, 1981.

(1) For the consolidated goodwill—to prepare all consolidated statements.
(2) For the equipment:
 (a) To prepare only a consolidated balance sheet.
 (b) To prepare all consolidated statements.
(3) For the intercompany merchandise transactions—to prepare all consolidated statements.
(4) For the note transactions—to prepare only a consolidated balance sheet.

(AICPA adapted)

# 14

# Consolidated Statements — Intercompany Stock Transactions

In the preceding chapters dealing with consolidated statements it has been assumed, either expressly or by implication, that the controlling interest in a particular subsidiary was obtained as the result of a single purchase or by parental formation. It was also assumed that this interest remained constant throughout the period(s) reported upon. This approach has been used in order to simplify the development of the basic problems involved in the preparation of consolidated statements. However, in any given situation these assumptions may or may not be valid. For example, control of a subsidiary may not always be obtained by a single purchase or by formation; instead, it may be obtained by piecemeal acquisition of its stock. Likewise, the controlling interest may not always remain unchanged. It may change at any time not only because of particular actions by the parent but also occasionally because of certain actions of the subsidiary involved. For example, the parent may acquire additional stock in a subsidiary or dispose of some already owned. On the other hand, a subsidiary may issue additional stock which may or may not affect the controlling interest, depending upon the given situation. Likewise, treasury stock transactions by a subsidiary may affect the controlling interest.

In this chapter several of the problems arising from intercompany stock transactions are considered. The effect of such transactions on the parent company's investment account, on the resultant minority interest, and on consolidated retained earnings will be emphasized. The student should relate the methods of analysis of these problems to those methods discussed in the preceding chapters.

# 14 / Consolidated Statements—Intercompany Stock Transactions

# ACQUISITION OF SUBSIDIARY STOCK

## Acquisition of Control and the Date of Acquisition

As has been stressed throughout the preceding chapters, the "date of acquisition" is an important time reference, and the periods of time prior to and after this date are important time frames in the preparation of consolidated statements. The date of acquisition must be known in order to determine the difference between the cost and the book value of the shares acquired, and to segregate the subsidiary's stockholders' equity into its pre- and post-acquisition components.

When control is obtained by one block acquisition of subsidiary company stock, either by purchase or formation, there is general unanimity among accountants as to what the date of acquisition is—the date that control was obtained.

When stock is acquired piecemeal, however, there is not as complete agreement. Some accountants contend that the date of acquisition is the date that control is obtained; others maintain that it is the several dates of acquisition. While recognizing the possibility that the former approach may be acceptable under some circumstances, in *Accounting Research Bulletin No. 51* the Institute recommends that, as a general rule, the latter approach be used.

The use of the date that control is obtained is supported, even when the subsidiary stock has been acquired in small amounts over a period of time, because of its relative simplicity. However, this approach can also be supported on the theoretical grounds that subsidiary stock acquired prior to the acquisition of control is similar to and should be treated as an investment in any other nonaffiliated company. In theory the use of the several dates of acquisition can be justified, especially if the intent of the parent when acquiring the stock on a piecemeal basis was eventually to acquire a controlling interest.

For comparative purposes both approaches are illustrated in the following example. Particular attention should be given to the effect the approach chosen has on the computation of goodwill and consolidated retained earnings.

Assume that Company A makes the various purchases of Company B stock at the times indicated and under the conditions given below.

The consolidating problem created when the several dates are used is illustrated on pages 400–401. For comparative purposes both approaches are illustrated.

|  |  |  | Company B's Stockholders' Equity |  |
|---|---|---|---|---|
| Date of Purchase | Percent Purchased | Cost | Retained Earnings | Capital Stock |
| January 1, 1979 | 10% | $15,000 | $20,000 | $100,000 |
| January 1, 1980 | 20% | 32,000 | 30,000 | 100,000 |
| January 1, 1981 | 40% | 65,000 | 40,000 | 100,000 |

Company A's retained earnings as of January 1, 1981, is $200,000.

(1) Date of acquisition considered to be the *date control acquired*:
   (a) Computation of goodwill

|  |  |
|---|---|
| Amount paid | $112,000 |
| Book value acquired | 98,000 (70% of $140,000) |
| Goodwill | $ 14,000 |

   (b) Consolidated retained earnings as of January 1, 1981:
       Company A's     $200,000

(2) Date of acquisition considered to be the *several dates of acquisition*:
   (a) Computation of goodwill:

*First purchase:*

|  |  |  |
|---|---|---|
| Amount paid | $ 15,000 | |
| Book value acquired | 12,000 (10% of $120,000) | |
| Goodwill | $ 3,000 | $ 3,000 |

*Second purchase:*

|  |  |  |
|---|---|---|
| Amount paid | $ 32,000 | |
| Book value acquired | 26,000 (20% of $130,000) | |
| Goodwill | $ 6,000 | 6,000 |

*Third purchase:*

|  |  |  |
|---|---|---|
| Amount paid | $ 65,000 | |
| Book value acquired | 56,000 (40% of $140,000) | |
| Goodwill | $ 9,000 | 9,000 |
| Total goodwill | | $ 18,000 |

   (b) Consolidated retained earnings as of January 1, 1981:

|  |  |
|---|---|
| Company A's | $200,000 |
| 10% of Company B's increase since January 1, 1979 | 2,000 |
| 20% of Company B's increase since January 1, 1980. | 2,000 |
| Consolidated retained earnings as of January 1, 1981 | $204,000 |

(1)

COMPANY A AND SUBSIDIARY COMPANY B

CONSOLIDATED WORKING PAPERS

STATEMENT OF FINANCIAL POSITION

JANUARY 1, 1981

|  | Company A | Company B | Adjustments & Eliminations Debit | Adjustments & Eliminations Credit | Consolidated Financial Position |
|---|---|---|---|---|---|
| Current assets | $ 400,000 | $ 50,000 | | | $ 450,000 |
| Investment in Co. B (carried at cost) | 112,000 | | | $98,000*A* | 14,000*G* |

**14 / Consolidated Statements—Intercompany Stock Transactions**

| | | | | | | |
|---|---|---|---|---|---|---|
| Fixed assets (net) | 610,000 | 100,000 | | | | 710,000 |
| | $1,122,000 | $150,000 | | | | $1,174,000 |
| Current liabilities | $ 22,000 | $ 10,000 | | | | $ 32,000 |
| Fixed liabilities | 100,000 | | | | | 100,000 |
| Stockholders' equity: | | | | | | |
| Company A: | | | | | | |
| Capital stock | 800,000 | | | | | 800,000 |
| Retained earnings | 200,000 | | | | | 200,000RE |
| Company B: | | | | | | |
| Capital stock | | 100,000 | $70,000A | | | 30,000MI |
| Retained earnings | | 40,000 | 28,000A | | | 12,000MI |
| | $1,122,000 | $150,000 | $98,000 | $98,000 | | $1,174,000 |

*A:* To eliminate 70% of Company B's stockholders' equity against the investment account.

(2)   COMPANY A AND SUBSIDIARY COMPANY B
CONSOLIDATED WORKING PAPERS
STATEMENT OF FINANCIAL POSITION
JANUARY 1, 1981

| | Company A | Company B | Adjustments & Eliminations Debit | Credit | Consolidated Financial Position |
|---|---|---|---|---|---|
| Current assets | $ 400,000 | $ 50,000 | | | $ 450,000 |
| Investment in Co. B (carried at cost) | 112,000 | | $ 4,000(1)* | 98,000A | 18,000G |
| Fixed assets (net) | 610,000 | 100,000 | | | 710,000 |
| | $1,122,000 | $150,000 | | | $1,178,000 |
| Current liabilities | $ 22,000 | $ 10,000 | | | $ 32,000 |
| Fixed liabilities | 100,000 | | | | 100,000 |
| Stockholders' equity: | | | | | |
| Company A: | | | | | |
| Capital stock | 800,000 | | | | 800,000 |
| Retained earnings | 200,000 | | | 4,000(1) | 204,000RE |
| Company B: | | | | | |
| Capital stock | | 100,000 | 70,000A | | 30,000MI |
| Retained earnings | | 40,000 | 28,000A | | 12,000MI |
| | $1,122,000 | $150,000 | $102,000 | $102,000 | $1,178,000 |

(1): To recognize Company A's share of the increase in Company B's retained earnings prior to the acquisition of controlling interest.

A: To eliminate 70% of Company B's stockholders' equity against the investment account.
*If the investment account were carried on the equity basis, this entry would have been entered in Company A's books. However, since the cost method is in use, it is a work sheet entry only.

In these examples the selection of the several dates of acquisition, rather than the date on which control is acquired, results in an additional $4,000 of goodwill with an offsetting $4,000 in consolidated retained earnings. When consolidating (as illustrated in set (2) of the working papers above) it is necessary to make an adjustment that increases both goodwill and consolidated retained earnings. Set (2) of working papers (where date of acquisition is considered to be the *several dates of acquisition*) should be compared with set (1) (where the date of acquisition is considered to be the *date control is acquired*).

## Purchase of Subsidiary Stock After Acquisition of Control

If a parent company purchases additional subsidiary stock after a controlling interest has been acquired, no new problems are encountered. Although the basic procedure remains the same, establishment of reciprocity and proof of goodwill may become a little more complicated.

When reciprocity is established through a work sheet adjustment if the investment account is carried at cost, or a book entry if the equity method is used, the problem is still one of recognizing the parent's share of any increase or decrease in the subsidiary's stockholders' equity since acquisition. To establish reciprocity for any given period of time, the parent should recognize as the increase or decrease the percent it owned during that time and still owns at the date of consolidation. For example, assume that the parent owned an 80% interest during the entire first half of 1980 and a 90% interest during the entire second half. When reciprocity is established as of December 31, 1980, the amount of the adjustment would equal 80% of any increase or decrease during the first six months plus 90% for the second six months.

Although several purchases of subsidiary stock may complicate the proving of goodwill, the problem is still a matter of determining the amount involved in each purchase by comparing the amount paid with the book value acquired as of the purchase date. The usual elimination whereby goodwill is determined by eliminating the parent's share of the subsidiary's stockholders' equity against the investment account remains the same. To prove the goodwill, however, the amount involved on each individual purchase must be determined.

The following examples as of December 31, 1979, January 1, 1980, and December 31, 1980, show (1) establishment of reciprocity, and (2) proof of goodwill where several purchases have taken place subsequent to the acquisition of control. For purposes of simplicity it is assumed that goodwill is not being amortized at this time. In addition to the specific facts given in the individual statements of financial position, also assume:

14 / Consolidated Statements—Intercompany Stock Transactions

|  |  |  | Co. B's Stockholders' Equity |  |
|---|---|---|---|---|
| Date of Purchase | Percent Purchased | Cost | Retained Earnings | Capital Stock |
| January 1, 1978 | 70% | $105,000 | $20,000 | $100,000 |
| January 1, 1979 | 10% | 16,000 | 30,000 | 100,000 |
| January 1, 1980 | 10% | 16,250 | 40,000 | 100,000 |
| December 31, 1980 | 5% | 9,000 | 48,000 | 100,000 |

As of December 31, 1979, the work sheet would be:

Company A and Subsidiary Company B

Consolidated Working Papers

Statement of Financial Position as of December 31, 1979

|  | Company A | Company B | Adjustments & Eliminations Debit | Adjustments & Eliminations Credit | Consolidated Financial Position |
|---|---|---|---|---|---|
| Current assets | $ 391,000 | $ 50,000 |  |  | $ 441,000 |
| Investment in Co. B (carried at cost) | 121,000 |  | $15,000(1) | $112,000A | 24,000G* |
| Fixed assets (net) | 610,000 | 100,000 |  |  | 710,000 |
|  | $1,122,000 | $150,000 |  |  | $1,175,000 |
| Current liabilities | $ 22,000 | $ 10,000 |  |  | $ 32,000 |
| Fixed liabilities | 100,000 |  |  |  | 100,000 |
| Stockholders' equity: |  |  |  |  |  |
| Company A: |  |  |  |  |  |
| Capital stock | 800,000 |  |  |  | 800,000 |
| Retained earnings | 200,000 |  |  | 15,000(1) | 215,000RE |
| Company B: |  |  |  |  |  |
| Capital stock |  | 100,000 | 80,000A |  | 20,000MI |
| Retained earnings |  | 40,000 | 32,000A |  | 8,000MI |
|  | $1,122,000 | $150,000 | $127,000 | $127,000 | $1,175,000 |

(1): To establish reciprocity by recognizing Company A's share of the increase in Company B's stockholders' equity since acquisition. Computed:

| Either | Or |
|---|---|
| 70% × $10,000 = $ 7,000† | 70% × $20,000 = $14,000 |
| 80% × 10,000 = 8,000† | 10% × 10,000 = 1,000 |
|  $15,000 |  $15,000 |

A: To eliminate 80% of Company B's stockholders' equity against the investment account.

*Goodwill proof:
*First purchase:*
| | | |
|---|---|---|
| Amount paid | $105,000 | |
| Book value acquired | 84,000 (70% of $120,000) | |
| Goodwill | $ 21,000 | $21,000 |

*Second purchase:*
| | | |
|---|---|---|
| Amount paid | $ 16,000 | |
| Book value acquired | 13,000 (10% of $130,000) | |
| Goodwill | $ 3,000 | 3,000 |
| Goodwill as of December 31, 1979 | | $24,000 |

†Recorded periodically when the equity method is used.

As of January 1, 1980, the work sheet would be:

COMPANY A AND SUBSIDIARY COMPANY B
CONSOLIDATED WORKING PAPERS
STATEMENT OF FINANCIAL POSITION
JANUARY 1, 1980

| | Company A | Company B | Adjustments & Eliminations Debit | Credit | Consolidated Financial Position |
|---|---|---|---|---|---|
| Current assets | $ 374,750 | $ 50,000 | | | $ 424,750 |
| Investment in Co. B (carried at cost) | 137,250 | | $15,000(1) | $126,000A | 26,250G* |
| Fixed assets (net) | 610,000 | 100,000 | | | 710,000 |
| | $1,122,000 | $150,000 | | | $1,161,000 |
| Current liabilities | $ 22,000 | $ 10,000 | | | $ 32,000 |
| Fixed liabilities | 100,000 | | | | 100,000 |
| Stockholders' equity: | | | | | |
| Company A: | | | | | |
| Capital stock | 800,000 | | | | 800,000 |
| Retained earnings | 200,000 | | | 15,000(1) | 215,000RE |
| Company B: | | | | | |
| Capital stock | | 100,000 | 90,000A | | 10,000MI |
| Retained earnings | | 40,000 | 36,000A | | 4,000MI |
| | $1,122,000 | $150,000 | $141,000 | $141,000 | $1,161,000 |

(1): To establish reciprocity by recognizing Company A's share of the increase in Company B's stockholders' equity since acquisition. Computed:

|  | *Either* |  |  | *Or* |  |
|---|---|---|---|---|---|
| 70% × | $10,000 = | $ 7,000† | 70% × | $20,000 = | $14,000 |
| 80% × | 10,000 = | 8,000† | 10% × | 10,000 = | 1,000 |
|  |  | $15,000 |  |  | $15,000 |

A: To eliminate 90% of Company B's stockholders' equity against the investment account.
*Goodwill proof:

*First purchase:*
| Amount paid | $105,000 |  |
|---|---|---|
| Book value acquired | 84,000 |  |
| Goodwill | $ 21,000 | $21,000 |

*Second purchase:*
| Amount paid | $ 16,000 |  |
|---|---|---|
| Book value acquired | 13,000 |  |
| Goodwill | $ 3,000 | 3,000 |

*Third purchase:*
| Amount paid | $ 16,250 |  |
|---|---|---|
| Book value acquired | 14,000 (10% of $140,000) |  |
| Goodwill | $ 2,250 | 2,250 |
| Goodwill as of January 1, 1980 |  | $26,250 |

†Recorded periodically when the equity method is used.

As of December 31, 1980, the work sheet would be:

Company A and Subsidiary Company B

Consolidated Working Papers
Statement of Financial Position

December 31, 1980

|  | Company A | Company B | Adjustments & Eliminations Debit | Adjustments & Eliminations Credit | Consolidated Financial Position |
|---|---|---|---|---|---|
| Current assets | $ 400,750 | $ 53,000 |  |  | $ 453,750 |
| Investment in Co. B (carried at cost) | 146,250 |  | $22,200(1) | $140,600A | 27,850G* |
| Fixed assets (net) | 650,000 | 100,000 |  |  | 750,000 |
|  | $1,197,000 | $153,000 |  |  | $1,231,600 |
| Current liabilities | $ 77,000 | $ 5,000 |  |  | $ 82,000 |
| Fixed liabilities | 100,000 |  |  |  | 100,000 |
| Stockholders' equity: |  |  |  |  |  |
| Company A: |  |  |  |  |  |
| Capital stock | 800,000 |  |  |  | 800,000 |
| Retained earnings | 220,000 |  |  | 22,200(1) | 242,200RE |

Company B:
Capital stock             100,000    95,000A                    5,000MI
Retained
  earnings                 48,000    45,600A                    2,400MI
                       $1,197,000  $153,000  $162,800  $162,800  $1,231,600

(1): To establish reciprocity by recognizing Company A's share of the increase in Company B's stockholders' equity since acquisition. Computed:

| Either | Or |
|---|---|
| 70% × $10,000 = $ 7,000† | 70% × $28,000 = $19,600 |
| 80% × 10,000 = 8,000† | 10% × 18,000 = 1,800 |
| 90% × 8,000 = 7,200† | 10% × 8,000 = 800 |
| $22,200 | $22,200 |

A: To eliminate 95% of Company B's stockholders' equity against the investment account.
*Goodwill proof:

First purchase: (as computed above)                           $21,000
Second purchase: (as computed above)                           3,000
Third purchase: (as computed above)                            2,250
Fourth purchase:
  Amount paid              $9,000
  Book value acquired       7,400 (5% of $148,000)
  Goodwill                 $1,600                              1,600
        Goodwill as of December 31, 1980                     $27,850

†Recorded periodically when the equity method is used.

## Purchase of Subsidiary Stock at Interim Dates

Only the parent's share of post-acquisition earnings of a subsidiary is properly included in consolidated retained earnings. Thus whenever stock of a subsidiary is acquired at some date other than the subsidiary's closing date, whether it be the acquisition of a controlling interest or additional stock acquisition after control has been acquired, a proration of the subsidiary's income may be necessary. Proration may be necessary not only to determine the subsidiary's income after the date of acquisition, but also to determine the amount of subsidiary's retained earnings as of the date of acquisition and the amount of any goodwill involved. If the subsidiary has an adequate system of interim reporting, the problem is simplified. However, if statement preparation by the subsidiary is not feasible as of the date of an interim purchase, proration based on approximation may be necessary.

Once the subsidiary's income for a period has been prorated between the pre- and post-acquisition periods, the problem of statement presentation arises. One of two methods may be used. The first includes both the pre- and post-acquisition earnings of the subsidiary in the consolidated statement of income as if the purchase had been made either prior to or as of the beginning of the year. The pre-acquisition earnings of the subsidiary are then deducted when proration takes

14 / *Consolidated Statements—Intercompany Stock Transactions*    **407**

place. The second method includes only the post-acquisition earnings of the subsidiary in the consolidated statement of income. The first method is generally preferred, not only because it facilitates comparision with subsequent statements, but also because the resultant statement is more indicative of the earning power of the affiliated group. This method is illustrated in the following examples.

Since the problems involved in interim acquisitions pertain not only to the acquisition of control but also to the acquisition of additional stock after the acquisition of control, both situations are illustrated. For comparison purposes a continuing situation is used.

**Interim Acquisition of Control.** In addition to the facts given in the respective statements, assume that:

1. On April 30, 1980, Company A purchases 80% of Company B's capital stock for $125,000.
2. As of December 31, 1979, Company B had retained earnings of $40,000.
3. During 1980, Company B's earnings of $30,000 were earned more or less uniformly throughout the year.
4. Goodwill is not being amortized at this time.

COMPANY A AND SUBSIDIARY COMPANY B
CONSOLIDATED WORKING PAPERS
STATEMENT OF FINANCIAL POSITION
DECEMBER 31, 1980

|  | Company A | Company B | Adjustments & Eliminations Debit | Adjustments & Eliminations Credit | Consolidated Financial Position |
|---|---|---|---|---|---|
| Current assets | $200,000 | $ 90,000 |  |  | $290,000 |
| Investment in Co. B (carried at cost) | 125,000 |  | $16,000(1) | $136,000A | 5,000G* |
| Fixed assets (net) | 500,000 | 100,000 |  |  | 600,000 |
|  | $825,000 | $190,000 |  |  | $895,000 |
| Current liabilities | $ 65,000 | $ 20,000 |  |  | $ 85,000 |
| Fixed liabilities | 100,000 |  |  |  | 100,000 |
| Stockholders' equity: |  |  |  |  |  |
| Company A: |  |  |  |  |  |
| Capital stock | 500,000 |  |  |  | 500,000 |
| Retained earnings | 160,000 |  |  | 16,000(1) | 176,000RE |
| Company B: |  |  |  |  |  |
| Capital stock |  | 100,000 | 80,000A |  | 20,000MI |
| Retained earnings |  | 70,000 | 56,000A |  | 14,000MI |
|  | $825,000 | $190,000 | $152,000 | $152,000 | $895,000 |

(1): To establish reciprocity by recognizing Company A's share of the increase in Company B's stockholders' equity since acquisition (80% × $30,000 × ⅔).

A: To eliminate 80% of Company B's stockholders' equity against the investment account.
*Goodwill proof:

| | |
|---|---|
| Amount paid | $125,000 |
| Book value acquired | 120,000 (80% of $150,000)† |
| Goodwill | $ 5,000 |

†$100,000 + $70,000 − (⅔ of $30,000) = $150,000
or $100,000 + $40,000 + (⅓ of $30,000) = $150,000

### COMPANY A AND SUBSIDIARY COMPANY B
### CONSOLIDATED WORKING PAPERS
### STATEMENT OF INCOME
### FOR THE YEAR 1980

| | Company A | Company B | Eliminations | Consolidated Income |
|---|---|---|---|---|
| *Credits:* | | | | |
| Net sales | $800,000 | $200,000 | $10,000A | $990,000 |
| Interest income | 6,000 | | | 6,000 |
| Totals | $806,000 | $200,000 | $10,000 | $996,000 |
| *Debits:* | | | | |
| Cost of sales | $560,000 | $110,000 | $10,000A | $660,000 |
| Depreciation | 80,000 | 20,000 | | 100,000 |
| Selling expense | 46,000 | 10,000 | | 56,000 |
| Taxes | 60,000 | 30,000 | | 90,000 |
| Net income | 60,000 | 30,000 | | 90,000 |
| Totals | $806,000 | $200,000 | $10,000 | $996,000 |
| Apportionment of net income: | | | | |
| Net income | | | | $ 90,000 |
| Minority interest (20% of $30,000) | | | $ 6,000 | |
| Parent's share of B's income earned prior to acquisition (80% of $10,000) | | | 8,000 | 14,000 |
| Consolidated net income (remainder) | | | | $ 76,000 |

A: To eliminate intercompany sales.

### COMPANY A AND SUBSIDIARY COMPANY B
### STATEMENT OF INCOME
### FOR THE YEAR 1980

*Income:*

| | | |
|---|---|---|
| Net sales | | $990,000 |
| Interest income | | 6,000 |
| | | 996,000 $996,000 |

*Deductions from Income:*

| | | |
|---|---|---|
| Cost of sales | | $660,000 |

|  |  | 100,000 |  |
|---|---|---|---|
| Depreciation |  | 100,000 |  |
| Selling expense |  | 56,000 |  |
| Taxes |  | 90,000 |  |
|  |  | 906,000 | 906,000 |
| Net income |  |  | $ 90,000 |
| Deduct: |  |  |  |
| Minority interest |  | $ 6,000 |  |
| Parent's share of B's income prior to acquisition |  | 8,000 | 14,000 |
| Consolidated net income |  |  | $ 76,000 |

**Interim Purchase Subsequent to Acquisition of Control.** In addition to the specific facts given in the respective statements and those given in the preceding example, assume that:

1. On April 30, 1981, Company A purchases an additional 10% of Company B's capital stock for $20,000.
2. During 1981, Company B earned $36,000 that was earned uniformly throughout the year.

COMPANY A AND SUBSIDIARY COMPANY B

CONSOLIDATED WORKING PAPERS

STATEMENT OF FINANCIAL POSITION

DECEMBER 31, 1981

|  | Company A | Company B | Adjustments & Eliminations Debit | Adjustments & Eliminations Credit | Consolidated Financial Position |
|---|---|---|---|---|---|
| Current assets | $225,000 | $126,000 |  |  | $351,000 |
| Investment in Co. B (carried at cost) | 145,000 |  | $47,200(1) | $185,400A | 6,800G* |
| Fixed assets (net) | 530,000 | 90,000 |  |  | 620,000 |
|  | $900,000 | $216,000 |  |  | $977,800 |
| Current liabilities | $ 70,000 | $ 10,000 |  |  | $ 80,000 |
| Fixed liabilities | 100,000 |  |  |  | 100,000 |
| Stockholders' equity: |  |  |  |  |  |
| Company A: |  |  |  |  |  |
| Capital stock | 500,000 |  |  |  | 500,000 |
| Retained earnings | 230,000 |  |  | 47,200(1) | 277,200RE |
| Company B: |  |  |  |  |  |
| Capital stock |  | 100,000 | 90,000A |  | 10,000MI |
| Retained earnings |  | 106,000 | 95,400A |  | 10,600MI |
|  | $900,000 | $216,000 | $232,600 | $232,600 | $977,800 |

(1): To establish reciprocity by recognizing Company A's share of the increase in Company B's stockholders' equity since acquisition. Computed:

| *Either* | | *Or* | |
|---|---|---|---|
| 80% ($106,000 − $50,000) = | $44,800 | 1980 (80% × $30,000 × ⅔) = | $16,000 |
| 10% × $36,000 × ⅔ = | 2,400 | 1981 (80% × $36,000 × ⅓) = | 9,600 |
| | $47,200 | (90% × $36,000 × ⅔) = | 21,600 |
| | | | $47,200 |

A: To eliminate 90% of Company B's stockholders' equity against the investment account.
*Goodwill proof:

| | | |
|---|---|---|
| First purchase (as computed above) | | $5,000 |
| Second purchase: | | |
|   Amount paid | $20,000 | |
|   Book value acquired | 18,200 (10% of $182,000)† | |
|   Goodwill | $1,800 | 1,800 |
| Goodwill as of December 31, 1981 | | $6,800 |

†$100,000 + $70,000 + (⅓ of $36,000) = $182,000.

COMPANY A AND SUBSIDIARY COMPANY B

CONSOLIDATED WORKING PAPERS

STATEMENT OF INCOME

FOR THE YEAR 1981

| | Company A | Company B | Eliminations | Consolidated Income |
|---|---|---|---|---|
| *Credits:* | | | | |
| Net sales | $840,000 | $210,000 | $20,000A | $1,030,000 |
| Interest income | 6,000 | | | 6,000 |
| | $846,000 | $210,000 | $20,000 | $1,036,000 |
| *Debits:* | | | | |
| Cost of sales | $570,000 | $115,000 | $20,000A | $ 665,000 |
| Depreciation | 80,000 | 15,000 | | 95,000 |
| Selling expense | 56,000 | 8,000 | | 64,000 |
| Taxes | 70,000 | 36,000 | | 106,000 |
| Net income | 70,000 | 36,000 | | 106,000 |
| | $846,000 | $210,000 | $20,000 | $1,036,000 |
| Apportionment of net income: | | | | |
|   Net income | | | | $ 106,000 |
|   Minority interest (10% of $36,000) | | | $ 3,600 | |
|   Parent's share of B's income earned prior to acquisition (10% × $36,000 × ⅓) | | | 1,200 | 4,800 |
|   Consolidated net income (remainder) | | | | $ 101,200 |

A: To eliminate intercompany sales.

14 / *Consolidated Statements—Intercompany Stock Transactions*

COMPANY A AND SUBSIDIARY COMPANY B

STATEMENT OF INCOME

FOR THE YEAR 1981

*Income:*

|  |  |  |
|---|---:|---:|
| Net sales | $1,030,000 | |
| Interest income | 6,000 | |
|  | 1,036,000 | $1,036,000 |

*Deductions from Income:*

|  |  |  |
|---|---:|---:|
| Cost of sales | $ 665,000 | |
| Depreciation | 95,000 | |
| Selling expense | 64,000 | |
| Taxes | 106,000 | |
|  | 930,000 | 930,000 |
| Net income |  | $ 106,000 |
| Deduct: | | |
| Minority interest | $ 3,600 | |
| Parent's share of B's income prior to acquisition | 1,200 | 4,800 |
| Consolidated net income |  | $ 101,200 |

## DISPOSAL OF SUBSIDIARY STOCK

*[handwritten note: don't state in prob use FIFO]*

The disposal of subsidiary stock, whether it be complete or partial, is similar to the disposal of any other asset. In disposing of subsidiary stock, as in disposing of any asset, the problem includes (1) recording any asset(s) received, (2) removing the carrying value of the asset disposed of from the appropriate account(s), and (3) recording any gain or loss on disposal. Since the determination of the value of the asset(s) received is normally not too difficult, and since the gain or loss is the difference between the value of the asset(s) received and the carrying value of the asset disposed of, the basic problem involved is one of determining the carrying value of the subsidiary stock disposed of.

In order to illustrate some of the ramifications of accounting for disposal of subsidiary stock, several different examples are presented. For purposes of comparison, both the cost and equity methods are illustrated. When the two methods are compared, it should be recognized that since the carrying value may vary, depending upon the method used, any gain or loss on disposal will also vary. The ultimate effect on consolidated retained earnings, however, will be the same. When the equity method is used, the ultimate effect will include not only any gain or loss on disposal but also the parent's share of all increases and decreases in the subsidiary's stockholders' equity since acquisition. Under the cost method the ultimate effect would include only the gain or loss on disposal. Reconciliation of the consolidated retained earnings is illustrated in the first example. In addition, it should be noted that a proportionate amount of goodwill is also disposed of since goodwill arising from consolidation attaches to the individual shares owned. When some of the shares are sold, goodwill on consolidation is also sold.

In addition to specific conditions given in each illustration, assume also the following general conditions. It should be emphasized that the illustrations are *not* continuous. Each is a separate situation based on the general and specific facts given.

1. As of January 1, 1979, Company A purchases 80% of Company B's capital stock for $80,000. As of that date, Company B had capital stock of $100,000 and a deficit of $10,000.
2. During 1979, Company B earns $20,000.
3. As of January 1, 1980, Company A purchases an additional 10% interest in Company B for $11,000.
4. As of May 1, 1980, Company A purchases another 10% interest in Company B for $11,000.
5. During 1980, Company B earns $30,000.
6. Assume that yearly earnings by Company B are earned more or less uniformly throughout the year.
7. Assume that goodwill is not being amortized at this time.

## Complete Disposal

In addition to the general conditions, assume that Company A sells all of its interest (80%) in Company B as of December 31, 1979, for $88,000. The entry to reflect the sale would be:

*Cost method:*
|   |   |   |
|---|---|---|
| Cash | $88,000 |   |
|     Investment in Company B (cost) |   | $80,000 |
|     Gain on disposal of subsidiary stock |   | 8,000* |

*Equity method:*
|   |   |   |
|---|---|---|
| Cash | $88,000 |   |
| Loss on disposal of subsidiary stock | 8,000* |   |
|     Investment in Company B |   | $96,000 |
|     [$80,000 + (80% × $20,000)] |   |   |

*The ultimate effect on consolidated retained earnings would be:

|   | Cost | Equity |
|---|---|---|
| Recognition of B's increase or (decrease) in stockholders' equity | –0– | $16,000 |
| Recognition of gain or (loss) on disposal | $8,000 | (8,000) |
| Ultimate effect | $8,000 | $ 8,000 |

## Partial Disposal

In addition to the general conditions, assume that on December 31, 1980, Company A sells a 10% interest in Company B for $15,000. The gain or loss on disposal may vary depending upon the accounting policy adopted for pricing out the stock investment sold. Since specific identification is one method that may be used to price the investment sold, the amount of gain or loss reported may be regulated

14 / *Consolidated Statements—Intercompany Stock Transactions* 413

to a certain extent by selecting the certificates delivered. In the following example, the specific identification method is assumed, and entries for all three blocks of stock are included:

|  | Certificates Delivered | | |
|---|---|---|---|
|  | 1st Purchase | 2nd Purchase | 3rd Purchase |
| *Cost method* | | | |
| Cash $15,000 | | | |
|   Investment in Company B | $10,000 | $11,000 | $11,000 |
|   Gain on disposal of stock | 5,000 | 4,000 | 4,000 |
| *Equity method:* | | | |
| Cash $15,000 | | | |
|   Investment in Company B | $15,000* | $14,000* | $13,000* |
|   Gain on disposal of stock | –0– | 1,000 | 2,000 |

*Computation of carrying value:

First purchase:
(1/8 × $80,000) + (1/10 × $50,000) = $15,000

Second purchase:
$11,000 + (1/10 × $30,000) = 14,000

Third purchase:
$11,000 + (1/10 × $30,000 × 2/3) = 13,000

**Partial Disposal at an Interim Date.** Disposal at an interim date creates no unusual problem if the investment account is carried at cost. However, if the equity method is in use, a proration of income similar to the proration problem involved when subsidiary stock is acquired at an interim date may be necessary. In addition to the general conditions, assume that as of July 1, 1980, Company A sells a 10% interest in Company B for $11,000.

|  | Certificates Delivered | | |
|---|---|---|---|
|  | 1st Purchase | 2nd Purchase | 3rd Purchase |
| *Cost method:* | | | |
| Cash $11,000 | | | |
|   Investment in Company B | $10,000 | $11,000 | $11,000 |
|   Gain (loss) | 1,000 | –0– | –0– |
| *Equity method:* | | | |
| Cash $11,000 | | | |
|   Investment in Company B | $13,500* | $12,500* | $11,500* |
|   Gain (loss) | (2,500) | (1,500) | (500) |

*Computation of carrying value:

First purchase:
(1/8 × $80,000) + (1/10 × $20,000) + (1/10 × $30,000 × 1/2) = $13,500

Second purchase:
$11,000 + (1/10 × $30,000 × 1/2) = 12,500

Third purchase:
$11,000 + (1/10 × $30,000 × 1/6) = 11,500

**Effect of Partial Disposals on Consolidated Goodwill.** As emphasized throughout the work on consolidated statements, the amount of goodwill determined at the date of purchase remains the same unless it is amortized or unless there is a change in the percent of ownership. As seen earlier in this chapter, an increase in the percent of ownership will affect the amount of consolidated goodwill, if the purchase price is anything other than book value of the interest acquired. A disposal of subsidiary stock likewise will affect consolidated goodwill, if there was any goodwill associated with the acquisition of the stock being disposed of.

In addition to the general conditions stated earlier, assume also that a 10% interest in Company B is sold by Company A for $14,000 on October 31, 1980. Assume further that the stock certificates delivered are from the January 1, 1979, purchase. The entry to record the sale would be:

|  |  | Cost | Equity |
|---|---|---|---|
| Cash | $14,000 |  |  |
|    Investment in Company B |  | $10,000 | $14,500* |
|    Gain (loss) on disposal |  | 4,000 | (500) |

*Computation of carrying value:
   1/8 × ($80,000 + $16,000 + $20,000)

*Goodwill prior to the disposal:*

   *First purchase (1/1/79):*
|  |  |  |
|---|---|---|
|      Paid | $80,000 |  |
|      Book value acquired | 72,000 [80% × ($100,000 − $10,000)] |  |
|      Goodwill | $ 8,000 | $8,000 |

   *Second purchase (1/1/80):*
|  |  |  |
|---|---|---|
|      Paid | $11,000 |  |
|      Book value acquired | 11,000 [10% × ($100,000 + $10,000)] |  |
|      Goodwill | $ −0− | −0− |

   *Third purchase (5/1/80):*
|  |  |  |
|---|---|---|
|      Paid | $11,000 |  |
|      Book value acquired | 12,000 [10% × ($100,000 + $20,000)] |  |
|      Goodwill | $(1,000) | (1,000) |

   Consolildated goodwill as of October 31, 1980, prior to sale     $7,000

Since the stock certificates were identified as being from the first purchase, one-eighth of the goodwill associated with that purchase was disposed of. Consequently, consolidated goodwill after the disposal should be $1,000 (1/8 × $8,000) less or a total of $6,000. Proof of this under both the cost and equity methods follows:

*Goodwill after disposal:*

|  | Cost | Equity |
|---|---|---|
| Carrying value after disposal (10/31/80) | $ 92,000[1] | $127,500[2] |
| Establishment of reciprocity (10/31/80) | 35,500[3] | −0− |

|  | | | $127,500 | $127,500 |
| --- | --- | --- | --- | --- |
| Elimination (90% × $135,000) | | | 121,500 | 121,500 |
| Goodwill | | | $ 6,000 | $ 6,000 |

### ¹Investment in Company B (Cost)

| 1st Purchase | $80,000 | Disposal | $10,000 |
| --- | --- | --- | --- |
| 2nd Purchase | 11,000 | | |
| 3rd Purchase | 11,000 | | |

### ²Investment in Company B (Equity)

| 1st Purchase | $80,000 | Disposal | $14,500 |
| --- | --- | --- | --- |
| 1979 Profit | 16,000 | | |
| 2nd Purchase | 11,000 | | |
| 3rd Purchase | 11,000 | | |
| 1980 Profit as of 10/31/80 | 24,000 | | |

³Establishment of reciprocity:

*Either*                                                                 *or*

```
1979 Profits 70% × $20,000          = $14,000      70% × $20,000           = $14,000
1980 Profits 80% × 30,000 × 5/6 =    20,000        80% × 30,000 × 1/3 =       8,000
             10% × 30,000 × 1/2 =     1,500        90% × 30,000 × 1/2 =     13,500
                                    $35,500                                 $35,500
```

**Effect of Partial Disposals on Subsequent Consolidations.** When the effect of a partial disposal on consolidated goodwill was illustrated in the preceding section, it was observed that a partial disposal affects subsequent consolidations if the cost method is used. For example, when reciprocity was established in the immediately preceding illustration, under the cost method the establishment of reciprocity was dependent not upon the percentage of subsidiary stock owned during a given period but upon the percentage owned during the period and retained to the date of consolidation. For instance, during 1979, Company A owned an 80% interest in Company B. However, since the 10% disposal was assumed to have been from the first purchase, when reciprocity was established after the disposal, only 70% of the profits for 1979 were recognized. Likewise, Company A owned a 90% interest during the first four months and a 100% interest during the next six months of 1980, but only 80% and 90% respectively were recognized when reciprocity was established after the sale.

Had the certificates delivered been identified as having been from the second or third purchase, the percentages to use in establishing reciprocity would have been as follows (for comparison purposes the first purchase is also included):

**416** EXPANSION OF THE BUSINESS ORGANIZATION

|  | Certificates Delivered | | |
|---|---|---|---|
|  | 1st Purchase | 2nd Purchase | 3rd Purchase |
| 1979 Profits | 70% | 80% | 80% |
| 1980 Profits: First 4 months | 80% | 80% | 90% |
| Next 6 months | 90% | 90% | 90% |

If the investment account is carried on the equity method, a partial disposal creates no unusual problem as far as subsequent consolidations are concerned. This is because increases and decreases in a subsidiary's stockholders' equity are recognized on the books of the parent, and the resulting gain or loss on disposal is affected accordingly.

Continuing the illustration from the preceding section, the consolidating process as of December 31, 1980, would reflect the following:

|  | Cost | Equity |
|---|---|---|
| Carrying value | $ 92,000 | $132,000[1] |
| Establishment of reciprocity | 40,000[2] | –0– |
|  | $132,000 | $132,000 |
| Elimination (90% × $140,000) | 126,000 | 126,000 |
| Goodwill | $ 6,000 | $ 6,000 |

[1] $127,500 + (90% × $30,000 × 1/6).
[2] 70% × $20,000 = $14,000
80% × 30,000 × 1/3 = 8,000
90% × 30,000 × 2/3 = 18,000
$40,000

Assuming that the 10% disposal was from the second or third purchase rather than the first, the consolidating process as of December 31, 1980, would reflect the following:

|  | Certificates Delivered | | | |
|---|---|---|---|---|
|  | 2nd Purchase | | 3rd Purchase | |
|  | Cost | Equity | Cost | Equity |
| Carrying value | $ 91,000 | $133,000 | $ 91,000 | $134,000 |
| Establishment of reciprocity | 42,000 | –0– | 43,000 | –0– |
|  | $133,000 | $133,000 | $134,000 | $134,000 |
| Elimination (90% of $140,000) | 126,000 | 126,000 | 126,000 | 126,000 |
| Goodwill* | $ 7,000 | $ 7,000 | $ 8,000 | $ 8,000 |

*The goodwill determined here should be reconciled with the goodwill determined prior to the disposal on page 414.

## SUBSIDIARY STOCK TRANSACTIONS

Preceding sections of this chapter have been concerned with intercompany stock-transaction problems created primarily by parental action. However, some intercompany stock-transaction problems are created primarily by subsidiary action, for instance, through (1) the subsidiary's issuance of additional shares of stock, or (2) its treasury stock transactions. Likewise, a problem may arise from the existence or creation of subsidiary preferred stock. These and similar problems are considered in this section.

### Issuance of Additional Shares of Subsidiary Stock

The issuance of additional shares of stock by a subsidiary may take the form of (1) a sale, or (2) a stock distribution.[1] When additional shares are sold by a subsidiary subsequent to the date of acquisition, the parent's equity in the subsidiary held before the sale may be affected depending upon circumstances. On the other hand, the parent's equity is generally not affected by a subsidiary stock distribution, although the composition of the subsidiary's stockholders' equity is affected.

**Issuance by Sale.** If subsequent to the date of acquisition a subsidiary sells additional stock at *book value*, a change in the percent of ownership by the parent may take place. (No change, however, would take place in the parent company's equity held prior to the sale, and no particular problem arises.) If an additional issue of stock is sold by a subsidiary subsequent to the date of acquisition at a price *other than book value*, however, not only may the percent of ownership change but a dilution or an increase in the parent company's equity held prior to the sale may result. The particular effect will depend upon the circumstances.

The following examples, although not exhaustive, illustrate the effect of an additional issue of a subsidiary stock by sale and the adjustments that may be necessary. Although only three general possibilities exist from the standpoint of the price received (at, above, or below book value), many possibilities exist from the standpoint of who acquires the new issue. For instance, the parent may buy some, none, or all of the stock issued. Since so many possible combinations exist, for illustrative purposes it is assumed that the parent buys either all or none. Assume also that Company A (the parent) acquired 80% of Company B's stock for $110,000 at a time when Company B had capital stock outstanding of $100,000 (par value—$100 per share) and retained earnings of $20,000. At the time of the additional issue of $20,000 par value stock, Company B's retained earnings was $60,000.

**Sale at Book Value.** If Company B issues $20,000 par value stock at book value, it will receive $32,000 [($160,000 ÷ 100,000) × 20,000].

---

[1] Both stock dividends and stock split-ups are included in the term "stock distribution" as used in this section.

418 EXPANSION OF THE BUSINESS ORGANIZATION

|  | New Issue Acquired by |  |  |  |
|---|---|---|---|---|
|  | Company A |  | Outsiders |  |
|  | Prior to Issuance | After Issuance | Prior to Issuance | After Issuance |
| Company B's stockholders' equity: |  |  |  |  |
| Capital stock | $100,000 | $120,000 | $100,000 | $120,000 |
| Retained earnings | 60,000 | 60,000 | 60,000 | 60,000 |
| Capital in excess of par |  | 12,000 |  | 12,000 |
| Total stockholders' equity | $160,000 | $192,000 | $160,000 | $192,000 |
| Company A's interest | 80% | 83⅓% | 80% | 66⅔% |
| Minority interest | 20% | 16⅔% | 20% | 33⅓% |
| Company A's equity | $128,000 | $160,000 | $128,000 | $128,000 |
| Pertaining to new issue |  | 32,000* |  |  |
| Pertaining to old issue | 128,000 | 128,000 | 128,000 | 128,000 |
| Increase (decrease) |  | –0– |  | –0– |

*16⅔% of $192,000.   83⅓ = (800 + 200) / (1000 + 250)

Although Company A's percent of ownership will change unless it acquires a proportionate amount of the new issue, the equity of the stock held prior to the new issue will not be affected. This is true whether Company A or outsiders acquire the new issue.

**Sale Above Book Value.** If Company B issues $20,000 par value stock at $175 per share, it will receive $35,000. In this instance Company A's percent of ownership will change unless it acquires a proportionate amount of the new issue. In addition, the equity of the shares held prior to the new issue will also change. As a consequence, the basic procedure involved when establishing reciprocity will include an adjustment for this change.

|  | New Issue Acquired by |  |  |  |
|---|---|---|---|---|
|  | Company A |  | Outsiders |  |
|  | Before Issuance | After Issuance | Before Issuance | After Issuance |
| Company B's stockholders' equity: |  |  |  |  |
| Capital stock | $100,000 | $120,000 | $100,000 | $120,000 |
| Retained earnings | 60,000 | 60,000 | 60,000 | 60,000 |
| Capital in excess of par |  | 15,000 |  | 15,000 |
| Total stockholders' equity | $160,000 | $195,000 | $160,000 | $195,000 |
| Company A's interest | 80% | 83⅓% | 80% | 66⅔% |
| Minority interest | 20% | 16⅔% | 20% | 33⅓% |
| Company A's equity | $128,000 | $162,500 | $128,000 | $130,000 |
| Pertaining to new issue |  | 32,500* |  |  |
| Pertaining to old issue | 128,000 | 130,000 | 128,000 | 130,000 |
| Increase or (decrease) |  | $2,000 |  | $2,000 |

*16⅔% of $195,000

83⅓% × 195,000
162,500 – 32,500

## 14 / Consolidated Statements—Intercompany Stock Transactions

**Basic Procedure.** Since Company A's equity in Company B as represented by the interest held prior to the additional issue has increased, the following entry (a work sheet entry if the investment is carried at cost, and a book entry if the equity method is used) is necessary when establishing reciprocity:

| | | |
|---|---|---|
| Investment in Company B | $2,000 | |
|     Capital in excess of par | | $2,000 |

The entry above recognizes the increase in the parent's equity in the subsidiary arising from the subsidiary's issuance of additional stock at more than book value. While it may be contended that the credit above should be to retained earnings, the credit to capital in excess of par appears to be more appropriate because the amount involved arose from a capital stock transaction. The need for the adjustment is clearly evident when the goodwill elements in existence before and after the additional issue are reconciled. (For illustrative purposes, it is assumed that goodwill on the original issue is not being amortized at this time.)

GOODWILL RECONCILIATION

| | | New Issue Acquired by | |
|---|---|---|---|
| | | Company A | Outsiders |
| *Goodwill determined at date of purchase:* | | | |
|   Original issue: | | | |
|     Paid | $110,000 | | |
|     Book value acquired | 96,000 | | |
|     Goodwill involved | $ 14,000 | $ 14,000 | $ 14,000 |
|   Additional issue: | | | |
|     Paid | $ 35,000 | | |
|     Book value acquired | 32,500 | | |
|     Goodwill involved | $ 2,500 | 2,500 | –0– |
|   Total goodwill | | $ 16,500 | $ 14,000 |
| *Goodwill determined by work sheet elimination:*\* | | | |
|   Carrying value: | | | |
|     Cost | | $145,000 | $110,000 |
|     (80% × $40,000 increase in B's retained earnings since acquisition—needed to establish reciprocity) | | 32,000 | 32,000 |
| | | $177,000 | $142,000 |
|   Elimination | | 162,500[1] | 130,000[2] |
|   Goodwill | | $ 14,500 | $ 12,000 |

\*Assuming no adjustment for the increase in equity.
[1] 83⅓% of $195,000.
[2] 66⅔% of $195,000.

Since the amount of goodwill determined by comparing cost with book value acquired on the purchase date, as compared with the amount determined by elimination after the additional stock issue, differs by $2,000 ($16,500 as compared with $14,500, and $14,000 as compared with $12,000), an adjustment is necessary.

To illustrate the overall effect on consolidated statements of a sale of subsidiary stock to *outsiders,* two work sheets in abbreviated form are presented below.

CONSOLIDATED WORKING PAPERS

BEFORE SALE OF NEW STOCK

|  | Company A | Company B | Adjustments & Eliminations Debit | Adjustments & Eliminations Credit | Consolidated Financial Position |
|---|---|---|---|---|---|
| Investment in B, at cost (80%) | $110,000 |  | $32,000(1) | $128,000A | $ 14,000G |
| Other assets | 702,000 | $160,000 |  |  | 862,000 |
|  | $812,000 | $160,000 |  |  | $876,000 |
| Capital stock, A | $800,000 |  |  |  | $800,000 |
| Retained earnings, A | 12,000 |  |  | 32,000(1) | 44,000RE |
| Capital stock, B |  | $100,000 | 80,000A |  | 20,000MI |
| Retained earnings, B |  | 60,000 | 48,000A |  | 12,000MI |
|  | $812,000 | $160,000 | $160,000 | $160,000 | $876,000 |

CONSOLIDATED WORKING PAPERS

AFTER SALE OF NEW STOCK

|  | Company A | Company B | Adjustments & Eliminations Debit | Adjustments & Eliminations Credit | Consolidated Financial Position |
|---|---|---|---|---|---|
| Investment in B, at cost (66⅔%) | $110,000 |  | $ 34,000(1) | $130,000A | $ 14,000G |
| Other assets | 702,000 | $195,000 |  |  | 897,000 |
|  | $812,000 | $195,000 |  |  | $911,000 |
| Capital stock, A | $800,000 |  |  |  | $800,000 |
| Capital in excess of par |  |  |  | 2,000(1) | 2,000 |
| Retained earnings, A | 12,000 |  |  | 32,000(1) | 44,000RE |
| Capital stock, B |  | $120,000 | 80,000A |  | 40,000MI |

| | | | | | |
|---|---|---|---|---|---|
| Retained earnings, B | | 60,000 | 40,000A | | 20,000MI |
| Capital in excess of par | | 15,000 | 10,000A | | 5,000MI |
| | $812,000 | $195,000 | $164,000 | $164,000 | $911,000 |

**Sale Below Book Value.** If Company B issues $20,000 par value stock at $130 per share, it will receive $26,000. In this instance, as in the preceding one, Company A's percent of ownership will change unless it acquires a proportionate amount of the new issue, and the equity of the shares held prior to the new issue will also change. As a consequence, the basic procedure involved when establishing reciprocity will again include an adjustment for this change. In this case, however, the change is a dilution in equity instead of an increase. (Again it is assumed that goodwill on the original issue is not being amortized at this time.)

| | New Issue Acquired by | | | |
|---|---|---|---|---|
| | Company A | | Outsiders | |
| | Before Issuance | After Issuance | Before Issuance | After Issuance |
| Company B's stockholders' equity: | | | | |
| Capital stock | $100,000 | $120,000 | $100,000 | $120,000 |
| Retained earnings | 60,000 | 60,000 | 60,000 | 60,000 |
| Capital in excess of par | | 6,000 | | 6,000 |
| Total stockholders' equity | $160,000 | $186,000 | $160,000 | $186,000 |
| Company A's interest | 80% | 83⅓% | 80% | 66⅔% |
| Minority interest | 20% | 16⅔% | 20% | 33⅓% |
| Company A's equity | $128,000 | $155,000 | $128,000 | $124,000 |
| Pertaining to new issue | | 31,000* | | |
| Pertaining to old issue | 128,000 | 124,000 | 128,000 | 124,000 |
| Increase or (decrease) | | ($4,000) | | ($4,000) |

*16⅔% of $186,000

**Basic Procedure.** Since Company A's equity, as represented by the interest held prior to the additional issue, has decreased, the following entry (a work sheet entry if the investment is carried at cost and a book entry if the equity method is in use) is necessary when establishing reciprocity.

| | | |
|---|---|---|
| Capital in excess of par | $4,000 | |
|     Investment in Company B | | $4,000 |
| (to recognize dilution in equity resulting from the issuance of additional stock at less than book value) | | |

GOODWILL RECONCILIATION

|  | | New Issue Acquired by | |
|---|---|---|---|
|  | | Company A | Outsiders |
| *Goodwill determined at date of purchase:* | | | |
| Original issue: | | | |
|   Paid | $110,000 | | |
|   Book value acquired | 96,000 | | |
|   Goodwill involved | $ 14,000 | $ 14,000 | $ 14,000 |
| Additional issue: | | | |
|   Paid | $ 26,000 | | |
|   Book value acquired | 31,000 | | |
|   Goodwill involved | (5,000) | $ (5,000) | $ −0− |
| Total Goodwill | | $ 9,000 | $ 14,000 |
| *Goodwill determined by work sheet elimination:* | | | |
| Carrying value: | | | |
|   Cost | | $136,000 | $110,000 |
|   (80% × $40,000 increase in B's retained earnings since acquisition—needed to establish reciprocity) | | 32,000 | 32,000 |
| | | $168,000 | $142,000 |
| Elimination | | 155,000* | 124,000† |
| Goodwill | | $ 13,000 | $ 18,000 |

*83⅓% of $186,000
†66⅔% of $186,000

Since the amount of goodwill determined by comparing purchase price and book value acquired, as contrasted with the amount determined by the elimination process, differs by $4,000 ($9,000 as compared with $13,000, and $14,000 as compared with $18,000), an adjustment is necessary.

## Subsidiary Stock Distributions

If, subsequent to acquisition, a subsidiary capitalizes part or all of its retained earnings accumulated since acquisition by means of a stock distribution or otherwise,[2] a problem arises as to the proper treatment of the amount so capitalized.

---

[2] Capitalization of retained earnings may be effected by a change in par or stated value as well as by a stock dividend or split-up. However, since the basic problem involved is similar in each instance, all possibilities will not be covered.

## 14 / Consolidated Statements—Intercompany Stock Transactions

Some accountants would consider the amount capitalized as part of consolidated paid-in capital, whereas others would treat it as part of consolidated retained earnings. According to one line of reasoning the amount capitalized should be considered as a part of consolidated paid-in capital because the capitalization is a legal fact. Other accountants maintain that, regardless of the form of account in which the subsidiary keeps the amount, it represents earnings to the combined entity and the amount so capitalized is properly included in consolidated retained earnings. Since the consolidating process varies slightly, depending upon the approach used, the basic procedure involved in both instances is illustrated.

In addition to the specific facts given in the illustration, assume that Company A purchased an 80% interest in Company B at a time when Company B's retained earnings were $40,000. In addition, assume that, subsequent to acquisition, Company B issued a 20% stock dividend and made the following entry:

| | | |
|---|---|---|
| Retained earnings | $20,000 | |
| Capital stock | | $20,000 |

### Capitalization Considered as Part of Consolidated Paid-in Capital.

COMPANY A AND SUBSIDIARY COMPANY B

CONSOLIDATED WORKING PAPERS
STATEMENT OF FINANCIAL POSITION
(DATE)

| | Company A | Company B | Adjustments & Eliminations Debit | Adjustments & Eliminations Credit | Consolidated Financial Position |
|---|---|---|---|---|---|
| Current assets | $200,000 | $ 90,000 | | | $290,000 |
| Investment in Co. B | | | | | |
| (carried at cost) | 125,000 | | $24,000(1) | $136,000A | 13,000G* |
| Fixed assets | 500,000 | 100,000 | | | 600,000 |
| | $825,000 | $190,000 | | | $903,000 |
| Current liabilities | $ 65,000 | $ 20,000 | | | $ 85,000 |
| Fixed liabilities | 100,000 | | | | 100,000 |
| Stockholders' equity: | | | | | |
| Company A: | | | | | |
| Capital stock | 500,000 | | | | 500,000 |
| Capital in excess of par | 60,000 | | | 16,000(1) | 76,000 |

16000 = .80 (20,000) Incr in B's cap st
(see above entry)

| | | | | | |
|---|---|---|---|---|---|
| Retained earnings 100,000 | | | | 8,000(1) | 108,000RE |
| Company B: | | | | | |
| Capital stock | 120,000 | 96,000A | | | 24,000MI |
| Retained earnings | 50,000 | 40,000A | | | 10,000MI |
| | $825,000 | $190,000 | $160,000 | $160,000 | $903,000 |

(1): To establish reciprocity by recognizing Company A's share of Company B's increase in stockholders' equity since acquisition.

A: To eliminate 80% of Company B's stockholders' equity against the investment account.

*Goodwill proof:

| | |
|---|---|
| Paid | $125,000 |
| Book value acquired | 112,000 [80% × ($100,000 + $40,000)] |
| Goodwill | $ 13,000 |

## Capitalization Considered as Part of Consolidated Retained Earnings.

COMPANY A AND SUBSIDIARY COMPANY B
CONSOLIDATED WORKING PAPERS
STATEMENT OF FINANCIAL POSITION
(DATE)

| | Company A | Company B | Adjustments & Eliminations Debit | Credit | Consolidated Financial Position |
|---|---|---|---|---|---|
| Current assets | $200,000 | $ 90,000 | | | $290,000 |
| Investment in Co. B (carried at cost) | 125,000 | | $ 24,000(1) | $136,000A | 13,000G* |
| Fixed assets (net) | 500,000 | 100,000 | | | 600,000 |
| | $825,000 | $190,000 | | | $903,000 |
| Current liabilities | $ 65,000 | $ 20,000 | | | $ 85,000 |
| Fixed liabilities | 100,000 | | | | 100,000 |
| Stockholders' equity: | | | | | |
| Company A: | | | | | |
| Capital stock | 500,000 | | | | 500,000 |
| Capital in excess of par | 60,000 | | | | 60,000 |
| Retained earnings | 100,000 | | | 24,000(1) | 124,000RE |
| Company B: | | | | | |
| Capital stock | | 120,000 | 96,000A | | 24,000MI |
| Retained earnings | | 50,000 | 40,000A | | 10,000MI |
| | $825,000 | $190,000 | $160,000 | $160,000 | $903,000 |

Although there is not complete unanimity among accountants as to whether or not the capitalization of retained earnings accumulated by a subsidiary after acquisition requires a transfer to capital in excess of par on consolidation, *Bulletin No. 51* indicates that such a transfer is not required.

## Treasury Stock Transactions

When a subsidiary acquires some of its own stock or sells some stock previously acquired, the parent company's percent of ownership will increase or decrease, depending upon whether the transaction is a sale or purchase. Likewise, as in the case of the issuance of additional stock, the parent company's equity in the subsidiary will change unless the treasury stock is purchased or sold at book value. If a change in the parent's equity results from a treasury stock transaction, an adjustment of the investment account is necessary in order to establish reciprocity. The following examples illustrate the effect of (1) a purchase of treasury stock by a subsidiary, and (2) a sale of treasury stock by a subsidiary. Although the adjusting entries, as such, and the proof of goodwill are not included, the procedure illustrated in the preceding examples of additional stock issues would apply.

In addition to the specific facts given in the illustrations, assume that 100 shares of treasury stock were *acquired* at:

1. $120 per share, or book value. (Illustration is on page 426.)
2. $210 per share, or above book value. (Illustration is on page 426.)
3. $75 per share, or below book value. (Illustration is on page 426.)

and 100 shares of treasury stock were *sold* at:

1. $120 per share, or book value. (Illustration is on page 427.)
2. $160 per share, or above book value. (Illustration is on page 427.)
3. $80 per share, or below book value. (Illustration is on page 427.)

## Preferred Stock

When a subsidiary having both common and preferred shares outstanding is consolidated, an additional problem arises. Since both the common and preferred interests have a claim against the stockholders' equity of the subsidiary, their respective claims must be recognized in order to prepare consolidated statements.

The four cases on pp. 428–429, although not exhaustive (especially since there are so many different types of preferred claims), illustrate the problem involved when allocating the stockholders' equity of a subsidiary between its common and preferred interests. Although the procedure is essentially the same whether consolidating at the date of acquisition or subsequent to that date, for comparative purposes both are illustrated. (Again it is assumed that goodwill is not being amortized at this time.)

## PURCHASE OF TREASURY STOCK

|  | At Book Value | | Above Book Value | | Below Book Value | |
|---|---|---|---|---|---|---|
|  | Before Purchase | After Purchase | Before Purchase | After Purchase | Before Purchase | After Purchase |
| Company B's stockholders' equity: | | | | | | |
| Capital stock | $100,000 | $100,000 | $100,000 | $100,000 | $100,000 | $100,000 |
| Retained earnings | 20,000 | 20,000 | 20,000 | 20,000 | 20,000 | 20,000 |
| Treasury stock |  | (12,000) |  | (21,000) |  | (7,500) |
| Total stockholders' equity | $120,000 | $108,000 | $120,000 | $ 99,000 | $120,000 | $112,500 |
| Company A's interest | 80% | 8/9 | 80% | 8/9 | 80% | 8/9 |
| Minority interest | 20% | 1/9 | 20% | 1/9 | 20% | 1/9 |
| Company A's equity | $ 96,000 | $ 96,000 | $ 96,000 | $ 88,000 | $ 96,000 | $100,000 |
| Increase or (decrease) | | –0– | | ($8,000) | | $4,000 |

## SALE OF TREASURY STOCK

| | At Book Value | | Above Book Value | | Below Book Value | |
|---|---|---|---|---|---|---|
| | Before Sale | After Sale | Before Sale | After Sale | Before Sale | After Sale |
| Company B's stockholders' equity: | | | | | | |
| Capital stock | $100,000 | $100,000 | $100,000 | $100,000 | $100,000 | $100,000 |
| Retained earnings | 20,000 | 20,000 | 20,000 | 20,000 | 20,000 | 20,000 |
| Premium (discount) on treasury stock | | | | 4,000 | | (4,000) |
| Treasury stock | (12,000) | | (12,000) | | (12,000) | |
| Total stockholders' equity | $108,000 | $120,000 | $108,000 | $124,000 | $108,000 | $116,000 |
| Company A's interest | 8/9 | 80% | 8/9 | 80% | 8/9 | 80% |
| Minority interest | 1/9 | 20% | 1/9 | 20% | 1/9 | 20% |
| Company A's equity | $ 96,000 | $ 96,000 | $ 96,000 | $ 99,200 | $ 96,000 | $ 92,800 |
| Increase or (decrease) | | –0– | | $3,200 | | ($3,200) |

## At Date of Acquisition.

*(handwritten: non-cum + non-particip)*

|  | Company B's Stockholders' Equity | Case 1 Common | Case 1 Preferred |
|---|---|---|---|
| Company B's stockholders' equity: |  |  |  |
| Common stock | $200,000 | $200,000 |  |
| Preferred stock, 6% | 100,000 |  | $100,000 |
| Retained earnings | 60,000 | 60,000 | –0– |
| Total equities | $360,000 | $260,000 | $100,000 |
| Company A's interest |  | 90% | 70% |
| Minority interest |  | 10% | 30% |
| Company A's equity |  | $234,000 | $ 70,000 |
| Computation of goodwill: |  |  |  |
| Paid |  | $240,000 | $ 80,000 |
| Book value acquired |  | 234,000 | 70,000 |
| Goodwill (Negative goodwill) |  | $ 6,000 | $ 10,000 |

*(handwritten notes:)*
Case 2: leftover 42000 = 60,000 – (6000 + 12000)
Pfd 6% × 100 × 1000 sh = 6000    Com: 6% × 100 × 2000 sh = 12000
42000 (1000/3000) = 14000    42,000 (2000/3000) = 28000
20,000    40000

## Subsequent to Date of Acquisition.*

|  | Company B's Stockholders' Equity | Case 1 Common | Case 1 Preferred |
|---|---|---|---|
| Company B's stockholders' equity: |  |  |  |
| Common stock | $200,000 | $200,000 |  |
| Preferred stock, 6% | 100,000 |  | $100,000 |
| Retained earnings | 90,000 | 90,000 | –0– |
| Total equities | $390,000 | $290,000 | $100,000 |
| Company A's interest |  | 90% | 70% |
| Minority interest |  | 10% | 30% |
| Company A's equity |  | $261,000 | $ 70,000 |
| Computation of goodwill: |  |  |  |
| Investment in Co. B (cost) |  | $240,000 | $ 80,000 |
| Establishment of reciprocity |  | 27,000 | –0– |
| Investment account as adjusted |  | $267,000 | $ 80,000 |
| Eliminate Co. A's equity |  | 261,000 | 70,000 |
| Goodwill (Negative goodwill) |  | $ 6,000 | $ 10,000 |

*One year later.

14 / *Consolidated Statements—Intercompany Stock Transactions*    **429**

*non-cum & fully particip*  |  *cum & non-particip*  |  *cum & fully particip*

|  | Case 2 |  | Case 3 |  | Case 4 |
|---|---|---|---|---|---|
| Common | Preferred | Common | Preferred | Common | Preferred |
| $200,000 |  | $200,000 |  | $200,000 |  |
|  | $100,000 |  | $100,000 |  | $100,000 |
| 40,000 | 20,000 | 48,000 | 12,000 | 32,000 | 28,000 |
| $240,000 | $120,000 | $248,000 | $112,000 | $232,000 | $128,000 |
| 90% | 70% | 90% | 70% | 90% | 70% |
| 10% | 30% | 10% | 30% | 10% | 30% |
| $216,000 | $ 84,000 | $223,200 | $ 78,400 | $208,800 | $ 89,600 |
| $240,000 | $ 80,000 | $240,000 | $ 80,000 | $240,000 | $ 80,000 |
| 216,000 | 84,000 | 223,200 | 78,400 | 208,800 | 89,600 |
| $ 24,000 | $ (4,000) | $ 16,800 | $ 1,600 | $ 31,200 | $ (9,600) |

Case 3:
2 yrs in arrears
6000 × 2

Case 4: Pfd In Arrears Current Part

Leftover = 30,000
12000
6000
10,000
28,000

Comm Current Part
12000
20,000
32,000

|  | Case 2 |  | Case 3 |  | Case 4 |
|---|---|---|---|---|---|
| Common | Preferred | Common | Preferred | Common | Preferred |
| $200,000 |  | $200,000 |  | $200,000 |  |
|  | $100,000 |  | $100,000 |  | $100,000 |
| 60,000 | 30,000 | 72,000 | 18,000 | 48,000 | 42,000 |
| $260,000 | $130,000 | $272,000 | $118,000 | $248,000 | $142,000 |
| 90% | 70% | 90% | 70% | 90% | 70% |
| 10% | 30% | 10% | 30% | 10% | 30% |
| $234,000 | $ 91,000 | $244,800 | $ 82,600 | $223,200 | $ 99,400 |
| $240,000 | $ 80,000 | $240,000 | $ 80,000 | $240,000 | $ 80,000 |
| 18,000 | 7,000 | 21,600 | 4,200 | 14,400 | 9,800 |
| $258,000 | $ 87,000 | $261,600 | $ 84,200 | $254,400 | $ 89,800 |
| 234,000 | 91,000 | 244,800 | 82,600 | 223,200 | 99,400 |
| $ 24,000 | $ (4,000) | $ 16,800 | $ 1,600 | $ 31,200 | $ (9,600) |

# EXPANSION OF THE BUSINESS ORGANIZATION

In addition to the specific facts given in the illustrations, also assume that in:

*Case 1,* the preferred shares are noncumulative and nonparticipating.
*Case 2,* the preferred shares are noncumulative but fully participating.
*Case 3,* the preferred shares are cumulative but nonparticipating.*
*Case 4,* the preferred shares are cumulative and fully participating.*

*Preferred dividends two years in arrears at date of acquisition.

The consolidating procedure at **date of acquisition** is illustrated in the following work sheet. Although the approach is the same in all cases, **Case 4**, in which the preferred stock is cumulative and fully participating, is selected for illustrative purposes.

COMPANY A AND SUBSIDIARY COMPANY B
CONSOLIDATED WORKING PAPERS
STATEMENT OF FINANCIAL POSITION
(DATE)

|  | Company A | Company B | Adjustments & Eliminations Debit | Adjustments & Eliminations Credit | Consolidated Financial Position |
|---|---|---|---|---|---|
| Current assets | $ 400,000 | $150,000 |  |  | $ 550,000 |
| Investment in Co. B common (cost) | 240,000 |  |  | $208,800A | 31,200G |
| Investment in Co. B preferred (cost) | 80,000 |  |  | 89,600B | (9,600)G |
| Fixed assets (net) | 1,580,000 | 240,000 |  |  | 1,820,000 |
|  | $2,300,000 | $390,000 |  |  | $2,391,600 |
| Current liabilities | $ 100,000 | $ 30,000 |  |  | $ 130,000 |
| Stockholders' equity: |  |  |  |  |  |
| Company A: |  |  |  |  |  |
| Capital stock | 2,000,000 |  |  |  | 2,000,000 |
| Retained earnings | 200,000 |  |  |  | 200,000RE |
| Company B: |  |  |  |  |  |
| Common stock |  | 200,000 | $180,000A |  | 20,000MI |
| Preferred stock |  | 100,000 | 70,000B |  | 30,000MI |
| Retained earnings |  | 60,000 | 19,600B |  |  |
|  |  |  | 28,800A |  | 11,600MI |
|  | $2,300,000 | $390,000 | $298,400 | $298,400 | $2,391,600 |

*A:* To eliminate 90% of common stock equity against the investment account.
*B:* To eliminate 70% of preferred stock equity against the investment account.

14 / *Consolidated Statements—Intercompany Stock Transactions*      **431**

**Subsequent to Date of Acquisition.** Assuming that during the next year Company B earns $30,000 and distributes no dividends, the same four cases are analyzed on pages 428–429 and, as above, Case 4 is used for the statement of financial position illustration.

COMPANY A AND SUBSIDIARY COMPANY B
CONSOLIDATED WORKING PAPERS
STATEMENT OF FINANCIAL POSITION
(DATE)

|  | Company A | Company B | Adjustments & Eliminations Debit | Adjustments & Eliminations Credit | Consolidated Financial Position |
|---|---|---|---|---|---|
| Current assets | $ 660,000 | $230,000 |  |  | $ 890,000 |
| Investment in Co. B common (cost) | 240,000 |  | $14,400(1) | $223,200A | 31,200G |
| Investment in Co. B preferred (cost) | 80,000 |  | 9,800(2) | 99,400B | (9,600)G |
| Fixed assets (net) | 1,400,000 | 210,000 |  |  | 1,610,000 |
|  | $2,380,000 | $440,000 |  |  | $2,521,600 |
| Current liabilities | $ 80,000 | $ 50,000 |  |  | $ 130,000 |
| Stockholders' equity: |  |  |  |  |  |
| Company A: |  |  |  |  |  |
| Capital stock | 2,000,000 |  |  |  | 2,000,000 |
| Retained earnings | 300,000 |  |  | 14,400(1) |  |
| Company B: |  |  |  | 9,800(2) | 324,200RE |
| Common stock |  | 200,000 | 180,000A |  | 20,000MI |
| Preferred stock |  | 100,000 | 70,000B |  | 30,000MI |
| Retained earnings |  | 90,000 | 43,200A |  |  |
|  |  |  | 29,400B |  | 17,400MI |
|  | $2,380,000 | $440,000 | $346,800 | $346,800 | $2,521,600 |

(1): To establish reciprocity by recognizing Company A's share in the increase in Company B's stockholders' equity pertaining to the common stock investment. (48,000 − 32,000).9

(2): To establish reciprocity by recognizing Company A's share in the increase in Company B's stockholders' equity pertaining to the preferred stock investment.

A: To eliminate 90% of Company B's common stock equity against the investment account.

B: To eliminate 70% of Company B's preferred stock equity against the investment account.

43,200 = .9 (480,000)
180,000 = .9 (200,000)

## PROBLEMS

### Problem 14-1

Company S had capital stock issued and outstanding of $50,000 and retained earnings of $30,000. Additional stock of a par value of $150,000 was issued to Company H, which had previously owned none of the Company S stock. Company H paid $250,000 for the stock.

Determine the amount of (1) goodwill (positive or negative), and (2) minority interest that would appear in a consolidated statement of financial position prepared as of the date of acquisition.

### Problem 14-2

From the following data, assuming that goodwill is not being amortized at this time, that each company has $100,000 capital stock of $100 par, and that profits are earned uniformly throughout the year, determine:

1. The amount that should be credited to the investment account for the May 1, 1980, sale if the investment is carried by:
    a. The cost method, and
    b. The equity method.
2. The amount of goodwill (positive or negative) that should be shown in the consolidated statement of financial position as of:
    a. December 31, 1979, and
    b. December 31, 1980.

INVESTMENT IN COMPANY S

| | | | |
|---|---|---|---|
| Jan. 1, 1979 (800 shares) | $116,000 | May 1, 1980 (175 shares) | ??? |
| Sept. 1, 1979 (100 shares) | 18,000 | | |

RETAINED EARNINGS (COMPANY S)

| | | | |
|---|---|---|---|
| Dec. 31, 1979 (dividends) | $12,000 | Jan. 1, 1979 balance | $60,000 |
| Dec. 31, 1980 (dividends) | 12,000 | Profits, 1979 | 15,000 |
| | | Profits, 1980 | 15,000 |

### Problem 14-3

The following facts were taken from the records of a parent company and its subsidiary on the dates indicated:

|  | Jan. 1 1979 | Dec. 31 1979 | Dec. 31 1980 | Dec. 31 1981 |
|---|---|---|---|---|

14 / Consolidated Statements – Intercompany Stock Transactions    433

|  | 1/1/79 | 12/31/79 | 12/31/80 | 12/31/81 |
|---|---|---|---|---|
| **Parent Company:** | | | | |
| Investment in subsidiary | $288,000 | $315,000 | $308,000 | $347,500 |
| Retained earnings | 240,000 | 290,000 | 276,000 | 280,000 |
| **Subsidiary Company:** | | | | |
| Capital stock ($100 par) | $200,000 | $200,000 | $200,000 | $200,000 |
| Retained earnings | 100,000 | 130,000 | 170,000 | 190,000 |

The parent company purchased 1,800 shares of subsidiary stock on January 1, 1979, sold 200 shares on January 1, 1980, and purchased 100 shares on January 1, 1981. Assuming that the investment account is carried on the *equity* basis and that it was *credited* for the *proceeds* of the stock sold, prepare statements showing the amounts of (1) goodwill, (2) retained earnings, and (3) minority interest that would appear on the consolidated statements of financial position as of January 1, 1979, and December 31, 1979, 1980, and 1981. Assume also that goodwill is not being amortized at this time.

## Problem 14-4

P Corporation acquired control of S Co. on June 30, 1979, by purchase in the market of 2,800 shares of its 4,000 issued shares of $100 par value common stock. At that time S had 500 shares of its own stock held as treasury stock and carried at par.

On January 1, 1981, P acquired 200 additional shares from a minority stockholder. On December 31, 1981, by agreement with the minority stockholders, P acquired the 500 shares held in the treasury of S.

The Investment account of P, carried at cost, shows the following debits:

| | |
|---|---|
| June 30, 1979, 2,800 shares of S | $394,800 |
| January 1, 1981, 200 shares of S purchased from outside interests | 35,000 |
| December 31, 1981, 500 shares of S obtained from S | 90,000 |
| Total | $519,800 |

The accounts of S contained the following items:

| Credits | Capital in excess of par | Retained Earnings |
|---|---|---|
| June 30, 1979 | $ 74,300 | $ 43,745 |
| Earnings 6/30 to 12/31/79 | — | 35,306 |
| Earnings 1980 | — | 65,754 |
| Earnings 1981 | — | 51,025 |
| Premium on sale of treasury stock | 40,000 | — |
| Total | $114,300 | $195,830 |

|  | *Debits* |  |  |
| --- | --- | --- | --- |
| Dividends paid 12/1/79 |  | — | $ 35,000 |
| Dividends paid 12/5/80 |  | — | 35,000 |
| Dividends paid 12/15/81 |  | — | 40,000 |
| Total |  |  | $110,000 |
| Balance 12/31/81 |  | $114,300 | $ 85,830 |

*Required:*
(1) Goodwill from consolidation as of 7/1/79.
(2) Minority interest as of 7/1/79.
(3) Goodwill from consolidation as of 1/2/81.
(4) Minority interest as of 1/2/81.
(5) Goodwill from consolidation as of 1/1/82.
(6) Minority interest as of 1/1/82.

## Problem 14-5

From the following data, prepare a consolidated statement of financial position as of December 31, 1980:

On January 1, 1980, the A Company purchased 90% of the stock of Company B and 80% of the stock of Company C. Wishing to acquire the remaining stock of the more profitable company (Company C), Company A on June 30, 1980, disposed of 200 shares of its holdings in Company B at a price of $160 per share, and on that date acquired an additional 10% of the stock of Company C in consideration of the entire proceeds from the shares of Company B stock disposed of.

The investment accounts on the books of Company A are carried at cost, except the account representing the investment in capital stock of Company B. This account has been credited with the proceeds of the 200 shares sold.

STATEMENTS OF FINANCIAL POSITION

DECEMBER 31, 1980

|  | A | B | C |
| --- | --- | --- | --- |
| *Assets* |  |  |  |
| Current assets | $152,500 | $150,000 | $105,000 |
| Investment in subsidiary companies: |  |  |  |
| Company B: |  |  |  |
| Capital stock | 220,000 |  |  |
| Advances | 25,000 |  |  |
| Company C: |  |  |  |
| Capital stock | 214,000 |  |  |
| Advances | 40,000 |  |  |
| Buildings and equipment (net) |  | 170,000 | 235,000 |
|  | $651,500 | $320,000 | $340,000 |

14 / *Consolidated Statements—Intercompany Stock Transactions*     435

| Equities | A | B | C |
|---|---|---|---|
| Capital stock: | | | |
|   Company A, 3,000 shares | $300,000 | | |
|   Company B, 2,000 shares | | $200,000 | |
|   Company C, 1,000 shares | | | $100,000 |
| Due to parent company | | 25,000 | 40,000 |
| Accounts payable | 235,000 | 40,000 | 25,000 |
| Retained earnings at beginning of year | 166,500 | 60,000 | 145,000 |
| Profit for the year | 20,000* | 15,000 | 40,000 |
| Dividends (paid December 31, 1980) | (70,000) | (20,000) | (10,000) |
| | $651,500 | $320,000 | $340,000 |

*Dividends received from subsidiary companies, less expenses of parent company. It is assumed that the profits of the companies for the year 1980 were earned uniformly throughout the year.

(AICPA adapted)

## Problem 14-6

From the following data, prepare consolidated working papers with separate columns for adjustments and eliminations.

The date on which A acquired capital stock of subsidiary companies was, in each case, the date on which the subsidiary company was organized. All investments are carried at cost.

| | |
|---|---|
| *A Company* | |
|   Investment in B Company: | |
|     Common stock, 800 shares, 80% interest | $ 80,000 |
|     Preferred stock, 400 shares, 40% interest | 40,000 |
|   Investment in C Company: | |
|     Common stock, 600 shares, 60% interest | 60,000 |
|   Investment in D Company: | |
|     Common stock, 1,000 shares, 66⅔% interest | 100,000 |
|     Preferred stock, 800 shares, 80% interest | 80,000 |
|   Investment in E Company: | |
|     Common stock, 1,900 shares, 95% interest | 190,000 |
|     Preferred stock, 400 shares, 80% interest | 40,000 |
|   Accounts receivable, C Company | 300,000 |
|   Other assets | 10,000 |
|   Capital stock | 500,000 |
|   Retained earnings | 400,000 |
| *B Company* | |
|   Assets | $350,000 |
|   Preferred stock, 6% noncumulative | 100,000 |
|   Common stock | 100,000 |
|   Retained earnings | 150,000 |

*C Company*

| | |
|---|---|
| Assets | $420,000 |
| Accounts payable, A Company | 300,000 |
| Common stock | 100,000 |
| Retained earnings | 20,000 |

*D Company*

| | |
|---|---|
| Assets | $244,000 |
| Preferred stock, 6% cumulative | 100,000 |
| Common stock | 150,000 |
| Retained earnings (deficit) | (6,000) |

*E Company*

| | |
|---|---|
| Assets | $285,000 |
| Preferred stock, 6% cumulative | 50,000 |
| Common stock | 200,000 |
| Retained earnings | 35,000 |

Dividends have not been paid on preferred stock outstanding as follows:

| | | |
|---|---|---|
| D | for 3 years | |
| E | for 4 years | (AICPA adapted) |

## Problem 14-7

The following balances appear on the books of a parent company and its subsidiary on the dates stated:

| | Jan. 1, 1979 | Dec. 31, 1979 | Dec. 31, 1980 | Dec. 31, 1981 |
|---|---|---|---|---|
| *Parent Company:* | | | | |
| Investment in subsidiary | $128,000 | $128,000 | $119,000 | $140,000 |
| Retained earnings | 135,000 | 160,000 | 148,000 | 155,000 |
| *Subsidiary:* | | | | |
| Capital stock | 100,000 | 100,000 | 100,000 | 100,000 |
| Retained earnings | 50,000 | 62,000 | 70,000 | 80,000 |

The subsidiary's capital stock consists of 1,000 shares of $100 par each. The parent company purchased 800 shares on January 1, 1979, sold 50 shares on January 1, 1980, and purchased 100 shares on January 1, 1981. Investment account was charged with the cost of stock purchased and credited with the proceeds from the stock sold. The parent company has made no other entries in the investment account and has credited income with all dividends received from the subsidiary.

Prepare statements showing the composition of the amounts of goodwill, retained earnings, and minority interest that would appear on the consolidated statements of financial position at December 31, 1979, 1980, and 1981.

(AICPA adapted)

14 / *Consolidated Statements – Intercompany Stock Transactions* 437

## Problem 14-8

Four years ago, The American Company acquired 50% of the preferred stock of the Banner Corporation for $55,000, and 90% of its common stock for $195,000. At acquisition date the Banner Corporation had retained earnings of $60,000, and dividends on the 5% cumulative preferred stock were not in arrears. The investments were recorded by The American Company at the book value shown by the Banner Corporation at date of acquisition.

Consolidated statements are now being prepared as of December 31, 1980, for The American Company and its subsidiary. The financial position of the individual companies was as follows on that date:

THE AMERICAN COMPANY

| | | | |
|---|---|---|---|
| Miscellaneous assets | $116,000 | Liabilities | $ 50,000 |
| Investments: | | Preferred stock (4%) | 100,000 |
| Banner preferred | 50,000 | Common stock | 100,000 |
| Banner common | 234,000 | Retained earnings | 150,000 |
| | $400,000 | | $400,000 |

BANNER CORPORATION

| | | | |
|---|---|---|---|
| Miscellaneous assets | $400,000 | Liabilities | $ 60,000 |
| | | Preferred stock (5%)* | 100,000 |
| | | Common stock | 200,000 |
| | | Retained earnings | 40,000 |
| | $400,000 | | $400,000 |

*The preferred stock dividends are three years in arrears. No dividends have been paid on common stock since acquisition by The American Company. Profit in 1977 was $8,000, but losses during the past three years have totaled $23,000.

You are to prepare a consolidated statement of financial position of the companies above as of December 31, 1980, in which all significant details given in the information above are fully disclosed. Present in good form schedules showing all computations needed.

Comment on any item which you feel requires explanation.

(AICPA adapted)

## Problem 14-9

On January 1, 1979, A Company purchased 800 shares of the stock of B Company @ 118. On January 1, 1980, A Company purchased an additional 150 shares of B's stock @ 125, and on January 1, 1981, sold 100 shares @ 130.

On December 31, 1981, the following data were obtained from the records of the two companies:

|  | A Company | B Company |
|---|---|---|
| Inventories, 1/1/81 | $ 80,000 | $ 30,000 |
| Investment in B Company | 101,350 | |
| Other assets (net) | 450,000 | 255,000 |
| Purchases | 520,000 | 275,000 |
| Expenses | 133,425 | 65,000 |
| Dividends | 10,000 | 6,000 |
|  | $1,294,775 | $631,000 |
| Sales | $ 754,000 | $375,000 |
| Dividends | 5,100 | |
| Liabilities | 136,000 | 76,000 |
| Capital stock ($100 par) | 200,000 | 100,000 |
| Retained earnings | 199,675 | 80,000 |
|  | $1,294,775 | $631,000 |
| Inventories, 12/31/81 | $ 86,000 | $ 28,000 |

RETAINED EARNINGS

|  | A Company | B Company |
|---|---|---|
| Balances, 1/1/79 | $ 26,675 | $50,000 |
| Profits, 1979 | 107,000 | 17,000 |
| Dividends, 1979 | (10,000) | (6,000) |
| Balances, 12/31/79 | 123,675 | 61,000 |
| Profits, 1980 | 86,000 | 25,000 |
| Dividends, 1980 | (10,000) | (6,000) |
| Balances, 12/31/80 | $199,675 | $80,000 |

During 1981, B Company sold to A Company for $100,000 merchandise that cost $50,000. Fifty percent of the merchandise remains in A's inventory on December 31, 1981.

*Required:*
Consolidated financial statements for the year ended December 31, 1981.

## Problem 14-10

From the following information, prepare a consolidated statement of financial position of H Co. and subsidiaries, A Co. and B Co., as of December 31, 1980.

H Co., an operating company, acquired 90% of the outstanding stock of B Co. on March 31, 1980, for $162,000. Previously, H Co. acquired 30% of the outstanding stock of A Co. on January 1, 1979, for $25,000. On July 1, 1980, H Co. purchased an additional 40% of the outstanding stock of A Co. for $42,000, thereby gaining effective control of A Co. as of that date. In order further to increase its stockholdings in A Co. without impairing working capital, H Co. sold 100 shares

14 / *Consolidated Statements – Intercompany Stock Transactions*

of B Co. stock on October 1, 1980, for $20,500 and immediately used $13,800 of the proceeds to secure an additional 15% of A Co. outstanding stock.

The statements of financial position of the respective companies as of December 31, 1980, are set forth as follows:

|  | H Co. | A Co. | B Co. |
|---|---|---|---|
| *Assets* |  |  |  |
| Cash in banks | $ 86,000 | $ 12,500 | $ 35,000 |
| Notes receivable | 18,000 | 6,000 | 8,000 |
| Accounts receivable (net) | 52,000 | 13,000 | 34,000 |
| Inventories | 89,500 | 16,000 | 51,000 |
| Investment in Company A (at cost) | 80,800 |  |  |
| Investment in Company B (at equity) | 149,320 |  |  |
| Plant and equipment (net) | 225,000 | 56,500 | 101,000 |
|  | $700,620 | $104,000 | $229,000 |
| *Equities* |  |  |  |
| Notes payable | $ 9,000 | $ 8,000 | $ 12,000 |
| Accounts payable | 73,600 | 22,400 | 46,200 |
| Accrued liabilities | 5,320 | 2,600 | 4,800 |
| Capital stock, common, $100 par | 400,000 | 60,000 | 100,000 |
| Retained earnings | 212,700 | 11,000 | 66,000 |
|  | $700,620 | $104,000 | $229,000 |

A summary of retained earnings (deficit) from January 1, 1979, to December 31, 1980, is as follows:

|  | H Co. | A Co. | B Co. |
|---|---|---|---|
| Balance at January 1, 1979 | $150,000 | $(10,000) | $40,000 |
| Net profit (or loss), 1979 |  |  |  |
| 1st quarter | 7,000 | (2,000) | 3,000 |
| 2nd quarter | 9,000 | 1,000 | 4,000 |
| 3rd quarter | 15,000 | 3,000 | 6,000 |
| 4th quarter | 12,000 | 6,000 | 5,000 |
| Total | $193,000 | $ (2,000) | $58,000 |
| Dividends declared and paid on July 1, 1979 | 12,000 |  | 3,000 |
| Balance at January 1, 1980 | $181,000 | $ (2,000) | $55,000 |
| Net profit (or loss), 1980 |  |  |  |
| 1st quarter | 6,000 | 2,500 | 4,500 |
| 2nd quarter | 11,500 | 3,000 | 7,000 |
| 3rd quarter | 13,000 | 3,600 | 6,200 |
| 4th quarter | 16,200 | 5,900 | 5,300 |
| Total | $227,700 | $ 13,000 | $78,000 |
| Dividends declared June 1, 1980 and paid on June 15, 1980 | 15,000 |  | 12,000 |

Dividends declared December 1, 1980 and paid
on December 15, 1980      2,000
Balance, December 31, 1980—
Retained earnings      $212,700      $ 11,000      $66,000

Net profit of H Co. for the fourth quarter of 1980 includes $2,500 representing the gain on the sale of 100 shares of B Co. stock. (Proceeds $20,500, less March 31, 1980, cost, $18,000.)

Inventories at December 31, 1980, include intercompany items as follows:

| Date of Transaction | Company Purchaser | Company Seller | Amount Inventory | Amount Seller's Cost |
|---|---|---|---|---|
| April 5, 1980 | H | A | $ 3,600 | $ 3,000 |
| August 15, 1980 | H | B | 5,000 | 4,500* |
| October 5, 1980 | H | A | 10,000 | 9,000 |
| May 15, 1980 | A | B | 7,000 | 6,200 |
| September 26, 1980 | A | B | 6,000 | 4,800 |
| November 12, 1980 | B | A | 16,000 | 14,000 |

*Acquired on July 20, 1980, by B from A, A's cost then being $4,200.

(AICPA adapted)

## Problem 14-11

Following are the statements of financial position of Company A and its subsidiaries B and C as of December 31, 1980:

|  | Companies A | B | C |
|---|---|---|---|
| **Assets** | | | |
| Investments: | | | |
| Preferred capital stock of Company B, 60% | $ 300,000 | | |
| Common capital stock of Company B, 90% | 800,000 | | |
| Common capital stock of Company C, 90% | 1,300,000 | | |
| Bonds of Company B at cost | 270,000 | | |
| Notes receivable: | | | |
| Company B | 20,000 | | |
| Other assets | 2,000,000 | $2,180,000 | $2,000,000 |
|  | $4,690,000 | $2,180,000 | $2,000,000 |

Equities

|  | | | |
|---|---|---|---|
| Capital stock: | | | |
| Preferred, 6% | $ 500,000 | $ 500,000 | $ 500,000 |
| Common | 1,100,000 | 150,000 | 500,000 |
| | $1,600,000 | $ 650,000 | $1,000,000 |
| Retained earnings: | | | |
| Balance, January 1, 1980 | $1,100,000 | $ 150,000 | $ 300,000 |
| Net profits for the year 1980 | 400,000 | 200,000 | 300,000 |
| Dividends deducted | $ 12,000 | $ 30,000 | $ 30,000 |
| | $1,488,000 | $ 320,000 | $ 570,000 |
| First mtge., 6% bonds outstanding | $1,000,000 | $ 600,000 | |
| Notes receivable discounted, Company B | 10,000 | | |
| Notes payable, Company A | | 20,000 | |
| Other liabilities | 592,000 | 590,000 | 430,000 |
| | $4,690,000 | $2,180,000 | $2,000,000 |

The dividends on the preferred stocks of the respective companies have all been paid through the year 1979.

The bonds of Company B, which mature December 31, 1987, were acquired by Company A on December 31, 1980, at 90.

Company A acquired its holdings of the stock in Companies B and C at the date of their incorporation and has taken up its share of the earnings of these companies.

From the foregoing, prepare a consolidated statement of financial position as of December 31, 1980. (AICPA adapted)

## Problem 14-12

Prepare a consolidated statement of financial position and a consolidated statement of income from the following data:

TRIAL BALANCES, DECEMBER 31, 1980

|  | A Company | B Company |
|---|---|---|
| *Debits* | | |
| Cash | $ 100,000 | $ 25,000 |
| Accounts receivable | 150,000 | 75,000 |
| Plant—cost less depreciation | 350,000 | 200,000 |
| Inventories | | |
| Raw materials | 60,000 | 40,000 |
| Work-in-process | 75,000 | 50,000 |

|  |  |  |
|---|---|---|
| Finished goods | 45,000 | 30,000 |
| Raw materials purchased | 400,000 | 250,000 |
| Manufacturing labor and expenses | 300,000 | 200,000 |
| Operating expenses | 225,000 | 150,000 |
| Dividends paid December 15, 1980 | 90,000 | 20,000 |
| Investment in stock of B Company (cost) | 275,000 |  |
| Totals | $2,070,000 | $1,040,000 |

*Credits*

|  |  |  |
|---|---|---|
| Sales | $1,095,000 | $ 750,000 |
| Dividends received | 18,000 |  |
| Capital stock | 900,000 | 200,000 |
| Retained earnings January 1, 1980 | 57,000 | 90,000 |
| Totals | $2,070,000 | $1,040,000 |

A Company acquired 80% of the stock of B Company on January 1, 1980, for $240,000, and an additional 10% on July 1, 1980, for $35,000.

In solving the problem, assume that profits were earned uniformly throughout the year and that the inventories on December 31, 1980, were as follows:

|  | A Company | B Company |
|---|---|---|
| Raw materials | $50,000 | $35,000 |
| Work-in-process | 65,000 | 25,000 |
| Finished goods | 35,000 | 10,000 |

## Problem 14-13

The following facts were taken from the records of a parent company and its subsidiary on the dates indicated:

|  | Jan. 1 1979 | Dec. 31 1979 | Dec. 31 1980 | Dec. 31 1981 |
|---|---|---|---|---|
| *Parent Company:* |  |  |  |  |
| Investment in subsidiary | $288,000 | $313,200 | $303,600 | $342,900 |
| Retained earnings | 240,000 | 290,000 | 276,000 | 280,000 |
| *Subsidiary Company:* |  |  |  |  |
| Capital stock ($100 par) | $200,000 | $200,000 | $200,000 | $200,000 |
| Retained earnings | 100,000 | 130,000 | 170,000 | 190,000 |

The parent company purchased 1,800 shares of subsidiary stock on January 1, 1979, sold 200 shares on January 1, 1980, and purchased 100 shares on January 1, 1981. Assuming that the investment account is carred on the *equity* basis and that it was *credited* for the *proceeds* of the stock sold, prepare statements showing the amounts of (1) goodwill, (2) retained earnings, and (3) minority interest that would appear on the consolidated statements of financial position as of January 1,

1979, and December 31, 1979, 1980, and 1981. Assume also that goodwill is being amortized on a straight-line basis over 10 years.

## Problem 14-14

The following balances appear on the books of a parent company and its subsidiary on the dates stated:

|  | Jan. 1, 1979 | Dec. 31, 1979 | Dec. 31, 1980 | Dec. 31, 1981 |
|---|---|---|---|---|
| *Parent Company:* |  |  |  |  |
| Investment in subsidiary | $128,000 | $127,200 | $119,000 | $140,000 |
| Retained earnings | 135,000 | 160,000 | 148,000 | 155,000 |
| *Subsidiary:* |  |  |  |  |
| Capital stock | 100,000 | 100,000 | 100,000 | 100,000 |
| Retained earnings | 50,000 | 62,000 | 70,000 | 80,000 |

The subsidiary's capital stock consists of 1,000 shares of $100 par each. The parent company purchased 800 shares on January 1, 1979, sold 50 shares on January 1, 1980, and purchased 100 shares on January 1, 1981. Investment account was charged with the cost of stock purchased and credited with the proceeds from the stock sold. The parent company has made no other entries in the investment account except for the amortization of goodwill on a straight-line basis over 10 years.

Prepare statements showing the composition of the amounts of goodwill, retained earnings, and minority interest that would appear on the consolidated statements of financial position at December 31, 1979, 1980, and 1981.

(AICPA adapted)

## Problem 14-15

Sterling, Inc., a domestic corporation having a fiscal year ending June 30, has purchased common stock in several other domestic corporations. As of June 30, 1980, the balance in Sterling's Investments accounts was $870,600, the total cost of stock purchased less the cost of stock sold. Sterling wishes to restate the Investments account to reflect the provisions of *APB Opinion No. 18,* "The Equity Method of Accounting for Investments in Common Stock."

Data concerning the investments follow:

|  |  | Turner, Inc. | Grotex, Inc. | Scott, Inc. |
|---|---|---|---|---|
| Shares of common stock outstanding |  | 3,000 | 32,000 | 100,000 |
| Shares purchased by Sterling | (a) | 300 | 8,000 | 30,000 |
|  | (b) | 810 |  |  |
| Date of purchase | (a) | July 1, 1977 | June 30, 1978 | June 30, 1979 |
|  | (b) | July 1, 1979 |  |  |

|  |  |  | July 1, 1979 | June 30, 1978 | June 30, 1979 |
|---|---|---|---|---|---|
| Cost of shares purchased | (a) | $ 49,400 |  | $ 46,000 | $ 670,000 |
|  | (b) | $ 142,000 |  |  |  |

Balance sheet at date indicated:

| Assets | July 1, 1979 | June 30, 1978 | June 30, 1979 |
|---|---|---|---|
| Current assets | $ 362,000 | $ 39,600 | $ 994,500 |
| Fixed assets, net of depreciation | 1,638,000 | 716,400 | 3,300,000 |
| Patent, net of amortization |  |  | 148,500 |
|  | $2,000,000 | $756,000 | $4,443,000 |

| *Liabilities and Capital* |  |  |  |
|---|---|---|---|
| Liabilities | $1,500,000 | $572,000 | $2,494,500 |
| Common stock | 260,000 | 80,000 | 1,400,000 |
| Retained earnings | 240,000 | 104,000 | 548,500 |
|  | $2,000,000 | $756,000 | $4,443,000 |

| | | | |
|---|---|---|---|
| Changes in common stock since July 1, 1977 | None | None | None |
| Average remaining life of fixed assets at date of balance sheet (above) | 12 years | 9 years | 22 years |
| Analysis of retained earnings: | | | |
| Balance, July 1, 1977 | $234,000 | | |
| Net income, July 1, 1977 to June 30, 1978 | 53,400 | | |
| Dividend paid—April 1, 1978 | (51,000) | | |
| Balance, June 30, 1978 | 236,400 | $104,000 | |
| Net income (loss), July 1, 1978 to June 30, 1979 | 55,600 | (2,000) | |
| Dividend paid—April 1, 1979 | (52,000) | | |
| Balance, June 30, 1979 | 240,000 | 102,000 | $548,500 |
| Net income, July 1, 1979 to June 30, 1980 | 25,000 | 18,000 | 330,000 |
| Dividends paid: | | | |
| December 28, 1979 | | | (150,000) |
| June 1, 1980 | | (5,600) | |
| Balance, June 30, 1980 | $265,000 | $114,400 | $728,500 |

Sterling's first purchase of Turner's stock was made because of the high rate of return expected on the investment. All later purchases of stock have been made to gain substantial influence over the operations of the various companies.

In December 1979, changing market conditions caused Sterling to reevaluate its relation to Grotex. On December 31, 1979, Sterling sold 6,400 shares of Grotex for $54,400.

For Turner and Grotex, the fair values of the net assets did not differ materially from the book values as shown in the balance sheets above. For Scott, fair values exceeded book values only with respect to the patent, which had a fair value of $300,000 and a remaining life of 15 years as of June 30, 1979.

At June 30, 1980, Sterling's inventory included $48,600 of items purchased from Scott during May and June at a 20% markup over Scott's cost.

*Required:*

Prepare a work sheet to restate Sterling's Investments account as of June 30, 1980, and its investment income by year for the three years then ended. Transactions should be listed in chronological order and supporting computations should be in good form. *Ignore income taxes.* Amortization of goodwill, if any, is to be over a 40-year period. Use the following columnar headings for your work sheet.

|  |  | Investments |  |  |  |  |
| --- | --- | --- | --- | --- | --- | --- |
|  |  | Turner | Grotex | Scott |  |  |
| Date | Description | Dr. (Cr.) | Dr. (Cr.) | Dr. (Cr.) |  |  |
|  | Investment Income, Year Ended June 30 |  |  | Other Accounts |  |  |
|  | 1978 | 1979 | 1980 |  | Amount | Name |
|  | Cr. (Dr.) | Cr. (Dr.) | Cr. (Dr.) |  | Dr. (Cr.) |  |

(AICPA adapted)

# 15

# Consolidated Statements — Indirect Ownership and Mutual Stockholdings

Occasionally a parent company may have an interest in a subsidiary(ies) that in turn has an interest in a subsidiary(ies) of its own, or a parent company may have two or more subsidiaries, one or more of which has an interest in one of the other subsidiaries. For example, Company A may own a 90% interest in Company B, which in turn owns an 80% interest in Company C, or Company A may own a 90% interest in Company B and a 70% interest in Company C, with Company B, in turn, owning a 20% interest in Company C. These and similar types of ownership are usually described as indirect ownership. Thus Company A's 72% indirect ownership of Company C in the first instance is a result of A's owning 90% of B, which in turn owns 80% of C. In the second situation, Company A's 88% effective interest in Company C is a result of Company A owning 70% directly and 18% (90% × 20%) indirectly through Company B. In the first situation, Company A is usually referred to as the major parent and Company B the minor parent; whereas in the second situation, Company B is usually referred to as a connecting affiliate.

In addition, the accountant may also occasionally be faced with situations where two or more affiliates in a consolidated group have an interest, represented by stockholdings, in each other. For example, Company A may own a 90% interest in Company B, which in turn owns a 5% interest in Company A. This type of relationship and others similar to it are usually referred to as mutual stockholdings.

Some of the problems involved in consolidating companies where indirect ownership and mutual stockholdings exist are considered in this chapter. Although there is no attempt to discuss all of the possibilities that may arise in the case of indirect ownership or mutual stockholdings, sufficient coverage is given to enable one to acquire an understanding of the particular problems involved. The basic consolidating procedure of (1) establishing reciprocity, (2) eliminating reciprocals, and (3) consolidating nonreciprocals remains the same, although the establishment of reciprocity may become a little more involved. Likewise, the apportionment of net income may become a little more difficult. For these reasons special emphasis is placed on the process of establishing reciprocity and the apportionment of net income in this chapter. The elimination and the consolidation of nonreciprocals, once reciprocity has been established, are somewhat routine and will not be emphasized.

As has been stressed throughout the preceding chapters, the date of acquisition is an important reference point when preparing consolidated statements. Although the date of acquisition assumes no additional significance when consolidating a group of companies in which indirect ownership or mutual stockholdings exist, its determination in a particular situation may require additional analysis. Since the date of acquisition in any given situation refers to the date of acquisition for consolidating purposes, this date may or may not be the one on which a particular subsidiary was acquired by an affiliate. For example, assume that Company A owns a 95% interest in Company B, which in turn owns an 85% interest in Company C. If Company B acquired its interest in Company C on or before the date on which Company A acquired its interest in Company B, the date of acquisition of Company C when consolidating A, B, and C is the date on which Company A acquired its interest in Company B. However, if Company B acquired its interest in Company C subsequent to the date Company A acquired its interest in Company B, the date of acquisition when consolidating C with A and B is the date Company B acquired its interest in Company C. It should be noted that the important date in situations of this nature, from a consolidating standpoint, is the date a particular affiliate enters the consolidated group. In the illustrations presented in this chapter, when the date of acquisition is referred to, it is assumed to be the date of acquisition for consolidating purposes.

## INDIRECT OWNERSHIP

When consolidating a group of companies in which some form of indirect ownership exists, whether it be a major and minor parent situation, a connecting affiliate relationship, or a combination of the two, it is essential that establishment of reciprocity start on the lowest strata or tier of subsidiaries. The establishment of reciprocity should then progress up to the top tier or apex where the major parent is found. It is likewise better to progress up the consolidation ladder rung by rung rather than to by-pass some of the rungs. For example, if Company A owns 90% of Company B and if Company B in turn owns 80% of Company C, the first step should be to establish reciprocity between B and C by recognizing B's 80% interest in C's increase or decrease in stockholders' equity since acquisition. Then reciprocity should be established between A and B by recognizing A's 90% interest in B's increase or decrease in stockholders' equity since acquisition, which would include B's appropriate share of C's increase or decrease.

## Major and Minor Parents

**First Illustration.** Assume that Company A owns a 90% interest in Company B, which, in turn, owns an 80% interest in Company C; that B's stockholders' equity has increased $20,000 (from its own operations) since date of acquisition; that C's stockholders' equity has increased $10,000 since the date of acquisition; and that all investment accounts are on the cost basis. Reciprocity would be established when consolidating by the following work sheet entries:

*First:*

| | | |
|---|---:|---:|
| Investment in Company C | $ 8,000 | |
|     Retained earnings (B's) | | $ 8,000 |
|     (to recognize Company B's 80% interest in the increase in Company C's stockholders' equity) | | |

*Second:*

| | | |
|---|---:|---:|
| Investment in Company B | $25,200 | |
|     Retained earnings (A's) | | $25,200 |
|     [to recognize Company A's 90% interest in the increase in Company B's stockholders' equity — 90% × ($20,000 + $8,000)] | | |

Assuming that in any given period Company A earns $100,000; Company B, $20,000; and Company C, $10,000, from their respective operations, net income would be apportioned as follows:

| | Company A | Company B | Company C | Total |
|---|---:|---:|---:|---:|
| Net income before apportionment | $100,000 | $20,000 | $10,000 | $130,000 |
| Apportionment: | | | | |
|   B's share of C's (80%) | | 8,000 | (8,000) | |
|   A's share of B's (90%) | 25,200 | (25,200) | | |
|   Balances | $125,200 | $ 2,800 | $ 2,000 | $130,000 |
| Consolidated net income | 125,200 | | | $125,200 |
| Minority interest, B | | 2,800 | | 2,800 |
| Minority interest, C | | | 2,000 | 2,000 |
| Total | | | | $130,000 |

**Second Illustration.** Assume that Company A owns a 90% interest in Company B, which, in turn, owns a 90% interest in Company C and a 70% interest in Company D; that from individual operations B's stockholders' equity has increased $30,000, and C's, $20,000, while D's has decreased $10,000 since the re-

## 15 / Consolidated Statements – Indirect Ownership and Mutual Stockholdings

spective dates of acquisition; and that all investment accounts are on the cost basis. Reciprocity would be established by the following work sheet entries:

*First:*

| | | |
|---|---:|---:|
| Retained earnings (B's) | $ 7,000 | |
|     Investment in Company D | | $ 7,000 |
| (to recognize Company B's 70% interest in the decrease in Company D's stockholders' equity) | | |

*Second:*

| | | |
|---|---:|---:|
| Investment in Company C | $18,000 | |
|     Retained earnings (B's) | | $18,000 |
| (to recognize Company B's 90% interest in the increase in Company C's stockholders' equity) | | |

*Third:*

| | | |
|---|---:|---:|
| Investment in Company B | $36,900 | |
|     Retained earnings (A's) | | $36,900 |
| [to recognize Company A's 90% interest in the increase in Company B's stockholders' equity —90% × ($30,000 + $18,000 − $7,000)] | | |

Assuming that in any given period Company A earns $100,000; Company B, $30,000; Company C, $20,000; and that Company D loses $10,000 from their respective operations, net income would be apportioned as follows:

| | Company A | Company B | Company C | Company D | Total |
|---|---:|---:|---:|---:|---:|
| Net income before apportionment | $100,000 | $30,000 | $20,000 | ($10,000) | $140,000 |
| Apportionment: | | | | | |
|   B's share of D's (70%) | | ( 7,000) | | 7,000 | |
|   B's share of C's (90%) | | 18,000 | (18,000) | | |
|   A's share of B's (90%) | 36,900 | ( 36,900) | | | |
| Balances | $136,900 | $ 4,100 | $ 2,000 | ($ 3,000) | $140,000 |
| Consolidated net income | 136,900 | | | | $136,900 |
| Minority interest, B | | 4,100 | | | 4,100 |
| Minority interest, C | | | 2,000 | | 2,000 |
| Minority interest, D | | | | (3,000) | (3,000) |
| Total | | | | | $140,000 |

Diagrams are frequently useful in following through various consolidated relationships and should be used whenever helpful. For instance, with arrows indicating the direction from which ownership flows, the aforementioned situations might be diagramed as follows:

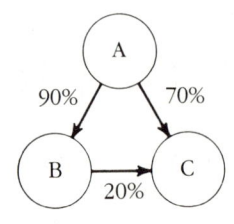

## Connecting Affiliates

**First Illustration.** Assume that Company A owns a 90% interest in Company B and a 70% interest in Company C, while Company B owns 20% of C; and B's stockholders' equity has increased $20,000 from its own operations since acquisition and that C's stockholders' equity has increased $10,000 since acquisition; that all investment accounts are on the cost basis; and that Company A and Company B acquired their interests in Company C at the same time. Reciprocity would be established by the following work sheet entries:

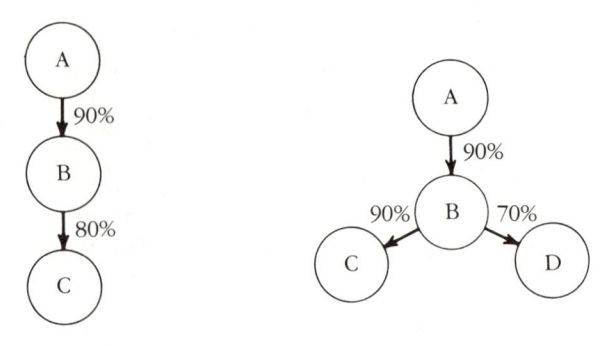

*First:*

| | | |
|---|---:|---:|
| Investment in Company C (A's) | $ 7,000 | |
| Investment in Company C (B's) | 2,000 | |
|    Retained earnings (A's) | | $ 7,000 |
|    Retained earnings (B's) | | 2,000 |
| (to recognize Company A's 70% and Company B's 20% interest in the increase in Company C's stockholders' equity) | | |

*Second:*

| | | |
|---|---:|---:|
| Investment in Company B | $19,800 | |
|    Retained earnings (A's) | | $19,800 |
| [to recognize Company A's 90% interest in increase in Company B's stockholders' equity — 90% × ($20,000 + $2,000)] | | |

## 15 / Consolidated Statements—Indirect Ownership and Mutual Stockholdings

Assuming that in any given period Company A earns $100,000; Company B, $20,000; and Company C, $10,000, from their separate operations, net income would be apportioned as follows:

|  | Company A | Company B | Company C | Total |
|---|---|---|---|---|
| Net income before apportionment | $100,000 | $20,000 | $10,000 | $130,000 |
| Apportionment: | | | | |
|   A's share of C's (70%) | 7,000 | | (7,000) | |
|   B's share of C's (20%) | | 2,000 | (2,000) | |
|   A's share of B's (90%) | 19,800 | (19,800) | | |
| Balances | $126,800 | $ 2,200 | $ 1,000 | $130,000 |
| Consolidated net income | 126,800 | | | $126,800 |
| Minority interest, B | | 2,200 | | 2,200 |
| Minority interest, C | | | 1,000 | 1,000 |
| Total | | | | $130,000 |

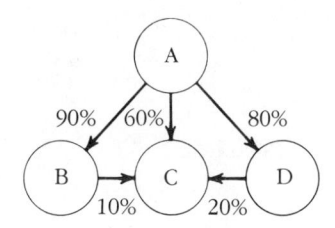

Connecting Affiliates

**Second Illustration.** Assume that Company A owns a 90% interest in Company B, a 60% interest in Company C, and an 80% interest in Company D; that Company B owns a 10% interest in Company C; that Company D owns a 20% interest in Company C; and that Company B's stockholders' equity has increased $30,000, C's, $20,000, and D's, $10,000, since acquisition from their own operations. Reciprocity would be established by the following work sheet entries:

*First:*

| | | |
|---|---|---|
| Investment in Company C (A's) | $12,000 | |
| Investment in Company C (D's) | 4,000 | |
| Investment in Company C (B's) | 2,000 | |
|   Retained earnings (A's) | | $12,000 |
|   Retained earnings (D's) | | 4,000 |
|   Retained earnings (B's) | | 2,000 |
| (to recognize Company A's 60%, D's 20%, and B's 10% interest in the increase in Company C's stockholders' equity) | | |

*Second:*

| | | |
|---|---|---|
| Investment in Company D | $11,200 | |
|     Retained earnings (A's) | | $11,200 |

[to recognize Company A's 80% interest in the increase in Company D's stockholders' equity—80% × ($10,000 + $4,000)]

*Third:*

| | | |
|---|---|---|
| Investment in Company B | $28,800 | |
|     Retained earnings (A's) | | $28,800 |

[to recognize Company A's 90% interest in the increase in Company B's stockholders' equity—90% × ($30,000 + $2,000)]

Assuming that in any given year (period) Company A earns $100,000; B, $30,000; C, $20,000; and D, $10,000, from their separate operations, net income would be apportioned as follows:

| | Company A | Company B | Company C | Company D | Total |
|---|---|---|---|---|---|
| Net income before apportionment | $100,000 | $30,000 | $20,000 | $10,000 | $160,000 |
| Apportionment: | | | | | |
| A's share of C's (60%) | 12,000 | | (12,000) | | |
| D's share of C's (20%) | | | (4,000) | 4,000 | |
| B's share of C's (10%) | | 2,000 | (2,000) | | |
| A's share of D's (80%) | 11,200 | | | (11,200) | |
| A's share of B's (90%) | 28,800 | (28,800) | | | |
| Balances | $152,000 | $ 3,200 | $ 2,000 | $ 2,800 | $160,000 |
| Consolidated net income | 152,000 | | | | $152,000 |
| Minority interest, B | | 3,200 | | | 3,200 |
| Minority interest, C | | | 2,000 | | 2,000 |
| Minority interest, D | | | | 2,800 | 2,800 |
| Total | | | | | $160,000 |

## Combination of Major and Minor Parents and a Connecting Affiliate

Assume that Company A owns a 90% interest in Company B and an 80% interest in Company C; that Company B, in turn, owns an 80% interest in Company D; that Company C owns a 70% interest in Company E; that Company D owns a 20% interest in Company E; that Company B's stockholders' equity has increased $20,000, C's, $30,000, D's, $20,000, and E's, $10,000 from their own operations since their respective acquisitions; that all investments are on the cost basis; and that Company C and Company D acquired their interests in Company E on the same date. Reciprocity would be established by the following work sheet entries:

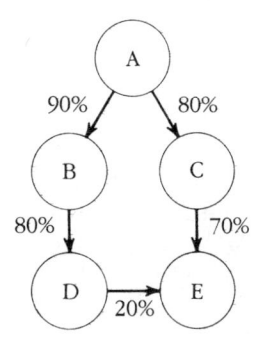

Combination of Major and Minor Parents and a Connecting Affiliate

*First:*

| | | |
|---|---|---|
| Investment in Company E (D's) | $ 2,000 | |
| Investment in Company E (C's) | 7,000 | |
|     Retained earnings (D's) | | $ 2,000 |
|     Retained earnings (C's) | | 7,000 |

(to recognize Company D's 20% and Company C's 70% interest in the increase in Company E's stockholders' equity)

*Second:*

| | | |
|---|---|---|
| Investment in Company D | $17,600 | |
|     Retained earnings (B's) | | $17,600 |

[to recognize Company B's 80% interest in the increase in Company D's stockholders' equity—80% × ($20,000 + $2,000)]

*Third:*

| | | |
|---|---|---|
| Investment in Company B | $33,840 | |
| Investment in Company C | 29,600 | |
|     Retained earnings (A's) | | $63,440 |

[to recognize Company A's 90% interest—90% × ($20,000 + $17,600)—in Company B's and 80% interest—80% × ($30,000 + $7,000)—in Company C's increases in stockholders' equities]

Assuming that in any given period Company A earns $100,000; B, $40,000; C, $30,000; D, $20,000; and E, $15,000, from their respective operations, net income would be apportioned as follows:

|  | Company A | Company B | Company C | Company D | Company E | Total |
|---|---|---|---|---|---|---|
| Net income before apportionment | $100,000 | $40,000 | $30,000 | $20,000 | $15,000 | $205,000 |
| Apportionment: | | | | | | |
| C's share of E's (70%) | | | 10,500 | | (10,500) | |
| D's share of E's (20%) | | | | 3,000 | (3,000) | |
| B's share of D's (80%) | | 18,400 | | (18,400) | | |
| A's share of B's (90%) | 52,560 | (52,560) | | | | |
| A's share of C's (80%) | 32,400 | | (32,400) | | | |
| Balances | $184,960 | $ 5,840 | $ 8,100 | $ 4,600 | $ 1,500 | $205,000 |
| Consolidated net income | 184,960 | | | | | $184,960 |
| Minority interest, B | | 5,840 | | | | 5,840 |
| Minority interest, C | | | 8,100 | | | 8,100 |
| Minority interest, D | | | | 4,600 | | 4,600 |
| Minority interest, E | | | | | 1,500 | 1,500 |
| Total | | | | | | $205,000 |

## MUTUAL STOCKHOLDINGS

The establishment of reciprocity and the apportionment of net income may be complicated slightly by the existence of mutual stockholdings. When reciprocity is being established, the increase or decrease in the stockholders' equity of one particular affiliate may depend upon the increase or decrease in the stockholders' equity of a second affiliate, whereas the second affiliate's change may depend upon the change in the first affiliate's increase or decrease. Likewise, in the apportionment of net income, one affiliate's income may be dependent upon another's, and vice versa. Although there are roundabout ways to handle problems of this kind, the most direct approach is to solve them algebraically.

### Mutual Stockholdings Between Subsidiaries

**First Illustration.** Assume that Company A owns an 80% interest in Company B and a 90% interest in Company C directly; that Company C owns a 20% interest in Company B, and Company B, in turn, owns a 10% interest in Company C; that from their respective operations Company B's stockholders' equity has increased $12,000 and Company C's $27,000 since acquisition; and that all investment ac-

15 / *Consolidated Statements – Indirect Ownership and Mutual Stockholdings*

counts are on the cost basis. Reciprocity would be established by the following work sheet entries:

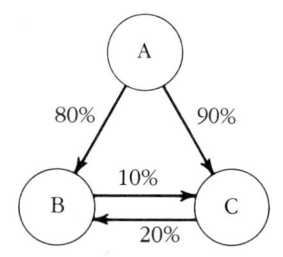

Mutual Stockholdings Between Subsidiaries

| | | |
|---|---:|---:|
| Investment in Company C (A's) | $27,000 | |
| Investment in Company C (B's) | 3,000 | |
|     Retained earnings (A's) | | $27,000 |
|     Retained earnings (B's) | | 3,000 |

(to recognize Company A's 90% and Company B's 10% interest in the increase in Company C's stockholders' equity)*

| | | |
|---|---:|---:|
| Investment in Company B (A's) | $12,000 | |
| Investment in Company B (C's) | 3,000 | |
|     Retained earnings (A's) | | $12,000 |
|     Retained earnings (C's) | | 3,000 |

(to recognize Company A's 80% and Company C's 20% interest in the increase in Company B's stockholders' equity)*

*Let B = Company B's increase in stockholders' equity on a consolidated basis.
Let C = Company C's increase in stockholders' equity on a consolidated basis.

$$B = \$12{,}000 + .1C$$
$$C = \$27{,}000 + .2B$$
$$B = \$12{,}000 + .1\,(\$27{,}000 + .2B)$$
$$B = \$12{,}000 + \$2{,}700 + .02B$$
$$.98B = \$14{,}700$$
$$B = \underline{\underline{\$15{,}000}}$$
$$C = \$27{,}000 + .2B$$
$$C = \$27{,}000 + .2\,(\$15{,}000)$$
$$C = \$27{,}000 + \$3{,}000$$
$$C = \underline{\underline{\$30{,}000}}$$

Assuming that in any given period Company A earns $100,000; B, $8,000; and C, $18,000, from their respective operations, net income would be apportioned as follows:

|  | Company A | Company B | Company C | Total |
|---|---|---|---|---|
| Net income before apportionment | $100,000 | $10,000* | $20,000* | $130,000 |
| Elimination of mutual income: | | | | |
|   C's share of B's (20%) | | (2,000) | | (2,000) |
|   B's share of C's (10%) | | | (2,000) | (2,000) |
| Apportionment: | | | | |
|   A's share of B's (80%) | 8,000 | (8,000) | | |
|   A's share of C's (90%) | 18,000 | | (18,000) | |
| Balances | $126,000 | –0– | –0– | $126,000 |
| Consolidated net income | $126,000 | | | $126,000† |
| Minority interest, B | | –0– | | |
| Minority interest, C | | | –0– | |
| Total | | | | $126,000 |

†Since, from the consolidated viewpoint, Company B and Company C are wholly owned, consolidated net income may be proved by merely adding arithmetically the separate incomes of the respective companies on a nonconsolidated basis ($100,000 + $8,000 + $18,000).

*Let B = Company B's net income on a consolidated basis.
Let C = Company C's net income on a consolidated basis.

$B = \$8,000 + .1C$
$C = \$18,000 + .2B$

$B = \$8,000 + .1 (\$18,000 + .2B)$
$B = \$8,000 + \$1,800 + .02B$
$.98B = \$9,800$
$B = \underline{\$10,000}$

$C = \$18,000 + .2B$
$C = \$18,000 + .2 (\$10,000)$
$C = \$18,000 + \$2,000$
$C = \underline{\$20,000}$

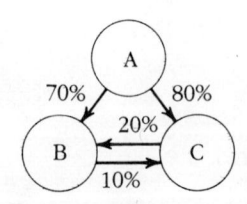

Mutual Stockholdings Between Subsidiaries

**Second Illustration.** Assuming the same facts used in the preceding illustration, except that Company A owns directly only an 80% interest in Company C and a 70% interest in Company B, the establishment of reciprocity and the apportionment of net income would be accomplished as follows:

| | | |
|---|---:|---:|
| Investment in Company C (A's) | $24,000 | |
| Investment in Company C (B's) | 3,000 | |
|     Retained earnings (A's) | | $24,000 |
|     Retained earnings (B's) | | 3,000 |
| (to recognize Company A's 80% and Company B's 10% interest in the increase in Company C's stockholders' equity) | | |
| Investment in Company B (A's) | $10,500 | |
| Investment in Company B (C's) | 3,000 | |
|     Retained earnings (A's) | | $10,500 |
|     Retained earnings (C's) | | 3,000 |
| (to recognize Company A's 70% and Company C's 20% interest in the increase in Company B's stockholders' equity) | | |

| | Company A | Company B | Company C | Total |
|---|---:|---:|---:|---:|
| Net income before apportionment | $100,000 | $10,000 | $20,000 | $130,000 |
| Elimination of mutual income: | | | | |
|   C's share of B's (20%) | | (2,000) | | (2,000) |
|   B's share of C's (10%) | | | (2,000) | (2,000) |
| Apportionment: | | | | |
|   A's share of B's (70%) | 7,000 | (7,000) | | |
|   A's share of C's (80%) | 16,000 | | (16,000) | |
| Balances | $123,000 | $ 1,000 | $ 2,000 | $126,000 |
| Consolidated net income | $123,000 | | | $123,000 |
| Minority interest, B (10%) | | $ 1,000 | | 1,000 |
| Minority interest, C (10%) | | | $ 2,000 | 2,000 |
| Total | | | | $126,000 |

## Mutual Stockholdings Between Parent and Subsidiary

Assume that Company A owns an 80% interest in Company B and that Company B, in turn, owns a 10% interest in Company A; that from their own operations Company B's stockholders' equity has increased $10,000 and Company A's $84,000 since date of acquisition; and that both investment accounts are on the cost basis. Reciprocity would be established by the following work sheet entry:

| | | |
|---|---:|---:|
| Investment in Company A (B's) | $10,000 | |
| Investment in Company B (A's) | 16,000 | |
|     Retained earnings (B's) | | $10,000 |
|     Retained earnings (A's) | | 16,000 |

```
        A
    ↑   ↓
 10%|   |80%
    |   ↓
        B
```

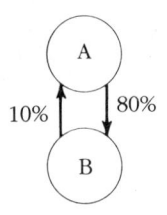

Mutual Stockholdings Between Parent and Subsidiary

(to recognize Company B's 10% interest in Company A's increase in stockholders' equity, and to recognize Company A's 80% interest in Company B's increase in stockholders' equity)*

*Let A = Company A's increase in stockholders' equity on a consolidated basis.
Let B = Company B's increase in stockholders' equity on a consolidated basis.

$$A = \$84{,}000 + .8B$$
$$B = \$10{,}000 + .1A$$

$$B = \$10{,}000 + .1(\$84{,}000 + .8B)$$
$$B = \$10{,}000 + \$8{,}400 + .08B$$
$$.92B = \$18{,}400$$
$$B = \$20{,}000$$

$$A = \$84{,}000 + .8B$$
$$A = \$84{,}000 + .8(\$20{,}000)$$
$$A = \$84{,}000 + \$16{,}000$$
$$A = \$100{,}000$$

Assuming that in any given period Company A earns $42,000, and Company B, $5,000, from their respective operations, net income would be apportioned as follows:

|  | Company A | Company B | Total |
|---|---|---|---|
| Net income before apportionment | $50,000* | $10,000* | $60,000 |
| Elimination of mutual income: |  |  |  |
|   A's share of B's (80%) |  | (8,000) | (8,000) |
|   B's share of A's (10%) | (5,000) |  | (5,000) |
| Balances | $45,000 | $ 2,000 | $47,000 |
|   Consolidated net income | $45,000 |  | $45,000 |
|   Minority interest, B (20%) |  | $ 2,000 | 2,000 |
| Total |  |  | $47,000 |

*Let A = A's net income on a consolidated basis.
Let B = B's net income on a consolidated basis.

15 / *Consolidated Statements – Indirect Ownership and Mutual Stockholdings*    **459**

$$A = \$42{,}000 + .8B$$
$$B = \$ 5{,}000 + .1A$$

$$A = \$42{,}000 + .8 (\$5{,}000 + .1A)$$
$$A = \$42{,}000 + \$4{,}000 + .08A$$
$$.92A = \$46{,}000$$
$$A = \underline{\underline{\$50{,}000}}$$

$$B = \$ 5{,}000 + .1A$$
$$B = \$ 5{,}000 + .1 (\$50{,}000)$$
$$B = \underline{\underline{\$10{,}000}}$$

## Mutual Stockholdings Between Subsidiaries and Between the Parent and Subsidiaries

Assume that Company A owns an 80% interest in Company B and a 90% interest in Company C directly; that Company B holds a 5% interest in Company A and a 10% interest in Company C; that Company C holds a 10% interest in both Company A and Company B; that from their own operations Company A's stockholders' equity has increased $100,000, Company B's, $20,000, and Company C's, $10,000, since the date of acquisition; and that all investment accounts are on the cost basis. Reciprocity would be established by the following work sheet entry:

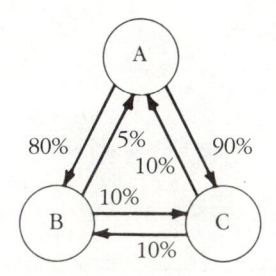

Mutual Stockholdings Between Subsidiaries and Between the Parent and Subsidiaries

| | | |
|---|---:|---:|
| Investment in Company A (B's) | $ 7,469 | |
| Investment in Company A (C's) | 14,938 | |
| Investment in Company B (A's) | 24,212 | |
| Investment in Company B (C's) | 3,027 | |
| Investment in Company C (A's) | 25,168 | |
| Investment in Company C (B's) | 2,796 | |
|    Retained earnings (A's) | | $49,380 |
|    Retained earnings (B's) | | 10,265 |
|    Retained earnings (C's) | | 17,965 |

(to recognize Company A's 80% interest in the increase in B's stockholders' equity and

90% interest in the increase in C's stockholders' equity; and Company B's 5% interest in A and 10% interest in C; and C's 10% interest in both A and B)

Although problems of this nature may be solved by means of simultaneous equations, as has been illustrated, more involved holdings with a greater number of subsidiaries may make the algebraic solution unduly complex. In such situations it is not uncommon to find the "successive allocation" method used to establish reciprocity or to apportion net income. The use of this method to establish reciprocity is illustrated below:

|  | Company A | Company B | Company C |
|---|---|---|---|
| *First allocation:* | | | |
| Separate company increases | $100,000 | $20,000 | $10,000 |
| Allocation of A (5% to B, 10% to C) | — | 5,000 | 10,000 |
| Allocation of B (80% to A, 10% to C) | 20,000 | — | 2,500 |
| Allocation of C (90% to A, 10% to B) | 20,250 | 2,250 | — |
| Total | $140,250 | $27,250 | $22,500 |
| | | | |
| *Second allocation:* | | | |
| Separate company increases | $100,000 | $20,000 | $10,000 |
| Allocation of A (140,250) | — | 7,012 | 14,025 |
| Allocation of B (27,250) | 21,800 | — | 2,725 |
| Allocation of C (26,750) | 24,075 | 2,675 | — |
| Total | $145,875 | $29,687 | $26,750 |

(Third through seventh allocation omitted.)

|  | | | |
|---|---|---|---|
| *Eighth allocation:* | | | |
| Separate company increases | $100,000 | $20,000 | $10,000 |
| Allocation of A (149,376) | — | 7,469 | 14,938 |
| Allocation of B (30,264) | 24,211 | — | 3,026 |
| Allocation of C (27,964) | 25,168 | 2,796 | — |
| Total | $149,379 | $30,265 | $27,964 |
| | | | |
| *Ninth allocation:* | | | |
| Separate company increases | $100,000 | $20,000 | $10,000 |
| Allocation of A (149,379) | — | 7,469 | 14,938 |
| Allocation of B (30,265) | 24,212 | — | 3,027 |

| | | | |
|---|---|---|---|
| Allocation of C (27,964)* | 25,168 | 2,796 | — |
| Total | $149,380 | $30,265 | $27,965 |

*Discrepancy of $1.00 due to rounding.

Since further allocations will give the same result, no further allocations are necessary. The work sheet entry to establish reciprocity would be based on the amounts determined in the ninth allocation.

## Mutual Stockholdings as Treasury Stock

A procedure well accepted in accounting practice is to treat the subsidiary's holdings of a parent company's stock as treasury stock. Supporting this treatment is the view that subsidiary ownership of parent company's stock is an investment by the subsidiary.

Consolidation procedure under this concept is simplified. Eliminations would be limited to the consolidated interest in the subsidiaries. A subsidiary's investment in the parent company's stock would be carried on the consolidated statement of financial position as treasury stock.

There is considerable support for the treasury stock point of view in practice. Its use is also recommended in *Accounting Research Bulletin No. 51*. The work sheet on pp. 462–463 and accompanying explanation illustrate the procedure involved. The amounts in the individual company statements are assumed and the adjustments to establish reciprocity are based on the illustration in the preceding section.

The increases in the stockholders' equities for Companies B and C on a consolidated basis, since acquisition, may be computed as follows:

Let B = Company B's increase in stockholders' equity on a consolidated basis.
Let C = Company C's increase in stockholders' equity on a consolidated basis.

$$B = \$20{,}000 + .1C$$
$$C = \$10{,}000 + .1B$$
$$B = \$20{,}000 + .1\,(\$10{,}000 + .1B)$$
$$B = \$20{,}000 + \$1{,}000 + .01B$$
$$.99B = \$21{,}000$$
$$B = \$21{,}212.12$$

$$C = \$10{,}000 + .1B$$
$$C = \$10{,}000 + 2{,}121.21$$
$$C = \$12{,}121.21$$

When subsidiary holdings of parent stock are treated as treasury stock, the results differ from the results obtained under the assumption of a mutual holding. The extent of this difference is revealed by a comparison of the work sheet entries to establish reciprocity in the preceding and following illustrations.

COMPANY A AND SUBSIDIARIES
CONSOLIDATED WORKING PAPERS
STATEMENT OF FINANCIAL POSITION
DECEMBER 31, 1980

| | Company A | Company B | Company C | Adjustments Debit | Adjustments Credit | Eliminations Debit | Eliminations Credit | Consolidated Financial Position |
|---|---|---|---|---|---|---|---|---|
| Current assets | $120,000 | $ 40,000 | $ 15,000 | | | | | $175,000 |
| Investment in A (Cost)— 5% | | 35,000 | | | | | | 35,000T/S |
| Investment in A (Cost)—10% | | | 90,000 | | | | | 90,000T/S |
| Investment in B (Cost)—80% | 125,000 | | | $16,970(3) | | | $136,970A | 5,000G |
| Investment in B (Cost)—10% | | | 15,000 | 2,121(1) | | | 17,121B | — |
| Investment in C (Cost)—90% | 120,000 | | | 10,909(4) | | | 127,909C | 3,000G |
| Investment in C (Cost)—10% | | 13,000 | | 1,212(2) | | | 14,212D | — |
| Fixed assets | 535,000 | 112,000 | 30,000 | | | | | 677,000 |
| Total | $900,000 | $200,000 | $150,000 | | | | | $985,000 |

15 / *Consolidated Statements—Indirect Ownership and Mutual Stockholdings*      463

| | | | | | | | |
|---|---|---|---|---|---|---|---|
| Current liabilities | $100,000 | $ 30,000 | $ 10,000 | | | | $140,000 |
| Capital stock—A | 500,000 | | | | | | 500,000 |
| Retained earnings—A, 12/31/80 | 300,000 | | | $16,970(3) | | | 327,879RE |
| | | | | 10,909(4) | | | |
| Capital stock—B | | 100,000 | | | $ 80,000A | | |
| | | | | | 10,000B | | 10,000MI |
| Retained earnings—B (at date acquired stock) | | 50,000 | | | 40,000A | | |
| | | | | | 5,000B | | 5,000MI |
| Retained earnings (since acquisition) | | 20,000 | | 1,212(2) | 16,970A | | |
| | | | | | 2,121B | | 2,121MI |
| Capital stock—C | | | 90,000 | | 81,000C | | |
| | | | | | 9,000D | | — |
| Retained earnings—C (at date acquired stock) | | | 40,000 | | 36,000C | | |
| | | | | | 4,000D | | — |
| Retained earnings (since acquisition) | | | 10,000 | 2,121(1) | 10,909C | | |
| | | | | | 1,212D | | |
| Total | $900,000 | $200,000 | $150,000 | $31,212 | $296,212 | $296,212 | $985,000 |

## Effect of Indirect Ownership and Mutual Stockholdings on Intercompany Profit Eliminations

Intercompany profit transactions, in the case of direct ownership, were discussed in Chapter Thirteen. Recognition was given to the general unanimity among accountants as to the need to eliminate intercompany profits and to the lack of agreement as to the amount to be eliminated or how it should be eliminated. Most accountants eliminate 100% of any intercompany profit unrealized at the date of consolidation. Some accountants, however, eliminate the entire amount from consolidated retained earnings. Others prorate the elimination between consolidated retained earnings and the minority interest.

The effect of indirect and mutual stockholdings upon the elimination of intercompany profits is illustrated in the following examples. In all cases, assume that as of the consolidating date Company B has merchandise in its inventory valued at $10,000 which it purchased from Company C. The merchandise had cost Company C $6,000.

**Indirect Ownership—Major and Minor Parent.** Assume, in addition to the general assumptions given above, that Company A owns a 90% interest in Company B, and that Company B, in turn, owns an 80% interest in Company C.

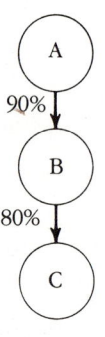

```
      A
   90% ↓
      B
   80% ↓
      C
```

Indirect Ownership—Major and Minor Parent

The intercompany profit elimination under the two basic approaches would be made as follows:

|  | 100% Elimination Not Prorated | | 100% Elimination Prorated | |
|---|---|---|---|---|
|  | Debit | Credit | Debit | Credit |
| Consolidated retained earnings | $4,000[4] |  | $2,880[1] |  |
| Minority interest, C | –0– |  | 800[2] |  |
| Minority interest, B | –0– |  | 320[3] |  |
| Inventory |  | $4,000[4] |  | $4,000[4] |

[1] 72% × $4,000 = $2,880
[2] 20% × $4,000 = 800

*15 / Consolidated Statements — Indirect Ownership and Mutual Stockholdings*

$$^3\ 8\% \times \$4{,}000 = \underline{\ \ 320^*\ \ }$$
$$^4 100\% \times \$4{,}000 = \underline{\$4{,}000}$$

*When establishing reciprocity, Company B would recognize $3,200 (80% × $4,000) of the intercompany profit and, in turn, Company A would recognize $2,880 (90% × $3,200), leaving $320 pertaining to the minority interest in Company B.

**Indirect Ownership — Connecting Affiliate.** Assume, in addition to the general assumptions, that Company A owns a 90% interest in Company B and an 80% interest in Company C, and that Company B, in turn, owns a 10% interest in Company C. The intercompany profit eliminations would be made as follows:

|  | 100% Elimination Not Prorated | | 100% Elimination Prorated | |
| --- | --- | --- | --- | --- |
|  | Debit | Credit | Debit | Credit |
| Consolidated retained earnings | $4,000[4] |  | $3,560[1] |  |
| Minority interest, C | –0– |  | 400[2] |  |
| Minority interest, B | –0– |  | 40[3] |  |
| Inventory |  | $4,000 |  | $4,000 |

$$^1\ 89\% \times \$4{,}000 = \$3{,}560$$
$$^2\ 10\% \times \$4{,}000 = \ \ \ 400$$
$$^3\ \ 1\% \times \$4{,}000 = \ \ \ \ \ 40^*$$
$$^4 100\% \times \$4{,}000 = \underline{\$4{,}000}$$

*When establishing reciprocity, Company B would recognize $400 (10% × $4,000) of the intercompany profit, and Company A in turn would recognize $360 (90% × $400) of this, leaving $40 pertaining to the minority interest in Company B. This figure represents 1% (10% × 10%) of the intercompany profit.

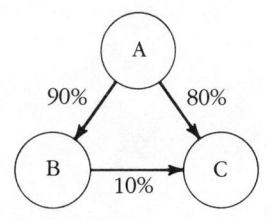

Indirect Ownership — Connecting Affiliate

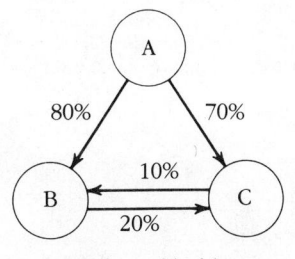

Mutual Stockholdings

**Mutual Stockholdings.** Assume, in addition to the general assumptions, that Company A owns an 80% interest in Company B and a 70% interest in Company C, that Company B holds a 20% interest in Company C, and that Company C, in turn, holds a 10% interest in Company B. The intercompany profit eliminations would be made as follows:

|  | 100% Elimination Not Prorated | | 100% Elimination Prorated | |
|---|---|---|---|---|
|  | Debit | Credit | Debit | Credit |
| Consolidated retained earnings | $4,000 |  | $3,510.21[1] |  |
| Minority interest, C | –0– |  | 408.16[2] |  |
| Minority interest, B | –0– |  | 81.63[3] |  |
| Inventory |  | $4,000 |  | $4,000 |

[1] The amount recognized by Company A when consolidating (see calculations below).

[2] 10% of $4,081.63, the amount recognized by Company C when consolidating (see calculations below).

[3] 10% of $816.33, the amount recognized by Company B when consolidating (see calculations below).

*Elimination algebraically determined:*

Let A = A's share of C's intercompany profit on a consolidated basis.
Let B = B's share of C's intercompany profit on a consolidated basis.
Let C = C's intercompany profit on a consolidated basis.

$$C = \$4{,}000 + .1B$$
$$B = .2C$$
$$A = .8B + .7C$$

$$B = .2 (\$4{,}000 + .1B)$$
$$B = \$800 + .02B$$
$$.98B = \$800$$
$$B = \underline{\underline{\$816.33}}$$

$$C = \$4{,}000 + .1B$$
$$C = \underline{\underline{\$4{,}081.63}}$$

$$A = .8 (\$816.33) + .7 (\$4{,}081.63)$$
$$A = \$653.07 + \$2{,}857.14$$
$$A = \underline{\underline{\$3{,}510.21}}$$

*Successive allocation method:*

|  | A | B | MI (B) | C | MI(C) |
|---|---|---|---|---|---|
| Intercompany profit |  |  |  | $4,000 |  |
| Allocation of intercompany profit | $2,800 | $800 |  | (4,000) | $400 |
| Allocation of B's share | 640 | (800) | $80 | 80 |  |
| Reallocation of C's share | 56 | 16 |  | (80) | 8 |
| Reallocation of B's share | 13 | (16) | 1 | 2 |  |
| Second reallocation of C's share | 2 |  |  | (2) |  |
| Total | $3,511 | –0– | $81 | –0– | $408 |

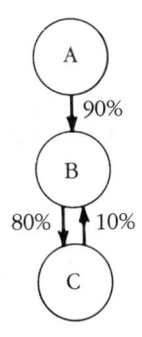

## 15 / Consolidated Statements—Indirect Ownership and Mutual Stockholdings

Combination of Indirect Ownership and Mutual Stockholdings

**Combination of Indirect Ownership and Mutual Stockholdings.** Assume, in addition to the general assumptions, that Company A owns a 90% interest in Company B, that Company B owns an 80% interest in Company C, and that Company C, in turn, holds a 10% interest in Company B. The intercompany profit eliminations would be made as follows:

|  | 100% Elimination Not Prorated ||  100% Elimination Prorated ||
| --- | --- | --- | --- | --- |
|  | Debit | Credit | Debit | Credit |
| Consolidated retained earnings | $4,000 |  | $3,130.43[1] |  |
| Minority interest, C | –0– |  | 869.57[2] |  |
| Minority interest, B | –0– |  | –0– |  |
| Inventory |  | $4,000 |  | $4,000 |

[1] The amount recognized by Company A when consolidating (see calculations below).
[2] 20% of $4,347.83, the amount recognized by Company C when consolidating (see calculations below).

*Elimination algebraically determined:*

Let C = C's intercompany profit on a consolidated basis.
Let B = B's share of C's intercompany profit on a consolidated basis.
Let A = A's share of C's intercompany profit on a consolidated basis.

$$C = \$4{,}000 + .1B$$
$$B = .8C$$
$$A = .9B$$

$$B = .8\,(\$4{,}000 + .1B)$$
$$B = \$3{,}200 + .08B$$
$$.92B = \$3{,}200.000$$
$$\underline{B = \$3{,}478.26}$$

$$C = \$4{,}000 + .1B$$
$$\underline{C = \$4{,}347.83}$$

$$A = .9B$$
$$\underline{A = \$3{,}130.43}$$

*Successive allocation method:*

|  | A | B | MI (B) | C | MI (C) |
|---|---|---|---|---|---|
| Intercompany profit |  |  |  | $4,000 |  |
| Allocation of intercompany profit |  | $3,200 |  | (4,000) | $800 |
| Allocation of B's share | $2,880 | (3,200) | –0– | 320 |  |
| Reallocation of C's share |  | 256 |  | (320) | 64 |
| Reallocation of B's share | 230 | (256) |  | 26 |  |
| Second reallocation of C's share |  | 21 |  | (26) | 5 |
| Second reallocation of B's share | 19 | (21) |  | 2 |  |
| Third reallocation of C's share | 2 |  |  | (2) |  |
| Total | $3,131 | –0– | –0– | –0– | $869 |

## PROBLEMS

### Problem 15-1

From the following data determine (1) the minority interest in the net income or loss of each company, and (2) consolidated net income.

Company A owns 90% of Company B and 80% of Company C. Company B owns 80% of Company D, and Company C owns 90% of Company E. During the current year the companies *individually* reported net income or loss as follows:

| Company | Net Income or Loss | Amount |
|---|---|---|
| A | Income | $50,000 |
| B | Income | 20,000 |
| C | Income | 22,000 |
| D | Income | 14,000 |
| E | Loss | 8,000 |

### Problem 15-2

From the following data determine (1) the minority interest in the net income or loss of each company, and (2) consolidated net income.

A Company owns 90% of B Company, 80% of C Company, and 70% of D Company. B Company owns 10% of D Company, and C Company owns 10% of D Company. During the current year the companies *individually* reported net income or loss as follows:

| Company | Net Income or Loss | Amount |
|---|---|---|
| A | Income | $40,000 |
| B | Loss | 10,000 |

|   |        |        |
|---|--------|--------|
| C | Income | 10,000 |
| D | Income | 20,000 |

## Problem 15-3

From the following data determine (1) the minority interest in the net income or loss of each company, and (2) consolidated net income.

Company A owns 80% of Company B and 90% of Company C. Company B owns 70% of Company D, and Company C owns 80% of Company E. Company E owns 20% of Company D. During the current year the companies *individually* reported net income or loss as follows:

| Company | Net Income or Loss | Amount |
|---------|--------------------|--------|
| A | Income | $100,000 |
| B | Loss | 20,000 |
| C | Income | 45,000 |
| D | Loss | 6,000 |
| E | Income | 9,000 |

## Problem 15-4

From the following data determine (1) the minority interest in the net income of each company, and (2) consolidated net income.

Company A owns 90% of Company B and 80% of Company C. Company B owns 10% of Company C, and Company C owns 10% of Company B. During the current year the companies *individually* reported net income or loss as follows:

| Company | Net Income or Loss | Amount |
|---------|--------------------|--------|
| A | Income | $100,000 |
| B | Income | 19,000 |
| C | Income | 8,000 |

## Problem 15-5

Company A controls Company B through the ownership of 75,600 shares of Company B's capital stock, out of a total of 96,000 shares outstanding at June 30, 1980. The authorized capital stock of Company B is 150,000 shares, all of one class.

Company B controls Company C through the ownership of 6,250 shares of the latter's capital stock, out of a total of 10,000 shares outstanding at June 30, 1980.

The sum of the capital stock and retained earnings of Company B at June 30, 1980, is $5,894,706, and of Company C, $2,132,470.

Company B wishes to acquire the minority interest in Company C through the issuance of shares of its capital stock at a value equal to its book value at June 30, 1980, taking into account the book value of capital stock of Company C. Company B's investment in Company C is carried on Company B's books at a total cost of $687,500.

*Required:*
(1) Determine the number of shares to be issued by Company B, ignoring fractional shares.
(2) Compute the percentage of control held by Company A after such shares have been issued. (AICPA adapted)

## Problem 15-6

The financial facts shown in Exhibit I below pertain to Corporations R and S, which had mutual holdings during and at the end of the fiscal year 1980.

There was no change in the mutual holdings during the year. Each corporation carries its investment account at cost.

EXHIBIT I

|  | Corporation R | Corporation S |
|---|---|---|
| Of the issued capital stock, | | |
| R owns | 10% | 50% |
| S owns | 20% | 10% |
| Net assets (exclusive of investment accounts), December 31, 1980 | $540,000 | $590,000 |
| Dividends declared during 1980 | ? | 18,000 |
| 1980 net income (after taxes), exclusive of dividends | 53,000 | 60,000 |

*Required:*
(1) Compute the dollar equity of outside stockholders in the total net assets of R and S, respectively.
(2) Compute the dollar amount of dividends declared in 1980 to which the outside stockholders of R are entitled, assuming that R declared as dividends its *total* 1980 net income after taxes. (AICPA adapted)

## Problem 15-7

From the following condensed statements of financial position of Company A, Company B, and Company C, prepared as of December 31, 1980, prepare a consolidated statement of financial position.

|  | Company A | Company B | Company C |
|---|---|---|---|
| Current assets | $1,234,567 | $ 691,282 | $340,274 |
| Investments: | | | |
| 80% of B stock, at cost | 1,400,000 | — | — |
| 75% of C stock, at cost | — | 580,200 | — |
| Fixed assets, net | 3,030,933 | 1,322,607 | 514,987 |
| Total | $5,665,500 | $2,594,089 | $855,261 |

15 / Consolidated Statements—Indirect Ownership and Mutual Stockholdings 471

| | | | |
|---|---|---|---|
| Current liabilities | $ 400,500 | $ 275,389 | $ 93,261 |
| Bonds payable | — | 750,000 | — |
| Reserve for redemption of bonds | — | 250,000 | — |
| Common stock, $100 par value | 3,000,000 | 1,000,000 | 600,000 |
| Capital in excess of par | 710,300 | — | 45,600 |
| Retained earnings | 1,554,700 | 318,700 | 116,400 |
| Total | $5,665,500 | $2,594,089 | $855,261 |

The stock of Company C was acquired by Company B on January 31, 1979. Since that date Company C has had total earnings of $28,400 and paid cash dividends of $40,000. Company B has credited all dividends received to its income account.

Company A acquired the stock of Company B on December 31, 1980.

(AICPA adapted)

## Problem 15-8 *work in pieces*

From the following financial statements and other data, prepare consolidated working papers with columns for income, retained earnings, minority interests, and financial position. *T/B approach*

STATEMENTS OF FINANCIAL POSITION

DECEMBER 31, 1980

| Assets | Phoenix Co. | Eastern Airports, Inc. | Potomac Airport Co. |
|---|---|---|---|
| Cash | $ 428,000 | $ 14,500 | $ 500 |
| Accounts receivable | | 45,000 | 8,500 |
| Prepayments and supplies | 5,000 | 26,500 | |
| Investment in U.S. Airlines Co. stock | 630,000 | | |
| Investment in Eastern, Inc. stock | 270,000 | | |
| Loans to Eastern, Inc. | 370,000 | | |
| Investment in Potomac Co. common stock | | 180,000 | |
| Land | | 284,000 | 215,500 |
| Buildings and equipment | | 310,000 | |
| Accumulated depreciation | | 50,000* | |
| | $1,703,000 | $810,000 | $224,500 |

| Liabilities | | | |
|---|---|---|---|
| Accounts payable | | $ 10,000 | |
| Taxes and other accruals | $ 15,000 | 24,000 | |
| Due Phoenix Co. | | 370,000 | |
| Due Potomac Co. | | 8,500 | |
| Capital stock—preferred | | | $ 40,000 |

|  |  |  |  |
|---|---|---|---|
| Capital stock—common | 500,000 | 225,000 | 200,000 |
| Capital in excess of par | 500,000 | 150,000 |  |
| Retained earnings | 688,000 | 22,500 | 15,500* |
|  | $1,703,000 | $810,000 | $224,500 |

*Deductions

### INCOME STATEMENTS—1980

|  | Phoenix Co. | Eastern Airports, Inc. | Potomac Airport Co. |
|---|---|---|---|
| *Income:* |  |  |  |
| Rent |  |  | $8,500 |
| Profit on sales of securities | $165,000 |  |  |
| Revenue from port activities |  | $ 75,000 |  |
| Dividends | 25,000 |  |  |
| Interest | 48,000 |  |  |
|  | $238,000 | $75,000 | $8,500 |
| *Expenses:* |  |  |  |
| Interest |  | $18,000 |  |
| General, including taxes | $ 75,000 | 46,000 | $2,000 |
| Loss on sale of hangar |  |  | 3,000 |
|  | $ 75,000 | $64,000 | $5,000 |
| Net Income | $163,000 | $11,000 | $3,500 |

*Other data:*

(1) Phoenix Co. owns 36,000 shares of the stock of Eastern Airports, Inc. Of this holding, 21,000 shares were acquired at $10 per share by subscription at the time Eastern was organized (January 1, 1977). An additional 3,000 shares of Eastern stock were purchased on December 31, 1978, at $20 per share; immediately after this transaction the stockholders' equity of Eastern stood as follows:

| Capital stock—stated value ($5 per share) | $150,000 |
|---|---|
| Capital in excess of par | 150,000 |
| Retained earnings | 100,000 |
|  | $400,000 |

As of January 1, 1979, Eastern Airports, Inc. declared a stock dividend of $75,000 (15,000 shares at $5 per share), which was appropriated from retained earnings.

(2) Eastern Airports, Inc., owns 90% of the common stock of Potomac Airport Co. acquired on December 31, 1978, at a total cost of $180,000. At this

time the accumulated operating deficit of Potomac was $14,000, but preferred dividends had been paid to date.
(3) No dividends were paid by Phoenix Co. in 1980.
(4) No dividends (other than the stock dividend referred to above) were declared by Eastern Airports, Inc., during the years 1979 and 1980.
(5) No dividends were declared on the peferred stock of Potomac Airport Co. for the two years, 1979-1980. This is a 6% cumulative stock.
(6) The interest charge on the books of Eastern Airports, Inc., is entirely applicable to the advances made by the Phoenix Co.
(7) All of the revenues of Potomac Airport Co. for 1980 are based on charges to Eastern Airports, Inc., not yet collected.
(8) All investment accounts are recorded on a cost basis, with no adjustments for intercompany profit, loss, or dividends.
(9) Assume that goodwill is not being amortized at this time.

(AICPA adapted)

## Problem 15-9

From the data shown below prepare a consolidated statement of financial position of the Top Holding Company and its subsidiaries R Company and S Company.

The investments in R Company stock are carried at cost less applicable portions of net losses since acquisition; the investments in S Company stock are carried at cost. The bonds were acquired at $1,500 discount and are carried at cost. The investments in R Company were made at a time when R Company had retained earnings of $1,500; the investments in S Company were made at a time when S Company had retained earnings of $5,000. (AICPA adapted)

STATEMENTS OF FINANCIAL POSITION

| Assets | Top Holding Company | R Company | S Company |
| --- | --- | --- | --- |
| Current assets | $150,000 | $30,000 | $118,110 |
| Property, less depreciation | 47,000 | 5,500 | 130,000 |
| Investment in R Company stock: | | | |
| 90% | 18,000 | | |
| 10% | | | 2,500 |
| Investment in S Company stock: | | | |
| 75% | 45,000 | | |
| 15% | | 9,000 | |
| Investment in S Company bonds | 41,500 | | |
| | $301,500 | $44,500 | $250,610 |

| Equities | | | |
|---|---|---|---|
| Current liabilities | $ 80,000 | $23,000 | $ 70,000 |
| Bonds payable | | | 100,000 |
| Capital stock | 200,000 | 30,000 | 50,000 |
| Retained earnings (deficit) | 21,500 | (8,500) | 30,610 |
| | $301,500 | $44,500 | $250,610 |

## Problem 15-10

From the following statements of financial position and additional data, prepare consolidated working papers as of December 31, 1980:

On December 31, 1979, the Rockford Electronics Company bought 90% of the $500,000 capital stock of the Elgin Supply Company for $370,080, and 80% of the $200,000 7% preferred stock of the Peoria Radio Company for $176,000.

The Elgin Supply Company had acquired previously (December 31, 1978) 90% of the $200,000 common stock of the Peoria Radio Company for $126,000.

ROCKFORD ELECTRONICS COMPANY

STATEMENT OF FINANCIAL POSITION

DECEMBER 31, 1980

| Assets | | Equities | |
|---|---|---|---|
| Investments | | Accounts payable | |
|   Elgin Co. | $ 397,080 |   Peoria Co. | $ 10,000 |
|   Peoria Co. | 187,200 | Capital stock | |
| Notes receivable | |   Preferred | 400,000 |
|   Peoria Co. | 20,000 |   Common | 800,000 |
| Other assets (net) | 708,520 | Retained Earnings | 102,800 |
| | $1,312,800 | | $1,312,800 |

1. Rockford consistently takes up on its books its share of Elgin's book profits.
2. The difference of $5,000 between the current accounts of Rockford and Peoria represents Peoria merchandise in transit to Rockford.

ELGIN SUPPLY COMPANY

STATEMENT OF FINANCIAL POSITION

DECEMBER 31, 1980

| Assets | | Equities | |
|---|---|---|---|
| Investments | | Notes receivable | |
|   Peoria Co. | $126,000 |   discounted | $ 10,000 |
| Notes receivable | | Capital stock | 500,000 |
|   Peoria Co. | 10,000 | Retained earnings | 26,000 |
| Other assets (net) | 400,000 | | |
| | $536,000 | | $536,000 |

15 / *Consolidated Statements—Indirect Ownership and Mutual Stockholdings*     **475**

3. Elgin does not take up on its books its share of the Peoria profits but credits to income the Peoria dividends when received.
4. Elgin made a profit of $50,000 in 1980, before considering income from its investment in Peoria, and on December 20, 1980, paid a dividend of 4% ($20,000) on its $500,000 capital stock.

PEORIA RADIO COMPANY
STATEMENT OF FINANCIAL POSITION
DECEMBER 31, 1980

| Assets | | Equities | |
|---|---|---|---|
| Goodwill | $ 20,000 | Notes payable | |
| Accounts receivable | |   Rockford Co. | $ 20,000 |
|   Rockford Co. | 15,000 |   Elgin Co. | 10,000 |
| Other assets (net) | 425,000 | Dividends payable | |
| | |   Preferred | 14,000 |
| | |   Common | 16,000 |
| | | Capital Stock | |
| | |   7% Preferred | 200,000 |
| | |   Common | 200,000 |
| | $460,000 | | $460,000 |

5. Peoria made a profit of $20,000 in 1979, which was paid out in dividends that were duly received by the stockholders before December 31, 1979.
6. Peoria made a profit of $30,000 in 1980 and on December 20, 1980, declared dividends of 7% on the preferred and 8% on the common stock, both payable January 10, 1981.
7. Goodwill (positive or negative) is not being amortized at this time.

(AICPA adapted)

### Problem 15-11

From the following data prepare a consolidated statement of financial position as of December 31, 1980:

| Assets | A | B | C |
|---|---|---|---|
| Investment in Company B 4,000 shares | $ 480,000 | | |
| Investment in Company C 1,500 shares | | $ 150,000 | |
| Other assets | 3,201,000 | 965,000 | $269,000 |
| | $3,681,000 | $1,115,000 | $269,000 |
| **Liabilities and Capital** | | | |
| Liabilities | $ 425,000 | $ 191,000 | $ 36,000 |
| Capital stock: | | | |
|   Number of shares | 22,000 | 6,000 | 2,000 |
|   Par or declared value | $ 100 | $ 90 | $ 100 |
|   Amount | $2,200,000 | $ 540,000 | $200,000 |
| Capital in excess of par | | $ 60,000 | |

Retained earnings:
|  |  |  |  |
|---|---:|---:|---:|
| At January 1, 1980 | $ 937,000 | $ 288,000 | $ 38,000 |
| Profit for 1980 | 559,000 | 54,000 | 3,000 |
| Total | $1,496,000 | $ 342,000 | $ 41,000 |
| Dividends declared in 1980 | 440,000 | 18,000 | 8,000 |
| At December 31, 1980 | $1,056,000 | $ 324,000 | $ 33,000 |
|  | $3,681,000 | $1,115,000 | $269,000 |

The investments in Companies B and C were acquired at the close of the year 1979, and the 1980 dividends paid or declared thereon have been credited to income. The capital in excess of par of Company B arose through the sale of its no-par capital stock at $100 per share, of which $90 was designated as its declared value, and the balance of $10 was credited to capital in excess of par.

There are no intercompany accounts or relations other than those that are indicated above.
(AICPA adapted)

## Problem 15-12

Akron, Inc., owns 80% of the capital stock of Benson Co. and 70% of the capital stock of Cashin, Inc. Benson Co. owns 15% of the capital stock of Cashin, Inc. Cashin, Inc., in turns, owns 25% of the capital stock of Akron, Inc. These ownership interrelationships are illustrated in the following diagram:

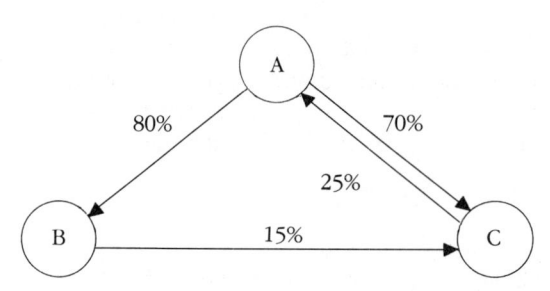

Net income before adjusting for interests in intercompany net income for each corporation follows:

| Akron, Inc. | $190,000 |
|---|---|
| Benson Co. | $170,000 |
| Cashin, Inc. | $230,000 |

The following notations relate to items 1 through 4. *Ignore all income tax considerations.*

$A_e$ = Akron's consolidated net income, i.e., its net income plus its share of the consolidated net incomes of Benson and Cashin.

$B_e$ = Benson's consolidated net income, i.e., its net income plus its share of the consolidated net income of Cashin.

$C_e$ = Cashin's consolidated net income, i.e., its net income plus its share of the consolidated income of Akron.

15 / *Consolidated Statements – Indirect Ownership and Mutual Stockholdings*  477

1. The equation, in a set of simultaneous equations, which computes $A_e$ is
    a. $A_e = .75 \, (190{,}000 + .8B_e + .7C_e)$.
    b. $A_e = 190{,}000 + .8B_e + .7C_e$.
    c. $A_e = .75 \, (190{,}000) + .8 \, (170{,}000) + .7 \, (230{,}000)$.
    d. $A_e = .75 \, (190{,}000) + .8B_e + .7C_e$.

2. The equation, in a set of simultaneous equations, which computes $B_e$ is
    a. $B_e = 170{,}000 + .15C_e - .75A_e$.
    b. $B_e = 170{,}000 + .15C_e$.
    c. $B_e = .2 \, (170{,}000) + .15 \, (230{,}000)$.
    d. $B_e = .2 \, (170{,}000) + .15C_e$.

3. Cashin's minority interest in consolidated net income is
    a. $.15 \, (230{,}000)$.
    b. $230{,}000 + .25A_e$.
    c. $.15 \, (230{,}000) + .25A_e$.
    d. $.15C_e$.

4. Benson's minority interest in consolidated net income is
    a. $34,316.
    b. $25,500.
    c. $45,755.
    d. $30,675.

(AICPA adapted)

# 16

# Consolidated Statements — Comprehensive Review

In the preceding chapters several problems that are likely to be encountered in the preparation of consolidated statements have been examined in detail. As a result, at any one time the reader's attention has been focused primarily on the solving of one particular type of problem. To provide an overall picture of consolidations, a comprehensive review is presented in this chapter. The review problem is based on the assumption that goodwill (either positive or negative) is not being amortized at this time and is developed in the following sequence:

1. Consolidation at the date of acquisition.
2. Consolidation subsequent to the date of acquisition.
3. Intercompany profit transactions.
4. Intercompany stock transactions.
5. Indirect ownership and mutual stockholdings.

## CONSOLIDATION AT DATE OF ACQUISITION

The review is predicated on the assumption that as of January 1, 1980, The Parent Company purchases an 80% interest in The Cost Company and a 90% interest in The Equity Company for $100,000 and $72,000, respectively. Immediately after the acquisitions the following statements of financial position are presented for consolidation:

THE PARENT COMPANY
STATEMENT OF FINANCIAL POSITION
AS OF JANUARY 1, 1980

| Assets | | Equities | |
|---|---|---|---|
| Current assets | $290,000 | Current liabilities | $ 62,000 |
| Investment in Cost Company | 100,000 | Fixed liabilities | 100,000 |

|  |  |  |  |
|---|---|---|---|
| Investment in Equity Company | 72,000 | Stockholders' equity: | |
| | | Capital stock | 1,000,000 |
| Fixed assets (net) | 900,000 | Retained earnings | 200,000 |
| | $1,362,000 | | $1,362,000 |

### THE COST COMPANY
### STATEMENT OF FINANCIAL POSITION
### JANUARY 1, 1980

| Assets | | Equities | |
|---|---|---|---|
| Current assets | $ 40,000 | Current liabilities | $ 10,000 |
| Fixed assets (net) | 130,000 | Fixed liabilities | 40,000 |
| | | Stockholders' equity: | |
| | | Capital stock | 100,000 |
| | | Retained earnings | 20,000 |
| | $170,000 | | $170,000 |

### THE EQUITY COMPANY
### STATEMENT OF FINANCIAL POSITION
### JANUARY 1, 1980

| Assets | | Equities | |
|---|---|---|---|
| Current assets | $ 30,000 | Current liabilities | $ 20,000 |
| Fixed assets (net) | 130,000 | Fixed liabilities | 50,000 |
| | | Stockholders' equity: | |
| | | Capital stock | 100,000 |
| | | Retained earnings | (10,000) |
| | $160,000 | | $160,000 |

**Summary.** Since reciprocity usually exists at the date of acquisition, consolidation at that time is primarily a matter of (1) eliminating the reciprocal elements, and (2) consolidating the nonreciprocal elements. However, if reciprocity does not exist (for instance, one or more of the affiliated group may not have recorded an intercompany transaction), it must be established before eliminating. It should also be remembered that consolidated retained earnings at the date of acquisition is composed of the parent company's retained earnings only. (See pages 482–483.)

## CONSOLIDATION SUBSEQUENT TO DATE OF ACQUISITION

In the work sheets on pp. 484–487 the individual statements reflect the financial position of the respective companies as of December 31, 1980, and the operating results of the respective companies for the year ending December 31, 1980. The consolidated statement columns show how the financial position and operating results would appear on a consolidated basis at that time.

**Summary.** When consolidating subsequent to the date of acquisition, it may be necessary to establish reciprocity before consolidating, especially when the investment is carried on the cost basis as illustrated in entry (1). In the foregoing situation reciprocity existed between The Parent Company and The Equity Company, since The Parent Company had recognized on its books its share of the increase in The Equity Company's stockholders' equity since the date of acquisition.

It should be noted that the goodwill elements ($4,000 positive as related to the investment in The Cost Company, and $9,000 negative as related to the investment in The Equity Company) remain the same. This condition should exist because there has been no change in the percent of ownership since the date of acquisition and no amortization has taken place.

It should also be noted that the consolidated retained earnings is composed of the retained earnings of The Parent Company and The Parent Company's share of the retained earnings that the subsidiaries have earned since acquisition.

|  | Retained Earnings 1/1/80 | Earnings Retained Since 1/1/80 | Parent's Share | Consolidated Retained Earnings 12/31/80 |
|---|---|---|---|---|
| The Parent Company | $200,000 | $80,000 | $80,000 | $280,000 |
| The Cost Company | 20,000 | 23,000 | 18,400 | 18,400 |
| The Equity Company | (10,000) | 20,000 | 18,000 | 18,000 |
| Consolidated retained earnings 12/31/80 |  |  |  | $316,400 |

## INTERCOMPANY PROFIT TRANSACTIONS

Intercompany profits and losses are defined as those profits and losses recognized by the selling affiliate at the time of sale, but which have not been realized from the consolidated viewpoint by transference to parties outside the affiliated group. It should be remembered that the Institute, in *Accounting Research Bulletin No. 51,* recommends that intercompany profits be (1) eliminated entirely from consolidated retained earnings, or (2) prorated between consolidated retained earnings and minority interest.

**Intercompany Profits in Inventories.** Assume that as of December 31, 1980, the inventories of the respective companies contain the following intercompany profit elements:

|  | P's Inventory | C's Inventory | E's Inventory | Total |
|---|---|---|---|---|
| Purchased from P |  | $10,000 | $15,000 | $ 25,000 |
| Purchased from C | $18,000 |  | 20,000 | 38,000 |
| Purchased from E | 25,000 | 12,000 |  | 37,000 |
| Totals | $43,000 | $22,000 | $35,000 | $100,000 |

## 16 / Consolidated Statements — Comprehensive Review

Work sheet entries to eliminate the intercompany profit in inventories under each of the alternatives are presented below:

1. One hundred percent elimination against consolidated retained earnings:

| | | |
|---|---|---|
| Consolidated retained earnings | $100,000 | |
| Inventory, Company P | | $43,000 |
| Inventory, Company C | | 22,000 |
| Inventory, Company E | | 35,000 |

2. One hundred percent elimination prorated between consolidated retained earnings and the minority interest:

| | | |
|---|---|---|
| Consolidated retained earnings | $88,700* | |
| Minority interest, C (20% × $38,000) | 7,600 | |
| Minority interest, E (10% × $37,000) | 3,700 | |
| Inventory, Company P | | $43,000 |
| Inventory, Company C | | 22,000 |
| Inventory, Company E | | 35,000 |

*$25,000 × 100% = $25,000
38,000 × 80% = 30,400
37,000 × 90% = 33,300
$88,700

**Intercompany Profits in Fixed Assets.** Although the treatment necessary for the elimination of intercompany profits in nondepreciating fixed assets and inventories is basically the same, the elimination necessary for intercompany profits in the case of depreciating fixed assets is somewhat different. The intercompany profit in depreciating assets is considered earned over the useful life of the asset as it is consumed and charged to production or to the cost of sales. The procedure involved is reviewed by assuming that as of the date of the intercompany fixed-asset transactions, December 31, 1980, the assets of the respective companies contained the following intercompany profit elements. Assume also that a 10-year useful life remained for all assets involved.

| | P's Assets | C's Assets | E's Assets | Total |
|---|---|---|---|---|
| Purchased from P (12/31/80) | | $20,000 | $30,000 | $50,000 |
| Purchased from C (12/31/80) | $35,000 | | 40,000 | 75,000 |
| Purchased from E (12/31/80) | 50,000 | 25,000 | | 75,000 |
| Totals | $85,000 | $45,000 | $70,000 | $200,000 |

Work sheet entries to eliminate the intercompany profit in fixed assets under each of the alternatives are presented on page 489.

THE PARENT COMPANY AND SUBSIDIARIES
CONSOLIDATED WORKING PAPERS
STATEMENT OF FINANCIAL POSITION
JANUARY 1, 1980

| Assets | The Parent Company | The Cost Company | The Equity Company | Adjustments & Eliminations | Consolidated Financial Position |
|---|---|---|---|---|---|
| Current assets | $ 290,000 | $ 40,000 | $ 30,000 | | $ 360,000 |
| Investment in C | 100,000 | | | $ 96,000A | 4,000G |
| Investment in E | 72,000 | | | 81,000B | (9,000)G |
| Fixed assets (net) | 900,000 | 130,000 | 130,000 | | 1,160,000 |
| | $1,362,000 | $170,000 | $160,000 | | $1,515,000 |

## 16 / Consolidated Statements — Comprehensive Review

| Equities | | | | | |
|---|---|---|---|---|---|
| Current liabilities | $ 62,000 | $ 10,000 | $ 20,000 | | $ 92,000 |
| Fixed liabilities | 100,000 | 40,000 | 50,000 | | 190,000 |
| Stockholders' equity: | | | | | |
| Capital stock: | | | | | |
| Parent Company | 1,000,000 | | | | 1,000,000 |
| Cost Company | | 100,000 | $ 80,000A | | 20,000MI |
| Equity Company | | | 100,000 | 90,000B | 10,000MI |
| Retained earnings: | | | | | |
| Parent Company | 200,000 | | | | 200,000RE |
| Cost Company | | 20,000 | 16,000A | | 4,000MI |
| Equity Company | | | (10,000) | 9,000B | (1,000)MI |
| | $1,362,000 | $170,000 | $160,000 | $186,000 | $1,515,000 |
| | | | | $186,000 | |

A: To eliminate 80% of The Cost Company's stockholders' equity against the investment account.
B: To eliminate 90% of The Equity Company's stockholders' equity against the investment account.

*Goodwill proof:*

| THE COST COMPANY | | THE EQUITY COMPANY | |
|---|---|---|---|
| Paid | $100,000 | Paid | $72,000 |
| Book value acquired | 96,000 | Book value acquired | 81,000 |
| Goodwill | $ 4,000 | Goodwill | $(9,000) |

## The Parent Company and Subsidiaries
### Consolidated Working Papers
### Statement of Financial Position
### December 31, 1980

| | The Parent Company | The Cost Company | The Equity Company | Adjustments & Eliminations | | Consolidated Financial Position |
|---|---|---|---|---|---|---|
| **Assets** | | | | | | |
| Current assets | $ 348,000 | $ 55,000 | $ 50,000 | | | $ 453,000 |
| Investment in C | 100,000 | | | $ 18,400(1) | $114,400A | 4,000G |
| Investment in E | 90,000 | | | | 99,000B | (9,000)G |
| Fixed assets (net) | 920,000 | 120,000 | 120,000 | | | 1,160,000 |
| | $1,458,000 | $175,000 | $170,000 | | | $1,608,000 |

## Equities

| | | | | | |
|---|---|---|---|---|---|
| Current liabilities | $ 50,000 | $ 12,000 | $ 10,000 | | $ 72,000 |
| Fixed liabilities | 110,000 | 20,000 | 50,000 | | 180,000 |
| Stockholders' equity: | | | | | |
| Capital stock: | | | | | |
| Parent Company | 1,000,000 | | | | 1,000,000 |
| Cost Company | | 100,000 | | 80,000*A* | 20,000MI |
| Equity Company | | | 100,000 | 90,000*B* | 10,000MI |
| Retained earnings: | | | | | |
| Parent Company | 298,000 | | | 18,400(1) | 316,400RE |
| Cost Company | | 43,000 | | 34,400*A* | 8,600MI |
| Equity Company | | | 10,000 | 9,000*B* | 1,000MI |
| | $1,458,000 | $175,000 | $170,000 | $231,800 $231,800 | $1,608,000 |

(1): To recognize P's 80% interest in C's increase in stockholders' equity since acquisition, 80% (143,000 − 120,000).
*A:* To eliminate 80% of C's stockholders' equity against the investment account.
*B:* To eliminate 90% of E's stockholders' equity against the investment account.

THE PARENT COMPANY AND SUBSIDIARIES
CONSOLIDATED WORKING PAPERS
STATEMENT OF INCOME AND RETAINED EARNINGS
YEAR ENDED DECEMBER 31, 1980

|  | The Parent Company | The Cost Company | The Equity Company | Eliminations | Consolidated Income | Consolidated Retained Earnings |
|---|---|---|---|---|---|---|
| *Credits* |  |  |  |  |  |  |
| Net sales | $800,000 | $210,000 | $200,000 |  | $1,210,000 |  |
| Interest income from C | 400 |  |  | $ 400*C* |  |  |
| Income from E | 18,000 |  |  | 18,000*D* |  |  |
|  | $818,400 | $210,000 | $200,000 | $18,400 | $1,210,000 |  |

486  EXPANSION OF THE BUSINESS ORGANIZATION

## 16 / Consolidated Statements—Comprehensive Review

| Debits | | | | |
|---|---|---|---|---|
| Cost of sales | $556,200 | $154,000 | $150,000 | | $ 860,200 |
| Depreciation | 80,000 | 10,000 | 10,000 | | 100,000 |
| Interest expense | 4,200 | 800 | 2,000 | $ 400C | 6,600 |
| Federal income taxes | 80,000 | 22,200 | 18,000 | | 120,200 |
| Net income | 98,000 | 23,000 | 20,000 | 18,000D | 123,000 |
| | $818,400 | $210,000 | $200,000 | $18,400 | $1,210,000 |
| Retained earnings, 1/1/80 | $200,000 | $ 20,000 | $(10,000) | | $200,000* |
| Net income | 98,000 | 23,000 | 20,000 | | |
| Retained earnings, 12/31/80 | $298,000 | $ 43,000 | $ 10,000 | | |

Apportionment of net income:

| | | | | | |
|---|---|---|---|---|---|
| Net income | | | | | $ 123,000 |
| Minority interest, C (20% × 23,000) | | | | $ 4,600 | |
| Minority interest, E (10% × 20,000) | | | | 2,000 | 6,600 |
| Consolidated net income—remainder (P's 98,000 × 80% of C's 23,000) | | | | | $ 116,400 |
| Consolidated retained earnings, 12/31/80 | | | | | $316,400 |

C: To eliminate intercompany interest income and interest expense.
D: To eliminate intercompany income.
*Parent's retained earnings at date of acquisition.

**Summary.** Although most accountants agree as to the necessity for eliminating intercompany profits in inventories and fixed assets, they do not always agree as to the amount that should be eliminated or as to how it should be eliminated. If the cost principle is to be followed, 100% elimination seems to be appropriate. Realistically, the elimination should be prorated between consolidated retained earnings and the minority interest (where appropriate). For practical reasons based on materiality, however, complete elimination from consolidated retained earnings may be justified in many instances.

## INTERCOMPANY STOCK TRANSACTIONS

Although intercompany stock transactions may take many different forms, the problems involved are perhaps best reviewed by an examination of the:

1. Disposal of subsidiary stock.
2. Acquisition of additional subsidiary stock.
3. Effect(s) of intercompany stock transactions upon the subsequent consolidations.

**Disposal of Subsidiary Stock.** As of January 1, 1981, when contemplating investing in the Foreign Company, the Parent Company sells a 10% interest in the Cost Company for $15,000 and a 10% interest in the Equity Company for $14,000. As was pointed out in Chapter 14, the disposal of subsidiary stock is recorded, as is any asset disposal, by (1) recording any asset(s) received, (2) removing the carrying value of the asset disposed of from the appropriate account(s), and (3) recording any gain or loss on disposal. The following entries would be made to record the sales listed above.

*Sale of the Cost Company stock:*

| | | |
|---|---|---|
| Cash | $15,000 | |
|     Investment in Cost Company | | $12,500 |
|     Gain on disposal of stock | | 2,500 |
| (to record sale of stock: carrying value 1/8 of $100,000 original cost) | | |

*Sale of the Equity Company stock:*

| | | |
|---|---|---|
| Cash | $14,000 | |
|     Investment in Equity Company | | $10,000 |
|     Gain on disposal of stock | | 4,000 |
| [to record sale of stock: carrying value 1/9 of $90,000 ($72,000 original cost + $18,000 increase)] | | |

It should also be noted that on the disposal of subsidiary stock a proportionate amount of any *unamortized* goodwill associated with the acquisition of the stock is also disposed of. For example, 1/8 of the *unamortized* $4,000 goodwill associ-

16 / *Consolidated Statements—Comprehensive Review* **489**

1. One hundred percent elimination against consolidated retained earnings:

|  | Date of Sale | | End of 1st Year | | End of 2nd Year | | End of 10th Year | |
|---|---|---|---|---|---|---|---|---|
|  | Debit | Credit | Debit | Credit | Debit | Credit | Debit | Credit |
| Consolidated retained earnings | $200,000 |  | $180,000 |  | $160,000 |  |  |  |
| Accrued depreciation (P) | — |  | 8,500 |  | 17,000 |  | $85,000 |  |
| Accrued depreciation (C) | — |  | 4,500 |  | 9,000 |  | 45,000 |  |
| Accrued depreciation (E) | — |  | 7,000 |  | 14,000 |  | 70,000 |  |
| Fixed assets (P) |  | $85,000 |  | $85,000 |  | $85,000 |  | $85,000 |
| Fixed assets (C) |  | 45,000 |  | 45,000 |  | 45,000 |  | 45,000 |
| Fixed assets (E) |  | 70,000 |  | 70,000 |  | 70,000 |  | 70,000 |

2. One hundred percent elimination prorated between consolidated retained earnings and minority interest:

|  | Date of Sale | | End of 1st Year | | End of 2nd Year | | End of 10th Year | |
|---|---|---|---|---|---|---|---|---|
|  | Debit | Credit | Debit | Credit | Debit | Credit | Debit | Credit |
| Consolidated retained earnings | $177,500 |  | $159,750 |  | $142,000 |  |  |  |
| Minority interest (C) | 15,000 |  | 13,500 |  | 12,000 |  |  |  |
| Minority interest (E) | 7,500 |  | 6,750 |  | 6,000 |  |  |  |
| Accrued depreciation (P) | — |  | 8,500 |  | 17,000 |  | $85,000 |  |
| Accrued depreciation (C) | — |  | 4,500 |  | 9,000 |  | 45,000 |  |
| Accrued depreciation (E) | — |  | 7,000 |  | 14,000 |  | 70,000 |  |
| Fixed assets (P) |  | $85,000 |  | $85,000 |  | $85,000 |  | $85,000 |
| Fixed assets (C) |  | 45,000 |  | 45,000 |  | 45,000 |  | 45,000 |
| Fixed assets (E) |  | 70,000 |  | 70,000 |  | 70,000 |  | 70,000 |

ated with the investment in the Cost Company and 1/9 of the unamortized $9,000 negative goodwill associated with the investment in the Equity Company has been disposed of.

**Acquisition of Additional Subsidiary Stock.** Although the recording of an acquisition of additional shares of subsidiary stock is more or less routine, for subsequent illustrative purposes assume that as of July 1, 1981, the Parent Company purchases an additional 5% interest in the Cost Company for $7,000. The purchase would be recorded by:

| | | |
|---|---|---|
| Investment in Cost Company | $7,000 | |
| Cash | | $7,000 |

**Effect(s) of Intercompany Stock Transactions upon Subsequent Consolidations.** The example on pp. 492–495 reviews the effect(s) of sales or purchases of subsidiary stock upon subsequent consolidations. The individual statements reflect the financial position of the respective companies as of December 31, 1981, and the operating results of the respective companies for the year then ended. The consolidated statement columns show how the financial position and operating results would appear on a consolidated basis at that time.

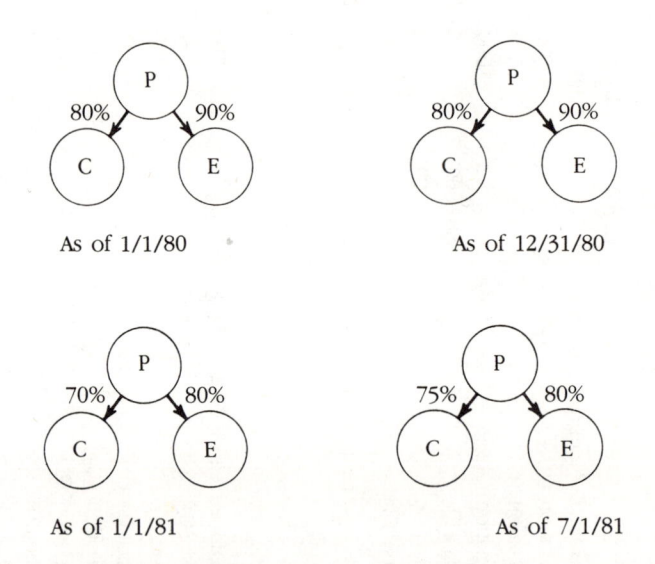

```
        P                          P
   80% / \ 90%               80% / \ 90%
      C   E                     C   E
   As of 1/1/80              As of 12/31/80

        P                          P
   70% / \ 80%               75% / \ 80%
      C   E                     C   E
   As of 1/1/81              As of 7/1/81
```

**Summary.** The disposal of a portion of a subsidiary's stock or the acquisition of additional subsidiary stock is recorded as any other asset disposal or acquisition. A disposal is recorded by (1) recording any asset(s) received, (2) removing the carrying value of the asset from the appropriate account(s), and (3) recording any gain or loss on disposal. The recording of the acquisition of additional shares of subsidiary stock is merely a matter of debiting and crediting the appropriate accounts. When consolidating subsequent to a change in the percent of ownership in a subsidiary, the earnings of the subsidiary in any given period can be reflected in consolidated retained earnings only to the extent of the ownership existing in that period that has been retained to the date of consolidation. It should also be emphasized that any *unamortized* goodwill (either positive or negative) involved in the acquisition of subsidiary stock is disposed of proportionately when the stock is disposed of.

## Indirect Ownership and Mutual Stockholdings

Although the basic procedure for consolidating remains the same when indirect ownership or mutual stockholdings exist, as pointed out in Chapter Fifteen the establishment of reciprocity may become a little more complicated. As a consequence, this phase of consolidated work is emphasized in the review at this time. The establishment of reciprocity is considered primarily from the standpoint of:

1. Major and minor parent.
2. Connecting affiliate.
3. Mutual stockholdings.

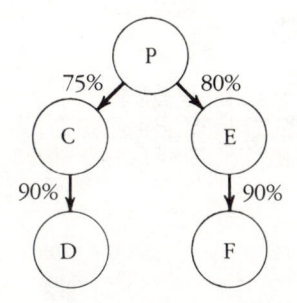

Major and Minor Parent

**Major and Minor Parent.** Assume that as of January 1, 1982, the Cost Company purchases a 90% interest in the D Company for $50,000 and the Equity Company purchases a 90% interest in the F Company for $40,000. Also assume that as of that date the D Company had net assets of $48,000 and the F Company $50,000. The example on pp. 496–499 illustrates the consolidating procedures as of December 31, 1982. The Equity Company carries the investment in the F Company on the equity basis, and the Cost Company carries the investment in the D Company on the cost basis.

## The Parent Company and Subsidiaries
### Consolidated Working Papers
### Statement of Financial Position
### December 31, 1981

| | The Parent Company | The Cost Company | The Equity Company | Adjustments & Eliminations | | Consolidated Financial Position |
|---|---|---|---|---|---|---|
| **Assets** | | | | | | |
| Current assets | $ 344,500 | $ 80,000 | $ 66,000 | | | $ 490,500 |
| Investment in C | 94,500 | | | | $122,250A | 2,850G |
| Investment in E | 96,000 | | | | 104,000B | (8,000)G† |
| Fixed assets (net) | 910,000 | 110,000 | 114,000 | | | 1,134,000 |
| | $1,445,000 | $190,000 | $180,000 | | | $1,619,350 |
| **Equities** | | | | | | |
| Current liabilities | $ 23,500 | $ 7,000 | $ 10,000 | | | $ 40,500 |
| Fixed liabilities | 55,000 | 20,000 | 40,000 | | | 115,000 |
| Stockholders' equity: | | | | | | |
| Capital stock: | | | | | | |
| Parent Company | 1,000,000 | | | | | 1,000,000 |
| Cost Company | | 100,000 | | 75,000A | | 25,000MI |
| Equity Company | | | 100,000 | 80,000B | | 20,000MI |
| Retained earnings: | | | | | | |
| Parent Company | 366,500 | | | | 30,600(1) | 397,100RE |
| Cost Company | | 63,000* | | 47,250A | | 15,750MI |
| Equity Company | | | 30,000 | 24,000B | | 6,000MI |
| | $1,445,000 | $190,000 | $180,000 | $256,850 | $256,850 | $1,619,350 |

*Assume that C's income for 1981 was earned uniformly throughout the year.
(1): To recognize P's interest in C's increase in stockholders' equity since acquisition.

$33,000 × 70% = $23,100
$10,000 × 75% = 7,500
$30,600

A: To eliminate 75% of C's stockholders' equity against the investment account.
B: To eliminate 80% of E's stockholders' equity against the investment account.
†*Proof of goodwill:*
Company E, (8/9 × $9,000) original = ($8,000)
Company C:
7/8 × $4,000 original = $3,500
5% acquisition:
   Cost    $7,000
   Acquired (5% × $153,000)    7,650    (650)
                                        $2,850

THE PARENT COMPANY AND SUBSIDIARIES
CONSOLIDATED WORKING PAPERS
STATEMENT OF INCOME AND RETAINED EARNINGS
YEAR ENDED DECEMBER 31, 1981

|  | The Parent Company | The Cost Company | The Equity Company | Eliminations | Consolidated Income | Consolidated Retained Earnings |
|---|---|---|---|---|---|---|
| *Credits* |  |  |  |  |  |  |
| Net sales | $790,000 | $200,000 | $195,000 |  | $1,185,000 |  |
| Interest income from C | 400 |  |  | $ 400C |  |  |
| Income from E | 16,000 |  |  | 16,000D |  |  |
|  | $806,400 | $200,000 | $195,000 | $16,400 | $1,185,000 |  |
| *Debits* |  |  |  |  |  |  |
| Cost of sales | $560,000 | $150,000 | $145,000 |  | $ 855,000 |  |
| Depreciation | 80,000 | 10,000 | 10,000 |  | 100,000 |  |
| Interest expense | 4,200 | 800 | 2,000 | $ 400C | 6,600 |  |
| Federal income taxes | 80,200 | 19,200 | 18,000 |  | 117,400 |  |
| Net income | 82,000 | 20,000 | 20,000 | 16,000D | 106,000 |  |
|  | $806,400 | $200,000 | $195,000 | $16,400 | $1,185,000 |  |
| Retained earnings, 12/31/80 | $298,000 | $ 43,000 | $ 10,000 |  |  | $314,100† |
| Net income | 82,000 | 20,000 | 20,000 |  |  |  |
| Dividends | (20,000) |  |  |  |  | (20,000) |
| Gain on sale of stock | 6,500 |  |  |  |  | 6,500 |
| Retained earnings, 12/31/81 | $366,500 | $ 63,000 | $ 30,000 |  |  |  |

Apportionment of net income:
Net income                                                                    $ 106,000
Minority interest—C (25% × 20,000)                              $ 5,000
P's 5% claim earned prior to acquisition (5% × 20,000 × ½)         500
Minority interest—E (20% × 20,000)                                4,000     9,500
Consolidated net income—remainder                                         $ 96,500*
Consolidated retained earnings, 12/31/81                                  96,500
                                                                          $397,100

C: To eliminate intercompany interest income and interest expense.
D: To eliminate P's share of E's income.

*Consolidated net income:
P's own earnings ($82,000 − $16,000) =    $66,000
C's: 70% × $20,000            = $14,000
5% × $20,000 × 1/2 =      500              14,500
E's own earnings (80% × 20,000) =          16,000
                                          $96,500

†Consolidated retained earnings as of 12/31/80 as shown on page 487 is $316,400. However, when disposing of a 10% interest in C, a 10% claim against the 1980 earnings of $23,000 was also disposed of. Therefore, consolidated retained earnings as of 12/31/80 after disposing of C stock was 314,100 [316,400 − (10% × 23,000)]. No problem of reconciliation is involved as far as the disposal of Equity stock is concerned, since the carrying value reflects the claim against the 1980 earnings and when the appropriate amount is removed from the investment account, this claim is reflected in the gain or loss on disposal.

## The Parent Company and Subsidiaries
### Consolidated Working Papers
### Statement of Income and Retained Earnings
### Year Ended December 31, 1982

|  | P | C | D | E | F | Eliminations | Consolidated Income | Consolidated Retained Earnings |
|---|---|---|---|---|---|---|---|---|
| *Credits* |  |  |  |  |  |  |  |  |
| Net sales | $800,000 | $210,000 | $50,000 | $200,000 | $30,000 |  | $1,290,000 |  |
| Interest income from C | 400 |  |  |  |  | $ 400*E* |  |  |
| Income from E | 17,200 |  |  |  |  | 17,200*F* |  |  |
| Income (loss) from F |  |  |  | (4,500) |  | (4,500)*F* |  |  |
|  | $817,600 | $210,000 | $50,000 | $195,500 | $30,000 | $13,100 | $1,290,000 |  |
| *Debits* |  |  |  |  |  |  |  |  |
| Cost of sales | $565,900 | $152,200 | $36,900 | $147,000 | $28,100 |  | $ 930,100 |  |
| Depreciation | 82,000 | 10,000 | 4,500 | 10,000 | 6,000 |  | 112,500 |  |
| Interest expense | 4,200 | 800 | 600 | 2,000 | 900 | $ 400*E* | 8,100 |  |
| Federal income taxes | 80,000 | 20,000 | 2,000 | 15,000 | –0– |  | 117,000 |  |
| Net income | 85,500 | 27,000 | 6,000 | 21,500 | (5,000) | 12,700*F* | 122,300 |  |
|  | $817,600 | $210,000 | $50,000 | $195,500 | $30,000 | $13,100 | $1,290,000 |  |

# 16 / Consolidated Statements—Comprehensive Review

| | | | | | |
|---|---|---|---|---|---|
| Retained earnings, 1/1/82 | $366,500 | $ 63,000 | $(2,000) | $ 30,000 | $10,000 |
| Net income | 85,500 | 27,000 | 6,000 | 21,500 | (5,000) |
| Dividends | (20,000) | | | | |
| Retained earnings, 12/31/82 | $432,000 | $ 90,000 | $ 4,000 | $ 51,500 | $ 5,000 |

Apportionment of net income:

| | | |
|---|---|---|
| Net income | | $ 122,300 |
| Minority interest in C (25% × 27,000) and (25% × 90% × 6,000) | $ 8,100 | |
| Minority interest in D (10% × 6,000) | 600 | |
| Minority interest in E (20% × 21,500) | 4,300 | |
| Minority interest in F [10% × (5,000)] | (500) | 12,500 |
| Consolidated net income—remainder | | $ 109,800 |

Consolidated retained earnings, 12/31/82

$397,100*
(20,000)
109,800
$486,900

*See page 495. *E:* To eliminate intercompany income and expense. *F:* To eliminate intercompany income.

THE PARENT COMPANY AND SUBSIDIARIES
CONSOLIDATED WORKING PAPERS
STATEMENT OF FINANCIAL POSITION
DECEMBER 31, 1982

|  | P | C | D |
|---|---|---|---|
| *Assets* | | | |
| Current assets | $ 350,000 | $ 50,000 | $25,000 |
| Investment in C | 94,500 | | |
| Investment in D | | 50,000 | |
| Investment in E | 113,200 | | |
| Investment in F | | | |
| Fixed assets (net) | 950,000 | 120,000 | 45,000 |
| | $1,507,700 | $220,000 | $70,000 |
| *Equities* | | | |
| Current liabilities | $ 25,700 | $ 10,000 | $ 6,000 |
| Fixed liabilities | 50,000 | 20,000 | 10,000 |
| Stockholders' equity: | | | |
| Capital stock: | | | |
| Company P | 1,000,000 | | |
| Company C | | 100,000 | |
| Company D | | | 50,000 |
| Company E | | | |
| Company F | | | |
| Retained earnings: | | | |
| Company P | 432,000 | | |
| Company C | | 90,000 | |
| Company D | | | 4,000 |
| Company E | | | |
| Company F | | | |
| | $1,507,700 | $220,000 | $70,000 |

(1): To recognize C's interest in D's increase in stockholders' equity since acquisition (90% × $6,000).

(2): To recognize P's interest in C's increase in stockholders' equity since acquisition

$33,000* × 70% = $23,100
42,400† × 75% =  31,800
                 $54,900

*Increase from 1/1/80 to 6/30/81.

†$10,000 increase from 7/1/81 to 12/31/81 and $32,400 ($27,000 + $5,400) increase during 1982.

## 16 / Consolidated Statements — Comprehensive Review

### The Parent Company and Subsidiaries
### Consolidated Working Papers
### Statement of Financial Position (Continued)

| E | F | Adjustments & Eliminations Debit | Adjustments & Eliminations Credit | Consolidated Financial Position |
|---|---|---|---|---|
| $ 40,000 | $20,000 |  |  | $ 485,000 |
|  |  | $ 54,900(2) | $146,550A | 2,850G |
|  |  | 5,400(1) | 48,600B | 6,800G |
|  |  |  | 121,200C | (8,000)G |
| 35,500 |  |  | 40,500D | (5,000)G |
| 129,500 | 60,000 |  |  | 1,304,500 |
| $205,000 | $80,000 |  |  | $1,786,150 |
|  |  |  |  |  |
| $ 13,500 | $20,000 |  |  | $ 75,200 |
| 40,000 | 15,000 |  |  | 135,000 |
|  |  |  |  |  |
|  |  |  |  | 1,000,000 |
|  |  | 75,000A |  | 25,000MI |
|  |  | 45,000B |  | 5,000MI |
| 100,000 |  | 80,000C |  | 20,000MI |
|  | 40,000 | 36,000D |  | 4,000MI |
|  |  |  |  |  |
|  |  |  | 54,900(2) | 486,900RE |
|  |  | 71,550A | 5,400(1) | 23,850MI |
|  |  | 3,600B |  | 400MI |
| 51,500 |  | 41,200C |  | 10,300MI |
|  | 5,000 | 4,500D |  | 500MI |
| $205,000 | $80,000 | $417,150 | $417,150 | $1,786,150 |

A: To eliminate 75% of C's stockholders' equity against the investment account.
B: To eliminate 90% of D's stockholders' equity against the investment account.
C: To eliminate 80% of E's stockholders' equity against the investment account.
D: To eliminate 90% of F's stockholders' equity against the investment account.

**The Parent Company and Subsidiaries**
**Consolidated Working Papers**
**Statement of Income and Retained Earnings**
**Year Ended December 31, 1983**

|  | P | C | D | E | F | Eliminations | Consolidated Income | Consolidated Retained Earnings |
|---|---|---|---|---|---|---|---|---|
| *Credits* |  |  |  |  |  |  |  |  |
| Net sales | $820,000 | $214,000 | $70,000 | $210,000 | $50,000 |  | $1,364,000 |  |
| Interest income from C | 400 |  |  |  |  | $ 400*F* |  |  |
| Income from E | 23,200 |  |  |  |  | 23,200*G* |  |  |
| Income from F |  |  |  | 9,000 |  | 9,000*G* |  |  |
|  | $843,600 | $214,000 | $70,000 | $219,000 | $50,000 | $32,600 | $1,364,000 |  |
| *Debits* |  |  |  |  |  |  |  |  |
| Cost of sales | $587,400 | $151,200 | $48,900 | $158,000 | $32,100 |  | $977,600 |  |
| Depreciation | 80,000 | 10,000 | 4,500 | 10,000 | 6,000 |  | 110,500 |  |
| Interest expense | 4,200 | 800 | 600 | 2,000 | 900 | $ 400*F* | 8,100 |  |
| Federal income tax | 82,000 | 22,000 | 4,000 | 20,000 | 1,000 |  | 129,000 |  |
| Net income | 90,000 | 30,000 | 12,000 | 29,000 | 10,000 | 32,200*G* | 138,800 |  |
|  | $843,600 | $214,000 | $70,000 | $219,000 | $50,000 | $32,600 | $1,364,000 |  |

## 16 / Consolidated Statements—Comprehensive Review

|  |  |  |  |  |  |  |
|---|---|---|---|---|---|---|
| Retained earnings, 1/1/83 | $432,000 | $ 90,000 | $ 4,000 | $ 51,500 | $ 5,000 | $486,900 |
| Net income |  | 90,000 | 12,000 | 29,000 | 10,000 |  |
| Dividends |  | (20,000) |  |  |  | (20,000) |
| Retained earnings, 12/31/83 | $502,000 | $120,000 | $16,000 | $ 80,500 | $15,000 |  |

Apportionment of income:

| Net income |  | $ 138,800 |
|---|---|---|
| Minority interest in C (15% × 30,000) + (15% × 90% × 12,000) | $ 6,120 |  |
| Minority interest in D (10% × 12,000) | 1,200 |  |
| Minority interest in E (20% × 29,000) + (20% × 10% × 30,000) |  |  |
| + (20% × 10% × 90% × 12,000) | 6,616 |  |
| Minority interest in F (10% × 10,000) | 1,000 | 14,936 |
| Consolidated net income—remainder |  | $ 123,864 |
| Consolidated retained earnings, 12/31/83 |  | 123,864 |
|  |  | $590,764 |

F: To eliminate intercompany income and expense.
G: To eliminate intercompany income.

The Parent Company and Subsidiaries

Consolidated Working Papers

Statement of Financial Position

December 31, 1983

|  | P | C | D |
|---|---|---|---|
| *Assets* | | | |
| Current assets | $ 410,000 | $ 90,000 | $40,500 |
| Investment in C | 94,500 | | |
| Investment in C | | | |
| Investment in D | | 50,000 | |
| Investment in E | 136,400 | | |
| Investment in F | | | |
| Fixed assets (net) | 930,000 | 110,000 | 40,500 |
| | $1,570,900 | $250,000 | $81,000 |
| *Equities* | | | |
| Current liabilities | $ 18,900 | $ 10,000 | $ 5,000 |
| Fixed liabilities | 50,000 | 20,000 | 10,000 |
| Stockholders' equity: | | | |
| Capital stock: | | | |
|   Company P | 1,000,000 | | |
|   Company C | | 100,000 | |
|   Company D | | | 50,000 |
|   Company E | | | |
|   Company F | | | |
| Retained earnings: | | | |
|   Company P | 502,000 | | |
|   Company C | | 120,000 | |
|   Company D | | | 16,000 |
|   Company E | | | |
|   Company F | | | |
| | $1,570,900 | $250,000 | $81,000 |

Footnotes on page 506.

## The Parent Company and Subsidiaries
### Consolidated Working Papers
### Statement of Financial Position
#### (Continued)

| | | Adjustments & Eliminations | | Consolidated Financial Position |
|---|---|---|---|---|
| E | F | | | |
| $ 35,000 | $36,000 | | | $ 611,500 |
| | | $85,500(2) | $177,150A | 2,850G |
| 20,000 | | 4,080(3) | 23,620B | 460G |
| | | 16,200(1) | 59,400C | 6,800G |
| | | 3,264(4) | 147,664D | (8,000)G |
| 44,500 | | | 49,500E | (5,000)G |
| 136,000 | 54,000 | | | 1,270,500 |
| $235,500 | $90,000 | | | $1,879,110 |
| | | | | |
| $ 15,000 | $20,000 | | | $ 68,900 |
| 40,000 | 15,000 | | | 135,000 |
| | | | | 1,000,000 |
| | | 10,000B | | |
| | | 75,000A | | 15,000MI |
| | | 45,000C | | 5,000MI |
| 100,000 | | 80,000D | | 20,000MI |
| | 40,000 | 36,000E | | 4,000MI |
| | | | 3,264(4) | |
| | | | 85,500(2) | 590,764RE |
| | | 13,620B | 16,200(1) | |
| | | 102,150A | | 20,430MI |
| | | 14,400C | | 1,600MI |
| 80,500 | | 67,664D | 4,080(3) | 16,916MI |
| | 15,000 | 13,500E | | 1,500MI |
| $235,500 | $90,000 | $566,378 | $566,378 | $1,879,110 |

Footnotes on page 506.

## The Parent Company and Subsidiaries
### Consolidated Working Papers
Statement of Financial Position as of December 31, 1984

|  | P | C | D |
|---|---|---|---|
| *Assets* | | | |
| Current assets | $ 489,900 | $114,000 | $48,000 |
| Investment in C | 94,500 | | |
| Investment in C | | | |
| Investment in D | | 50,000 | |
| Investment in D | | | |
| Investment in E | 166,520 | | |
| Investment in F | | | |
| Investment in F | | | 6,000 |
| Fixed assets (net) | 900,000 | 110,000 | 40,000 |
| | $1,650,920 | $274,000 | $94,000 |
| *Equities* | | | |
| Current liabilities | $ 20,000 | $ 11,000 | $ 5,000 |
| Fixed liabilities | 50,000 | 10,000 | 10,000 |
| Stockholders' equity: | | | |
| Capital stock: | | | |
| Company P | 1,000,000 | | |
| Company C | | 100,000 | |
| Company D | | | 50,000 |
| Company E | | | |
| Company F | | | |
| Retained earnings: | | | |
| Company P | 580,920 | | |
| Company C | | 153,000 | |
| Company D | | | 29,000 |
| Company E | | | |
| Company F | | | |
| | $1,650,920 | $274,000 | $94,000 |

Footnotes on pages 506–507.

## The Parent Company and Subsidiaries
### Consolidated Working Papers
Statement of Financial Position (Continued)

| E | F | Adjustments & Eliminations | | Consolidated Financial Position |
|---|---|---|---|---|
| $ 52,000 | $ 45,000 | | | $ 748,900 |
| | | $120,375(3) | $212,025D | 2,850G |
| 20,000 | | 8,730(7) | 28,270F | 460G |
| | | 29,700(2) | 72,900C | 6,800G |
| | 7,000 | 1,500(4) | 8,100A | 400G |
| | | 6,984(8) | 182,584G | (8,000)G |
| | | 1,080(6) | | |
| 61,150 | | 1,350(5) | 67,500E | (5,000)G |
| | | 2,000(1) | 7,500B | 500G |
| 130,000 | 50,000 | | | 1,230,000 |
| $263,150 | $102,000 | | | $1,976,910 |
| | | | | |
| $ 15,000 | $ 13,500 | | | $ 64,500 |
| 30,000 | 15,000 | | | 115,000 |
| | | | | |
| | | | | 1,000,000 |
| | | 10,000F | | 15,000MI |
| | | 75,000D | | |
| | | 45,000C | | |
| | | 5,000A | | |
| 100,000 | | 80,000G | | 20,000MI |
| | 40,000 | 36,000E | | |
| | | 4,000B | | |
| | | | 6,984(8) | 709,359RE |
| | | | 1,080(6) | |
| | | | 120,375(3) | |
| | | 18,270F | 29,700(2) | 27,405MI |
| | | 137,025D | | |
| | | 27,900C | 2,000(1) | |
| | | 3,100A | | |
| 118,150 | | 102,584G | 8,730(7) | 25,646MI |
| | | | 1,350(5) | |
| | 33,500 | 31,500E | 1,500(4) | |
| | | 3,500B | | |
| $263,150 | $102,000 | $750,598 | $750,598 | $1,976,910 |

Footnotes on pages 506–507.

Footnotes for pages 502–503

(1): To recognize C's interest in D's increase in stockholders' equity since acquisition (90% × $18,000).

(2): To recognize P's interest in C's increase in stockholders' equity since acquisition:

$$\begin{array}{r} \$33{,}000^* \times 70\% = \$23{,}100 \\ 83{,}200\dagger \times 75\% = \underline{\phantom{0}62{,}400} \\ \underline{\$85{,}500} \end{array}$$

*Increase from 1/1/80 to 6/30/81.

†$10,000 increase from 7/1/81 to 12/31/81, $32,400 ($27,000 + $5,400) increase during 1982, and $40,800 ($30,000 + $10,800) increase during 1983.

(3): To recognize E's interest in C's increase in stockholders' equity since acquisition. Since E only owns a 10% interest in C, its interest in C's change in stockholders' equity has not been recognized (10% × $40,800) = $4,080.

(4): To recognize P's 80% interest in E's 10% interest in C's increase in stockholders' equity (80% × $4,080).

A: To eliminate 75% of C's stockholders' equity against the investment account.
B: To eliminate 10% of C's stockholders' equity against the investment account.
C: To eliminate 90% of D's stockholders' equity against the investment account.
D: To eliminate 80% of E's stockholders' equity against the investment account.
E: To eliminate 90% of F's stockholders' equity against the investment account.

---

Footnotes for pages 504–505

(1) To recognize D's 10% interest in the increase in F's stockholders' equity since acquisition (10% × $20,000*).

*Let F = Company F's increase in stockholders' equity since acquisition on a consolidated basis.

Let D = Company D's increase in stockholders' equity since acquisition on a consolidated basis.

$F = \$18{,}500 + .1D$
$D = \$13{,}000 + .1F$
$F = \$18{,}500 + .1\,(13{,}000 + .1F)$     $D = \$13{,}000 + .1F$
$F = \$18{,}500 + \$1{,}300 + .01F$     $D = \$13{,}000 + .1\,(20{,}000)$
$.99F = \$19{,}800$     $D = \$13{,}000 + \$2{,}000$
$F = \underline{\$20{,}000}$     $D = \underline{\$15{,}000}$

## 16 / Consolidated Statements — Comprehensive Review

(2): To recognize C's 90% interest in the increase in D's stockholders' equity since acquisition:

$$\begin{array}{r}\text{Prior to 1984, } 90\% \times \$18,000 = \$16,200 \\ 1984, 90\% \times \$15,000 = \underline{13,500} \\ \$29,700 \end{array}$$

(3): To recognize P's 75% interest in the increase in C's stockholders' equity since acquisition:

$$\begin{array}{r}\text{Prior to 1984, } \$ 85,500 \\ 1984, \quad 24,750 \ (\$33,000 \times 75\%) \\ \underline{10,125} \ (\$13,500 \times 75\%) \\ \$120,375 \end{array}$$

(4): To recognize F's 10% interest in the increase in D's stockholders' equity since acquisition (10% × $15,000).

(5): To recognize E's 90% interest in F's 10% interest in the increase in D's stockholders' equity since acquisition (90% × $1,500).

(6): To recognize P's 80% interest in E's 90% interest in F's 10% interest in the increase in D's stockholders' equity since acquisition [see (5) above].

(7): To recognize E's 10% interest in C's increase in stockholders' equity since acquisition. Since E has only a 10% interest in C this interest has not been recognized by E.

$$\begin{array}{r}\text{Prior to 1984, } \$4,080 \\ 1984, \quad 3,300 \ (\$33,000 \times 10\%) \\ \underline{1,350} \ (\$13,500 \times 10\%) \\ \$8,730 \end{array}$$

(8): To recognize P's 80% interest in E's 10% interest in C. [Same reason as (7) above.] 80% × $8,730 = $6,984.

A: To eliminate 10% of D's stockholders' equity against the investment account (F's investment in D).

B: To eliminate 10% of F's stockholders' equity against the investment account (D's investment in F).

C: To eliminate 90% of D's stockholders' equity against the investment account (C's investment in D).

D; To eliminate 75% of C's stockholders' equity against the investment account (P's investment in C).

E: To eliminate 90% of F's stockholders' equity against the investment account (E's investment in F).

F: To eliminate 10% of C's stockholders' equity against the investment account (E's investment in C).

G: To eliminate 80% of E's stockholders' equity against the investment account (P's investment in E).

THE PARENT COMPANY AND SUBSIDIARIES

CONSOLIDATED WORKING PAPERS

STATEMENT OF INCOME AND RETAINED EARNINGS

YEAR ENDED DECEMBER 31, 1984

|  | P | C | D |
|---|---|---|---|
| *Credits* | | | |
| Net sales | $840,000 | $220,000 | $70,000 |
| Interest income from C | 400 | | |
| Income from E | 30,120 | | |
| Income from F | | | |
| | $870,520 | $220,000 | $70,000 |
| *Debits* | | | |
| Cost of sales | $599,400 | $151,400 | $47,200 |
| Depreciation | 78,000 | 10,000 | 4,200 |
| Interest expense | 4,200 | 600 | 600 |
| Federal income tax | 90,000 | 25,000 | 5,000 |
| Net income | 98,920 | 33,000 | 13,000 |
| | $870,520 | $220,000 | $70,000 |
| Retained earnings, 1/1/84 | $502,000 | $120,000 | $16,000 |
| Net income | 98,920 | 33,000 | 13,000 |
| Dividends | (20,000) | | |
| Retained earnings, 12/31/84 | $580,920 | $153,000 | $29,000 |

Apportionment of net income:

Net income

Minority interest in C

Minority interest in E

Consolidated net income — remainder.

Consolidated retained earnings, 12/31/84

*H:* To eliminate intercompany income and expense.

*I:* To eliminate intercompany income.

*Minority interest in C has a claim against the following earnings:

| | |
|---|---|
| 15% × $33,000 (earned by C) | $4,950 |
| 15% × 90% × $15,000 (D's earnings on a consolidated basis) | 2,025 |
| | $6,975 |

## The Parent Company and Subsidiaries
### Consolidated Working Papers
### Statement of Income and Retained Earnings
(Continued)

| E | F | Eliminations | Consolidated Income | Consolidated Retained Earnings |
|---|---|---|---|---|
| $230,000 | $60,000 |  | $1,420,000 |  |
|  |  | $ 400 H |  |  |
|  |  | 30,120 I |  |  |
| 16,650 |  | 16,650 I |  |  |
| $246,650 | $60,000 | $47,170 | $1,420,000 |  |
|  |  |  |  |  |
| $175,700 | $28,600 |  | $1,002,300 |  |
| 9,800 | 6,000 |  | 108,000 |  |
| 1,500 | 900 | $ 400 H | 7,400 |  |
| 22,000 | 6,000 |  | 148,000 |  |
| 37,650 | 18,500 | 46,770 I | 154,300 |  |
| $246,650 | $60,000 | $47,170 | $1,420,000 |  |
| $80,500 | $15,000 |  |  | $590,764 |
| 37,650 | 18,500 |  |  |  |
|  |  |  |  | (20,000) |
| $118,150 | $33,500 |  |  |  |
|  |  |  | $ 154,300 |  |
|  |  | $ 6,975 * |  |  |
|  |  | 8,730 † | 15,705 |  |
|  |  |  | $ 138,595 | 138,595 |
|  |  |  |  | $709,359 |

†Minority interest in E has a claim against the following earnings:
20% × $37,650 (recognized by E) — $7,530
20% × 10% × $33,000 (earned by C) — 660
20% × 10% × 90% × $15,000 (D's earnings on a consolidated basis) — 270
20% × 90% × $1,500 [F's earnings on a consolidated basis not initially recognized by E (see adjustment 5)] — 270
$8,730

## The Parent Company and Subsidiaries
## Consolidated Working Papers
### December 31, 1984

| Debits | P | C | D | E | F | Adjustments & Eliminations* | | Consolidated Income | Consolidated Retained Earnings | Minority | Consolidated Financial Position |
|---|---|---|---|---|---|---|---|---|---|---|---|
| Current assets | $ 489,900 | $114,000 | $ 48,000 | $ 52,000 | $ 45,000 | | | | | | $ 748,900 |
| Investment in C | 94,500 | | | | | | $ 85,500(3) | | | | 2,850G |
| Investment in C | | | | | | | 4,080(7) | | | | 460G |
| Investment in D | | 50,000 | | 20,000 | | | 16,200(2) | | | | 6,800G |
| Investment in D | | | | | 7,000 | | | | | | 400G |
| Investment in E | 166,520 | | | | | | 6,600A | | | | |
| | | | | | | | 30,120(9) | | | | |
| Investment in F | | | | 61,150 | | 3,264(8) | 147,664G | | | | (8,000)G |
| | | | | | | | 16,650(10) | | | | |
| Investment in F | | | | | | | 49,500E | | | | (5,000)G |
| | | | | | | | 5,500B | | | | 500G |
| Fixed assets (net) | 900,000 | 110,000 | 40,000 | 130,000 | 50,000 | | | | | | 1,230,000 |
| Cost of sales | 599,400 | 151,400 | 47,200 | 175,700 | 28,600 | | | $1,002,300 | | | |
| Depreciation | 78,000 | 10,000 | 4,200 | 9,800 | 6,000 | | | 108,000 | | | |
| Interest expense | 4,200 | 600 | 600 | 1,500 | 900 | | 400H | 7,400 | | | |
| Federal income taxes | 90,000 | 25,000 | 5,000 | 22,000 | 6,000 | | | 148,000 | | | |
| Dividends paid | 20,000 | | | | | | | | $ 20,000 | | |
| | $2,442,520 | $461,000 | $151,000 | $472,150 | $143,500 | | | | $ 20,000 | —0— | $1,976,910 |
| Credits | | | | | | | | | | | |
| Sales (net) | $ 840,000 | $220,000 | $ 70,000 | $230,000 | $ 60,000 | | | $1,420,000 | | | |
| Interest income from C | 400 | | | | | 400H | | | | | |
| Income from E | 30,120 | | | | | 30,120(9) | | | | | |
| Income from F | | | | 16,650 | | 16,650(10) | | | | | |
| Current liabilities | 20,000 | 11,000 | 5,000 | 15,000 | 13,500 | | | | | | $ 64,500 |
| Fixed liabilities | 50,000 | 10,000 | 10,000 | 30,000 | 15,000 | | | | | | 115,000 |
| Stockholders' equity: | | | | | | | | | | | |
| Capital stock: | | | | | | | | | | | |
| Company P | 1,000,000 | | | | | | | | | | 1,000,000 |
| Company C | | 100,000 | | | | 75,000D | | | | | |

|  |  |  |  |  |  |  |  |  |
|---|---|---|---|---|---|---|---|---|
| Company D |  |  |  | 10,000F |  |  | $15,000 |  |
|  |  | 50,000 |  | 45,000C |  |  |  |  |
|  |  |  |  | 5,000A |  |  |  |  |
| Company E |  |  | 100,000 | 80,000G |  |  | 20,000 |  |
| Company F |  |  |  | 36,000E |  |  |  |  |
|  |  |  | 40,000 | 4,000B |  |  |  |  |
| Retained earnings, 1/1/84: |  |  |  |  |  |  |  |  |
| Company P | 502,000 |  |  |  | 3,264(8) | $590,764 |  |  |
| Company C |  | 120,000 |  |  | 85,500(3) |  |  |  |
| Company D |  |  |  | 102,150D | 16,200(2) |  | 20,430 |  |
|  |  |  |  | 13,620F |  |  |  |  |
|  |  | 16,000 |  | 14,400C |  |  |  |  |
|  |  |  |  | 1,600A |  |  |  |  |
| Company E |  |  | 80,500 | 67,664G | 4,080(7) |  | 16,916 |  |
| Company F |  |  |  | 13,500E |  |  |  |  |
|  |  |  | 15,000 | 1,500B |  |  |  |  |
|  | $2,444,520 | $461,000 | $151,000 | $472,150 | $143,500 | $625,648 | $625,648 |  |
| Income credits |  |  |  |  |  | $1,420,000 |  |  |
| Income debits |  |  |  |  |  | 1,265,700 |  |  |
| Net income |  |  |  |  |  | $ 154,300 |  |  |
| Apportionment of net income: |  |  |  |  |  |  |  |  |
| Minority interest: |  |  |  |  |  |  |  |  |
| C's 15% |  |  |  |  |  | 6,975 | 6,975 |  |
| E's 20% |  |  |  |  |  | 8,730 | 8,730 |  |
|  |  |  |  |  |  | $ 138,595 |  |  |
| Consolidated net income (remainder) |  |  |  |  |  |  | 138,595 |  |
|  |  |  |  |  |  |  | $729,359 |  |
|  |  |  |  |  |  |  | 20,000 |  |
|  |  |  |  |  |  |  | $709,359 |  |
| Consolidated retained earnings, 12/31/84 |  |  |  |  |  |  |  | 709,359RE |
| Minority interest |  |  |  |  |  |  | $88,051 | 88,051MI |
|  |  |  |  |  |  |  |  | $1,976,910 |

*The eliminations are lettered to correspond with the lettering in the preceding illustration. The adjustments were numbered where possible as the adjustments were numbered in the preceding illustration. However, on the work sheet there are no adjustments similar to 1, 4, 5, and 6 on the preceding statement approach. Likewise, the adjustments numbered 9 and 10 are peculiar to the trial balance approach.

**Connecting Affiliate.** Assume that as of January 1, 1983, the Equity Company acquires a 10% interest in the Cost Company for $20,000. As of December 31, 1983, the financial statements would be consolidated as shown on pages 500–503.

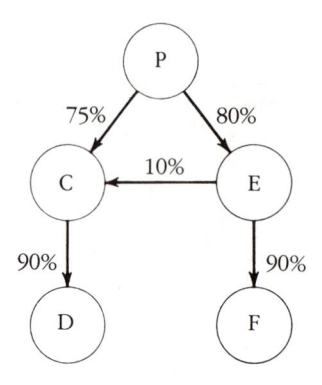

Connecting Affiliate

**Mutual Stockholdings.** Assume that as of January 1, 1984, the F Company acquires a 10% interest in the D Company for $7,000 and that the D Company, in turn, acquires a 10% interest in the F Company for $6,000. As of December 31, 1984, the financial statements would be consolidated as shown on pages 504–509.

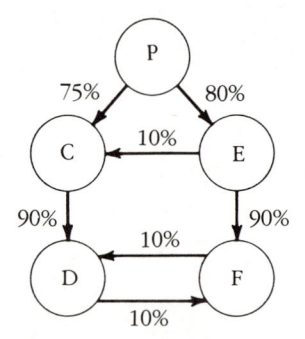

Mutual Stockholdings

**Summary.** When consolidating a group of companies in which some form of indirect ownership or mutual stockholdings exists, it is essential that the establishment of reciprocity start on the lowest strata or tier of subsidiaries. The establishment of reciprocity should then progress up to the top tier or apex where the major parent is found. It is likewise better to progress up the consolidation ladder rung by rung rather than to bypass some of the rungs.

## Trial Balance Approach

The preceding illustrations in this chapter have been based primarily on the assumption that the consolidated statements were being prepared from the financial statements of the companies involved. The trial balance approach is reviewed in the working papers on pages 510–511. For comparative purposes, the situation illustrated is the same as the immediately preceding one where the statements were being consolidated for the year ending December 31, 1984.

**Summary.** When the trial balance approach is used, reciprocity must be established as of the beginning of the period rather than as of the end of the period, as is the procedure when the statement approach is used. This modification in the basic procedure is necessary because consolidated net income is added to the beginning balance of consolidated retained earnings in the working papers. If reciprocity were established as of the end of the period, the parent company's share of a subsidiary's earnings for the period would be taken into consolidated retained earnings twice.

## PROBLEMS

### Problem 16-1

During the current year, Company P acquired an 80% interest in the capital stock of two existing companies: S and T. Company P issued 100,000 shares of its $50 par value common stock in exchange for 40,000 shares of the $25 par value common stock of Company S. P Company acquired 800 shares of T Company no-par common for $400,000 in cash. The investment in S was recorded at the par value of the stock issued and the investment in T at the cash price.

In the process of consolidating the three companies, it is determined that as of the date of acquisition the book value of the investment in S and in T is smaller than the book value of an 80% interest in the net assets of the respective companies as follows: S Company—$800,000; T Company—$160,000. At the time of the acquisition the approximate quoted market values of the common shares of the three companies were as follows: P—$60-65; S—$150-160; T—$480-495.

1. Explain the possible reasons why the cost of stock of a subsidiary can be less than the book value of the underlying net assets on the books of the subsidiary, and recommend how these amounts should be handled on the consolidated financial statements in each situation, giving reasons for your recommendation.
2. Discuss the specific situation of consolidating S Company and T Company in view of the data given and the reasons you present in (1) above.

(AICPA adapted)

## Problem 16-2

A corporation with one wholly owned subsidiary does not wish to prepare consolidated financial statements primarily on the grounds that the investment in the capital stock of the subsidiary is less than 1% of the total assets of the parent. Indicate circumstances under which it would be proper to follow the parent's wishes, and circumstances under which it would be necessary to insist upon consolidation of statements. Give particular thought to the financial affairs of the subsidiary and the relations between parent and subsidiary. (AICPA adapted)

## Problem 16-3

The P Corporation has made substantial advances of cash to S Corporation, its wholly owned subsidiary. S uses some of the cash to purchase a block of P Corporation stock in the open market. S also issues some of its own stock, which it sells to P, using the cash received to repay the advances received from P.

You are to give your opinion of each of the following practices:

1. The stock of P owned by S is shown as an "Investment" on the consolidated statement of financial position of P and S.
2. Dividends on the stock of S are shown as a nonoperating income on the income statement of P.
3. The total of dividends declared but not paid on the stock of P are shown as a current liability on the consolidated statement of financial position of P and S.

(AICPA adapted)

## Problem 16-4

The following data pertain to a parent company and its subsidiary on the dates indicated:

|  | Jan. 1, 1979 | Dec. 31, 1979 | Dec. 31, 1980 | Dec. 31, 1981 |
|---|---|---|---|---|
| *Parent Company:* | | | | |
| Investment in subsidiary | $256,000 | $256,000 | $238,000 | $280,000 |
| Retained earnings | 270,000 | 320,000 | 296,000 | 310,000 |
| *Subsidiary Company:* | | | | |
| Capital stock ($100 par) | 200,000 | 200,000 | 200,000 | 200,000 |
| Retained earnings | 100,000 | 124,000 | 140,000 | 160,000 |

The parent company purchased 1,600 shares of subsidiary stock on January 1, 1979, sold 100 shares on January 1, 1980, and purchased 200 shares on January 1, 1981. The investment account was charged with the cost of stock purchased and credited with the proceeds from the stock sold. The parent company has made no other entries in the investment account.

### Required:

Prepare statements showing the amounts of (1) goodwill, (2) retained earnings, and (3) minority interest that would appear on the consolidated statements of financial position as of January 1, 1979, and December 31, 1979, 1980, and 1981. (Assume that goodwill is not being amortized at this time.)

## Problem 16-5

The following data pertain to a parent company and its subsidiaries on the dates indicated:

|  | Jan. 1, 1979 | Dec. 31, 1979 | Dec. 31, 1980 | Dec. 31, 1981 |
|---|---|---|---|---|
| *Parent Company:* | | | | |
| Investment in S-1 | $198,000 | $198,000 | $138,000 | $183,000 |
| Investment in S-2 | 180,000 | 164,000 | 206,000 | 142,000 |
| Retained earnings | 420,000 | 470,000 | 460,000 | 490,000 |
| *Subsidiary S-1:* | | | | |
| Capital stock ($100 par) | 100,000 | 100,000 | 100,000 | 100,000 |
| Retained earnings | 110,000 | 110,000 | 140,000 | 165,000 |
| *Subsidiary S-2:* | | | | |
| Capital stock ($100 par) | 100,000 | 100,000 | 100,000 | 100,000 |
| Retained earnings | 110,000 | 90,000 | 120,000 | 100,000 |

The parent company purchased 900 shares of S-1 stock on January 1, 1979, sold 150 shares on January 1, 1980, and purchased 100 shares on January 1, 1981. The S-1 investment account was charged with the cost of the stock purchased and credited with the proceeds from the stock sold. The parent company has made no other entries in the S-1 investment account.

The parent company purchased 800 shares of S-2 stock on January 1, 1979, and 100 shares on January 1, 1980. The parent company sold 200 shares of S-2 stock on January 1, 1981. The S-2 investment account is carried on the *equity* basis, except that it was credited with the proceeds from the stock sold.

*Required:*
Prepare statements showing the amounts of (1) goodwill, (2) retained earnings, and (3) minority interest that would appear on the consolidated statements of financial position as of January 1, 1979, and December 31, 1979, 1980, and 1981. (Assume that goodwill is not being amortized at this time.)

## Problem 16-6

From the following information relative to the X Company and its wholly owned subsidiary, the Y Company, prepare:
(1) A consolidated statement of financial position, and (2) a consolidated statement of income and retained earnings.

|  | X Company | Y Company |
|---|---|---|
| Cash | $ 250,000 | $ 130,000 |
| Marketable securities | 400,000 | 150,000 |

| | | |
|---|---:|---:|
| Accounts receivable, customers | 1,250,000 | 540,000 |
| Allowance for doubtful accounts | (25,000) | (10,000) |
| Subsidiary current account | 100,000 | |
| Inventories | 1,100,000 | 600,000 |
| Treasury stock | 50,000 | |
| Stock of Y company (at cost) | 150,000 | |
| Advances to subsidiary | 420,000 | |
| Plant, property, and equipment (net) | 1,525,000 | 710,000 |
| | $ 5,220,000 | $2,120,000 |
| Accounts payable | $ 575,000 | $ 185,000 |
| Accrued expenses | 350,000 | 100,000 |
| Due to X Company | | 90,000 |
| Estimated federal taxes | 525,000 | 275,000 |
| Advances from parent | | 420,000 |
| Capital stock | 1,000,000 | 150,000 |
| Retained earnings, 1/1/80 | 2,420,000 | 825,000 |
| Net income | 650,000 | 250,000 |
| Dividends paid | (300,000) | (175,000) |
| | $ 5,220,000 | $2,120,000 |
| Net sales | $10,000,000 | $4,600,000 |
| Cost of goods sold | (6,700,000) | (3,210,000) |
| Selling, general and administrative | (2,400,000) | (900,000) |
| Other income (net) | 250,000 | 20,000 |
| Estimated federal income taxes | (500,000) | (260,000) |
| Net income | $ 650,000 | $ 250,000 |

*Additional information:*

(1) Marketable securities of the subsidiary includes $20,000 cost of shares of the parent company's stock acquired for payment of bonuses.
(2) Merchandise billed at $10,000 in transit from the parent to the subsidiary has not been recorded by the subsidiary.
(3) It has been determined that there is intercompany profit of $20,000 in the portion of the subsidiary's inventory purchased from the parent. The equivalent figure at December 31, 1979 was $10,000.
(4) The parent's equity in the subsidiary was $200,000 at the date of acquisition.
(5) Sales by the parent to the subsidiary in 1980 totaled $1,700,000.
(6) The parent has made a service charge of $50,000 to the subsidiary which is included in other income of the parent and in administrative expenses of the subsidiary.

(AICPA adapted)

## Problem 16-7

Following are trial balances of A Company and its subsidiary, B Company, as of December 31, 1980. From them and the other information given, prepare consolidated working papers.

## 16 / Consolidated Statements — Comprehensive Review

| Debits | A Company | B Company |
|---|---|---|
| Cash | $   545,200 | $   267,300 |
| Receivables, customers | 187,000 | 375,400 |
| Temporary investments | 1,575,300 | 556,000 |
| Inventories | 398,200 | 146,800 |
| Investment, B Company | | |
|   Bonds | 198,000 | |
|   Capital stock | 300,000 | |
|   Advances | 226,600 | |
| Investment, A Company bonds (at par) | | 30,000 |
| Fixed assets | 2,311,000 | 714,700 |
| Unamortized bond discount | | 2,700 |
| Goodwill | | 90,000 |
| Cost of sales | 3,280,500 | 1,676,100 |
| Selling and administrative expense | 333,000 | 261,000 |
| Depreciation expense | 184,000 | 42,600 |
| Interest expense | 24,000 | 19,700 |
| Bond discount amortized | | 300 |
| Amortization of premium on B Company bonds owned | 2,000 | |
| Provision for income taxes | 600,000 | 420,000 |
| Dividends paid | 100,000 | 20,000 |
| | $10,264,800 | $4,622,600 |

| Credits | | |
|---|---|---|
| Accounts payable | $     79,200 | $     69,500 |
| Accrued income taxes | 624,800 | 431,400 |
| Other accrued expense | 10,000 | 4,000 |
| Advances from A | | 226,600 |
| Allowance for bad debts | 2,500 | 3,200 |
| Allowance for depreciation | 1,420,600 | 302,300 |
| Allowance for product warranty | 1,000,000 | 445,000 |
| First-mortgage 3% bonds | 800,000 | |
| First-mortgage 4% bonds | | 200,000 |
| Capital stock | 1,000,000 | 200,000 |
| Capital in excess of par | 50,200 | |
| Retained earnings, 12/31/79 | 424,700 | 90,200 |
| Sales | 4,797,300 | 2,644,500 |
| Interest: temporary investments | 20,400 | 5,000 |
|     intercompany bonds | 7,200 | 900 |
|     advances to B | 11,700 | |
| Dividend received | 16,200 | |
| | $10,264,800 | $4,622,600 |

A Company on January 1, 1972, purchased from security holders its 81% interest in the capital stock of B Company and 90% interest in B Company bonds, the total consideration being $516,000, of which $216,000 was allocated to the bonds. The purpose of the purchase was to obtain additional manufacturing facilities and B Company's established markets for products similar to A Company's regular line. The retained earnings of B Company as shown by its books on December 31, 1971, was $150,000. The 25-year first-mortgage 4% bonds had been originally marketed on December 31, 1964 to net 96¼.

For several years a part of the output of B Company has been an intermediate product sold to A Company at a uniform markup of 20% (on sales). Sales of this character recorded on B Company's books were $258,000 for 1980, of which $64,500 remained in A Company's inventory at the end of the year; the corresponding amount in A Company's inventory at the beginning of the year was $82,000.

A Company has made advances to B Company on which the latter pays interest semi-annually at the rate of 6% per annum. During 1980 (on July 1) an additional $50,000 was advanced.

A Company constructed a building, at a cost of $100,000, which, on January 1, 1975, was turned over to B Company for its use at a price of $120,000. Depreciation of 3% has been accrued thereon since that date. (AICPA adapted)

## Problem 16-8

Midway Sales, Inc., and Kent Realty Corp. are wholly owned subsidiaries of the Davis Manufacturing Co., Inc. The parent corporation manufactures electric refrigerators, electric ranges, and various other electric appliances. The refrigerators and ranges are sold only to Midway Sales, Inc., which acts as a distributor. Other appliances are sold directly to outside distributors.

The parent and the subsidiary sales corporation are tenants of property owned by Kent Realty Corp.

The intercompany accounts on the books of each company as of December 31, 1980, were as follows:

### Davis Manufacturing Co., Inc.

|  | Debit | Credit |
|---|---|---|
| Investment in Midway Sales, Inc. (at cost) | $100,000.00 |  |
| Investment in Kent Realty Corp. (at cost) | 175,000.00 |  |
| Due from Midway Sales, Inc. | 86,175.97 |  |
| Due to Kent Realty Corp. |  | $ 1,475.00 |
| Capital stock issued and outstanding, 100,000 shares, no par value |  | 1,000,000.00 |
| Retained earnings |  | 410,169.50 |

### Midway Sales, Inc.

|  |  |  |
|---|---|---|
| Due to Kent Realty Corp. |  | $ 800.00 |
| Due to Davis Manufacturing Co., Inc. |  | 33,910.00 |
| Capital stock issued and outstanding, 1,000 shares, par value $100 per share |  | 100,000.00 |
| Retained earnings |  | 62,501.10 |

KENT REALTY CORP.

| | | |
|---|---|---|
| Due from Davis Manufacturing Co., Inc. | $ 6,575.00 | |
| Due to Midway Sales, Inc. | | $ 2,800.00 |
| Capital stock issued and outstanding, | | |
| 1,000 shares, no par value | | 175,000.00 |
| Retained earnings | | 34,109.50 |

An audit of the books of the three companies for the year ended December 31, 1980, revealed the following:

1. The minute books of the three companies indicate the following with respect to dividends:
   (a) The board of directors of Davis Manufacturing Co., Inc., at a meeting on January 4, 1981, declared a regular quarterly dividend of 50 cents per share, payable January 31, 1981, to stockholders of record on January 23, 1981.
   (b) The board of directors of Midway Sales, Inc., at a meeting on December 28, 1980, declared a 1% dividend payable in cash on January 15, 1981, to stockholders of record on December 31, 1980.
   (c) The board of directors of Kent Realty Corp. at a meeting on December 1, 1980, declared a dividend of $1.00 per share, payable January 2, 1981, to stockholders of record on December 15, 1980.

No effect has been given to these dividend declarations on the books of the parent company as of December 31, 1980. The subsidiary companies recorded the dividend declarations pertaining to their respective companies at date of declaration.

2. Midway Sales received from one of its customers a check for $4,200 covering its own invoices aggregating $2,400 and invoices of Davis Manufacturing aggregating $1,800. The sales corporation recorded this transaction as follows:

   | | | |
   |---|---|---|
   | Cash | $4,200 | |
   |     Accounts receivable | | $4,200 |

3. Midway Sales, Inc., advanced $5,000 in cash to Kent Realty Corp. and made the following entry:

   | | | |
   |---|---|---|
   | Davis Manufacturing Co., Inc. | $5,000 | |
   |     Cash | | $5,000 |

4. On September 15, 1980, Davis Manufacturing shipped 100 appliances of a new design on consignment at $20 each to Midway Sales. Midway made no entry upon receipt of the goods. During October, 1980, Midway sold all of these appliances at $25 each, crediting sales for the total thereof. Davis Manufacturing made no entries on its books, but included the 100 appliances in its inventory at December 31, 1980, at its cost of $14 each.
5. The parent corporation filed a consolidated federal income tax return for the year ended December 31, 1979. The results of operations for the respective companies that year, before consolidation, were as follows:

|   |   |
|---|---|
| Davis Manufacturing Co., Inc., net loss | $13,280 |
| Midway Sales, Inc., net profit | 42,260 |
| Kent Realty Corp., net profit | 21,130 |

The federal income tax, amounting to $21,000, was paid by the parent corporation, which recorded the transaction as follows:

| | | |
|---|---|---|
| Federal income taxes payable | $21,000 | |
|     Cash | | $21,000 |

An agreement in the files indicates that federal income taxes should be apportioned among the companies on the basis of consolidated net profit. A company having a loss year does not pay any tax or charge the other companies for the benefit derived from the use of its loss in the return. The proper liability of each company was recorded as of December 31, 1979.

6. Kent Realty sold certain of its furniture to Midway Sales at current market value, which was 75 percent of net book value. The realty corporation had purchased the furniture for $3,500 exactly two years prior to the date of sale and had taken depreciation at the rate of 10 percent per annum. It billed Midway Sales, Inc., for $2,800 and recorded the transaction as follows:

| | | |
|---|---|---|
| Midway Sales, Inc. | $2,800 | |
|     Furniture and fixtures | | $2,800 |

Midway Sales recorded the purchase as follows:

| | | |
|---|---|---|
| Furniture and fixtures | $2,800 | |
|     Kent Realty Corp. | | $2,800 |

7. As of December 31, 1980, the books of the parent corporation and the sales subsidiary do not reflect rent for the month of December, 1980, in the amounts of $6,100 and $1,400, respectively, due to Kent Realty Corp.
8. Midway Sales, Inc., had not recorded December, 1980, purchase invoices submitted by the parent corporation in the amount of $48,265.97.

*Required:*
(1) Prepare an itemized reconciliation of the intercompany accounts.
(2) Prepare the adjusting journal entries necessary to correct each set of books.  (AICPA adapted)

## Problem 16-9

*Required:*
From the data below prepare:
a. A work sheet for a consolidated statement of financial position as of December 31, 1980.
b. A consolidated statement of financial position as of December 31, 1980.
   (1) Post-closing trial balances as of December 31, 1980:

## 16 / Consolidated Statements—Comprehensive Review

|  | Company P | Company S-1 | Company S-2 |
|---|---|---|---|
| Investment in Company S-1 (acquired January 1, 1979) |  |  |  |
| Common stock (90%) | $200,000 |  |  |
| Preferred stock (40%) | 40,000 |  |  |
| Investment in Company S-2 (70% acquired January 1, 1980) | 59,300 |  |  |
| Current assets | 50,000 | $ 50,000 | $ 40,000 |
| Machinery and equipment | 40,000 | 20,000 | 30,000 |
| Allowance for depreciation |  |  |  |
| Machinery and equipment | (20,000) | (15,000) | (10,000) |
| Bonds of Company S-2 (Par $10,000) | 10,100 |  |  |
| All other assets | 600 | 313,000 | 70,180 |
| Current liabilities | (20,000) | (20,000) | (20,000) |
| Bonds payable—10 yrs., 4%, due December 31, 1985 |  |  | (30,000) |
| Premium on bonds payable |  |  | (180) |
| Capital stock—Common, par $100 | (300,000) | (250,000) | (60,000) |
| Capital stock—Preferred, 5%, par $100, cumulative and nonparticipating |  | (100,000) |  |
| Premium on preferred stock |  | (10,000) |  |
| Retained earnings | (60,000) | 12,000 | (20,000) |
|  | –0– | –0– | –0– |

(2) The investment accounts are carried at cost.

(3) At acquisition, dividends on preferred stock for 1977 and 1978 were in arrears. Preferred stock has a liquidation value of par plus dividends in arrears and is nonvoting.

(4) On January 1, 1980, Company S-1 declared a common stock dividend of $50,000 from Premium on Preferred Stock accounts.

(5) The Retained Earnings accounts showed the following:

|  | S-1 | S-2 |
|---|---|---|
| January 1, 1979 Balance | $(10,000) | $14,000 |
| Profits 1979 | 7,000 | 7,000 |
| Cash dividends 1980— |  |  |
| on January 1, 1980 | (5,000) |  |
| on December 31, 1980 |  | (6,000) |
| Profit and loss 1980 | (4,000) | 5,000 |
| Balance December 31, 1980 | (12,000) | 20,000 |

(6) Inventory of Company P includes $5,000 merchandise purchased from S-2; cost to S-2 is marked up 25%.

522      EXPANSION OF THE BUSINESS ORGANIZATION

(7) Inventory of Company S-2 includes $2,000 merchandise purchased from S-1; markup by S-1 is 10% on selling price.
(8) Current Liabilities include the following: Company S-1 owes Company P $1,000; Company S-2 owes Company P $2,000; Company S-1 owes Company S-2 $3,000; and Company P owes Company S-1 $2,000.
(9) Machinery having a life of 10 years was purchased by Company P from Company S-1 on January 1, 1979, for $10,000. Cost to S-1 was $7,000.
(10) Company S-2 neglected to amortize Premium on Bonds Payable for 1980.      (AICPA adapted)

## Problem 16-10

The financial statements of John Doe Manufacturing Company and its wholly owned subsidiary, Blank Sales Company, were submitted as shown below.

Also the following information was given:

1. In June, 1980, the authorized capital stock of John Doe Manufacturing Company was changed from 100,000 shares of $10 to 250,000 shares of $5 each and the shareholders agreed to exchange their stock on the basis of 1¾ shares of the new for each share of the old stock. Accordingly, all the 75,000 outstanding shares of the old $10 stock were exchanged for 131,250 shares of the new $5 stock on July 1, 1980.
2. On July 1, 1980, the company acquired all the outstanding 15,000 shares of Blank Sales Company for 75,000 shares of its new $5 stock.
3. Immediately after July 1, 1980, certain stockholders of John Doe Manufacturing Company disposed of a portion of their holdings to an underwriter, receiving $20 per share. The shares were offered to the public at $22.50.

In view of the wider distribution of its stock after the public offering, the company arranged to list its common shares on the stock exchange and agreed to pay all expenses of listing and of registering the stock under the Securities Act of 1933, amounting to $15,000.

STATEMENTS OF FINANCIAL POSITION
DECEMBER 31, 1980

| Assets | John Doe Mfg. Co. | Blank Sales Co. | Combined |
|---|---|---|---|
| Cash | $ 150,000 | $ 75,000 | $ 225,000 |
| U.S. Government bonds, as cost | 300,000 | 100,000 | 400,000 |
| Trade accounts receivable: | | | |
|   Customers, less reserves | 10,000 | 650,000 | 660,000 |
|   Blank Sales Co. | 490,000 | | 490,000 |
| Inventories | 600,000 | 200,000 | 800,000 |
| Investment in Blank Sales Co. | 375,000 | | 375,000 |
| Investment in 1,000 shares of John Doe Mfg. Co., $5 par stock, at cost | | 20,000 | 20,000 |

|  | | | |
|---|---:|---:|---:|
| Other assets | 25,000 | 30,000 | 55,000 |
| Property, plant, and equipment, at cost | 950,000 | 275,000 | 1,225,000 |
| Prepaid expenses | 35,000 | 25,000 | 60,000 |
| Expenses of registration and listing of stock | 15,000 | | 15,000 |
| | $2,950,000 | $1,375,000 | $4,325,000 |

### Equities

|  | | | |
|---|---:|---:|---:|
| Notes payable | $ 200,000 | $ 100,000 | $ 300,000 |
| Accounts payable | 325,000 | 665,000 | 990,000 |
| Federal taxes on income | 150,000 | 35,000 | 185,000 |
| Allowance for depreciation | 250,000 | 75,000 | 325,000 |
| Common stock, $10 par value | 750,000 | 150,000 | 900,000 |
| Common stock, $5 par value | 375,000 | | 375,000 |
| Retained earnings | | | |
| At January 1, 1980 | $ 596,250 | | |
| At July 1, 1980 | | $ 355,000 | $ 951,250 |
| Net profit per income statement | 510,000 | 115,000 | 625,000 |
| | $1,106,250 | $ 470,000 | $1,576,250 |
| Dividends paid | 206,250 | 120,000 | 326,250 |
| | $ 900,000 | $ 350,000 | $1,250,000 |
| | $2,950,000 | $1,375,000 | $4,325,000 |

4. The inventories of Blank Sales Company included merchandise bought from John Doe Manufacturing Company at the latter's regular sales prices, as follows:

|  |  |
|---|---:|
| January 1, 1980 | $50,000 |
| June 30, 1980 | 30,000 |
| December 31, 1980 | 40,000 |

5. The net sales of John Doe Manufacturing Company included net sales to Blank Sales Company as follows:

|  |  |
|---|---:|
| January 1, to June 30, 1980 | $1,500,000 |
| July to December 31, 1980 | 2,500,000 |

### Statements of Income

|  | John Doe Mfg. Co. Year ended Dec. 31, 1980 | Blank Sales Co. Six months to Dec. 31, 1980 | Combined |
|---|---:|---:|---:|
| Net sales | $4,200,000 | $3,300,000 | $7,500,000 |
| Cost of goods sold | 3,570,000 | 3,025,000 | 6,595,000 |
| | $ 630,000 | $ 275,000 | $ 905,000 |

|   |   |   |   |
|---|---:|---:|---:|
| Selling and administrative expenses | 75,000 | 140,000 | 215,000 |
|  | $ 555,000 | $ 135,000 | $ 690,000 |
| Other income: |  |  |  |
| Commission earned |  | $ 25,000 | $ 25,000 |
| Dividends received | $ 120,000 | 1,000 | 121,000 |
| Miscellaneous | 5,000 | 4,000 | 9,000 |
|  | $ 125,000 | $ 30,000 | $ 155,000 |
|  | $ 680,000 | $ 165,000 | $ 845,000 |
| Miscellaneous deductions from income | $ 20,000 | $ 15,000 | $ 35,000 |
| Federal taxes on income | 150,000 | 35,000 | 185,000 |
|  | $ 170,000 | $ 50,000 | $ 220,000 |
| Net income | $ 510,000 | $ 115,000 | $ 625,000 |

6. Commissions earned by the Blank Sales Company included $2,000 received from John Doe Manufacturing Company and charged to the latter's selling expenses.
7. Dividends received had been credited to income.
8. Throughout the year the rate of gross profit on sales remained the same.
9. All depreciation had been charged to production cost, the office equipment having been written down to nominal value in previous years.
10. No entries had been made to record the conversion of the John Doe Manufacturing Company capital stock.

From the foregoing data prepare a columnar work sheet distinctly showing the consolidated income and financial position of John Doe Manufacturing Company and its wholly owned subsidiary, Blank Sales Company. Show or mention how the 1,000 shares of John Doe Manufacturing Company stock owned by the Blank Sales Company should be treated. (AICPA adapted)

## Problem 16-11

From the information given, you are required to furnish the following:

1. Consolidated statement of retained earnings for P Company and subsidiary for the year ended December 31, 1980.
2. Eliminating and consolidating entries.
3. Any footnote or disclosure that you consider to be needed for statement presentation.

Submit all supporting computations in good form.

Consolidated retained earnings at December 31, 1979, were $12,347,300. Of this amount, $11,613,170 represented retained earnings of the parent and $734,130 represented retained earnings of the subsidiary. Book income of the parent company for the year ended December 31, 1980, was $487,537 and income for the subsidiary was $134,540.

Under government Certificates of Necessity, portions of the costs of the parent's expansion program, which was completed and put into operation on January 1,

1980, are being amortized for both book and income tax purposes over a period of sixty months. Depreciation computed at normal rates based on the estimated useful life of the properties was $1,143,350 less than the amount of amortization and depreciation taken into the accounts. The prevailing income tax rate is assumed to be 52%.

The parent company's investment in its 100%-owned subsidiary (a Delaware corporation) is recorded at cost of $100,000. During the year the subsidiary paid the parent $150,000 in cash dividends, together with a stock dividend of one new share of common stock for each share outstanding. The amount transferred from retained earnings to the capital stock account on the books of the subsidiary was $100,000, based on 1,000 shares with a par value of $100 a share. There were no other intercompany accounts or transactions.

During the year the parent company issued a stock dividend of one share for each 10 shares outstanding, or a total of 100,000 shares with a par value of $10 a share. The fair value of the additional shares issued was $15 a share. The issuance of the additional shares did not materially reduce the share market value.

The company, in order to state consolidated retained earnings on a realistic basis and to provide for all income taxes, both known and contingent, wants you to set up a separate reserve out of consolidated retained earnings equal to the amount of taxes that would be due at the prevailing income tax rates if the retained earnings as shown on the books of the subsidiary was distributed to the parent in the form of cash dividends. For income tax purposes, separate returns are filed and the dividends received credit is assumed to be 85%.

The bond indenture relating to the long-term debt of the parent company imposes a restriction on the payment of cash dividends and provides that no cash dividends can be paid out of the parent's retained earnings accumulated at December 31,1980.  (AICPA adapted)

# 17

# Consolidated Statements Reexamined

In the preceding chapters, consolidated statements have been viewed primarily from the standpoint of technique and methodology. In this chapter the basic reasoning underlying the technique and methodology is reexamined. In addition legal and economic considerations affecting consolidated statements are examined.

As indicated in *Accounting Research Bulletin 51,* and elaborated on in Chapter Nine, the primary justification for consolidated statements is the assumption that more meaningful information is disclosed by consolidated reports than is revealed by the financial statements of the separate companies. The reasoning in support of this assumption holds that the assets and equities underlying the investment account of a parent company should be revealed since these items are effectively used by top management in earning an income for the company as a consolidated group.

**Limitations.** Although consolidated statements have many advantages over separate company reports, such statements also have their limitations. For example, the variety and volume of data collected and reported upon in a consolidated statement may have to be condensed to such a degree that the brevity and conciseness afforded by the consolidated report may be misleading. The extent of the condensation in a typical consolidated report is often not realized. It may appear unusual, however, that roughly the same accounts and the same amount of space are needed for a statement of financial position on General Motors as for the Korner Grocery Store. If the growth and diversification of large companies are recognized, it becomes evident that an item such as inventory in a large company may encompass a much greater variety and volume of items than would be contained in the somewhat homogeneous inventory account of a typical small company. The question may well be raised as to whether the growth of large business organizations, even if a composition of a group of separate legal companies, suggests that accounting reports should be expanded in scope to provide more information for interested parties.

**Disclosure.** Most limitations of consolidated statements revolve around the problem of adequate disclosure of enterprise activity. As business organizations become more decentralized and as stock ownership becomes more widespread, the disclosure problem becomes a topic of increasing concern to accountants. In an attempt to overcome the disclosure limitation inherent in typical financial statements, footnotes and other supplementary data have been used to an increasing degree. Especially has this development been reflected in the use of footnotes. In part, the use and development of footnotes reflects an improvement in accounting reporting. In part, however, it has been used merely as a device enabling accountants to meet the demands placed upon accounting for additional information.

It is the opinion of the authors that footnotes may become an undesirable method for reporting if overused. Without suggesting any change that would omit the information typically revealed in a footnote, it is suggested that improvements in financial reporting are needed. For example, possible additional statements or supplementary data could be developed to enhance interpretation of the conventional reports. When the disclosure problem is examined, it is apparent that it applies to accounting reports in general but particularly to consolidated statements. Although there has been an increase in the amount of supplementary data included in the annual reports of a number of companies, such as financial reviews and financial statistics over a period of years, such data as are reported are frequently not uniform or systematic either in content or in form of presentation.

**Additional Problems.** In addition to the disclosure problem common to all reporting, other problems are unique to the consolidated area. For purposes of reexamination, the following problems special to the area of consolidation are considered further:

1. Problems related to consolidation policies:
   a. Criteria for consolidation.
   b. Meaning of control.
2. Problems related to statement presentation:
   a. Valuation of assets.
   b. Intercompany gains and losses.
   c. Minority interests.
   d. Retained earnings.
   e. Change in composition of the consolidated entity.
   f. Unconsolidated subsidiaries.

## CONSOLIDATION POLICIES

### Criteria for Consolidation

As indicated previously, consolidation is normally considered appropriate whenever the resulting information is more useful than if it were presented in unconsolidated statements. By more useful is meant:

1. More informative for investors and prospective investors.
2. More informative for creditors and others interested in limited investment in the company.
3. More informative for top management, which is concerned with reports on the results of overall operations.
4. More informative for governmental agencies concerned with problems of antitrust regulation, fair trade regulation, and similar problems.

A number of limiting factors, however, bear on the problem of when consolidation is appropriate. For example, legal considerations may encourage or discourage consolidation under certain situations. In addition, economic considerations, including accepted accounting conventions, may preclude consolidation for which one group, such as a governmental agency, may feel a need. Although usefulness is the underlying objective, the limiting factors have considerable force in establishing a consolidation policy on the appropriate consolidated accounting entity.

**Legal Considerations.** The Clayton Act of 1914, as amended, prohibits the acquisition of stock of another company where the result might be a lessening of competition. Section 7 provides:

> ... No corporation shall acquire, directly or indirectly, the whole or any part of the stock or other share capital and no corporation subject to the jurisdiction of the Federal Trade Commission shall acquire the whole or any part of the assets of one or more corporations engaged in commerce, where in any line of commerce in any section of the country, the effect of such acquisition, of such stock or assets, or the use of such stock by the voting or granting of proxies or otherwise, may be substantially to lessen competition, or to tend to create a monopoly.

The effect of this act appears to be to allow noncompeting companies to be consolidated, but to discourage the purchase of stock of competing companies. In effect this law seems to allow vertical combinations through stock ownership, but discourages horizontal combinations.

The idea that a combination of an integrated economic entity is necessary before consolidation is appropriate is reflected in Section 11 of the Public Utility Act of 1935, as follows:

> To require by order, after notice and opportunity for hearing, that each registered holding company, and each subsidiary company thereof, shall take such action as the Commission shall find necessary to limit the operations of the

holding-company system of which such company is a part to a single integrated public-utility system, and to such other businesses as are reasonably incidental, or economically necessary or appropriate to the operations of such integrated public-utility system. . . .

The implication of these two acts appears to be that a consolidated entity should not be allowed to come into existence unless it represents an integrated economic unit.

Rule 4-20(a) of Regulation S-X issued by the Securities and Exchange Commission states the basic rule for consolidation, which requires over 50% ownership of the stock of the subsidiary as justification for consolidation, as follows:

The registrant shall not consolidate any subsidiary which is not a majority-owned subsidiary.

Throughout the legal considerations the idea prevails that consolidation is not appropriate unless the subsidiary is controlled through stock ownership. Unless control exists, the stock ownership is considered an investment. The distinction made by the Clayton Act between an investment and acquisition of control is revealed by the following portion of Section 7:

. . . This section shall not apply to corporations purchasing such stock solely for investment and not using the same by voting or otherwise to bring about, or in attempting to bring about, the substantial lessening of competition.

The distinction between an investment and control is found in other areas of the law as well. The significance of the distinction is to invalidate the concept that consolidation is appropriate merely because the parent *effectively owns* the subsidiary.

**Economic Considerations.** The main economic considerations on consolidation policy revolve around the distinction between effective ownership and control. The concept of effective ownership is that stock ownership represents a claim to the assets of the subsidiary. When the stock ownership is such that the parent company effectively owns the assets of the subsidiary, from the economic standpoint consolidation is essentially the process of replacing the investment account with the underlying assets of the subsidiary. The distortion resulting from bringing into the consolidated statement the assets and equities represented by outside ownership of the subsidiary, as well as the assets and equities represented by the parent ownership, is assumed not to be material. Effective ownership might exist even though control is not applicable, as for example when an insurance company buys a substantial portion of the stock of a particular company. Effective ownership might exist but control might not be applicable because the stock owned is held as an investment, and no action is taken by the owners of the stock to control operations of the company. Since in situations of this kind it does not appear that effective ownership is in itself a proper basis for consolidation, some other criteria for consolidation must be appropriate. From an economic point of view the major criterion for consolidation is the existence of control or right to control the subsidiary rather than effective ownership.

As indicated in Chapter Nine, various other economic considerations may influence a decision on the appropriateness of consolidation. Some of these considerations are:

1. Subsidiary not an integral part of operating group, such as a realty corporation owned by a department store or a railroad owned by a cement company.
2. Foreign subsidiary with economic restrictions, such as a restriction on the transfer of currency.
3. Difference in accounting periods.
4. Senior securities of subsidiary outstanding.
5. Insolvent or bankrupt subsidiary.

## The Meaning of Control

A distinction is normally drawn between the ability to control a subsidiary by ownership of over 50% of the voting stock, and the exercise of control over the subsidiary. The ability to control is not necessarily sufficient basis for consolidation, as noted in the preceding section. Control must be exercised. To be exercised, control requires election or retention of a sufficient number of the board of directors of the subsidiary company to dictate policy for the subsidiary. It does not require that the operating actions of the subsidiary be planned and controlled by the parent company.

In those instances where the board of directors effectively surrenders its power to set policies for the subsidiary, such as might be the case under bankruptcy, it is assumed that control does not exist and consolidation is inappropriate.

The insistence on over 50% voting stock ownership before control may be assumed to exist is obviously not always in accord with the facts of the situation. In many cases control is effected with far less than 50% stock ownership.

**Reexamination of the Control Concept.** It may be difficult to justify the elimination from a consolidated report of assets effectively owned and completely controlled under a lease agreement and at the same time include in a consolidated report assets controlled through ownership of the stock of a subsidiary. What is the nature of the difference in the two types of control? In both cases the controlling company has control of the *uses* to which the assets can be directed. In both cases the company may have the right to sell the assets or the rights to the assets. The similarity is definite, yet the procedures of preparing consolidated statements are such that only the assets controlled by stock ownership of a subsidiary are included in the consolidated reports. Assets controlled by a lease agreement have not been generally included in consolidated reports.

On legal grounds, the concept of ownership may be used to justify inclusion of assets owned by a subsidiary and exclusion of those not owned although controlled by a lease agreement. Thus the control concept as used in consolidated reports appears to be influenced by legal as well as economic considerations.

**Large Block of Minority Interest.** There appears to be a reluctance on the part of some companies to consolidate whenever there is a large block of minority interest of a size relatively equal to the equity of the parent company stockholders. Such a situation may exist when a parent company uses substantially all of its assets to buy a fraction over 50% of the stock of a subsidiary. On consolidation the minority interest may be almost equal to the parent company's stockholders' equity in the consolidated report. Normally, separate statements are considered appropriate in such situations. This appears to represent a partial departure from the accepted control concept for consolidations.

### Conclusion on Consolidation Policy

The need for objective standards in deciding whether or not consolidation is appropriate is well recognized. It is true that the current rule of over 50% ownership of the voting stock meets the requirement of being objective. It is also evident that were the standard lowered to less than 50% ownership, the assets of one company might appear on the consolidated statements of two or more companies. For example, if the percentage of ownership required for consolidation were reduced to 20%, the assets and liabilities of a given company could well appear on the consolidated statements of five different companies.

Thus if control with less than 50% stock ownership were to be accepted as the standard for consolidation, control would have to be defined on some basis other than the percent of voting stock owned by the parent company. In general, current accounting practice supports consolidation for those subsidiaries in which over 50% voting stock ownership exists, *providing* the existence of various economic considerations does not make such consolidation appear inappropriate.

**STATEMENT PRESENTATION**

At times the question is raised as to when a parent company should issue separate statements if a consolidated report is rendered. In general, three of the major reasons for preparation of separate statements are:

1. To provide useful information for management.
2. To comply with statement requirements of bonds and other indentures.
3. To comply with Regulation S-X of the SEC where the parent company does not qualify to use consolidated statements only.

The preparation of separate company statements is generally based upon the needs of the various users of such statements. As a general rule, no particular problems of statement presentation arise for the separate company statement except for the presentation of investment accounts. In the preparation of consolidated statements, however, various special problems of statement presentation must be resolved. Some of these problems are considered in the following sections.

### Valuation of Consolidated Assets

**Dual Valuation.** A problem may arise in the valuation of consolidated assets when a parent company acquires an interest in a subsidiary at a price other than the book value of the stock acquired. When consolidating, the subsidiary assets may be valued at either their cost to the subsidiary or their cost to the consolidated entity. For example, if Company A pays $80,000 to acquire net assets of a subsidiary carried at $60,000, on a consolidated statement of financial position, the specific assets could be valued at the $60,000 cost to the subsidiary and supported by a separate goodwill item of $20,000. Alternatively the specific assets could be valued at their cost to the consolidated entity of $80,000. In the latter event, the excess of cost over subsidiary book value would be allocated to the specific assets and would not appear as a separate item on the consolidated statement of financial position.

When less than 100% of the outstanding stock of a subsidiary is acquired, the procedure of allocating the excess of cost over book value of stock acquired to specific assets may give a dual valuation basis to the consolidated assets. To illustrate, assume that Company A acquired 60% of the voting stock of Company B at a price of $50,000 above the book value of the stock acquired. In such a purchase it must be assumed that the net assets acquired were worth their book value plus $50,000. An objective investigation may reveal that the $50,000 excess should be allocated to specific assets in order to reflect properly their cost to the consolidated entity. If the excess were allocated, some assets would be valued on a dual basis on the consolidated statement of financial position. The portion of the assets to which the allocation has been made would be valued at cost to the consolidated entity, while the portion to which no allocation was made would be valued at cost to the subsidiary.

**Imputed Valuation.** Some accountants support a third valuation based on the fair value of the assets at the time they become a part of the consolidated entity. Continuing the illustration above, assume that an examination indicates that $3,000 of the $50,000 excess should be allocated to a particular asset carried by the subsidiary at a book value of $20,000. This means that Company A paid $15,000 for book value of $12,000 (60% × $20,000). Accountants supporting the imputed valuation concept would support a $25,000 valuation of the particular asset, determined as follows:

|  | Fair Value (Imputed from Cost to the Parent) |
|---|---|
| Valuation of 60% of the asset | $15,000 |
| Valuation of 40% of the asset (40/60 × $15,000) | 10,000 |
| Total | $25,000 |

The $25,000 valuation of the asset might be justified on the grounds that it represents an approximation of the value of the asset at the time the consolidated entity was formed and that it therefore conforms to the basic rule that assets should be valued at their fair value at the time they are contributed to a new entity (the consolidated entity). Although this position has merit, it becomes unrealistic when the parent's investment is acquired over a period of time by a series of purchases of subsidiary stock. Under these conditions parent company cost may not be representative of the fair value prevailing on the date when the consolidated entity came into existence.

**Unresolved Valuation Problems.** The view that the consolidated entity is a separate and distinct entity from the underlying legal entities appears not to be entirely accepted by the accounting profession. At least this appears to be true on questions regarding the proper valuation of consolidated assets. Considerable support exists for the view that assets should be valued either at their cost to the subsidiary entity or at their cost to the parent company. For assets acquired after the consolidated entity has come into existence, consolidated cost and separate company cost may be identical, but for assets acquired by the separate companies prior to emergence of a consolidated entity, problems may exist. Questions which may well be raised regarding the valuation of consolidated assets include:

1. Why should subsidiary assets be revalued upward upon consolidation (by an allocation of the excess of cost of an investment over the book value of the subsidiary stock acquired) when parent company assets continue to be carried at cost?
2. Why should part of an asset be valued on one basis and part of the asset on another basis?
3. Why is it assumed that because a parent company pays more for the stock of a subsidiary company than can be allocated to the valuation of the underlying assets the excess payment represents goodwill?

**Amortization of Goodwill.** Implicit in the traditional procedure of preparing consolidated reports is the view that any "goodwill" arising when subsidiary stock is purchased at a cost above book value should not be written off. The reluctance to amortize consolidated "goodwill" is claimed by some accountants to result in an understatement of the expense of the consolidated entity.

If the excess of cost over book value of assets acquired were apportioned to specific assets, the gradual absorption of these assets as operating charges would produce an expense not recognized if the "goodwill" element remains unamortized. Thus, the reasoning follows, understatement of expense arises from nonamortization of goodwill. On the other hand, other accountants claim that since the goodwill exists only to the consolidated entity, amortization would result in an expense not recorded by the separate entities.

According to some accountants, there does not appear to be any justification for treating goodwill from consolidation differently from any other type of purchased goodwill. Because the general conception of purchased goodwill is that it represents a payment for excess earnings that will accrue to the buying company in the future, proper matching of cost and revenue would require that goodwill, like any other cost, be amortized against the appropriate earnings of the future as they are realized.

**Reexamination of the Valuation of Consolidated Assets.** As indicated in the foregoing discussion, the generally accepted basis for valuing consolidated assets appears to be cost to the parent company. For those assets not acquired by the parent company, i.e., the assets of the subsidiary company(ies) represented by equities not acquired by the parent company (subsidiary company liabilities and minority interest), cost to the subsidiary is accepted as the appropriate valuation.

An exception to the foregoing rule is generally recognized when an asset is acquired directly from an affiliated company. In those instances, cost to the affiliate, adjusted for transportation and other costs normally capitalized when an item is transferred from one segment of an enterprise to another, is the accepted valuation basis.

The dual valuation basis for consolidated assets creates some rather unusual situations. For example, assume a 60% owned subsidiary whose only asset is an apartment building with a book value of $100,000. If the parent company pays $70,000 for 60% of the subsidiary's stock, the asset might be valued at $110,000 on the consolidated report, assuming that the excess of cost over book value is allocated to the asset on the consolidated report. The $110,000 has limited meaning, since part (60%) of the building is valued at cost to the parent and another part (40%) at cost to the subsidiary.

## Intercompany Gains and Losses

Another unusual situation might arise if a subsidiary traded machinery it has on its own books at $50,000 for machinery the parent has on its books at $60,000. To the parent company the machinery might be inventory. To the subsidiary the machinery might represent fixed assets. The parent would record the new asset at $60,000, thus recognizing no loss, while the subsidiary would enter its new asset at $50,000 and would recognize no gain on the sale of the exchange. No intercompany profit or loss is recognized, but it is evident that the proper valuation of the assets would require a decrease of inventory by $10,000 and an increase in fixed assets by $10,000

A somewhat similar situation arises in the classification of inventories as materials, work-in-process, and finished goods when the finished product of the subsidiary is used as raw material by the parent company. Should the finished goods of the subsidiary be included as part of the consolidated finished goods? In general, a negative answer is appropriate. The finished goods of the subsidiary are in reality work-in-process from a consolidated point of view. A work sheet adjustment would be necessary to reclassify the finished goods of the subsidiary as work-in-process or as raw materials, depending upon the nature of the parent's manufacturing operations.

## Valuation of Minority Interest

Traditionally, minority interest has been valued on the basis of its equity as revealed on the separate company report of the subsidiary. In addition, minority interest traditionally has been classified on the statement of financial position as a separate item between the liability section and the parent company stockholders' equity section.

Recently the views have shifted. Today, as indicated in Chapter Thirteen, it is not uncommon to find the minority interest valued at the separate company equity after adjustment for any intercompany profit eliminations that might apply to the minority interest. Also there appears to be growing recognition of the fact that the minority interest, as with preferred stock of the parent company, is part of the stockholders' equity section of the consolidated statement of financial position. In a sense, it represents a special class of stock outstanding.

In those rare instances where the minority interest is negative, there is a supposition that it should be deducted from the consolidated equity of the parent company. The reasoning involved is that the parent company will normally make good to subsidiary creditors any deficit in their "buffer" as represented by the stockholders' equity section.

Although minority interest is normally valued at its equity in the separate subsidiary company report, adjusted for intercompany profit or loss that might apply to the minority interest, one type of intercompany transaction should be considered further. It is the consolidated gain or loss that accrues to a parent or subsidiary when a liability of the other company is liquidated at an amount different from the amount at which it is carried on the books.

**Illustration.** To illustrate the situation above, assume that Company A has bonds payable outstanding at par of $50,000. Company B, 60% owned by A, acquires $30,000 of these bonds in the open market for $27,000. From the consolidated point of view, a gain of $3,000 has been realized. The question is: To whom does the gain accrue and when should it be recognized? If B holds the bonds to maturity, $30,000 will be received from A so that ultimately the $3,000 gain may be said to accrue to B's stockholders. It is often contended that the gain should be recognized immediately and not deferred until A pays B at maturity. To treat the gain as immediate income of the subsidiary would increase the minority interest by 40% of $3,000 or $1,200. To treat the gain as deferred income of the subsidiary would result in an allocation of the gain over the remaining life of the bonds. Many accountants would recognize immediately the portion of the $3,000 gain accruing to the parent company (60% of $3,000) and would defer the portion accruing to minority interest ($1,200) to future periods.

## Valuation of Consolidated Retained Earnings

As emphasized in preceding sections, retained earnings in a consolidated statement properly includes:

1. All undistributed retained earnings of the parent company.
2. The parent company's share of the increase or decrease in stockholders' equity of the subsidiary since the date of acquisition.

It does not include that portion of subsidiary retained earnings which pertains to the minority interest. However, consolidated retained earnings may include as earnings an element that might normally be treated as unrealized income from the point of view of the parent company. That is, income from investments in general is considered as unrealized until a distribution in the form of dividends is received. However, from the point of view of the parent company's stockholders, the consolidated report advances the date when earnings of subsidiaries are treated as income.

Another aspect of consolidated retained earnings is that it may change if the parent company increases or decreases its percent of equity in a subsidiary company. It should be the function of the statement of changes in consolidated retained earnings to show all changes in this account from one period to the next.

## Statement of Changes in Consolidated Retained Earnings—Illustrated.

Assume that Company A acquires an 80% interest in Company B on January 1, 1980, when B's stockholders' equity is composed of $100,000 of capital stock and $40,000 of retained earnings. At that time A's retained earnings as a separate company were $70,000. On a consolidated statement of financial position prepared on the date of acquisition, the $40,000 of retained earnings of the subsidiary would be partially eliminated ($32,000) and partially consolidated as minority interest ($8,000). As a result, consolidated retained earnings on that date would be $70,000.

Assume that during 1980 Company A earns an income from its own operations of $50,000 and pays a $40,000 dividend, and during the same period Company B reports an income of $30,000 and pays a $20,000 dividend.

STATEMENT OF CHANGES IN CONSOLIDATED

RETAINED EARNINGS

COMPANIES A AND B

| | | | | |
|---|---|---|---|---|
| Balance, January 1, 1980 | | | | $ 70,000 |
| Add: Income for 1980: | | | | |
| A's operations | | $50,000 | | |
| 80% of B's dividend | $16,000 | | | |
| 80% of B's equity increase, 1980 | 8,000 | 24,000 | | 74,000 |
| Total | | | | $144,000 |
| Deduct: A's dividends paid, 1980 | | | | 40,000 |
| Balance, December 31, 1980 | | | | $104,000 |
| Add: Income for 1981: | | | | |
| A's income | | $40,000 | | |
| 70% of B's dividend | $14,000 | | | |
| 70% of B's equity increase, 1981 | 17,500 | 31,500 | | 71,500 |
| Total | | | | $175,000 |
| Deduct: Loss on sale of investment in B | | $ 3,000 | | |
| Loss of 10% of B's equity increase since January 1, 1980 (10% × $10,000) | | 1,000 | | |
| A's dividends paid, 1981 | | 40,000 | | 44,000 |
| Balance, December 31, 1981 | | | | $131,500 |

## 17 / Consolidated Statements Reexamined

|  |  |  |  |  |
|---|---|---|---|---|
| *Add:* | A's income for 1982 |  | $52,000 |  |
|  | 70% of B's dividend | $21,000 |  |  |
|  | 70% of B's equity increase, 1982 | 7,000 | 28,000 | 80,000 |
|  | Total |  |  | $211,500 |
| *Deduct:* | A's dividends paid, 1982 |  |  | 50,000 |
| Balance, December 31, 1982 |  |  |  | $161,500* |

*If the stock dividend received by A (70% of $25,000) were to be excluded from consolidated retained earnings, the December 31, 1982, balance would be $144,000.

On January 1, 1981, Company A sells a 10% interest in Company B at a loss of $3,000, the difference between cost and selling price of the stock. During 1981, Company A earns an income from its own operations of $40,000 and pays a $40,000 dividend. During the same period Company B reports an income of $45,000 and pays a $20,000 dividend.

On January 1, 1982, B distributes a stock dividend that transfers $25,000 from retained earnings to the Capital Stock account. During 1982, Company A earns an income from its own operations of $52,000 and pays a $50,000 dividend, and during the same period Company B reports an income of $40,000 and pays a $30,000 dividend.

A continuing statement of changes in consolidated retained earnings would reflect the information as follows:

<table>
<tr><th colspan="5">Retained Earnings<br>Separate Company Statements</th></tr>
<tr><th></th><th colspan="2">Company A</th><th colspan="2">Company B</th></tr>
<tr><td>Balance, January 1, 1980</td><td></td><td>$ 70,000</td><td></td><td>$ 40,000</td></tr>
<tr><td>1980 income</td><td></td><td>50,000</td><td></td><td>30,000</td></tr>
<tr><td>Dividends received</td><td></td><td>16,000</td><td></td><td></td></tr>
<tr><td>Total</td><td></td><td>$136,000</td><td></td><td>$ 70,000</td></tr>
<tr><td>  *Deduct:* Dividends paid, 1980</td><td></td><td>40,000</td><td></td><td>20,000</td></tr>
<tr><td>Balance, December 31, 1980</td><td></td><td>$ 96,000</td><td></td><td>$ 50,000</td></tr>
<tr><td>1981 income</td><td></td><td>40,000</td><td></td><td>45,000</td></tr>
<tr><td>Dividends received</td><td></td><td>14,000</td><td></td><td></td></tr>
<tr><td>Total</td><td></td><td>$150,000</td><td></td><td>$ 95,000</td></tr>
<tr><td>  *Deduct:* Dividends paid, 1981</td><td>$40,000</td><td></td><td></td><td>20,000</td></tr>
<tr><td>    Loss on sale of B's stock</td><td>3,000</td><td>43,000</td><td></td><td></td></tr>
<tr><td>Balance, December 31, 1981</td><td></td><td>$107,000</td><td></td><td>$ 75,000</td></tr>
<tr><td>1982 income</td><td></td><td>52,000</td><td></td><td>40,000</td></tr>
<tr><td>Dividends received</td><td></td><td>21,000</td><td></td><td></td></tr>
<tr><td>Total</td><td></td><td>$180,000</td><td></td><td>$115,000</td></tr>
<tr><td>  *Deduct:* Stock dividend paid, 1982</td><td></td><td></td><td>$25,000</td><td></td></tr>
<tr><td>    Dividends paid, 1982</td><td></td><td>50,000</td><td>30,000</td><td>55,000</td></tr>
<tr><td>Balance, December 31, 1982</td><td></td><td>$130,000</td><td></td><td>$ 60,000</td></tr>
</table>

*Elimination:*

|  |  |  |  |
|---|---|---|---|
| Retained earnings at acquisition |  | $40,000 |  |
| Minority interest 30% of increase since acquisition |  | 6,000 | 46,000 |
| To consolidated retained earnings | 14,000 |  | $ 14,000 |
| *Add:* A's share of B's stock dividend | 17,500 |  |  |
| Consolidated retained earnings, December 31, 1982 | $161,500 |  |  |

**Change in Parent Company's Percent of Ownership of Subsidiary.** The impact of a change in the parent company's proportionate interest in a subsidiary can best be reexamined by an illustration. Assume that abbreviated statements of financial position of Company A and Company B, on January 1, 1980, were as follows:

COMPANY A

| Assets | $1,000,000 | Capital stock | $1,000,000 |
|---|---|---|---|

COMPANY B

| Assets | $ 300,000 | Capital stock | $ 300,000 |
|---|---|---|---|

On January 2, 1980, Company A purchases an 80% interest in Company B for $264,000. The statements immediately after the purchase would be:

COMPANY A

| Investment in B | $ 264,000 |  |  |
|---|---|---|---|
| Other assets | 736,000 | Capital stock | $1,000,000 |
|  | $1,000,000 |  | $1,000,000 |

COMPANY B

| Assets | $ 300,000 | Capital stock | $ 300,000 |
|---|---|---|---|

A consolidated statement of financial position prepared as of January 2, 1980, would reflect the following:

CONSOLIDATED STATEMENT OF FINANCIAL POSITION

| Assets | $1,036,000 | Minority interest | $ 60,000 |
|---|---|---|---|
| Goodwill | 24,000 | Capital stock | 1,000,000 |
|  | $1,060,000 |  | $1,060,000 |

Following the preferable consolidation procedure, the "Goodwill" of $24,000 would be allocated to other assets. As a result, the consolidated statement on January 2, 1980, might be:

## 17 / Consolidated Statements Reexamined

CONSOLIDATED STATEMENT OF FINANCIAL POSITION

| Assets | $1,060,000 | Minority interest | $   60,000 |
|---|---|---|---|
|  |  | Capital stock | 1,000,000 |
|  | $1,060,000 |  | $1,060,000 |

For illustrative purposes assume that during 1980 the only consolidated activity was Company B's operations, which provided an income of $40,000, all of which was retained by Company B. Assuming that Company A carries the investment at cost and that goodwill is not being amortized at this time, the statements on December 31, 1980, would appear as follows:

COMPANY A

| Investment in B | $   264,000 | Capital stock | $1,000,000 |
|---|---|---|---|
| Other assets | 736,000 |  |  |
|  | $1,000,000 |  | $1,000,000 |

COMPANY B

| Assets | $ 340,000 | Capital stock | $ 300,000 |
|---|---|---|---|
|  |  | Retained earnings | 40,000 |
|  | $ 340,000 |  | $ 340,000 |

CONSOLIDATED

| Assets | $1,100,000 | Minority interest | $   68,000 |
|---|---|---|---|
|  |  | Capital stock | 1,000,000 |
|  |  | Consolidated retained earnings | 32,000 |
|  | $1,100,000 |  | $1,100,000 |

Assume that on January 2, 1981, Company A sells one-eighth of its holdings of Company B stock for $33,000, the same price that Company A paid for the stock. Statements prepared on this date would appear as follows:

COMPANY A

| Investment in B | $ 231,000 | Capital stock | $1,000,000 |
|---|---|---|---|
| Other assets | 769,000 |  |  |
|  | $1,000,000 |  | $1,000,000 |

COMPANY B

| Assets | $ 340,000 | Capital stock | $ 300,000 |
|---|---|---|---|
|  |  | Retained earnings | 40,000 |
|  | $ 340,000 |  | $ 340,000 |

CONSOLIDATED

| | | | |
|---|---|---|---|
| Assets (including $21,000 of allocated "goodwill") | $1,130,000 | Minority interest (30%) | $  102,000 |
| | | Capital stock | 1,000,000 |
| | | Consolidated retained earnings | 28,000 |
| | $1,130,000 | | $1,130,000 |

Two pertinent observations may be drawn from the preceding illustration:

1. The consolidated statement of financial position on December 31, 1980, values the subsidiary assets at $24,000 above their cost to the subsidiary company, whereas the January 2, 1981, consolidated statement values the same assets at only $21,000 above the subsidiary company's cost. Allocated "Goodwill" was reduced from $24,000 to $21,000 by the sale of one-eighth of Company A's holdings in Company B.
2. Consolidated retained earnings declined from $32,000 on December 31, 1980, to $28,000 on January 2, 1981. The $4,000 decline was due to:

   (a) Revaluation of consolidated assets downward—allocated
   "Goodwill" declined from $24,000 to $21,000.     $3,000
   (b) Minority interest acquired an additional $34,000 book value
   equity in exchange for $33,000.     1,000
   Total decline in consolidated retained earnings     $4,000

## Change in Composition of Consolidated Entity

The impact of the sale by the parent of a substantial amount of the stock of a subsidiary may be such that it changes the composition of the consolidated entity. As a result, successive consolidated statements of financial position, income, and retained earnings may not be comparable over a period of time.

To illustrate, assume that Company A on January 1, 1980, owns 90% of Company B, 80% of Company C, and B owns 70% of Company D. These investments have been held for some time. On January 1, 1981, Company A sells eight-ninths of its investment in B, thus eliminating B and D from the consolidated group. For simplification purposes, assume that operating incomes for the separate companies in 1981 were identical with the 1980 earnings. Abbreviated consolidated statements of financial position and income might appear as follows:

CONSOLIDATED INCOME STATEMENTS

| | 1980 | 1981 |
|---|---|---|
| Sales | $890,000 | $490,000 |
| Cost of sales | 510,000 | 300,000 |
| Margin | $380,000 | $190,000 |
| Operating expenses | 230,000 | 120,000 |
| Income | $150,000 | $ 70,000 |
| Minority interest | 21,400 | 8,000 |
| Consolidated income | $128,600 | $ 62,000 |

## 17 / Consolidated Statements Reexamined

### CONSOLIDATED STATEMENTS OF FINANCIAL POSITION

|  | 1980 | 1981 |
|---|---|---|
| Current assets | $190,000 | $400,000 |
| Investment in B (cost) |  | 14,000 |
| Fixed assets | 641,000 | 431,000 |
| Goodwill | 61,000 | 25,000 |
| Total | $892,000 | $870,000 |
| Current liabilities | $120,000 | $ 80,000 |
| Fixed liabilities | 20,000 | 20,000 |
| Minority interest | 83,400 | 36,000 |
| Capital stock | 500,000 | 500,000 |
| Retained earnings | 168,600 | 234,000 |
| Total | $892,000 | $870,000 |

Any attempt to draw conclusions from comparative statements when a change in the composition of the consolidated entity has resulted between the dates of the two statements is questionable. Various suggestions have been made to overcome the problems arising from a change in the composition of a consolidated entity. As a minimum, it is suggested that footnotes be used to explain major changes in the composition of the entity. If data are available, adjusted statements that are comparable might be appropriate.

Disclosure of the effect of the disposition of a subsidiary on consolidated retained earnings should be disclosed in the statement of changes in consolidated earnings, if material, as shown below.

### COMPANY A
### CONSOLIDATED STATEMENT OF RETAINED EARNINGS
### FOR 1981

| | |
|---|---:|
| Balance, December 31, 1980 | $168,600 |
| Add: Gain on sale of 80% of B's stock | 3,400 |
| Balance, after adjustment for disposition of 80% of B's stock | $172,000 |
| Add: 1981 consolidated income | 62,000 |
| Balance, December 31, 1981 | $234,000 |

There should be no attempt to restate the December 31, 1980, balance of retained earnings to the amount it would have been had the composition of the 1980 entity been the same as the composition of the 1981 entity. Instead, all changes in consolidated retained earnings should be reflected in the consolidated statement of retained earnings. In computing the gain or loss on the sale of B's stock, it may be desirable to disclose the elements of the gain or loss in the following manner.

| | | |
|---|---|---:|
| Sale price of 80% of B's stock | | $xxxx |
| Less: | | |
| Cost of 80% of B's stock | $xxx | |

|  |  |  |
|---|---|---|
| 80% of B's increase in stockholders' equity since acquisition | xxx | |
| 10% of B's increase in stockholders' equity since acquisition | xxx | xxx |
| Net increase in consolidated retained earnings due to sale of B's stock | | $3,400 |

## Unconsolidated Subsidiaries

Although the proper valuation of investments in general is at cost, as indicated in *Bulletin 51*, two methods of dealing with investments in unconsolidated subsidiaries in consolidated statements are found in practice.

To illustrate, assume that Company A carries two investments on its books, as follows:

1. "Investment in B" acquired on January 1, 1980, when 60% of B's voting stock was acquired for $120,000. On that date B's stockholders' equity was $190,000, composed of $150,000 of capital stock and $40,000 of retained earnings.
2. "Investment in C" acquired on January 1, 1981, when 90% of C's voting stock was acquired for $380,000.

On January 1, 1981, the statements of financial position of the three companies were as follows:

|  | Company A | Company B | Company C |
|---|---|---|---|
| *Assets* | | | |
| Investment in B (60%) | $120,000 | | |
| Investment in C (90%) | 380,000 | | |
| Other assets | 440,000 | $250,000 | $400,000 |
| Total | $940,000 | $250,000 | $400,000 |
| *Equities* | | | |
| Liabilities | $100,000 | $ 40,000 | $ 20,000 |
| Capital stock | 800,000 | 150,000 | 300,000 |
| Retained earnings | 40,000 | 60,000 | 80,000 |
| Total | $940,000 | $250,000 | $400,000 |

Assume that Company B does not meet the standards for consolidation required by the consolidation policy of Company A. When Company C is acquired and does meet the standards for consolidation, however, consolidated statements may be prepared. In a consolidated statement of financial position, the investment in B may be reported as $120,000 with a footnote disclosure that the undistributed earnings of B since acquisition of the stock by A amounts to $20,000 ($210,000 − $190,000), and that 60% of this amount or $12,000 accrues to the investment. According to *APB Opinion No. 18*, the proper method, however, is to adjust the $120,000 investment upward by $12,000 with an offsetting credit through income to the retained earnings of Company A. A consolidated statement of financial position prepared on January 1, 1981, could be developed as follows:

COMPANY A AND SUBSIDIARY

CONSOLIDATED WORKING PAPERS

STATEMENT OF FINANCIAL POSITION

AS OF JANUARY 1, 1981

|  | Company A | Company C | Adjustments & Eliminations Debit | Adjustments & Eliminations Credit | Consolidated Financial Position |
|---|---|---|---|---|---|
| *Assets* | | | | | |
| Investment in B | $120,000 | | $ 12,000(1) | | $ 132,000 |
| Investment in C | 380,000 | | | $342,000A | 38,000G |
| Other assets | 440,000 | $400,000 | | | 840,000 |
| Total | $940,000 | $400,000 | | | $1,010,000 |
| *Equities* | | | | | |
| Liabilities | $100,000 | $ 20,000 | | | $ 120,000 |
| Capital stock | 800,000 | | | | 800,000 |
| Retained earnings | 40,000 | | | 12,000(1) | 52,000RE |
| Capital stock | | 300,000 | 270,000A | | 30,000MI |
| Retained earnings | | 80,000 | 72,000A | | 8,000MI |
| Total | $940,000 | $400,000 | $354,000 | $354,000 | $1,010,000 |

(1): To revalue upward the investment in the unconsolidated subsidiary by the amount of the parent's share of the subsidiary's undistributed earnings since January 1, 1980.

A: To eliminate 90% of C's stockholders' equity against the investment account.

## PROBLEMS

### Problem 17-1

The problem of consolidated working paper adjustments for intercompany bond holdings may be solved in accordance with a variety of assumptions, such as:

1. The consolidated gain or loss on reacquiring bonds may be assumed to accrue to both the purchasing company and the issuing company.
2. The consolidated gain or loss on reacquiring bonds may be assumed to accrue entirely to the issuing company (company having the bonds outstanding).
3. The consolidated gain or loss on reacquiring bonds may be assumed to accrue entirely to the purchasing company (company carrying the bonds as an investment).

*Required:*
(1) In the case below, give the journal entry or entries required to adjust for intercompany bondholding in the consolidated working papers under the three assumptions.
(2) How is consolidated retained earnings affected under each procedure?

STATEMENTS OF FINANCIAL POSITION

DECEMBER 31, 1980

|  | Company A | Company B |
|---|---|---|
| Investment in B Stock (80%) | $110,000 | |
| Investment in A Bonds ($10,000) | | $ 9,600 |
| Bond Discount | 6,000 | |
| Other Assets | 244,000 | 130,400 |
|  | $360,000 | $140,000 |
| Bonds Payable | $100,000 | |
| Capital Stock | 200,000 | $100,000 |
| Retained Earnings | 60,000 | 40,000 |
|  | $360,000 | $140,000 |

## Problem 17-2

Company P acquired control of Company S over a 15-year period, as follows:

|  |  |  | Subsidiary | |
|---|---|---|---|---|
| Date | Stock Acquired | Price Paid | Capital Stock | Retained Earnings |
| 1/1/66 | 10% | $ 45,000 | $500,000 | $100,000 |
| 1/1/70 | 2% | 12,000 | 500,000 | 130,000 |
| 1/1/72 | 10% | 75,000 | 500,000 | 160,000 |
| 1/1/76 | 10% | 90,000 | 500,000 | 210,000 |
| 1/1/78 | 13% | 120,000 | 500,000 | 250,000 |
| 1/1/81 | 20% | 200,000 | 500,000 | 300,000 |

On January 1, 1981, the retained earnings of Company P was $160,000. Having acquired control of Company S on January 1, 1981, the Company has decided to prepare a consolidated statement of financial position. Two amounts have been suggested for consolidated retained earnings: $160,000 and $212,900.

*Required:*
(1) Give the theory supporting each amount.
(2) How much "goodwill" should be recognized on the consolidated statement of financial position?
(3) Would your answer be different if the acquisitions were made as follows: 1/1/66 (10%), 1/1/70 (2%); 1/1/81 (53%). The price paid for the last acquisition was $530,000. The other prices were as given in the date above.

## Problem 17-3

On January 1, 1980, Company P acquired 80% of the stock of Company S for $55,000. On that date the statements of financial position of the two companies appeared as follows:

|  | Company P | | Company S | |
|---|---|---|---|---|
|  | Dr. | Cr. | Dr. | Cr. |
| Investment in S (80%) | $ 55,000 | | | |
| Other assets | 545,000 | | $210,000 | |
| Liabilities | | $ 60,000 | | $165,000 |
| Capital stock | | 500,000 | | 100,000 |
| Retained earnings | | 40,000 | | (55,000) |
| Total | $600,000 | $600,000 | $210,000 | $210,000 |

During 1980 neither company paid dividends. Financial statements of the separate companies on December 31, 1980, contained the following information.

|  | Company P | | Company S | |
|---|---|---|---|---|
|  | Dr. | Cr. | Dr. | Cr. |
| Investment in S (80%) | $ 55,000 | | | |
| Other assets | 585,000 | | $180,000 | |
| Liabilities | | $ 50,000 | | $200,000 |
| Capital stock | | 500,000 | | 100,000 |
| Retained earnings | | 90,000 | | (120,000) |
| Total | $640,000 | $640,000 | $180,000 | $180,000 |

*Required:*
Prepare a consolidated statement of financial position as of December 31, 1980.

## Problem 17-4

Company P owns 60% of Company S. Statements of financial position, as of December 31, 1980, reveal the following information:

|  | Company P | | Company S | |
|---|---|---|---|---|
|  | Dr. | Cr. | Dr. | Cr. |
| Investment in S (60%) | $480,000 | | | |
| Other assets | 35,000 | | $990,000 | |
| Liabilities | | $115,000 | | $ 90,000 |
| Capital stock | | 400,000 | | 800,000 |
| Retained earnings | | — | | 100,000 |
| Total | $515,000 | $515,000 | $990,000 | $990,000 |

Company P acquired the 60% interest in Company S on January 1, 1980, for $480,000 when Company S's retained earnings were zero. (Separate earnings of Company P for 1980 were zero.)

*Required:*
(1) Prepare a consolidated statement of financial position.
(2) Point out some limitations to the consolidated report that would be overcome by separate company reports.

## Problem 17-5

Company P acquired 90% of the stock of Company S by issuing its own stock in payment. The market value of the stock issued was $120,000; the market value of the stock acquired was $118,000; and the book value of the stock acquired was $54,000. The par value ($100 per share) of the stock issued was $100,000. Total assets of Company S were $75,000. The stock issued by Company P represents 10% of its total stock outstanding which has been issued on an average at 15% above par. Liabilities of Company P are $400,000.

*Required:*
Prepare a consolidated statement of financial position under each of the following assumptions:

(1) Subsidiary assets are to be valued at cost to the subsidiary.
(2) Subsidiary assets are to be valued at the cost prevailing when the parent company acquired the subsidiary.
(3) Assets claimed by parent company stockholders are valued at cost to the parent. Assets claimed by minority interest are valued at cost to the subsidiary.

## Problem 17-6

Company A purchased on January 1, 1980, 80% of Company S for $100,000 when Company S's stockholders' equity was $100,000 of capital stock and $10,000 of retained earnings. On this same date, S acquired a 10% interest in Company A for $40,000. At this time, Company A's stockholders' equity was capital stock of $300,000 and retained earnings of $60,000. Liabilities of the two companies on this date were: A, $70,000; S, $20,000. Earnings for 1980, all retained by each company, were: A, $30,000; S, $10,000. Liabilities on December 31, 1980, were A, $80,000; S, $25,000.

*Required:*
(1) Prepare a consolidated statement of financial position as of 12/31/80.
  (a) Assuming that the investment of S in A is considered a mutual holding.
  (b) Assuming that the investment of S in A is considered treasury stock.
(2) Prepare a statement reconciling the two views.

## Problem 17-7

Company A purchased 90% of Company S on January 1, 1980, for $160,000 when S's stockholders' equity was capital stock, $100,000, and retained earnings, $50,000. On this date, A's retained earnings were $70,000.

During 1980, S earned $20,000 and paid a cash dividend of $10,000. A earned from its own operations $15,000.

On January 1, 1981, A sold 2/9 of its holdings of S's stock for $32,000. During 1981, earnings and dividends were as follows:

|  | A | S |
|---|---|---|
| 1981 earnings | $20,000 | $24,000 |
| Cash dividend paid | 30,000 | 10,000 |
| Stock dividend paid (12/31/81) |  | 20,000 |

*Required:*
Prepare a statement of changes in consolidated retained earnings for 1980 and 1981.

## Problem 17-8

Comparative consolidated statements of financial position for Companies A and B on January 2 and January 3 were as follows. The change is due entirely to A's sale of 10% of B's stock.

|  | Jan. 2 | Jan. 3 |
|---|---|---|
| Assets (includes $16,000 goodwill on Jan. 2) | $880,000 | $905,000 |
| Minority interest | 48,000 | 72,000 |
| Capital stock | 700,000 | 700,000 |
| Retained earnings | 132,000 | 133,000 |
| Total | $880,000 | $905,000 |

*Required:*
Prepare a statement explaining the change in consolidated retained earnings.

## Problem 17-9

Condensed statements of financial position of Company P and Company S on January 1, 1980, appear as follows:

|  | Company P | Company S |
|---|---|---|
| Assets | $600,000 | $300,000 |
| Capital stock | 500,000 | 200,000 |
| Retained earnings | 40,000 | 50,000 |
| Liabilities | 60,000 | 50,000 |
| Total | $600,000 | $300,000 |

On January 2, Company P purchased 80% of the stock of Company S for $160,000. An examination of the difference between the price paid for the stock and its book value reveals the following information:

1. Assets of S are overvalued by $30,000
2. Additional costs required (none of which can be capitalized) for integrating the operations of P and S to be paid by P   25,000
3. Unrecorded liability of Company S   5,000

*Required:*
Prepare a consolidated statement of financial position as of January 2, 1980.

## Problem 17-10

Company S has 1,000 shares of stock outstanding. On January 2, 1980, H acquired 800 of these shares for $320,000. On that date S's stockholders' equity was

| | |
|---|---:|
| Capital stock (1,000 shares) | $100,000 |
| Retained earnings | 250,000 |
| Total | $350,000 |

Consolidated retained earnings on January 2, 1980, was $280,000.

During 1980, Company S earned an income of $50,000, all of which was retained in the business.

On January 2, 1981, Company S issued an additional 200 shares of stock to investors. None of this was purchased by Company H.

*Required:*
Compute consolidated retained earnings as of January 2, 1981, and explain the changes in it since January 2, 1980, assuming

  (a) The new stock is sold at $200 per share.
  (b) The new stock is sold at $400 per share.
  (c) The new stock is sold at $500 per share.

## Problem 17-11

Select the best answer for each of the following items relating to *APB Opinion No. 17* and *No. 18*. Assume that all investments were purchased after October 31, 1979, that the reporting periods begin after December 31, 1980, and that any amortization of goodwill is by the straight-line method for a 40-year period. Ignore income taxes.

1. On January 1, 1981, Investor Corporation purchased for $20,000 a 15% common stock interest in Investee Corporation, whose total common stock equity had a fair and a book value of $100,000. The investment is accounted for by the cost method. If Investee's net income during 1981 is $30,000 and Investor receives dividends of $5,000 from Investee, for 1981, Investor Corporation should report income from this investment of:

17 / Consolidated Statements Reexamined 549

    a. $5,000.
    b. $4,875.
    c. $4,500.
    d. $4,375.
    e. None of the above or not determinable from the facts above.
2. Assume the same facts as those in Item 1 except that Investor Corporation pays $50,000 for a 40% common stock interest in Investee Corporation, accounts for the investment by the equity method, and received $13,333 in dividends from Investee during 1981. For 1981, Investor Corporation should report as income from this investment the single amount of:
    a. $13,333.
    b. $13,083.
    c. $12,000.
    d. $11,750.
    e. None of the above or not determinable from the facts above.
3. The investment described in Item 2 should be reported as a long-term investment in Investor Corporation's balance sheet at December 31, 1981, as a single amount of:
    a. $63,083.
    b. $50,000.
    c. $48,667.
    d. $48,417.
    e. None of the above or not determinable from the facts above.
4. Assume that Operating Corporation purchases a 10% common stock interest in Service Corporation for $10,000 on January 1, 1981, and an additional 20% interest for $22,000 on January 1, 1982. The balance sheets of Service Corporation, which pays no dividends, follow:

|  | December 31, 1982 | December 31, 1981 | January 1, 1981 |
|---|---|---|---|
| Cash | $130,000 | $110,000 | $100,000 |
| Total Assets | $130,000 | $110,000 | $100,000 |
| Common stock | $100,000 | $100,000 | $100,000 |
| Retained earnings | 30,000 | 10,000 | –0– |
| Total owners' equity | $130,000 | $110,000 | $100,000 |

During 1981, Operating Corporation carries this investment under the cost method and on January 1, 1982, adopts the equity method. For 1982, Operating Corporation should report as income from this 30% investment the single amount of:
    a. $9,000.
    b. $7,000.
    c. $6,000.
    d. $5,950.
    e. None of the above or not determinable from the facts above.

5. The investment described in Item 4 should be reported as a long-term investment in Operating Corporation's balance sheet at December 31, 1982, as a single amount of:
   a. $41,000.
   b. $39,000.
   c. $38,000.
   d. $37,900.
   e. None of the above or not determinable from the facts above.

   (AICPA adapted)

## Problem 17-12

Select the *best* answer for each of the following items:

1. Investor, Inc., owns 40% of Alimand Corporation. During the calendar year 1979, Alimand had net earnings of $100,000 and paid dividends of $10,000. Investor mistakingly recorded these transactions using the cost method rather than the equity method of accounting. What effect would this have on the investment account, net earnings, and retained earnings, respectively?
   a. Understate, overstate, overstate.
   b. Overstate, understate, understate.
   c. Overstate, overstate, overstate.
   d. Understate, understate, understate.
2. Drab, Inc., owns 40% of the outstanding stock of Gloom Company. During 1979, Drab received a $4,000 cash dividend from Gloom. What effect did this dividend have on Drab's 1979 financial statements?
   a. Increased total assets.
   b. Decreased total assets.
   c. Increased income.
   d. Decreased investment account.

*Items 3 and 4 are based on the following information:*

Apex Company acquired 70% of the outstanding stock of Nadir Corporation. The separate balance sheet of Apex immediately after the acquisition and the consolidated balance sheet are as follows:

|  | Apex | Consolidated |
|---|---|---|
| Current assets | $106,000 | $146,000 |
| Investment in Nadir (cost) | 100,000 | — |
| Goodwill | — | 8,100 |
| Fixed assets (net) | 270,000 | 370,000 |
|  | $476,000 | $524,100 |
| Current liabilities | $ 15,000 | $ 28,000 |
| Capital stock | 350,000 | 350,000 |
| Minority interest | — | 35,100 |
| Retained earnings | 111,000 | 111,000 |
|  | $476,000 | $524,100 |

Ten thousand dollars of the excess payment for the investment in Nadir was ascribed to undervaluation of its fixed assets; the balance of the excess payment was ascribed to goodwill. Current assets of Nadir included a $2,000 receivable from Apex that arose before they became related on an ownership basis.

The following two items relate to Nadir's separate balance sheet prepared at the time Apex acquired its 70% interest in Nadir.

3. What was the total of the current assets on Nadir's separate balance sheet at the time Apex acquired its 70% interest?
   a. $38,000.
   b. $40,000.
   c. $42,000.
   d. $104,000.

4. What was the total stockholders' equity on Nadir's separate balance sheet at the time Apex acquired its 70% interest?
   a. $64,900.
   b. $70,000.
   c. $100,000.
   d. $117,000.

5. When the equity method of accounting for an investment in a subsidiary is used, dividends from the subsidiary should be accounted for by the parent corporation as
   a. Revenue unless paid from retained earnings of the subsidiary earned before the date of acquisition.
   b. Revenue so long as the dividends were declared from retained earnings.
   c. A reduction of the carrying value of the investment account.
   d. A deferred credit.

6. What would be the effect on the financial statements if an unconsolidated subsidiary is accounted for by the equity method, but consolidated statements are being prepared with other subsidiaries?
   a. All of the unconsolidated subsidiary's accounts will be included individually in the consolidated statements.
   b. The consolidated retained earnings will *not* reflect the earnings of the unconsolidated subsidiary.
   c. The consolidated retained earnings will be the same as if the subsidiary had been included in the consolidation.
   d. Dividend revenue from the unconsolidated subsidiary will be reflected in consolidated net income.

7. On January 1, 1979, the Swing Company purchased at book value 100,000 shares (20%) of the voting common stock of Harpo Instruments, Inc., for $1,200,000. Direct costs associated with the purchase were $50,000. On December 1, 1979, the board of directors of Harpo declared a dividend of $2 per share payable to holders of record on December 28, 1979. The net income of Harpo for the year ended December 31, 1979, was $1,600,000.

What should be the balance in Swing's "Investment in Harpo Instruments, Inc.," account at December 31, 1979?

a. $1,200,000.
b. $1,250,000.
c. $1,370,000.
d. $1,520,000.

8. Which of the following describes the amount at which a parent company should carry its unconsolidated domestic subsidiary on its separate financial statements in periods subsequent to acquisition?
   a. Original cost of the investment to the parent company.
   b. Original cost of the investment adjusted for the parent's share of the subsidiary's earnings, losses, and dividends.
   c. Current market value of the investment adjusted for dividends received.
   d. Current market value of the investment.

9. In a parent's unconsolidated financial statements, which accounts, other than cash, are affected when reflecting a subsidiary's earnings and dividends?
   a. Dividend revenue, equity in earnings of subsidiary, and retained earnings.
   b. Dividend revenue and retained earnings.
   c. Investment in subsidiary, equity in earnings of subsidiary, dividend revenue, and retained earnings.
   d. Investment in subsidiary, equity in earnings of subsidiary, and retained earnings.

10. How is the portion of consolidated earnings to be assigned to minority interest in consolidated financial statements determined?
    a. The net income of the parent is subtracted from the subsidiary's net income to determine the minority interest.
    b. The subsidiary's net income is extended to the minority interest.
    c. The amount of the subsidiary's earnings recognized for consolidation purposes is multiplied by the minority's percentage ownership.
    d. The amount of consolidated earnings determined on the consolidated working papers is multiplied by the minority interest percentage at the balance sheet date.

*Items 11 and 12 are based on the following information:*

On June 30, 1979, Axel, Inc., acquired Belle, Inc., in a business combination properly accounted for as a pooling of interests. Axel exchanged six of its shares of common stock for each share of Belle's outstanding common stock. June 30 was the fiscal year-end for both companies. There were *no* intercompany transactions during the year. The balance sheets immediately before the combination follow:

|  | Axel Book Value | Belle Book Value | Belle Fair Value |
| --- | --- | --- | --- |
| Current assets | $ 40,000 | $ 30,000 | $ 45,000 |
| Equipment (net) | 150,000 | 120,000 | 140,000 |
| Land | 30,000 | — | — |
|  | $220,000 | $150,000 | $185,000 |

|  |  |  |  |
|---|---|---|---|
| Current liabilities | $ 35,000 | $ 15,000 | $ 15,000 |
| Notes payable | 40,000 | — | — |
| Bonds payable | — | 100,000 | 100,000 |
| Common stock ($1 par) | 75,000 | — | — |
| Common stock ($5 par) | — | 50,000 | — |
| Retained earnings | 70,000 | (15,000) | — |
|  | $220,000 | $150,000 |  |

11. What was the retained earnings balance on the combined balance sheet at June 30, 1979?
    a. $45,000.
    b. $55,000.
    c. $70,000.
    d. $80,000.
12. How should the combined net income for the year be computed?
    a. Use only Axel's income because the combination occurred on the last day of the fiscal year.
    b. Use only Belle's income because the combination occurred on the last day of the fiscal year.
    c. Add together both companies' incomes even though the combination occurred on the last day of the fiscal year.
    d. Add together both companies' incomes and subtract the annual amortization of goodwill.
    (AICPA adapted)

# 18

# Expansion by Foreign Operations

History shows that as an economy matures and its business enterprises expand, businessmen often look abroad for wider markets and additional investment possibilities. The economy of the United States has been no exception. Today American business organizations operate throughout the world with some form of an organization in practically every country of the world.

The problems involved when accounting for foreign operations can best be examined by studying the problems peculiar to the various types of foreign operations. Foreign operations, as a general rule, can be classified in one of the following categories:

1. Domestic company with foreign transactions.
2. Foreign branches.
3. Foreign subsidiaries.

### Domestic Company with Foreign Transactions

When a domestic company sells or buys merchandise abroad, it may bill or be billed either in the domestic currency or in the foreign currency. If the company bills or is billed in domestic currency, no peculiar problems arise. However, if the company bills or is billed in the foreign currency, an exchange gain or loss may arise as the result of fluctuations in exchange rates between the date of sale or purchase and the date of settlement. If the exchange rate in effect at the date of settlement is the same as it was at the date of sale or purchase, no exchange gain or loss is involved. If the rates at these dates are not the same, an exchange gain or loss will arise.

**Foreign Sales.** Assuming that a United States company sells merchandise for $10,000 to a British company and bills the British company in dollars, no exchange gain or loss is involved from the standpoint of the United States company, as the following entries illustrate:

```
Date of sale:
    British company                         $10,000
        Sales (foreign)                                 $10,000

Date of settlement:
    Cash                                    $10,000
        British company                                 $10,000
```

However, if the United States company bills the British company in pounds, an exchange gain or loss will arise if the rate of exchange at the date of settlement is not the same as it was at the date of sale. For example, assume, in addition to the facts given above, that the rate of exchange at the date of sale was 1.675 (that is, $1.675 per pound) and at the date of settlement 1.640.

```
Date of sale:
    British company (£5,970)                $10,000
        Sales (foreign)                                 $10,000

Date of settlement:
    Cash (£5,970)                           $ 9,791
    Exchange gain or loss                       209
        British company                                 $10,000
```

**Foreign Purchases.** Assuming that a United States company buys $28,000 worth of merchandise from a British company and is billed by the British company in dollars, no exchange gain or loss is involved from the standpoint of the United States company, as the following entries illustrate:

```
Date of purchase:
    Purchases                               $28,000
        British company                                 $28,000

Date of settlement:
    British company                         $28,000
        Cash                                            $28,000
```

If, however, the United States company is billed in pounds instead of dollars, an exchange gain or loss will arise if the rate of exchange at the date of settlement is not the same as it was at the date of purchase. For example, assume that a United States company purchases merchandise worth 10,000 pounds from a British company at a time when the exchange rate is 1.640 and settles the obligation when the rate is 1.675.

| | | |
|---|---|---|
| Date of purchase: | | |
| Purchases | $16,400 | |
| British company (£10,000) | | $16,400 |
| Date of settlement: | | |
| British company | $16,400 | |
| Exchange gain or loss | 350 | |
| Cash (£10,000) | | $16,750 |

**Realized Versus Unrealized Exchange Gain or Loss.** The foregoing illustrations have dealt with realized exchange gains and losses. In contrast to realized exchange gains and losses are unrealized exchange gains and losses that come into being when financial statements are prepared before a transaction has been completed.

To illustrate, assume that a United States company, American Sales, Inc., sells to a British company, British Exchange, Ltd., on December 18, merchandise for $10,000 billed in pounds when the exchange rate was $1.675 per pound. The account was settled on April 15 when the exchange rate was $1.658 per pound ($9,899). American Sales prepared financial statements on December 31, when the exchange rate was $1.640 per pound ($9,791). On December 31, American Sales had an unrealized loss of $209 ($10,000 − $9,791). Under the provisions of *FASB Statement No. 8*, "Accounting for Translation of Foreign Currency Transactions and Foreign Currency Financial Statements," this unrealized loss would be reported as a loss at December 31, generally classified as a nonoperating item. The following entries would arise:

| | | |
|---|---|---|
| Date of Sale: | | |
| Due from British Exchange (£5,970) | $10,000 | |
| Sales | | $10,000 |
| December 31: | | |
| Exchange gain or loss | $   209 | |
| Due from British Exchange | | $   209 |

At the settlement date on April 15, when the exchange rate has moved up to $1.658 per pound (from $1.640 per pound at December 31), American Sales will receive £5,970, which has a dollar value of $9,899. Although American Sales incurs a foreign exchange loss of $101 ($10,000 − $9,899) on the now-completed transaction, it will report a foreign exchange gain of $108 ($209 − $101) at April 15. The gain arises because of the recovery of the pound from December 31, when £5,970 was worth $9,791 to April 15, when £5,970 was worth $9,899. The following entry would arise at April 15:

| | | |
|---|---|---|
| Cash (£5,970) | $9,899 | |
|     Due from British Exchange | | $9,791 |
|     Exchange gain or loss | | 108 |

From a practical point of view, the application of *FASB Statement No. 8* eliminates any distinction between a realized foreign exchange gain or loss and an unrealized foreign exchange gain or loss. Prior to the adoption of *Statement No. 8*, unrealized foreign exchange gains were commonly deferred as a suspense account reported on the balance sheet. Unrealized foreign exchange losses were also sometimes deferred in a similar fashion, but more commonly, unrealized losses were charged to income in the period of loss. In terms of the previous example, the FASB concluded that at December 31 the change in the exchange rate requires an adjustment to the receivable, "Due from British Exchange," and the offset to that adjustment reflects a loss associated with a market decline of a receivable.

**Assets Transmitted for Sale in a Foreign Country.** At times, a domestic company may ship goods to a foreign country for subsequent sale in the foreign country. Normally, this involves the use of an associated firm in the foreign country which will handle the goods for the domestic company.

It is normally assumed for accounting purposes that the goods shipped for sale will be sold at a price other than the cost valuation that was attached to them at the time of shipment. This raises a problem regarding any unrealized exchange gain or loss on unsold goods at any reporting date. Some accountants contend that no unrealized exchange gain or loss comes into existence until there is definite reason to believe a currency exchange is involved. These accountants maintain that no realized or unrealized exchange gain or loss is possible until the goods are sold and the probability of currency transmission increased. Essentially, this group contends that the proper translation rate for unsold goods is the rate that prevailed when the goods were shipped.

Other accountants maintain, however, that the cost of any unsold goods on any reporting date should be translated at the exchange rate prevailing at that date. This procedure, sometimes referred to as a one-transaction perspective, is based on the reasoning that the transaction involving the shipment of goods for sale in another country is incomplete until the amount in dollars necessary to settle the transaction is determined. These accountants regard the initial amount recorded in dollars as an estimate until final settlement. As a result, they would recognize an exchange gain or loss related to the unsold portion of the shipment as an adjustment of the costs of goods shipped but unsold.

In *Statement No. 8*, the FASB concluded that the former concept is the more appropriate one. Thus, the Board recognizes that gains and losses on assets accounted for at cost (e.g., inventories) are usually deferred until the assets are sold or their costs are otherwise deducted from operating revenues. No adjustment would be made at a reporting date for unrealized gain or loss on unsold merchandise when the merchandise is reported on the cost basis.

To illustrate, assume that U.S. Supply, a United States company, ships to a British company, British Provisions, goods that had cost the United States company $10,000. British Provisions picked up the goods at £5,750 (exchange rate of 1.739). On December 31, British Provisions reports that one-half of the goods had been sold at a net price of £4,000 on November 19, when the exchange rate was $1.632 per pound. On December 31, the rate of exchange is $1.640 per pound. On April 15, British Provisions transmits the £4,000 when the exchange rate is $1.658 and reports that the other half of the goods is unsold. Assuming that the cost of the unsold goods is translated at the rate prevailing when the goods were shipped, the following would record the transactions above:

Date shipped:
    Goods shipped British Provisions      $10,000
        Merchandise      $10,000

November 19, 1979:
    Due from British Provisions (£4,000 × 1.632)      $ 6,528
    Cost of sales      5,000
        Goods shipped to British Provisions      $ 5,000
        Sales      6,528
[to record the sale reported by British Provisions and the related cost of sales. The British Provisions report would be:
    Sales      £ 4,000
    Cost of sales (one-half £5,750)      2,875
    Gross margin      £ 1,125

If these amounts were translated to dollars at the exchange rate prevailing at the date of sales, the translated amounts would be:
    Sales £4,000 at 1.632      $ 6,528
    Cost of sales £2,875 at 1.632      4,692

Recording cost of sales at $5,000 instead of $4,692 is supported by the reasoning that holds that the cost of sales should be translated at the exchange rate prevailing at the date the goods were shipped:
    £2,875 at $1.739 = $5,000]
December 31, 1979:
    Due from British Provisions      $ 32
        Exchange gain or loss      $ 32
[to record the increase in cash since the sale date which would be received if British Provisions were to pay on

*18 / Expansion by Foreign Operations*

December 31 the £2,500 [4000] owed U.S. Supply. The computation would be:

Valuation of receivable from British Provisions:
| | |
|---|---|
| December 31, 1979—£4,000 @ 1.640 = | $6,560 |
| November 19, 1979—£4,000 @ 1.632 = | 6,528 |
| Increase in receivable since November 19 because of exchange fluctuation | $ 32 |

Although it may be suggested that an unrealized exchange loss exists on the unsold merchandise (£2,875 recorded at $5,000), accountants who believe that the cost of unsold merchandise should be translated at the exchange rate prevailing when the goods were shipped would give no recognition to the exchange fluctuations of the unsold goods.]

April 15, 1980:

| | | |
|---|---|---|
| Cash | $6,632 | |
| Due from British Provisions | | $ 6,560 |
| Exchange gain or loss | | 72 |

(to record the realized exchange gain when British Provisions pays the £2,500 [4000]. The computations would be:

| | | |
|---|---|---|
| Cash received £4,000 @ 1.658 | = | $6,632 |
| Valuation of receivable on December 31, 1979 £4,000 @ 1.640 | = | 6,560 |
| Realized exchange fluctuation gain | | $ 72 |

Because of the recognition of the unrealized exchange gain on December 31, which revalued the receivable to $6,560, the exchange gain on the settlement reflects only the currency fluctuation following December 31.)

**Assets Transmitted for Use in a Foreign Country.** Machinery and other fixed assets may be shipped by a domestic company to a foreign country for use by a branch or foreign associate and not for sale. Since these assets may have long lives and their contribution to sales in the foreign country may extend over a long period of time, the rate at which they are translated is normally the rate prevailing on the date these assets are shipped. This position on translation of fixed assets is consistent with the valuation of fixed assets at acquisition cost. Fluctuations in the values of assets committed to relatively long periods of use are normally not reflected in accounting records. It has also been contended that translation at exchange rates prevailing on the reporting date implies that this is the rate at which the fixed assets will be translated to currency and transmitted to the domestic country. Since it is obvious that this rate is not proper, it appears logical to conclude that the rate prevailing at the reporting date should not be used. Likewise, since it is impossible to forecast future exchange rates that will prevail when these assets are translated to currency, expected future rates should not be used. The most objective basis for translation appears to be the rate prevailing on the date the resources were shipped.

**Assets Transmitted Versus Assets Acquired in a Foreign Country.** No distinction should be drawn between assets shipped by a domestic company to a foreign associate for sale or use and similar assets acquired by the associate for sale or use for the benefit of the domestic company. Assets should be translated at similar exchange rates whether shipped from the domestic country or acquired in the foreign country. The exchange rate on the acquisition date is substituted for the exchange rate on the shipment date for acquired assets.

**Foreign Operations.** Before the procedures for translating branch accounts and subsidiary company accounts are discussed, certain aspects of foreign operations should be noted. First, many domestic companies have experienced difficulty in getting funds out of some foreign countries as a result of a variety of restrictions. Inclusion of income earned in a foreign country as part of the income of the United States company may be misleading if such income cannot be transmitted to the domestic company.

In some instances, different foreign exchange rates exist at the same time. A foreign government may decree an official exchange rate, and the free market may establish another rate. The selection of the most appropriate rate for translation should be realistic in terms of the rate that will prevail for the particular company.

### Foreign Branches

In Chapter Eight, when domestic branches were discussed, it was pointed out that it is not uncommon for companies to establish branches in foreign countries. Attention was also directed to the accounting procedures to be followed for such branches. Essentially the same procedures apply for foreign branches as for domestic branches, except when combined statements are prepared. For combined statements it is necessary to translate branch account balances from the foreign currency into the domestic currency.

**Translation Rates.** The Financial Accounting Standards Board in *Statement of Financial Accounting Standards No. 8* recommends the use of the following rates when translating foreign accounts into domestic currency:

**Monetary Assets and Liabilities.** Cash and amounts receivable or payable that are denominated in other than the local currency should be translated at the exchange rate prevailing on the reporting date. This rate is frequently referred to as the *current rate*.

**Nonmonetary Assets and Liabilities.** Inventories, fixed assets, investments not providing for redemption at a specified amount, and other nonmonetary assets should be translated using a rate consistent with the appropriate measurement basis for the asset. Certain assets, such as inventory and fixed assets, are generally measured at a past exchange price (historical cost). Those assets should be translated at rates prevailing when such assets were acquired or constructed, the historical exchange rate. Other assets, such as certain investments in securities, are generally measured at a current exchange price (replacement cost or market value). Those assets should be translated at the current exchange rate at the reporting date. Since fixed assets are translated at the rate prevailing when such assets were acquired or constructed, depreciation (not only the charge for the period, but also the accumulated amount) should also be translated at the historical rate.

**Reciprocal Accounts.** Branch accounts that are reciprocal to home office accounts should be translated to the balances shown by the respective home office accounts. For example:

"Home Office" account is translated to the same amount as shown in "Branch Office" account.

"Merchandise from Home Office" is translated to the same amount as shown in the "Merchandise Shipments to Branch" account.

"Remittances to Home Office" is translated to the same amount as shown in the "Remittances from Branch" account.

"Remittances from Home Office" is translated to the same amount as shown in the "Remittances to Branch" account.

**Nominal Accounts.** Income and expense accounts, except for depreciation, should be translated in a manner that produces approximately the same dollar amounts that would have resulted had the underlying transactions been translated into dollars on the dates they occurred. A practical approach is to translate the accounts at the average rate applicable to each month or on the basis of a carefully weighted average. This rate is usually referred to as the *average rate*. Depreciation, as was pointed out above, should be translated at the rates prevailing when the related assets were acquired or constructed.

**Exchange Gain or Loss.** When foreign accounts are translated into domestic currency, the use of several rates usually results in a discrepancy between the total debits and credits. This represents an exchange gain or loss, depending upon whether the debits exceed the credits (a gain) or whether the credits exceed the debits (a loss). Under the provisions of FASB Statement No. 8, both realized and unrealized exchange gains and losses are to be charged to operations.

**Realized Gains and Losses.** Realized gains or losses result if the rate of exchange prevailing when the cash transfer is made differs from the rate of exchange prevailing when the cash was advanced or earned. For example, a realized gain or loss would result if a branch made sales and incurred expenses that were translated at an average rate. When the cash arising from any income reported is transmitted to the home office, the rate of exchange may be different from the average rate at which the income was originally translated. In general, realized gains or losses arise from a delay in transmitting earnings after the date earned or in returning cash advances. The earlier illustrations of exchange gain or loss arising on foreign sales or purchases suggest the nature of realized gains and losses.

To illustrate more fully, assume that Branch B transferred £2,000 of income to the home office in the United States when the exchange rate was $1.70 per pound. The earnings were the result of £5,000 of sales and £3,000 of expenses. The average exchange rate during the period when the sales were made and the expenses incurred was $1.68 per pound. The translated income statement in abbreviated form would appear as follows:

|  | Pounds | Rate | Dollars |
|---|---|---|---|
| Sales | 5,000 | 1.68 | 8,400 |
| Expenses | 3,000 | 1.68 | 5,040 |
| Income | 2,000 | 1.68 | 3,360 |

Upon receipt of the report, the home office would record the income by the following entry:

| | | |
|---|---|---|
| Branch office (foreign) | $3,360 | |
|     Branch income | | $3,360 |

When the cash resulting from the operations (£2,000) is transmitted, however, the home office would receive a total of $3,400 (£2,000 @ $1.70). The entry to record the cash receipt would be:

| | | |
|---|---|---|
| Cash | $3,400 | |
|     Branch office (foreign) | | $3,360 |
|     Exchange gain or loss | | 40 |

**Unrealized Gains and Losses.** Unrealized gains or losses result from the translation of the accounts of a foreign branch to domestic currency, since different rates may be used in translating various interrelated accounts. Typical examples of unrealized gains or losses are:

1. Unremitted cash (translated at the rate prevailing at the reporting date) valued differently from the offsetting credit. (If the credit were to an income account,

the translation rate would *not* necessarily be that prevailing at the reporting date.)
2. An asset translated at one rate and the credit at another, which might result if a fixed asset were purchased with the credit going to a current liability, or if a current asset arose as a result of a credit to the Home Office account, as when the home office ships merchandise to the branch.

Thus various transactions may result in unrealized gains or losses. As noted previously, these unrealized gains or losses are reported in the current period's operating results.

To illustrate, assume the same facts as those in the example above except that the cash was not transmitted to the United States and the translation rate was $1.67 on the reporting date. In work sheet form, assuming that these are the only items to be translated, the result would be:

|  | Pounds |  | Translation | Dollars |  |
|---|---|---|---|---|---|
| Account | Dr. | Cr. | Rate | Dr. | Cr. |
| Cash | 2,000 |  | 1.67 | 3,340 |  |
| Income |  | 2,000 | 1.68 |  | 3,360 |
| Exchange gain or loss |  |  |  | 20 |  |
| Total | 2,000 | 2,000 |  | 3,360 | 3,360 |

The exchange loss would be charged to operations and the entry to pick up branch earnings would be:

| Branch office (foreign) | $3,340 |  |
|---|---|---|
| Exchange gain or loss | 20 |  |
| Branch income |  | $3,360 |

Of course, in an actual case, many other accounts would exist. The unrealized gain or loss is the amount needed to balance the translated amounts.

## Foreign Branch Accounting Illustrated

Assume that a United States company establishes a branch in England and that the following transactions occur during the first month of operation:

(1) January 1. The home office establishes the English branch by transferring $7,500 [5100] cash and $10,000 [6500] worth of merchandise to the branch.
(2) January 2. The home office purchases in England and turns over to the branch equipment costing £2,000.
(3) January 5. The branch purchases merchandise costing £1,000.
(4) January 10. The branch sells merchandise for £3,000 cash.

(5) January 20. The branch purchases £2,000 worth of merchandise on account.
(6) January 20. The branch sells merchandise on account for £4,000.
(7) January 31. The branch pays expenses for January totaling £2,000.
(8) January 31. The branch remits £1,000 to the home office.
(9) January 31. The branch submits its trial balance as of January 31 to the home office.
(10) January 31. The home office translates the branch trial balance and combines it with that of the home office.

The following rates of exchange were in effect during the month:

| | |
|---|---|
| January 1 | 1.700 |
| January 2 | 1.710 |
| January 5 | 1.712 |
| January 10 | 1.715 |
| January 20 | 1.720 |
| January 31 | 1.728 |
| Average January rate | 1.715 |

| BRANCH BOOKS | | | HOME OFFICE BOOKS | | |
|---|---|---|---|---|---|
| Jan. 1 | Cash | £3,000 | | Branch office | $11,900 | |
| | Merchandise from | | | Cash | | $ 5,100 |
| | home office | £4,000 | | Merchandise ship- | | |
| | Home office | | £7,000 | ments to branch | | $ 6,800 |
| Jan. 2 | Equipment | £2,000 | | Branch office | $ 3,420 | |
| | Home office | | £2,000 | Cash | | $ 3,420 |
| Jan. 5 | Purchases | £1,000 | | No entry | | |
| | Cash | | £1,000 | | | |
| Jan. 10 | Cash | £3,000 | | No entry | | |
| | Sales | | £3,000 | | | |
| Jan. 20 | Purchases | £2,000 | | No entry | | |
| | Accounts payable | | £2,000 | | | |
| Jan. 20 | Accounts receivable | £4,000 | | No entry | | |
| | Sales | | £4,000 | | | |
| Jan. 31 | Expenses | £2,000 | | No entry | | |
| | Cash | | £2,000 | | | |
| Jan. 31 | Remittances to home office | £1,000 | | Cash | $ 1,728 | |
| | Cash | | £1,000 | Remittances from branch | | $ 1,728 |

As of January 31, the branch submits the following trial balance to the home office:

18 / *Expansion by Foreign Operations*

BRANCH TRIAL BALANCE
AS OF JANUARY 31

| | | |
|---|---:|---:|
| Cash | £ 2,000 | |
| Merchandise from home office | 4,000 | |
| Equipment | 2,000 | |
| Purchases | 3,000 | |
| Accounts receivable | 4,000 | |
| Expenses | 2,000 | |
| Remittances to home office | 1,000 | |
| Home office | | £ 9,000 |
| Sales | | 7,000 |
| Accounts payable | | 2,000 |
| | £18,000 | £18,000 |

Merchandise on hand January 31, £2,000.

Translation of the branch trial balance would be as follows:

BRANCH TRIAL BALANCE
AS OF JANUARY 31

| | Pounds Dr. | Pounds Cr. | Translation Rate | Dollars Dr. | Dollars Cr. |
|---|---:|---:|---:|---:|---:|
| Cash | 2,000 | | 1.728C | 3,456 | |
| Merchandise from home office | 4,000 | | R | 6,800 | |
| Equipment | 2,000 | | 1.710D | 3,420 | |
| Purchases | 3,000 | | 1.715A | 5,145 | |
| Accounts receivable | 4,000 | | 1.728C | 6,912 | |
| Expenses | 2,000 | | 1.715A | 3,430 | |
| Remittances to home office | 1,000 | | R | 1,728 | |
| Home office | | 9,000 | R | | 15,320 |
| Sales | | 7,000 | 1.715A | | 12,005 |
| Accounts payable | | 2,000 | 1.728C | | 3,456 |
| | 18,000 | 18,000 | | | |
| Exchange gain or loss | | | | | 110 |
| | | | | 30,891 | 30,891 |
| Merchandise on hand January 31, £2,000 | | | 1.728C | 3,456 | |

A: Average rate.
C: Current rate.
D: Rate prevailing at date equipment was acquired.
R: Reciprocal.

Combination of the translated branch trial balance with the home office accounts would be as follows:

## U.S. Company and English Branch
### Combined Working Papers
#### January 31

| Debits | U.S. Company | English Branch | Adjustments & Eliminations | Income | Combined Financial Position |
|---|---|---|---|---|---|
| Cash | $ 20,000 | $ 3,456 | | | $ 23,456 |
| Accounts receivable | 30,000 | 6,912 | | | 36,912 |
| Inventory, January 1 | 40,000 | | | $ 40,000 | |
| Branch office | 15,320 | | $15,320A | | |
| Merchandise from home office | | 6,800 | 6,800B | | |
| Remittances to home office | | 1,728 | 1,728C | | |
| Equipment | | 3,420 | | | 3,420 |
| Other assets | 49,952 | | | | 49,952 |
| Purchases | 140,000 | 5,145 | | 145,145 | |
| Expenses | 25,056 | 3,430 | | 28,486 | |
| | $320,328 | $30,891 | | | |
| Inventories, January 31 | | | $33,456(1) | $213,631 | 33,456 |
| | | | | | $147,196 |

## 18 / Expansion by Foreign Operations

| Credits | | | | | | |
|---|---|---|---|---|---|---|
| Accounts payable | $ 15,000 | $ 3,456 | | | | $ 18,456 |
| Home office | | 15,320 | 15,320A | | | |
| Merchandise shipments to branch | 6,800 | | 6,800B | | | |
| Remittances from branch | 1,728 | | 1,728C | | | |
| Sales | 200,000 | 12,005 | | 212,005 | | |
| Exchange gain or loss | | 110 | | 110 | | |
| Capital stock | 80,000 | | | | | 80,000 |
| Retained earnings | 16,800 | | | | | 16,800 |
| | $320,328 | $30,891 | | | | |
| Inventories, January 31 | $ 30,000 | $ 3,456 | | 33,456 | 33,456(1) | |
| | | $57,304 | $57,304 | $245,571 | | |
| Income credits | | | | 213,631 | | |
| Income debits | | | | $ 31,940 | | 31,940 |
| Combined net income | | | | | | $147,196 |

## Foreign Subsidiaries

As indicated earlier, domestic companies may have subsidiaries in countries all over the world. These subsidiaries may be formed by their respective parent companies or they may be obtained through acquisition by the parent companies. In general, accounting for a foreign subsidiary is similar to accounting for a foreign branch. Consequently, only such areas as are peculiar to the subsidiary are stressed here.

**Translation Rates.** As a general rule, foreign subsidiary accounts are translated into domestic currency by using the same rates as are used when translating foreign branch accounts. However, there are certain accounts that are peculiar to the home office-branch relationship, whereas others are peculiar to the parent-subsidiary relationship. For instance, the branch office and home office accounts are replaced by the parent company's investment account and subsidiary's stockholders' equity section. In general, the following rates are used when translating the accounts of a foreign subsidiary into domestic currency:

1. *Monetary assets* and *monetary liabilities* at the current rate.
2. *Nonmonetary assets* and *nonmonetary liabilities* at the rates prevailing when the assets were acquired and the liabilities were incurred.
3. *Nominal accounts* (income and expense), except depreciation, in a manner that produces approximately the same dollar amounts that would have resulted had the underlying transactions been translated into dollars on the dates they occurred. A practical approach often followed is to translate these accounts at an average rate for the period. Depreciation, as indicated earlier, should be translated on the same basis as the related asset.
4. *Stockholders' equity accounts:*
    a. *Capital stock.* As a general rule, capital stock should be translated at the rate prevailing when the subsidiary was formed, if formed by the parent company, or at the date of acquisition, if acquired by the parent subsequent to formation.
    b. *Capital in excess of par.* If a parent company forms a foreign subsidiary, any capital in excess of par created by the formation should be translated at the rate prevailing at the date of formation. If the parent acquires a foreign subsidiary subsequent to its formation, any capital in excess of par in existence as of the date of acquisition should be translated at the rate prevailing at that time. Capital in excess of par created subsequent to either formation or acquisition should be translated at the rate(s) prevailing when such excess was created.
    c. *Retained earnings.* When a statement approach is employed, retained earnings may be either forced or translated using the current rate. If forced after all other real accounts are translated, retained earnings is considered to be the balancing amount. However, any exchange gain or loss is hidden when this method is used. If, under a statement approach,

retained earnings is translated at the current rate, the balancing amount is the exchange gain or loss. When a trial balance approach is employed, retained earnings at the beginning of a period must be the same as it was at the end of the preceding period.

## Consolidation of Foreign Subsidiaries Illustrated

When consolidating a foreign subsidiary with its parent, either a statement or trial balance approach may be used. Both methods are illustrated, using for comparison purposes the same basic data.

Assume that Company A, an American company, acquired a 90% interest in a British firm, Company B, for $130,000 on January 1, 1979, when Company B's $96,000 translated stockholders' equity was composed of $64,000 of capital stock and $32,000 retained earnings. In addition to the specific data given in the statements and trial balances, assume also that goodwill is not being amortized at this time and that the following exchange rates prevailed during the period:

*Prevailing rates*

| | |
|---|---|
| January 1, 1979 | 1.600 |
| December 31, 1979 | 1.630 |
| Average | 1.615 |
| At date fixed assets acquired | 1.610 |

**STATEMENT APPROACH**

COMPANY A AND SUBSIDIARY COMPANY B
CONSOLIDATED WORKING PAPERS
STATEMENT OF FINANCIAL POSITION
As of DECEMBER 31, 1979

|  | Co. B Pounds | Translation Rate | Co. B Translated | Company A | Adjustments and Eliminations | | Consolidated Financial Position |
|---|---|---|---|---|---|---|---|
| *Assets* | | | | | | | |
| Current assets | 30,000 | 1.630 | $ 48,900 | $ 100,000 | | | $ 148,900 |
| Investment in Company B | | | | 130,000 | $ 29,880(1) | $116,280A | 43,600(G) |
| Fixed assets (net) | 80,000 | 1.610 | 128,800 | 800,000 | | | 928,800 |
| | 110,000 | | $177,700 | $1,030,000 | | | $1,121,300 |
| *Equities* | | | | | | | |
| Current liabilities | 20,000 | 1.630 | $ 32,600 | $ 60,000 | | | $ 92,600 |
| Fixed liabilities | 10,000 | 1.630 | 16,300 | 100,000 | | | 116,300 |
| Stockholders' equity: | | | | | | | |
| Capital stock: | | | | | | | |
| Company A | | | | 500,000 | | | 500,000 |
| Company B | 40,000 | 1.600 | 64,000 | | 57,600A | | 6,400MI |
| Retained earnings: | | | | | | | |
| Company A | | | | 370,000 | 360(2) | 29,880(1) | 399,520RE |
| Company B | 40,000 | 1.630 | 65,200 | | 58,680A | 360(2) | 6,520MI |
| Exchange gain (loss) | | | (400) | | | | (40)MI |
| | 110,000 | | $177,700 | $1,030,000 | $146,520 | $146,520 | $1,121,300 |

(1) To recognize A's share of the increase in B's stockholders' equity (90% of $33,200).
(2) To recognize A's share of the exchange loss (90% of $400).
A: To eliminate 90% of B's stockholders' equity against the investment account.

## STATEMENT APPROACH (Continued)

**COMPANY A AND SUBSIDIARY COMPANY B**
**CONSOLIDATED WORKING PAPERS**
**STATEMENT OF INCOME AND RETAINED EARNINGS**
**YEAR ENDED DECEMBER 31, 1979**

|  | Co. B Pounds | Translation Rate | Co. B Translated | Company A | Income | Retained Earnings |
|---|---|---|---|---|---|---|
| *Credits* | | | | | | |
| Sales | 100,000 | 1.615 | $161,500 | $900,000 | $1,061,500 | |
|  | 100,000 | | $161,500 | $900,000 | $1,061,500 | |
| *Debits* | | | | | | |
| Cost of sales | 60,000 | 1.615 | $96,900 | $500,000 | $596,900 | |
| Depreciation | 10,000 | 1.610 | 16,100 | 90,000 | 106,100 | |
| Other expenses | 10,000 | 1.615 | 16,150 | 40,000 | 56,150 | |
| Net income | 20,000 | balance | 32,350 | 270,000 | 302,350 | |
|  | 100,000 | | $161,500 | $900,000 | $1,061,500 | |
| Retained earnings, 1/1/79 | 20,000 | 1.600 | $32,000 | | | $100,000 |
| Net income | 20,000 | as above | 32,350 | | | |
| Exchange gain or loss | | | 850 | | | 405* |
| Balance, 12/31/79 | 40,000 | 1.630 | $65,200 | | | |
| Apportionment of net income: | | | | | | |
| Net income | | | | | $302,350 | |
| Minority interest (10% of $32,350) | | | | | 3,235 | |
| Consolidated net income (remainder) | | | | | $299,115 | 299,115 |
| Retained earnings | | | | | | $399,520 |

*90% of $850 gain minus $400 loss (see statement of financial position).

## Trial Balance Approach

### Company A and Subsidiary Company B
### Consolidated Working Papers, As of December 31, 1979

|  | Co. B Pounds | Translation Rate | Co. B Translated | Company A |
|---|---:|---:|---:|---:|
| *Debits* | | | | |
| Current assets | 30,000 | 1.630 | $ 48,900 | $ 100,000 |
| Investment in Company B | | | | 130,000 |
| Fixed assets (net) | 80,000 | 1.610 | 128,800 | 800,000 |
| Cost of sales | 60,000 | 1.615 | 96,900 | 500,000 |
| Depreciation | 10,000 | 1.610 | 16,100 | 90,000 |
| Other expenses | 10,000 | 1.615 | 16,150 | 40,000 |
|  | 190,000 | | $306,850 | $1,660,000 |
| *Credits* | | | | |
| Current liabilities | 20,000 | 1.630 | $ 32,600 | $ 60,000 |
| Fixed liabilities | 10,000 | 1.630 | 16,300 | 100,000 |
| Sales | 100,000 | 1.615 | 161,500 | 900,000 |
| Stockholders' equity: | | | | |
|   Capital stock: | | | | |
|     Company A | | | | 500,000 |
|     Company B | 40,000 | 1.600 | 64,000 | |
|   Retained earnings: | | | | |
|     Company A, 1/1/79 | | | | 100,000 |
|     Company B, 1/1/79 | 20,000 | 1.600 | 32,000 | |
|     Exchange gain or loss | | | 450 | |
|  | 190,000 | | $306,850 | $1,660,000 |

Income credits
Income debits
Net income

Apportionment of net income:

  Minority interest:

| | | |
|---|---:|---|
|     Income credits, Co. B | $161,500 | |
|     Income debits, Co. B | 129,150 | |
|   Net income, Co. B | 32,350 | |
|     Minority interest (10%) | 3,235 | |

  Consolidated net income (remainder)

Retained earnings

Minority interest

## 18 / Expansion by Foreign Operations

TRIAL BALANCE APPROACH (Continued)

| Adjustments & Eliminations | | Income | Retained Earnings | Minority Interest | Consolidated Financial Position |
|---|---|---|---|---|---|
| | | | | | $ 148,900 |
| $ 86,400A | | | | | 43,600G |
| | | | | | 928,800 |
| | | $ 596,900 | | | |
| | | 106,100 | | | |
| | | 56,150 | | | |
| | | $ 759,150 | −0− | −0− | $1,121,300 |
| | | | | | $ 92,600 |
| | | | | | 116,300 |
| | | $1,061,500 | | | |
| | | | | | 500,000 |
| $ 57,600A | | | | $ 6,400 | |
| | | | $100,000 | | |
| 28,800A | | | | 3,200 | |
| | | | 405 | 45 | |
| $ 86,400 | $ 86,400 | | | | |
| | | $1,061,500 | | | |
| | | 759,150 | | | |
| | | $ 302,350 | | | |
| | | 3,235 | | 3,235 | |
| | | $ 299,115 | $299,115 | | |
| | | | $399,520 | | 399,520RE |
| | | | | $12,880 | 12,880MI |
| | | | | | $1,121,300 |

A: To eliminate 90% of B's stockholders' equity against the investment account.

## PROBLEMS

### Problem 18-1

During the year the Domestic Company (an American organization) made the following purchases from the British Company:

|  |  | Rate of Exchange* |  |  |
|---|---|---|---|---|
| Date of Purchase | Amount | Date of Purchase | Date of Payment | lbs |
| January 15 | $14,000 | 1.60 | 1.60 | 8750 |
| April 15 | 21,000 | 1.60 | 1.61 | 13125 |
| July 15 | 28,100 | 1.61 | 1.62 | 17453 |
| October 15 | 56,400 | 1.62 | 1.60 | 34815 |

*Dollars per pound.

*Required:*

Journal entries on the Domestic Company's books to record the payments of the purchases above, assuming that the billings were:
(1) In dollars.
(2) In pounds.

### Problem 18-2

Prepare in journal entry form all entries necessary to record the following transactions on the books of the American Company and its branch in Spain:

(1) January 1. American establishes the Spanish branch by transferring $10,000 cash to the branch.
(2) January 5. Home office purchases in Spain and turns over to the branch equipment costing 735,000 pesetas.
(3) January 10. The branch purchases merchandise for 200,000 pesetas.
(4) January 15. The branch sells merchandise for 100,000 pesetas.
(5) January 15. The branch purchases 120,000 pesetas worth of merchandise on account.
(6) January 20. The branch sells merchandise on account for 60,000 pesetas.
(7) January 30. The branch pays expenses for January totaling 40,000 pesetas.
(8) January 30. The branch remits 100,000 pesetas to the home office.

The following rates of exchange were in effect during the month:

Pesetas Per Dollar

| January 1 | 50 |
| January 5 | 49 |
| January 10 | 48 |
| January 15 | 46 |
| January 20 | 48 |
| January 30 | 52 |

18 / *Expansion by Foreign Operations*

## Problem 18-3

On the basis of the following information, translate the branch trial balance of the English Company into dollars:

|  | Pounds | Pounds |
|---|---|---|
| Cash | 1,400 |  |
| Accounts receivable | 2,800 |  |
| Inventory, Jan. 1 | 1,800 |  |
| Remittances to home office | 36,500 |  |
| Accounts payable |  | 1,100 |
| Remittances from home office |  | 3,000 |
| Home office |  | 33,300 |
| Sales |  | 46,500 |
| Merchandise from home office | 24,000 |  |
| Purchases | 2,400 |  |
| Expenses | 15,000 |  |
|  | 83,900 | 83,900 |

Inventory, Dec. 31   3,400 pounds

BRANCH OFFICE

| Balance, Jan. 1 | $13,956 | Remittances | $58,637 |
|---|---|---|---|
| Shipments to branch | 38,684 |  |  |
| Remittances | 4,860 |  |  |

Rates of exchange:
- January 1 — 1.63
- December 31 — 1.60
- Average for year — 1.61

## Problem 18-4

1. State the rule followed by a company in translating foreign currency into U.S. dollars on:

    (a) Fixed assets of branches in foreign countries.
    (b) Inventory of merchandise bought by the foreign branch in that country.
2. If your basis of translation differs as to the two items listed in (1), explain why there is such difference, including a discussion of the accounting principles that are involved.

(AICPA adapted)

## Problem 18-5

Translate the following trial balances into dollars prior to consolidating them with the parent company—The U.S. Company. When translating, round off to the nearest dollar.

|  | Argentina Company (pesos) | Brazil Company (cruzeiros) | Panama Company (balboas) | Venezuela Company (bolivares) |
|---|---:|---:|---:|---:|
| *Debits* | | | | |
| Inventories, 1/1/80 | 1,600,000 | 3,300,000 | 40,000 | 99,000 |
| Other current assets | 4,800,000 | 9,900,000 | 50,000 | 136,000 |
| Fixed assets | 8,000,000 | 16,100,000 | 130,000 | 603,000 |
| Purchases | 6,000,000 | 12,200,000 | 120,000 | 525,000 |
| Expenses | 1,500,000 | 3,350,000 | 30,000 | 140,000 |
|  | 21,900,000 | 44,850,000 | 370,000 | 1,503,000 |
| *Credits* | | | | |
| Sales | 8,000,000 | 16,080,000 | 140,000 | 720,000 |
| Current liabilities | 600,000 | 1,100,000 | 30,000 | 130,000 |
| Accumulated depreciation | 2,000,000 | 4,200,000 | 20,000 | 200,000 |
| Capital stock | 10,000,000 | 20,000,000 | 100,000 | 300,000 |
| Retained earnings, 1/80 | 1,300,000 | 3,470,000 | 80,000 | 153,000 |
|  | 21,900,000 | 44,850,000 | 370,000 | 1,503,000 |
| Inventories 12/31/80 | 2,100,000 | 3,900,000 | 70,000 | 110,000 |
| *Prevailing rates:* | Pesos* | Cruzeiros* | Balboas* | Bolivares*, |
| Jan. 1, 1980 | 37.00 | 68.00 | 1.00 | 3.30 |
| Dec. 31, 1980 | 40.00 | 66.00 | 1.00 | 3.40 |
| Average | 38.00 | 67.00 | 1.00 | 3.36 |
| Date fixed assets acquired | 36.00 | 70.00 | 1.00 | 3.35 |
| Date investment acquired | 37.00 | 68.00 | 1.00 | 3.30 |

*In terms of dollars.

## Problem 18-6

Using the data in Problem 18-5 and the following facts, prepare consolidated working papers for the U.S. Company and its foreign subsidiaries for the year ended December 31, 1980. The U.S. Company carries the investments at *cost*.

U.S. COMPANY
TRIAL BALANCE
AS OF DECEMBER 31, 1980

| *Debits* | |
|---|---:|
| Inventories, 1/1/80 | $ 600,000 |
| Other current assets | 900,000 |
| Investments in foreign subsidiaries (90% acquired 1/1/80) | 930,000 |
| Fixed assets | 2,000,000 |

18 / *Expansion by Foreign Operations*  577

|   |   |
|---|---|
| Purchases | 1,600,000 |
| Expenses | 200,000 |
|  | $6,230,000 |

*Credits*

|   |   |
|---|---|
| Sales | $2,400,000 |
| Current liabilities | 1,200,000 |
| Accumulated depreciation | 800,000 |
| Capital stock | 1,000,000 |
| Retained earnings, 1/1/80 | 830,000 |
|  | $6,230,000 |
| Inventories, 12/31/80 | $ 500,000 |

## Problem 18-7

The ABC Manufacturing Corporation during the current year opened a manufacturing and selling branch in X country. At the year-end the official rate of currency exchange with country X was 12 to $1 and the unofficial free market rate was 15 to $1.

1. In combining the statements of the branch with those of the parent at year-end, at what value would the following branch accounts be reflected in the combined statement of financial position?
   (a) Accounts receivable.
   (b) Fixed assets.
   (c) Inventories.
   (d) Short-term debt.
   (e) Long-term debt.
2. How is the gain or loss resulting from the translation of the foreign currency into U.S. currency reflected in the financial statements of ABC Corporation at year-end?
3. On June 30, 1981, ABC sold merchandise costing $75,000 to Z, located in Y country, taking a note payable in Y currency. At the official rate of exchange on the date of sale the note had a fair market value of $100,000. On December 31, 1981, the note was worth $75,000 owing to a change in the rate of exchange. On March 15, 1982, the note was paid in full and when immediately converted to U.S. dollars, ABC received $125,000. What journal entries are required at June 30, 1981, December 31, 1981, and March 15, 1982? Explain.

(AICPA adapted)

## Problem 18-8

Company A (an American company) owns 90% of the stock of Company B (a British company), which it acquired January 1, 1980. Company A bought the stock from various stockholders in England and carries the investment at *cost*. The following data were taken from the books and records of the respective companies as of December 31, 1980:

**578** EXPANSION OF THE BUSINESS ORGANIZATION

|  | Co. A (dollars) | Co. B (pounds) |  |
|---|---|---|---|
| Inventories, 1/1/80 | 120,000 | 20,000 | 1.65 |
| Other current assets | 200,000 | 20,000 | 1.68 |
| Investment in Company B | 140,000 |  |  |
| Fixed assets | 860,000 | 30,000 | 1.64 |
| Purchases | 700,000 | 120,000 | 1.66 |
| Depreciation | 34,400 | 1,200 | 1.64 |
| Other expenses | 400,000 | 90,000 | 1.66 |
|  | 2,454,400 | 281,200 |  |
| Sales | 1,700,000 | 182,200 | 1.66 |
| Accumulated depreciation | 344,000 | 9,000 | 1.64 |
| Capital stock | 300,000 | 80,000 | 1.65 |
| Retained earnings, 1/1/80 | 110,400 | 10,000 | 1.65 |
|  | 2,454,400 | 281,200 |  |
| Inventories, 12/31/80 | 140,000 | 70,000 | 1.68 |

Company A regularly sells merchandise to Company B. There was no intercompany profit in inventories at the beginning of the year, but Company B's inventory at the end of the year contained merchandise acquired from Company A at $25,000 above A's cost. During the year, Company A sold merchandise to Company B at a billed price of $210,000 [116,000].

Rates of exchange were as follows:

| January 1, 1980 | 1.65 |
| December 31, 1980 | 1.68 |
| Date of purchase of fixed assets | 1.64 |
| Average rate for the year | 1.66 |

*Required:*

Prepare consolidated working papers with columns for income, retained earnings, minority interest, and financial position for the year ended December 31, 1980.

## Problem 18-9

Trial balances as of December 31, 1979, of the parent company and its two subsidiaries were:

|  | Parent Company |  | Domestic Subsidiary |  | Mexican Subsidiary Pesos |  |
|---|---|---|---|---|---|---|
|  | Dr. | Cr. | Dr. | Cr. | Dr. | Cr. |
| Cash | $10,000 |  | $ 1,500 |  | 16,000 |  |
| Accounts receivable, trade | 30,000 |  | 8,000 |  | 56,000 |  |

18 / *Expansion by Foreign Operations*

| | | | | | | |
|---|---:|---:|---:|---:|---:|---:|
| Accounts receivable, merchandise in transit to domestic subsidiary | 4,000 | | | | | |
| Inventories | 20,000 | | | | 132,800 | |
| Investments at cost: | | | | | | |
| Domestic subsidiary 900 shares acquired 12/31/78 | 9,000 | | | | | |
| Foreign subsidiary 1,000 shares acquired 12/31/78 | 12,000 | | | | | |
| Fixed assets | 45,000 | | 3,500 | | 262,500 | |
| Goodwill | | | 2,000 | | | |
| Cost of sales | 300,000 | | 15,000 | | 466,667 | |
| Depreciation | 3,000 | | 200 | | 10,500 | |
| Taxes | 15,000 | | 400 | | 23,333 | |
| Selling expense | 42,000 | | 2,400 | | 42,000 | |
| Administrative and general expenses | 35,000 | | 2,000 | | 28,000 | |
| Dividends declared | | | 1,000 | | | |
| Sales, trade | | $400,000 | | $21,000 | | 593,600 |
| Sales, domestic subsidiary | | 10,000 | | | | |
| Accounts payable, trade | | 25,000 | | | | 11,200 |
| Dividend payable | | | | 1,000 | | |
| Long-term debt due 1/1/82 | | | | | | 160,000 |
| Accumulated depreciation | | 15,000 | | 2,000 | | 112,500 |
| Capital stock | | 50,000 | | *10,000 | | *150,000 |
| Retained earnings, 1/1/79 | | 25,000 | | 2,000 | | 10,500 |
| | $525,000 | $525,000 | $36,000 | $36,000 | 1,037,800 | 1,037,800 |

*1,000 shares issued and outstanding.

*Data:*

In April 1979, the Mexican peso was devalued from U.S. $.08, the prevailing rate of exchange on December 31, 1978, to $.05 which was also the prevailing rate of exchange on December 31, 1979.

*Required:*
(1) Prepare working trial balance in U.S. dollars for the Mexican subsidiary. (Round to nearest whole dollar.)
(2) Prepare working papers for consolidated statements.   (AICPA adapted)

## Problem 18-10

The Wiend Corporation acquired The Dieck Corporation on January 1, 1980 by the purchase at book value of all outstanding capital stock. The Dieck Corporation is located in a Central American country whose monetary unit is the peso. The Dieck Corporation's accounting records were continued without change; a trial balance, in pesos, of the balance sheet accounts at the purchase date follows:

THE DIECK CORPORATION
TRIAL BALANCE (IN PESOS)
JANUARY 1, 1980

|  | Debit | Credit |
|---|---|---|
| Cash | P 3,000 | |
| Accounts receivable | 5,000 | |
| Inventories | 32,000 | |
| Machinery and equipment | 204,000 | |
| Allowance for depreciation | | P 42,000 |
| Accounts payable | | 81,400 |
| Capital stock | | 50,000 |
| Retained earnings | | 70,600 |
| | P244,000 | P244,000 |

The Dieck Corporation's trial balance, in pesos, at December 31, 1980 follows:

THE DIECK CORPORATION
TRIAL BALANCE (IN PESOS)
DECEMBER 31, 1980

|  | Debit | Credit |
|---|---|---|
| Cash | P 25,000 | |
| Accounts receivable | 20,000 | |
| Allowance for bad debts | | P 500 |
| Due from The Wiend Corporation | 30,000 | |
| Inventories, December 31, 1980 | 110,000 | |
| Prepaid expenses | 3,000 | |
| Machinery and equipment | 210,000 | |
| Allowance for depreciation | | 79,900 |
| Accounts payable | | 22,000 |
| Income taxes payable | | 40,000 |
| Notes payable | | 60,000 |
| Capital stock | | 50,000 |
| Retained earnings | | 100,600 |
| Sales—domestic | | 170,000 |
| Sales—foreign | | 200,000 |
| Cost of sales | 207,600 | |
| Depreciation | 22,400 | |
| Selling and administrative expenses | 60,000 | |
| Gain on sale of assets | | 5,000 |
| Provision for income taxes | 40,000 | |
| | P728,000 | P728,000 |

## 18 / Expansion by Foreign Operations

The following additional information is available:

1. All of The Dieck Corporation's export sales are made to its parent company and are accumulated in the account, Sales—Foreign. The balance in the account, Due from The Wiend Corporation, is the total of unpaid invoices. All foreign sales are billed in U.S. dollars. The reciprocal accounts on the parent company's books show total 1980 purchases as $471,000 and the total of unpaid invoices as $70,500.
2. Depreciation is computed by the straight-line method over a 10-year life for all depreciable assets. Machinery costing P20,000 was purchased on December 31, 1979, and no depreciation was recorded for this machinery in 1979. There have been no other depreciable assets acquired since January 1, 1979, and no assets are fully depreciated.
3. Certain assets that were in the inventory of fixed assets at January 1, 1979 were sold on December 31, 1979. For 1980 a full year's depreciation was recorded before the assets were removed from the books. Information regarding the sale follows:

| | |
|---|---:|
| Cost of assets | P14,000 |
| Accumulated depreciation | 4,900 |
| Net book value | 9,100 |
| Proceeds of sale | 14,100 |
| Gain on sale | P 5,000 |

4. Notes payable are long-term obligations that were incurred on December 31, 1979.
5. No entries have been made in the Retained Earnings account of the subsidiary since its acquisition other than the net income for 1979. The Retained Earnings account at December 31, 1979 was translated to $212,000.
6. The prevailing rates of exchange follow:

| Dollars per Peso | |
|---|---:|
| January 1, 1979 | 2.00 |
| 1979 average | 2.10 |
| December 31, 1979 | 2.20 |
| 1980 average | 2.30 |
| December 31, 1980 | 2.40 |

*Required:*

Prepare a work sheet to translate the December 31, 1980 trial balance of The Dieck Corporation from pesos to dollars. The work sheet should show the untranslated trial balance, the translation rate, and the translated trial balance. (Do not extend the trial balance to statement columns. Supporting schedules should be in good form.)   (AICPA adapted)

## Problem 18-11

Dhia Products Company was incorporated in the state of Florida in 1970 to do business as a manufacturer of medical supplies and equipment. Since incorporating, Dhia has doubled in size about every three years and is now considered one of the leading medical supply companies in the country.

During January 1976, Dhia established a subsidiary, Ban, Ltd., in the emerging nation of Shatha. Dhia owns 90% of the outstanding capital stock of Ban; the remaining 10% of Ban's outstanding capital stock is held by Shatha citizens, as required by Shatha constitutional law. The investment in Ban, accounted for by Dhia by the equity method, represents about 18% of the total assets of Dhia at December 31, 1979, the close of the accounting period for both companies.

*Required:*
(1) What criteria should Dhia Products use in determining whether it would be appropriate to prepare consolidated financial statements with Ban, Ltd., for the year ended December 31, 1979? Explain.
(2) Independently of your answer to (1), assume that it has been appropriate for Dhia and Ban to prepare consolidated financial statements for each year 1976 through 1979. But before consolidated financial statements can be prepared, the individual account balances in Ban's December 31, 1979, adjusted trial balance must be translated into the appropriate number of United States dollars. For each of the ten (10) accounts listed below, taken from Ban's adjusted trial balance, specify what exchange rate (for example, average exchange rate for 1979, current exchange rate at December 31, 1979, etc.) should be used to translate the account balances into dollars and explain why that rate is appropriate. Letter your answers to correspond with each account listed below.
   a. Cash in Shatha National Bank.
   b. Trade accounts receivable (all from 1979 revenues).
   c. Supplies inventory (all purchased during the last quarter of 1979).
   d. Land (purchased in 1976).
   e. Short-term note payable to Shatha National Bank.
   f. Capital stock (no par or stated value and all issued in January 1976).
   g. Retained earnings, January 1, 1979.
   h. Sales revenue.
   i. Depreciation expense (on buildings).
   j. Salaries expense.
(3) Identify the standards of financial statement disclosure of foreign currency translations that Dhia must consider as required by the *Financial Accounting Standards Board Statement No. 8*.                (AICPA adapted)

## Problem 18-12

Select the *best* answer for each of the following items:

1. The Dease Company owns a foreign subsidiary with 3,600,000 local currency units (LCU) of property, plant, and equipment before accumulated deprecia-

tion at December 31, 1979. Of this amount, 2,400,000 LCU were acquired in 1977 when the rate of exchange was 1.6 LCU to $1, and 1,200,000 LCU were acquired in 1978 when the rate of exchange was 1.8 LCU to $1. The rate of exchange in effect at December 31, 1979, was 2 LCU to $1. The weighted average of exchange rates that were in effect during 1979 was 1.92 LCU to $1. Assuming that the property, plant, and equipment are depreciated using the straight-line method over a 10-year period with *no* salvage value, how much depreciation expense relating to the foreign subsidiary's property, plant, and equipment should be charged in Dease's income statement for 1979?
   a. $180,000.
   b. $187,500.
   c. $200,000.
   d. $216,667.
2. The Clark Company owns a foreign subsidiary which had net income for the year ended December 31, 1979, of 4,800,000 local currency units (LCU), which was appropriately translated into $800,000. On October 15, 1979, when the rate of exchange was 5.7 LCU to $1, the foreign subsidiary paid a dividend to Clark of 2,400,000 LCU. The dividend represented the net income of the foreign subsidiary for the six months ended June 30, 1979, during which time the weighted average of exchange rates was 5.8 LCU to $1. The rate of exchange in effect at December 31, 1979, was 5.9 LCU to $1. What rate of exchange should be used to translate the dividend for the December 31, 1979, financial statements?
   a. 5.7 LCU to $1.
   b. 5.8 LCU to $1.
   c. 5.9 LCU to $1.
   d. 6.0 LCU to $1.

(AICPA adapted)

# 19

# Expansion by Combination

Expansion of a business enterprise may be accomplished in various ways. Some of these methods have been discussed in preceding chapters. In addition, expansion may be effected by what is called a "business combination." This term, as used in accounting, encompasses certain types of more rigorously defined combinations, such as merger, consolidation, pooling of interests, acquisition, and purchase. Generally a business combination is "any transaction whereby one economic unit obtains control over the assets and properties of another economic unit, regardless of the legal avenue by which such control is obtained and regardless of the resultant form of the economic unit emerging from the combination transaction."[1]

When two or more business entities are joined by means of a combination, one of the predecessor entities (commonly referred to as the surviving entity) normally takes over the assets and liabilities of the other entities in the combination (hence, the term "takeover" is sometimes used to describe the transaction). The entities that have been "taken over" may lose their identity, as when they are legally merged into the surviving entity or when their former legal structure is eliminated by liquidation. Frequently, the entities taken over remain in existence as operating subsidiaries of the surviving entity. On occasion, an entirely new entity may be formed to take over the assets and liabilities of all the combining organizations.

The accounting problems created by a business combination transaction are often complex. One problem is the classification of the transaction according to the type of business combination involved. The decision on classification has consequences of an accounting nature that have a long-run impact on financial results

[1] Wyatt, Arthur R., *A Critical Study of Accounting for Business Combinations,* American Institute of Certified Public Accountants, New York, 1963, p. 12.

of the enterprise. Another problem involves recording and valuation decisions for the combination transaction. If a given entity that has been taken over remains in existence as a subsidiary, many of the problems discussed in the several preceding chapters will assume importance. The emphasis in the ensuing sections centers on the classification of a business combination and on the accounting problems that must be resolved once a classification has been made.

## PRECOMBINATION CONSIDERATIONS

During the last 20 years or so a special area of expertise has evolved in business dealing with the area of "mergers and acquisitions." Public accounting firms, management consulting firms, investment bankers, and others have special divisions or units that devote much or all of their time to merger and acquisition activities. Many corporations have merger and acquisition groups or staff specialists.

These individuals play various roles in the drama of producing a business combination. Some seek out and identify potential merger candidates. Others evaluate the manner in which identified candidates will fit, both operationally and in financial terms. Some assist in negotiations and offer advice on the numerous variables requiring resolution before a combination is completed.

For a proposed merger to have a predictable chance of success, considerable data, much of it financially oriented, must be considered and evaluated. The accountant's role in this process is an important and challenging one, important because factual data are critical, and challenging because numerous alternatives must be anticipated, often on the tightest possible time schedule. In this area the accountant makes wide use of pro forma financial presentations. He puts together the financial data of separate entities to present a picture of financial position and results of operations as if the two entities were one. Frequently, adjustments are necessary to conform diverse accounting methods, to eliminate effects of duplicate facilities, or to give recognition to anticipated changed conditions following consummation of the proposed combination.

Accountants also become significantly involved in the problems of reporting on the combination after it has been consummated. This responsibility includes both review of the combination transaction characteristics to evaluate the proposed accounting classification of the combination and determination of the most appropriate accounting reflection of the combination consequences.

### Types of Business Combinations

Any type of business organization—proprietorship, partnership, or corporation—may be a constituent of a business combination, but the majority by far are corporations. Thus, the discussions and examples that follow are in terms of corporations.

For accounting purposes, business combinations are generally classified in one of two broad categories.

1. Pooling of interests.
2. Purchase.

As these two concepts emerged in the 1940's, business combinations were classified at the time of the transaction as either a pooling of interests or as a purchase, and this classification determined the appropriate accounting treatment. Starting in the 1950's, however, the difference in concept between the two classes of business combinations became less well defined. At the same time, two clearly different methods of accounting for business combinations emerged in practice. These two accounting methods, also called pooling of interests and purchase, soon came to be determinative of the classification of a given business combination. Thus, while we may view the business combination accounting problem as, first, a determination of the kind of combination that has been consummated and, then, as a determination of the appropriate accounting treatment, the two parts are commonly reversed in practice. That is, the accounting treatment decision is made first, and this decision governs the classification of the transaction. The difference between the two types of business combinations insofar as accounting treatment is concerned is covered in some detail in a later section.

**Definitions.** In concept, a *pooling of interests* is a business combination in which the holders of all or substantially all of the common stock interests in the combining entities continue as holders of common stock interests in the entity that results or emerges from the combination. The resultant enterprise owns the assets and businesses of the constituent organizations, either directly or through ownership of the stock. A *purchase* is a business combination in which all or an important part of the common stock interests in one or more of the constituent entities is eliminated, that is, is no longer in a common stock ownership position.

## Basic Accounting Distinctions

Two principal accounting distinctions exist between the accounting entries for a pooling of interests and those used for a purchase. One distinction lies in the accounting for the assets of the taken-over company, and the other concerns the accounting for retained earnings, or more broadly, stockholders' equity. These accounting distinctions both rest on a concept underlying the distinction between a pooling of interests and a purchase. This concept is that in a pooling-of-interests type of combination nothing of real economic substance has occurred. That is, the people who were stockholders prior to the business combination are still stockholders; the assets in use are unchanged; the relative interests of the various parties, if changed, are changed only in relatively minor respects. In a purchase combination, on the other hand, changes of economic substance have occurred. One group of stockholders has actually bought out another. Some previous ownership interests have been replaced, and one or more other quite substantive changes has occurred. These conceptual distinctions lead rather naturally to the two important differences in accounting treatment.

## Pooling-of-Interests Accounting

Since nothing of real substance is deemed to have occurred in a pooling of interests, the accounting entries necessary to give effect to the combination leave existing relationships basically undisturbed. The basis of accountability for the taken-over entity is the book value of the net assets of that entity at the date of combination. This means that the company effecting the combination will either debit various asset accounts for amounts as stated in the taken-over entity's ledger (in the situation in which that entity goes out of existence) or debit an investment account for the book value of the net assets (in the situation in which the taken-over entity will continue to operate as a subsidiary). The fair market value of the shares issued to effect the combination is of no consequence to the accounting entries. Certain exceptions to the generalizations above are permitted in order to place like assets of each company's books on a consistent basis. For example, inventories may be restated to move LIFO to FIFO if this is the pricing basis used by the dominant company in the combination.

The credit entries emerging from the transaction likewise tend to continue existing relationships. Here, however, some adjustments are commonly necessary because of legal requirements. In *general,* however, the retained earnings of the taken-over entity become a credit to Retained Earnings on the dominant or surviving company's books. Capital Stock is credited for the par or stated value of the shares issued to effect the combination. Any additional credit necessary to make the entry balance goes to a capital surplus account (Capital in Excess of Par). If the credits to Retained Earnings and Capital Stock as determined above exceed the book value of the net assets, the amount credited to Retained Earnings is normally scaled down to balance the entry. We can conclude that in a pooling of interests the retained earnings of the taken-over entity become retained earnings of the resultant enterprise in the absence of changes caused by legal requirements or adjustments to achieve consistency in asset bases.

## Purchase Accounting

A combination classified as a purchase is accounted for like any other purchase or acquisition. The fair value of the consideration given or the fair value of the consideration acquired, whichever is more clearly evident, becomes the basis of accountability. In most business combinations the fair value of the consideration given, cash or shares of stock with a ready marketability, provides a valid starting point for determining the basis of accounting. In some situations a thorough consideration of all negotiations leading to the eventual combination may provide a more valid basis of accountability than the market value of shares given.

Although this principle has many applications and is fairly simple in concept, in practice its application to a business combination may involve certain difficulties. The most significant difficulty probably lies in a determination of the proper accounting for the difference between the fair market value of the shares issued, or other basis of accountability, and the book value of the net assets acquired. Prior to 1971 the simple expedient of calling this difference "goodwill" was commonly followed. At present, this practice is unacceptable, and efforts must be made to assign appropriate fair values to the assets acquired and liabilities assumed.

The overall problem is one that arises any time a group of assets is purchased at a lump-sum price. Little justification appears to exist for the acquiring company to use the book values of the assets on the acquired company's books in accounting for the purchase. Rather, serious effort should be made to determine the fair values of the various assets acquired, and these values should become the basis of accountability on the acquiring company's books. Any difference between the purchase price and the sum of the fair values of the various identifiable assets, tangible and intangible, acquired could be labeled "goodwill." If the acquired company is to remain in existence as a subsidiary, the acquiring company should debit an Investment account for the fair value of the consideration given. The problem of allocating this cost to specific assets will become important at the date of consolidation.

The credit entries for a purchase combination are relatively simple to make. No portion of the credit can be made to Retained Earnings in a purchase combination. A long-standing and widely accepted rule of the American Institute of Certified Public Accountants states that the retained earnings of a subsidiary created prior to acquisition does not form a part of the consolidated retained earnings.[2]

The justification for crediting Retained Earnings in a pooling combination, as discussed above, lies in the concept that the pooling combination is not an acquisition, but merely the continuation of formerly separate entities as one entity. In a purchase combination Capital Stock is credited for the par or stated value of the shares given, and any amount necessary to balance the entry is credited to Capital in Excess of Par. Of course, if cash or other assets are used to consummate the transaction, rather than stock, those assets would be credited.

**Summary.** The accounting treatment distinctions between a pooling-of-interests combination and a purchase combination are rather well defined and widely accepted. One should recognize, however, that significantly different results may be determined from the accounting records if a given combination is considered a pooling of interests rather than a purchase, or vice versa. The example on pages 592–596 highlights this difference.

### Classification of the Combination Transaction

The primary importance of the classification of a given combination transaction becomes clear once we grasp the implications of the two methods of accounting

---

[2] American Institute of Certified Public Accountants, Committee on Accounting Procedure, *Accounting Research Bulletin No. 43,* Chapter 1a, "Rules Adopted by the Membership," p. 11, 1953. However, in a merger or consolidation effected legally at a date subsequent to acquisition, retained earnings of the subsidiary accumulated since acquisition may become part of the consolidated retained earnings.

and recognize that the methods produce quite different results in accounting records and reports. Several attempts have been made to develop guidelines useful for classifying a combination as a purchase or as a pooling of interests. The official pronouncement of the American Institute of Certified Public Accountants on this topic is *Accounting Principles Board Opinion No. 16* issued in September 1970. *Opinion No. 16* supersedes official positions taken in earlier pronouncements and sets forth a number of criteria, all of which must be met for a business combination to be accounted for as a pooling of interests. If any of the criteria are not met, the combination must be accounted for as a purchase.

Although the criteria are somewehat complex, the overriding principle is that a business combination qualifies as a pooling of interests only when the common stock ownership interests of the separate companies prior to combination are also common stock ownership interests in essentially an unaltered relationship to one another following the combination. The numerous criteria were considered necessary to prevent evasions of this concept and to correct abuses that had existed in practice prior to issuance of *Opinion No. 16*. The complexity of the criteria has led to issuance of numerous "interpretations" of them by the AICPA in the *Journal of Accountancy*. The criteria, in a summarized form, are:

1. Each of the combining companies must be autonomous and cannot have been a subsidiary or division of another corporation within two years before the plan of combination is initiated. However, a subsidiary that has at least a 20% minority interest outstanding at November 1, 1970, and has at least a 20% minority interest outstanding when a plan of combination is initiated may combine in a pooling of interests prior to November 1, 1975*. Also, a wholly owned subsidiary may effect a combination by issuing its parent company's stock and follow pooling-of-interests accounting.
2. Each of the combining companies must be independent of the other combining companies. Being independent means that no combining company owns more than 10% of the oustanding stock of another combining company. (The merger of a parent and its subsidiary or of two subsidiaries is not considered to be a business combination, and the provisions of *Opinion No. 16* do not pertain to such a merger.)
3. The combination is effected in a single transaction or is completed in accordance with a specified plan within one year after the plan is initiated.
4. A corporation can issue only common stock with rights identical to those of the majority of its outstanding voting common stock in exchange for substantially all (90% or more) of the voting common interest of another company.
5. No combining company may change its voting common stock interests in contemplation of a combination, and any change within two years prior to

---

*In 1975, the Financial Accounting Standards Board issued its Statement No. 10 that extended indefinitely the November 1, 1975, date. The FASB has had the entire subject of accounting for business combinations on its agenda since 1974 and issued a Discussion Memorandum on the issues in 1976.

initiation of a plan of combination is presumed to be in contemplation of the plan unless the facts indicate otherwise.

6. Each of the combining companies can reacquire shares of voting common stock (treasury stock) only for purposes other than use in poolings of interest, and no more than a normal number of shares can be acquired after the date a pooling-of-interests plan is initiated.
7. The exchange of stock in a combination does not alter the interest of an individual common stockholder relative to any other common stockholder in a combining company.
8. Only the stockholders (not a voting trust, for example) may exercise the voting rights of the common stock ownership interest in the resulting corporation, and no stockholder can be deprived of or restricted in exercising those rights.
9. No provisions of the plan of combination can relate to the issuance of securities or other consideration on a contingent basis (or to the contingent return of shares issued) except to give effect to settlement subsequent to combination to a contingency existing at the date of combination on a basis different from that recorded by a combining company.
10. The combined company cannot agree directly or indirectly to retire or reacquire all or part of the common stock issued in the combination.
11. The combined company can make no financial arrangement for the benefit of the former stockholders of a combining company, for example, a guaranty of loans secured by the stock issued.
12. The combined company can have no plan or intention to dispose of a significant part of the assets of the combining companies within two years after the combination, except to eliminate duplicate facilities, excess capacity, or assets that would have been disposed of in the ordinary course of business of the separate companies.

## Practice Since *APB Opinion No. 16*

Accounting practice since the issuance of *Opinion No. 16* has generally adhered to the criteria specified in the *Opinion*. Borderline issues have been resolved in part by "interpretations" issued by the AICPA and in part by interpretations of individual accountants and firms of accountants. In addition, the Securities and Exchange Commission has issued several Accounting Series Releases and Staff Accounting Bulletins that amend certain aspects of *Opinion No. 16* in some cases and interpret it in others. Certain criteria are under attack as being more punitive in nature to business than consistent with the pooling-of-interests concept. *Opinion No. 16* is merely the latest in a series of official pronouncements of the AICPA on accounting for business combinations, and many believe that further pronouncements will need to be issued by the Financial Accounting Standards Board to cope adequately with changing business practices in the merger and acquisition area.

## Pro Forma Statements

"Pro Forma" statements are often called "as if" or "giving effect" statements. The rules of professional conduct of the public accounting profession generally prohibit a public accountant from attaching his name to financial statements that involve predictions of future earnings or events, but pro forma statements are acceptable in some circumstances. Most generally they are used to report the accounting effect of some contemplated specific transaction or set of transactions. They come into use in the business combination area when securities are to be issued to effect the combination. Requirements of the New York Stock Exchange and of the Securities and Exchange Commission deal with the issuance of a prospectus prior to the issuance or sale of a block of stock. When a proposed business combination is to be effected by an exchange of shares, one part of the prospectus is a pro forma balance sheet.

A typical proposal to consummate a business combination may involve presentation in columnar form of:

1. The financial statements of the combining companies
2. The changes to be effected in the combination process
3. Pro forma statements giving effect to the proposed combination.

Although practicing public accountants are not permitted to express opinions on financial statements going to the public which involve predictions of future earnings or events, accountants regularly assist management in the preparation of pro forma financial data. During the investigations and negotiations that precede any business combination, pro forma projections would regularly be a part of the data that management uses as a basis for negotiation and the ultimate decision. Hence, accountants are an integral part of the merger and acquisition team of an acquisition-minded company. The pro forma statements prepared frequently provide a point of departure for discussions as negotiations proceed. Pro forma statements are also useful to management in areas of decision-making other than that of business combinations. Thus, while the principal focus of an accountant is to report the results of consummated transactions, he has an important, and sometimes vital, role in the planning and decision-making activities that precede the consummation of the transaction.

**Pro Forma Statement—Illustrated.** Companies A, B, and C decided to pool their resources and continue operations on a combined basis. To effect the combination, Company A agreed to issue its common stock in exchange for the oustanding common stock of the other two companies. The basis for the exchange of stock was determined by considering relative market values, relative profitability of the three companies, and various other factors. The combination agreement provided that 1 share of A's stock would be issued for each 3 shares of B's, and that 1 share of A's would be issued for each 2 shares of C's stock. The combination was considered to have met the requirements necessary to be classified as a pooling of interests.

COMPANIES A, B, AND C
STATEMENT OF FINANCIAL POSITION
PROPOSED COMBINATION

| Items | Co. A | Co. B | Co. C | Adjustments | Pro forma |
|---|---|---|---|---|---|
| Cash | $ 30,000 | $ 20,000 | $ 25,000 | | $ 75,000 |
| Receivables | 60,000 | 50,000 | 40,000 | | 150,000 |
| Merchandise | 70,000 | 40,000 | 50,000 | | 160,000 |
| Fixed assets (net) | 240,000 | 315,000 | 196,000 | | 751,000 |
| Total assets | $400,000 | $425,000 | $311,000 | | $1,136,000 |
| Payables | $ 50,000 | $ 40,000 | $ 60,000 | | $ 150,000 |
| Common stock (1,000 shares) | 100,000 | | | +500,000 | 600,000 |
| Common stock (par $50) | | 300,000 | | −300,000 | — |
| Common stock (par $50) | | | 200,000 | −200,000 | — |
| Retained earnings | 250,000 | | | +136,000 | 386,000 |
| Retained earnings | | 85,000 | | − 85,000 | — |
| Retained earnings | | | 51,000 | − 51,000 | — |
| Total equities | $400,000 | $425,000 | $311,000 | | $1,136,000 |

In some reports the data in the right-hand column are presented in statement form.

## Accounting for Business Combination — An Example

Agreement has been reached in principle for a business combination involving the Pitcher Company and the Vaughn Company. Negotiations have taken place over a period of months. The combination is to be effected by an exchange of common shares, and subsequent to the exchange the Vaughn Company is to be dissolved. The following data along with various other information were considered in the negotiations:

| | Price Range of Common Stock | | Earnings per Share | |
|---|---|---|---|---|
| | Pitcher | Vaughn | Pitcher | Vaughn |
| 1978 | 26–32 | 7–11 | $2.10 | $ .70 |
| 1979 | 31–54 | 10–18 | 2.60 | 1.05 |
| 1980 | 46–65 | 16–33 | 3.00 | 1.45 |

Agreement was reached that the Pitcher Company would issue 800,000 shares of its $5 stated value common stock in exchange for the 2,000,000 outstanding shares of the Vaughn Company's $3 par value common stock, the exchange to be made on the basis of .4 share of Pitcher for each share of Vaughn stock exchanged. The exchange ratio of .4 to 1 was determined after lengthy negotiations. The relative price ranges of the common stock and the relative earnings per share were particularly important in the determination of the exchange ratio.

Other aspects of the combination remain unresolved, and the independent certified public accountants for the Pitcher Company have been asked to prepare pro forma statements as if the transaction were either a purchase or a pooling of interests. An understanding has been reached that the Securities and Exchange Commission will permit pooling-of-interests accounting if the independent accountants conclude the transaction meets the criteria of *Opinion 16*.

The condensed statements of financial position of the two companies presented below were prepared as a basis for discussions concerning the combination. A pro forma statement of financial position giving effect to the combination under each accounting alternative is to be prepared. Under the purchase alternative, the board of directors of the Pitcher Company has determined that a fair value for the shares to be issued in the combination is $51.25 per share.

In the pooling-of-interest columns of the pro forma statement all items except Common Stock and Capital in Excess of Stated Value have been determined by combining (or pooling) like items in the separate company statements of financial position. This result is consistent with the pooling concept that nothing of economic substance happens in a combination. Even the new balance of Retained Earnings combines the balances of Retained Earnings on the separate company statements. The noncombination of the Common Stock and Capital in Excess of Stated Value items for each company results from legal rather than from accounting considerations. The Pitcher Company gave up 800,000 shares of $5 stated value stock and, therefore, should credit Common Stock for $4,000,000. However, the par value of the Vaughn Company stock was $6,000,000. The excess of the par value of the Vaughn Company stock over the stated value of the Pitcher Company stock given in exchange ($2,000,000) is classified as Capital in Excess of Stated Value on the pro forma statement. Under the pooling concept the agreed fair value per share of the Pitcher stock given in the combination has no bearing on the accounting procedures. It is apparent in the pro forma statement that the objective of pooling is to effect a statement of financial position as similar as possible to the combined precombination statements.

PITCHER COMPANY AND VAUGHN COMPANY
CONDENSED STATEMENTS OF FINANCIAL POSITION
DECEMBER 31, 1980

| Assets | Pitcher Co. | Vaughn Co. |
|---|---|---|
| Cash | $ 2,500,000 | $ 800,000 |
| Receivables | 12,500,000 | 3,200,000 |
| Inventories | 21,000,000 | 6,000,000 |
| Investments | 14,000,000 | — |
| Fixed assets (net) | 42,000,000 | 12,000,000 |
| Goodwill | 2,400,000 | — |
| Other assets | 3,600,000 | 800,000 |
| | $ 98,000,000 | $ 22,800,000 |

## Equities

| | | |
|---|---|---|
| Current payables | $ 14,000,000 | $ 3,800,000 |
| Long-term debt | 22,000,000 | — |
| Common stock | 36,000,000 | 6,000,000 |
| Capital in excess of stated value | 4,200,000 | 4,000,000 |
| Retained earnings | 21,800,000 | 9,000,000 |
| | $ 98,000,000 | $ 22,800,000 |

PITCHER-VAUGHN COMBINATION
PRO FORMA STATEMENT OF FINANCIAL POSITION
DECEMBER 31, 1980

### Assets

| | Pooling of Interests | Purchase |
|---|---|---|
| Cash | $ 3,300,000 | $ 3,300,000 |
| Receivables | 15,700,000 | 15,700,000 |
| Inventories | 27,000,000 | 27,000,000 |
| Investments | 14,000,000 | 14,000,000 |
| Fixed assets (net) | 54,000,000 | 54,000,000 |
| Goodwill | 2,400,000 | 24,400,000 |
| Other assets | 4,400,000 | 4,400,000 |
| | $120,800,000 | $142,800,000 |

### Equities

| | | |
|---|---|---|
| Current payables | $ 17,800,000 | $ 17,800,000 |
| Long-term debt | 22,000,000 | 22,000,000 |
| Common stock ($5 stated value) | 40,000,000 | 40,000,000 |
| Capital in excess of stated value | 10,200,000 | 41,200,000 |
| Retained earnings | 30,800,000 | 21,800,000 |
| | $120,800,000 | $142,800,000 |

Several differences appear in the column presenting the combination as a purchase on a pro forma basis. Among the assets, the only item of difference is the Goodwill amount. On a pro forma basis, it is stated at $22,000,000 greater than the combined Goodwill of the two companies (and also $22,000,000 greater than the Goodwill on a pro forma pooling basis). This $22,000,000 is determined as follows: the fair value of the 800,000 shares of the Pitcher Company stock transferred in the combination, $41,000,000 (800,000 × $51.25), less the book value of the net assets of the Vaughn Company, $19,000,000. In many actual combinations effected during periods of rising prices, the difference between the fair value of the shares given in the combination transaction and the book value of the net assets acquired is substantial. In the illustration, this excess is classified as Goodwill in accounting for the combination, based on the assumption that the fair value of the assets acquired is equal to their book value.

Another difference exists in the amount reported as Retained Earnings. Under the purchase assumption, the pro forma statement shows $21,800,000 as Retained Earnings, or the same amount as reported separately by the Pitcher Company. The $9,000,000 Retained Earnings of the Vaughn Company is not carried forward as retained earnings, but is classified as Capital in Excess of Stated Value. The Capital in Excess of Stated Value amount under the purchase assumption is $41,200,000 on a pro forma basis, whereas it was $10,200,000 on a pro forma pooling basis. The difference of $31,000,000 is accounted for by the Goodwill increase ($22,000,000) and by the Retained Earnings decrease ($9,000,000) under the purchase assumption.

The pro forma statement under the purchase assumption gives effect to the purchase concept by recording assets on the basis of the fair value of the consideration given and by carrying forward as retained earnings only the amount so reported on the acquiring company's statements.

This illustration of the pro forma statement under the purchase assumption is oversimplified. The oversimplification lies in the treatment of the entire excess of the fair value of the shares transferred over the book value of the net assets acquired as Goodwill. While this conclusion was reached many times in practice prior to the issuance of *Opinion 16,* under that *Opinion* the appropriate approach is to attempt to allocate any excess among specific assets, tangible and intangible, that appear undervalued. In a purchase combination, little justification exists for carrying forward the asset book values that appear on the acquired company's books. For example, assume that an appraisal of the Vaughn Company assets indicated that replacement values for inventories and fixed assets (net) were $9,000,000 and $23,000,000, respectively. We might conclude that the undervaluation on the books for these assets could be one of the causes of the price difference between the value of the shares given and the book value of the assets. If this were the case, the pro forma statement of financial position might appear as follows:

PITCHER VAUGHN COMBINATION
PRO FORMA STATEMENT OF FINANCIAL POSITION (PURCHASE)

DECEMBER 31, 1980

| Assets | | Equities | |
|---|---|---|---|
| Cash | $ 3,300,000 | Current payables | $ 17,800,000 |
| Receivables | 15,700,000 | Long-term Debt | 22,000,000 |
| Inventories | 30,000,000 | Common Stock | 40,000,000 |
| Investments | 14,000,000 | Capital in Excess | |
| Fixed Assets (net) | 65,000,000 | of Stated Value | 41,200,000 |
| Goodwill | 10,400,000 | Retained Earnings | 21,800,000 |
| Other Assets | 4,400,000 | | |
| | $142,800,000 | | $142,800,000 |

As previously noted, any adjustments necessary to place the accounting records of the two companies on a uniform basis are permissible under both the purchase and the pooling concepts.

Since the assumption was made that the Vaughn Company was to be dissolved, the Pitcher Company would make entries in its ledger accounts to give effect to the combination transaction. The entries made would result in new account balances as represented in the pro forma statements. This is true under either the pooling or the purchase accounting treatment.

If the Vaughn Company were to be operated as a subsidiary, on the other hand, the Pitcher Company would debit a new account—Investment in Vaughn Company—for the appropriate exchange value. In the pooling case the debit to the investment account would be $19,000,000, while in the purchase example the debit would be for $41,000,000. In each situation a consolidated balance sheet would be prepared at the end of each fiscal period, following procedures discussed in earlier chapters.

## Impact on Subsequent Financial Statements

From the examples presented in the preceding section it is apparent that for some business combinations the two alternative methods of accounting produce widely different statements of financial position. This conclusion is true in practice for a substantial portion of the combinations effected by American businesses. While the differences in financial position as illustrated can lead to different interpretations of financial position, the significance of the alternative accounting methods lies in the impact each has on the operating results of subsequent fiscal periods.

The results of operations subsequent to a business combination can vary, of course, from the sum of the results of the separate companies for a wide variety of reasons. Managerial efficiencies, production efficiencies, marketing efficiencies, and many other factors may improve operating results in periods subsequent to the combination. The reverse can also result from a variety of unanticipated inefficiencies or uneconomical events. Disregarding all of these for the moment, the results of operations may be influenced purely by the accounting treatments accorded the combination transaction.

If the combination is accounted for as a pooling of interests, the accounting treatment will have a minimal effect on operating results of future periods. All deferred items carried forward as assets on the combined balance sheet would be the same as would have been reported on the separate company statements. Amortizations and other charges to operations in future periods would not be affected by the accounting entries. Since the accounting entries for the pooling did not alter previously existing book values, subsequent earnings statements on a combined basis would approximate the aggregate of the separate company earnings statements, disregarding other effects that the combination event could produce on the operations of the various companies.

A similar conclusion was reached in practice for many purchase combinations prior to the issuance of *APB Opinion No. 17,* "Intangible Assets," in September

1970. Thus, for example, under the first purchase assumption presented in the preceding section, all deferred items carried forward as assets in the combined balance sheet are the same as would have been reported on the separate company statements, except for goodwill, an intangible asset. Prior to *Opinion No. 17,* goodwill was commonly carried forward on the balance sheet from period to period without amortization. Under this practice the subsequent earnings statements on a combined basis would approximate the aggregate of the separate company earnings statements, disregarding the other effects on operations that the combination event might produce. In effect, the only asset difference between purchase and pooling accounting was sterilized in that it had no effect on future earnings.

*APB Opinion No. 17* concluded that goodwill arising from business combinations initiated after October 31, 1970, should not be carried forward without amortization. Instead, goodwill should be amortized by systematic (generally on a straight-line basis) charges to income over a period not to exceed 40 years. Therefore, except in those rare combinations in which the price paid for a company is equal to its book value and the book values of all assets and liabilities are equal to their fair values, operating results following a purchase combination will differ from those that would result under pooling accounting. When the price paid exceeds the book value, earnings subsequent to the combination will be lower if the combination is accounted for as a purchase than they will be if the combination is accounted for as a pooling. The amount of the difference will be directly attributable to the manner of accounting for the combination transaction. To the extent that the specific tangible or intangible assets are subject to periodic amortization, results of operations in subsequent periods will be affected by the amortization.

Referring to the Pitcher-Vaughn combination, the following comparisons can be made (goodwill amortization is not deductible for income tax purposes, and a 50% tax rate is assumed for fixed asset and inventory adjustments):

|  | | Purchase Accounting | |
| --- | --- | --- | --- |
|  | | | New Goodwill Amortized—40 Years |
|  | Pooling Accounting | Asset Book Values Assumed to Be Fair Values | New Fixed Asset Life—15 Years. Inventory on FIFO Basis |
| Shares outstanding after combination | 8,000,000 | 8,000,000 | 8,000,000 |
| 1980 combined net income | $24,500,000 | $24,500,000 | $24,500,000 |
| 1980 earnings per share combined basis | $3.06 | $3.06 | $3.06 |
| 1981 pro forma net income | $24,500,000 | $23,950,000 | $22,433,333 |
| 1981 pro forma earnings per share | $3.06 | $2.99 | $2.80 |

The impact on subsequent earnings of the decision on how to accomplish a business combination should be apparent from this oversimplified illustration. Considerable evidence exists that awareness of these subsequent effects has had a significant impact on decisions on how to accomplish a given business combination. In some cases otherwise unacceptable provisions of a combination plan are agreed to meet the pooling criteria and, therefore, to overcome the depressing income effect of purchasing accounting.

## Accounting for Combinations—A Reevaluation

Any discussion of accounting for business combinations embodies a number of issues:

1. *Proper accounting for goodwill.* Once goodwill has been determined to exist in a given transaction, a problem arises in accounting for this item in subsequent periods. Prior to *APB Opinions No. 16 and 17,* goodwill was frequently considered to be the excess of cost over book value of the acquired company, and such goodwill was carried forward indefinitely so long as no limitation on its useful life was apparent. These two *Opinions* now require (1) that any excess of cost over book value of the acquired company in a purchase combination be allocated to the assets acquired and liabilities assumed on the basis of their fair values at the date of acquisition, (2) that only a residual amount not otherwise assignable be designated as goodwill, and (3) that the goodwill be amortized by charges to income over a period not to exceed 40 years. Whether an arbitrary requirement to amortize goodwill by charges to income, even in the face of evidence that the goodwill value remains undiminished, is sound and capable of withstanding practical pressures remains to be seen.

2. *Determination of value in exchange transactions.* As previously indicated, accountants have long followed a principle of valuation in noncash transactions which stipulates the appropriate value of assets received as the fair value of the consideration given or the fair value of the consideration received, whichever is more clearly evident. When the consideration given is stock that is traded in a reasonably broad market, the value of this stock provides an apparently valid basis for valuing the consideration received. However, even in a reasonably broad market, prices of shares of stock may have rather wide variations for obscure reasons. Further, listed prices commonly relate to the trading value of shares in relatively small quantities, certainly smaller than the number of shares issued to effect a combination. When purchase accounting is appropriate, serious consideration should be given to establishing a fair value for accountability. The fair value of the shares issued as determined from the stock market should be no more than a point of departure in determining the exchange value. Likewise, the problem of determining the fair value of the assets acquired and liabilities assumed frequently is difficult to resolve, but it is critical if income statements following a purchase combination are to be fair reflections of operating results.

3. *The nature of a transaction.* Insofar as accounting entries are concerned, accountants are principally concerned with business transactions. Business trans-

# 19 / Expansion by Combination

actions generally embody some exchange of values, and the accountant must explain this exchange. Most accountants would agree that a business combination is a business transaction and that it involves an exchange of values. Those accountants who support pooling-of-interests accounting, however, hold that in the combination transaction nothing of economic substance has happened. As a result, these accountants account for the combination *as if* no transaction occurred. While *APB Opinion No. 16* provides further support to pooling-of-interests accounting, that *Opinion* restricts severely the use of such accounting as compared with pre-*Opinion No. 16* practice. Whether the criteria of *Opinion 16* will withstand better than its predecessors the pressures of attrition only time will tell.

## Distribution of Securities

In some business combinations various types of securities are issued. To illustrate different methods for distributing securities in exchange when a combination is formed, assume the following facts:

|  | Company A | Company B | Company C | Total |
|---|---|---|---|---|
| Adjusted book value of assets contributed: |  |  |  |  |
| Fixed assets | $100,000 | $300,000 | $100,000 | $500,000 |
| Current assets | 100,000 | 100,000 | 200,000 | 400,000 |
| Total assets | $200,000 | $400,000 | $300,000 | $900,000 |
| Book value of equities: |  |  |  |  |
| Current liabilities | $ 50,000 | $ 50,000 | $100,000 | $200,000 |
| Fixed liabilities | — | 100,000 | — | 100,000 |
| Stockholders' equity | 150,000 | 250,000 | 200,000 | 600,000 |
| Total equities | $200,000 | $400,000 | $300,000 | $900,000 |
| Annual earnings: |  |  |  |  |
| 1980 | $ 25,000 | $ 20,000 | $ 21,000 | $ 66,000 |
| 1979 | 23,000 | 18,000 | 17,000 | 58,000 |
| 1978 | 19,500 | 22,000 | 14,500 | 56,000 |
| Average annual earnings | $ 22,500 | $ 20,000 | $ 17,500 | $ 60,000 |
| Average rate of return on stockholders' equity | 15% | 8% | 8.75% | 10% |

It is estimated that total average earnings will increase to $75,000 per year and that the competitive position of the three companies will be improved by the combination.

Plans under consideration for distributing securities to the three companies by a newly formed Company D, in exchange for the stockholders' rights in the separate companies, are:

1. Common stock with a par value of $600,000 to be issued in the ratio of relative stockholder equity contributed.

C/S for Earnings Pfd St for assets



2. Common stock with a par value of $600,000 to be issued in the ratio of former earning power.
3. Excess earning power (over 8%) to be capitalized at 16% and treated as goodwill, and common stock to be issued in the ratio of relative stockholder equity plus the goodwill contributed. Total capital of the three companies was $600,000, and an 8% return on this would have been $48,000. Since $60,000 was earned, the excess is $12,000, to be capitalized at 16%. Common stock to be issued is $600,000 plus $75,000 ($12,000 ÷ .16), or $675,000.
4. Preferred stock (6%), to be issued in payment for the stockholder equity contributed, and common stock to be issued for the earning power contributed (earnings in excess of 6% to be capitalized at 16%). Here the excess earnings are $24,000 ($60,000 − 6% of $600,000). When capitalized at 16%, $24,000 = $150,000.
5. Bonds to be issued in payment for 50% of the portion of the stockholder equity represented by fixed assets; preferred stock to be issued in payment for any balance of the stockholder equity contributed; Class A Common Stock to be issued for the goodwill, computed as excess of past earnings over 8% capitalized at 8%, contributed by each company ($60,000 − 8% of $600,000 = $12,000 ÷ .08 = $150,000); and Class B Common Stock to be issued equally to each company for the anticipated increase in earnings due to the combination capitalized at 20%.

The proposed distribution of securities under each plan would be as shown below. Any evaluation of the relative merits of the five plans for distributing securities should as a minimum give consideration to the following analysis:

*Plan 1.* Although this plan gives an equitable allocation of the net assets to the contributing companies, future earnings of the combined companies will not be allocated to stockholder interests in the manner they would have been if the companies had not merged. Companies B and C would receive a greater proportion while Company A's share would be reduced.

| | Company A | Company B | Company C | Total |
|---|---|---|---|---|
| *Plan 1:* | | | | |
| Common stock | $150,000 | $250,000 | $200,000 | $600,000 |
| *Plan 2:* | | | | |
| Common stock | $225,000 | $200,000 | $175,000 | $600,000 |
| *Plan 3:* | | | | |
| Common stock | | | | |
| For equity | $150,000 | $250,000 | $200,000 | $600,000 |
| For goodwill (excess earnings over 8% capitalized at 16%) | 65,625 | −0− | 9,375 | 75,000 |
| Total | $215,625 | $250,000 | $209,375 | $675,000 |

*Plan 4:*

|  |  |  |  |  |
|---|---|---|---|---|
| Preferred stock (6%) | $150,000 | $250,000 | $200,000 | $600,000 |
| Common stock (excess earnings over 6% capitalized at 16%) | 84,375 | 31,250 | 34,375 | 150,000 |
| Total | $234,375 | $281,250 | $234,375 | $750,000 |

*(handwritten note: → same as Plan 1)*

*Plan 5:*

|  |  |  |  |  |
|---|---|---|---|---|
| Bonds (50% of fixed assets) | $ 50,000 | $150,000 | $ 50,000 | $250,000 |
| Preferred stock | 100,000 | 100,000 | 150,000 | 350,000 |
| Class A, Common | 131,250 | –0– | 18,750 | 150,000 |
| Class B, Common | 25,000 | 25,000 | 25,000 | 75,000 |
|  | $306,250 | $275,000 | $243,750 | $825,000 |

*Plan 2.* This plan will allocate earnings on an equitable basis as represented by past earnings of the separate companies, but the stockholdings acquired by each company will not be in proportion to the assets contributed by each company. If the combination were to be liquidated, Company B might not receive an equitable share of the assets distributed whereas Company A might receive an excessive share of the distributed assets.

*Plan 3.* Unless the goodwill can be realized in case the combination is liquidated, this plan is subject to the same reservation as Plan 2. In addition, it may involve including an amount of goodwill as an asset of the combination. If goodwill is not recorded on the books of the combination, this plan is a compromise between Plan 1 and Plan 2.

*Plan 4.* Provided the preferred stock is participating, this plan has merit. It provides a means of giving the new stockholders an equity claim for assets contributed which will be returned to them upon dissolution of the business through the preferred stock. By making the preferred stock preferred as to dividends in an amount equal to a fair earnings rate on assets, common stock needs to be distributed only to companies contributing earning power in excess of the basic rate. As a result of this arrangement, earnings will be distributed among the various stockholder interests in the same proportion as they would have if the combination had not been formed. Should the combined entity produce income in excess of what had previously been the total normal earnings of the separate companies, it is equitable that such excess earnings should be distributed to both the new preferred stockholders and the new common stockholders. This can be accomplished by making the preferred stock participating with the common stock in all distributions of earnings in excess of the amount that it appears would have been earned had the companies remained as separate entities.

A variation of this plan used by one company was to issue common stock on the basis of relative earning power contributed by the separate companies, and to issue convertible preferred stock to stockholders for the book value of the assets not covered by the common stock. To illustrate the procedure, assume that Companies A, B, and C contribute net assets of $100,000 each to a new company and earning power of $1,000, $5,000, and $10,000, respectively. The distribution of the common stock would be on the ratio of 1:5:10. The earnings of the company with the highest rate of return is C, with a 10% return. Capitalizing the earnings of each company at 10% indicates the amount of common stock to be issued as follows:

|   | Earnings | Capitalized Value |
|---|---|---|
| A | $ 1,000 | $ 10,000 |
| B | 5,000 | 50,000 |
| C | 10,000 | 100,000 |
| Common stock to be issued | | $160,000 |

If the $160,000 of common stock is distributed as indicated and earnings are paid only on common stock (the preferred stock would normally be assigned a dividend rate but to keep the illustration simple, assume that the preferred receives no dividend and is preferred as to assets on dissolution only), earnings of the combination will be distributed in accordance with the earning power contributed by the separate companies.

To provide for the assets contributed by the separate companies for which common stock is not issued, convertible preferred stock may be issued, as follows:

|   | A | B | C |
|---|---|---|---|
| Assets contributed | $100,000 | $100,000 | $100,000 |
| Common stock issued | 10,000 | 50,000 | 100,000 |
| Preferred stock | $ 90,000 | $ 50,000 | $ –0– |

The idea involved in this plan was that if the assets not covered by the common stock should start earning greater income, the market price of the common stock would react accordingly, and by converting the preferred stock, the preferred stockholders would receive the earnings arising as a result of their contribution of assets.

*Plan 5.* This plan represents an attempt to equalize the risk of loss, provide for equitable rights to assets contributed on liquidation, distribute future earnings equal in amount to past earnings of the separate companies as such earnings would have been distributed had the combination not taken place, and provide for an equal distribution of excess earnings due to the combination. It is based on an assumption that future earnings will be greater than, or at least equal to, past combined earnings.

Under the plan the bonds provide the greatest protection against loss for the company contributing proportionately more fixed assets than the other companies. The preferred stock assures the various stockholders of protection against unfair distribution at liquidation of their contributed assets. The Class A common stock assures a fair distribution of earning power contributed by each company, while the Class B common stock provides for a fair distribution of excess earnings among the stockholders.

A variation of this plan, when only one class of common stock is issued, was used by a company a few years ago. Under this plan the common stock was issued for the goodwill, but a provision in the combination agreement provided that the additional shares would be issued on the basis of future excess earnings, attributable to the combined contributed assets. This method was used because it was felt that the record of past earnings was not representative of earning power.

There are, of course, many variations from these five plans to be found in practice. The selection and presentation of a suitable plan for the distribution of securities in a business combination requires considerable experience and judgment.

## PROBLEMS

### Problem 19-1

The balance sheets of the J. K. Foster Co. and the P. C. Baker Co. as of October 31, 1979, are presented below. On that date, following a lengthy period of negotiations, a merger of the two companies was effected, with the resulting company to be known as Foster-Baker, Inc. In the merger, the J. K. Foster Co. was to exchange 250,000 of its authorized, but unissued, shares in exchange for all the shares of the Baker Co., on the basis of 1¼ shares of Foster for each share of Baker. Market values of the respective shares on October 31 were:

|  |  |
|---|---|
| J. K. Foster Co. stock, | 20 |
| P. C. Baker Co. stock, | 25 |

During the preceding three months the respective shares had traded in the following ranges: Foster, 18½-22; Baker 22-26¾.

|  | Foster Co. | Baker Co. |
|---|---|---|
| Cash | $ 1,200,000 | $ 400,000 |
| Receivables | 1,400,000 | 600,000 |
| Inventories | 4,000,000 | 800,000 |
| Fixed assets (net) | 11,400,000 | 2,000,000 |
|  | $18,000,000 | $3,800,000 |
| Payables | $ 3,000,000 | $ 800,000 |
| Common stock (par $10) | 10,000,000 | 2,000,000 |
| Capital in excess of par | 1,000,000 | -0- |
| Retained income | 4,000,000 | 1,000,000 |
|  | $18,000,000 | $3,800,000 |

*Required:*
(1) Present a statement of financial position for Foster-Baker, Inc., on the assumption that the business combination is a pooling of interests.

(2) Present a statement of financial position of Foster-Baker, Inc., on the assumption that the business combination is a purchase.

## Problem 19-2

The Bess Co. has been negotiating several months to effect a combination with the Tate Co. The book value of the net assets of the Tate Co. at the present time is $8,000,000. At current market prices the Bess Co. would issue about $12,000,000 in common stock in exchange for all the common stock of the Tate Co. Of this difference about one-half can be attributed to undervalued assets (inventory and properties) on the Tate Co. books, and the other half represents the Tate Co.'s favorable earning capacity. Several unresolved questions remain, including whether to operate Tate as a subsidiary, how to account for the combination, and effect on future earnings.

*Required:*
Write a brief discussion which might be helpful to the Bess Co. management on the following points:

(1) How would the Bess Co. statement of financial position differ if the Tate Co. were operated as a subsidiary as opposed to being a division in a merged company?
(2) What would be the principal differences in accounting if the combination were considered to be a pooling of interests as opposed to a purchase?
(3) Would the decision made as to a pooling of interests or a purchase affect subsequent income statements? Why?

## Problem 19-3

Presented below are condensed balance sheets of three companies as of May 31, 1979. All companies are in the same industry. Effective as of that date, the Regis Co. obtained control of both the Tippit Co. and the Peoples Co. through exchanges of stock with the respective stockholders. In both instances, the management of the two acquired companies were to continue to operate their former companies as departments of the Regis Co. The stockholders of both Tippit and Peoples agreed not to sell their newly acquired Regis Co. shares for a period of at least two years.

|                                | Regis Co.     | Tippit Co.   | Peoples Co.  |
| --- | --- | --- | --- |
| Cash                           | $  2,000,000  | $   200,000  | $   400,000  |
| Receivables                    | 18,000,000    | 600,000      | 700,000      |
| Inventories                    | 42,000,000    | 1,400,000    | 1,000,000    |
| Investments                    | 30,000,000    | 300,000      | –0–          |
| Plant, property, and equipment | 85,000,000    | 2,600,000    | 1,500,000    |
| Other assets                   | 6,000,000     | 400,000      | –0–          |
| Goodwill                       | 8,000,000     | –0–          | –0–          |
|                                | $191,000,000  | $5,500,000   | $3,600,000   |

| | | | |
|---|---:|---:|---:|
| Current liabilities | $ 20,000,000 | $1,300,000 | $ 500,000 |
| Bonds payable | 40,000,000 | –0– | –0– |
| Common stock—par $20 | 100,000,000 | –0– | –0– |
| Common stock—par $100 | –0– | 3,000,000 | 2,500,000 |
| Capital in excess of par | 4,000,000 | 900,000 | –0– |
| Retained earnings | 27,000,000 | 300,000 | 600,000 |
| | $191,000,000 | $5,500,000 | $3,600,000 |

Separate negotiations were conducted with the boards of directors of the Tippit Co. and the Peoples Co. Each agreement indicated that the Regis Co. would issue 140,000 shares of its $20 par value common stock to the stockholders of the respective companies in exchange for their shares. During the 90 days prior to May 31, 1979, the common stocks of the three companies had traded in the following ranges:

| | |
|---|---|
| Regis Co. | 28–32 |
| Tippit Co. | 90–124 |
| Peoples Co. | 116–163 |

The board of directors of the Regis Co. decided: (1) to account for the Tippit combination as a purchase, using the average of the range of market prices for the Regis Co. stock during the 90 days prior to May 31, 1979 as a basis for the accounting; and (2) to account for the Peoples combination as a pooling of interests. The Regis Co.'s independent auditors and the SEC approved these decisions.

*Required:*
(1) Prepare a statement of financial position of the Regis Co. giving effect to the Tippit Co. combination only.
(2) Prepare a statement of financial position of the Regis Co. giving effect to the Peoples Co. combination only.
(3) Prepare a statement of financial position for the Regis Co. giving effect to both the Tippit and Peoples combinations.
(4) Why would the board of directors of the Regis Co. decide to account for the two combinations in the manner indicated? As their independent auditor, how would you support your decision to approve the board actions?
(5) Why might the Regis Co. pay the same price for both companies?

## Problem 19-4

On January 1, 1979, Corporation Z acquired all of the outstanding stock of Corporation M in order to combine the two businesses. Z issued $100,000 par value of its stock (which had a market value of $300,000) to the stockholders of M in exchange for their stock. Immediately upon the exchange of the stock, Corporation M was dissolved and Z took over the net assets. As of January 1, 1979, Corporation M had $100,000 of stock outstanding; $100,000 of capital in excess of par; and $100,000 of retained earnings.

*Required:*
(1) Give two ways that these transactions may be recorded on the books of Corporation Z.
(2) State the circumstances under which each of the two treatments would be appropriate and give the reasoning supporting each treatment.

(AICPA adapted)

## Problem 19-5

Effective December 31, 1979, Wesco Corporation proposes to acquire, in exchange for common stock, all of the assets and liabilities of Southco Corporation and Eastco Corporation, after which Southco and Eastco will distribute the Wesco stock to their stockholders in complete liquidation and dissolution. Wesco proposes to increase its outstanding stock for purposes of these acquisitions. Balance sheets of each of the corporations immediately prior to merger on December 31, 1979 are given below. The assets are deemed to be worth their book values.

|  | Wesco | Southco | Eastco |
|---|---|---|---|
| Current assets | $ 2,000,000 | $ 500,000 | $ 25,000 |
| Fixed assets (net) | 10,000,000 | 4,000,000 | 200,000 |
|  | $12,000,000 | $4,500,000 | $225,000 |
| Current liabilities | $ 1,000,000 | $ 300,000 | $ 20,000 |
| Long-term debt | 3,000,000 | 1,000,000 | 105,000 |
| Capital stock ($10 par) | 3,000,000 | 1,000,000 | 50,000 |
| Retained earnings | 5,000,000 | 2,200,000 | 50,000 |
|  | $12,000,000 | $4,500,000 | $225,000 |
| Other data relative to acquisition: |  |  |  |
| Shares outstanding | 300,000 | 100,000 | 5,000 |
| Fair market value per share | $40 | $40 | $30 |
| Number of shares Wesco stock to be exchanged: |  |  |  |
| for Southco assets |  | 100,000 |  |
| for Eastco assets |  |  | 5,000 |
| Old management to continue |  | Yes | No |
| Old stockholders to elect director on Wesco board |  | Yes | No |

*Required:*
(1) The terms *purchase* and *pooling of interests* describe two methods designating the results of bringing together two or more corporations into a combination for the purpose of carrying on the previously conducted businesses. Define the terms *purchase* and *pooling of interests* as used to designate business combinations.
(2) Describe the accounting treatment in each case.
(3) Prepare Wesco's journal entries from the data above to record the combination of Wesco, Southco, and Eastco.

(AICPA adapted)

## Problem 19-6

Mr. J. T. Hendrix owns three corporations, A, B, and C. The three companies are in different industries, have different managements, and operate independently of each other. At times Mr. Hendrix has borrowed money from one company and loaned it to another company. Also, he sold 10% of his interest in B to C for $20,000 and loaned that money to B. The financial statements of the three companies on December 31, 1979, are as follows:

|  | A | B | C |
|---|---|---|---|
| Due from J. T. Hendrix | $ 10,000 | | |
| Investment in B (10%) | | | $ 20,000 |
| Due from A | | $ 6,000 | |
| Other assets | 370,000 | 184,000 | 430,000 |
| Total assets | $380,000 | $190,000 | $450,000 |
| Due to J. T. Hendrix | | $ 25,000 | $ 5,000 |
| Other liabilities | $ 40,000 | 15,000 | 95,000 |
| Capital stock | 300,000 | 100,000 | 300,000 |
| Retained earnings | 40,000 | 50,000 | 50,000 |
| Total equities | $380,000 | $190,000 | $450,000 |

*Required:*
Prepare a combined statement of financial position, showing Mr. Hendrix a composite picture of his holdings.

## Problem 19-7

A news release of the SEC is presented below:

Futterman-Dupont Hotel Company, 580 Fifth Ave., *New York,* filed a registration statement (File 2-15148) with the SEC, seeking registration of $1,706,900 of Limited Partnership Interests.

The company is a limited partnership consisting of Robert A. Futterman, I. Theodore Leader and M. Joshua Aber, as General Partners, and Rosalie Futterman, Beatrice Leader, and eight other individuals as original Limited Partners. The partnership has purchased the land and the Dupont Plaza Hotel at Dupont Circle in Washington, D.C., from Sidney B. Fink as trustee for the stockholders of Dupont Plaza, Inc. The purchase price was $4,565,000, of which $1,565,000 was paid in cash and the balance by taking title subject to a $3,000,000 mortgage. The partnership is offering $975,000 of Limited Partnership interests to repay monies borrowed for the purposes of closing title and paying incidental acquisition costs. The original Limited Partners also are offering their Limited Partnership interests in the amount of $731,900. The offering is to be made in $25,000 units. The properties are leased for slightly over 21 years to Dupont Plaza, Inc., The Babin Company, Clinton B. Synder, Max Siegal, and Paul M. Schreibman.

*Required:*
(1) What effect will the consummation of this plan have on the financial position of Dupont Plaza, Inc.?
(2) Should this be considered a business combination for reporting purposes? Would your answer be the same if the Futterman-Dupont Hotel Company held other assets besides the hotel?

## Problem 19-8

Company A and Company B have considered a merger. At issue is the proper ratio at which their shares shall be exchanged. Neither stock is listed on any stock exchange. Earnings and book value of the two companies are:

|  | A | B |
|---|---|---|
| Book value of capital stock (10,000 shares for A and 5,000 shares for B) | $900,000 | $400,000 |
| Average annual earnings | 80,000 | 80,000 |

In addition, A has an asset that will reduce B's future annual expenses by $20,000 a year for 5 years, if the merger is accomplished. A requests and receives B's approval to treat the $20,000 annual cost savings as an asset, by discounting it at the rate of earnings currently enjoyed by B.

*Required:*
Suggest a basis for exchanging the stock for the merger. Assume that A's stock is to be surrendered for new stock of B.

## Problem 19-9

The Argonat Company and the Bassilla Company are considering a merger under which all of the Bassilla outstanding stock would be sold to Argonat in exchange for stock of Argonat. The basis of exchange of the stock is 1 share of Argonat for 1.3 shares of Bassilla. Fractional shares shall be paid in cash at $130 per share. The agreement has to be approved by the stockholders. Condensed financial statements of the two companies are:

|  | Argonat | Bassilla |
|---|---|---|
| Cash | $ 60,000 | $ 50,000 |
| Receivables | 100,000 | 180,000 |
| Merchandise | 100,000 | 200,000 |
| Fixed assets | 800,000 | 400,000 |
| Allowance for depreciation | (300,000) | (100,000) |
| Total assets | $760,000 | $730,000 |
| Liabilities | $150,000 | $200,000 |
| Capital stock (par $100) | 500,000 | 500,000 |
| Retained earnings | 110,000 | 30,000 |
| Total equities | $760,000 | $730,000 |

Adjustments needed to value the assets of both companies on a consistent basis are:

1. Increase Bassilla's merchandise by $20,000.
2. Decrease Argonat's accumulated depreciation by $10,000.
3. Increase Argonat's liabilities by $20,000.

*Required:*
Prepare a report showing adjustments and eliminations and a pro forma statement of financial position, assuming a pooling of interest.

## Problem 19-10

Company A purchased 90% of the stock of Company B, paying for the stock by issuing 2 shares of A's stock for 1 share of B's stock. Financial statements of the two companies immediately prior to the exchange of stock, in condensed form, were:

|  | A | B |
|---|---|---|
| Assets | $800,000 | $400,000 |
| Liabilities | $100,000 | $ 20,000 |
| Capital stock (no par) | 600,000 | 200,000 |
| Retained earnings | 100,000 | 180,000 |
| Total | $800,000 | $400,000 |

The market prices of the stock on the date agreed upon for the exchange were:

|  | Price per Share | Number of Shares Outstanding |
|---|---|---|
| Company A | $ 80 | 12,000 |
| Company B | $160 | 4,000 |

*Required:*
(1) Prepare a consolidated statement of financial position assuming that:
   (a) The merger is considered a purchase by A.
   (b) The merger is considered a pooling of interests of the two companies.
(2) Which procedure is more realistic?

## Problem 19-11

On April 30, 1979, Investment Co. agrees to purchase the common stock of Consolidated Co. for a tentative price of $180,000. The purchase price is to be reduced by the amount, if any, by which the total book value of the shares of Consoliated Co. as of January 31, 1979 exceeded the total book value as of April 30, 1979.

The balance sheets of Consolidated Co. were as follows:

|  | April 30, 1979 | January 31, 1979 |
|---|---|---|
| *Assets* | | |
| Current assets | $ 55,000 | $ 56,000 |
| Fixed assets, less accumulated depreciation | 76,000 | 78,000 |
| Investment in and advances to Industries, Inc. | 20,200 | 14,100 |
| | $151,200 | $148,100 |
| *Liabilities and Owners' Equity* | | |
| Current liabilities | $ 27,000 | $ 30,000 |
| Capital stock | 17,000 | 17,000 |
| Retained earnings | 107,200 | 101,100 |
| | $151,200 | $148,100 |

The balance sheets of Industries, Inc., subsidiary of Consolidated Co., were as follows:

|  | April 30, 1979 | January 31, 1979 |
|---|---|---|
| *Assets* | | |
| Current assets | $ 10,000 | $ 18,100 |
| Other assets | 1,200 | 1,200 |
| Fixed assets, less accumulated depreciation | 4,300 | 18,600 |
| | $ 15,500 | $ 37,900 |
| *Liabilities and Owners' Equity* | | |
| Notes payable | $ 5,000 | $ 14,300 |
| Accounts payable—trade | 5,800 | 8,600 |
| Accrued liabilities | 2,000 | 2,200 |
| | $ 12,800 | $ 25,100 |
| Long-term debt: | | |
| Notes payable | $ 18,500 | $ 19,400 |
| Advance from Consolidated Co. | 250 | 6,400 |
| | $ 18,750 | $ 25,800 |
| Capital stock | 700 | 1,000 |
| Paid-in capital | 19,250 | 10,000 |
| Deficit | (36,000) | (24,000) |
| | $ 15,500 | $ 37,900 |

The agreement provided that the book value of Consolidated Co. should be determined in accordance with generally accepted accounting principles except that the shares of Industries, Inc., should be included at their book value, if any. In the absence of a book value, the liabilities of Consolidated Co. are to be increased by a proportionate amount of the excess of the liabilities of Industries, Inc., over its assets; the proportion shall be the percentage of outstanding stock owned. The excess of liabilities over assets shall be reduced by any loss sustained by Industries, Inc., in the transfer of certain assets to its sole minority stockholder in cancellation of its promissory note.

During the period from January 31, 1979 to April 30, 1979, accumulated advances made by Consolidated Co. in the amount of $12,250 were transferred to Paid-in Capital by Industries, Inc.

On March 31, 1979, Industries, Inc., sold certain assets to its minority stockholder in consideration of the cancellation of a note payable to him. The transaction resulted in a book loss of $6,100. As part of this transaction the minority stockholder surrendered all of his stock, 30% of the outstanding stock, to Industries, Inc., for cancellation.

*Required:*
(1) Prepare schedules showing the net book value of Consolidated Co. at January 31, 1979 and April 30, 1979, computed in accordance with the terms of the sales agreement.
(2) Compute the adjustment, if any, to the tentative purchase price.

(AICPA adapted)

## Problem 19-12

Financial statements of the Orange Corporation and the Blue Corporation appear below:

STATEMENTS OF FINANCIAL POSITION
JUNE 30, 1979

| Assets | Orange Corporation | Blue Corporation |
|---|---|---|
| Cash | $ 25,500 | $ 1,500 |
| Receivables, net | 24,500 | 7,500 |
| Inventories | 42,000 | 8,800 |
| Due from Blue Corporation | 7,600 | |
| Fixed assets, less depreciation | 59,500 | 35,800 |
| Other assets | 4,500 | 200 |
| | $163,600 | $ 53,800 |
| *Liabilities* | | |
| Accounts and notes payable | $ 22,600 | $ 35,400 |
| Due to Orange Corporation | | 7,600 |
| Accrued expenses | 1,500 | 2,200 |
| Federal income tax payable | 9,500 | |
| Total liabilities | 33,600 | 45,200 |
| Capital stock, $10 par value | 50,000 | |
| Capital stock, $100 par value | | 25,000 |
| Capital contributed in excess of par value | 30,000 | 32,000 |
| Retained earnings, December 31, 1978 | 43,000 | (42,300) |
| Net income (loss) from January 1, 1979 | 9,500 | (6,100) |
| Dividends paid | (2,500) | |
| Total stockholders' equity | 130,000 | 8,600 |
| | $163,600 | $ 53,800 |

STATEMENTS OF INCOME AND EXPENSE
FOR THE SIX MONTHS ENDED JUNE 30, 1979

|  | Orange Corporation | Blue Corporation |
|---|---|---|
| Sales | $150,000 | $ 60,000 |
| Cost of sales | 105,000 | 54,000 |
| Gross profit | 45,000 | 6,000 |
| Operating expenses | 31,000 | 8,200 |
| Operating profit (loss) | 14,000 | (2,200) |
| Other income (deductions) | 5,000 | (3,900) |
| Net income (loss) before taxes | 19,000 | (6,100) |
| Provision for income taxes | 9,500 |  |
| Net income after taxes | $ 9,500 | $ (6,100) |

The net incomes (losses) before income taxes for the two corporations for the last six years are as follows (net income per books and net taxable income are the same):

|  | Orange Corporation | Blue Corporation |
|---|---|---|
| 1973 | $18,000 | $(10,000) |
| 1974 | (7,500) | 4,000 |
| 1975 | 12,600 | (15,000) |
| 1976 | 14,900 | (6,000) |
| 1977 | 31,200 | (7,000) |
| 1978 | 28,900 | (11,100) |

*Start here* → 1975

On July 1, 1979, the Blue Corporation transferred to Orange Corporation all of its assets, subject to all liabilities, in exchange for unissued Orange Corporation capital stock. Both corporations have been owned since their inceptions in 1973 by the same group of stockholders, although in different proportions as to individuals. The terms of the merger provided that the fair value of the stock in each case is to be its book value except that an allowance is to be made for the value of any net operating carry-forward losses. Obtaining the benefit of the loss carryover deduction was not the principal purpose for the merger. (Assume a 50% tax rate.)

*Required:*
(1) Compute (*a*) the number of shares of Orange Corp. to be distributed to stockholders of Blue Corp., and (*b*) the number of shares of Orange Corp. stock to be exchanged for each share of Blue stock.
(2) Prepare the journal entry for the books of Orange Corp. recording the merger with Blue Corp. as a pooling of interests.
(3) Prepare the journal entries for the books of Blue Corp. recording the merger with Orange Corp. and the distribution of Orange Corp. stock to the stockholders of Blue Corp.            (AICPA adapted)

19 / *Expansion by Combination*     613

## Problem 19-13

Prior to January 1, 1980, the stockholders of Large Co. and Small Co. approved the merger of the two companies. On January 1, 1980, 5,000 shares of Large Co. common stock were issued to the Small Co. stockholders in exchange for the 3,000 shares of Small Co. common stock outstanding.

The December 31, 1979 postclosing statements of financial position of the two companies are as follows:

LARGE COMPANY AND SUBSIDIARY
POSTCLOSING STATEMENTS OF FINANCIAL POSITION
DECEMBER 31, 1979

|  | Large Company | Small Company |
|---|---|---|
| Cash | $ 36,400 | $ 28,200 |
| Notes receivable | 22,000 | 9,000 |
| Accounts receivable | 20,900 | 21,700 |
| Accruals receivable | 13,000 | 3,300 |
| Inventories | 81,200 | 49,600 |
| Plant and equipment | 83,200 | 43,500 |
| Accumulated depreciation | (12,800) | (9,300) |
| Investment in Small Co. | 50,000 |  |
|  | $293,900 | $146,000 |
|  |  |  |
| Notes payable | $ 4,000 | $ 12,000 |
| Accounts payable | 42,000 | 19,600 |
| Dividends payable |  | 4,500 |
| Accruals payable | 2,600 | 2,100 |
| Notes receivable discounted | 8,100 |  |
| Capital stock, $10 par value | 120,000 |  |
| Capital stock, $20 par value |  | 60,000 |
| Capital in excess of par | 28,500 | 20,000 |
| Retained earnings | 88,700 | 27,800 |
|  | $293,900 | $146,000 |

The following additional information is available:

(a) Net income for 1979 (disregard income taxes):

| Large Company | $21,700 |
|---|---|
| Small Company | 10,200 |

(b) On December 31, 1979, Small Co. owed Large Co. $16,000 on open account and $8,000 in interest-bearing notes. Large Co. discounted $3,000 of the notes received from Small Co. with the First State Bank.

(c) On December 31, 1979, Small Co. accrued interest payable of $120 on the notes payable to Large Co.; $40 on the notes of $3,000 discounted with the bank and $80 on the remaining notes of $5,000. Large Co. did not accrue interest receivable from Small Co.

(d) During 1979, Large Co. sold merchandise that cost $30,000 to Small Co. for $40,000. Small Company's December 31st inventory included $10,000 of this merchandise priced at Small Company's cost.

(e) On July 1, Small Co. sold equipment that had a book value of $15,000 to Large Co. for $17,000. Large Co. recorded depreciation on it in the amount of $850 for 1979. The remaining life of the equipment at the date of sale was 10 years.

(f) Small Co. shipped merchandise to Large Co. on December 31, 1979 and recorded an account receivable of $6,000 for the sale. Small Company's cost for the merchandise was $4,800. Because the merchandise was in transit, Large Company did not record the transaction. The terms of the sale were FOB shipping point.

(g) Small Co. declared a dividend of $1.50 per share on December 30, 1979, payable on January 10, 1980. Large Co. made no entry for the declaration.

*Required:*

Prepare a consolidated statement of financial position work sheet. The consolidation is to be accounted for as a pooling of interests. Formal journal entries are not required. (AICPA adapted)

## Problem 19-14

The managements of the Kelly Co. and the Foster Co. are discussing a combination of their companies. The tentative agreement reached is for the Kelly Co. to issue its common stock in exchange for all the common stock of the Foster Co. The exchange ratio has been tentatively set at 0.8 share of Kelly for each share of Foster. However, Foster management wants to include in the plan either of two provisions: (1) that if the postcombination earnings of the Foster Co. exceed $1,000,000 in each of the first three years following the combination, the exchange ratio will be adjusted to 0.9 shares of Kelly for each share of Foster, or (2) that if the market price of Kelly stock (at present $30 per share) fails to reach $40 per share within the first three years following combination, the exchange ratio will be adjusted to 0.9 share of Kelly for each share of Foster.

*Required:*

Would the combination qualify as a pooling of interests assuming neither of the two additional provisions is included in the plan? Would either provision preclude the use of pooling-of-interests accounting? Why? Does either additional provision make business sense? Why? Does either of these provisions conflict with a general concept of a pooling of interests?

## Problem 19-15

On January 2, 1979, Asch Corporation paid $1,000,000 cash for all of Bacher Company's outstanding stock. The recorded amount (book value) of Bacher's net assets on January 2 was $880,000. Both Asch and Bacher have operated profitably for many years, both have December 31 accounting year-ends, and both have only one class of stock outstanding. This business combination should be accounted for by the purchase method in which Asch should follow certain principles in allocating its investment cost to the assets acquired and liabilities assumed.

*Required:*
(1) Describe the principles that Asch should follow in allocating its investment cost to the assets purchased and liabilities assumed for a January 2, 1979, consolidated balance sheet. Explain.
(2) Independent of your answer to part (1), assume that on January 2, 1979, Asch acquired all of Bacher's outstanding stock in a stock-for-stock exchange and that all other conditions prerequisite to a pooling of interests were met. Describe the principles that Asch should follow in applying the pooling of interests method to this business combination when combining the balance sheet accounts of both companies in the preparation of a consolidated balance sheet on January 2, 1979. (AICPA adapted)

## Problem 19-16

Select the *best* answer for each of the following items. *Items 1, 2,* and *3* are based on the following information:

Presented below are the balance sheets of two companies prior to their combination:

January 1, 1979

|  | Co. P | Co. S |
|---|---|---|
| Cash | $ 3,000 | $ 100 |
| Inventory (at FIFO cost, which approximates fair value) | 2,000 | 200 |
| Fixed assets (net) | 5,000 | 700* |
| Total assets | $10,000 | $1,000 |
| Current liabilities | $ 600 | $ 100 |
| Common stock ($1 par value) | 1,000 | 100 |
| Additional paid-in capital | 3,000 | 200 |
| Retained earnings | 5,400 | 600 |
| Total equities | $10,000 | $1,000 |

*Fair value at January 1, 1979, is $1,500.

1. On January 1, 1979, Co. P acquires 100% of the common stock of Co. S by issuing, in a tax-free exchange, 200 shares of its (Co. P's) common stock, which has a fair value of $10 per share on that date.

    The requirements for use of pooling-of-interests accounting are met and will be followed. A balance sheet of the two companies combined as of January 1, 1979, is to be prepared. The amount of "additional paid-in capital" that would be shown on this consolidated balance sheet is

a. $3,000.
b. $3,100. ⊙
c. $3,200.
d. $3,900.

2. On January 1, 1979, Co. P acquires 100% of the common stock of Co. S in a taxable purchase by payment of $2,000 cash. The amount that would be shown as "goodwill" on the consolidated balance sheet as of January 1, 1979, is
   a. $200.
   b. $900.
   c. $1,100.
   d. $300. ⊙

3. On January 1, 1979, Co. P acquires 100% of the common stock of Co. S in a taxable purchase by payment of $1,500 cash. The amount that would be shown as "fixed assets" in the consolidated balance sheet is
   a. $5,700.
   b. $6,500.
   c. $6,300. ⊙
   d. $6,700.

4. L Co. acquires the net assets of M Co. in a business combination accounted for as a purchase. As a result, goodwill will be recorded. For tax purposes, the business combination is a tax-free merger.

   One of the assets of M Co. acquired by L Co. is a building with an appraised fair value of $100,000 at the date of the business combination. It had been recorded on the books of M Co. at $80,000. Because M Co. had used accelerated depreciation for tax purposes, the building had a tax basis to M Co. (and, as a result of the merger, to L Co.) of $60,000. L Co. is in a 48% corporate income tax bracket.

   The amount at which L Co. will record the building on its books as a result of its acquisition of M Co. is
   a. $100,000.
   b. $60,000.
   c. $52,000. ⊙
   d. $80,800.

5. In a business combination accounted for as a pooling of interests, the combined corporation's retained earnings usually equals the sum of the retained earnings of the individual combining corporations. Assuming there is *no* contributed capital other than capital stock at par value, which of the following describes a situation where the combined retained earnings must be increased or decreased?
   a. Increased if the par value dollar amount of the outstanding shares of the combined corporation exceeds the total capital stock of the separate combining companies.
   b. Increased if the par value dollar amount of the outstanding shares of the combined corporation is less than the total capital stock of the separate combining companies.

c. Decreased if the par value dollar amount of the outstanding shares of the combined corporation exceeds the total capital stock of the separate combining companies.
d. Decreased if the par value dollar amount of the outstanding shares of the combined corporation is less than the total capital stock of the separate combining companies.

## Problem 19-17

The boards of directors of Kessler Corporation, Bar Company, Cohen, Inc., and Mason Corporation are meeting jointly to discuss plans for a business combination. Each of the corporations has one class of common stock outstanding; Bar also has one class of preferred stock outstanding. Although terms have not as yet been settled, Kessler will be the acquiring or issuing corporation. Because the directors want to conform to generally accepted accounting principles, they have asked you to attend the meeting as an advisor.

*Required:*
Consider each of the following questions independently of the others and answer each in accordance with generally accepted accounting principles. Explain your answers.
(1) Assume that the combination will be consummated August 31, 1979. Explain the philosophy underlying the accounting and how the balance-sheet accounts of each of the four corporations will appear on Kessler's consolidated balance sheet on September 1, 1979, if the combination is accounted for as a
   (a) Pooling of interests.
   (b) Purchase.
(2) Assume that the combination will be consummated August 31, 1979. Explain how the income-statement accounts of each of the four corporations will be accounted for in preparing Kessler's consolidated income statement for the year ended December 31, 1979, if the combination is accounted for as a
   (a) Pooling of interests.
   (b) Purchase.
(3) Some of the directors believe that the terms of the combination should be agreed upon immediately and that the method of accounting to be used (whether pooling-of-interests, purchase, or a mixture) may be chosen at some later date. Others believe that the terms of the combination and the method to be used are very closely related. Which position is correct?
(4) Kessler and Mason are comparable in size; Cohen and Bar are much smaller. How do these facts affect the choice of accounting method?
(5) Bar was formerly a subsidiary of Tucker Corporation, which has no other relationship to any of the four companies discussing combination. Eighteen months ago Tucker voluntarily spun off Bar. What effect, if any, do these facts have on the choice of accounting method?

(6) Kessler holds 2,000 of Bar's 10,000 outstanding shares of preferred stock and 15,000 of Cohen's 100,000 outstanding shares of common stock. All of Kessler's holdings were acquired during the first three months of 1979. What effect, if any, do these facts have on the choice of accounting method?

(7) It is almost certain that Mrs. Victor Mason, Sr., who holds 5% of Mason's common stock, will object to the combination. Assume that Kessler is able to acquire only 95% (rather than 100%) of Mason's stock, issuing Kessler common stock in exchange.
  (a) Which accounting method is applicable?
  (b) If Kessler is able to acquire the remaining 5% at some future time — in five years, for instance — in exchange for its own common stock, which accounting method will be applicable to this second acquisition?

(8) Since the directors feel that one of Mason's major divisions will not be compatible with the operations of the combined company, they anticipate that it will be sold as soon as possible after the combination is consummated. They expect to have no trouble in finding a buyer. What effect, if any, do these facts have on the choice of accounting method?

(AICPA adapted)

# PART FOUR
# Contraction of the Business Organization

# 20
# Disinvestment

The earlier sections of this textbook have dealt with some of the important accounting problems involved in the formation, maintenance, and expansion of a business enterprise. There are times, however, when even the best managements find that the wisest course of action is to retrench the scope of operations. At times such retrenchment may actually be the first step in total liquidation of the enterprise. Other situations may arise in the life cycle of the enterprise, such as improper management, unsettled economic conditions in general, changes in customer habits, failure to meet competition, and many other specific detrimental occurrences which may bring about a period of contraction, or even of eventual liquidation, for a business enterprise. This section of the book will consider some of the accounting problems incident to the contraction of a going enterprise. The following section of the book will treat some of the accounting problems arising from business liquidations.

**Enterprise Contraction.** A business enterprise may contract the scope of its operations voluntarily, wherein management (board of directors or owners) may decide that, of several alternatives available under the circumstances, contraction is the most desirable. On occasion the enterprise may find that, in effect, contraction has been decreed involuntarily through the working of outside forces upon the enterprise. In any event, such contraction may be a temporary condition in a long-run growth pattern of the enterprise, it may be the turning point of past growth and the start of a more stabilized period of operations, or it may presage the eventual liquidation of the enterprise in the reasonably near future. Thus, a contraction of the scope of operations does not necessarily indicate a decision to liquidate the enterprise. Frequently, long-run growth patterns may be achieved only by living through periods of retrenchment in which the basic strengths of the enterprise are further developed and past weaknesses are eliminated. Thus, while contraction of the firm nearly always precedes actual liquidation of the firm, contraction does not necessarily mean that liquidation will be forthcoming in the near future.

**Accounting for Contraction.** In accounting for decisions to contract the scope of operations the accountant should, in general, be governed by the same basic theory that is applicable to maintenance and expansion decisions of a business enterprise. During the period of contraction one cannot know with a high degree of certainty what the events of the future will bring. Thus, it is generally unwise to use predictions of future events to any great extent in determining accounting actions during a contraction phase of the enterprise. The accounting actions taken must strive to account for the decisions made, and the guding principles previously discussed are generally applicable to most business contraction situations.

Previous discussion has pointed out that during the maintenance and expansion phases of the life of an enterprise accounting actions may occasionally deviate from a strictly theoretical soundness. Likewise, during the contraction phase of an enterprise it may be necessary to modify some of the guiding principles of accounting. This section and the following section will deal with some of the modifications of the guiding principles. Generally such modifications are necessitated by an alteration in one of the basic assumptions on which accounting for the enterprise is based. For example, if full or partial liquidation is imminent, the going-concern concept of accounting for enterprise actions may no longer be valid. Those principles which rest primarily on this assumption may therefore require modification in such situations.

In the discussion that follows it must be recognized that the accounting treatment accorded the various events in contraction and in liquidation may involve departures from the concepts previously presented. Attempts will be made to justify these departures in relation to the conditions involved and to support the deviations as being proper or suitable under the circumstances.

## ASSET REALIZATION

An enterprise may dispose of a portion of its assets in various ways and for a variety of reasons. The sale of a plant site or a producing facility may be dictated by over-expansion in the past. Likewise, the disposition of productive facilities, or even an operating division, may be necessary because of the loss of a key customer or because of changes in government procurement. At times the sale of productive facilities may develop from changing consumer habits, from lack of raw materials, or from an absence of a favorable labor market. While these are only a few of the reasons for contraction of productive facilities, the important problem from the accountant's point of view involves the accounting treatment to be accorded the various dispositions.

### Accounting for Asset Realization

**Sale for Cash and for Interest-Bearing Securities.** The accounting problems are fairly simple if the disposition involves an outright sale for cash or for interest-bearing securities. Thus, if the A Corporation were to dispose of its plant and part of its equipment at Danville, Illinois, by a sale to the Bell Corporation, the basis of the property sold would be removed from the records, and a gain or loss would arise based upon the difference between such basis and the assets received in exchange. If the assets sold were carried on the books as follows:

| | | |
|---|---|---|
| Plant | $450,000 | |
| Allowance for depreciation of plant | | $288,000 |
| Machinery | 122,000 | |
| Allowance for depreciation of machinery | | 90,000 |

and if these assets were sold for $100,000 in cash and $60,000 of notes receivable due in four years at 7% interest, the following entry would be made (assuming the 7% rate is reasonable and no imputation is necessary):

| | | |
|---|---|---|
| Cash | $100,000 | |
| Notes receivable | 60,000 | |
| Allowance for depreciation of plant | 288,000 | |
| Allowance for depreciation of machinery | 90,000 | |
| Loss on disposal of fixed assets | 34,000 | |
| Plant | | $450,000 |
| Machinery | | 122,000 |

The cash received may be used for a variety of purposes, depending upon the existing needs of the business. For example, the cash may be temporarily invested until it may be employed profitably in a venture in a new field or in the development of a new plant site in a more favorable location. If the contraction is in reality the initial stage of a disinvestment or liquidation process, the cash may be used as a partial liquidating dividend to the stockholders in a corporate organization, as a partial return of invested capital for a partnership, or be applied in other ways to reduce a portion of the equities of the enterprise.

**Sale for Noninterest-Bearing Securities.** The problem becomes somewhat more complicated if the sale is not made for cash. Thus, if the A Corporation were to sell the assets described in the example above to the Bell Corporation for 10-year, noninterest-bearing serial notes having a face value of $227,804.10, the following entry might appear to be appropriate:

| | | |
|---|---|---|
| Notes receivable | $227,804.10 | |
| Allowance for depreciation of plant | 288,000.00 | |
| Allowance for depreciation of machinery | 90,000.00 | |
| Plant | | $450,000.00 |
| Machinery | | 122,000.00 |
| Gain on disposal of fixed assets | | 33,804.10 |

From this entry it appears that the A Corporation made a profit on the disposal, whereas in the sale for cash and interest-bearing notes the Corporation suffered a loss. A closer study of this situation, however, leads to the conclusion that the entry above is not proper and that no profit was earned.

In the sale for cash and interest-bearing notes the A Corporation receives assets having a present value of $160,000, assuming that 7% is the market rate of interest. In the sale for noninterest-bearing serial notes in the face amount of $227,804.10, the A Corporation receives no immediate cash, but will receive cash over a 10-year period at $22,780.41 per year. It appears logical to conclude that the face amount of the notes includes an interest element, since no interest is explicit in the transaction.

**Determination of Cash Equivalent of Securities.** Referring to Chapter Two and the concepts on the valuation of assets discussed at that point, as well as the principles established in *APB Opinion No. 21*, "Interest on Receivable and Payables," the serial notes are more properly valued at their cash equivalent value at the date of receipt. The present value of the notes becomes the basis for the assets, and the interest implicit in the face of the notes is taken up as income as the serial notes are paid. If the present value of the notes received is to be used as the basis for their valuation, a problem arises in the determination of their value. The problem is to determine the present value of 10 payments of $22,780.41 each, assuming that 7% is the market rate of interest. Referring to the Present Value of an Annuity of 1 Table in the Appendix, the present value of an annuity of $1 at 7% for 10 periods is found to be 7.02358154. If this value is multiplied by the $22,780.41 payments that will be made each year, the result should be the value today of an annuity of 10 payments or $22,780.41 at 7%. The present value of the notes received which results from the multiplication is $160,000. Using this amount as the basis of the notes, the following entry would be made:

| | | |
|---|---|---|
| Notes receivable | $160,000 | |
| Allowance for depreciation of plant | 288,000 | |
| Allowance for depreciation of machinery | 90,000 | |
| Loss on disposal of fixed assets | 34,000 | |
| Plant | | $450,000 |
| Machinery | | 122,000 |

The entry above results in the same dollar loss from disposal of the assets that resulted when it was assumed that the assets were sold for a cash equivalent of $160,000 composed of cash and 7% interest-bearing notes.

This example illustrates the general principle underlying *APB Opinion No. 21*. Whenever notes or other securities transferred in a transaction bear interest at rates other than the going rate for similar securities issued or received in similar transactions, it will be necessary to impute a proper rate of interest to determine the present value of the securities. Unless present value is so determined and the interest element in the securities is properly determined, the gain or loss on the transaction will be improperly determined and the security itself will be erroneously valued. Thus the computation of interest would have been appropriate in the illustration above if the noninterest-bearing serial notes had been interest-bearing but at a rate that differed in any significant degree from 7%, the market rate of interest assumed appropriate for this transaction.

**Interest Earned — Straight-line Approach.** Assuming that $160,000 is the proper basis for the notes received in the sale transaction, another problem arises at the end of the first year when the first payment is received. The amount received will be 1/10 of the face amount of the serial notes, or $22,780.41. The entry to record the receipt of cash could be:

| | | |
|---|---|---|
| Cash | $22,780.41 | |
| Notes receivable | | $16,000.00 |
| Interest income | | 6,780.41 |

The credit to the Notes Receivable account equals 1/10 of the basis upon which the notes were recorded, since 1/10 of the face value was received. The entry above would be made for each of the 10 payments on the serial notes.

**Interest Earned — Actuarial Approach.** One criticism of the entry above is that the interest income reported would be the same for each of the 10 years, even though the amount of the debt unpaid decreases each year. It does not appear logical to conclude that the interest earned on $160,000 during the first year should be the same as the interest earned on roughly one-tenth of this amount during the tenth year. One method of overcoming this criticism is to take up as income the interest earned on the amount of debt unpaid. Under this method of determining the interest earned the present value of the serial notes is determined at the start of the year and also at the end of the year. The difference represents the interest income for the period.

The foregoing discussion indicates that the present value of an annuity of 10 payments of $22,780.41 at 7% is $160,000. One year later the present value would have to be increased by the amount of interest for the one year. Thus, the present value of the serial notes just prior to the payment of the first installment would equal $171,200 or $160,000 plus one year's interest on the $160,000 at 7%. The increase in present value from the start of the year, $11,200, represents the interest income for that year. Actuarially, the present value could be determined as follows:

| | |
|---|---|
| Present value of an annuity of 9 payments of $22,780.41 at 7% = (22,780.41 × 6.51523224) | = $148,419.59 |
| Present value of one payment of $22,780.41 due immediately | = 22,780.41 |
| Total present value | = $171,200.00 |

If the increase in present value during the year is considered to be the interest earned, the following entry would be made:

| | | |
|---|---|---|
| Cash | $22,780.41 | |
| Notes receivable | | $11,580.41 |
| Interest income | | 11,200,00 |

At the end of the second year a similar entry would be made, but the interest earned would be less since the second year's interest would be based upon the present value of the unpaid notes at the start of the second year, or $148,419.59 ($160,000 − $11,580.41). Thus the credit to interest income would be progressively less in each of the 10 years, and the credit to notes receivable would increase in each of the 10 years. The total interest income over the 10 years would be $67,804.10, or the same total income that would be reported if the interest income were recorded at $6,780.41 per year.

By recording the notes at their present value at the date of their receipt in exchange for the assets, and by determining interest income as a percentage of the present value of the notes at the start of the year, the accounting records will provide more accurate information both on asset bases and on income earned. APB Opinion No. 21 requires the actuarial approach to amortization unless the amount involved is not material, in which case the straight-line method is acceptable.

**Sale for Stock of Acquiring Corporation.** Another possibility in the sale of assets is to receive stock of the acquiring enterprise in exchange for the assets sold. The problem here is somewhat different from that arising if cash, interest-bearing notes, or noninterest-bearing notes or bonds are involved. Assume that the A Corporation sells the assets in the example above for 2,000 shares of Bell Corporation $50 par value common stock. At the date of the sale, the Bell Corporation stock has a market value of $80 per share, and the fair value of the assets exchanged is $156,000. Once again the problem involves determination of the proper accounting basis for the asset received in exchange for the operating assets sold. At least four alternative methods for valuing the stock received may be considered.

1. Record the stock on the basis of the book value of the assets exchanged for the stock:

|  |  |  |
|---|---|---|
| Stock of Bell Corporation | $194,000 |  |
| Allowance for depreciation of plant | 288,000 |  |
| Allowance for depreciation of machinery | 90,000 |  |
| Plant |  | $450,000 |
| Machinery |  | 122,000 |

If this entry is made no gain or loss is recognized on the sale of the assets. In the absence of objective evidence as to the fair value of the assets sold, *and* in the absence of a ready market and therefore an existing market value for the stock, the entry above may be the only practical solution. In the entry it is assumed that the value, or basis, of the stock is equal to the book value, or undepreciated cost, of the assets sold. Rarely would such a relationship exist, and if this relationship is known not to exist, the entry above is not advisable.

2. Record the stock on the basis of the fair value of the assets exchanged for the stock:

|  |  |
|---|---|
| Stock of Bell Corporation | $156,000 |
| Allowance for depreciation of plant | 288,000 |

| | | |
|---|---|---|
| Allowance for depreciation of machinery | 90,000 | |
| Loss on sale of assets | 38,000 | |
| Plant | | $450,000 |
| Machinery | | 122,000 |

Valuation of the stock received at the fair value of the assets given up in exchange for the stock may be appropriate when the fair value has an objective basis. The use of fair value would appear to be more appropriate than the use of book value of the assets exchanged whenever the fair value may be determined with a reasonable degree of objectivity, as by an independent appraisal, for example.

3. Record the stock on the basis of the par value of the stock:

| | | |
|---|---|---|
| Stock of Bell Corporation | $100,000 | |
| Allowance for depreciation of plant | 288,000 | |
| Allowance for depreciation of machinery | 90,000 | |
| Loss on sale of assets | 94,000 | |
| Plant | | $450,000 |
| Machinery | | 122,000 |

Valuation of stock received in the sale transaction at par value will result in recognition of a loss or a gain, depending on whether the book value of the assets sold exceeds or is less than the par value of the stock. Other than some minor legal justification, the use of par value as a basis for recording stock has little support. Par value bears no necessary relationship to the inherent worth of the stock, and therefore its use as a basis for asset recordation is not recommended.

4. Record the stock on the basis of the market value of the stock at the date of the sale:

| | | |
|---|---|---|
| Stock of Bell Corporation | $160,000 | |
| Allowance for depreciation of plant | 288,000 | |
| Allowance for depreciation of machinery | 90,000 | |
| Loss on sale of assets | 34,000 | |
| Plant | | $450,000 |
| Machinery | | 122,000 |

If the entry above is made, the assets received are recorded on the basis of their value existing at the date of the transaction. The loss or gain which may arise is determined by comparison of the value of the assets received and the book value of the assets sold. Recognition of loss or gain in such a manner is commonly the most appropriate procedure to follow. Assuming that the market value of the stock is based on a reasonable amount of trading, such market value is the best measure of the present value of that stock.

If a sound basis exists to determine the value of the consideration received in a sale transaction, such basis should be used as the basis for recording the transaction. If a sound basis for valuation of the consideration received does not exist, the fair value of the assets given up in the transaction may be the most appropriate basis to use. If neither the fair value of the consideration given up nor the fair value of the assets received is available, the book value of the assets given up in exchange may be the most appropriate basis to use. Rarely, if ever, is par value appropriate as a basis for valuation of stock received and held as an asset.

From the foregoing discussion the conclusion can be drawn that there is little relationship between the reason supporting a disinvestment situation through the realization of assets and the accounting for the disinvestment. Of far more importance from an accounting viewpoint is the manner in which the disinvestment is consummated. The objective in accounting for disinvestments through asset realization is consistent with the objectives of accounting for assets as previously discussed. That is, the entry to reflect the disinvestment should remove from the accounting records the bases of the properties disposed of and should record any assets received in exchange at the cash or cash equivalent value of the assets at the date of the transaction.

## ASSET REVALUATION

A few of the accounting problems arising when an enterprise purposely disposes of a portion of its productive facilities were considered in the preceding section. At this point a different type of disinvestment situation will be considered. A disinvestment may be accomplished not only by management plan or decision, but also without the awareness of management or in spite of management planning. In fact, an erosion of asset values may develop so slowly that management may become aware of the disinvestment only after it has become rather severe.

**Decline in Economic Values.** A decline in economic values in the economy generally, or a decline in economic values within an industry, or even a decline in economic values in a locality affecting various industries in the locality may produce a noticeable, or even a substantial, decline in the value of the assets of a given enterprise. The decline in value may be rather abrupt, or it may be a relatively slow process requiring several years. Regardless of the degree of abruptness of the change in economic value, at any time when such a decline has occurred and when the extent of the decline is subject to reasonably objective measurement, accounting recognition of the decline may be appropriate.

**Accounting for Decline in Economic Values.** As previously discussed, assets are normally recorded at the cash or cash equivalent value of the asset at the date of its acquisition. Changes in the acquisition value of an asset are not commonly reflected in the accounting records except for those changes which are closely related to the passage of time or to the physical consumption or utilization of the asset. Recognizing that the accountant assumes the enterprise is a going concern, periodic fluctuations in economic values in general are not recorded in the accounting records. This fact alone may contribute to a rather sudden awakening as to the degree of decline in economic values that may have developed over a period of years. Thus, if the economic values of the assets of an enterprise have been declining for a number of years, and if no accounting recognition has been made of this situation, after several years the extent of the decline could be substantial. While adherence to acquisition costs in the accounting records is the traditional valuation policy for service resources, in circumstances indicating a relatively permanent decline in economic values of such resources, revaluation may well be necessary if the accounting data and reports of the company are to be useful and not misleading.

If the decline in economic values has been substantial, if the decline appears to have a relative degree of permanence, and if the decline may be measured quantitatively in some relatively objective manner, recognition of the decline in economic values in the accounting records is advisable. At times the recording of such a decline in values is accomplished as a part of a quasi reorganization of the enterprise. The subject of quasi reorganizations is discussed more fully in the next chapter. In other instances, the decline in economic values may be recorded to put the accounting bases in more realistic terms. In any event, the recording of a decline in economic values gives accounting recognition to a disinvestment process that may have been developing for several years.

Once sufficient evidence as to the nature and extent of the decline in economic values has been accumulated, the actual accounting entries are not very complicated. The various asset accounts which are being carried at excessive values would be credited to reflect their decline in value. The total (or net) effect of the decline would be charged to a loss account, appropriately described, and reported as an extraordinary item in results of operations. Full disclosure would require complete discussion of the action taken in any reports issued for public consumption.

**Decline in Value Due to Obsolescence.** In addition to a general decline in economic values, an enterprise may find that a specific asset has lost its economic usefulness rather abruptly or at least somewhat in advance of previous expectations. Thus a given asset or unit of productive facilities may become obsolete under a variety of circumstances. If an asset becomes obsolete, the enterprise has in reality suffered a disinvestment of assets, and this disinvestment should receive accounting recognition.

The possibility of obsolescence may have some effect upon the depreciation policy which an enterprise adopts in its fixed asset accounting. Thus, an asset with a physical life of 15 years, but which is expected to have a useful life to the enterprise of eight years because of technological progress or other causes of obsolescence, would be depreciated over the eight-year period. At times, however, the economic usefulness of the asset may disappear even more quickly than had originally been anticipated. Or, after usage for a few years it may become evident that the remaining period of useful life will be somewhat less than had been previously expected.

**Accounting for Decline Due to Obsolescence.** Under either of these situations the accounting records should reflect the decline in economic usefulness. If the obsolescence occurs rather suddenly so that the asset is scrapped, sold, or traded in on a newer asset, the entry to be made would be as follows:

| | | |
|---|---|---|
| Cash (or other asset) | $xxxx | |
| Allowance for depreciation of asset | xxxx | |
| Loss on disposal of fixed asset | xxxx | |
| Fixed asset | | $xxxx |

If obsolescence is recognized in advance of its actual final impact, an entry may be prepared at the date of recognition to reflect the reduced economic usefulness of the asset. The loss recognized may be viewed as an adjustment of prior years' depreciation on the reasoning that, had the obsolescence been foreseen at the date of acquisition, the depreciation charges in the past years would have been greater. Thus the entry to recognize the obsolescence might appear as follows:

| | | |
|---|---|---|
| Loss from obsolescence of fixed assets | $xxxx | |
| Allowance for depreciation of fixed assets | | $xxxx |

Each of the entries above produces a decrease in the book value of the assets of the enterprise, and therefore recognizes a disinvestment for the firm. It should be noted at this point that obsolescence of fixed assets does not necessarily produce a disinvestment, because on some occasions the obsolete assets are replaced with more modern equipment. The net result of the change may be an additional investment in assets for the firm. Closely related to the decline in value due to the obsolescence problem is the change in an accounting estimate (see *APB Opinion No. 20*).

## DEBT RETIREMENT

The preceding two sections have dealt briefly with some of the accounting problems arising from contraction of the operations of an enterprise through asset realizations or revaluations. As was noted, realization of assets does not necessarily result in enterprise contraction nor in disinvestment. The realization of operating assets in cash or cash equivalent may be an early phase of an expansion program or change in product mix. On the other hand, the cash received from the realization of assets may be applied to the retirement of various equity interests—claims of short-term creditors, bonds outstanding, partnership contributions, or all or portions of one or more classes of stock outstanding. Use of the proceeds of realization to effect equity retirements normally accomplishes firm contraction or disinvestment.

**Retirement of Short-term Debt.** Debt retirement is commonly a characteristic of disinvestment, and the accounting problems arising from some debt retirements are not too complicated. In particular, the retirement of short-term obligations normally involves an entry similar to the settlement of payables in the normal course of business.

**Early Extinguishment of Long-term Debt.** Long-term debt is often extinguished before its maturity. The early extinguishment can be accomplished (1) by the use of accumulated funds, (2) by the use of funds derived from asset dispositions, (3) by the use of funds derived from the issuance of equity securities, or (4) by the use of funds derived from the issuance of other debt securities. The early extinguishment may be made at a price equal to the par or face value of the debt extinguished, at a price less than par, or at a price greater than par.

The manner in which the early extinguishment of debt is financed is not significant to the accounting for the early extinguishment. The key accounting issue is how to report the differential between the amount paid to effect the extinguishment and the face value (par) or other carrying amount of the debt extinguished. Should this differential be deferred and amortized over some future period, or should the differential be included in the current period's income? If the differential is to be reported in current period income, should the amount be included in operating income or be reported as an extraordinary item?

The principal guidance for the first of these issues is found in *APB Opinion No. 26*. Prior to issuance of that *Opinion* in 1972, various methods of accounting for the differential arising from early extinguishment had been used. In some cases, generally when the early extinguishment arose from the issuance of new debt securities (generally called a refunding), the differential was reported in the balance sheet and amortized either over the remaining life of the old debt issue or over the life of the new debt issue. In other situations, as well as in some refundings, the differential was reported as a gain or loss in the period of the early extinguishment.

*Opinion No. 26* specified that the differential between the amount paid to effect the extinguishment and the carrying amount of the debt extinguished should be reported as a gain or loss in the period of extinguishment. These gains or losses were to be separately reported in the income statement, sometimes as extraordinary items and sometimes as a component of operating income. When *APB Opinion No. 30* was issued in 1973, however, these gains or losses from early extinguishment could rarely qualify as extraordinary items. Finally, in 1975 the FASB issued its *Statement No. 4*, which specified that gains and losses from the early extinguishment of debt be aggregated in a period and, if material, be classified as an extraordinary item in the statement of income. Although *Statement No. 4* does not alter the criteria for the classification of other types of gains or losses as extraordinary items, it defines the gain or loss from early extinguishment of debt as an extraordinary item.

The following terms used in *Opinion No. 26* are essential to a thorough understanding of the accounting treatment for gains or losses on the early extinguishment of debt.

**Net Carrying Amount.** The amount due on the debt at maturity, adjusted for unamortized premium or discount and costs of issuance.

**Reacquisition Price.** The amount paid on early extinguishment, including any call premium and costs of acquisition. When early extinguishment is achieved by a direct exchange of new securities, the reacquisition price is the present value of the new securities.

**Difference.** The excess of the reacquisition price over the net carrying amount, or, the excess of the net carrying amount over the reacquisition price.

The following three examples illustrate various aspects of accounting for the early extinguishment of debt.

**Retirement of Bonds Outstanding—at Par.** Assume the Y Corporation sold $1,000,000 of 8% bonds on January 2, 1970. The bonds were due December 31, 1989, were sold at 97, and the interest on them was payable on January 2 and July 1. The entry to record the sale, under usual accounting practice, would have been:

| | | |
|---|---|---|
| Cash | $970,000 | |
| Unamortized bond discount | 30,000 | |
| Bonds payable | | $1,000,000 |

On April 1, 1979, the Y Corporation completes the sale, for cash, of certain productive facilities and desires to use the proceeds of the sale to retire the bonds outstanding. At this date the Unamortized Bond Discount account contains a balance of $16,125 ($30,000 less 9¼ annual amortization entries of $1,500 each.) The net carrying amount of the bonds is $983,875 ($1,000,000 less $16,125), the reacquisition price is $1,000,000 (exclusive of interest due) and the difference is a loss of $16,125. The entry to record the retirement, assumed in this instance to be accomplished at face value, would be:

| | | |
|---|---|---|
| Bonds payable | $1,000,000 | |
| Interest expense | 20,000 | |
| Loss on retirement of bonds | 16,125 | |
| Unamortized bond discount | | $ 16,125 |
| Cash | | 1,020,000 |

The loss on retirement would be reported in the income statement as an extraordinary item.

**Retirement of Bonds Outstanding—at a Premium.** If the bond indenture provided that the bonds could be retired prior to maturity only by payment of a call premium, the loss on retirement would be increased by the amount of the premium. Thus, if the bonds above were callable in the January 1, 1979, to January 1, 1981, period at 102½, the following entry would reflect the retirement on April 1, 1979:

| | | |
|---|---|---|
| Bonds payable | $1,000,000 | |
| Interest expense | 20,000 | |

| | | |
|---|---|---|
| Loss on retirement of bonds (16,125 + 25,000) | 41,125 | |
| Unamortized bond discount | | $ 16,125 |
| Cash | | 1,045,000 |

In this situation the net carrying amount is also $983,875, but the reacquisition price is $1,025,000. The difference ($41,125) is a loss to be reported as an extraordinary item.

**Refunding of Bonds Outstanding.** In a refunding situation, new bonds are sold to provide the proceeds to retire outstanding bonds. When a refunding occurs prior to the maturity date of the outstanding bonds, the motivation is consciously to reduce the amount of outstanding liability. When interest rates have increased sharply from the time the outstanding bonds were issued, the outstanding bonds are often selling at a deep discount in the market and may, therefore, be acquired from the proceeds of sale of a lesser face amount of new bonds.

Assume that Fledermaus Corporation has outstanding an issue of 6% debentures in the amount of $8,000,000 which mature July 1, 1986. Unamortized debt discount and costs of issuance amount to $300,000 on July 1, 1979. At that date, Fledermaus Corporation effects an exchange of its 10% debentures in the face amount of $6,000,000, due July 1, 1999, for the entire issue of the 6% debentures. Costs incurred to effect this exchange total $320,000.

In this situation, if the 10% interest rate on the new debentures represents the fair market rate of interest for these debentures on July 1, 1979, the reacquisition price is $6,320,000 (present value of new debentures plus the costs of issuance). Since the net carrying amount of the debt extinguished is $7,700,000 ($8,000,000 less $300,000), the early extinguishment results in a difference of $1,380,000, an extraordinary gain. The entry to reflect the early extinguishment would be:

| | | |
|---|---|---|
| Debentures payable (old) | $8,000,000 | |
| Debentures payable | | $6,000,000 |
| Cash (for expenses of issuance) | | 320,000 |
| Unamortized debt discount | | 300,000 |
| Gain on retirement of bonds | | 1,380,000 |

A more thorough treatment of the accounting problems arising from the retirement of long-term indebtedness prior to maturity is found in most intermediate accounting textbooks.

**Alternatives to Debt Retirement.** As with most areas of accounting, accountants may be called upon in the area of disinvestment, and particularly in the debt retirement phase, to provide the bases upon which to make decisions among alternative plans of action. For example, in the first two illustrations above, alternative uses could have been made of the cash realized from the sale of the assets. It is possible that one or more of these alternatives would prove to be more advisable than the retirement of the bonds outstanding.

After completing the asset retrenchment previously decided upon, company officials may be faced with these alternatives, among others: (1) retirement of outstanding indebtedness, as described above; (2) retirement of portions of equity interests or payment of a partial liquidating dividend, as discussed in the following section; (3) acquisition of new assets or the controlling interest in a going concern, as described in Part III of this textbook; (4) acquisition of temporary investments to hold until a more permanent decision is made or until debt retirement conditions become more favorable.

For example, a company may generate funds through the disposition of assets or other operations that are not needed in current operations. If the company has outstanding a debt issue that matures within a short time and that carries a relatively low rate of interest, say, 5½%, the company may elect to invest the funds temporarily if they can obtain a return greater than 5½%. The investment alternative becomes even more advisable when the existence of a call premium is considered. Most bond indentures that contain a call premium provide for a declining premium to maturity. Thus, a call price three years prior to maturity might be 103, with that amount declining to 100 at maturity. When the call premium is considered along with the income that can be realized from temporary investment of the funds available, it is often more economical to acquire temporary investments and delay the retirement of the debt until maturity.

A similar situation may exist if the bonds do not have a callable provision, but may be retired prior to maturity only through acquisitions on the open market. Because of the vagaries of the market situation, company officials may deem it advisable to hold off making open-market acquisitions until market prices for the bonds are more favorable. During the interim, a period of unknown duration, temporary investments of the cash available to retire the bonds may be advisable.

The decision on which of the various alternative uses of the cash is most advisable must be made by the responsible management officials; however, the accounting staff may be expected to provide management with dollar evaluations of the alternatives available.

## RESIDUAL EQUITY RETIREMENTS

As already mentioned, the realization in cash of assets previously committed to operations may result in the retirement of portions of the residual equity interests, among other possibilities. For purposes of this discussion we can divide residual equity retirements into the following areas: (1) retirement or sale of partnership interest; (2) payment of corporate liquidating dividends; (3) acquisition by the corporation of its own shares; and (4) acquisition and elimination of one or more classes of outstanding stock.

**Retirement or Sale of Partnership Interest.** In Chapter Two the accounting for the purchase of an interest and for the purchase of an investment in a partnership was discussed. At that point the most important problem raised concerned the proper valuation of the assets of the partnership at the date of admission of a new partner. Since the admission of a new partner creates a new partnership, adjustments of existing asset values to correspond to their value to the new entity are generally advisable. In the sale of a partnership interest the same problem arises, since the sale is merely the other side of the purchase transaction.

It has been also noted previously that the true profit or loss of an enterprise can be known only at the time that enterprise is liquidated or dissolved. When a partner sells his interest or when a partner retires, in reality a dissolution of an enterprise has occurred, and it would seem desirable to determine as accurately as possible the final profit of that enterprise. This is particularly true when a partner retires, since there may not be an objective bargaining basis upon which to base the retirement settlement. When a partner sells his interest, on the other hand, a buyer exists, and the worth of the interest being transferred is at least indicated by the exchange price.

Since the sale of a partnership interest has been discussed previously, and since the sale does not generally result in a contraction of the firm's operations or in a disinvestment situation, only the problems of accounting for a retirement of a partner will be considered here.

**Basis of Settlement with Retiring Partner.** The basic problem when a partner retires lies in the determination of the proper settlement to him. While it might appear simple enough to settle with a partner on the basis of the equity represented by his capital, drawing, and loan accounts, various reasons could exist to cause the fair value of this equity to be different from the value as reflected in these accounts. For example, the existing market values of the assets in use may be somewhat different from the acquisition costs or amortized-acquisition costs (book value) of those assets. Likewise, either excessively conservative or excessively liberal accounting policies in areas involving estimates may, at the date of retirement, result in the statement of financial position providing an improper basis for determining the value of the retiring partner's equity. Unrecorded assets may exist, the most commonly noted of which is goodwill. Any of these conditions may require that the statement values of the partnership be modified in order to achieve an equitable settlement with a retiring partner.

When a partner retires it would seem that the settlement with him by the partnership should be based upon the value of the partnership at the date of retirement. Although the theory of using this value as a settlement basis is usually acceptable, its application may be accomplished only by solving some of the problems in valuing assets that were discussed in Chapter Two. If at the date of retirement inventories, fixed assets, or other properties of the partnership have current values different from their book values, some adjustment of the book values may be necessary to achieve an equitable settlement with the retiring partner. Even if the partners who continue in the partnership are agreeable to a settlement with the retiring partner based on current values of the assets, the recognition of these values in the accounting records of the partnership may still pose some problems.

***Illustration.*** To illustrate the accounting treatment of some of the problems that may arise from partner retirement, assume the following partnership situation:

ABC Partnership
Financial Position
December 31, 1979

| | | | |
|---|---:|---|---:|
| Cash | $110,000 | Payables | $ 30,000 |
| Receivables | 40,000 | A, Capital | 90,000 |
| Inventory (Fair value, $68,000) | 60,000 | B, Capital | 90,000 |
| Fixed assets (Fair value, $109,000) | 90,000 | C, Capital | 90,000 |
| | $300,000 | | $300,000 |

Partner A desires to withdraw from the partnership for personal reasons, and in anticipation of this withdrawal, the partnership has conserved its working capital so that it is now in a position to effect the retirement. At the date of retirement, December 31, 1979, the fair market value of the inventory is $8,000 in excess of the cost, and the fair market value of the fixed assets is $19,000 in excess of amortized cost. The partners agree that settlement with A should be based upon the current values. The partners share profits and losses equally, so that one-third of the increase in the market value of $27,000 is allocable to A. Therefore, A will be paid $99,000—$90,000 for his book equity plus $9,000 for his share of the increase in market value of the assets.

***Adherence to Cost Principle.*** The accounting treatment of the $9,000 excess over book equity paid to A and of the market value increases in general is open to some differences of opinion. On one hand, there is support for the following entry when settlement is effected with A:

| | | |
|---|---:|---:|
| A, Capital | $90,000 | |
| Inventory | 2,667 | |
| Fixed assets | 6,333 | |
|     Cash | | $99,000 |

This entry would find support from those who place considerable emphasis on the cost principle. Since a going business will remain in operation, the cost of the inventory and fixed assets to B and C has increased by a total of $9,000 because of the retirement settlement with A. Recognition of the additional increase in market values of $18,000 would introduce unrealized profit into the accounts and result in the statement of assets at amounts in excess of their cost.

***Revaluation of Assets.*** On the other hand, some accountants would argue that the following entry is proper to record the retirement of A:

| | | |
|---|---:|---:|
| A, Capital | $90,000 | |
| Inventory | 8,000 | |

| | | |
|---|---|---|
| Fixed assets | 19,000 | |
| Cash | | $99,000 |
| B, Capital | | 9,000 |
| C, Capital | | 9,000 |

This entry would find support from those who would view the new partnership involving B and C as a new enterprise. In accordance with the principles of valuation of assets for a new enterprise, as previously discussed, each partner is entitled to receive credit for his share of the proper value of the assets contributed. Here recognition of the entire increase in market value is necessary to value properly the assets of the new business and to credit the new partners for the fair value of the assets contributed at the date of organization of the enterprise. Modification of the cost principle is justified on the basis that a new enterprise is established and the going-concern assumption that existed previously is now inapplicable as far as these assets are concerned.

It appears that the latter reasoning is preferable, providing the fair market values determined for the assets are subject to reasonably objective verification. If the remaining partners must pay the retiring partner an amount in excess of his book equity because of increases in market values of assets of the enterprise, it appears that the remaining partners are entitled to capital credits in the new enterprise based upon the values of the assets agreed upon in the settlement with the retiring partner.

**Recognition of Goodwill.** A problem similar to that discussed above arises if the partners agree that goodwill, previously unrecognized, exists at the time a partner retires. Thus, if in the illustration above the current values for the various assets were unknown, or if the current values were essentially the same as the book values, the partners might agree to recognize the existence of goodwill in effecting the settlement with A. Assume that the goodwill is valued at $27,000. Since the general rule is that goodwill should be divided among the partners in their profit and loss sharing ratio, each partner would be entitled to $9,000 of the goodwill. Two alternatives exist as to the recognition of the goodwill.

| | | |
|---|---|---|
| Goodwill | $9,000 | |
| A, Capital | | $9,000 |

This entry records on the books A's portion of the goodwill since this is the only portion that the enterprise is paying for at this time.

| | | |
|---|---|---|
| Goodwill | $27,000 | |
| A, Capital | | $9,000 |
| B, Capital | | 9,000 |
| C, Capital | | 9,000 |

This entry records on the books the goodwill agreed on and credits the partners for their appropriate portions of the goodwill.

The determination of which of these two entries is the more acceptable rests very largely upon the degree of objectivity with which the goodwill value has been determined. In the two preceding sections it was assumed that the fair values determined for the inventory and fixed assets were subject to reasonably objective verification. The determination, objectively, of a fair value for goodwill is frequently a more difficult problem than is such a determination for tangible assets. The second entry above would be preferable if the goodwill value were subject to objective verification. The first entry would likely be preferred by most accountants, however, because of the subjective nature of the valuation of goodwill in most instances. Thus, the choice between the alternatives appears to rest upon the degree of objectivity with which the goodwill value has been determined.

**Bonus to Retiring Partner.** Another alternative is available to A, B, and C at the date that A retires. The partners may agree that A is to receive $99,000 for his equity in the partnership, but they may agree that no increases in asset values are appropriate and that no goodwill exists, or if it exists, it is to remain unrecognized. In this alternative B and C are in reality paying a $9,000 bonus to A, and the entry to effect A's retirement would be:

| | | |
|---|---|---|
| A, Capital | $90,000 | |
| B, Capital | 4,500 | |
| C, Capital | 4,500 | |
| Cash | | $99,000 |

So long as B and C continue to share profits in the same relationship after the retirement of A as they did prior to his retirement, neither will be affected by the decision to use the bonus treatment rather than goodwill, or vice versa. After recording the bonus in the entry above, each partner has a balance of $85,500 in his capital account. If the goodwill recorded in either of the entries above subsequently proves to be nonexistent and is written off, B and C will each have a capital balance of $85,500. If the goodwill is recorded and if B and C change their profit and loss relationship prior to the date that the goodwill is written off, the end result will be different from that produced by the use of the bonus treatment, as noted in Chapter Two.

**Deferred Settlement on Retirement.** In the illustrations above it has been assumed that the partnership had sufficient assets to effect the settlement with retiring partner A. The settlement, of course, reduces the properties and the equities of the enterprise, and thus results in a disinvestment by the firm. On some occasions a partner may decide to retire, but the partnership may not have sufficient assets to pay the retiring partner in full for his agreed settlement price. In some instances the settlement may be deferred until the value of certain assets can be determined with finality through their actual realization. In either instance, when the agreed settlement is deferred, it would seem preferable to eliminate the retiring partner's capital account and to transfer the amount due him in settlement to a payable account, clearly described.

## Payment of Corporate Liquidating Dividend

In a corporate disinvestment situation the contraction of the assets of an enterprise may proceed in various ways, one of which involves a distribution to the stockholders of a portion of their capital contributions. Such a distribution is commonly referred to as a liquidating dividend.

While the term "liquidating dividend" might seem to imply that this type of distribution would be made only during the actual liquidation phase of the enterprise, the term might also be used properly to describe a distribution of assets arising from asset realizations in a disinvestment phase of the life of the enterprise. Since a liquidating dividend is paid from capital contribution rather than from earnings, certain legal requirements must be satisfied prior to the payment of the dividend. The legal requirements vary from state to state, but they generally provide for action by the board of directors, ratification by the various classes of stockholders, and full disclosure to all dividend recipients that they were receiving a return of their invested capital and not a distribution from earnings of the corporation.

**Accounting for a Liquidating Dividend.** When a liquidating dividend is paid, it would appear to be preferable to record the distribution as a charge to a special account rather than as a charge against the existing capital accounts. The dividend does not redeem any shares of stock, but merely involves a pro rata return to the stockholders of a portion of the contributed capital. Thus, if a corporation declares a $90,000 dividend and notifies the stockholders that $30,000 of the dividend comes from earnings of the business and $60,000 involves a return of contributed capital no longer needed in the operations of the enterprise, the following entry could be made:

| | | |
|---|---|---|
| Retained earnings | $30,000 | |
| Capital distribution to stockholders | 60,000 | |
| Dividends payable (Cash) | | $90,000 |

The special account charged for the $60,000 return of contributed capital could be reported in the stockholders' equity section of the statement of financial position as a deduction from the contributed capital items.

In making a liquidating dividend distribution, a corporation should notify the stockholders as to the nature of the dividend they are receiving. Dividends received from earnings of the corporation are income to the stockholders, whereas dividends received from capital contributions are reductions in the basis of the investment carried by the stockholder.

It should also be noted that corporate officials must be conversant with the appropriate income tax regulations in a decision to declare a liquidating dividend. Certain provisions of the tax law stipulate the requirements that must be met for a distribution to be considered a liquidating dividend from an income tax point of view. These requirements should be considered in arriving at a decision as to the form of the distribution.

A liquidating dividend may effect a disinvestment by an enterprise, since assets realized in cash are returned to the investors through the medium of the dividend. The distribution may be made in contemplation of eventual liquidation or it may be made at a time when the corporate officials intend to continue operations of the enterprise.

### Reacquisition of Corporation's Own Stock

The various reasons why a corporation might reacquire its own shares and the possible accounting treatments for the reacquired shares are discussed rather thoroughly in most intermediate accounting textbooks. At this point the discussion will be limited to the reacquisition of a corporation's own stock in order to effect a disinvestment.

As an alternative to the payment of a liquidating dividend, the board of directors of a corporation that has excess cash assets available may decide to acquire on the open market, or directly from some of the existing stockholders, a portion of the stock outstanding. The stock so acquired, generally referred to as treasury stock, might be retired in a legal sense, although legal retirement of the shares would not be necessary.

**Reporting of Stock Reacquired.** While there may be some justification under certain circumstances for reporting treasury stock as an asset, such reporting would not be proper for treasury stock acquired in order to effect a disinvestment for the enterprise. If the intention of the board of directors is to acquire the shares in order to retire them, either legally or effectively, proper reporting of the reacquired shares would be as a deduction in the stockholders' equity section of the statement of financial position. Likewise, any legal restriction on dividend distributions resulting from the acquisition of the treasury shares should be reported.

Although remaining stockholders may have a gain or loss when stock is reacquired above or below *book value,* for recording purposes accountants are concerned primarily with a comparison of the reacquisition price with the *issue price.*

To illustrate, assume that the Bow Corporation has the following stockholders' equity section on May 31, 1979:

| | |
|---|---:|
| Stockholders' equity: | |
| Common stock, 300,000 shares, $100 par | $30,000,000 |
| Excess of issue price over par value | 6,000,000 |
| Total contributed capital | 36,000,000 |
| Retained earnings | 14,000,000 |
| Total stockholders' equity | $50,000,000 |

The board of directors of the Bow Corporation decides to acquire 50,000 shares of its own stock in order to effect a disinvestment and to strengthen the market position of the shares that will remain outstanding. In acquiring these shares, the Bow Corporation may:

1. Acquire 50,000 shares for exactly $6,000,000, the pro-rata portion of the contributed capital applicable to the 50,000 shares.
2. Acquire 50,000 shares for less than $6,000,000, for example, $5,000,000.
3. Acquire 50,000 shares for more than $6,000,000, for example, $8,000,000.

**Stock Reacquired at Issue Price.** In the first possibility above, the cost of the treasury shares, $6,000,000, should be deducted from the total of the contributed capital on the statement of financial position. The resulting balance of $30,000,000 might be labeled "contributed capital of outstanding shares." If the effective disinvestment is completed from a legal point of view by retiring the shares, the Common Stock account would be reduced by $5,000,000 and the "Excess" account would be reduced by $1,000,000.

**Stock Reacquired at Less than Issue Price.** In the second possibility above, many accountants maintain that the $5,000,000 cost of the treasury shares should be deducted from the total of the contributed capital, leaving $31,000,000 contributed capital applicable to the outstanding shares. The excess of the contributed capital applicable to the shares reacquired over the acquisition cost of those shares should still be properly labeled contributed capital. A problem arises, however, if these shares are retired. Should the $1,000,000 excess of contributed capital over the cost of the shares retired remain in the "Excess" account, or should this amount be removed from the "Excess" account and be credited to Retained Earnings? Some accountants would argue that the $1,000,000 is contributed capital and the fact that the shares to which it applies have been retired does not change this fact. Following this reasoning the $1,000,000 should remain as a part of the contributed capital. Other accountants would argue that, upon retirement of stock that cost less to reacquire than the initial contribution, the difference becomes an addition to retained earnings. The sale and acquisition of the stock were accomplished at a profit to the corporation, and are as much a profit as income from operations. Hence, following this line of reasoning, the $1,000,000 should be transferred out of contributed capital into retained earnings. The weight of authority, however, at present supports the reporting of the $1,000,000 as a part of contributed capital. Accountants generally do not approve inclusion of "profit" on treasury stock transactions in the income statement, and likewise are hesitant to treat such "profits" as a part of retained earnings.

**Stock Reacquired at More Than Issue Price.** When treasury stock is acquired for more than the portion of contributed capital attributable to such stock, as in the third possibility above, the reporting of the cost of the treasury stock is not so clear as in the situations above. Some accountants would argue that the total cost, $8,000,000 in the illustration, should be deducted from contributed capital, leaving $28,000,000 as contributed capital. Other accountants would limit the amount of the deduction from contributed capital to the pro rata portion of the contributed capital applicable to the shares reacquired. Any excess would be charged against retained earnings and be considered as a partial distribution of such retained earnings. In the example above, this treatment would result in reporting $30,000,000 contributed capital and $12,000,000 retained earnings.

The deduction of the total price paid to reacquire the share from the contributed capital is consistent with the discussion above regarding the excess of contributed capital over the cost of reacquired shares. The resulting balance of contributed capital would then represent the original contributions, less amounts paid to reacquire a portion of the shares sold. The amount would not indicate the contributed capital attributable to the shares remaining outstanding. Accountants who support this procedure would argue that if profits from reacquiring (and retiring) a corporation's own shares are not included in retained earnings, it would hardly appear to be logical to charge "losses" from such acquisitions to the retained earnings account.

However, most authorities support the charge to retained earnings of any excess paid to reacquire the shares.[1] Presumably, the action by the board of directors to reacquire the shares was in the best interests of the remaining stockholders, and if the price paid to effect the retirement was greater than the amount previously paid in for those shares, the difference may be looked upon as a distribution of retained earnings for the benefit of the remaining stockholders. The authors support this alternative as being the preferable treatment when shares have been reacquired at a cost in excess of the capital contributed applicable to the shares.

In the third possibility discussed above, a reporting problem arises at the time the shares are reacquired, whether or not they are retired. At the date of retirement the problem must be resolved in the accounting records as well as in the reports. It appears preferable to charge the excess discussed above to the Retained Earnings account at the date of retirement.

In each of the three possibilities discussed the accountant must be cognizant of applicable state incorporation laws. If the state law so provides, either a parenthetical notation, a footnote, or a segregation of retained earnings must be made to indicate the extent to which the retained earnings is restricted as to dividends because of the treasury stock acquisitions.

## Retirement of One or More Classes of Stock

Another method of effecting a disinvestment of a corporation is the retirement or elimination of one or more of the classes of stock outstanding. This method is related to the acquisition of treasury shares discussed above, but differs in that *all* of the shares of a class are retired, not just a portion of the class.

If the corporation has liquid assets that will not be required for operating purposes in the foreseeable future, such assets may be applied to the retirement of

---

[1] *Accounting and Reporting Standards for Corporate Financial Statements and Preceding Statements and Supplements,* American Accounting Association, 1957 Revision, p. 7: "Preferably, the outlay by a corporation for its own shares is reflected as a reduction of the aggregate of contributed capital, and any excess of outlay over the pro-rata portion of contributed capital as a distribution of retained earnings."

one class of stock for various reasons. A given class of stock may have certain objectionable features, such as a fixed dividend rate, a high dividend rate, or possibly an unfavorable conversion feature which may become operative in the near future. Retirement of a class of stock may be desired to simplify the corporate capital structure. At times the retirement might eliminate from "nuisance control" those individuals holding the shares of the class to be retired. Thus retirement of a class of stock may be desirable even though disinvestment is not particularly desirable. The coexistence of excess liquid assets and the desire to eliminate a given class of stock may result in both disinvestment and elimination of the objectionable capital element.

**Exercise of Call Option.** The retirement of a class of stock may arise under two conditions. The covenants of the stock issue may provide that the stock be callable at a certain price or prices at various dates in the future. If such a covenant exists, and if the board of directors calls the stock for redemption, the stock issue will be retired with a minimum of inconvenience. Thus, if the Arrow Corporation has outstanding 1,000 shares of Class A Stock, par value $100, and if the stock is presently callable at 103, the following entry could be made at retirement:

| | | |
|---|---|---|
| Class A stock | $100,000 | |
| Stock retirement expense (Retained earnings) | 3,000 | |
| Cash | | $103,000 |

The $3,000 excess of redemption price over par (assuming here par was also the amount paid in upon the original sale) may be charged to income or to retained earnings, depending upon the materiality of the item. If the stock had been sold at more or less than par originally, any paid-in surplus account should be removed in the entry to record the redemption.

**Use of an Agent to Effect Retirement.** At times a corporation may avail itself of an agent to handle the details of the retirement. If the Class A Stock above were retired through an agent, and if the agent's fee for handling such retirement were set at $2,500, the following entry would record the deposit with the agent:

| | | |
|---|---|---|
| Stock retirement fund deposit | $105,500 | |
| Cash | | $105,500 |

As the canceled stock certificates are turned over to the company, or as the disposal certificates are received, the following entry would be made:

| | | |
|---|---|---|
| Class A stock | $xxxx | |
| Stock retirement expense | xxxx | |
| Stock retirement fund deposit | | $xxxx |

After a reasonable period of time any cash deposited for shares not redeemed should be returned to the corporation.

**Retirement without a Call Option.** A given class of stock may also be retired even though the covenants of the stock do not provide for calling the stock for redemption immediately. For example, the board of directors may vote to retire the Class A stock, and if the various classes of stockholders approve (depending on the law of the various states), the retirement could proceed although complete retirement could take some time. A general announcement would be made of the retirement plans and of the price set for redemption. In addition, specific notices would normally be sent to the stockholders involved. Each would be urged to submit his shares for redemption immediately. However, for various reasons some of the stockholders may refuse to send in their stock for redemption. Thus, although a large percentage of the shares may be redeemed in a short period of time, total retirement could take several years.

Retirement of a class of stock might also proceed on a piecemeal basis over a period of years through the purchase by the corporation of shares of the given class of stock on the open market. In some instances these shares might be carried as treasury shares until a substantial amount is accumulated, particularly if the corporation officials did not want to disclose their intentions to retire the class of stock.

Regardless of the accounting and reporting procedures followed for treasury stock during the period prior to retirement of the shares, it would appear proper to account for the retirement of the shares in the manner discussed above. That is, any excess of the retirement outlay over the original capital contribution attributable to the class of stock involved should be charged against retained earnings upon retirement of the shares. Logically, it would appear proper to credit retained earnings for any excess of the original capital contribution over the cost of acquiring the shares at retirement. However, the hesitancy of the accounting profession to recognize an increase in retained earnings, whether through the income statement or not, from dealings in the enterprise's own stock is likely to persist for some time.

**SUMMARY**

Disinvestment by an enterprise normally involves the realization in cash of some of the existing operating assets. The cash so realized is then used to eliminate or reduce a portion of the equities of the enterprise, either creditorship or ownership. To the extent that any equity interests are retired above or below book value, the disinvestment also involves a redistribution of the remaining equity. That is, the remaining equity interests are decreased or increased from their former interests by the disinvestment. On completion of the realization-equity retirement cycle, the enterprise may well be in a strong financial and operating condition. On the other hand, a given disinvestment situation may be merely one in a chain of events leading to reorganization or liquidation. In the following chapters, some of the problems of reorganization and liquidation will be considered.

## PROBLEMS

### Problem 20-1

The Barclay Corporation has the following balance sheet as of June 30, 1979, at which date the books have been closed:

THE BARCLAY CORPORATION
BALANCE SHEET, JUNE 30, 1979

| | | | |
|---|---|---|---|
| Cash | $ 400,000 | Payables | $ 2,200,000 |
| Receivables | 600,000 | Current accruals | 250,000 |
| Finished goods | 1,200,000 | 5% First-mortgage bonds | |
| Work in process | 500,000 | due June 30, 1988 | 1,750,000 |
| Raw materials | 800,000 | Preferred stock | 2,500,000 |
| Buildings (net) | 3,540,000 | Common stock, 50,000 shares | |
| Machinery (net) | 4,500,000 | auth., 38,000 outstanding | 3,800,000 |
| Unamortized bond discount | 60,000 | Retained income | 1,100,000 |
| | $11,600,000 | | $11,600,000 |

Profits in recent years have been declining, and the management is now planning more aggressively for the future. Certain unprofitable operations are to be sold or otherwise disposed of, the capital structure is to be modified, and possible new acquisitions are to be studied, although none is under consideration at present.

The glass-making facilities at Portsmouth have been a particularly heavy loser, and the sale of these facilities has been decided upon. The facilities to be sold include:

| | | |
|---|---|---|
| Buildings, at cost | $1,700,000 | |
| Less allowance | 800,000 | $ 900,000 |
| Machinery, at cost | 2,000,000 | |
| Less allowance | 800,000 | 1,200,000 |
| Finished goods, at cost | | 400,000 |
| Raw materials, at cost | | 300,000 |
| Book value of facilities to be sold | | $2,800,000 |

None of the glass-making facilities is subject to the mortgage.

The Acme Glass Co. has evidenced an interest in acquiring these facilities and has presented four optional plans for the acquisition:

1. Cash of $2,500,000.
2. Acme Glass Co. common stock, 100,000 shares of $20 par, market value currently ranging from 25½ to 27. Acme is largely controlled by one family, and this block of stock would represent about 5% of the total outstanding stock and about 12% of the stock generally considered available for trading on the market.

3. A serial note issue, face value $3,600,000, with interest included in the face, the notes maturing $300,000 per year beginning June 30, 1983.
4. Convertible bonds, face value $2,800,000, interest at 4%, due on June 30, 1994, and convertible into Acme Co. Common stock at prices ranging from 38 to 50, beginning January 1, 1983. During the five years prior to June 30, 1979, Acme Common traded in a range of $12 to $36 per share.

The Barclay management is undecided as to which option to accept. Part of the indecision arises from a lack of agreement on the use of any proceeds from the sale. The "Payables" balance contains $750,000 of 6% bank notes, which have been outstanding for 18 months. The notes have a six-month maturity, but they have been renewed each six months, on January 1 and July 1, for the past two years. The First Mortgage bonds are callable at 103 until January 1, 1981, and at declining call premiums thereafter until maturity. The Preferred stock pays dividends of $5 per year on a cumulative basis, has no arrearage, and is redeemable at 105 until January 1, 1984, and at declining call premiums thereafter.

*Required:*

The management of the Barclay Corporation would like an evaluation of the options presented by the Acme Glass Co., assuming that they decide (1) to make no equity adjustments at present, but to invest any cash received at an expected market rate of interest of 5%; (2) to eliminate the bank notes and bonds from the balance sheet; or (3) to redeem the preferred stock. They would also like a recommendation on the total course of action to follow.

## Problem 20-2

The William Saw Co. has accepted an offer from the Morten Tool Co. for the sale of its plant and facilities at Menasha. The William Saw Co. will receive 25,000 shares of Morten Tool $100 par value common stock in exchange for the facilities. The assets sold are carried on the William Saw Co. books at the date of sale as follows:

| | | |
|---|---:|---:|
| Building | $2,500,000 | |
| Less accrued depreciation | 1,600,000 | $ 900,000 |
| Machinery and equipment | 3,750,000 | |
| Less accrued depreciation | 2,250,000 | 1,500,000 |
| Inventories | | 600,000 |
| | | $3,000,000 |

Operations at the Menasha plant had not been profitable to the William Saw Co. and it was felt that the sale of these facilities would remove a drain on profits. Review of the asset values shortly before the date of the sale indicated the following appraised values for the Menasha facilities:

| | |
|---|---:|
| Building (net) | $1,000,000 |
| Machinery and equipment (net) | 1,200,000 |
| Inventories | 450,000 |

20 / *Disinvestment*

The Morten Tool Co. common stock trades in a rather narrow market, with a price range during the two years preceding the sale of $90 to $135 per share. Just prior to announcement of the acquisition of the Menasha facilities, the stock was quoted at $112. On the sale date the stock had fallen back to $105 per share.

*Required:*
Consider the several possible bases for recording the receipt of the Morten Tool Co. stock and prepare a journal entry to record the sale of assets in exchange for the stock. Justify your entry as best reflecting the valuation of the stock received.

## Problem 20-3

The Niblick Corporation has been carrying on negotiations for the sale of one of its operating divisions at Greenbriar. The negotiations have reached a point where the Niblick management must decide which of several alternative offers to accept. The basic decision to sell has already been reached. The offers available and under consideration are:

1. Cash of $1,500,000, payable one-third at date of sale and the balance in quarterly installments, the first due three months after date of sale.
2. Cash of $300,000 and $1,250,000 in 8-year 4% notes, the notes due in full eight years from the date of sale.
3. Cash of $500,000 and $1,200,000 in 8-year noninterest-bearing serial notes, the first series payable one year from the date of sale.

The assets involved in the sale negotiations have a book value of $1,350,000.

The management has no specific plans in mind for employment of cash derived from the sale, but investment of such cash to earn 6% is considered the most likely usage. You agree that 6% appears to be a reasonable market rate of interest.

*Required:*
Determine which of the three options is most advisable from the viewpoint of the Niblick Co., disregarding all considerations other than the sale price.

## Problem 20-4

During the last months of 1979 the Sawbill Co. reviewed carefully its various asset values and determined that of total assets of $1,000,000 the inventories were overvalued $80,000 on a lower of cost or market basis, and the fixed properties were overvalued $140,000 on a depreciated cost basis. The Company had capital stock outstanding of $400,000 stated value and retained income of $160,000. Fixed assets totaled $620,000 at cost on which depreciation of $200,000 had been recorded by the end of 1979. These assets had an average estimated life of 10 years.

Company officials cannot agree on the action to take with regard to the overvalued assets. Profits for the past three years have averaged $20,000 on sales averaging $1,000,000.

You have been asked by the Sawbill management to discuss with them some of the implications of their overvalued asset condition, including consideration of recording the write-downs indicated, effects on retained income and dividend possibilities, and effects on future earnings.

## Problem 20-5

The Waldie Corporation recently completed the sale of a plant site and various assets for cash. The balance sheet at December 31, 1979, appears below:

THE WALDIE CORPORATION

BALANCE SHEET, DECEMBER 31, 1979

| | | | |
|---|---|---|---|
| Cash | $2,500,000 | Accounts payable | $ 400,000 |
| Receivables | 500,000 | 20-year, 6% Notes Payable, | |
| Inventories | 1,300,000 | due 12/31/1984 | 2,000,000 |
| Plant and machinery (net) | 4,000,000 | $5.50 Preferred stock, | |
| Other assets | 200,000 | $100 par | 2,000,000 |
| | | Common stock | 2,500,000 |
| | | Retained income | 1,600,000 |
| | $8,500,000 | | $8,500,000 |

Several alternative uses are available for the cash on hand. The management feels that approximately $2,000,000 in cash is not required for business purposes at the existing level of operations. No immediate acquisitions or expansion plans are contemplated, although the management is not opposed to considering such plans as they might develop.

The present rate of interest for short-term investments is approximately 5%. The notes payable are redeemable at 103 prior to December 31, 1982, at 101.5 prior to December 31, 1985, and at par thereafter. The preferred stock is callable at par.

*Required:*

Prepare a summary for management evaluating several possible uses of the excess cash available, placing primary emphasis on cost savings.

## Problem 20-6

The partnership of Bolstad, Kepler, and Fitch has the following balance sheet at December 31, 1980:

BOLSTAD, KEPLER, & FITCH

BALANCE SHEET, DECEMBER 31, 1980

| | | | |
|---|---|---|---|
| Cash | $120,000 | Payables | $ 50,000 |
| Receivables | 40,000 | Bolstad Capital (50%) | 120,000 |
| Inventories | 60,000 | Kepler, Capital (30%) | 70,000 |

| Fixed assets (net) | 80,000 | Kepler, Drawing | (10,000) |
|---|---|---|---|
|  |  | Fitch, Capital (20%) | 65,000 |
|  |  | Fitch, Drawing | 5,000 |
|  | $300,000 |  | $300,000 |

The partners share profits in the ratios indicated above. Fitch desires to withdraw from the partnership, and the partners agree to settle with him in cash for his equity. Prior to the settlement, the following facts are determined as of December 31, 1980:

1. Purchases in transit and unrecorded, 12/31/80       $6,000
2. Inventory pricing errors, understatement, net       5,000
3. Miscellaneous accrued expenses unrecorded          3,000
4. Salary unrecorded for Fitch, an expense of the partnership    2,000

Settlement with Fitch is to be based on his equity, after considering any adjustments in the figures above, at 12/31/1980.

*Required:*

Prepare a schedule to determine the amount of the settlement with Fitch. If Fitch were paid $74,000, how much "Goodwill" might be recorded? How much bonus would be involved in a settlement of $74,000, assuming that no goodwill is to be recorded?

## Problem 20-7

Black, Boots, and Drake have been operating a partnership in which profits and losses have been shared equally. On October 31, 1980, the balances in their capital accounts appeared as follows:

| Black, Capital | $30,000 |
|---|---|
| Boots, Capital | 36,000 |
| Drake, Capital | 38,000 |

In addition, during 1980, Black and Boots had each drawn $6,000 from the business, while Drake had withdrawn $2,000. Drake's salary for September and October, which is normally recorded as an expense of the partnership and an adjustment of his drawing account, had not been recorded. His salary is $1,000 per month.

On October 31, Black desires to withdraw from the partnership. If the partners agree to pay him on the basis of his equity as of October 31, and if he is paid $29,000, how much profit had the partnership earned in the first 10 months of 1980?

If the partners agree to pay Black $32,000, and if the profits per the books as of closing on October 31, 1980, were $20,000, prepare journal entries to record Black's retirement, assuming:

1. That inventories have been improperly valued to the extent reflected in the settlement price with Black.
2. That goodwill is to be recorded for Black only.
3. That goodwill is to be recorded on the basis of the amount indicated by the settlement with Black.
4. That a "bonus" entry is to be made.

## Problem 20-8

Roddy, Rees, and Rowe have been in partnership for several years, sharing profits in the ratio of 2:4:4. Rowe, the senior partner and founder of the firm, is to retire as of December 31, 1980. On this date the following balance sheet is prepared:

RODDY, REES, & ROWE

BALANCE SHEET, DECEMBER 31, 1980

| | | | |
|---|---|---|---|
| Cash | $ 80,000 | Accounts payable | $ 20,000 |
| Receivables | 30,000 | Due to Rowe | 20,000 |
| Inventory | 60,000 | Roddy, Capital | 40,000 |
| Fixed assets (net) | 75,000 | Rees, Capital | 80,000 |
| Goodwill | 5,000 | Rowe, Capital | 90,000 |
| | $250,000 | | $250,000 |

The partners agree that no specific asset values require modification. They also agree that Rowe is to receive $120,000 in full settlement of his partnership claims, one-half of which is payable in cash and one-half in notes payable in five equal annual installments, beginning January 1, 1982, with interest at 5% on the unpaid balance.

*Required:*

Prepare three alternative entries possible to record the retirement of Rowe. Evaluate the propriety of each solution.

## Problem 20-9

Brewer, Swain, and Brown had been operating as a partnership for several years, and at December 31, 1979, the partners agreed that Brown would retire from active interest in the partnership. Profits and losses had been shared equally. The following balance sheet was prepared at December 31, 1979:

BREWER, SWAIN, & BROWN

BALANCE SHEET, DECEMBER 31, 1979

| | | | |
|---|---|---|---|
| Cash | $ 58,000 | Payables | $ 40,000 |
| Receivables | 20,000 | Brewer, Capital | 148,000 |
| Inventories | 60,000 | Swain, Capital | 130,000 |
| Buildings (net) | 180,000 | Swain, Drawing | 25,000 |

| Equipment (net)        | 120,000   | Brown, Capital  | 125,000   |
| Autos and trucks (net) | 30,000    | Brown, Drawing  | 10,000    |
| Other assets           | 10,000    |                 |           |
|                        | $478,000  |                 | $478,000  |

The terms of settlement with Brown are as follows: Inventories, at lower of cost or market, are valued at $50,000; the Buildings account, which relates to two buildings, should contain a net value of $95,000 for Building A and $100,000 for Building B; Equipment has an appraisal value of $107,000; Autos and trucks contains 5 trucks, each with a net value of $4,200; and 3 autos, each with a value of $2,400; Other assets are worthless. Brown is to receive one auto, Building A (which he had owned prior to formation of the partnership), and cash of $35,000. The partners agree that the settlement with Brown involves a goodwill element and desire to recognize on their books the total goodwill implied in the settlement with Brown.

*Required:*
Prepare journal entries to reflect the facts above. Prepare a balance sheet giving effect to your entries.

## Problem 20-10

The Bradford Corporation had the following stockholder equities at December 31, 1979:

| | | |
|---|---|---|
| Class A Common, 10,000 shares, par value $100 | | $1,000,000 |
| Excess of issue price over par of Class A Common | | 600,000 |
| | | 1,600,000 |
| Class B Common, 150,000 shares, $10 stated value | $1,500,000 | |
| Excess of issue price over stated value | 400,000 | 1,900,000 |
| Retained income | | 1,000,000 |
| Total | | $4,500,000 |

The Class A Common is nonvoting, and management's desire is to retire this class of stock gradually. On January 3, 1980, the management acquired on the open market 2,000 shares of the Class A Common at $125 per share. The shares were not immediately retired. The state of incorporation limits dividend payments if treasury stock is held.

*Required:*
(1) Prepare a journal entry to record the acquisition of the treasury shares. Prepare an equity section of the Bradford Corporation balance sheet subsequent to the acquisition of the treasury shares. Support your treatment.
(2) Prepare a journal entry to record the acquisition of the Class A Common shares assuming that they are immediately retired. Prepare an equity section of the Bradford Corporation balance sheet subsequent to the retirement of the shares. Support your treatment.

## Problem 20-11

The capital and surplus section of the Jones Company's balance sheet at December 31, 1979, was as follows:

| | |
|---|---:|
| Common Stock—$100 par (Authorized 50,000 shares, issued and outstanding 10,000 shares) | $1,000,000 |
| Capital in excess of par | 200,000 |
| Retained earnings | 100,000 |
| | $1,300,000 |

On January 2, 1980, having idle cash, the Company repurchased 400 shares of its stock for $50,000. During the year it sold 100 of the reacquired shares at $135 per share, sold 100 shares at $122.50 per share, and legally retired the remaining 200 shares.

*Required:*
(1) Discuss the accounting principles involved in handling these transactions, including consideration of possible alternatives.
(2) Prepare journal entries for each transaction in accordance with the principles which you believe should be applied. (AICPA adapted)

## Problem 20-12

The Ecton Company proposes to sell all of its assets except Cash and Receivables to the Jones Company on July 31, 1980. The sales price will be $10,000,000 adjusted by the change in book value from December 31, 1979 to May 31, 1980 for Inventories and Property. The May 31 book values of Prepaid Expenses and Other Assets are to be added to the sales price.

The settlement shall be:

a. Jones Company 4% note for $3,000,000 payable in semi-annual installments of $150,000 commencing January 31, 1981.
b. Assumption of all liabilities except the Estimated Federal Income Taxes Payable and Long-Term Debt.
c. Balance payable in cash immediately.

The Company intends to retire the preferred stock and establish a $300,000 reserve for contingencies. The net income for June and July is estimated at $150,000 before taxes (assume that a 50% tax rate has been in effect since 1975).

The last preferred stock dividend was declared on December 31, 1979. The regular common stock dividend was paid on June 15, 1980.

Taxable income for the past four years follows:

| | |
|---:|---:|
| 1976 | $1,481,000 |
| 1977 | 412,400 |
| 1978 | 639,600 |
| 1979 | 842,500 |

Presented below are statements of financial position for December 31, 1979 and May 31, 1980:

ECTON COMPANY

STATEMENTS OF FINANCIAL POSITION

| Assets | December 31, 1979 | May 31, 1980 |
|---|---|---|
| Cash | $ 1,038,000 | $ 472,000 |
| Receivables | 2,550,000 | 3,105,000 |
| Inventories | 5,592,000 | 6,028,000 |
| Prepaid expenses | 308,000 | 297,000 |
| Total current assets | 9,488,000 | 9,902,000 |
| Property (net) | 6,927,000 | 6,804,000 |
| Other assets | 635,000 | 604,000 |
| Total assets | $17,050,000 | $17,310,000 |
| **Liabilities and Capital** | | |
| Accounts payable | $ 2,427,000 | $ 3,052,500 |
| Current maturities—long-term debt | 600,000 | 600,000 |
| Accrued liabilities | 1,096,000 | 922,000 |
| Dividends payable—preferred stock | 63,000 | –0– |
| Estimated federal income taxes | 417,000 | 333,500 |
| Total current liabilities | 4,603,000 | 4,908,000 |
| Long-term debt | 4,200,000 | 4,050,000 |
| Stockholders' equity: | | |
| Preferred cumulative stock—21,000 shares of $100 par, 3%, outstanding. Redeemable at $102 | 2,100,000 | 2,100,000 |
| Common stock—100,000 shares of $10 par outstanding | 1,000,000 | 1,000,000 |
| Capital contributed in excess of par value of common stock | 587,000 | 587,000 |
| Retained earnings | 4,560,000 | 4,665,000 |
| Total liabilities and capital | $17,050,000 | $17,310,000 |

*Note:*

The increase in Retained Earnings is net of a dividend of $.20 per share paid March 15, 1980 on common stock.

*Required:*

(1) Compute the total sales price and settlement to be made.
(2) Compute Ecton Company's gain or loss on the sale giving effect to income taxes.
(3) Prepare a work sheet with column headings "Per Books," "Adjustments," and "Estimated Statement of Financial Position, July 31, 1980" giving effect to the proposed sale and other information given. Support your adjustments with schedules or computations you deem necessary.

(AICPA adapted)

# 21

# Reorganizations

In the preceding chapter some of the accounting problems encountered when an enterprise contracts its scope of operations were considered. In most of the situations considered it was presumed that the enterprise would continue operations somewhat as it had in the past, although on a reduced scale. In addition, it was presumed that existing ownership interests would not be severely upset. At times, however, an enterprise may require a rather drastic overhauling if it is to continue as an operating enterprise. The enterprise that emerges from the overhauling may bear the same name, but it frequently will have a new look, a new management, a new financial structure, and in some instances, a substantially new ownership equity. This chapter will deal with some of the accounting problems arising from various forms of enterprise reorganization. In general, the reorganizations considered will have been preceded by a period in which the enterprise has had financial difficulties. The basic earning potential may still exist, but its emergence awaits various changes and modifications in the enterprise financial structure.

The problems to be considered could relate to all types of business organizations; they are found to some degree in proprietorships, partnerships, and corporations. The type of business organization, however, will not be an important aspect of the problem in most instances. The primary areas of interest in reorganization lie in the various equity interests and in the elimination of the causes of the financial difficulties of an enterprise.

The residual owners of a business which has had past financial difficulties, but which has a basic earning potential, may decide that the simplest procedure to eliminate existing problems is to dissolve the existing enterprise and to begin a new enterprise with the remains of the old. Frequently, such a procedure involves certain legal requirements, considerable time, and even a diminution or gradual erosion of the basic earning potential.

The dissolution of the existing enterprise and emergence of a new enterprise may be accomplished by meeting certain legal requirements pertaining to dissolution of an existing business and formation of a new business. On the other hand, a similar result may be obtained through the employment of certain accounting entries and without a legal dissolution.

**Legal Background.** A corporate enterprise may find the reorganization procedure somewhat easier to accomplish than will a proprietorship or a partnership. Thus a new corporation may be formed legally to take over the assets of an existing enterprise, the latter being legally dissolved in the process. Since the new corporation is a new entity, the values attached to the assets and the equities of the new corporation need not be related in any way to the values attached to the same assets and equities in the old enterprise. For example, the valuation of the inventories taken over by the new enterprise would depend upon the "cost" of those assets to the new enterprise, and this cost might be far different from the basis, or unrecovered cost, at which the inventories were carried on the preceding corporation's books.

Of course, the concept underlying the coincident establishment of a new corporate entity to replace a dissolved predecessor may involve a departure from the acquisition-cost basis of the assets of the old enterprise. Generally, if the legal reorganization is completed for some reason other than existing financial or operating difficulties, the prior cost bases are retained. However, in reorganizations undertaken to facilitate the turnaround of a problem situation, asset values are commonly restated. This does not mean that the assets of the new corporation may be stated at any convenient basis desired by the new equity interests. The assets are valued normally by appraisal of fair market value or in some similar manner. While it may appear that this is a devious means of avoiding adherence to the acquisition cost principle, the fact remains that legally a new entity exists, and the new entity should not necessarily be bound by values carried by the predecessor entity, particularly when experience shows that those values are not realizable.

**Accounting Background.** The above-described procedure of legally dissolving an existing enterprise and creating a new enterprise to take its place may be somewhat costly and may also be impractical in some instances. Justification for a restatement of various asset and equity interests should not turn upon a legal nicety such as the dissolution-creation procedure described. Thus in practice the revaluation of assets downward, and the resulting realignment of equity interests, has been an accepted accounting procedure when there is reason to think the enterprise might otherwise legally reorganize and find legal support for the revaluations. The process by which accountants record revaluations of assets without a formal reorganization is sometimes referred to as a quasi reorganization. The term indicates that the same results as those of a formal reorganization are accomplished, but the legal processes of the formal reorganization are absent. The quasi reorganization is also sometimes referred to as the "fresh start."

## QUASI REORGANIZATION

**Characteristics.** Quasi reorganizations should be limited to rather unusual business situations and should possess all or most of the following characteristics:

1. *A new management.* When a new management assumes control of an enterprise that has had financial difficulties, the new management should be relieved of responsibility for the mistakes of the former management if such mistakes are reflected in overstated asset values. Since the asset values carried forward would eventually flow through an income statement, the new management may be entitled to assume asset values that are more in line with actualities at the time it assumes control.

2. *Overstated asset values.* If an enterprise has had a period of operating losses, but if it also has a valid potential earning capacity, and if in spite of the operating losses the asset valuations are still excessive in relation to current values, it would appear that justification exists for asset write-downs. Continued adherence to the existing asset values may distort depreciation charges in the coming periods and thereby prevent the reported income from being a realistic measure of the operating efficiency of management.

3. *Overstated equity values.* If asset values are excessive, it follows that some equity interests are also overvalued. Normally, the equity of the residual owners (stockholders in the case of a corporation) is overstated. The inaccurate picture presented generally has arisen from a failure in the past to recognize all losses that have occurred.

4. *A brighter future.* If operating losses have been incurred in the past, or if such losses have not been reported but actually exist in overstated asset and equity values, an enterprise may find that its financial statements do not disclose a fair picture of its earning potential. Development of new products, emergence of new markets, institution of new management, elimination of past inefficiencies, and other developments may make the future appear brighter, even from an objective viewpoint. While a new enterprise may not be a legal reality, the future may be so much different from the past that the new enterprise *appears* to exist. If this situation exists, accounting adjustments to effect the new enterprise may be warranted.

**Upward Versus Downward Revaluations.** The discussion above has not dealt with the situation where a "fresh start" is warranted and the existing asset and equity interests are undervalued. The question may be raised: Do accountants utilize the quasi-reorganization procedure to include upward revaluation of assets as well as downward adjustments? In one sense it is difficult to justify the downward adjustment and reject the upward revaluation of assets. Both represent an attempt to correct valuations on the accounting records. It has previously been emphasized, however, that accountants are reluctant to depart from the acquisition-cost principle. This reluctance is reflected in the view that revaluation of assets should normally be recorded only when an objective transaction takes place. The adherence to acquisition cost appears to be more tenacious on the part of accountants when the possible revaluation is upward than when it is downward. Losses are more often recognized prior to an actual transaction occurrence than are gains. Thus many accountants at the present time support the quasi-reorganization procedure when assets are overvalued, but do not support a similar procedure to correct the accounts for assets that are undervalued.

Many reasons have been cited to support the accounting procedure of recognizing losses prior to a transaction occurrence, but most of them appear more in the nature of attempts to justify the procedure rather than to explain the reason for the procedure. It seems likely that the reason behind the advance recognition of losses (without a similar advance recognition of gains) lies in the historical conservatism of accountants. Most of the outside pressures on accountants during the early part of the century—the period of emergence of accounting as an important service to business—originated from conservative sources, bankers and other credit grantors. Since their primary concern was an absence of overvaluation, it is not surprising that write-downs were somewhat prevalent. While accountants today do not generally approve indiscriminate write-downs, the past effect of conservatism probably makes write-downs to appropriate values more acceptable than write-ups to appropriate values. The accountant probably has not overcome completely his past conditioning to accept conservative departures from otherwise acceptable standards.

**Revaluations in a Quasi Reorganization.** If a management decides that an accounting, or quasi, reorganization is warranted, the first step would be to determine the fair market values of the various assets that will be employed in the future operations of the enterprise. While some accountants would contend that only the fixed assets should be revalued, the quasi reorganization procedure should probably be a thoroughgoing one and include revaluation of all the assets. If it is realized that the justification for the quasi-reorganization procedure lies in the "fresh start" which the enterprise is contemplating, it appears only logical that the reorganization should include a review and adjustment of all asset and equity elements. The following illustration indicates the process of revaluation in a quasi reorganization.

## Illustration of Quasi Reorganization

Assume that the EXY Corporation has been in operations for several years, that for the past few years operating results have not been satisfactory, and that assets are currently overvalued. However, certain new products have been perfected from a marketability viewpoint, and the officers are convinced that profitable operations will exist in the coming months. The statement of financial position of the EXY Corporation on December 31, 1979, follows, on page 658, with current fair values of the assets shown parenthetically.

**Adjustment of Assets.** Assuming that the fair market values as shown are reasonable and that the management wishes to proceed with a revaluation of the assets, the accountant would record the revaluation as follows:

| | | |
|---|---|---|
| Inventory | $ 1,000 | |
| Loss on revaluation of assets | 25,000 | |
|     Receivables | | $ 1,000 |
|     Building | | 20,000 |
|     Machinery | | 5,000 |
| (to record revaluation of assets to fair market value) | | |

The effect of the entry above is to place the assets at a proper value for future operating periods of the enterprise. The loss on revaluation of assets should be reflected on the 1979 income statement as a special charge. Full disclosure of the quasi reorganization is essential.

EXY CORPORATION
FINANCIAL POSITION AS OF DECEMBER 31, 1979
*Assets*

| | |
|---|---|
| Cash ($40,000) | $ 40,000 |
| Receivables ($89,000) | 90,000 |
| Inventories ($21,000) | 20,000 |
| Building ($80,000) | 100,000 |
| Machinery ($45,000) | 50,000 |
| Total assets | $300,000 |

*Equities*

| | |
|---|---|
| Current liabilities | $ 60,000 |
| Capital stock (par value $100) | 200,000 |
| Retained earnings | 40,000 |
| Total equities | $300,000 |

**Adjustment of Equities.** The quasi reorganization in the example above involved only a revaluation of assets. Now assume that the assets of the EXY Corporation as shown at cost on the statement of financial position above are proper valuations. Thus $300,000 does measure the fair value of the assets of the Corporation. Also assume that the equity section of the statement appears as follows:

*Equities*

| | |
|---|---|
| Current liabilities | $ 60,000 |
| Capital stock (par value $100) | 400,000 |
| Retained earnings (Deficit) | (160,000) |
| Total equities | $300,000 |

Since the future outlook for the EXY Corporation is relatively bright, the management may decide that the existing deficit should be eliminated if possible so that the expected profits of the future may be available for dividends without having to overcome the large deficit. One means of eliminating this deficit would be to reduce the par value of the common stock from $100 a share to $60 a share. The reduction of the par value would create "additional paid-in capital" against which the deficit could be charged. This procedure would eliminate the deficit and permit dividends to be paid out of future earnings.

If the par value of the capital stock is reduced to $60 per share, the following entry would be made:

| | | |
|---|---|---|
| Capital stock | $160,000 | |
|     Additional paid-in capital | | $160,000 |
| (to reduce par value per share from $100 to $60, or $40 per share on 4,000 shares outstanding = $160,000) | | |

The existing deficit could then be charged off against the additional paid-in capital created in the entry above:

| | | |
|---|---|---|
| Additional paid-in capital | $160,000 | |
|     Retained earnings (deficit) | | $160,000 |

After these entries have been made, the equity section of the statement of financial position of the EXY Corporation would be:

*Equities*

| | |
|---|---|
| Current liabilities | $ 60,000 |
| Capital stock (par value $60) | 240,000 |
| Retained earnings | –0– |
| Total equities | $300,000 |

It should be noted that it is not necessary for the reduction in par of the capital stock to equal exactly the deficit to be eliminated. Thus, the par value above could have been reduced to $50 per share, creating additional pain-in capital of $200,000. After eliminating the deficit, $40,000 of additional paid-in capital would remain.

The above entries give effect to a quasi reorganization even though no asset adjustments were involved. Thus a revaluation of assets is not necessary to effect a quasi reorganization. If the assets are already properly valued and the various losses have been recorded previously through the normal accounting procedure, the result may have been to produce the deficit that was assumed to exist above. The quasi reorganization then becomes a problem in elimination of the deficit.

**Adjustments of Both Assets and Equities.** Most quasi reorganizations involve both the adjustment of asset values and the adjustment of equity interests. Thus assume that the EXY Corporation in the previous examples has a statement of financial position reporting assets at acquisition cost of $300,000, but with the fair values as indicated on page 658. Also assume the equities to be those in the preceding section, with a $160,000 deficit existing from past operations.

In this situation the EXY Corporation accountant should first record the write-down of the assets to their fair values (see entry on page 658), and should charge the resulting loss to the Retained Earnings (Deficit) account. After recording the asset revaluation, the deficit would be $185,000. At this point the board of directors of the Corporation would probably decide to write down the par value of the capital stock sufficiently to absorb the entire $185,000 deficit by the additional paid-in capital created in the write-down of par. Assuming that the par is to be reduced to $50 per share, the following series of entries would be made to record the quasi reorganization:

| | | |
|---|---|---|
| Inventory | $ 1,000 | |
| Loss on revaluation of assets | 25,000 | |
|    Receivables | | $ 1,000 |
|    Building | | 20,000 |
|    Machinery | | 5,000 |
| Retained earnings (deficit) | $ 25,000 | |
|    Loss on revaluation of assets | | $ 25,000 |
| Capital stock | $200,000 | |
|    Additional paid-in capital | | $200,000 |
| Additional paid-in capital | $185,000 | |
|    Retained earnings (deficit) | | $185,000 |

The statement of financial position of the EXY Corporation after giving effect to the quasi reorganization would be:

EXY CORPORATION

FINANCIAL POSITION AS OF DECEMBER 31, 1979

*Assets*

| | |
|---|---|
| Cash | $ 40,000 |
| Receivables | 89,000 |
| Inventories | 21,000 |
| Building | 80,000 |
| Machinery | 45,000 |
| Total assets | $275,000 |

*Equities*

| | |
|---|---|
| Current liabilities | $ 60,000 |
| Capital stock (par value $50) | 200,000 |
| Additional paid-in capital | 15,000 |
| Total equities | $275,000 |

A thorough explanation of the reorganization procedure should accompany the statement to enable the reader to interpret properly the results of the reorganization.

**Dating of Retained Earnings.** If the EXY Corporation reports profitable operations in 1980, such profits would be closed to the Retained Earnings account in the normal manner. However, a statement of financial position prepared at December 31, 1980, should disclose that the retained earnings reported has been accumulated since December 31, 1979, the effective date of the quasi reorganization. In order to put the statement reader on notice that a reorganization has occurred and that the amount in the Retained Earnings account represents only undistributed earnings since reorganization, the Retained Earnings account should be dated for several years. It is unlikely that the date would have significance after a period of 10 years, and in some instances the date of the amount could be discontinued at the conclusion of a period of less than 10 years.[1]

## FINANCIAL REORGANIZATIONS

Business enterprises in financial difficulty may employ various other means to alleviate their financial problems. Certain available methods involve modifications in the financial structure of the enterprise; such modifications are implemented by the existing management or by representatives of existing equity interests, and are discussed at this point. Other procedures involve modifications in the financial structure of the enterprise; such modifications are implemented by a court, trustee, or other agency outside the existing enterprise management or equity interests, and are considered in the final portion of this chapter. Finally, some procedures involve plans to liquidate the enterprise. Accounting problems involved in liquidations will be considered in the final section of the book, beginning with Chapter Twenty-two.

### Securing an Extension of Time for Payments to Creditors

When the financial difficulty arises from a temporary shortage of cash occasioned by having too much of the equity contributions tied up in noncash assets, it is often possible to secure from creditors an extension of the time period over which the debts will be paid. Creditors are aware that, if they resort to legal procedures to collect their claims against the enterprise, considerable time and expense may be involved. Thus the creditors may prefer to grant an extension of time to the debtor in the hope that the amount due will be paid in full, within a reasonable time, and without incurring the ill will that may arise in a legal action.

In addition to gaining an extension of time, debtors may also be able to negotiate either a temporary suspension of interest payments or even a reduction in the previously stipulated interest rate. Either of these alternatives may be granted by a creditor in recognition of cash-availability problems of the debtor. In some instances, the interest abatement is restored when the debtor's financial status recovers, and in other cases, the restoration may be contingent on certain specified

---

[1] *Accounting Research Bulletin No. 46,* American Institute of Certified Public Accountants, February, 1956.

later developments. As a general rule, no accounting recognition is given to modifications in terms of indebtedness such as these, and future periods will simply reflect reduced interest charges for debtors.

The accounting personnel of an enterprise in financial difficulty may be asked to aid in the solution of problems of this nature in the following ways:

1. The development of a cash budget or cash forecast to accompany the request for an extension of time. If the creditors can see that the enterprise in financial difficulty has a well-thought-out plan of reducing its indebtedness, they may be more amenable to granting the suggested extension of time.
2. The development of a schedule for the payment of various creditors. This becomes particularly important if the extension of time is granted only by certain creditors.

## Asset Exchange for Debt

In addition to gaining various modifications of debt agreements, debtors may effect an exchange of assets for debts that have matured. Transactions of this nature generally arise when the debtor is unable to settle maturing debt in the conventional way, and the creditor prefers to accept other assets rather than work out a modification of the debt agreement.

Assume that the Gerard Co. has outstanding $1,000,000 of debt on which $120,000 interest has accrued. Gerard does not have adequate cash flow to meet either interest payments or settlement of the debt. The lender, however, is willing to accept in full settlement of the debt and interest a land parcel on Gerard's books at a cost of $200,000 and other real estate that had a cost of $1,200,000 and has accumulated depreciation of $500,000. Responsible appraisers indicate that the current value of the land is $275,000 and the current value of the other real estate is $600,000. The entries to record the transfer of these assets in exchange for the release of indebtedness would be:

| | | |
|---|---|---|
| Land | $75,000 | |
| Loss on revaluation of assets | 25,000 | |
|    Real Estate | | $100,000 |
| (to recognize the fair value of assets to be transferred to settle indebtedness) | | |
| | | |
| Debt | $1,000,000 | |
| Interest payable | 120,000 | |
| Accumulated depreciation | 500,000 | |
|    Land | | $275,000 |
|    Real Estate | | 1,100,000 |
|    Gain on extinguishment of debt | | 245,000 |
| (to account for exchange of assets for debt and accrued interest) | | |

These entries indicate that (1) assets used to settle the indebtedness should be adjusted to current values at the date of settlement, and (2) the settlement itself involves recognition of a gain arising from a release from indebtedness in excess of the fair values of the assets used in the settlement. Both entries are consistent with the general principle that exchange transactions should be accounted for at the fair values of the consideration used in the exchange.

## Refinancing of Debt

At times financial difficulty may arise from, or at least be partially the result of, heavy interest or financing charges on existing bonds or other debt obligations. Thus a company may have a bond issue outstanding on which it is paying 9% interest, when under present conditions a similar bond issue could be sold at 5½ or 6% interest. If the company could replace the existing bonds with bonds carrying the lower interest rate, at least one factor contributing to the financial difficulty would be removed. In other situations a company may have a bond issue coming due but not have available funds with which to meet the retirement of the debt. Depending upon the going rate of interest, the company might well be able to sell a new bond issue, possibly at a lower interest rate, and use the proceeds to retire the bonds that are currently maturing. This process of replacing an existing indebtedness with a new indebtedness is generally referred to as refinancing or refunding. It should be noted here that refinancing or refunding of debt may arise in enterprises that are financially sound, as well as in enterprises that are in financial difficulty. The conditions surrounding the refinancing are not significant from the accounting viewpoint.

Certain aspects of refinancing of debt prior to its maturity date, sometimes called the early extinguishment of debt, were considered in Chapter 20 on pages 631 to 633. Those aspects should be reviewed at this time, inasmuch as they will not be considered further in the following sections.

**Refinancing at Face Value.** In the simplest situation, Zee Company may have outstanding $1,000,000 of first mortgage 6% bonds, which were issued at par 10 years ago and which have 15 years remaining until maturity. In addition, the bond indenture of these bonds provides that they are callable at par any time prior to maturity. In order to reduce the interest charges, the company may decide to call this bond issue and to replace the indebtedness with an issue of $1,000,000 first mortgage bonds, with interest at 4%. Assuming that the new bond issue could be sold at exactly the face amount, the following entry summarizes the transaction:

| | | |
|---|---|---|
| Bonds payable | $1,000,000 | |
| Bonds payable | | $1,000,000 |

The net effect of the refinancing would be to reduce the interest charges by $20,000 a year (from $60,000 to $40,000). Since the old bonds have 15 years of life remaining, a saving of $300,000 may be gained over the 15 years. As this saving would build up annually in $20,000 increments, investment of the increments would produce an additional saving. Offsetting this saving would be the cost of refinancing, which would include the costs of printing and selling the new bonds, and of calling and retiring the old bonds.

**Refinancing with a Call Premium.** Assume that the Zee Company has outstanding $1,000,000 of first-mortgage, 6% bonds, which were issued at par 10 years ago. Because of the decline in the market rate of interest, the management believes that it will be advisable to call the old bonds and to issue new bonds bearing 4% interest to replace them. However, the existing bonds are not currently callable at par. The call price at the date decided on is 103.

Assuming that the Company does not have any excess cash available to help retire the bonds, it is apparent that the new bonds will have to yield an amount in excess of $1,000,000 if the old bonds are to be retired. The sale of the new bonds must yield at least $1,030,000 (103% of par). The management of the Zee Company must evaluate several alternatives in arriving at a decision on how to retire the 6% bonds. Assume that the decision is finally made to set the interest rate at 4% on the new bonds. If at the date of sale the 4% bonds sell at 99, the Zee Company will have to sell in excess of $1,040,000 par value bonds of the new issue in order to realize enough cash to retire the old bonds. Assume that they decide to issue bonds of $1,050,000 par value at 99. This would provide cash of $1,039,500, of which $1,030,000 would be necessary to retire the outstanding bonds. The entries to record these events could be made as follows:

| | | |
|---|---|---|
| Cash | $1,039,500 | |
| Unamortized bond discount | 10,500 | |
| Bonds payable | | $1,050,000 |
| (to record the sale and issuance of new bonds) | | |
| Bonds payable | $1,000,000 | |
| Loss on retirement of bonds | 30,000 | |
| Cash | | $1,030,000 |
| (to record retirement of original issue of bonds) | | |

The loss on retirement of the bonds ($30,000) and the bond discount ($10,500) would in effect be recovered over the years through the reduction in interest costs from $60,000 a year to $40,000 a year.

**Unamortized Discount or Premium on Issue Outstanding.** Another problem that sometimes exists in the refinancing of an existing bond issue has to do with any unamortized discount or premium on the original bond issuance that is still being carried at the time of the refinancing. Thus, for example, the Zee Company might have sold initially the $1,000,000 of first mortgage, 6% bonds at 97½, or for $975,000. If the life of these bonds is assumed to be 25 years, and if the refinancing arises 10 years after the initial sale, $15,000 of unamortized discount exists at the date of the refinancing.

Three alternatives are commonly suggested as possibilities for handling this discount:

1. The discount (or premium if such existed) could be written off immediately to income as a gain or loss on retirement of the bonds.
2. The discount (premium) could be amortized over the remaining period of the life of the original bond issue. In the example above, the discount would be written off over 15 years, the remaining life of the bonds retired.
3. The discount (premium) could be amortized over the life of the new bonds. Thus, if the 4% bonds that the Zee Company is selling to retire the original bonds has a life of 25 years, the $15,000 unamortized discount would be written off over this 25-year period.

Referring to the illustration above, if the Zee Company retired at 103 their 6% bonds, which had $15,000 unamortized discount and 15 years to maturity, and if the retirement were effected by the sale at 99 of $1,050,000 of 4% bonds, the following entry could be made under the first alternative above:

| | | |
|---|---|---|
| Cash | $ 9,500 | |
| Loss on retirement of bonds | 45,000 | |
| Unamortized bond discount | 10,500 | |
| Bonds payable | 1,000,000 | |
| Unamortized bond discount | | $ 15,000 |
| Bonds payable | | 1,050,000 |

The loss on retirement of bonds is composed of the $15,000 unamortized discount on the bonds retired, plus the $30,000 premium required to call the old bonds in order to retire them.

Under the second and third alternatives above, the entry at the date of retirement of the 6% bonds would charge the $30,000 call premium required to retire the old bonds to unamortized bond discount. Subsequent periods would be charged for a portion of the $45,000 ($3,000 per year under the second alternative, and $1,800 a year under the third alternative).

**Immediate Write-off.** Numerous arguments have been advanced over the years in support of the three alternatives. The direct charge to income for the unamortized discount or premium treats this item in a manner similar to the issue cost or redemption premium on the bonds retired. The basic question seems to rest on the time when the gain or loss on retirement is to be recognized. The immediate elimination of the redemption premium, issue cost, and unamortized discount or premium on the bonds retired may be justified by reasoning that the retirement of the bonds brings to a close a series of entries arising from those bonds. Since the bonds are no longer carried forward, all costs (income) related to those bonds should also be closed to income. The fact that the bonds were replaced by similar bonds is not significant in determining the accounting treatment for the retirement of the old bonds.

**Amortization Over Life of Original Issue.** The second alternative has been supported on the grounds that the cost of borrowing money was established at the date of the issuance of the original bonds. Thus, unless future periods are charged or credited with "their share" of the gain or loss on retirement of the bonds, an overstatement or an understatement of income will exist in the future periods. The benefit to the future periods from the lower interest charges on the new bonds must be offset by the portion of the loss (gain) arising from the retirement of the original issue.

**Amortization Over Life of New Issue.** The third alternative does not appear to have much theoretical support. There seems to be little justification for charging unamortized costs of one bond issue over a period unrelated to that bond issue.

It is the opinion of the authors that the first alternative, the charging off of the unamortized discount and the redemption premium as a loss on retirement is the most appropriate procedure. This procedure is consistent with other accounting procedures that recognize gains and losses at the time of their occurrence. If the second procedure were used, a logical extension of it into the area of fixed asset accounting would require that gains or losses on assets replaced should not be recognized until such time as the assets would have been fully depreciated.

Refinancing of debt may involve either an increase or a decrease in the amount of debt previously outstanding. Likewise, refinancing may well arise at times when the enterprise is in a sound financial condition. However, enterprises that are in financial difficulty may well be able to convince various equity interests that, through refinancing, the causes or some of the causes of the financial difficulty may be eliminated.

**Creditor Committee.** The process of turning the business over to a committee representing the creditors is, in reality, more in the nature of a change in management than it is a reorganization. Likewise, the formation of a creditor committee, and its assumption of control of the business operations, may frequently follow certain legal proceedings. At times, however, a group of creditors may organize to advise, on a voluntary basis, the existing management. In any event, the end effect desired is to eliminate the causes of financial difficulty and to rehabilitate the business prior to the resumption of control by the former management. At times a legal reorganization is effected before the business is returned to the ownership equities. No particular accounting problems arise from the existence of a creditor committee. Any actions taken or transactions entered into by the committee would be recorded in the same manner as if the previous management had taken the action or entered into the transaction.

**Equity Receivership.** An alternative to the formation of a creditor committee may involve the filing of a petition in a court requesting the court to protect the business during a period of financial difficulty or planning preceding reorganization. As with a creditor committee, the request for the protection of the court may be voluntary on the part of the management of the enterprise, or it may be involuntarily imposed at the request of one or more equity interests. If the court deems such action desirable, it may appoint either an individual or a corporation to act as receiver. The receiver is an agent of the court, and since the purpose of appointment of the receiver is to preserve the interests of the various equity groups of the corporation, the period during which the receiver has control of the operations of the enterprise is generally referred to as a period of equity receivership.

**Legal Procedures.** In an equity receivership the court appoints the receiver, provides the receiver with certain instructions, and in general assumes responsibility for the protection of the assets and of the equity interests of the corporation. The receiver is generally charged with the responsibility of attempting to eliminate the causes of financial difficulty, and at the same time he must retain the goodwill of the various equity interests. If the receiver is unable to remove the causes of difficulty, or if he is unable to get the various parties to agree to a particular plan of reorganization, he may recommend to the court that liquidation proceedings be instituted. If such action does result, the receiver may supervise the liquidation. Likewise, during the period of receivership, one or more of the equity interests may petition the court for institution of liquidation proceedings. As discussed in the following chapter, the institution of receivership proceedings, either voluntary or involuntary, when the debtor is insolvent under the terms of bankruptcy law is an act of bankruptcy. As such, any creditor who may so desire may institute bankruptcy proceedings. If the debtor business is found to be bankrupt, the receivership proceedings are terminated.

Equity receiverships may proceed under state courts or under federal courts, depending upon the circumstances. Although receiverships may begin in an atmosphere of cooperation, various conflicts of interest may arise as the receivership period progresses. The resolution of the conflicts to the satisfaction of the varied parties at interest is frequently a difficult and time-consuming problem. At times the parties at conflict cannot reach a suitable agreement, and, if this situation does result, complete reorganization or even liquidation may be necessary.

**Accounting Procedures.** Although the accounting problems of a receivership are discussed in more detail in Chapter Twenty-four, it should be noted at this point that a receiver must maintain thorough records of the various actions taken during the period of receivership. Just as business management has the responsibility of maintaining adequate records for the information of the various equity interests of the enterprise, so the receiver must maintain similarly detailed records to discharge his responsibilities to the court as well as to the existing equity interests.

In recent years, since the amendment to the Bankruptcy Act of 1933, equity receivership proceedings have become relatively uncommon. The procedure was unduly time consuming and costly, and provisions of the Bankruptcy Act afford comparable relief which, at least in theory, may be accomplished in a more economical and less time-consuming manner.

## Reorganizations under the Bankruptcy Act

Amendments to the Bankruptcy Act in 1938 (as well as those adopted in 1933 and 1934) dealt to a considerable degree with relief provisions for debtors. Chapter X of the 1938 amendment (Chandler Act) governs those corporate reorganizations wherein revisions of the capital structure are proposed. In general, corporate reorganizations other than those involving adjustment of unsecured obligations only fall within the framework of Chapter X.

**Legal Procedures.** The action preliminary to a reorganization is somewhat similar to that preceding an equity receivership. The petition to effect a reorganization plan may be filed with the court by the corporation or by any of the equity interests or their representatives. The filing of the reorganization petition is not an act of bankruptcy, however, and the court may approve the petition even though bankruptcy proceedings may be pending against the corporation. Depending on the size of the corporation, the court may appoint one or more trustees (comparable in duties and responsibilities to receivers) to administer the assets of the corporation, or the existing management may continue in control.

After the trustee assumes control, or after management is approved to retain control under the petition, a reorganization plan is prepared and filed with the court. The court will hold a hearing on the plan, and if the plan is fair, equitable, and feasible, it will be approved. At this point the plan is submitted to the various equity interests for their approval. Approval must be obtained from the holders of two-thirds of the amount of the equity in each equity class that has had its claim allowed by the court. A majority of each class of stockholders must also approve the plan if the corporation is solvent. After the approvals of the various equity interests have been obtained, the court will hold another hearing on the plan and, providing the plan is still considered to be fair, equitable, and feasible, the court will order the plan confirmed. The plan is then binding on all parties, and the trustee or management in control will execute the various terms of the plan. After the various provisions of the plan have been carried out, the court will enter an order discharging the corporation from its liabilities and discharging the trustee from his responsibilities.

As mentioned above, the reorganization provisions of Chapter X of the Chandler Act have largely rendered equity receivership obsolete. Although the expected savings in time and costs under the reorganization procedure probably have not been realized, this procedure has been effective in rehabilitating financially troubled corporations. Under the equity receivership procedure, the court (and the receiver) was in the position of being a guardian of the corporation, with its main duty being to preserve the rights of the various parties at issue until the management resumed control or until liquidation proceedings began. Under reorganization procedure, the court largely assumes the responsibilities of corporate management, and its main duty is to preserve the fundamental values of the various properties in order for each equity interest to obtain the fairest and most equitable adjustment of its claims.

# 21 / Reorganizations

**Accounting Procedures.** The accounting problems arising in a reorganization plan may be divided into two groups:

1. Those arising from the assumption of control by a trustee or other court-appointed official. The trustee is in a position comparable to that of the receiver in an equity receivership, and he should maintain such records as will permit him to render a thorough and accurate report to the court and the equity interests regarding the actions taken during the period of his control. This problem area is discussed in greater detail in Chapter Twenty-four.
2. Those arising from the sales, disposals, or adjustments made to the various asset values of the corporation, and from the settlements, agreements, or adjustments made with the various equity interests of the corporation.

In addition to the problems in these two groups, it must be recognized that the advice and counsel of accountants are solicited on a widespread basis in reorganization planning. Problems of asset valuation, projections of future earning probabilities, and evaluations of the equity in the various phases of the reorganization plan are all areas in which the accountant may render valuable service.

While it is quite difficult to generalize regarding reorganization plans, the following example indicates a few of the readjustments in the equity structure that might be made. In the illustration it is necessary to recognize that a considerable amount of discussion, proposal, and counterproposal preceded the plan finally decided upon. Likewise, the plan itself could have been varied in a number of respects. The primary interest here lies in the accounting treatment accorded the various provisions of the reorganization plan as agreed upon. It might also be desirable to compare the discussion in the following example with the plan of reorganization discussed on pages 656–661, to see the differences in a rather thoroughgoing financial reorganization and a quasi reorganization.

**Illustration.** *Reorganization of F Corporation.* The F Corporation is a manufacturer of machine tools. During its early life the Corporation incurred steady losses, but in 1978 and 1979 the operations generated $800,000 total profit after interest charges and taxes. The future outlook is promising, but the Corporation has certain restrictive covenants in some of the equity provisions that will impede growth. Throughout 1979 representatives of the various equity interests met and finally agreed on a reorganization plan which has been approved by the proper court officials. The plan is to be made effective on January 1, 1980. The statement of financial position of the F Corporation on December 31, 1979, appears below. Following the statement are the various provisions of the reorganization plan.

THE F CORPORATION<br>
FINANCIAL POSITION DECEMBER 31, 1979<br>
*Assets*

| | |
|---|---:|
| Cash | $ 600,000 |
| Receivables | 1,800,000 |

|  |  |
|---|---:|
| Inventories | 3,440,000 |
| Plant and equipment | 10,300,000 |
| Unamortized bond discount | 60,000 |
| Total assets | $16,200,000 |

*Equities*

|  |  |
|---|---:|
| Current payables | $ 2,000,000 |
| 8% First-mortgage bonds payable, due 1/1/90 | 6,000,000 |
| 6% Cumulative preferred stock, $50 par value, 100,000 shares outstanding (Dividends in arrears since 1/1/71) | 5,000,000 |
| Common stock, no par, 120,000 shares outstanding, assigned value of $40 per share | 4,800,000 |
| Accumulated operating deficit | (1,600,000) |
| Total equities | $16,200,000 |

1. No revision in the carrying value of the assets is to be made. Review of current values indicates that the assets are reasonably stated.
2. Current payables will be paid in full as they fall due. The corporation has been slow in paying its current debt, but has paid all such debt in full in the past. The various current payables have agreed to a reasonable extension of time of payments on a temporary basis.
3. The bondholders have agreed to surrender their 8% first-mortgage bonds on the following terms: Each $1,000 bond will be exchanged for one $1,000, 6% first-mortgage bond, due January 1, 1990, plus five shares of new Class B common stock.
4. Preferred stockholders have agreed that 6% preferred stock be reduced from $50 par value per share to $40 par value; that it continue to be preferred for $3 per share dividends on a cumulative basis; and that it be preferred in liquidations at $50 per share. In settlement of the dividends in arrears, cash of $400,000 is to be paid and 125,000 shares of Class B common stock are to be issued. Class B common has a $10 par value, is nonvoting, and is not entitled to dividends. In addition, the Class B common is redeemable at $25 per share and entitled to $25 per share after preferred but prior to Class A common in liquidation. The Class B common is to be retired through a redemption fund to be created by yearly deposits equal to 50% of net profits in excess of preferred dividend requirements. No dividend will be paid on the Class A common until the Class B common has been fully retired.
5. The common stock is to be exchanged for Class A common on a share for share basis, but the stated value of the new Class A common is to be $10 per share.

Entries to give effect to the plan:

(*a*) 8% First-mortgage bonds payable     $6,000,000
       Reorganization surplus     360,000

|  |  |
|---|---|
| 6% First-mortgage bonds payable | $6,000,000 |
| Class B common stock | 300,000 |
| Unamortized bond discount | 60,000 |

This entry gives effect to the transfer of the 8% bonds for 6% bonds and Class B common stock. The unamortized discount is written off, although this amount could be carried forward on the reasoning that the bonds to which it was related are, in effect, still outstanding. However, a write-off appears advisable at this time on the reasoning that a new equity structure exists and no discount arose in its formation. The Reorganization Surplus account is a temporary account used only to effect the equity changes. It is disposed of in the final entry below.

|  |  |  |
|---|---|---|
| (b) 6% Cumulative preferred stock | $1,000,000 |  |
| Reorganization surplus |  | $1,000,000 |

This entry records the reduction in the par value of the preferred stock and the reorganization surplus created by the write-down in par value.

|  |  |  |
|---|---|---|
| (c) Reorganization surplus | $1,650,000 |  |
| Cash |  | $ 400,000 |
| Class B common stock |  | 1,250,000 |

This entry records the settlement of the preferred dividend arrearage. The Class B common is recorded at its par value rather than at its redemption value. The redemption value and terms of redemption must be fully disclosed on the statement of financial position.

|  |  |  |
|---|---|---|
| (d) Common stock | $4,800,000 |  |
| Class A common stock |  | $1,200,000 |
| Reorganization surplus |  | 3,600,000 |

This entry records the transfer of the old common for the new Class A common and the write-down in par value from $40 per share to $10 per share.

|  |  |  |
|---|---|---|
| (e) Reorganization surplus | $1,600,000 |  |
| Accumulated operating deficit |  | $1,600,000 |

This entry eliminates the existing operating deficit by a charge against the reorganization surplus established through the write-downs of par of the preferred and common stock.

|  |  |  |
|---|---|---|
| (f) Reorganization surplus | $990,000 |  |
| Additional paid-in capital |  | $990,000 |

This entry closes the Reorganization Surplus account and transfers the balance to Additional Paid-In Capital. Any retained earnings resulting from profitable operations in the future should be dated from 1/1/80.

After the entries above have been made, the statement of financial position of the F Corporation would appear as follows:

THE F CORPORATION

FINANCIAL POSITION, JANUARY 1, 1980

*Assets*

| | |
|---|---:|
| Cash | $ 200,000 |
| Receivables | 1,800,000 |
| Inventories | 3,440,000 |
| Plant and equipment | 10,300,000 |
| Total assets | $15,740,000 |

*Equities*

| | |
|---|---:|
| Current payables | $ 2,000,000 |
| 6% First mortgage bonds payable, due 1/1/90 | 6,000,000 |
| 6% Cumulative preferred stock, $40 par value—100,000 shares outstanding (Note 1) | 4,000,000 |
| Class B common stock, par value $10 per share, 155,000 shares outstanding (Notes 2 and 4) | 1,550,000 |
| Class A common stock, stated value $10 per share, 120,000 shares outstanding (Note 3) | 1,200,000 |
| Additional paid-in capital (excess of equity write-downs at reorganization of 1/1/80 over existing operating deficit) | 990,000 |
| Total equities | $15,740,000 |

*Note 1.* Stock is entitled to $50 per share in liquidation.

*Note 2.* Stock is not entitled to dividends, is redeemable at $25 per share, and is preferred over Class A Common as to assets in liquidation at $25 per share.

*Note 3.* The liquidating preference of the preferred stock amounting to $5,000,000 and of the Class B common stock amounting to $3,875,000 exceeds the entire stockholders' equity of the company and creates a deficiency to the Class A common stock amounting to $1,135,000 as of January 1, 1980. No dividends may be paid on the Class A common stock as long as any Class B common stock remains outstanding.

*Note 4.* The Class B common stock is to be retired through accumulation of a cash fund equal to 50% of the net profits in excess of dividend requirements on preferred stock. The stock will be retired as funds are available at a price of $25 per share.

**Summary.** While the illustration above is merely indicative of the treatment in the accounting records of a reorganization plan, it does indicate the thoroughgoing nature of such a plan. The reorganization of a business enterprise that has suffered a period of financial difficulty is a complex process. Even though a sound plan is worked out and is acceptable to all interests concerned, there is no assurance that the plan will eliminate the causes of the difficulty. Unless the basic cause or causes of the past financial difficulties are eliminated, a plan of reorganization may merely provide a short breathing period prior to eventual liquidation of the enterprise. A sound plan or reorganization accompanied by a suitable economic climate and the elimination of the causes of financial distress may well result in a rehabilitated company, one in which the various equity interests will fare far better than they would through a liquidation of the enterprise. If the enterprise does recuperate, its subsequent problems will be similar to those discussed in earlier sections of this textbook. If the enterprise is not able to reestablish a firm financial base, liquidation may be the next and final stage of its life. Some of the problems arising in the liquidation of business enterprises will be considered in the following chapters.

## PROBLEMS

### Problem 21-1

The Foley Company presented the following condensed balance sheet on March 31, 1979.

THE FOLEY COMPANY

BALANCE SHEET, MARCH 31, 1979

| | | | |
|---|---|---|---|
| Cash and receivables | $110,000 | Current payables | $130,000 |
| Inventories | 180,000 | First mortgage bonds | |
| Fixed assets (net) | 480,000 | payable, 5% | 250,000 |
| | | Common stock, authorized and issued 100,000 shares at $5 par value | 500,000 |
| | | Retained income (deficit) | (110,000) |
| | $770,000 | | $770,000 |

The Company is in need of additional cash, but the balance sheet above is not conducive to borrowing or to the successful sale of additional stock. Thus, the directors have decided to proceed with a quasi reorganization. By May 31, 1979, the necessary approvals of the suggested plan have been received, and the principal points of the plan are presented below:

1. The par value attaching to the shares will be eliminated, the number of shares increased to 500,000, and a stated value per share of $1.00 adopted.
2. Three shares of the new stock are to be exchanged for each share of $5.00 par value stock.
3. Inventories are to be reduced to $160,000 to bring their value down to the lower of cost or market.
4. Bondholders agreed to accept 30,000 shares of the new common stock in lieu of two years' interest accrued but unpaid.

5. Fixed assets no longer in use with a book value of $26,000 are to be written off.
6. No deficit is to exist at May 31, 1979.

*Required:*

Prepare journal entries to give effect to the items above and prepare a balance sheet as of May 31, 1979, after preparation of the entries above.

## Problem 21-2

The Cainbrake Corporation was formed in July 1979. At date of incorporation it issued $1,000,000 of $100 par value common stock at par for cash. Operations during the remainder of 1979 resulted in $60,000 net income. As a result of its operating experience, it was decided that $800,000 of contributed capital would be adequate to meet foreseeable operating needs and provide for reasonable expansion. At a directors' meeting in January, the following independent suggestions were made to take care of the excess capitalization:

1. Reduce shares from $100 to $80 par value.
2. Invest $200,000 of excess cash in the firm's own shares.
3. Distribute a cash dividend of $20 per share.
4. Resort to a quasi reorganization and write-down various assets by $200,000.

*Required:*

Explain the soundness and reasonableness of each of these suggestions in relation to the accomplishment of the desired purpose.     (AICPA adapted)

## Problem 21-3

The Mancett Corporation had $105,000 of dividends in arrears on its preferred stock as of March 31, 1979. While retained earnings were adequate to meet accumulated dividends, the Corporation's management did not wish to weaken its working capital position. They also realized that a portion of the fixed assets was no longer used or useful in their operation. Therefore, they proposed the following reorganization, which was approved by stockholders to be effected as of April 1, 1979:

1. The preferred stock was to be exchanged for $300,000 of 5% debenture bonds. Dividends in arrears were to be settled by the issuance of $120,000 of $10 par value, 5% noncumulative preferred stock.
2. Common stock was to be assigned a value of $50 per share.
3. Goodwill was to be written off.
4. Property, plant, and equipment were to be written down, on the basis of appraisal and estimates of useful value, by a total of $103,200 consisting of $85,400 increase in allowance for depreciation and $17,800 decrease in certain assets.
5. Current assets were to be written down by $10,460 to reduce certain items to expected realizable values.
6. The condensed balance sheet as of March 31, 1979 appears below:

## Assets

| | | |
|---|---|---|
| Cash | | $ 34,690 |
| Other current assets | | 252,890 |
| Property, plant, and equipment | $1,458,731 | |
| Allowance for depreciation | 512,481 | 946,250 |
| Goodwill | | 50,000 |
| | | $1,283,830 |

## Liabilities and Capital

| | |
|---|---|
| Current liabilities | $ 136,860 |
| 7% Cumulative preferred stock ($100 par)* | 300,000 |
| Common stock (9,000 shares, no par) | 648,430 |
| Premium on preferred stock | 22,470 |
| Retained earnings | 176,070 |
| | $1,283,830 |

*$105,000 dividends in arrears.

### Required:

You are to prepare:
(1) The journal entries to give effect to the reorganization as of April 1, 1979. Give complete explanations with each entry and comment on any possible options in recording the reorganization.
(2) A balance sheet as of April 30, 1979, assuming that net income in April was $10,320 after provision for taxes. The operations resulted in $5,290 increase in cash, $10,660 increase in other current assets, $2,010 increase in current liabilities, and $3,620 increase in allowance for depreciation.

(AICPA adapted)

## Problem 21-4

The Vance Corporation encountered a series of loss years after several prior years of profits. As of January 1, 1980, the stockholders' equity section of the balance sheet of the Vance Corporation was as follows:

| | |
|---|---|
| Preferred stock, $25 par value, authorized 10,000 shares, outstanding 6,000 shares | $150,000 |
| Common stock, $5 par value, authorized and outstanding 15,000 shares | 75,000 |
| Retained income (deficit) | (40,000) |
| Total | $185,000 |

During the year various revisions were made in Vance's articles of incorporation, with the result that the Corporation's new authorized capital consisted of 1,000 shares of $100 par value preferred stock and 50,000 shares of common stock with no par value.

On October 1, 1980, 36,000 shares of the new common stock were issued on the following basis: 4 shares of the new common for each share of the outstanding preferred stock; 8/10 of a share of the new common for each share of the then outstanding common stock. The remaining authorized shares of new common were not issued. Four hundred shares of the new preferred stock were sold at par value.

An analysis of Retained Income at December 31, 1980, is presented below:

| | |
|---|---:|
| Balance, January 1, 1979 | $ (5,000) |
| Net loss for 1979 | (25,000) |
| | (30,000) |
| Provision for doubtful accounts receivables | (10,000) |
| Balance, December 31, 1979 | (40,000) |
| Net loss for 1980 | (12,000) |
| Balance, December 31, 1980 | $(52,000) |

At December 31, 1980, you are called in to prepare a balance sheet for the Vance Corporation. You find that no earnings information is available for any interim date during the year.

*Required:*

Prepare a stockholders' equity section for the Vance Corporation at December 31, 1980, assuming that the capital adjustments effected constitute a quasi reorganization. In addition, discuss any features of the data presented which might cause you to modify your presentation or on which you would want additional information prior to preparation of the balance sheet.

## Problem 21-5

The Johnson Company issued 5%, 25-year debenture bonds totaling $10,000,000 face value on January 2, 1972 at 97. The bonds were callable for redemption at 105 prior to January 1, 1978, at 104 from January 1, 1978, to January 1, 1983, and at 103 subsequently. Discount on issuance was amortized on a straight line basis to maturity.

On March 31, 1983, the company issued at 4%, 30-year convertible debentures totaling $10,000,000 face value at 101½ plus accrued interest. The proceeds were used to call the 5%, 25-year bonds at that date.

Interest on both bond issues was payable January 2 and July 1.

*Required:*

Prepare all journal entries required during the year 1983, assuming that the Company's fiscal year ends December 31. Support your entry(ies) for March 31, 1983, as being preferable to possible alternatives.

## Problem 21-6

1. The X Company has outstanding $2,000,000 of 20-year 5% bonds which were issued 10 years ago. Unamortized discount and expense of $120,000 remains

on the books. The bonds are callable at 105. The Company has the opportunity to refinance, by issuing at par, $2,150,000 of 4%, 10-year bonds. Expenses that would be incurred in connection with the issue are estimated to be $50,000. Interest on both issues is payable semi-annually.

Determine whether refinancing would be desirable. Show your computations in good form and explain the basis used in reaching your conclusion. Ignore any tax difference that might arise out of the refinancing. Refer to the appropriate tables in the Appendix.

2. If X Company carries out the refunding of the long-term debt, a decision must be made concerning the accounting treatment to be accorded the unamortized portion of discount and expense pertaining to the old bonds. Three different treatments of this item have received support from various accountants.

Describe these treatments and give a brief statement of the central argument offered in support of each of them. (AICPA adapted)

## Problem 21-7

The Herbert Sherman Company issued $3,000,000 of 4% first mortgage bonds on September 30, 1972, at 96 and accrued interest. The bonds were dated June 30, 1972; interest payable semi-annually; redeemable after June 30, 1977 and to June 30, 1979 at 104, and thereafter until maturity at 102; and convertible into $100 par value common stock as follows:

Until June 30, 1977, at the rate of 6 shares for each $1,000 of bonds.
From July 1, 1977 to June 30, 1980, at the rate of 5 shares for each $1,000 of bonds.
After June 30, 1980, at the rate of 4 shares for each $1,000 of bonds.

Expenses of issue were $6,360, which is to be combined with the premium or discount, and the total is to be amortized over the life of the bonds from date of issue. The bonds mature in 10 years from their date. The Company adjusts its books monthly and closes as of December 31 each year.

The following transactions occur in connection with the bonds:

(*a*) July 1, 1978—$500,000 of bonds were converted into stock.
(*b*) December 30, 1979—$500,000 face amounts of bonds were reacquired by purchase on the market at 99¼ and accrued interest. These were immediately retired.
(*c*) June 30, 1980—Because of favorable market conditions and interest rates, the management had instituted and publicized a plan to retire the remainder of the bonds. The remaining bonds were called for redemption. A $2,000,000 issue of 2¾% bonds were sold to effect this redemption. The sale price was 98¾, the bonds were dated June 30, 1980 and were due in 20 years.

*Required:*

Prepare in journal form the entries necessary for the Company in connection with the transactions above, including monthly adjustments where appropriate, as of each of the following dates: (1) September 30, 1972; (2) December 31, 1972; (3) July 1, 1978; (4) December 30, 1979; (5) June 30, 1980.   (AICPA adapted)

## Problem 21-8

The board of directors of the Nelson Company authorized a $1,000,000 issue of 5% convertible 20-year bonds dated March 1, 1980. Interest is payable on March 1 and September 1 of each year. The conversion agreement provides that until March 1, 1985, each of $1,000 of bonds may be converted into 6 shares of $100 par value common stock and that interest accrued to date of conversion will be paid in cash. After March 1, 1985, each $1,000 of bonds is convertible into 5 shares of common.

The Company sold the entire bond issue on June 30, 1980, at 98 and accrued interest. Deferrable costs incurred in making the sale amounted to $8,320. The Company adjusts its books at the end of each month and closes them on December 31 of each year. Interest is paid as due. On February 1, 1982, a holder of $20,000 of bonds converts them into common stock.

You are to prepare entries in journal form to reflect the transactions arising out of the existence of these bonds on each of the following dates:

> June 30, 1980
> September 1, 1980
> December 31, 1981 (including closing entries)
> February 1, 1982
> December 31, 1982 (including closing entries)

In support of the entries above, prepare a summary analysis of the unamortized bond discount and expense account for the period to December 31, 1982.

(AICPA adapted)

## Problem 21-9

The president of the Bankrola Company, F. A. Bank, is planning to retire. By agreement with the other stockholders of the Company he will exchange his capital stock and other voting rights for nonvoting preferred stock.

The Bankrola Company has no preferred stock in its capitalization. The capital stock is held as follows:

> 100 shares held by F. A. Bank, President
> 350 shares held by J. R. Fenn, Executive Vice-President
> 150 shares held by M. A. Rola, Vice-President in charge of sales
> 150 shares held in treasury of Company
> 750 shares, total capital stock issued

21 / *Reorganizations* 679

The stockholders' equity section of the Company's statement of financial position follows:

| | |
|---|---:|
| Capital stock ($100 par value) | $ 75,000 |
| Premium on stock | 37,500 |
| Retained earnings | 17,500 |
| Total | 130,000 |
| Treasury stock, at cost | 10,000 |
| Total stockholders' equity | $120,000 |

Under the terms of the agreement the Company will be reorganized as follows:

a. The treasury stock will be cancelled.
b. Two new stock issues will be authorized, common and 5% cumulative nonvoting preferred. Both will be $100 par value per share.
c. The stockholders will surrender their capital stock for cancellation and will receive the newly authorized issues as follows:
  1. F. A. Bank will receive only preferred stock.
  2. J. R. Fenn will receive 60% of the common stock and the remainder of the preferred.
  3. M. A. Rola will receive 40% of the common.
d. The combined total number of shares of common and preferred stock outstanding after the exchange will be the same as the total number of shares authorized and outstanding before the transfer (after giving effect to the retirement of the treasury stock). *ie 600 sh total*

*Required:*
(1) Prepare the journal entry to cancel the treasury stock account on the books of the Company.
(2) Prepare a schedule computing the amount of each stockholder's equity in the Company before recapitalization.
(3) Compute the number of new common stock and new preferred stock shares to be issued.
(4) Prepare a schedule computing the number of shares of each type of newly issued stock that each stockholder must receive so that he will have the same equity in the Company after the exchange as before the exchange.

(AICPA adapted)

## Problem 21-10

Following a series of creditor committee meetings, stockholder meetings, and conferences with other individuals and management representatives, officers of the Small Corporation agreed to the following plan of action:

1. Sale of the assets of the Hoop Division to the Downey Corporation for $300,000 cash, plus $1,500,000 in 4%, 8-year notes, due June 30, 1989. Assets of the Hoop Division taken over by the Downey Corporation include, at book value:

|  |  |
|---|---|
| Inventories | $ 400,000 |
| Machinery and Equipment | 1,600,000 |
| Supplies and Parts | 50,000 |

The Downey Company also assumed the lease terms and obligations for the building that housed the Hoop Division operations.

2. Reduction in par value of the common stock outstanding from $25 per share to $10 per share, with an increase in authorized shares from 300,000 to 600,000.
3. Redemption of the outstanding 6% serial bond issue on the following terms: Payment of six months' accrued interest; redemption of the bonds at 80% face value, in cash, plus issuance of 30 shares of new common for each $1,000 bond outstanding. Existing call price covenants of the serial issue were waived by the bondholders.
4. Redemption of the outstanding $7, $100 par value preferred stock on the following terms: 1 new share of $5 convertible $100 par value preferred stock for each share of $7 preferred outstanding, plus 3 shares of new common for each share of $7 preferred stock outstanding, in lieu of three years' dividends in arrears and reduction of the dividend rate on the new preferred.
5. Issuance of 1 share of new $10 par value common stock for each share of old $25 par value common stock.
6. Discounting of the 8-year notes received from the Downey Company, at 6%, at the First National Bank.
7. Elimination of any deficit on the books of the Small Corporation at June 30, 1981.

The plan above was properly approved by all necessary groups, including the court of jurisdiction, and became effective June 30, 1981.

The Small Corporation balance sheet, after closing, but prior to implementation of the plan above, on June 30, 1981, was as follows:

THE SMALL CORPORATION

BALANCE SHEET, JUNE 30, 1981

| | | | |
|---|---|---|---|
| Cash | $ 500,000 | Current payables | $ 600,000 |
| Receivables | 610,000 | 6% Serial bonds, due | |
| Inventories | 1,350,000 | 1981 | 1,750,000 |
| Supplies and parts | 110,000 | $7 Preferred stock, par | |
| Buildings (net) | 1,200,000 | $100 | 2,000,000 |
| Machinery and equipment | 4,000,000 | Common stock, $25 par | |
| Unamort. discount on | | value, 200,000 shares | |
| bonds | 30,000 | outstanding | 5,000,000 |
| | | Retained income | |
| | | (deficit) | (1,550,000) |
| | $7,800,000 | | $7,800,000 |

## 21 / Reorganizations

*Required:*
(1) Prepare a work sheet to give effect to the plan above of reorganization, including necessary journal entries.
(2) Prepare a balance sheet for the Small Corporation, after the reorganization plan has been effected.

## Problem 21-11

The assets shown on the balance sheets at September 30, 1980 of three summer resorts on Waverly Lake are shown below. The appraisal data opposite the book values for land and depreciable assets summarize an independent appraisal made in September, 1980, as a basis for negotiations to combine the three resorts under one management. The appraisal was made on the basis of reproduction cost less depreciation.

| Description | Book Value | Appraised Value (Reproduction Cost Less Depreciation) |
|---|---|---|
| *Assets of Waverly Hotel Co.* | | |
| Current | $15,000 | — |
| Land | 5,000 | $10,000 |
| Hotel building | 12,500 | 38,000 |
| Boathouse | 600 | 2,000 |
| Kitchen equipment | 1,000 | 1,000 |
| Other equipment | 4,000 | 29,000 |
| Total | $38,100 | $80,000 |
| *Assets of Rustic Camps* (Orville Johnsen, Proprietor) | | |
| Current | $ 3,000 | — |
| Land | 1,000 | $ 1,500 |
| Lodge | 4,000 | 9,500 |
| Boathouse | 600 | 700 |
| Kitchen equipment | 2,500 | 2,500 |
| Other equipment | 1,000 | 800 |
| Total | $12,100 | $15,000 |
| *Assets of Lakeview Cottages* (Burgess & Crayton, A Partnership) | | |
| Current | $ 6,800 | — |
| Land | 3,000 | $ 1,600 |
| Lodge | 8,000 | 9,400 |
| Cottages | 15,000 | 32,000 |
| Lodge kitchen equipment | 2,000 | 2,000 |
| Other equipment | 3,500 | 5,000 |
| Total | $38,300 | $50,000 |

Total appraised value of land and
depreciable assets $145,000

Operating statements for the year ended September 30, 1980 are as follows:

|  | Waverly Hotel | Rustic Camps | Lakeview Cottages |
|---|---|---|---|
| Revenue | $17,281 | $13,698 | $8,740 |
| Deduct: | | | |
| Officers' salaries | $ 3,600 | — | — |
| Partners' drawings | — | — | $5,500 |
| Depreciation | 1,590 | $ 850 | 2,300 |
| Interest on notes | 600 | — | — |
| Other expenses | 8,112 | 5,224 | 1,868 |
| Total | $13,902 | $ 6,074 | $9,668 |
| Net income (loss) | $ 3,379 | $ 7,624 | ($ 928) |

The hotel's clientele has been declining in recent years, so Mr. Holt, the principal stockholder and manager, decided to retire. The Rustic Camp's profit is attributable to Mr. Johnsen's facility with people and knack for organized recreation. Burgess and Crayton provide light-housekeeping cottages and serve dinner in the lodge, but provide no organized recreation.

The three businesses agree to combine by organizing a new corporation, Waverly Resorts, Inc. This corporation is to have authorized capital of 2,000 shares of 5% cumulative preferred stock of $100 par value and 1,000 shares of no-par common stock. The new corporation will take over the land and depreciable assets of the three businesses. It will also take over from the hotel at $10,000 and from the partnership at $5,000 certain assets classed as current, but which are carried on their books at $10,500 and $4,800, respectively. All liabilities are to be paid off by the separate businesses and all other current assets retained by them.

In exchange for the assets acquired, the corporation is to issue to the Hotel Company $50,000 of first mortgage 4% bonds and preferred stock having $32,500 par value. Rustic Camps is to receive $25,000 of preferred stock and Lakeview Cottages is to receive $55,000 of preferred stock. The differences between the appraisal values of the properties taken over and the bonds and stock issued are to adjust for the low income earned on the hotel property and the high income that Mr. Johnsen has been receiving from his camps as a result of his ability to attract patronage.

Common stock is all to be issued and divided to the nearest share among the three businesses in the ratio of their net operating profits for the year ended September 30, 1980, adjusted as follows:

As an approximation of correct depreciation, the depreciation charges for the past year are to be recomputed. In recomputing, use rates of 4% per annum for building and 10% for equipment applied to the September 30, 1980, appraised values. The new corporation will use the 10% and 4% annual rates, applied to the balances in the asset accounts at the first of each quarter-year period.

As a result of a specific request for information as to the adequacy of past maintenance, the appraiser reported that maintenance on the hotel had been inadequate over the past 10 years to the extent of approximately $500 per year. Adjustment is to be made for the annual deficiency.

It is also agreed that for the purpose of restating profits, each business should have $3,000 a year charged as the reasonable value of the services of the officers or owners.

The businesses were combined on October 1, 1980 as planned. Transactions for the three months ended December 31, 1980 are summarized below:

Received $6,500 from guests.

Paid $1,800 to Tom and Lee Wilson, whose time was spent as follows: one-half installing equipment to convert the Rustic Camp's lodge to a bar and dance pavilion; one-third moving the camp's boathouse next to the hotel boathouse; and one-sixth moving wooden floors for tents from the camps to a location near the cottages.

Equipment for the pavilion was purchased for $1,500, of which $1,200 was paid.

The principal maintenance work needed on the hotel was done in December at a cost of $4,500. Payment for this work was made by issuing a 12-month note.

Three hundred dollars appraised value of kitchen equipment in the lodge by the cottages was moved to the hotel, and the remaining $1,700 of equipment was sold for $550.

Orville Johnsen's monthly salary of $400 was paid for October and November.

Other expenses amounted to $3,000, of which $2,750 was paid.

You are to prepare a work sheet for the Waverly Resorts, Inc., with columns showing the acquisition of the assets on October 1, 1980; the transactions from October 1 to December 31; the Income Statement figures for the three months ended December 31, and Balance Sheet figures for December 31, 1980. In a separate schedule you are to show the distribution of the common stock among the three business units. Give an explanation and justification for your treatment of any transaction where you consider the treatment to be debatable.

(AICPA adapted)

## Problem 21-12

The president of Wooddee Corporation, your client, has asked you for an explanation of a "quasi reorganization." He is unfamiliar with the procedure and is concerned that a competitor might have an advantage since undergoing a "quasi reorganization."

*Required:*

Prepare a report for the president explaining the "quasi reorganization." Your report should include the following points:
(1) Definition and accounting features of the procedure.
(2) The purpose of the procedure. Under what conditions should it be considered?
(3) Authorization necessary.
(4) Disclosure required in financial statements.
(5) Does the competitor have an advantage? Discuss briefly.

(AICPA adapted)

## Problem 21-13

The Saucer Corporation had operated on a profitable basis for a number of years prior to 1973. Starting with 1973, however, the Corporation suffered a series of loss years, and by December 31, 1979, a sizable deficit existed. Representatives of the various equity interests worked out a plan to eliminate the deficit and to effect a balance sheet that might meet with favorable reaction in efforts to raise new capital investment. The reorganization group felt that the worst was past and that the operating outlook in coming months was again favorable.

At December 31, 1979, the equity portion of the Saucer Corporation balance sheet appeared as follows:

| | |
|---|---:|
| Current liabilities | $140,000 |
| Bonds payable, 6% interest | 250,000 |
| Preferred stock, 6%, par value $100, cumulative, 2,000 shares outstanding | 200,000 |
| Common stock, $10 par value, 25,000 shares outstanding | 250,000 |
| Retained income (deficit) | (75,000) |
| | $765,000 |

The following plan was agreed on:

1. The 6% bonds payable were exchanged for new 4% bonds payable plus 20 shares of new common stock for each $1,000, 6% bond outstanding.
2. Preferred stockholders received three shares of new common stock for each share of $100 par preferred in lieu of $12,000 dividends in arrears, and in exchange for elimination of the cumulative feature from the preferred shares outstanding.
3. Each old common share, par $10, was exchanged for 3 shares of the new no-par common, stated value $2 per share, 150,000 shares authorized.
4. No asset write-downs were considered necessary at the date of reorganization, since recent review of the asset values indicated that book values were generally in line with current values. Inventory write-downs had been made periodically in recent years.

## Required:

Prepare entries to give effect to the foregoing features of the quasi reorganization. Prepare an equity section of a balance sheet as of March 31, 1980, assuming that first-quarter net income for 1980 was $2,600.

# PART FIVE:
# Liquidation of the Business Organization

# 22

# Proprietorship Liquidation

The final stage in the life cycle of a business entity, and the ultimate in the contraction of a business organization, is liquidation. Liquidation of a business enterprise includes the process of winding up business affairs, converting assets into cash, paying the various priority equity claims, and finally distributing any remaining cash or other assets among the ownership equity interests. Throughout this process the business is generally said to be in liquidation.

A business in the liquidation stage presents many peculiar accounting problems, several of which are discussed in this and succeeding chapters. By and large, most of the problems arise because one of the basic assumptions underlying accounting decisions for a "going concern" is no longer valid. This assumption, that the business entity will have an indefinite life (so-called going-concern concept), is not warranted when the business is anticipating or is involved in liquidation. Because the business no longer anticipates indefinite life, a new assumption is applied in lieu of the going-concern concept; an assumption of imminent liquidation. Subsequent portions of this book will consider the effect which the assumption of liquidation has on accounting actions and financial statements.

**Reasons for a Business Liquidation.** Liquidation of a business enterprise may take place for various reasons, some voluntary and some involuntary. A single proprietorship, for example, may well be liquidated upon the death of the owner. Death of a partner may also result in liquidation of a partnership. Completion of the predetermined term of life of a partnership or corporation will result in liquidation. In addition, the results of past business activity, if of a generally adverse nature, may produce a situation requiring liquidation. Situations such as the following may precede liquidation: (1) overextension of credit, (2) excessive stockpiling of inventories, (3) undue investment in plant and equipment, (4) excessive borrowing, and (5) continued operating losses. The results of any of the preceding situations may cause liquidation of a proprietorship, partnership, or corporation. In addition, other acts over which the business entity may not have complete control may precipitate liquidation, such as fires, floods, thefts, or fraud. Other forces working on a business organization may encourage liquidation, such as the pressure of competition, loss of markets, personality conflicts in management, and excessive government taxation or regulation. And, of course, there are times when a businessman or a group of businessmen just decide to quit and liquidate their operations and retire.

**Liquidation Procedures.** In general, the first step in the liquidation procedure is either a decision by the owner(s) of the business entity to liquidate or an act or series of acts by the business enterprise that will force liquidation. Thus the single proprietor, partners, or stockholders may decide to liquidate their business venture, or through the operation of the law, in situations such as those resulting from death or bankruptcy, the decision to liquidate is, in effect, made for the owners.

Once the decision to liquidate the enterprise has been made, the owners must make plans to provide for the realization of the business assets. Realization of the assets may proceed on a piecemeal basis over a period of time, or it may be accomplished largely or wholly through sale to one purchaser. In either event the aim is to secure as much cash, or claims to cash, as possible for the assets of the business. It should be noted that even during the period of asset realization, the enterprise may continue to conduct business somewhat as in the past, though normally on a reduced scale of operations. In fact, many times continued business activity is essential to the realization of maximum value for the assets. This is particularly true where large dollar amounts are invested in inventories at various stages of completion at the time the enterprise decides to liquidate.

Concurrently with the realization of the assets, the enterprise will gradually liquidate or pay off the various creditor claims. In some instances creditors may accept assets such as inventory, equipment, notes, or other assets in lieu of cash in settlement of their claims. Thus realization of a particular asset in cash would not occur, although realization to the extent the asset satisfies or liquidates a creditorship claim does result. No particular problems arise in the process of liquidating creditor claims, except in liquidations arising under bankruptcy statutes. Some of these problems are discussed further in a subsequent section.

When realization of assets is completed and when the various creditorship claims are settled in full, any remaining assets will be distributed among the ownership interests in the enterprise. Such distribution will be made to the owners in accordance with their various interests in the organization.

The procedure of realizing the assets, liquidating the liabilities, and distributing the excess assets among the ownership interests may take place under the supervision of the proprietor, one or several of the partners, or the management or board of directors of a corporation. Many liquidations, however, are supervised by an outside party such as an executor, a trustee, a receiver, a third party appointed by the court, or someone agreed upon by members of the business organization. The accounting problems vary somewhat with the type of supervision in a liquidation situation.

## Bankruptcy

As previously noted, business enterprises may be liquidated voluntarily by the owners or involuntarily because of action of the law or because of adverse past operating results and an inability of the enterprise to pay its debts as they mature. When an enterprise is unable to pay its maturing obligations, it is normally considered from a practical standpoint to be in an *insolvent* financial condition. Technical insolvency, however, within the framework of the National Bankruptcy Act embraces only those organizations whose aggregate liabilities exceed their assets at a fair valuation.

**Insolvency Versus Bankruptcy.** A clear distinction should be made between an insolvent business enterprise and one that is bankrupt. An organization may be insolvent in the general sense (as well as within the meaning of most state statutes) in that it cannot meet its maturing obligations. Or, it may be insolvent in the technical sense of the National Bankruptcy Act, as noted above. Neither of these conditions of insolvency means that the enterprise is necessarily bankrupt. An enterprise is not bankrupt, under the provisions of the National Bankruptcy Act, unless (1) adjudged a bankrupt, or a petition has been filed by a creditor or creditors, a petition has been filed voluntarily by the enterprise, asking that it be alleging commission of an act of bankruptcy by the enterprise; and (2) an adjudication that the enterprise is bankrupt has been delivered.

**Involuntary Bankruptcy.** The Bankruptcy Act permits any person except a municipal, railroad, insurance, or banking corporation or a building and loan association to file a petition asking to be adjudged a voluntary bankrupt. The law also permits creditors to file a petition against any natural person, except a wage earner or a farmer, any unincorporated company, and any moneyed business or commercial corporation, except a municipal, railroad, insurance, or banking corporation or a building and loan association, with debts of $1,000 or more, asking that the person be adjudged an *involuntary bankrupt*. Thus, under the Act, either the debtor may seek discharge from his debts or his creditors may seek a fair distribution of the bankrupt's assets. From an accounting viewpoint, there is little difference between a voluntary bankrupt and an involuntary bankrupt.

**Acts of Bankruptcy.** The Bankruptcy Act sets forth certain *acts of bankruptcy,* one or more of which must have been committed by the debtor within four months prior to the filing of the petition requesting adjudication as a bankrupt. It should be noted that specific acts of bankruptcy are required, and the condition of technical insolvency alone is not sufficient grounds for filing a petition for bankruptcy. A debtor has committed an act of bankruptcy if he has:

1. Conveyed, transferred, concealed, or removed, or permitted to be concealed or removed, any of his property with the intent to hinder, delay, or defraud his creditors.
2. Transferred, while insolvent, any portion of his property to one or more of his creditors with intent to prefer such creditors over his other creditors.
3. Suffered, or permitted, while insolvent, any creditor to obtain a lien upon any of his property through legal proceedings, and not having vacated or discharged such lien within 30 days, or at least within 5 days before the date set for any sale or other disposition of such property.
4. Made a general assignment for the benefit of creditors.
5. While insolvent or unable to pay his debts as they matured, procured, permitted, or suffered, voluntarily or involuntarily, the appointment of a receiver or trustee to take charge of his property.
6. Admitted in writing his inability to pay his debts and his willingness to be adjudged a bankrupt.

**General Bankruptcy Procedure.** The filing of the voluntary or involuntary petition with the bankruptcy court indicates the grounds for the petition and is the initial step in the liquidation of the business. As previously noted, liquidation of a business may frequently require a considerable period of time. Liquidation through bankruptcy proceedings is no exception. While no fixed pattern follows from the filing of a petition to be adjudged a bankrupt, the normal sequence of events would be somewhat along the following line. The court appoints a receiver or custodian to take charge of the assets of the bankrupt organization and manage its operations pending action on the petition. If the debtor is adjudged a bankrupt, either the creditors agree on a trustee or the court appoints one or more. In some cases the receiver becomes the trustee. The trustee acquires all of the bankrupt's rights, titles, and interests in property, real or personal, tangible or intangible. The trustee then proceeds with the liquidation of the enterprise under the general supervision of a *referee,* an officer appointed by the court, who reviews the activities of the trustee and authorizes the distribution of the proceeds from the sale of the bankrupt's property. Liquidation of the creditorship claims according to their rights proceeds to the extent that the realized assets permit. Further discussion of the creditors' rights and priority of liquidation is presented in Chapter Twenty-four.

Adjudication as a bankrupt of any person except a corporation operates as an application for a discharge in bankruptcy. A corporate debtor, however, may file an application for a discharge within six months after the adjudication. In the absence of any valid objections to a discharge in bankruptcy filed within a time fixed by the court, the court will grant a discharge that serves to release the bankrupt from all his provable debts except for certain debts specifically not dischargeable under the Bankruptcy Act.

Throughout the liquidation proceedings the services of accountants may be utilized frequently. Accountants may be called upon to aid in the preparation and presentation of various financial reports. In addition, accountants are frequently called upon to aid the receiver and the trustee in the proper discharge of their reporting responsibilities under the law.

**Summary.** In summary, liquidation of an enterprise through bankruptcy proceedings consists of a judicial determination that the debtor is a bankrupt, a grouping or marshaling of the debtor's assets, the realization of these assets, the distribution of the proceeds of the realization to the creditors according to their priority, and the discharge of the bankrupt from the liabilities that cannot be paid.

Not all liquidations of business organizations arise through bankruptcy proceedings. The discussion above indicates (1) that a liquidation may be voluntary or involuntary on the part of the organization, (2) that a liquidation is a time-consuming process accomplished with due care and accountability, (3) that liquidation proceedings are sometimes handled by individuals not connected with the organization, and (4) that some reasons for liquidation apply alike to proprietorships, partnerships, and corporations. Liquidations because of bankruptcy are considered further in Chapter Twenty-four, at which time an example involving a corporate bankruptcy is considered. The legal form of the business enterprise involved in bankruptcy affects only negligibly the accounting problems involved.

## LIQUIDATION OF PROPRIETORSHIPS

Single proprietorships may be liquidated for a number of reasons. The general procedure if the proprietor has been adjudged a bankrupt has already been considered. Among the other reasons for a proprietorship liquidation, death of the proprietor is probably the most prevalent. Although the proprietor's widow, children, or other relatives may continue operation of the business, death of the proprietor frequently causes liquidation of the business. This is particularly true when there are numerous heirs, each of whom is to share in the estate of the proprietor.

### Liquidation Because of Death of the Proprietor

The death of any person normally creates a problem of control and administration of the property of the deceased until appropriate distribution of such property can be made. The problem may be more complicated, however, when the deceased is the owner of a going business. As in the case where a proprietor is adjudged a bankrupt, liquidation of a proprietorship because of the death of the owner frequently requires considerable time.

Various legal procedures must be observed, and during this period the property of the deceased must be conserved and administered according to the provision of the will of the deceased and good business practice.

**Role of the Accountant.** Occasionally an accountant will be called upon for advice or to take charge of the accountability for the property involved. Because of his financial background, the accountant is often in a position to give helpful advice on matters relating to valuation and realization of assets and on matters dealing with the optimum manner of liquidating liabilities. In addition, accountants are being called upon with increasing frequency in connection with estate planning of individuals, both with and without ownership interests in going business organizations. Thus the accountant should be familiar with the more important laws and legal decisions relating to the administration of estates.

**General Legal Procedures.** If the decedent has left a will directing the disposal of his estate, he is said to have died *testate,* and the property should be disposed of in accordance with the terms of the will. If he has left no will, he is said to have died *intestate,* and the property should be disposed of in accordance with the *laws of descent and distribution*. The law of descent governs the disposition of real property, whereas the law of distribution governs the disposition of personal property. For a will to become operative, it must be *probated* or proved in a court of probate jurisdiction. Such a court is variously known as a *probate, surrogate,* or *orphan's* court. This court governs the administration and disposition of the decedent's property.

If the decedent has left a will, he normally will have named therein an individual to serve as *executor* (or *executrix*) of the estate. The executor is expected to carry out the terms of the will. If no executor is named in the will, or if the person named is not satisfactory to the court, the court will appoint an *administrator* (or *administratress*) to settle the estate. His duties are similar to those of an executor.

**Duties of Executor.** The executor or administrator obtains control of the property of the decedent upon admission of the will to probate. The executor must first take an inventory of the property of the decedent, as he will be accountable for such property. He must likewise establish records that will permit him to keep the estate properties separate from his own. If the decedent owned a business that is to be liquidated, the executor would normally value the business assets according to the values expressed on the books of the owner. The original valuation by the executor is made primarily to get a complete listing of the items of property owned and is later adjusted upward or downward to reflect fair values of the various inventoriable items. The eventual valuation of the business property may depend largely on whether the business is to be sold piecemeal or as a going concern.

During the administration of the estate, the executor is expected to continue to seek out and take possession of any property belonging to the estate. He is expected to manage prudently all properties coming under his control and to protect and conserve such properties until they are realized and utilized in settlement of debts arising from the estate or in satisfaction of the terms of the will or laws of the state involved.

The executor also has the responsibility of paying various debts and obligations of the decedent. Most state laws fix a limited period within which creditors must file their claims or otherwise forfeit any legal rights they have against the estate. The executor should exercise care in examining all claims against the estate and should liquidate only those which are valid. If the properties of the estate are not sufficient to meet all liabilities, the applicable state laws will indicate the priority of payment. In general, the following priority is applicable: (1) funeral and administrative expenses, including expenses connected with the last illness and with the administration of the estate, (2) certain allowances to support and maintain the decedent's family for a limited period, (3) debts entitled to preference under laws of the United States and of the state, (4) government claims and taxes, (5) any judgment creditors, and (6) all other debts.

***Realization and Liquidation by an Executor.*** The executor normally realizes the properties and liquidates the valid claims against the estate. Many times only properties sufficient to pay the claims against the estate are realized, the remaining properties being maintained for distribution among the heirs of the estate. On other occasions all properties may be realized in cash prior to distribution to the heirs. In any event, the executor pays the claims against the estate and then takes steps to distribute the remaining properties. Personal property disposed of in accordance with the will is known as a *legacy* or *bequest*. Real property disposed of in accordance with the will is known as a *devise*. The will may provide for specific *legacies* (e.g., an automobile to a son), *demonstrative legacies* (e.g., $1,000 out of the First National Bank account to the gardener), *general legacies* (e.g., $5,000 to the State University), and *residuary legacies* (includes all personal property remaining after payment of other legacies).

The executor normally takes title to all personal property of the decedent except life insurance proceeds when the beneficiary is other than the estate. In addition, the executor takes title to real estate of the decedent if the terms of the will so provide or if the court orders sale of the real estate to provide funds to pay existing debts. Thus the executor would take title to all business property of a proprietorship (including inventory, fixed assets, etc.) except the real estate and would, in some cases, take title to the latter as well. The executor must account for all properties with care and must also recognize that estate expenses and debts of the decedent take priority over legacies stipulated in the will. If the executor should distribute assets as legacies and then be unable to meet estate or creditor claims, he may be held personally liable to the unsatisfied creditors.

Consequently, an executor should itemize with care the various creditorship claims against the estate of a deceased, both personal and business. If the payment of various claims does not leave a sufficient amount of assets to pay all legacies provided for in the will, the terms of the will are met by a scaling down (*abatement*) of legacies in the following order: (1) residuary legacies, (2) general legacies, (3) demonstrative and specific legacies. As mentioned above, when the personal property is insufficient to satisfy the claims of the estate, the court may approve the sale, mortgage, or lease of any real property owned by the decedent.

## Accounting for Estate Liquidation

As previously emphasized, an executor must maintain careful records of any property that he controls for the settlement of the estate. The accounts that an executor should maintain are based upon a different accounting equation from the one that applies to commercial operations. The executor is interested in safeguarding the property, realizing proceeds from its sale, and distributing the property or its proceeds in accordance with the will or the state law. Thus the set of accounts should show the property over which the executor has control and his disposition of that property. The equation

$$\text{Assets} = \text{Accountability}$$

is more appropriate to the executor's records than the standard equation

$$\text{Assets} = \text{Equities}$$

**Opening Accountability Records.** The executor opens his books by recording the properties of the estate to which he takes title. The various properties should be recorded in appropriately named asset accounts at the valuations shown by the inventory prepared by the executor and accepted by the court. Sufficient accounts should be maintained to permit a proper classification of the assets. The executor's accountability should be recorded initially in an account normally called "Estate Corpus" or "Estate Principal." Subsequent changes in his accountability should be recorded in separate accounts. Thus, if additional assets are discovered after recording the initial inventory, the executor should debit an appropriate asset account and credit an accountability account normally called "Assets Subsequently Discovered." Even though this latter account is an accountability account, similar to Estate Corpus, the use of a separate account is desirable since it facilitates the preparation of the executor's reports to the court. Instead of having to analyze several entries in the Estate Corpus account to determine how his accountability has changed during his executorship, the executor can use the various supplementary accountability accounts to provide this information. No liabilities of the decedent are recorded at the time the executor assumes control of the decedent's properties. However, liquidation of liabilities will necessitate an entry. This requirement applies to liquidation of liabilities of the proprietorship which the deceased owned as well as to liquidation of the decedent's personal obligations.

**Entries in Accountability Records.** The executor's accountability changes whenever an asset is sold at a gain or a loss. When an asset is disposed of, the asset account should be credited at its carrying value, a new asset account debited, and any gain should be credited to an account such as "Gain on Realization," and any loss debited to an account such as "Loss on Realization." Both the gain and the loss accounts are accountability accounts similar in nature to Assets Subsequently Discovered.

When the executor settles or liquidates any of the claims against the deceased or claims arising from estate operations, he should credit the appropriate asset and debit an accountability account. Thus, if funeral or administrative expenses are paid, instead of charging Estate Corpus, the executor should charge an appropriately named expense account. In small estates one account, sometimes titled

"Funeral and Administrative Expense," is used. In larger or complex estates the executor may wish to use several accounts for the several types of administrative expenses that arise.

When the executor settles liabilities incurred by the decedent, either through his business operations or his personal activities, the accountability of the executor is likewise decreased. An entry is necessary, crediting the asset used and debiting an account such as "Debts of Decedent Paid," including the name of the creditor, as "Debts of Decedent Paid—Jones Produce Co." If numerous creditors exist, the Debts of Decedent Paid account may serve as a controlling account. In any event, the account will provide the executor with information necessary to satisfy his reporting responsibilities as to the discharge of his accountability.

In addition to discharging his accountability for the decedent's property through liquidation of the various claims against the estate, the executor also decreases his accountability through payment of legacies. As legacies are paid, the executor charges an account such as "Legacies Paid" and credits the asset transferred to the legatee. Depending upon the number of legacies involved, the executor may wish to use several accounts for the legacies paid. While legacies may be paid any time after the executor takes charge of the estate, payment of legacies should normally be deferred until the executor has determined that the estate is sufficient to pay existing debts. Payment of legacies that reduce the estate below an amount sufficient to pay debts of the decedent and the estate may involve the executor in personal liability to creditors.

The new accounts discussed above—Assets Subsequently Discovered, Gain on Realization, Loss on Realization, Funeral and Administrative Expenses, Debts of Decedent Paid, Legacies Paid—are all temporary accountability accounts designed to provide the executor with necessary reporting information. After his report has been accepted by the court, the executor closes these accounts to Estate Corpus.

**Pro Forma Entries for Estate Liquidation.** The preceding sections introduced several accounts peculiar to estate accounting. The following entries summarize relatively common transactions arising in the liquidation of an estate.

($a$) Dr. Assets (various)    xxxx
    Cr. Estate corpus (or Estate principal)    xxxx
  (to record assumption by the executor of responsibility for estate assets)

($b$) Dr. Assets (specific asset discovered)    xxxx
    Cr. Assets subsequently discovered    xxxx
  (to record discovery of an asset not known to exist at inventory date)

($c$) Dr. Asset (newly acquired)    xxxx
    Cr. Asset (at inventory carrying value)    xxxx
      Gain on realization    xx
  (to record disposition of an asset in inventory, at a gain)

($d$) Dr. Asset (newly acquired)    xxxx
    Loss on realization    xx

|  |  |  |  |
|---|---|---|---|
|  | Cr. Asset (at inventory carrying value) |  | xxxx |
|  | (to record disposition of an asset in inventory, at a loss) |  |  |
| (e) | Dr. Funeral and administrative expense | xxxx |  |
|  | Cr. Assets (Cash, generally) |  | xxxx |
|  | (to record payment of funeral and administrative expenses) |  |  |
| (f) | Dr. Debts of decedent paid | xxxx |  |
|  | Cr. Assets (Cash, generally) |  | xxxx |
|  | (to record payment of liabilities incurred by the decedent) |  |  |
| (g) | Cr. Assets (various) |  | xxxx |
|  | Dr. Legacies paid |  | xxxx |
|  | (to record payment of legacies as provided in the will) |  |  |
| (h) | Dr. Gain on realization | xx |  |
|  | Estate corpus | xxxx |  |
|  | Cr. Loss on realization |  | xx |
|  | Funeral and administrative expense |  | xxxx |
|  | Debts of decedent paid |  | xxxx |
|  | Legacies paid |  | xxxx |
|  | (to close temporary accountability accounts to "Estate corpus" *after* executor's report is submitted) |  |  |

**Estate Principal Versus Estate Income.** While the primary purpose of an executor is to conserve the assets of the decedent and to liquidate the estate, the executor frequently must account for transactions that may involve income (expense) on estate assets. The distinction between estate principal (or estate corpus) and income is particularly important if the will of the decedent provides that part or all of the principal of the estate should be maintained by a trustee (the executor or a different party), with the income from the assets of the trust going to one class of beneficiaries during a given period of time and with the estate principal eventually passing over to another class of beneficiaries at a later date. Although accounting for the operations of a trust is not under consideration at this time, the importance of a clear distinction between principal and income warrants further discussion.

The executor (or trustee) should maintain records that will distinguish principal and income. Thus, any income from estate assets should be credited to an income account, or accounts, the numbers of which will depend upon the variety of incomes that the estate generates. Likewise, expenses deductible from income may be charged to one account, generally called "Expense-Income," or to as many separate accounts as the executor deems necessary. Any cash collected from income and later distributed to beneficiaries should be charged to an account such as "Distributions to Income Beneficiaries."

**Estate Principal and Income Problems.** Certain problems arise in distinguishing between estate principal and income. If the trust provisions provide specifically for a method of distinguishing principal and income, the provisions of the trust must be followed. If the trust makes no provision for distinguishing principal and income, the appropriate state law or ruling of the court must be followed. While it is difficult to generalize because of the variety of state laws and court rulings, the following statements suggest some of the general rules governing the apportionment of estate property between principal and income:

1. Interest generally accrues, with interest accrued up to and including the date of death of the decedent being considered principal, and interest accruing subsequent to the date of death being considered income.
2. Dividends do not accrue. Cash dividends declared prior to the date of death are generally principal, and dividends in cash declared subsequent to the date of death are income. The date of collection is not significant. *Ordinary* stock dividends are commonly treated in a manner similar to that used for cash dividends. *Extraordinary* cash or stock dividends may be similarly treated or may be subject to apportionment between principal and income. The apportionment of an extraordinary dividend is made in such a manner that the book value of the stock after the payment of the dividend, plus the portion of the dividend allocated to principal, is equal to the book value at the date of death.
3. Rents become due on the rent date. Rents due prior to the date of death are principal, and rents falling due after death are income.
4. Taxes generally do not accrue, but are payable out of principal if the assessment became a lien prior to death, and payable out of income if the assessment became a lien subsequent to death.
5. Other possible accruals are generally handled in a manner that relates the item to the passage of time. If the item involved accrues in a reasonably direct relationship to the passage of time, in general it will be accrued on this basis for estate purposes. If such accrual-time relationship does not exist, there will normally have to be a determination of the status of the item at the date of death. For example, partnership profits do not accrue but must be determined as of the date of death unless provided for otherwise in the partnership agreement.

**Classification of Estate Expenditures.** A problem related to the distinction between principal and income concerns the classification of certain expenditures made by the executor or the trustee. Some of the expenditures mentioned previously are properly chargeable against principal, such as debts of decedent, expenses of the decedent's last illness, and funeral and administrative expenses. Other expenditures generally chargeable to principal include various legal fees, costs of probating the will, defending it against various claimants, and preserving the principal of the estate. In addition, federal and state estate and inheritance taxes are generally chargeable against principal.

Ordinary operating expenses of the estate are normally chargeable against the income of the estate and, as mentioned earlier, these items should be charged to an account such as "Expense-Income" or to several such accounts. Expenditures falling within this area include ordinary repairs, fees for collection and distribution of income, wages of people caring for the property, legal fees arising from matters pertaining to earning income, and generally insurance premiums on income-producing property.

Many varied problems may arise in the area of distinguishing principal and income because of the wide variety of properties that may comprise an estate. The proper treatment of specific items frequently requires reference to the intentions of the decedent, to applicable state and federal laws, and to court rulings. Because of the possibility of differences of opinion on the treatment of many items of receipt and expenditure for an estate, it is essential that the executor or trustee maintain careful records detailing the treatment accorded the various items.

## Accounting for Proprietorship Liquidation

Proprietorships are, of course, liquidated for reasons other than bankruptcy or death of the owner, as discussed in preceding sections. For example, a proprietor may merely tire of continuing in business and decide either to sell his business or to liquidate. In either situation, the accounting problems involved are not particularly complex. The liquidation process may cover a considerable period of time during which operations proceed in a more or less normal fashion, although possibly on a reduced scale. During the liquidation period sales and purchases are normally accounted for as in the usual operations. Disposal of non-inventoriable assets will normally involve gains or losses, but accounting for these gains and losses is no different from that encountered in normal business operations.

When a business proprietorship is to be liquidated because of the death of the proprietor, a dual accounting problem arises. One aspect relates to the accounting for the business assets, and the problems here are no different from those arising in a liquidation for other reasons. The other aspect relates to the accounting for personal assets. The problem here is that of estate accounting, and one of the inventoriable assets of the estate would be the decedent's equity in his business. Although the illustrative situation that follows combines the two problems of accounting for the liquidation of a proprietorship and for the estate of the deceased proprietor, it should be recognized that either aspect of the problem could exist separately from the other.

The following liquidation situation illustrates some of the accounting and reporting procedures involved in the liquidation of a proprietorship because of the death of the proprietor. The accounting records of the proprietorship should be closed as of the date of death in order to establish accountability at that date. The executor should maintain records sufficient to enable the court to determine whether or not he has fulfilled his fiduciary responsibility. Assume that the following statement of financial position was taken from the ledger of James Andrews, Grocer, as of October 8, 1979, the date of the death of Mr. Andrews.

In his will Mr. Andrews named D. F. Keck, a close personal friend, as executor of his estate. Andrews was married and had four children, three of whom were married, but none of whom had an active part in his business. His widow and all children survive. His will included the following provisions:

1. Household effects and automobile to his widow.
2. Cash of $5,000 to each married child; cash of $3,000 to his single child; cash of $1,000 to D. F. Keck, in lieu of fee for services as executor.
3. Remainder to his widow.

JAMES ANDREWS, GROCER
FINANCIAL POSITION
OCTOBER 8, 1979

ASSETS

| | | | | |
|---|---|---|---|---|
| *Current assets:* | | | | |
| Cash in bank | | | | $ 3,400 |
| Petty cash | | | | 100 |
| Accounts receivable | | | | 1,600 |
| Inventory | | | | 31,880 |
| Unexpired insurance | | | | 120 |
| Total current assets | | | | $37,100 |
| *Fixed assets:* | | | | |
| | Cost | Accumulated Depreciation | Net | |
| Showcases and fixtures | $ 2,800 | $1,700 | $ 1,100 | |
| Refrigeration equipment | 7,200 | 3,200 | 4,000 | |
| Total | $10,000 | $4,900 | | 5,100 |
| TOTAL ASSETS | | | | $42,200 |

EQUITIES

| | | |
|---|---|---|
| *Liabilities:* | | |
| Accounts payable | | $ 4,200 |
| Notes payable to bank | | 5,000 |
| Total liabilities | | $ 9,200 |
| *Owners' equity:* | | |
| James Andrews, Equity, 1/1/79 | $30,470 | |
| Net profit through 10/8/79 | 2,530 | |
| James Andrews, Equity, 10/8/79 | | 33,000 |
| TOTAL EQUITIES | | $42,200 |

It was decided to liquidate the grocery business. November 30, 1979, was set as a target date for completing the sale of the inventory and other assets. In order to facilitate the liquidation of the business, the heirs agreed to apply to the court to have Mr. Keck appointed temporary administrator of the estate. Approval was received and the operations of the store were continued October 9 without having to await probating of the will some 10 days later. Keck agreed that the statement of financial position as of October 8 would serve as the basis for inclusion of the business equity in the inventory of assets filed with the court subject to final approval by the executor. Keck also authorized Mr. Andrews' butcher to wind up the store affairs under his supervision.

On the following pages the events in the liquidation process are presented. The executor records the equity of the business as it is reflected on the books of the business. The executor's records need not reflect in detail each step in the liquidation process, but they should reveal what has transpired each time he makes a report to the court. On the other hand, the books of the store should reflect the step-by-step process in the liquidation of the grocery business. The illustration does not include consideration of any federal or state income, inheritance, or estate taxes. The tax laws applicable in the jurisdiction involved would require the attention of the executor.

### Events in the Liquidation of the James Andrews Estate

(1) Oct. 9 — Court approved D. F. Keck as a temporary administrator.

(2) Oct. 19 — The will was admitted to probate and D. F. Keck was duly approved (issued letters testamentary) to act as executor.

(3) Oct. 22 — The executor filed the following inventory with the court:

| | |
|---|---:|
| Cash | $ 1,200 |
| Life insurance, payable to the estate | 15,000 |
| Co. X bonds (5%) | 2,400 |
| Accrued interest on Co. X bonds, July 1 to October 7 | 32 |
| Y Co. preferred stock | 1,000 |
| Z Co. common stock | 3,400 |
| Household effects | 2,600 |
| Automobile | 1,900 |
| Equity in grocery business (*a*) | 33,000 |
| Total | $60,532 |

(*a*) Amount equals equity per statement of financial position as of October 8, 1979. The books of the grocery business were closed as of October 8, 1979, to establish the cut-off point for the executor's responsibility.

(4) Oct. 22 — A summary of grocery store operations since death includes the following: cash sales, $9,000; collections on account, $700; purchases for cash, $1,200; payments on account, $3,000; payments of expenses, including salaries, $700.

(5) Oct. 25 — The executor collected the $15,000 life insurance.

(6) Nov. 1 — Y Company stock was sold for $1,100.

(7) Nov. 3 — Paid various liabilities filed against the estate:

| | |
|---|---:|
| Jones Auto Repair | $65 |
| Gorman Haberdashery | 90 |

(8) Nov. 5 — Summary of grocery store operations since 10/22/79: cash sales, $13,000; collections on account, $800; purchases for cash, $2,100; payments on account, $1,200; payment of notes, $5,000; payment of expenses, including interest on notes, $750.

(9) Nov. 8 — Sold X Company bonds for $2,200, plus accrued interest of $42.

## 22 / Proprietorship Liquidation

(10) Nov. 10—Received dividend on Z Company stock, declared October 10, 1979, $150.
(11) Nov. 12—Discovered a savings account having a balance of $860.
(12) Nov. 15—Paid funeral expenses, $400.
(13) Nov. 16—Paid various administrative and legal expenses, $150.
(14) Nov. 18—Executor turned over household furniture and automobile to the widow. He also paid her $100 cash.
(15) Nov. 19—Summary of store operations since November 5, 1979: cash sales, $7,000; collections on account, $60; purchases for cash, $1,600; payments of expenses, $500.
(16) Nov. 26—Received $10,000 from grocery store account.
(17) Nov. 27—Paid legacies to the four children, as provided in the will.
(18) Nov. 30—Final report on store operations showed the following: cash sales, $8,500; purchases for cash, $800; payments of expenses, $900; sale of showcases, fixtures, etc., $500; sale of refrigeration equipment, $5,500; refund on insurance, $50; cash balance transferred to Estate Cash account.
(19) Nov. 30—Executor received his $1,000 bequest and rendered his report to the court.

Presented below are cash journals and a general journal in which the executor might have recorded the events listed above. Events 1, 2, 4, 8, and 15 would not require any entries in the executor's journals. Entries for all other events numbered may be found by reference to the various journals. Events 4, 8, 15, 16, and 18 would require entries in the grocery store records, and these entries are presented following the executor's journals.

### D. F. KECK
#### EXECUTOR'S JOURNAL

|   |   |   | Dr. | Cr. |
|---|---|---|-----|-----|
| (3) | Oct. 22 | Cash—Principal (√) | $ 1,200 | |
| | | Insurance policies | 15,000 | |
| | | Co. X. bonds | 2,400 | |
| | | Interest receivable | 32 | |
| | | Y Co. preferred stock | 1,000 | |
| | | Z Co. common stock | 3,400 | |
| | | Household effects | 2,600 | |
| | | Automobile | 1,900 | |
| | | Equity in grocery business | 33,000 | |
| | |     Estate corpus | | $60,532 |
| | | (to record assets, per inventory) | | |
| (14) | Nov. 18 | Legacies paid—Mrs. Andrews | $4,500 | |
| | |     Household effects | | $ 2,600 |
| | |     Automobile | | 1,900 |
| | | (payment of legacy, as provided in will) | | |

## D. F. Keck Executor's Cash Receipts Journal

| Date | | L.F. | Account Credited | Explanation | Principal Credit | Loss | Gain | Cash | Income Cash |
|---|---|---|---|---|---|---|---|---|---|
| (3) Oct. | 22 | (✓) | Estate corpus | Cash, per inventory | $ 1,200 | | | $ 1,200 | |
| (5) " | 25 | | Insurance policies | Face of policies collected | 15,000 | | | 15,000 | |
| (6) Nov. | 1 | | Y Co. preferred stock | Sold | 1,000 | | $100 | 1,100 | |
| (9) " | 8 | | Co. X bonds | Sold | 2,400 | $ 200 | | 2,200 | |
| (9) " | 8 | | Interest receivable | Interest collected | 32 | | | 32 | |
| (9) " | 8 | | Income | Interest from 10/8/79 | | | | | $ 10 |
| (10) " | 10 | | Income | Dividend on Z Co. stock | | | | | 150 |
| (11) " | 12 | | Assets subsequently discovered | Savings account discovered | 860 | | | 860 | |
| (16) " | 26 | | Equity in grocery business | Transfer of cash | 10,000 | | | 10,000 | |
| (18) " | 30 | | Equity in grocery business | Transfer of cash (final) | 23,000 | 2,140 | | 20,860 | |
| | | | | | $53,492 | $2,340 | $100 | $51,252 | $160 |

## D. F. Keck Executor's Cash Disbursements Journal

| Date | | L.F. | Account Debited | Explanation | Principal | Income |
|---|---|---|---|---|---|---|
| (7) Nov. | 3 | | Debts of decedent paid | Jones Auto Repair | $ 65 | |
| (7) " | 3 | | Debts of decedent paid | Gorman Haberdashery | 90 | |
| (12) " | 15 | | Funeral expenses | Funeral expenses | 400 | |
| (13) " | 16 | | Administrative expenses | Administrative and legal expenses | 150 | |
| (14) " | 18 | | Distributions to income beneficiary | Payment of cash to widow | | $100 |
| (17) " | 27 | | Legacies paid | Cash payments to children, per will | 18,000 | |
| (19) " | 30 | | Legacies paid | D. F. Keck, for services | 1,000 | |
| | | | | | $19,705 | $100 |

## 22 / Proprietorship Liquidation

Entries to be made on the books of the Andrews Grocery Store giving effect to the liquidation:

| | | | | |
|---|---|---|---|---|
| (4) | Oct. 22 | Cash | $ 9,700 | |
| | | Purchases | 1,200 | |
| | | Accounts payable | 3,000 | |
| | | Expenses | 700 | |
| | |     Cash | | $ 4,900 |
| | |     Sales | | 9,000 |
| | |     Accounts receivable | | 700 |
| (8) | Nov. 5 | Cash | $13,800 | |
| | | Purchases | 2,100 | |
| | | Accounts payable | 1,200 | |
| | | Notes payable | 5,000 | |
| | | Expenses | 750 | |
| | |     Cash | | $ 9,050 |
| | |     Sales | | 13,000 |
| | |     Accounts receivable | | 800 |
| (15) | Nov. 19 | Cash | $ 7,060 | |
| | | Purchases | 1,600 | |
| | | Expenses | 500 | |
| | |     Cash | | $ 2,100 |
| | |     Sales | | 7,000 |
| | |     Accounts receivable | | 60 |
| (16) | Nov. 26 | James Andrews, Equity | $10,000 | |
| | |     Cash | | $10,000 |
| (18) | Nov. 30 | Cash | $14,550 | |
| | | Purchases | 800 | |
| | | Expenses | 900 | |
| | |     Cash | | $ 1,700 |
| | |     Sales | | 8,500 |
| | |     Showcases and fixtures | | 500 |
| | |     Refrigeration equipment | | 5,500 |
| | |     Unexpired insurance | | 50 |
| | 30 | Expenses (loss on receivables and unexpired insurance) | $ 110 | |
| | | Accumulated depreciation— | | |
| | |   Showcases and fixtures | 1,700 | |
| | | Accumulated depreciation— | | |
| | |   Refrigeration equipment | 3,200 | |
| | |     Accounts receivable | | $ 40 |
| | |     Showcases and fixtures | | 2,300 |
| | |     Refrigeration equipment | | 1,700 |
| | |     Unexpired insurance | | 70 |
| | |     Gain on sale of equipment | | 900 |

(to write off remaining uncollectible accounts and unexpired insurance; to remove remaining asset and allowance balances and take up gain on sale from previous transaction)

| | | | | |
|---|---|---|---|---|
| 30 | James Andrews, Equity | $ 2,140 | | |
| | Sales | 37,500 | | |
| | Gain on sale of equipment | 900 | | |
| | Inventory | | $31,880 | |
| | Purchases | | 5,700 | |
| | Expenses | | 2,960 | |

(to close the cost, expense, and income accounts and the loss on liquidation to the capital account)

| | | | | |
|---|---|---|---|---|
| 30 | James Andrews, Equity | $20,860 | | |
| | Cash | | $20,760 | |
| | Petty cash | | 100 | |

(to record transfer of cash from grocery business to executor)

## Executor's Report to the Court

The exact form of the statements that an executor will render is generally prescribed by the court to which he will report. An example of a charge and discharge statement based upon the preceding facts is presented below. Requirements of this type of report vary from state to state, and as a result several variations in form may be found. The statements presented below indicate the information which a fiduciary (executor or administrator) is generally required to submit, although not necessarily in the form in which the information would be submitted.

ESTATE OF JAMES ANDREWS

D. F. KECK, EXECUTOR

CHARGE AND DISCHARGE STATEMENT

AS TO PRINCIPAL

OCTOBER 8, 1979 TO NOVEMBER 30, 1979

*I Charge Myself with*

| | | |
|---|---|---|
| Assets per inventory (Schedule A) | | $60,532 |
| Assets subsequently discovered—savings account | | 860 |
| Gain on realization of assets (Schedule B) | | 100 |
| Total Charges | | $61,492 |

*I Credit Myself with:*

| | | |
|---|---|---|
| Debts of decedent paid (Schedule C) | $ 155 | |
| Funeral expenses | 400 | |

|  |  |  |
|---|---:|---:|
| Administrative expenses | 150 | |
| Legacies paid (Schedule D) | 23,500 | |
| Loss on realization of assets (Schedule B) | 2,340 | |
| Total credits | | 26,545 |
| Balance as to principal | | $34,947 |
| Balance consists of: | | |
| Z Co. common stock | $ 3,400 | |
| Cash | 31,547 | |
| Total | $34,947 | |

*Schedule A*

### Assets per Inventory, October 8, 1979

| | |
|---|---:|
| Cash | $ 1,200 |
| Insurance policies | 15,000 |
| Co. X bonds | 2,400 |
| Interest receivable | 32 |
| Y Co. preferred stock | 1,000 |
| Z Co. common stock | 3,400 |
| Household effects | 2,600 |
| Automobile | 1,900 |
| Equity in grocery business | 33,000 |
| Total assets per inventory | $60,532 |

*Schedule B*

### Realization of Assets

| | Per Inventory | Cash on Realization | Gain | Loss |
|---|---:|---:|---:|---:|
| Insurance policies | $15,000 | $15,000 | | |
| Y Co. preferred stock | 1,000 | 1,100 | $100 | |
| Co. X bonds | 2,400 | 2,200 | | $ 200 |
| Interest receivable | 32 | 32 | | |
| Equity in grocery business (See Schedule B-1) | 33,000 | 30,860 | | 2,140 |
| | $51,432 | $49,192 | $100 | $2,340 |

*Schedule B-1*

### Summary of James Andrews Grocery Business Liquidation
### October 8, 1979 to November 30, 1979

| | | | |
|---|---:|---:|---:|
| Equity per inventory | | | $33,000 |
| Sales | | $37,500 | |
| Less cost of sales: | | | |
| Inventory | $31,880 | | |
| Purchases | 5,700 | | |

|  |  |  |
|---|---:|---:|
| Cost of goods sold | | 37,580 |
| Gross loss on sales | | $(  80) |
| Expenses: | | |
|   Uncollectible receivables | $    40 | |
|   Insurance expired | 70 | |
|   Various | 2,850 | |
|     Total expenses | | $ 2,960 |
| Net operating loss | | $(3,040) |
| Gain on disposal of assets | | 900 |
| Net loss | | (2,140) |
| Equity of grocery business, as realized | | $30,860 |

*Schedule C*

### Debts of Decedent Paid

| | |
|---|---:|
| Jones Auto Repair | $   65 |
| Gorman Haberdashery | 90 |
|   Total | $  155 |

*Schedule D*

### Legacies Paid

|  |  |  |
|---|---:|---:|
| Mrs. James Andrews: | | |
|   Household Effects | $2,600 | |
|   Automobile | 1,900 | $ 4,500 |
| Tom Andrews | | 5,000 |
| Richard Andrews | | 5,000 |
| Harry Andrews | | 5,000 |
| Vernon Andrews | | 3,000 |
| D. F. Keck | | 1,000 |
|   Total | | $23,500 |

Estate of James Andrews
D. F. Keck, Executor
Charge and Discharge Statement
as to Income
October 8, 1979 to November 30, 1979

| | |
|---|---:|
| *I Charge Myself with:* | |
|   Interest on Co. X bonds, October 8, 1979, | |
|     to November 8, 1979 | $    10 |
|   Dividends received on Z Co., common stock | 150 |
|     Total Charges | $  160 |
| *I Credit Myself with:* | |
|   Distribution to income beneficiary, | |
|     Mrs. J. Andrews | 100 |
| Balance as to income | $    60 |
| Balance consists of: Cash | $   60 |

## PROBLEMS

### Problem 22-1

Prepare entries in general journal form to record the following events relating to the estate of L. Johnson, who died October 1, 1979.

a. Semi-annual interest is collected on the 5% bonds of the A Company, face value $30,000. One-third of this interest had accrued at the date of death and was included in the inventory of the estate.
b. The executor sold bonds of the B Company, face value $10,000, interest 6%, for 104 and two months accrued interest. These bonds were valued at $10,250 at the date of the inventory. Date of the sale was December 1, 1979.
c. The executor sold some of the decedent's personal effects for $500. These items had been included in the inventory of the estate at a value of $125.
d. The executor sold 200 shares of the Acme Corporation common stock for $60 per share, plus a $.50 dividend. The dividend was declared on October 6, 1979. The stock was carried in the inventory at $12,400.
e. A dividend check for $100 was received on November 6 relating to 100 shares of the Greater Corporation common stock. Investigation revealed that this stock was in a locked box, the existence of which was unknown until November 6. The stock had a value of $8,000 at October 1, 1979, and the dividend declaration was September 20, 1979.

### Problem 22-2

On July 20, 1980, A. N. Phillip died, leaving the following items in his estate. G. Vance was named executor.

| | |
|---|---:|
| Cash in checking account | $ 1,450 |
| Cash in savings account | 2,475 |
| Automobile | 2,600 |
| Household effects | 1,750 |
| Stock in GD Co., 400 shares | 14,400 |
| Bonds of AB Co., face value $8,000 | 8,075 |
| U.S. Savings Bonds, Series E, valued at | 9,275 |

Mr. Phillip's will provided for the following legacies:

| | |
|---|---:|
| To his son, Andrew: Cash | $ 2,000 |
|     Automobile | |
|     200 shares of GD Stock | |
| To University Achievement Fund: | $ 2,500 |
| To his widow: Remainder of the estate | |

During the period in which the executor administered the estate, the following transactions occurred:

1. Funeral expenses were paid, $950.
2. U.S. Savings Bonds, Series E, were redeemed for $9,350.

3. Debts of the decedent were paid, $2,150.
4. A dividend of $120 was received on the GD stock.
5. The legacy to the University Achievement Fund was paid.
6. The legacy to the son, Andrew, was distributed.
7. Interest on the AB Co. bonds was collected, $200, ¾ earned subsequent to the date of death.
8. Administrative fees and expenses of the executor, $1,200 were approved and paid.
9. The balance of the estate was turned over to the widow, December 1, 1980.

*Required:*
Prepare journal entries to record the events above for the executor.

## Problem 22-3

On June 10, 1980, J. B. Whitson, a retired businessman, died, leaving the following assets in his estate:

| | |
|---|---|
| Cash in 2nd National Bank | $ 7,240 |
| Preferred stock of Gable Corp., 200 shares | 20,000 |
| 1979 automobile, valued at | 3,100 |
| Life insurance policies payable to the estate | 25,000 |
| U.S. Government Bonds, face value $10,000 | 8,975 |
| Household effects | 1,050 |

The items above were included in the inventory filed with the court, and the following events subsequently took place:

a. Various liabilities owed by Whitson as of June 10, 1980, were paid, totaling $3,400.
b. An additional certificate for 20 shares of preferred stock of the Gable Corporation was discovered. The stock had a value of $100 per share at June 10, 1980.
c. Funeral and other related expenses of $1,450 were paid.
d. A dividend of $1.25 per share was received on the Gable Corporation preferred stock. The dividend was declared June 30, 1980.
e. The U.S. Government bonds were redeemed for $9,035. The difference in redemption price and inventory value represents interest earned after the date of the inventory.
f. One-half the Gable Corporation preferred stock was sold at 101½.
g. Personal property taxes of $42 were paid. These taxes related to the automobile and had been assessed in April, 1980.

*Required:*
Prepare entries in general journal form to record the foregoing events relating to the estate of Mr. Whitson.

## Problem 22-4

Robert Hill died on August 10, 1980, and his will designated Richard Hill as the executor. Richard Hill established a general journal and appropriate cash journals in which to record the transactions of the estate. Record the following events as they might appear in such journals.

1. The following items constituted the inventory of the estate filed with the probate court:

    | | |
    |---|---|
    | Cash | $ 4,050 |
    | Stock of ABC Co. | 25,000 |
    | Bonds of ABC Co., 4%, interest A & O, par value | 18,000 |
    | Automobile | 1,800 |
    | Note receivable, 5% | 3,000 |
    | Accrued interest on note | 200 |
    | Bonds of LMN Co., 4½%, interest M & S, par value | 10,000 |

2. The following collections of cash were made in 1980:
    - a. Sept. 1 Interest on LMN Co. bonds — $ 225
    - b. Oct. 1 Interest on ABC Co. bonds — 360
    - c. Oct. 10 Note receivable — 1,000
        - Interest on note receivable — 225
    - d. Nov. 1 Dividend on ABC Co. stock (declared September 1, 1980) — 800
    - e. Nov. 10 Note receivable — 500
    - f. Dec. 1 Sale of automobile — 1,650

3. The following cash disbursements were made in 1980:
    - a. Aug. 15 Miscellaneous debts — $1,200
    - b. Sept. 1 Funeral expenses — 950
    - c. Sept. 10 Hospital and physician's bills — 1,650
    - d. Oct. 10 Legal expenses in connection with will — 200
    - e. Nov. 1 Safe deposit box rental to 11/1/81 — 10

4. On December 10, 1980, the LMN Co. bonds were sold for $10,900, net, including interest.

5. On December 1, 1980, special bequests were paid, as follows:
    - Steven Hill, a nephew — $2,000
    - Jackson Hill, a brother — 4,000

6. All interest income collected was transferred to the widow on the date of collection.
7. On December 31, 1980, all cash on hand was transferred to the widow.

## Problem 22-5

The following items arose in connection with the estate of B. L. Brothers, who died on August 1, 1979. For each item determine the portion of the amount properly allocable to the principal of the estate and the portion properly allocable to the income of the estate.

*a.* A dividend of $3,200 was received from the XYZ Realty Company in October 1979. The dividend was declared in September 1979. Attached to the dividend check was a notation that 60% of the dividend represented earnings of the Company, and the remainder represented a return of capital.

*b.* An uncashed check for $4,500 was included in the inventory of assets. The check had been received by Mr. Brothers on July 1, 1979, and represented the rental payment for the third quarter of 1979 on a building owned by Brothers and included as a part of the estate.

*c.* Bonds of the Vinella Production Company were included in the inventory. Par value of the bonds was $30,000, interest rate was 5%, and the bonds were inventoried at the market value on August 1, 1979, of 98. On November 1, 1979, the bonds were sold for 100 plus accrued interest. Interest was payable February 1 and August 1.

*d.* Bonds of the Pinella Co., face value of $5,000, were discovered on October 1, 1979. These bonds had not been inventoried because their presence was not known at August 1, 1979. On October 1, 1979, the semi-annual interest check for $137.50 was received.

## Problem 22-6

Mr. G. G. Frey, a haberdasher in Catlin, Illinois, died on February 20, 1979, leaving an estate consisting of the following:

| | |
|---|---:|
| Cash in bank | $ 6,950 |
| Cash on his person | 120 |
| Household goods | 2,000 |
| Building at 1 Main St., leased on a quarterly basis, at $1,800 per quarter, in advance | 68,000 |
| City of Catlin Improvement Bonds, 4%, interest payable January 1 and July 1 | 9,000 |
| Equity in haberdashery, per books | 52,500 |

The will made the following provisions: The widow was to receive $10,000 plus all household goods; a married daughter, Jane Simmer, was to receive the City of Catlin bonds; the executor, A. R. Combes, was to receive $1,500; the remaining estate was to be established as a trust fund, the income to be payable to the widow for life. The principal of the estate would pass in equal shares to the heirs of Jane Simmer upon death of the widow.

The executor paid funeral expenses of $1,100, debts existing at February 20, 1979, of $3,200, and legal and accounting fees of $1,250. Rents were collected on April 1 and July 1. Interest on the City of Catlin bonds was collected on July 1. On July 10, all legacies prescribed in the will were paid. In addition, the widow was paid $800 on March 15 and on May 15.

The executor, and the widow, decided to accept a lump-sum offer for the equity in the haberdashery—cash of $30,000 received March 15, 1979, and $25,000 in 5% notes received March 15, 1979. Interest and one-fifth of the face of the notes would be due March 15, 1980, and each succeeding March 15 for 5 years.

## 22 / Proprietorship Liquidation

*Required:*
Record the events above in the appropriate journals of the executor, A. R. Combes. List the assets to be turned over to the trustee on July 15.

### Problem 22-7

The trial balance below was taken from the records of L. Landt, executor for the estate of W. Ridley, on October 31, 1979. Landt had acted as executor since the date of Ridley's death, June 12, 1979.

*Required:*
1. Prepare the proper statements for the estate of W. Ridley, and
2. Prepare journal entries as of November 1, 1979, to close the executor's accounts and to transfer the remaining assets to Helga Ridley, widow, on that date.

L. Landt<br>Trial Balance<br>October 31, 1979

| | | |
|---|---:|---:|
| Cash: Principal | $ 4,400 | |
| Cash: Income | 680 | |
| Debts of decedent paid | 1,120 | |
| Loss on realization | 460 | |
| Funeral and administrative expenses | 850 | |
| Automobile | 1,750 | |
| Bonds | 20,000 | |
| Legacy paid: Martha Ridley | 2,500 | |
| Gain on Realization | | $   960 |
| Assets subsequently discovered | | 1,450 |
| Expense — Income | 290 | |
| Distribution to income beneficiary: | | |
|    Helga Ridley | 1,070 | |
| Estate Corpus | | 28,670 |
| Income | | 2,040 |
| | $33,120 | $33,120 |

### Problem 22-8

William Hite died on March 31, 1980. His will provided for two executors, Paul Mortensen and William Sawtell, to administer his estate. In addition to providing for the payment of the normal funeral expenses and other debts, the will included the following bequests:

| | |
|---|---:|
| Local Church | $ 2,500 |
| University Achievement Fund | 4,000 |
| Brother, Ernest | 10,000 |
| Executors (in lieu of fees, $2,500 each) | 5,000 |

The inventory of assets, as presented to the court by the executors, was as follows at the date of death:

| | |
|---|---:|
| Cash in First National Bank | $ 6,500 |
| Real property, valued by appraisal at | 41,400 |
| Convertible debenture bonds of KC Corporation, 4½%, Interest January 1 and July 1, par (and market) | 60,000 |
| Stock investments: | |
|   KC Corporation, 600 shares common, value | 36,500 |
|   GSG Mining Corp., 1,000 shares, no par, value | –0– |
|   AD Corporation, 200 shares common, value | 12,500 |
| Furniture and household items | 5,000 |
| Accrued interest (KC Corp. bonds) | 675 |

The following transactions relating to the estate were consummated by the executors:

April 15. Paid funeral expenses, $2,100; debts of decedent, $4,000.
April 30. Sold KC Corp. bonds at 102, plus accrued interest.
May 10. Paid all specific bequests, except executors' fees.
May 15. Received dividends on KC Corp. stock, $260, and on AD Corp. stock, $400, both being income items.
May 20. Sold GSG Mining stock for $.0425 per share.
May 22. Received check from M. Mills, $2,500 in repayment of personal loan made by Mr. Hite before death.
May 24. Paid estate administration expenses, totaling $7,800, of which $300 was allocable to income.
May 27. ½ furniture and household items were sold for $1,000, and other ½ donated to charitable organizations.
May 31. Paid bequests to executors.

On May 31, the executors requested release from their charge and turned over the remainder of the estate to the trustee provided in the will. Income from the trust was to be paid equally to Mr. Hite's two children.

*Required:*
Prepare charge and discharge statements as to principal and income for the period March 31, 1980 to May 31, 1980. Supporting schedules should be prepared where necessary.

## Problem 22-9

E. W. Smith died on January 13, 1980. His will appointed C. W. Bowen as the executor to administer the estate. At the date of death the decedent possessed the following assets: cash, $40,000; amount loaned to associates, $12,000; bonds of OC Corporation, 5%, interest payable January 1 and July 1, par $24,000, market value $26,000; Stock of SA Company, 1,000 shares, no par, cost $15,500, market value $71,000; Stock of CU Development Co., 50 shares, par value $50, cost $2,500, market value, nominal; City of Kenyon Bonds, 4%, par value $18,000, market value, $16,200, interest March 1 and September 1; clothing, $1,500; jewelry, $5,700, accrued interest, (?).

The will provided for the payment of funeral and other necessary expenses, and for the following bequests:

| City Cemetery | $ 5,000 |
| Civic Auditorium | 5,000 |
| Brother, W. E. Smith | 10,000 |
| Executor, in lieu of fees | 4,000 |

From January 13, 1980, to March 31, 1980, the executor completed the following transactions relating to the E. W. Smith estate:

Collected amounts advanced to associates, $10,500, with the balance considered uncollectible; sold OC Corporation bonds on March 1, 1980, at 110, plus interest; received dividend of $.50 per share on SA Company stock, payable to stockholders of record on December 29, 1979, received January 21, 1980; received interest on City of Kenyon bonds March 1; paid funeral expenses, $2,000, administrative expenses, $6,150 ($6,000 applicable to principal), debts of decedent, $8,750, legal and accounting fees, $3,600; purchased SA Corporation bonds, par value $20,000, interest 5½%, for 103, plus 3 months interest on March 15, 1980; paid all bequests in full, with brother W. E. Smith accepting jewelry at inventory value, $4,000 in cash, and the CU Development stock in full settlement of his bequest; gave clothing to charity; sold golf equipment found in country club locker to neighbor for $150.

*Required:*

Prepare charge and discharge statements as to principal and income for the period January 13, 1980, to March 31, 1980. Prepare supporting schedules where necessary.

## Problem 22-10

Arthur Taine died in an accident on May 31, 1980. His will, dated February 28, 1979, provided that all just debts and expenses be paid and that his property be disposed of as follows:

Personal residence—devised to Bertha Taine, widow.
United States Treasury bonds and Puritan Company stock—to be placed in trust. All income to go to Bertha Taine during her lifetime, with right of appointment on her death.
Seneca Co. mortgage notes—bequeathed to Elaine Taine Langer, daughter.
Cash—a bequest of $10,000 to David Taine, son.
Remainder of estate—to be divided equally between the two children, Elaine Langer and David Taine.

The will further provided that during the administration period Bertha Taine was to receive $300 a month out of estate income. Estate and inheritance taxes are to be borne by the residue. David Taine was named as executor and trustee.

An inventory of the decedent's property was prepared. The fair market value of all items as of the date of death was determined. The preliminary inventory, before the computation of any appropriate income accruals on inventory items, follows:

| | |
|---|---:|
| Personal residence property | $ 45,000 |
| Jewelry—diamond ring | 9,000 |
| York Life Insurance Co.—term life policy on life of Arthur Taine. Beneficiary—Bertha Taine, widow. | 120,000 |
| Granite Trust Co.—3% savings bank account, Arthur Taine, in trust for Philip Langer (grandchild), interest credited January and July 1; balance May 31, 1980. | 400 |
| Fidelity National Bank—checking account; balance May 31, 1980 | 143,000 |
| $100,000 United States Treasury Bonds, 3%, 2007, interest payable March 1 and September 1 | 100,000 |
| $9,700 Seneca Co. first mortgage notes, 6%, 1984, interest payable May 31 and November 30 | 9,900 |
| 800 shares Puritan Co. common stock | 64,000 |
| 700 shares Meta Manufacturing Co. common stock | 70,000 |

The executor opened an estate bank account to which he transferred the decedent's checking account balance. Other deposits, through July 1, 1981, were as follows:

| | |
|---|---:|
| Interest collected on bonds: | |
| $100,000 United States Treasury | |
| September 1, 1980 | $ 1,500 |
| March 1, 1981 | 1,500 |
| Dividends received on stock: | |
| 800 shares Puritan Co. | |
| June 15, 1980 declared May 7, 1980 payable to holders of record May 27, 1980 | 800 |
| September 15, 1980 | 800 |
| December 15, 1980 | 1,200 |
| March 15, 1981 | 800 |
| June 15, 1981 | 800 |
| Net proceeds of June 19, 1980 sale of 700 shares of Meta Mfg. Co. | 68,810 |

Payments were made from the estate's checking account through July 1, 1980 for the following:

| | |
|---|---:|
| Funeral expenses | $ 2,000 |
| Assessments for additional 1978 federal and state income tax ($1,700) plus interest ($110) to May 31, 1980 | 1,810 |
| 1980 income taxes of Arthur Taine for the period January 1, 1980 through May 31, 1980, in excess of amounts paid by the decedent on declarations of estimated tax | 9,100 |

| | |
|---|---:|
| Federal and state fiduciary income taxes, fiscal years ending June 30, 1980 ($75) and June 30, 1981 ($1,400) | 1,475 |
| Federal and state estate taxes | 58,000 |
| Monthly payments to Bertha Taine: 13 payments of $300 | 3,900 |
| Attorney's and accountant's fee | 25,000 |

The executor waived his commission, but he wished to receive his father's diamond ring in lieu of the $10,000 specific legacy. All parties agreed to this in writing, and the court's approval was secured. All other specific legacies were delivered by July 15, 1981.

*Required:*

Prepare a Charge and Discharge Statement as to Principal and Income, and its supporting schedules, to accompany the attorney's formal court accounting on behalf of the executor of the estate of Arthur Taine for the period May 31, 1980 through July 1, 1981. (Arthur Taine was not a resident of a community property state.) The following supporting schedules should be included:

1. Original Capital of Estate.
2. Gain on Disposal of Estate Assets.
3. Loss on Disposal of Estate Assets.
4. Funeral, Administration and Other Expenses.
5. Debts of Decedent Paid.
6. Legacies Paid or Delivered.
7. Assets (Corpus) on Hand, July 1, 1981.
8. Proposed Plan of Distribution of Estate Assets.
9. Income Collected.
10. Distribution of Income.  (AICPA adapted)

## Problem 22-11

For several years John Kibler had operated a clothing store in Central City. Aside from part-time help, his only full-time employee was an older brother, Sam. On February 16, 1980, John Kibler died, leaving a will in which he appointed Don MacArthur executor of his estate, provided for the payment of funeral and other expenses, and made the following special bequests:

| | |
|---|---|
| First Church | $1,500 |
| Sam Kibler | 3,000 |
| Susan Kibler, his wife | their home and furnishings |
| Marie MacArthur, his daughter | 5,000 |
| Executor, in lieu of fees | 2,000 |

The remainder of his estate was to become a trust, the income of which was to go to his widow during her lifetime, with the trust being divided in equal shares among his grandchildren after the death of Susan Kibler.

The executor listed the following assets of John Kibler:

| | |
|---|---|
| Home and furnishings, valued at | $26,500 |
| Cash, personal | 1,500 |
| U.S. Govt. Bonds, Series E, redemption value | 12,750 |
| MG Corporation stock, 200 shares, value | 18,600 |
| Life insurance policy, Susan Kibler beneficiary | 20,000 |
| Equity in Kibler Clothing Store | (?) |

Sam Kibler drew a trial balance from the records of the Kibler Clothing Store on February 17, 1980, the store being closed that day. This trial balance showed the following:

### KIBLER CLOTHING STORE
### TRIAL BALANCE, FEBRUARY 17, 1980

| | | |
|---|---:|---:|
| Cash | $ 2,100 | |
| Accounts receivable | 8,400 | |
| Inventory as of Jan. 1, 1980 | 26,250 | |
| Fixtures, net | 3,600 | |
| Prepaid expenses | 400 | |
| Accounts payable | | $ 8,000 |
| Accrued liabilities | | 750 |
| Kibler, Capital | | 25,700 |
| Purchases | 16,000 | |
| Sales | | 28,000 |
| Advertising | 1,100 | |
| Salaries | 1,400 | |
| Rent | 1,200 | |
| Various expenses | 2,000 | |
| | $62,450 | $62,450 |

Past experience indicated that gross profit on sales was normally 25%, and this was agreed upon as the basis for determining the inventory on February 17, 1980. It was similarly agreed that Sam Kibler would operate the store on a liquidation basis, reporting periodically to the executor. The books were not closed. It was estimated that the liquidation would be completed by April 15, 1980. New purchases would be limited to fast-moving items.

On April 15, 1980, the executor disposed of the U.S. Government bonds for $13,000; collected a dividend on the MG Corporation stock, declared March 1, 1980, $200; paid all bequests, except his own. He had also given the widow $150 from the income collected. He paid funeral and administrative costs of $1,200 and paid other debts of $1,800. On April 15, Sam Kibler presented the following trial balance of the Kibler Clothing Store:

| | |
|---|---:|
| Cash | $25,520 |
| Accounts receivable | 700 |
| Inventory, as of Jan. 1, 1980 | 26,250 |
| Fixtures, net | –0– |

## 22 / Proprietorship Liquidation

|  |  |  |
|---|---:|---:|
| Prepaid expenses | 50 |  |
| Accounts payable |  | $ –0– |
| Accrued liabilities |  | 20 |
| Kibler, Capital |  | 25,700 |
| Purchases | 24,000 |  |
| Sales |  | 64,000 |
| Advertising | 3,100 |  |
| Salaries | 3,800 |  |
| Rent | 2,600 |  |
| Various expenses | 3,000 |  |
| Loss on sale of fixtures | 700 |  |
|  | $89,720 | $89,720 |

No further operations are contemplated, even though there is about $800 of inventory on hand. About $400 of the receivables will be collectible, but no recovery from the prepayments is anticipated. The accrued liabilities are paid by the executor, and he turns over all remaining properties to the trustee on April 17, 1980, after paying himself the bequest provided in the will.

*Required:*

Prepare the charge and discharge statements as to principal and income for the period February 17, 1980, to April 17, 1980. Ignore all federal and state income, estate, and inheritance taxes. Prepare supporting schedules for all necessary amounts.

## Problem 22-12

The Eells Print Shop in Hamilton had been operated continuously by the Eells family since 1832. On September 15, 1979, William Eells died, leaving his widow but no children or grandchildren to succeed him in operation of the family business. Eells' will appointed Dave Brown executor of the estate and provided that, upon settlement of the estate, a trust would be established, the income from which would go to the widow, with the trust principal passing to various educational and charitable sources upon the widow's death.

In addition to his equity in the Eells Print Shop, William Eells possessed the following properties over which the executor assumed control:

|  |  |
|---|---:|
| Cash in personal account | $ 1,800 |
| AB Corporation 4% bonds, face value $30,000 interest F & A, value | 31,375 |
| Accrued interest on AB Corp. bonds | 150 |
| BO Corporation 6% cumulative preferred stock, 200 shares, $100 par, dividends unpaid since October 31, 1977, value | 16,400 |
| Property at One Green Street, housing Eells Print Shop and two other businesses, value | 40,000 |
| Personal effects | 1,500 |
| Equity in Eells Print Shop | 65,000 |

A balance sheet of the Eells Print Shop, prepared after closing the books as of September 15, 1979, follows:

EELLS PRINT SHOP
BALANCE SHEET AS OF SEPTEMBER 15, 1979

| | | | |
|---|---|---|---|
| Cash | $ 4,000 | Accounts payable | $ 3,400 |
| Accounts receivable | 8,500 | Note due at bank | 5,000 |
| Paper stock | 16,400 | Misc. accruals | 2,000 |
| Unbilled order, completed | 3,600 | Total liabilities | 10,500 |
| Supplies | 1,500 | | |
| Mach. and equip., net | 41,500 | Eells, Capital | 65,000 |
| | $75,500 | | $75,500 |

During the latter part of September, negotiations were completed for the sale of the Eells Print Shop business to J. K. Foster on the following terms: Foster takes over all the assets except cash and receivables; assumes all liabilities; agrees to pay $48,000, ⅓ on October 1, 1979, ⅓ on January 2, 1980, and ⅓ on June 1, 1980, with interest at 6% upon default of any payment; and agrees to a monthly rental of $240 on the Print Shop building.

The executor also completes the following transactions by December 1, 1979, on which date he transfers the estate to the trustee:

1. Takes control of cash and receivables of the Eells Print Shop.
2. Collects rent from other tenants, $200 on each of the following dates, a month in advance: September 15, October 15, November 15.
3. Collects $8,200 of receivables of Eells Print Shop, remainder deemed uncollectible.
4. On October 1, 1979, receives a check from J. K. Foster for $16,240.
5. Sells AB Corp. Bonds on November 15 for $32,000 and accrued interest.
6. Receives $2,400 dividend on BO Corporation stock, declared October 1, 1979.
7. Paid following items: funeral expenses, $1,500; personal debts of Eells at time of death, $2,400; legal fees, $1,500; executor's fee, determined by court, $2,500.
8. Receives rental checks of $240 on November 1 and December 1.
9. Buys, on November 15, 1979, 300 shares of TA & A stock, cost $33,675, per agreement with widow and approval of the court.
10. Personal effects were donated to charity except for a few items of little intrinsic value.
11. Pays widow three checks of $400 from income and pays $250 of expenses in connection with income.

*Required:*

Prepare a charge and discharge statement as to principal and as to income for the period September 15, 1979, to December 1, 1979. Ignore all federal and state income, estate, and inheritance taxes. Supporting schedules should be included where necessary.

## Problem 22-13

On April 15, 1980, Craig Stewart, for many years operator of Stewart's Book Shop, died. In his will, Ralph Reno was named executor of his estate. The book store had not been prospering sufficiently in recent years to attract the interest of any of Stewart's three children, James, Paul, and Larry. It was decided that the executor should proceed with the liquidation of the business, with one son, James, supervising much of the actual liquidation operation.

The executor decided to set up necessary journals and ledgers to account for the estate operations, and he assumed control of the business properties as of April 15, 1980. The balance sheet, after closing, on that date showed:

STEWART BOOK STORE

BALANCE SHEET AS OF APRIL 15, 1980

| | | | |
|---|---|---|---|
| Cash in bank | $ 3,700 | Due to book companies | $ 4,600 |
| Accounts receivable | 400 | Misc. accrued debts | 1,400 |
| Inventory of books (net) | 42,600 | Rent payable | 150 |
| Inventory of novelties (net) | 12,800 | Total liabilities | 6,150 |
| Showcases and equipment (net) | 4,200 | Stewart, Capital | 57,550 |
| | $63,700 | | $63,700 |

In addition to the book store, Stewart possessed the following properties, per inventory:

| | |
|---|---|
| Automobile | $ 2,200 |
| Cash in bank | 4,000 |
| Real estate, per appraisal | 38,400 |
| Household effects | 4,200 |
| Bonds of XYZ Co. 4%, $30,000 par value, interest January 1 and July 1, valued at | 31,000 |
| Accrued interest | 350 |

Mr. Stewart's will provided for certain bequests, listed below. The estate, including any income arising during the period of executorship, was to be divided equally among the three sons. It was estimated that about five months would be required to liquidate the book store. The sons agreed that James Stewart would be paid $1,500 for his services in supervising the store liquidation. The bequests provided:

| | |
|---|---|
| University Achievement Fund | $2,500 |
| Local hospital | 5,000 |
| Executor, in lieu of fee | 2,500 |

Ralph Reno, executor, paid the bequests above, funeral expenses of $1,800, debts of Mr. Stewart existing at the date of death, $2,500, legal and accounting fees, $3,000. The real estate was sold for $35,000 net. The household effects were divided equally among the three sons. Bond interest of $600 was collected July 1. Paul Stewart agreed, the other brothers concurring, to accept the automobile at

$2,000 in partial settlement of his legacy. On October 1, the bonds had not been sold. By that date Ralph Reno had received the following reports from James Stewart:

|  | Apr.– May | June | July | August | September |
|---|---|---|---|---|---|
| Sales of merchandise | $27,000 | $16,000 | $11,000 | $ 6,500 | $ 4,000 |
| Expenses paid, incl. | | | | | |
| Liquidator's fee | 4,000 | 3,000 | 2,600 | 2,000 | 2,000 |
| Cash collections | 26,800 | 16,100 | 10,800 | 6,900 | 6,800 |
| Cash payments | 6,000 | 4,000 | 4,200 | 3,050 | 2,500 |
|  | May 31 | June 30 | July 31 | Aug. 31 | Sept. 30 |
| Cash on hand | $24,500 | $36,600 | $43,200 | $47,050 | $51,350 |
| Inventory of books | 29,000 | 19,000 | 12,000 | 6,000 | 500 |
| Inven. of novelties | 6,800 | 3,000 | 2,000 | 800 | 200 |

Items other than those above pertaining to the business on September 30, 1980, were: Receivables estimated collectible, $200; sales value of inventory, $200. Included in September cash collections was $2,800 received from the sale of all showcases and equipment. No obligations remained outstanding, and all cash was transferred to the executor on October 1, 1980:

*Required:*
(1) Determine the gain or loss on liquidation of the Stewart Book Store, accepting the values above as proper at September 30, 1980. Prepare an operating statement and a balance sheet to reflect the liquidation proceedings and results thereof.
(2) Prepare a charge and discharge statement and supporting schedules.
(3) Determine the division of the remaining properties at October 1, 1980.

# 23

# Partnership Liquidation

In the preceding chapter a few of the reasons why a business might be liquidated were mentioned. In this chapter the accounting problems involved in the liquidation of a partnership are covered more completely.

In Chapter One it was pointed out that a partnership is an association of two or more persons to carry on a business for profit. A partnership rests upon a contractual foundation, and the life period of a partnership may therefore be somewhat hazardous, depending in part on the moods and relationships of the various partners. When the contract that establishes a partnership is terminated, the partnership is dissolved. Thus dissolution of a partnership arises when the contractual relationship comes to an end. Dissolution may occur under a variety of circumstances. It should be noted that dissolution and liquidation, as related to partnerships, are not synonymous. A partnership is *dissolved* when a partner withdraws, regardless of the reason. A partnership is *liquidated* when the business is terminated with the assets being converted into cash, liabilities being paid, and the remaining cash being distributed among the partners. Thus a partnership may be dissolved without being liquidated. For example, this situation would exist when one or more of the old partners continues the operation of the business upon the withdrawal of a partner or partners.

Although this chapter deals primarily with the accounting problems of liquidations, a brief digest of the causes or reasons for partnership dissolution is necessary. Dissolution *may* result in liquidation of the partnership, whereas liquidation *always* results in dissolution. As a result, all the following causes of dissolution may also be causes for partnership liquidation.

## Causes of Partnership Dissolution

The various causes of partnership dissolution may be classified as:
I. Dissolution caused by acts of the parties to the partnership agreement:
   A. Termination of the time stipulated in the contract. When a definite time for termination is stated in the partnership agreement, the passage of

the agreed time terminates the contract, and the partnership dissolves. If the partners decide to continue the partnership beyond the termination time stipulated, the partnership is known as a "partnership at will," and any partner may withdraw at any time.
   B.  Accomplishment of the purpose stipulated in the contract. When the contract states that the partnership was formed for the accomplishment of a specific task or purpose, the accomplishment of this stated task or purpose fulfills the contract and dissolves the partnership.
   C.  Mutual agreement of the partners. In a partnership contract, as with any contract, the parties at interest may at any time mutually agree to terminate the contract.
   D.  Withdrawal of a partner. A partner has the power to withdraw from a partnership at any time; that is, a partner cannot be forced to continue in a business venture against his will. However, when a partner withdraws from a partnership at a time other than when he has a *right* to do so (e.g., when agreed-upon time has elapsed, when stated purpose has been accomplished, or when partners mutually agree to the withdrawal), he violates the partnership contract and thus becomes liable to his prior copartners for any damages sustained because of his withdrawal from the partnership.

II.  Dissolution caused by operation of the law:
   A.  Death of a partner. A partnership is automatically dissolved upon the death of any partner.
   B.  Bankruptcy of the partnership or of any partner.
   C.  Illegality of purpose. The partnership is dissolved when legislation is enacted that makes the business of the firm illegal.
   D.  Entrance into war. If one or more of the partners of a partnership are citizens or subjects of different warring countries, the partnership is dissolved or suspended during the war.

III.  Dissolution caused by judicial decree. Any of the following circumstances may become the basis for a decree dissolving the partnership, such decree being issued by a court of equity upon the application of any partner:
   A.  Insanity or other incapacity of a partner to fulfill his duties.
   B.  Misconduct of a partner that tends to interfere with successful operations of the business.
   C.  Internal dissension among the partners, which interferes with successful operations of the business.
   D.  Inability of the business to make profits.
   E.  Fraudulent representations that induced the complaining partner to become a partner.

## Accounting for Liquidation of a Partnership

Although the cause of partnership dissolution does have some effect on the events preceding the final liquidation of a partnership, the similarities of liquidations flowing from all causes are more significant than the differences. The procedure in liquidation involves the sale or other realization of the assets into cash, the apportionment of any gains or losses upon realization to the partners in the proper ratio, the liquidation of any liabilities, and the payment of partners' interests.

Certain rules should be followed by individuals handling the liquidation of a partnership and by the accountant maintaining the records of the liquidation. The first rule involves the accounting allocation of any gain or loss arising from the realization of partnership assets. Simply stated, the rule is, *always allocate any gains or losses to the proper partners' accounts prior to distributing any cash to the partners*. Violation of this rule can subject the liquidator or administrator of the partnership liquidation to liability for improper distribution of partnership assets. Profits and losses upon realization of assets are allocated to the partners in the appropriate profit and loss sharing ratios, and this allocation must be accomplished prior to any cash distribution to the partners for return of their loans, investments, or accumulated profits. After gains and losses on realization have been allocated to the partners' accounts, cash may be distributed to the various equity interests. As a general rule, all outside creditors must be paid first. When these claims have been settled, the remaining cash is distributed to the partners in their latest equity ratio.

## Death of a Partner

The death of a partner automatically dissolves the existing partnership. At the same time, as we have seen in the previous chapter, death creates a problem of control and administration of the property of the deceased until appropriate distribution of such property can be made. In a partnership the problem may be more complicated than with a proprietorship, since the partnership agreement may contain various provisions bearing upon events subsequent to the death of a partner. While the executor of the deceased is interested in as rapid and equitable liquidation of the estate as is feasible, the remaining partners may not be interested in actual liquidation of the partnership.

For example, a partnership agreement may provide that surviving partners are to continue in business as a new partnership. Even though this may be the situation, the estate of the decedent is entitled to a determination of the interest of the decedent partner at the date of his death. Such a valuation of the equity of the decedent may have to be tentative at the date of death, subject to later determination at the close of the partnership fiscal period, or at some other agreed-upon date.

Because there is frequently a conflict of interests between the estate of the decedent, which desires a cash settlement for the equity of the deceased partner in the shortest possible time, and the surviving partners, who desire to retain the business assets for continued business operation, many partnerships carry insurance on the partners. Proceeds of the life insurance policies are used to settle the equity of the deceased partner with his estate.

When the death of a partner results in actual liquidation (as well as dissolution) of the partnership, the accounting problems of the partnership are similar to those discussed on the following pages. The accounting problems of the deceased partner's heirs or executors are similar to those discussed in the preceding chapter.

## Liquidation of a Partnership After Complete Realization of Assets

In the following several examples it is assumed that the partnership is dissolved and all assets are realized in cash before any distribution of assets is made to the partners. Because various situations may arise from the realization of assets, the following illustrations are organized into three groups:

*Group 1.* Allocation of realization losses does not produce a debit balance in any partner's equity, as represented by his capital, loan, and drawing accounts.

*Group 2.* Allocation of realization losses produces a debit balance in one or more (but not all) of the partners' equities, as represented by capital, loan, and drawing accounts.

*Group 3.* Allocation of realization losses renders the partnership insolvent, that is, it produces a net debit balance in partners' equities, as represented by capital, loan, and drawing accounts.

**Group I Illustrations.** For the two examples in this group, assume that the ABC Partnership has three partners who share profits and losses as follows: A, 30%; B, 30%; and C, 40%. The following statement of financial position was prepared just prior to dissolution and subsequent liquidation:

ABC Partnership
Financial Position
October 15, 1979

|  |  |  |  |
|---|---|---|---|
| Cash | $ 4,000 | Liabilities | $40,000 |
| Other assets | 90,000 | A, Loan | 3,000 |
|  |  | B, Loan | 6,000 |
|  |  | A, Capital | 12,000 |
|  |  | B, Capital | 15,000 |
|  |  | C, Capital | 18,000 |
|  | $94,000 |  | $94,000 |

**Illustration 1-1.** For purposes of illustration, assume that the other assets were sold for $75,000 cash. The loss to be allocated among the partners is $15,000. This loss must be allocated to the partners' equity accounts before distributing any cash. Existing cash is then applied in accordance with the general rule previously stated to outside creditors and to partners' equities. The following entries illustrate the accounting procedures involved.

(1) Cash $75,000
 Loss on realization of assets 15,000

## 23 / Partnership Liquidation

|     | Other assets | | $90,000 |
| --- | --- | --- | --- |
|     | (to record the sale of other assets at a $15,000 loss) | | |
| (2) | A, Capital | $ 4,500 | |
|     | B, Capital | 4,500 | |
|     | C, Capital | 6,000 | |
|     | Loss on realization of assets | | $15,000 |
|     | (to allocate the loss to partners in their profit and loss ratio) | | |
| (3) | Liabilities | $40,000 | |
|     | Cash | | $40,000 |
|     | (to record payment of liabilities) | | |
| (4) | A, Loan | $ 3,000 | |
|     | B, Loan | 6,000 | |
|     | Cash | | $ 9,000 |
|     | (to record payment of partners' loans) | | |
| (5) | A, Capital | $ 7,500 | |
|     | B, Capital | 10,500 | |
|     | C, Capital | 12,000 | |
|     | Cash | | $30,000 |
|     | (to record payment of partners' remaining capital balances) | | |

A tabular arrangement to portray the liquidation of this partnership might appear as follows on page 730.

This illustration shows that the distribution of cash does not present a difficult problem when the capital of each partner is large enough to absorb his share of the loss from realization of assets. It should be noted at this point that gains or losses from realization should *always* be allocated among the partners in their profit and loss sharing ratio, or in the same manner as gains or losses from operations are allocated.

**Illustration 1-2.** Assume the assets were sold for $45,000. The following entries would be made:

| (1) | Cash | $45,000 | |
| --- | --- | --- | --- |
|     | Loss on realization of assets | 45,000 | |
|     | Other assets | | $90,000 |
| (2) | A, Capital | $13,500 | |
|     | B, Capital | 13,500 | |
|     | C, Capital | 18,000 | |
|     | Loss on realization of assets | | $45,000 |
| (3) | Liabilities | $40,000 | |
|     | Cash | | $40,000 |

| | | | |
|---|---|---|---|
| (4) | A, Loan | $1,500 | |
| | A, Capital | | $1,500 |
| | (to transfer from A's loan account to his capital account an amount required to absorb his capital deficit) | | |
| (5) | A, Loan | $1,500 | |
| | B, Loan | 6,000 | |
| | Cash | | $7,500 |
| (6) | B, Capital | $1,500 | |
| | Cash | | $1,500 |

A tabular arrangement to portray the liquidation of this partnership would appear as follows on page 731.

From this tabular presentation the following points should be noted: (1) the loss from realization is allocated to the partners' capitals in their profit and loss ratio, even though one partner's capital balance (A) is not sufficient to absorb the loss; (2) the allocation of the loss from the realization takes place prior to any cash distributions; and (3) an adjustment of the partners' loan accounts takes place prior to the liquidation of the loans. A partner should not be paid in full for his loan if his capital account contains a debit balance. In reality the debit balance in the partner's capital account represents a debt owning to the partnership, while the loan account credit balance represents a debt owing from the partnership to the partner. In step (4) enough of the loan credit is transferred to the capital account to eliminate the debit balance in the capital account. This procedure is called exercising the *right of offset,* and after it is completed, the remaining balance in the loan account represents a claim against the partnership. After the offset of part of A's loan against his capital deficit, the remaining loan balances are paid, and finally, the balances in the partners' capitals are liquidated.

**Group 2 Illustrations.** For the two illustrations and their alternatives in this group, assume the same statement of financial position and related facts as those used for the previous group of illustrations.

This group of illustrations portrays the accounting treatment for partnership liquidations in which allocation of loss upon realization produces a debit balance in one or more, but not all, of the partners' equities.

***Illustration 2-1.*** The first illustration in this group would arise whenever the loss upon realization of the assets was great enough to produce a debit balance in *one* partners' equity, the equity being the sum of the partners' capital, drawing, and loan accounts. For this example, assume a sale of the other assets for $43,000, with a resulting loss of $47,000 to be allocated to the partners. The following entries would be made:

(1)

| | | |
|---|---|---|
| Cash | $43,000 | |
| Loss on realization of assets | 47,000 | |
| Other assets | | $90,000 |

## 23 / Partnership Liquidation

|  | (2) |  |  |
|---|---|---|---|
| A, Capital |  | $14,100 |  |
| B, Capital |  | 14,100 |  |
| C, Capital |  | 18,800 |  |
|    Loss on realization of assets |  |  | $47,000 |

|  | (3) |  |  |
|---|---|---|---|
| Liabilities |  | $40,000 |  |
|    Cash |  |  | $40,000 |

(The entries above are similar to those in the preceding illustrations)

A tabular arrangement to portray the liquidation events to this point would appear as on page 732.

At this point the tabulation reveals that $7,000 cash is available for distribution to the partners; and A's equity is $900 (the net balance of his $3,000 loan and the $2,100 debit in his capital account); that B's equity is $6,900 (the sum of his loan and capital accounts); and that C has a negative equity of $800. In other words, C owes the ABC Partnership $800.

Three alternative solutions are possible in this type of situation depending upon the action taken by C.

***Alternative 1.*** C may pay the partnership the $800 that he owes. If C pays the $800, the partnership is able to proceed with the liquidation in a manner similar to that in previous illustrations. The following entries would be made:

|  | (4) |  |  |
|---|---|---|---|
| Cash |  | $ 800 |  |
|    C, Capital |  |  | $ 800 |
| (to record C's payment to the partnership) |  |  |  |

|  | (5) |  |  |
|---|---|---|---|
| A, Loan |  | $ 2,100 |  |
|    A, Capital |  |  | $ 2,100 |
| (to offset A's capital deficit against his loan account) |  |  |  |

|  | (6) |  |  |
|---|---|---|---|
| A, Loan |  | $ 900 |  |
| B, Loan |  | 6,000 |  |
|    Cash |  |  | $ 6,900 |

|  | (7) |  |  |
|---|---|---|---|
| B, Capital |  | $ 900 |  |
|    Cash |  |  | $ 900 |

The preceding tabular arrangement could then be completed as on page 733.

## ABC Partnership
### Statement of Liquidation
### October, 1979

|  | Cash | Other Assets | Liabilities | Loans A | Loans B | Capitals A (30%) | Capitals B (30%) | Capitals C (40%) |
|---|---|---|---|---|---|---|---|---|
| Profit and loss ratio |  |  |  |  |  | 30% | 30% | 40% |
| Balances per statement | $ 4,000 | $90,000 | $40,000 | $ 3,000 | $ 6,000 | $12,000 | $15,000 | $18,000 |
| (1, 2) Sale of assets and allocation of loss | 75,000 | (90,000) |  |  |  | (4,500) | (4,500) | (6,000) |
| Balances | $79,000 | — | $40,000 | $ 3,000 | $ 6,000 | $ 7,500 | $10,500 | $12,000 |
| (3) Payment to creditors | (40,000) |  | (40,000) |  |  |  |  |  |
| Balances | $39,000 | — | — | $ 3,000 | $ 6,000 | $ 7,500 | $10,500 | $12,000 |
| (4) Payment of loans | (9,000) |  |  | (3,000) | (6,000) |  |  |  |
| Balances | $30,000 | — | — | — | — | $ 7,500 | $10,500 | $12,000 |
| (5) Distribution to partners | (30,000) |  |  |  |  | (7,500) | (10,500) | (12,000) |
| Balances | –0– | –0– | –0– | –0– | –0– | –0– | –0– | –0– |

## ABC Partnership
### Statement of Liquidation
### October, 1979

|  | Cash | Other Assets | Liabilities | Loans A | Loans B | Capitals A 30% | Capitals B 30% | Capitals C 40% |
|---|---|---|---|---|---|---|---|---|
| Profit and loss ratio |  |  |  |  |  | 30% | 30% | 40% |
| Balances per statement | $4,000 | $90,000 | $40,000 | $3,000 | $6,000 | $12,000 | $15,000 | $18,000 |
| (1, 2) Sale of assets and allocation of loss | 45,000 | (90,000) |  |  |  | (13,500) | (13,500) | (18,000) |
| Balances | $49,000 | — | $40,000 | $3,000 | $6,000 | $(1,500) | $1,500 | — |
| (3) Payment to creditors | (40,000) |  | (40,000) |  |  |  |  |  |
| Balances | $9,000 | — | — | $3,000 | $6,000 | $(1,500) | $1,500 | — |
| (4) Offset of A's capital deficit against loan account |  |  |  | (1,500) |  | $1,500 |  |  |
| Balances | $9,000 |  |  | $1,500 | $6,000 | — | $1,500 | — |
| (5) Payment of loans | (7,500) |  |  | (1,500) | (6,000) |  |  |  |
| Balances | $1,500 |  |  | — | — |  | $1,500 | — |
| (6) Distribution to partners | (1,500) |  |  |  |  |  | (1,500) |  |
| Balances | —0— |  |  | —0— | —0— | —0— | —0— | —0— |

## ABC Partnership
### Statement of Liquidation (Partial)
### October, 1979

|  | Cash | Other Assets | Liabilities | Loans A | Loans B | Capitals A 30% | Capitals B 30% | Capitals C 40% |
|---|---|---|---|---|---|---|---|---|
| Profit and loss ratio |  |  |  |  |  | 30% | 30% | 40% |
| Balances per statement | $ 4,000 | $90,000 | $40,000 | $3,000 | $6,000 | $12,000 | $15,000 | $18,000 |
| (1, 2) Sale of assets and allocation of loss | 43,000 | (90,000) |  |  |  | (14,100) | (14,100) | (18,800) |
| Balances | $47,000 | — | $40,000 | $3,000 | $6,000 | $(2,100) | $ 900 | $ (800) |
| (3) Payment to creditors | (40,000) |  | (40,000) |  |  |  |  |  |
| Balances (see subsequent statements) | $ 7,000 | -0- | -0- | $3,000 | $6,000 | $(2,100) | $ 900 | $ (800) |

## ABC Partnership
### Statement of Liquidation (Completed)
### October, 1979

| | Cash | Other Assets | Liabilities | Loans A | Loans B | Capitals A 30% | Capitals B 30% | Capitals C 40% |
|---|---|---|---|---|---|---|---|---|
| Profit and loss ratio | | | | | | 30% | 30% | 40% |
| Balances per preceding partial statement | $7,000 | -0- | -0- | $3,000 | $6,000 | $(2,100) | $900 | $(800) |
| (4) Cash from C | 800 | — | — | | | | | 800 |
| Balances | $7,800 | — | — | $3,000 | $6,000 | $(2,100) | $900 | -0- |
| (5) Offset A's capital debit against loan | | — | — | (2,100) | | 2,100 | | |
| Balances | $7,800 | — | — | $ 900 | $6,000 | — | $900 | — |
| (6) Payment of loans | (6,900) | | | (900) | (6,000) | | | |
| Balances | $ 900 | — | — | — | — | | $900 | — |
| (7) Distribution to partners | (900) | | | | | | (900) | |
| Balances | -0- | -0- | -0- | -0- | -0- | -0- | -0- | -0- |

**Alternative 2.** C may be unable to pay the $800 owed the partnership. To the other partners the $800 represents a loss to the partnership and should be shared by the remaining partners in their respective profit and loss ratio. Since A and B share in the profits and losses to the extent of 30% each, they would share the $800 loss equally (30/60 to each). The following entry would be necessary to record the additional loss suffered by A and B:

(4)

| | | |
|---|---|---|
| A, Capital | $ 400 | |
| B, Capital | 400 | |
|   C, Capital | | $ 800 |
| (to record A's and B's share of C's uncollectible equity balance) | | |

Entries similar to (5), (6), and (7) in Alternative 1 would then be made reflecting the appropriate amounts. Completion of the tabular arrangement would proceed as on page 736.

**Alternative 3.** Partners A and B may decide to distribute the remaining cash ($7,000) before it is known whether Partner C will pay the partnership his $800 debt. Under this situation the problem facing the partners is how to distribute the $7,000 cash between the equity of A of $900 ($3,000 loan minus $2,100 capital deficit) and the equity of B of $6,900 ($6,000 loan plus $900 capital balance), or a total equity of $7,800.

Here it must be recognized that if C cannot pay his $800 obligation, the other partners will have to absorb C's capital deficit in their relative profit and loss ratio. Therefore, before any cash distribution should be made to the partners, the amount necessary to absorb any *possible* future loss must be calculated for each partner. The loss calculated must then be subtracted from each partner's equity to arrive at the balance of each partner's equity which can be paid. The cash may then be distributed accordingly. After distribution of the cash, the partners' equities on the partnership's books would contain credit balances exactly equal to their respective shares of the possible loss from nonpayment by the partner with the debit balance in his capital account.

The key to the solution of a situation where cash is to be distributed before all possible losses are known is to recognize that provision *must* be made to restrict each partner's equity for his possible loss *prior* to the distribution of any cash to the partners.

Referring again to the partial statement of liquidation on page 732, under Alternative 3 the possible loss from the nonpayment by C must be computed and deducted from the remaining partners' equities. (Such deductions are calculations only and not the basis of an entry affecting the ledger accounts.) After the deduction, the amount properly payable to each partner is the balance of each partner's equity.

## ABC Partnership
### Schedule 1
### Computation of Payments to Partners
### October, 1979

|  | Partners' Equities |  |  |
|---|---|---|---|
|  | A | B | C |
| Profit and loss ratio | 30% | 30% | 40% |
| Capital account balances, per statement on page 732. | ($2,100) | $ 900 | $(800) |
| Add: Loan balances | 3,000 | 6,000 |  |
| Partners' total equities | $ 900 | $6,900 | $(800) |
| Amount of restriction of equity for possible loss from nonpayment of C. (A and B share in a 30 : 30 ratio) | $ (400) | $ (400) | $ 800 |
| Net equity | $ 500 | $6,500 | –0– |

After this calculation has been made, the $7,000 cash can be distributed: $6,000 to pay B's loan, $500 to pay a portion of the remaining balance of A's loan, and $500 to pay a portion of B's remaining capital account credit balance. Entries similar to (4), (5), and (6), for the first alternative under this group would then be made. Completion of the tabular arrangement would appear as on page 737.

If C subsequently pays in the $800, A and B would use the $800 to settle their respective equities. If C subsequently finds it impossible to pay, the remaining balances would be eliminated by an appropriate entry.

This alternative also illustrates that the general rule to the effect that partners' loan accounts are to be liquidated before payments are made on capital accounts does not necessarily hold true. The only equitable distribution in the illustration above is to pay B $6,000 to liquidate his loan completely, pay B an additional $500 on his capital contribution, and pay A $500 in partial settlement of his loan. Payment of A's loan in full at this point would be inequitable to B, particularly if A subsequently refused, or was unable, to make good his capital deficit.

***Illustration 2-2.*** This illustration indicates the accounting procedure necessary whenever the loss upon realization of the assets is great enough to produce a deficit in *more* than *one* partners' equity accounts. This situation may arise in one of two ways. First, the loss on realization itself may produce only one equity deficit, but absorption of this deficit by the remaining partners may produce another equity deficit. Second, the loss on realization itself may produce more than one equity deficit.

Using the statement of financial position and related data previously used, and assuming that the other assets were sold for $41,000, the following entries would be made:

## ABC Partnership
### Statement of Liquidation (Completed)
### October, 1979

|  | Cash | Other Assets | Liabilities | Loans A | Loans B | Capitals A 30% | Capitals B 30% | Capitals C 40% |
|---|---|---|---|---|---|---|---|---|
| Profit and loss ratio | | | | | | 30% | 30% | 40% |
| Balances per preceding partial statement | $7,000 | –0– | –0– | $3,000 | $6,000 | $(2,100) | $900 | $(800) |
| (4) Record loss on noncollection from partner C | | | | | | (400) | (400) | 800 |
| Balances | $7,000 | — | — | $3,000 | $6,000 | (2,500) | $500 | — |
| (5) Offset A's capital debit against loan | | | | (2,500) | | 2,500 | | |
| Balances | $7,000 | — | — | $ 500 | $6,000 | — | $500 | — |
| (6) Payment of loans | (6,500) | | | (500) | (6,000) | | | |
| Balances | $ 500 | — | — | — | — | — | $500 | — |
| (7) Distribution to partners | (500) | | | | | | (500) | |
| Balances | –0– | –0– | –0– | –0– | –0– | –0– | –0– | –0– |

## 23 / Partnership Liquidation

**ABC Partnership**
**Statement of Liquidation (Completed)**
**October, 1979**

|  | Cash | Assets | Liabilities | Loans A | Loans B | Capital A (30%) | Capital B (30%) | Capital C (40%) |
|---|---|---|---|---|---|---|---|---|
| Profit and loss ratio |  |  |  |  |  | 30% | 30% | 40% |
| Balances per preceding partial statement | $7,000 | –0– | –0– | $3,000 | $6,000 | $(2,100) | $900 | $(800) |
| (4) No entry to be made (see computation of payment to partners) |  |  |  |  |  |  |  |  |
| (5) Offset of A's capital debit against loan |  |  |  | $(2,100) |  | $2,100 |  |  |
| Balances | $7,000 | — | — | $ 900 | $6,000 | — | $900 | $ (800) |
| (6, 7) Settlement of loans and capital accounts, per computation of payment to partners | (7,000) |  |  | (500) | (6,000) |  | (500) | 400 |
| Balances | –0– | –0– | –0– | $ 400 | –0– | –0– | $400 | $(800) |

(1)

| | | |
|---|---|---|
| Cash | $41,000 | |
| Loss on realization of assets | 49,000 | |
|    Other assets | | $90,000 |

(2)

| | | |
|---|---|---|
| A, Capital | $14,700 | |
| B, Capital | 14,700 | |
| C, Capital | 19,600 | |
|    Loss on realization of assets | | $49,000 |

(3)

| | | |
|---|---|---|
| Liabilities | $40,000 | |
|    Cash | | $40,000 |

A tabular arrangement to portray the liquidation events to this point would appear as on page 740.

At this point the tabulation reveals that there is $5,000 cash available for distribution to the partners and that the following equities (loans plus capitals) exist:

$$\begin{aligned} A &= \$\ 300 \\ B &= 6{,}300 \\ C &= (1{,}600) \\ \text{Total} &= \$5{,}000 \end{aligned}$$

***Alternative 1-A.*** If C pays the amount he owes, cash will be increased to $6,600, and A will receive $300 and B will receive $6,300.

***Alternative 2-A.*** If C is unable to pay the $1,600, A and B must share this loss in their profit and loss ratio. Completion of the Statement of Liquidation for this illustration would appear as on page 741.

At this point A owes the partnership $500 and if he pays this amount into the partnership, B will receive the entire $5,500 in full settlement of the remaining balance in his loan account. If A cannot pay in this $500, B will receive only the $5,000 cash on hand.

***Alternative 3-A.*** In this alternative, as in Alternative 3, it is possible that partners A and B may desire to distribute the cash before it is known whether C can pay in the $1,600 balance he owes. In this situation, all possible losses to each partner must be computed before deciding how the $5,000 will be distributed. Therefore, after preparing the Statement of Liquidation (partial), the following schedule would be prepared:

## ABC PARTNERSHIP
### SCHEDULE 1
#### COMPUTATION OF PAYMENTS TO PARTNERS
##### OCTOBER, 1979

|  | Partners' Equities |  |  |
|---|---|---|---|
|  | A | B | C |
| Profit and loss ratio | 30% | 30% | 40% |
| Capital account balance, per statement on page 740 | $(2,700) | $ 300 | $(1,600) |
| Add: loan balances | 3,000 | 6,000 |  |
| Partners' total equities | $ 300 | $6,300 | $(1,600) |
| Allocation of possible loss from nonpayment by C (A and B now share in a 30 : 30 ratio) | $ (800) | (800) | 1,600 |
| Net equities | $ (500) | $5,500 | — |
| Allocation of possible loss from nonpayment by A | 500 | (500) |  |
| Net equity | –0– | $5,000 | –0– |

This schedule reveals that at this point the only equitable method for distributing the $5,000 is to distribute it all to B. Although the loss on realization of assets did not eliminate A's equity in the partnership entirely, his share of that loss, plus his share of the possible loss arising from nonpayment by C, did create an equity deficit for A although it may be temporary.

If the $5,000 were distributed to B at this time, the following completion of the Statement of Liquidation started would result, as on page 742.

If C subsequently pays in the $1,600 he owes, A and B would use the $1,600 to settle their respective equity interests. If C subsequently finds it impossible to pay, the remaining equity balances would be eliminated by an appropriate entry.

**Group 3 Illustrations.** For the two illustrations and their alternatives in this group, assume the same statement of financial position and related facts as those used for the previous illustrations.

This group of illustrations portrays the accounting treatment for those partnership liquidations in which the distribution of the loss upon realization of the assets renders the partnership insolvent, that is, produces a net debit balance in partners' equities. The two basic illustrations in this group deal with the situations that exist when a partnership is insolvent and (1) all partners are individually solvent, or (2) one or more partners is individually insolvent.

**Illustration 3-1.** Situations falling within Group 3 will arise, under the basic facts assumed, whenever realization of the assets produces less than $36,000 cash or, conversely, whenever realization results in a loss in excess of $54,000, the sum

## ABC Partnership
### Statement of Liquidation (Partial)
### October, 1979

|  | Cash | Other Assets | Liabilities | Loans A | Loans B | Capitals A 30% | Capitals B 30% | Capitals C 40% |
|---|---|---|---|---|---|---|---|---|
| Profit and loss ratio |  |  |  |  |  | 30% | 30% | 40% |
| Balances per statement | $ 4,000 | $90,000 | $40,000 | $3,000 | $6,000 | $12,000 | $15,000 | $18,000 |
| (1, 2) Sale of assets and allocation of loss | 41,000 | (90,000) |  |  |  | (14,700) | (14,700) | (19,600) |
| Balances | $45,000 | — | $40,000 | $3,000 | $6,000 | $(2,700) | $ 300 | (1,600) |
| (3) Payment to creditors | (40,000) |  | (40,000) |  |  |  |  |  |
| Balances | $ 5,000 | –0– | –0– | $3,000 | $6,000 | $(2,700) | $ 300 | $(1,600) |

## 23 / Partnership Liquidation

### ABC PARTNERSHIP
### STATEMENT OF LIQUIDATION (CONTINUATION)
### OCTOBER, 1979

|  | Cash | Other Assets | Liabilities | Loans A | Loans B | Capitals A 30% | Capitals B 30% | Capitals C 40% |
|---|---|---|---|---|---|---|---|---|
| Profit and loss ratio |  |  |  |  |  |  |  |  |
| Balances per preceding partial statement | $5,000 | –0– | –0– | $3,000 | $6,000 | $(2,700) | $ 300 | $(1,600) |
| (4) Allocation of C's deficit |  |  |  |  |  | (800) | (800) | 1,600 |
| Balances | $5,000 | —— | —— | $3,000 | $6,000 | $(3,500) | $ (500) | —— |
| (5) Offset capital deficits against loan accounts |  |  |  | (3,000) | (500) | 3,000 | 500 |  |
| Balances | $5,000 | –0– | –0– | –0– | $5,500 | $ (500) | –0– | –0– |

## ABC Partnership
### Statement of Liquidation (Completed)
### October, 1979

|  | Cash | Other Assets | Liabilities | Loans A | Loans B | Capitals A 30% | Capitals B 30% | Capitals C 40% |
|---|---|---|---|---|---|---|---|---|
| Profit and loss ratio |  |  |  |  |  | 30% | 30% | 40% |
| Balance per preceding partial statement, p. 740 | $5,000 | –0– | –0– | $3,000 | $6,000 | $(2,700) | $300 | $(1,600) |
| (4) No entry necessary (see Computation of payment to partners) |  |  |  |  |  |  |  |  |
| (5) Offset of A's capital deficit against his loan account |  |  |  | (2,700) |  | 2,700 |  |  |
| Balances | $5,000 | –0– | –0– | $ 300 | $6,000 | –0– | $300 | $(1,600) |
| (6, 7) Partial settlement of B's Loan, per Schedule 1 | (5,000) |  |  |  | (5,000) |  |  |  |
| Balances | –0– | –0– | –0– | $ 300 | $1,000 | –0– | $300 | $(1,600) |

of the partners' equities. Assume a sale of other assets for $30,000, with a resulting loss of $60,000. The entries to record the realization and allocation of the resulting loss would be as previously illustrated, and the Statement of Partnership Liquidation would appear as on page 744.

For this illustration, assume in addition that all the individual partners are solvent. This being the case, any of the three partners may be called upon to pay the remaining $6,000 owed to the creditors, since partners are jointly and severally liable for any partnership debts.

***Alternative 1-B.*** If A pays the $6,000 balance of liabilities, the partners' equities after the payment would appear as follows:

$$
\begin{aligned}
\text{A's equity} &= \$3{,}000 \text{ (increased from \$}{-}3{,}000 \text{ by payment)} \\
\text{B's equity} &= 3{,}000 \\
\text{C's equity} &= (6{,}000)
\end{aligned}
$$

If C can pay in his negative equity, A and B can be paid in full. If C cannot pay in his negative equity, A and B will stand a $3,000 loss each.

***Alternative 2-B.*** If B pays the $6,000 of liabilities, the partners' equities after the payment would appear as follows:

$$
\begin{aligned}
\text{A's equity} &= \$(3{,}000) \\
\text{B's equity} &= 9{,}000 \text{ (increased from \$3{,}000 by payment)} \\
\text{C's equity} &= (6{,}000)
\end{aligned}
$$

If both A and C can make payments, B will take such payments in settlement of his $9,000 equity. However, if A can make his payment and C cannot, there must be a further division of C's loss between A and B in their profit and loss ratio. Thus, if C cannot pay, A's and B's equities would appear as below:

$$
\begin{aligned}
\text{A's equity} &= \$(6{,}000) \\
\text{B's equity} &= 6{,}000
\end{aligned}
$$

A and B would share the $6,000 loss from nonpayment by C in their profit and loss ratio of $^{30}/_{60}$ and $^{30}/_{60}$. Thus, A would owe B a total of $6,000, $3,000 for his original negative equity and $3,000 for his share of C's nonpayment.

On the other hand, if C can settle his deficit and A cannot, there must be a division of the loss from A's nonpayment between B and C in their profit and loss ratio. Thus, if A cannot pay, B's and C's equities would appear as below:

$$
\begin{aligned}
\text{B's equity} &= \$7{,}714 \\
\text{C's equity} &= (7{,}714)
\end{aligned}
$$

B and C would share the $3,000 loss from nonpayment by A in their profit and loss ratio of $^{30}/_{70}$ and $^{40}/_{70}$. Thus, C would owe B a total of $7,714, $6,000 for his deficit and $1,714 for his 4/7 share of A's nonpayment.

## ABC Partnership
### Statement of Liquidation (Partial)
### October, 1979

|  | Cash | Other Assets | Liabilities | Loans A | Loans B | Capitals A 30% | Capitals B 30% | Capitals C 40% |
|---|---|---|---|---|---|---|---|---|
| Profit and loss ratio |  |  |  |  |  | 30% | 30% | 40% |
| Balances per statement | $4,000 | $90,000 | $40,000 | $3,000 | $6,000 | $12,000 | $15,000 | $18,000 |
| Sale of assets and allocation of loss | 30,000 | (90,000) |  |  |  | (18,000) | (18,000) | (24,000) |
| Balances | $34,000 | — | $40,000 | $3,000 | $6,000 | $(6,000) | $(3,000) | $(6,000) |
| Payment to creditors | (34,000) |  | (34,000) |  |  |  |  |  |
| Balances | — | — | $ 6,000 | $3,000 | $6,000 | $(6,000) | $(3,000) | $(6,000) |
| Offset of partners' capital deficits against loans |  |  |  | (3,000) | (3,000) | 3,000 | 3,000 |  |
| Balances | -0- | -0- | $ 6,000 | -0- | $ 3,000 | $(3,000) | -0- | $(6,000) |

**Alternative 3-B.** If C pays the $6,000 of liabilities, the partners' equities after the payment would appear as follows:

A's equity = $(3,000)
B's equity = 3,000
C's equity = –0–        (decreased from $ −6,000 by payment to creditors)

If A can pay his negative equity, B will receive the $3,000 in settlement of his claim. However, if A cannot pay his $3,000 negative equity, the amount that A owes to the partnership and cannot pay must be shared by B and C in their profit and loss ratio. Thus, if A cannot pay, B's and C's equities would appear as follows:

B's equity = $1,714
C's equity = (1,714)

B's equity would absorb 3/7 of the $3,000 loss, or $1,286, while C's equity would be charged with 4/7, or $1,714. Thus, C would owe B $1,714, his share of the loss arising from A's inability to pay his capital deficit.

**Illustration 3-2.** For this illustration, assume the same conditions with regard to realization of partnership assets as those in the preceding illustrations in this group. This would leave the following balances on the partnership books:

|  | Dr. | Cr. |
|---|---|---|
| Liabilities |  | $6,000 |
| B, Loan |  | 3,000 |
| A, Capital | $3,000 |  |
| C, Capital | 6,000 |  |

Assume also that each of the partners has personal assets and liabilities, in addition to their partnership claims and debts, as follows:

|  | Assets | Liabilities |
|---|---|---|
| A | $ 4,000 | $3,000 |
| B | 4,000 | 9,000 |
| C | 14,000 | 2,000 |

From the data above it can be seen that A's personal assets are sufficient to settle fully his personal obligations, but the excess is not sufficient to settle his obligation as evidenced by his partnership capital account.

B's personal assets will not meet his personal debts, and the $3,000 due him from the partnership is insufficient to make up the difference. C has sufficient assets to meet his personal debts as well as to meet the obligations arising from his partnership interest.

Certain legal rules, which are generally referred to as marshaling of assets, govern situations in which a partnership and one or more of the partners are insolvent. These rules, although subject to some exceptions, in essence provide:

1. That creditors of the partnership have the right to payment in full from partnership assets before any of the partners' personal creditors can claim partnership assets. However, if all partnership obligations have been paid, personal creditors of any partner may receive settlement from partnership assets, through a court-obtained charging order, to the extent of that partner's remaining equity.
2. That personal creditors of a partner have the right to payment in full from the partner's personal assets before creditors of the partnership can claim payment from these assets. However, once the personal creditors have been paid, the unpaid partnership creditors may obtain settlement from the balance of the partners' personal assets, regardless of the capital balance a given partner has in the partnership.

In this illustration all proceeds from the sale of partnership assets have been used to pay partnership creditors, and those creditors still have claims of $6,000 against the partnership. These creditors cannot look to B at this time for payment, since his assets are insufficient to cover his personal debts. They can look to A for only $1,000 of the $6,000 due, since A must apply $3,000 of his personal assets to settle his personal debts. The unsatisfied partnership creditors can, however, look to C for full payment, as his assets are sufficient to make such payment. These creditors will be able to obtain payment from C regardless of whether he has a debit or credit balance in his partnership equity account.

If the partnership creditors collect $6,000 from C, the balances on the partnership books would then be:

|  | Dr. | Cr. |
|---|---|---|
| B, Loan |  | $3,000 |
| A, Capital | $3,000 |  |

All partnership creditors would now be satisfied, but the personal obligations of each partner remain unsettled. The remaining partnership question concerns what to do about B's $3,000 loan and A's $3,000 capital deficit.

Under the Uniform Partnership Act, A's personal creditors would receive the first $3,000 from his personal assets. The remaining $1,000 of A's assets would be paid by A to the partnership in partial settlement of his $3,000 capital account deficit. Since A has no additional assets at this time, his remaining $2,000 deficit may be considered a loss by the partnership. The following table shows the accounts as they would appear on the partnership books assuming the conditions above.

|  | Cash | B Loan | A Capital | C Capital |
|---|---|---|---|---|
| Balances after C pays the partnership creditors, but before any receipt of cash from A |  | $3,000 | $(3,000) |  |
| Receipts of cash from A | $1,000 |  | 1,000 |  |
| Balances | 1,000 | 3,000 | (2,000) |  |

| | | | | |
|---|---|---|---|---|
| Loss on A's remaining balance, in profit and loss ratio of 30:40 | | (857) | 2,000 | $(1,143) |
| Balances | $1,000 | $2,143 | –0– | $(1,143) |

This table reveals that B has a $2,143 interest in the partnership. Since B owes his personal creditors $9,000 and has personal assets of only $4,000, B's personal creditors have unsatisfied claims of $5,000. In satisfaction of these claims these creditors have a right to any interest that B may have in the partnership, or $2,143 as indicated. Thus, B's personal creditors would be entitled to the $1,000 cash of the partnership and would also have a claim against the partnership for the $1,143 that C must pay in as his share of A's nonpayment. C's assets are sufficient to pay his personal creditors, to pay the $6,000 unsatisfied partnership claims, and also to allow him to contribute to the partnership his portion of any nonpayment by A, or $1,143.

B and C would each retain a claim against A, of $857 and $1,143 respectively, because of his failure to be able to meet the terms of the partnership agreement.

## Liquidation of a Partnership by Installment

Frequently, partnership assets are not realized through an instantaneous sale but are realized in a piecemeal fashion over a period of time. Under such circumstances the partners may prefer not to wait until realization of all assets has been completed before they begin to distribute the cash resulting from realization. Whereas the preceding illustrations have been concerned with the distribution of the cash available after all assets have been realized, the following illustrations indicate the procedure for the distribution of cash to the partners prior to the completion of the realization of all assets. This type of partnership liquidation is generally referred to as "liquidation by installments."

**General Rules for Distribution of Cash.** Preceding illustrations have emphasized the considerable care required in liquidation of a partnership in order to assure an equitable distribution of assets. Such care is equally important in the partial liquidation of a partnership prior to complete realization of assets. In a situation of this nature partners receive payments in installments, the payments being made before knowledge exists of the complete loss from realization. In order to assure equitable treatment among the partners, and also to protect any individuals charged with the responsibility of approving the installment payments, no payments should be made to any partner at any time when his equity (capital, loan, and drawing accounts) is insufficient to bear his share of any *possible* loss from subsequent asset realizations or from failure of a fellow partner to contribute the amount of any debit balance which may result in his equity.

In addition to the rule above, which should guide liquidations by installments, no distributions of assets to the partners should be made until all liabilities are either (1) paid in full or (2) provided for through retention of cash sufficient to complete their liquidation. Therefore, each of the following conditions must exist before a partner should receive any cash in the liquidation procedure:

1. All liabilities should be liquidated, or cash retained sufficient to accomplish their total liquidation.
2. The capital, loan, and drawing accounts of the partners must contain sufficient total credit balances to absorb all *possible* losses in the future.

**Illustrations.** Three illustrations are presented to indicate the manner in which liquidation proceeds under varying conditions. These illustrations do not, of course, cover all possible alternatives, but merely indicate some of the problems encountered and how the rules above are applied to meet these problems.

For these illustrations assume the same ABC partnership that was used in the previous series of illustrations. A, B, and C share profits and losses in a 30 : 30 : 40 relationship, respectively. The following statement of financial position was prepared immediately prior to the start of the liquidation process.

ABC PARTNERSHIP
STATEMENT OF FINANCIAL POSITION
OCTOBER 15, 1979

| | | | |
|---|---:|---|---:|
| Cash | $ 4,000 | Liabilities | $40,000 |
| Other assets | 90,000 | A, Loan | 3,000 |
| | | B, Loan | 6,000 |
| | | A, Capital | 12,000 |
| | | B, Capital | 15,000 |
| | | C, Capital | 18,000 |
| | $94,000 | | $94,000 |

***Illustration 4-1.*** In the first illustration in this section assume that realization of the assets proceeds in the three stages set forth below. In addition, as cash becomes available from the realization of assets, it is used to liquidate liabilities and to make distributions to the partners.

1. Assets carried at $30,000 are sold for $25,000. All cash on hand after the sale, $29,000, is used to liquidate liabilities.
2. Assets carried at $40,000 are sold for $30,000. Cash of $11,000 is used to liquidate remaining liabilities, and $19,000 is distributed to the partners.
3. Remaining assets are sold for $10,000.

Entries to record these events are similar to those previously presented. A statement of partnership liquidation would appear as in Exhibit A on page 751.

The first phase of the liquidation statement, (1), should be completed without difficulty. The second phase, (2), also can be completed down to the "Payment to partners" without any complications arising. In order to complete the "Payment to partners" line, it is necessary to determine the total possible loss that each partner may have to bear if the remaining assets prove to be a total loss. A schedule to organize this information may be prepared as in Schedule 1 as follows:

Schedule 1

ABC PARTNERSHIP
COMPUTATION OF BALANCES AFTER PROVIDING
FOR POSSIBLE LOSSES

|  | Loans A | Loans B | Capitals A | Capitals B | Capitals C |
|---|---|---|---|---|---|
| Profit and loss ratio |  |  | 30% | 30% | 40% |
| (2) Balances after liquidation of liabilities | $3,000 | $6,000 | $7,500 | $10,500 | $12,000 |
| Possible loss from nonrealization of remaining Other Assets ($20,000), per Exhibit A |  |  | (6,000) | (6,000) | (8,000) |
| Balances after deducting all possible losses (payment to partners) | $3,000 | $6,000 | $1,500 | $4,500 | $4,000 |

The balances shown, which total $19,000, represent the amount that may be safely paid to the partners. The payments are safe in that after deducting them from the partners' equities, which exist after liquidation of the liabilities, each partner has a remaining equity balance equal to his share of all possible future loss from nonrealization of the assets.

The final phase of the liquidation statement, (3), poses no problem. The partners' equities at this point are sufficient to bear their respective shares of any possible loss. After each partner is charged with his share of the actual loss in the final phase, the cash realized in the final phase would be distributed, with each partner receiving the balance of his equity after deducting his share of the actual loss.

The foregoing liquidation of the ABC partnership by installments has the same result as if no distributions had been made to the partners until the final realization phase was completed. No party was harmed by the liquidation by installments because (1) all liabilities were liquidated before any cash was distributed to the partners, and (2) payments were made to partners only to the extent that their partnership equities were sufficient to cover all possible losses.

**Illustration 4-2.** In this illustration, assume that realization of the assets proceeds in the following three stages:

1. Assets carried at $30,000 are sold for $25,000. All cash on hand after the sale, $29,000, is used to liquidate liabilities.
2. Assets carried at $40,000 are sold for $22,000. Cash of $11,000 is used to liquidate the remaining liabilities, and $11,000 is distributed to the partners.
3. Remaining assets are sold for $10,000.

This illustration again indicates the exception to the general rule that partners' loan accounts are to be paid before their capital accounts. The right of offset has been dealt with in previous illustrations whereby a debit balance in a partner's capital account may be offset against his loan account. When partners are to receive cash for their partnership interests prior to complete realization of the assets, care must be taken to provide for all possible losses for each partner prior to distributing any cash to the partners. The total possible loss for each partner should be compared with that partner's equity (capital, drawing, and loan) to see if the equity is sufficient to bear the loss. Only then should the liquidation proceed.

The following statement of partnership liquidation on page 752 presents the liquidation under the assumptions above.

As in the preceding illustration, Phase (1) of the liquidation should be completed without difficulty. All cash realized from the partial sale of assets is used to liquidate liabilities. In the second phase, however, a problem arises after final liquidation of liabilities. The statement can be completed only down to the "Payment to partners" line under (2), without making supplementary calculations to determine the safe payments to partners at this point. The schedule showing this computation would appear as follows:

*Schedule 1*

### ABC Partnership
#### Computation of Balances after Providing for Possible Losses

|  | Loans A | Loans B | Capitals A | Capitals B | Capitals C |
|---|---|---|---|---|---|
| Profit and loss ratio |  |  | 30% | 30% | 40% |
| (2) Balances, after payment of creditors | $3,000 | $6,000 | $5,100 | $8,100 | $8,800 |
| Possible loss from nonrealization of remaining other assets, ($20,000) per Exhibit A |  |  | (6,000) | (6,000) | (8,000) |
| Balances | $3,000 | $6,000 | $(900) | $2,100 | $ 800 |
| Offset of capital debit of A against loan account | (900) |  | 900 |  |  |
| Balances after deduction of all possible losses (payments to partners) | $2,100 | $6,000 | –0– | $2,100 | $ 800 |

As the schedule reveals, partners B and C receive payment of a portion of their capitals even though partner A does not receive full return of his loan. Any other distribution of the available cash would not provide fully for the possibility of nonrealization of the remaining "Other Assets."

*Exhibit A*

## ABC PARTNERSHIP
### STATEMENT OF LIQUIDATION
### OCTOBER, 1979

|  | Cash | Other Assets | Liabilities | Loans A | Loans B | Capitals A 30% | Capitals B 30% | Capitals C 40% |
|---|---|---|---|---|---|---|---|---|
| Profit and loss ratio | | | | | | 30% | 30% | 40% |
| Balances per statement | $4,000 | $90,000 | $40,000 | $3,000 | $6,000 | $12,000 | $15,000 | $18,000 |
| (1) Realization and loss | 25,000 | (30,000) | | | | (1,500) | (1,500) | (2,000) |
| Balances | $29,000 | $60,000 | $40,000 | $3,000 | $6,000 | $10,500 | $13,500 | $16,000 |
| Payment to creditors | (29,000) | | (29,000) | | | | | |
| Balances | — | $60,000 | $11,000 | $3,000 | $6,000 | $10,500 | $13,500 | $16,000 |
| (2) Realization and loss | $30,000 | (40,000) | | | | (3,000) | (3,000) | (4,000) |
| Balances | $30,000 | $20,000 | $11,000 | $3,000 | $6,000 | $7,500 | $10,500 | $12,000 |
| Payment to creditors | (11,000) | | (11,000) | | | | | |
| Balances | $19,000 | $20,000 | — | $3,000 | $6,000 | $7,500 | $10,500 | $12,000 |
| Payment to partners (Schedule 1): | | | | | | | | |
| Loans | (9,000) | | | (3,000) | (6,000) | | | |
| Capitals | (10,000) | | | | | (1,500) | (4,500) | (4,000) |
| Balances | — | $20,000 | | — | — | $6,000 | $6,000 | $8,000 |
| (3) Realization and loss | $10,000 | (20,000) | | | | (3,000) | (3,000) | (4,000) |
| Balances | $10,000 | — | | — | — | $3,000 | $3,000 | $4,000 |
| Payments to partners | (10,000) | | | | | (3,000) | (3,000) | (4,000) |
| Balances | –0– | –0– | | –0– | –0– | –0– | –0– | –0– |

*Exhibit A*

## ABC PARTNERSHIP
### STATEMENT OF LIQUIDATION
### OCTOBER, 1979

|  | Cash | Other Assets | Liabilities | Loans A | Loans B | Capitals A 30% | Capitals B 30% | Capitals C 40% |
|---|---|---|---|---|---|---|---|---|
| Profit and loss ratio |  |  |  |  |  | 30% | 30% | 40% |
| Balances per statement | $4,000 | $90,000 | $40,000 | $3,000 | $6,000 | $12,000 | $15,000 | $18,000 |
| (1) Realization and loss | 25,000 | (30,000) |  |  |  | (1,500) | (1,500) | (2,000) |
| Balances | $29,000 | $60,000 | $40,000 | $3,000 | $6,000 | $10,500 | $13,500 | $16,000 |
| Payment to creditors | (29,000) |  | (29,000) |  |  |  |  |  |
| Balances | — | $60,000 | $11,000 | $3,000 | $6,000 | $10,500 | $13,500 | $16,000 |
| (2) Realization and loss | $22,000 | (40,000) |  |  |  | (5,400) | (5,400) | (7,200) |
| Balances | $22,000 | $20,000 | $11,000 | $3,000 | $6,000 | $5,100 | $8,100 | $8,800 |
| Payment to creditors | (11,000) |  | (11,000) |  |  |  |  |  |
| Balances | $11,000 | $20,000 | — | $3,000 | $6,000 | $5,100 | $8,100 | $8,800 |
| Payment to partners (Schedule 1): |  |  |  |  |  |  |  |  |
| Loans | (8,100) |  |  | (2,100) | (6,000) |  |  |  |
| Capitals | (2,900) |  |  |  |  |  | (2,100) | (800) |
| Balances | — | $20,000 |  | $900 | — | $5,100 | $6,000 | $8,000 |
| (3) Realization and loss | $10,000 | (20,000) |  |  |  | (3,000) | (3,000) | (4,000) |
| Balances | $10,000 | — |  | $900 | — | $2,100 | $3,000 | $4,000 |
| Payment to partners: |  |  |  |  |  |  |  |  |
| Loans | (900) |  |  | (900) |  |  |  |  |
| Capitals | (9,100) |  |  |  |  | (2,100) | (3,000) | (4,000) |
| Balances | —0— |  |  | —0— | —0— | —0— | —0— | —0— |

Phase (3) of the liquidation causes no problem in determining how much to pay the partners, regardless of the amount realized on the final $20,000 of assets. Provision was made in the schedule above to absorb a 100% loss. Any loss of less than 100% can thus be absorbed by the partners, with cash being distributed for whatever equity interests remain.

***Illustration 4-3.*** In each of the preceding illustrations each partner has had some equity in the partnership at the time of the first cash distribution to the partners, even after providing for possible losses from nonrealization of remaining assets. This illustration deals with the situation that arises when one or more partners do not have an equity remaining after providing for all possible loss from realization of remaining assets. In this illustration, assume that realization of the assets proceeds in the following three stages:

1. Assets carried at $30,000 are sold for $25,000. All cash on hand after the sale, $29,000, is used to liquidate liabilities.
2. Assets carried at $40,000 are sold for $18,000. Cash of $11,000 is used to liquidate remaining liabilities, and $7,000 is distributed to the partners.
3. Remaining assets are sold for $10,000.

In this illustration, it should be noted that after liquidation of all liabilities in Phase (2), Partner C should not receive any of the $7,000 cash remaining because his partnership equity is not sufficient to bear his share of the possible loss on nonrealization of the remaining $20,000 of Other Assets. The amount to be distributed to Partners A and B cannot be determined until after provision is made in their equities for (1) their share of the possible loss from nonrealization of Other Assets, and (2) their share of the possible loss from the failure of C to make good his debit balance, that would exist if a total loss on the remaining assets did arise.

The following statement of partnership liquidation, Exhibit A on page 754, illustrates the liquidation procedure under the assumptions above.

Again, no problems arise in liquidation until the point of determining payments to partners in Phase (2) is encountered. Cash of $7,000 is available for distribution, and partners' equities total $27,000. Only after provision is made for the possible loss of $20,000 from nonrealization of remaining assets can the liquidation proceed. In this illustration, as Schedule 1 on page 755 reveals, additional provision must be made for possible nonrealization of C's debit balance before the cash can be distributed appropriately.

In this same schedule it should be noted that offsets of capital debit balances against loans should be made before providing for additional losses from noncollection of other partners' debit balances.

After payment of the amounts indicated on the final line of the cited schedule, A and B will each have remaining equities of $6,400 (see Exhibit A). This is the equity required for each to absorb his share of the possible loss from nonrealization of assets and from noncollection from C.

*Exhibit A*

## ABC PARTNERSHIP
### STATEMENT OF LIQUIDATION
### OCTOBER, 1979

|  | Cash | Other Assets | Liabilities | Loans A | Loans B | Capitals A 30% | Capitals B 30% | Capitals C 40% |
|---|---|---|---|---|---|---|---|---|
| Profit and loss ratio |  |  |  |  |  | 30% | 30% | 40% |
| Balances per statement | $ 4,000 | $90,000 | $40,000 | $3,000 | $6,000 | $12,000 | $15,000 | $18,000 |
| (1) Realization and loss | 25,000 | (30,000) |  |  |  | (1,500) | (1,500) | (2,000) |
| Balances | $29,000 | $60,000 | $40,000 | $3,000 | $6,000 | $10,500 | $13,500 | $16,000 |
| Payments to creditors | (29,000) |  | (29,000) |  |  |  |  |  |
| Balances | — | $60,000 | $11,000 | $3,000 | $6,000 | $10,500 | $13,500 | $16,000 |
| (2) Realization and loss | $18,000 | (40,000) |  |  |  | (6,600) | (6,600) | (8,800) |
| Balances | $18,000 | $20,000 | $11,000 | $3,000 | $6,000 | $ 3,900 | $ 6,900 | $ 7,200 |
| Payment to creditors | (11,000) |  | (11,000) |  |  |  |  |  |
| Balances | $ 7,000 | $20,000 | — | $3,000 | $6,000 | $ 3,900 | $ 6,900 | $ 7,200 |
| Payment to partners (Schedule 1): |  |  |  |  |  |  |  |  |
| Loans | (6,500) |  |  | (500) | (6,000) |  |  |  |
| Capitals | ( 500) |  |  |  |  |  | (500) |  |
| Balances | — | $20,000 |  | $2,500 | — | $ 3,900 | $ 6,400 | $ 7,200 |
| (3) Realization and loss | $10,000 | (20,000) |  |  |  | (3,000) | (3,000) | (4,000) |
| Balances | $10,000 | — |  | $2,500 | — | $ 900 | $ 3,400 | $ 3,200 |
| Payments to partners: |  |  |  |  |  |  |  |  |
| Loans | (2,500) |  |  | (2,500) |  |  |  |  |
| Capitals | (7,500) |  |  |  |  | ( 900) | (3,400) | (3,200) |
| Balances | —0— | —0— | —0— | —0— | —0— | —0— | —0— | —0— |

## Schedule 1

### ABC Partnership
#### Computation of Balances after Providing for Possible Losses

|  | Loans | | Capitals | | |
| --- | ---: | ---: | ---: | ---: | ---: |
|  | A | B | A | B | C |
| Profit and loss ratio |  |  | 30% | 30% | 40% |
| (2) Balances after payment to creditors | $3,000 | $6,000 | $3,900 | $6,900 | $7,200 |
| Possible loss from nonrealization of remaining Other Assets of $20,000 per Exhibit A |  |  | (6,000) | (6,000) | (8,000) |
| Balances | $3,000 | $6,000 | $(2,100) | $ 900 | $( 800) |
| Offset of A's capital debit against loan account | (2,100) |  | 2,100 |  |  |
| Balances | $ 900 | $6,000 | — | $ 900 | $( 800) |
| Possible additional loss from noncontribution by C of debit balance (in 30 : 30 ratio) | ( 400) |  |  | ( 400) | 800 |
| Balance after deduction of all possible losses (payments to partners) | $ 500 | $6,000 | –0– | $ 500 | –0– |

## Miscellaneous Problems

The amounts determined to be safe payments under the general rules for distribution of cash discussed in the preceding sections might not be acceptable to each of the partners concerned. For example, in Illustration 4-3, A might feel that B was being treated preferentially if, in Phase (2) of the realization and liquidation, B received return in full of his $6,000 loan and also $500 return of his capital while A received only $500 of his $3,000 loan. If the liquidator or individual charged with administering the liquidation could not convince A that the proposed payments were the only ones that could be made properly at that time, the liquidator should refrain from making any payments until the assets are fully realized. Since the liquidator may be held liable for any improper installment payments, he should not make any payments prior to full realization of assets if the partners cannot agree to his plan of payment.

**Advance Planning for Cash Distributions.** When a partnership's assets are realized on a piecemeal basis over a period of time, it may be desirable to determine in advance the order or priority in which any cash realized from the sale of assets will be applied in settlement of the existing claims. To develop an advance plan of cash distribution, the liquidator must consider the extent of loss

## ABC Partnership
### Statement of Liquidation (Partial)

|  | Cash | Other Assets | Liabilities | Loans A | Loans B | Capitals A 30% | Capitals B 30% | Capitals C 40% |
|---|---|---|---|---|---|---|---|---|
| Profit and loss ratio | | | | | | 30% | 30% | 40% |
| Balances | $4,000 | $90,000 | $40,000 | $3,000 | $6,000 | $12,000 | $15,000 | $18,000 |
| Loss, as above | | (45,000) | | | | (13,500) | (13,500) | (18,000) |
| Balances | $4,000 | $45,000 | $40,000 | $3,000 | $6,000 | $(1,500) | $1,500 | –0– |

The liquidator must now determine how much additional loss would be needed to extinguish the equities of A and B ($1,500 and $7,500, respectively). Since they share profits in a 30:30 relationship or 50% each, an additional loss of $3,000 would eliminate A. The partial Statement of Liquidation above would be continued as follows:

|  | Cash | Other Assets | Liabilities | Loans A | Loans B | Capitals A | Capitals B | Capitals C |
|---|---|---|---|---|---|---|---|---|
| Balances, as above | $4,000 | $45,000 | $40,000 | $3,000 | $6,000 | (1,500) | $1,500 | –0– |
| Loss, as above to be shared by A and B only | | (3,000) | | | | (1,500) | (1,500) | |
| Balances | $4,000 | $42,000 | $40,000 | $3,000 | $6,000 | $(3,000) | – | – |
| Offset A's debit balance against loan | | | | (3,000) | | 3,000 | | |
| Balances | $4,000 | $42,000 | $40,000 | –0– | $6,000 | –0– | –0– | –0– |

## 23 / Partnership Liquidation

that would be necessary to eliminate each partner's equity. After determining the loss required to eliminate each partner from any cash distribution, the liquidator may plan his cash distribution.

For example, assume that partnership ABC has $94,000 of assets prior to realization, $40,000 in liabilities, and total equities for A, B, and C of $15,000, $21,000, and $18,000, respectively. Since A, B, and C share profits in a 30 : 30 : 40 relationship, the loss that would extinguish each partner's equity may be determined by dividing his profit and loss percentage into his equity.

A — $15,000 ÷ 30% = $50,000 loss required to extinguish A's equity.
B — $21,000 ÷ 30% = $70,000 loss required to extinguish B's equity.
C — $18,000 ÷ 40% = $45,000 loss required to extinguish C's equity.

Since C's equity would be eliminated by the smallest loss, if realization of the assets brought $49,000 cash causing a $45,000 loss, C would receive no payments on his equity. (See liquidation statement on page 756.)

From this illustration, it should be noted:

1. The general rule of priority of partners' loans in liquidation is of little consequence when installment liquidation is to be followed. In liquidation by installments, partner equity (loans, drawings, and capital) is of prime importance.
2. The order of cash distribution is the reverse of the order of losses necessary to extinguish each partner's equity in the partnership. Before the plan can be prepared, the liquidator must determine for each partnership interest, in turn, the loss necessary to extinguish such interest. This determination proceeds until all partner interests have been eliminated.
3. By working back through the illustration, the liquidator could prepare a plan to guide his liquidation similar to the following one.

### ABC PARTNERSHIP IN LIQUIDATION
#### Plan for Distribution of Cash

|  | Total Assets | Liabilities | A | B | C |
|---|---|---|---|---|---|
| Balances prior to realization | $94,000 | $40,000 | $15,000 | $21,000 | $18,000 |
| Order of distribution of cash: |  |  |  |  |  |
| First $40,000 | $40,000 | $40,000 |  |  |  |
| Next $6,000 | 6,000 |  |  | $ 6,000 |  |
| Next $3,000 | 3,000 |  | $ 1,500 | 1,500 |  |
| Next $45,000, in profit and loss ratio* | 45,000 |  | 13,500 | 13,500 | 18,000 |
| Total | $94,000 | $40,000 | $15,000 | $21,000 | $18,000 |

*Any additional cash realized in liquidation would be distributed in the profit and loss ratio.

## PROBLEMS

### Problem 23-1

Green, Brown, and White are partners with capital balances of $12,000, $9,000, and $7,000, respectively. On November 10, 1979, the partners agree to liquidate their business. At this date they have assets of $47,000 and liabilities of $22,000, including an amount due to Brown of $2,000. On November 10 they accept an offer of $35,000 for the assets of their business, the partners agreeing to settle all partnership obligations.

*Required:*
Prepare a liquidation statement for the partnership showing how the cash arising from the sale of assets is to be distributed.

### Problem 23-2

Burnside and Brewer decided to liquidate their partnership business on August 1, 1979. The partners had been sharing profits and losses in a 60 : 40 ratio. The following balance sheet was prepared on the day liquidation began.

BURNSIDE AND BREWER
BALANCE SHEET, AUGUST 1, 1979

| | | | |
|---|---|---|---|
| Cash | $ 6,000 | Accounts payable | $14,000 |
| Receivables | 25,000 | Burnside, Loan | 8,000 |
| Inventory | 30,000 | Burnside, Capital (60%) | 34,000 |
| Other assets (net) | 28,000 | Brewer, Drawing | 3,000 |
| | | Brewer, Capital (40%) | 30,000 |
| | $89,000 | | $89,000 |

During August, one-half the receivables were collected at a loss of $1,000; $20,000 of inventory was sold at an average of 75% of book value; all the "other assets" were sold for $20,000.

*Required:*
Prepare a liquidation statement and accompanying schedule to show how the cash on hand would be distributed on August 31, 1979.

### Problem 23-3

Adams, Denny, and Paul operated a partnership, sharing profits in a 5 : 3 : 2 ratio. On October 31, 1980, the balance sheet of their partnership showed the following:

ADAMS, DENNY, & PAUL PARTNERSHIP
BALANCE SHEET 10/31/80

| | | | |
|---|---|---|---|
| Cash | $ 5,000 | Liabilities | $ 45,000 |
| Other Assets | 145,000 | Due to Adams | 10,000 |

|                  |           |
|------------------|-----------|
| Adams, Capital   | 35,000    |
| Denny, Capital   | 30,000    |
| Paul, Capital    | 30,000    |
| $150,000         | $150,000  |

The partnership agreement also provided for a $1,000 per month salary payable to Denny and chargeable to operations as an expense. Salaries have not been paid or accrued since December 31, 1979. On October 31, 1980, the partners realize that their assets are overvalued. Because of pressing demands from creditors, they accept an offer of $79,000 for the "Other Assets" shown above.

*Required:*
(1) Prepare a statement of partnership liquidation that will reflect the facts above and show how the cash resulting would be distributed.
(2) How would the cash resulting from the sale have been distributed if the proceeds of the sale had been only $49,000, and if Adams were personally insolvent? Prepare a statement to support your conclusion.

## Problem 23-4

Keenan, Opal, and Peters, each of whom had personal assets well in excess of their personal debts, decided to liquidate their partnership on August 31, 1980. On that date the equities of each partner were as follows:

| Loan from Keenan   | $15,000      |
|--------------------|--------------|
| Loan from Peters   | 5,000        |
| Keenan, Capital    | 35,000       |
| Keenan, Drawing    | 5,000 Cr.    |
| Opal, Capital      | 30,000       |
| Opal, Drawing      | 5,000 Dr.    |
| Peters, Capital    | 15,000       |

The partners shared profits equally. Liabilities of the partnership at August 31, 1980, exclusive of the partners' claims, were equal to 50% of the book value of the assets. Opal insisted, and the other partners agreed, that upon sale the assets of the partnership had to realize an amount sufficient to provide him with $5,000 cash. A buyer was found who agreed to buy the assets at a price just sufficient to meet Opal's demands.

*Required:*
Prepare a statement of partnership liquidation with supporting calculations where necessary. Show how cash from the sale of the assets would be distributed.

## Problem 23-5

The partners of Sims and Company agreed to dissolve their partnership and to begin liquidation on February 1, 1980. Rowe was designated as the partner in charge of liquidation. It was agreed that distributions of cash to the partners were to be made on the last day of each month during liquidation, provided that there was sufficient cash available.

The partnership agreement provided that profits and losses were to be shared on the following basis: Quinn 20%, Rowe 30%, Sims 30%, and Toth 20%. The firm's condensed balance sheet on February 1, 1980 was as follows:

| Cash | $33,440 | Accounts payable | $ 7,120 |
|---|---|---|---|
| Goodwill | 20,000 | Loan from Quinn | 5,000 |
| Other assets | 44,510 | Capital: | |
| | | Quinn | 8,040 |
| | | Rowe | 32,160 |
| | | Sims | 36,340 |
| | | Toth | 9,290 |
| | $97,950 | | $97,950 |

The liquidating transactions for February and March, other than cash distributions to partners, are summarized by months below:

|  | Cash | |
|---|---|---|
|  | February | March |
| Realization of assets with a book value of: | | |
| $22,020 | $16,440 | |
| $14,950 | | $16,110 |
| Paid liquidation expenses as incurred | 2,740 | 2,460 |
| Paid to Creditors on account | 5,910 | 1,210 |

*Required:*

Prepare a schedule showing the total amounts of cash distributed to the partners at the end of February and March, and the amounts received by each partner in each distribution. Assume that Rowe made the distributions in such a manner that eventual overpayment was precluded. (AICPA adapted)

### Problem 23-6

Kolar, Leddy, and Martin are partners sharing profits in the ratio of 4, 3, and 2, respectively. The partnership and two of the partners are currently unable to pay their creditors. The firm balance sheet and personal status of the partners are as follows:

KOLAR, LEDDY, & MARTIN PARTNERSHIP

BALANCE SHEET

| Assets | | Liabilities | |
|---|---|---|---|
| Cash | $ 500 | Accounts and Bills Payable | $37,000 |
| Other Assets | 60,500 | Capital: Kolar | 10,000 |
| | | Leddy | 6,000 |
| | | Martin | 8,000 |
| | $61,000 | | $61,000 |

### Personal Status of Partners
(Excluding Partnership Interests)

| Partner | Cash and cash value of personal assets | Liabilities |
|---------|----------------------------------------|-------------|
| Kolar   | $31,000                                | $20,000     |
| Leddy   | 9,450                                  | 11,900      |
| Martin  | 4,000                                  | 5,000       |

*Required:*
(1) Prepare a work sheet showing distribution to partnership and personal creditors in the event of dissolution under the provisions of the Uniform Partnership Act, assuming that the "Other Assets" are sold for $33,500.
(2) Prepare a computation showing the minimum amount that must be realized from the sale of the partnership assets other than cash, so that the personal creditors of Leddy would receive full settlement of their claims.

(AICPA adapted)

### Problem 23-7

The balance sheet of the Button, Conroy, and Tolle partnership just prior to the sale of the partnership assets is:

**BUTTON, CONROY & TOLLE**
**Balance Sheet as of July 15, 1980**

| Cash              | $ 20,000 | Payables        | $ 75,000 |
|-------------------|----------|-----------------|----------|
| Receivables       | 40,000   | Conroy, Loan    | 15,000   |
| Inventory         | 60,000   | Button, Capital | 49,000   |
| Fixed assets (net)| 60,000   | Conroy, Capital | 25,000   |
|                   |          | Tolle, Capital  | 16,000   |
|                   | $180,000 |                 | $180,000 |

Button, Conroy, and Tolle share profits and losses in a 4 : 3 : 3 ratio, respectively. Sale of the noncash assets realizes a total of $60,000. The personal financial position of each partner, in addition to their partnership status, is shown below:

|        | Assets   | Liabilities |
|--------|----------|-------------|
| Button | $90,000  | $100,000    |
| Conroy | 70,000   | 30,000      |
| Tolle  | 30,000   | 36,000      |

*Required:*
(1) Prepare a statement of partnership liquidation to show how the cash realized from the sale of the assets will be distributed, assuming (*a*) that the Uniform Partnership Act is applicable, *and* (*b*) assuming that common law is applicable.
(2) Prepare journal entries to record the facts above under assumption (*a*) in (1) above.

## Problem 23-8

Sawtell, Mortensen, and Halasz have decided to dissolve their partnership. On March 1, 1980, the partners had the following equities and profit and loss sharing ratios:

| Partner | Loan Acct. | Capital Acct. | P & L |
|---|---|---|---|
| Sawtell | $20,000 | $42,000 | 40% |
| Mortensen | — | 26,000 | 30% |
| Halasz | 10,000 | 31,000 | 30% |
| | $30,000 | $99,000 | |

On March 1, 1980, all liabilities except $11,000 had been paid and cash on hand amounted to $5,000. During March, assets with a book value of $65,000 were sold for $50,000; during April, additional assets with a book value of $40,000 were sold for $28,000; during May, the remaining assets were sold for $10,000. Expenses of realization were $4,000, $3,000, and $2,000 in March, April, and May, respectively. All liabilities were paid at March 31, and cash realized was distributed to partners at the end of each month. The partners had no personal assets.

*Required:*
(1) Prepare a liquidation statement, with supporting schedule, to show how the cash available should be paid out on March 31, April 30, and May 31.
(2) Prepare journal entries to record the events of the three months.

## Problem 23-9

The partners of the Three-Ten Company agree to dissolve their partnership and to begin the realization of assets on August 1, 1980. The partners agreed to distribute to themselves at the end of each month all cash resulting from realization of assets except any cash needed to liquidate unpaid liabilities, plus $5,000 to be reserved for the following month's expenses. On completion of the realization of the assets, all existing cash was distributed.

The partners had been in business for many years and had been sharing profits and losses as follows: Brown, 40%; Herman, 40%; Schwartz, 20%. A balance sheet prepared on August 1, 1980, disclosed the following financial condition:

THREE-TEN COMPANY

BALANCE SHEET, AUGUST 1, 1980

| | | | |
|---|---|---|---|
| Cash | $ 6,000 | Payables | $ 20,000 |
| Other Assets | 106,000 | Brown, Loan | 5,000 |
| Herman, Drawing | 6,000 | Herman, Loan | 10,000 |
| Schwartz, Drawing | 2,000 | Brown, Capital | 23,000 |
| | | Herman, Capital | 40,000 |
| | | Schwartz, Capital | 22,000 |
| | $120,000 | | $120,000 |

The following table summarizes the results of realization over a three-month period:

|  | Assets Realized | Cash Received | Liabilities Paid |
|---|---|---|---|
| August | $30,000 | $20,000 | $12,000 |
| September | 30,000 | 18,000 | 8,000 |
| October | 46,000 | 22,000 |  |

### Required:

Prepare a statement of partnership liquidation and a supporting schedule to show how the cash available at the end of the three months was distributed.

## Problem 23-10

On September 1, 1980, Berns, a partner in the firm of Berns, Giller, and Ulrich, discovers that the books of the partnership do not reflect an accurate state of partnership affairs. Ulrich has been in charge of the partnership records, and Berns' discovery reveals that certain personal transactions of Ulrich have been merged with the partnership affairs, while other partnership transactions have not been recorded properly. The three men began business by contributing equal capitals of $30,000, and they share profits and losses equally. A balance sheet prepared on September 1, 1980, before reflecting any of the findings of Berns, follows:

### BERNS, GILLER, & ULRICH
### BALANCE SHEET, SEPTEMBER 1, 1980

| Cash | $ 6,000 | Accounts payable | $ 55,000 |
|---|---|---|---|
| Receivables | 30,000 | Berns, Loan | 15,000 |
| Inventory | 50,000 | Berns, Capital | 23,000 |
| Other assets | 70,000 | Giller, Capital | 25,000 |
|  |  | Ulrich, Capital | 38,000 |
|  | $156,000 |  | $156,000 |

After a thorough examination of the records of the partnership, the following discrepancies are determined to exist:

1. Over a period of years, Ulrich made purchases of items for his personal use through the partnership, totaling $12,000, and he charged "Purchases" for these items.
2. Ulrich has "borrowed" funds from the partnership totaling $15,000 over several years. Of this amount, $6,000 is currently included in the balance of "Receivables" above, while the other $9,000 has been charged off as a loss in previous years.
3. Giller had loaned $5,000 to the partnership, but Ulrich had taken the amount for his personal use and had not recorded the loan. This amount was unpaid at September 1, 1980.

4. Purchases of merchandise made in late August, 1980, totaling $4,500 had not been recorded prior to closing the books at the end of August, although the merchandise was on hand and included in the inventory September 1, 1980.

Berns and Giller agree to continue in business after acquiring the interest of Ulrich. The partners agree that, in addition to the corrections required from the facts above, the proper values for the other assets and inventories are $60,000 and $45,000, respectively. Ulrich is to bear no penalty for his actions.

*Required:*
(1) How much will Ulrich receive for his partnership interest?
(2) Prepare entries to reflect the facts above, including an entry to set up as a liability the amount due to Ulrich for liquidation of his partnership interest.
(3) What is the corrected balance of Berns' capital? Of Giller's capital?

## Problem 23-11

*Part A.* The partnership of Adams, Baker, and Crane has called you to assist them in winding up the affairs of their partnership. You are able to gather the following information:

1. The trial balance of the partnership at June 30, 1979 is as follows:

|  | Debit | Credit |
|---|---|---|
| Cash | $ 6,000 | |
| Accounts receivable | 22,000 | |
| Inventory | 14,000 | |
| Plant and equipment (net) | 99,000 | |
| Adams, loan | 12,000 | |
| Crane, loan | 7,500 | |
| Accounts payable | | $ 17,000 |
| Adams, capital | | 67,000 |
| Baker, capital | | 45,000 |
| Crane, capital | | 31,500 |
| | $160,500 | $160,500 |

2. The partners share profits and losses as follows: Adams, 50%; Baker, 30%; Crane, 20%.
3. The partners are considering an offer of $100,000 for the accounts receivable, inventory, and plant and equipment as of June 30. The $100,000 would be paid to the partners in installments, the number and amounts of which are to be negotiated.

*Required:*
Prepare a cash distribution schedule as of June 30, 1979, showing how the $100,000 would be distributed as it becomes available.

*Part B.* Assume the same facts as in Part A except that the partners have decided to liquidate their partnership instead of accepting the offer of $100,000. Cash is to be distributed to the partners at the end of each month.

A summary of the liquidation transactions follows:

*July*
    $16,500 — collected on accounts receivable, balance is uncollectible.
    10,000 — received for the entire inventory.
    1,000 — liquidation expenses.
    8,000 — cash retained in the business at end of the month.

*August*
    $ 1,500 — liquidation expenses paid.
            As part payment of his capital, Crane accepted a piece of special equipment that he developed which had a book value of $4,000. The partners agreed that a value of $10,000 should be placed on the machine for liquidation purposes.
    2,500 — cash retained in the business at end of the month.

*September*
    $75,000 — received on sale of remaining plant and equipment.
    1,000 — liquidation expenses paid.
            No cash retained in the business.

*Required:*

Prepare a schedule of cash payments as of September 30, 1979, showing how the cash was actually distributed.           (AICPA adapted)

## Problem 23-12

You are engaged to assist in terminating the affairs of T and A Discount Sales, a partnership under liquidation. Allen owns Toy Wholesalers and contributed $10,000 in inventory for a 50% interest in T and A Discount Sales on January 2, 1980. Ball owns Appliance Wholesalers and contributed $2,000 cash and $8,000 in inventory for a 50% interest on the same date. All profits and losses are to be shared equally.

T and A Discount Sales was an unsuccessful operation, so it was decided to dissolve the partnership after the Christmas shopping season.

In the course of your examination, you determine the following facts:

1. An incompetent part-time bookkeeper had discarded all cash register tapes and invoices for expenses and purchases. He was also the bookkeeper for Appliance Wholesalers.
2. The partners state that the only existing payables are to themselves, as follows:

| | |
|---|---:|
| Toy Wholesalers | $ 9,740 |
| Appliance Wholesalers | 5,260 |
| | $15,000 |

3. You are able to prepare the following summary of cash transactions from bank statements and cancelled checks:

| | | |
|---|---:|---:|
| Opening cash balance | | $ 2,000 |
| Receipts: | | |
|   Sales | $70,000 | |
|   Inventory liquidation | 7,000 | 77,000 |
| | | 79,000 |
| Disbursements: | | |
|   Purchases | 36,000 | |
|   Operating expenses | 26,000 | |
|   Leasehold improvements (5-year lease) | 6,000 | |
|   Liquidating expense | 4,000 | 72,000 |
| Balance, December 31, 1980 | | $ 7,000 |

4. On December 31, 1980, $7,000 was paid to the partners, $3,500 to each, to apply on the $15,000 liability.
5. The partners state that the dollar amounts of regular sales of toys and appliances were approximately equal and that the dollar amounts of liquidating sales of toys and appliances were also approximately equal. There was a uniform markup of 40% of cost on toys and 25% of cost on appliances. All sales were for cash. The ending inventory of shopworn merchandise was liquidated on December 31, 1980 for 50% of the retail sales price.
6. The partners believe that some appliances may have been returned to Appliance Wholesalers but the bookkeeper failed to record the returns on the books of either organization.

*Required:*
(1) Compute the unrecorded amount of appliances returned to Appliance Wholesalers, if any.
(2) Prepare an income statement for T and A Discount Sales for the period January 2 to December 31, 1980.
(3) Prepare a statement of partners' capital accounts.    (AICPA adapted)

## Problem 23-13

The XYZ Partnership is being dissolved. All liabilities have been liquidated. The balance of assets on hand is being realized gradually. Shown below are details of partners' accounts:

| | Capital Account (Original Investment) | Current Account (Undistributed Earnings Net of Drawings) | Profit and Loss Ratio |
|---|---:|---:|---:|
| X | $20,000 | $1,500 Cr. | 4 |
| Y | 25,000 | 2,000 Dr. | 4 |
| Z | 10,000 | 1,000 Cr. | 2 |

*Additional information:*
X loaned $15,000 to the partnership and Z loaned $5,000. Y made no loan to the partnership.

*Required:*
Prepare a schedule showing how cash payments should be made to the partners as assets are realized. (AICPA adapted)

## Problem 23-14

Bowers, Levan, and Miller have agreed to dissolve their partnership as of November 1, 1980. They plan to proceed with a gradual liquidation of the business in hopes of reducing the loss upon realization to a minimum. As cash from realization becomes available, the partners plan to have partial distributions in settlement of their interests. The following balance sheet was prepared on October 31, 1980:

BOWERS, LEVAN, & MILLER
BALANCE SHEET, OCTOBER 31, 1980

| | | | |
|---|---|---|---|
| Cash | $ 10,000 | Current liabilities | $ 30,000 |
| Other assets | 170,000 | Bowers, Loan | 20,000 |
| | | Bowers, Capital | 62,000 |
| | | Levan, Capital | 24,000 |
| | | Miller, Capital | 44,000 |
| | $180,000 | | $180,000 |

The partners have been sharing profits and losses in the following manner: Bowers, 50%; Levan, 30%; Miller, 20%.

*Required:*
Prepare a cash distribution showing the proper distribution of cash as it becomes available.

## Problem 23-15

The partners of Able, Bright, Cool, and Dahl have decided to dissolve their partnership. They plan to sell the assets gradually in order to minimize losses. They share profits and losses as follows: Able, 40%; Bright, 35%; Cool, 15%; and Dahl, 10%. Presented below is the partnership's trial balance as of October 1, 1979, the date on which liquidation begins:

| | Debit | Credit |
|---|---|---|
| Cash | $ 200 | |
| Receivables | 25,900 | |
| Inventory, October 1, 1979 | 42,600 | |
| Equipment (net) | 19,800 | |
| Accounts Payable | | $ 3,000 |
| Able, Loan | | 6,000 |

|  |  |  |
|---|---|---|
| Bright, Loan |  | 10,000 |
| Able, Capital |  | 20,000 |
| Bright, Capital |  | 21,500 |
| Cool, Capital |  | 18,000 |
| Dahl, Capital |  | 10,000 |
|  | $88,500 | $88,500 |

*Required:*
(1) Prepare a statement as of October 1, 1979, showing how cash will be distributed among partners by installments as it becomes available.
(2) On October 31, 1979, cash of $12,700 becomes available to creditors and partners. How should it be distributed?
(3) If, instead of being dissolved, the partnership continued operations and earned a profit of $23,625, how should that profit be distributed if, in addition to the aforementioned profit-sharing arrangement, it was provided that Dahl receive a bonus of 5% of the net income from operations after treating such bonus as an expense? (AICPA adapted)

## Problem 23-16

The following balance sheet is for the partnership of Able, Boyer and Cain:

| Cash | $ 20,000 | Liabilities | $ 50,000 |
|---|---|---|---|
| Other assets | 180,000 | Able, Capital (40%) | 37,000 |
|  |  | Boyer, Capital (40%) | 65,000 |
|  |  | Cain, Capital (20%) | 48,000 |
|  | $200,000 |  | $200,000 |

Figures shown parenthetically reflect agreed profit and loss sharing percentages.

1. If the assets are fairly valued on the balance sheet above and the partnership wishes to admit Day as a new 1/6 partner without recording goodwill or bonus, Day should contribute cash or other assets of
   a. $40,000.
   b. $36,000.
   c. $33,333.
   d. $30,000.
2. If assets on the initial balance sheet are fairly valued, Able and Boyer consent and Day pays Cain $51,000 for his interest; the revised capital balances of the partners would be
   a. Able, $38,500; Boyer, $66,500; Day, $51,000.
   b. Able, $38,500; Boyer, $66,500; Day, $48,000.
   c. Able, $37,000; Boyer, $65,000; Day, $51,000.
   d. Able, $37,000; Boyer, $65,000; Day, $48,000.
3. If the firm, as shown on the original balance sheet, is dissolved and liquidated by selling assets in installments, the first sale of noncash assets having a book

value of $90,000 realizes $50,000 and all cash available after settlement with creditors is distributed; the respective partners would receive (to the nearest dollar)
 a. Able, $8,000; Boyer, $8,000; Cain, $4,000.
 b. Able, $6,667; Boyer, $6,667; Cain, $6,666.
 c. Able, $0; Boyer, $13,333; Cain, $6,667.
 d. Able, $0; Boyer, $3,000; Cain, $17,000.
4. If the facts are as in Item 3 above except that $3,000 cash is to be withheld, the respective partners would then receive (to the nearest dollar)
 a. Able, $6,800; Boyer, $6,800; Cain, $3,400.
 b. Able, $5,667; Boyer, $5,667; Cain, $5,666.
 c. Able, $0; Boyer, $11,333; Cain, $5,667.
 d. Able, $0; Boyer, $1,000; Cain, $16,000.
5. If each partner properly received some cash in the distribution after the second sale, the cash to be distributed amounts to $12,000 from the third sale, and unsold assets with an $8,000 book value remain; ignoring Items 3 and 4, the respective partners would receive
 a. Able, $4,800; Boyer, $4,800; Cain, $2,400.
 b. Able, $4,000; Boyer, $4,000; Cain, $4,000.
 c. Able, 37/150 of $12,000; Boyer, 65/150 of $12,000; Cain 48/150 of $12,000.
 d. Able, $0; Boyer, $8,000; Cain, $4,000. (AICPA adapted)

## Problem 23-17

Flint, Durant, and Nash are partners in a wholesale business. On January 1, 1979, the total capital was $48,000, divided as follows: Flint, $10,000; Durant, $8,000; Nash, $30,000. Their 1979 drawings were $6,000, $4,000 and $2,000, respectively. Through the failure of debtors they lose heavily and are compelled to liquidate. After exhausting the partnership assets, including those arising from an operating profit of $7,200 in 1979, they still owe $8,400 to creditors on December 31, 1979. Flint has no personal assets but the others are well off.

*Required:*
 Prepare:
 (1) Computation of partnership's liquidating loss.
 (2) Statement of partnership's liquidation.
 (3) Profit and loss and partners' accounts, closed out after liquidation.
 (AICPA adapted)

# 24

# Corporate Liquidation

This chapter deals primarily with some of the accounting and reporting problems faced by a corporation that is in the process of liquidation. Certain related legal and tax considerations will be noted from time to time to indicate some of the complications involved in a corporate liquidation situation.

The preceding two chapters have dealt with the liquidation problems of proprietorships and partnerships. In those chapters some of the reasons for business liquidations were noted. Corporate liquidations arise for some of the same reasons, and, in addition, for reasons peculiar to the corporate form of organization. The following situations may precipitate corporate liquidation: bankruptcy, occasioned by sustained operating losses, overinvestment in fixed assets, excessive accumulation of inventories, excessive borrowing, as well as a variety of other reasons; theft, fraud, or improper managerial manipulations: losses from floods, fires, or other "acts of God"; excessive taxation or undue legal or administrative stringencies imposed by governmental rulings; and loss of sales potential because of success of competitors, developing of new products, or changes in consumer demand.

Since a corporation is in reality a creature of the state, that is, it is organized and operated only under the jurisdiction of a state law, it follows that liquidation and dissolution of a corporation would proceed according to the provision of the statutes of the state of incorporation. Although a corporation is legally terminated only when its franchise is extinguished and its charter is terminated, for all practical purposes the corporation is terminated when it goes out of business.

**Reasons for Corporate Dissolution.** Ballantine lists the following ways in which a corporation may be legally dissolved:[1]

[1] Ballantine's *Manual on Corporation Law and Practice,* 1930, Callaghan & Co., p. 775.

1. By an act of the legislature repealing or withdrawing its charter, provided the legislature, in granting the charter, has reserved the power to repeal the same, but not otherwise.
2. By the expiration of a time *limited* in its charter for the continuance of its corporate existence.
3. By the happening of some contingency prescribed in its charter or by statute.
4. By a surrender of its charter, provided the surrender is authorized or accepted by the state.
5. By the forfeiture of its charter in a judicial proceeding by the state.
6. By decree of court of equity in some states.

**Corporate Liquidation Versus Dissolution.** As in the two preceding chapters, the primary emphasis in this chapter will be on liquidation of the business entity rather than on its dissolution. While neither bankruptcy nor receivership in equity necessarily results in legal dissolution, each of these will frequently result in corporate liquidation. A corporation may be liquidated, that is, its assets may be sold and its liabilities liquidated, without necessarily being dissolved in a legal sense. From an accounting point of view, corporate liquidation is more significant than dissolution.

The distinction between liquidation and dissolution is particularly important as far as corporations are concerned, because the period of liquidation may extend well beyond the legal date of corporate dissolution. The statutes of most states permit a corporation to continue in existence for an interval (frequently three years) after filing notice of dissolution with the state. During this period of existence, certain officials are empowered to collect the corporate assets, pay its liabilities, and distribute remaining assets to the stockholders. In addition, lawsuits may be brought, continued, or defended, and any other actions undertaken which are necessary to wind up the corporate affairs.

## Tax Considerations

In addition to meeting the various legal requirements of a corporate dissolution, the officers of a corporation that faces liquidation should plan their actions carefully so that the stockholders will suffer minimum tax disadvantages. The basic problem for officials of a corporation considering liquidation is to plan their actions leading up to liquidation, and generally legal dissolution, in such a manner that distributions to stockholders are considered to be distributions in carrying out a "plan of liquidation" and are not considered to be distributions in the nature of dividends. Collateral problems exist in distinguishing between certain types of statutory reorganizations, stock redemption plans, and corporate liquidation plans.

As a general rule, taxing authorities appear to take the position that the question of whether a corporation is or is not liquidating is one of intention or fact. In any questionable liquidation situation, they seem to attempt to determine the intent of the corporate officials and use this intent as the basis for deciding what, in fact, has been done. An attempt is generally made to determine whether the overall plan of liquidation is a device to deprive the taxing authority of tax revenue to which it is entitled.

**Types of Corporate Liquidations.** A corporate liquidation may be consummated completely in a single-step transaction with the proceeds being distributed to the stockholders, or the liquidation may proceed piecemeal with distributions being made periodically to stockholders. The latter alternative creates the greater number of problems from a tax viewpoint. When corporate liquidation is contemplated, one of the main tax considerations is whether the distribution is a liquidation distribution, wherein the stockholder-taxpayer does not include any amounts received as income until the basis of his holdings is recovered, or whether the distribution is essentially equivalent to a taxable dividend, wherein the stockholder-taxpayer includes the distribution as ordinary income from dividends. To be treated as a liquidation distribution, the amount paid out by a corporation must be in full settlement of *all* outstanding stock or it must be in accordance with a plan of gradual liquidation that is directed toward eventual complete liquidation of the corporation. The existence of either of these alternatives is a matter of fact to be determined by review of the intent underlying the distributions made.

**Corporate Liquidation by Trustee.** Corporate liquidations, particularly when a large corporation is involved, frequently require a considerable period of time. In addition, it may be desirable for the liquidation to be carried out by trustees specifically appointed for the purpose. The trustee (or trustees) takes control of the assets and acts in the place of the regular corporate officials. The trustee(s) acts in a fiduciary capacity, being compensated for his services normally through a fee arrangement. When liquidation proceeds under the direction of a trustee, the corporation is faced with several alternative tax possibilities. For instance, its operations during the liquidation period may be taxed on a regular corporate basis, on a trust association basis, or on a strict trust arrangement basis. The detailed form of the trustee's organization, duties, and responsibilities would establish the factual situation that would be the basis for determination of the tax method applicable.

**Significance of Current Values.** When a corporation is insolvent or faces bankruptcy, a statement of financial position prepared in accordance with generally accepted principles of accounting may not present a fair representation of the financial position of the company. The primary reason for the shortcomings of regular statements of financial position under conditions of imminent liquidation is the fact that the statement is normally presented from a "going-concern" point of view. The assets are reported on the basis of acquisition cost, less applicable amortization, to the corporation. Little attempt is made to report the current value of the various assets. The current value of an asset assumes greater importance when the corporate officials contemplate that the asset will be severed from corporate use through sale, trade, or abandonment.

A corporation facing liquidation is more interested in the current value of its various assets than in their book value. A statement presenting financial position in terms of current realizable values is frequently more useful than a statement prepared on the basis of traditional accounting concepts. In substance, reporting on a company under conditions that suggest that dissolution and liquidation are probable should focus principally on the realization probabilities under conditions of liquidation.

A statement of financial position based on current realizable values can take many forms. However, the statement should be labeled clearly so that the reader will understand the basis on which it has been prepared. Since the reader is interested in the manner in which assets may be realized and liabilities may be liquidated, the statement may present related assets and liabilities as offsets, even though offset reporting is not generally accepted in traditional reporting.

**Example of Presentation.** For example, a company may have a 7% first mortgage bond issue outstanding totaling $3,000,000. The property mortgaged as security for the bond issue cost $4,000,000 and has been depreciated by $800,000. The realizable value of the property in liquidation is estimated to be $2,500,000. In a traditional statement of financial position this information might be reported as follows:

ASSETS

| | |
|---|---|
| Property, plant and equipment (Note X) | $4,000,000 |
| Less accumulated depreciation | 800,000 |
| | $3,200,000 |

LIABILITIES

| | |
|---|---|
| Long-term debt: | |
| First mortgage bonds, 7%, due 1998 (Note X) | $3,000,000 |

Note X would describe more fully the first mortgage bond indenture and the property pledged as security.

In a statement of financial position prepared in terms of current realizable values for the company contemplating liquidation, this information might be reported as follows:

ASSETS

| | |
|---|---|
| Property, plant and equipment, pledged against First mortgage bonds, $2,500,000 realizable value (Note X) | –0– |

LIABILITIES

| | |
|---|---|
| Long-term debt: | |
| First mortgage bonds, 7%, due 1998 | $3,000,000 |
| Less: realizable value of property, plant, and equipment pledged (Note X) | 2,500,000 |
| Balance, not secured | $ 500,000 |

Note X would describe more fully the first mortgage bond indenture the property pledged as security, and the basis for the estimate of net realizable value for the property.

**Reporting Deficiency in Resources.** The following illustration presents a going-concern statement of financial position along with supplementary information that indicates realizable values. The corporation is insolvent. A statement of financial position based on realizable values could, as previously noted, take various forms. A summary of the deficiency in available resources may also be presented, and this summary is illustrated following the presentation of the basic data.

ABC CORPORATION
STATEMENT OF FINANCIAL POSITION
AS OF OCTOBER 31, 1980

| Assets | | Equities | | |
|---|---:|---|---:|---:|
| Current assets: | | Current liabilities: | | |
| Cash | $ 1,000 | Accounts payable | | $ 36,000 |
| Accounts receivable | 16,000 | Notes payable | | 10,000 |
| Inventory | 24,000 | Accrued wages | | 800 |
| Prepayments | 1,200 | Accrued interest | | 450 |
| Total current assets | $ 42,200 | Total current liabilities | | $ 47,250 |
| Investment in stock of X Co. | 12,000 | 5% bonds payable | | 36,000 |
| Property, plant, & equipment | 56,000 | Common stock | $35,000 | |
| Goodwill | 10,000 | Retained earnings | 1,950 | 36,950 |
| | $120,200 | | | $120,200 |

On October 31, 1980, the corporation contemplates liquidation because of a deteriorating sales market, poor current financial position, and recent operating losses. At this date the following data must also be considered to view properly the financial position of the company from a possible liquidation point of view:

1. The notes payable are due to the First National Bank and are secured by the X Co. stock as collateral. Market value of the X Co. stock at October 31, 1980, is $8,000.
2. The bonds payable are secured by the property, plant, and equipment, which are estimated to be worth $40,000 at October 31, 1980.
3. The receivables contain $1,500 of uncollectible accounts and $4,000 of accounts from which 50% collectibility is expected. All other accounts are considered wholly collectible.
4. The inventory is not pledged and is estimated to be worth $18,000.
5. The prepayments will yield about $400 cash upon sale or rebate.

When the realizable value of an asset pledged as security for a debt equals or exceeds the amount of the debt, the debt is considered to be fully secured. In liquidation, one of two alternatives may arise. The creditor may sell the pledged assets, deduct the amount of his claim, and remit the excess to the receiver or trustee responsible for the liquidation. Or, the corporate officials may arrange for the sale of the assets, using the proceeds to liquidate the secured debt, with any remainder flowing into the corporate treasury.

When the realizable value of an asset pledged as security for a debt is less than the amount of the debt, the debt is considered to be partially secured. The asset pledged as security will not, upon realization, fully satisfy the creditor claims. No excess exists to be used to settle unsecured claims. A portion of the debt itself is in reality unsecured, and this portion would be reported as a liability as in the illustration in the preceding section.

Under bankruptcy law, certain liabilities have a preferential or prior claim upon liquidation. The priority order, in general, under bankruptcy law is somewhat as follows:

1. Liabilities incurred by receivers or trustees in preserving and administering the assets of the business.
2. Amounts due wage earners for services rendered, not to exceed $600 per employee, and provided that the wages have been earned within the last three months.
3. Amounts claimed by creditors for reimbursement of funds expended to defeat alternative, and thus presumably less reasonable, settlement plans.
4. Taxes.
5. Amounts owing for rent or to governmental units that have been granted priority under state or federal statute.

Any liabilities falling within the categories above must be settled in full before any payments may be made on unsecured claims. Liabilities not secured and having no priority are classified as unsecured liabilities.

**Deficiency to Unsecured Creditors.** A deficiency exists when the amounts due unsecured creditors exceed the assets not otherwise pledged or required to settle priority claims. If these assets exceed the unsecured claims, no deficiency to unsecured creditors exists and assets will be available for stockholders' claims.

The deficiency to unsecured creditors may be further analyzed in terms of its causes. On the basis of data in the illustration, the estimated deficiency may be analyzed as follows:

ABC CORPORATION

DEFICIENCY ACCOUNT

OCTOBER 31, 1980

| | | | |
|---|---|---|---|
| Estimated loss on: | | Equity interests bearing loss: | |
| Accounts receivable | $ 3,500 | Common stock | $35,000 |
| Inventory | 6,000 | Retained earnings | 1,950 |
| Prepayments | 800 | Unsecured creditors | |
| Stock of X Co. | 4,000 | (deficiency) | 3,350 |
| Property, plant, and equipment | 16,000 | | |
| Goodwill | 10,000 | | |
| | $40,300 | | $40,300 |

The left side of the account details the losses estimated on realization of the various assets. On the right side the equity interests that will bear the estimated loss are listed in the order in which they will bear the loss. If gains arise on the realization of particular assets, the gains would appear on the right side of the account, separately reported.

**Additional Considerations.** At times, more than one asset may be pledged as security for a given liability. When this situation exists, the assets so pledged would be reported under the appropriate heading and the liability deducted from the total estimated realizable value. Likewise, more than one liability may be secured by a specific asset.

A company may pledge only a part of an asset as security for a given liability. For example, a portion of the X Co. stock may have been pledged as collateral for the note payable to the bank. If this had been done, the portion of the asset pledged would be deducted from the note payable and the remaining portion would be reported as an asset.

A more difficult problem arises in the reporting of assets that will require an additional expenditure prior to their realization. This condition frequently exists when determining realizable value for a goods in process inventory. Assume the following data:

|  | Book Value | Realizable Value |
|---|---|---|
| Goods in process | $12,000 | $15,000 |
| Raw materials | 20,000 | 15,000 |

For the goods in process to realize $15,000, however, the following additional costs must be incurred:

| | |
|---|---|
| Additional raw material, cost (at realizable value, $1,500) | $2,000 |
| Additional labor cost | 2,500 |
| Additional other costs | 500 |

Assuming that neither the goods in process nor the raw materials are pledged, the information above could be reported in the following manner:

| | | | |
|---|---|---|---|
| Goods in process: | | | |
| Estimated realization upon completion | | 15,000 | |
| Less: Costs of completion: | | | |
| Raw materials (75% of cost) | 1,500 | | |
| Labor costs | 2,500 | | |
| Other costs | 500 | 4,500 | 10,500 |
| Raw materials: | | | |
| Used in completing goods in process (cost of $2,000) | | | 1,500 |
| Available for sale (cost of $18,000) | | | 13,500 |

This procedure reveals the proceeds on realization of both goods in process and the raw materials. In addition, the wages and other costs necessary to complete the goods in process are deducted directly from the estimated proceeds of the sale of this asset.

## RECEIVERSHIP IN EQUITY

Some corporate liquidations are accomplished by the same corporate officials who formerly managed the organization. Others are accomplished under the supervision of a third party, often a receiver in equity. Liquidation under the direction of a receiver in equity arises through a court order and may come about from a variety of reasons. Likewise, a receiver is sometimes appointed by the courts to take charge of the operations of a going concern. In either instance it is usually advisable for the receiver to establish a new set of accounting records in order to record his activities in directing the corporate affairs. The following sections deal with the accounting procedures that a receiver should follow, with emphasis primarily directed at the liquidation proceedings.

As is the case when any person is charged with responsibility for property, a receiver should maintain records that will enable him to report clearly the results of his activities while he has control of the property. The records that a receiver should maintain are not substitutes for the regular corporate records, but are in addition to them. In general, a receiver should take up on his records the various assets over which he assumes control, as well as the related valuation accounts. The assets are recorded at the same values at which they appear on the corporate records. Normally, no existing liabilities are recorded by the receiver on his books. However, liabilities subsequently incurred by the receiver are entered on his books. Thus, a distinction is clearly drawn between debts existing prior to the receivership period and debts incurred by the receiver. The receiver also sets up an accountability account for the net assets taken over. The accountability account title frequently used includes the corporation name, such as "ABC Corporation— in receivership."

On the corporate books the asset and valuation accounts turned over to the receiver are closed out, and a new receivable-type account opened for the net assets transferred such as "John Jones—receiver." No change is made in existing liability accounts.

### Receivership Accounting

**General Concepts.** After the receiver assumes control of the corporate properties, a dual accounting problem arises. Entries must be recorded on the receiver's books for any change in the assets over which he has assumed control and for any change in liabilities incurred by him. Likewise, entries must be made on the corporation's books for any change in the liability accounts existing prior to the receivership period. Some transactions, such as payments by the receiver of a prior liability, require entries in each set of records.

If the receiver is charged solely with winding up the affairs of the corporation, that is, if he is not authorized to continue the regular business activities of the corporation, the problem is relatively simple. Entries need to be made only to record cash received for assets realized, cash paid out for liabilities liquidated, and for any gains or losses on realization. Eventually all assets will be realized in cash, all liabilities will be liquidated, and appropriate cash distributions made to stockholders.

The receiver may also be charged with the responsibility of operating the corporation, pending either (1) eventual liquidation, with the continued operation primarily designed to preserve asset values, or (2) eventual improvement in financial condition, with the subsequent return of operating control to the corporate officials. Except for a difference in scale of operations and for the entries to record final liquidation under (1), the accounting problems under these two alternatives are similar.

### Basic Procedures.

***(1) Payment of liabilities existing at the date the receiver assumes control of the corporation.*** As previously stated, the receiver does not include in his records any liabilities owing by the corporation at the date the receiver assumes responsibility. However, he may pay these liabilities, either in the normal course of operating the corporation or under court order to pay. The payment of liabilities of this nature reduces the assets for which the receiver is accountable, and also reduces the receiver's responsibility to the corporation. A receiver generally finds it preferable not to record changes in his accountability in "ABC Corporation—in receivership," the same account that was used to record his initial accountability. The use of a temporary accountability account facilitates the preparation of subsequent reports. For example, if a receiver pays $10,000 of accounts payable that the corporation had incurred prior to the assumption of control by the receiver, the following entry would be made on the receiver's books:

|  |  |  |
|---|---|---|
| ABC Corporation—Accounts payable paid | $10,000 |  |
|     Cash |  | $10,000 |

An entry also must be made on the corporation books to reflect the liability liquidation, as follows:

|  |  |  |
|---|---|---|
| Accounts payable | $10,000 |  |
|     John Jones—Receiver |  | $10,000 |

It should be noted that the account credited on the corporation's books is the "receivable" account set up to record the receiver's initial accountability.

**(2) Incurrence and payment of liabilities incurred subsequent to the date of receivership.** No particular problems arise in this situation. If purchases are made or expenses incurred by the receiver, the appropriate purchase or expense account is charged and "accounts payable" credited on the receiver's books. No entry is necessary on the corporation's books. Likewise, the receiver records payment of the liability in the usual manner, and no entry would be made on the corporation's books.

**(3) Increase in liability existing at the date receiver assumes control, and subsequent payment thereof.** Interest that accrues on a note or mortgage liability on the corporation's books should be recorded periodically. Since the liability is reflected on the corporation's books, the entry to record the accrual of interest should also be made on the corporation's books. No entry need be made on the receiver's books for the accrual. When the interest is paid, entries similar to those in (1) above would be made on both the corporation's books and the receiver's books.

**(4) Operating transactions.** If the corporation continues operations in a normal manner under the receivership, the receiver should record all operating transactions on his records. The account classification should follow closely that previously used by the corporation. No entries for the operating results need be recorded on the corporation's books. At the end of the accounting period the receiver closes his books and determines any profit or loss. The net profit or loss is also recorded on the corporation's books by adjusting the accountability account (receivable) with the receiver.

**Receiver's Reports.** Periodically the receiver may desire or be required to report on the results of corporate activities under his supervision. Since it is generally desirable to report on total corporate activities, the receiver combines the data from his records and from the corporation records by means of a work sheet. The resulting information should enable the receiver to prepare reports, statement of financial position, and income statement, which can be compared with prior corporation reports. A statement designed to report on what has been accomplished in the realization and liquidation of an insolvent business is illustrated later in this chapter.

**Termination of Receivership.** A receivership may be terminated when a corporation's assets have been realized. Termination may also arise when a corporation regains a solvent state while under the receiver's control. In either situation, the receiver closes his books by returning to the corporation the various assets for which he is accountable. Likewise, any unpaid liabilities incurred by the receiver are transferred to the corporation's books. The entries made on the receiver's books and on the corporation's books closely parallel the entries made to establish the receivership. The receiver's accountability account with the corporation and the corporation's receivable-type account with the receiver are closed. The corporation thereafter accounts for its transactions in the normal manner.

## Realization and Liquidation Statement

As noted previously, corporate liquidations often require a considerable period of time to accomplish. Frequently it is desirable during the liquidation period to have prepared reports that indicate the progress of the liquidation. Periodic reports are particularly desirable when the corporation is continuing operations in a normal or semi-normal manner, even though on a reduced scale, during the period of liquidation. A statement of particular usefulness to report this type of information is the *realization and liquidation statement,* or, as it is commonly called because of its form of presentation, the *realization and liquidation account.*

This statement contains information concerning the events that have occurred during the liquidation operations. It is designed to indicate the initial accountability of the individual who assumed control over the assets and liabilities of the enterprise being liquidated, the effect of actions taken under his supervision in regard to these properties and liabilities, and the resultant accountability of this individual at the date the statement is prepared.

This statement, which may be prepared by a receiver, a trustee, or an individual responsible for the corporate activities during the realization of the assets and the liquidation of the liabilities, is organized in the manner shown on page 781. Depending on the results of operations during the period covered by the report, a net gain would appear as a balancing amount on the left side of the statement, whereas a net loss would appear as a balance amount on the right side of the statement. The net gain or loss results from (1) the realization of assets at more or less than their book value, (2) the liquidation of liabilities for less (or more) than their book value, and (3) the excess of supplementary credits over supplementary charges, or vice versa.

In addition to the statement on page 781, a cash account or a summary of cash changes during the period is generally presented. A memorandum capital account would also be necessary to complete the reporting picture, as owners' equities are not included in the realization and liquidation statement.

From the information in the realization and liquidation statement, a realization profit and loss statement may be prepared. A statement of financial position as of the final date of the period covered by the realization and liquidation statement may also be prepared from the following data: (1) all items in the final sections of the statement (liabilities not liquidated and assets not realized), (2) ending cash balance from the cash account, and (3) ending capital from the memorandum capital account. The information for the realization and liquidation statement may be prepared from analyses of the information contained in a regular ledger maintained by a trustee or receiver, or the statement may be prepared from memoranda of various transactions made by the trustee or receiver during the period.

## ABC CORPORATION
### Realization and Liquidation Statement

*Assets to be realized*:
All assets other than cash are listed at their respective book (carrying) values as of the beginning of the period covered by the statement. ........ xxxxx

*Assets subsequently acquired*:
All assets other than cash that were discovered or acquired during the period covered by the report are listed here. ........ xxxxx

*Supplementary charges*:
All expenses are listed here, *except* asset expirations and losses arising from the realization of specific assets. ........ xxxxx

*Liabilities liquidated*:
All liabilities settled are listed here. ........ xxxxx

*Liabilities not liquidated*:
All liabilities not liquidated at the end of the period covered by the statement are listed here. ........ xxxxx

*Liabilities to be liquidated*:
All liabilities as of the beginning of the period covered by the statement are listed here. ........ xxxxxx

*Liabilities subsequently assumed*:
All liabilities incurred or discovered during the period covered by the report are listed here. ........ xxxxx

*Supplementary credits*:
All revenue is listed here, *except* gains on the realization of specific assets. ........ xxxx

*Assets realized*:
The proceeds from the realization of the various assets are listed here. ........ xxxxx

*Assets not realized*:
All assets not realized at the end of the period covered by the statement are listed here at their book (carrying) values. ........ xxxxx

**Illustration.** In the following illustration it is assumed that the corporation, Johnson Sales Co., is placed in receivership under Vernon Griffin on March 1, 1980. Griffin operates the company for the remainder of the year, and on December 31, 1980, prepares a realization and liquidation statement and other data in order to report on the results of the corporate activities under his supervision. The following statement of financial position reveals the condition of the corporation on March 1, 1980:

JOHNSON SALES CO.<br>STATEMENT OF FINANCIAL POSITION<br>MARCH 1, 1980<br>Assets

| | | | |
|---|---|---|---|
| Current assets: | | | |
|   Cash | | | $ 1,060 |
|   Receivables | | | 55,820 |
|   Finished goods | | | 37,840 |
|   Raw materials | | | 41,660 |
|     Total current assets | | | $136,380 |
| Fixed assets: | | | |
|   Land | | $10,000 | |
|   Building | $100,000 | | |
|     Less: Depreciation | 47,000 | 53,000 | |
|   Equipment | $ 50,000 | | |
|     Less: Depreciation | 19,600 | 30,400 | |
|     Total fixed assets | | | 93,400 |
| Organization cost | | | 6,980 |
| | | | $236,760 |

Equities

| | | |
|---|---|---|
| Current liabilities | | |
|   Accounts payable | | $ 79,540 |
|   Notes payable | | 33,020 |
|   Accrued interest payable | | 520 |
|     Total current liabilities | | $113,080 |
| Fixed liabilities: | | |
|   Mortgage payable | | 48,000 |
| Stockholders' equity: | | |
|   Common stock | $80,000 | |
|   Deficit | (4,320) | 75,680 |
| | | $236,760 |

The various transactions of the receiver during the remainder of the year are summarized below. The transaction summaries, identified by the number opposite each summary, are journalized as they would appear on the records of the receiver and the corporation.

## 24 / Corporate Liquidation

1. March 1. The receiver takes over the assets at the values shown on the statement of financial position.
2. The receiver purchases additional merchandise on account, $5,280.
3. Sales on account total $137,500.
4. Of the receivables on the books on March 1, $50,800 is collected after allowing discounts of $520.
5. Collections are made on all accounts receivable arising from the receiver's sales, except on $14,200. Discounts of $1,900 are allowed on the accounts collected.
6. Payments for labor and other costs total $22,400.
7. All old accounts payable are paid; discounts amount to $1,600.
8. All new accounts payable are paid in full.
9. Payment on notes payable total $30,020.
10. Payments on the mortgage total $10,000.
11. Mortgage interest accrued from March 1 to December 31 totals $2,400. All mortgage interest is paid at December 31, 1980.
12. Depreciation for the year is as follows: on building, $2,600; on equipment, $2,800.
13. The receiver submits a bill for his services of $10,000, and is paid.
14. All organization costs are written off.
15. An allowance for uncollectibles amounting to one-half the remaining old accounts receivable is set up.
16. The inventories on hand at December 31, 1980, are: raw materials, $6,800; finished goods, $3,560.

Vernon Griffin — Receiver

Journal

| | | | |
|---|---|---|---|
| (1) | Cash | $ 1,060 | |
| | Receivables — old | 55,820 | |
| | Raw materials | 41,660 | |
| | Finished goods | 37,840 | |
| | Land | 10,000 | |
| | Buildings | 100,000 | |
| | Equipment | 50,000 | |
| | Organization cost | 6,980 | |
| |     Accumulated depreciation of building | | $ 47,000 |
| |     Accumulated depreciation of equipment | | 19,600 |
| |     Johnson Sales Co. — In receivership | | 236,760 |
| |         (to open receiver's books) | | |
| (2) | Purchases | $ 5,280 | |
| |     Accounts payable | | $ 5,280 |
| |         (to record purchase of merchandise) | | |
| (3) | Accounts receivable — new | $137,500 | |
| |     Sales | | $137,500 |
| |         (to record sales of finished goods) | | |

| | | | |
|---|---|---|---|
| (4) | Cash | $ 50,800 | |
| | Sales discount | 520 | |
| | Accounts receivable—old | | $ 51,320 |
| | (to record collections of old receivables) | | |
| (5) | Cash | $121,400 | |
| | Sales discount | 1,900 | |
| | Accounts receivable—new | | $123,300 |
| | (to record collections of new receivables) | | |
| (6) | Labor and other costs | $ 22,400 | |
| | Cash | | $ 22,400 |
| | (to record payment of labor and other costs) | | |
| (7) | Johnson Sales Co.—Accounts payable paid | $ 79,540 | |
| | Purchase discount | | $ 1,600 |
| | Cash | | 77,940 |
| | (to record payment of old accounts payable) | | |
| (8) | Accounts payable | $ 5,280 | |
| | Cash | | $ 5,280 |
| | (to record payment of new accounts payable) | | |
| (9) | Johnson Sales Co.—Notes payable paid | $ 30,020 | |
| | Cash | | $ 30,020 |
| | (to record payment on notes payable) | | |
| (10) | Johnson Sales Co.—Mortgage payable paid | $ 10,000 | |
| | Cash | | $ 10,000 |
| | (to record payment on mortgage payable) | | |
| (11) | (No entry to record additional interest. Entry to be made on corporation's books.) | | |
| | Johnson Sales Co.—Interest paid | $ 2,920 | |
| | Cash | | $ 2,920 |
| | (to record payment of interest on mortgage) | | |
| (12) | Depreciation on building | $ 2,600 | |
| | Depreciation on equipment | 2,800 | |
| | Accumulated depreciation of building | | $ 2,600 |
| | Accumulated depreciation of equipment | | 2,800 |
| | (to record depreciation provisions for the year) | | |
| (13) | Receiver's expenses | $ 10,000 | |
| | Cash | | $ 10,000 |
| | (to record payment of receiver's fee) | | |

24 / *Corporate Liquidation*

| | | | |
|---|---|---|---|
| (14) | Loss on organization expense | $ 6,980 | |
| |     Organization cost | | $ 6,980 |
| |         (to write off organization costs) | | |
| (15) | Bad debts expense | $ 2,250 | |
| |     Allowance for uncollectibles | | $ 2,250 |
| |         (to record estimated uncollectibles, ½ of old accounts receivable) | | |

JOHNSON SALES CO.

JOURNAL

| | | | |
|---|---|---|---|
| (1) | Vernon Griffin — Receiver | $236,760 | |
| | Accumulated depreciation of building | 47,000 | |
| | Accumulated depreciation of equipment | 19,600 | |
| |     Cash | | $ 1,060 |
| |     Receivables | | 55,820 |
| |     Raw materials | | 41,660 |
| |     Finished goods | | 37,840 |
| |     Land | | 10,000 |
| |     Buildings | | 100,000 |
| |     Equipment | | 50,000 |
| |     Organization cost | | 6,980 |
| |         (to close accounts for which receiver took responsibility) | | |
| (7) | Accounts payable | $ 79,540 | |
| |     Vernon Griffin — Receiver | | $ 79,540 |
| |         (to record payment of old accounts payable by the receiver) | | |
| (9) | Notes payable | $ 30,020 | |
| |     Vernon Griffin — Receiver | | $ 30,020 |
| |         (to record payment of notes payable by receiver) | | |
| (10) | Mortgage payable | $ 10,000 | |
| |     Vernon Griffin — Receiver | | $ 10,000 |
| |         (to record payment on mortgage payable by the receiver) | | |
| (11) | Mortgage interest expense | $ 2,400 | |
| |     Accrued interest payable | | $ 2,400 |
| |         (to accrue interest to December 31, 1980) | | |
| | Accrued interest payable | $ 2,920 | |
| |     Vernon Griffin — Receiver | | $ 2,920 |
| |         (to record payment of accrued interest on the mortgage by the receiver) | | |

The Johnson Sales Co. — in Receivership
Vernon Griffin, Receiver
Realization and Liquidation Statement
March 1, 1980 to December 31, 1980

| | | | | | |
|---|---|---|---|---|---|
| *Assets to be realized:* | | | *Liabilities to be liquidated:* | | |
| (1) Receivables — old | | $55,820 | Accounts payable | $ 79,540 | |
| (1) Raw materials | | 41,660 | Notes payable | 33,020 | |
| (1) Finished goods | | 37,840 | Interest on mortgage payable | 520 | |
| (1) Land | | 10,000 | Mortgage payable | 48,000 | $161,080 |
| (1) Building | $100,000 | | *Liabilities subsequently assumed:* | | |
| Less: allowance | 47,000 | 53,000 | (2) Accounts payable for purchases | | $ 5,280 |
| (1) Equipment | 50,000 | | (11) Accrued interest on mortgage, from 3/1/80 to 12/31/80 | 2,400 | 7,680 |
| Less: allowance | 19,600 | 30,400 | | | |
| (1) Organization cost | | 6,980 | $235,700 | *Supplementary credits:* | | |
| *Assets subsequently acquired:* | | | (3) Sales | $137,500 | |
| (3) Accounts receivable — new | | 137,500 | (7) Purchase discounts | 1,600 | 139,100 |
| *Supplementary charges:* | | | *Assets realized:* | | |
| (2) Purchases | | $ 5,280 | (4) Accounts receivable — old | $ 51,320 | |
| (4) (5) Discounts on sales | | 2,420 | (5) Accounts receivable — new | 123,300 | 174,620 |
| (6) Labor and other costs | | 22,400 | *Assets not realized:* | | |
| (11) Mortgage interest expense | | 2,400 | Accounts receivable — old | $ 4,500 | |
| (13) Receiver's expense | | 10,000 | 42,500 | Less: allowance | 2,250 | 2,250 |
| *Liabilities liquidated:* | | | Accounts receivable — new | 14,200 | |
| (7) Accounts payable — old | $79,540 | | Raw materials | 6,800 | |
| (8) Accounts payable — new | 5,280 | | Finished goods | 3,560 | |
| (9) Notes payable | 30,020 | | Land | 10,000 | |
| (10) Mortgage payable | 10,000 | | Buildings | $100,000 | |
| (11) Interest on mortgage, to 3/1/80 | $ 520 | | Less: allowance | 49,600 | 50,400 |
| Interest on mortgage, 3/1/80 to 12/31/80 | 2,400 | 127,760 | Equipment | 50,000 | |
| *Liabilities not liquidated:* | | | Less: allowance | 22,400 | 27,600 | 114,810 |
| Notes payable | | $ 3,000 | | | $597,290 |
| Mortgage payable | | 38,000 | 41,000 | | |
| Gain for the period | | | 12,830 | | |
| | | | $597,290 | | |

At this point the results of operations under the receivership have been journalized. The reports on page 786 and that follow are based upon the foregoing entries and are reports that Vernon Griffin might render at December 31, 1980. At this point assume that the receiver continues to control the affairs of the Johnson Sales Co. beyond December 31, 1980.

THE JOHNSON CO. — IN RECEIVERSHIP
VERNON GRIFFIN, RECEIVER
ANALYSIS OF CASH ACCOUNT
MARCH 1, 1980 TO DECEMBER 31, 1980

| | | | | | |
|---|---|---|---|---|---|
| Balance, 3/1/80 | | $ 1,060 | (6) Labor and other costs | | $ 22,400 |
| (4) Accounts receivable — old | | 50,800 | (7) Accounts payable — old | | 77,940 |
| (5) Accounts receivable — new | | 121,400 | (8) Accounts payable — new | | 5,280 |
| | | | (9) Notes payable | | 30,020 |
| | | | (10) Mortgage payable | | 10,000 |
| | | | (11) Mortgage interest | | 2,920 |
| | | | (13) Receiver's fees | | 10,000 |
| | | | Balance, 12/31/80 | | 14,700 |
| | | $173,260 | | | $173,260 |

MEMORANDUM CAPITAL ACCOUNT

| | | | | |
|---|---|---|---|---|
| Deficit, 3/1/80 | $ 4,320 | Common stock, 3/1/80 | | $ 80,000 |
| Balance, 12/31/80 | 88,510 | Gain for the period | | |
| | | (see income statement) | | 12,830 |
| | $ 92,830 | | | $ 92,830 |

THE JOHNSON SALES CO. — IN RECEIVERSHIP
VERNON GRIFFIN, RECEIVER
INCOME STATEMENT
MARCH 1, 1980 TO DECEMBER 31, 1980

| | | |
|---|---|---|
| Sales | | $137,500 |
| Cost of sales: | | |
|   Beginning inventory of raw materials | $ 41,660 | |
|   Add: purchases | 5,280 | |
|     Cost of materials available | $ 46,940 | |
|   Ending inventory of raw materials | 6,800 | |
|     Cost of materials used | $ 40,140 | |
|   Labor and other costs | 22,400 | |
|     Total costs incurred | $62,540 | |
|   Add: Finished goods inventory, 3/1/80 | 37,840 | |
|     Cost of goods available for sale | $100,380 | |
|   Less: Finished goods inventory, 12/31/80 | 3,560 | |

|  |  |  |
|---|---:|---:|
| Cost of goods sold | | 96,820 |
| Gross profit on sales | | $ 40,680 |
| Operating expenses: | | |
|     Receiver's expenses | $ 10,000 | |
|     Discount on sales | 2,420 | |
|     Depreciation on building | 2,600 | |
|     Depreciation on equipment | 2,800 | |
|     Estimated loss on bad debts | 2,250 | 20,070 |
| | | $ 20,610 |
| Discount on purchases | | 1,600 |
| Net income on sales | | $ 22,210 |
| Write-off of organization cost | | 6,980 |
| Net gain before mortgage interest | | $ 15,230 |
| Less: Mortgage interest expense | | 2,400 |
| Net gain for the period | | $ 12,830 |

In reviewing the statements (including the one shown below) and their relationship to the transactions during the period of the receivership, the following comments may help clarify certain areas:

***Purchases and Sales of Products.*** The continued operations of the business must be reported in the Statement of Realization and Liquidation. In the illustration above the purchases were included as supplementary charges and the sales as supplementary credits. The treatment is logical since it results in the inclusion of the operating transactions in the supplementary charge and credit sections. An alternative treatment would report the purchases as assets acquired, and the sales as assets realized.

THE JOHNSON CO. — IN RECEIVERSHIP
VERNON GRIFFIN, RECEIVER
STATEMENT OF FINANCIAL POSITION
DECEMBER 31, 1980

*Assets*

|  |  |  |  |
|---|---:|---:|---:|
| Current assets: | | | |
|   Cash | | | $ 14,700 |
|   Receivables—old | | $ 4,500 | |
|     Less: uncollectibles | | 2,250 | 2,250 |
|   Receivables—new | | | 14,200 |
|   Finished goods | | | 3,560 |
|   Raw materials | | | 6,800 |
|     Total current assets | | | $ 41,510 |
| Fixed assets: | | | |
|   Land | | | $10,000 |
|   Buildings | $100,000 | | |
|     Less: allowance | 49,600 | | 50,400 |

|  |  |  |  |  |
|---|---|---|---|---|
| Equipment | | 50,000 | | |
| Less: allowance | | 22,400 | 27,600 | |
| Total fixed assets | | | | 88,000 |
| | | | | $129,510 |

### Equities

|  |  |  |  |
|---|---|---|---|
| Current liabilities: | | | |
| Notes payable | | | $ 3,000 |
| Fixed liabilities: | | | |
| Mortgage payable | | | 38,000 |
| Stockholders' equity: | | | |
| Common stock | | $80,000 | |
| Retained earnings | | 8,510 | 88,510 |
| | | | $129,510 |

**Old and New Accounts.** In transaction (3), the account debited was "Accounts receivable—new." The distinction between accounts receivable existing at the date the receiver assumes control and those resulting from the receiver's operation of the business is important because the receiver has a different degree of responsibility for the two types of receivables. The receiver is responsible only for diligent collection action on the old accounts receivable, but is responsible for an appraisal of credit risks in granting credit to new customers.

Separate accounts are of necessity maintained for old and new accounts payable, since the liabilities existing when the receiver assumes control remain on the corporation's books, while new liabilities incurred are recorded on the receiver's books. The separation is significant because of the priority of rights enjoyed by those creditors whose claims arise from dealings with the receiver.

**Cash Discounts.** Transactions (4), (5), and (7) involved cash discounts. In each transaction the amount of the discount was reported as a supplementary charge (sales discount) or as a supplementary credit (purchase discount). Reporting discounts in this manner necessitates showing the realization proceeds from collection or the liabilities liquidated by payment at the gross amounts rather than at the amount of the cash involved. An alternative treatment of discounts follows, with transaction (4) used as an example:

| *Supplementary Charges:* | *Assets Realized:* |
|---|---|
| No entry | Accounts receivable—old |
| | $50,800 |

Under this method of reporting, the discount is not separately shown, but becomes a part of the net gain or loss on realization for the period. Entry (4) on page 784 would be the same except that the $520 discount would not be entered in a separate expense account.

***Accrued Interest.*** Transaction (11) involves interest accrued during the receiver's period of operation. As noted previously, if the accrued interest results from a liability existing at the date the receivership began, the entry for the additional interest is made on the corporation's books. However, since the statement of realization and liquidation reflects all transactions of the receivership period, the effect of the additional interest is reported in the statement. The additional interest is reported both as a supplementary charge and as a liability assumed. Payment of the previously existing accrued interest plus the addition this period is reported under liabilities liquidated.

An alternative treatment reports the additional accrual only as a supplementary charge. When payment takes place, only the liability existing at the date the receiver took charge would be reported as liquidated. This method appears less preferable than the other.

Other accrued expenses are handled in a manner similar to that used in handling interest charges, and accrued incomes are reported, preferably, as assets acquired and as supplementary credits.

***Depreciation.*** Periodic depreciation does not appear on the realization and liquidation statement although it is reported on the receiver's income statement. On the realization and liquidation statement the assets to be realized are reported, less any accumulated depreciation, and the assets not realized are reported similarly. The period depreciation is considered as part of the realization gain or loss for the period.

***Bad Debts.*** Any increase in the allowance for uncollectibles is handled in a manner similar to that used for depreciation. Write-offs of specific accounts against a previously established allowance do not affect the realization and liquidation statement or the gain or loss for the period. Such write-offs were, in effect, reported as losses at the time the allowance was established.

***Asset Write-offs.*** Since gains and losses on realization of assets are not reported separately on the realization and liquidation statement, asset write-offs do not appear as separate amounts. The effect of an asset write-off, as illustrated in the write-off of organization cost, appears in the gain or loss for the period as part of the balancing amount on the statement.

***Closing Out the Receivership.*** When a receivership is terminated, the receiver closes all accounts remaining on his books, and the corporation records the return of the various assets and liabilities in its books. In the illustration, the receiver would credit the asset accounts appearing on the statement of financial position, would debit the valuation accounts, and would debit The Johnson Co.—In Receivership for $129,510 to close that account. The corporation would make the reverse of this entry, crediting Vernon Griffin, Receiver for $129,510.

## PROBLEMS

### Problem 24-1

The Machine Manufacturing Company has been forced into bankruptcy as of April 30, 1980. The following balance sheet was prepared by the company bookkeeper as of April 30, 1980:

*Assets*

| | |
|---|---:|
| Cash | $ 2,700 |
| Accounts receivable | 39,350 |
| Notes receivable | 18,500 |
| Inventories: | |
|     Raw materials | 19,600 |
|     Work in process | 35,100 |
|     Finished goods | 12,000 |
|     Supplies | 6,450 |
|     Tools | 14,700 |
| Prepaid expenses | 950 |
| Plant and property: | |
|     Land | 20,000 |
|     Buildings | 75,000 |
|     Machinery | 80,900 |
| | $325,250 |

*Liabilities and Capital*

| | |
|---|---:|
| Note payable to the First Bank | $ 15,000 |
| Notes payable to suppliers | 51,250 |
| Accounts payable | 52,000 |
| Accrued liabilities: | |
|     Accrued salaries and wages | 8,850 |
|     Accrued property taxes | 2,900 |
|     Employees' taxes withheld | 1,150 |
|     Accrued wage taxes | 600 |
|     Accrued interest on bonds | 1,800 |

| | |
|---|---|
| First-mortgage bonds payable | 90,000 |
| Allowance for depreciation, Buildings | 33,750 |
| Allowance for depreciation, Machinery | 32,100 |
| Common stock ($100 par value) | 75,000 |
| Deficit | (39,150) |
| | $325,250 |

*Additional information:*
1. Of the total accounts receivable, $10,300 are believed to be good. The other accounts are doubtful, but it seems probable that 20% finally can be collected.
2. A total of $15,000 of the notes receivable have been pledged to secure the note payable to the First Bank. All except $2,500 of these appear to be good. Interest of $800 is accrued on the $12,500 of good notes pledged, and $300 is accrued on the $15,000 payable to the bank. The remaining notes are not considered collectible.
3. The finished machines are expected to be sold for one-third above their cost, but expenses of disposing of them will equal 20% of their sales price. Work in process can be completed at an additional cost of $15,400, of which $3,700 would be material used from the raw material inventory. The work in process, when completed, will probably sell for $40,000 and costs of selling this will be 20% of sales price. The raw material not used will realize $8,000. Most of the value of tools consists of special items. After completion of work in process, the tools should sell for $3,000. The supply inventory that will not be needed to complete work should sell for $1,000.
4. Land and buildings are mortgaged as security for bonds. They have an appraised value of $95,000. The company recently purchased $20,000 of machinery on a conditional sales contract. It still owes $12,000 principal on this contract, which is included in the notes payable. These machines have a current used value of $10,000. Depreciation taken on these machines amounts to $1,800. The remaining machinery is believed to be salable at $10,000, but cost of selling may be $1,000.

*Required:*
(1) Prepare a statement of financial position in contemplation of liquidation, and compute the percent of probable payment to the $52,000 accounts payable.
(2) Prepare a statement showing the estimated deficiency to unsecured creditors, indicating clearly the causes of the deficiency. Omit consideration of any expenses of liquidation that are not specifically mentioned.

(AICPA adapted)

## Problem 24-2

The Hardhyt Corporation is in financial difficulty because of low sales. Its stockholders and principal creditors want an estimate of the financial results of the liquidation of the assets and liabilities and the dissolution of the Corporation. The Corporation's trial balance follows:

## 24 / Corporate Liquidation

HARDHYT CORPORATION<br>
POSTCLOSING TRIAL BALANCE<br>
DECEMBER 31, 1980

| | | |
|---|---:|---:|
| Cash | $ 1,000 | |
| Accounts receivable | 20,500 | |
| Allowance for bad debts | | $ 350 |
| Inventories | 40,000 | |
| Supplies inventory | 3,000 | |
| Downhill Railroad 5% bonds | 5,000 | |
| Accrued bond interest receivable | 750 | |
| Advertising | 6,000 | |
| Land | 4,000 | |
| Building | 30,000 | |
| Accumulated depreciation—building | | 5,000 |
| Machinery and equipment | 46,000 | |
| Accumulated depreciation—machinery and equipment | | 8,000 |
| Accounts payable | | 26,000 |
| Notes payable—bank | | 25,000 |
| Notes payable—officers | | 20,000 |
| Payroll taxes payable | | 800 |
| Wages payable | | 1,500 |
| Mortgage payable | | 42,000 |
| Mortgage interest payable | | 500 |
| Capital stock | | 50,000 |
| Retained earnings | 29,100 | |
| Allowance for product guarantees | | 6,200 |
| | $185,350 | $185,350 |

The following information has been collected in anticipation of a meeting of the stockholders and principal creditors to be held on January 2, 1981.

1. Cash includes a $300 protested check from a customer. The customer stated that he would have funds to honor the check in about two weeks.
2. Accounts receivable include accounts totaling $10,000 that are fully collectible and have been assigned to the bank in connection with the notes payable. Included in unassigned receivables is an uncollectible account of $150. The Allowance for Bad Debts account of $350 now on the books will adequately provide for other doubtful accounts.
3. Purchase orders totaling $9,000 are on hand for the Corporation's products. Inventory with a book value of $6,000 can be processed at an additional cost of $400 to fill these orders. The balance of the inventory, which includes obsolete materials with a book value of $1,200, can be sold for $10,500.
4. In transit at December 31 but not recorded on the books was a shipment of defective merchandise being returned by a customer. Mr. Hardhyt, president of the Corporation, had authorized the return and the refund of the purchase price of $250 after the merchandise had been inspected. Mr. Hardhyt

knows of no defective merchandise, other than this return, that would bear on the Allowance for Product Guarantees account. The merchandise being returned has no salvage value.
5. The Supplies Inventory is comprised of advertising literature, brochures, and other sales aids. These could not be replaced for less than $3,700.
6. The Downhill Railroad bonds are recorded at face value. They were purchased in 1969 for $600, and the adjustment to face value was credited to Retained Earnings. At December 31, 1980, the bonds were quoted at 18 dealt in flat.
7. The Advertising account represents the future benefits of a 1980 advertising campaign. Ten percent of certain advertising expenditures were placed in the account. Mr. Hardhyt stated that this percentage was too conservative and that 20% would result in a more realistic measure of the market that was created.
8. The land and building are in a downtown area. A firm offer of $50,000 has been received for the land, which would be used as a parking lot; the building would be razed at a cost of $12,000 to the buyer. Another offer of $40,000 was received for the real estate, which the bidder stated would be used for manufacturing that would probably employ some Hardhyt emmployees.
9. The highest of the offers received from used machinery dealers was $18,000 for all of the machinery and equipment.
10. One creditor, whose account for $1,000 is included in the accounts payable, confirmed in writing that he would accept 90 cents on the dollar if the Corporation paid him by January 10.
11. Wages payable include year-end adjustments of $325 payable to certain factory employees for their overtime during the busy season.
12. The mortgage payable is secured by the land and building. The last two monthly principal payments of $200 each were not made.
13. Estimated liquidation expenses amount to $3,200.
14. For income tax purposes the Corporation has the following net operating loss carryovers: (The tax rate is 50%.)

| | |
|---|---|
| 1978 | $10,000 |
| 1979 | 12,000 |
| 1980 | 8,000 |

*Required:*
(1) Prepare a statement of financial condition on contemplation of liquidation.
(2) Prepare a schedule that computes the estimated settlement per dollar of unsecured liabilities.  (AICPA adapted)

## Problem 24-3

The Hamilton Company entered receivership on July 31, 1980. The following trial balance is taken from the company records on that date:

## 24 / Corporate Liquidation

THE HAMILTON COMPANY
TRIAL BALANCE, JULY 31, 1980

| | | |
|---|---:|---:|
| Cash | $ 20,000 | |
| Notes receivable | 25,000 | |
| Accounts receivable | 90,000 | |
| Inventories | 40,000 | |
| Land | 30,000 | |
| Buildings | 240,000 | |
| Accumulated depreciation—buildings | | $110,000 |
| Equipment | 200,000 | |
| Accumulated depreciation—equipment | | 90,000 |
| Unexpired insurance | 5,000 | |
| Accounts payable | | 150,000 |
| Notes payable | | 55,000 |
| Accrued wages | | 6,000 |
| Accrued interest on bonds | | 2,000 |
| First mortgage bonds, 4% | | 120,000 |
| Common stock | | 100,000 |
| Retained earnings | | 17,000 |
| | $650,000 | $650,000 |

Additional analyses of the Hamilton Company's financial position and discussions with responsible officials disclosed the following information:

| | |
|---|---:|
| Realizable value of assets: | |
| Notes receivable | $17,000 |
| Accounts receivable | 65,000 |
| Inventories | 45,000 |
| Land | 25,000 |
| Buildings | 100,000 |
| Equipment | 60,000 |
| Unexpired insurance | 1,000 |

*Other Information:*

1. The first mortgage bonds are secured by a mortgage on the land and buildings.
2. The Company is liable under certain product guarantees. No entry has been made to reflect this contingency, but it is estimated that $15,000 will be necessary to settle claims that will arise.
3. The inventories have been pledged as collateral for the notes payable.
4. All accrued wages are of recent origin.
5. Expenses of liquidation are expected to total $7,000.

*Required:*
  (1) Prepare a statement of financial condition in contemplation of liquidation.
  (2) Prepare a deficiency account.

## Problem 24-4

The partnership of Brody, Mason, and Soule was placed in receivership on September 1, 1980. At that date the receiver took control, and the following balance sheet of the partnership was prepared:

Brody, Mason, & Soule Partnership
Balance Sheet, September 1, 1980

| | | | | |
|---|---:|---|---:|---:|
| Cash | $ 600 | Accounts payable | | $124,000 |
| Accounts receivable | 90,000 | Notes payable | | 45,000 |
| Marketable securities | 30,000 | Wages payable | | 4,400 |
| Inventories | 84,000 | Taxes payable | | 1,500 |
| Prepaid insurance | 900 | Interest payable on mortgage | | 600 |
| Land | 30,000 | Mortgage payable | | 120,000 |
| Buildings (net) | 165,000 | Partners' capitals: | | |
| | | Brody | $60,000 | |
| | | Mason | 30,000 | |
| | | Soule | 15,000 | 105,000 |
| | $400,500 | | | $400,500 |

Other information pertinent to the financial condition of the partnership appears below:

1. The mortgage payable is secured by the land and buildings.
2. The marketable securities have been pledged as collateral for the notes payable.
3. On liquidation, the assets are expected to realize the following amounts:

Accounts receivable:
1/3, fully collectible
1/2, collectible at 66⅔%
1/6, uncollectible
Marketable securities — $34,000
Inventories — $41,000
Prepaid insurance — $225
Land — $24,000
Buildings — $120,000

*Required:*
(1) Prepare a statement of financial condition for the partnership, based on the data above.
(2) Prepare a deficiency account.

## Problem 24-5

The Adams-Story Partnership, of which Adams is manager, has had difficulty in meeting its obligations as the debts matured. If the business is dissolved, it will

## 24 / Corporate Liquidation

require six months to complete the dissolution. The bookkeeper prepared the trial balance as shown below.

An analysis of the accounts revealed the following:

1. Cash in First Bank, $8,000; in Second Bank, $12,000.
2. Of the accounts receivable, 60% are good and fully collectible, 30% are doubtful and considered to be only 80% collectible, the remaining 10% are worthless.
3. All notes are good and are pledged as security on notes payable to the Factor House of $50,000 with accrued interest of $500.
4. Of the notes that were discounted at the Manning Bank, it is estimated that one, amounting to $2,000, will not be paid at maturity or thereafter.
5. All finished goods will be sold for 20% less than their cost. Work in process cannot be sold until finished and can be completed by incurring labor and material costs of $9,000, of which $3,000 will be from raw material inventory. The balance of raw material inventory will realize $5,000.
6. The prepaid insurance, which expires October 15, has a short-term cancellation value on April 15, 1980 of $900.
7. Property held in trust is in the form of stocks and bonds with realizable value of $24,000. The partnership is entitled to a fee of $600 per year, payable April 15, for their services. Cash was not available in the trust for the payment; therefore, the fee was not recorded.
8. The machinery and equipment with a book value of $8,000 will realize $5,000.
9. The land and building may be sold for $38,000; however, the mortgage holder has indicated a willingness to cancel the debt and assume all encumbrances for the surrender of the title to the real estate. Interest on the mortgage was paid on January 15, 1980.
10. The wages and commissions were last paid in full on December 31, 1979. Commission salesmen were dismissed on February 15, 1980. Accrued wages in the trial balance are:

| | |
|---|---:|
| Burke, bookkeeper (to April 15) | $1,400 |
| Commission salesman (to February 15) | 300 |
| Adams, manager (to April 15) | 1,750 |
| | $3,450 |

### ADAMS-STORY PARTNERSHIP
### TRIAL BALANCE, APRIL 15, 1980

| | | |
|---|---:|---:|
| Cash in banks | $ 20,000 | |
| Accounts receivable | 100,000 | |
| Allowance for bad debts | | $ 4,000 |
| Notes receivable | 58,000 | |
| Notes receivable discounted | | 12,000 |
| Raw materials | 9,000 | |

| | | |
|---|---:|---:|
| Work in process | 20,000 | |
| Finished goods | 15,000 | |
| Prepaid insurance | 1,200 | |
| Property held in trust | 18,000 | |
| Machinery and equipment, cost | 9,000 | |
| Building | 33,000 | |
| Land | 12,000 | |
| Accumulated depreciation | | 6,000 |
| Interest receivable | 700 | |
| Payroll taxes payable | | 200 |
| Real estate taxes | | 1,200 |
| Wages payable | | 3,450 |
| Notes payable | | 60,000 |
| Accounts payable | | 125,700 |
| Mortgage payable, 4% | | 40,000 |
| Equipment contract payable (purchased on a conditional sales contract) | | 6,400 |
| Interest payable | | 1,000 |
| Adams, Capital | | 15,975 |
| Story, Capital | | 1,975 |
| Trust, Capital | | 18,000 |
| | $295,900 | $295,900 |

11. The partnership owes the Second Bank a note of $10,000.
12. The estimated administrative expenses are $3,000.
13. Adams has personal liabilities that are approximately equal to his personal assets, but Story's personal assets exceed his personal liabilities by $2,800.

*Required:*
(1) Prepare a statement showing the estimated deficiency, if any, to the unsecured creditors.
(2) Prepare a schedule summarizing the estimated amounts available for each class of creditors. (AICPA adapted)

## Problem 24-6

The Alpha Corporation, currently in financial difficulty, has the following inventory amounts on hand:

| | |
|---|---:|
| Raw materials | $60,000 |
| Work-in-process | 45,000 |
| Finished goods | 40,000 |

The work-in-process will require the application of $12,000 of raw materials and expenditure of $14,000 for labor and other costs in order to process the goods to a finished condition. The remaining raw materials will be sold at a discount of 20% from their book value. It is estimated that all finished goods will be sold for cost plus 10%.

*Required:*

How would the information above be reported on a statement of financial condition prepared in contemplation of liquidation?

## Problem 24-7

The Neversink Corporation advises you that it is facing bankruptcy proceedings. As the company's CPA, you are aware of its condition.

The statement of financial position of the Neversink Corporation at June 30, 1980 and supplementary data are presented below:

*Assets*

| | |
|---|---:|
| Cash | $ 2,000 |
| Accounts receivable, less allowance for bad debts | 70,000 |
| Inventory, raw material | 40,000 |
| Inventory, finished goods | 60,000 |
| Marketable securities | 20,000 |
| Land | 13,000 |
| Buildings, less allowance for depreciation | 90,000 |
| Machinery, less allowance for depreciation | 120,000 |
| Goodwill | 20,000 |
| Prepaid expenses | 5,000 |
| Total assets | $440,000 |

*Liabilities and Capital*

| | |
|---|---:|
| Accounts payable | $ 80,000 |
| Notes payable | 135,000 |
| Accrued wages | 15,000 |
| Mortgage payable | 130,000 |
| Common stock | 100,000 |
| Retained earnings (deficit) | (20,000) |
| Total liabilities and capital | $440,000 |

Supplementary data:

1. Cash includes a $500 travel advance that has been expended.
2. Accounts receivable of $40,000 have been pledged in support of bank loans of $30,000. Credit balances of $5,000 are netted in the accounts receivable total.
3. Marketable securities consisted of government bonds costing $10,000 and 500 shares of Bartlett Company stock. The market value of the bonds is $10,000 and the stock is $18 per share. The bonds have accrued interest due of $200. The securities are collateral for a $20,000 bank loan.

4. Appraised value for raw materials is $30,000 and $50,000 for finished goods. For an additional cost of $10,000, the raw materials would realize $70,000 as finished goods.
5. The appraisal of fixed assets is: Land, $25,000; Buildings, $110,000; Machinery, $75,000.
6. Prepaid expenses will be exhausted during the liquidation period.
7. Accounts payable include $15,000 withheld payroll taxes and $6,000 for creditors, who had been reassured by the president they would be paid. There are unrecorded employer's taxes in the amount of $500.
8. Wages payable are not subject to any limitations under bankruptcy laws.
9. Mortgages payable consist of $100,000 on land and buildings, and $30,000 chattel mortgage on machinery. Total unrecorded accrued interest for these mortgages amounted to $2,400.
10. Estimated legal fees and expenses in connection with the liquidation are $10,000.
11. Probable judgment on a pending damage suit is $50,000.
12. You have not rendered an invoice for $5,000 for last year's audit, and you estimate a $1,000 fee for liquidation work.

*Required:*
  (1) Prepare a statement of financial condition reflecting the data above.
  (2) Compute the estimated settlement per dollar of unsecured liabilities.

(AICPA adapted)

## Problem 24-8

The Sellow Furniture Company, Inc., has been finding it more and more difficult to meet its obligations. Although its sales volume appeared to be satisfactory and it was showing a profit, the requirements for capital for inventory and time contracts were greater than the Company could provide. Finally, after pledging all of its installment accounts, it found itself unable to meet the bills falling due on October 10, 1980. It is the opinion of the management that if it could obtain an extension of time in which to pay its obligations, it could meet its liabilities in full. The Company has arranged for a meeting of creditors to determine whether it should be granted an extension or be forced into bankruptcy.

You have been asked to assist the Company by:

1. Preparing a statement of financial position in contemplation of liquidation.
2. Preparing a statement of estimated deficiency to unsecured creditors.
3. Computing the percentage of recovery by the unsecured creditors if the Company were to be forced into bankruptcy.

You find the trial balance for the current calendar year of Sellow on September 30, 1980, is as shown on page 801.

From further investigation you obtain the following additional data:

*a.* Depreciation, bad debts, prepaid and accrued items had all been adjusted as of September 30, 1980.

24 / Corporate Liquidation

*b.* All installment contracts had been pledged with the bank on September 30, 1980; the bank had deducted its interest to date and had increased the Company's loan to equal 75% of face amount of the contracts in accordance with a loan agreement. It was estimated that a forced liquidation would result in a loss of $40,000 from the face amount of the contracts.

*c.* Thirty-day accounts receivable were not pledged, and it was estimated that they would provide $16,500 on a liquidation basis.

*d.* It was estimated that since January 1, 1980, the Company had made a gross profit of 33⅓%, but that the inventory on hand would provide only $100,000 on a forced liquidation.

*e.* Cancellation of the insurance would provide $990.

*f.* All the autos and trucks were covered by a chattel mortgage, and their total market value was $8,000.

*g.* The store had been remodeled in 1979, and the furniture and equipment had been acquired on contract. Because of its special utility, it was estimated that on a forced sale no more than $5,000 could be expected.

THE SELLOW FURNITURE COMPANY, INC.
TRIAL BALANCE, SEPTEMBER 30, 1980

| | | |
|---|---:|---:|
| Cash on hand | $ 500 | |
| Cash in bank | 1,620 | |
| Installment contracts, pledged | 215,000 | |
| Allowance for bad contracts | | $ 13,440 |
| Accounts receivable, 30 days | 20,830 | |
| Allowance for bad debts | | 1,050 |
| Inventories, January 1, 1980 | 151,150 | |
| Unexpired insurance | 1,490 | |
| Autos and trucks | 22,380 | |
| Allowance for depreciation, autos and trucks | | 14,960 |
| Furniture and equipment | 12,500 | |
| Allowance for depreciation, furniture and equipment | | 2,140 |
| Buildings | 89,760 | |
| Allowance for depreciation, buildings | | 7,530 |
| Land | 10,240 | |
| Organization expense | 880 | |
| Trade accounts payable | | 132,100 |
| Contract payable, furniture and equipment | | 5,800 |
| Chattel mortgage on autos and trucks | | 10,000 |
| Bank loan, secured by installment contracts | | 161,250 |
| Taxes payable | | 14,220 |
| Accrued salaries and wages | | 4,680 |
| Accrued interest | | 10,990 |
| Notes payable, stockholder | | 100,000 |
| First mortgage | | 49,000 |
| Capital stock | | 100,000 |

| | | |
|---|---:|---:|
| Retained earnings | 65,290 | |
| Sales | | 708,900 |
| Purchases | 527,630 | |
| Expenses and miscellaneous income (net) | 216,790 | |
| | $1,336,060 | $1,336,060 |

*h.* The land and buildings were subject to a 6% first mortgage on which interest had been paid to July 30, 1980. It was estimated that the property could be sold for $75,000.

*i.* The notes payable to stockholders had not been subordinated to general creditors. The notes carried a 6% rate of interest, but no interest had been paid since December 31, 1978.

*j.* Since prior income tax returns disclosed a large available net operating loss carry-over, no current income tax need be considered.

*k.* The cost of a liquidation proceedings was estimated to be $5,000.

*l.* There appeared to be no other values on liquidation and no unrecorded liabilities. (AICPA adapted)

## Problem 24-9

The Bielby Corporation was placed in receivership on August 31, 1980, at which date Frank Herhold was appointed receiver. On assuming control of the Bielby Corp., Herhold prepared the following trial balance.

THE BIELBY CORPORATION — IN RECEIVERSHIP
FRANK HERHOLD, RECEIVER
TRIAL BALANCE, AUGUST 31, 1980

| | | |
|---|---:|---:|
| Cash | $ 3,000 | |
| Accounts receivable | 18,400 | |
| Stock of Niehus Co., at cost | 12,200 | |
| Inventory | 17,600 | |
| Machinery and equipment | 42,200 | |
| Allowance for depreciation of mach. and equip. | | $27,400 |
| Accounts payable | | 40,600 |
| Accrued wages | | 3,600 |
| Accrued taxes | | 2,800 |
| Common stock | | 20,000 |
| Retained income | 1,000 | |
| | $94,400 | $94,400 |

During the three months ended November 30, 1980, the receiver entered into various transactions, the results of which are summarized below:

(*a*) Cash receipts:
Collections of accounts receivable as of 8/31/80 ............ $12,000

| | |
|---|---:|
| Collections of accounts receivable arising in receivership | 31,000 |
| Sale of equipment (cost, $10,000, 60% depreciated) | 2,800 |
| (b) Cash disbursements: | |
|     Payment of accrued wages | 3,600 |
|     Payment of accrued taxes | 2,800 |
|     Payment of accounts payable as of 8/31/80 | 30,000 |
|     Payment of accounts payable arising in receivership | 8,200 |
|     Payment of receivership operating expenses | 4,500 |
| (c) Purchases on account | 10,000 |
| (d) Sales on account | 34,000 |
| (e) Inventory of unsold merchandise at November 30, 1980 | 1,700 |
| (f) Depreciation of machinery and equipment for 3 months | 1,100 |
| (g) Balance of accounts receivable as of 8/31/80 is not collectible. | |

*Required:*

Prepare a statement of realization and liquidation. Analyze the net gain or loss for the period.

## Problem 24-10

The Gorman Dental Equipment Co. has suffered a series of declining profit years, and the management of the company has decided to liquidate the business. On April 30, 1980, the following balance sheet was taken from the ledger of the company:

GORMAN DENTAL EQUIPMENT CO.
BALANCE SHEET, APRIL 30, 1980

| | | | |
|---|---:|---|---:|
| Cash | $ 4,220 | Accounts payable | $ 52,400 |
| Accounts receivable | 32,400 | Notes payable | 21,000 |
| Notes receivable | 8,600 | Accrued wages | 3,600 |
| Finished goods | 18,350 | Interest payable on notes | 150 |
| Materials and supplies | 7,480 | Mortgage payable, 6% | 25,000 |
| Land and building (net) | 60,000 | Common stock | 50,000 |
| Equipment and tools (net) | 26,800 | Retained earnings | 5,700 |
| | $157,850 | | $157,850 |

During the three months ended July 31, 1980, the officers designated to supervise the liquidation operations sold all the finished goods, $6,200 for cash and $18,400 on account. The materials and supplies realized $4,000, and at July 31 an estimated $1,200 remained on hand. Collections on accounts amounted to $44,000, with only $4,200 of the receivables arising in the three-month period remaining uncollected and collectible. All accounts written off existed at April 30, 1980. Notes collected totaled $6,000, with 50% of the remaining balance estimated to be uncollectible. The major portion of the equipment and tools was sold for $16,000, with equipment on hand July 31 valued at $2,000.

Payments were made as follows: expenses during the period, $7,500; on accounts payable, $46,500; on notes and interest, $21,400, settled in full; on accrued wages, $3,600; on mortgage interest, $125.

On June 1 the land and buildings were taken over by the mortgagee in settlement of his claim. In addition, the mortgagee agreed to pay the Gorman Co. $20,000, payment to be made prior to January 1, 1981.

Accounts payable remaining unpaid totaled $4,700.

*Required:*

Prepare a statement of realization and liquidation for the period ended July 31, 1980.

## Problem 24-11

Keenan and Mosher, a partnership, were unable to obtain working capital sufficient to carry on their business. On May 15, 1980, the creditors convened and appointed a friendly receiver to take over the business immediately. The books were closed and the following balance sheet was prepared:

### KEENAN AND MOSHER
### BALANCE SHEET, MAY 15, 1980

| | | | | | | |
|---|---|---|---|---|---|---|
| Cash | | $ 356 | Accounts payable | | | $38,560 |
| Notes receivable | | 4,500 | Notes payable | | | 6,500 |
| Accounts receivable | $32,546 | | Keenan, Capital | $6,986 | | |
| Less Allowance | 3,250 | 29,296 | Keenan, Drawing | 2,228 | 4,758 | |
| Furn. and fixtures | 750 | | Mosher, Capital | 7,166 | | |
| Less Accumulated depreciation | 150 | 600 | Mosher, Drawing | 2,232 | 4,934 | |
| Goodwill | | 20,000 | | | | |
| | | $54,752 | | | | $54,752 |

A review of the records discloses that an inventory of merchandise exists, totaling $3,250. This amount had not been considered when the books were closed on May 15.

During the next 5½ months the receiver operated the business and collected the following amounts on the accounts above: $3,900 on notes receivable; $27,470 on accounts receivable. At November 1, 1980, the balance of the notes and accounts were considered to be uncollectible. All notes payable were paid, and all old accounts payable were settled at $.80 on the dollar. In addition, the following summary presents other operations of the receiver:

| | |
|---|---|
| Sales on account | $56,000 |
| Purchases on account | 28,000 |
| Operating expenses paid | 13,600 |
| Receiver's expenses | 5,600 |
| Collections on sales made | 51,600 |

|                              |        |
|------------------------------|--------|
| Payments on purchases made   | 24,500 |
| Unsold merchandise as 11/1/80 | 3,400  |

*Required:*

Prepare a realization and liquidation statement.

## Problem 24-12

The Specialty Shops Company was unable to meet its obligations. As a result, John Mann was appointed receiver on February 5, 1980. The trial balance below was taken from the books as of that date.

In the period from February 5, to April 30, 1980, the receiver's actions resulted in the following:

1. An audit of the accounts receivable disclosed that there were an additional $423 of accounts receivable that had not been brought on the books.
2. Merchandise costing $8,310 was sold for cash.
3. A portion of the fixtures, which cost $5,376 and had accumulated depreciation credits of $942, was sold.
4. Accounts receivable totaling $1,882 were collected. Other accounts, amounting to $741, have been determined to be worthless.
5. Claims have been approved and paid for $903 of the wages and taxes that were accrued at February 5. Wage claims for $125 that were unrecorded on February 5 have also been approved and paid. Other claims have not yet been paid.

THE SPECIALTY SHOPS COMPANY

TRIAL BALANCE, FEBRUARY 5, 1980

|                              |          |          |
|------------------------------|----------|----------|
| Cash                         | $ 764    |          |
| Accounts receivable          | 5,928    |          |
| Merchandise                  | 16,536   |          |
| Prepayment of expenses       | 704      |          |
| Fixtures                     | 12,342   |          |
| Accounts payable             |          | $15,987  |
| Notes payable                |          | 3,500    |
| Accrued wages, taxes, etc.   |          | 1,275    |
| Accrued rent                 |          | 600      |
| Accumulated depreciation     |          | 3,803    |
| Capital stock                |          | 10,000   |
| Retained earnings            |          | 1,109    |
|                              | $36,274  | $36,274  |

6. Expenses for wages and supplies used in liquidating the business to April 30 amounted to $1,245. Fees for the receiver need not be considered.
7. Rent under leases has continued to accrue in the amount of $900. Interest of $70 has accrued on notes payable.
8. Cash receipts and cash disbursements show the following:

### Cash Receipts
| | |
|---|---|
| Collection of accounts | $1,882 |
| Sales of merchandise | 9,108 |
| Sale of fixtures | 1,000 |

### Cash Disbursements
| | |
|---|---|
| Accrued wages and taxes | $1,028 |
| Expenses of the receivership | 1,245 |

*Required:*

Prepare a statement of realization and liquidation and related gain and loss account for the period February 5 to April 30, 1980. (AICPA adapted)

## Problem 24-13

The Deake Toy Company finds itself in financial difficulty, because it is unable to meet its obligations to its general creditors. The following balance sheet was prepared on October 16, 1980.

DEAKE TOY COMPANY
BALANCE SHEET, OCTOBER 16, 1980

| | | | | |
|---|---|---|---|---|
| Cash | $ 15,240 | Accounts payable | | $156,000 |
| Receivables | 73,324 | Accrued wages | | 8,220 |
| Inventories | 44,778 | Notes payable | | 96,800 |
| Prepaid insurance | 7,120 | Capital stock | $30,000 | |
| Equipment (net) | 151,080 | Retained income | 552 | 30,522 |
| | $291,542 | | | $291,542 |

The general creditors have been negotiating for a suitable settlement with the stockholders-managers of the Company. The best offer they have received to date involves a settlement at 42½ cents on the dollar, with 20 cents payable immediately and the balance in three bi-monthly installments, beginning December 15, 1980. Acceptance of this plan may permit the Deake Company to raise additional capital and thereby to strengthen further the financial structure of the Company.

Accountants for the general creditors have agreed that the following represent reasonable liquidation values for the various assets: receivables, $50,000; inventories, $40,000; prepaid insurance, $4,000; equipment, $98,000. The notes payable are secured by the equipment. Costs estimated to be incurred if liquidation materializes are $18,000.

*Required:*

Prepare a report that will indicate to the general creditors the advisability of accepting the offer of the Deake Co. officials, or starting liquidation proceedings.

# APPENDIX A

# Actuarial Science: Compound Interest and Probability

An understanding of the basic ideas of compound interest and probability as applied to accounting is essential if the accountant is to perform with maximum effectiveness in his profession. In particular, it is necessary to have an understanding of the field of actuarial science, which is the mathematical science based upon compound interest and upon insurance probabilities. Although most of the accounting applications of actuarial science are concerned with compound interest and annuities, there is increasing use of probability measures. In several areas of this textbook it is assumed that the student has a working knowledge of these topics. For students not familiar with the application of these methods to accounting, it seems appropriate to provide at this point an elementary discussion of the essentials of compound interest, probability, and annuities. Students who have had previous exposure to the mathematics of finance should have less need for a thorough study of the following material.

**INTEREST**

Interest may be defined as the payment for the use of money. In this sense it represents an excess payment over and above the principal loaned or borrowed. For example, if A were to lend B $1,000 with the understanding that B would repay $1,100, the excess over $1,000 would represent interest, computed as follows:

| | |
|---|---:|
| Proceeds from loan | $1,100 |
| Amount lent | 1,000 |
| Interest on loan | $ 100 |

The amount of interest to be paid is generally stated as a rate over a specific period of time. For example, if B were to have the use of the money for 1 year before repaying the principal plus interest, the rate of interest would be 10% per year. That is, the interest is 10% of the principal each year. The custom of expressing interest as a rate is well established. In fact, decisions are made on the basis of the *rate* of interest involved rather than on the actual dollar amount of interest that will have to be paid.

**Rate of Interest.** The period of 1 year is rather well established as the period to which the rate of interest applies. Thus, a rate of interest of 6% is assumed to represent a rate of 6% per year unless stipulated otherwise. In fact, the statement that a company will pay bond interest of 6%, payable semi-annually, means a rate of 3% every 6 months, not 6% each 6 months. There is no necessary reason, of course, why the rate must be expressed at so much a year. In fact, some small finance companies generally refer to their interest rate as 1% per month to give an appearance of a low rate when it really represents a rate of about 12% a year.

To illustrate the difference in the manner in which interest rates are expressed, assume that A borrowed $1,000 in cash with an interest rate of 12% payable at the end of the year, and that B borrowed $1,000 with an interest rate of 1% per month payable at the end of each month. The total repayment required to settle the debt would be:

|  | A | B |
|---|---|---|
| Payable during year: |  |  |
| 11 payments at $10 |  | $ 110 |
| Payable at end of year: |  |  |
| 1 payment at $10 |  | 10 |
| 1 payment at $120 | $ 120 |  |
| Principal borrowed | 1,000 | 1,000 |
| Total payment | $1,120 | $1,120 |

Actually, it may be noted that A will have a slight advantage over B in that A gets to keep the entire $1,000 borrowed until the end of the year, whereas B has to use $110 for interest payments during the year.

## Simple Interest

Simple interest is the term used to describe interest that is computed on the amount of the principle only. The illustrations in the sections above were in terms of simple interest, since the rate was always applied to the principal. For example, if the $1,000 A borrowed in the illustration above were for a 5-year period, with a simple interest rate of 12% per year, the total interest A would have to pay would be $600 ($120 times 5 years).

Appendix A / Actuarial Science

**Symbols for Simple Interest.** The following symbols are commonly used in presenting data on simple interest:

$i$ — rate of interest for a single period.
$n$ — number of periods.
$P$ — principal.

If $i$ equals the rate of interest per period of time, $n$ the number of periods, and $P$ the principal, simple interest on a sum of money may be expressed as:

$$\text{Interest} = P \times i \times n$$

In the foregoing illustration of a rate of 1% per month for 1 year, the computation would be:

$$\begin{aligned}\text{Interest} &= \$1{,}000 \times .01 \times 12 \\ &= \$1{,}000 \times .12 \\ &= \underline{\underline{\$120}}\end{aligned}$$

## Compound Interest

Simple interest, as indicated above, is interest on principal only. Compound interest is the term used to describe interest that is computed on principal and on any interest earned that has not been paid. To illustrate the difference, assume you borrow $1,000 from Bank A, agreeing to pay simple interest of 6% per year, and you borrow another $1,000 from Bank B, agreeing to pay compound interest of 6% per year compounded annually. Assume that you pay no interest until the maturity date of the loan, which may be assumed to be 3 years. The calculation of the interest to be paid would be as follows:

|  |  | Simple Interest<br>Bank A | Compound Interest<br>Bank B |
|---|---|---|---|
| First year | ($ 1,000 × 6%) | $ 60.00 | $ 60.00 |
| Second year | ($ 1,000 × 6%) | 60.00 | 60.00 |
|  | ($ 60 × 6%) | — | 3.60 |
| Third year | ($ 1,000 × 6%) | 60.00 | 60.00 |
|  | ($123.60 × 6%) | — | 7.42 |
| Total interest, 3-year period |  | $180.00 | $191.02 |

The amount of compound interest in the illustration above is $191.02, whereas the amount of simple interest is only $180. The difference in amounts is due to the calculation of interest on interest in the case of the compound interest. Compound interest is the type of interest, normally used in business. For practical purposes in computing compound interest, it may be assumed that unpaid interest earned becomes a part of the principal and is entitled to interest. In the illustration above, the computation of compound interest under this assumption would be:

|  | Principal | Interest Rate | Amount |
|---|---|---|---|
| First year | $1,000 | 6% | $ 60.00 |
| Second year | $1,060 (1,000 plus 60) | 6% | 63.60 |
| Third year | $1,123.60 (1,000 plus 60 plus 63.60) | 6% | 67.42 |
| Total interest |  |  | $191.02 |

**Compound Interest Tables.** Every loan made by a lender is made on the assumption that the lender will receive back the principal loaned plus any interest. Each period the loan is outstanding the amount due increases by the amount of interest. Thus if $1.00 is loaned at a rate of 6% per year, the $1.00 will increase to $1.06 at the end of the year. Each subsequent year the previous amount due will increase to 1.06 of the amount due at the beginning of the period. In compound interest terminology, 1 plus the rate of interest expressed as a decimal (.06) gives the *ratio of increase*. Under compound interest, the interest is computed on the balance of principal and interest accumulated at the end of the previous period, so that the second year's interest will be 6% of the $1.06 to which the amount due had accumulated at the end of the first year. Stated another way, the ratio of increase for the 2 periods may be multiplied together to get the ratio of increase for the 2-year period as one amount. To illustrate:

|  |  |
|---|---|
| Ratio of increase — 1st year | 1.06 |
| Ratio of increase — 2nd year | 1.06 |
|  | 636 |
|  | 000 |
|  | 106 |
| Ratio of increase for 2 years | 1.1236 |

To demonstrate, assume that Mr. A puts $1.00 on deposit to receive compound interest of 6% compounded annually and that he leaves the money on deposit for 2 years.

|  |  |
|---|---|
| Principal | $1.00 |
| Interest — 1st year ($1.00 @ 6%) | .06 |
| Interest — 2nd year ($1.06 @ 6%) | .0636 |
| Total amount due at end of 2 years | $1.1236 |

Using the computed ratio of increase, the amount to which the $1.00 will accumulate may be computed by multiplying $1.00 directly by 1.1236 to arrive at the $1.1236. Since there is a need on the part of a great number of people to know how much a sum invested at a certain rate of compound interest will amount to over a period of time, tables have been constructed to show how much $1 invested at various compound rates of interest will amount to at the end of various periods. Compound interest tables are presented at the end of this appendix. The excerpt below illustrates the nature of such tables by showing the amount of 1 at the end of each of the periods given.

AMOUNT OF 1 AT COMPOUND INTEREST

| Periods | 3% | 4% | 5% |
|---|---|---|---|
| 1 | 1.030000 | 1.040000 | 1.050000 |
| 2 | 1.060900 | 1.081600 | 1.102500 |
| 3 | 1.092727 | 1.124864 | 1.157625 |
| 4 | 1.125509 | 1.169859 | 1.215506 |
| 5 | 1.159274 | 1.216653 | 1.276282 |

Interpreting the table, if $1.00 is invested for 3 periods at a compound interest rate of 3% per period, the $1.00 will amount to $1.09 (1.092727 × $1.00); if the investment were for 5 periods it would amount to $1.16. If $1 were invested at 5%, at the end of 4 periods, it would amount to $1.22; at the end of 5 periods it would equal $1.28. If the investment were $100 instead of $1.00, the amounts would be as follows:

If invested for 3 periods at 3% ($100 × 1.092727) = $109.27.
If invested for 4 periods at 5% ($100 × 1.215506) = $121.55.
If invested for 5 periods at 4% ($100 × 1.216653) = $121.67.

For any sum invested, the amount to which 1 would accumulate may be multiplied by the amount invested to determine the amount to which the sum invested would accumulate.

**Symbols for Compound Interest.** The following symbols are commonly used in presenting data on compound interest:

$i$—rate of interest for a single period.
$n$—number of periods.
$r$—periodic ratio of increase (1 plus $i$).
$s$—compound amount of 1.
$P$—principal.

## Amount of 1

Frequently an individual or a business enterprise that has an amount available for investment wants to know how much the investment will accumulate to at a given rate of interest compounded periodically. The amount to which 1 will accumulate may be expressed as a formula:

$$s = (1 + i)^n$$

To illustrate, assume that $1.00 is invested at 6% interest for 3 periods. The amounts to which $1.00 will accumulate at the end of each period are expressed as follows:

$s = (1.06)^1$ for the end of the 1st period.
$s = (1.06)^2$ for the end of the 2nd period.
$s = (1.06)^3$ for the end of the 3rd period.

If tables are available, there is no need to apply the formula, since the formula is the basis for the construction of the table.

**Amount of 1 Table.** In using the tables for the amount of 1, care must be exercised to distinguish between the stated rate of interest per year and the actual rate of interest per period implicit in a given problem. Thus a loan that stipulates a stated rate of interest of 6% per year, the interest compounded twice a year for 10 years, is in reality a loan at an interest rate of 3% per period for 20 periods. Assuming that the loan is for $1,000 at the end of the 10-year period, the amount payable would be equal to:

$1,000 × amount of 1 for 20 periods at 3%,
(1.80611123), or a total of $1,806.11.

It would be incorrect to compute the future amount of the $1,000 at the stated rate of 6% per year for 10 years. Using the 6% rate for 10 years, the incorrect computation would be:

$1,000 × amount of 1 for 10 years at 6%,
(1.79084770), or a total of $1,790.85.

Because the amount is compounded semi-annually rather than annually, the future amount is $15.26 ($1,806.11 − $1,790.85) greater.

As the foregoing illustration indicates, the number of *periods* involved in a computation is not merely the number of *years* involved in the investment. For example, $1,000 invested at 6% per year compounded *monthly* for 5 years, represents 60 periods (5 × 12) at ½% interest per period.

**EXAMPLE**

QUESTION: What amount will be accumulated in 5 years if $400 is loaned at 6% compounded quarterly?

*Solution:* Since the interest is compounded quarterly, the stated rate of 6% per year becomes an actual rate of 1½% per quarterly period (6% divided by 4). Likewise, the 5-year period becomes 20 periods on a quarterly basis. To compute the amount to which $400 would accumulate in 5 years at 6% compounded quarterly, select the amount of 1 table for which the interest rate is 1½% and determine the amount in this table for 20 periods. This amount would be 1.34685501 (the amount of 1 for 20 periods at 1½% interest). When this amount is multiplied by $400, the result is $538.74, or the amount to which $400 would accumulate in 5 years at 6% interest compounded quarterly.

*Appendix A / Actuarial Science*  813

## Present Value of 1

Sometimes an individual wants to know how much should be deposited now to amount to a given sum in the future. Thus, if an individual needs $1,000 in 10 years, and if the current rate of interest at which money can be invested is 6% per year, the problem is to determine how much he would have to invest now to have $1,000 in 10 years. This type of problem is known as the determination of the *present value* of a future amount. The present value is always a smaller amount than the known future amount because interest will be earned and accumulated on the present value to the future date.

The present value of an amount may be computed by dividing 1 by the amount of 1 for a like number of periods and a like rate of interest and multiplying the result by the known future amount. To illustrate, assume that $1,000 is needed in 10 years and funds can be invested currently at 6% per year. Using the table of amount of 1, it can be seen that $1.00 invested for 10 periods at 6% will equal $1.79084770. If $1.00 is divided by this amount (1.79084770), the result equals the present value of 1 due in 10 years if invested at 6% per year, or $0.55839478. This means that an investment of approximately $0.56 now at 6% will equal approximately $1.00 in 10 years. Since $1,000 is needed, the amount to be invested would be 1,000 times $0.55839478 or $558.39.

**Present Value of 1 Tables.** Because there is frequently need for quick computations of present values, tables have been developed showing how much would have to be invested at various compound interest rates for various periods of time to equal 1 at a future date. Excerpts from such tables are illustrated below, and more complete tables appear in Appendix T.

PRESENT VALUE OF 1 AT COMPOUND INTEREST

| Periods | 3% | 4% | 5% |
|---|---|---|---|
| 1 | 0.97087379 | 0.96153846 | 0.95238095 |
| 2 | 0.94259591 | 0.92455621 | 0.90702948 |
| 3 | 0.91514166 | 0.88899636 | 0.86383760 |
| 4 | 0.88848705 | 0.85480419 | 0.82270247 |
| 5 | 0.86260878 | 0.82192711 | 0.78352617 |

The present value of 1 tables may be constructed from the general formula:

$$v = 1 \div s$$

where $s$ is the amount of 1 and $v$ is the present value of 1. To illustrate, assume that it is desired to determine the present value of $1 at compound interest of 5% for 4 periods. Referring to the amount of 1 table on p. 811, the amount of 1 at 5% compound interest for 4 periods = 1.215506. To determine the present value, the formula above becomes:

$$v = \frac{1}{1.215506} = \$0.82270247$$

or the amount that must be invested now to equal $1.00 in 4 years at 5% compound interest. In the table above, this same amount may be found in the 5% column on the 4-period line.

The tables of present value give the amount that would have to be invested at a specified rate of interest for a period of time to equal 1 at the end of the period of time. For example, the table indicates that an investment of 0.86383760 at 5% for 3 years will equal 1. To validate the table, a computation may be made of the increase that would take place each period to see if the accumulation would amount to 1 at the end of the 3-year period, as follows:

| | |
|---|---|
| Present value at start of investment | 0.86383760 |
| Interest—1st year (5% × 0.86383760) | 0.04319188 |
| Value at end of 1st year | 0.90702948 |
| Interest—2nd year (5% × 0.90702948) | 0.04535147 |
| Value at end of 2nd year | 0.95238095 |
| Interest—3rd year (5% × 0.95238095) | 0.04761905 |
| Value at end of 3rd year | 1.00000000 |

To illustrate the use of the table, assume that a young man has the opportunity to make a substantial investment now at 6% interest compounded annually for a 42-year period. At the end of the 42-year period, the young man plans to retire. He has decided that he will require $100,000 to meet his retirement needs. He wants to know how much he should invest now in order to have $100,000 at the end of the 42 years. By referring to the tables of present value, he would find that approximately $0.08 (0.08652740) invested now will yield $1.00 in 42 years. Since he needs $100,000 instead of $1.00, he must multiply the 0.08652740 by $100,000. The multiplication indicates that he should invest $8,652.74 now in order to have the needed $100,000 at retirement time.

## ANNUITIES

Life insurance companies have made a great contribution to the American way of life by encouraging people to save a regular sum of money. That is, a person may pay a premium every week, month, quarter, or year which then accumulates to a given amount at the end of a specified number of periods. Such a process of periodic saving represents the accumulation through an annuity of a sum of money. By definition an annuity is a series of equal payments made at equal intervals of time. It should be emphasized that an annuity requires the periodic payment always be the same amount and that the interval between payments always be the same.

### Amount of an Annuity

The amount of an annuity is the sum of the payments (called rents) and the accumulated compound interest on them. To illustrate, assume that a man starts an annuity of $1,000 a year for 3 years and earns on all investments 5% compound

Appendix A / Actuarial Science

interest. An annuity of $1,000 a year means that this sum is invested each year for 3 years. It should be noted that the annual $1,000 investment may be made at either the *beginning* or the *end* of the year. To distinguish annuity investments under these two alternatives, an annuity is classified as either an *ordinary annuity* or an *annuity due*.

In an ordinary annuity, the payments are made at the *end* of the period. In an annuity due, the payments are made at the *beginning* of the period.

The distinction between the two kinds of annuities may be noted by the solution to the illustration noted above, as follows:

|  | Ordinary Annuity | Annuity Due |
|---|---|---|
| 1st year's investment | $1,000.00 | $1,000.00 |
| 1st year's interest | –0– | 50.00 |
| Balance at end of 1st year | $1,000.00 | $1,050.00 |
| 2nd year's investment | 1,000.00 | 1,000.00 |
| 2nd year's interest: |  |  |
| $1,000 @ 5% | 50.00 |  |
| $2,050 @ 5% |  | 102.50 |
| Balance at end of 2nd year | $2,050.00 | $2,152.50 |
| 3rd year's investment | 1,000.00 | 1,000.00 |
| 3rd year's interest: |  |  |
| $2,050 @ 5% | 102.50 |  |
| $3,152.50 @ 5% |  | 157.63 |
| Balance at end of 3rd year | $3,152.50 | $3,310.13 |

Thus, the amount to which an annuity of $1,000 a year for 3 years at 5% will accumulate depends upon whether it is an ordinary annuity or an annuity due. When investments are made during the middle of a calendar year, they are converted to an ordinary annuity or to an annuity due by using a fiscal year starting at the time of the investment, rather than a regular calendar year, so that the annual payment falls either at the end (ordinary annuity) or at the beginning (annuity due) of the fiscal year.

**Annuity Tables.** Tables have been developed similar to those used for the amount of 1 and the present value of 1 for both an ordinary annuity and an annuity due. Because an annuity due table is easily constructed from an ordinary annuity table, this textbook presents only tables for an ordinary annuity. An explanation of the process for converting an ordinary annuity table into a table for an annuity due will be presented later.

An understanding of annuities requires familiarity with the method by which compound interest tables are constructed. It will be recalled that the amount of 1 table was constructed from the general formula:

$$s = (1 + i)^n$$

Thus, if $1.00 is deposited for 4 periods at 5%, the formula becomes $s = (1.05)^4$ or $(1.05 \times 1.05 \times 1.05 \times 1.05)$, which gives 1.21550625 (the amount indicated in the amount of 1 table), or approximately $1.22.

The table for an ordinary annuity of 1 can be constructed from an amount of 1 table. The procedure:

1. Determine the compound amount of 1 at the given rate of interest for the number of periods involved, using the formula $s = (1 + i)^n$, or find this amount in the amount of 1 table.
2. Compute the compound interest by subtracting 1 from the amount derived in Step (1). In formula form this is $I = s - 1$.
3. Divide the compound interest ($I$) by the interest rate ($i$) to obtain the amount of the annuity of 1. The formula is: $I \div (i) = (s_{ni})$, where $s_{ni}$ represents the amount of an annuity of 1 for $n$ periods at $i$ rate of interest.
4. Multiply the amount of an annuity of 1 by the number of dollars in each rent. In formula form this is: $R \times s_{ni}$, where $R$ equals the amount of each rent.

## EXAMPLE

QUESTION: To what amount will an ordinary annuity of $1 for 4 periods at 5% accumulate?

Solution: From the table of amount of 1:

| | | |
|---|---|---:|
| (1) | Amount of 1 for 4 periods at 5% | 1.215506 |
| (2) | Deduct 1 | −1.000000 |
| (2) | Compound interest | .215506 |
| (3) | Divide by the interest rate | .05 |
| (3) | Amount of annuity of 1 for 4 periods at 5% | 4.310125 |

A table of the amount of an annuity of 1 which might be constructed from a series of solutions similar to that illustrated above is shown below:

AMOUNT OF ANNUITY OF 1

| Periods | 3% | 4% | 5% |
|---|---|---|---|
| 1 | 1.000000 | 1.000000 | 1.000000 |
| 2 | 2.030000 | 2.040000 | 2.050000 |
| 3 | 3.090900 | 3.121600 | 3.152500 |
| 4 | 4.183627 | 4.246464 | 4.310125 |
| 5 | 5.309136 | 5.416323 | 5.525631 |

**Relation of Compound Interest and Annuities** An analysis of compound interest tables reveals that the amount of 1 table is composed of three elements:

1. The principal of 1.
2. The annual regular addition of simple interest on the principal.
3. The interest on the interest.

This may be illustrated by the following tabulation, on a 5% basis:

Appendix A / Actuarial Science

|  | Principal | Simple Interest | Interest on Interest | Total |
|---|---|---|---|---|
| Investment beginning of period | 1.000000 |  |  | 1.000000 |
| 1st period: |  |  |  |  |
| Simple interest |  | .0500 |  | .050000 |
| Interest on interest |  |  | — |  |
| 2nd period: |  |  |  |  |
| Simple interest |  | .0500 |  | .050000 |
| Interest on interest |  |  | .0025 | .002500 |
| 3rd period: |  |  |  |  |
| Simple interest |  | .0500 |  | .050000 |
| Interest on interest |  |  | .005125 | .005125 |
| 4th period: |  |  |  |  |
| Simple interest |  | .0500 |  | .050000 |
| Interest on interest |  |  | .007881 | .007881 |
| Total | 1.000000 | .200000 | .015506 | 1.215506 |

The sum of the three elements, 1.215506, agrees with the amount in the table of the amount of 1 for 4 periods at 5%. If the principal is deducted from this amount, the remainder is the compound interest ($I$) of .215506. From the tabulation it can be seen that the .215506 is accumulated by regular deposits of simple interest of $.05 each period, plus interest on the deposits. Compound interest is thus the same as an annuity of .05 each period of time. If an annuity of .05 equals a total of .215506 in 4 periods if invested at 5%, it may be concluded that an annuity of 1 could be computed by dividing the accumulation of .215506 by .05. The result would be 4.310125, which is the amount of an annuity of 1 for 4 periods at 5%. A review of this analysis will show that it followed the steps set forth in the preceding section for developing a table of an amount of ordinary annuity of 1.

**Amount of an Annuity of 1 Tables.** The uses to which an amount of an ordinary annuity table may be applied are extensive. Listed below are two illustrations of the use of annuity tables in the business world.

1. How much should a young man deposit each year for 30 years if he wants to have $100,000 at the end of the period and if he can invest all deposits at 5% interest compounded annually?
   According to the amount of an ordinary annuity table, if he were to deposit $1.00 a period for 30 periods at 5%, he would have a total of $66.43884750. If $1.00 a period gives him over $66, he may divide the $100,000 by $66.43884750 and determine that the annual deposit he should make would be $1,505.14.
2. A borrower promises to pay back to a lender the sum of $100,000 in 30 years, if the lender will lend him $2,000 a year at the end of each year. What

rate of interest would the lender earn on the investment assuming yearly compounding?

Dividing the $100,000 by 2,000, it can be seen that $1 loaned each period will return a total of $50 at the end of the 30 years. Referring to the table of the amount of an annuity of 1, it can be seen that for 30 periods at a rate of 3%, the $1 annuity would yield $47.58, whereas a rate of 3½% will yield $51.62. If each of the values in the table is multiplied by $2,000 the following results are obtained:

> At 3%, an annuity of $2,000 will yield $95,150.83.
> At 3½%, an annuity of $2,000 will yield $103,245.35.

From this, by interpolation an approximation from the table shows that the lender would obtain a rate of return on his investment of between 3% and 3½%.

**Relationship of Annuity Due to Ordinary Annuity Table.** It has been noted that under an annuity due the periodic payments, termed "rents" in actuarial terminology, are made at the beginning of the period. Payments under an ordinary annuity are made at the end of the period. This means an annuity due will accumulate interest on the first year's payment in the first year, whereas an ordinary annuity payment will earn no interest during the first year. Stated in general terms, the periodic interest earnings under an ordinary annuity will always be less by one period's interest than the interest earned by an annuity due. To illustrate the relationship of the two types of annuities, the following tabulated comparison accumulates the interest and payments of $1,000 a period for 5 periods at 6%.

|        | ORDINARY ANNUITY |          |                              | ANNUITY DUE |          |                              |
|--------|------------------|----------|------------------------------|-------------|----------|------------------------------|
| Period | Payment          | Interest | End of Period Accumulation   | Payment     | Interest | End of Period Accumulation   |
| 1      | $1,000           | $ 0      | $1,000.00                    | $1,000      | $ 60.00  | $1,060.00                    |
| 2      | 1,000            | 60.00    | 2,060.00                     | 1,000       | 123.60   | 2,183.60                     |
| 3      | 1,000            | 123.60   | 3,183.60                     | 1,000       | 191.02   | 3,374.62                     |
| 4      | 1,000            | 191.02   | 4,374.62                     | 1,000       | 262.48   | 4,637.10                     |
| 5      | 1,000            | 262.48   | 5,637.10                     | 1,000       | 338.23   | 5,975.33                     |

The illustration emphasizes the fact that an ordinary annuity for 5 periods earns interest for only 4 periods. This is so because the payments are always made at the end of the period. The annuity due, however, earns 4 periods' interest in 4 periods. This relationship suggests the basis for converting an ordinary annuity table to an annuity due table. If the last rent payment in an ordinary annuity is deducted from the end of period accumulation, the residual will represent the amount of an annuity due for 1 less period. For example, if 1 payment is deducted from the ordinary annuity of 5 periods at 6%, in the preceding illustration, the result will be the amount of an annuity due of 4 periods at 6%, as follows:

(1) Amount of ordinary annuity of $1,000 a
period for 5 periods at 6%          $5,637.10
(2) Deduct last payment          1,000.00
(3) Amount of annuity due of $1,000 a
period for 4 periods at 6%          $4,637.10

## EXAMPLE

PROBLEM: Convert a table of the amount of an ordinary annuity of 1 to a table of the amount of an annuity due of 1 for 4 periods at an interest rate of 4%.

| Ordinary Annuity | | | Annuity Due | |
|---|---|---|---|---|
| 1st period | 1.000000 | | | |
| 2nd period | 2.040000 | −1 | 1st period | 1.040000 |
| 3rd period | 3.121600 | −1 | 2nd period | 2.121600 |
| 4th period | 4.246464 | −1 | 3rd period | 3.246464 |
| 5th period | 5.416323 | −1 | 4th period | 4.416323 |

**Use of Annuity Due Illustrated.** Mr. Zim plans to deposit $2,000 at six-month intervals, starting with his 35th birthday, at 6% interest compounded semiannually. He wants to know the amount he will have accumulated on his 50th birthday. He plans to make no payment on his 50th birthday.

Since the first payment is made on his 35th birthday, he will make a total of 30 payments over the life of the annuity. These payments will all be made at the beginning of the periods, so the payments represent an annuity due.

Referring to the amount of an ordinary annuity for 31 periods at 3% and deducting 1 to arrive at the annuity due for 30 periods, the solution would be as follows:

(1) Amount of an ordinary annuity of 1 for
31 periods at 3%          50.00267818
(2) Deduct 1 payment          1.00000000
(3) Amount of an annuity due of 1 for
30 periods at 3%          49.00267818
(4) Periodic payment          × $2,000
(5) Accumulated amount on 50th birthday          $98,005.36

## Present Value of an Annuity

A simple way to look at the idea of the present value of an annuity is to consider what lump sum needs to be deposited now at a specified rate of interest in order to receive back an annuity of so much a period for so many periods. More formally, the present value of an ordinary annuity is the sum which, if earning compound interest, will provide the periodic rents of an annuity contract as they become due. The present value is always computed as of the beginning of the first period.

**Computing Present Value of an Annuity—Method One.** The future payments to be received as an annuity may be treated individually as the present value of a series of separate amounts. For example, an annuity of $1.00 a year to be received at the end of each year for 5 years may be looked upon as separate amounts and the present value of each computed from the table of present value of 1. If the interest rate is 6%, the present value of the annuity above might be computed as follows:

End of Year in Which $1.00 Is to Be Received

| Present Value | 1 | 2 | 3 | 4 | 5 |
|---|---|---|---|---|---|
| $ .9434 | $1.00 | | | | |
| .8900 | | $1.00 | | | |
| .8396 | | | $1.00 | | |
| 7921 | | | | $1.00 | |
| .7473 | | | | | $1.00 |
| $4.2124 | Total (Present value of annuity of $1.00 for 5 periods at 6% interest rate) | | | | |

**Computing Present Value of an Annuity—Method Two.** Method One, a variation of which can also be used for computing the amount of an annuity by using an amount of 1 table, becomes cumbersome and subject to error if the annuity covers a great number of periods. As a consequence, Method Two is often used. The procedure under this method is as follows:

1. Compute the compound discount ($D$) on 1 (this is the difference between 1 and the present value of 1) for the number of periods involved at the stated rate of interest. The formula to be used is: $(1 - v^n) = D$, where $v^n$ represents the present value of 1 and may be taken from the table of present value of 1.
2. Divide the compound discount by the rate of interest used. The quotient will be the present value of an annuity of 1. The formula is: $D \div i = a_{ni}$, where $a_{ni}$ represents the present value of an annuity of 1 for $n$ periods at $i$ rate of interest.
3. Multiply the present value of the annuity of 1 by the number of dollars in each rent. In formula form, this is: $R \times a_{ni}$.

**EXAMPLE**

QUESTION: What amount should be deposited now at 4% annual interest to receive an annuity of $3,000 a year, starting at the end of the first year, for 15 years?

## Solution:

| | | |
|---|---|---|
| (1) | Start with 1 | 1.000000 |
| (1) | Deduct the present value of 1 at 4% for 15 years ($v^{15}$) | .555265 |
| (1) | Compound discount ($D$) | .444735 |
| (2) | Rate of interest ($i$) | .04 |
| (2) | Present value of ordinary annuity of 1 at 4% for 15 years ($D$ divided by $i$) | 11.118387 |
| (3) | Number of dollars in each rent ($R$) | 3,000 |
| (3) | Present value of annuity of $3,000 at 4% for 15 periods | $33,355.16 |

**Construction of Present Value of Annuity of 1 Table.** A table of present value of an annuity of 1 may be constructed quite easily by Method Two, as illustrated below:

| Period | Table of present value of 1 at 4% | $D$, or $(1 - v^n)$ | Divide by $i$ | Present value of ordinary annuity of 1 at 4% |
|---|---|---|---|---|
| 1 | .961538 | .038462 | .04 | .961538 |
| 2 | .924556 | .075444 | .04 | 1.886100 |
| 3 | .888996 | .111004 | .04 | 2.775100 |
| 4 | .854804 | .145196 | .04 | 3.629900 |

From several calculations such as this for various rates of interest and periods, the table may be constructed. Excerpts from such a table are illustrated below:

PRESENT VALUE OF ANNUITY OF 1

| Periods | 3% | 4% | 5% |
|---|---|---|---|
| 1 | .970874 | .961538 | .952381 |
| 2 | 1.913470 | 1.886095 | 1.859410 |
| 3 | 2.828611 | 2.775091 | 2.723248 |
| 4 | 3.717098 | 3.629895 | 3.545951 |
| 5 | 4.579707 | 4.451822 | 4.329477 |

**Present Value of Ordinary Annuity of 1 Table.** One of the many uses to which a table of present value of an ordinary annuity of 1 may be applied is illustrated in the following example:

Mr. X died, leaving to his wife an insurance policy contract that provided that the beneficiary (the wife) could choose any one of the three following options:

(a) $100 every three months payable at the end of each quarter, for 12 years.
(b) $1,000 immediate cash and $100 every three months for 9 years.
(c) $200 every three months for 3 years and $100 a quarter for the following 26 quarters.

If money is worth 1% per quarter, compounded quarterly, which option should the wife exercise?

*Solution:*

|  |  | OPTION |  |
|---|---|---|---|
|  | a | b | c |
| (1) Immediate cash | –0– | $1,000.00 | –0– |
| (2) P.v. of $100 a quarter for 48 quarters at 1% interest per quarter | $3,797.40 | –0– | –0– |
| (3) P.v. of $100 a quarter for 36 quarters at 1% interest per quarter | –0– | 3,010.75 | –0– |
| (4) P.v. of $100 a quarter for 38 quarters at 1% interest per quarter | –0– | –0– | $3,148.47 |
| (5) P.v. of $100 a quarter for 12 quarters at 1% interest per quarter | –0– | –0– | 1,125.51 |
| Present value of option | $3,797.40 | $4,010.75 | $4,273.98 |

From the facts above, Option (c) appears to be the best option on the basis of the dollar amounts involved.

**Present Value of an Annuity Due.** In an annuity due, payments or withdrawals are made at the beginning of the period. As a result, in the present value of an annuity due the first withdrawal will be made immediately and will have no opportunity to earn interest. The second withdrawal will have earned interest for one period before it is made at the start of the second period. In an ordinary annuity, however, because withdrawal takes place at the end of the period, the first withdrawal will have earned interest for one period before it is made. This means a smaller deposit will have to be made for the first period's withdrawal in an ordinary annuity than in an annuity due. The difference between the interest accumulations may be illustrated by noting the interest periods in each annuity, as follows:

|  | Ordinary Annuity | Annuity Due |
|---|---|---|
| Initial deposit (present value) | xxxxxxxx | xxxxxxxx |
| Beginning of period—1st withdrawal |  | 1.00 |
| Interest on 1st withdrawal | yes | no |
| End of period—1st withdrawal | 1.00 |  |
| Beginning of 2nd period withdrawal |  | 1.00 |
| Interest on 2nd withdrawal | yes | yes |
| End of 2nd period withdrawal | 1.00 |  |

The presentation illustrates that in an ordinary annuity that is to be withdrawn, the number of interest periods and the number of withdrawals are the same (two in the illustration), whereas in an annuity due, the number of interest periods is always one less than the number of withdrawals. This suggests the basis for converting a table of present value of an ordinary annuity of 1 to a table of present value of an annuity due of 1. The procedure would involve adding 1 withdrawal to the present value of an ordinary annuity of one less period than that of the annuity due as follows:

| | |
|---|---|
| Present value of an ordinary annuity of 1 for 5 rents at 6% | 4.212364 |
| Add 1 | 1.000000 |
| Present value of an annuity due of 1 for 6 rents at 6% | 5.212364 |

The steps in computing the present value of an annuity due are:

1. Compute, or take from a table, the present value of an ordinary annuity of 1 at the specified rate of interest for one less period than the desired number of annuity periods.
2. To the result of (1) add 1. The result is the present value of an annuity due of 1 for the desired number of periods.
3. Multiply the present value of an annuity due of 1 by the number of dollars in each rent.

**EXAMPLE**

PROBLEM: Convert a table of the present value of an ordinary annuity of 1 to a table of the present value of an annuity due of 1 to 6 periods at an interest rate of 4%.

*Solution:*

| Ordinary Annuity | | | Annuity Due | |
|---|---|---|---|---|
| | | +1 | 1st period | 1.000000 |
| 1st period | .961538 | +1 | 2nd period | 1.961538 |
| 2nd period | 1.886095 | +1 | 3rd period | 2.886095 |
| 3rd period | 2.775091 | +1 | 4th period | 3.775091 |
| 4th period | 3.629895 | +1 | 5th period | 4.629895 |
| 5th period | 4.451822 | +1 | 6th period | 5.451822 |

**Use of Present Value of an Annuity Due.** Typical of the use of present value of an annuity is the situation in which a homeowner buys a home and mortgages it, for example, for $18,000 at 5% a year interest under a direct-reduction type of loan, so that the mortgage is to be paid off in 15 annual payments of equal amounts. The first payment is to be made immediately. The problem is to determine the required amount of the equal annual payments.

From a table of present value of an ordinary annuity of 1:

(1) Determine the present value of 14 rents of 1 at 5%                  9.898641
(2) Add                                                                 1.000000
(3) Present value of an annuity due of 1 for 15 periods at 5%          10.898641
(4) If $10.898641 is the present value of an annuity of $1.00 for 15 periods at 5%, to determine the amount of the periodic rent of an annuity due for 15 periods at 5% for which the present value is $18,000, divide the $18,000 by $10.898641. The result is $1,651.59, the amount of each annual payment, and the first payment is due immediately.

## Summary of Compound Interest Tables

1. An amount of 1 table indicates the amount to which 1 will accumulate if it is deposited now at a specified rate of interest and left for a specified number of periods.
2. A present value of 1 table indicates the amount that must be deposited now at a specified rate of interest to amount to 1 at the end of a specified number of periods.
3. An amount of an annuity of 1 table indicates the amount to which periodic payments of 1 will accumulate if the payments are invested at a specified rate of interest and are continued for a specified number of periods. If the payment is made at the start of each period, the series of payments is called an annuity due; if made at the end of each period, it is called an ordinary annuity.
4. A present value of an annuity of 1 table indicates the amount that must be deposited now at a specified rate of interest to permit withdrawals of 1 at regular periodic intervals for the specified number of periods. If withdrawal is made at the start of each period, the annuity is called an annuity due; if made at the end of each period, it is called an ordinary annuity.

Various combinations of these tables may be used to solve such problems as (1) deferred annuities, (2) the price to pay for a bond, (3) sinking fund accumulations, (4) annuity method of depreciation, (5) valuation of leaseholds, and (6) amortization of a variety of investments.

## SPECIAL APPLICATIONS

### Deferred Annuity

A deferred annuity is an annuity in which the periodic payments are deferred a specified number of periods before the initial payment is made. Thus a deferred annuity of 10 periods deferred 6 periods means the annuity will not start for 6 periods.

The amount of a deferred annuity is identical to the amount of an annuity that is not deferred. This is so because the amount of any annuity does not begin to accumulate until the initial payment is made, and the initial payment in a deferred annuity will not be made until the deferred periods have passed.

## Appendix A / Actuarial Science

The present value of a deferred annuity is the value now of an annuity in which the initial payment will be made later. Thus, it involves a deposit now, a waiting period, and then the start of the withdrawal payments. The present value of a deferred annuity will not be identical to the present value of an annuity that is not deferred, as the following two methods for computing the present value of a deferred annuity will indicate.

## Method One

1. Select from the table the present value of an ordinary annuity of 1 at the specified rate and the number of periods for which payments are to be made.
2. Multiply the result of (1) by the amount of each rent.
3. Multiply the result of (2) by the present value of 1 for the number of deferred periods.

**Illustration.** Determine the present value of an annuity of $1,000 a year for 12 years at 6% deferred 5 years.

| | | |
|---|---|---|
| (1) | P.v. of ordinary annuity of 1 for 12 periods at 6% | 8.383844 |
| (2) | Amount of each rent | $1,000 |
| (2) | P.v. of ordinary annuity of $1,000 for 12 periods at 6% | $8,383.84 |
| (3) | P.v. of 1 at 6% for 5 periods | .747258 |
| (3) | P.v. of annuity of $1,000 a period for 12 periods at 6% deferred 5 periods ($8,383.84 multiplied by .747258) | $6,264.89 |

## Method Two

1. Select from the table the present value of an ordinary annuity of 1 at the specified rate and the number of periods equal to the sum of the deferred periods and the payment periods.
2. Select from the table the present value of an ordinary annuity of 1 at the specified rate and number of periods equal to the deferred periods.
3. Subtract (2) from (1).
4. Multiply (3) by the amount of each payment (rent).

**Illustration.** Determine the present value of an annuity of $1,000 a year for 12 years at 6% deferred 5 years.

| | | |
|---|---|---|
| (1) | P.v. of ordinary annuity of 1 for 17 years at 6% | 10.477260 |
| (2) | P.v. of ordinary annuity of 1 for 5 years at 6% | 4.212364 |
| (3) | P.v. of ordinary annuity of 1 for 12 periods at 6% deferred 5 periods | 6.264896 |
| (4) | Annual rent | $1,000 |
| (4) | P.v. of ordinary annuity of $1,000 for 12 years at 6% deferred 5 years | $6,264.89 |

## Computing the Price of a Bond

Bonds are normally issued with a promise (1) to pay at a designated future date a stated sum of money called the par, maturity, or face value of the bond, and (2) to pay at regular intervals cash interest computed as a specified percent of the face of the bond. The cash interest paid at the regular intervals is referred to as the "nominal" rate of interest.

The proper price to pay for a bond depends not upon the par or face value of the bond but upon the present value of the interest annuity and the present value of the par, maturity, or face value that the bond will provide.

To illustrate, assume that the SAF Board Company issues a $1,000, 5% bond on April 1, 1980, due on April 1, 2000, with interest payable each October 1 and April 1. At the time the bond is issued, investors may be earning more or less than the nominal rate that the SAF bond is to pay. If investors are earning 3% every six months on investments of risk comparable to that of the SAF bond, investors will not pay $1,000 for the SAF bond. If an investor did pay $1,000 for the bond, he would earn only 2½% interest every six months. To realize an effective rate of interest of 3% every six months on a SAF bond, the investor would have to pay something less than $1,000.

The solution to the problem of the appropriate price for the bond rests on the realization that ownership of the bond will provide $1,000 on April 1, 2000, plus $25 every six months for the 20-year period. Since the investor wants to earn 3% every six months on the investment, the price of the bond will be the present value of the future $1,000 plus the present value of the $25 annuity of 40 six-month periods. The process of discounting these amounts at 3% every six months is presented below:

(1) P.v. of $1,000 discounted at 3% for 40 periods:
　　P.v. of 1 @ 3% for 40 periods　　　　　　　　　　　　　　　.306557
　　Times　　　　　　　　　　　　　　　　　　　　　　　$ 1,000　　$306.56
(2) P.v. of annuity of $25 for 40 periods at 3%:
　　P.v. of annuity of 1 at 3% for 40 periods　　　　　　　　　23.11477
　　Times　　　　　　　　　　　　　　　　　　　　　　　$     25　　 577.87
Price to be paid for a $1,000, 5% bond to yield an effective
rate of return of 3% every 6 months for 40 periods　　　　　　　　　　$884.43

**Accounting for Bond Amortization—Effective Rate Method.** Proper accounting requires that the premium or discount, the difference between the face of the bond ($1,000) and the price of the bond ($884.43), be amortized over the life of the bond. The amount involved ($115.57) may be amortized on a straight-line basis, in which case the total discount ($115.57) or premium will be divided by the number of periods before maturity of the bonds (40 periods) to determine the amount to write off each period ($2.89 each six months). The entry to amortize the discount each period and to recognize the cash interest received would be:

|                     |          | $25.00 |        |
|---------------------|----------|--------|--------|
| Cash                |          | 2.89   |        |
| Bond investment     |          |        |        |
| Interest income     |          |        | $27.89 |

The straight-line method of amortization is widely used in accounting practice, but a more accurate procedure, and one that is used by many investors with large holdings of bonds, is the effective rate method of amortization.

The effective rate method for amortizing bond discount or bond premium is based on the realization that bond interest income, or bond interest expense in the case of the issuing company, should be computed at the effective rate at which the bonds were purchased or issued. In the preceding illustration, the bond was purchased to yield 3% every six months on the money invested. For the first six months this would be 3% of $884.43, or $26.53. Since only $25 of this income would be in cash, the remaining $1.53 would represent the amortization of the discount for that period. The entry to record the interest for the six months would be:

| Cash            | $25.00 |        |
|-----------------|--------|--------|
| Bond investment | 1.53   |        |
| Interest income |        | $26.53 |

At the start of the second six-month period, the bond would be carried at $885.96 ($884.43 plus $1.53), and the second six months' interest income would be 3% of $885.96, or $26.58. This income would be recorded in a manner similar to that shown for the first six-month period. If the procedure of the effective rate method is followed carefully, the amortization of the bond discount in the 40th six-month period will bring the bond up to par, face, or maturity value at the maturity or due date.

When the effective rate method is used for amortizing bond discount or premium, a schedule is typically prepared to facilitate recording the periodic income. Such a schedule, illustrating the purchase at a premium of $35.85 of a $1,000 bond paying nominal interest of 3% every six months but yielding an effective rate of only 2½% every six months, is presented above.

SCHEDULE OF AMORTIZATION
6% BOND BOUGHT TO YIELD 5%

| Date | Debit Cash | Credit Interest Income | Credit Bond Account | Carrying Value of Bond |
|------|-----------|------------------------|---------------------|------------------------|
| Purchase date  | —       | —       | —      | $1,035.85 |
| End 1st 6 mos. | $ 30.00 | $ 25.90 | $ 4.10 | 1,031.75  |
| End 2nd 6 mos. | 30.00   | 25.79   | 4.21   | 1,027.54  |
| End 3rd 6 mos. | 30.00   | 25.69   | 4.31   | 1,023.23  |
| End 4th 6 mos. | 30.00   | 25.58   | 4.42   | 1,018.81  |
| End 5th 6 mos. | 30.00   | 25.47   | 4.53   | 1,014.28  |
| End 6th 6 mos. | 30.00   | 25.36   | 4.64   | 1,009.64  |

|  |  |  |  |  |
|---|---|---|---|---|
| End 7th 6 mos. | 30.00 | 25.24 | 4.76 | 1,004.88 |
| End 8th 6 mos. | 30.00 | 25.12 | 4.88 | 1,000.00 |
|  | $240.00 | $204.15 | $35.85 |  |

## Sinking-Fund Accumulations

It is not uncommon for business organizations to accumulate funds for specific purposes. In fact, many indentures under which bonds are issued may require a company to accumulate a fund to redeem the bonds upon their maturity. Funds built up or being accumulated are often referred to as sinking funds to indicate that the resources invested in the fund are tied up or "sunk" and not available for normal business operations.

**Bond Sinking—Fund Contributions.** In the case of sinking funds to redeem outstanding bonds at their maturity, a third party called a trustee may be designated as the person to whom the sinking-fund payments are to be made. To illustrate the problem involved, assume that the Lini Book Company issues $100,000 of bonds due in 20 years. The bond indenture provides that the Company shall deposit annually in a sinking fund, with the First National Bank as trustee, an amount which when invested at 6% will provide a fund of $100,000 to retire the bonds at their maturity date in 20 years.

The amount of the annual payment to be made may be computed by dividing the $100,000 by the amount of an annuity of 1 for 20 years at 6% (36.78559120). The result ($2,718.46) indicates the approximate amount that should be deposited in the fund each year. Actually, this might be rounded off to $2,720, or $2,700 for purposes of the accumulation.

**Sinking-Funding Depreciation.** Some accountants have suggested that the sinking-fund concept be applied to the measurement of depreciation of fixed assets. In fact, some public utility companies have used the sinking-fund concept to determine annual depreciation charges. Under the sinking-fund concept, the annual depreciation is the amount of the periodic deposit that would have to be made *if* a sinking fund were being accumulated plus the interest on the accumulated balance. Thus, from the illustration above, the first year's depreciation entry on a $100,000 asset with a useful life of 20 years would be:

| | | |
|---|---|---|
| Depreciation expense | $2,718.46 | |
|     Allowance for depreciation | | $2,718.46 |

This first year's entry would be for the amount of the periodic deposit only, since no interest would have been earned. The second year's depreciation, however, would be for the periodic deposit plus interest (at 6%) on the accumulated depreciation to date. The interest for the second year would be $163.11, and the depreciation entry at the end of the second year would be:

| | | |
|---|---|---|
| Depreciation expense | $2,881.57 | |
|     Allowance for depreciation | | $2,881.57 |

Appendix A / Actuarial Science

The effect of this method of depreciation is to increase gradually the depreciation charge each period. It has not been used extensively in practice, and, when used, has seldom been used along with a voluntary sinking-fund accumulation.

## Annuity Method of Depreciation

The sinking-fund method of depreciation looks upon the cost of the asset as the amount of an annuity to be accumulated from annual deposits. Depreciation is considered to be the process of accumulating a sum of money equal to the cost of the asset (less scrap value) being depreciated. On the other hand, the annuity method of depreciation looks upon the cost of the asset as the present value of a future annuity that will be received. Depreciation is considered to be the amount of the rents foregone by investing in the asset rather than by purchasing the annuity. The distinction between the two methods may best be explained by a comparison of the procedures to be followed and the results of an illustrative example:

## Procedure

### Sinking-Fund Method

1. Deduct scrap value from the cost of the asset to determine depreciable cost.
2. Divide depreciable cost by the *amount* of any ordinary annuity of 1 at the sinking-fund interest rate for the number of years of useful life of the asset.
3. To the periodic sum determined in (2), add a sum equal to the interest on the accumulated balance in the "Allowance for Depreciation" account. This gives the periodic depreciation charge.

### Annuity Method

1. Deduct scrap value from the cost of the asset to determine depreciable cost.
2. Divide depreciable cost by the *present value* of an annuity of 1 at the specified interest rate for the number of years of useful life of asset.
3. Compute the annual interest on the scrap value for one year at the specified rate of interest.
4. The sum of (2) and (3) is the annual depreciation charge.
5. Imputed interest on the undepreciated cost is recorded, reducing the credit for accumulated depreciation.

**Illustration.** The Shrud-&-Coy Company purchases for $11,000 a machine having an estimated useful life of four years and an estimated scrap value at the end of the four years of $1,000. Had the Company not invested in the asset, it could have earned interest at 5% a year and can earn this same rate on any future investments it might make. The depreciation entries that would be made over each of the four years of useful life of the machine, using both the sinking-fund method and the annuity method of depreciation, are presented below:

## Annuity Method

(1) Cost $11,000
 Scrap value 1,000
 Depreciable cost $10,000
(2) $10,000 divided by the present value of an ordinary annuity of 1 at 5% for 4 years (3.5459505) gives $2,820.12.
(2) Annual interest on scrap value is $1,000 × .05 or $50.00.
(4) $2,820.12 plus $50 gives $2,870.12, the annual depreciation charge.

*Summary of depreciation:*

| Year | Depreciation Expense | Interest Income | Allowance for Depreciation |
|---|---|---|---|
| 1 | $2,870.12 | $550.00 | $ 2,320.12 |
| 2 | 2,870.12 | 433.99 | 2,436.13 |
| 3 | 2,870.12 | 312.19 | 2,557.93 |
| 4 | 2,870.12 | 184.29 | 2,685.83 |
|   |           |        | $10,000.01 |

### Entries

*Year 1*

Depreciation $2,870.12
  Allowance for depreciation $2,320.12
  Interest income 550.00

*Year 2*

Depreciation $2,870.12
  Allowance for depreciation $2,436.13
  Interest income 433.99

*Year 3*

Depreciation $2,870.12
  Allowance for depreciation $2,557.93
  Interest income 312.19

*Year 4*

Depreciation $2,870.12
  Allowance for depreciation $2,685.83
  Interest income 184.29

## Sinking-Fund Method

(1) Cost $11,000
 Scrap value 1,000
 Depreciable cost $10,000
(2) $10,000 divided by the amount of an ordinary annuity of 1 at 5% for 4 years (4.310125) gives $2,320.12, the first year's depreciation.
(3) The depreciation charge by years would be

Appendix A / *Actuarial Science* 831

| | |
|---|---:|
| 1st year: | $ 2,320.12 |
| 2nd year: $2,320.12 plus 5% of 2,320.12 ($116.01) = | $ 2,436.13 |
| 3rd year: $2,320.12 plus 5% of 4,756.25 ($237.81) = | $ 2,557.93 |
| 4th year: $2,320.12 plus 5% of 7,314.18 ($365.71) = | $ 2,685.83 |
| Total | $10,000.01 |

ENTRIES

*Year 1*

| | | |
|---|---|---|
| Depreciation | $2,320.12 | |
|    Allowance for depreciation | | $2,320.12 |

*Year 2*

| | | |
|---|---|---|
| Depreciation | $2,436.13 | |
|    Allowance for depreciation | | $2,436.13 |

*Year 3*

| | | |
|---|---|---|
| Depreciation | $2,557.93 | |
|    Allowance for depreciation | | $2,557.93 |

*Year 4*

| | | |
|---|---|---|
| Depreciation | $2,685.83 | |
|    Allowance for depreciation | | $2,685.83 |

## Valuation of Leaseholds

A leasehold arises from a tenure contract that provides for the use of property by the lessee in exchange for a specified sum of money payable at various times. The owner of the property, called the lessor, commonly has inserted in the contract a provision that a lump-sum deposit shall be made at the time of signing of the tenure contract. Such a deposit or direct advance payment of rent essentially represents a prepayment of a future rental payment(s). In reaching agreement regarding the amount to be paid in the form of a deposit for prepaid rent, the lessor and lessee not infrequently resort to the use of compound interest tables.

**Illustration.** To illustrate, assume that Mr. A., the lessor, and Mr. B., the lessee, reach the following rental agreement:

1. The rental payments shall be:
   (a) $8,000 a year for the 1st 5 years.
   (b) $10,000 a year for the next 5 years.
   (c) $12,000 a year for the last 5 years.
2. Payments are to be made as follows:
   (a) $5,000 cash shall be paid at the beginning of each year.
   (b) A deposit shall be made immediately of an amount which, when deposited at 5% per year, shall provide for the payment of the balance of the annual rent due at the beginning of each year.

The question of the amount of the leasehold prepayment resolves itself into one of determining the amount of the present value of annuities due for:

(1) $3,000 a year for 5 years.
(2) $5,000 a year for 5 years deferred 5 years.
(3) $7,000 a year for 5 years deferred 10 years.

1. P.v. of an annuity due of $3,000 a year for 5 years at 5%:
   P.v. of ordinary annuity of 1 for 4 years at 5% — 3.54595
   Add — 1.00000
   P.v. of annuity due of 1 for 5 years at 5% — 4.54595
   Times — $3,000 — $13,637.85

2. P.v. of an annuity due of $5,000 a year for 5 years at 5% deferred 5 years:
   P.v. of ordinary annuity of 1 for 9 years at 5% — 7.10782
   Add — 1.00000
   P.v. of annuity due of 1 for 10 years at 5% — 8.10782
   Less P.v. of annuity due of 1 for 5 years at 5% (above) — 4.54595
   P.v. of annuity due of 1 for 5 years at 5% deferred 5 years — 3.56187
   Times — $5,000 — 17,809.35

3. P.v. of an annuity due of $7,000 a year for 5 years at 5% deferred 10 years:
   P.v. of ordinary annuity of 1 for 14 years at 5% — 9.89864
   Add — 1.00000
   P.v. of annuity due of 1 for 15 years at 5% — 10.89864
   Less P.v. of annuity due of 1 for 10 years at 5% (above) — 8.10782
   P.v. of annuity due of 1 for 5 years at 5% deferred 10 years — 2.79082
   Times — $7,000 — 19,535.74

Deposit to be made (total) — $50,982.94*

*Notice that this computation is a variation of Method Two on page 825.

When the deposit or advance upon the purchase of the leasehold is made, an entry similar to the following would be made to record the acquisition of the asset, "Leasehold":

   Leasehold        $50,982.94
     Cash                          $50,982.94

A schedule for the amortization of the leasehold might be set up as follows:

Appendix A / Actuarial Science

### AMORTIZATION SCHEDULE

| Start of Period | Interest Earned | Withdrawal | Annual Amortization | Balance of "Leasehold" |
|---|---|---|---|---|
| 0 | — | — | — | $50,982.94 |
| 1 | — | $3,000 | $3,000.00* | 47,982.94 |
| 2 | $2,399.15 | 3,000 | 600.85 | 47,382.09 |
| 3 | 2,369.10 | 3,000 | 630.90 | 46,751.19 |
| 4 | 2,337.56 | 3,000 | 662.44 | 46,088.75 |
| 5 | 2,304.44 | 3,000 | 695.56 | 45,393.19 |
| 6 | 2,269.66 | 5,000 | 2,730.34 | 42,662.85 |
| 7 | 2,133.14 | 5,000 | 2,866.86 | 39,795.99 |
| 8 | 1,989.80 | 5,000 | 3,010.20 | 36,785.79 |
| 9 | 1,839.29 | 5,000 | 3,160.71 | 33,625.08 |
| 10 | 1,681.25 | 5,000 | 3,318.75 | 30,306.33 |
| 11 | 1,515.31 | 7,000 | 5,484.69 | 24,821.64 |
| 12 | 1,241.08 | 7,000 | 5,758.92 | 19,062.72 |
| 13 | 953.13 | 7,000 | 6,046.87 | 13,015.85 |
| 14 | 650.79 | 7,000 | 6,349.21 | 6,666.64 |
| 15 | 333.36 | 7,000 | 6,666.64 | –0– |

*Actually, the $3,000 for the first year's payment would seldom be included as a cost of the leasehold. Normally, it would be charged directly to leasehold expense for the first year. As a result, the initial valuation of the leasehold would be $47,982.94.

## Miscellaneous Problems

**Compound Interest for Fractional Part of a Period.** Sometimes a deposit may be left at compound interest for a specified number of periods, plus a fraction of another period. The problem of determining the compound interest on the fractional period is settled in practice by using simple interest for the fractional period.

To illustrate, assume that Mr. K. T. Belsley deposited $1,000 at 6% and plans to leave it for 8 years and 3 months, or 8¼ years. Interest is compounded annually. The solution to determine the amount of the fund at the end of the 8 years and 3 months would be:

(1) Amount of 1 for 8 periods at 6% is     1.593848
      Times     $1,000
(2) Amount of $1,000 for 8 periods at 6%     $1,593.85
(3) Interest on $1,593.85 at 6% per year
      for 3 months is     23.91
(4) Amount of $1,000 for 8 years and 3
      months at 6%     $1,617.76

**Computing the Number of Periods in an Annuity.** The practice of leaving a sum of money on deposit at a specified rate of interest with provisions for periodic withdrawals is not uncommon. The unsolved problem in such situations may be to determine the number of periodic payments that will be made. Normally, a close approximation may be made, as illustrated below.

## EXAMPLE

Mr. A. T. Halsey left the sum of $27,180 on deposit at 6% annual interest with a provision that $2,000 a year could be withdrawn at the end of each year. He wished to know how many withdrawals could be made.

*Solution:*

1. Divide the deposit of $27,180 by $2,000 to arrive at the present value of an annuity of 1 for $x$ periods at 6% interest. The result is 13.59.
2. Locate in the present value of an annuity of 1 table at 6% the amount nearest 13.59. The table indicates that for 29 periods the present value of an annuity of 1 at 6% is 13.59072102. From this the conclusion is drawn that the annuity of $2,000 a year will last approximately 29 years.

**Perpetuity.** A perpetuity is an annuity that is to run indefinitely. As an example, the problem involved would arise if a person wanted to leave a deposit at 7% annual interest that would provide $1,400 a year indefinitely. The solution involves dividing the annuity by the rate of interest ($1,400 ÷ .07 = $20,000), or determining the present value of $1,400 for an indefinitely long period, as illustrated in Chapter Six.

The amount of the endowment fund would be $20,000 and it would remain unchanged as long as the annuity conditions remained constant. To illustrate, the $20,000 at 7% a year would increase the fund by $1,400 a year. Since the $1,400 is then withdrawn, the fund reverts to $20,000 to start the next period.

## PROBABILITY

Probability may be defined as the relative frequency with which one event out of all possible events occurs. For example, the probability that a newly acquired machine will last six (6) years, when a sampling of the lives of similar machines indicates that the possible lives are 3, 4, 5, 6, 7, 8, or 9 years, would be the frequency or number of machines lasting 6 years relative to the total number of similar machines. Thus, if a representative sample of 100 similar machines indicated lives as follows:

| Number of Machines | Years of Life | Relative Frequency | Probability |
|---|---|---|---|
| 9 | 3 | 9/100 | .09 |
| 16 | 4 | 16/100 | .16 |

Appendix A / Actuarial Science

|  |  |  |  |  |
|---|---|---|---|---|
|  | 22 | 5 | 22/100 | .22 |
|  | 26 | 6 | 26/100 | .26 |
|  | 15 | 7 | 15/100 | .15 |
|  | 9 | 8 | 9/100 | .09 |
|  | 3 | 9 | 3/100 | .03 |
| Total | 100 |  | 100/100 | 1.00 |

then the probability that a new machine would have a life of six (6) years is 26 out of 100 or .26. Note that the sum of all possible probabilities is 1.00 and that the probability of any one event is between .00 and 1.00.

Stated in slightly different terms, the probability of an event is the number of ways the event can occur divided by the sum of the ways it can occur plus the ways it cannot occur. In the illustration above, there are 26 ways for the event of a life of six (6) years to occur and 74 (9 + 16 + 22 + 15 + 9 + 3) ways for it not to occur. The probability would be

$$\frac{26}{26 + 74} = .26$$

Actually, the probability above is an estimate and is valid only if the sample is representative of all possible similar machines that have been or will be available. Practically, because the total number of possible outcomes (available machines) cannot be known in advance (a priori), statistical sampling of past experience is used to develop a probability of future events. When all possible outcomes are known in advance (a priori), such as the results of the throw of a six-sided die, precise probabilities may be computed. Thus, the probability of throwing a six (6) on one throw of a die would be

$$\frac{1}{1 + 5} = .167$$

These precise probabilities are typically not available and the estimated empirically derived probabilities are used. In the illustration above, the probabilities of the life of a machine would be the .09, .16, .22, .26, .15, .09, .03, and the average or "expected" life of the 100 machines would be computed as follows:

|  | Number of Machines | Years of Life | Number of Machine Years |
|---|---|---|---|
|  | 9 | 3 | 27 |
|  | 16 | 4 | 64 |
|  | 22 | 5 | 110 |
|  | 26 | 6 | 156 |
|  | 15 | 7 | 105 |
|  | 9 | 8 | 72 |
|  | 3 | 9 | 27 |
| Total | 100 |  | 561 |

Average life of the 100 machines (561/100) is 5.61 years. Note that the computation is eased and the average or "expected value" is universally accepted if the probabilities are substituted for the actual number of machines. Since the probabilities total 1, division is simpler, and since the probabilities are derived from a representative sample of all machines, the average is indeed the "expected value" (life) of the new machine.

One more illustration will help clarify the notion of "expected value," which plays such an important role in accounting measures. Assume that the manager of the sales division needs an estimate of next year's sales for planning purposes. He doesn't know what will occur but, on the basis of his experience and reports from his salesmen, he estimates sales with the following probabilities:

| Estimated Sales | Estimated Probabilities | Probable Sales |
|---|---|---|
| $10,000 | .20 | $ 2,000 |
| 15,000 | .30 | 4,500 |
| 20,000 | .30 | 6,000 |
| 25,000 | .20 | 5,000 |
| Expected value of next year's sales | | $17,500 |

The $17,500 is the long-run average sales that will occur if the probabilities are representative of the true state of affairs. Assume that the manager knows he needs sales of $18,000 to avoid a loss. If he uses "expected value" for decision-making, he would probably not operate, even though there is a 20% chance sales might be $25,000. On the other hand, he might "feel" that the expected value was not appropriate for the current year's decision and decide to operate. From an accounting point of view, the actual decision is not relevant, but making available the "expected value" to management to use in deciding may be a desirable accounting measure.

The development of probabilities and expected value is only part of the statistics that can be used in deciding such things as the appropriate depreciation life of a machine, the collectibility of receivables, or an estimate of next year's sales. Another useful measure is the degree of dispersion of the possible outcomes from the expected value. The typical measure of this dispersion is the standard deviation. Standard deviation is the square root of the sum of the products when the relative frequency of each possible event is multiplied by the squared deviations of each possible outcome from the expected value. The standard deviation ($\alpha$) of the estimated life of the new machine in the earlier illustration would be computed as follows:

| Life of Machine | Deviation from Expected Value | Deviation Squared | Probability of Occurrence | Product |
|---|---|---|---|---|
| 3 | −2.61 | 6.81 | .09 | .613 |
| 4 | −1.61 | 2.59 | .16 | .414 |
| 5 | − .61 | .37 | .22 | .081 |

Appendix A / Actuarial Science

| | | | | |
|---|---|---|---|---|
| 6 | + .39 | .15 | .26 | .039 |
| 7 | +1.39 | 1.93 | .15 | .290 |
| 8 | +2.39 | 5.71 | .09 | .514 |
| 9 | +3.39 | 11.49 | .03 | .345 |
| | | | | 2.296 |

Variance ($\alpha^2$)

The standard deviation ($\alpha$) is the square root of the variance, or $\sqrt{2.296}$, or 1.515.

The interpretation of the standard deviation is normally based on the assumption of a normal curve dispersion of the possible outcomes from the expected value. Appendix TH provides a measure of the area under one side of the normal curve, and this area reflects the percentage or probability of occurrence of events that vary from the expected value expressed in terms of standard deviation. Reading from the table of areas under the normal curve, the area between one standard deviation from the expected value and expected value (5.61 − 1.51 and 5.61) or between a life of 4.1 years and 5.61 years would be the probability that the new machine would have a life within these two life spans. The table in the Appendix shows that in 34.13% of the cases the actual life of the machine would fall between 4.1 and 5.61 years. If the standard deviation were added to the expected value, indicating machine lives between 5.61 years and 7.12 years, the probability that actual life would fall between 4.1 and 7.12 years would be double the 34.13%, or 68.26%.

## EXAMPLES

(1) Assuming that the estimated expected value of a pending lawsuit is $180,000 with an estimated standard deviation of $30,900, what is the probability that the actual liability on the lawsuit will exceed $200,000?

*Solution:*

Since the $20,000 variation from the expected value is only ⅔ of one standard deviation, the probability that the actual liability will be less than $200,000 is 50% plus 24.86% (the area under the normal curve between the expected value and .67 of one standard deviation). So the expected probability that the loss will exceed $200,000 is 25.14%.

(2) Uncollectibles for the Short Department Store for the past five (5) years are believed to be typical of uncollectibles for the store. Actual uncollectibles were

19×1 = .0051 on sales of $3,000,000
19×2 = .0040 on sales of $2,000,000
19×3 = .0048 on sales of $2,500,000
19×4 = .0053 on sales of $3,500,000
19×5 = .0045 on sales of $2,800,000

*Required:*

What provision should the Short Store make in 19×6 when sales are $2,863,000 if the store has a policy of assuming a risk of no more than 20% that actual uncollectibles will exceed the provision?

*Solution:*

The possible uncollectibles per $1,000,000 of sales would be $5,100; $4,000; $4,800; $5,300; and $4,500. Since actual sales over the five-year period were 13.8 million, the probability distribution of the sales would be

$$19\times1 = .217 \ (3/13.8)$$
$$19\times2 = .145$$
$$19\times3 = .181$$
$$19\times4 = .254$$
$$19\times5 = .203$$
$$\text{Total} \quad 1.00$$

From this, the expected value of the uncollectibles per $1,000,000 of sales would be computed as follows:

|  | Uncollectibles | Probability | Expected Value |
|---|---|---|---|
| 19×1 | 5,100 | .217 | $1,106.70 |
| 19×2 | 4,000 | .145 | 580.00 |
| 19×3 | 4,800 | .181 | 868.80 |
| 19×4 | 5,300 | .254 | 1,346.20 |
| 19×5 | 4,500 | .203 | 913.50 |
|  | Expected value |  | $4,815.20 |

Since actual sales for 19×6 were $2,863,000, the expected value of the uncollectibles on 19×6 sales would be:

$$2.863 \text{ times } \$4,815.20 \text{ or } \$13,785.92$$

Since the Short Store wants to provide for uncollectibles sufficient to assure that it runs a risk that only in one-fifth (20%) of the cases would actual uncollectibles exceed the provision, the standard deviation of the actual uncollectibles from expected value per $1,000,000 of sales has to be calculated as follows:

| Year | Deviation from Expected Value | Deviation Squared | Probability of Occurrence | Product |
|---|---|---|---|---|
| 19×1 | 284.80 | 81,111 | .217 | 17,601 |
| 19×2 | −815.20 | 664,551 | .145 | 96,360 |
| 19×3 | − 15.20 | 231 | .181 | 42 |
| 19×4 | 484.80 | 235,031 | .254 | 59,698 |
| 19×5 | −315.20 | 99,351 | .203 | 20,168 |
|  |  | Variance |  | 193,869 |
|  |  | Standard deviation ($\alpha$) |  | 440 |

For sales of $2,863,000, the standard deviation would be 440 times 2.863, or $1,259.72. From the table of the area under the normal curve, the provision to cover 80% of the cases of actual uncollectibles would be

| | |
|---|---:|
| 50% (expected value) | $13,785.92 |
| 30% (.84178 times $\alpha$ of $1,259.72) | 1,060.41 |
| Provision for uncollectibles desired | $14,846.33 |

## PROBLEMS

### Problem AP-1

Adams borrowed $1,200 from a friend who agreed to lend him money at the monthly rate of 1% of $1,200 each month ($12 a month), provided Adams paid off the loan at the rate of $100 a month. The friend then withheld $100 of the $1,200 loan as a financing charge. Adams paid the loan off ($112 a month) in the 12-month period.

*Required:*
What was the effective rate of interest Adams paid?

### Problem AP-2

Using the table of normal curve areas, compute blank spaces in the following table.

| Case No. | Expected Value | Standard Deviation | Range of one Standard Deviation | Values above 1.50 Standard Deviation |
|---|---|---|---|---|
| 1 | $10,000 | $ 3,000 | _____ | _____ |
| 2 | $10,000 | $ 500 | _____ | _____ |
| 3 | $10,000 | $10,000 | _____ | _____ |

### Problem AP-3

Using the tables of amount of 1, compute the amount the following sums would accumulate to at compound interest by the end of the designated periods at the specified rate of interest:

1. $1,000 for 10 years at 6% per year.
2. $1,000 for 10 years at 3% every 6 months.
3. $1,000 for 5 years at 1% every month.
4. $1,000 for 5 years at 5% per year, then at 6% per year for another 5 years.
5. $1,000 for 4 years at 2% per quarter.
6. $633.33 for 9 years at 5% per year.
7. $1,000 each year for 5 years at 4% per year.

## Problem AP-4

Using the tables of present value of 1, compute the amount to be deposited now at compound interest to provide the desired sum at the end of the designated periods at the specified rate of interest.

1. Invested for 10 years at 6% per year to amount to $1,000.
2. Invested for 10 years at 3% every 6 months to amount to $1,000.
3. Invested for 5 years at 6% per year, then invested at 5% per year for another 10 years to amount to $10,000.
4. To be invested now at 6% per year until retirement (33 years) to have $100,000.

## Problem AP-5

Compute the amount Smith would have at the end of 2005 if the following investments were made.

1. $1,000 a year at the end of each year 1980 through 1989.
2. Nothing in 1990.
3. $2,000 a year at the end of each year 1991 through 2000.
4. Nothing in 2001, 2002, and 2003.
5. $5,000 a year at the end of each year 2004 and 2005. The investments earned compound interest at the following rates:

$$1980 \text{ through } 1991 - 7\%$$
$$1992 \text{ through } 2002 - 6\%$$
$$2003 \text{ through } 2005 - 4\%$$

## Problem AP-6

Mr. Black wants to retire at the end of this year. His life expectancy is 20 years from the present. He wants to know how much he should deposit now at 7% to be able to withdraw $5,000 at the end of each year for the next 20 years.

## Problem AP-7

The expected value of next year's receipts are estimated at $100,000 with a standard deviation of $8,000. Actual receipts were $75,000. What is the probability that the large variance from expected value was due entirely to chance (assume that the normal curve is valid for this solution).

## Problem AP-8

Mr. C. A. Dorner deposits $1,000 a year, starting on his 40th birthday, until retirement on his 70th birthday, at which time he starts withdrawing $3,000 a year. (His last deposit was on his 69th birthday.) Interest is constant by a contract with an insurance company at 5% per year.

Appendix A / Actuarial Science

*Required:*
For how many periods could Mr. Dorner make his $3,000 annual withdrawals?

## Problem AP-9

1. Compute the amount of an annuity due for $3,000 a year for 10 years at 5% interest.
2. What would the amount be if it were an ordinary annuity?

## Problem AP-10

How much should be deposited at 6% annual interest to provide an annuity of $10,000 a year for 20 years, if the start of the annuity is deferred 40 years?

## Problem AP-11

A sample of times required to complete a job is to be used to establish a standard time for similar jobs. The sample consisted of 50 trials with the following results:

| Time required | No. of cases |
|---|---|
| 90 minutes | 5 |
| 80 minutes | 25 |
| 70 minutes | 10 |
| 60 minutes | 8 |
| 50 minutes | 2 |
| Total Cases | 50 |

During the month of January, the actual time required to complete a similar job was 88 minutes. Assuming that the company considers any performance that varies from expected value by more than one standard deviation as being out of control, are the company's operations out of control? What is the probability that the actual performance was due to chance?

## Problem AP-12

Company P leases a store building to Company R on a 10-year lease. The lease calls for rent the first 5 years of $15,000 per year, and $20,000 per year for the last 5 years. Company R pays the entire 10 years' rent in advance at 8% discount. How much is the payment?

## Problem AP-13

Your client has made annual payments of $2,500 into a fund at the close of each year for the past 9 years. The fund balance immediately after the ninth payment totaled $26,457. He has asked you how many more $2,500 annual payments will be required to bring the fund to $50,000, assuming that the fund continues to earn interest at 4% compounded annually. Compute the number of full payments required and the amount of the final payment, if it does not require the entire $2,500. Carefully label all computations supporting your answer.

## Problem AP-14

Your client wishes to provide for the payment of an obligation of $200,000 due on July 1, 1988. He plans to deposit $20,000 in a special fund each July 1 for 8 years, starting July 1, 1981. He wishes to make an initial deposit on July 1, 1980, of an amount which, with its accumulated interest, will bring the fund up to $200,000 at the maturity of the obligation.

## Problem AP-15

The BBB Company leased property from the CCC Company. The lease contract provides that annual rentals shall be paid in advance in January of each year. The lease runs for 10 years with payments according to the following schedule:

> Years 1 through 2—$2,000 per year.
> Years 3 through 4—$4,000 per year.
> Years 5 through 10—$5,000 per year.

1. What single immediate sum will pay all of these annual rentals if they are discounted at 5%?
2. Assuming that the amounts computed above were set up to be used as a fund to pay the annual rentals, what amount would be in the fund after the payment on the first day of the fourth year?

## Problem AP-16

Company Q purchased a 10-year, $1,000 bond on the date it was issued at a price that yielded 2% on a semi-annual basis. At the end of the fourth year, the following entry was made to record the receipt of 6 months' interest:

|  | | |
|---|---|---|
| Cash | $18.75 | |
| Bond investments | .97 | |
| Interest income | | $19.72 |

What price did the Company pay for the bond?

## Problem AP-17

A six-year $1,000, 8% bond with interest payable annually is bought to net 7%. What is the price of the bond?

## Problem AP-18

A ten-year $1,000, 7% bond with interest payable semi-annually is bought to yield 8%. What is the price of the bond?

## Problem AP-19

A 10-year $20,000, 9% bond with interest payable annually is bought to yield 7%. What is the price of the bond?

## Problem AP-20

A 10-year $10,000, 7% bond with interest payable annually is bought to yield 8%. What is the price of the bond?

## Problem AP-21

A 3-year $5,000, 6% bond with interest payable semi-annually is bought to yield 4%. (a) What is the price of the bond? (b) Prepare the amortization schedule.

## Problem AP-22

A 3-year $5,000, 4% bond with interest payable semi-annually is bought to yield 6%. (a) What is the price of the bond? (b) Prepare the amortization schedule.

## Problem AP-23

How much should be deposited now at 4% semi-annual interest to provide an annuity of $8,000 a year for 20 years, if the start of the annuity is deferred 10 years? If the start of the annuity is deferred 15 years?

## Problem AP-24

How much must be deposited now at 4% annual interest to provide an annuity of $5,000 a year for 4 years, if the start of the annuity is deferred 17 years? If the start of the annuity is deferred 12 years?

## Problem AP-25

Your client has agreed to sell a property for $60,000. He is to receive $20,000 cash at date of sale and 20 notes of equal amount that will not bear interest. The notes are due serially, one each 6 months starting six months from date of sale. It is agreed that the notes will include in their face an amount that will equal 7% interest to be compounded semi-annually.

Compute to the nearest dollar the amount of each note. Show your computations in good form, with each part explained or labeled. (AICPA adapted)

## Problem AP-26

Jones, an employee of the Union Company, asks your advice on the following matter:

He is eligible to participate in a company insurance and retirement plan. His payment into the company plan would amount to $500 each 6 months for the next 10 years, and starting with the eleventh year he would receive an annual payment of $1,080 for life. He does not need insurance protection and states that he can save and invest each 6 months the amounts to be paid into the company plan so that he will earn 6% compounded semi-annually. Also, he can continue to earn the same rate on his capital after retirement. He would like to have an equal amount per year of funds for 15 years after retirement.

Assuming that he can carry out his personal saving and investing plan, how much can he expect to have available each 6 months for the 15 years following his retirement? Compute to the nearest dollar and show your computations in good form.  (AICPA adapted)

## Problem AP-27

Reproduced below are the first three lines from the 25 columns of each of several tables of mathematical values. For each of the following items you are to select from among these fragmentary tables the one from which the amount required can be obtained *most directly* (assuming that the complete table was available in each instance):

1. The amount to which a single sum would accumulate at compound interest by the end of a specified period (interest compounded annually).
2. The amount that must be appropriated at the end of each of a specific number of years in order to provide for the accumulation, at annually compounded interest, of a certain sum of money.
3. The amount that must be deposited in a fund that will earn interest at a specified rate, compounded annually, in order to make possible the withdrawal of certain equal sums annually over a specified period starting 1 year from date of deposit.
4. The amount of interest that will accumulate on a single deposit by the end of a specified period (interest compounded semiannually).
5. The amount, net of compound discount, which if paid now would settle a debt of larger amount due at a specified future date.

| Periods | Table A | Table B | Table C | Table D | Table E | Table F |
|---|---|---|---|---|---|---|
| 0 | 1.0000 |  | 1.0000 |  |  |  |
| 1 | 0.9804 | 1.0200 | 1.0200 | 1.0000 | 0.9804 | 1.0200 |
| 2 | 0.9612 | 2.0604 | 1.0404 | 0.4950 | 1.9416 | 0.5150 |
| 3 |  | 3.1216 |  | 0.3268 | 2.8839 | 0.3468 |

(AICPA adapted)

## Problem AP-28

A loan is made with the proviso that on each interest date a payment shall be made on account of principal equal to the amount of interest then paid. This arrangement is to continue until the principal is reduced to approximately one-half of the original loan, when a new arrangement will be made.

Appendix A / Actuarial Science    845

1. Show by formula the number of payments required under the first arrangement.
2. How many payments would be required to pay off the entire loan under the first arrangement? Give formula.              (AICPA adapted)

## Problem AP-29

The C Company is planning a pension system for certain of its employees. It wishes to provide funds for meeting the payments under the pension plan and asks your assistance.

The Company does not contemplate making any pension payments under the plan until January, 1986. Payments in 1986 and thereafter to the present group of covered employees are expected to be as follows:

|  |  |
|---|---|
| January 1, 1986 | $ 5,000 |
| January 1, 1987 | 7,000 |
| January 1, 1988 | 10,000 |
| January 1, 1989 | 14,000 |
| January 1, 1990 | 16,000 |
| January 1, 1991 | 20,000 |
| January 1, 1992 | 25,000 |
| January 1, 1993 | 22,000 |
| January 1, 1994 | 17,000 |
| January 1, 1995 | 12,000 |
| January 1, 1996 | 8,000 |
| January 1, 1997 | 5,000 |
| January 1, 1998 | 2,000 |
| January 1, 1999 | 2,000 |

Starting on January 1, 1981, and continuing for 10 years, the Company will deposit $10,000 a year in a special fund. On January 1, 1980, the Company wishes to make a lump-sum deposit of an amount sufficient to provide the remaining funds needed for meeting the pensions. It is expected that all the funds above will earn 5% interest compounded annually during the entire life of the fund.

*Required:*

Compute the amount of payment that should be made on January 1, 1980. Show all supporting computations in good form.              (AICPA adapted)

## Problem AP-30

In 1980, J-P Bowling Company entered into an agreement with a bank for an unsecured long-term loan of $2,000,000. The loan agreement provides for interest at 8% and lump-sum repayment in 1990. Certain terms of the loan agreement placing restrictions on incurring additional long-term debt and on payment of dividends are presented here in summary:

A. Additional long-term debt shall not be incurred unless the net tangible assets (investments, plant, and equipment), adjusted to include the proceeds of such long-term debt, will be at least 225% of the total long-term debt after incurring such additional debt.
B. Long-term debt shall mean the total of all debt outstanding for a period of one year or longer plus an amount equal to the "Capitalized Rent" on unexpired long-term leases of real property. "Capitalized Rent" shall be computed by discounting the aggregate rental obligations under the long-term lease, by years, to the date of the computation at the rate of 8% per annum.
C. Payment of cash dividends during the period of the loan shall be subject to the following limitations:

1. Working capital of at least $6,500,000 shall be maintained.
2. Cash dividends shall not exceed earnings subsequent to December 31, 1979, except that the payment of cash dividends in 1980 may exceed 1980 net income by an amount that is not more than 50% of the net income for 1979.
3. In 1981 and subsequent years, cash dividends shall be limited to 25% of the prior year's net income.
4. The total annual cash dividends shall not exceed $2 per share of stock outstanding at the end of any year.
5. Should cash dividends be paid in excess of restrictions, such excess shall be applied in determining the amounts of dividends that may be paid in subsequent years.

The condensed balance sheet of J-P Bowling Company at December 31, 1981 follows:

*Assets*

| | |
|---|---:|
| Current assets | $16,787,000 |
| Investments | 300,000 |
| Plant and equipment | 5,000,000 |
| Goodwill and patents | 400,000 |
| | $22,487,000 |

*Liabilities and Owners' Equity*

| | |
|---|---:|
| Current liabilities | $ 8,290,000 |
| Note payable to bank | 2,000,000 |
| Capital stock (par value, $50) | 3,131,000 |
| Contributed capital in excess of par value | 2,485,000 |
| Retained earnings | 6,581,000 |
| | $22,487,000 |

An analysis of the Company's retained earnings for 1979, 1890, and 1981 discloses the following:

| | |
|---|---:|
| Balance, December 31, 1978 | $5,445,000 |
| Net income for 1979 | 422,100 |
| Balance, December 31, 1979 | 5,867,000 |

Appendix A / Actuarial Science

|  |  |
|---|---|
| Net income for 1980 | 507,000 |
| Cash dividends paid in 1980 | (98,000) |
| Balance, December 31, 1980 | 6,276,000 |
| Net income for 1981 | 522,000 |
| Cash dividends paid in 1981 | (124,000) |
| 1% stock dividend—at market value of shares issued | (93,000) |
| Balance, December 31, 1981 | $6,581,000 |

The Company has a 10-year lease for a warehouse on which the last annual rental payment is due December 31, 1985. The annual rental is $40,000 until December 31, 1982, and $50,000 thereafter. Under an option, the lease may be extended for another 10 years, or portion thereof, at an annual rental of $60,000.

*Required*:
(1) The amount of cash dividends that may be paid under the loan agreement in 1982, including an indication of the application of each of the limitations contained in the loan agreement.
(2) The amount of additional long-term debt that may be incurred under the loan agreement as of December 31, 1981.   (AICPA adapted)

## Problem AP-31

Select the *best* answer for each of the following items:

1. A businessman wants to invest a certain sum of money at the end of each year for five years. The investment will earn 6% compounded annually. At the end of five years, he will need a total of $30,000 accumulated. How should he compute his required annual investment?
   a. $30,000 times the amount of an annuity of $1 at 6% at the end of each year for five years.
   b. $30,000 divided by the amount of an annuity of $1 at 6% at the end of each year for five years.
   c. $30,000 times the present value of an annuity of $1 at 6% at the end of each year for five years.
   d. $30,000 divided by the present value of an annuity of $1 at 6% at the end of each year for five years.
2. The figure .9423 is taken from the column marked 2% and the row marked three periods in a certain interest table. From what interest table is this figure taken?
   a. Amount of $1.
   b. Amount of annuity of $1.
   c. Present value of $1.
   d. Present value of annuity of $1.
3. A businessman wants to withdraw $3,000 (including principal) from an investment fund at the end of each year for five years. How should he compute his required initial investment at the beginning of the first year if the fund earns 6% compounded annually?

a. $3,000 times the amount of an annuity of $1 at 6% at the end of each year for five years.
b. $3,000 divided by the amount of an annuity of $1 at 6% at the end of each year for five years.
c. $3,000 times the present value of an annuity of $1 at 6% at the end of each year for five years.
d. $3,000 divided by the present value of an annuity of $1 at 6% at the end of each year for five years.

4. An accountant wishes to find the present value of an annuity of $1 payable at the *beginning* of each period at 10% for eight periods. He has only a present-value table which shows the present value of an annuity of $1 payable at the *end* of each period. To compute the present-value factor he needs, the accountant would use the present-value factor in the 10% column for
    a. Seven periods.
    b. Seven periods and add $1.
    c. Eight periods.
    d. Nine periods and subtract $1.

*Items 5 and 6 are based on the following information:*

On January 2, 1979, Kirk Manufacturing Company leased some equipment from Quarter Corporation. This lease was noncancelable and was in substance an installment purchase. The initial term of the lease was twelve years with title passing to Kirk at the end of the twelfth year upon payment of $1. Annual rental to be paid by Kirk is $10,000 at the beginning of each year. The first rental payment was made on January 2, 1979, and *no* deposit was required. The equipment has an estimated useful life of twenty years with *no* anticipated salvage value. The prevailing interest rate for Kirk on similar financing arrangements is 8%.

*Present Value of an Annuity in Advance of $1 at 8%*

| | |
|---|---|
| 11 years | $ 7.710 |
| 12 years | 8.139 |
| 19 years | 10.372 |
| 20 years | 10.604 |

5. At what amount should Kirk have capitalized this equipment?
    a. $77,100.
    b. $81,390.
    c. $103,720.
    d. $106,040.
6. If the equipment had been capitalized at $90,000 and all other facts remain as originally stated, how much interest expense should Kirk have recorded in 1979?
    a. Zero.
    b. $6,400.

c. $7,200.
d. $9,600.

7. Gorch Company sold some machinery that was *not* merchandise. Gorch received a noninterest-bearing note to be paid $1,000 per year for 10 years. A fair rate of interest for this transaction is 8%. The present value of $1.00 at 8% after 10 periods is $.463. The present value of an annuity in arrears of $1.00 at 8% for 10 periods is $6.710. What discount should Gorch record on this transaction?
   a. Zero.
   b. $3,290.
   c. $4,630.
   d. $6,710.

8. A company sold bonds on July 1, 1979, with a face value of $100,000 and due in ten years. The stated annual interest rate is 6%, payable semi-annually on June 30 and December 31. These bonds were sold to yield 8%. The present value of $1 for twenty periods at 4% is $0.4563. The present value of an annuity of $1 in arrears for twenty periods at 4% is $13.5903. For how much did these bonds sell on July 1, 1979 (rounded to nearest dollar?
   a. $86,401.
   b. $91,542.
   c. $100,000.
   d. $127,172.

9. Foster Company wants to finance some long-term assets by selling bonds. Management projects the earnings *before* deducting bond interest expense and income taxes as $1,166,000 per year. Foster's income tax rate is 40%. Management wants its net earnings *after* deducting bond interest expense and income taxes to be ten times the bond interest expense. Assuming that the bonds can be sold at face value, what amount should Foster issue at 8%?
   a. Approximately $560,580.
   b. Exactly $583,000.
   c. Exactly $825,000.
   d. Exactly $874,500.

10. Herman Company acquired an asset at a cost of $46,600. It had an estimated life of ten years. Annual after-tax net cash benefits are estimated to be $10,000 at the end of each year. The following amounts appear in the interest table for the present value of an annuity of $1 at year-end for ten years:

    | 16% | 4.83 |
    | 18% | 4.49 |
    | 20% | 4.19 |

    What is the maximum interest rate that could be paid for the capital employed over the life of this asset without loss on this project?
    a. 16%.
    b. 17%.

c. 18%.
d. 19%.

*Items 11 and 12* apply to the appropriate use of present-value tables. Given below are the present-value factors for $1.00 discounted at 8% for one to five periods. Each of the following items is based on 8% interest compounded annually from day of deposit to day of withdrawal.

| Periods | Present value of $1 discounted at 8% per period |
|---|---|
| 1 | 0.926 |
| 2 | 0.857 |
| 3 | 0.794 |
| 4 | 0.735 |
| 5 | 0.681 |

11. If an individual put $3,000 in a savings account today, what amount of cash would be available two years from today?
    a. $3,000 × 0.857.
    b. $3,000 × 0.857 × 2.
    c. $\dfrac{\$3,000}{0.857}$.
    d. $\dfrac{\$3,000}{0.926} \times 2$.

12. What is the present value today of $4,000 to be received six years from today?
    a. $4,000 × 0.926 × 6.
    b. $4,000 × 0.794 × 2.
    c. $4,000 × 0.681 × 0.926.
    d. *Cannot* be determined from the information given.

(AICPA adapted)

# APPENDIX B
# Governmental (Fund) Accounting

As indicated in the preface, the material in this appendix is included for one reason and one reason only—to help the well-qualified, serious candidate pass the governmental portion of the Uniform CPA Examination.

In the last ten years six candidates using this material have placed first nationally, four have placed second nationally, and over one hundred have received honorable mention. On two of the examinations, both the number one and number two candidates used the material.

Although the candidate who is well prepared in governmental accounting may enjoy a slight advantage in this area, based on past performance a reasonable understanding of the underlying theory and practical application of the basic governmental accounting principles and procedures will suffice for the candidate who is well versed in enterprise accounting but who is perhaps not as well prepared in governmental accounting.

**Governmental Accounting Principles and Procedures.** The National Committee on Governmental Accounting in its manual entitled *Municipal Accounting and Auditing* recommends the following principles and procedures as being applicable to governmental accounting:

## PRINCIPLES

1. A municipal accounting system must make it possible (1) to show that *legal provisions* have been complied with and (2) to reflect the *financial condition* and financial operations of the municipality.
2. If legal and sound accounting provisions conflict, legal provisions must take precedence. It is, however, the finance officer's duty to seek changes in the law which will make such law in harmony with sound accounting principles.

3. The general accounting system should be on a double-entry basis with a general ledger in which all financial transactions are recorded in detail or in summary. Additional subsidiary records should be kept where necessary.
4. Every municipality should establish the *funds* called for either by law or by sound financial administration. It should be recognized, however, that funds introduce an element of inflexibility in the financial system. Accordingly, consistent with legal provisions and requirements of sound financial administration, as few funds as possible should be established.
5. Depending on the legal and financial requirements mentioned immediately above, the following types of funds are recognized: (1) General, (2) Special Revenue, (3) Intragovernmental Service, (4) Special Assessment, (5) Bond, (6) Sinking, (7) Trust and Agency, and (8) Utility or Other Enterprise. This classification of funds to the extent required should be followed in the budget document and in the municipality's financial reports.
6. A complete balancing *group of accounts* should be established for each fund. This group should include all of the accounts necessary to set forth the financial condition and financial operations of the fund and to reflect compliance with legal provisions.
7. A clear segregation should be made between the accounts relating to current assets and liabilities and those relating to fixed assets and liabilities. With the exception of Intragovernmental Service, Utility or Other Enterprise, or Trust Funds, fixed assets should not be carried in the same fund with the current assets but should be set up in a self-balancing group of accounts known as the General Fixed Asset Group of Accounts. Similarly, except in Special Assessment and Utility Funds, long-term liabilities should not be carried with the current liabilities of any fund but should be shown in a separate self-balancing group of accounts forming part of the General Bonded Debt and Interest group of accounts.
8. The *fixed asset accounts* should be maintained on the basis of original cost, or the estimated cost if the original cost is not available, or, in the case of gifts, the appraised value at the time received.
9. *Depreciation* on general municipal fixed assets should not be computed unless cash for replacements can legally be set aside. Depreciation on such assets may be computed for unit cost purposes even if cash for replacements cannot legally be set aside, providing these depreciation charges are used for memorandum purposes only and are not reflected in the accounts.
10. The accounting system should provide for *budgetary control* for both revenues and expenditures, and the financial statements should reflect, among other things, budgetary information.
11. The use of the *accrual basis* in accounting for revenues and expenditures is recommended to the extent applicable. Revenues, partially offset by provisions for estimated losses, should be taken into consideration when earned, even though not received in cash. Expenditures should be recorded as soon as liabilities are incurred.

Appendix B / Governmental (Fund) Accounting

12. *Revenues* should be classified by fund and source; and *expenditures* by fund, function, department, activity, character, and by main classes of objects, in accordance with standard classification.
13. *Cost accounting systems* should be established wherever costs can be measured. Each cost accounting system should provide for the recording of all the elements of cost incurred to accomplish a purpose, to carry on an activity or operation, or to complete a unit of work or a specific job. Although depreciation on general municipal assets may be omitted in the general accounts and reports, it should be considered in determining unit costs if a cost accounting system is used.
14. A common *terminology and classification* should be used consistently throughout the budget, the accounts, and the financial reports.

## PROCEDURES

1. The accounts should be centralized under the direction of one officer. He should be responsible for keeping or supervising all accounts and for preparing and issuing all financial reports.
2. A *budget* should be prepared by every municipality even if not required by law, because such budgets are essential to the proper management of its financial affairs. A distinction between the different funds must be made in such budget.
3. As soon as purchase orders or *contracts* are signed, the resulting obligations should be recorded at once as encumbrances of the funds and appropriations affected.
4. *Inventories* of both consumable and permanent property should be kept in subsidiary records controlled by accounts in the general accounting system. Physical inventories of both consumable and permanent property should be taken at least annually and the accounts and records should be made to agree with such inventories.
5. The accounting for municipal *business enterprises* should follow the standard classifications employed by similar private enterprises. Each college, hospital, library, and other public institution should follow the standard classification for such institution.
6. Financial reports should be prepared monthly or oftener, to show the current condition of the budgetary accounts and other information necessary to control operations. At least once each year a general *financial report* should be prepared and published.
7. There should be general uniformity in the financial reports of all municipalities of similar size and type.
8. A *periodic audit* by independent accountants is desirable.

**The Fund Concept.** The only major difference between governmental accounting and private enterprise accounting is the use of the fund as the basic accounting entity. As defined by the National Committee on Governmental Accounting, a fund is

> ... an independent fiscal and accounting entity with self-balancing set of accounts recording cash and/or other resources together with all related liabilities, obligations, reserves, and equities which are segregated for the purpose of carrying on specific activities or attaining certain objectives in accordance with special regulations, restrictions, or limitations.

The establishment of the fund as a separate accounting entity necessitates the creation of an independent system of self-balancing accounts for each fund from which financial statements may be prepared periodically—normally at the end of each accounting period.

To establish uniformity in the financial reports of governmental bodies, the National Committee has recommended that the following classification of funds be used.

(*Note:* Some of the titles in the following list are relatively new. Where appropriate, the old title(s) is given parenthetically. Since we are still in the transition period, you may encounter either term on the examination.)

1. *The General Fund* (Current Fund or Operating Fund) to account for all financial transactions not properly accounted for in another fund.
2. *Special Revenue Fund* to account for the proceeds of specific revenue sources (other than special assessments) or to finance specified activities as required by law or administrative regulation.
3. *Capital Projects Fund* (Bond Fund) to account for the receipt and disbursement of monies used for the acquisition of capital facilities other than those financed by special assessments and enterprise funds.
4. *Debt Service Fund* (Sinking Fund) to account for the payment of interest and principal on long-term debt other than special assessment and revenue bonds (includes serial and term bonds).
5. *Enterprise Fund* (Utility Fund) to account for the financing of services to the general public where all or most of the costs involved are paid in the form of charges by users of such services.
6. *Intragovernmental Service Fund* (Working Capital Fund) to account for the financing of special activities and services performed by a designated organizational unit with a governmental jurisdiction for other organizational units within the same jurisdiction.
7. *Special Assessment Fund* to account for special assessments levied to finance public improvements or services deemed to benefit the properties against which the assessments are levied.
8. *Trust and Agency Fund* to account for assets held by a governmental unit as trustee or agent for individuals, private organizations, and other governmental units.

Appendix B / Governmental (Fund) Accounting

**Depreciation in Governmental Accounting.** In explanation of the position taken on depreciation the manual states that:

1. A municipality, except in the case of utilities or other self-supporting enterprises, is not concerned with profits or losses.
2. Since the general fixed assets are not presumed to produce tax or other general revenues, charging current operations with depreciation has the effect of reducing revenues by costs to which they did not give rise, in violation of the principle of matching costs with their relevant revenues.
3. Unless cash can be set aside out of current revenues, depreciation charges cannot be included in the budget.

**Fund Accounting Illustrated.** In fund accounting, the basic procedures are essentially the same regardless of the particular fund involved. Since the General Fund and the Intragovernmental Service Fund appear most often on the examination, they are the two selected for illustrative purposes.

*The General Fund.* The accounts of the *general fund* of Aztec City as of the beginning of the current year were as follows:

| | |
|---|---|
| Cash | $ 2,500 |
| Taxes receivable—delinquent | 20,000 |
| Accounts payable | 17,500 |
| Reserve for encumbrances | 3,000 |
| Fund balance | 2,000 |

The following transactions took place during the current year:

1. The budget that was adopted for the current year provided for taxes of $600,000, special assessments of $150,000, fees of $25,000, and license revenues of $15,000. Appropriations were $650,000 for general fund operations, and $100,000 for the purpose of establishing a working capital fund.
2. All taxes and special assessments became receivable.
3. Cash receipts included the following:

| | |
|---|---|
| Taxes—current | $570,000 |
| Special assessments | 150,000 |
| Fees | 27,000 |
| Licenses | 17,500 |
| Taxes receivable—delinquent* plus interest of $800 | 15,800 |

*Tax liens were obtained on the remainder of the delinquent taxes.

4. Contracts amounting to $96,000 were let by the general fund.
5. Services rendered by the working capital fund, $50,000.
6. The following cash disbursements were made:

|   |   |
|---|---|
| Working capital fund | $100,000 |
| Accounts payable of the preceding year | 17,500 |
| Outstanding orders at beginning of year were all received and paid for | 3,600 |
| Expenses of fund incurred during year | 130,000 |
| Stores purchased for central storeroom established during year | 8,000 |
| Contracts let during year | 36,000 |
| Services performed by working capital fund | 40,000 |
| Salaries paid during year | 45,000 |

7. All unpaid taxes become delinquent.
8. Stores inventory in general fund amounted to $3,000 as of the end of the current year.

The entries to record the above general fund data would be as follows:

(1)

| | | |
|---|---|---|
| Estimated revenues | $790,000 | |
|     Appropriations | | $750,000 |
|     Fund Balance | | 40,000 |

(To record estimated revenues and expenditures.)

(2)

| | | |
|---|---|---|
| Taxes receivable—current | 600,000 | |
| Special assessments receivable | 150,000 | |
|     Revenues | | 750,000 |

(To record accrual of taxes and assessments.)

(3)

| | | |
|---|---|---|
| Cash | 780,300 | |
|     Taxes receivable—current | | 570,000 |
|     Special assessments receivable | | 150,000 |
|     Taxes receivable—delinquent | | 15,000 |
|     Revenues | | 45,300 |
| Tax liens | 5,000 | |
|     Taxes receivable—delinquent | | 5,000 |

(To record cash receipts and to reclassify delinquent taxes as tax liens.)

(4)

| | | |
|---|---|---|
| Encumbrances | 96,000 | |
|     Reserve for encumbrances | | 96,000 |

(To record encumbering of appropriations.)

Appendix B / Governmental (Fund) Accounting

(5)

| | | |
|---|---|---|
| Expenditures | 50,000 | |
|     Due to intragovernmental service fund | | 50,000 |
|     (To record expenditures.) | | |

(6)

| | | |
|---|---|---|
| Expenditures | 319,000 | |
| Accounts payable | 17,500 | |
| Reserve for encumbrances | 3,000 | |
| Fund balance | 600 | |
| Due to intragovernmental service fund | 40,000 | |
|     Cash | | 380,100 |
| Reserve for encumbrances | 36,000 | |
|     Encumbrances | | 36,000 |

(To record cash disbursements. Since only $3,000 had been provided in the Reserve for Encumbrances account as of the beginning of the period, the excess $600 is charged against the Fund Balance account.)

(7)

| | | |
|---|---|---|
| Taxes receivable—delinquent | 30,000 | |
|     Taxes receivable—current | | 30,000 |

(To reclassify taxes from a current status to a delinquent status.)

| | | |
|---|---|---|
| Stores inventory | 3,000 | |
|     Reserve for stores inventory | | 3,000 |

(To record the stores inventory.)

(*Instructional Note:* As is the case with fund titles, the terminology used in account titles is in a transitional phase. For example, *Unappropriated Surplus,* the old title of the Fund Balance account, is still in use. Likewise, you might encounter an account entitled *Appropriation Expenditures* which was the old title of the account now labeled simply *Expenditures.*)

The trial balance that follows results from the above data:

AZTEC CITY
Trial Balance
General Fund

| | Debit | Credit |
|---|---|---|
| Cash | $ 402,700 | |
| Taxes receivable—delinquent | 30,000 | |
| Tax liens | 5,000 | |
| Stores inventory | 3,000 | |

| | | |
|---|---:|---:|
| Estimated revenues | 790,000 | |
| Expenditures | 369,000 | |
| Encumbrances | 60,000 | |
| Due to intragovernmental service fund | | $ 10,000 |
| Revenues | | 795,300 |
| Appropriations | | 750,000 |
| Reserve for stores inventory | | 3,000 |
| Reserve for encumbrances | | 60,000 |
| Fund balance | | 41,400 |
| | $1,659,700 | $1,659,700 |

The following *closing entries* would be made from the preceding trial balance, assuming it is the end of the accounting period:

(1)

| | | |
|---|---:|---:|
| Revenues | $795,300 | |
|     Estimated revenues | | $790,000 |
|     Fund balance | | 5,300 |

(To close out the estimated and actual revenue accounts.)

(2)

| | | |
|---|---:|---:|
| Appropriations | 750,000 | |
|     Expenditures | | 369,000 |
|     Encumbrances | | 60,000 |
|     Fund balance | | 321,000 |

(To close out the appropriation, expenditure, and encumbrance accounts.)

After the closing entries are posted, the balance sheet of the general fund would appear as follows:

Aztec City

General Fund

Balance Sheet

*Assets*

| | |
|---|---:|
| Cash | $402,700 |
| Taxes receivable—delinquent | 30,000 |
| Tax liens | 5,000 |
| Stores inventory | 3,000 |
| | $440,700 |

*Liabilities, Reserves, and Fund Balance*

| | |
|---|---:|
| Due to intragovernmental service fund | $ 10,000 |
| Reserve for stores inventory | 3,000 |
| Reserve for encumbrances | 60,000 |
| Fund balance | 367,700 |
| | $440,700 |

Since the general fund is a nonprofit-oriented entity, income statements are not prepared. In lieu thereof, however, a statement analyzing changes in the fund balance is ordinarily submitted. Based on the above data, the statement would appear somewhat as follows:

AZTEC CITY<br>
Analysis of Changes in Fund Balance<br>
General Fund

|  | Estimated | Actual | Actual Over (Under) |
|---|---|---|---|
| Fund balance, beginning | $ 2,000 | $ 2,000 | $ — |
| Add: Reserve for encumbrances, beginning | 3,000 | 3,000 | — |
| Revenues | 790,000 | 795,300 | $ 5,300 |
| Total additions | $795,000 | $800,300 | $ 5,300 |
| Deduct: |  |  |  |
| Expenditures | $750,000 | $369,000 | ($381,000) |
| Expenditures chargeable against Reserve for encumbrances of prior year | 3,000 | 3,600 | 600 |
| Reserve for encumbrances | — | 60,000 | 60,000 |
| Total deductions | $753,000 | $432,600 | $320,400 |
| Fund balance, ending | $ 42,000 | $367,700 | $325,700 |

**The Intragovernmental Service Fund.** On January 1 of the current year, Aztec City established a working capital fund to finance the operation of a central equipment department.

(*Instructional Note:* As indicated earlier, an intragovernmental service fund is an intermediary fiscal entity through which some of the expenditures of other departments are made. Activities covered by such funds might include such miscellaneous services as printing and duplicating, centralized motor pools, or laundries. An intragovernmental service fund should be accounted for as if it were a private enterprise, with monies received from other departments accounted for as revenue to be offset by the costs incurred in earning such revenue. If long-lived assets are necessary to provide the services covered by the fund, they are maintained as fund assets, and depreciation is recorded in order to maintain the integrity of the fund. A Capital account is set up to record the amount contributed to establish the fund, and any profits, are recorded in a Retained Earnings account.)

The following transactions took place during the current year:

1. Aztec City initiated operations of the intragovernmental service fund by transferring $100,000 from its general fund.

2. Services rendered by the working capital fund to other departments included the following: General fund, $50,000; Utility fund, $30,000; and Special assessment fund, $20,000.
3. Cash receipts included:

| | |
|---|---:|
| From general fund—capital | $100,000 |
| From general fund—services | 40,000 |
| From utility fund—services | 20,000 |
| From special assessment fund—services | 15,000 |

4. The following cash disbursements were made:

| | |
|---|---:|
| Purchase of equipment (estimated useful life 10 years) | $ 50,000 |
| Purchase of materials and supplies of which ¼ remained at end of year | 30,000 |
| Salaries and wages as follows: | |
| Direct labor | 12,000 |
| Office salaries | 9,000 |
| Superintendent's salary | 8,000 |
| Heat, light, and power | 1,800 |
| Office expenses | 1,200 |

The entries to record the preceding *intragovernmental service fund* data would be as follows:

(1)

| | | |
|---|---:|---:|
| Cash | $100,000 | |
|     Capital | | 100,000 |

(2)

| | | |
|---|---:|---:|
| Due from general fund | 50,000 | |
| Due from utility fund | 30,000 | |
| Due from special assessments fund | 20,000 | |
|     Billings for services | | 100,000 |

(3)

| | | |
|---|---:|---:|
| Cash | 75,000 | |
|     Due from general fund | | 40,000 |
|     Due from utility fund | | 20,000 |
|     Due from special assessments fund | | 15,000 |

(4)

| | | |
|---|---:|---:|
| Equipment | 50,000 | |
| Inventory of materials and supplies | 7,500 | |
| Cost of materials and supplies used | 22,500 | |
| Direct labor | 12,000 | |
| Office salaries | 9,000 | |
| Superintendent's salary | 8,000 | |

Appendix B / Governmental (Fund) Accounting

| | | |
|---|---|---|
| Heat, light, and power | 1,800 | |
| Office expenses | 1,200 | |
| Cash | | 112,000 |
| Depreciation—equipment | 5,000 | |
| Accumulated depreciation—equipment | | 5,000 |

The trial balance that follows results from the preceding data:

AZTEC CITY

Trial Balance

Intragovernmental Service Fund

| | | |
|---|---|---|
| Cash | $ 63,000 | |
| Due from general fund | 10,000 | |
| Due from utility fund | 10,000 | |
| Due from special assessments fund | 5,000 | |
| Inventory of materials and supplies | 7,500 | |
| Equipment | 50,000 | |
| Billings for services | | $100,000 |
| Cost of materials and supplies used | 22,500 | |
| Direct labor | 12,000 | |
| Office salaries | 9,000 | |
| Superintendent's salary | 8,000 | |
| Heat, light, and power | 1,800 | |
| Office expenses | 1,200 | |
| Depreciation—equipment | 5,000 | |
| Accumulated depreciation—equipment | | 5,000 |
| Capital | | 100,000 |
| | $205,000 | $205,000 |

The following closing entries would be made from the preceding trial balance, assuming it is the end of the accounting period:

(1)

| | | |
|---|---|---|
| Billings for services | $100,000 | |
|     Retained earnings | | $100,000 |
| (To close out revenue account.) | | |

(2)

| | | |
|---|---|---|
| Retained earnings | 59,500 | |
|     Cost of materials and supplies used | | 22,500 |
|     Direct labor | | 12,000 |
|     Office salaries | | 9,000 |
|     Superintendent's salary | | 8,000 |
|     Heat, light, and power | | 1,800 |
|     Office expenses | | 1,200 |
|     Depreciation—equipment | | 5,000 |
| (To close out expense accounts.) | | |

After the closing entries are posted, the balance sheet and statement of operations of the intragovernmental service fund would appear as follows:

AZTEC CITY
Intragovernmental Service Fund
Balance Sheet

*Assets*

| | | |
|---|---:|---:|
| Cash | | $ 63,000 |
| Due from general fund | | 10,000 |
| Due from utility fund | | 10,000 |
| Due from special assessments fund | | 5,000 |
| Inventory of materials and supplies | | 7,500 |
| Equipment | $ 50,000 | |
| Less: Accumulated depreciation | 5,000 | 45,000 |
| | | $140,500 |

*Liabilities, Capital, and Retained Earnings*

| | |
|---|---:|
| Capital | $100,000 |
| Retained earnings | 40,500 |
| | $140,500 |

AZTEC CITY
Intragovernmental Service Fund
Statement of Operations

| | | |
|---|---:|---:|
| Billings for service | | $100,000 |
| Less: Cost of materials and supplies used | $ 22,500 | |
| Direct labor | 12,000 | |
| Office salaries | 9,000 | |
| Superintendent's salary | 8,000 | |
| Heat, light, and power | 1,800 | |
| Office expenses | 1,200 | |
| Depreciation—equipment | 5,000 | 59,500 |
| Excess of billings over costs | | $40,500 |

**General Comments.** As with any question or problem on the CPA examination, read the governmental problem carefully before attempting a solution. Unless a work sheet is specifically required, journal entries or "T" accounts will normally suffice for data analysis and considerable time may be saved if this is possible. When reading the governmental problem, be on the alert for answers to the following questions:

1. Does the problem involve (a) opening the books, (b) recording transactions during a particular period, (c) adjusting and/or closing the books, or (d) the preparation of financial statements?

Appendix B / Governmental (Fund) Accounting

2. Does the problem specifically identify the fund (or funds) as to type or must this be determined from the context and nature of the transactions? If the latter, what type of fund (or funds) is involved in the problem?
3. Does the problem require the use of budgetary accounts?
4. Does the problem involve multiple funds? If so, are there any inter-fund transactions? If there are inter-fund transactions, note these transactions and list the funds involved in each when drawing up your solution outline.
5. Does the problem specifically require the preparation of a work sheet, "T" accounts, journal entries, or financial statements, or is the choice of method and form of presentation left up to the candidate? In case of the latter, what method and form of presentation are most appropriate considering the time available and your capabilities in the area?

## PROBLEMS

### Number 1 (Estimated time—40 to 60 minutes)

The City of Linde, organized on January 1, 1968, has never kept accounts on a double-entry system. During 1978 the city council employed you to install a system of accounts. You made a study and determined the values of assets and liabilities in order to inaugurate the proper system as of January 1, 1979, the beginning of the city's fiscal year, as follows:

1. City Taxes Receivable—1978 and prior years
   (including 10% considered uncollectible)      $ 21,900
2. Investment in Securities
   a. Earmarked to Bond Retirement      136,680
   b. Donated by J. Stark on July 1, 1978, the net income from which to supplement Library operations. The cost of all the stock to Stark was $50,000. Appraised value on July 1      65,400
3. Cash
   a. For general operations, including $3,000 in petty cash      18,000
   b. Earmarked to investments for bond retirement (represents interest earned over the actuarial estimate)      840
   c. Balance of cash donated by J. Stark, the net income from which to supplement Library operations      12,000
   d. Undistributed balance of cash received from J. Stark investments and apartment rents      3,000
4. Buildings
   a. For general operations      235,000
   b. Apartment building donated by J. Stark on July 1, 1978. Net income to be used in the operation of the Library. Cost of completion to Stark, July 1, 1968, $96,000 (exclusive of cost of land) with estimated life of 50 years, no salvage. Appraised value on July 1, 1978      90,000

5. Equipment
   a. For general use — 280,000
   b. Apartment furniture purchased with donated cash, October 1, 1978, estimated life 10 years, no salvage. Cost — 36,000
6. Streets and curbs built by special assessment funds in prior years. (All collected.) The City contributed one-third of the cost — 300,000
7. Land
   a. For general use — 60,000
   b. For apartment building site — 10,000
8. Supplies
   a. For general operation — 1,800
   b. For apartment house operation, purchased by income cash — 300
   c. Originally purchased for general operations were transferred to and used in library operations; no settlement has been made — 2,400
9. Vouchers Payable — for general operations — 16,000
10. 3%-30-year bonds payable, due on December 31, 1995. (Issued for purchase of land, buildings and equipment) — 400,000

*Required:*

List the *funds* or *group titles* that would be required for the City on the basis of the above information, leaving at least 15 lines between each title. Under each title make one summary journal entry that will record all of the required accounts and amounts in the appropriate fund.

## Number 2 (Estimated time — 65 to 90 minutes)

From the following information concerning the City of Langdon, you are to prepare as of December 31, 1978:

a. A work sheet reflecting the transactions, closing entries and balance sheet for its *general fund.*
b. A statement of operations for its *working capital fund.*
c. A balance sheet for its *working capital fund.*

The accounts of the *general fund* as of January 1, 1978 were as follows:

| | |
|---|---|
| Cash | $ 1,000 |
| Taxes receivable — delinquent | 8,000 |
| Accounts payable | 7,000 |
| Reserve for encumbrances | 1,500 |
| Fund balance | 500 |

The following transactions for the current year are to be considered:

Appendix B / Governmental (Fund) Accounting

1. The budget which was adopted for 1978 provided for taxes of $275,000, special assessments of $100,000, fees of $15,000, and license revenues of $10,000. Appropriations were $290,000 for general fund operations, and $100,000 for the purpose of establishing a working capital fund.
2. All taxes and special assessments became receivable.
3. Cash receipts for the general fund included:

| | |
|---|---:|
| Taxes from 1978 | $260,000 |
| Special assessments | 100,000 |
| Fees | 16,000 |
| Licenses | 9,500 |
| Taxes receivable—delinquent plus interest of $500. Tax liens were obtained on the remainder of the delinquent taxes | 5,500 |

4. Contracts amounting to $75,000 were let by the general fund.
5. Services rendered by the working capital fund to other departments included: General fund, $40,000; Utility fund, $20,000 of which $5,000 remained uncollected at the end of the year.
6. The following cash disbursements were made by the general fund:

| | |
|---|---:|
| Working capital fund | $100,000 |
| Accounts payable of the preceding year | 7,000 |
| Outstanding orders at beginning of year were all received and paid for | 2,000 |
| Expenses of fund incurred during year | 145,000 |
| Stores purchased for central storeroom established during year | 5,000 |
| Contracts let during year | 30,000 |
| Permanent advance to newly created petty cash fund | 1,000 |
| Services performed by working capital fund | 35,000 |
| Salaries paid during year | 30,000 |

7. The following cash disbursements were made by the *working capital fund*:

| | |
|---|---:|
| Purchase of equipment (Estimated useful life 10 years) | $ 60,000 |
| Purchase of materials and supplies of which 1/5 remained at end of year | 40,000 |
| Salaries and wages as follows: | |
|   Direct labor | 9,000 |
|   Office salaries | 2,000 |
|   Superintendent's salary | 4,000 |
| Heat, light & power | 2,000 |
| Office expenses | 500 |

8. All unpaid taxes become delinquent.
9. Stores inventory in general fund amounted to $2,000 on December 31, 1978.

## Number 3 (Estimated time—40 to 60 minutes)

On January 1, 1978 Medium City established a working capital fund for operating a central motor vehicle pool. It transferred $100,000 from the general fund.

Immediately upon establishment, a fleet of trucks was purchased as follows:

| Type | Number | Cost per Truck |
|---|---|---|
| 4-ton GMC | 4 | $3,500 |
| 3-ton Ford | 4 | 2,500 |
| 3-ton Mack | 4 | 2,200 |
| 1-ton Dodge | 5 | 1,500 |

Operating each of the three- and four-ton trucks requires a driver and a helper who are paid standard wage rates of $2.00 and $1.50 per hour, respectively. The one-ton trucks do not require a helper.

All trucks are depreciated on a straight-line basis over a 5-year period with 5% residual salvage value.

Trucks are rented to the general fund on an hourly basis and the following usage and gasoline costs were reported for the year ended December 31, 1978:

| Type | Rental Rate per Hour | Total Number of Hours Used | Cost of Gasoline Used |
|---|---|---|---|
| 4-ton GMC | $5.50 | 6,000 | $2,400 |
| 3-ton Ford | 5.00 | 8,000 | 2,400 |
| 3-ton Mack | 5.00 | 8,000 | 2,800 |
| 1-ton Dodge | 3.00 | 15,000 | 3,000 |

The following additional costs were incurred in operation of the fleet:

1. Drivers and helpers wages were paid for exactly the hours the trucks were used. There was no unpaid payroll at the end of the year.
2. Unpaid gasoline invoices at December 31, 1978 aggregated $1,500.
3. Other indirect costs incurred were as follows:

| | |
|---|---|
| Supervision | $15,000 |
| Repairs | 10,000 |
| Tires and tubes purchased | 1,600 |

There were no unpaid bills at December 31, 1978 pertaining to the above items; however, at the end of the year the fund had on hand an inventory of new tires costing $500.

During the year the general fund paid the vehicle pool $95,000 on its account for services rendered.

a. You are to prepare the journal entries to open the fund, to record the transactions in it for 1978, and to close the fund at December 31st.
b. Prepare a balance sheet in good form for the fund as of December 31, 1978. (A work sheet is *not acceptable* in meeting this requirement. It is suggested that the statement be prepared from the entries and the use of skeleton "T" accounts.)

Appendix B / Governmental (Fund) Accounting

## Number 4 (Estimated time—50 to 75 minutes)

From the following information about the Water Department of the City of X, *prepare a work sheet* showing the original trial balance, adjustments, and the extended profit and loss and balance sheet accounts. Also prepare in proper form a fund balance sheet and operating statement for the year ended December 31, 1978, for the Water Department.

*Ledger Balances December 31, 1978*

| | | | |
|---|---:|---|---:|
| Cash—operating fund | $ 588,800 | Accounts payable—trade | $ 47,000 |
| Cash—consumers' deposits | 17,000 | Accounts payable—township | 56,000 |
| Postage on meter | 1,000 | Water consumers' deposits | 67,000 |
| Accounts receivable: | | Revenue bonds payable | 300,000 |
|   Consumer billing | 65,000 | Accumulated depreciation | 1,200,000 |
|   Service | 17,000 | Surplus | 4,500,000 |
|   Sundry | 700 | Revenue | 1,500,000 |
| Due from other funds | — | Expense: | |
| Supplies inventory | 140,000 |   Production | 340,000 |
| Merchandise on order and in | |   Distribution | 151,000 |
|   transit | 145,000 |   Office | 90,000 |
| Investments—consumers' | |   Administrative and | |
|   deposits | 50,000 |     general | 105,000 |
| Property | 6,000,000 | Cost of installations, | |
| Unfilled orders and contracts | 145,000 |   repairs and parts | 140,000 |
| Warrants payable | 50,100 | Interest on consumers' | |
| Due to other funds | — |   deposits | 600 |
| Advance service payments | | Interest on bonds | 9,000 |
|   (continued) | | Allowance and adjustments | 5,000 |

*Note:* Revenue bonds mature serially $30,000 each year.

*Examination of the records discloses the following additional data:*

(1) Included in error in accounts payable—trade:
  a.  For reimbursement of metered postage    $ 500
  b.  Due to other City funds    18,500
(2) Items included in book inventory that were not received until 1979    2,000
(3) Computation of inventory items chargeable to distribution expense understated    1,000
(4) Classified as accounts payable trade, should be accounts payable township    10,000
(5) Unfilled orders not of record    1,000
(6) 1979 expense purchases recorded as 1978 liabilities and charged to expense as follows:
    a.  Production expense    $500
    b.  Distribution expense    500
    c.  Office expense    500
    d.  Administrative expense    500

| | |
|---|---:|
| (7) Included in accounts receivable—service, but actually due from other funds | 500 |
| (8) Credit balances included in accounts receivable—service, are advance service payments | 1,000 |
| (9) Included in accounts receivable sundry but due from other City funds | 50 |
| (10) Required adjustment to reduce unfilled orders and contracts to proper estimates | 2,600 |
| (11) Purchase order included in unfilled orders and contracts. This order a duplication of previously recorded expenditure | 40,000 |
| (12) Unrecorded receivable from township for water consumed | 5,000 |

## Number 5 (Estimated time—40 to 50 minutes)

### Instructions

Select the *best* answer for each of the following items relating to fund accounting. *Mark only one answer for each item.* Your grade will be determined from your total of correct answers.

### Items to be Answered

1. The operations of a public library receiving the majority of its support from property taxes levied for that purpose should be accounted for in:
   a. The general fund.
   b. A special revenue fund.
   c. An enterprise fund.
   d. An intragovernmental service fund.
   e. None of the above.

2. The liability for general obligation bonds issued for the benefit of a municipal electric company and serviced by its earnings should be recorded in:
   a. An enterprise fund.
   b. The general fund.
   c. An enterprise fund and the general long-term debt group.
   d. An enterprise fund and disclosed in a footnote in the statement of general long-term debt.
   e. None of the above.

3. The liability for special assessment bonds which carry a secondary pledge of a municipality's general credit should be recorded in:
   a. An enterprise fund.
   b. A special revenue fund and general long-term debt group.
   c. A special assessment fund and the general long-term debt group.
   d. A special assessment fund and disclosed in a footnote in the statement of general long-term debt.
   e. None of the above.

Appendix B / Governmental (Fund) Accounting

4. The proceeds of a federal grant made to assist in financing the future construction of an adult training center should be recorded in:
   a. The general fund.
   b. A special revenue fund.
   c. A capital projects fund.
   d. A special assessment fund.
   e. None of the above.

5. The receipts from a special tax levy to retire and pay interest on general obligation bonds issued to finance the construction of a new city hall should be recorded in a:
   a. Debt service fund.
   b. Capital projects fund.
   c. Revolving interest fund.
   d. Special revenue fund.
   e. None of the above.

6. The operations of a municipal swimming pool receiving the majority of its support from charges to users should be accounted for in:
   a. A special revenue fund.
   b. The general fund.
   c. An intragovernmental service fund.
   d. An enterprise fund.
   e. None of the above.

7. The fixed assets of a central purchasing and stores department organized to serve all municipal departments should be recorded in:
   a. An enterprise fund and the general fixed assets group.
   b. An enterprise fund.
   c. The general fixed assets group.
   d. The general fund.
   e. None of the above.

8. The monthly remittance to an insurance company of the lump sum of hospital-surgical insurance premiums collected as payroll deductions from employees should be recorded in:
   a. The general fund.
   b. An agency fund.
   c. A special revenue fund.
   d. An intragovernmental service fund.
   e. None of the above.

9. Several years ago a city provided for the establishment of a sinking fund to retire an issue of general obligation bonds. This year the city made a $50,000 contribution to the sinking fund from general revenues and realized $15,000 in revenue from securities in the sinking fund. The bonds due this year were retired. These transactions require accounting recognition in:
   a. The general fund.
   b. A debt service fund and the general long-term debt group of accounts.
   c. A debt service fund, the general fund and the general long-term debt group of accounts.

d. A capital projects fund, a debt service fund, the general fund and the general long-term debt group of accounts.
e. None of the above.

10. A city realized large capital gains and losses on securities in its library endownment fund. In the absence of specific instructions from the donor or state statutory requirements, the general rule of law holds that these amounts should be charged or credited to:
    a. General fund income.
    b. General fund principal.
    c. Trust fund income.
    d. Trust fund principal.
    e. None of the above.

11. The activities of a central motor pool which provides and services vehicles for the use of municipal employees on official business should be accounted for in:
    a. An agency fund.
    b. The general fund.
    c. An intragovernmental service fund.
    d. A special revenue fund.
    e. None of the above.

12. A transaction in which a municipal electric utility paid $150,000 out of its earnings for new equipment requires accounting recognition in:
    a. An enterprise fund.
    b. The general fund.
    c. The general fund and the general fixed assets group of accounts.
    d. An enterprise fund and the general fixed assets group of accounts.
    e. None of the above.

13. In order to provide for the retirement of general obligation bonds, a city invests a portion of its general revenue receipts in marketable securities. This investment activity should be accounted for in:
    a. A trust fund.
    b. The enterprise fund.
    c. A special assessment fund.
    d. A special revenue fund.
    e. None of the above.

14. The activities of a municipal employee retirement plan which is financed by equal employer and employee contributions should be accounted for in:
    a. An agency fund.
    b. An intragovernmental service fund.
    c. A special assessment fund.
    d. A trust fund.
    e. None of the above.

15. A city collects property taxes for the benefit of the local sanitary, park and school districts and periodically remits collections to these units. This activity should be accounted for in:

Appendix B / Governmental (Fund) Accounting

    a. An agency fund.
    b. The general fund.
    c. An intragovernmental service fund.
    d. A special assessment fund.
    e. None of the above.

16. A transaction in which a municipal electric utility issues bonds (to be repaid from its own operations) requires accounting recognition in:
    a. The general fund.
    b. A debt service fund.
    c. Enterprise and debt service funds.
    c. An enterprise fund, a debt service fund and the general long-term debt group of accounts.
    e. None of the above.

17. A transaction in which a municipality issued general obligation serial bonds to finance the construction of a fire station requires accounting recognition in the:
    a. General fund.
    b. Capital projects and general funds.
    c. Capital projects fund and the general long-term debt group of accounts.
    d. General fund and the general long-term debt group of accounts.
    e. None of the above.

18. Expenditures of $200,000 were made during the year on the fire station in item 17. This transaction requires accounting recognition in the:
    a. General fund.
    b. Capital projects fund and the general fixed assets group of accounts.
    c. Capital projects fund and the general long-term debt group of accounts.
    d. General fund and the general fixed assets group of accounts.
    e. None of the above.

## Number 6 (Estimated time—25 to 30 minutes)

Select the *best* answer for each of the following items relating to fund accounting. *Mark only one answer for each item.* Your grade will be based on your total correct answers.

1. What type of account is used to earmark the fund balance to liquidate the contingent obligations of goods ordered but *not* yet received?
    a. Appropriations.
    b. Encumbrances.
    c. Obligations.
    d. Reserve for encumbrances.

2. Premiums received on general obligation bonds are generally transferred to what fund or group of accounts?
    a. Debt service.
    b. General long-term debt.

c. General.
d. Special revenue.
3. Self-supporting activities that are provided on a user charge basis are accounted for in what fund?
   a. Agency.
   b. Enterprise.
   c. Intragovernmental service.
   d. Special revenue.
4. A statement of changes in financial position is prepared for which fund?
   a. Enterprise.
   b. Intragovernmental service.
   c. Special assessment.
   d. Trust.
5. A city should record depreciation as an expense in its
   a. General fund and enterprise fund.
   b. Intragovernmental service fund and general fixed-assets group of accounts.
   c. Enterprise fund and intragovernmental service fund.
   d. Enterprise fund and capital-projects fund.
6. Authority granted by a legislative body to make expenditures and to incur obligations during a fiscal year is the definition of an
   a. Appropriation.
   b. Authorization.
   c. Encumbrance.
   d. Expenditure.
7. An account for expenditures does *not* appear in which fund?
   a. Capital projects.
   b. Enterprise.
   c. Special assessment.
   d. Special revenue.
8. Part of the general obligation bond proceeds from a new issuance was used to pay for the cost of a new city hall as soon as construction was completed. The remainder of the proceeds was transferred to repay the debt. Entries are needed to record these transactions in the
   a. General fund and general long-term debt group of accounts.
   b. General fund, general long-term debt group of accounts, and debt-service fund.
   c. Trust fund, debt-service fund, and general fixed-assets group of accounts.
   d. General long-term debt group of accounts, debt-service fund, general fixed-assets group of accounts, and capital-projects fund.
9. Cash secured from property tax revenue was transferred for the eventual payment of principal and interest on general obligation bonds. The bonds had been issued when land had been acquired several years ago for a city

park. Upon the transfer, an entry would *not* be made in which of the following?
   a. Debt-service fund.
   b. General fixed-assets group of accounts.
   c. General long-term debt group of accounts.
   d. General fund.
10. Equipment in general governmental service that had been constructed ten years before by a capital-projects fund was sold. The receipts were accounted for as unrestricted revenue. Entries are necessary in the
   a. General fund and capital-projects fund.
   b. General fund and general fixed-assets group of accounts.
   c. General fund, capital-projects fund, and enterprise fund.
   d. General fund, capital-projects fund, and general fixed-assets group of accounts.

## Number 7 (Estimated time — 40 to 60 minutes)

The City of Bergen entered into the following transactions during the year 1978:

1. A bond issue was authorized by vote to provide funds for the construction of a new municipal building which it was estimated would cost $500,000. The bonds were to be paid in ten equal installments from a sinking fund, payments being due March 1 of each year. Any balance of the bond fund is to be transferred directly to the sinking fund.
2. An advance of $40,000 was received from the General Fund to underwrite a deposit on the land contract of $60,000. The deposit was made.
3. Bonds of $450,000 were sold for cash at 102. It was decided not to sell all of the bonds because the cost of the land was less than was expected.
4. Contracts amounting to $390,000 were let to Michela and Company, the lowest bidder, for the construction of the municipal building.
5. The temporary advance from the General Fund was repaid and the balance on the land contract was paid.
6. Based on the architect's certificate, warrants were issued for $320,000 for the work completed to date.
7. Warrants paid in cash by the treasurer amounted to $310,000.
8. Due to changes in the plans the contract with Michela and Company was revised to $440,000; the remainder of the bonds were sold at 101.
9. Before the end of the year the building had been completed and additional warrants amounting to $115,000 were issued to the contractor in final payment for the work. All warrants were paid by the treasurer.

*Required:*
   (1) Record the above and closing entries in *bond fund* T-accounts. Designate the entries in the T-accounts by the numbers which identify the data.

(2) Prepare applicable fund balance sheets as of December 31, 1978, considering only the proceeds and expenditures from *bond fund* transactions.

## Number 8 (Estimated time — 40 to 60 minutes)

The following information pertains to the operation of the *water fund* of the city of M. Included in the operations of this fund are those of a special replacement fund for the water department, the accounts of which are a part of the accounts of the water fund.

The balances in the accounts of this fund on January 1, 1978 were as follows:

| | |
|---|---:|
| Cash | $ 6,126 |
| Accounts receivable | 7,645 |
| Stores | 13,826 |
| Investments of replacement fund | 21,700 |
| Permanent property | 212,604 |
| Accounts payable | 4,324 |
| Customers' deposits | 1,500 |
| Replacement fund reserve | 21,700 |
| Operating surplus | 21,773 |
| Bonds payable | 60,000 |
| Capital surplus | 152,604 |

The following items represent the total transactions of the fund for the year ended December 31, 1978:

| | | |
|---|---|---:|
| (1) | Services billed | $146,867 |
| (2) | Accounts collected | 147,842 |
| (3) | Uncollectible accounts of prior years written off | 1,097 |
| (4) | Invoices and payrolls approved for current expense | 69,826 |
| (5) | Invoices approved for purchase of water department stores | 31,424 |
| (6) | Stores issued for use in operation | 32,615 |
| (7) | Supplies secured from general fund stores and used in operation (cash transferred to general fund) | 7,197 |
| (8) | Vouchers approved for payment of bonds and interest of $3,000 | 23,000 |
| (9) | Depreciation entered as charge against current income and credited to replacement reserve | 10,600 |
| (10) | Deposits received | 400 |
| | Deposits refunded | 240 |
| (11) | Invoices approved for replacement of equipment which cost $6,200 | 7,800 |
| (12) | Invoices approved for additions to plant | 12,460 |
| (13) | Vouchers approved for purchase of securities necessary to fully invest the replacement fund | compute |
| (14) | Income received on investments | 1,102 |
| (15) | Warrants drawn for invoices, payrolls and vouchers approved | 147,316 |

*Appendix B / Governmental (Fund) Accounting* **875**

From the above information you are to prepare:

a. A balance sheet of the fund as of December 31, 1978.
b. An operating statement of the water department for 1978.
c. An analysis of the operating surplus of the department for 1978.

# APPENDIX T

# Tables of Amounts and Present Values

## AMOUNT OF 1
$s = (1 + i)^n$

| Periods | ½% | 1% | 1½% | 2% | 2½% | 3% | 3½% |
|---|---|---|---|---|---|---|---|
| 0 | 1. | 1. | 1. | 1. | 1. | 1. | 1. |
| 1 | 1.005 | 1.01 | 1.015 | 1.02 | 1.025 | 1.03 | 1.035 |
| 2 | 1.010025 | 1.0201 | 1.030225 | 1.0404 | 1.050625 | 1.0609 | 1.071225 |
| 3 | 1.01507512 | 1.030301 | 1.04567838 | 1.061208 | 1.07689063 | 1.092727 | 1.10871788 |
| 4 | 1.02015050 | 1.04060401 | 1.06136355 | 1.08243216 | 1.10381289 | 1.12550881 | 1.14752300 |
| 5 | 1.02525125 | 1.05101005 | 1.07728400 | 1.10408080 | 1.13140821 | 1.15927407 | 1.18768631 |
| 6 | 1.03037750 | 1.06152015 | 1.09344326 | 1.12616242 | 1.15969342 | 1.19405230 | 1.22925533 |
| 7 | 1.03552939 | 1.07213535 | 1.10984491 | 1.14868567 | 1.18868575 | 1.22987387 | 1.27227926 |
| 8 | 1.04070704 | 1.08285671 | 1.12649259 | 1.17165938 | 1.21840290 | 1.26677008 | 1.31680904 |
| 9 | 1.04591057 | 1.09368527 | 1.14338998 | 1.19509257 | 1.24886297 | 1.30477318 | 1.36289735 |
| 10 | 1.05114013 | 1.10462213 | 1.16054083 | 1.21899442 | 1.28008454 | 1.34391638 | 1.41059876 |
| 11 | 1.05639583 | 1.11566835 | 1.17794894 | 1.24337431 | 1.31208666 | 1.38423387 | 1.45996972 |
| 12 | 1.06167781 | 1.12682503 | 1.19561817 | 1.26824179 | 1.34488882 | 1.42576089 | 1.51106866 |
| 13 | 1.06698620 | 1.13809328 | 1.21355244 | 1.29360663 | 1.37851104 | 1.46853371 | 1.56395606 |
| 14 | 1.07232113 | 1.14947421 | 1.23175573 | 1.31947876 | 1.41297382 | 1.51258972 | 1.61869452 |
| 15 | 1.07768273 | 1.16096896 | 1.25023207 | 1.34586834 | 1.44829817 | 1.55796742 | 1.67534838 |
| 16 | 1.08307115 | 1.17257864 | 1.26898555 | 1.37278571 | 1.48450562 | 1.60470644 | 1.73398604 |
| 17 | 1.08848650 | 1.18430443 | 1.28802033 | 1.40024142 | 1.52161826 | 1.65284763 | 1.79467555 |
| 18 | 1.09398283 | 1.19614748 | 1.30734064 | 1.42824625 | 1.55965872 | 1.70243306 | 1.85748920 |
| 19 | 1.09939858 | 1.20810895 | 1.32695075 | 1.45681117 | 1.59865019 | 1.75350605 | 1.92250132 |
| 20 | 1.10489557 | 1.22019004 | 1.34685501 | 1.48594740 | 1.63861644 | 1.80611123 | 1.98978886 |
| 21 | 1.11042005 | 1.23239194 | 1.36705783 | 1.51566634 | 1.67958185 | 1.86029457 | 2.05943147 |
| 22 | 1.11597215 | 1.24471586 | 1.38756370 | 1.54597967 | 1.72157140 | 1.91610341 | 2.13151158 |
| 23 | 1.12155201 | 1.25716302 | 1.40837715 | 1.57689926 | 1.76461068 | 1.97358651 | 2.20611448 |
| 24 | 1.12715977 | 1.26973465 | 1.42950281 | 1.60843725 | 1.80872595 | 2.03279411 | 2.28332849 |
| 25 | 1.13279557 | 1.28243200 | 1.45094535 | 1.64060599 | 1.85394410 | 2.09377793 | 2.36324498 |
| 26 | 1.13845955 | 1.29525631 | 1.47270953 | 1.67341811 | 1.90029270 | 2.15659127 | 2.44595856 |
| 27 | 1.14415185 | 1.30820888 | 1.49480018 | 1.70688468 | 1.94780002 | 2.22128901 | 2.53156711 |
| 28 | 1.14987261 | 1.32129097 | 1.51722218 | 1.74102421 | 1.99649502 | 2.28792768 | 2.62017196 |
| 29 | 1.15562197 | 1.33450388 | 1.53998051 | 1.77584469 | 2.04640739 | 2.35656551 | 2.71187798 |
| 30 | 1.16140008 | 1.34784892 | 1.56308022 | 1.81136158 | 2.09756758 | 2.42726247 | 2.80679370 |
| 31 | 1.16720708 | 1.36132740 | 1.58652642 | 1.84758882 | 2.15000677 | 2.50008035 | 2.90503148 |
| 32 | 1.17304311 | 1.37494068 | 1.61032432 | 1.88454059 | 2.20375694 | 2.57508276 | 3.00670759 |
| 33 | 1.17990833 | 1.38869009 | 1.63447918 | 1.92223140 | 2.25885086 | 2.75233524 | 3.11194235 |
| 34 | 1.18480287 | 1.40257699 | 1.65899637 | 1.96067603 | 2.31532213 | 2.73190530 | 3.22086033 |
| 35 | 1.19072689 | 1.41660276 | 1.68388132 | 1.99988955 | 2.37320519 | 2.81386245 | 3.33359045 |
| 36 | 1.19668052 | 1.43076878 | 1.70913954 | 2.03988734 | 2.43253532 | 2.89827833 | 3.45026611 |
| 37 | 1.20266392 | 1.44507647 | 1.73477663 | 2.08068509 | 2.49334870 | 2.98522668 | 3.57102543 |
| 38 | 1.20867721 | 1.45952724 | 1.76079828 | 2.12229879 | 2.55568242 | 3.07478348 | 3.69601132 |
| 39 | 1.21472063 | 1.47412251 | 1.78721025 | 2.16474477 | 2.61957448 | 3.16702698 | 3.82537171 |
| 40 | 1.22079423 | 1.48886373 | 1.81401841 | 2.20803966 | 2.68506384 | 3.26203779 | 3.95925972 |
| 41 | 1.22689820 | 1.50375237 | 1.84122868 | 2.25220046 | 2.75219043 | 3.35989893 | 4.09783381 |
| 42 | 1.23303269 | 1.51878989 | 1.86884712 | 2.29724447 | 2.82099520 | 3.46069589 | 4.24125799 |
| 43 | 1.23919786 | 1.53397779 | 1.89698982 | 2.34318936 | 2.89152008 | 3.56451677 | 4.38970202 |
| 44 | 1.24539385 | 1.54931757 | 1.92533302 | 2.39005314 | 2.96380808 | 3.67145227 | 4.54334160 |
| 45 | 1.25162082 | 1.56481075 | 1.95421301 | 2.43785421 | 3.03790328 | 3.78159584 | 4.70235855 |
| 46 | 1.25787892 | 1.58045885 | 1.98352621 | 2.48661129 | 3.11385086 | 3.89504273 | 4.86694110 |
| 47 | 1.26416831 | 1.59626344 | 2.01327910 | 2.53634351 | 3.19169713 | 4.01189503 | 5.03728404 |
| 48 | 1.27048916 | 1.61222608 | 2.04347829 | 2.58707039 | 3.27148956 | 4.13225188 | 5.21358898 |
| 49 | 1.27684160 | 1.62834834 | 2.07413046 | 2.63881179 | 3.35327680 | 4.25621944 | 5.39606459 |
| 50 | 1.28322581 | 1.64463182 | 2.10524242 | 2.69158803 | 3.43710872 | 4.38390602 | 5.58492686 |
| 55 | 1.31562897 | 1.72852457 | 2.26794398 | 2.97173067 | 3.88877303 | 5.08214859 | 6.63314114 |
| 60 | 1.34885015 | 1.81669670 | 2.44321978 | 3.28103079 | 4.39978975 | 5.89160310 | 7.87809090 |
| 65 | 1.38291030 | 1.90936649 | 2.63204158 | 3.62252311 | 4.97795826 | 6.82998273 | 9.35670068 |
| 70 | 1.41783052 | 2.00676337 | 2.83545629 | 3.99955822 | 5.63210286 | 7.91782191 | 11.11282526 |
| 75 | 1.45373252 | 2.10912847 | 3.05459171 | 4.41583546 | 6.37220743 | 9.17892567 | 13.19855038 |
| 80 | 1.49033856 | 2.21671522 | 3.29066279 | 4.87543916 | 7.20956782 | 10.64089056 | 15.67573754 |
| 85 | 1.52797148 | 2.32978997 | 3.54497838 | 5.38289878 | 8.15696424 | 12.33570855 | 18.61585881 |
| 90 | 1.56655467 | 2.44863267 | 3.81894851 | 5.94313313 | 9.22885633 | 14.30046711 | 22.11217595 |
| 95 | 1.60611214 | 2.57353755 | 4.11409214 | 6.56169920 | 10.44160385 | 16.57816077 | 26.26232856 |
| 100 | 1.64666849 | 2.70481383 | 4.43204565 | 7.24464612 | 11.81371635 | 19.21863198 | 31.19140798 |

## AMOUNT OF 1
$s = (1 + i)^n$

| Periods | 4% | 4½% | 5% | 6% | 7% | 8% | 9% |
|---|---|---|---|---|---|---|---|
| 0 | 1. | 1. | 1. | 1. | 1. | 1. | 1. |
| 1 | 1.04 | 1.045 | 1.05 | 1.06 | 1.07 | 1.08 | 1.09 |
| 2 | 1.0816 | 1.092025 | 1.1025 | 1.1236 | 1.144 | 1.166 | 1.188 |
| 3 | 1.124864 | 1.14116613 | 1.157625 | 1.191016 | 1.225043 | 1.259712 | 1.295029 |
| 4 | 1.16985856 | 1.19251860 | 1.21550625 | 1.26247696 | 1.31079601 | 1.36048896 | 1.41158161 |
| 5 | 1.21665290 | 1.24618194 | 1.27628156 | 1.33822558 | 1.40255173 | 1.46932807 | 1.53862395 |
| 6 | 1.26531902 | 1.30226012 | 1.34009564 | 1.41851911 | 1.50073035 | 1.58687432 | 1.67710011 |
| 7 | 1.31593178 | 1.36086183 | 1.40710042 | 1.50363026 | 1.60578147 | 1.71382426 | 1.82803912 |
| 8 | 1.36856905 | 1.42210061 | 1.47745544 | 1.59384807 | 1.71818617 | 1.85093021 | 1.99256264 |
| 9 | 1.42331181 | 1.48609514 | 1.55132822 | 1.68947896 | 1.83845921 | 1.99900462 | 2.17189327 |
| 10 | 1.48024428 | 1.55296942 | 1.62889463 | 1.79084770 | 1.96715135 | 2.15892499 | 2.36736367 |
| 11 | 1.53945406 | 1.62285305 | 1.71033936 | 1.89829856 | 2.10485195 | 2.33163899 | 2.58042640 |
| 12 | 1.60103222 | 1.69588143 | 1.79585633 | 2.01219647 | 2.25219158 | 2.51817011 | 2.81266478 |
| 13 | 1.66507351 | 1.77219610 | 1.88564914 | 2.13292826 | 2.40984500 | 2.71962372 | 3.06580461 |
| 14 | 1.73167645 | 1.85194492 | 1.97993160 | 2.26090396 | 2.57853415 | 2.93719362 | 3.34172702 |
| 15 | 1.80094351 | 1.93528244 | 2.07892818 | 2.39655819 | 2.75903154 | 3.17216911 | 3.64248245 |
| 16 | 1.87298125 | 2.02237015 | 2.18287459 | 2.54035168 | 2.95216374 | 3.42594264 | 3.97030588 |
| 17 | 1.94790050 | 2.11337681 | 2.29201832 | 2.69277279 | 3.15881521 | 3.70001805 | 4.32763341 |
| 18 | 2.02581652 | 2.20847877 | 2.40661923 | 2.85433915 | 3.37993227 | 3.99601949 | 4.71712041 |
| 19 | 2.10684918 | 2.30786031 | 2.52695020 | 3.02559950 | 3.61652753 | 4.31570105 | 5.14166125 |
| 20 | 2.19112314 | 2.41171402 | 2.65329771 | 3.20713547 | 3.86968446 | 4.66095714 | 5.60441076 |
| 21 | 2.27876807 | 2.52024116 | 2.78596259 | 3.39956360 | 4.14056237 | 5.03383371 | 6.10880773 |
| 22 | 2.36991879 | 2.63365201 | 2.92526072 | 3.60353742 | 4.43040174 | 5.43654041 | 6.65860043 |
| 23 | 2.46471554 | 2.75216635 | 3.07152376 | 3.81974966 | 4.74052986 | 5.87146364 | 7.25787447 |
| 24 | 2.56330416 | 2.87601383 | 3.22509994 | 4.04893464 | 5.07236695 | 6.34118073 | 7.91108317 |
| 25 | 2.66583633 | 3.00543446 | 3.38635494 | 4.29187072 | 5.42743264 | 6.84847519 | 8.62308066 |
| 26 | 2.77246978 | 3.14067901 | 3.55567269 | 4.54938296 | 5.80735292 | 7.39635321 | 9.39915791 |
| 27 | 2.88336858 | 3.28200956 | 3.73345632 | 4.82234594 | 6.21386762 | 7.98806146 | 10.24508213 |
| 28 | 2.99870332 | 3.42969999 | 3.92012914 | 5.11168670 | 6.64883836 | 8.62710638 | 11.16713952 |
| 29 | 3.11865145 | 3.58403649 | 4.11613560 | 5.41838790 | 7.11425704 | 9.31727489 | 12.17218208 |
| 30 | 3.24339751 | 3.74531813 | 4.32194238 | 5.74349117 | 7.61225504 | 10.06265688 | 13.26767846 |
| 31 | 3.37313301 | 3.91385745 | 4.53803949 | 6.08810064 | 8.14511289 | 10.86766944 | 14.46176953 |
| 32 | 3.50805875 | 4.08998104 | 4.76494147 | 6.45338668 | 8.71527079 | 11.73708299 | 15.76332878 |
| 33 | 3.64838110 | 4.27403018 | 5.00318854 | 6.84058988 | 9.32533975 | 12.67604963 | 17.18202838 |
| 34 | 3.79431634 | 4.46636154 | 5.25334797 | 7.25102529 | 9.97811353 | 13.69013360 | 18.72841093 |
| 35 | 3.94608899 | 4.66734781 | 5.51601537 | 7.68608600 | 10.67658148 | 14.78534429 | 20.41396791 |
| 36 | 4.10393255 | 4.87737846 | 5.79181614 | 8.14725220 | 11.42394218 | 15.96817183 | 22.25122503 |
| 37 | 4.26808986 | 5.09686049 | 6.08140694 | 8.63608712 | 12.22361814 | 17.24562558 | 24.25383528 |
| 38 | 4.43881345 | 5.32621921 | 6.38547729 | 9.15425235 | 13.07927141 | 18.62527563 | 26.43668045 |
| 39 | 4.61636599 | 5.56589908 | 6.60475115 | 9.70350749 | 13.99482041 | 20.11529768 | 28.81598170 |
| 40 | 4.80102063 | 5.81636454 | 7.03998871 | 10.28561794 | 14.97445783 | 21.72452149 | 31.40942005 |
| 41 | 4.99306145 | 6.07810094 | 7.39198815 | 10.90286101 | 16.02266988 | 23.46248321 | 34.23626785 |
| 42 | 5.19278391 | 6.35161548 | 7.76158756 | 11.55703677 | 17.14425678 | 25.33948187 | 37.31753196 |
| 43 | 5.40049527 | 6.63743818 | 8.14966693 | 12.25045463 | 18.34435475 | 27.36664042 | 40.67610984 |
| 44 | 5.61651508 | 6.93612290 | 8.55715028 | 12.98548191 | 19.62845958 | 29.55597165 | 44.33695972 |
| 45 | 5.84117568 | 7.24824843 | 8.98500779 | 13.76461083 | 21.00245175 | 31.92044939 | 48.32728610 |
| 46 | 6.07482271 | 7.57441961 | 9.43425818 | 14.59048748 | 22.47262338 | 34.47408534 | 52.67674185 |
| 47 | 6.31781562 | 7.91526849 | 9.90597109 | 15.46591673 | 24.04570701 | 37.23201216 | 57.41764862 |
| 48 | 6.57052824 | 8.27145557 | 10.40126965 | 16.39387178 | 25.72890650 | 40.21057314 | 62.58523699 |
| 49 | 6.83334937 | 8.64367107 | 10.92133313 | 17.37750403 | 27.52992996 | 43.42741899 | 68.21790832 |
| 50 | 7.10668335 | 9.03263627 | 11.46739979 | 18.42015427 | 29.45702506 | 46.90161251 | 74.35752007 |
| 55 | 8.64636692 | 11.25630817 | 14.63563092 | 24.65032159 | 41.31500148 | 68.91385611 | 114.40826161 |
| 60 | 10.51962741 | 14.02740793 | 18.67918589 | 32.98769085 | 57.94642683 | 101.25706366 | 176.03129196 |
| 65 | 12.79873522 | 17.48070239 | 23.83990056 | 44.41497165 | 81.27286124 | 148.77984662 | 270.84596262 |
| 70 | 15.57161835 | 21.78413558 | 30.42642554 | 59.07593018 | 113.98939219 | 218.60640590 | 416.73008617 |
| 75 | 18.94525466 | 27.14699629 | 38.83268592 | 79.05692079 | 159.87601930 | 321.20452995 | 641.19089332 |
| 80 | 23.04979907 | 33.83009643 | 49.56144107 | 105.79599348 | 224.23438757 | 471.95483426 | 986.55166812 |
| 85 | 28.04360494 | 42.15845513 | 63.25435344 | 141.57890449 | 314.50038238 | 693.45648896 | 1517.93202932 |
| 90 | 34.11933334 | 52.53710530 | 80.73036505 | 189.46451123 | 441.10297987 | 1018.91508927 | 2335.52658223 |
| 95 | 41.51138594 | 65.47079168 | 103.03467645 | 253.54625498 | 618.66974784 | 1497.12054855 | 3593.49714673 |
| 100 | 50.50494818 | 81.58851803 | 131.50125785 | 339.30208351 | 867.71632556 | 2199.76125634 | 5529.04079182 |

**PRESENT VALUE OF 1**

$$v^n = \frac{1}{(1+i)^n} = (1+i)^{-n}$$

| Periods | ½% | 1% | 1½% | 2% | 2½% | 3% | 3½% |
|---|---|---|---|---|---|---|---|
| 0 | 1. | 1. | 1. | 1. | 1. | 1. | 1. |
| 1 | 0.99502482 | 0.99009901 | 0.98522167 | 0.98039216 | 0.97560976 | 0.97087379 | 0.96618357 |
| 2 | 0.99007450 | 0.98029605 | 0.97066175 | 0.96116878 | 0.95181440 | 0.94259591 | 0.93351070 |
| 3 | 0.98514875 | 0.97059015 | 0.95631699 | 0.94232233 | 0.92859941 | 0.91514166 | 0.90192471 |
| 4 | 0.98024752 | 0.96098034 | 0.94218423 | 0.92384543 | 0.90595064 | 0.88848705 | 0.87144223 |
| 5 | 0.97537066 | 0.95146569 | 0.92826033 | 0.90573081 | 0.88385429 | 0.86260878 | 0.84197317 |
| 6 | 0.97051807 | 0.94204524 | 0.91454219 | 0.88797138 | 0.86229687 | 0.83748426 | 0.81350064 |
| 7 | 0.96568962 | 0.93271805 | 0.90102679 | 0.87056018 | 0.84126524 | 0.81309151 | 0.78599096 |
| 8 | 0.96088520 | 0.92348322 | 0.88771112 | 0.85349037 | 0.82074657 | 0.78940923 | 0.75941156 |
| 9 | 0.95610468 | 0.91433982 | 0.87459224 | 0.83675527 | 0.80072836 | 0.76641673 | 0.73373097 |
| 10 | 0.95134794 | 0.90528695 | 0.86166723 | 0.82034830 | 0.78119840 | 0.74409391 | 0.70891881 |
| 11 | 0.94661486 | 0.89632372 | 0.84893323 | 0.80426304 | 0.76214478 | 0.72242128 | 0.68494571 |
| 12 | 0.94190533 | 0.88744923 | 0.83638742 | 0.78849318 | 0.74355589 | 0.70137988 | 0.66178330 |
| 13 | 0.93721924 | 0.87866260 | 0.82402702 | 0.77303253 | 0.72542038 | 0.68095134 | 0.63940415 |
| 14 | 0.93255646 | 0.86996297 | 0.81184928 | 0.75787502 | 0.70772720 | 0.66111781 | 0.61778179 |
| 15 | 0.92791687 | 0.86134947 | 0.79985150 | 0.74301473 | 0.69046556 | 0.64186195 | 0.59689062 |
| 16 | 0.92330037 | 0.85282126 | 0.78803104 | 0.72844581 | 0.67362493 | 0.62316694 | 0.57670591 |
| 17 | 0.91870684 | 0.84437749 | 0.77638526 | 0.71416256 | 0.65719506 | 0.60501645 | 0.55720378 |
| 18 | 0.91413615 | 0.83601731 | 0.76491159 | 0.70015937 | 0.64116591 | 0.58739461 | 0.53836114 |
| 19 | 0.90958821 | 0.82773992 | 0.75360747 | 0.68643076 | 0.62552772 | 0.57028603 | 0.52015569 |
| 20 | 0.90506290 | 0.81954447 | 0.74247042 | 0.67297133 | 0.61027094 | 0.55367575 | 0.50256588 |
| 21 | 0.90056010 | 0.81143017 | 0.73149795 | 0.65977582 | 0.59538629 | 0.53754928 | 0.48557090 |
| 22 | 0.89607970 | 0.80339621 | 0.72068763 | 0.64683904 | 0.58086467 | 0.52189250 | 0.46915063 |
| 23 | 0.89162159 | 0.79544179 | 0.71003708 | 0.63415592 | 0.56669724 | 0.50669175 | 0.45328563 |
| 24 | 0.88718566 | 0.78756613 | 0.69954392 | 0.62172149 | 0.55287535 | 0.49193374 | 0.43795713 |
| 25 | 0.88277180 | 0.77976844 | 0.68920583 | 0.60953087 | 0.53939059 | 0.47760557 | 0.42314699 |
| 26 | 0.87837991 | 0.77204796 | 0.67902052 | 0.59757928 | 0.52623472 | 0.46369473 | 0.40883767 |
| 27 | 0.87400986 | 0.76440392 | 0.66898574 | 0.58586204 | 0.51339973 | 0.45018906 | 0.39501224 |
| 28 | 0.86966155 | 0.75683557 | 0.65909925 | 0.57437455 | 0.50087778 | 0.43707675 | 0.38165434 |
| 29 | 0.86533487 | 0.74934215 | 0.64935887 | 0.56311231 | 0.48866125 | 0.42434636 | 0.36874815 |
| 30 | 0.86102973 | 0.74192292 | 0.63976243 | 0.55207089 | 0.47674269 | 0.41198676 | 0.35627841 |
| 31 | 0.85674600 | 0.73457715 | 0.63030781 | 0.54124597 | 0.46511481 | 0.39998715 | 0.34423035 |
| 32 | 0.85248358 | 0.72730411 | 0.62099292 | 0.53063330 | 0.45377055 | 0.38833703 | 0.33258971 |
| 33 | 0.84824237 | 0.72010307 | 0.61181568 | 0.52022873 | 0.44270298 | 0.37702625 | 0.32134271 |
| 34 | 0.84402225 | 0.71297334 | 0.60277407 | 0.51002817 | 0.43190534 | 0.36604490 | 0.31047605 |
| 35 | 0.83982314 | 0.70591420 | 0.59386608 | 0.50002761 | 0.42137107 | 0.35538340 | 0.29997686 |
| 36 | 0.83564491 | 0.69892495 | 0.58508974 | 0.49022315 | 0.41109372 | 0.34503243 | 0.28983272 |
| 37 | 0.83148748 | 0.69200490 | 0.57644309 | 0.48061093 | 0.40106705 | 0.33498294 | 0.28003161 |
| 38 | 0.82735072 | 0.68515337 | 0.56792423 | 0.47118719 | 0.39128492 | 0.32522615 | 0.27056194 |
| 39 | 0.82323455 | 0.67836967 | 0.55953126 | 0.46194822 | 0.38174139 | 0.31575355 | 0.26141250 |
| 40 | 0.81913886 | 0.67165314 | 0.55126232 | 0.45289042 | 0.37243062 | 0.30655684 | 0.25257247 |
| 41 | 0.81506354 | 0.66500311 | 0.54311559 | 0.44401021 | 0.36334695 | 0.29762800 | 0.24403137 |
| 42 | 0.81100850 | 0.65841892 | 0.53508925 | 0.43530413 | 0.35448483 | 0.28895922 | 0.23577910 |
| 43 | 0.80697363 | 0.65189992 | 0.52718153 | 0.42676875 | 0.34583886 | 0.28054294 | 0.22780590 |
| 44 | 0.80295883 | 0.64544546 | 0.51939067 | 0.41840074 | 0.33740376 | 0.27237178 | 0.22010231 |
| 45 | 0.79896401 | 0.63905492 | 0.51171494 | 0.41019680 | 0.32917440 | 0.26443862 | 0.21265924 |
| 46 | 0.79498907 | 0.63272764 | 0.50415265 | 0.40215373 | 0.32114576 | 0.25673653 | 0.20546787 |
| 47 | 0.79103390 | 0.62646301 | 0.49670212 | 0.39426836 | 0.31331294 | 0.24925876 | 0.19851968 |
| 48 | 0.78709841 | 0.62026041 | 0.48936170 | 0.38653761 | 0.30567116 | 0.24199880 | 0.19180645 |
| 49 | 0.78318249 | 0.61411921 | 0.48212975 | 0.37895844 | 0.29821576 | 0.23495029 | 0.18532024 |
| 50 | 0.77928606 | 0.60803882 | 0.47500468 | 0.37152788 | 0.29094221 | 0.22810708 | 0.17905337 |
| 55 | 0.76009277 | 0.57852808 | 0.44092800 | 0.33650425 | 0.25715052 | 0.19676717 | 0.15075814 |
| 60 | 0.74137219 | 0.55044962 | 0.40929597 | 0.30478227 | 0.22728359 | 0.16973309 | 0.12693431 |
| 65 | 0.72311269 | 0.52373392 | 0.37993321 | 0.27605069 | 0.20088557 | 0.14641325 | 0.10687528 |
| 70 | 0.70530291 | 0.49831486 | 0.35267692 | 0.25002761 | 0.17755358 | 0.12629736 | 0.08998612 |
| 75 | 0.68793177 | 0.47412949 | 0.32737599 | 0.22645771 | 0.15693149 | 0.10894521 | 0.07576590 |
| 80 | 0.67098847 | 0.45111794 | 0.30389015 | 0.20510973 | 0.13870457 | 0.09397710 | 0.06379285 |
| 85 | 0.65446247 | 0.42922324 | 0.28208917 | 0.18577420 | 0.12259463 | 0.08106547 | 0.05371187 |
| 90 | 0.63834350 | 0.40839119 | 0.26185218 | 0.16826142 | 0.10835579 | 0.06992779 | 0.04522395 |
| 95 | 0.62262152 | 0.38857020 | 0.24306699 | 0.15239955 | 0.09577073 | 0.06032032 | 0.03807735 |
| 100 | 0.60728677 | 0.36971121 | 0.22562944 | 0.13803297 | 0.08464737 | 0.05203284 | 0.03206011 |

**PRESENT VALUE OF 1**

$$v^n = \frac{1}{(1+i)^n} = (1+i)^{-n}$$

| Periods | 4% | 4½% | 5% | 6% | 7% | 8% | 9% |
|---|---|---|---|---|---|---|---|
| 0 | 1. | 1. | 1. | 1. | 1. | 1. | 1. |
| 1 | 0.96153846 | 0.95693780 | 0.95238095 | 0.94339623 | 0.93457943 | 0.92592592 | 0.91743119 |
| 2 | 0.92455621 | 0.91572995 | 0.90702948 | 0.88999644 | 0.87343872 | 0.85733882 | 0.84167999 |
| 3 | 0.88899636 | 0.87629660 | 0.86383760 | 0.83961928 | 0.81629787 | 0.79383224 | 0.77218348 |
| 4 | 0.85480419 | 0.83856134 | 0.82270247 | 0.79209366 | 0.76289521 | 0.73502985 | 0.70842521 |
| 5 | 0.82192711 | 0.80245105 | 0.78352617 | 0.74725817 | 0.71298617 | 0.68058319 | 0.64993138 |
| 6 | 0.79031453 | 0.76789574 | 0.74621540 | 0.70496054 | 0.66634222 | 0.63016962 | 0.59626732 |
| 7 | 0.75991781 | 0.73482846 | 0.71068133 | 0.66505711 | 0.62274974 | 0.58349039 | 0.54703424 |
| 8 | 0.73069021 | 0.70318513 | 0.67683936 | 0.62741237 | 0.58200910 | 0.54026888 | 0.50186627 |
| 9 | 0.70258674 | 0.67290443 | 0.64460892 | 0.59189846 | 0.54393374 | 0.50024896 | 0.46042777 |
| 10 | 0.67556417 | 0.64392768 | 0.61391325 | 0.55839478 | 0.50834929 | 0.46319348 | 0.42241080 |
| 11 | 0.64958093 | 0.61619874 | 0.58467929 | 0.52678753 | 0.47509279 | 0.42888285 | 0.38753285 |
| 12 | 0.62459705 | 0.58966386 | 0.55683742 | 0.49696936 | 0.44401195 | 0.39711375 | 0.35553472 |
| 13 | 0.60057409 | 0.56471264 | 0.53032135 | 0.46883902 | 0.41496444 | 0.36769792 | 0.32617864 |
| 14 | 0.57747508 | 0.53997286 | 0.50506795 | 0.44230096 | 0.38781724 | 0.34046104 | 0.29924646 |
| 15 | 0.55526450 | 0.51672044 | 0.48101710 | 0.41726506 | 0.36244601 | 0.31524170 | 0.27453804 |
| 16 | 0.53390818 | 0.49446932 | 0.45811152 | 0.39364628 | 0.33873459 | 0.29189046 | 0.25186976 |
| 17 | 0.51337325 | 0.47317639 | 0.43629669 | 0.37136442 | 0.31657439 | 0.27026895 | 0.23107317 |
| 18 | 0.49362812 | 0.45280037 | 0.41552065 | 0.35034379 | 0.29586391 | 0.25024902 | 0.21199374 |
| 19 | 0.47464242 | 0.43330179 | 0.39573396 | 0.33051301 | 0.27650833 | 0.23171206 | 0.19448966 |
| 20 | 0.45638695 | 0.41464286 | 0.37688948 | 0.31180473 | 0.25841900 | 0.21454820 | 0.17843088 |
| 21 | 0.43883360 | 0.39678743 | 0.35894236 | 0.29415540 | 0.24151308 | 0.19865574 | 0.16369806 |
| 22 | 0.41295539 | 0.37970089 | 0.34184987 | 0.27750510 | 0.22571316 | 0.18394050 | 0.15018171 |
| 23 | 0.40572633 | 0.36335013 | 0.32557131 | 0.26179726 | 0.21094688 | 0.17031528 | 0.13778138 |
| 24 | 0.39012147 | 0.34770347 | 0.31006791 | 0.24697855 | 0.19714661 | 0.15769933 | 0.12640494 |
| 25 | 0.37511680 | 0.33273060 | 0.29530277 | 0.23299863 | 0.18424917 | 0.14601790 | 0.11596783 |
| 26 | 0.36068923 | 0.31840248 | 0.28124073 | 0.21981003 | 0.17219549 | 0.13520176 | 0.10639250 |
| 27 | 0.34681657 | 0.30469137 | 0.26784832 | 0.20736795 | 0.16093036 | 0.12518682 | 0.09760780 |
| 28 | 0.33347747 | 0.29157069 | 0.25509364 | 0.19563014 | 0.15040221 | 0.11591371 | 0.08954844 |
| 29 | 0.32065141 | 0.27901502 | 0.24294632 | 0.18455674 | 0.14056281 | 0.10732751 | 0.08215453 |
| 30 | 0.30831867 | 0.26700002 | 0.23137745 | 0.17411013 | 0.13136711 | 0.09937733 | 0.07537113 |
| 31 | 0.29646026 | 0.25550241 | 0.22035947 | 0.16425484 | 0.12277300 | 0.09201604 | 0.06914783 |
| 32 | 0.28505794 | 0.24449991 | 0.20986617 | 0.15495740 | 0.11474112 | 0.08520004 | 0.06343837 |
| 33 | 0.27409417 | 0.23397121 | 0.19987254 | 0.14618622 | 0.10723469 | 0.07888893 | 0.05820034 |
| 34 | 0.26355209 | 0.22389589 | 0.19035480 | 0.13791153 | 0.10021934 | 0.07304530 | 0.05339481 |
| 35 | 0.25341547 | 0.21425444 | 0.18129029 | 0.13010522 | 0.09366293 | 0.06763654 | 0.04898606 |
| 36 | 0.24366872 | 0.20502817 | 0.17265741 | 0.12274077 | 0.08753545 | 0.06262457 | 0.04494134 |
| 37 | 0.23429685 | 0.19619921 | 0.16443563 | 0.11579318 | 0.08180883 | 0.05798571 | 0.04123059 |
| 38 | 0.22528543 | 0.18775044 | 0.15660536 | 0.10923885 | 0.07645685 | 0.05369048 | 0.03782623 |
| 39 | 0.21662061 | 0.17966549 | 0.14914797 | 1.10305552 | 0.07145500 | 0.04971340 | 0.03470296 |
| 40 | 0.20828904 | 0.17192870 | 0.14204568 | 0.09722219 | 0.06678038 | 0.04603093 | 0.03183758 |
| 41 | 0.20027793 | 0.16452507 | 0.13528160 | 0.09171905 | 0.06241157 | 0.04262123 | 0.02920879 |
| 42 | 0.19257493 | 0.15744026 | 0.12883962 | 0.08652740 | 0.05832857 | 0.03946410 | 0.02679705 |
| 43 | 0.18516820 | 0.15066054 | 0.12270440 | 0.08162962 | 0.05451268 | 0.03654083 | 0.02458445 |
| 44 | 0.17804635 | 0.14417276 | 0.11686413 | 0.07700908 | 0.05094643 | 0.03383411 | 0.02255454 |
| 45 | 0.17119841 | 0.13796437 | 0.11129651 | 0.07265007 | 0.04761348 | 0.03132787 | 0.02069224 |
| 46 | 0.16461386 | 0.13202332 | 0.10599668 | 0.06853781 | 0.04449858 | 0.02900729 | 0.01898371 |
| 47 | 0.15828256 | 0.12633810 | 0.10094921 | 0.06465831 | 0.04158746 | 0.02685860 | 0.01741624 |
| 48 | 0.15219476 | 0.12089771 | 0.09614211 | 0.06099840 | 0.03886668 | 0.02486908 | 0.01597820 |
| 49 | 0.14634112 | 0.11569158 | 0.09156391 | 0.05754566 | 0.03632410 | 0.02302692 | 0.01465890 |
| 50 | 0.14071262 | 0.11070965 | 0.08720373 | 0.05428836 | 0.03394775 | 0.02132122 | 0.01344853 |
| 55 | 0.11565551 | 0.08883907 | 0.06832640 | 0.04056742 | 0.02420428 | 0.01451086 | 0.00874062 |
| 60 | 0.09506040 | 0.07128901 | 0.05353552 | 0.03031434 | 0.01725731 | 0.00987385 | 0.00568080 |
| 65 | 0.07813272 | 0.05720594 | 0.04194648 | 0.02265264 | 0.01230423 | 0.00672134 | 0.00369213 |
| 70 | 0.06421940 | 0.04590497 | 0.03286617 | 0.01692737 | 0.00877274 | 0.00457443 | 0.00239963 |
| 75 | 0.05278367 | 0.03683649 | 0.02575150 | 0.01264911 | 0.00625484 | 0.00311328 | 0.00155959 |
| 80 | 0.04338433 | 0.02955948 | 0.02017698 | 0.00945215 | 0.00445961 | 0.00211884 | 0.00101363 |
| 85 | 0.03565875 | 0.02372003 | 0.01580919 | 0.00706320 | 0.00317964 | 0.00144205 | 0.00065879 |
| 90 | 0.02930890 | 0.01903417 | 0.01238691 | 0.00527803 | 0.00226704 | 0.00098143 | 0.00042816 |
| 95 | 0.02408978 | 0.01527399 | 0.00970547 | 0.00394405 | 0.00161637 | 0.00066794 | 0.00027828 |
| 100 | 0.01980004 | 0.01225663 | 0.00760449 | 0.00294723 | 0.00115245 | 0.00045459 | 0.00018086 |

**AMOUNT OF AN ORDINARY ANNUITY OF 1**

$$s_{n\,i} = \frac{(1+i)^n - 1}{i}$$

| Periods | ½% | 1% | 1½% | 2% | 2½% | 3% | 3½% |
|---|---|---|---|---|---|---|---|
| 1 | 1.00000000 | 1. | 1. | 1. | 1. | 1. | 1. |
| 2 | 2.00500000 | 2.01 | 2.015 | 2.02 | 2.025 | 2.03 | 2.035 |
| 3 | 3.01502500 | 3.0301 | 3.045225 | 3.0604 | 3.075625 | 3.0909 | 3.106225 |
| 4 | 4.03010012 | 4.060401 | 4.09090338 | 4.121608 | 4.15251563 | 4.183627 | 4.21494288 |
| 5 | 5.05025062 | 5.10100501 | 5.15226693 | 5.20404016 | 5.25632852 | 5.30913581 | 5.36246588 |
| 6 | 6.07550187 | 6.15201506 | 6.22955093 | 6.30812096 | 6.38773673 | 6.46840988 | 6.55015218 |
| 7 | 7.10587938 | 7.21353521 | 7.32299419 | 7.43428338 | 7.54743015 | 7.66246218 | 7.77940751 |
| 8 | 8.14140878 | 8.28567056 | 8.43283911 | 8.58296905 | 8.73611590 | 8.89233605 | 9.05168677 |
| 9 | 9.18211582 | 9.36852727 | 9.55933169 | 9.75462843 | 9.95451880 | 10.15910613 | 10.36849581 |
| 10 | 10.22802640 | 10.46221254 | 10.70272167 | 10.94972100 | 11.20338177 | 11.46387931 | 11.73139316 |
| 11 | 11.27916654 | 11.56683467 | 11.86326249 | 12.16871542 | 12.48346631 | 12.80779569 | 13.14199192 |
| 12 | 12.33556237 | 12.68250301 | 13.04121143 | 13.41208973 | 13.79555297 | 14.19202956 | 14.60196164 |
| 13 | 13.39724018 | 13.80932804 | 14.23682960 | 14.68033152 | 15.14044179 | 15.61779045 | 16.11303030 |
| 14 | 14.46422638 | 14.94742132 | 15.45038205 | 15.97393815 | 16.51895284 | 17.08632416 | 17.67698636 |
| 15 | 15.53654751 | 16.09689554 | 16.68213778 | 17.29341692 | 17.93192666 | 18.59891389 | 19.29568088 |
| 16 | 16.61423025 | 17.25786449 | 17.93236984 | 18.63928525 | 19.38022483 | 20.15688130 | 20.97102971 |
| 17 | 17.69730140 | 18.43044314 | 19.20135539 | 20.01207096 | 20.86473045 | 21.76158774 | 22.70501575 |
| 18 | 18.78578791 | 19.61474757 | 20.48937572 | 21.41231238 | 22.38634871 | 23.41443537 | 24.49969130 |
| 19 | 19.87971685 | 20.81089504 | 21.79671636 | 22.84055863 | 23.94600743 | 25.11686844 | 26.35718050 |
| 20 | 20.97911543 | 22.01900399 | 23.12366710 | 24.29736980 | 25.54465761 | 26.87037449 | 28.27968181 |
| 21 | 22.08401101 | 23.23919403 | 24.47052211 | 25.78331719 | 27.18327405 | 28.67648572 | 30.26947068 |
| 22 | 23.19443106 | 24.47158598 | 25.83757994 | 27.29898354 | 28.86285590 | 30.53678030 | 32.32890215 |
| 23 | 24.31040322 | 25.71630183 | 27.22514364 | 28.84496321 | 30.58442730 | 32.45288370 | 34.46041373 |
| 24 | 25.43195524 | 26.97346485 | 28.63352080 | 30.42186247 | 32.34903798 | 34.42647022 | 36.66652821 |
| 25 | 26.55911501 | 28.24319950 | 30.06302361 | 32.03029972 | 34.15776393 | 36.45926432 | 38.94985669 |
| 26 | 27.69191059 | 29.52563150 | 31.51396896 | 33.67090572 | 36.01170803 | 38.55304225 | 41.31310168 |
| 27 | 28.83037014 | 30.82088781 | 32.98667850 | 35.34432383 | 37.91200073 | 40.70963352 | 43.75906024 |
| 28 | 31.12439460 | 32.12909669 | 34.48147867 | 37.05121031 | 39.85980075 | 42.93092252 | 46.29062734 |
| 29 | 29.97452199 | 33.45038766 | 35.99870085 | 38.79223451 | 41.85629577 | 45.21885020 | 48.91079930 |
| 30 | 32.28001657 | 34.78489153 | 37.53868137 | 40.56807921 | 43.90270316 | 47.57541571 | 51.62267728 |
| 31 | 33.44141666 | 36.13274045 | 39.10176159 | 42.37944079 | 46.00027074 | 50.00267818 | 54.42947098 |
| 32 | 34.60862374 | 37.49406785 | 40.68828801 | 44.22702961 | 48.15027751 | 52.50275852 | 57.33450247 |
| 33 | 35.78166686 | 38.86900853 | 42.29861233 | 46.11157020 | 50.35403445 | 55.07784128 | 60.34121005 |
| 34 | 36.96057519 | 40.25769862 | 43.93309152 | 48.03380160 | 52.61288531 | 57.73017652 | 63.45415240 |
| 35 | 38.14537807 | 41.66027560 | 45.59208789 | 49.99447763 | 54.92820744 | 60.46208181 | 66.67401274 |
| 36 | 39.33610496 | 43.07687836 | 47.27596921 | 51.99436719 | 57.30141263 | 63.27594427 | 70.00760318 |
| 37 | 40.53278548 | 44.50764714 | 48.98510874 | 54.03425453 | 59.73394794 | 66.17422259 | 73.45786930 |
| 38 | 41.73544941 | 45.95272361 | 50.71988538 | 56.11493962 | 62.22729664 | 69.15944927 | 77.02889472 |
| 39 | 42.94412666 | 47.41225085 | 52.48068366 | 58.23723841 | 64.78297906 | 72.23423275 | 80.72490604 |
| 40 | 44.15884729 | 48.88637336 | 54.26789391 | 60.40198318 | 67.40255354 | 75.40125973 | 84.55027775 |
| 41 | 45.37964153 | 50.37523709 | 56.08191352 | 62.61002284 | 70.08761737 | 78.66329753 | 88.50953747 |
| 42 | 46.60653974 | 51.87898946 | 57.92314100 | 64.86222330 | 72.83980781 | 82.02319645 | 92.60737128 |
| 43 | 47.83957244 | 53.39777936 | 59.79198812 | 67.15946777 | 75.66080300 | 85.48389234 | 96.84862928 |
| 44 | 49.07877030 | 54.93175715 | 61.68886794 | 69.50265712 | 78.55232308 | 89.04840911 | 101.23833130 |
| 45 | 50.32416415 | 56.48107472 | 63.61420096 | 71.89271027 | 81.51613116 | 92.71986139 | 105.78167290 |
| 46 | 51.57578497 | 58.04588547 | 65.56841398 | 74.33056447 | 84.55403443 | 96.50145723 | 110.48403145 |
| 47 | 52.83366389 | 59.62634432 | 67.55194018 | 76.81717576 | 87.66788530 | 100.39650095 | 115.35097255 |
| 48 | 54.09783221 | 61.22260777 | 69.56521929 | 79.35351927 | 90.85958243 | 104.40839598 | 120.38825659 |
| 49 | 55.36832138 | 62.83483385 | 71.60869758 | 81.94058966 | 94.13107199 | 108.54064785 | 125.60184557 |
| 50 | 56.64516298 | 64.46318218 | 73.68282804 | 84.57940145 | 97.48434879 | 112.79686729 | 130.99791016 |
| 55 | 63.12577496 | 72.85245735 | 84.52959893 | 98.58653365 | 115.55092136 | 136.07161972 | 160.94688984 |
| 60 | 69.77003050 | 81.66696986 | 96.21465171 | 114.05153942 | 135.99158995 | 163.05343680 | 196.51688288 |
| 65 | 76.58206183 | 90.93664882 | 108.80277215 | 131.12615541 | 159.11833027 | 194.33275782 | 238.76287650 |
| 70 | 83.56610549 | 100.67633684 | 122.36375295 | 149.97791114 | 185.28411421 | 230.59406374 | 288.93786459 |

## AMOUNT OF AN ORDINARY ANNUITY OF I

$$s_{n\,i} = \frac{(1+i)^n - 1}{i}$$

| Periods | 4% | 4½% | 5% | 6% | 7% | 8% | 9% |
|---|---|---|---|---|---|---|---|
| 1 | 1. | 1. | 1. | 1. | 1.00000000 | 1.00000000 | 1.00000000 |
| 2 | 2.04 | 2.045 | 2.05 | 2.06 | 2.07000000 | 2.08000000 | 2.09000000 |
| 3 | 3.1216 | 3.137025 | 3.1525 | 3.1836 | 3.21490000 | 3.24640000 | 3.27810000 |
| 4 | 4.246464 | 4.278191113 | 4.310125 | 4.374616 | 4.43994300 | 4.50611200 | 4.57312900 |
| 5 | 5.41632256 | 5.47070973 | 5.52563125 | 5.63709296 | 5.75073901 | 5.86660096 | 5.98471061 |
| 6 | 6.63297546 | 6.71689166 | 6.80191281 | 6.97531854 | 7.15329074 | 7.33592903 | 7.52333456 |
| 7 | 7.89829448 | 8.01915179 | 8.14200845 | 8.39383765 | 8.65402109 | 8.92280335 | 9.20043467 |
| 8 | 9.21422626 | 9.38001362 | 9.54910888 | 9.89746791 | 10.25980256 | 10.63662762 | 11.02847379 |
| 9 | 10.58279531 | 10.80211423 | 11.02656432 | 11.49131598 | 11.97798874 | 12.48755783 | 13.02103643 |
| 10 | 12.00610712 | 12.28820937 | 12.57789254 | 13.18079494 | 13.81644796 | 14.48656246 | 15.19292971 |
| 11 | 13.48635141 | 13.84117879 | 14.20678716 | 14.97164264 | 15.78359931 | 16.64548746 | 17.56029339 |
| 12 | 15.02580546 | 15.46403184 | 15.91712652 | 16.86994120 | 17.88845127 | 18.97712646 | 20.14071979 |
| 13 | 16.62683768 | 17.15991327 | 17.71298285 | 18.88213767 | 20.14064285 | 21.49529657 | 22.95338457 |
| 14 | 18.29191119 | 18.93210937 | 19.59863199 | 21.01506593 | 22.55048786 | 24.21492030 | 26.01918919 |
| 15 | 20.02358764 | 20.78405429 | 21.57856359 | 23.27596988 | 25.12902201 | 27.15211392 | 29.36091621 |
| 16 | 21.82453114 | 22.71933673 | 23.65749177 | 25.67252808 | 27.88805355 | 30.32428304 | 33.00339867 |
| 17 | 23.69751239 | 24.74170689 | 25.84036636 | 28.21287976 | 30.84021729 | 33.75022568 | 36.97370455 |
| 18 | 25.64541288 | 26.85508370 | 28.13238467 | 30.90565253 | 33.99903251 | 37.45024373 | 41.30133796 |
| 19 | 27.67122940 | 29.06356246 | 30.53900391 | 33.75999170 | 37.37896478 | 41.44626323 | 46.01845838 |
| 20 | 29.77807858 | 31.37142277 | 33.06595410 | 36.78559120 | 40.99549232 | 45.76196429 | 51.16011964 |
| 21 | 31.96920172 | 33.78313680 | 35.71925181 | 39.99272668 | 44.86517678 | 50.42292144 | 56.76453040 |
| 22 | 34.24796979 | 36.30337795 | 38.50521440 | 43.39229028 | 49.00573915 | 55.45675515 | 62.87333814 |
| 23 | 36.61788858 | 38.93702996 | 41.43047512 | 46.99582769 | 53.43614089 | 60.89329556 | 69.53193857 |
| 24 | 39.08260412 | 41.68919631 | 44.50199887 | 50.81557735 | 58.17667076 | 66.76475921 | 76.78981305 |
| 25 | 41.64590829 | 44.56521015 | 47.72709882 | 54.86451200 | 63.24903771 | 73.10593995 | 84.70089622 |
| 26 | 44.31174462 | 47.57064460 | 51.11345376 | 59.15638272 | 68.67647035 | 79.95441514 | 93.32397688 |
| 27 | 47.08421440 | 50.71132361 | 54.66912645 | 63.70576568 | 74.48382323 | 87.35076836 | 102.72313480 |
| 28 | 49.96758298 | 53.99333317 | 58.40258277 | 68.52811162 | 80.69769091 | 95.33882982 | 112.96821693 |
| 29 | 52.96628630 | 57.42303316 | 62.32271191 | 73.63979832 | 87.34652927 | 103.96593621 | 124.13535646 |
| 30 | 56.08493775 | 61.00706966 | 66.43884750 | 79.05818622 | 94.46078632 | 113.28321111 | 136.30753854 |
| 31 | 59.32833526 | 64.75238779 | 70.76078988 | 84.80167739 | 102.07304136 | 123.34586800 | 149.57521701 |
| 32 | 62.70146867 | 68.66624524 | 75.29882937 | 90.88977803 | 110.21815426 | 134.21353744 | 164.03698654 |
| 33 | 66.20952742 | 72.75622628 | 80.06377084 | 97.34316471 | 118.93342506 | 145.95062043 | 179.80031533 |
| 34 | 69.85790851 | 77.03025646 | 85.06695938 | 104.18375460 | 128.25876481 | 158.62667007 | 196.98234371 |
| 35 | 73.65222486 | 81.49661800 | 90.32030735 | 111.43477987 | 138.23687835 | 172.31680367 | 215.71075465 |
| 36 | 77.59831385 | 86.16396581 | 95.83632272 | 119.12086666 | 148.91345805 | 187.10214797 | 236.12472256 |
| 37 | 81.70224640 | 91.04134427 | 101.62813886 | 127.26811866 | 160.33740202 | 203.07031981 | 258.37594759 |
| 38 | 85.97033626 | 96.13820476 | 107.70954580 | 135.90420578 | 172.56102016 | 220.31594539 | 282.62978288 |
| 39 | 90.40914971 | 101.46442398 | 114.09502309 | 145.05845813 | 185.64029157 | 238.94122102 | 309.06646334 |
| 40 | 95.02551570 | 107.03032306 | 120.79977424 | 154.76196562 | 199.63511198 | 259.05651871 | 337.88244504 |
| 41 | 99.82653633 | 112.84668760 | 127.83976295 | 165.04768356 | 214.60956982 | 280.78104020 | 369.29186509 |
| 42 | 104.81959778 | 118.92478854 | 135.23175110 | 175.95054457 | 230.63223971 | 304.24352342 | 403.52813295 |
| 43 | 110.01238169 | 125.27640402 | 142.99333866 | 187.50757724 | 247.77649649 | 329.58300529 | 440.84566492 |
| 44 | 115.41287696 | 131.91384220 | 151.14300559 | 199.75803188 | 266.12085125 | 356.94964572 | 481.52177476 |
| 45 | 121.02939204 | 138.84996510 | 159.70015587 | 212.74351379 | 285.74931083 | 386.50561737 | 525.85873449 |
| 46 | 126.87056772 | 146.09821353 | 168.68516366 | 226.50812462 | 306.75176259 | 418.42606676 | 574.18602060 |
| 47 | 132.94539043 | 153.67263314 | 178.11942185 | 241.09861210 | 329.22438597 | 452.90015211 | 626.86276245 |
| 48 | 139.26320604 | 161.58790163 | 188.02539294 | 256.56452882 | 353.27009299 | 490.13216427 | 684.28041107 |
| 49 | 145.83373429 | 169.85935720 | 198.42666259 | 272.95840055 | 378.99899950 | 530.34273742 | 746.86564807 |
| 50 | 152.66708366 | 178.50302828 | 209.34799572 | 290.33590458 | 406.52892947 | 573.77015641 | 815.08355639 |
| 55 | 191.15917299 | 227.91795938 | 272.71261833 | 394.17202657 | 575.92859262 | 848.92320141 | 1260.09179572 |
| 60 | 237.99068520 | 289.49795398 | 353.58371788 | 533.12818089 | 813.52038335 | 1253.21329584 | 1944.79213289 |
| 65 | 294.96838045 | 366.23783096 | 456.79801118 | 719.08286076 | 1146.75516063 | 1847.24808275 | 2998.28847357 |
| 70 | 364.29045876 | 461.86967955 | 588.52851071 | 967.93216905 | 1614.13417425 | 2720.08007377 | 4619.22317975 |

## PRESENT VALUE OF AN ORDINARY ANNUITY OF 1

$$a_{n\,i} = \frac{1 - \dfrac{1}{(1+i)^n}}{i} = \frac{1 - v^n}{i}$$

| | ½% | 1% | 1½% | 2% | 2½% | 3% | 3½% |
|---|---|---|---|---|---|---|---|
| 1 | .99502487 | 0.99009901 | 0.98522167 | 0.98039216 | 0.97560976 | 0.97087379 | 0.96618357 |
| 2 | 1.98509937 | 1.97039506 | 1.95588342 | 1.94156094 | 1.92742415 | 1.91346970 | 1.89969428 |
| 3 | 2.97024813 | 2.94098521 | 2.91220042 | 2.88388327 | 2.85602356 | 2.82861135 | 2.80163698 |
| 4 | 3.95049565 | 3.90196555 | 3.85438465 | 3.80772870 | 3.76197421 | 3.71709840 | 3.67307921 |
| 5 | 4.92586632 | 4.85343124 | 4.78264497 | 4.71345951 | 4.64582850 | 4.57970719 | 4.51505238 |
| 6 | 5.89638440 | 5.79547647 | 5.69718717 | 5.60143089 | 5.50812536 | 5.41719144 | 5.32855302 |
| 7 | 6.86207403 | 6.72819453 | 6.59821396 | 6.47199107 | 6.34939060 | 6.23028296 | 6.11454398 |
| 8 | 7.82295923 | 7.65167775 | 7.48592508 | 7.32548144 | 7.17013717 | 7.01969219 | 6.87395554 |
| 9 | 8.77906392 | 8.56601758 | 8.36051732 | 8.16223671 | 7.97086553 | 7.78610892 | 7.60768651 |
| 10 | 9.73041186 | 9.47130453 | 9.22218455 | 8.98258501 | 8.75206393 | 8.53020284 | 8.31660532 |
| 11 | 10.67702672 | 10.36762825 | 10.07111779 | 9.78684805 | 9.51420871 | 9.25262411 | 9.00155104 |
| 12 | 11.61893206 | 11.25507747 | 10.90750521 | 10.57534122 | 10.25776460 | 9.95400399 | 9.66333433 |
| 13 | 12.55615131 | 12.13374007 | 11.73153222 | 11.34837375 | 10.98318497 | 10.63495533 | 10.30273849 |
| 14 | 13.48870777 | 13.00370304 | 12.54338150 | 12.10624877 | 11.69091217 | 11.29607314 | 10.92052028 |
| 15 | 14.41662464 | 13.86505252 | 13.34323301 | 12.84926350 | 12.38137773 | 11.93793509 | 11.51741090 |
| 16 | 15.33992502 | 14.71787378 | 14.13126405 | 13.57770931 | 13.05500266 | 12.56110203 | 12.09411681 |
| 17 | 16.25863186 | 15.56225127 | 14.90764931 | 14.29187188 | 13.71219772 | 13.16611847 | 12.65132059 |
| 18 | 17.17276802 | 16.39826858 | 15.67256089 | 14.99203125 | 14.35336363 | 13.75351308 | 13.18968173 |
| 19 | 18.08235624 | 17.22600850 | 16.42616837 | 15.67846201 | 14.97889134 | 14.32379911 | 13.70983742 |
| 20 | 18.98741914 | 18.04555297 | 17.16863879 | 16.35143334 | 15.58916229 | 14.87747486 | 14.21240330 |
| 21 | 19.88797925 | 18.85698313 | 17.90013673 | 17.01120916 | 16.18454857 | 15.41502414 | 14.69797420 |
| 22 | 20.78405895 | 19.66037934 | 18.62082437 | 17.65804820 | 16.76541324 | 15.93691664 | 15.16712484 |
| 23 | 21.67568055 | 20.45582113 | 19.33086145 | 18.29220412 | 17.33211048 | 16.44360839 | 15.62041047 |
| 24 | 22.56286622 | 21.24338726 | 20.03040537 | 18.91392560 | 17.88498583 | 16.93554212 | 16.05836760 |
| 25 | 23.44563803 | 22.02315570 | 20.71961120 | 19.52345647 | 18.42437642 | 17.41314769 | 16.48151459 |
| 26 | 24.32401794 | 22.79520366 | 21.39863172 | 20.12103576 | 18.95061114 | 17.87684242 | 16.89035226 |
| 27 | 25.19802780 | 23.55960759 | 22.06761746 | 20.70689780 | 19.46401087 | 18.32703147 | 17.28536451 |
| 28 | 26.06768935 | 24.31644316 | 22.72671671 | 21.28127236 | 19.96488866 | 18.76410823 | 17.66701885 |
| 29 | 26.93302423 | 25.06578530 | 23.37607558 | 21.84438466 | 20.45354991 | 19.18845459 | 18.03576700 |
| 30 | 27.79405396 | 25.80770822 | 24.01583801 | 22.39645555 | 20.93029259 | 19.60044135 | 18.39204541 |
| 31 | 28.65079996 | 26.54228537 | 24.64614582 | 22.93770152 | 21.39540741 | 20.00042849 | 18.73627576 |
| 32 | 29.50328354 | 27.26958947 | 25.26713874 | 23.46833482 | 21.84917796 | 20.38876553 | 19.06886547 |
| 33 | 30.35152591 | 27.98969255 | 25.87895442 | 23.98856355 | 22.29188094 | 20.76579178 | 19.39020818 |
| 34 | 31.19554817 | 28.70266589 | 26.48172849 | 24.49859172 | 22.72378628 | 21.13183668 | 19.70068423 |
| 35 | 32.03537132 | 29.40858009 | 27.07559458 | 24.99861933 | 23.14515734 | 21.48722007 | 20.00066110 |
| 36 | 32.87101623 | 30.10750504 | 27.66068431 | 25.48884248 | 23.55625107 | 21.83225250 | 20.29049381 |
| 37 | 33.70250372 | 30.79950994 | 28.23712740 | 25.96945341 | 23.95731812 | 22.16723544 | 20.57052542 |
| 38 | 34.52985444 | 31.48466330 | 28.80505163 | 26.44064060 | 24.34860304 | 22.49246159 | 20.84108736 |
| 39 | 35.35308900 | 32.16303298 | 29.36458288 | 26.90258883 | 24.73034443 | 22.80821513 | 21.10249987 |
| 40 | 36.17222786 | 32.83468611 | 29.91584520 | 27.35547924 | 25.10277505 | 23.11477197 | 21.35507234 |
| 41 | 36.98729140 | 33.49968922 | 30.45896079 | 27.79948945 | 25.46612200 | 23.41239997 | 21.59910371 |
| 42 | 37.79829990 | 34.15860814 | 30.99405004 | 28.23479358 | 25.82060683 | 23.70135920 | 21.83488281 |
| 43 | 38.60527353 | 34.81000806 | 31.52123157 | 28.66156233 | 26.16644569 | 23.98190213 | 22.06268870 |
| 44 | 39.40823237 | 35.45545352 | 32.04062223 | 29.07996307 | 26.50384945 | 24.25427392 | 22.28279102 |
| 45 | 40.20719639 | 36.09450844 | 32.55233718 | 29.49015987 | 26.83302386 | 24.51871254 | 22.49545026 |
| 46 | 41.00218546 | 36.72723608 | 33.05648983 | 29.89231360 | 27.15416962 | 24.77544907 | 22.70091813 |
| 47 | 41.79321937 | 37.35369909 | 33.55319195 | 30.28658196 | 27.46748255 | 25.02470783 | 22.89943780 |
| 48 | 42.58031778 | 37.97395949 | 34.04255365 | 30.67311957 | 27.77315371 | 25.26670664 | 23.09124425 |
| 49 | 43.36350028 | 38.58807871 | 34.52468339 | 31.05207801 | 28.07136947 | 25.50165693 | 23.27656450 |
| 50 | 44.14278634 | 39.19611753 | 34.99968807 | 31.42360589 | 28.36231168 | 25.72976401 | 23.45561787 |
| 55 | 47.98144535 | 42.14719216 | 37.27146681 | 33.17478752 | 29.71397928 | 26.77442764 | 24.26405323 |
| 60 | 51.72556075 | 44.95503841 | 39.38026889 | 34.76088668 | 30.90865649 | 27.67556367 | 24.94473412 |
| 65 | 55.37746108 | 47.62660777 | 41.33778618 | 36.19746555 | 31.96457705 | 28.45289152 | 25.51784916 |
| 70 | 58.93941756 | 50.16851435 | 43.15487183 | 37.49861929 | 32.89785698 | 29.12342135 | 26.00039664 |
| 75 | 62.41364542 | 52.58705124 | 44.84160034 | 38.67711433 | 33.72274044 | 29.70182628 | 26.40668868 |
| 80 | 65.80230538 | 54.88820611 | 46.40732349 | 39.74451359 | 34.45181722 | 30.20076345 | 26.74877567 |
| 85 | 69.10750491 | 57.07767600 | 47.86072218 | 40.71128999 | 35.09621486 | 30.63115103 | 27.03680373 |
| 90 | 72.33129958 | 59.16088148 | 49.20985452 | 41.58692916 | 35.66576848 | 31.00240714 | 27.27931564 |
| 95 | 75.47569434 | 61.14298002 | 50.46220054 | 42.38002254 | 36.16917089 | 31.32265592 | 27.48350415 |
| 100 | 78.54264476 | 63.02887877 | 51.62470367 | 43.09835164 | 36.61410526 | 31.59890534 | 27.65542540 |

## PRESENT VALUE OF AN ORDINARY ANNUITY OF I

$$a_{n\ i} = \frac{1 - \dfrac{1}{(1+i)^n}}{i} = \frac{1 - v^n}{i}$$

| Periods | 4% | 4½% | 5% | 6% | 7% | 8% | 9% |
|---|---|---|---|---|---|---|---|
| 1 | 0.96153846 | 0.95693780 | 0.95238095 | 0.94339623 | .93457943 | .92592592 | .91743119 |
| 2 | 1.88609467 | 1.87266775 | 1.85941043 | 1.83339267 | 1.80801816 | 1.78326474 | 1.75911118 |
| 3 | 2.77509103 | 2.74896435 | 2.72324803 | 2.67301195 | 2.62431604 | 2.57709698 | 2.53129466 |
| 4 | 3.62989522 | 3.58752570 | 3.54595050 | 3.46510561 | 3.38721125 | 3.31212684 | 3.23971987 |
| 5 | 4.45182233 | 4.38997674 | 4.32947667 | 4.21236379 | 4.10019743 | 3.99271003 | 3.88965126 |
| 6 | 5.24213686 | 5.15787248 | 5.07569206 | 4.91732433 | 4.76653965 | 4.62287966 | 4.48591859 |
| 7 | 6.00205467 | 5.89270094 | 5.78637340 | 5.58238144 | 5.8928940 | 5.60537005 | 5.03295283 |
| 8 | 6.73274487 | 6.59588607 | 6.46321276 | 6.20979381 | 5.97129850 | 5.74663894 | 5.53481911 |
| 9 | 7.43533161 | 7.26879050 | 7.10782168 | 6.80169227 | 6.51523224 | 6.24688791 | 5.99524689 |
| 10 | 8.11089578 | 7.91271818 | 7.72173493 | 7.36008706 | 7.02358154 | 6.71008139 | 6.41765770 |
| 11 | 8.76047671 | 8.52891692 | 8.30641422 | 7.88687458 | 7.49867433 | 7.13896425 | 6.80519055 |
| 12 | 9.38507376 | 9.11858076 | 8.86325164 | 8.38384394 | 7.94268629 | 7.53607801 | 7.16072527 |
| 13 | 9.98564785 | 9.68285242 | 9.39357299 | 8.85268296 | 8.35765074 | 7.90377594 | 7.48690392 |
| 14 | 10.56312293 | 10.22282528 | 9.89864094 | 9.29498393 | 8.74546798 | 8.24423698 | 7.78615038 |
| 15 | 11.11838743 | 10.73954573 | 10.37965804 | 9.71224899 | 9.10791400 | 8.55947868 | 8.06068842 |
| 16 | 11.65229561 | 11.23401505 | 10.83776956 | 10.10589527 | 9.44664860 | 8.85136915 | 8.31255819 |
| 17 | 12.16566885 | 11.70719143 | 11.27406625 | 10.47725969 | 9.76322299 | 9.12163810 | 8.54363136 |
| 18 | 12.65929697 | 12.15999180 | 11.68959690 | 10.82760348 | 10.05908690 | 9.37188713 | 8.75562510 |
| 19 | 13.13393940 | 12.59329359 | 12.08532086 | 11.15811649 | 10.33550524 | 9.60359920 | 8.95011477 |
| 20 | 13.59032634 | 13.00793645 | 12.46221034 | 11.46992122 | 10.59401424 | 9.81814740 | 9.12854566 |
| 21 | 14.02915995 | 13.40472388 | 12.82115271 | 11.76407662 | 10.83552733 | 10.01680315 | 9.29224373 |
| 22 | 14.45111533 | 13.78442476 | 13.16300258 | 12.04158172 | 11.06124049 | 10.20074366 | 9.44242544 |
| 23 | 14.85684167 | 14.14777489 | 13.48857388 | 12.30337898 | 11.27218738 | 10.37105894 | 9.58020682 |
| 24 | 15.24696314 | 14.49547837 | 13.79864179 | 12.55035753 | 11.46933400 | 10.52875828 | 9.70661176 |
| 25 | 15.62207994 | 14.82820896 | 14.09394457 | 12.78335616 | 11.65358317 | 10.67477618 | 9.82257960 |
| 26 | 15.98276918 | 15.14661145 | 14.37518530 | 13.00316619 | 11.82577867 | 10.80997795 | 9.92897211 |
| 27 | 16.32958575 | 15.45130282 | 14.64303362 | 13.21053414 | 11.98670903 | 10.93516477 | 10.02657992 |
| 28 | 16.66306322 | 15.74287351 | 14.89812726 | 13.40616428 | 12.13711125 | 11.05107849 | 10.11612836 |
| 29 | 16.98371463 | 16.02188853 | 15.14107358 | 13.59072102 | 12.27767406 | 11.15840601 | 10.19828290 |
| 30 | 17.29203330 | 16.28888854 | 15.37245103 | 13.76483115 | 12.40904181 | 11.25778334 | 10.27365404 |
| 31 | 17.58849356 | 16.54439095 | 15.59281050 | 13.92908599 | 12.53181419 | 11.34979939 | 10.34280187 |
| 32 | 17.87355150 | 16.78889088 | 15.80267667 | 14.08404339 | 12.64655521 | 11.43499943 | 10.40624025 |
| 33 | 18.14764567 | 17.02286207 | 16.00254921 | 14.23022961 | 12.75379001 | 11.51388836 | 10.46444059 |
| 34 | 18.41119776 | 17.24675796 | 16.19290401 | 14.36814114 | 12.85400936 | 11.58693367 | 10.51783541 |
| 35 | 18.66461323 | 17.46101240 | 16.37419429 | 14.49824636 | 12.94767230 | 11.65456821 | 10.56682147 |
| 36 | 18.90828195 | 17.66604058 | 16.54685171 | 14.62098713 | 13.03520775 | 11.71719279 | 10.61176282 |
| 37 | 19.14257880 | 17.86223979 | 16.71128734 | 14.73678031 | 13.11701659 | 11.77517851 | 10.65299341 |
| 38 | 19.36786423 | 18.04999023 | 16.86789271 | 14.84601916 | 13.19347345 | 11.82886899 | 10.69081964 |
| 39 | 19.58448484 | 18.22965572 | 17.01704067 | 14.94907468 | 13.26492846 | 11.87858240 | 10.72552261 |
| 40 | 19.79277388 | 18.40158442 | 17.15908635 | 15.04629687 | 13.33180884 | 11.92461333 | 10.75736019 |
| 41 | 19.99305181 | 18.56610949 | 17.29436796 | 15.13801592 | 13.39412401 | 11.96723456 | 10.78656898 |
| 42 | 20.18562674 | 18.72354975 | 17.42320758 | 15.22454332 | 13.45244898 | 12.00669867 | 10.81336604 |
| 43 | 20.37079494 | 18.87421029 | 17.54591198 | 15.30617294 | 13.50696166 | 12.04323951 | 10.83795049 |
| 44 | 20.54884129 | 19.01838305 | 17.66277331 | 15.38318202 | 13.55790810 | 12.07707362 | 10.86050504 |
| 45 | 20.72003970 | 19.15634742 | 17.77406982 | 15.45583209 | 13.60552158 | 12.10840150 | 10.88119728 |
| 46 | 20.88465356 | 19.28837074 | 17.88006650 | 15.52436990 | 13.65002017 | 12.13740879 | 10.90018099 |
| 47 | 21.04293612 | 19.41470884 | 17.98101571 | 15.58902821 | 13.69160764 | 12.16426740 | 10.91759724 |
| 48 | 21.19513088 | 19.53560654 | 18.07715782 | 15.65002661 | 13.73047443 | 12.18913648 | 10.93357545 |
| 49 | 21.34147200 | 19.65129813 | 18.16872173 | 15.70757227 | 13.76679853 | 12.21216341 | 10.94823436 |
| 50 | 21.48218462 | 19.76200778 | 18.25592546 | 15.76186064 | 13.80074629 | 12.23348464 | 10.96168290 |
| 55 | 22.10861218 | 20.24802057 | 18.63347196 | 15.99054297 | 13.93993881 | 12.31861412 | 11.01399302 |
| 60 | 22.62348997 | 20.63802204 | 18.92928952 | 16.16142771 | 14.03918115 | 12.37655182 | 11.04799102 |
| 65 | 23.04668199 | 20.95097913 | 19.16107033 | 16.28912272 | 14.10993956 | 12.41598324 | 11.07008738 |
| 70 | 23.39451498 | 21.20211187 | 19.34267665 | 16.38454387 | 14.16038934 | 12.44281960 | 11.08444850 |
| 75 | 23.68040834 | 21.40363360 | 19.48496995 | 16.45584810 | 14.19635933 | 12.46108398 | 11.09378224 |
| 80 | 23.91539185 | 21.56534493 | 19.59646048 | 16.50913077 | 14.22200543 | 12.47351441 | 11.09984853 |
| 85 | 24.10853116 | 21.69511035 | 19.68381623 | 16.54894668 | 14.24029075 | 12.48197435 | 11.10379121 |
| 90 | 24.26727759 | 21.79924075 | 19.75226174 | 16.57869944 | 14.25332793 | 12.48773204 | 11.10635367 |
| 95 | 24.39775559 | 21.88280030 | 19.80589059 | 16.60093244 | 14.26262326 | 12.49165063 | 11.10801910 |
| 100 | 24.50499900 | 21.94985274 | 19.84791020 | 16.61754623 | 14.26925070 | 12.49431756 | 11.10910152 |

# APPENDIX TH

# Table of Area Under Normal Curve

| z | .00 | .01 | .02 | .03 | .04 | .05 | .06 | .07 | .08 | .09 |
|---|---|---|---|---|---|---|---|---|---|---|
| 0.0 | .0000 | .0040 | .0080 | .0120 | .0160 | .0199 | .0239 | .0279 | .0319 | .0359 |
| 0.1 | .0398 | .0438 | .0478 | .0517 | .0557 | .0596 | .0636 | .0675 | .0714 | .0753 |
| 0.2 | .0793 | .0832 | .0871 | .0910 | .0948 | .0987 | .1026 | .1064 | .1103 | .1141 |
| 0.3 | .1179 | .1217 | .1255 | .1293 | .1331 | .1368 | .1406 | .1443 | .1480 | .1517 |
| 0.4 | .1554 | .1591 | .1628 | .1664 | .1700 | .1736 | .1772 | .1808 | .1844 | .1879 |
| 0.5 | .1915 | .1950 | .1985 | .2019 | .2054 | .2088 | .2123 | .2157 | .2190 | .2224 |
| 0.6 | .2257 | .2291 | .2324 | .2357 | .2389 | .2422 | .2454 | .2486 | .2517 | .2549 |
| 0.7 | .2580 | .2611 | .2642 | .2673 | .2704 | .2734 | .2764 | .2794 | .2823 | .2852 |
| 0.8 | .2881 | .2910 | .2939 | .2967 | .2995 | .3023 | .3051 | .3078 | .3106 | .3133 |
| 0.9 | .3159 | .3186 | .3212 | .3238 | .3264 | .3289 | .3315 | .3340 | .3365 | .3389 |
| 1.0 | .3413 | .3438 | .3461 | .3485 | .3508 | .3531 | .3554 | .3577 | .3599 | .3621 |
| 1.1 | .3643 | .3665 | .3686 | .3708 | .3729 | .3749 | .3770 | .3790 | .3810 | .3830 |
| 1.2 | .3849 | .3869 | .3888 | .3907 | .3925 | .3944 | .3962 | .3980 | .3997 | .4015 |
| 1.3 | .4032 | .4049 | .4066 | .4082 | .4099 | .4115 | .4131 | .4147 | .4162 | .4177 |
| 1.4 | .4192 | .4207 | .4222 | .4236 | .4251 | .4265 | .4279 | .4292 | .4306 | .4319 |
| 1.5 | .4332 | .4345 | .4357 | .4370 | .4382 | .4394 | .4406 | .4418 | .4429 | .4441 |
| 1.6 | .4452 | .4463 | .4474 | .4484 | .4495 | .4505 | .4515 | .4525 | .4535 | .4545 |
| 1.7 | .4554 | .4564 | .4573 | .4582 | .4591 | .4599 | .4608 | .4616 | .4625 | .4633 |
| 1.8 | .4641 | .4649 | .4656 | .4664 | .4671 | .4678 | .4686 | .4693 | .4699 | .4706 |
| 1.9 | .4713 | .4719 | .4726 | .4732 | .4738 | .4744 | .4750 | .4756 | .4761 | .4767 |
| 2.0 | .4772 | .4778 | .4783 | .4788 | .4793 | .4798 | .4803 | .4808 | .4812 | .4817 |
| 2.1 | .4821 | .4826 | .4830 | .4834 | .4838 | .4842 | .4846 | .4850 | .4854 | .4857 |
| 2.2 | .4861 | .4864 | .4868 | .4871 | .4875 | .4878 | .4881 | .4884 | .4887 | .4890 |
| 2.3 | .4893 | .4896 | .4898 | .4901 | .4904 | .4906 | .4909 | .4911 | .4913 | .4916 |
| 2.4 | .4918 | .4920 | .4922 | .4925 | .4927 | .4929 | .4931 | .4932 | .4934 | .4936 |
| 2.5 | .4938 | .4940 | .4941 | .4943 | .4945 | .4946 | .4948 | .4949 | .4951 | .4952 |
| 2.6 | .4953 | .4955 | .4956 | .4957 | .4959 | .4960 | .4961 | .4962 | .4963 | .4964 |
| 2.7 | .4965 | .4966 | .4967 | .4968 | .4969 | .4970 | .4971 | .4972 | .4973 | .4974 |
| 2.8 | .4974 | .4975 | .4976 | .4977 | .4977 | .4978 | .4979 | .4979 | .4980 | .4981 |
| 2.9 | .4981 | .4982 | .4982 | .4983 | .4984 | .4984 | .4985 | .4985 | .4986 | .4986 |
| 3.0 | .4987 | .4987 | .4987 | .4988 | .4988 | .4989 | .4989 | .4989 | .4990 | .4990 |

# INDEX

Abatement, 695
Account, deficiency, 775–776
  realization and liquidation, 780
Accountability, 696
Accountability records, 696–698
Accounting, entities, 3–21
  nature of, 3
  postulates, 5–7
  principles, 7–8
  role of, 3–4
    in investment decisions, 200
    social significance of, 8–9
Accounting data for expansion plans, 200–205
Accounting environment, 4–5
Accounting, fund, 851
Accounting, governmental, 851
Accounting information, uses of, 3–4
*Accounting Principles Board Opinion 8,* 111–112
*Accounting Principles Board Opinion 16,* 290, 589–590, 593–599
*Accounting Principles Board Opinion 17,* 290, 596, 598
*Accounting Principles Board Opinion 18,* 264, 334
*Accounting Principles Board Statement 3,* 162, 163
*Accounting Research Bulletin 46,* 661
*Accounting Research Bulletin 51,* 259, 261, 366, 399, 461, 526, 542
Accounts payable, amount of, 69–70
Accounts receivable, new, 789
  valuation of 37–38
Acquisition cost, 30–31
Acquisition of control, 399–402, 406–411
Acts of bankruptcy, 691–692
Actuarial sciences, 807–839
Adjunct account, 78

Administration of income, 123–141
Affiliated companies, 315
Allocation of income, capital ratio, 126–127
  corporations, 132–133
  estates and trusts, 133–135
  interest allowance, 130–132
  partnerships, 126–132
  salary allowance, 128–130
  specified ratios, 127–128
Amount of an annuity, 814–815
Amount of annuity of 1 tables, 881–882
Amount of 1, 811–812
Annuities, 814–825, 834, 881–884
  amount of, 814–820
  deferred, 824–825
  number of periods, 834
  present value of, 819–823
  relation to compound interest, 816–817
  tables of, 881–884
Annuity due, 814–816
  present value of, 822–823
Annuity method of depreciation, 179, 829–831
Annuity tables, 877–884
  construction of, 821
Appraisal, valuation by, 155–157
Appraisals, accounting for, 156
Appreciation, unrecognized, 82
Appropriated income, 132–133
"As if" statements, 591–592
Asset classification, 46–47
Asset realization, 622–628
  cash equivalent, 624
  by cash sale, 622
  by sale for securities, 622–623
  by sale for stock, 626–628
    at book value, 626
    at fair value, 626–627

# Index

at market value, 627–628
at par value, 627
Asset recognition, 47
Asset revaluation, 628–630
  decline in economic value, 628–629
  due to obsolescence, 629
Asset valuation, 30–54
  methods of, 149–165
  problems of, 31
  quasi-reorganization, 656–661
Assets, pledged, 774–775
  realized, 781
  subsequently acquired, 781
  to be realized, 781
Authorized stock, 15–16

Balance sheet, supplementary data, 82
Bankruptcy, 668–672, 691–693
  accounting for, 669–672
  acts, 691–692
  involuntary, 691
  procedures, 668–669, 692–693
Bequest, 695
Bond amortization, effective rate method, 826–828
  straight-line basis, 827
Bond discount, 64, 175
Bond discount retirement, 664–666
  amortize, over new issue life, 666
    over original issue life, 666
  immediate write-off, 665
Bond dividend, 139–140
Bond premium, 175, 664–665
Bond pricing, 175–176, 826
Bond refunding, accounting for, 174–175
  planning for, 173–174
Bond retirement, accounting for, 174
  at call premium, 664
  discount write-off, 664–665
  at face value, 663, 664
Bonds, 32, 34–36
Bonds payable, valuation of, 175
Bonus procedure, 214–216
Branch accounting, 233–246
Branch operations, 231–246
Branch shipments, 238–239
Branches, foreign, 245–246
Business combinations, accounting for, 592–596
  accounting revaluations, 598–599
  definitions of, 584
  pooling, 586–587, 591–592
  purchase, 586, 587–588
  types of, 585–586

Business contraction, 621–622
Business expansion, methods, 221
  role of accounting in, 199–205
  through combinations, 584–603
Business interruption insurance, 99–100
Business liquidation, procedure, 690–691
  reasons for, 689–690
Business organizations, 3–21
  types of, 11

Call option, 643–644
Capital ratios, 126–127
Capitalizing retained earnings, 209–213
  accounting entries, 210
Cash, 32
  claims to, 32–42
  equivalent, 624
  surrender value, 36, 119–121
    accounting for, 101–103
    reporting, 104
  valuation of, 32–37
Charge and discharge statement, 706–708
  as to income, 133–135
  as to principal, 706–707
Coinsurance clause, 96–97
Combination transaction, 586–588
  impact on statements, 596–598
Combined statements, branch and home office, 243–245
Common dollar valuation, 157–165
Compound interest, 809–814
  fractional periods, 833
Compound interest tables, 877–884
Connecting affiliate, 512
Consolidated assets, dual valuation of, 531–532
  goodwill amortization, 533
  imputed valuation, 532–533
  valuation problems, 533
Consolidated goodwill, 281, 414–416
Consolidated income statement, 315–325
  preparation illustrated, 316–325, 344–349
Consolidated retained earnings statement, 535–540
  preparation illustrated, 344–349
  valuation of, 535–536
Consolidated statements, comprehensive review, 478–513
  cost and equity methods compared, 344
  date of acquisition, 274–281, 383–384
  dual valuation, 531–532
  economic aspects, 529
  indirect ownership, 447–454

Consolidated statements *(Continued)*
  connecting affiliates, 450–452
  major and minor parents, 448–450, 452–454
 intercompany bonds, 375–383
 intercompany fixed assets, 370–375, 481
  depreciating assets, 373–375
  nondepreciating assets, 371–373
 intercompany inventory, 365–370, 480
  elimination of profit, 366–370
  illustration, 369–370
  minority interest, 367
  retained earnings charge, 366
 intercompany profit, 364–383, 464–488, 480–488
 intercompany stock, 398–399, 488–491
 investment, carried at cost, 301
  basic procedure, 301
  establishing reciprocity, 302
  carried at equity, 335–336
 legal aspects, 528–529
 limitations of, 262–264, 526–527
 mutual stockholdings, 454–468
  as treasury stock, 461–463
  between subsidiaries, 454–457, 459–461
  between subsidiaries and parent, 457–461
 problems of, 527
 reexamined, 530–543
 subsequent consolidation, 479
 theories of, 265–267
 types of, 274
Consolidated retained earnings, 288–289
Consolidated working papers, 320–325, 350–355
Consolidated procedures, basic, 272
 full (100%) ownership, 275–281, 302–309, 336–340
  cost above book value, 277–278, 305–307, 337–338
  cost below book value, 278–281, 307–309, 339–340
  cost equal to book value, 275–276, 302–305, 336–337
 less than 100% ownership, 281–288, 309–315, 340–344
  cost above book value, 281–283, 341–342, 311–313
  cost below book value, 286–287, 313–314, 343–344
  cost equal to book values, 281–284, 309–311, 340–341
 preferred stock, treatment of, 425–430
 trial balance approach, 320–326, 349–356, 368–370, 513

Consolidation, conditions for, 259–260
 entity theory of, 265–267
 proprietary theory of, 265–266
 standards for, 267
Consolidation policies, composition of entity, 540–542
 conclusion of, 531
 control, meaning of, 530
 criteria for consolidation, 528
 ownership percentage change, 538–540
 valuation problems, 531–533
Continuity postulate, 7
Contra account, 78
Contributed assets, valuation of, 43–44
Contribution clause, fire insurance, 98
Control, acquisition of, 399–402, 406–411
 meaning of, 530
Controlling interest, 260
Cooperative, 18
Corporate charter, 15
Corporate dissolution, reasons for, 770–771
Corporate formation, 13–16
 accounting for, 15–16
 legal aspects, 14–15
Corporate liquidation, 770–791
 tax considerations, 771–772
 trustees for, 772
 types of, 772
Cost, acquisition, 30–31
 differential, 201–202
 utilization, 202–203
Cost and book value, variations in, 289–291
Creditor committee, 666
Creditors, secured and unsecured, 774–775
Creditorship equities, recognition date, 66
 retirement, 69–70
 valuation of, 64–66
Criteria for consolidation, 528
Currency translation rates, 560–561
Curve, normal, 885

Dated retained earnings, 661
Debt retirement, 630–634
 alternatives to, 633–634
 bonds, at par, 632
  at premium, 632–633
Deferred annuity, 824–825
Deficiency account, 776
Demonstrative legacies, 695
Depreciation and funds, 208–210
Depreciation and governmental accounting, 855
Depreciation methods, 178–179

# Index

annuity method, 829–831
sinking fund method, 829–831
Devise, 695
Differential costing, 201–202
Discounting, 178–179
Discounts, 789
trade, 42
Distribution of income, 135–141
nature of, 138
valuation of, 140–141
Dividends, in kind, 140–141
liquidating, 639
recognition date, 139–140
scrip, 139
stock dividend, 139–140
valuation, 140–141, 209–212

Earning power valuation method, 150–155
Economic aspects of consolidation, 529–530
Economic value decline, 628–629
Effective interest, 176–177
Employee participating insurance, 100–101
Enterprise, valuation of, 53–54
Enterprise valuation, adjustment of, 169–172
partnership goodwill, 170–171
Entity postulate, 6
Entity theory, 9–11
Equities, 64–82
definition of, 64
valuation for quasi-reorganization, 657–661
Equity standards, 5
Equity valuation, 72
Estate, income, 698–700
liquidation, 695–696
accounting for, 696–698
principal, 698–700
"Estate Corpus," 696
Estimated liabilities, 68–69
Exchange transaction, nature of, 598–599
Exchanges, valuation of, 42–43
Executor, duties of, 694–695
report, 706–708

Factory ledger, 232
Fidelity bond, 108–109
Fiduciary, 16
Financial ratios, 263–264
Financial reorganization, 661–673
debt refinancing, 663–666
extension of time for payment, 661–662
under bankruptcy, 668–673
Financing, distribution of securities, 599–603

external sources, 213–218
types of securities, 599–600
Financing plans, 207–221
Financing the entity, 78–79
Fire insurance, 94–99
coinsurance clause, 96–98
contribution clause, 98
mortgage clause, 99
Fire loss, accounting for, 94–96
measurement of, 95–96
Fixed assets, valuation of, 178–179
Foreign assets, translation of, 560–561
Foreign branches, 245–246
accounting for, 563–567
translation rates, 560
Foreign exchange gain or loss, 556–557
realized, 556–557, 562
Foreign operations, 554–573
Foreign subsidiaries, 568–573
account translation rates, 568–569
consolidation, illustrated, 569–573
Foreign transactions, 554–560
assets shipped, for sale, 557–559
for use, 559–560
purchases, 555–556
sales, 554–555
"Fresh" start, 657
Fund accounting, 851
agency fund, 854
bond fund, 854
capital projects fund, 854
debt service fund, 854
enterprise fund, 854
general bonded debt and interest group of accounts, 852
general fixed asset group of accounts, 852
general fund, 852, 854, 855
intragovernmental service fund, 852, 854, 859
special assessment fund, 852, 854
special revenue fund, 852, 854
trust fund, 852, 854
utility fund, 852, 854
Fund concept, 853

General legacies, 695
Going concern postulate, 7
Goodwill, 49–53, 216–218, 598
amortization of, 533
consolidated, 281
corporation, 51–52
definition of, 50
partnership, 50–51

# 890

*Index*

Goodwill *(Continued)*
　partner's retirement, 637–638
Governmental accounting, 851
Governmental accounting principles and procedures, 851
Gross profit method, 96
Group insurance plans, 104–105

Health insurance, 105
Home office account, 235

Imputed interest, 178
Imputed valuation, 532–533
Income, administration of, 123–141
　allocation of, 126–135
　　corporation, 132–133
Income, estates and trusts, 133–135
　　partnership, 126–132
　distribution of, 135–141
　　asset severance, 138
　　methods, 138–140
　　valuation of, 140–141
　undistributed, 136–138
　　accounting for, 136–138
　　disclosure, 137–138
Income realization, 334
Incremental revenue, 206
Index numbers, use of, 157–165
Indirect ownership, 415–418, 447–454, 491–512
　effect on profit, 464–468
Insolvency, 691
Insurable asset risks, 94–100
Insurable employee risks, 100–108
　fidelity bond, 108–109
　health, 105
　liability, 106–108
　life, 100–105
Insurance clauses, coinsurance clause, 96–98
　contribution clause, 98
　mortgage clause, 99
Insurance policies, cash surrender value, 101–103
　valuation of, 36
Intercompany gains and losses, 534
Intercompany items, 288
Intercompany profit, 364–383
　on bonds, 375–383
　on fixed assets, 370–375
　on inventories, 365–370
Interest, 807–839
　compound, 809–814
　rate, 808

　simple, 808–809
　tables, 809–811, 877–884
Interest charges, as distribution of income, 124–125
　as expense, 125
Interest cost, accounting for, 177
Interest earned, 625–626
Internal financing, 208–213
Intestate, 694
Investments in subsidiaries, cost method, 300–326
　equity method, 334–356

Joint venture, 20–21
　accounting for, 20–21
　nature of, 20
　reporting, 21
　uncompleted, 20–21

Laws of descent, 694
Lease, liability, 67
　valuation of, 44–46
Leasehold, valuation of, 831–833
Legacies, 695
Leverage, 80
Liabilities, classification of, 73–75
　estimated, 68–70
　lease, 67
　priority, 775
　product guarantee, 69
　unsecured, 775
Life insurance, 100–105
　group, 104
　ordinary life, 101–104
　settlement, 104
Liquidating dividend, 639–640
Liquidating preference, 672
Liquidation statement, 730–731, 732–733, 736, 737, 740–741, 742, 744, 751–752

Market value, 35
Marshaling of assets, 745–747
Materiality, 33
Minority interest, large block of, 530–531
　nature of, 260–261, 283
　valuation of, 534–535
Mutual stockholdings, 454–468, 502–509, 512
　effect on intercompany profit, 466–468

National Committee on Governmental Accounting, 851
Nominal interest, 175

# Index

Normal curve, 885
Notes receivable, valuation of, 38–40

Objective evidence, 82
Obsolescence, accounting for, 629–630
Offset, right of, 728
Ordinary annuity, 818–820
Owner's equities, classification of, 70–73, 75–81
  valuation of, 70–73

Partner admission, at book value, 167–168
  bonus recognized, 214–216
  by investment, 213–218
  goodwill recognized, 216–218
  at less than book value, 168–170
  at more than book value, 168, 170
Partner's deficit, accounting for, 743–745
Partnership, capital, 77–78
  income allocation, 126–132
  interest provision, 130
  loss allocation, 128
  partner admission, 165–172
  salary provisions, 127–130
  sale of interest, 165–166
  valuation of, 165–172
Partnership dissolution, 723
  causes of, 723–724
  death of partner, 725
Partnership formation, 12–13
  accounting for, 13
  bonus, 52–53
  goodwill, 50–51, 52–53
  legal aspects, 12–13
  valuation of, 47–49
Partnership liquidation, 723–757
  accounting for, 724–725
  cash distribution planning, 755–757
  cash distribution rules, 747–748
  installment liquidation, 747–755
  realization losses, 726–747
Partnership retirement, 634–638
  bonus, 638
  goodwill recognition, 637–638
  settlement basis, 637–638
Pension plans, funded, 111
  unfunded, 111
Pensions costs, 110–112
  past service cost, 111–112
Periodicity postulate, 7
Perpetuity, 834
Planning reports, 200–205
Plant expansion reserve, 209–210
Pooling of interests, 586–587

  criteria for, 589–590
Postulates, 5–7
Preferred stock, in consolidation, 425–431
Present value concept, 151–153
Present value of 1, 813–814, 879–880
Present value of annuity, 819–824
Price-level adjustments, 157–165
Price postulate, 6–7
Principles of accounting, 7–8
Private ledger, 232
Probate, 694
Product guarantee liability, 69
Proforma statements, 591
  illustrated, 591–592
Proprietary theory, 9–10
Proprietorship formation, 11–12
  accounting for, 11
  legal aspects, 11
Proprietorship liquidation, 693–708
  accounting for, 700–706
  at death, 693–695
  executor duties, 694–695
Provision for exchange fluctuation, 557–559
Provision for self insurance, 109–110
Prudent conduct, 5

Quasi-reorganization, 656–661
  characteristics of, 656
  illustration of, 657–661
  revaluations in, 657

Rate of return, 79–80, 204–205
Rational conduct, 5
Realizable value, 31–34
Realization and liquidation statement, 780–782
  form, 781, 786
Realized gains and losses, 562
Receivables, long-term, 34–35, 40–42
  valuation procedures, 34–35
Receiver reports, 779
  analysis of cash, 787
  income statement, 787–788
  realization and liquidation statement, 786
Receivership, accounting, 777–791
  in equity, 666–667, 777
  termination of, 779–780
Reciprocal accounts, 272–273
Referee, 692
Refinancing, 663–666
Reorganization surplus, 670–671
Reorganizations, 654–673
  accounting aspects, 655

Reorganizations *(Continued)*
  legal aspects, 655
Replacement cost, 204
Residuary legacies, 695
Retained earnings, as source of funds, 209
  capitalization of, 209–213
Retirement, of partners, 634–639
  of stock, 642–644
Revaluations, losses, 656–657
  upward, 656
Right of offset, 728
Risk management, 93–94

Sales agency, 231
Salvage, 96
Scarce means, impact of, 4–5
Scrip dividend, 139
Self-insurance, accrual basis, 109–110
  nonaccrual basis, 110
Service resources, valuation of, 31, 42–47
Severance of assets, 135–141
  legal aspects, 138–139
  time of, 138–139
Shareholder's equity, classification of, 80–81
Sinking fund depreciation method, 179, 829–831
Social significance of accounting, 8–9
Stock discount, 65
Stock dividend, accounting for, 137, 139–140
  valuation of, 137, 209–211
Stock reacquisition, at issue price, 641
  at less than issue price, 641
  at more than issue price, 641–642
  reporting of, 640–641
Stock retirement, 642–644
  at call option, 643
  by stockholder action, 644
  use of agent for, 643
Stock split, 211–212
Subsidiary company, concept of, 257–259
Subsidiary stock, acquired after control obtained, 402–406
  acquisition date, 399–402
  change in relative equity, 417–425, 488–491
  disposal, 411–416, 488–490
  interim acquisitions, 406–411
Supplementary data, 82

*Tables, interest,* 877–884
Testate, 694
Trading on the equity, 79–80
Transaction postulate, 6
Transfers, interbranch, 242–245
Translation rates, 560–561, 568–569
Treasury stock, 425–427, 461–463
Trust formation, 16–17
  accounting for, 17–18
  powers of trustees, 16–17
Trustee, 16, 692

Unamortized bond discount, 664–666
Unconsolidated subsidiaries, 264–265, 542–543
Undistributed income, accounting for, 136–138
Uniform Partnership Act, 746
Unrealized gains and losses, 562–563
Unrealized profit, in fixed assets, 370–375
  in inventory, 239, 365–370
Usefulness postulate, 14
Utilization cost, 202–204
  measurement of, 203–204
Utilization costing, 202–203

Valuation methods, 149–165
Valuation of consolidated assets, dual, 531–532
  imputed, 532–533
Venture accounting, 20
Venture combinations, 21

Working fund, 234–235
Workmen's compensation, 106–108